Handbook of Research on Individualism and Identity in the Globalized Digital Age

F. Sigmund Topor
Keio University, Japan

A volume in the Advances in Human and Social Aspects of Technology (AHSAT) Book Series

www.igi-global.com

Published in the United States of America by
    IGI Global
    Information Science Reference (an imprint of IGI Global)
    701 E. Chocolate Avenue
    Hershey PA, USA 17033
    Tel: 717-533-8845
    Fax: 717-533-8661
    E-mail: cust@igi-global.com
    Web site: http://www.igi-global.com

Library of Congress Cataloging-in-Publication Data

Names: Topor, Francis Sigmund, 1957- editor.
Title: Handbook of research on individualism and identity in the globalized
  digital age / Francis Sigmund Topor, editor.
Description: Hershey : Information Science Reference, 2016. | Includes
  bibliographical references and index.
Identifiers: LCCN 2016017808| ISBN 9781522505228 (hardcover) | ISBN
  9781522505235 (ebook)
Subjects: LCSH: Information technology--Economic aspects. | Internet--Social
  aspects. | Mass media and education. | Globalization--Social aspects. |
  Social changes.
Classification: LCC HC79.I55 H3336 2016 | DDC 303.48/33--dc23 LC record available at https://lccn.loc.gov/2016017808

This book is published in the IGI Global book series Advances in Human and Social Aspects of Technology (AHSAT) (ISSN: 2328-1316; eISSN: 2328-1324)

British Cataloguing in Publication Data
A Cataloguing in Publication record for this book is available from the British Library.

For electronic access to this publication, please contact: eresources@igi-global.com.

Advances in Human and Social Aspects of Technology (AHSAT) Book Series

Ashish Dwivedi
The University of Hull, UK

ISSN: 2328-1316
EISSN: 2328-1324

MISSION

In recent years, the societal impact of technology has been noted as we become increasingly more connected and are presented with more digital tools and devices. With the popularity of digital devices such as cell phones and tablets, it is crucial to consider the implications of our digital dependence and the presence of technology in our everyday lives.

The **Advances in Human and Social Aspects of Technology (AHSAT) Book Series** seeks to explore the ways in which society and human beings have been affected by technology and how the technological revolution has changed the way we conduct our lives as well as our behavior. The AHSAT book series aims to publish the most cutting-edge research on human behavior and interaction with technology and the ways in which the digital age is changing society.

COVERAGE

- End-User Computing
- Philosophy of technology
- Activism and ICTs
- Technology Dependence
- Human Development and Technology
- Technology Adoption
- Technology and Freedom of Speech
- Computer-Mediated Communication
- Cyber Behavior
- Public Access to ICTs

IGI Global is currently accepting manuscripts for publication within this series. To submit a proposal for a volume in this series, please contact our Acquisition Editors at Acquisitions@igi-global.com or visit: http://www.igi-global.com/publish/.

Titles in this Series

For a list of additional titles in this series, please visit: www.igi-global.com

Handbook of Research on Human-Computer Interfaces, Developments, and Applications
João Rodrigues (University of Algarve, Portugal) Pedro Cardoso (University of Algarve, Portugal) Jânio Monteiro (University of Algarve, Portugal) and Mauro Figueiredo (University of Algarve, Portugal)
Information Science Reference • copyright 2016 • 663pp • H/C (ISBN: 9781522504351) • US $330.00 (our price)

Human Development and Interaction in the Age of Ubiquitous Technology
Hakikur Rahman (BRAC University, Bangladesh)
Information Science Reference • copyright 2016 • 384pp • H/C (ISBN: 9781522505563) • US $185.00 (our price)

Examining the Evolution of Gaming and Its Impact on Social, Cultural, and Political Perspectives
Keri Duncan Valentine (West Virginia University, USA) and Lucas John Jensen (Georgia Southern University, USA)
Information Science Reference • copyright 2016 • 456pp • H/C (ISBN: 9781522502616) • US $190.00 (our price)

Handbook of Research on Human Social Interaction in the Age of Mobile Devices
Xiaoge Xu (Botswana International University of Science and Technology, Botswana)
Information Science Reference • copyright 2016 • 548pp • H/C (ISBN: 9781522504696) • US $325.00 (our price)

Defining Identity and the Changing Scope of Culture in the Digital Age
Alison Novak (Rowan University, USA) and Imaani Jamillah El-Burki (Lehigh University, USA)
Information Science Reference • copyright 2016 • 316pp • H/C (ISBN: 9781522502128) • US $185.00 (our price)

Gender Considerations in Online Consumption Behavior and Internet Use
Rebecca English (Queensland University of Technology, Australia) and Raechel Johns (University of Canberra, Australia)
Information Science Reference • copyright 2016 • 297pp • H/C (ISBN: 9781522500100) • US $165.00 (our price)

Analyzing Digital Discourse and Human Behavior in Modern Virtual Environments
Bobbe Gaines Baggio (American University, USA)
Information Science Reference • copyright 2016 • 320pp • H/C (ISBN: 9781466698994) • US $175.00 (our price)

Overcoming Gender Inequalities through Technology Integration
Joseph Wilson (University of Maiduguri, Nigeria) and Nuhu Diraso Gapsiso (University of Maiduguri, Nigeria)
Information Science Reference • copyright 2016 • 324pp • H/C (ISBN: 9781466697737) • US $185.00 (our price)

Cultural, Behavioral, and Social Considerations in Electronic Collaboration
Ayse Kok (Bogazici University, Turkey) and Hyunkyung Lee (Yonsei University, South Korea)
Business Science Reference • copyright 2016 • 374pp • H/C (ISBN: 9781466695566) • US $205.00 (our price)

www.igi-global.com

701 E. Chocolate Ave., Hershey, PA 17033
Order online at www.igi-global.com or call 717-533-8845 x100
To place a standing order for titles released in this series, contact: cust@igi-global.com
Mon-Fri 8:00 am - 5:00 pm (est) or fax 24 hours a day 717-533-8661

Editorial Advisory Board

List of Contributors

Table of Contents

Section 4
Globalization

Section 5
Wellness and Healthcare

Detailed Table of Contents

Section 1
Information Technology

Chapter 1
Art Bangert, Montana State University, USA
Mabark Fayaz Alshahri, Imam Mohammed Ibn Saud Islamic University, Saudi Arabia

Research related to differences in how Saudi and US faculty use Information and Technology Communication
(ICT) tools is discussed as well as their perceptions of ICT applications and ICT use. Saudi faculty from
six universities in KSA and US faculty from five US universities completed a questionnaire designed
to identify the ICT tools most frequently used and their perceptions toward the use of these tools. In
addition, a path analysis Technology Acceptance Model was conducted to investigate the relationships
between faculty attitudes toward ICT applications and actual ICT use. Findings from this study suggest
that both Saudi faculty social media most often while US faculty use productivity tools more often. Both
Saudi and US faculty and would benefit from training in the use of these applications for use within a
Learning Management System.

Chapter 2
Amanda Sue Schulze, Pepperdine University, USA
Doug Leigh, Pepperdine University, USA
Paul Sparks, Pepperdine University, USA
Elio Spinello, Pepperdine University, USA

Millions of adults have registered for massive open online courses, known as MOOCs, yet little research
exists on how effective MOOCs are at meeting the needs of these learners. Critics of MOOCs highlight
that completion rates can average fewer than 5%. Such low completion rates raise questions about the
effectiveness of MOOCs and whether all adults have the skills and abilities needed for success. MOOCs
have the potential to be powerful change agents for universities and students, but it has previously been

unknown whether these online courses serve more than just the most persistent, self-directed learners. This study explored the relationship between self-directed learning readiness and MOOC completion percents among adults taking a single Coursera MOOC. By examining self-directed learning - the ability to take responsibility for one's own educational experiences - and MOOC completion rates, this research may help to confirm the knowledge and skills needed to be a successful adult learner in the 21st century, as well as how to improve online education offered to adult learners.

Chapter 3

Michelle F. Wright, Masaryk University, Czech Republic

Children and adolescents grow up in a constantly connected digital world. They maintain active involvement in the digital world through the creation of blogs, communication via social networking sites, and watching videos. Despite the opportunities seeming almost limitless in a digitally connected world, there is a darker side to electronic technology usage. Cyberbullying is a darker side to children's and adolescents' immersion in a digital world. Incorporating research from around the world and across multiple disciplines, the aim of this chapter is to describe the nature, extent, causes, and consequences associated with children's and adolescents' cyberbullying involvement. The chapter concludes with solutions and recommendations in order to further cyberbullying intervention and prevention. Such an approach is important as cyberbullying is a phenomenon occurring throughout the world. Future research directions are also given, with the aim of furthering research on cyberbullying in an effort to improve the world's understanding of these behaviors.

Chapter 4

Eric Niemi, Northern Illinois University, USA

This chapter conveys the results of a study examining how male students use video games to construct their masculinity. Applying a critical discourse methodology, the study provides insight into how men construct their masculinity within video game discourse communities and how the construction applies to other discourses. It examines how men enter the discourse, what they learn in the discourse, and then how they apply that learning to other discourse communities. It concludes with recommendations and suggestions regarding how video games are a critical part of popular culture that facilitates construction of an identity through the multitude of encounters and relationships within the discourse.

Chapter 5

Gregory C. Gardner, George Mason University, USA

Smartphones bring major changes to the way people gather information and interact. While smartphone use unleashes productivity it also has worrying implications. This study focused on the most important aspects of user experiences of smartphones in an Army work environment. Theory U and systems theory guided the research. This phenomenological study was based on interviews with soldiers of a variety of ages, ranks, and duty positions. While the findings are consistent with other research, it is clear that smartphone use ties to a number of complex leadership challenges. Paradoxical aspects of smartphone use are apparent as it also fosters stress and anxiety. More concerning, such use jeopardizes the development of the traditional military culture of the unit. Current Army policies do not address the concerns expressed by respondents. The results of the study are a call to action for Army leaders and offer a compelling case for transformative change.

Chapter 6

Randy L. Burkhead, Capella University, USA

In today's culture organizations have come to expect that information security incidents and breaches are no longer a matter of if but when. This shifting paradigm has brought increased attention, not to the defenses in place to prevent an incident but, to how companies manage the aftermath. Using a phenomenological model, organizations can reconstruct events focused on the human aspects of security with forensic technology providing supporting information. This can be achieved by conducting an after action review for incidents using a phenomenological model. Through this approach the researcher can discover the common incident management cycle attributes and how these attributes have been applied in the organization. An interview guide and six steps are presented to accomplish this type of review. By understanding what happened, how it happened, and why it happened during incident response, organizations can turn their moment of weakness into a pillar of strength.

Section 2
Education

Chapter 7

Şahin Gökçearslan, Gazi University, Turkey
Ebru Solmaz, Gazi University, Turkey
Burcu Karabulut Coşkun, Gazi University, Turkey

The aim of this study is to identify the new trends on technology use in developing critical thinking skills. By this purpose, the researches published between 2008-2014 in Science Direct database were examined by using content analysis. Also study was completed in three main parts. The first part consists of the conceptual framework about, technology use in education, critical thinking, the effect of technology on critical thinking and new technologies used to develop critical thinking skills. In the second part the content analysis method was used to examine the researches published in Science Direct database. In the final part, the conclusion and recommendations were given about the research and future studies.

Chapter 8

Irina Khoutyz, Kuban State University, Russia

The purpose of this research is to establish a connection between the effects of globalization on contemporary societies and the increase in individualist attributes in former collectivist societies. To achieve it, the chapter presents the study of the experiences of Russian students participating in academic mobility programs. A two-step survey conducted among the Russian university students reveals, by means of cultural dimension analysis, individualist attributes in their academic behavior while studying overseas and at a home university. The interest towards academic mobility programs expressed by the students of various years of study, their desire for independence and self-development as well as an enjoyable process of acquiring a diploma are examples of individualist attributes. The conclusion is made that individuals trying to find their place in a globalized world acquire more individualist attributes in their behavior and world perception.

Critical Thinking (CT) in the nurse graduate continues to be a topic of concern in the academic and acute care settings. Few studies focus on early evaluation of Critical Thinking Skills (CTS). The purpose of this chapter is to show how the non-experimental, explanatory, quantitative study, the Kaplan CTIT, was employed to determine if a transformation in the level of CTS occurs within the first semester of associate degree nursing students. Participants completed the pretest in the first three weeks of classes. Posttests were given after course finals. A significant transformation in the level of CT occurred. The estimated change in CT test scores was 2.04, with 95% confidence. Implications for early measurement of CTS in nursing programs reveals if teaching methodology is providing the necessary input for developing CTS or if evaluation and changes are needed.

Chapter 10

The unity of humanity has placed the role of culture in maintaining wellness and coping with illness under examination in biomedical research. The qualitative methodology, which is the method most widely used in healthcare research, been placed under the globalization microscope for its role in intercultural biomedical research. Neither does the etiology of diseases such as, for example, the common cold, the adenovirus and influenza respiratory viruses, among others, nor treatments of such ailments distinguish between the religious, geographic, and linguistic dissimilarities that violate the unity of humanity. The subjectivity that clods investigators of various cultural backgrounds and disciplinary stripes, deems it expedient that stakeholders be provided with the means to ontologically verify research findings. Researchers employing the qualitative methodology can mitigate subjectivity and enhance objectivity by being culturally cognizant. The unity of humanity is manifested in healthcare and transcends national borders, laws, ethics, and customs.

This chapter will discuss a study that set out to determine if knowledge of the structure of language and self-efficacy of pre-service and in-service teachers was impacted by whether the course was taken in a face to face or online format. Results of the study showed there was a statistically significant change in the Teacher Knowledge Assessment: Structure of Language (TKA: SL) for participants in the online courses, but not for students taking the course face to face. To determine whether or not self-efficacy increased, the Teacher Efficacy Scale: short form (TES) was used, The TES includes two subscales:

teacher efficacy and personal efficacy. Results showed no statistical significance on the overall TES score between participants; however, on the personal efficacy score, there was a statistically significant change in pre and post test scores of participants who took the course face to face.

Section 3
Individualism

Chapter 12

Derek Cooley, Godwin Heights Public Schools, USA
Elizabeth Whitten, Western Michigan University, USA

Special education administrators provide leadership to guide the identification of learners with exceptionalities and ensure that staff working with special education students delivers instructional best practice. In order to execute these responsibilities, special education administrators must be effective leaders who collaborate with a variety of stakeholder including. Contrary to their general education counterparts, special education administrators must possess a specific body of procedural knowledge to identify low-performing groups of students. These procedures are often referred to Response to Intervention (RTI) or Multi-Tier Systems of Support (MTSS). Under IDEA (2004), students with and without disabilities can benefit from the same system of interventions and supports. This intersection has necessitated coordination of RTI models by both general and special education administrators. Special education and general education leaders will be challenged to blend models of leadership to address the high-stakes environment in our K-12 schools.

Chapter 13

Sandra J. Aguirre, George Washington University, USA

Globalization presents an array of challenges and opportunities for today's leaders. Recurring corporate and government malfeasance on a global scale as well as the morally complex environments of organizations are imposing more significant demands on organizational actors. Authentic leadership is an emerging leadership category that is gaining much interest due to the demand for more authentic leaders. Authentic leaders attain greater performance from their followers and this is considered a leadership multiplier that produces a virtuous cycle of performance and learning for leaders, followers, and organizations. This chapter discusses a completed study that addresses the following research question: How do experiences inform authentic leadership development across the 4 dimensions of the authentic leadership multidimensional construct of self-awareness, balanced processing, relational transparency, and internalized moral/ethical perspectives?

Chapter 14

Ellen Brook, Cuyahoga Community College, USA

The purpose of the study was to describe the experiences adult learners have while solving mathematical word problems. The focus of the study was on how these adult students used prior mathematical knowledge and how their past experiences with mathematics influenced their solving of mathematics word problems.

The study found that the attitudes, feelings and beliefs that adult students in the study hold toward mathematics and problem solving are an integral part of their mathematics learning experience. This study also reports on the particular pattern observed within the participants' attitude toward mathematics education during their schooling years beginning from elementary school till college. The adult students participated in the study lacked the necessary knowledge of such concepts as motion and concentration. Finally, the study found that even after learning the topic during the college class, the participants had difficulties with applying algebraic approaches to word problem solving.

Section 4
Globalization

Chapter 15

As life approaches expectancy and senescence actualizes, the regenerative capacity of the vital organs and their functionality is reduced. Such a reality gives rise the need to identify with a better purpose in life. Religion and spirituality assume a central role in the wellness and healthcare in such circumstances. Although societies and civilizations differ in their religious and spiritual orientations, all peoples everywhere ascribe to some God or gods. The globalization of religion was initiated sometime between the late Bronze Age and late classical antiquity. The pivotal point was characterized by a conversion from polytheism, or primary religions as practiced by the Ancient Egyptians; Phoenicians; Babylonians; Greek; and Romans on the one hand, to monotheism—secondary religions characterized by the worship of one supreme God. Religion and spirituality has now become the one and remaining source of solace for the terminally ill.

Chapter 16

The chapter purpose is to examine Employee Wellness Programs (EWP) internationally. The review of previous literature and discovery of outcomes and recommendations for future research are explored. Additionally, developing culturally competent international EWPs and training the development team are presented. The importance of intercultural communication, interpersonal and intrapersonal competence, and indigenous and cross-cultural psychology applications offer the foundation for the development of effective EWPs internationally. Issues, controversies, and problems, along with solutions and recommendations for the development of culturally competent EWPs are reviewed.

Chapter 17

Internet, eHealth and digitalization have opened information access for patients and medical health users. Digitalization provides an opportunity for telemedicine, storage of Electronic Patient Records (EPRs) and net communication for both medical staff and patients with access. Digitalization and technical improvement have increased the usage of Internet based technologies and telephones for positive health coaching and digital-learning applications for all medical users, school staff, and students. The effect of Information Technology on healthcare and medical services can be described as revolutionary. Increasingly, the utilization of digital equipment and medical technology are employed in patients' homes.

Chapter 18

Nilsa I. I. Elias, Capella University, USA
Terry W. Walker, Capella University, USA

The use of e-training in healthcare has experienced considerable growth. The results of this study provide insights regarding the importance of technology compatibility attributes to behavioral intentions to continue the use of e-training by healthcare professionals. A model based on the technology acceptance literature has been used. The model adds the construct of healthcare practice compatibility to the Technology Acceptance Model as a predictor of behavioral intention to continued use of e-training by healthcare professionals. Using Partial Least Squares Structural Equation Modeling (PLS-SEM), findings suggest that perceived practice compatibility, perceived workflow compatibility, and perceived task compatibility in e-training are essential to healthcare professionals' intent to continue use of e-training. The parsimonious model in this study is a more predictive model than the basic TAM model in explaining users' intentions to continue use of e-training.

Section 5
Wellness and Healthcare

Chapter 19

Donna Reed, Southwest Independent School District, USA

This qualitative case study describes global studies education and curriculum, global citizenship, and the impact of a global studies education and curriculum on students after graduation. What life choices might be influenced by what the students learned through global studies? Did they choose their university studies based on globalized thinking? These are difficult questions to answer, because there are so many variables in the life of an adolescent when making choices after high school graduation. This study discovers the impact of a global studies education with a global citizenship emphasis on graduates of a global studies high school through student voice and experience—backwards mapping.

Chapter 20

Elise Kiregian, TCI, USA

This chapter looks at the transformation of Post-Soviet Russian business education. The extraordinary metamorphosis shapes the new generation of Russians profoundly. Russians are now far more likely to speak English, to hold personal investment portfolios and to be able to work outside of Russia in global businesses. The old-fashioned idea of central control of every aspect of life is largely gone as are business courses extolling the virtues of Marxism. Research shows the wide acceptance of western business concepts such as strategic planning and case analysis and the rapid growth of the Master of Business Administration (MBA) degree. One unexpected outcome is the rise of Russian women to management positions in Russian corporations.

Under the context of English as a Lingua Franca, this chapter explores the use of English prepositional verbs in writing by Chinese university students in comparison with that by their American and British counterparts. A written learner corpus compiled by the author and four native comparable corpora were used for both quantitative and qualitative analysis. The overall frequency of prepositional verbs in the five corpora shows that Chinese learners use fewer prepositional verbs in comparison with their American and British counterparts. Qualitative analysis, on the other hand, shows that Chinese learners are capable of producing an adequate number of prepositional verbs that stylistically appropriate. Moreover, differences are also found between the native novice writers in regard to both the frequency and the stylistic features of the prepositional verbs in the four native corpora. The results lead to critical discussion about the use of native corpora as the benchmark in learner corpus research.

Can globalization be socially inclusive through new 2.0 digital initiatives? This is the thought-provoking question we ask in this article, with a special focus on the Republic of Moldova. Part 1 begins with a reflection on the intersection between globalization, development studies and the current Moldovan context. Part 2 is devoted to the promising field of emergent tourism, and more particularly, tourism 2.0, a blossoming concept that we try to uncover. Part 3 presents a concrete application with the example of Moldova Tours 2.0, a digital initiative in the field of tourism 2.0 in the Republic of Moldova. Various aspects of this project are highlighted and analyzed.

Foreword

Globalization has many facets, institutional, economic, social, political, but like all phenomena it has no real meaning until experienced directly by human beings. The impact of informational technology on globalization is essentially personal. Not long ago I Skyped my daughter in New York from 33,000 feet on a flight from Narita to Dulles. Having a wireless device in my hand that enabled me to talk to someone at that distance during a flight and for no cost felt no more miraculous to me than making a phone call. Neither does talking to my phone while in my car to get driving directions. These things are not mindboggling; but that they are not is in and of itself mind-boggling. When I first moved to Japan 40 years ago, my communications with friends and family were pretty much limited to a blue flimsy Aerogramme once a week, information was confined to selected depositories, phones were confined to verbal communication, and watches told time. Now I have instantaneous communication all over the globe, at very low cost, and can access an almost infinite amount of information from any of seven different devices that I own including my phone, my watch, my music player and, soon, my glasses. Why is that not mind-boggling? We have become acclimated to, or numbed by, a stunning rate of innovation and technological change and, as with all shocks to the collective system, the ultimate ramifications of these changes have yet to be fully understood. But one can accurately say that almost all of what is happening in the world today is fundamentally affected by globalization manifested as information and communication technological development.

Globalization is an outcome of the processing and communication of information made possible by the information technology revolution. It has happened so rapidly that we have let it wash over us like a wave of bytes and pixels, avidly soaking up all the advances that make our lives so much easier and more difficult. And that is the rub; this change has been so extreme in such a short period of time that our reaction to it has created extreme positives and extreme negatives. Let me use another personal example from this flight from Narita to Dulles. Over 40 years I have made the east coast-to-Tokyo and return many times and for most of those flights there was 12-14 hours of mixed relaxation, boredom and contemplation. It was time out of time. Now the advent of laptop computers, electrical outlets and on-board Wi-Fi make the flight much less boring, and yet they also have ended the time out of time element as I, and my colleagues, expect that I will be doing my emails and working.

It is the incremental (albeit rapid) increase of information, communication and transportation technologies that have numbed the sense of wonder and change. As we all moved from Tandy 2000s to Macs or PCs to laptops, the ability to somehow connect them to an interface that could access everyone and everything that exists now, and has existed in the past, did not seem so strange. Similarly, we were all equally accepting the idea that less industrialized societies that struggled with landline communications technologies for decades could leapfrog those problems by individual use of cellular phones. The fundamental point is that from the early 1980s to the mid-1990s societies around the globe went from limited intercommunication and limited access to information to unlimited intercommunication and unlimited access to information; i.e., globalization

The Internet connects everyone in the world who has the mechanical capability to connect to it, but it does so in a very constrained and individual way. We as individuals sit in our coffee shops and offices and bedrooms with our ears to the small end of an infinite listening tube. That is globalized individuality.

The human mind cannot cope with an infinite amount of information so we rely on internal and external mediators and filters: our religion, our desires, our prejudices, our knowledge, our state. The mediators have an impact on two basic human social desires, the urge to standardize, the comfort of the similarity and homogeneousness, and the desire to be seen as an individual, to differentiate ourselves from others. New information technologies can create the same type of anomie that Durkhiem describes in the late 19th century as the result of leaving comfortable and known structures and being overwhelmed with the new. For those who experience this change as anomie, globalization allows us to bring the egalitarianism of standardization to a whole new level. One can use the Internet to discover the warmth of the same; Christians, Moslems and Jews like cute kitten videos. It allows us to experience direct communication with others worlds away geographically, culturally, religiously, and politically.

But one of the most fundamental aspects of increased communication between humans, especially cross-cultural and cross-national communication, that that we also discover things we don't like about them, or reconfirm preconceived prejudices we held against them. In this case ubiquitous means of communication for all people in the world can empower individual or group reactions against what is perceived as the all-powerful "other", whatever guise that may take. So while globalized communication through the Internet may bring the hope/fear of uniformity and homogenization, it also gives a voice to any individual or group who can put up a website. The Internet is uniformity shattered into a million shards.

In my opinion, this is what the *Handbook of Research on Individualism and Identity in the Globalized Digital Age* is all about. To return to my original points, globalization is meaningless unless understood as the ability of people around the globe to instantaneously communicate with one another while having access to an almost infinite amount of information. And no matter how old or savvy we are as individuals, as a species, and as a global society, we are still learning to cope with this new, and literally awesome, condition.

Do we use it to come together or break apart? Educate or obfuscate? Share health and wellness or control for profit? Enjoy or fear? Or all of the above? I don't have the answer but I do know that the more we know about this new and awesome condition of Globalization, the more we can manage it to enhance the positives and suppress the negatives.

Bruce Stronach
Temple University, Japan Campus, Japan

Bruce Stronach *is currently Dean of Temple University, Japan Campus (Tokyo, Japan). His other current functions include: Organization Member Director, Executive Board, JAFSA (Japan Network for International Education), and Member of the Tsukuba University Management Council. His previous functions include; President, Yokohama City University (Yokohama, Japan), Acting President, Becker College (MA: USA), Provost and Chief Operating Officer, Becker College Visiting Professor, Darden Graduate School of Business Administration, University of Virginia (VA, USA), Dean and Professor of Japanese Studies, Graduate School of International Relations, International University of Japan (Niigata, Japan), Associate Professor of Japanese Studies, Graduate School of International Relations, International University of Japan, Assistant Professor of Political Science, Merrimack College (MA, USA), Chairman, New England-Japan Seminar, Lecturer, International Center, Keio University (Tokyo, Japan), Chairman, School of International Studies, International Education Center (Tokyo, Japan), Visiting Scholar, Economics Observatory (Sangyo Kenkyujo), Keio University, Visiting Researcher, Institute for Communications Research, Keio University, Member, External Advisory Board for International Affairs, Osaka University, and Vice-Chairman of the Board of Trustees, Japan University Accreditation Association.*

Preface

This book is a product of demand, the demand for knowledge. This book traversed a lengthy passage that commenced from conception, progressed through deliberations, reflections, research, and was produced in its current form. Such a progression has been the motivation of scholars to actualize the realities of the 21st Century. The life of a 21st Century individual is foregrounded by a heightened desire for individual wellness as punctuated by the Age of Information Technology and Globalization.

This handbook encompasses all subject matters of relevance in the education and empowerment of information-oriented 21st Century individuals. The intention of this handbook is to illustrate precisely what is needed for individuals to ably participate in the current milieu of globalization.

There is indeed a growing global market for healthcare professionals, accompanied by scarcity in both developed and developing countries. Such growth on the one hand scarcity on the other, signifies some of the many ramifications of the intercultural integration of education, healthcare, production and consumption, and the like, all of which are subsumed under the term *globalization*. Healthcare services, which, in developed countries, are typically conducted by national governments, are now seen as being in dying need of reform. Among the many social, political, and administrative reasons are mismanagement, ineffective leadership, disequilibrium between demand and supply, and diminishing supply of professionals. Yet, dissimilarities between local and foreign ailments are somehow becoming extinct.

The current globalization phenomenon, which threatens localities with the prospect of losing their abilities to impose limits on the activities of 21st century individuals, cannot be completely ignored. For centuries, the lack of transport facilities confined ordinary people to their various geographic homelands. Nonetheless, such inadequacies failed to entirely prevent migration and cross-cultural trade in the ancient world. Push and pull factors, such as poverty, employment or unemployment opportunities, liberalization, and standardizations and the like, have always facilitated cross-cultural and international migration. Notwithstanding, Information Technology and modern transportation systems continue to now intensify global interaction.

This book is not for you, should you prefer asceticism or self-denial while living in the current global operational environment of knowledge that is generated by interdisciplinary researcher. All chapters in this book represent independent research by twenty authors.

OBJECTIVE

These pages brim with issues of concern to both senior investigators as well as becoming scholar-practitioners in academia, corporate enterprise, government, and other institutions interested in solutions-oriented questions. Handbook of Research on Individualism and Identity in the Globalized Digital Age is particularly appropriate for those who affirm the necessity of partaking in the current global climate of scholarship, characterized by the coactions of Educational, Information Technology, Sociocultural, and Wellness (healthcare) among the world's peoples.

As you go through the pages of this book, I expect that you will appreciate the works for the many scholars and that you will be in agreement with the suggestion that adequate education enables individuals to critically process information. I draw on Benjamin S. Bloom

in defining adequacy as, among other things, the ability to discern, explain, interpret, and extrapolate information through critical assessment.

THE 21ST CENTURY INDIVIDUAL

A 21st Century individual will need the ability to critically and independently contemplate, deliberate, innovate, conduct intercultural communication and collaborate, employ digital aptitude, be healthy, and be prepared to learn and lead. Call centers, which were the initial manifestations of a globalized workforce and workplace, were and still require intercultural awareness. The Internet exemplifies standardization, which facilitates globalization.

The syntax, context, and formats involved in online learning employ Internet protocols that are standardized to ensure global communication. Hence, Information Technology is integral to the 21st century global individual. Education engulfs a borderless worldwide workforce from India, the Philippines, and elsewhere to respond to outsourced customer inbound service calls across the globe to English-speaking customers.

The term globalization connotes wide-ranging differences and varieties of customs, laws, creeds, languages, and other values or institutions. Research presented in this book will show that inequalities in such areas as healthcare, education, access to technology, and other basic items, attest to the fact, although globalization tends to facilitate or promote the homogenization of hegemony, it is by no means universal.

Globalized Pitfalls

Different reasons account for shortages of healthcare professionals in both developed and developing countries. Such differences include healthcare educators and programs, working conditions and incentives, supply of medicine and equipment, patient to physician ratios, among others.

Contextual dissimilarities among cultures account for the sole source of confusion, often resulting in unsmiling ramifications, the least of which include trade disputes as promulgated by trade imbalances, disputes, individual exploitation, and some. Contrarily, distinctions between local and foreign ailments are quickly becoming extinct. The SARS outbreak of 2003, followed by the 2009 H1N1 influenza "A" pandemic, and the recent Ebola outbreak in West Africa are but a few examples of the globalization of local diseases.

Globalization fuels the need to reexamine of all that have heretofore remained locally moored in terms of education, personhood, wellness, age, and employment. Being foregrounded, globalization has besieged cultural institutions and such socio-cultural elements such as religion, spirituality through medical tourism.

Among the many ramifications of globalization is the growing global market for healthcare professionals, accompanied by scarcity in both developed and developing countries. The main cause of such shortages is migration of nurses, physicians, pharmacists, technologists, and other practitioners from poor to wealthy countries, while others migrate between economically affluent countries. Emigration has a negative impact on the ability of governments in less developed and developing countries to deliver vital services due to brain drain.

Developed countries are likewise affected by demographic changes as their aging populations contribute to increases in demand for services while supply of professionals dwindle.

OVERVIEW OF THE CONTENTS

The book is primarily concerned with the subject of education. It is comprised of five sections, covering five subjects: Information Technology, Education, Individualism, Wellness or Healthcare, and Globalization. It must be noted that the issues covered in most of the twenty chanters entwine with the subject matter of others chapters; the fulcrum being education. For example, discussion of Massive Open Online Courses (MOOCs) in chapter 2 will explore IT, Globalization, and Education, whereas such subjects constitute separate topics by different authors. This is symptomatic of the interdisciplinary nature of the subject matter of this book.

Information Technology

Chapters 1-6 deal with Information Technology in the context of education.

The term *education* is a loaded word with the complexities of culture, politics, and economics embedded. It has different meaning depending on the country or society to which it is applied. Defining aspects of education include differences based on gender, health, and recreation. For countries with over 90% literacy and numeracy, education connotes lifelong learning since almost adults have achieved basic education. This is different for less developed countries where lifelong learning includes adults that are yet to acquire basic education. The educational challenge for 21st century remains a standard that is wanting.

Massive Open Online Courses (MOOCs) now threaten the sustenance of traditional brick-and-mortar classrooms. Although such Internet-enabled educational enterprise offers free education to the global masses, ethical questions are raised respecting assessment, identity, anonymity, confidentiality, and cultural impact, all of which are absent in the pedagogy of MOOCs.

The contestants of MOOCs typically transcend a single epistemic learning culture. For example, validation of knowledge in the Western culture, is accompanied by the analysis and synthesis of given facts that a learner has acquired, whereas, Eastern-oriented Confucius cultures espouse the facts unaltered by critical analysis and synthesis. In such diverse learning environment, any benefits contained in the MOOC pedagogical practice could arguably be obnubilated by dissimilarities in the epistemologies of the targeted constituents.

Education

Chapters 7-11 deal with Education.

All chapters in this book deal with the subject of education as an aspect of the specific topics being explored. The age-old requirements for learning remain in place as long as humans remain with memory and other cognitive faculties. The two significant changes to the definition and meaning of education include Information Technology and globalization. Nonetheless, learners still need to remember what they have learned; they must also be motivated and engaged in critical thinking. For these reasons the subject of education permeates all of the chapters in this book.

Challenges for specialized educational programs are foregrounded by the emergence and transcendence of multiple cultural epistemologies as facilitated by several elements, including globalization, the Internet, and a new lingua franca. The reader's attention is drawn to the need to overcome and harmonize global research methodologies.

The educational challenge for the 21st century individual is the means by which educational programs, pedagogic, and materials are designed, developed and delivered to meet and transcend multiple cultural epistemologies in a globalized market place.

Individualism

Chapters 12-14 deal with Individualism

Although a definitional debate over such concepts as personhood, birth, death, wellness and other remain unabated, intercultural communication has come into prominence in the worldwide deportment of globalization.

In birth, most civilizations, with some dissent, believe that humans come into being at conception. For some religions, any tempering with stem cells that lead to their destruction is tantamount to a pre-natal sin of homicide. Based on the Gregorian calendar of 28-31 days, the rest of the world seems to concur that pregnancies last for an average duration of forty weeks *full-term* gestation, which is approximately nine months. Infants born less than 37 weeks gestation are *pre-term*; those born over 42 weeks gestation are *post-term*. Conversely, using the traditional lunar calendar months of precise 28 days, Japanese women are conceived for ten months rather than the nine months as referenced by the rest of the world. Beyond these distinctions lie the tasks awaiting those individuals that are born.

While the end of life results to death, a precise definition or meaning of death is also subject to debate according to dissimilar cultures and customs. Does a person cease to be a human being when the heart stops pumping blood or when the brain stops functioning? Consequences for organs donation and transplantation are invoked in the brain vs. cardiac death debate. The unity of humanity requires a global conception of wellness. The current confusion, disagreement and adoption of anecdotal and/or socio-cultural interpretations associated with personhood promote distinctiveness.

Unlike Eastern philosophy, which posits the unity or inseparability of the body and mind, Western philosophy espouses a Cartesian dualism of mind and body as constituents of an individual. Eastern oriented Buddhism and Confucianism espouse holistic interconnectedness, interdependence, and harmonious symmetry between *yin*–female, passive, negative, and *yang*–positive, active, male.

The technology that effectuates lifelong learning will have to accommodate people living longer, particularly those in Europe, Asia and the United States where most centenarians are deemed to reside. Innovative wellness or healthcare management will be needed in all societies, clearly those with growing numbers of centenarians, such as Japan. Although longevity is said to be indicative of good health, improvements in the cognitive capacity of the elderly will become imperative given the reality of age-related defects as typified by processing constraints–restrictions of declarative, procedural, and strategic knowledge.

Ageing and Wellness

Wellness is undergoing renewed conceptualizations as life expectancy and old age are redefined. Wellness issues relating to centenarian are expected to occupy center stage in the 21st century. Because the elderly is specifically susceptible to aches, pain, and other incurable illness such as cancer, centenarians of the 21st century will require specific healthcare or wellness products and services. Given that illness inhabits learning, information about wellness is thus an aspect of an educated individual in the 21st century.

Globalization

Chapters 15-18 deal with Globalization.

Topics on globalization in this book relate to education, healthcare, and information technology. As such, readers should look elsewhere for issues dealing with the environment and it degradation, trade, and other business matters.

With succulent enticements of economic growth and development, often with clear evidence of cultural and environmental degradation and other ills, all countries, including the developed, developing, and the less developed, have shown their failure to ably respond to questions regarding education, health, and other aspects that contribute the life in a globalized and worldwide interconnected world.

Globalization, which began in the nineteenth century, is a phenomenon with nebulous definitions, often imbued with the proclivity of luring reluctant national governments into contracts that invoke interdependencies with ramifications that remain clearly misconceived by some nations or peoples. Nonetheless, the significance of the ubiquitous soi-disant globalization phenomenon and its effects on the lives of all individuals living in the 21st Century cannot be overestimated.

Globalization is a lose-win phenomenon for poorer economies and individuals. Changes instituted by this globalization within North America and Europe were socioeconomic and psychosocial. There were corporate downsizing or rightsizing—metaphors for redundancies or layoffs. Globalization facilitated mergers; bankruptcies, outsourcing, temporary employment; pension defaults; extensive transfer or relocation of capital and technology to foreign countries; medical tourism, and other aftereffects.

Wellness and Healthcare

Chapters 19-22 deal with Wellness and Healthcare.

These pages contain research that investigates problems with healthcare, specifically those relating to access, cost, quality, and availability. The 21st Century challenge is the global harmonization of wellness and healthcare services. Unlike tangible products that are transferred across geographic regions, wellness involves such issues as parents' confidentiality, dissimilarities in the meaning of wellness, education, and biomedical ethics, among others.

While individual existence is acknowledged, agreement of a standard definition and meaning of wellness remains elusive. Thus, a global approach to healthcare is desired given the current scheme of things. To ensure universal treatment and the wellness of individuals, empirical data should be preferred to the anecdotal accounts that has so far exist based on an individual country and epistemologies.

Bovine Spongiform Encepholopathy (BSE), commonly known as Mad Cow Disease, is a disease that causes a degeneration of the brain. The disease originally affected cows in the United Kingdom (UK) in 1986. However, the effect and potential dangers of the infectious and progressive neurological disease on humans quickly became a matter of global concern. Similar global concerns came about in 2015, regarding the SARS (Severe Acute Respiratory Syndrome) outbreak of 2003 in China Canada, South Korea. Other local diseases that sparked global fears and concerns were the H1N1 influenza pandemic in 2009 and the recent Ebola outbreak of 2014 in West Africa.

An increasing trend toward the internationalization of healthcare is manifested by *medical tourism*. There is a need to entertain the harmonization of the multiplicity of educational programs, pedagogic practices, and material diversities that currently pervade sociocultural institutions here and there, if meaningful intercultural communication and cooperation are to be attained. Curriculum design, development and delivery need to converge. The 21st Century individual needs to transcend multiple cultural epistemologies in order to achieve global proficiency.

ACKNOWLEDGMENT

The generosity of all members of the Editorial Advisory Board (EAB) and Reviewers is hereby acknowledged. Special thanks to those EAB members who work professionally outside of the academy and were still willing and able to spare their valuable time in ensuring the successful production of a book that contributes to humanity. Because of their plenteous generosity readers, researchers, and other professionals can now be informed about issues on Individualism and Identity in the Globalized Digital Age.

We are also grateful to IGI Global for its continuous attention to quality research in order to meet the needs and demands of the academic and professional communities. Despite a burgeoning deployment of digital or Online media, coupled with the challenges posed by e-books, IGI Global has incessantly responded to the needs of individuals, especially those that have yet to gain access to the Internet and telecommunication technologies, by providing books in both printed and digital formats. Thus, making it possible for almost all individuals to read this book.

F. Sigmund Topor
Keio University, Japan

Section 1
Information Technology

Chapter 1

A Comparison of Saudi and United States Faculty Use of Information and Communication Technology Tools

Art Bangert
Montana State University, USA

Mabark Fayaz Alshahri
Imam Mohammed Ibn Saud Islamic University, Saudi Arabia

ABSTRACT

Research related to differences in how Saudi and US faculty use Information and Technology Communication (ICT) tools is discussed as well as their perceptions of ICT applications and ICT use. Saudi faculty from six universities in KSA and US faculty from five US universities completed a questionnaire designed to identify the ICT tools most frequently used and their perceptions toward the use of these tools. In addition, a path analysis based on Davis's (1993) Technology Acceptance Model was conducted to investigate the relationships between faculty attitudes toward ICT applications and actual ICT use. Findings from this study suggest that both Saudi faculty social media most often while US faculty use productivity tools more often. Both Saudi and US faculty and would benefit from training in the use of these applications for use within a Learning Management System.

INTRODUCTION

A diverse range of new and existing Information and Communication Technology tools now support collaborative interactions that were limited by time and space. In particular, these ICT tools have been integrated into schools and universities in efforts to support and enhance instruction. However, educational organizations are struggling to overcome the difficulty of effectively utilizing appropriate tech-

DOI: 10.4018/978-1-5225-0522-8.ch001

nologies that are designed to support instruction (Daher, 2014). According to Daher (2014), "teachers and professors need to adapt in order to better connect with their students and more effectively lead their classes" (p. 42). Access to technologies that support the use of audio, video, web conferencing, and the Internet are providing many learning opportunities that were not available to students in the past. The vast amount of information accessible with a simple mouse click allows teachers and students to access and experience information from countless resources.

While the use of Information and Communication Technologies such as online learning management systems and social media are being used internationally to support learning, there are few ICT supported learning resources available to students in Saudi universities. According to Al-Shawi and Al-Wabil (2013),

The widespread adoption of Internet applications in Saudi Arabia started in the late 1990s. Universities were among the first adopters of the technology and years later the Internet witnessed an unparalleled spread across campuses. Despite increased Internet connectivity in Saudi Arabian higher education institutions, there is little empirical research investigating the factors associated with the use of the Internet by faculty in teaching, research, and communication. (p. 81)

It is clear that the United States, as well as in other developed countries, have well-established ICT systems that support university degree programs available to most postsecondary students (Anderson, 2008). The use of ICT tools to support online coursework provides numerous benefits for students, including the convenience of accessing the courses at any time and place to engage with their instructor and other learners, both asynchronously and synchronously. In addition, ICT systems support a more meaningful learning environment by providing students with opportunities to gain knowledge and skills situated within the context of their work or other personalized environments. For instructors, tutoring can be done at any time, materials can be updated immediately for learner access, and learning activities can be more customizable based on individual needs.

The Saudi Ministry of Higher Education (MHE) has "encouraged the use of information technology (IT) for teaching and learning among its faculties and students" and the Ministry is continuously developing projects to "provide adequate IT infrastructure as well as content development for higher education students" (Alebaikan & Troudi, 2010, p. 49). The Ministry is striving to integrate web-based and traditional instruction across Saudi universities. Despite support from the MHE, and the fact that there are many new technologies available to support learning, there are few studies that have investigated how university faculty in developing and developed countries use ICT tools such as learning management systems, social media technologies, and other productivity software to support learning in higher education.

This chapter reports on results of a descriptive study conducted by the authors to identify the differences and similarities in the types of Information and Communication Technology tools used by university faculty in the United States and Saudi Arabia to support learning. In addition, results investigating the relationships between actual use of ICT tools and faculty attitudes toward their use will also be discussed. Davis's Technology Acceptance Model (1993) was used as the model for investigating these relationships.

Although a developing country technologically, Saudi Arabia has the resources to provide new technologies, including interactive classroom management systems and social media, which can enhance their educational systems at both the K-12 and university level. However, there are still barriers to online learning that puts Saudi postsecondary students at a disadvantage (Al Mulhem, 2014). These barriers likely contribute to the significant gap between educational opportunities in Saudi Arabia and the United States. The demand for higher education and cultural differences contribute significantly to the differences in access to educational opportunities (Hamdan, 2014).

The Kingdom of Saudi Arabia's (KSA) Ministry of Higher Education (MHE) was "established in 1975 to implement the Kingdom's higher education policy in the rapidly expanding sphere of postsecondary education. Prior to 1975, higher education was supervised by the Ministry of Education (MoE) along with K-12 schools (Al-Maliki, 2013). Despite the 40-year existence of the MHE, the capacity of universities and colleges in Saudi Arabia cannot accommodate the rapid growth of students applying for college education (Alebaikan & Troudi, 2010). However, Saudi Arabia does have the resources to provide new technologies, including interactive course room management systems and social media, which can enhance their educational systems at both the K-12 and university level. Utilization of existing resources and the adoption of such technologies would provide increased learning opportunities for Saudi citizens who reside in remote and isolated areas, and would accommodate the educational needs of a population of over 29 million (29,000,000) in a country with only 25 universities. Currently, individuals from more remote areas must move to larger cities to earn degrees in higher education (Saudi Ministry of Higher Education, n.d.). The significant gap between KSA and USA in education is due to the differences between the population and the number of students. According to Saudi National Center for Education statistics, the number of U.S. students in higher education in 2011 was 21.0 million and the number of U.S. universities was 2,680.

Due to the increase in the number of Saudi students in higher education, the use of technology is very important to provide opportunities for all students. According to the Saudi Higher Education Statistic Center, in 2013 the number of students in higher education reached 1,932,208 students (www.mohe. gov.sa/ar/default.aspx). Also, the Saudi government struggles to improve education by sending many students to many countries through the Custodian of the Two Holy Mosques Program Foreign Scholarship. Since the program's inception in 2005, the number of scholarships for Saudis jumped from 5,000 scholarships to the United States to more than 150,000 student scholarships dispersed over more than 30 countries in 2014 (Saudi Ministry of Higher Education, n.d.).

BACKGROUND

Information and Communication Technology (ICT) tools have the potential to solve complex instructional issues related to interacting with students and delivering effective instruction. The Saudi government is central for determining teachers' use of ICT tools in their K-12 schools and in higher education. The Ministry of Education, the Ministry of Higher Education, and the General Organization for Technical Education and Vocational Training jointly manage the Saudi educational system (Almalki & Williams, 2012). However, collectively these governmental bodies have been slow to recognize the potential of online learning and the use of other electronic tools to increase educational access. On the other hand, the American educational and cultural systems operate in an entirely different fashion. In the United States, education is highly decentralized and instructional delivery is not controlled by the federal government, whereas in Saudi Arabia, the K-12 and higher education systems are overseen by the Saudi government. Although the use of online learning platforms and other ICT tools to deliver instruction is not regulated by the United States government or state governments, universities are still required to meet criteria set forth by regional and national accrediting bodies.

Most countries see ICT tools as a gateway for raising educational standards (Noor-Ul-Amin, 2013). Today both developed and developing countries not only recognize the value of ICT tools for improving education but also as important to their economic development. Developed countries such as the United

States spend more than 13 billion dollars annually in educational technology in public schools (Nagel, 2014), while Australia spends more than eight billion dollars annually (Lane, 2012). The sparse use of ICT tools instructionally in Saudi colleges and universities may originate with the strategies that the Saudi Ministry of Education uses to manage ICT use in Saudi Arabia's K-12 schools. Hew and Brush (2007) identified the main barriers to the use of ICT in K-12 schools as (a) lack of resources, (b) institutional factors, (c) subject culture, (d) attitudes and beliefs, and (e) knowledge and skills.

In terms of resources, the Saudi government has made huge investments with a view to developing public education. For example, in 2007 the Saudi government invested almost three billion dollars in reforming and improving education using modern technologies (Albugami & Ahmed, 2015). However, in spite of this massive spending and governmental support, Saudi Arabia still lags behind other countries in their use of ICT to support learning in K-12 environments (Ageel, 2011). Studies related to ICT use in Saudi schools revealed that the Saudi government, in addition to financial support, needs to develop an effective strategy for developing K-12 ICT infrastructure and training (Oyaid, 2009; Almalki & Williams, 2012; Al-Harbi, 2014).

Research conducted by Alwani and Soomro (2010), found evidence to support lack of resources from the Saudi Ministry of Education to support the use of ICT for instructional purposes. Their study of 284 science teachers from Yanbu Kingdom found their schools had no funds to purchase hardware or, more importantly, no specific budget to support ICT infrastructure. In another study, Al-Oteawi (2002) found most teachers and administrators who responded to his study reported that there is no planning for current technology in schools. They added that ICT cannot be effectively integrated without the development of a clear ICT policy and plan to facilitate its implementation into education. One administrator commented that "if there is no plan, it is difficult to utilise [*sic*]information technology in schools" (Al-Oteawi, 2002, p. 246).

In addition to financial support, institutional factors such as support from school leaders has been identified as a determinant to the use of ICT in Saudi schools. For example, Al-Harbi (2014) and Ghamrawi (2013) found that school leaders must provide adequate support and encouragement to teachers in order to create an instructional environment that motivates teachers to experiment with ICT in their classrooms. Their conclusions are supported by Levin and Wadmany's (2005) research which suggests that school leaders with negative attitudes toward ICT use will have a negative influence on teachers' attitudes and beliefs toward ICT use. For example, Bingimlas (2010) investigated the use of ICT supported learning practices by Saudi primary school science teachers. A major outcome of his study was that a majority of teachers (n = 241) participating in the study felt their principal's negative attitudes toward ICT limited their use of ICT supported instructional practices. For example, Saudi teachers commented that they were prevented from using ICT devices because principals were afraid teachers and students would lose or break the devices. One principal felt the use of ICT devices for laboratory activities would cause confusion and waste instructional time.

The limitation of Internet access in Saudi schools may be attributed to religious or cultural beliefs (Barzilai-Nahon & Barzilai, 2005). Burkhart and Older (2003) reported that more than 2,000 websites containing pornography or information on faiths other than Islam have been restricted by Saudi authorities. Rather than portray the Internet as a threat to cultural and religious beliefs by severely limiting its use, solutions such as the use of the latest internet security could be installed on school computers to monitor and filter student Internet use.

Islam dominates all aspects of life, including culture and education in Saudi Arabia (Robertson & Al-Zahrani, 2012). Islamic religious education constitutes a cultural component by which individuals must exist. Religious socialization restricts any social interactions between men and women in Saudi Arabia. The development and use of ICT infrastructure in Saudi public schools is no exception. For example, males and females attend separate high schools and universities. There is a large body of research that suggests learning may be dependent on gender (Banks-Wallace, 2000Joiner et al., 2011Yau & Cheng, 2012; Weil, 2008, Many Saudi universities lack adequate numbers of female faculty, leaving most academic majors to be taught by men. The only institutions of higher education established exclusively for women are located in the capital city of Riyadh and Jeddah. These institutions create educational opportunities for urban women while ignoring those women in rural areas (Alhareth, McBride, Prior, Leigh & Flick, 2013). The current gender-divided system, as well as the lack of female professors, limits educational opportunities for women and reduces opportunities for the diverse classroom interactions that typically occur in gender-neutral cultures such as the Unites States and other countries, thus reducing the effectiveness of instruction (Curseu & Pluut, 2013).

Information and Communication Technology tools such as those that are used with learning management systems would offer a solution for delivering education outside of the major cities and allow a greater number of female students to interact with the smaller number of Saudi female faculty. The use of ICT tools along with learning managements systems by Saudi faculty may serve to reduce issues related to female university students' anxiety related to interacting with males outside of their immediate family and reduce the need to travel or relocate to urban centers to attend classes.

The main reason for widespread use of Information and Communication Technologies in the United States, such as those used for online learning, is due to the relative ease with which teachers and students are able to access online courses and other online learning resources. As compared to the traditional classroom model, online courses are not dependent on time and space. Students can study asynchronously on their own or cooperatively by accessing content when it is convenient and appropriate to their learning. Use of electronic instruction has became widespread in U.S. universities with estimates as high as seven million students enrolled in at least one online course during the 2014 academic year (Allen & Seaman, 2015) . That marks an increase of 560,000 students over the number reported the previous year, or 31% of all higher education students take at least one course online during their time as a student.

Although U.S. faculty may perceive online courses as taking considerably more time to teach, they understand the benefits of online instruction. A study conducted by Hilsop and Ellis (2004) found that almost all (99%) of faculty valued flexible access to courses for students and faculty. United States faculty overwhelmingly agreed that it is important for them to have the flexibility to offer courses online that would provide educational opportunities for underserved student populations. Importantly, Hislop and Ellis's study further indicated that U.S. faculty felt that students were actively involved in learning when enrolled in online coursework (95%), that the technology they use is reliable (93%), and that they looked forward to teaching their next online course (93%).

Although the use of ICT tools by U.S. universities has increased dramatically over the past few years, U.S. faculty still fear that abandoning traditional, face-to-face settings will disrupt student involvement and create a less personal and accessible environment for students (Tanner, Noser, & Tataro, 2009). Wasilik and Bollinger (2009) found that technology-related problems, lack of face-to-face contact with students, and limited student involvement in the online environment are three concerns that faculty have about online teaching. In addition, their study found that participants were also concerned about students cheating and limited interaction with their colleagues. While these fears must be taken into consideration, it is equally important to acknowledge the ubiquitous use of ICT tools by students. More than ever, students in the United States have access to smartphones, laptops, tablets, and computers. Professors have the choice to either ignore the new technologies that students are familiar with or find meaningful ways to embrace these technologies to support their instruction by increasing student engagement.

United States faculty are aware of the benefits and ubiquity of social media among the general population. Moran, Seaman, and Tinti-Kane (2011), for example, note that over 90% of faculty report they are familiar with social media applications such as Myspace, Facebook, Twitter, YouTube, and blogs. Roblyer, McDaniel, Webb, Herman and Witty (2010) suggest that faculty who see teaching as establishing a relationship with students may view social media technologies as an efficient or even a business-like way to interact with students to establish relationships. Their research further indicates that faculty and students do not differ in the frequency with which they check their social media applications for messages. This finding suggests that although some faculty may bemoan the use of technology in their classrooms, they remain equally as connected to their social media accounts as their students.

Using social media applications to promote greater faculty-student interactions seems like an obvious next step to further support student learning. Moran et al. (2011) report that while more than 80% of faculty is aware of common social media applications such as Twitter and Facebook, less than half of faculty report familiarity with applications such as "SlideShare", a presentation-sharing site. While it is encouraging that faculty are becoming more aware of social media applications, their awareness of other ICT tools that would benefit instruction is still limited.

Roblyer et al. (2010) assert that the adoption of technology in education has been much slower in Saudi Arabia than in the United States. As the adoption of ICT tools and other learning technologies increases in the U.S., it remains stagnant or slow in Saudi Arabia, creating a gap in educational opportunities. Aljabre (2012) describes this as "the digital divide," stating, "[T[he digital divide continues to haunt the world on a global level, separating the developing from the developed and on the national level dividing the haves from the have nots" (p. 133). For Saudi Arabia, the digital divide is exaggerated because of extremely remote areas with limited internet access, cultural barriers related to gender interactions, and a growing number of students in urban centers that universities are unable to adequately accommodate.

The sparse use of ICT tools by Saudi faculty is due in large part to a lack of resources and access for students. Although access to the Internet by the Saudi public has increased dramatically since 1999, the use of technologies by faculty and students for instruction and communication has decreased (Alebaikan & Troudi, 2010). However, 84% of Saudi universities have purchased or acquired some type of learning management system. This finding suggests that the trend toward the use of online learning platforms by Saudi universities should increase over the next decade. Early investigations of Saudi faculty's use of the Internet as a resource suggest that faculty members are in the early stages of adoption . However, Internet use by Saudi faculty is dependent on academic major and expertise. For example, research by Al-Shawi and Al-Wabil (2013) suggests that those working in technologically focused majors spent more time using electronic tools, while other majors spent less time with these tools.

In addition to slow adoption of Internet use as a way to communicate, Saudi Arabia faces other challenges around the use of technology for communication and instruction. Alhareth et al. (2013 identified cultural beliefs and the nature of the education system as a major barrier to the use of ICT tools for e-learning in Saudi Arabia. One major feature of this society is the dichotomy that exists between the adoption of modern technology and the preservation of beliefs and religious values. The importance of preserving traditional religious values is a distinction that clearly differentiates Internet use in Saudi Arabia versus the United States. By 2002, 59% of people in the U.S. were using the Internet as compared to only 38.1% of Saudi citizens (Altawil, 2012). Even among students in Saudi Arabia, a division exists around the perceived benefits that online learning would have for Saudi Arabians. For example, 44.3%

of Saudi students felt that it would not be difficult to offer online learning in Saudi universities while 37.8% felt it would be very difficult for Saudi universities to offer online courses (Altawil, 2012).

In the last few years Saudi Arabia has been working toward improving higher education by incorporating more technology. For example, in 2011 the Ministry of Education established the Electronic University that exclusively uses electronic tools, such as the Blackboard software, to teach and communicate with students ("About the Saudi Electronic University," n.d.). Creation of this online university is an effort by the Ministry of Education to work toward greater acceptance and adoption of electronic learning management systems as a means of improving classroom environments, curriculum, and education as a whole. However, a major limitation and barrier to widespread acceptance of electronic tools lies in the attitudes of professors toward the value of these systems for supporting instruction.

Research studies indicate a clear relationship between use of technology and instructor attitudes. Al-Kahtani, Ryan, and Jefferson (2006) investigated female Saudi faculty attitudes toward the use of electronic tools like the Internet for instruction. His study found that although the majority of the female instructors have positive attitudes toward the Internet, their use of the Internet for instruction is likely to be impacted by the subject area they teach. For example, the majority of the Saudi female science faculty perceived the Internet positively. However, the relationship was not entirely straightforward. While all faculty reported positive attitudes toward the use of the Internet, those who did not use the Internet also reported positive attitudes. For Saudi faculty teaching in religious studies, not surprisingly, those who do not use the Internet have clearly negative attitudes toward Internet use; however, those faculty who use the Internet have mixed perceptions with some indicating positive perceptions of the Internet while others perceive its use negatively. These perceptions clearly contribute to the divide that exists between faculty who teach different content and also between male and female Saudi faculty.

Research by Al Kahtani et al. (2006) further found that female faculty who have mixed perceptions about the benefits of using the Internet were influenced by websites that contain offensive or inappropriate material. While there are obvious benefits for religion classes, such as looking at various translations of a text or exploring the history of religion and the various leaders and influences, these female Saudi faculty remain skeptical. The use of the Internet for instruction in this case is clearly based on unique individual attitudes influenced by the discipline they teach. Nevertheless, there are opportunities within all subjects to incorporate electronic tools to enhance greater communication between students and faculty and to support instruction.

It has been suggested that Saudi faculty members lack the experience using ICT tools for instruction because they do not have adequate training. Al-Jarf (2007) for example, reported that interviews with Saudi university vice-presidents, college deans, vice deans, and department heads indicated that Saudi faculty who received training in the use of ICT tools were more likely to engage in online instruction as compared to those faculty not trained. However, Al-Shawi and Al-Wabil (2013) suggest that professors are simply unaware of many of the tools available, and instead continue using those programs already comfortable to them—including e-mail and basic Microsoft Office applications.

In addition to lack of training, Saudi primary school teachers and higher education faculty cite a lack of time to integrate ICT tools into their teaching. For example, Alwani & Soomro (2010) found that Saudi primary school teachers' lack of time to prepare for instruction using ICT tools was just as problematic as lack of training when considering the use of ICT to support instruction. A study by Al Kahtani et al. (2006) found that 53% of female Saudi faculty interviewed cited lack of release time as a major consideration that strongly influenced their decisions about using online instruction. Taking time to train and understand new concepts and tools is difficult for Saudi K-12 teachers and university professors who are often already overwhelmed by the amount of work they have. In terms of universities, one solution might be to provide training during the summer months when many Saudi professors teach less and have more time to learn the instructional advantages of using ICT tools. Continued training of Saudi preservice teachers in the use of ICT will provide the confidence they need to successfully use ICT to support instruction and to overcome barriers that untrained teachers may not be able to overcome (Robertson & Al-Zahrani, 2012).

A final barrier for Saudi faculty and K-12 teachers alike is a lack of technical support (Al-Jarf, 2007). Research by Al-Jarf (2007) found the technological infrastructure at Saudi universities could not accommodate all the ICT needs of students and faculty. Many departments do not have computer labs, and when they are available, they are not equipped with sufficient numbers of computers, software, or Internet connections. Computers are often in disrepair and the network is very slow due to bandwidth limitations. A combination of slow network speeds and slow or limited response to technical problems, in addition to a lack of resources, creates a sense of uncertainty that may cause Saudi faculty to shy away from the use of the Internet and other associated technologies to enhance their instruction.

While educational facilities grow, expand, and develop across Saudi Arabia, technology continues to lag behind. Al Shaer (2007) writes,

Achieving excellence in the teaching and learning processes requires the use of information and communication technology (ICT) inside and outside the school environment, making it a fundamental element in the performance of the school, its administrative and teaching staff, and students. (p. 7)

Without proper support, whether for resources within educational environments or people with adequate knowledge to train professors and students to use technology for learning, the problems will only be exacerbated rather than solved. The potential benefits of technology are numerous, but limited acceptance and access prevent Saudi professors, faculty, and students from experiencing these advantages.

A COMPARISON OF SAUDI AND U.S. FACULTY USE OF ICT TOOLS

Research Design and Research Questions

A cross-sectional survey design was used to collect data characterizing Saudi and United States faculty use of Information and Communication Technology tools. In addition, faculty from both countries were asked to answer questions related to their attitudes toward the use of ICT tools. The relationships between actual ICT tool use and attitudes toward ICT tool use were explored for both Saudi and U.S. faculty using path analysis. The research questions posed for this study were:

a.   What Information and Communication Technology tools do Saudi and United States faculty indicate that they use most frequently for communicating with students and for instruction?

b.   How many hours per week do Saudi and United States faculty estimate they use ICT tools to communicate with their students and for instruction?

c.   How do Saudi and United States faculty perceptions of ease of use, perceived value, attitude toward the use of Information and Communication Technology and actual ICT use relate to one another?

Table 1. Universities of Saudi and United States Faculty

Saudi Universities	United States Universities
King Saud University	Minot State University
King Khalid University	Montana State University
Imam Muhammad Ibn Saud University	Stanford University
Umm Al-qura University	University of Michigan
Taibah University	Washington State University
	Wayne State University

Participant Characteristics

A convenience sample of Education faculty from five Saudi universities and six universities from the United States completed a questionnaire designed to gather perceptions of their use of electronic tools for communication with students and instruction. The questionnaire was completed by 305 Saudi faculty and 268 United States faculty. The 11 institutions representing the 573 faculty participants are reported in Table 1.

Faculty experience using ICT tools for both Saudi and U.S. faculty is reported in Table 2. Sixty five percent of U.S. faculty taught all or part of a course online as compared to only 26% of Saudi faculty. In addition, nearly 60% of Saudi faculty reported never teaching an online course as compared to only 13% of U.S. faculty. The most frequently reported learning management systems used by Saudi faculty were Blackboard (82%) followed by Moodle (10%). Similarly, the United States faculty participants reported using the learning management system Blackboard (50%) most frequently followed by Moodle (34%) and Desire2Learn (28%).

Table 2. Saudi and United States Faculty Experience using Electronic Tools

	Saudi Arabia		United States	
	f	%	*f*	%
Taught Part or All of an Online Course				
Yes	76	26%	169	65%
No	217	74%	90	35%
Learning Management System Use				
Desire-to-Learn	16	6%	73	28%
Blackboard	85	29%	128	50%
Moodle	28	10%	89	34%
Other	27	9%	43	17%
Never Used	165	57%	33	13%

Instrument

The questionnaire used for this research was based on the work of Payette and Verreault (2007). In addition, questions related to faculty's perception of the ease of use, value, and attitude toward the use of electronic tools was based on the work of Ajjan and Hartstone (2008) and Tabata and Johnsrud (2008). The first part of the questionnaire asked respondents to indicate their gender, age, experience teaching, and their experience with electronic tools used for communicating with students and teaching. The second section consisted of multiple choice that asked faculty to rate how often they use electronic tools for communication and teaching using the descriptors: 1 = Never, 2 = Seldom, 3 = Sometimes, 4 = Often, and 5 = Always. In addition, faculty were asked to estimate the hours they used electronic tools per week for communication and teaching. The final part of the questionnaire consisted of questions designed to elicit faculty perceptions of value, ease of use, and attitudes toward the use of ICT tools. In addition to the fixed response questions, three open-ended questions were posed to capture more in-depth descriptions of faculty's perceptions related to their use of electronic tools for connecting with students and teaching.

The content and construct validity of the questionnaire was established by having an expert panel review the items to further enhance construct validity (American Educational Research Association, 2014; DeVillis, 2011). Three professors of educational technology were asked to review items to evaluate their relevancy, clarity, and conciseness (DeVillis, 2011). The survey was piloted with a small group of Saudi and United States faculty to gather additional feedback about the clarity and relevance of the items. In addition to the expert panel review and pilot study, results for both the Saudi and United States faculty responses to the items written to measure perceptions of ease of use, usefulness, and attitude were factor analyzed using principal components analysis.

Results

Saudi and U.S. Faculty ICT Tool Use

Both Saudi and United States faculty were asked to choose descriptors representing the frequency with which they used 18 different Information and Communication Technology (ICT) tools using the following Likert scale: 1 = "Never" (Not at all), 2 = "Rarely" (Less than weekly), 3 = "Sometimes" (Multiple times per week but not daily), and 4 = "All of the Time" (Daily). Table 3 reports the means and standard deviations for the ICT tools rated by Saudi and United States faculty. Results show that for Saudi faculty the most often used ICT tools were E-mail (M = 4.14, SD = 1.33) and Word Processing (M = 4.14, SD = 1.17) followed by Social Media Applications (M = 3.39, SD = 1.62). United States faculty also rated E-mail (M = 4.29, SD = .96) and Word Processing Tools as the most frequently used ICT tools followed by Presentation Tools (M = 3.87, SD = 1.09). Results from independent samples *t*-tests (α = .05) found that the largest discrepancy between Saudi and United States faculty was in social media applications where Saudi Faculty indicated they used social media applications significantly more often than United States faculty. In addition, Saudi faculty reported that they used Google Documents, Photos, and Website links significantly more often than United States faculty. However, United States faculty indicated their use of podcasts and text documents significantly more often than Saudi faculty.

Saudi and U.S. faculty were also asked to estimate the number of actual hours they used four broad categories of ICT tools for communication with students and instruction. Descriptive statistics for the estimated hours as well as independent samples t-tests were used to compare Saudi and United States

Table 3. Means and Standard Deviations for Frequency of ICT Use for Saudi and Unites States Faculty

ICT Application	Saudi Faculty			United States Faculty			
	n	M	SD	n	M	SD	P
Email	277	4.14	1.33	250	4.28	.96	.148
Social Media	274	3.39	1.62	248	1.93	1.23	.001*
Video Conferencing	289	2.18	1.26	252	2.38	1.18	.057
Word Processing	290	4.14	1.11	251	4.01	1.08	.227
Spreadsheets	290	3.03	1.41	250	3.00	1.38	.991
Presentations (e.g. PowerPoint)	288	3.92	1.21	250	3.86	1.09	.702
Videos	284	3.24	1.45	252	3.07	1.17	.188
Podcasts	288	1.68	1.09	250	1.90	1.22	.030*
Screencasts	288	2.04	1.30	251	1.89	1.32	.168
Photos	282	3.47	1.43	253	2.92	1.32	.000*
Google Documents	280	2.79	1.50	248	2.47	1.29	.021
Portable Document Files	287	3.70	1.41	248	3.62	1.19	.600
Instructor Created Webpages	288	1.69	1.13	250	1.89	1.22	.050
Webinars	285	1.77	1.01	2552	1.71	1.19	.565
Text Documents	282	2.65	1.45	250	2.99	1.44	.002*
Website links	290	2.77	1.45	251	3.39	1.22	.000*
Concept Maps	288	2.10	1.28	251	1.93	1.21	.172
Blogs	289	1.90	1.21	251	1.87	1.11	.599

faculty's estimated weekly use of ICT applications for communicating with students and instruction. Results reported in Table 4 show that Saudi faculty on average used social media for instruction (M = 17.37, SD = 28.24) and e-mail for communication (M=16.74, SD = 25.86) more hours per week than the other categories of ICT tools. However, e-mail for instruction (M = 16.36, SD = 26.79) and the use of social media tools for communication (M = 15.78, SD = 25.97) were found to be used less often per week but more hours per week than video or audio ICT tools. U.S. faculty reported using social media applications for communication (M = 14.75, SD = 27.58) and instruction (M = 14.57, SD = 28.50) as well as e-mail for communication (M = 14.14, SD = 19.02) more hours per week than the other ICT tools but less hours per week than Saudi faculty. The only significant finding from independent sample t-tests ($\alpha = .05$) was for the comparison of the use of email for instruction. Saudi faculty indicated they used email on average significantly more hours per week than United States faculty.

Attitude Toward ICT Tool Use

A principal component analysis of Saudi responses to the questionnaire found that the ICT attitude items loaded on similar constructs they were written to measure. The principal components analysis using oblique rotation methods that allowed factors to correlate yielded four interpretable factors. The first interpreted as "Perceived Value" captured three of four perceived value items and one attitude item. The second factor was comprised of two attitude items and one item written to tap ease of electronic tool

Table 4. Means and Standard Deviations for Hours of Actual ICT Use for Saudi and United States Faculty

ICT Application Category	Saudi Faculty			United States Faculty			
	n	M	SD	n	M	SD	P
Communication							
Email	270	16.74	25.826	245	14.14	19.02	.266
Social Media	220	15.78	25.97	115	14.57	28.50	.755
Video Conferencing	169	12.69	23.38	108	10.62	22.32	.361
Audio	131	8.449	19.39	89	12.17	14.25	.219
Instruction							
Email	250	16.36	26.79	194	10.51	20.44	.015*
Social Media	210	17.37	28.24	95	14.75	27.8	.467
Video Conferencing	158	13.37	24.43	135	10.30	21.58	.349
Audio	122	7.48	17.90	84	13.42	26.53	.059

Note. *p < .05

use. The third factor, Ease of Use, captured three of the four items written to tap respondents' perceptions of ease of use of Information and Communication Technology. The fourth factor, Attitude, was comprised of one item written to assess attitude, one to measure Ease of Use, and one item written to assess Perceived Value. The internal consistency reliabilities for the items comprising each factor were as follows: Perceived Value = .83, Skills and Access = .81, Ease of Use = .60, and Attitude = .70. Item factor loadings, Means and Standard Deviations are reported in Table 5.

United States faculty results from the principal components analysis of ICT attitude items found that not all of the items loaded on the constructs they were written to measure. The exploratory factor analysis using principal components extraction and oblique rotation methods constrained to extract three factors produced three underlying dimensions adequate for assessing the three constructs related to Ease of Use, Perceived Value, and Attitude Toward Use of ICT. The first factor was interpreted as "Perceived Value" and captured all four perceived value items explaining 31% of the variance of the data structure. The second factor, Ease of Use, was comprised of two Ease of Use items and one item written to tap Attitude toward electronic tool factor were as follows: Perceived Value = .81, Ease of Use = .60 and Attitude = .70 Item factor loadings, Means and Standard Deviations for the US faculty are reported in Table 6.

The results of the path analysis for Saudi faculty conducted to explore the relationships between Perceived Value, Ease of Use, Attitudes Toward ICT Use and Actual ICT Tool Use is presented in Figure 1. The Skills and Access identified by the principal components analysis of the Saudi ICT attitude items was not used in the analysis because it did not align with Davis' Technology Acceptance Model. System was measured by how often faculty indicated they used E-mail (System 1), Social Media (System 2), Web Conferencing (System 3), and Audio (System 4) (Never, Rarely, Sometimes, Often, Always). The latent traits of Perceived Value, Ease of Use, and Attitude were measured using the items identified from the principal component factor analysis. Use of Social Media was measured by the number of hours that Saudi faculty indicated they actually used E-mail, Web Conferencing, Video, and Audio per week. Audio was not included in this analysis because less than one third of Saudi faculty indicated that they used Audio for communication or instruction. The path coefficients are reported in Figure 1.

Table 5. Factor Loadings, Means and Standard Deviations for Saudi Faculty ICT Attitude Items

ITEMS BY FACTOR	n	1	2	3	4	M	SD
Perceived Usefulness							
Using electronic tools in my course will help students better learn the material.	268	**.882**	-.043	.007	-.018	3.90	1.01
The advantages of using electronic tools outweighs the disadvantages of not using them.	263	**.868**	.053	-.003		4.03	.886
Using electronic tools will improve student satisfaction with the course.	266	**.763**	-.105	.112	.021	4.10	.843
The use of technological tools is important for conducting professional work.	265	**.433**	-.307	-.021	.169	4.32	.842
Skills and Access							
I have the basic skills for navigating the Internet.	262	-.009	**.901**	-.057	.034	4.56	.723
I have access to a computer with productivity software.	265	-.043	**.879**	-.045	.040	4.52	.749
Using productivity software for communicating with students and for instruction is easy.	269	.108	**.640**	.120	.054	4.47	.804
Ease of Use							
Using courseroom management systems (e.g. Blackboard, D2L, Moodle) for communicating with students and instruction is easy.	268	.085	-.314	**.737**	-.243	3.90	1.10
Using Web conferencing software (e.g. Skype, Webex) for communicating with students and instruction is easy.	268	-.023	.022	**.732**	.211	3.47	1.10
Using social media tools and other electronic tools to communicate with students and for instruction is stressful.	264	.023	.137	**.664**	.043	3.36	1.15

Table 6. Factor Loadings, Means and Standard Deviations for United States Faculty ICT Attitude Items

ITEMS BY FACTOR	n	1	2	3	M	SD
Perceived Usefulness						
Using electronic tools in my course will help students better learn the material.	239	**809**	-.150	-.044	3.82	.861
The advantages of using electronic tools outweights the disadvantages of not using them.	238	**.761**	-.290	-.170	3.75	.872
Using electronic tools will improve student satisfacation with the course.	239	**.720**	-.240	-.029	3.76	.966
Using electronic tools such as Facebook, Podcasts, Videos, Skype to communicate with students and for instruction is a good idea.	239	**.740**	.166	.061	3.42	.949
Ease of Use						
Using productivity sofware for communicating with students and instruction is easy.	237	.115	**-.733**	.002	4.27	.778
I have access to a computer with productivity software.	241	-.031	**-.733**	.107	4.57	.739
Using Learning Management systems or communciating with students and instruction is easy.	237	.200	**-.576**	-.011	3.89	.943
Attitude Towart ICT Use						
I have the basic skills to use social netowrking software like Facebook or Twitter.	242	-.152	-.348	**.829**	3.86	1.13
I am skillful in using social media and productivity electronic tools for communicating with students and for Instruction.	242	.007	-.150	**.821**	3.86	1.20
Using social media tools for communicating with students and instruction is easy.	236	.326	.354	**.543**	3.10	1.08

Figure 1.

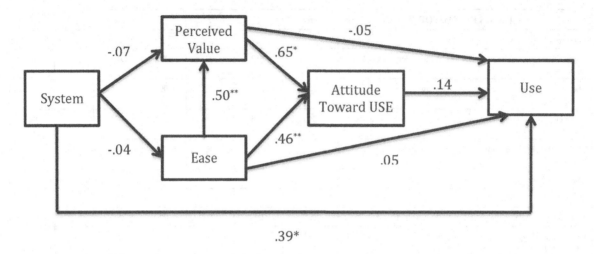

Results from the path analysis did not identify any significant relationships between Perceived Value, Ease of Use, Attitude and Actual Use of Electronic Tools for Saudi Faculty. However, System use was found to have a significant effect on Actual ICT Use (β=. 39). In addition, Ease of Use had a significant effect on Perceived Value (β =. 50), while Perceived Value was significantly related to Attitude Toward ICT Use (β =. 65). A significant indirect effect of Ease of Use was found on Attitude when passing through Perceived Value (β =. 33).

Similar results were found for U.S. faculty. System use for the U.S. faculty was measured by an overall of the hours they estimated they used ICT tools each week for communicating and instruction and an average rating of how often "Never" - Not at all, "Rarely" - Less than weekly, "Sometimes"- Multiple times per week but not daily, and "All of the Time"- Daily) they used email for communicating with students. This approach is similar to how Davis (1993) measured system use for his original study of the Technology Acceptance Model. The latent traits of Perceived Value, Ease of Use, and Attitude were measured using the items identified in Table 4 resulting from the principal component factor analysis. The path coefficients for the United States faculty analysis are reported in Figure 2.

Results from the path analysis for United States faculty found there was no significant relationship between Perceived Value, Ease of Use, Attitude, and Actual Use of ICT tools. However, System Use was found to be significantly related to Actual ICT Use (β =.73). In addition, Perceived Value was found to have a significant effect on Attitude (β =.41). No significant indirect effects were found for System on Perceived Value and Use, nor were their significant indirect effects for Ease of Use on Attitude or Use. Lastly, there were no significant indirect effects for Perceived Value on Use.

CONCLUSION

Access to Information Communication Technologies that support the use of audio, video, web conferencing, and the Internet are providing many learning opportunities that were not available to students in the past. Over the past two decades the use ofcComputer and Internet technology for instructional purposes has grown dramatically in higher education (Buchanan, Sainter, & Saunders, 2013). Leaning manage-

Figure 2. United States Faculty Path Diagram

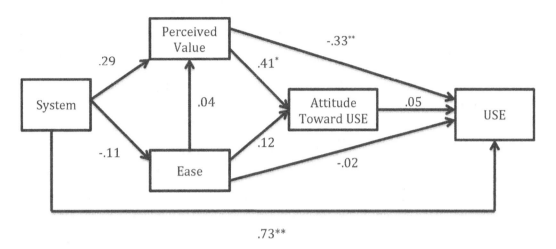

ment systems such as Blackboard, Desire2Learn, and Moodle have integrated the use of ICT tools to allow faculty to create effective learning environments that will provide educational opportunities for students at a distance (Al-Zaidiyeen, Mei, & Fook, 2010). However, the potential instructional, cultural, and institutional benefits of these ICT tools cannot be realized unless faculty use them. The use of ICT applications are dependent on faculty perceptions such as the ease of use of ICT applications and their value for improving learning and instruction.

Saudi faculty reported most frequently using e-mail, word processing, and social media applications. U.S. faculty also rated e-mail and word processing tools as their most frequently used ICT tools followed by presentation tools (e.g., PowerPoint). Results from comparisons using independent samples t-tests revealed that Saudi faculty rated their use of social media applications significantly more often than United States faculty. Saudi faculty also rated their use of Google documents and photos significantly more often than United States faculty. However, United States faculty rated their use of podcasts and text documents significantly more often than Saudi faculty.

In addition to frequency of ICT tool use, both Saudi and United States faculty were asked to estimate their actual hours of use per week for four broad ICT applications—which included email, social media, video, and audio—for interacting with students and for instruction. Saudi faculty estimated they used e-mail, social media, and video conferencing more hours per week on average than did United States faculty. However, United States faculty reported using audio applications more often per week than Saudi faculty. The average hours per week of audio use was the only ICT category of application where Saudi and United States faculty differed significantly. These results are similar to those reported by Keengwe (2007) who found that U.S. faculty use web-browsers and multimedia presentation tools that integrate both video and audio multiple times per week. Similar to results reported by this study, Alenzi (2012) found that Saudi faculty reported most experience using productivity, presentation software, and Microsoft Word.

Interestingly, Saudi faculty reported using social media applications significantly more often that United States faculty. Ghannam (2011) posited that the pervasive use of social media applications in higher education and informally by Saudi faculty and university students alike is not surprising when considering that 50% of the population of Saudi Arabia, Yemen, Oman, Jordan, Morocco, and Egypt are currently estimated to be under 25 years of age. He characterized this group as belonging to the "net generation." Moran et al. (2011) surveyed more than 1,900 United States faculty to investigate their use of social media tools. Their report found the most frequently used social media application for instruction by 80% faculty surveyed was online video. However, the use of online video is different from how data on the use of social media applications were assessed for this study. The report by Moran et al. found that only 11% of United States faculty used social media applications like Facebook or Twitter weekly for communicating with others. These findings are similar to results from this research which found that United States faculty use social media applications several times per week.

Results of the path analyses for both Saudi and U.S. faculty did not find significant relationships between actual ICT use and perceptions of ease of use, value, or general attitudes toward ICT. Interestingly, Perceived Value for U.S. faculty had a significant and negative effect on Actual ICT Use, which suggests that United States faculty may value the use of more complex ICT technologies but do not use them as often because of the training requirements and time required to implement them. Although Davis (1993) found a positive relationship between Perceived Value of ICT use and Actual Use, his sample was small and consisted only of professional and managerial employees, while ICT applications were limited to only e-mail and a text editor.

Results for the Saudi path analysis found some similarities to findings from Davis' (1993) seminal study which investigated the relationships between perceptions of technology ease of use, perceived value and general attitude toward technology. The path analysis for Saudi faculty found that Ease of Use of ICT tools had a significant effect on Perceived Value of ICT tools. Likewise, Perceived Value of ICT tools had a significant effect on Attitude Toward ICT tool use. However, there was no relationship between Attitude Toward ICT use and actual use of ICT tools as Davis found in his study. Similarly, results from this study were similar to those of Ajjan and Hartshorne's (2012) research examining factors related to faculty decisions to use Web 2.0 technologies. Their study found that Perceived Ease of Use and Perceived Usefulness were positively related to attitude toward the use of Web 2.0 applications. More specifically, as was the case with this study, Perceived Usefulness had a much stronger effect on Attitude Toward Use than did Perceived Ease of Use. Ajjan and Hartshorne, however, did not examine the relationship between Perceived Ease of Use and Perceived Value within the context of Web 2.0 tools. Their research found that Attitude Toward Use was significantly related to Intention to use Web 2.0 applications, which in turn was a significant determinant of actual Web 2.0 use. This study, however, did not find a significant relationship between attitude toward use of ICT tools and actual use of ICT tools for either Saudi or United States faculty.

RECOMMENDATIONS

Although ICT tools can be used independently for instructional purposes, they provide much more enriched student interactions and learning experiences when integrated with learning management systems such as Blackboard, Desire2Learn, and Moodle for online and hybrid learning environments. However, 74%of Saudi faculty and 35% of U.S. faculty indicated they had used not learning management system for instruction. This finding is surprising when considering the large percentage of Saudi faculty's use of social media for productivity, instruction and communicating with students. Some of the barriers cited for Saudi faculty's lack of use of learning management systems may be due to past experiences with the Jusur Learning Management System developed by Saudi Arabia's National Center for E-Learning and Distance Learning (NCEL) (Al-Khalifa, 2010). For example, Al-Khalifa (2010) found that Jusur users reported difficulties in downloading course materials and uploading course files. In addition, Jusur discussion forums are difficult to browse when attempting to interact with other users. Administratively, the Jusur system does not allow faculty to remove or add students independently, and it is not integrated with university registration or academic portals. The difficulties that Saudi faculty may have experienced in the past with the Jusur learning management system may be responsible for the small percentage who use learning management systems and may have influenced their attitudes toward the use of more integrated ICT tools for instructional purposes.

Although the use by faculty of learning management systems such as Blackboard or Desire-To-Learn is commonplace, there is still concern about availability of training and institutional support (Tabata & Johnsrud, 2008). This concern is well-founded because faculty cannot effectively integrate technology into their teaching and learning activities if they lack the skills to use ICT tools effectively in the classroom (Keengwe, Kidd & Kyei-Blankson, 2009). Training and technical support will help faculty overcome the anxieties associated with the use of ICT applications for instruction and help them to realize the value of these tools for improving instruction, thus increasing their effectiveness as instructors (Johnson, Wisniewski, Kuhlemeyer, Isaacs, & Kryzkowski, 2008). Although, U.S. faculty predominately use ICT tools in the category of productivity software, training related to the application of Social Media for instruction is recommended. Saudi Faculty, on the other hand, would benefit from training related to integrated social media tools with learning management systems. Research related to the Technology Acceptance Model (Alenzi, 2012; Ajjan & Hartshone, 2008; Davis, 1993) suggests that ease of ICT use and perceived value have large influences on faculty attitudes to engage in the use of ICT application to support their instruction. However, when training and support is not available, ease of use is compromised, thus reducing the likelihood that faculty will integrate ICT tools into their instruction.

FUTURE RESEARCH DIRECTIONS

It is recommended the more current indicators of attitude toward the use of ICT tools (ease of use, perceived value, and attitude toward ICT use) be developed to capture a more accurate representation of the relationships between faculty attitude and their actual use of ICT applications for communication and learning. The use of focus group interviews and observations may help to create a questionnaire that captures attitudes toward ICT use based on the use of current ICT applications.

The use of social media as a broad category was clearly important to Saudi faculty and somewhat less so for U.S. faculty. However, it would be interesting to identify how frequent Saudi and U.S. faculty use specific social media applications such as Facebook, Twitter, SnapChat, and other unique forms of social media for interacting with students and for instruction. Much of the published research considers ICT applications such as Facebook, Twitter, YouTube, and Instagram as one extensive category of social media applications, whereas others classify Facebook and Twitter as communication tools and YouTube as a multimedia application. These applications need to be more precisely defined and investigated in terms of their use for creating effective learning environments. In addition, when modeling the relationships represented by the Technology Acceptance Model, factors such as gender, self-efficacy, and facilitating conditions could also be added to the model to determine their relationships with ease of use, perceived value, attitude toward ICT use, and actual integration of ICT instructionally.

CONCLUSION

Results from this study find that in general, Saudi faculty and United States faculty use ICT tools similarly for communication and learning. However, Saudi faculty attitudes toward the use of ICT tools are different from those of United States faculty. United States faculty reported use of ICT applications in general had a much larger effect on their actual ICT use as compared to Saudi faculty. However, for Saudi faculty, ease of ICT tool use and perceived value of ICT tool use were found to be important factors in determining their use of ICT tools. One reason for this may be that faculty in the U.S. reported much more access to ICT technologies and have had access to multiple ICT applications for a longer period of time than Saudi faculty. The importance of training to build confidence and competence is critical to the successful use of ICT applications. However, the literature suggests that although this is a barrier for all faculty related to the use of ICT, it is even more so for Saudi faculty.

REFERENCES

About, Saudi electronic university. (n.d.). Retrieved from https://www.seu.edu.sa/sites/en/AboutSEU/Pages/HistoryTimeline.aspx

Ageel, M. (2011). The ICT proficiencies of university teachers in Saudi Arabia: A case study to identify challenges and encouragements. *Hummingbird, University of Southampton's Doctoral Research Journal*, *21*(8), 55–60.

Ajjan, H., & Hartshorne, R. (2008). Investigating Faculty Decisions to Adopt Web 2.0 Technologies: Theory and Empirical Tests. *The Internet and Higher Education*, *11*(2), 71–80. doi:10.1016/j.iheduc.2008.05.002

Al Harbi, H. (2014), *Towards successful implementation of ICT in education*. Paper presented at the 2014 WEI International Academic Conference, Vienna, Austria. Retrieved from http://www.westeastinstitute.com/wp-content/uploads/2014/05/Hanaa-Eid-Al-harbi-Full-Paper.pdf

Al-Jarf, R. (2007). E-integration challenges for rectors and deans in higher education. *Computer and Advanced Technology in Education Conference Proceedings*. ACTA.

Al-Kahtani, N. K. M., Ryan, J. J. C. H., & Jefferson, T. I. (2006). How Saudi female faculty perceive internet technology usage and potential. *Information, Knowledge, Systems Management*, *5*, 227–243.

Al-Khalifa, S. H. (2009, October). The state of distance education in Saudi Arabia. *eLearn Magazine*. Retrieved from http://elearnmag.acm.org/archive.cfm?aid=1642193

Al-Maliki, S. (2013). Information and communication technology (ICT) investment in the kingdom of Saudi Arabia: Assessing strengths and weaknesses. *Journal of Knowledge Management*, *213*, 1–15.

Al Mulhem, A. (2014). Common Barriers to E-learning Implementation in Saudi Higher Education Sector: A Review of Literature. In M. Searson & M. Ochoa (Eds.), *Proceedings of Society for Information Technology & Teacher Education International Conference 2014* (pp. 830-840). Chesapeake, VA: Association for the Advancement of Computing in Education (AACE).

Al-Oteawi, S. (2002). *The perceptions of administrators and teachers in utilizing information technology in instruction, administrative work, technology planning and staff development in Saudi Arabia (Doctoral Dissertation).* Ohio University.

Al Shaer, A. I. (2007). *Education for all programmes in the Kingdom of Saudi Arabia.* Paper commissioned for the EFA Global Monitoring Report 2008, Education for All by 2015: will we make it? Retrieved from http://unesdoc.unesco.org/images/0015/001554/155498e.pdf

Al-Shawi, A., & Al-Wabil, A. (2013). Internet usage by faculty in Saudi higher education. *International Journal of Computer Science Issue, 10*(3), 81–87.

Al-Zaidiyeen, N. J., Mei, L. L., & Fook, F. S. (2010). Teachers' attitudes and levels of technology use in classrooms: The case of Jordan schools. *International Education Studies, 3*(2), 211–218. doi:10.5539/ ies.v3n2p211

Albugami, S. & Ahmed, V. (2015). Success factors for ICT implementation in Saudi secondary schools: From the perspective of ICT directors, head teachers, teachers and students. *International Journal of Education and Development using Information and Communication Technology, 11*(1), 36-54.

Alebaikan, R., & Troudi, S. (2010). Blended learning in Saudi universities: Challenges and perspectives. *Research in Learning Technology, 18*(1), 49–59. doi:10.1080/09687761003657614

Alenzi, A. M. (2012). *Faculty members' perceptions of e-learning in the Kingdom of Saudi Arabia (KSA).* (Unpublished doctoral dissertation). Texas Tech University, Lubbock, TX.

Alhareth, Y., McBride, N., Prior, M., Leigh, M., & Flick, C. (2013, July). *Saudi women and e-learning.* Paper presented at the third annual meeting of The Future of Education International Conference. Retrieved from http://conference.pixel-online.net/foe2013/common/download/Paper_pdf/142-ELE15-FP-Alhareth-FOE2013.pdf

Aljabre, A. (2012). An exploration of distance learning in Saudi Arabian universities: Current practices and future possibilities. *International Journal of Business Human Technology, 2*(132), 132–137.

Allen, E. I., & Seaman, J. (2015). *Grade level: Tracking online education in the United States, 2014.* Babson Park, MA: Babson Survey Research Group.

Almalki, G., & Williams, N. (2012). A strategy to improve the usage of ICT in the kingdom of Saudi Arabia primary school. *International Journal of Advanced Computer Science & Application, 3*(10), 42–49. doi:10.14569/IJACSA.2012.031007

Altawil, A. N. (2012). The perceptions of Saudi students on using fully online courses at university level (Unpublished master's thesis). Chico, CA: California State University. Retrieved from http://www.academia.edu/8616172/The_perceptions_of_Saudi_students_on_using_fully_online_courses_at_university_level

Alwani, A., & Soomro, S. (2010). Barriers to effective use of information technology in science education at Yanbu Kingdom of Saudi Arabia. In S. Soomro (Ed.), E-Learning Experiences and the Future. Rijeka, Croatia: InTech. doi:10.5772/8809

American Educational Research Association, American Psychological Association, & National Council on Measurement in Education. (2014). *Standards for educational and psychological testing*. Washington, DC: Authors.

Anderson, T. (2008). Toward a theory of online learning. In T. Anderson (Ed.), *The theory and practice of online learning* (pp. 45–74). Edmonton: AU Press.

Banks-Wallace, J. (2000). Womanist ways of knowing: Theoretical considerations for research with African American women. *ANS. Advances in Nursing Science*, *22*(3), 33–45. doi:10.1097/00012272-200003000-00004 PMID:10711803

Barzilai-Nahon, K., & Barzilai, G. (2005). Cultured technology: The Internet and religious fundamentalism. *The Information Society*, *21*(1), 25–40. doi:10.1080/01972240590895892

Bingimlas, K. A. (2010). *Evaluating the quality of science teachers' practices in ICT-supported learning and teaching environments in Saudi primary schools*. (Unpublished dissertation). RMIT University, Melbourne, Australia.

Buchanan, T., Sainter, P., & Saunders, G. (2013). Factors affecting faculty use of learning technologies: Implications for models of technology adoption. *Journal of Computing in Higher Education*, *25*(1), 1–11. doi:10.1007/s12528-013-9066-6

Burkhart, G. E., & Older, S. (2003). *The information revolution in the Middle East and North Africa. National Defense Research Institute*. RAND.

Curseu, P. L., & Pluut, H. (2013). Student groups as learning entities: The effect of group diversity and teamwork quality on groups' cognitive complexity. *Studies in Higher Education*, *38*(1), 87–103. doi:10.1080/03075079.2011.565122

Daher, T., & Lazarevic, B. (2014). Emerging instructional technologies: Exploring the extent of faculty use of web 2.0 tools at a midwestern community college. *TechTrends*, *58*(6), 42–50. doi:10.1007/s11528-014-0802-1

Davis, F. D. (1989). Perceived usefulness, perceived ease of use, and user acceptance of information technology. *Management Information Systems Quarterly*, *13*(3), 319–340. doi:10.2307/249008

Davis, F. D. (1993). User acceptance of information technology: System characteristics, user perceptions and behavioral impacts. *International Journal of Man-Machine Studies*, *38*(3), 475–487. doi:10.1006/imms.1993.1022

DeVillis, R. F. (2011). *Scale development: Theory and applications*. Thousand Oaks, CA: Sage.

Fahrni, P., Rudolph, J., & De Schutter, A. (2004). Vendor-Assisted Evaluation of a Learning Management System. *International Review of Research in Open and Distance Learning*, *5*(1), 1–4.

Gay, L. R., Mills, G. E., & Airasian, P. (2012). *Educational research: Competencies for analysis and applications*. Boston, MA: Pearson.

Ghamraw, N. (2013). The relationship between the leadership styles of Lebanese public school principals and their attitudes toward ICT versus the level of ICT use by their teachers. *Open Journal of Leadership*, 2(1), 11–20. doi:10.4236/ojl.2013.21002

Ghannam, J. (2011). Social media in the Arab world: Leading up to the uprisings of 2011. Washington, DC: Center for International Media Assistance. Retrieved from http://www.databank.com.lb/docs/Social%20Media%20in%20the%20Arab%20World%20Leading%20up%20to%20the%20Uprisings%20of%202011.pdf

Hamdan, A. (2014). The Reciprocal and correlative relationship between learning Culture and Online education: A case from Saudi Arabia. *The International Review of Research in Open and Distributed Learning, 15*(1). Retrieved from http://www.irrodl.org/index.php/irrodl/article/view/1408

Heirdsfield, A., Walker, S., Tambyah, M., & Beutel, D. (2011). Blackboard as an Online Learning Environment: What Do Teacher Education Students and Staff Think? *Australian Journal Of Teacher Education, 36*(7), 1–16. doi:10.14221/ajte.2011v36n7.4

Hew, K. F., & Brush, T. (2007). Integrating technology into k-12 teaching and learning: Current knowledge gaps and recommendations for future research. *Educational Technology Research and Development, 55*(3), 223–252. doi:10.1007/s11423-006-9022-5

Hilsop, G. W., & Ellis, H. C. J. (2004). A study of faculty effort in online teaching. *The Internet and Higher Education, 7*(1), 15–31. doi:10.1016/j.iheduc.2003.10.001

Johnson, T., Wisniewski, M. A., Kuhlemeyer, G., Isaacs, G., & Kryzkowski, J. (2008). Technology adoption in higher education: Overcoming anxiety through faculty bootcamp. *Journal of Asynchronous Learning Networks, 16*(2), 63–72.

Joiner, R., Iacovides, J., Owen, M., Gavin, C., Clibbery, S., Darling, J., & Drew, B. (2011). Digital games, gender and learning in engineering: Do females benefit as much as males? *Journal of Science Education and Technology, 20*(2), 178–185. doi:10.1007/s10956-010-9244-5

Keengwe, J. (2007). Faculty integration of technology into instruction and students' perceptions of computer technology to improve student learning. *Journal of Information Technology, 6*, 169–17.

Keengwe, J., Kidd, T., & Kyei-Blankson, L. (2009). Faculty and technology: Implications for faculty training and technology leadership. *Journal of Science Education and Technology, 18*(1), 23–28. doi:10.1007/s10956-008-9126-2

Lane, J. M. (2012). Developing the vision: Preparing teachers to deliver a digital world-class education system. *Australian Journal of Teacher Education, 37*(4), 59–74. doi:10.14221/ajte.2012v37n4.7

Levin, T., & Wadmany, R. (2005). Changes in educational beliefs and classroom practices of teachers and students in rich technology-based classrooms. *Technology, Pedagogy and Education, 14*(3), 281–307. doi:10.1080/14759390500200208

Levin, T., & Wadmany, R. (2005). Changes in educational beliefs and classroom practices of teachers and students in rich technology-based classrooms. *Technology, Pedagogy and Education, 14*(3), 281–307. doi:10.1080/14759390500200208

Mejiuni, O., & Obilade, O. (2006). The dialectics of poverty,educational opportunities, and ICTs. In A. Oduaran & H. S. Bhola (Eds.), *Widening Access to Education As Social Justice* (pp. 139–148). The Netherlands: Springer. doi:10.1007/1-4020-4324-4_9

Moran, M., Seaman, J., & Tinti-Kane, H. (2011). Teaching, learning, and sharing: How today's higher education faculty use social media. *The Educational Resources Information Center*. Retrieved from http://eric.ed.gov/?id=ED535130

Nagel, D. (2014, June). Spending on instructional tech to reach $19 billion within 5 years. *THE Journal*. Retrieved from https://thejournal.com/Articles/2014/06/11/Spending-on-Instructional-Tech-To-Reach-19-Billion-Within-5-Years.aspx?p=1

Noor-Ul-Amin, S. (2013). An effective use of ICT for education and learning by drawing on worldwide knowledge, research and experience: ICT as a change agent for education. *Scholarly Journal of Education*, *2*(4), 38–54.

Oyaid, A. (2009). *Education policy in Saudi Arabia and its relation to secondary school teachers' ICT use, perceptions, and views of the future of ICT in education.* (Unpublished dissertation). University of Exeter, Exeter, UK.

Payette, D. L., & Verreault, D. (2007). Teaching methods and technologies: Aggregated faculty analysis, conclusions and recommendations phase IV. *Journal of College Teaching and Learning*, *4*(6), 43–60.

Powers, L., Alhussain, R., Averbeck, C., & Warner, A. (2012). Perspectives on distance education and social media. *Quarterly Review of Distance Education*, *13*, 241–245.

Robertson, M., & Al-Zahrani, A. (2012). Self-efficacy and ICT integration into initial teacher education in Saudi Arabia: Matching policy with practice. *Australasian Journal of Educational Technology*, *28*(7), 1136–1151. doi:10.14742/ajet.793

Roblyer, M. D., McDaniel, M., Webb, M., Herman, J., & Witty, J. V. (2010). Findings on Facebook in higher education: A comparison of college faculty and student uses and perceptions of social networking sites. *The Internet and Higher Education*, *13*(3), 134–140. doi:10.1016/j.iheduc.2010.03.002

Saudi Ministry of Higher Education. (n.d.). Retrieved from http://he.moe.gov.sa/en/default.aspx

Tabata, L. N., & Johnsrud, L. K. (2008). The impact of faculty attitudes toward technology, distance education and innovation. *Research in Higher Education*, *49*(7), 625–646. doi:10.1007/s11162-008-9094-7

Tanner, J. R., Noser, T. C., & Totaro, M. W. (2009). Business faculty and undergraduate students' perceptions of online learning: A comparative study. *Journal of Information Systems*, *20*(1), 29–40.

Ward, M., Peters, G., & Shelley, K. (2010). Student and Faculty Perceptions of the Quality of Online Learning Experiences. *International Review of Research in Open and Distance Learning*, *11*(3), 57–77.

Wasilik, O., & Bollinger, D. U. (2009). Faculty satisfaction in the online environment: An institutional study. *The Internet and Higher Education*, *12*(3-4), 173–178. doi:10.1016/j.iheduc.2009.05.001

Weil, E. (2008). Teaching boys and girls separately. *New York Times*. Retrieved from http://nytimes.com/2008/03/02/magazine/02sex3-t. html

Yau, H. K., & Cheng, A. F. (2012). Gender difference of confidence in using technology for learning. *Journal Of Technology Studies*, *38*(2), 74–79.

KEY TERMS AND DEFINITIONS

Asynchronous Online Learning: Is online learning that does not apply to audio/video communication, but instead relies solely on a text-based, written discussion format for communication (Ward, Peters, Shelley, 2010).

Blackboard Learning Management System: Is an online learning management system that provides instructional tools and other resources to create a virtual learning environment (Heirdsfield, Walker, Tambyah & Beutel, 2011).

Desire2Learn Incorporated (D2L) (Also Known as Desire2Learn): Is an integrated online learning management system (LMS), which provides synchronous and asynchronous interaction between students, teachers, and learning content (Fahrni, Rudolph, & De Schutter, 2004).

Information and Communication Technology (ICT): Is the electronic and non-electronic technologies and infrastructure systems used to create, store, manipulate, retrieve, and communicate or disseminate information (Mejiuni & Obilade, 2006).

Synchronous Online Learning (SOL): Is online learning that applies live audio/video communication to an online class (Ward et al., 2010).

Path Analysis: Is a technique that uses regression methods to provide a visual representation of the relationships between variables being studied (Gay, Mills, & Airasian, 2012).

Technology Acceptance Model (TAM): Was developed by Davis (1993) and theorized that attitude toward using technology is a function of two beliefs: perceived usefulness and perceived ease of use.

Chapter 2

Massive Open Online Courses and Completion Rates:
Are Self-Directed Adult Learners the Most Successful at MOOCs?

Amanda Sue Schulze
Pepperdine University, USA

Paul Sparks
Pepperdine University, USA

Doug Leigh
Pepperdine University, USA

Elio Spinello
Pepperdine University, USA

ABSTRACT

Millions of adults have registered for massive open online courses, known as MOOCs, yet little research exists on how effective MOOCs are at meeting the needs of these learners. Critics of MOOCs highlight that completion rates can average fewer than 5%. Such low completion rates raise questions about the effectiveness of MOOCs and whether all adults have the skills and abilities needed for success. MOOCs have the potential to be powerful change agents for universities and students, but it has previously been unknown whether these online courses serve more than just the most persistent, self-directed learners. This study explored the relationship between self-directed learning readiness and MOOC completion percents among adults taking a single Coursera MOOC. By examining self-directed learning - the ability to take responsibility for one's own educational experiences - and MOOC completion rates, this research may help to confirm the knowledge and skills needed to be a successful adult learner in the 21st century, as well as how to improve online education offered to adult learners.

INTRODUCTION

Online courses for adult learners have traditionally suffered from lower course completion rates than face-to-face classroom courses (Rovai, 2002). Dropout rates for online university courses have been found to be 10% to 20% higher than traditional college classroom courses (Carr, 2000). Barriers to completion of university and continuing education online courses for adult learners are often linked to

DOI: 10.4018/978-1-5225-0522-8.ch002

feelings of isolation, lack of support from the learning community and instructor, and challenges with persistence (Rovai, 2002). Massive open online courses, called MOOCs, are a new platform and online course structure being used to deliver instruction simultaneously to thousands of learners. Yet, completion rates for MOOCs are not nearly as high as what has been found for similar university classroom or online courses (Watters, 2012).

There are three unique features of MOOCs that may contribute to the low completion rates and corresponding high enrollment numbers that other online courses offered at universities do not have. First, in terms of cost, MOOCs are free of charge, which removes the barrier that higher education is only available to the wealthy. When examining the universities that offer MOOCs, such as Harvard, Massachusetts Institute of Technology (MIT), and Stanford, it seems likely that MOOC learners now have access to education from Ivy League universities that many may have never thought possible (Pappano, 2012). Second, MOOCs are usually taken asynchronously when individuals have time, making them a flexible education option for working adults, parents, and anyone with a busy schedule. However, MOOCs are still only available for a scheduled period of time. If a leaner registers, but has scheduling conflicts during the MOOC period, then that learner cannot complete the course. Third, MOOCs are open and accessible to anyone with an Internet connection, making them available to adults located across the globe. Given these three criteria alone, MOOCs may be the beginning to the various challenges facing universities today. However, while these three factors may be some of the reasons why MOOCs are attracting large numbers of registrants, they may also offer insight into why low numbers of learners complete MOOCs.

Though millions of adult learners have registered for MOOCs, there are few empirical studies at this time that examine MOOCs and their value for learning. Critics cannot help but point out that MOOC completion rates can average fewer than 5% of those registered (Kolowich, 2012; Pappano, 2012; Balch, 2013). A recent unofficial study examined enrollment and completion rates of MOOC learners from data made available to the public. This study reported enrollments for MOOCs were typically around 50,000 learners with most MOOCs having completion rates lower than 10% (Jordan, 2013). Such evidence raises questions about the effectiveness of the MOOC learning environment for adult learners, and whether all adults have the skills and abilities needed to succeed within MOOCs.

Different theories exist to explain these low MOOC completion rates. For example, adult learners may find MOOCs challenging because the courses are massive, meaning that one course can contain hundreds of thousands of learners. Because of these enormous class sizes, the design of MOOCs may not allow for a single instructor to direct, guide, or assist the participants, leaving learners to take charge of the learning environment for themselves. Fortunately, self-directed learners are often able to take responsibility for their own learning, and these self-guided learners may not always need the physical presence of an instructor to direct the learning process (Knowles, 1975). However, adult learners who are not familiar with how MOOCs are structured or how to manage their own learning experiences with self-directed learning are likely to struggle within such environments (Koutropoulos & Hogue, 2012). In one study, some learners expressed the desire for more direction and guidance throughout their MOOC experience (Kop, 2011). Kop (2011) also noted that to be successful at MOOCs participants needed confidence in their abilities, competence with the technology tools, and the capability to take charge of their own learning experience. If MOOCs are not designed to support and motivate learners with varying degrees of self-direction then, given the low threshold for entry compounded with the struggles some may face with these courses, dropping out could be a predicable outcome for the majority of learners (Balch, 2013).

A more thorough investigation of the traits of MOOC adult learners is needed. By studying self-directed learning, new strategies may be identified to increase MOOC completion and learning. Knowing more about those learners that complete MOOCs and those that do not can provide insight into how to improve the design and development of MOOCs so that more adult learners can experience success. MOOCs have the potential to be powerful change agents for universities and adult learners, but these courses should serve more than just the most persistent, self-directed learners.

Purpose and Nature of the Study

The purpose of this study was to determine the extent to which, if at all, there was a relationship between the degree of self-directed learning readiness among adult learners and the degree of their MOOC completion. In addition, this study explored the extent to which, if at all, there were differences in the demographics of adult learners that completed MOOCs compared with those learners that did not. Lastly, this study examined the extent to which, if at all, adult learner demographics mediated the relationship between self-directed learning readiness and degree of MOOC completion.

Research Questions

This research study explored the relationship between self-directed learning and MOOC completion percentages among adult learners taking a single Coursera MOOC in the fall of 2013. The following research questions were answered:

1.   To what extent, if at all, was there a relationship between the degree of self-directed learning readiness of adult learners and the degree of their MOOC completion?
2.   To what extent, if at all, were there differences in the demographics of adult learners that completed a MOOC compared with those that did not complete a MOOC?
3.   To what extent, if at all, did adult learner demographics mediate the relationship between self-directed learning readiness and degree of MOOC completion?

Hypothesis

This research study explored three different hypotheses based on each of the research questions presented. The first hypothesis was that the more competent adult learners were at self-directed learning, the more likely these learners would be to successfully complete a greater percent of the MOOC examined in this study. Course completion is a measure or educational outcome often used to assess quality and effectiveness of an online course (Bonk & Kim, 2006). Low completion rates may be a sign that participants are facing challenges, or that the educational options being provided may not be meeting their needs (California Community Colleges Chancellor's Office, 2012). A survey of online instructors and higher education administrators found that self-regulation of learning by university students was identified as the most important success factors for students of online university courses (Bonk & Kim, 2006). It was expected that adult learners stronger in self-directed learning were more capable and successful in a MOOC because of the characteristics of the MOOC and how it was designed.

The second hypothesis explored was that those adult learners with previous experience taking a MOOC would be more likely to complete the MOOC examined in this study. One of the demographic questions found on the survey for this research study asked participants to indicate if they had previously taken a MOOC, other than the one for which this study examined. Previous empirical research has found that the experience a learner has with university distance education is related to the likelihood that the learner will complete or drop out of a distance learning course (Parker, 1999). This suggests that the more distance education courses learners have taken, the more likely they are to succeed and complete distance learning courses in the future. In addition, Candy (1991) found that learners may be strong in self-directed learning for topics with which they are familiar, or in contexts that are similar to a prior experience. Also, Eisenberg and Dowsett (1990) and Erhman (1990) found that university students taking online education for the first time did not have all the necessary skills needed to be successful in those courses.

The third hypothesis explored in this study assumed that adult learners in their thirties and forties, who are female, with high levels of education, previous MOOC experience, strong English language skills, and with no physical disability or impairment that may interfere with completing an online course, would be stronger self-directed learners and more likely to complete a greater percentage of the MOOC examined in this study. To explore this hypothesis this study collected participant data on several demographics including age, gender, level of education completed, previous MOOC experience, English language ability, and a disability or impairment, in addition to measuring self-directed learning and MOOC completion.

With all of the changes occurring in higher education, MOOCs are a relatively new education solution that may or may not be able to meet the needs of universities, adult learners, and instructors. MOOCs have the potential to bring well-known universities to a global audience and provide life-long learners with numerous opportunities to continue their education in a flexible, convenient format. However, as stated previously, a more thorough investigation of MOOCs is needed since little research has been conducted on this learning environment to determine if it is an effective learning solution. Nevertheless, the data that has been previously collected highlights that the completion rates for MOOCs are less than stellar. The high drop out rates of MOOC participants could indicate that there are issues underlying these online courses that need to be addressed.

By studying the relationship between self-directed learning and MOOC completion percents, new strategies may be identified to lower drop out rates by MOOC participants. Knowing more about adult learners that complete MOOCs and those that do not can also provide insight into how to improve the design and development of MOOCs so more adult learners can be successful. MOOCs have the potential to be powerful change agents for universities and adult learners, but these courses should serve more than just the most persistent, self-directed learners.

BACKGROUND

The conceptual framework selected for this research study was adult learning theory because within this theory the concept of self-directed learning is found. In the 1970s, it was Knowles that introduced American research to the concept of andragogy, which was an acknowledgment that adults learn differently than children. Through research of adult education it was shown that adults have unique attributes that shape their educational growth and development (Knowles, 1980). Knowles began what is still an active field of research by adult educators to explore andragogy as part of adult learning theory (Knowles, Holton, & Swanson, 2011). Though there is no one theory or principle that captures all the pieces of how adults learn, two key components of adult learning theory emerged. These components are andragogy and self-directed learning. These two foundational principles have remained critical to adult learning theory over time and self-directed learning is explored next.

Self-Directed Learning

Knowles (1975) is credited as an early contributor to self-directed learning and defined self-directed learners as those that take the initiative to plan, organize, and conduct their own learning. These individuals complete learning tasks without the assistance of others, are able to set their own learning objectives, and can locate the resources and materials needed to learn. Self-directed learners are also able to evaluate their learning progress and outcomes. Knowles also reasoned that self-directed learners may learn more and to a greater extent then reactive and passive learners that depend on others. He also believed that self-directed learners were more motivated and as a result retained more new knowledge than passive learners.

Though there are many definitions and views of self-directed learning found throughout the adult learning research, Knowles (1975) is the most widely cited and his definition is used for this research study. Knowles said,

In its broadest meaning, 'self-directed learning' describes a process in which individuals take the initiative, with or without the help of others, in diagnosing their learning needs, formulating learning goals, identifying human and material resources for learning, choosing and implementing appropriate learning strategies, and evaluating learning outcomes. (p. 18)

Self-Directed Learning Traits in Online Learning Contexts

From the literature it is clear that studies have focused on the traits that learners need to be successful in online learning or how the context of online education impacts self-directed learning. Several studies have found that self-directed learning, or one of the many traits related to self-directed learning, can have an impact on the success of online learners (Dillon & Gabbard, 1998). Though not directly related to self-directed learning, prior knowledge or experience with online learning environments is often cited as being critical for online learning success. However, a learners' ability to manage and control the learning process has also been noted as critical in online learning environments. The management and control of the learning process can be traced directly to self-directed learning. Unfortunately, examining learner attributes in online learning environments is a critical part of adult learning research that has not kept pace with all of the new technology-supported learning environments that continue to appear. Hartley and Bendixen (2001) noted that various online learning environments such as online courses, discussion boards, and online spaces where learners interact and collaborate rely on the active engagement of learners to build new knowledge in these spaces. These researchers looked specifically at the individual attribute of self-regulation, which they described as one's ability to use their cognitive skills to plan and monitor learning activities, and determined that self-regulation was a critical skill needed to mediate success in these types of online learning environments. Their results were inline with other researchers that have concluded that online learning environments tend to give more control to learners during the online education process (Garrison, 2003).

Attrition in Online Learning Environments

Unfortunately, attrition rates for online learning initiatives are often greater than traditional, face-to-face classes. Some studies show that attrition rates for online undergraduate college courses are 10% to 20% higher than those of traditional courses (Carr, 2000). Many reasons have been documented for possible causes of the higher attrition rates in online courses. Some of those reasons include learners registering for courses for knowledge and not completion, and the physical separation from other students, which can lead to feelings of isolation and lack of motivation to complete an online course (Rovai, 2002). As online learning opportunities become a more popular solution for universities, it is reasonable that improving completion rates within online courses should be a goal of universities.

One online education initiative that is receiving increased attention because of high attrition rates is the MOOC. MOOCs have reported attrition rates as high as 95%, meaning that only around five percent of the registrants completed all the course requirements (Watters, 2012). Beginning to research these online course environments is critical to understanding the traits of those taking MOOCs and if instructional methods can be applied to MOOCs to increase completion rates. Increasing completion rates of MOOCs is one strategy that may be needed to ensure that this type of education option remains available for learners across the globe wishing to take advantage of quality education for little to no cost.

In an attempt to learn more about MOOCs and completion rates, this study examined the hypothesis that those strongest in self-directed learning were more likely to complete a higher percent of a MOOC. The next section reviews the few MOOC studies that include references to learner traits related to self-directed learning, and also explores the connection between MOOCs and the open education movement.

The Open Education Movement, MOOCs, and Self-Directed Learning

This section considers a possible relationship between the open education movement, MOOCs, and self-directed learners. Hiemstra (1994) believed that from the attention and research given to adults as self-directed learners, organizations have had to re-imagine how they design and develop adult education opportunities, and as a result, have developed open learning initiatives, online learning offerings, individualized study programs, and other innovate education solutions for self-directed adult learners. Though self-directed learners may be some of the thrust for expansions in open education, there are many challenges higher education is facing that open education may solve.

For example, there are more potential students than can be taught in traditional higher education settings, making alternative education options necessary. Another challenge is that learning is a lifelong process that adults are continuously involved in, which does not stop after graduation. These learners continuously desire access to quality education, which may not always be available. Another challenge is that the cost of attending a university to obtain a degree remains out of reach for many, making free education necessary. In addition, adult learners want flexible ways to learn that fit into their busy lifestyles. These and other challenges have perpetuated the demand for open education, which can be defined as education that is flexible, allows greater access, and gives learners choices (Iioyoshi & Kumar, 2008).

Characteristics of the open education movement include opening up content, empowering all people through education, equality in access to information, and inviting all to participate (Iioyoshi & Kumar, 2008). These are similar characteristics to MOOCs. For example, MOOCs give a global, massive audience access to education that they may otherwise never have been able to afford. Yet, it is important to note that many involved in the offering of MOOCs may be interested in developing new revenue streams for cash-strapped institutions. Some institutions offer MOOCs as part of the open education movement, yet other organizations are looking to eventually make a profit from MOOCs (Yuan & Powell, 2013). Though links can be made between the open education movement and MOOCs, some questions remain about the current state and longevity of MOOCs.

Similar principles that have guided the Open University, which caters to adult learners with self-directed principles, can be linked to the organizations that offer MOOCs. The ideas from self-directed learning such as adult learners want to continuously learn, make their own decisions about their learning plans, and seek out learning opportunities that meet their needs, fit well with the learning context of MOOCs. Many MOOCs lack a familiar structure, and an instructor is rarely, if ever, available, making MOOCs similar to self-directed learning environments (Yuan & Powell, 2013).

To learn more about the relationship between self-directed learning and MOOC environments more research is needed. In addition, more information is needed to determine if MOOCs support those strong in self-directed learning as well as those weaker in self-directedness. MOOC platforms such as Coursera leave the design and development of each MOOC primarily up to the instructor or university offering the MOOC, which leaves quality to chance. To further highlight how this can be an issue, a correlation was found to exist between self-directed learning readiness and the structure of a learning environment. Wiley (1983) conducted a study of university students and administered the SDLRS/LPA (Guglielmino, 1977). The study showed that individuals that score low in terms of readiness for self-directed learning preferred a more structured learning environment when given a self-directed learning project. In another study, O'Kell (1988) was able to match an individual's readiness for self-directed learning with instructional strategies. For example, those with low scores of readiness for self-directed learning preferred instructor-led discussions and lectures to independent project work. If only the strongest self-directed learners can successfully complete MOOCs, then more time and effort should likely be invested into the design and development of MOOCs to meet the needs of many learners. If this is not done, MOOC completion rates could continue to suffer and new open education solutions of higher quality may appear, making MOOCs a short-lived solution.

Self-directed learning and open education have long been linked. Tuman (1988) discussed the fact that learning in open environments requires complex skills that not everyone has an opportunity to develop. Tuman believed that self-direction should be explicitly taught, otherwise open education will only be useful for the strongest self-directed learners (Tuman, 1988).

The final studies in this section focus specifically on MOOCs. In one of a handful of research studies on MOOCs, Kop (2011) highlighted that MOOCs give learners an open, online learning environment. Yet, the researcher cautioned educators to learn more about these open learning environments and suggested that not all learners are going to have a quality learning experience when taking a MOOC. According to Kop (2011), cMOOCs place the instructor in the role of facilitating the learning process. The MOOC is therefore learner-centered and new knowledge is not passed from the instructor to learners, but knowledge is created when learners interact with resources distributed throughout the Internet. One of the key challenges the researcher highlighted to this type of learning context is that learners are expected to be self-directed. In a traditional course the instructor sets the learning goals, objectives, timelines, and evaluates the learning progress. In a MOOC, learners are expected to take on these responsibilities themselves. Learners cannot depend on an instructor to assist them in the learning process but are expected to be autonomous within a MOOC.

Kop (2011) surveyed participants, observed behaviors, and conducted focus groups on two cMOOCs held in 2010. The study revealed that those participants that had not engaged in this type of MOOC previously reported feeling overwhelmed and confused with the learning environment and process. In terms of self-directed learning, some participants enjoyed the autonomy provided by the MOOC and felt that the instructors or facilitators were equal contributors with the participants within the MOOC. Kop (2011) believed the participants of the MOOC were split on their comfort of the course. Half were comfortable being in control of their learning experience, and the other half indicated more support and direction would have been appreciated. Kop (2011) concluded that for MOOCs to be successful, especially the cMOOCs, learners must be self-directed and that there are conditions that can be created within MOOCs to encourage and assist learners through the course.

In a study of MOOC participants by Mackness, Mak, and Williams, (2010) some participants in the MOOC struggled with the lack of structure with the learning environment and some indicated a need for more guidance during the MOOC. Mackness et al. (2010), suggested that MOOCs are a paradox for learners in that the more MOOCs are designed for independent learning, the more learners must rely on each other to complete the MOOC. The researchers found that participants had a tendency to fall back on traditional methods of learning such as group formation to get them through the MOOC. More research is needed to find the ideal balance between open learning environments such as MOOCs, and structure and support.

Kop and Fournier (2010) conducted another study of a cMOOC to examine learner control. The researchers identified time management, goal setting, and a person's availability to participate in learning as three critical factors that influenced learners' abilities to participate in the MOOC. Participants cited reviewing resources critically and being able to learn actively with an open mindset as challenges they faced during the MOOC. The researchers concluded that participants of MOOCs should not have an aversion to risk or change if they are to be successful in MOOCs.

McAuley, Stewart, Siemens, and Cormier (2010) argued that MOOCs may be challenging for participants because they break the participants' traditional notion of what it means to be in a course. For example, the roles of instructor and student are not what may be expected, and this could be stressful to those experiencing a MOOC for the first time. Within a MOOC a learner takes on the responsibility for the learning goals and how the goals will be achieved. As a result, the researchers suggested that the high attrition rates in MOOCs occurred because participants did not understand the role they would have to play in the MOOC, and they likely did not have the academic experience or appropriate background to work within the MOOC. As a result, learners may dropout of MOOCs.

One of the key questions answered in the McAuley et al. (2010) study was what skills participants of MOOCs need. The researchers identified that MOOCs are self-guided because there are thousands of participants in each MOOC. Successful MOOC participants therefore should be self-starters that can collaborate, make decisions, and take charge of the learning process. Another research question explored in this study was to identify the factors that limit learner participation in MOOCs. The researchers noted that those participants most comfortable in traditional learning environments are likely to struggle in MOOCs. The researchers suggested that learners new to MOOCs will likely find their first MOOC challenging because of the lack of support and scaffolding offered (McAuley et al., 2010).

To summarize, at this time MOOCs are only one single solution to the challenges that higher education is currently facing. However, if more learners are not able to successfully meet the goals of a MOOC, it is likely that other open education initiatives may provide a better education alternative and MOOCs may not continue to exist. On the other hand, MOOCs should be viewed as a starting point to motivate universities into new educational opportunities, and to further innovate and develop meaningful open education for global learners. In addition, MOOCs could be the beginning of new policies, business models, and teaching practices for higher education, which are all in need of change (Yuan & Powell, 2013).

Self-directed learning remains a viable means of study as part of adult learning theory (Merriam, 2001), and regardless of criticism, self-directed learning is one of the most studied and practiced areas within adult education (Brockett & Donaghy, 2005). As new learning contexts such as MOOCs appear within higher education, from the literature review, it is logical to examine these online courses and their relationship with self-directed learners.

Because MOOCs have only been part of American university offerings for approximately two years, little research exists on the effectiveness of these online courses. If more is known about the adult learners that persist and complete MOOCs, as compared to those that do not complete MOOCs, steps can be taken to improve MOOCs for many different types of learners, especially those not strong in self-directed learning. Studies have found that matching a learner's readiness for self-directed learning to the proper educational delivery method can lead to optimal learning outcomes (Grow, 1991). More information is needed about MOOC completion and the learners that take these courses if MOOCs are to prevail and be a successful educational offering for many years to come.

RESEARCH METHODS AND DATA

This chapter provides a look at the research methods used to study the relationship between adult learners' readiness for self-directed learning and MOOC completion percents. To accomplish this, the research subjects and population are described, along with the instrument that was used to measure the identified variables. Also included in this chapter is a description of the approach used to gather and analyze data collected for this study and the summary of the data results.

Research Approach

Using quantitative research methods this was a relational study with a single-group design, resulting in a non-experimental study. Participants registered for a single Coursera MOOC titled Disaster Preparedness were invited to participate in the study. Coursera was selected as the MOOC platform for this study because it was one of the largest providers of massive online courses (Young, 2013) offering over 200 MOOCs on more than 20 different subjects ("The big three," 2012). In addition to its large MOOC offering, Coursera has two and half million registrants taking its MOOCs (Morrison, 2013). Such a popular MOOC provider seemed ideal to reach a large MOOC audience for this study.

Phenomena Investigated

Several variables were examined in this study including self-directed learning readiness, MOOC completion percents, and the demographic variables of age, gender, highest level of education completed, previous MOOC experience, reason for taking the course, English language ability, possible interference with course completion from a disability or impairment, and reasons for not completing this course. The independent variable in this study was an individual's readiness for self-directed learning methods, which was measured using a self-directed learning instrument administered through the first self-reporting online survey. From this first survey participants answered 40 questions on their readiness for self-directed learning experiences and then were assigned a score between 40 and 200 based on their responses. This score indicated their readiness for self-directed learning.

The dependent variable for this study was MOOC completion percent, which was self-reported through an online survey sent to those who completed the first survey. All the study participants were asked to estimate their completion percents from zero to 100 once the MOOC ended.

Population

This study had a single population of adults, defined as those 18 and older, with at least a minimal ability to read English, registered for the MOOC on the Coursera platform. As of early 2013, more than two and a half million people were registered for one or more of the over 200 MOOCs offered at Coursera. Of those registered with Coursera, approximately 28% were located within Europe and 35% lived in North America. From this population, 80% have college degrees, and half of this group has formal education beyond a bachelor's degree (Morrison, 2013). Based on these general statistics of Coursera MOOC participants, the population for this study was identified. It was estimated that between 20,000 and 50,000 adults would register for the Disaster Preparedness MOOC. Approximately 21,000 did register. From this group it was estimated that the majority of registrants would have college degrees and be located within the United States.

Sampling Method

The sample for this study was drawn from a single Coursera MOOC called Disaster Preparedness, which began on August 26, 2013 and ran for six weeks. All registrants of this MOOC were invited to participate in this study making this a census since the researcher was not sampling the population.

Summary of Study Participants

Using a sample size calculator, it was estimated that, with a confidence level of 95%, a confidence interval of five and population of 21,912, that the minimum sample size needed was 378. Given that 583 MOOC registrants participated in this study, the results should be a representative sample of the Disaster Preparedness MOOC registrants, though they cannot be declared a representative sample of all adult MOOC learners. To learn more about the 583 study participants, descriptive statistics were calculated for the eight demographic questions collected through the first online survey (see Table 1).

Also part of the first online survey, participants were asked to select the reasons they chose to enroll in the Disaster Preparedness MOOC. Respondents could choose as many responses as applied. The two most popular reasons chosen were, "to gain specific skills to do my current job better" (28%) and "a curiosity about the online course" at (26%). However, 60% indicated that another reason was responsible for their registration in this specific MOOC. Participants had the option to select "other" and type in a more specific response. These responses were reviewed and most that typed in a response indicated a curiosity about the subject matter or felt the content would assist them with their current positions, which reflects the two most popular options already highlighted. For the complete list of reasons the participants enrolled in the MOOC, view Table 2.

Table 1. Study Participant Demographics

Variable	n and percent
Gender • Male • Female	 273 (46.8%) 310 (53.2%)
Age • 18 to 19 years old • 20 to 24 years old • 25 to 29 years old • 30 to 34 years old • 35 to 39 years old • 40 to 44 years old • 45 to 49 years old • 50 to 54 years old • 55 to 59 years old • 60 to 64 years old • 65 to 74 years old • 75 to 84 years old • 85 years and over	 2 (0.3%) 35 (6.05%) 64 (11%) 78 (13.4%) 63 (10.8%) 70 (12%) 64 (11%) 60 (10.3%) 74 (12.7%) 35 (6%) 37 (6.3%) 1 (0.2%) 0 (0%)
Education • Secondary/Middle School • High School/GED • Associate's Degree • Bachelor's Degree • Master's Degree • Ph.D./Doctorate	 5 (0.9%) 101 (17.3%) 65 (11.1%) 198 (34%) 174 (29.8%) 40 (6.9%)
Previous MOOC Experience • Yes • No	 415 (71.2%) 168 (28.8%)
English Speaking Ability • Proficient • Advanced • Moderate • Low • None	 418 (71.7%) 78 (13.4%) 78 (13.4%) 9 (1.5%) 0 (0%)
English Literacy Ability • Proficient • Advanced • Moderate • Low • None	 438 (75.1%) 94 (16.1%) 49 (8.4%) 2 (0.3%) 0 (0%)
Disability or Impairment • Yes • No • Prefer not to say	 19 (3.3%) 552 (94.7%) 12 (2.1%)

Self-Directed Learning Readiness

The first online survey contained the 40-question assessment used to measure a person's readiness for self-directed learning, called the Self-Directed Learning Readiness Scale (Fisher, King, & Tague, 2001). This scale measures one's ability for readiness to take charge and manage educational experiences. Scores of the SDLRS can range from 40 points, the lowest possible score, to 200 points, the highest score possible. All participants who scored 150 and over were said to be ready for self-directed learning

Table 2. Reasons for Enrolling in the MOOC

Variable	n and percent
Reasons for Enrolling in MOOC	
• Skills for current job	163 (28.4%)
• Skills for new job	82 (14.1%)
• It was recommended	35 (6%)
• Professor	9 (1.5%)
• Univ. of Pittsburgh	29 (5%)
• Knowledge for degree	21 (3.6%)
• Curiosity	149 (25.6%)
• Other	352 (60%)
• None of these	27 (4.6%)

according to Fisher et al. (2001). Those that scored less than 150 on the SDLRS were categorized as not being ready for self-directed learning.

All 583 study participants completed the 40 questions of the SDLRS and a cumulative score was calculated for each participant. For the SDLRS scores, the average score was 165.62, the mean score. The standard deviation of scores was 16.149. The most common score in the data, the mode, was a score of 166, and the number in the middle of the data set, the median, was 165. The range was found to be 100, with the lowest or minimum score being 100 and the highest score being 200. Based on these numbers, the scores formed a roughly bell-shaped curve. See Figure 1 for a bar chart that represents the frequency of each score and the number of participants that obtained each score.

In addition, the participants were divided into two groups, those considered "ready" for self-directed learning strategies and those "not ready" for self-directed learning. Based on the data, 81% of the participants fell into the "ready" category. While 13% of the study participants were grouped "not ready". The mean score of those "ready" for self-directed learning was 169.80 and the mean score of those "not ready" was 139.84.

MOOC Completion Percents

Participants of the study were asked to estimate the percent of the MOOC they completed. Participants were given three opportunities to estimate their MOOC completion on the second survey. Ideally, all three of these questions would have been answered with data directly downloaded from the Coursera LMS, but instead, participants were asked to estimate their MOOC completion. Again, 583 participants completed this four-question survey. The first question asked participants if they completed all the MOOC requirements by passing all six quizzes and completing the final project. All participants in the study responded and 61.2% indicated they completed all the MOOC requirements, 37% estimated they did not complete the MOOC requirements, and 1.7% were not sure if they completed all the requirements.

The second question asked participants to select the individual MOOC requirements that were successfully completed. Again, 61% indicated they completed the final project, which was the final required component of the MOOC. This percent matched the 61% that indicated they completed all the MOOC requirements in the first survey question. For an overview of MOOC requirements completed as indicated by the first two survey questions, view Table 3.

The third question on the survey instructed participants to estimate the percent of the MOOC they completed. Completion could range from 0% to 100%. The mean, or average completion percent indicated, was 70.98%. The standard deviation was calculated to be 37.980. The most common percent of

Figure 1. SDLRS scores

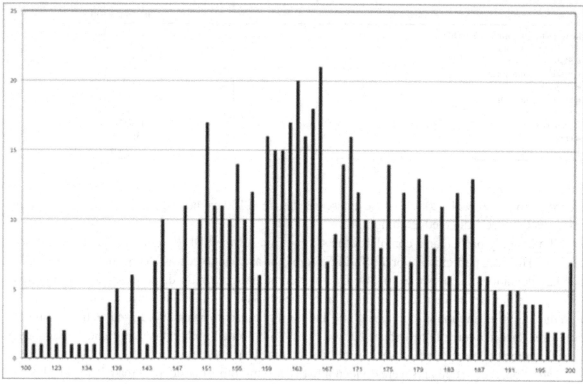

completion indicated, the mode, was 100%, and the number in the middle of the data set, the median, was 99%. The range was 100, with the lowest or minimum percent indicated 0% complete, and the highest end of the range being 100% complete. See Figure 2 for a pie chart representing the percent of completion grouped from 0% to 49% complete (26.40%), from 50% to 99% complete (22.70%), and those that estimated 100% of the course requirements were completed (50.90%). Note on the chart that 297 respondents, or 50.90%, indicated they completed 100% of the course. This completion percent was slightly lower than the 60% that indicated in the first two questions that they completed all the MOOC requirements. When reviewing the raw data, there were several participants that indicted they completed the MOOC on the first survey question, that they completed the final project, but then only estimated they completed 90% of the MOOC requirements, for example.

To summarize the data collected on MOOC completion, for the first survey question, approximately 61.2% of the study participants indicated they completed all of the MOOC requirements, for the second survey question, 60.9% estimated they completed the final project, and for the third survey question, 50.9% estimated they completed 100% of the MOOC requirements. These were only estimates, but they appear inflated for MOOC learners in general, and specifically for those that registered for the Disaster Preparedness MOOC on Coursera. Of the 21,912 registrants for the MOOC, in reality only 1,475 completed all the MOOC requirements, approximately 7%. The 7% completion, while typical for a MOOC, was not represented in the data collected, as around 60% of the study participants indicated they completed all the requirements. Figure 3 compares the estimated MOOC completion for each of the three survey questions.

Table 3. MOOC Requirements Completed

Variable	n and percent
Completed all requirements? • Yes • No • Not Sure	357 (61.2%) 216 (37%) 10 (1.7%)
Completed Week 1 Quiz • Yes • No	488 (83.7%) 95 (16.3%)
Completed Week 2 Quiz • Yes • No	469 (75.4%) 114 (18.3%)
Completed Week 3 Quiz • Yes • No	447 (76.7%) 136 (23.3%)
Completed Week 4 Quiz • Yes • No	423 (72.6%) 160 (27.4%)
Completed Week 5 Quiz • Yes • No	407 (69.8%) 176 (30.2%)
Completed Week 6 Quiz • Yes • No	400 (68.6%) 183 (31.4%)
Completed Final Project • Yes • No	355 (60.9%) 228 (39.1%)
Completed No Components • Yes • No	81 (13.9%) 502 (86.1%)

For the final question of the second survey, participants chose reasons, if they did not complete the Disaster Preparedness MOOC. Respondents could choose as many responses as applied. The three most selected reasons were time constraints, 28%, all the information needed was obtained, 9.3%, and the choice other, 14.8%. The other choice allowed participants to write in responses. These responses were reviewed and participants wrote about events that interfered with their completion such as having a baby, they also wrote that they were not comfortable completing the final assignment, and participants indicated that all the information they required was obtained. Many of the responses written would likely fit into the choices provided. View Table 4 for a list of the choices and the percents assigned to each.

SOLUTIONS AND RECOMMENDATIONS

This study explored the relationship between self-directed learning readiness and MOOC completion among adult learners taking a single Coursera MOOC in the fall of 2013. Through two online surveys administered by the researcher, the participants completed the SDLRS developed by Fisher et al. (2001) to measure readiness for self-directed learning, and self-reported their MOOC completion percent. Data was also collected on the MOOC participants to uncover their reasons for registering for the MOOC

Figure 2. MOOC completion percents

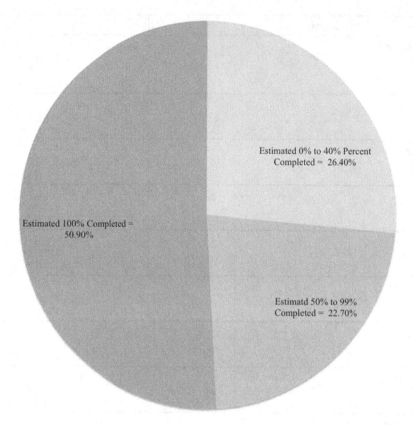

as well as their reasons for not completing the MOOC. After conducting the data analysis, several key findings were identified. First, and most importantly, a statistical significance was found between higher scores on the SDLRS and higher MOOC completion percents, as well as those that completed 100% of the MOOC. Though the effect sizes were small to near moderate, there were statistically significant relationships between the degree of self-directed learning readiness of adult learners and the degree of their MOOC completion, or their MOOC completion status. Second, English speaking ability was a variable that found statistical significance with MOOC completion status, as well as had a mediating effect between both SDLRS scores and MOOC completion percent. Third, those participants with proficient or advanced English speaking abilities tended to be more ready for self-directed learning. One finding that did not materialize after analyzing the data was the expectation that those with previous MOOC experience would be more likely to complete the MOOC. These results and others are discussed in more detail in this chapter.

Research Question 1: Conclusions

The first research question was, "to what extent, if at all, was there a relationship between the degree of self-directed learning readiness of adult learners and the degree of their MOOC completion?". The hypothesis was that the more competent adult learners were at self-directed learning, the more likely these learners were to successfully complete a greater percent of a MOOC. Based on this hypothesis, the

Figure 3. Three survey questions for estimated MOOC completion

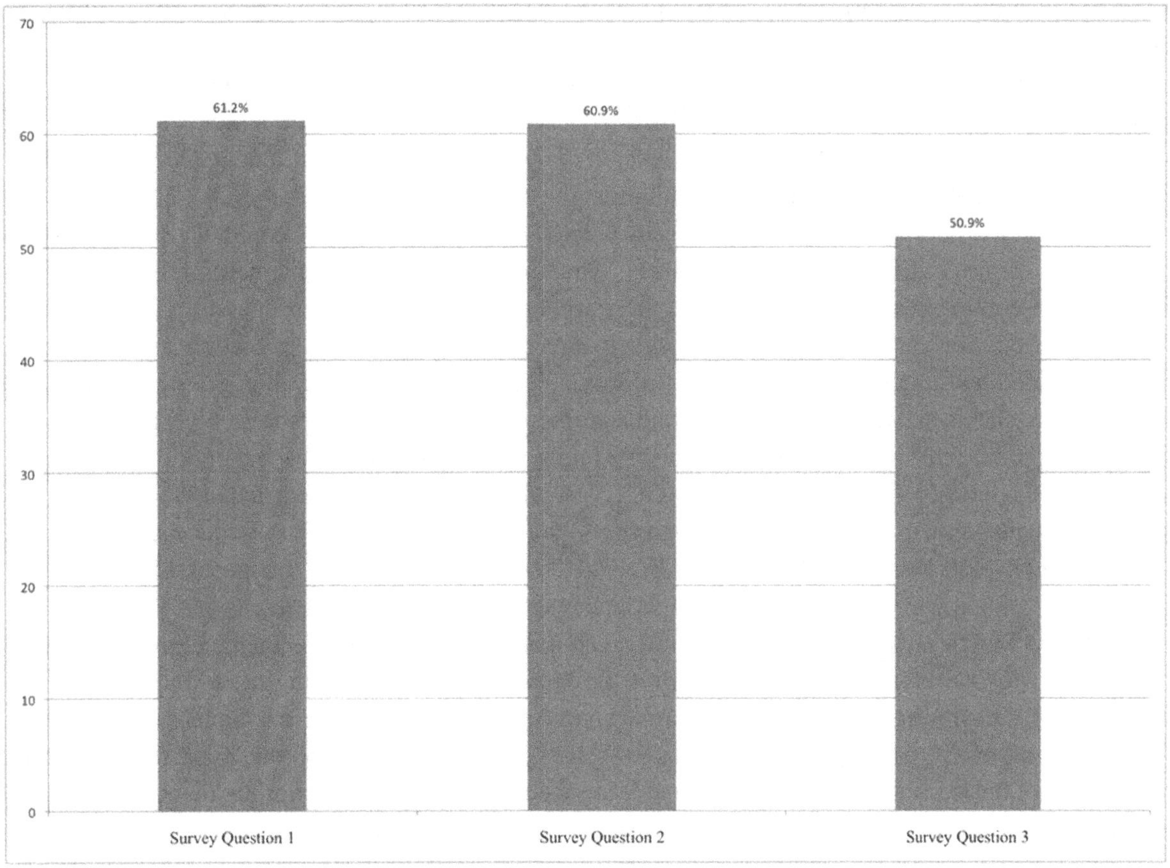

Table 4. Reasons for Not Completing the MOOC

Variable	n and percent
Reasons for Not Completing MOOC	
• Time constraints	175 (30.0%)
• Got all information needed	58 (9.9%)
• Content not what expected	39 (6.7%)
• Challenging to navigate	8 (1.3%)
• Language was a barrier	10 (1.7%)
• Technical problems	13 (2.2%)
• Assignments increasingly hard	10 (1.7%)
• No college credit offered	7 (1.2%)
• Did not feel comfortable	16 (2.7%)
• Course requirements unclear	6 (1.0%)
• Needed more assistance	2 (0.3%)
• Other	86 (14.8%)

two variables measured were self-directed learning readiness scores and MOOC completion percents. From the hypothesis, the researcher expected that those that scored higher on the SDLRS would have completed a greater percent of the MOOC.

The first hypothesis was supported and it was found that a significant relationship, though small effect size, existed between readiness for self-directed learning and MOOC completion percent. In other words, those with greater SDLRS scores completed more of the MOOC requirements. Support for this hypothesis can be found in research that highlighted the autonomy learners face while taking a MOOC and that these learners were expected to be self-directed (Kop, 2011; Bonk, Lee, Sheu, & Kou, 2013). The results of the SDLRS (Fisher et al., 2001), which measured self-management, desire for learning, and self-control, seemed to indicate that these were the skills needed to successfully complete the MOOC studied. Several studies indicated that self-directed learning, or one of the many traits related to self-directed learning, had an impact on the success of online learners (Dillon & Gabbard, 1998). For example, Garrison (2003) found that online learning environments gave more control to learners as compared to traditional learning environments. Assuming MOOCs would offer the opportunity for this same kind of control, to be successful in a MOOC, one might conclude that participants would need to be able to manage their own progress through the MOOC, stay motivated throughout the experience, and work independently to complete the MOOC. Kop (2011) concluded that to be successful at MOOCs, learners participating in these educational experiences should be self-directed. Yuan and Powell (2013) also believed that motivation for learners could be an issue as they started and then had to persevere to complete a MOOC. From this study, as well as the literature, it seemed being ready for self-directed learning, and thus having a strong desire to learn, should have assisted learners in completion of MOOCs.

Successful MOOC participants may need to be self-starters that can collaborate, make decisions, and take charge of the learning process. The studies referenced here supported the finding that those stronger in self-directed learning were more successful at completing the MOOC identified for this study.

This section discusses the implications for individual learners, MOOC designers, and the universities offering MOOCs based on the findings of the first hypothesis. First, more opportunities for developing self-directed learning skills should be considered. Given that self-directed learners may be more successful at MOOCs, it seems logical to examine whether or not all learners are being prepared to participate in educational contexts such as MOOCs. An argument could be made that education needs to focus on making learners independent in their inquiry and more autonomous. This could be done by implementing teaching strategies and methods, such as those referenced in the field of andragogy. Individuals exposed to this independent type of education grow to seek out learning experiences, enjoy learning new things, and embrace changes as an opportunity to learn (Knowles, 1980).

If higher education continues to develop offerings such as MOOCs, then developing independent and autonomous learners may need to be a priority. Adults should be actively participating in their own educational activities, and as more non-traditional students emerge, there need to be educational opportunities for them such as MOOCs. For example, the highest ranked reason the study participants indicated for wanting to take the MOOC in this study was to develop new skills. Adult learners that want to enhance their careers and build new skills need opportunities to access education solutions that are affordable and flexible. MOOCs are one option that adult learners are seeking out to fill their educational needs. Those wanting to learn from MOOCs may need assistance in developing their self-directed learning skills to be successful at MOOCs.

The second implication is for those designing MOOCs. If adults that are strong in self-directed learning are succeeding, then it may be that those not self-directed are struggling with MOOCs. Different design strategies could be applied to MOOCs to offer those requiring more assistance, additional opportunities to be successful. For example, MOOCs lack structure and must be designed for thousands of learners, which limits student access to the instructor. This is a very different model than traditional higher education courses (Yuan & Powell, 2013). Again, for those strong in self-directed learning, this learning context may be an ideal learning environment. However, for those not comfortable with self-directed learning, they may feel overwhelmed and need more access to content experts or assistance moving within the MOOC. Studies have found that matching a learner's readiness for self-directed learning to the proper educational delivery method can lead to optimal learning outcomes (Grow, 1991). One idea is for MOOC designers to offer different delivery options for learners or build more structured options for those that may need extra assistance and guidance. A few changes, even something as simple as an online MOOC orientation, an online syllabus or road-map for completion, may allow more types of adult learners to be successful at MOOCs. Another suggestion may be to have facilitators available to those taking MOOCs. These facilitators, though not content experts like instructors, perhaps could be experts in taking MOOCs and offer guidance in MOOC completion.

Another strategy that could be useful is for MOOC designers to document and apply specific online course development standards or criteria to ensure that MOOCs meet minimum standards of quality. For example, Johnson and Aragon (2003) identified seven criteria that all online learning environments should meet. These criteria include addressing the individual needs of learners, motivating learners, providing opportunities for engagement, and more. Following specific standards such as these could enable designers to more consistently develop quality MOOCs that can be taken and completed by many different types of learners.

The third implication is at the university level. Universities that offer MOOCs need to be aware of who is taking their MOOCs and who is successfully completing them. MOOCs were originally intended to drive down the costs of higher education for students by providing quality education online for free. If universities are going to continue to invest in MOOC development, then they may eventually require higher completion rates. For example, if the business model for MOOCs is to be self-sustaining, then one opportunity for making money is to charge a fee for obtaining a course completion certificate (Yuan & Powell, 2013). As data continues to show, the majority of learners are not completing MOOCs, which should be a cause for concern when trying to build a sustainable business model for universities such as the one in this study. In addition, if learners continue to register for MOOCs, but not complete them, then platforms of MOOCs like Coursera may have to look for new sources of income such as charging for registration or requesting higher fees from the universities that are hosting MOOCs on their platforms.

An opposing view to increasing MOOC completion rates should also be discussed. As this study noted, it is critical to understand the reasons a learner is enrolling in a MOOC in order to better know how to best meet that person's learning needs within the educational context. Participants in this study indicated they wanted to learn new skills for their current jobs, 28%, or develop their skills for a future job, 14%. Very few, only around 4%, selected they were taking the MOOC as part of working toward a degree. The fact that learners are out to gain new skills may translate into lower MOOC completion rates because the incentive to complete academic requirements of a course may not be needed (Kolowich, 2014). With over 70% of the participants in this study already having a bachelor's, master's, or doctorate degree, it may be unlikely that these attendees felt compelled to complete all the MOOC requirements. These learners may simply access a MOOC to get at the content found within the course. This idea could cause one to reconsider measuring MOOC effectiveness through completion rates. Universities may need to reassess how they define successful MOOCs based on the needs of the audiences taking their MOOCs.

While the results for this first hypothesis indicated that those strong in self-directed learning may be successful at MOOCs, unfortunately one may find that those not strong in self-directed learning will not be successful at MOOCs. Implications to consider include long-term investment in developing self-directed learning skills, designing MOOCs so that many learners can be successful, and focusing how universities view MOOCs, not as a marketing tool, but as a sustainable business model for many different types of adult learners.

Research Question 2: Conclusions and Implications

The second research question was, "to what extent, if at all, were there differences in demographics of adult learners that completed a MOOC compared with those that did not complete a MOOC?". The hypothesis was that adult learners with previous experience taking a MOOC were more likely to complete a MOOC. When examining the results of the data analysis, no significant relationship was found between previous MOOC experience and MOOC completion status. In a study by Shih, Munoz, and Sanchez (2006), students' previous experience with online tools was measured with their experiences in an undergraduate online classroom. The researchers determined that regardless of previous experience with online tools, participants rated the online course as a positive learning experience. In other words, previous MOOC experience may or may not have been helpful when it came to completing the specific MOOC in this study.

Several different possibilities were considered to explain this finding. One explanation was that the number of registrants that self-reported completing the MOOC was inflated. Of the 21,912 registrants for the MOOC, in reality only 1,475 completed all the MOOC requirements, approximately 7%. The 7% completion, while typical for a MOOC (Yuan & Powell, 2013), is not represented in the data collected, as over 60% of the study participants indicated they completed all the requirements. Again, more than 60% indicated they completed the final project, which was the final required component of the MOOC. This validates the 60% that indicated they completed 100% of the MOOC requirements. It may be that those participants that completed the MOOC were the ones that participated in the study, or that these participants overestimated their completion. It is important to consider that since only 2.7% of the total MOOC registrants participated in this study, the results of this research question may have been due to self-selection. Another explanation for the lack of previous MOOC experience being significant was that the specific Coursera MOOC identified for this study could have been intuitive for learners to complete, and no previous experience was necessary. Therefore, there may be a relationship between previous MOOC experience and MOOC completion. Additional research using other MOOCs is needed to determine if this finding is an outlier of the research.

The last significant relationship found for the second research question was the enrollment reason that stated, the MOOC was recommended by someone the learner knew. If participants selected they enrolled in the MOOC because it was recommended by someone they knew, then they were more likely to complete the MOOC. Around 7% of the study respondents indicated that someone they knew recommended the MOOC to them and these registrants then went on to complete the MOOC. Obviously, having a course recommended is valuable for registration, but its effect on persistence through completion needs further study. One explanation for this is that perhaps some of the registrants looking to build new skills had the MOOC recommended by their work supervisors. These employees may have felt obligated to complete the MOOC as part of a work requirement. Another thought is that if a peer recommended the course, then perhaps both learners were taking the MOOC together and they were able to motivate each other to complete all the requirements. More research is needed to determine if having the MOOC recommended by someone you know is a good indicator for completion.

Research Question 3: Conclusions

The third research question was, "to what extent, if at all, did adult learner demographics mediate the relationship between self-directed learning readiness and degree of MOOC completion?". The third hypothesis was that adult learners in their thirties and forties, who were female, with high levels of education, previous MOOC experience, strong English language skills, and with no physical disability or impairment that may interfere with completing an online course, would have higher scores in self-directed learning readiness and therefore have higher MOOC completion percents. Again, self-directed learning readiness scores were measured using the SDLRS and MOOC completion percents were gathered from the self-reported data collected on the second online survey.

All eight demographic variables collected were analyzed against self-directed learning readiness scores and MOOC completion percents. It should be noted that most of the variables in the hypothesis were not found to be significant between self-directed learning and MOOC completion percents. The only variable that had a significant mediating effect between both percent of MOOC completed and SDLRS score was English speaking ability. Those that rated themselves proficient or advanced in English speaking were found to have higher SDLRS scores and completed a greater percent of the MOOC than those that rated themselves as moderate, low, or with no English speaking ability. Of those that participated in the study, 85% indicated they were proficient or advanced in English speaking.

This section discusses the implications for individual learners, MOOC designers, and the universities offering MOOCs based on the findings of the third hypothesis. The first implication is that MOOCs may not be accessible to all learners, especially those that do not speak English. The second implication is that designers of MOOCs may need to develop MOOCs that are more manageable to learners in different cultures, and the third implication is that universities should further examine if they are reaching the intended audiences for their MOOCs.

In addition, there are claims that MOOCs are supposed to benefit third world countries where people wanting access to education do not have opportunities to attend a quality university. Yet, the majority of MOOCs are currently developed by western universities and may not be culturally appropriate for all learners (Rivard, 2013). It may be that MOOCs are only being accessed by those proficient in the English language, or that only those proficient in English can successfully complete them. If MOOCs are being designed by western universities, then these courses are likely best suited for English speaking cultures as well. Those not as familiar with western ideas and learning practices may not be able to successfully complete MOOCs. A recommendation from this study would be to have MOOC designers consider additional support and instructional strategies to assist learners who are not proficient in the English language. Universities should also consider placing more emphasis on reaching different audiences to include those not proficient in English.

This study highlights the possibility that to be successful at MOOCs, one should likely be advanced or proficient in speaking English and even listening to English given all the instructional videos in many MOOCs. This leaves out a large percent of the world's population that MOOCs were originally targeted to reach. More research should be conducted on those that take MOOCs, with the idea of comparing these results to the audiences not proficient in speaking English. Designers should be aware that all learners are not going to be successful at MOOCs if their culture and language was not considered from the conception of the development of each course.

Unfortunately, guidelines for developers that should assist in overcoming accessibility barriers such as language are often complex to understand and challenging to implement (Pearson & Koppi, 2002). Designers may need training and education on how to design and develop culturally appropriate MOOCs. If learners have negative experiences with online education, then their perceptions of online courses are likely not positive, which can lead to them dropping out of future online courses (Carr, 2000). Better understanding the barriers learners face should allow for more effective online course design and development.

In addition, universities need to carefully design and market MOOCs to their intended audiences. This means that more should be done to design accessible MOOCs and then promote them to non-native English speakers. One recommendation might be for universities to carefully document their marketing and promotion strategies of MOOCs to make sure that the intended audiences have the knowledge needed to decide which MOOCs they would like to participate in.

In summary, there were several implications surrounding English speakers and their ability to complete MOOCs and obtain high SDLRS scores. Unfortunately, MOOCs may not be accessible to all learners, especially those that are not proficient in the English language. As a result, designers of MOOCs should focus on making MOOCs more accessible, while universities should further examine if they are reaching the intended audiences for their MOOCs.

FUTURE RESEARCH DIRECTIONS

Given there were several significant relationships found between variables, future research should continue to examine these same relationships to determine if the results can be generalized to other populations. First, a statistically significant relationship was found to exist between self-directed learning and MOOC completion percents. The SDLRS should be administered to registrants in other MOOCs, and on different platforms. These results should then be compared to the MOOC completion percents, which should not be self-reported, but downloaded from the learning management system. Next, MOOC learner demographic data should be examined to determine if there are variables that have relationships between self-directed learning and MOOC completion.

Second, more data is needed to better understand why learners register for MOOCs and why they do not complete them. It is important to study those learners who are successful and complete MOOCs, as well as those that do not complete MOOCs. Having a better understanding of the specific point a person leaves a MOOC and knowing why that person left, would be valuable data to collect. This research study found that time constraints was the primary reason a learner did not complete the MOOC. This insight, if confirmed by other researchers, could support the development of new types of MOOCs such as massive, open, online, content, not courses. It may be that some learners are only accessing a MOOC to examine the content and are not interested in taking an actual course. This type of content MOOC focuses on smaller chunks of information that may be easier to complete and then apply (Lue, 2013). In addition, if there were no time constraints on accessing the MOOC materials, non-native speakers of English would have additional time to listen and comprehend videos, and read materials, instead of perhaps rushing to complete content and not fully comprehending the information. New forms of

MOOCs, along with other ideas for how best to evolve current MOOCs, should be based on research to meet specific problems that learners have.

Third, it would be interesting to further explore the relationship between MOOC completion and having the MOOC recommended by someone you know. Additional research should be conducted to determine if a learner has a friend or colleague recommend a MOOC, and possibly takes the MOOC with that person, then the learner is more likely to complete the MOOC. If this relationship continues to exist in other MOOCs, then many new strategies could be used to increase the likelihood of completion. For example, invitations to register for MOOCs could be based on getting a personal invite from a friend that is already attending the MOOC. Another idea is that MOOC attendance could be linked to social media where individuals could invite their friends to attend a MOOC. Getting MOOC registrants to recommend and then attend a MOOC with a friend would be an idea worth further study.

By examining more MOOCs, data can continue to be collected to assess whether registrants must be self-directed learners to successfully complete MOOCs. Such high dropout rates as MOOCs show, could begin to negatively impact universities from a quality and financial viewpoint (Angelino, Williams, & Natvig, 2007). Coming up with solutions to attrition in online education could be critical to the future success of online education initiatives such as MOOCs.

CONCLUSION

This study explored the relationship between self-directed learning readiness and MOOC completion among adult learners taking a single Coursera MOOC. The hypothesis that the more competent adult learners were at self-directed learning, the more likely these learners were to successfully complete a greater percent of a MOOC, was found to be statistically significant. This finding was supported in the literature, confirming that to be successful in a MOOC, learners were expected to be self-directed (Kop, 2011; Bonk et al., 2013). Given that alternative explanations could have resulted in this significant relationship, additional research is needed to measure the self-directed learning readiness of other MOOC registrants. These results should then be compared to the MOOC completion percents, which ideally would be downloaded from a learning management system, and not self-reported. MOOC learner demographic data should also be examined to determine if there are variables that have statistically significant relationships between self-directed learning and MOOC completion, such as English speaking ability did for this study.

Though some statistically significant relationships between variables were found, other hypotheses were not supported by the findings of this study. For example, the second hypothesis was not supported; previous MOOC experience and MOOC completion status were not statistically significant. The researcher expected that having previous exposure to the MOOC learning environment would positively impact the ability to complete the MOOC in this study. Therefore, it is recommended that additional research on factors that influence MOOC completion is warranted to better understand the skills and experiences needed to be successful in a MOOC. Lastly, to further improve the completion rates for MOOCs, more information about those that drop out, when they drop out, and why, should be studied. These research results and others can then be compiled to create solutions for improving the effectiveness and therefore the completion rates of MOOCs.

REFERENCES

Angelino, L. M., Williams, F. K., & Natvig, D. (2007). Strategies to engage online students and reduce attrition rates. *The Journal of Educators Online*, *4*(2). Retrieved from http://www.thejeo.com/Volume4Number2/Angelino%20Final.pdf

Balch, T. (2013). *About MOOC completion rates: The importance of student investment* [Web log post]. Retrieved from http://augmentedtrader.wordpress.com/2013/01/06/about-mooc-completion-rates-the-importance-of-investment/

Bonk, C. J., & Kim, K. J. (2006). The future of online teaching and learning in higher education: The survey says…. *EDUCAUSE Quarterly*, *4*, 22–30. Retrieved from http://www.educause.edu/ero/article/future-online-teaching-and-learning-higher-education-survey-says%E2%80%A6

Bonk, C. J., Lee, M. M., Sheu, F. R., & Kou, X. (2013). *Self-directed online learning: MOOCs, open education, and beyond.* Retrieved from http://www.courseshare.com/pdfs/Self-Directed_Lrng_MOOCs_Open_Ed_AECT_Bonk_et_al_Friday_paper_session.pdf

Brockett, R. G., & Donaghy, R. C. (2005, June). *Beyond the inquiring mind: Cyril Houle's contribution to self-directed learning.* Paper presented at the meeting of Proceedings of the 46th Annual Adult Education Research Conference, Athens, GA. Retrieved from http://www.sdlglobal.com/IJSDL/IJSDL9.2.pdf

California Community Colleges Chancellor's Office, California Community Colleges Student Success Task Force. (2012). *Advancing Student Success in the California Community Colleges.* Retrieved from http://californiacommunitycolleges.cccco.edu/PolicyinAction/StudentSuccessTaskForce.aspx

Candy, P. (1991). *Self-direction for lifelong learning: A comprehensive guide to theory and practice.* San Francisco, CA: Jossey-Bass.

Carr, S. (2000). As distance education comes of age, the challenge is keeping the students. *The Chronicle of Higher Education*, *46*(23), A39–A41. Retrieved from http://chronicle.com/article/As-Distance-Education-Comes-of/14334

Dillon, A., & Gabbard, R. (1998). Hypermedia as an educational technology: A review of the quantitative research literature on learner comprehension, control, and style. *Review of Educational Research*, *68*(3), 322–349. doi:10.3102/00346543068003322

Ehrman, M. (1990). Psychological factors and distance education. *American Journal of Distance Education*, *4*(1), 10–23. doi:10.1080/08923649009526688

Eisenberg, E., & Dowsett, T. (1990). Student dropout from a distance education project course: A new method analysis. *Distance Education*, *11*(2), 231–253. http://files.eric.ed.gov/fulltext/EJ853871.pdf doi:10.1080/0158791900110205

Fisher, M., King, J., & Tague, G. (2001). Development of a self-directed learning readiness scale for nursing education. *Nurse Education Today*, *21*(7), 516–525. doi:10.1054/nedt.2001.0589 PMID:11559005

Garrison, D. R. (2003). Self-directed learning and distance education. In M. G. Moore & W. Anderson (Eds.), *Handbook of distance education* (pp. 161–168). Mahwah, NJ: Routledge.

Grow, G. (1991). Teaching learners to be self-directed: A stage approach. *Adult Education Quarterly*, *41*(3), 125–149. doi:10.1177/0001848191041003001

Guglielmino, L. M. (1977). *Development of the self-directed learning readiness scale* (Doctoral dissertation). Available from ProQuest Information & Learning. (No. 38)

Hartley, K., & Bendixen, L. D. (2001). Educational research in the Internet age: Examining the role of individual characteristics. *Educational Researcher*, *30*(9), 22–26. doi:10.3102/0013189X030009022

Hiemstra, R. (1994). Self-directed adult learning. In T. Husen & T. N. Postlethwaite (Eds.), *International encyclopedia of education* (2nd ed.; pp. 9–19). Oxford, UK: Pergamon Press.

Iiyoshi, T., & Kumar, M. S. V. (2008). *Opening up education: The collective advancement of education through open technology, open content, and open knowledge*. MIT Press. Retrieved from https://mitpress. mit.edu/sites/default/files/titles/content/9780262515016_ Open_Access_Edition.pdf

Johnson, S. D., & Aragon, S. R. (2003). An instructional strategy framework for online learning environments. *Facilitating learning in online environments*, (pp. 31-43). San Francisco: Jossey-Bass. Retrieved from http://www.editlib.org/noaccess/15267

Jordan, K. (2013). *MOOC completion rates: The data* [Web log post]. Retrieved from http://www.katy-jordan.com/MOOCproject.html

Knowles, M. S. (1975). *Self-directed learning*. New York, NY: Association Press.

Knowles, M. S. (1980). *The modern practice of adult education: From pedagogy to andragogy revised and updated*. New York, NY: The Adult Education Company.

Knowles, M. S., Holton, E. F., & Swanson, R. A. (2011). *The adult learner* (7th ed.). Oxford, UK: Elsevier.

Kolowich, S. (2012, September). The MOOC survivors: edX explores demographics of most persistent MOOC students. *Inside Higher Education*. Retrieved from http://www.insidehighered.com/news/2012/09/12/edx-explores-demographics-most-persistent-mooc-students

Kolowich, S. (2014, January 22). *Completion rates aren't the best way to judge MOOCs, researchers say* [Web log post]. Retrieved from http://chronicle.com/blogs/wiredcampus/completion-rates-arent-the-best-way-to-judge-moocs-researchers-say/49721

Kop, R. (2011). The challenges to connectivist learning on open online networks: Learning experiences during a massive open online course. *International Review of Research in Open and Distance Learning*, *12*(3), 19–38. Retrieved from http://www.irrodl.org/index.php/irrodl/article/view/882

Kop, R., & Fournier, H. (2010). New dimensions to self-directed learning in an open networked learning environment. *International Journal of Self-Directed Learning*, *7*(2), 1–13. Retrieved from http://selfdirectedlearning.com/documents/Kop&Fournier2010.pdf

Koutropoulos, A., & Hogue, R. (2012). How to succeed in a MOOC: Massive online open course. *Learning Solutions Magazine*. Retrieved from http://www.learningsolutionsmag.com/articles/1023/how-to-succeed-in-a-massive-online-open-course-mooc

Lue, R. (2013, December 16). *Massive Open Online Courses, MOOC's: The Future of Education?* [Audio podcast]. Retrieved from http://www.kcrw.com/news/programs/tp/tp131216massive_open_online_

Mackness, J., Mak, S. F. J., & Williams, R. (2010). The ideals and reality of participating in a MOOC. Proceedings of the Seventh International Conference on Networked Learning. Lancaster, MI: University of Lancaster. Retrieved from http://www.lancs.ac.uk/fss/organisations/netlc/past/nlc2010/abstracts/Mackness.html

McAuley, A., Stewart, B., Siemens, G., & Cormier, D. (2010). *The MOOC model for digital practice.* Unpublished manuscript, University of Prince Edward Island. Retrieved from http://www.elearnspace.org/Articles/MOOC_Final.pdf

Merriam, S. B. (1993). Taking Stock. *New Directions for Adult and Continuing Education, 1993*(57), 105–110. doi:10.1002/ace.36719935712

Merriam, S. B. (2001). Andragogy and self-directed learning: Pillars of adult learning theory. *New Directions for Adult and Continuing Education, 2001*(89), 3–14. doi:10.1002/ace.3

Morrison, J. (2013, January 2). *MOOCs: Daphne Koller of Coursera shares insights* [Web log post]. Retrieved from http://digitalpresent.myblog.arts.ac.uk/2013/02/01/moocs-daphne-koller-of-coursera-shares-insights/

O'Kell, S. P. (1988). A study of the relationships between learning style, readiness for self-directed learning, and teaching preference of learner nurses in one health district. *Nurse Education Today, 8*(4), 197–204. doi:10.1016/0260-6917(88)90149-9 PMID:3419409

Pappano, L. (2012, November 2). The year of the MOOC. *The New York Times.* Retrieved from http://www.nytimes.com/2012/11/04/education/edlife/massive-open-online-courses-are-multiplying-at-a-rapid-pace.html?pagewanted=all

Parker, A. (1999). A Study of Variables that Predict Dropout from Distance Education. *International Journal of Educational Technology, 1*(2). Retrieved from http://www.ascilite.org.au/ajet/ijet/v1n2/parker/

Pearson, E. J., & Koppi, T. (2002). Inclusion and online learning opportunities: Designing for a Accessibility. *ALT-J, 10*(2), 17–28. doi:10.1080/0968776020100203

Pratt, D. D. (1993). Andragogy after twenty-five years. In S. B. Merriam (Ed.), *An update on adult learning theory. New directions for adult and continuing education* (Vol. 57). San Francisco, CA: Jossey-Bass.

Rivard, R. (2013). The world is not flat. *Inside Higher Education.* Retrieved from http://www.insidehighered.com/news/2013/04/25/moocs-may-eye-world-market-does-world-want-them

Rovai, A. (2002). Building sense of community at a distance. *International Review of Research in Open and Distance Learning, 4*(1), 1–9. Retrieved from http://www.irrodl.org/index.php/irrodl

Shih, P., Munoz, D., & Sanchez, F. (2006). The effect of previous experience with information and communication technologies on performance in a Web-based learning program. *Computers in Human Behavior, 22*(6), 962–970. doi:10.1016/j.chb.2004.03.016

The big three, at a glance. (2012, November 2). *The New York Times*. Retrieved from http://www.nytimes.com/2012/11/04/education/edlife/the-big-three-mooc-providers.html

Tuman, M. C. (1988). Class, codes, and composition: Basil Bernstein and the critique of Pedagogy. *College Composition and Communication, 39*(1), 42. doi:10.2307/357815

Watters, A. (2012a). *6.003z: A learner-created MOOC spins out of MITx* [Web log post]. Retrieved from http://www.hackeducation.com/2012/08/14/6.003z-learner-organized-mooc/

Wiley, K. (1983). Effects of a self-directed learning project and preference for a structure on self-directed learning readiness. *Nursing Research, 32*(3), 181–185. doi:10.1097/00006199-198305000-00011 PMID:6551780

Young, J. R. (2013). *Coursera announces details for selling certificates and verifying identities.* [Web log post]. Retrieved from http://chronicle.com/blogs/wiredcampus/coursera-announces-details-for-selling-certificates-and-verifying-identities/41519

Yuan, L., & Powell, S. (2013). MOOCs and open education: Implications for higher education. *Center for Educational Technology & Interoperability Standards* [Whitepaper]. Retrieved from http://publications.cetis.ac.uk/wp-content/uploads/2013/03/MOOCs-and-Open-Education.pdf

KEY TERMS AND DEFINITIONS

Adult Learner: Those that have taken on adult roles, such as a parent or spouse, and are responsible for their own lives.

Andragogy: A key component of adult learning theory and describes how adults learn and adult preferences for learning.

Course Completion: A measure of course success.

MOOC: A massive, open, online course about a specific topic, guided by an expert. Learners access free resources on the subject presented in the course.

Open Education: Free education that is accessible to all.

Scaffolding: Instructional strategies that can be used to move students successfully through a course.

Self-Directed Learners: Are responsible for planning, managing, and evaluating their own learning experiences.

Chapter 3
Cyberbullying:
Bullying in the Digital Age

Michelle F. Wright
Masaryk University, Czech Republic

ABSTRACT

Children and adolescents grow up in a constantly connected digital world. They maintain active involvement in the digital world through the creation of blogs, communication via social networking sites, and watching videos. Despite the opportunities seeming almost limitless in a digitally connected world, there is a darker side to electronic technology usage. Cyberbullying is a darker side to children's and adolescents' immersion in a digital world. Incorporating research from around the world and across multiple disciplines, the aim of this chapter is to describe the nature, extent, causes, and consequences associated with children's and adolescents' cyberbullying involvement. The chapter concludes with solutions and recommendations in order to further cyberbullying intervention and prevention. Such an approach is important as cyberbullying is a phenomenon occurring throughout the world. Future research directions are also given, with the aim of furthering research on cyberbullying in an effort to improve the world's understanding of these behaviors.

INTRODUCTION

Fully embracing electronic technologies (e.g., cell phones, the Internet, gaming consoles, computers), around 92% of children and adolescents utilize some form of technology daily (Lenhart, 2015). Electronic technologies allow children and adolescents many opportunities in their lives, including communication with friends and family, looking up information for personal, leisure, and school purposes, watching videos, and creating content, like blogs and wikis. Although electronic technologies allow many opportunities, there are also risks associated with this usage, including being exposed to fake or incorrect information, identity theft, sexual predators, and viewing unwanted and/or gory electronic content via videos, images, text messages, and writing. Cyberbullying is another risk factor related to children's and adolescents' electronic technology usage. Conceptualized as an extension of traditional face-to-face bullying, cyberbullying involves bullying through electronic technologies, including email, instant mes-

DOI: 10.4018/978-1-5225-0522-8.ch003

saging, social networking sites, text messaging via mobile devices, gaming consoles, and video content (Grigg, 2010, 2012; Nocentini et al., 2010). Being able to remain anonymous in the cyber context allows cyberbullies the flexibility to harm their victims without threat or fear of the consequences associated with their actions as they are able to hide their identity, often avoiding retribution from victims (Wright, 2014b). The anonymity created by the cyber context leads to the online disinhibition effect. This effect leads children and adolescents to do or say things to others in the cyber context that they would never do or say in the offline world (Moore, Nakano, Enomoto, & Suda, 2012; Suler, 2004; Wright, 2014a). The cyber context allows cyberbullies to harm their victims much quicker (e.g., it could take less than a minute or so to spread a rumor in the online world versus several hours or days to do so in the offline world), as much as they want (e.g., bullying in the online world often follows victims into their homed, whereas traditional face-to-face school bullying is usually localized to the school environment, allowing the victim to escape once he or she is home), and involve various people or bystanders in the bullying incident (e.g., posting a video online can receive thousands of watches and be shared multiple times by other people in the cyber context).

The aim of this chapter is to describe cyberbullying among children and adolescents, while incorporating research from psychology, education, media studies, communication, sociology, social work, human development, and computer science. The research also includes qualitative and quantitative studies as well as cross-sectional and longitudinal designs and those that incorporate cross-cultural and cross-national samples. Organized into nine sections, this chapter includes:

1. A description of cyberbullying, including the definition, types of electronic technologies used, anonymity, and prevalence rates of children's and adolescents' involvement in these behaviors,
2. An explanation of the predictors of children's and adolescents' perpetration of cyberbullying and cyber victimization,
3. A discussion of the role of parents in their children's cyberbullying involvement as perpetrators and/or victims,
4. A description of the role of schools and peers in children's and adolescents' cyberbullying involvement,
5. A review of the consequences (e.g., psychological, behavioral, academic) related to children's and adolescents' cyberbullying perpetration and cyber victimization,
6. A discussion of the cross-cultural differences in children's and adolescents' cyberbullying involvement,
7. An explanation of the solutions and recommendation for preventing and intervening in cyberbullying involvement as well as public policy recommendations for the intervention and prevention of these behaviors,
8. A description of possible future research directions regarding children's and adolescents' cyberbullying involvement,
9. A conclusion regarding the current state of the literature on children's and adolescents' cyberbullying perpetration and cyber victimization.

CYBERBULLYING

Researchers define cyberbullying as children's and adolescents' utilization of electronic technologies in order to hostilely and intentionally harass, embarrass, and intimidate others, including their peers and strangers (Ferdon & Hertz, 2007; Joinson, 1998; Kowalski & Limber, 2007; Slonje & Smith, 2008;

Topcu, Erdur-Baker, & Aydin, 2008; Wolak, Mitchell, & Finkelhor, 2007; Ybarra, West, & Leaf, 2007). Hostility and intentionality are essential to the definition of cyberbullying as these behaviors must include malicious, intentionally harmful acts in order to be classified as cyberbullying. Similar to the definition of traditional face-to-face bullying, cyberbullying involves repetition as well as an imbalance of power between the victim and the bully. The repetition of bullying behaviors in the cyber context is unique as cyberbullying can involve bullying the victim multiple times by sharing a humiliating video or text message with one person or multiple people, and in turn this person or people can further share the content multiple times (Vandebosch & Van Cleemput, 2008). This perpetuates the cycle of cyberbullying victimization as the cyberbullying behavior is shared over and over, potentially revictimizing the victim.

The difference between the definition of traditional face-to-face bullying and cyberbullying is the inclusion of electronic technology in the definition of cyberbullying (Olweus, 1999). Such behaviors can be carried out via various electronic technologies. The most frequently used electronic technologies for cyberbullying behaviors include gaming consoles, instant messaging, social networking sites, and text messages via mobile phones (Arslan, Savaser, Hallett, & Balci, 2012; Mouttapa, Valente, Gallagher, Rohrbach, & Unger, 2004). Although not an exhaustive list of cyberbullying behaviors and mediums, these behaviors can include sending unkind text messages and emails, stealing identity information, impersonating or pretending to be someone else on social media or email, making anonymous, harassing phone calls, revealing secrets about someone by posting the secret online or sending it to someone else, spreading untrue rumors about someone using social networking sites or text messages, threatening to harm someone in the offline world, or maliciously and intentionally posting an embarrassing picture or video of someone (Wolak et al., 2007; Wright & Li, 2012; Ybarra & Mitchell, 2004). Other forms of cyberbullying include similar behaviors as those perpetrated in the offline world, such as repeated harassment, nasty insults, verbal attacks, malicious teasing, physical threats, ostracism, and humiliation (Chisholm, 2006). Furthermore, cyberbullying can involve sending explicit, degrading, or embarrassing videos of someone via different mediums, like social networking sites, text messages, and email as well as creating malicious websites to defame and humiliate someone, making fake social networking site profiles using someone's identity, happy slapping (i.e., involves a group of people who insult someone at random while filming the incident with a mobile phone), and flaming (i.e., posting provocative or offensive messages and/or content in a public forum or chatroom with the intent of provoking a hostile response and/or argument) (Gillepsi, 2006; Rideout et al., 2005; Smith, Mahdavi, Carvalho, Fisher, Russell, & Tippett, 2008).

As children's and adolescents' electronic technology consumption has increased over the years, researchers began to recognize the importance of examining their involvement in cyberbullying. Earlier investigations of cyberbullying focused on the prevalence rates of children's and adolescents' cyberbullying perpetration and cyber victimization. In 2006, Patchin and Hinduja found that 29% of adolescents in their sample from the United States reported cyber victimization, while 47% had witnessed someone else be the victim of cyberbullying. Wolak and colleagues (2007) also conducted one of the earliest studies on cyberbullying among children and adolescents in the United States. They found that 50% of their participants reported cyber victimization. That same year, Kowalski and Limber (2007) also published a study on the prevalence rates of cyber victimization in the United States. Kowalski and Limber's study included 3,767 middle school students (aged 11-14), and they found that 11% of the sample were cybervictims, 4% were cyberbullies, and 7% were both cybervictims and cyberbullies. Most of these earlier studies involved early adolescence (ages 11-14), but some also include older samples. In particular, Goebert and colleagues (2011) found that 56.1% of their participants from Hawaii in grades 9th through 12th were victims of cyberbullying. Hinduja and Patchin (2012) reported that 4.9% of adolescents in grades 6th through 12th in their sample perpetrated cyberbullying within the last 30 days, while Cappadocia and colleagues (2013) found that only 2.1% of the Canadian 10th graders in their sample were cyberbullying perpetrators, 1.9% were classified as cybervictims, and 0.6% were both cyberbullies and cybervictims. One difference between Hinduja and Patchin's (2012) and Cappadocia and colleagues' (2013) studies is the country of origin for adolescents. However, Bonnanno and Hymel (2013) found prevalence rates more aligned with Hinduja and Patchin (2012) as 6% of their sample of Canadian 8th through 10th graders perpetrated cyberbullying, 5.8% were cybervictims, and 5% were both cyberbullies and cybervictims. Differences in prevalence rates might reflect variations in sampling techniques, measurement techniques, definitions used, and country of origin. Despite these differences, it is clear that cyberbullying is a concern, and consequently additional attention should be given to understanding the predictors of children's and adolescents' involvement in cyberbullying behaviors as perpetrators and/or victims.

PREDICTORS OF CYBERBULLYING

Nowadays, research on cyberbullying has moved beyond comparing prevalence rates among samples as many questions remained regarding the nature, extent, and measurement of these behaviors. Therefore, attention shifted from prevalence rates to the predictors of children's and adolescents' involvement in cyberbullying. Much of this research began by investigating age-related predictors of cyberbullying perpetration and cyber victimization. Among this research, some patterns seemed to emerge. For instance, early adolescents were revealed as experiencing the highest levels of cyber victimization when compared to children, older adolescents, and young adults. However, older adolescents were more often the perpetrators of cyberbullying. In one study, Williams and Guerra (2007) found that physical forms of cyberbullying, like hacking, peaked in middle school, with rates declining in high school. Unlike the previous studies on age, some research has found that age is not a consistent predictor of cyberbullying among children and adolescents. For instance, Wade and Beran's (2011) study revealed that 9th graders in their sample had the highest rates of cyberbullying involvement in comparison to adolescents from middle school. A lack of longitudinal research on age-related differences in cyberbullying has made it difficult to fully understand age as a predictor of children's and adolescents' involvement in these behaviors.

Like age, researchers also focused their attention on understanding gender as a predictor of cyberbullying perpetration and cyber victimization. Boulton and colleagues (2012) as well as Li (2007) and Ybarra et al. (2007) concluded that boys from their samples were most often the perpetrators of cyberbullying when compared to girls. Other research has suggested that girls were more likely to experience cyberbullying as victims when compared to boys (e.g., Adams, 2010; Hinduja & Patchin, 2007; Kowalski & Limber 2007). In related research, using similar ages, some researchers concluded that girls were more often engaged in cyberbullying, whereas boys experienced more victimization by cyberbullying (Akbulut, Sahih, & Eristi, 2010; Dehue, Bolman, & Vollink, 2008; Erdur-Baker, 2010; Huang & Chou, 2010; Pornari & Wood, 2010). Yet some research has revealed no gender differences in children's and adolescents' cyberbullying involvement (e.g., Beran & Li, 2005; Didden, Scholte, Korzilius, de Moore, Vermeulen, O'Reilly, Lang, & Lancioni, 2009; Fredrick, 2010; Marcum, Higgins, Freiburger, & Ricketts, 2012; Wright & Li, 2013b).

As active consumers of electronic technology, researchers began to theorize that children and adolescents are connected to their online world in similar ways as they are to their offline world. Therefore, it was proposed that their behaviors in the cyber context are similar and linked to their behaviors in the offline environment. As a result of these connections, another heavily researched predictor of cyberbullying is children's and adolescents' involvement in traditional face-to-face bullying. Among these studies, researchers have found positive associations between cyberbullying perpetration and traditional face-to-face bullying perpetration, cyber victimization and traditional face-to-face victimization, and traditional face-to-face victimization and cyberbullying perpetration (Barlett & Gentile, 2012; Cappadocia et al., 2013; Corcoran, Connolly, & O'Moore, 2012; Heirman & Walrave, 2012; Mitchell et al., 2007; Steffgen, Konig, Pfetsch, & Melzer, 2011; Fanti, Demetriou, & Hawa, 2012).

Because children and adolescents have active digital lives, studies have focused on examining electronic technology usage as a predictor of cyberbullying perpetration and cyber victimization. Greater usage of electronic technologies related positively to cyberbullying involvement among cyberbullies and cybervictims (Aricak, Siyahhan, Uzunhasanoglu, Saribeyoglu, Ciplak, Yilmaz, & Memmedov, 2008; Ybarra & Mitchell, 2004). In comparison to nonvictims, cybervictims utilize instant messaging, email, blogging sites, and online gaming more often (Smith et al., 2008; Ybarra & Mitchell, 2004). To explain the linkage between electronic technology usage and cyberbullying involvement, Ybarra and colleagues (2007) hypothesized that this relationship can be explained by the amount of children's and adolescents' disclosure of personal information online. Therefore, children and adolescents who more freely disclosed personal information online, such as geographical location, were more likely to experience cyberbullying.

Less attention has been given to the associations of internalizing difficulties (e.g., depression, anxiety, loneliness) and externalizing difficulties (e.g., alcohol use, theft) to children's and adolescents' cyberbullying involvement. For instance, Cappadocia and colleagues (2013) found positive associations of alcohol and drug use to cyberbullying perpetration, while adolescents with higher levels of depression experienced cyber victimization. Given that these difficulties reduce victims' ability to cope, researchers suggest that this makes them more vulnerable to attacks, like victimization by cyberbullying (Cappadocia et al., 2013; Mitchell et al., 2007; Ybarra & Mitchell, 2004).

Some research has found that higher levels of normative beliefs regarding traditional face-to-face bullying and cyberbullying were associated positively with cyberbullying perpetration (e.g., Ang, Tan, & Mansor, 2010; Burton, Florell, & Wygant, 2013; Wright & Li, 2013a). Therefore, these results suggest that perpetrators of cyberbullying have favorable attitudes concerning the perpetration of bullying behaviors, making them more likely to engage in these behaviors when compared to other children and adolescents with lower levels of normative beliefs. Furthermore, holding less provictim attitudes (i.e., believing that bullying is appropriate and acceptable, and that standing up for the victim is not valuable), having lower peer attachment, less self-control and empathy, and greater moral disengagement were related positively with cyberbullying perpetration (Elledge, Williford, Boulton, DePaolis, Little, & Salmivalli, 2013; Jang, Song, & Kim, 2014; Lazuras et al., 2013; Robson & Witenberg, 2013; Steffgen et al., 2011; Wright, Kamble, Lei, Li, Aoyama, & Shruti, 2015).

Most of the research on the predictors of cyberbullying involvement have utilized concurrent research designs. Such designs make it difficult to understand the long-term associations of these predictors to cyberbullying perpetration and cyber victimization. In one study that utilized a longitudinal design, Wright and Li (2013) found that normative beliefs about cyberbullying were associated with cyberbullying perpetration six months later. In addition, Wright (2014a) found that perceived stress from parents, peers, and academics increased adolescents' risk of cyberbullying perpetration one year later. In another study with a longitudinal design, Fanti and colleagues (2012) examined the associations of children's and adolescents' exposure to violent media content, their callous and unemotional traits, and their cyberbullying involvement, assessed one year later. The findings revealed that exposure to media violence predicted later victimization by cyberbullying. The most current research on cyberbullying perpetration and cyber victimization has focused on the role of parents in children's and adolescents' cyberbullying involvement.

PARENTS AND CYBERBULLYING

Ample attention has been given to the linkages of parental monitoring and various parenting styles to children's and adolescents' involvement in traditional face-to-face bullying. In this research, permissive parenting styles were associated with less knowledge concerning children's and adolescents' offline activities, which increased their risk for face-to-face bullying involvement (Marini, Dane, Bosacki, & Ylc-Cura, 2006). The indifferent-uninvolved parenting style as well as inconsistent monitoring of children's and adolescents' activities were associated with their involvement in face-to-face traditional bullying as bully-victims and increased their risk of cyberbullying involvement (Aoyama, Utsumi, & Hasegawa, 2011; Duncan, 2004; Totura, MacKinnon-Lewis, Gesten, Gadd, Divine, Dunham, & Kamboukos, 2009). Children and adolescents from overprotective families are also at an increased risk of experiencing face-to-face traditional bullying victimization (Smith, Madsen, & Moody, 1999). Such families do not allow their children to become autonomous, assertive, or practice social skills, which increases their risk of being targets of face-to-face traditional bullying.

Parents also engage in various levels of monitoring of children's online activities. In one study, Mason (2008) found that, despite 30% of children and adolescents in his sample utilizing the internet often (around three hours or more daily), only about 50% of his participants reported that parents monitored their online activities. Parental monitoring of online activities is important as Wright (2015b) found that adolescents who experienced the most mediation of electronic technology usage by their parents had lower levels of cyber victimization and psychosocial adjustment difficulties (i.e., depression, anxiety, loneliness) resulting from this victimization one year later. Therefore, she proposed that parental mediation might serve as a buffer against the negative psychological consequences associated with cyber victimization. Some research does not support the benefits of parental monitoring on children's and adolescents' online risk exposure. In particular, Aoyama and colleagues (2013) found that parental mediation and monitoring of their children's online activities were not related to cyberbullying perpetration or cyber victimization. To explain these results, they suggested that many parents lack the technological skills to efficiently and effectively monitor their children's online activities, and because they lack these skills they find it difficult to know when and how to intervene. Aoyama and colleagues also found that when parents did have procedures for making the internet safer for their children that they often failed to follow-up and implement these procedures. When parents do not follow through on these procedures, this can give children and adolescents the impression that their parents are unconcerned with their online activities, increasing their risk of perpetrating cyberbullying. Given that many parents do not follow through on the procedures they implement to mediate their children's online activities, they are also not likely to revise these procedures as their children become more independent electronic technologies users and when new technologies are developed and utilized by their children. The available research on this topic suggests that parents are often unsure of what their children are up to online and that they are not certain of how to pose the topic of appropriate online activities with their children (Rosen, 2007). In addition, many parents overestimate the amount of electronic technology monitoring that they engage in. For instance, McQuade and colleagues (2009) found that 93% of parents in their sample reported to having set limits on their children's online activities as well as discussed appropriate online activities. However, their children had a different perspective, with only 37% of their children reporting that they were given rules from their parents about their usage of electronic technologies. There are a few explanations of these contrasting perceptions, including parents over reporting the extent of monitoring they engage in, that their implemented procedures for monitoring are ineffective, leading their children to believe that no procedures have been implemented, or that children recognize that their parents have inconsistent monitoring procedures, making it difficult for them to take these procedures seriously.

Other family characteristics have been examined in association with cyberbullying involvement. Poor caregiver monitoring and poor emotional bonds with caregivers were related to children's and adolescents' cyberbullying perpetration and cyber victimization (Ybarra & Mitchell, 2004). Furthermore, Ybarra and Mitchell found no associations of family income, parental education, and marital status of caregivers or parents to children's and adolescents cyberbullying involvement. Some research (i.e., Arslan et al., 2012) has linked parental unemployment to children's and adolescents' cyberbullying perpetration and victimization. This linkage might be explained by increases in stress and decreases in coping strategies among children and adolescents. In one study, neglectful parenting style increased children's and adolescents' risk of cyberbullying involvement when compared to children and adolescents who experienced authoritative parenting style (Dehue, Bolman, Vollink, & Pouwelse, 2012). The failure of parents to monitor their children's electronic technology usage or to set rules pertaining to such usage had children with an increased risk of experiencing cyber victimization (Mesch, 2009; Navarro, Serna, Martinez, & Ruiz-Oliva, 2013). When parents monitor their children's electronic technology usage, they have more opportunity to discuss the risks associated with electronic technology usage, like cyberbullying. Furthermore, children and adolescents who believed that their parents would discipline them for engaging in negative online behaviors, including cyberbullying, were less likely to engage in cyberbullying or experience cyber victimization (Hinduja & Patchin, 2013). Each of these studies reveal the important role of parents in mitigating their children's involvement in risky online behaviors. Moving beyond the focus on parents, some research has focused on the role of schools and peers in children's and adolescents' cyberbullying perpetration and cyber victimization.

THE ROLE OF SCHOOLS AND PEERS IN CYBERBULLYING INVOLVEMENT

There is much debate regarding schools' role in the monitoring and punishing of children's and adolescents' involvement in cyberbullying. This debate is centered on most incidences of cyberbullying occurring off school grounds, making it difficult for schools to know when these incidences happen. This is especially important as many victims do not tell anyone about their plight (deLara, 2012; Mason, 2008). Furthermore, because many schools are unsure of their role in implementing consequences associated with cyberbullying, their code of conduct might not include any information about children's and adolescents' involvement in these behaviors. It is important for schools to acknowledge that many incidences of cyberbullying involve children and adolescents who attend the same school, which further complicates schools' role in handling these incidences. Because the cyberbully and cybervictim might attend the same school, there is the increased chance that the cyberbullying incident might spread to the school environment, potentially causing further negative interactions while on school grounds, thereby disrupting the learning process. Despite the potential for the effects of cyberbullying incidences to "spill over" onto school grounds, many administrators and teachers have limited awareness of cyberbullying (Kochenderfer-Ladd & Pelletier, 2008). Some administrators and teachers do not believe that cyberbullying incidences are serious, problematic, or occur among their students. These administrators and teachers who do not recognize the negative impacts of cyberbullying are likely to believe that physical forms of bullying are much more serious and harmful when compared to covert forms of bullying behavior, including cyberbullying and relational bullying (Sahin, 2010). Tangen and Campbell (2010) found that when teachers encouraged the development of intervention and prevention programs at their school they were more likely to focus on programs used to reduce physical forms of bullying. Being uninformed about the consequences of cyberbullying is oftentimes the result of ineffective teacher training, which does not inform teachers on how to properly deal with and recognize these behaviors. Cassidy and colleagues (2012a) found that Canadian teachers' unfamiliarity with newer technologies made it extremely difficult for them to recognize cyberbullying incidences and to deal effectively with these behaviors as they were often unsure of how to respond to the incidence or on which strategies to implement in an effort to alleviate the situation. On the other hand, when teachers were concerned with cyberbullying at their school, there were rarely programs and policies developed at the school level, which made it incredibly difficult for them to implement solutions and strategies (Cassidy, Brown, & Jackson, 2012b). Schools must recognize the importance of developing and implementing policies and training aimed at dealing effectively with cyberbullying as these behaviors can hinder children's and adolescents' learning (Shariff & Hoff, 2007). Schools and teachers need to take the implementation of policies seriously as perpetrators and victims of cyberbullying perceive their school environment as less positive when compared to uninvolved children and adolescents (Bayar & Ucanok, 2012). Victims of cyberbullying fear that their classmates might be cyberbullies, which hinders their ability to concentrate on learning, reducing their academic attainment and performance (Eden, Heiman, & Olenik-Shemesh, 2013). They also feel less connected to their school, have lower school commitment, and perceive their school climate as more negative (Williams & Guerra, 2007). Longitudinal research links adolescents' cyberbullying perpetration and cyber victimization to poor academic functioning and negative classroom behaviors (Wright, 2015a).

It is important that administrators and teachers receive training to increase their awareness of cyberbullying. The ultimate aim of this training is for them to develop policies at the school level in an effort to reduce their students' involvement in these behaviors. Training can help to increase administrators' and teachers' confidence concerning their abilities and lead to a stronger commitment to their school, making them more likely to learn about cyberbullying (Eden et al., 2013). The more they learn about cyberbullying the more knowledge that administrators and teachers have about preventing children's and adolescents' cyberbullying perpetration and cyber victimization. As teachers' confidence increases, they are more likely to intervene in cyberbullying incidences, which protects their students from experiencing these behaviors (Elledge et al., 2013). Teachers' motivation for learning about cyberbullying decreases from elementary school to middle school (Ybarra et al., 2007). This is problematic as cyberbullying involvement increases in the middle school years. Therefore, teacher training programs should strive to raise awareness of cyberbullying, especially in middle school.

The social norms of the peer group determine acceptable and unacceptable behaviors. Consequently, children and adolescents engage in these unacceptable behaviors, even if these behaviors are perceived as negative (Miller & Prentice, 1996). As a result of these social norms, one of the best predictors of cyberbullying involvement is classrooms with the highest levels of cyberbullying perpetration and cyber victimization (Festl, Schwarkow, & Quandt, 2013). The climate of the classroom encourages students to engage in certain behaviors. Furthermore, when children and adolescents reported that their friends engaged in cyberbullying, they also perpetrated higher levels of these behaviors (Hinduja & Patchin, 2013). The effects of classroom norms and friends' behaviors on cyberbullying involvement might be explained by the peer contagion effect. This effect suggests that the engagement in negative behaviors perpetrated by one's friends or peers "spread" to other children and adolescents, which leads to these individuals also engaging in these negative behaviors (Dishion & Tipsord, 2011; Sijtsema, Ashwin, Simona, & Gina, 2014). Peer attachment also relates to children's and adolescents' cyberbullying involvement. This form of attachment represents children's and adolescents' beliefs about their peers and whether they believe that their peers will be there for them when they need it. Poor peer attachment promotes more negative interactions among children and adolescents. In particular, lower levels of peer attachment relate positively to cyberbullying perpetration and cyber victimization (Burton et al., 2013). Some research has linked cyberbullying involvement to children's and adolescents' experience of peer rejection (Sevcikova, Machackova, Wright, Dedkova, & Cerna, 2015; Wright & Li, 2013b). A possible explanation for this relationship was offered by Wright and Li (2012). They argued that peer rejection triggers negative emotions, which leads to cyberbullying involvement as victims and/or perpetrators. Other research has focused on higher levels of social standing in the peer group, and how social standing might relate to cyberbullying involvement. In this research, Wright (2014c) found that higher levels of perceived popularity (i.e., reputational form of popularity in the peer group) was related positively to cyberbullying perpetration among adolescents six months later. Wright proposed that electronic technologies might be used as tools to promote and maintain children's and adolescents' social standing in their peer group.

THE CONSEQUENCES ASSOCIATED WITH YOUTHS' INVOLVEMENT IN CYBERBULLYING

Because of findings linking children's and adolescents' cyberbullying perpetration and cyber victimization to negative psychological and behavior consequences, researchers began to focus increased attention on these behaviors. Victimization by cyberbullying produces negative emotional experiences among children and adolescents. Cybervictims reported lower levels of global happiness, school satisfaction, general school happiness, family satisfaction, and self-satisfaction (Navarro et al., 2013). Furthermore, cybervictims reported more feelings of anger, sadness, and fear when compared to uninvolved children and adolescents (Beran & Li, 2005; Dehue et al., 2008; Patchin & Hinduja, 2006). Not only does victimization by cyberbullying relate to emotional harm among children and adolescents, but it also hinders their academic performance. Both cyberbullies and cybervictims are at an increased risk of academic difficulties at school (Balae & Hall, 2007; Beran & Li, 2007). They have less motivation for school, poorer academic performance, lower levels of academic attainment, and more school absences. Lower school functioning is also associated with cyberbullying perpetration and cyber victimization. In particular, cyberbullies and cybervictims experience poor academic performance, greater absences, and more classroom problem behaviors (Wright, 2015a).

A lot of research attention has focused on the risk of internalizing and externalizing problems among cyberbullies and cybervictims (e.g., Arslan et al., 2012; Campbell, Spears, Slee, Butler, & Kift, 2012; Gamez-Guadiz, Orue, Smith, & Calvete, 2013; Laftman, Modin, & Ostberg, 2013; Li, 2007; Mitchell, Ybarra, & Finkelhor, 2007; Olenik-Shemesh, Heiman, & Eden, 2012; Patchin & Hinduja, 2006; Perren, Dooley, Shaw, & Cross, 2010; Wright, 2014b; Ybarra, Diener-West, & Leaf, 2007). They also experience suicidal thoughts and attempt suicide more often when compared to uninvolved children and adolescents (Bauman, Toomey, & Walker 2013). In addition, cybervictims and cyerbullies are also at an increased risk of experiencing mental health difficulties, like psychiatric and psychosomatic problems (Beckman et al., 2012; Sourander et al., 2010). Despite receiving a lot of research focus, many of these investigations do not account for children's and adolescents' involvement in traditional face-to-face bullying when examining the associations between cyberbullying involvement and psychosocial adjustment difficulties. The inclusion of children's and adolescents' involvement in traditional face-to-face bullying is important as this behavior is highly correlated with the involvement in cyberbullying, and that both forms of bullying relate to adjustment difficulties (Williams & Guerra, 2007; Wright & Li, 2013b). Such a focus is important because findings from one study suggested that cyberbullying perpetration and cyber victimization were worse experiences for children and adolescents when compared to the involvement in traditional face-to-face bullying. In this study, Bonanno and colleagues (2013) found that adolescents who were involved in cyberbullying reported more depressive symptoms and suicidal ideation after controlling for face-to-face traditional bullying involvement. Some research has considered the conjoint effects of face-to-face traditional bullying and cyberbullying on children's and adolescents' psychological and behavioral outcomes. In a pair of studies, Gradinger and colleagues (2009) and Perren and colleagues (2012) found that victims of both types of bullying had more internalizing symptoms when compared to children and adolescents who experienced only one type of victimization. Thus, experiencing multiple types of bullying behaviors might worsen children's and adolescents' experiences of depression, anxiety, and loneliness. These findings underscore the importance of considering children's and adolescents' experiences of both offline and online bullying in order to understand more about these relationships and how to intervene.

CROSS-CULTURAL DIFFERENCES IN CYBERBULLYING INVOLVEMENT

Cyberbullying is a global problem, occurring in many countries across the world. The evidence is mounting that children and adolescents are involved in cyberbullying in Africa, Asia, Australia, Europe, North America, and South America. Some of this research has investigated cross-cultural differences in cyberbullying involvement. Research indicates that children and adolescents from the United States reported higher rates of cyberbullying involvement when compared to Japanese children and adolescents (Aoyama et al., 2011; Barlett, Gentile, Anderson, Suzuki, Sakamoto, Yamaoka, & Katsura, 2013). Furthermore, Austrian children and adolescents also reported more cyberbullying perpetration and cyber victimization when compared to Japanese children and adolescents (Strohmeier, Aoyama, Gradinger, & Toda, 2013). Similar results were found among Chinese and Canadian children and adolescents. In this research, Li (2008) found that Chinese children and adolescents engaged in less cyberbullying perpetration when compared to Canadian children and adolescents. However, children and adolescents from both countries did not differ on their experience of cyber victimization. In contrast to this result, Li's (2006) study revealed that Chinese children and adolescents reported more cyber victimization. Other research from Canada focused on the motivations for cyberbullying perpetration among Canadian and East Asian adolescents from Canada (Shapka & Law, 2013). The findings revealed that East Asian adolescents perpetrated cyberbullying for proactive purposes (i.e., to obtain a goal), while Canadian adolescents engaged in cyberbullying perpetration for reactive purposes (i.e., response to provocation).

Most of the cross-cultural research is conducted in Australia, Canada, Europe, and the United States, with very little focus on cyberbullying involvement among children and adolescents from Africa, India, and South America. Focusing on cyberbullying involvement among Indian adolescents, Wright and colleagues (2015) found that these adolescents reported more cyberbullying perpetration and cyber victimization in comparison to adolescents from China and Japan. Chinese adolescents reported more cyberbullying involvement when compared to Japanese adolescents. Other research investigated gender differences across these countries as well. In one study, Genta and colleagues (2012) found that Italian adolescent males perpetrated more cyberbullying when compared to Spanish and English adolescent males. Furthermore, Indian adolescent boys were involved in cyberbullying more often than boys from China and Japan (Wright et al., 2015). The review of this literature suggests that cyberbullying involvement is a concern for many countries across the world.

SOLUTIONS AND RECOMMENDATIONS

Everyone, including communities, researchers, educations, and children and adolescents themselves, needs to be concerned with cyberbullying involvement. School curriculum needs to be designed with lessons focused on teaching children and adolescents about cyberbullying, digital literacy, and citizenship in both the offline and online worlds (Cassidy et al., 2012b). This curriculum should also highlight the positive uses of electronic technology, and instill empathy, self-esteem, and social skills in children and adolescents. Schools should also strive to improve school climate by learning children's and adolescents' names, recognizing and praising good behavior, and keeping up-to-date on technology (Hinduja & Patchin, 2012). In addition, schools need to create a code of conduct which includes policies related to appropriate technology usage. Furthermore, administrators and teachers need to advocate and enforce these policies. Parents also need to take responsibility for helping to address cyberbullying involvement. They need to team-up with their children's schools and increase their awareness and knowledge of electronic technologies as well as stay up-to-date on new technologies (Cassidy et al., 2012a; Diamanduros & Downs, 2011). When parents are knowledgeable of electronic technologies, they are better able to understand their children's behaviors in the cyber context as well as the potential risks associated with their children's electronic technology usage. Increased knowledge of electronic technologies will also help parents implement monitoring strategies that could potentially diminish their children's risk of experiencing cyberbullying. Parents also need to recognize the importance of modeling appropriate electronic technologies usage and online behavior in an effort to serve as role models for their children. It is also important that parents maintain open communication with their children concerning appropriate and safe electronic technology usage. They should discuss the amount of time their children spend online and utilize electronic technologies as well as how their children should act in the online environment and with technologies. The role of communities in helping to reduce cyberbullying is important. Many of us go about our day as bystanders within our communities. We might notice someone needing help within our community, and believe that others will help him or her. Therefore, it is imperative that we recognize the importance of helping, and not expect others to do it. Doing this, will help to model approach behaviors for everyone in our communities, including children and adolescents. Society must recognize the threat of cyberbullying and understand what everyone can do to intervene. Communities must unite to effectively deal with these behaviors. The governments across the world need to recognize the importance of stopping cyberbullying and the need to develop initiatives to fund studies devoted to the prevention of these behaviors. When we understand more about cyberbullying, we are better able to develop strategies to prevent these behaviors and encourage positive interactions.

FUTURE RESEARCH DIRECTIONS

After reviewing the literature, there are some limitations that need to be addressed through future research in order to advance our knowledge of children's and adolescents' involvement in cyberbullying. Although researchers are quick to acknowledge the role of anonymity in children's and adolescents' cyberbullying perpetration, little attention has been devoted to this topic. Future research on this topic should focus on children's and adolescents' perceptions of anonymous behaviors online, and what factors might motivate them to engage in anonymous forms of cyberbullying. Research should also focus on examining differences between non-anonymous forms of cyberbullying and anonymous forms of cyberbullying in order to better reveal the motivators associated with children's and adolescents' involvement in these behaviors. A lot of the studies discussed in this literature review use concurrent research designs, which makes it difficult to understand the long-term consequences associated with cyberbullying perpetration and cyber victimization across various age groups. Many studies on cyberbullying involvement focus on early and late adolescents, with little attention given to cyberbullying perpetration and cyber victimization among elementary school-aged children or young adults, even though both age groups have access to electronic technologies, a risk factor associated with these behaviors (Madden et al., 2013; Ybarra et al., 2007). Directing attention on younger age groups can also produce a better understanding of the developmental trajectory of traditional face-to-face bullying and cyberbullying involvement. This research can also help to provide information about the temporal ordering of face-to-face and cyberbullying behaviors.

CONCLUSION

Altogether, the literature on cyberbullying provides a solid foundation for understanding the predictors and consequences associated with children's and adolescents' involvement in these behaviors. Although the study of cyberbullying is in its infancy, it has begun to move beyond examining prevalence rates associated with cyberbullying, and instead direct more attention to the causes and consequences of children's and adolescents' involvement in these behaviors. Researchers are beginning to understand the causes related to cyberbullying involvement, but little attention is given to the role of parents, schools, peers, and communities in children's and adolescents' perpetration and victimization by these behaviors. Consequently, the aim of future research should be on these individuals and entities in an increasing effort to acknowledge that cyberbullying is a global concern, warranting involvement from countries across the world. Such a focus is important as cyberbullying impacts all components of our society, potentially undermining ethical and moral values. Thus, it is imperative that we unite as global citizens in order to do our part to reduce children's and adolescents' involvement in cyberbullying.

REFERENCES

Adams, C. (2010). Cyberbullying: How to make it stop. *Instructor, 120*(2), 44–49.

Akbulut, Y., Sahin, T. L., & Eristi, B. (2010). Cyberbullying victimization among Turkish online social utility members. *Journal of Educational Technology & Society, 13*, 192–201.

Ang, R. P., Kit-Aun, T., & Mansor, A. T. (2010). Normative beliefs about aggression as a mediator of narcissistic exploitativeness and cyberbullying. *Journal of Interpersonal Violence, 26*(13), 2619–2634. doi:10.1177/0886260510388286 PMID:21156699

Aoyama, I., Barnard-Brak, L., & Talbert, T. L. (2011). Cyberbullying among high school students: Cluster analysis of sex and age differences and the level of parental monitoring. *International Journal of Cyber Behavior, Psychology and Learning, 1*(1), 1–11. doi:10.4018/ijcbpl.2011010103

Aoyama, I., Utsumi, S., & Hasegawa, M. (2011). Cyberbullying in Japan: Cases, government reports, adolescent relational aggression and parental monitoring roles. In Q. Li, D. Cross, & P. K. Smith (Eds.), *Bullying in the global playground: Research from an international perspective*. Oxford, UK: Wiley-Blackwell.

Aricak, T., Siyahhan, S., Uzunhasanoglu, A., Saribeyoglu, S., Ciplak, S., Yilmaz, N., & Memmedov, C. (2008). Cyberbullying among Turkish adolescents. *Cyberpsychology & Behavior, 11*(3), 253–261. doi:10.1089/cpb.2007.0016 PMID:18537493

Arslan, S., Savaser, S., Hallett, V., & Balci, S. (2012). Cyberbullying among primary school students in Turkey: Self-reported prevalence and associations with home and school life. *Cyberpsychology, Behavior, and Social Networking, 15*(10), 527–533. doi:10.1089/cyber.2012.0207 PMID:23002988

Barlett, C. P., & Gentile, D. A. (2012). Long-term psychological predictors of cyber-bullying in late adolescence. *Psychology of Popular Media Culture, 2*, 123–135. doi:10.1037/a0028113

Barlett, C. P., Gentile, D. A., Anderson, C. A., Suzuki, K., Sakamoto, A., Yamaoka, A., & Katsura, R. (2013). Cross-cultural differences in cyberbullying behavior: A short-term longitudinal study. *Journal of Cross-Cultural Psychology, 45*(2), 300–313. doi:10.1177/0022022113504622

Bauman, S., Toomey, R. B., & Walker, J. L. (2013). Associations among bullying, cyberbullying, and suicide in high school students. *Journal of Adolescence, 36*(2), 341–350. doi:10.1016/j.adolescence.2012.12.001 PMID:23332116

Bayar, Y., & Ucanok, Z. (2012). School social climate and generalized peer perception in traditional and cyberbullying status. *Educational Sciences: Theory and Practice, 12*, 2352–2358.

Beckman, L., Hagquist, C., & Hellstrom, L. (2012). Does the association with psychosomatic health problems differ between cyberbullying and traditional bullying? *Emotional & Behavioural Difficulties, 17*(3-4), 421–434. doi:10.1080/13632752.2012.704228

Beran, T., & Li, Q. (2005). Cyber-harassment: A new method for an old behavior. *Journal of Educational Computing Research, 32*(3), 265–277. doi:10.2190/8YQM-B04H-PG4D-BLLH

Beran, T., & Li, Q. (2007). The relationship between cyberbullying and school bullying. *Journal of Student Wellbeing*, *1*, 15–33.

Bonanno, R. A., & Hymel, S. (2013). Cyber bullying and internalizing difficulties: Above and beyond the impact of traditional forms of bullying. *Journal of Youth and Adolescence*, *42*(5), 685–697. doi:10.1007/s10964-013-9937-1 PMID:23512485

Boulton, M., Lloyd, J., Down, J., & Marx, H. (2012). Predicting undergraduates' self-reported engagement in traditional and cyberbullying from attitudes. *Cyberpsychology, Behavior, and Social Networking*, *15*(3), 141–147. doi:10.1089/cyber.2011.0369 PMID:22304402

Brighi, A., Guarini, A., Melotti, G., Galli, S., & Genta, M. L. (2012). Predictors of victimisation across direct bullying, indirect bullying and cyberbullying. *Emotional & Behavioural Difficulties*, *17*(3-4), 375–388. doi:10.1080/13632752.2012.704684

Burton, K. A., Florell, D., & Wygant, D. B. (2013). The role of peer attachment and normative beliefs about aggression on traditional bullying and cyberbullying. *Psychology in the Schools*, *50*(2), 103–114. doi:10.1002/pits.21663

Campbell, M., Spears, B., Slee, P. H., Butler, D., & Kift, S. (2012). Victims' perceptions of traditional and cyberbullying, and the psychosocial correlates of their victimisation. *Emotional & Behavioural Difficulties*, *17*(3-4), 389–401. doi:10.1080/13632752.2012.704316

Cappadocia, M. C., Craig, W. M., & Pepler, D. (2013). Cyberbullying: Prevalence, stability and risk factors during adolescence. *Canadian Journal of School Psychology*, *28*, 171–192.

Cassidy, W., Brown, K., & Jackson, M. (2012a). "Making kind cool": Parents' suggestions for preventing cyber bullying and fostering cyber kindness. *Journal of Educational Computing Research*, *46*(4), 415–436. doi:10.2190/EC.46.4.f

Cassidy, W., Brown, K., & Jackson, M. (2012b). "Under the radar": Educators and cyberbullying in schools. *School Psychology International*, *33*(5), 520–532. doi:10.1177/0143034312445245

Chisholm, J. F. (2006). Cyberspace violence against girls and adolescent females. *Annals of the New York Academy of Sciences*, *1087*(1), 74–89. doi:10.1196/annals.1385.022 PMID:17189499

Corcoran, L., Connolly, I., & O'Moore, M. (2012). Cyberbullying in Irish schools: An investigation of personality and self-concept. *The Irish Journal of Psychology*, *33*(4), 153–165. doi:10.1080/0303391 0.2012.677995

Dehue, F., Bolman, C., & Vollink, T. (2008). Cyberbullying: Youngsters' experiences and parental perception. *CyberPscyhology & Behavior*, *11*(2), 217–223. doi:10.1089/cpb.2007.0008 PMID:18422417

Dehue, F., Bolman, C., Vollink, T., & Pouwelse, M. (2012). Cyberbullying and traditional bullying in relation to adolescents' perceptions of parenting. *Journal of Cyber Therapy and Rehabilitation*, *5*, 25–34.

deLara, E. W. (2012). Why adolescents don't disclose incidents of bullying and harassment. *Journal of School Violence*, *11*(4), 288–305. doi:10.1080/15388220.2012.705931

Diamanduros, T., & Downs, E. (2011). Creating a safe school environment: How to prevent cyberbullying at your school. *Library Media Connection*, *30*(2), 36–38.

Didden, R., Scholte, R. H. J., Korzilius, H., de Moor, J. M. H., Vermeulen, A., O'Reilly, M., & Lancioni, G. E. et al. (2009). Cyberbullying among students with intellectual and developmental disability in special education settings. *Developmental Neurorehabilitation*, *12*(3), 146–151. doi:10.1080/17518420902971356 PMID:19466622

Dishion, T. J., & Tipsord, J. M. (2011). Peer contagion in child and adolescent social and emotional development. *Annual Review of Psychology*, *62*(1), 189–214. doi:10.1146/annurev.psych.093008.100412 PMID:19575606

Duncan, D. R. (2004). The impact of family relationships on school bullies and victims. In D. L. Espelage & S. M. Swearer (Eds.), *Bullying in American schools* (pp. 277–244). London: Lawrence Erlbaum Associates.

Eden, S., Heiman, T., & Olenik-Shemesh, D. (2013). Teachers' perceptions, beliefs and concerns about cyberbullying. *British Journal of Educational Technology*, *44*(6), 1036–1052. doi:10.1111/j.1467-8535.2012.01363.x

Elledge, L. C., Williford, A., Boulton, A. J., DePaolis, K. J., Little, T. D., & Salmivalli, C. (2013). Individual and contextual predictors of cyberbullying: The influence of children's provictim attitudes and teachers' ability to intervene. *Journal of Youth and Adolescence*, *42*(5), 698–710. doi:10.1007/s10964-013-9920-x PMID:23371005

Erdur-Baker, O. (2010). Cyberbullying and its correlation to traditional bullying, gender and frequent and risky usage of internet-mediated communication tools. *New Media & Society*, *12*(1), 109–125. doi:10.1177/1461444809341260

Fanti, K. A., Demetriou, A. G., & Hawa, V. V. (2012). A longitudinal study of cyberbullying: Examining risk and protective factors. *European Journal of Developmental Psychology*, *8*(2), 168–181. doi:10.1080/17405629.2011.643169

Ferdon, C. D., & Hertz, M. F. (2007). Electronic media, violence, and adolescents. An emerging public health problem. *The Journal of Adolescent Health*, *41*(6), 1–5. doi:10.1016/j.jadohealth.2007.08.020 PMID:17577527

Festl, R., Schwarkow, M., & Quandt, T. (2013). Peer influence, internet use and cyberbullying: A comparison of different context effects among German adolescents. *Journal of Children and Media*, *7*(4), 446–462. doi:10.1080/17482798.2013.781514

Fredrick, K. (2010). Mean girls (and boys): Cyberbullying and what can be done about it. *School Library Media Activities Monthly*, *25*(8), 44–45.

Gamez-Guadix, M., Orue, I., Smith, P. K., & Calvete, E. (2013). Longitudinal and reciprocal relations of cyberbullying with depression, substance use, and problematic internet use among adolescents. *The Journal of Adolescent Health*, *53*(4), 446–452. doi:10.1016/j.jadohealth.2013.03.030 PMID:23721758

Gillespie, A. A. (2006). Cyber-bullying and harassment of teenagers: The legal response. *Journal of Social Welfare and Family Law*, *28*(2), 123–136. doi:10.1080/09649060600973772

Goebert, D., Else, I., Matsu, C., Chung-Do, J., & Chang, J. Y. (2011). The impact of cyberbullying on substance use and mental health in a multiethnic sample. *Maternal and Child Health Journal*, *15*(8), 1282–1286. doi:10.1007/s10995-010-0672-x PMID:20824318

Gradinger, P., Strohmeier, D., & Spiel, C. (2009). Traditional bullying and cyberbullying. *The Journal of Psychology*, *217*, 205–213.

Grigg, D. W. (2010). Cyber-aggression: Definition and concept of cyberbullying. *Australian Journal of Guidance & Counselling*, *20*(02), 143–156. doi:10.1375/ajgc.20.2.143

Grigg, D. W. (2012). Definitional constructs of cyberbullying and cyber aggression from a triagnulatory overview: A preliminary study into elements. *Journal of Aggression, Conflict and Peace Research*, *4*(4), 202–215. doi:10.1108/17596591211270699

Heirman, W., & Walrave, M. (2012). Predicting adolescent perpetration in cyberbullying: An application of the theory of planned behavior. *Psicothema*, *24*, 614–620. PMID:23079360

Hinduja, S., & Patchin, J. W. (2007). Offline consequences of online victimization. *Journal of School Violence*, *6*(3), 89–112. doi:10.1300/J202v06n03_06

Hinduja, S., & Patchin, J. W. (2008). Cyberbullying: An exploratory analysis of factors related to offending and victimization. *Deviant Behavior*, *29*(2), 129–156. doi:10.1080/01639620701457816

Hinduja, S., & Patchin, J. W. (2010). Bullying, cyberbullying, and suicide. *Archives of Suicide Research*, *14*(3), 206–221. doi:10.1080/13811118.2010.494133 PMID:20658375

Hinduja, S., & Patchin, J. W. (2012). Cyberbullying: Neither and epidemic nor a rarity. *European Journal of Developmental Psychology*, *9*(5), 539–543. doi:10.1080/17405629.2012.706448

Hinduja, S., & Patchin, J. W. (2013). Social influences on cyberbullying behaviors among middle and high school students. *Journal of Youth and Adolescence*, *42*(5), 711–722. doi:10.1007/s10964-012-9902-4 PMID:23296318

Huang, Y., & Chou, C. (2010). An analysis of multiple factors of cyberbullying among junior high school students in Taiwan. *Computers in Human Behavior*, *26*(6), 1581–1590. doi:10.1016/j.chb.2010.06.005

Joinson, A. (1998). Causes and implications of behavior on the Internet. In J. Gackenbach (Ed.), *Psychology and the Internet: Intrapersonal, interpersonal, and transpersonal implications* (pp. 43–60). San Diego, CA: Academic Press.

Kochenderfer-Ladd, B., & Pelletier, M. (2008). Teachers' views and beliefs about bullying: Influences on classroom management strategies and students' coping with peer victimization. *Journal of School Psychology*, *46*(4), 431–453. doi:10.1016/j.jsp.2007.07.005 PMID:19083367

Kowalski, R. M., & Limber, S. P. (2007). Electronic bullying among middle school students. *The Journal of Adolescent Health*, *41*(6), 22–30. doi:10.1016/j.jadohealth.2007.08.017 PMID:18047942

Laftman, S. B., Modin, B., & Ostberg, V. (2013). Cyberbullying and subjective health: A large-scale study of students in Stockholm, Sweden. *Children and Youth Services Review, 35*(1), 112–119. doi:10.1016/j. childyouth.2012.10.020

Lazuras, L., Barkoukis, V., Ourda, D., & Tsorbatzoudis, H. (2013). A process model of cyberbullying in adolescence. *Computers in Human Behavior, 29*(3), 881–887. doi:10.1016/j.chb.2012.12.015

Li, Q. (2007). Bullying in the new playground: Research into cyberbullying and cybervictimization. *Australasian Journal of Educational Technology, 23*(4), 435–454. doi:10.14742/ajet.1245

Li, Q. (2008). A cross-cultural comparison of adolescents' experience related to cyberbullying. *Educational Research, 50*(3), 223–234. doi:10.1080/00131880802309333

Madden, M., Lenhart, A., Duggan, M., Cortesi, S., & Gasser, U. (2013). *Teens and technology 2013*. Retrieved from: http://www.pewinternet.org/2013/03/13/teens-and-technology-2013/

Marcum, C. D., Higgins, G. E., Freiburger, T. L., & Ricketts, M. L. (2012). Battle of the sexes: An examination of male and female cyber bullying. *International Journal of Cyber Criminology, 6*(1), 904–911.

Marini, Z., Dane, A., Bosacki, S., & Ylc-Cura, Y. (2006). Direct and indirect bully-victims: Differential psychosocial risk factors associated with adolescents involved in bullying and victimization. *Aggressive Behavior, 32*(6), 551–569. doi:10.1002/ab.20155

Mason, K. (2008). Cyberbullying: A preliminary assessment for school personnel. *Psychology in the Schools, 45*(4), 323–348. doi:10.1002/pits.20301

McQuade, C. S., Colt, P. J., & Meyer, B. N. (2009). *Cyber bullying: Protecting kids and adults from online bullies*. Westport: Praeger.

Mesch, G. S. (2009). Parental mediation, online activities, and cyberbullying. *Cyberpsychology & Behavior, 12*(4), 387–393. doi:10.1089/cpb.2009.0068 PMID:19630583

Mitchell, K. J., Ybarra, M., & Finkelhor, D. (2007). The relative importance of online victimization in understanding depression, delinquency, and substance use. *Child Maltreatment, 12*(4), 314–324. doi:10.1177/1077559507305996 PMID:17954938

Moore, M. J., Nakano, T. N., Enomoto, A., & Suda, T. (2012). Anonymity and roles associated with aggressive posts in an online forum. *Computers in Human Behavior, 28*(3), 861–867. doi:10.1016/j. chb.2011.12.005

Mouttapa, M., Valente, T., Gallagher, P., Rohrbach, L. A., & Unger, J. B. (2004). Social network predictor of bullying and victimization. *Adolescence, 39*, 315–335. PMID:15563041

Navarro, R., Serna, C., Martinez, V., & Ruiz-Oliva, R. (2013). The role of Internet use and parental mediation on cyberbullying victimization among Spanish children from rural public schools. *European Journal of Psychology of Education, 28*(3), 725–745. doi:10.1007/s10212-012-0137-2

Nocentini, A., Calmaestra, J., Schultze-Krumbholz, A., Scheithauer, H., Ortega, R., & Menesini, E. (2010). Cyberbullying: Labels, behaviours and definition in three European countries. *Australian Journal of Guidance & Counselling, 20*(02), 129–142. doi:10.1375/ajgc.20.2.129

Olenik-Shemesh, D., Heiman, T., & Eden, S. (2012). Cyberbullying victimisation in adolescence: Relationships with loneliness and depressive mood. *Emotional & Behavioural Difficulties*, *17*(3-4), 361–374. doi:10.1080/13632752.2012.704227

Olweus, D. (1999). Sweden. In K. Smith, Y. Morita, J. Junger-Tas, D. Olweus, R. Catalano, & P. Slee (Eds.), *The nature of school bullying: A cross-national perspective* (pp. 7–27). New York, NY: Routledge.

Patchin, J. W., & Hinduja, S. (2006). Bullies move beyond the schoolyard: A preliminary look at cyberbullying. *Youth Violence and Juvenile Justice*, *4*(2), 148–169. doi:10.1177/1541204006286288

Perren, S., Dooley, J., Shaw, T., & Cross, D. (2010). Bullying in school and cyberspace: Associations with depressive symptoms in Swiss and Australian adolescents. *Child and Adolescent Psychiatry and Mental Health*, *4*(1), 1–10. doi:10.1186/1753-2000-4-28 PMID:21092266

Pornari, C. D., & Wood, J. (2010). Peer and cyber aggression in secondary school students: The role of moral disengagement, hostile attribution bias, and outcome expectancies. *Aggressive Behavior*, *36*(2), 81–94. doi:10.1002/ab.20336 PMID:20035548

Rideout, V. J., Roberts, D. F., & Foehr, U. G. (2005). *Generation M: Media in the lives of 8-18-year-olds: Executive summary*. Menlo Park, CA: Henry J. Kaiser Family Foundation.

Robson, C., & Witenberg, R. T. (2013). The influence of moral disengagement, morally based self-esteem, age, and gender on traditional bullying and cyberbullying. *Journal of School Violence*, *12*(2), 211–231. doi:10.1080/15388220.2012.762921

Rosen, L. D. (2007). *Me, Myspace, and I: Parenting the Net Generation*. New York: Palgrave Macmillan.

Sahin, M. (2010). Teachers' perceptions of bullying in high schools: A Turkish study. *Social Behavior and Personality*, *38*(1), 127–142. doi:10.2224/sbp.2010.38.1.127

Sevcikova, A., Machackova, H., Wright, M. F., Dedkova, L., & Cerna, A. (2015). Social support seeking in relation to parental attachment and peer relationships among victims of cyberbullying. *Australian Journal of Guidance & Counselling*, *15*, 1–13. doi:10.1017/jgc.2015.1

Shapka, J. D., & Law, D. M. (2013). Does one size fit all? Ethnic differences in parenting behaviors and motivations for adolescent engagement in cyberbullying. *Journal of Youth and Adolescence*, *42*(5), 723–738. doi:10.1007/s10964-013-9928-2 PMID:23479327

Shariff, S., & Hoff, D. L. (2007). Cyber bullying: Clarifying legal boundaries for school supervision in cyberspace. *International Journal of Cyber Criminology*, *1*, 76–118.

Sijtsema, J. J., Ashwin, R. J., Simona, C. S., & Gina, G. (2014). Friendship selection and influence in bullying and defending. *Effects of moral disengagement. Developmental Psychology*, *50*(8), 2093–2104. doi:10.1037/a0037145 PMID:24911569

Slonje, R., & Smith, P. K. (2008). Cyberbullying another main type of bullying? *Scandinavian Journal of Psychology*, *49*(2), 147–154. doi:10.1111/j.1467-9450.2007.00611.x PMID:18352984

Smith, P. K., Madsen, K. C., & Moody, J. C. (1999). What cause the age decline in reports of being bullied at school? Towards a developmental analysis of risks of being bullied. *Educational Research, 41*(3), 267–285. doi:10.1080/0013188990410303

Smith, P. K., Mahdavi, J., Carvalho, M., Fisher, S., Russell, S., & Tippett, N. (2008). Cyberbullying: Its nature and impact in secondary school pupils. *Journal of Child Psychology and Psychiatry, and Allied Disciplines, 49*(4), 376–385. doi:10.1111/j.1469-7610.2007.01846.x PMID:18363945

Sourander, A., Brunstein, A., Ikonen, M., Lindroos, J., Luntamo, T., Koskelainen, M., & Helenius, H. et al. (2010). Psychosocial risk factors associated with cyberbullying among adolescents: A population-based study. *Archives of General Psychiatry, 67*(7), 720–728. doi:10.1001/archgenpsychiatry.2010.79 PMID:20603453

Steffgen, G., Konig, A., Pfetsch, J., & Melzer, A. (2011). Are cyberbullies less empathic? Adolescents' cyberbullying behavior and empathic responsiveness. *Cyberpsychology, Behavior, and Social Networking, 14*(11), 643–648. doi:10.1089/cyber.2010.0445 PMID:21554126

Strohmeier, D., Aoyama, I., Gradinger, P., & Toda, Y. (2013). Cybervictimization and cyberaggression in Eastern and Western countries: Challenges of constructing a cross-cultural appropriate scale. In S. Bauman, D. Cross, & J. L. Walker (Eds.), *Principles of cyberbullying research: Definitions, measures, and methodology* (pp. 202–221). New York: Routledge.

Suler, J. (2004). The online disinhibition effect. *Cyberpsychology & Behavior, 7*(3), 321–326. doi:10.1089/1094931041291295 PMID:15257832

Tangen, D., & Campbell, M. (2010). Cyberbullying prevention: One primary school's approach. *Australian Journal of Guidance & Counselling, 20*(02), 225–234. doi:10.1375/ajgc.20.2.225

Topcu, C., Erdur-Baker, O., & Capa, A. Y. (2008). Examination of cyber-bullying experiences among Turkish students from different school types. *Cyberpsychology & Behavior, 11*(6), 644–648. doi:10.1089/cpb.2007.0161 PMID:18783345

Totura, C. M. W., MacKinnon-Lewis, C., Gesten, E. L., Gadd, R., Divine, K. P., Dunham, S., & Kamboukos, D. (2009). Bullying and victimization among boys and girls in middle school: The influence of perceived family and school contexts. *The Journal of Early Adolescence, 29*(4), 571–609. doi:10.1177/0272431608324190

Vandebosch, H., & van Cleemput, K. (2008). Defining cyberbullying: A qualitative research into the perceptions of youngsters. *Cyberpsychology & Behavior, 11*(4), 499–503. doi:10.1089/cpb.2007.0042 PMID:18721100

Wade, A., & Beran, T. (2011). Cyberbullying: The new era of bullying. *Canadian Journal of School Psychology, 26*(1), 44–61. doi:10.1177/0829573510396318

Wright, M. F. (2013). The relationship between young adults' beliefs about anonymity and subsequent cyber aggression. *Cyberpsychology, Behavior, and Social Networking, 16*(12), 858–862. doi:10.1089/cyber.2013.0009 PMID:23849002

Wright, M. F. (2014a). Cyber victimization and perceived stress: Linkages to late adolescents' cyber aggression and psychological functioning. *Youth & Society.*

Wright, M. F. (2014b). Predictors of anonymous cyber aggression: The role of adolescents' beliefs about anonymity, aggression, and the permanency of digital content. *Cyberpsychology, Behavior, and Social Networking, 17*(7), 431–438. doi:10.1089/cyber.2013.0457 PMID:24724731

Wright, M. F. (2014c). Longitudinal investigation of the associations between adolescents' popularity and cyber social behaviors. *Journal of School Violence, 13*(3), 291–314. doi:10.1080/15388220.2013.849201

Wright, M. F. (2015b). Cyber victimization and adjustment difficulties: The mediation of Chinese and American adolescents' digital technology usage. *CyberPsychology: Journal of Psychosocial Research in Cyberspace, 1*(1), article 1. Retrieved from: http://cyberpsychology.eu/view.php?cisloclanku=2015 051102&article=1

Wright, M. F., Kamble, S., Lei, K., Li, Z., Aoyama, I., & Shruti, S. (2015). Peer attachment and cyberbullying involvement among Chinese, Indian, and Japanese adolescents. *Societies, 5*(2), 339–353. doi:10.3390/soc5020339

Wright, M. F., & Li, Y. (2012). Kicking the digital dog: A longitudinal investigation of young adults' victimization and cyber-displaced aggression. *Cyberpsychology, Behavior, and Social Networking, 15*(9), 448–454. doi:10.1089/cyber.2012.0061 PMID:22974350

Wright, M. F., & Li, Y. (2013a). Normative beliefs about aggression and cyber aggression among young adults: A longitudinal investigation. *Aggressive Behavior, 39*(3), 161–170. doi:10.1002/ab.21470 PMID:23440595

Wright, M. F., & Li, Y. (2013b). The association between cyber victimization and subsequent cyber aggression: The moderating effect of peer rejection. *Journal of Youth and Adolescence, 42*(5), 662–674. doi:10.1007/s10964-012-9903-3 PMID:23299177

Wright, M. F. (2015b). Adolescents' cyber aggression perpetration and cyber victimization: The longitudinal associations with school functioning. Social Psychology of Education, 18(4), 653-666. doi: 10.1007/s11218-015-9318-6

Ybarra, M. L., Diener-West, M., & Leaf, P. (2007). Examining the overlap in internet harassment and school bullying: Implications for school intervention. *The Journal of Adolescent Health, 1*(6), 42–50. doi:10.1016/j.jadohealth.2007.09.004 PMID:18047944

Ybarra, M. L., & Mitchell, K. J. (2004). Online aggressor/targets, aggressors, and targets: A comparison of associated youth characteristics. *Journal of Child Psychology and Psychiatry, and Allied Disciplines, 45*(7), 1308–1316. doi:10.1111/j.1469-7610.2004.00328.x PMID:15335350

ADDITIONAL READING

Bauman, S. (2011). *Cyberbullying: What counselors need to know*. Alexandria, VA: American Counseling Association.

Bauman, S., Cross, D., & Walker, J. (2013). *Principles of cyberbullying research: Definitions, measures, and methodology*. New York, NY: Routledge.

Feinberg, T., & Robey, N. (2010). Cyberbullying: Intervention and prevention strategies. Retrieved from: http://www.nasponline.org/resources/bullying/cyberbullying.pdf

Hinduja, S., & Patchin, J. W. (2015). *Bullying beyond the schoolyard: Preventing and responding to cyberbullying*. Thousand Oaks, CA: Sage Publications.

Li, Q., Cross, D., & Smith, P. K. (2012). *Cyberbullying in the global playground*. Malden, MA: Blackwell Publishing. doi:10.1002/9781119954484

Menesini, E., & Spiel, C. (2012). *Cyberbullying: Development, consequences, risk and protective factors*. New York, NY: Psychology Press.

Shariff, S., & Churchill, A. H. (2010). *Truths and myths of cyber-bullying: International perspectives on stakeholder responsibility and children's safety*. New York, NY: Peter Lang Publishing, Inc.

Tokunaga, R. S. (2010). Following you home from school: A critical review and synthesis of research on cyberbullying victimization. *Computers in Human Behavior*, 26(3), 277–287. doi:10.1016/j.chb.2009.11.014

Chapter 4
The Games Men Play:
How Students Use Video Games to Construct Masculinity

Eric Niemi
Northern Illinois University, USA

ABSTRACT

This chapter conveys the results of a study examining how male students use video games to construct their masculinity. Applying a critical discourse methodology, the study provides insight into how men construct their masculinity within video game discourse communities and how the construction applies to other discourses. It examines how men enter the discourse, what they learn in the discourse, and then how they apply that learning to other discourse communities. It concludes with recommendations and suggestions regarding how video games are a critical part of popular culture that facilitates construction of an identity through the multitude of encounters and relationships within the discourse.

INTRODUCTION

There is a common misconception that video game players are overweight, social awkward individuals that reside in their parents basement either shunning human interaction or living as ticking human time-bombs waiting and planning to express their rage in angry outbursts of violence. Likewise, the misconception exists that video games not only encourage this behavior but stick men playing these games into a place where they eschew adult responsibilities and fail to reach their human potential. In either case, video games are a cause for the regression and stunting of men and masculinity development (Kimmel, 2008).

These assumptions and misconceptions are, of course, false. This study examines the traditional problems associated with video games and men to uncover if and how men are able to construct a masculine identity within these discourse communities. Given so many public misconceptions about video games and men, this study investigates the relationship to determine interactions and effects between the two.

Research about video games and media suggests these are rich and fecund sites of semiotics representation (Gee, 2004; Jenkins, 2008). What it does not explore, however, is how these video impact the development and constructions of masculinity. Hence, the purpose of this study is to investigate and

DOI: 10.4018/978-1-5225-0522-8.ch004

inquire about how two-year college men construct their masculinity using referents and encounters from video game discourse communities. It situates itself at the intersection of semiotics, video games, and college men and masculinity to examine how each relate to and impact one other. Importantly, it seeks to understand how constructions of masculinity lead to the development of identity and leads to the challenging and resistance of hegemony.

What follows is a brief outline of significant concepts and research that comprise the background literature for this study. Next, there is a brief overview of the study's design and participant selection. This is followed by findings related to how the participants entered video game discourse communities, what they learned and internalized, and then how they applied that learning. Finally, it concludes with discussion and recommendations for further study.

UNDERSTANDING THE GAMES

Semiotics

Paul Cobley (2015) makes the assertion that there is a "sublime position growing out of the definition of the humanities as fostering harmony or standing against de-humanization" (p.210). While conventional wisdom and perceptions see technology as repressive and dehumanizing, taking a semiotic perspective can emphasis the individual person and the associated identity within the cacophony. Individuality, then, emerges from the conglomeration and configuration of signs, referents, and meaning produced through this interaction. The individual, then, is the acknowledgement of human agency: "human agency is the *Umwelt*; we are within the products of semiosis that make up the objects of the humanities" (Cobley, 2015, p. 217). From this position within the *umwelt*, individuals are able to interact and potential change the lifeworld and, thereby, control their own identity. The individual does not passively exist within this process of semiotic mediation; they actively interpret and internalize signs to create their own meaning.

This exchange of information is central to communication theory and communicative action. Habermas (1985) interrogated this process to warn about the colonization of the lifeworld, which he defined as those things on the peripheral of human awareness. Advertisements on the side of the road, for example, are part of the lifeworld because drivers recognize and read them. These drivers, however, may not be actively aware of this process; it is part of the background. So, Habermas believed that acts of hegemony and hegemonic control leech into the lifeworld to create subversive ideology that limits the replication of meanings until only one remains. Of course, this sole remaining hermeneutic supports the dominate ideology and maintains repressive power structures in society.

To this end, Habermas echoes Horkheimer and Adorno's (1999) critique of the Culture Industry. Culture is intentionally manipulated through these culture industries to control the sign-systems that produce meaning. Horkeimer and Adorno theorized that culture would become sites of hegemonic control where the definition of 'normal' would be created and replicated. Individuals existing within these culture industries would believe this definition to be natural and, thus, internalize and accept it. Their own identity, therefore, would blend into this ooze and any sense of individuality would be lost. As the lifeworld is colonized by these hegemonic culture industries, the sense of the individuality and the individual diminishes due to these hegemonic influences. They become automatons.

While theorists from the Frankfurt School wrote in opposition to culture industry, Walter Benjamin proposed an alternative point of view. In his seminal essay "Digital Art in the Age of Mechanical Reproduction", he argues that texts cannot hold a monolithic definition—the textual aura of a test changes dependent on the culture consuming it (Benjamin, 2008). As a cultural artifact or referent, a text cannot hold a monolithic definition. As the culture surrounding a text changes, the meaning of that text changes, too. Texts become polysemic and dependent on culture to produce meaning. So, while a culture industry can attempt to produce a single definition and limit meaning, members of the individual culture have the ability to resist or subvert this meaning. Hegemony can never establish a strong foothold because of this inherent slipperiness: as different individuals bring different referents to the text they produce different meanings. The aura of the text is constantly changing and evolving with the culture that consumes it. Throughout this process, the individual and their unique culture interacts with the text and affects its meaning.

To conclude, the act of humanization places the individual within the center of the umwelt and meaning-making process. While some theories argue this leads to repressive acts of hegemony that repress the individual, the process of interpretation involved with the creation of meaning depends upon the culture of the individual. This culture, then, prevents monolithic stabilization of meaning because the culture is always changing. Interpretation is a dialogue, not a monologue. The dialogic process involved depends upon an exchange of information between the individual and specific culture and the text itself.

Video Games

Curiously, video games encourage this dialogic process as central to the act of meaning. Video games are a part of popular culture and, therefore, function as cultural artifacts that people use to define and construct meaning (Storrey, 2009). Much like film, television, and books, video games are part of the lifeworld that have become semiotic referents used to construct meaning. They are like any other narrative experiences that are able to reflect and refract culture and they are also able to touch upon abstract concepts to become "the new myth-makers for many of us" (Hung, 2011, p. 2013). More so, when discussing the positionality of the player and their individuality in video games, Bradford (2010) articulates this process clearly:

When young people play video games they do so as embodied subjects whose identities are shaped by the culture in which they are situated, the circumstances of their lived experiences, and the particularities of their dispositions, actions, and interests. . . . no two players, any more than readers or viewers are the same (p. 54).

Certainly they are part of our culture, and suspect to being a culture industry, but the aura generated by video games is less stable that other texts because games depend on actions from the individual to produce meaning.

Two theorists outline and define the process of making meaning in video games. Gee's (2004) makes the argument that video games act as a vehicle to literacy and should be studied like other popular culture texts; likewise, Jenkins (2008) observes that media, of which he includes video game, is participatory and their meaning depends upon the exchange of information between peers to be actualized. They both note that games depend upon the placement of the individual in the discourse because they have control over the signifier in the game. Through this process, the individual experiences a number of encounters with referents that produce meaning during the playing of video games, and these encounters are internalized by the individual and used to produce their own meaning (Gee, 2004; Jenkins, 2008). They develop an identity through playing video games and the exchange of information with others. More importantly, individuals can internalize or reject meaning from these encounters as they develop their identity, and the identity developed on-line can differ from their identity in reality.

Verifying the relationship between video games and learning are studies conducted by Barab and associates (2009, 2010). These studies examine how video games can provide a digital scenario for learning within a controlled, formal learning environment. The Quest Atlantis project created fictional, scientific scenarios that allowed students the freedom to explore and apply concepts to solve problems. Within this learning space, students could work independently and work together in this learning space. More advanced scenarios allowed for the scaffolding of cognitive and socio-cultural skills as the problems were more complex and intricate for an individual to solve. The results of these studies evinced the notion that learning and the transfer of knowledge occurs within these semiotic domains. Experiencing problems and dialogue with other gamers allows for the internalization of knowledge and the production of an identity. The scenarios are designed around a specific problem and the players are students with a specific skills-set tailored for this problem.

Some of the current research concerning video games and learning supports an idea that learning can occur in non-formal learning spaces. In this regard, learning occurs in social discourses where learners are not directed to a specific scenario or directed to acquire specific knowledge. Partington (2010) explores some of the social dynamics to note how a mentor-figure often emerges in video games to help newer players navigate them. With the multiplicity of options afforded to players in many video games, experienced members of the community can act as a guide. Gee and Hayes (2010) use *The Sims,* a simulation of real life, to explore how players apply learning from the game to their reality and apply skills from reality to the game. This shows a transfer of information and knowledge that impacts both the video game and reality. Of note in both these studies in the role of the individual: in Gee and Hayes' study they are applying learning to their own culture, and Partington uncovers players are helping players. Both resist the idea that a monolithic culture industry is controlling the production of meaning and limiting options.

College Men and Masculinity

To this point, there has been little research examining the development of masculinity and a masculine identity in video game discourse communities. While there is learning and identity development occurring (Gee, 2004), these issues are largely absent from the discussion. Kimmel (2008) criticizes video games as a device that traps college men in luminal space he labels 'Guyland': a space that traps men between boyhood and adulthood. This space prevents them from developing into independent, responsible men and reaching their full potential. Rather, they are placated with repressive images and meanings, or they are encouraged to replicate harmful vestiges of the status quo.

Other prominent researchers ask questions related to the development of college men and masculinity. Central amongst them is how certain aspects of masculinity are replicated and rewarded, while others are marginalized and repressed. Drawing from research from Connell (2005), the questions asked examine how men can resist hegemonic masculinity and develop their own identity. Hegemonic masculinity contains the representations and values that support traditional, patriarchal forms of masculinity. Hence, these aspects of hegemonic masculinity are promoted by culture industries in the lifeworld to encourage replication of specific aspect of masculinity that promotes the established social order. Wark (2008) further provides evidence and connection between hegemonic masculinity and video games by describing the military entertainment complex developed within popular war simulators to encourage pro-military ideologies and perpetuating the man-as-soldier archetype in society. He argues that playing these games replicates virtues associated with soldering and warfare to encourage a mindset conducive to violent conquest. Encountering these representations of men encourages their acceptance and replication in society.

Aspects of hegemonic masculinity also seep into the development of college men. Along with the anxieties expressed by Kimmel, men also face challenges with their masculinity. First, certain masculine scripts are developed to appear as 'natural' vestiges of masculinity: certain vocations and professions are privileged because (hegemonic) masculinity (Brown & McDonald, 2008; Mahalik, Perry, Coonerty-Femiano & Land, 2006; Sayman, 2007); it creates challenges with receiving aid and assistance for feelings or mental health issues are repressed and ignored (Addas & Mahalik, 2003; Blazina, Settle, & Eddins, 2008); and, it encourages a code of silence concerning acts of sexual violence (Kelly & Erickson, 2007). In short, hegemonic masculinity privileges certain actions and social constructions that favor the status quo, while marginalizing those constructions of masculinity that resist it.

The tension created between hegemonic masculinity and other social constructions is a concern found in the research. Many wish to challenge the idea that masculinity is a monolithic construct and promote the notion that masculinity is a nuanced, complicated identity (Kimmel, 2011; Harper and Harris, 2010). Fundamentally, there is a challenge in how men are able to develop their unique identity, which may differ from the dominant construction of masculinity. Davis (2002) provides evidence of gender role conflict occurring when masculinity differs from the majority. Men choose to develop masculine aligning with hegemonic masculinity because they desire acceptance from the social group and desire the privileges associated with it. Conversely, men may hide their masculinity to pass amongst social groups or avoid retribution by wearing 'gender masks' that present a form of masculinity in alignment with dominate constructions in a social group (Edwards & Jones, 2009).

While the construction of masculinity amongst college students is complicate, intricate, but critical, it is paramount that social networks and influences are examined to determine how video games affect this construction. While Kimmel (2008) condemns them, Harris (2010) observes that "multiple masculinities are situated within socio-cultural contexts" and examines how male peer group interactions are part of these contexts (p. 299). He defines video games as part of these peer groups and a site where masculinity is practiced, developed, and replicated. Just as video game players do not experience the narratives in isolation, men do not develop masculinity in isolation either. Harris' Model of Masculinity Development provides insight into the social network and discourse communities that college men experience. He observes that men, rightly so, bring their individual culture to college campuses, but these cultures are mixed and shared through a reciprocal process of communication.

METHODOLOGY

Participants

One obvious gap in the research is the lack of studies conducted on two-year college students. When studied, the research often focuses on concerns related to academic success and the transfer process (Gardernshire, Collado, Marin, & Castro, 2010; Sanchez, Huerta, Venesgas, 2012, Sontam & Gabiel, 2012; Strayhom, 2013; Winter, 2009). In these studies, there is a lack of examination of two year students beings situated in culture or specific discourse communities. Importantly, two-year students do not fit the traditional definition of 'student': they often have full or part time jobs, family needs, and they often focus on practical needs (Cohen & Brawer, 2008).

For these reasons, this qualitative study used a targeted sampling and snowball technique to gather participants who self-identified as two-year students and as someone who plays video games. Participants needed to have life experiences from both of these areas to qualify. To generate the initial list, area business were researched to establish their connection to the video game community and, once verified, flyers were posted. Flyers were also posted at a mid-western two-year institution. Names of future potential participants were gathered at the end of the semi-structured interviews.

As a result of these actions, the 13 participants were used in the study: 11 participants were between the ages of 21 and 16, one participant was 34, and one participant was over 40. This final participant was the only person to disclose having children. Further, all participants were white. The presence of only a single race is identified as a limitation to the study, but the dominance of a single race reflects composition of the area.

Question Design

The study examined the relationship between an individual and a particular discourse community; thus, a critical discourse analysis was employed to understand this relationship. Gee (2011) articulates that Discourse is "the ways of combining and integrating language, actions, interactions, ways of thinking, believing, valuing, and various symbols, tools, and objects to enact a particular sort of socially recognizable identity" (p. 29); Fairclough (2001) argues the internalization of these symbols can lead to an internalization of power dynamics that prevent resistance to authority and, consequently, hegemony. The multitude of referents and sign systems engaged within this discourse impact the epistemological and hermeneutical development of players. Hence, questions were designed to understand how men construct this identity through the interactions and learning opportunity engaged within video game communities. Players come to ascribe attributes and value to actions from these experiences, and, due to the colonization of the life world, some are valued higher and privileged more than others because of the hegemonic influences.

The questions employed in the interview, then, seek to uncover the criticality and semiotics associated with the social goods and power dynamics present within the communicative actions of the discourse community (Fairclough, 2001; Gee, 2011). To this end, the methodology for a critical discourse analysis described by Gee was used to highlight the relationship between subject and discourse. First, questions were used to establish the initial entry of the subject into this discourse community. Then, questions were asked to establish some of the significant aspects of this community and how an identity was developed. It was important to note how the participants ascribed meaning to cultural artifacts and to note how that meaning affected their construction of masculinity. This significance was then examined in conjunction to other relationships and connections made by the participant in the discourse community. In effect, the studied asked participants how they entered the discourse, what was learned within the discourse, and then how they applied this learning to other discourses. Finally, because discourse contain permeable boundaries and are never static, concluding questions asked about intertextual relationships created within multiple discourses (Gee, 2011).

One important aspect of this study is the inflections and emphasis placed on words as they are being spoken. Language extends beyond the mere usage of a word, body language, tonal inflection, and pauses can also provide insight into how meaning is generated and ascribed. To document this process, certain words containing emphasis or de-emphasis in the interview were noted during the coding process, as was notable body language or gestures while answering.

FINDINGS

What is a Man?

A theme emerging from the participants concerned the concept of 'responsibility' and its connection to constructing a masculine identity. The notion of 'responsibility' was mentioned directly by 5 of the 13 participants in the interviews. By mentioning this concept so predominately, the connection a connection between 'responsible' and 'masculine' can be drawn. Adam B. provided a significant quote that indicates the importance of this concept: "it's like being responsible for yourself to a point where you can be responsible for others". He further qualified a hierarchy that indicates he considered work most important, family the next important, and, finally, video games were the least important. Other participants echoed this hierarchy, too, to indicate that other concepts are valued higher than video games.

While video games are a part of this identity, other aspects trump them. Nate, for example, indicated that he learned more from his family then from video games. Additionally, participants Brent, Jake, and Adam S. construct masculine in relationship to being responsible for a family, or other people of value. These observations align with Adam B. and his construction of masculinity and being responsible for family. With this, the word 'provide' is used repeatedly, indicating that a man's responsibility for the family extends to caring for needs.

Rooted in this construction is an emphasis on action: masculinity depends on being actively responsible for others. As such, several participants decoupled the idea of masculinity and responsible, suggesting that this connection moves beyond men. Three participants noted a belief that gender is defined at a genetic level, such as Josh's statement, "the only real definition that I've come across is just that you have X and Y genes". Spencer, too, succinctly stated, "it's the floppy bits" as a defining characteristic of gender. Yet, even this de-emphasis of masculinity yields evidence that actions, such as responsibility, come to define men and masculinity. It is the actions that men take which define their masculinity.

This notion of action runs parallel to representations of men and masculinity in video games. When asked about specific characters or video games, participants noted a range of cultural artifacts, but all of the men mentioned were the protagonists in the narratives. Further, the male characters were classified into three archetypes, which emerged from this data.

First, representations of male characters were classified as the man-as-warrior archetypes. This archetypes depends upon a straight-forward and direct approach to action, typically through open battle or feats of strengths. Characters mentioned in this archetype were either military figures or hyper-masculine figures with enlarged muscles and physical prowess in battle. Second, the archetype of the man-as-assassin emerged as another construction of masculinity. These archetypical characters depend upon stealth and guile as their form of problem solving. While they avoid direct conflict and prefer stealth, they are a capable in combat; however, they prefer to remain hidden or deceive their opponents. Lastly, the man-as-athlete archetype appeared through references to sports and sports simulators. Citing popular simulators, like the NFL Football simulator *Madden*, participants mentioned how sports and athletes promote responsibility to maintain health and awareness to defeat opponents and popularize virtues associated with professional competitions.

A running theme amongst these archetypes is the physical prowess and form of the characters in game. Dan mentioned that men in video games are "defined [as] more masculine"; Adam S. described how they all look "like bodybuilders". Interestingly, while the representations of men invoke depictions of an ideal masculine form, no participants noted this form in their definitions of their own masculinity. There were no comments about a desire or wish to achieve the bodies represented in the narratives. A comment from Josh summarizes this sentiment, "men are getting more realistic portrayals of actual people instead of this stereotypical big guy with muscles". So, while representations of men are depictions of an ideal form, there does not seem to be an internalization of this standard; in fact, there is some movement away from it.

In conclusion, participants noted how their construction of masculinity depends upon a concept of responsibility, most often invoked in conjunction with family, to establish a masculine identity. These men articulate a construction of masculinity that depends upon relationships with others, and their being active in encouraging and maintaining this relationship. More so, representations of men found in video games encourage this activity. The characters mentioned are responsible either as the protagonists of a narrative or as icons of popular sports-celebrities.

Learning to Act Like a Man

Following the responses documenting a masculine identity and how it is constructed in the discourse, there are also data indicated specific actions and activities that are associated with masculinity. These actions and activities are encouraged and internalized through video game playing experiences, too.

Chivalry. This concept of responsibility extended to ideas about chivalry. Nate stated it as, "the sense of chivalry [is] being respectful to others"; Jake noted, 'don't do anything dumb that hurts your family". Additionally, participants noted strong themes of chivalry in video games associated with medieval or fantasy narratives. These types of narratives help produce the man-as-warrior archetype and often place that archetype in a world of knights and heroism. While closely related to the concept of responsibility, associating masculinity with the concept of chivalry indicates a sense of morality and duty—it is larger than a person's individual responsibility because it extends out to a social code and protocols for behavior. Adam B. provides evidence for this by mentioning a notion of civic duty and masculinity, which is emblematic for the relationship expressed by others.

Social Skills. Overwhelmingly, 12 of the 13 participants notes learning social dynamics and customs through the interactions with others in video games. Nate and Mark both directly stated how the increased on-line video games depend upon social interactions and communities. This leads to teamwork, problem solving, and the development of intra-personal relationships and habits.

Interactions, in this regard, lead to the development of communities. There is a social cohesion developed through on-line interactions and relationships. Spencer comments how video games can promote and maintain friendship in a global community, and Nate discussed how video games are components of conversations. Finally, John comments how "on-line games give [people] a way to be social" to evince how introverts can develop relationships in these on-line communities. They are social outlets and texts that people can use to communicate with others.

Male Bonding. As part of social bonding rituals, participants noted how men will boast and brag about their accomplishments to establish dominance. Participants qualified this as a sign of friendship, and as something that transcended discursive lines. For example, actions performed in video games could become part of workplace conversations as video games become part of the social network and conversation pieces. Mark and John, for example, recall discussing video games and their meanings with workplace colleagues. While many noted that this bonding occurs in the spirit of camaraderie, some, like Matt, noted how it could lead to bullying. Thus, there is an ethic of care and not condemnation that needs to be maintained. Nick describes how his teammates will often help new players, or players below their skill level, but he did describe some negative encounters where "people would waste time" being angry at others. Further, both Mark and John note how some video games encounters are disrespectful and bigoted; however, these actions are often policed by members of the group and disallowed and discouraged.

Exercise and Health. A connection between exercise and physical appearance emerged from the data. This connection is important because participants frequently noted the peak physical appearance of men represented in games, and they noted the stereotype of the overweight male gamer. Matt was passionate about mentioning he defied stereotypes and was able to run marathons in addition to playing video games. He passionately wanted to challenge this stereotype. Both Adam B. and Jake, too, mentioned the importance of exercise and physical appearance. Jake even went so far as to suggest how some people "look like a gamer" because of their physical stature or apparel.

John and George commented on the role of drugs and alcohol in video games, too. They rejected the construction that smoking and drinking are connected to masculinity, but noted how many popular characters glorify smoking and drinking. John commented that alcohol could restore health in the game *Dues Ex*. George connected drinking and masculinity because men want "big drinks and shots" to establish their masculinity. He also notes how drinking and driving can lead to complications. In an effort to promote physical wellness, these participants noted that some representations of men in video games should not be replicated. Much like the physical prowess represented in the appearance of men, these representations of smoking and drinking do not transfer to their constructions of masculinity. More so, they are expressively rejected.

Anxieties. Some of the actions indicated anxiety on the part of the participants about which actions developed in video games should be internalized and replicated, and which should be rejected. Brent rejected the idea of partying and this type of lifestyle in games, even mentioning how "people don't take things seriously" to demonstrate men avoiding responsibility. Dan noted how he wanted his kids to feel "it's alright to cry if you are a boy," and John noted that "men are not usually portrayed in a very good, respectful way". Most importantly, John concluded that his portrayal is a result of a 'brainwashing society to give an idea of what society thinks men should be like". He also mentioned how video games encourage these portrayals. Adam B., furthermore, expressed concerns about how men should appear both in video games and in reality. He established, "just for the record, I've never gotten a manicure or a pedicure".

Other types of anxiety appeared in the form of ambivalence or uncertainty about how to develop as a man. George angrily noted how social pressures, such as 'listening to his mother', produced anxiety because he felt compelled to act in a certain way. Adam S., noted how he wonders, "what should I do? What do I want to be like?" as he considers how to construct his masculinity. Josh notes, too, that "it would be really hard to say this is how a man acts". Interestingly, both Adam S. and Josh mentioned video game narratives that involve the male protagonist coming-of-age and accepting adulthood and being a man. They both specifically note a transition from childhood to adulthood in these narratives.

Acting like a Man

Findings using this tool uncover connection between discourses. Identities and actions developed within these video game communities do not stay in the community—they link to others. More importantly, the discourses and their linkages reveal some of the underlying power dynamics and social good associated with this epistemological development.

Work. Connections between masculinity and work also emerged from the data. Men, to be able to maintain their responsibilities, develop actions and relationships and apply them to their career or job to succeed in the workforce. Additionally, Spencer noted how some of the changes in stereotypes regarding 'male professions' open up new opportunities and challenges. Once consider a profession for women, nursing, for example, represents new opportunities for men, Spencer notes, but also challenges because of these traditional stereotypes that state heterosexual men do not become nurses. He also notes how society is changing to accept women as the leaders of international business and as community leaders, too. Adam S provides a historical context by discussing changes in the workplace from the 1950 to the 2010. Like Spencer, the changes in the workplace and acceptable professions lead to new opportunities and challenges to construct masculinity.

Video games, too, connect to the workforce because they represent professions deemed acceptable for men and because actions and abilities practiced in the discourse apply to the workforce. Participants noted that men in these video games are leaders, and they note how many of the popular simulators enforce constructions of masculinity in relationship to soldiering or professional athleticism. Dan noted the popularity of war simulators, like *Call of Duty*, encourages acceptance of the military. He also noted that strategies learned in sports simulators can be used in wagers: "I like betting people on what the next [football] play is going to be in a game." Mark, too, provides connection for how abilities developed in the game can apply to the workplace. He notes, "I remember the small details. I remember visuals. I never used that skill professionally before. I was practicing for this playing video games without really knowing it".

Social Stereotypes. 6 participants describes the stereotypical gamer as 'anti-social' and 'over-weight'. As discussed earlier, this is the stereotypical depiction of the average gamer; however, as discussed earlier, too, participants noted a dedication to exercise and social relationships to challenge this stereotype. More so, both Matt and Adam B vehemently described actions to avoid being defined by this stereotype in social networks.

There was also a growing theme about the popularity of gamers and how this popularity challenges the stereotype. Overwhelmingly, participants noted that this increase of popularity, and marketing, expands the number of people playing games, which expands the community. Thus, the more people in the community lead to more interactions and dispelling of stereotypes and stereotypical beliefs. Due to the emphasis of corporate influence and promotion of video games, the stereotypes has been challenged and changed. People know, and develop relationships with, video gamers.

Women. A notable theme, too, that relates to challenging of stereotypes is the increase of female players. Spencer, Mark, and Matt made comments about the presence of women in video game communities affects behaviors. Male players act differently and there is a change in stereotypical behaviors. More so, the presence of women in this discourse also affects the construction of masculinity and masculine actions. The participants, especially Matt, noted a development of stronger bond and relationships both in video games and out of video games.

Active Resistance. Along with challenges to stereotypes associated with being a gamer, stereotypes associated with being a man were also challenged. In part, the inclusion of women led to these challenges. Overwhelming, the construction that masculinity must equate with aggressive behavior was resisted and challenged. This includes acts of violence and asserting dominance over others. Dan and Brent noted these stereotypes were challenged and no longer socially valued. Meanwhile, John and George noted challenges to associations of smoking, drugs, and alcohol. A quote provided by Spencer summarizes the ethos expressed by the participants: "men don't have to be one thing anymore".

In particular, the construction of man-as-leader was challenged because female gamers do not automatically accept this construction. They, too, desire leadership, and this desire challenges typical male behavior. Mark noted this also challenge tradition 'aggressive' and 'territorial' actions, and Matt astutely noted challenges to 'womanizing' and patriarchal order. Interestingly, George noted how some men now shift to a subservient role by "paying the bills. [He] get's the door for the girl. [He] does everything for the women". He questioned this emerging stereotype and shift in power dynamics.

Parents. Another emergent theme concerned the role of parents and politics associated with parenting. Many participants noted that it was a parent or surrogate parent which helped them into the discourse. Often, participants noted their first video game system as a gift or something shared with their parent-figure. So, they extended this relationship to their ideas about raising children. They viewed the role of the parent as analogous to mentors in the video game: just as experienced players would coach and guide novice players in video game communities, parents should coach and guide children. Adam B provided a critical quote: "video games don't kill people, you know, parenting is what affects, ultimately, your child. The emphasis is on the parent to guide the development of their children. Others described how parents would limit the games available for play, such as not allowing teen-agers to play *Mortal Kombat*. Finally, Nick offers this quote that shows that family can be more influential than video games: "I grew up in a house where gender wasn't stressed. I'd just, kind off, learned that it didn't take anything else along those lines from video games".

DISCUSSION

There are several important epistemological, hermeneutical, and pedagogical considerations to contemplate.

Culture Industries

Clearly, these video games are sites of culture replication and internalization that men use to construct their social reality and masculinity. While culture industries are indicted as producing hegemony, many participants notes resistance or challenged hegemonic ideals (Horkheimer and Adorno, 1999). There was more alignment with Benjamin (1936) and his concept of textual aura. These men integrated the video games with their own culture, challenging notions of textual dominance: the presence of both hegemonic and counter-hegemonic narratives within these video games challenges notion of monolithic supremacy. As each individual participant encountered these texts through their own cultural lens, the shifted and changed the meaning of that text. The video games themselves, nor the culture industry that created them, appear to possess sole control over the meaning-making process. Direct influence over the participants was not clearly noted; they were able to maintain and develop their own identity and definition of masculinity.

Of importance, however, is the role of other figures, not texts, to this meaning-making process. These social encounters with other players both in-game and out-of-game appeared to elicit more power over the participant than the actual game or text. For example, interaction with women in-game caused men to re-evaluate and challenge certain behaviors; furthermore, family members also exerted influence of the participants, often more than the game itself. This does align with Parrington's (2010) observation that mentors or mentor-figures increase the development of participants. Thus, the encounters that these participants experienced suggest that other people act as mentors and, thusly, influence how they construct knowledge. Interestingly, though, is that the notion that mentors often did not help with cognitive understanding regarding the rules of procedures associated with the game, but rather they helped participants navigate cultural expectations and mores.

Ultimately, these encounters within video games text offer approaches to challenge hegemony and raise the critical consciousness of the participants. They form pockets of resistance, and participants because active within them. They do not respond passively, but are active within both the games and its social relationships. Thus, the experiences within these particular discourse communities afford the participants to both challenge and change hegemonic constructs.

Learning about Men and Masculinity

The data indicates that learning and development occurs within these video game discourse communities. They are not idle fancies or wastes of times, but they are sites of cultural replication and production that affects meaning. Video games, indeed, are part of the popular cultural topos, and they are subject to issues related to the production of and resistance to hegemony and ideology. The semantics and semiotics associated with video games are internalized and integrated with an identity, particularly an identity associated with masculinity.

Vocation. To this end, the connection between the discourse of video games and the discourse of work was interesting. Participants noted transference of skills and attitudes developed in video games discourse communities to the workplace. This professional discourse, curiously, also contained cognitive and social benefits due to their interaction with these cultural artifacts. Unlike some of the current beliefs about video games being devoid of meaning or value, these participants revealed a connection between work and play. Skills developed in one impacted the other.

Tangent to this connection is the concept of vocation and its positioning within a masculine identity. Not only was there findings connecting work and play, there was also suggestion that work and being responsible were central to developing a masculine identity. Of course, this aligns with the notion that men define themselves through their profession (Connell, 2005), but it also uncovers the hegemonic power dynamics operating within this section of the lifeworld. Importantly, no singular profession or field of study emerged from this data—a hegemonic hold did not take effect. While present, hegemonic masculinity was not predominate in the data, and many participants showed resistance or disbelief to its effects. Options were not limited, and there was liberation expressed in being able to choose traditionally non-masculine fields of study, like nursing.

Pride and acceptance for their choose profession were the presiding emotions, not marginalization or persecution. Possibly connecting to the notions of chivalry expressed, these participants integrated their vocation (or intended vocation) strongly into their identity. This both affirms and challenges hegemonic masculinity. For example, while many noted representations of soldering, no participants expressed a desire to be a soldier. Certainly men having an identity connected to their work represent traditional, hegemonic constructions; however, the particular professions and field of studies are no long limited to traditional, hegemonic constructions. Men appear to possess the ability to transgress against these expectations, and experiences within video game discourses facilitate this act. Participants in this study did not accept hegemonic masculinity; they acknowledged the relationship between masculinity and work, but also integrated it with an ethos of responsibility and care for others. Vocations are not chosen based upon the accumulation of wealth and power, but the accumulation of resources to care and provide for others.

Other Scripts. While scripts and identities associated with vocation are the most predominant, there were other indications of scripts. While there is a traditional construction that men cannot and should not discuss their feelings, no data supported this position. Participants freely talked about their feelings and anxieties; one even expressed his desire to have his son cry and work through his feelings. Additionally, these participants did not express constructions about asserting or accepting sexual violence, or any other kind of violence. Participants actively denounced bigotry and sexism and, despite the mention of physical aggression as a form of conflict resolution appearing in the games, no participants encouraged violent retaliation. Men, furthermore, did not express, and appear to discourage, adherence to any codes of silence. They were active and vocal about challenging bigotry and sexism.

Multiple Masculinities

Video games are an integral and embedded part of popular culture and the modern media-scape. With specific attention addressed to hegemonic masculinity in video games, it must be stated that no singular construction of masculinity emerged from this data. Hegemonic masculinity did not take hold over the participants due to experiencing these video games; in fact, it appears the opposite may be occurring. Playing games encourages exploration and development of other forms of masculinity. As many of the participants noted, definitions and constructions of masculinity is changing. Liberation from hegemony can occur in these discourse communities because of the number of encounters and experiences present within the games. There is a diversity of ideas and philosophies that can be constructed because of the diversity of players and cultures experienced through the games. Of course, not all are positives—many participants observed bigoted comments; however, participants also observed ways to challenge bigotry and assist other gamers. In this regard, participants helped other gamers transgress against hegemonic cultural boundaries.

While gender role conflict was expressed by some participants, many more expressed comfort and acceptance of their masculine roles. If anything, potential hesitancy or anxiety about expressing a definition or construction for masculinity occurred because of the multiple definitions and constructions of masculinity present. There is no singular construction of masculinity, and many of the participants acknowledge this in their responses. Further, no participants noted desire or actions related to wearing 'gender masks'. Men were comfortable and freely discussed their masculinity and how it related to their identity.

A predominate theme emerging was this notion of the 'floppy bits' defining gender constructions. Rather than constructing specific gender definitions, participants expressed the belief that gender moves beyond binary constructions of men equate to masculinity and women equate to femininity—the belief in 'floppy bits' presumes a belief that both men and women can share and develop masculine and feminine attributes. The implicit suggestion to these observations is that potential differences between genders are based along biological lines and not sociological lines. Importantly, these cultural lines and boundaries are permeable because of the frequent exchanges of culture and information within these discourses that encourage transgression, and, additionally, both men and women can internalize the same texts and cultural repositories to construct their individual, gendered identity.

IMPLICATIONS AND RECOMMENDATIONS FOR FURTHER STUDY

First and foremost, the notion that video games relegate men to a socio-cultural wasteland must be rejected and ignored. Video games and their associative discourse communities are rich with information and meaning that promote learning and development. Rather than eschewing video games as part of Guyland, there must be more critical examination about how video games define a critical male peer group interaction, which leads to their development of a masculinity identity. The interactions and relationships formed within these groups are highly influential to the development of socio-cultural constructions. Because identity is based upon the situated reality of the learner, the situations of relationships and interactions must also be considered. The studies conducted by Gee and Hayes (2010) and Barab and associates (2009, 2010) provide crucial evidence that learning and transference of knowledge can occur, so more research and examination must be conducted to understand how positive identities and constructions of masculinity (and others) are produced and replicated.

More so, the fear of culture industries and globalization marginalizing or repressing the individual may be unfounded. While an ever-present threat, the multiplicity of encounters and relationships challenges the notion that hegemony can take a permanent foothold in this discourse. Counter-hegemonic narratives emerge, too, and individual participants select and choose with signifiers are internalized and replicated. With meaning being dependent on the unique culture and social positionality of the individual, a monologic and didadic exchange of information is constantly being challenges and/or reframed. Meaning is constantly being constructed due to the limitless semiotics involved within this discourse; new referants are constantly being introduced and encountered.

The relationship between video games and work must also be studied further. Admittedly, two-year college students value work with more emphasis and passion than other types of students (Cohen and Brawer, 2008). Yet, these participants situated work and their masculinity identity closely, and, additionally, they integrated video game discourse communities into this process. Their insistence that skills and relationships developed within video games can apply to their workplace and vocation is a connection worthy of more significant research.

With this, too, is the emphasis on the notion of responsibility being central—if not critical—to the construction of masculinity. While a subjective term, the notion of 'being responsible' emerge too strongly to be ignored; furthermore, it impacted the development and application of other scripts. Taking responsibility for their actions put emphasis on positive constructions of masculinity that operate in opposition to many negative representations of it. They resisted connections to unhealthy lifestyles, for example, and many participants expressly and passionately noted how they actively work to challenge and confront these stereotypes.

Better understanding about how this form of masculinity can be developed, too, would alleviate the gender role conflict. This is an area where more research can be conducted to determine for to alleviate the anxieties and pressures developed when the individual construction of masculinity is perpendicular to the group's construction of masculinity. To this end, better understanding the role, position, and influence of women and femininity may help relieve this type of conflict.

In close, this study opened up avenues for future studies into video games, (college) men and masculinity, and semiotics connect to one another. While the connections and constructions are potentially limitless, it is important to note the strong emphasis on responsibility as a critical part to constructions of masculinity. If anything, the idea of ownership and investment to another person, place, or thing seems to engage men in construction of masculinity and their identity. More so, they resist hegemony in their pursuit of being able to enact their definition of responsible.

REFERENCES

Addis, M., & Mahalik, J. (2003). Men, masculinity, and the contexts of help seeking. *The American Psychologist*, *58*(1), 5–14. doi:10.1037/0003-066X.58.1.5 PMID:12674814

Barab, S., Goldstone, R., & Zulker, S. (2009). Transformational play as a curricular scaffold: Using videogames to support science education. *Journal of Educational Technology*, *18*(4), 305–320. doi:10.1007/s10956-009-9171-5

Barab, S., Gresalfi, M., & Ingram-Goble, A. (2010). Transformational play: Using games to position person, content, and context. *Educational Researcher*, *39*(7), 525–536. doi:10.3102/0013189X10386593

Benjamin, W. (2008). *The work of art in the age of mechanical reproduction and other essays on the media*. Cambridge, MA: Harvard UP.

Blazina, C., Settle, A., & Eddins, R. (2008). Gender role conflict and separation-individuation difficulties: Their impact on college men's loneliness. *Journal of Men's Studies*, *16*(1), 69–81. doi:10.3149/jms.1601.69

Bradford, C. (2010). Looking for my corpse: Video games and player positioning. *Australian Journal of Language and Literacy*, *33*(1), 54–64.

Brown, S., & Macdonald, D. (2003). Masculinities in physical recreation: The (re)production of masculinist discourses in vocation education. *Sport Education and Society*, *13*(1), 19–37. doi:10.1080/13573320701780506

Cobley, P. (2015). What the humanities are for: A semiotic perspective. *American Journal of Semiotics*, *30*(3/4), 205–228.

Cohen, A., & Brawer, F. (2008). *The American community college* (5th ed.). San Francisco, CA: Jossey Bass.

Connell, R. W. (2005). *Masculinities* (2nd ed.). Berkeley, CA: UC Berkeley Press.

Davis, T. L. (2002). Voices of gender role conflict: The social construction of college men's identity. *Journal of College Student Development*, *43*, 508–521.

Edwards, K., & Jones, S. (2009). "Putting my man face on": A grounded theory of college men's gender identity development. *Journal of College Student Development*, *50*(2), 210–228. doi:10.1353/csd.0.0063

Fairclough, N. (2001). *Language and power* (2nd ed.). New York, NY: Longman Press.

Gardenshire-Crooks, A., Collado, H., Martin, K., & Castro, A. (2010). Terms of Engagement: Men of Color Discuss Their Experiences in Community College. *Achieving the Dream, I*, c.

Gee, J. (2004). *What video games have to teach us about learning and literacy*. New York, NY: Palgrave Macmillan.

Gee, J. (2011). *Introduction to discourse analysis* (3rd ed.). New York, NY: Routledge.

Gee, J., & Hayes, E. (2010). *Women and gaming: The Sims and 21st century learning*. New York, NY: Palgrave Macmillan. doi:10.1057/9780230106734

Habermas, J. (1985). The theory of communicative action: Vol. 2. *Lifeworld and system*. Beacon Press.

Harper, S., & Harris, F. (2010). *College men and masculinities: Theory, research, and implications for practice*. San Francisco, CA: Jossey-Bass.

Harris, F. (2008). Deconstructing masculinity: A qualitative study of college men's masculine conceptualizations and gender performance. *NASPA Journal, 45*(4), 453–474.

Horkheimer, T., & Adorno, M. (1999). *The dialectic of enlightenment*. New York, NY: Continuum.

Hung, A. C. Y. (2011). *The work of play: meaning-making in videogames*. New York, NY: Hill & Wang Press.

Jenkins, H. (2008). *Convergence culture*. New York, NY: New York University Press.

Kelly, T., & Erickson, C. (2007). An examination of gender role identity, sexual self-esteem, sexual coercion, and sexual victimization in a university sample. *Journal of Sexual Aggression, 13*(3), 235–245. doi:10.1080/13552600701794366

Kimmel, M. (2008). *Guyland: The perilous place where boys become men*. New York, NY: Harper Collins.

Kimmel, M. (2011). *Manhood in America* (3rd ed.). Cambridge, UK: Oxford University Press.

Mahalik, J. R., Good, G. E., & Englar-Carlson, M. (2003). Masculinity scripts, presenting concerns, and help seeking: Implications for practice and training. *Professional Psychology, Research and Practice, 34*(2), 123–132. doi:10.1037/0735-7028.34.2.123

Partington, A. (2010). Game literacy, gaming cultures, and media education. *English Teaching, 9*(1), 73–86.

Sanchez, S., Huerta, A., & Venesgas, K. (2012). Latino males and college preparation programs: Examples of increased access. *Metropolitan Universities, 22*(3), 27–45.

Sayman, D. (2007). The elimination of sexism and stereotyping in occupational education. *Journal of Men's Studies, 15*(1), 19–30. doi:10.3149/jms.1501.19

Sontam, V., & Gabiel, G. (2012). Student engagement at a large suburban community college: Gender and race differences. *Community College Journal of Research and Practice, 36*(10), 808–820. doi:10.1080/10668926.2010.491998

Storey, J. (2009). *Cultural theory and popular culture: An introduction* (5th ed.). London, UK: Pearson.

Strayhorn, T. (2013). Satisfaction and retention among African American Men at two-year community colleges. *Community College Journal of Research and Practice*, *36*(5), 358–375. doi:10.1080/10668920902782508

Wark, M. (2007). *Game Theory*. Cambridge, MA: Harvard University Press.

Winter, B. (2009). Gender related attitudes toward achievement in college. *Community College Enterprise*, *15*(1), 83–91.

Chapter 5
The Lived Experience of Smartphone Use in a Unit of the United States Army

Gregory C. Gardner
George Mason University, USA

ABSTRACT

Smartphones bring major changes to the way people gather information and interact. While smartphone use unleashes productivity it also has worrying implications. This study focused on the most important aspects of user experiences of smartphones in an Army work environment. Theory U and systems theory guided the research. This phenomenological study was based on interviews with soldiers of a variety of ages, ranks, and duty positions. While the findings are consistent with other research, it is clear that smartphone use ties to a number of complex leadership challenges. Paradoxical aspects of smartphone use are apparent as it also fosters stress and anxiety. More concerning, such use jeopardizes the development of the traditional military culture of the unit. Current Army policies do not address the concerns expressed by respondents. The results of the study are a call to action for Army leaders and offer a compelling case for transformative change.

INTRODUCTION

The simple truth is that the Web, the Internet does one thing. It speeds up the retrieval and dissemination of information, partially eliminating such chores as going outdoors to the mailbox, or having to pick up the phone to get ahold of your stock broker or some old buddies to shoot the breeze with. That one thing the Internet does and only that. The rest is Digibabble. – Tom Wolfe, "Hooking Up"

Mr. Wolfe got it wrong. The global connectivity of internetted communications has now extended to mobile devices so ubiquitous that almost 100% of the teenagers and adults in the United States carry one (CTIA, 2014). That connectivity is bringing major changes not just to the way Americans gather and exchange information but also to the way in which they interact with one another and with the organizations they are part of. Indeed, smartphones are now being used like a "digital Swiss Army Knife,"

DOI: 10.4018/978-1-5225-0522-8.ch005

replacing possessions like watches, cameras, books, and even laptops (Chappuis, Gaffey, & Parvizi, 2011, p. 21). In fact, voice communications are now only the fifth most used function of smartphones (Johnson, 2012, para 4). While there is little doubt that mobile information communications technologies (ICTs), commonly called smartphones, enable individuals and machines to much more efficiently exchange information, a variety of research indicates that the ubiquity of these devices and the associated entangled, adaptive network of people and machines leads to a number of increasingly more stressful, more worrying implications (Hillis, 2010). These include changes in how users think, how they interact, how they consider time, and how they deal with the gnawing insecurity resulting from conflicting information, unexpected disconnection, and expectations of immediate response. Those changes also affect organizational cultures, even society as a whole (Gharajedaghi, 2011; Rushkoff, 2013).

Those cultural aspects are especially important in military units where strong interpersonal bonds of camaraderie and esprit-de-corps are the hallmarks of effective combat outfits. What happens to those bonds when young soldiers are more comfortable "living" on their smartphones and would rather send a text message than endure the "real time" commitment of even a phone call much less a face-to-face conversation (Turkle, 2011, p. 202)?

This study, which focuses on the lived experience of smartphone usage in an Army unit, addresses those questions and many more. More importantly, it explores the importance of embracing organizational change and transformation in order to confront the implications of the ubiquity of information and constant connectivity in a distracted present. Even more concerning are the long-term degradation of individual intellect and collective culture that some attribute to the widespread use of those devices (Carr, 2010; Turkle, 2011). Indeed, change in this area is so rapid and the accompanying "survival anxiety" (Schein, 2013, p.100) is so great that long-held habits and processes of communications and information sharing must be unlearned and new approaches relearned (Gharajedaghi, 2011; Schein, 2013). This study argues that to deal with the smartphone phenomenon, leaders must let go of their deeply-held beliefs, open their minds, hearts, and wills, and lead from the future as it emerges (Scharmer, 2009).

Background of the Study

Organizations of all types have gained great advantages in productivity efficiencies and worker effectiveness through the implementation and assimilation of mobile information communications technologies (Kudya & Diwan, 2002). The benefits of this technology, including timeliness, flexibility, ubiquity, competitive advantage, and the ability to carry out otherwise impossible tasks are well documented (Kakabadse, Kousmin, & Kakabadse, 2000; Powell & Dente-Micallef, 1997). Military commentators, including General Officers, often note the revolutionary impacts modern information technology (IT) on military operations (Friedman & Mandelbaum, 2011). In fact, many of the benefits of ICTs or smartphones stem from the ability to foster innovation and creativity.

Complexity, ambiguity and chaos - the unintended consequences of smartphone usage – may, however, also bring counterproductive effects. The strains on users from technology-related stress – technostress – are linked to significant behavior and health issues (Ayyagari, Grover, & Purvis, 2011; Brod, 1984; Weil & Rosen, 1997). Persons experiencing technostress have lower productivity, lower job satisfaction and decreased commitment to the organization (Tarafdar, Tu, Ragu-Nathan, B., & Ragu-Nathan, T., 2007). Other studies suggest that technostress can lead to the ineffective acceptance and usage of new technologies (Sami & Pangannaiah, 2005). Interestingly, the most innovative organizations often exhibit the highest user technostress (Wang, Shu, & Tu, 2008). In sum, the continually evolving smartphone user experience is varied, complex, chaotic, and often ambiguous.

Heidegger (1996) adds an important caveat to that understanding. His substantive position is consistent with an argument that addresses the tensions in technology usage including both its paradoxical nature and the ironic implications of its supposed advantages. As a result, he lays a useful groundwork for analysis of technology-based stress. Reduced to its most basic aspects, Heidegger's position is that we comprehend and understand the world through a technological lens: specifically, he notes, technology of itself does not answer questions, satisfy demands, or increase any particular capacity. Conversely, it is much more fundamental, framing the world in such a manner that both question and answer are changed, that both direction and mechanism are impacted, and that need and gratification are no longer the same. For example, the word processor and the electronic calculator are far more than simply more efficient, more effective methods of writing or doing mathematics. In fact, they fundamentally change what it is to write and to manipulate numbers. The framing of information technologies, like the mobile phone, in ironic and paradoxical terms, allows the complexity and ambiguity of a social situation to be recognized, analyzed, and addressed (Arnold, 2003). Organizational leaders may then take action to intervene.

The conflicting experiences of ICTs, including smartphones, are rather graphically described as a "mess" (Ackoff, 1999, p.14). A mess does not have a straightforward solution. It is ambiguous and often chaotic: it contains considerable complexity and uncertainty, is interwoven and bounded by significant constraints, is seen differently from different points of view, contains many value conflicts, and is often illogical (Horn, 2001). Gharajedaghi (2011) argues that a mess must be mapped to make sense of the key themes, relationships, and interactions existing in the system. The process of mapping is accomplished through the use of causal linkages (Maani & Cavana, 2000). Once mapped, the mess can be dissolved "through focused and concerted transformational effort" (Gharajedaghi, 2011, p. 179).

Statement of the Problem

The research problem is that smartphone-related user experiences in an Army work environment provide evidence of the complex, systemic "mess" of technology usage (Ackoff, 1999, p.14). While these experiences are often positive, the chaos and ambiguity of this situation affect the social relationships amongst Army smartphone users and thus complicate paths to success for the individual, the organization, and society. A systemic causal link map of the user experience and associated technostress caused by smartphones is diagramed in Figure 1.

Research Question

This study is based on one comprehensive research question. It is, "What are the most important aspects of the holistic smartphone user experience in an Army work environment?"

Limitations and Assumptions

While of significant utility, the conduct of the research within the limited confines of a military unit is also its most significant weakness. Accordingly, the research takes great care with both interview questions and analysis to ensure the results are as widely applicable as possible.

Figure 1. Mapping the Systemic Mess of User Technostress in an O rganizational Context. Adapted from Systems Thinking: Managing Chaos and Complexity by J. Gharajedaghi, 2011, New York: Elsevier. Copyright 2011 by Elsevier, Inc.

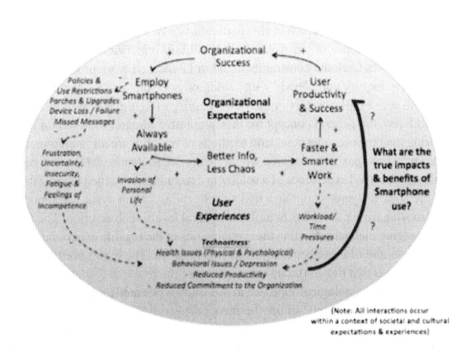

The study has a number of other limitations. It is qualitative in nature, examining the lived experiences of only a very small number of soldiers in what existing research shows is an exceptionally complex phenomenon. Accordingly, the results cannot be directly extrapolated to other organizations. The participants were all soldiers and while they do reflect a diverse population, they do not reflect society as a whole.

METHODOLOGY

The hermeneutical phenomenological approach to qualitative inquiry presents an opportunity to increase the understanding of the lived experience of smartphones in an Army unit. Qualitative research studies seek to understand the phenomenon, perspectives and meanings people attach to their experiences (Creswell, 2007; Creswell, 2009; Denzin & Lincoln, 1998; Taylor & Bogdan, 1998). These types of studies allow for a focus on learning the true experiences of subjects of the study as opposed to the meaning the researcher brings to the effort (Creswell, 2009). Qualitative research in particular affords the opportunity to explore and probe the views of the participants to gain a view into and understanding of what real life is like. This in turn provides both contextual richness and a means of determining categories of meaning and salient themes (Miles & Huberman, 1994; Taylor & Bogdan, 1998).

Research Design

The design of this qualitative study begins with the broad assumptions central to qualitative inquiry, the worldview and theoretical lens that shape the study (Giorgi, 1997). An advocacy / participatory worldview informs the practice of research in this particular study. The key features include a focus on understanding the lived experience of smartphones in a military organization, helping individuals understand and free themselves from the constraints found in IT-focused work procedures, and executing a practical, collaborative inquiry completed "with" soldiers vice "on" or "to" them. In this construct, the participants are all active collaborators in their own inquiries (Kemmis & Wilkinson, 1998, p. 22).

Within that worldview, the general concept for this qualitative research is based on methodological congruence; ensuring the purpose, questions, and methods of research are all interconnected and interrelated so that the study emerges as a cohesive whole (Morse & Richards, 2002). The core concept of the research focuses on the lived experience of a soldier in a technology enabled organization. The study includes detailed methods, a rigorous approach to data collection, data analysis, and report writing. The data was analyzed moving from particulars to multiple general levels of abstraction. The report was then drafted in a clear, engaging manner reflecting the complexities of the real life experiences of the soldiers and groups he interviews and offering believable, realistic findings. The report is ethical, addressing all aspects of the ethical issues that thread through each phase of the research (Natanson, 1997).

The hermeneutical phenomenological approach in this study is oriented toward lived experience (phenomenology) and interpreting the "texts" of life (hermeneutics) (van Maanen, 1990, p. 4). This approach involves dynamic interplay between numerous research activities. The "abiding concern" (van Maanen, 1990, p. 31) was first addresses, in this case the lived experience of daily smartphone usage in a military unit reflect on the essential themes that constitute the nature of this lived experience. A researcher writes a description of the phenomenon, maintaining a strong relation to the topic of inquiry and balancing parts of the writing to the whole. Most importantly, hermeneutical phenomenology includes not only a description of lived experiences, but is also an analytical process in which the researcher interprets or "mediates" between different meanings of the lived experiences. Key questions, including, "What changes take place within you as a result of the change experience when using the devices?" and "What attitude does that change engender in you and what actions do you take as a result of those thoughts and feelings?" help determine the lived experience (van Maanen, 1990, p. 26).

The proliferation of information technology (IT) in the workplace offers an extraordinary opportunity for access to information and new ways of working. At the same time, however, smartphone usage presents work-related and social challenges that leadership/management have to contend with and that published literature has yet to fully acknowledge, particularly in military units. The literature reveals that there are two majority streams dealing with IT in organizations; the IT-enabling stream and the IT-consequences stream.

The consequences of IT linked to behavioral changes include: Absenteeism, aggressiveness, negativism, withdrawal, argumentativeness and denigration of colleagues (Bichteler, 1987). Information overload and the ubiquity of smartphones and other ICTs lead to lower productivity, including lower motivation, extreme dissatisfaction with the job, burn out, and emotional breakdown (McGee, 1996). Further, a variety of physical health issues, including: psycho-social behavior exemplified by depression, repetitive stain injuries, and chronic fatigue syndrome (Amicil & Celentanino, 1991; Herrmann, 1999). Mitigating those costs while preserving the benefits of IT can have significant benefits to a wide variety of organizations, especially military units.

Sample and Setting

This study focuses on one unit of the United States Army, a command consisting of approximately 2500 soldiers. Twenty-eight members of the unit were interviewed to ensure an in-depth understanding of the smartphone phenomenon. This unit is stationed in the Continental United States and contains a number of members who have previously served in Iraq and Afghanistan. The unit is well resourced employing a broad range of wired and wireless ICTs, including a variety of government issued and personal smartphones. The unit conducts missions ranging from routine garrison activities to field training. As an integral part of this study, the researcher became familiar with the policies and practices that govern the use of smartphones in this unit.

Accordingly, interviewees included a representational cross-section of senior and mid-grade commissioned and non-commissioned officers as well as soldiers in a variety of roles across the command. Purposeful sampling ensured that each participant was pre-screened to ensure that he or she is a frequent user of smartphones and had significant personal experience with these devices (Moustakas, 1994). Only persons with that experience participated in the interviews.

A maximal variation sampling strategy was followed to ensure that diverse individuals are chosen who are expected to hold different perspectives on smartphone usage (Giorgi, 1997). Members from each segment of the unit's population were solicited in compliance with this strategy.

Instrumentation/Measures

The ATLAS.ti 7 qualitative data analysis software tool was then used to assist with transcription analysis for this study, as the software provides an efficient means for coding storing and locating qualitative data. Additionally, the researcher maintained a journal as an additional resource to document information provided by the participants during the telephonic interviews (Friese, 2012).

The data collection process and flow are shown in Figure 2.

Data analysis was guided by semi-structured interview questions and a search for patterns (Patton, 1987). In inductive analysis, the categories emerge directly from the participant interview responses augmented by the researcher's journal notes. The data collected from each participant was first reviewed individually for thoroughness and completeness. After completing, validating, and annotating individual transcripts, the researcher loaded each into ATLAS.ti 7, a qualitative data analysis software tool used to assist with text synthesis of information by identifying meaning units or themes derived from statements. The process the researcher followed to analyze the interview results is the iterative Noticing/Collecting/Thinking (NCT) model of qualitative data analysis (Siedel, 1998; Freise, 2012).

Once the data was coded, related items were grouped to form patterns. As patterns began to form, data that corresponded to specific patterns was combined. Journal notes complemented and clarified direct quotes by participants. All patterns were then reviewed for the emergence of comprehensive themes, combining patterns into themes as appropriate. Importantly, this process was repeated three times until a logical pattern of themes emerged.

Once all transcripts were analyzed, themes were arranged in a matrix with all supporting patterns. This enabled easy, logical access to supporting categories when crafting the write-up for each theme. A detailed abstract analysis was then recorded for each theme, summarizing the scope and substance was identified.. As a final step, conclusions were drawn based on the analysis of the data providing a summary and conclusion to the research question (Freise, 2012; Patton, 1987).

Figure 2. Data Collection and Process Flow. Adapted from "Qualitative Data Analysis with ATLAS.ti," by S. Friese, 2012, Thousand Oaks, CA: Sage. Copyright 2012 by Susanne Friese.

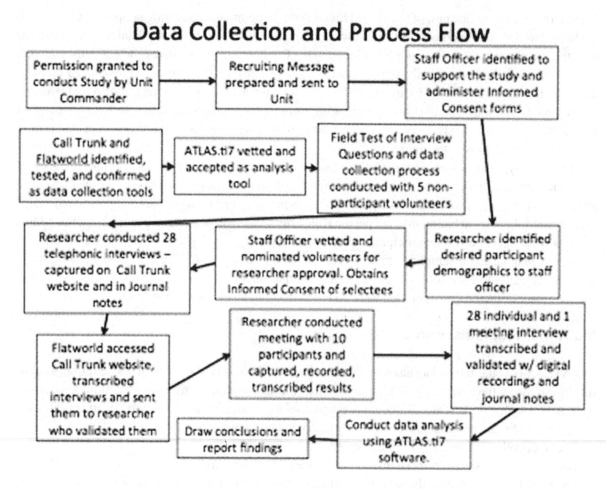

RESULTS

At the end of the individual interviews, the researcher met face-to-face with 10 of the participants in a review session that was also recorded and transcribed. This session verified and validated a number of the comments captured in individual interviews.

Per agreement with the unit commander, that unit is not identified. Volunteers came from the unit's headquarters as well as a number of subordinate organizations. A specific summary is at Table 1.

Of those surveyed, 11 (39%) participants were officers, 9 (32%) were NCO's, and 8 (29%) were enlisted soldiers. Their identified Military Occupational Specialties (MOS) ranged from Infantry and IT to Food Service and Legal. One was a Chaplain's Assistant. Not surprisingly, 26 (93%) of the respondents were men, reflecting the general demographics of this predominantly male organization.

The age mix of the participants ranged from 19 to 41; 3 (11%) are still in their teens, 9 (32%) are in their 20s, 13 (46%) were in their 30s, and one (4%) is over 40. Turkle (2011) asserts that these age cohorts will demonstrate significant differences in perceptions of smartphone usage.

Table 1. Participant Demographics

Participant #	Position	Officer / NCO / Enlisted	Rank	Gender	Age	Years of Service	Education Level
P1	Staff	O	CPT	M	31	10	BS
P2	IT	E	SPC	M	23	4	Certs
P3	Personnel	N	SFC	M	33	8	48 credits
P4	Infantry	E	SPC	M	32	7	30 credits
P5	IT	N	SFC	M	29	10	AA
P6	Transportation	O	CPT	M	27	6	BS
P7	Chemical	O	CPT	M	32	10	BS
P8	Infantry	N	1SG	M	35	17	AA
P9	Infantry	N	SFC	M	32	12	AA
P10	Legal	N	SSG	M	28	10	BS
P11	Infantry	O	1LT	M	26	4	BS
P12	IT	E	PFC	M	21	1	HS
P13	Military Police	N	SFC	M	38	19	AA
P14	Food Service	N	SFC	M	35	10	AA
P15	Chaplain's Asst	N	SGT	M	30	13	AA
P16	Headquarters	E	SPC	M	19	2	35 credits
P17	IT	E	PFC	M	19	2	24 credits
P18	Headquarters	E	PFC	M	19	2	12 credits
P19	Infantry	O	LTC	M	41	20	MA
P20	Infantry	O	MAJ	M	37	15	BS
P21	Public Affairs	O	MAJ	M	39	13	BS
P22	Staff	O	MAJ	M	37	19	MS
P23	Personnel	O	1LT	F	26	5	BS
P24	IT	E	SPC	F	26	9	AA
P25	Headquarters	E	SPC	M	29	5	HS
P26	Staff	N	SGT	M	30	4	HS
P27	Infantry	O	CPT	M	30	10	BS
P28	Personnel	O	1LT	M	31	13	BS

Both young soldiers/junior officers and senior NCOs/Field Grade officers have similar years of service. Of the participants, 9 (32%) have 5 years or less military service, 10 (36%) have between 6 and 10 years in the military and the remaining 9 (32%) have from 12 to 20 years of service.

The education mix of the study participants was closely tied to their age and rank. Both Field Grade officers have Master's Degrees. Every other officer and one NCO, a total of 10 participants (36%), have Bachelor's degrees. In a testament to the education level of the average soldier in today's U.S. Army, 12 (42%), including the youngest enlisted soldiers, had either Associates Degrees or a number of college credits. Just 3 respondents (11%) reported only a High School diploma.

Inductive Analysis

Inductive analysis is a complementary process used to focus on identifiable themes and patterns across a data set to find repeated patterns of meanings (Denzin & Lincoln, 1998; Patton, 1987; Taylor & Bogdan, 1998). This evaluation approach is inductive to the extent that one is able to make sense of the data without imposing pre-existing knowledge or categories prior to data collection.

After completing, validating, and annotating individual transcripts, each was loaded into ATLAS.ti 7, a qualitative data analysis software tool used to assist with text synthesis of information by identifying meaning units or themes derived from statements. The iterative Noticing/Collecting/Thinking (NCT) model of qualitative data analysis (Siedel, 1998; Freise, 2012) was employed in the data analysis..

Often coding/collecting must be modified as the thinking process evolves and the process must be repeated to properly tease out the patterns in the data. The integrated, iterative nature of the NCT process is shown in Figure 3.

On reflection, these codes did not coincide with the key themes of the data and were insufficient to address the research question. Accordingly, a second code pattern was established, grouping and consolidating items as interview transcripts were reviewed. Throughout this noticing/coding/thinking process, insights emerged leading to the addition of new codes. The process of adding and modifying codes continued until the process ran its course (Miles & Huberman, 1994).

This second coding turn was quite valuable as it brought the coding model much closer to a form that clearly addressed the research question. Nevertheless, it still lacked the necessary clarity, simplicity, and rigor to develop insights and generate theoretical understandings.

After more reflection and still following the NCT process, the full data set was reordered. The matrix of these categories with supporting codes and frequencies is shown at Table 2.

Figure 3. The NCT Model of Qualitative Data Analysis. Adapted from "Qualitative Data Analysis with ATLAS.ti," by S. Friese, 2012, Thousand Oaks, CA: Sage. Copyright 2012 by Susanne Friese.

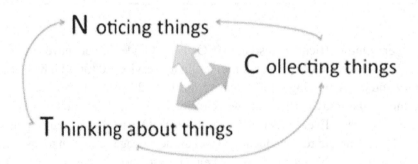

The third coding turn provided the necessary information. After this turn, it became clear that the specific codes fell into five general themes: Productivity, Individual Behaviors, Collective Behaviors, Anxiety, and Policy. When compiled under these categories, the codes both supported the research aim and enabled a rigorous, structured analysis of the data. This detailed analysis led to the identification of the scope and substance of each theme supported by direct quotations from the data. The ATLAS.ti 7 software enabled the coding, storing and locating of the qualitative data. The data was synthesized to form a summary and conclusion concerning the research question. Figure 4 reflects the data reduction, analysis, and synthesis process.

Themes

As the iterative analytical process progressed, the researcher became immersed in the data and began to recognize specific coding moments or sense emerging themes from the data (Swanson & Holton, 2005). The data was examined multiple times until themes were revealed during the data synthesis process. The themes associated with the third set of codes are shown in Table 3. They reflect five major themes: Productivity, Individual Behaviors, Collective Behaviors, Anxieties, and Policy.

Those five themes mapped back to the research question, the conceptual theorists and the research area of focus in the exploratory qualitative inquiry.

Productivity

By a large margin (89%), participants overwhelmingly endorse the significant productivity improvements afforded by their smartphones. The productivity section examined four aspects of smartphone use that subjects highlighted as increasing their work-related productivity. The freedom and increased productivity that attend the use of smartphones make them so attractive to every subject in this study.

Table 2. Final Set of Code Frequencies From All Interview Transcripts and Notes

Code	Frequency	Code	Frequency
Ability to share information	41	Access to information	60
Accessibility	45	Ease of Communications	32
Cultural change	47	Text to share information	57
Distraction	31	Immediacy	36
Impersonal	26	Multitask	31
Prefer to Text	48	Use Social Media	45
Constant availability	49	Loss of device	14
Missed calls	11	Overwhelmed with information	15
General lack of policy	23	Lack of consistent usage policy when deployed	20
Resource Shortfalls	7	Security concerns impede productivity	53

Figure 4. Data Reduction, Analysis, and Synthesis Process. Adapted from "Qualitative Data Analysis with ATLAS.ti," by S. Friese, 2012, Thousand Oaks, CA: Sage. Copyright 2012 by Susanne Friese.

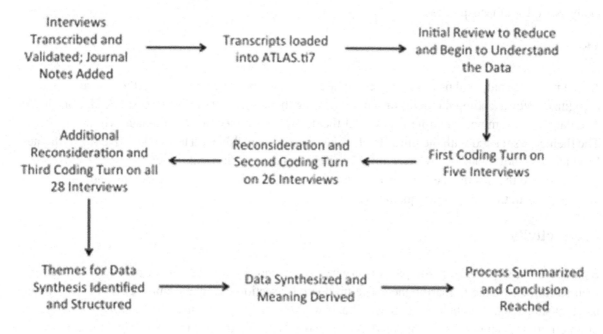

Data Reduction, Analysis, and Synthesis Process

Table 3. Third Set of Code Frequencies in Relationship to the Five Themes

Productivity	Individual Behaviors	Collective Behaviors	Anxiety	Policy
Ability to Share Information (41)	Distraction (31)	Text To Share Information (57)	Constant Availability (49)	General Lack of Policy (23)
Access to Information (60)	Immediacy (36)	Cultural Change (47)	Loss of Device (14)	Lack of Consistent Usage Policy When Deployed (20)
User Availability (45)	Impersonal (26)		Missed Calls (11)	Security Concerns Impede Productivity (53)
Ease of Communications (32)	Multi-Task (31)		Overwhelmed with Information (15)	Resource Shortfalls (7)
	Prefer to Text (48)			
	Use Social Media (45)			

Individual Behaviors

Many (in the range of 50%) noted changes wrought by smartphones to the individual behaviors of themselves and those around them. Those range from a sense of immediacy and distraction caused by the messages on their devices to the impersonal nature of electronic messages, to a preference for text messaging, the use of social media, and, among a large number of subjects, multi-tasking.

Collective Behaviors

A majority (67%) expressed concerns that the use of smartphones was impacting the culture of their unit. The particular nature of this observation focused on changes in the unique camaraderie long been associated with military service. Even more respondents (86%) cited the high frequency of text message usage for work-related information sharing throughout the unit. More than just random individual behavior, it had become a common approach across the unit.

Anxiety

A significant majority (75%) attributed stress and anxiety of one form or another to their smartphone use. Those feelings fell into four categories: the stress caused by constant availability, the deep anxiety that attends the loss of a device, the fear of missing a message or call, and, finally, the overwhelming amount of information a smartphone presents to the user.

Policy Issues and Group Discussion

Well over half of the respondents (67%) found shortfalls in current policies attending smartphones and saw the need for others that would increase the utility of those devices. The group discussion generally confirmed this assessment. Collectively, participants are so enamored with smartphones that they will not work without them, however, they are quite frustrated with the lack of policies that could make them so much more effective.

DISCUSSION, IMPLICATIONS, RECOMMENDATIONS

The understanding of the dynamics and implications of information access and sharing through the use of smartphones is enhanced by this phenomenological qualitative study. While the research focuses on one Army unit, the findings have broader organizational and societal implications. The results of the study offer a call to action for 21st century leaders to realize the pervasive implications of the ownership and work-related use of smartphones by every individual in their organizations. It offers compelling evidence for transformative change with respect to the policies related to the use of these devices to optimize the effectiveness of organizational information sharing in the emerging future (Scharmer, 2009).

Summary of the Results

The research problem is that smartphone-related user experiences in an Army work environment are evidence of the complex, systemic "mess" of technology usage (Ackoff, 1999b, p.14). While these experiences are often positive, the chaos and ambiguity of this situation affects social relationships amongst smartphone users and thus complicates paths to success for both the individual and the organization (Gharajedaghi, 2011). This phenomenological study identifies the systemic linkages connecting user experiences of personal smartphones in a military organization by deconstructing the multi-dimensional principles and properties that form emergent roadblocks to organizational success. A systems theory view is critical as aspects of complexity and chaos are the defining characteristics of individual communications technologies in contemporary organizations that must be resolved over and over (Gharajedaghi, 2011).

The significance of this study is that it addresses the holistic issue of the user experience of smartphone usage and resultant benefits and stresses from the perspective of a systems theory approach dealing with the chaos and complexity of the current organizational reality. The real value of a systemic perspective of the user experience in an organization is that it enables a richer learning context for developmental resiliency with the potential for decreasing the negative and increasing the positive experiences of smartphone usage to enhance organizational success (Gharajedaghi, 2011). This study expands on the existing literature that addresses the microcosm of the user experience, it offers a new understanding in recognizing several systemic constructs, and provides fertile ground for a more sophisticated understanding of the implications of smartphone use by organizational leaders. In doing so, it enhances transformational systemic change signaling a new innovative perspective to what has become a remarkably interconnected system (Scharmer, 2009; Scharmer & Kaufer, 2013).

The literature reviewed for this study covered the dynamics of mobile device/smartphone usage, including productivity (Friedman & Mandelbaum, 2011; Kakabadse et al., 2000; Kudya & Diwan, 2002; Powell & Dente-Micallef, 1997), complexity, ambiguity, and stress (Ayyagari et al., 2011; Brod, 1984; Tarafdar et al., 2007; Weil & Rosen, 1997), and the effects of mobile devices / smartphones in the workplace (Sami & Pangannaiah, 2005; Wang et al., 2008). Arnold (2003) drew on the work of Heidegger (1969) to describe the dynamic of these devices as ironic and paradoxical. Gharadeghi (2011) and Horn (2011) build on Ackoff (1999b, p. 14) to frame this situation as a "mess" that does not have a straightforward solution. Conversely, they argue, it is ambiguous and often chaotic, contains considerable complexity and uncertainty, is interwoven and bounded by significant constraints, is seen differently from different points of view, contains many value conflicts, and is often illogical. Contemporary studies by Turkle (2011) and Rushkoff (2013) on young people, organizations, and society confirm these dynamics (Gharajedaghi, 2011).

Framework for Assessment and Discussion of Results

The results of this study reinforce the paradoxes of smartphone use. If the implications of those paradoxes are fixed-mobility, independent-dependence, busy-availability and so on, then a framework for assessment must address the inherent complexity, chaos, and ambiguity of smartphone use in this Army unit. This section identifies a framework for analysis and details specific results under five interdependent themes: Productivity, Individual Behaviors, Collective Behaviors, Anxiety, and Policy.

Based on close study of the Atlas.ti 7 results, Scharmer's Theory U was selected as the framework for analysis. This approach recognizes that the evolution of smartphone technologies and the rapid adoption of the device by the military community are evidence of an emerging future first referenced by Scharmer (2009). Clearly, policy issues referenced by many are evidence of a leadership "Blind Spot" (Scharmer, 2009, p. 21). The interview results also revealed the enormous potential of smartphones as a tool for both personal and organizational productivity and creativity is significantly limited by the combination of shortcomings in leadership attention and intention and complicated still more by the barriers existent in judgment, cynicism, and fear. Theory U provides both a basis for understanding the phenomenon and, more importantly, a way forward.

Scharmer (2009) describes four different sources of attention, or states of awareness and consciousness, from which social action can emerge. Every action emerges from one of these four, yet, as Scharmer notes, most members of the organization remain unaware of their very existence. The first field structure of attention is acting from the center inside one's organizational boundaries, characterized by general politeness and reenacting past patterns. The findings revealed this "downloading" state was most in evidence. Some participants and certainly the group session moved to "debate", a more open and confrontational way of expressing perspectives and interests and focusing on disconfirming data. In no case, however, was there "dialogue" (Scharmer, 2009, p. 234). Participants did not realize that they, in fact, embody the system they are criticizing. They were not, "asking about one another's viewpoints and experiences and reflecting on how they had collectively enacted a system that no one really wanted" (Scharmer, 2009, p. 236). With no dialogue, group members could not reflect and relate to one another in order to incorporate an emerging set of rules. Not surprisingly, no awareness at the fourth or "presencing" level was found where the organization looks to the future and collective creativity and innovation take place (Scharmer, 2009, p. 234).

Related to these states of attention is the never-ending process of learning, unlearning and relearning both within and beyond conventional frameworks (Gharajedaghi, 2011). Without dialogue and without attention and awareness, members of the unit will not unlearn the old behaviors that have led to the current mess. Only when they do will they be mentally and emotionally ready to leverage smartphone technologies to enhance creativity and productivity while optimizing organizational development in the emerging future.

In the conduct of this study, the comments of officers and non-commissioned officers were often indistinguishable from those of their soldiers. This is particularly noteworthy as, "meeting and dealing with the voice of fear is the very essence of leadership" (Scharmer, 2009, p. 43). While some may jump to the conclusion that unit leaders are failing, a different determination was reached. A combination of the newness of the dynamics of pervasive smartphone usage combined with a lack of policy guidance from higher organizational levels created a variety of paradoxes that the unit leadership may be just beginning to understand and deal with. Indeed, Turkle (2011), who believes society has reached a point of inflection and can begin to see a way forward, nevertheless warns that smartphone users are "in an experiment in which we are the human subjects." She wonders, "Are we guinea pigs who can no longer tolerate the slightest solitude? And is that a new norm we're willing to embrace?" (p. 296). Yet Rushkoff (2013) concludes that the digital reality of smartphones "is just plain incompatible with the way most institutions operate" (p. 219). In sum, the situation is complex and chaotic (Gharajedagi, 2011); there is much more work to be done.

A theme-by-theme discussion follows. Importantly, these discussions took the form of downloading and tentative debates with no deep dialogue or presencing (Scharmer, 2009). The themes identified in this study track closely with the general trends related to smartphone use in society. Turkle (2011) and Rushkoff (2013) provide excellent framing insights into the societal impacts of modern technology.

A measure of chaos, ambiguity, and complexity are apparent throughout (Gharajedaghi, 2011). These contemporary perspectives provide a baseline for discussion of the findings of this study. Citations from these authors, and others, accompany the analysis of each theme.

Productivity

The consensus of the participants in this study was that the ability to share information (75% of respondents), access information (89%), contact other users (82%), and easily communicate (54%) were the aspects of smartphone usage that most improved the productivity of the members of this unit. Clearly, smartphones do enhance each of these attributes. Although the amount of productivity improvement may decrease over time as the use of smartphones becomes routine, nevertheless, the success metric is the relativity to what one could accomplish were they not connected (Turkle, 2011).

There is broad agreement amongst study participants that the information sharing capabilities stemming from smartphones do indeed radically improve the productivity of both the individuals in this organization and of the organization as a whole (Prahalad and Krishnan, 2008). Those benefits include faster, more informed decision-making, increased flexibility, better time management, and the ability to execute tasks that might otherwise be exceptionally difficult or impossible (Kakabadse et al., 2000).

Individual Behaviors

Subjects uniformly pointed out that smartphones significantly influenced their thoughts, feelings, and personal behaviors and those of their fellow unit members. Those phones and the messages they convey often preoccupied them. That preoccupation includes a sense that they need to immediately respond to a message received on their phone (43%), regardless of the fact that they found those messages significantly distracting (57%) and noticeably impersonal (36%). Nevertheless, 86% prefer the efficiency of smartphone-enabled text messages to other forms of electronic, voice, or face-to-face communications and 93% routinely employ social media on their smartphones.

Of particular interest is the resulting dynamic of multi-tasking. While a modest majority of respondents (64%) admit to this behavior to deal with the frequency and variety of information they receive, collective comments from all participants imply that the practice is widespread. Multi-tasking has mixed implications. Certainly, "It is a lot more convenient and a lot more gets done," as participant P14 notes, others, however, like P20, find it rude and annoying. While often mentioning the modest excitement of receiving a message, respondents on the whole opined that multi-tasking inhibited reflection and deep thought. A number noted that too many of their peers seemed to prefer electronic messages to human interaction (Carr, 2010; Rushkoff, 2013; Turkle, 2011).

While the jury is still out on the specific meaning of these observations, the tentative conclusion is that many of the individual behaviors engendered by the information sharing capabilities of smartphones are at odds with the interpersonal interactions expected in normal civil discourse. This is another form of smartphone-related tension that deserves much more debate and dialogue within the unit (Scharmer, 2009).

Collective Behavior

Participants made two general comments about the impacts of smartphones on their unit. First, a significant majority (86% of respondents) commented on the routine use of text messages for work-related information sharing across the unit. This included both messages exchanged between individuals as well as those shared with text-message groups and transmitted as directives by senior members of the chain of command. By all accounts, this has become a common approach across the unit. While Borg (2010) argues the importance of visual cues in interpersonal communications, Turkle (2011) maintains that text messages offer "just the right amount of access, just the right amount of control" (p. 15). Certainly, although participants cite occasional technical and procedural issues passing or confirming texts, this means of direct communication, particularly as it carries a consistent message simultaneously to all the members of an organization, fills a void not addressed by other communications means and appears to have significant value.

More worrisome, however, is the fact that a majority of respondents (67%) expressed concern, and backed their assertions with specific observations, that fundamental changes in the culture of the organization were taking place due to the proliferation of smartphones. While this collective behavior may dovetail with the observations of young people by Turkle (2011) on the streets of New York and Rushkoff (2013) in waiting lines at Disneyland, the implications here are vastly more significant.

At issue is the unique camaraderie found in military units in general and the Army in particular. These bonds, formed over time and based on the collective value of hundreds of minor interactions, are the basis for the trust that, as General Dempsey, the Chairman of the Joint Chiefs of Staff says, "stands out as the defining element that enabled our military to overcome adversity and endure the demands of extended combat" (Department of Defense, 2012b, page 1). The fact so many respondents pointed out, as P4 and P20 did, that "no one talks to one another anymore," and that "face-to-face talking has died away," as P9 says, should be concerning to military leaders at all levels. While it is reassuring that a number of respondents find this situation unsatisfactory, there is no evidence that this issue is being seriously debated within the unit. In the analytical construct of Scharmer (2009), this is evidence both of the limited state of awareness and attention in the unit and of the Judgmental Barrier that prevents leaders from seeing the situation with fresh eyes. This issue is so important it deserves further focus and study.

Anxiety

Most of the respondents to this study attributed some level of stress or anxiety to the use of their smartphones. Those feelings fell into four categories: the stress caused by constant availability (75% of respondents), the anxiety that attends the loss of a mobile device (50%), concerns over missing or not responding quickly enough to a text, email or call (32%) and, finally, the fact that the capability of the smartphone to deliver vast amounts of information can sometimes overwhelm the user (39%).

In addition to reinforcing the comments on smartphone-based stress made by Turkle (2011) and Rushkoff (2013) and cited above, the comments on anxiety in this study, particularly when considered in light of the considerable productivity benefits cited by almost every smartphone user in this unit, dovetail with the technostress research of Ayyagari et al. (2011) who concluded that the costs of smartphones and other ICTs are both significant and not always apparent. They also ring true to the findings of Ragu-Nathan et al. (2008) who argue that most organizations do not understand the pervasive impacts of technology-based stress on their members.

The study's findings also reinforce the work of Arnold (2003) who contends that the nature of smartphone use is remarkably paradoxical: the user is liberated yet leashed, independent yet co-dependent, distant yet present and so on. The comment by P22 that the "negative aspect of all these wonderful devices is the fact that there's never ever, ever a chance that you're away from work," and P24's frustration with frequent dinner disturbances, confirm the relevance of paradox to this study. Moreover, these comments also point to the importance of Scharmer's (2009) argument that overcoming the Barrier of Fear with significantly increased discussion and dialogue within the unit is key to addressing issues of stress and anxiety resulting from these paradoxes and leading from the future as it emerges. Those discussions are not taking place in the unit today.

Policy

It is important to note that, collectively, participants of all ranks are so enamored with smartphone-related productivity and organizational effectiveness that they will work around ineffective policies to use their devices. Nevertheless, respondents were also quite frustrated with the absence of policies that could improve their productivity. The capstone DoD Mobile Device Policy (2013) is focused strictly on security and does not address the paradoxes or stresses identified in this study. A logical, comprehensive strategy that addresses, in addition to security, a wide variety of issues including consistent policies for smartphone use in deployed units, the official recognition of individual smartphones, and procedures and standards for messaging and smartphone use that would mitigate stress and anxiety would go a long way to addressing the concerns expressed by study participants.

Clearly, mobile technologies will continue to evolve and policies will attempt to keep pace. The study findings, considered in light of Scharmer's Theory U (2009) point to the importance of both resolving the Barrier of Judgment related to mobile devices and significantly increasing reflective inquiry and dialogue. Failing to address smartphone-related issues with a related communication strategy suggests to members of the unit that leadership is not attentive and does not understand their concerns (Scharmer, 2009; Schein, 2010).

Limitations of the Study

While this study is valuable in comparing military experiences of smartphone use to the broader general population studies of researchers like Turkle (2011) and Rushkoff (2013), as well as the technostress studies of teams like Ayyagari et al. (2011) and Ragu-Nathan et al. (2008), the fact that this research was conducted in one particular unit of the U.S. Army is its most significant weakness. There are no guarantees that the findings extend to other Army units, to other military organizations of the United States or other countries, or to any other non-military organization.

The nature of this hermeneutical phenomenological study is also a limitation. It is qualitative in nature examining the lived experiences of a small sample of soldiers in what existing research (Giorgi, 1997) shows is an exceptionally complex phenomenon. The value of this research has yet to be proven. Qualitative research is assessed based on the extent other researchers accept its method, purpose, analysis and results. Consistency, dependability, and systemic methodology are highly valued (Giorgi & Giorgi, 2003; Swanson & Holton, 2005). Transferability and analytical generalizations are the only possible forms of generalization in qualitative research (Lincoln & Guba, 1985; Miles & Huberman, 1994; Swanson & Holton, 2005).

Structurally, the study has several other limitations. The researcher worked with a relatively small sample of 28 soldiers. While care was taken to ensure that these volunteers generally reflected the diverse population of this unit, they certainly do not reflect society, even military society, as a whole. Additionally, while great care was taken to bracket personal observations and assessments from the study, the researcher is a former career military officer and his subtle biases may well have crept in.

Implications of Study Results

The dominant implication from this study is that smartphone use is inextricably linked to a number of specific and complex challenges for the leaders of the military unit studied. Those challenges are not being addressed today.

Recommendations for Further Research

This study explored the lived experience of smartphone use in an Army unit. Future researchers interested in better understanding the broader implications of the proliferation of personal smartphones in military organizations should consider expanding the findings of this study initially by conducting both quantitative and qualitative studies involving greater numbers of service members in a larger number and wider variety of Army units, both deployed and in garrison. This will enable researchers to validate and expand upon the findings of this study. A subsequent step would then be further study in military organizations of other Services. In each case, the implications of smartphone use on traditional military culture should be examined.

This study has shown that the current Defense Department policy (DoD Commercial Mobile Device Policy, 2013) inadequately addresses the issues that attend the day-to-day use of smartphones in at least one representative Army unit. Essentially, they are blind to the smartphone-related realities that appear to exist at the unit level (Scharmer, 2009). The Department of Defense and the Military Services should recognize the ubiquity of these devices and consider commissioning formal studies into personal smartphone use by both service members and civilian employees to determine optimal policies for their employment in the emerging future. In doing so, these organizations will significantly enhance the dialogue on this subject and move their organizations down the path to transformational change (Scharmer, 2009).

In a more general sense, the findings of this study indicate there is significant value in the rigorous study of smartphone use and its implications in a wide variety of forums from public sector and healthcare organizations to academia to private business. While many appreciate the productivity benefits of smartphone use, the paradoxes, tensions, and anxieties associated with smartphones would likely have implications that have not yet been considered.

CONCLUSION

The hermeneutical phenomenological approach in this study was oriented toward the lived experiences of smartphones in an Army unit and interpreting the related "texts" of those experiences (van Maanen, 1990, p. 4). Overall, the findings in this study were consistent with literature related to the subject, including studies into the dynamics of smartphone use in general society, studies of technology related stress, and work by theorists in areas of productivity, systems theory, and transformational change. Data collection and analysis led to findings that reinforced assessments of the productivity of smartphones while revealing significant issues associated with individual and collective behaviors, stress/anxiety, and lack of comprehensive policy.

A number of important results emerged from this study. Not surprisingly, as soldiers are drawn from and live in the general society, the results of this Army unit study track closely with contemporary studies of American organizations (Rushkoff, 2013) and young people (Turkle, 2011). The study confirmed that every soldier in this unit does, in fact, have some sort of personal smartphone and those devices are used daily to exchange work-related information. The paradoxical aspects of smartphone use increase the ambiguity and complexity of both personal and organizational communications within the unit. Smartphones use often increases interpersonal tensions as users attempt to balance face-to-face discussions with the insistent demands of the electronic messages delivered by their devices. A number of respondents fear that the proliferation of smartphones and associated individualistic behaviors are jeopardizing the cultural development of their unit. This study found that the anxieties and stresses associated with smartphones use are significant and underappreciated and that the policies related to the use of smartphones in this unit inadequately address the issues and concerns expressed by respondents.

As those issues remain unresolved, the findings of this study suggest a useful connection to both systems theory (Gharajedagi, 2011) and Theory U (Scharmer, 2009). Systems' thinking is the art of reducing complexity. It is about seeing through chaos, managing interdependency, managing choice, and getting a handle on problems before trying to solve them (Ackoff, 1999; Gharajedaghi, 2011). This study may provide a first step to understanding the complexity and details of smartphone usage in one Army unit. Importantly, however, to design a solution to the issues and concerns raised in this study, one must "start with an exciting vision of the future and work backward to the existing system" (Gharajedagi, 2011, p. 336).

Scharmer (2009) and Scharmer and Kaufer (2013) make a similar argument. Transformational change, they argue, allows leaders to meet existing challenges, such as the paradoxes of smartphone usage, through knowledge sharing in the organization. However, leaders must first learn how to operate from the emerging future, versus recycling patterns of past experiences. Downloading, debate, dialogue, and presencing are the four different sources of attention, or states of awareness and consciousness, from which social action emerges (Scharmer, 2009). Every leadership action derives from one of these four, yet the participants in this study were unaware of their very existence. Accordingly, this study reinforces Scharmer's argument; in no case did participants realize that they, in fact, embody the system they are criticizing. They did not "ask about one another's viewpoints and experiences and reflect on how they had collectively enacted a system that no one really wanted" (Scharmer, 2009, p. 236).

Resistance to improved awareness and attention comes from several powerful forces. Scharmer (2009) identifies three "voices" (p. 246) that restrict an organization's ability to grow. The most important of these is the Voice of Judgment characterized by old and limiting patterns of thought and behavior. This mental barrier blocks the ability to embrace change. In the study, particularly in the areas of individual and collective behaviors and in participant comments on unresponsive policy, it was determined that participants ineffectively reacted to the emerging technologies of smartphones by employing the same routine processes they had used in the past.

The results of the study, therefore, serve as a call to action for leaders to realize the pervasive implications of the ownership and work-related use of smartphones by every individual in their organization. It offers a compelling case for transformative change, leader involvement, and thoughtful policies so that smartphones can productively optimize organizational information sharing (Scharmer, 2009).

REFERENCES

Ackerman, S. (2013, April). Army practices poor data hygiene on its new smartphones, tablets. *Wired*. Retrieved from www.wired.com/dangerroom/2013/04/army-data-hygiene

Ackoff, R. L. (1999). On learning and the systems that facilitate it. *Reflections: The SoL Journal, 1*(1), 14–24. doi:10.1162/152417399570250

Allen, D. (2012, March 18), When technology overwhelms, get organized. *New York Times*, p. B4.

Amicil, B. C., & Celentano, D. D. (1984). Human factors epidemiology: An integrated approach to the study of health issues in office work. In B. G. F. Cohen (Ed.), *Human aspects of office automation* (pp. 78–82). Amsterdam, The Netherlands: Elsevier.

Anderson, S., & Rutherford, H. (2013, June). DoD's commercial mobile device implementation plan: Enabling the mobile workforce. *CHIPS*. Retrieved from http://www.privacy.navy.mil/CHIPS/Article-Details.aspx?id=4534

Arnold, M. (2003, October). On the phenomenology of technology: The "janus-faces" of mobile phones. *Information and Organization, 13*(4), 231–256. doi:10.1016/S1471-7727(03)00013-7

ATLAS.ti. (2012). *Scientific software development corporation*. Retrieved from http://www.atlasti.com/index.html

Avery, G. C., & Baker, E. (2002). Reframing he infomated household-workplace. *Information and Organization, 12*(2), 109–134. doi:10.1016/S1471-7727(01)00013-6

Ayyagari, R. (2007). *What and why of technostress: Technology antecedents and implications.* (Unpublished doctoral dissertation). Clemson, SC: Clemson University.

Ayyagari, R., Grover, V., & Purvis, R. (2011). Technostress: Technological antecedents and implications. *Management Information Systems Quarterly, 35*(4), 831–858.

Bannister, F., & Remenyi, D. (2009). Multitasking: The uncertain impact of technology on knowledge workers and managers. *The Electronic Journal Information Systems Evaluation, 12*(1), 1 – 12.

Bichteler, J. (1987). Technostress in libraries: Causes, effects and solutions. *The Electronic Library, 5*(5), 282–287. doi:10.1108/eb044766

Borg, J. (2010). Body language: 7 easy lessons to master the silent language. Upper Saddle River, NJ: FT.

Borgmann, A. (1987). *Technology and the character of contemporary life: A Philosophical inquiry.* Chicago, IL: University of Chicago Press.

Bowers, J. M. (1991). The janus face of design: Some critical questions for CSCW. In J. M. Bowers, & S. D. Benford (Eds.), Studies in computer supported cooperative work (pp. 333–350). Elsevier Science.

Bowman, R. J. (1997). High technology: Dream or nightmare? *Distribution, 96*(13), 30–34.

Boyd, D. (2014, March). How to take an email sabbatical. *Fast Company*. Retrieved from http://www.fastcompany.com/3027058/work-smart/how-to-take-an-email-sabatical

Brewin, R. (2014, January). The army wants more smartphones on the battlefield. *Defense One*. Retrieved from http://www.defenseone.com/technology/2014/01/army-wants-more-smartphones-battlefield/77657/print/

Brod, C. (1984). *Technostress: The human cost of the computer revolution*. Reading, MA: Addison-Wesley.

Brooks, M. E. (2012, September). Death of secular saint Steve Jobs in a theologically devoid culture. *The Christian Post*. Retrieved from http://www.christianpost.com/news/death-of-secular-saint-steve-jobs-in-a-theologically-devoid-culture-59595/

Caelli, K., Ray, L., & Mill, J. (2003). Clear as mud: Toward greater clarity in generic qualitative research. *International Journal of Qualitative Methods, 2*(2). Article 1. Retrieved from http://www.ualberta.ca/~iiqm/backissues/pdf/caellietal.pdf

Carey, R. J. (2014). *Response to TechAmerica CIO survey: IT in periods of rapid change*. Unpublished manuscript.

Carr, N. (2010). *The shallows: What the internet is doing to our brains*. New York, NY: Norton.

Chappuis, B., Gaffey, B., & Parvizi, P. (2011). Are your customers becoming digital junkies? *The McKinsey Quarterly*, (3): 20–23.

Christensen, C. M., & Overdorf, M. (2000, March-April). Meeting the challenge of disruptive change. *Harvard Business Review, 2*(2), 88–101.

Clark, K., & Kalin, S. (1996). Technostressed out: How to cope in the digital age. *Library Journal, 121*(13), 30–35.

Columbus, L. (2013, September). IDC: 87% of connected devices sales by 2017 will be tablets and smartphones. *Forbes On-line Edition*. Retrieved from http://www.forbes.com/sites/louiscolumbus/2013/09/12/idc-87-of-connected-devices-by-2017-will-be-tablets-and-smartphones/

Cooper, C. R., & Schindler, P. S. (2011). *Business research methods* (11th ed.). Boston, MA: McGraw-Hill.

Cooper, S. (2002). *Technoculture and critical theory: In the service of the machine?* London, UK: Routledge. doi:10.4324/9780203167021

Creswell, J. W. (2003). *Research design: Qualitative, quantitative, and mixed-methods approaches* (2nd ed.). Thousand Oaks, CA: Sage.

Creswell, J. W. (2007). *Qualitative inquiry and research design: Choosing among five approaches*. Thousand Oaks, CA: Sage.

Creswell, J. W. (2008). *Educational research: Planning, conducting, and evaluating quantitative and qualitative research* (3rd ed.). Upper Saddle River, NJ: Pearson.

Creswell, J. W. (2009). *Research design: Qualitative, quantitative, and mixed methods approaches* (3rd ed.). Thousand Oaks, CA: Sage.

CTIA. (2014). *The wireless association: Policy and initiatives, accessibility and assistive technologies*. Retrieved from http://www.ctia.org/policy-initiatives/policy-topics/accessibility-and-assistive-technology

Daly, J. (2013, September 13). Mobility is about data, devices, and demand. *Fed Tech*. Retrieved from http://www.fedtechmagazine.com/article/2013/09/mobility-about-data-devices-and-demand

Defense Information Systems Agency. (2013). *Apple iOS 6 security technical implementation guide (STIG) Version 1*. Fort Meade, MD: Chief Information Assurance Executive.

Denzin, N. K., & Lincoln, Y. S. (1998). *Strategies of qualitative inquiry*. Thousand Oaks, CA: Sage.

Department of Defense. (2012a). *Managing for official use only information on commercial mobile devices*. Washington, DC: Office of the Chief Information Officer.

Department of Defense. (2012b). Capstone concept for joint operations: Joint force 2020. Washington, DC: Chairman of the Joint Chiefs of Staff.

Department of Defense. (2013). *Department of defense commercial mobile device implementation plan*. Washington, DC: Office of the Chief Information Officer.

Department of the Army. (2013). *U.S Army guidance on the use of commercial mobile devices (CMD)*. Washington, DC: Office of the Secretary of the Army.

Department of the Army. (2014). *Army regulation 670-1 (Wear and appearance of Army uniforms and insignia)*. Washington, DC: Headquarters, Department of the Army.

Depraz, N., Varela, F., & Vermersch, P. (Eds.). (2003). *On becoming aware: Pragmatics of experiencing*. Philadelphia, PA: John Benjamins. doi:10.1075/aicr.43

Eisenhardt, K. M. (2000). Introduction to special topic forum: Paradox, spirals, ambivalence: The new language of change and pluralism. *Academy of Management Review*, *25*(4), 703–705. doi:10.5465/AMR.2000.3707694

Elliot, J. (1998, June 2). Bill Gates calling or maybe not. *The Daily Telegraph*, p. 6.

Ellul, J. (1967). *The technological society* (J. Wilkinson, Trans.). New York, NY: Knopf/Vintage.

Ephron, D. (2012, June 19). Upgrade hell. The *Wall Street Journal*, p. A13.

Evans, B. (2013, December 13). *What does mobile scale mean?* [Web log comment]. Retrieved from http://ben-es.com/benedictevans/2013/12/18/what-does-mobile-scale-mean

Fabre, J., Jenkin, K., Thompson, C., & Senjen, R. (1999). *Trial of future wireless broadband services: Insights into customer behaviour* (Report 99–19). Retrieved from Telstra website: http://www.telstra.com.au/business-enterprise/

Feenberg, A. (1999). *Questioning technology*. London, UK: Routledge.

Friedman, T., & Mandelbaum, M. (2011). *That used to be us: How America fell behind the world it invented and how we can come back*. New York, NY: Farrar.

Friese, S. (2012). *Qualitative data analysis with ATLAS.ti*. Thousand Oaks, CA: SAGE.

Frissen, V. A. J. (2000). ICTs in the rush hour of life. *The Information Society*, *16*(1), 65–75. doi:10.1080/019722400128338

Ganzel, R. (1998). Feeling squeezed by technology? *Training (New York, N.Y.), 35*(4), 62–70.

Garfinkel, S. (2005). *Design principles and patterns for computer systems that are simultaneously secure and usable.* (Doctoral Dissertation). Retrieved from http://hdl.handle.net/1721.1/33204

Gatewood, B. (2012, November). The nuts and bolts of making BYOD work. *Information & Management, 46*(6), 26–30.

Gayomali, C. (2014, April 10). The French move to protect workers from after-hours email. *Fast company.* Retrieved from http://www.fastcompany.com/3028945/work-smart/france-just-made-it-illegal-to-answer-work-emails-after-6pm

Gharajedaghi, J. (2011). *Systems thinking, managing chaos and complexity: A platform for designing business architecture* (3rd ed.). Amsterdam: Elsevier.

Gillard, P., Wale, K., & Bow, A. (1997). Prediction of future demand from current telecommunications uses in the home. *Telecommunications Policy, 21*(4), 329–339. doi:10.1016/S0308-5961(97)00013-X

Giorgi, A. (1997). The theory, practice and evaluation of phenomenological methods as a qualitative research procedure. *Journal of Phenomenological Psychology, 28*(2), 235–281. doi:10.1163/156916297X00103

Giorgi, A. P., & Giorgi, B. M. (2003). The descriptive phenomenological psychological method. In P. M. Camic, J. E. Rhodes, & L. Yardley (Eds.), *Qualitative research in psychology: Expanding perspectives in methodology and design* (pp. 243–273). Washington, DC: American Psychological Association. doi:10.1037/10595-013

Habermas, J. (1984). The theory of communicative action: Vol. 1. *Reason and the rationalization of society.* Boston, MA: Beacon.

Hallowell, E. (1999, January). The human moment at work. *Harvard Business Review, 77*(1), 58–152. PMID:10345392

Hanley, M., & Boostrom, R. (2011). How the smartphone is changing college student mobile content usage and advertising acceptance: An IMC perspective. *International Journal of Integrated Marketing Communications,* 49-64.

Hannakaisa, L., Jose, M. P., & Mika, K. (2000). Collective stress and coping in the context of organizational culture. *European Journal of Work and Organizational Psychology, 9*(4), 527–559. doi:10.1080/13594320050203120

Haraway, D. (1985). A manifesto for cyborgs: Science, technology, and socialist feminism in the1980s. *Socialist Review, 80,* 65–107.

Haraway, D. (1991). *A cyborg manifesto in simians, cyborgs, and women: The reinvention of nature.* New York, NY: Rutledge.

Hatch, J. A. (2002). *Doing qualitative research in educational settings.* Albany, NY: State University of New York Press.

Hehn, S. (2013, December 9). Teens dig digital privacy. *National Public Radio*. Retrieved from http://www.npr.org/blogs/alltechconsidered/2013/12/10/249731334/teens-dig-digital-privacy-if-snapchat-is-any-indication

Heidegger, M. (1950). *A question concerning technology*. New York, NY: Harper & Row.

Heidegger, M. (1969). *Discourse on thinking*. New York, NY: Harper & Row.

Heller, J. (2013, March). Call signs. *Hemispheres Magazine*, 15.

Heron, J., & Reason, P. (1997). A participatory inquiry paradigm. *Qualitative Inquiry*, *3*(3), 274–279. doi:10.1177/107780049700300302

Herrmann, P. (1999). Electro-magnetic radiation. *International Well Being Magazine Annual, 74*, 45–46.

High, P. (2013, October). Gartner: Top 10 strategic technology trends for 2014. *Forbes On-line*. Retrieved from http://www.forbes.com/sites/peterhigh/2013/10/14/gartner-top-10-strategic-technology-trends-for-2014/

Hillis, W. (2010, July 18). *Re: The knowledge web* [Web log comment]. Retrieved from http://edge.org/conversation/the-hillis-knowledge-web

Hind, P. (1998, September). Captured by technology. *CIO Magazine*, 22-23.

Holmes, E. (2014, April 1). People for whom one cellphone isn't enough. *Wall Street Journal On-line*. Retrieved from http://online.wsj.com/news/article_email/SB10001424052702304432604579475303715000912-lMyQjAxMTA0MDAwNzEwNDcyWj

Horn, R. E. (2001, May). *Knowledge mapping for complex social messes*. A presentation to the David and Lucile Packard Foundation, Stanford University, Palo Alto, CA.

Hu, E. (2013, September 5). Our cultural addiction to phones, in one disconcerting video. *National public radio*. Retrieved from http://www.npr.org/blogs/alltechconsidered/2013/09/05/219266779/our-cultural-addiction-to-phones-in-one-disconcerting-video

Hu, E. (2014, March 27). Pay attention: Your frustration over smartphone distraction. *National Public Radio*. Retrieved from http://www.npr.org/blogs/alltechconsidered/2014/03/27/294842209/pay-attention-your-frustration-over-smartphone-distraction

Husserl, E. (1970). *Logical investigation*. New York, NY: Humanities.

IDC Press Release. (2013, September 11). Tablet shipments forecast to top total PC shipments in the fourth quarter of 2013 and annually by 2015. *According to IDC*. Retrieved from http://www.idc.com/getdoc.jsp?containerId=prUS24314413

Ihde, D. (1990). *Technology and the lifeworld: From garden to earth*. Bloomington, IN: Indiana University Press.

Ito, M. (2010). *Hanging out, messing around, and geeking out: Kids learning and living with new media*. Cambridge, MA: MIT Press.

Jackson, M. (2008). *Distracted: The erosion of attention and the coming dark age*. New York, NY: Prometheus.

Jendricke, U., & Markotten, D. (2005). *Usability meets security: The identity-manager as your personal security manager for the internet*. Unpublished paper, Albert-Ludwigs University of Freiberg, Germany.

Jenkins, H. (2009, November 16). The Skill of the future: In a word 'multitasking'. *Public Broadcasting Service*. Retrieved from www.pbs.org/wgbh/pages/frontline/digitalnation/living-faster/split-focus/the-skill-of-the-future.html

Jenner, D., Reynolds, V., & Harrison, G. (1980). Catechlomine excretion rates and occupation. *Ergonomics, 23*(2), 237–246. doi:10.1080/00140138008924737 PMID:7428768

Johnson, D. (2012, June 29). Making calls has become fifth most frequent use for smartphone for newly-networked generation of users. *The Blue*. Retrieved from http://news.o2.co.uk/?press-release=making-calls-has-become-fifth-most-frequent-use-for-a-smartphone-for-newly-networked-generation-of-users

Kakabadse, N. K., Kouzmin, A., & Kakabadse, A. K. (2000). Technostress: Over-Identification with information technology and its impact on employees and managerial effectiveness. In N. K. Kakabadse & A. K. Kakabadse (Eds.), *Creating futures: Leading change through information systems* (pp. 259–296). Hampshire, UK: Ashgate.

Kemmis, S., & Wilkinson, M. (1998). Participatory action research and the study of practice. In B. Atweh, S. Kemmis, & P. Weeks (Eds.), *Action research in practice: Partnerships for social justice in education* (pp. 21–36). New York, NY: Routledge.

Khalaf, S. (2014, April 22). The Rise of the mobile addict. *Flurry Research*. Retrieved from http://www.flurry.com/bid/110166/the-rise-of-the-mobile-addict#.U2adya1dXMg

Klein, G. (2008). Naturalistic decision making. *Human Factors, 50*(3), 456–460. doi:10.1518/001872008X288385 PMID:18689053

Korn, M. (2014, February 6). Smartphones make you tired and unproductive, study says. *Wall Street Journal On-line*. Retrieved from http://blogs.wsj.com/atwork/2014/02/06/smartphones-make-you-tired-and-unproductive-study-says/?mod=e2fb

Kostere, K., & Percy, W. H. (2008). *Qualitative research approaches*. Unpublished manuscript, Capella University, Minneapolis, MN.

Kudya, S., & Diwan, R. (2002). The Impact of information technology on U.S. industry. *Japan and the World Economy, 14*(3), 321–333. doi:10.1016/S0922-1425(01)00074-3

Kvale, S. (1996). *InterViews: An introduction to qualitative research interviewing*. Thousand Oaks, CA: Sage.

Lacroix, A. (1984). Occupational exposure to high demand / local control work and coronary heart disease incidence at the Framingham cohort. *Dissertation Abstracts International, 45*(2521B), 575–579.

Lane, W., & Manner, C. (2011). The impact of personality traits on smartphone ownership and use. *International Journal of Business and Social Science, 2*(17), 22–28.

Latour, B. (1987). *Science in action*. Milton Keynes, UK: Open University Press.

Lewis, M. W. (2000). Exploring paradox: Towards a more comprehensive guide. *Academy of Management Review, 25*(4), 760–766.

Lincoln, Y. S., & Guba, E. G. (1985). *Naturalistic Inquiry*. Beverly Hills, CA: Sage.

Maani, K. E., & Cavana, R. Y. (2000). *Systems thinking and modeling: Understanding change and complexity*. Auckland, New Zealand: Pearson.

MacKenzie, D., & Wajcman, J. (1999). *The social shaping of technology* (2nd ed.). Buckingham, UK: Open University Press.

Macmillan, D. (2014, January 3). Andreessen: Bubble believers 'don't know what they're talking about'. *Wall Street Journal On-line*. Retrieved from http://online.wsj.com/news/articles/SB100014240527023 03640604579298330921690014

Manjoo, F. (2013, December 31). Stop pouting about tech's next big thing, it's here, *Wall Street Journal On-line*. Retrieved from http://online.wsj.com/news/articles/SB1000142405270230364060457929833 0921690014

Mankin, D., Bikson, T., & Gutek, B. (1982). The office of the future: Prison or paradise? *The Futurist, 16*(3), 333–337.

Marshall, C., & Rossman, G. B. (2006). *Designing qualitative research* (4th ed.). Thousand Oaks, CA: Sage.

Marshall, E. (1995). *Transforming the way we work: The power of the collaborative workplace*. New York, NY: Amacom.

McCormick, P., & Elliston, F. (Eds.). (1981). *Husserl: Shorter works*. South Bend, IN: University of Notre Dame Press.

McGarry, B. (2013, March 27). Army set to introduce smartphones into combat. *Military.com*. Retrieved from www.military.com/daily-news/2013/03/27/army-set-to-introduce-smartphones-into-combat.html

McGee, M. K. (1996, March4). Burnout. *Information Week, 56*(9), 34–40.

McKee, R. (1997). *Story, substance, style, and the principles of screenwriting*. New York, NY: Regan.

McLuhan, M. (1967). *Understanding media: The extension of man*. London, UK: Sphere.

Meeker, M., & Wu, L. (2013, May 29). *Internet trends*. Presentation to the D11 conference. Abstract retrieved from http://www.kpcb.com/insights/2013-internet-trends

Merleau-Ponty, M. (1962). *Phenomenology of perception*. London, UK: Routledge.

Meservy, T. (2013, September 5). *Re: Lying in a text message? Response delay trips people up*. [Web log post]. Retrieved from http://www.science20.com/news_articles/lying_text_message_response_delay_trips_people-119823

Miles, M. B., & Huberman, A. M. (1994). *Qualitative data analysis* (2nd ed.). Thousand Oaks, CA: Sage.

Morse, J. M., & Richards, L. (2002). *Readme first for a users guide to qualitative methods*. Thousand Oaks, CA: Sage.

Mossberg, W. (2013, April 10). Facebook gets a hold on phones. *Wall Street Journal*, p. D1.

Moustakas, C. (1994). *Phenomenological research methods*. Thousand Oaks, CA: Sage.

Murphy, L. R. (1987). A review of organizational stress management research: Methodological considerations. *Journal of Organizational Behavior Management, 8*(2), 215–227. doi:10.1300/J075v08n02_13

Natanson, M. (Ed.). (1973). *Phenomenology and the social sciences*. Evanston, IL: Northwestern University Press.

Nightengale, K. (2014, 14 February). *Re: The Army and IT*. [Online forum comment]. Retrieved from http://www.warlordloop.org/

Orlikowski, W. J. (1991). Integrated information environment or matrix of control?: The contradictory implications of information technology. *Accounting, Management, and Information Technology, 1*(1), 9–42. doi:10.1016/0959-8022(91)90011-3

Park, N., & Lee, H. (2012). Social implications of smartphone use: Korean college students' smartphone use and psychological well-being. *Cyberpsychology, Behavior, and Social Networking, 15*(9), 491–497. doi:10.1089/cyber.2011.0580 PMID:22817650

Patton, M. Q. (1987). *How to use qualitative methods in evaluation*. Thousand Oaks, CA: Sage.

Patton, M. Q. (1990). *Qualitative evaluation and research methods* (2nd ed.). Newbury Park, CA: Sage.

Poole, S. M., & Van De Ven, A. H. (1989). Using paradox to build management and organization theories. *Academy of Management Review, 14*(4), 562–578.

Powell, T. C., & Dente-Micallef, A. (1997). Information technology as competitive advantage: The role of human, business, and technology resources. *Strategic Management Journal, 18*(5), 375–403. doi:10.1002/(SICI)1097-0266(199705)18:5<375::AID-SMJ876>3.0.CO;2-7

Prahalad, C. K., & Krishnan, M. S. (2008). *The New Age of Innovation: Driving Co-Created Value Through Global Networks*. New York, NY: McGraw-Hill.

Prahalad, C. K., & Ramaswamy, V. (2004). Co-creating unique value with customers. *Strategy and Leadership, 32*(3), 4–9. doi:10.1108/10878570410699249

Presencing Institute. (2010). *Theory u*. Retrieved from http://www.presencing.com/theoryu

Ragu-Nathan, T. S., Tarafdar, M., Tu, Q., & Ragu-Nathan, B. S. (2008, December). The Consequences of technostress for end users in organizations: Conceptual development and empirical validation. *Information Systems Research, 19*(4), 471–433. doi:10.1287/isre.1070.0165

Richtel, M. (2010, July 7). Your brain on computers; Hooked on gadgets and paying a mental price. *New York Times*. Retrieved from http://community.nytimes.com/comments/www.nytimes.com/2010/06/07/technology/07brain.html

Rifkin, J. (2011). *The third industrial revolution: How lateral power is transforming energy, the economy, and the world.* New York, NY: Palgrace Macmillan.

Robey, D., & Boudreau, M. C. (1999). Accounting for the contradictory organizational consequences of information technology: Theoretical directions and methodological implications. *Information Systems Research, 10*(2), 167–185. doi:10.1287/isre.10.2.167

Rogers, E. M. (1995). *Diffusion of innovations.* New York, NY: Free.

Rushkoff, D. (2013). *Present shock: When everything happens now.* New York, NY: Penguin.

Sami, L. K., & Pangannaiah, N. B. (2006). Technostress: A literature survey on the effect of information technology on library users. *Library Review, 55*(7), 429–439. doi:10.1108/00242530610682146

Sawyer, S., & Eschenfelder, K. R. (2002). Social informatics: Perspectives, examples, and trends. In B. Cronin (Ed.), Annual review of information science and technology. Medford, NJ: Information Today Inc./ASIST.

Scharmer, C. O. (2009). *Theory u: Leading from the future as it emerges.* San Francisco, CA: Barrett-Koehler.

Scharmer, C. O. (2011). *The future of change management: 13 propositions draft 1.0.* Paper presented to the Zeitschrift fur Organisationsentwicklung, Berlin, Germany.

Scharmer, C. O. (2013, September 10). *Re: Implementation of theory u.* [Web log post]. Retrieved from http://www.blog.ottoscharmer.com/?p=557

Scharmer, C. O., & Kaufer, K. (2013). *Leading from the emerging future: From ego-system to eco-system economies.* San Francisco, CA: Berrett-Koehler.

Schein, E. H. (2010). *Organizational culture and leadership.* San Francisco, CA: Jossey-Bass.

Schein, E. H. (2013). *Humble inquiry: The gentle art of asking instead of telling.* San Francisco, CA: Berrett-Kohler.

Senge, P. (1990). *The fifth discipline: The art and practice of the earning organization.* New York, NY: Random House.

Shirkey, C. (2008). *Here comes everybody: The power of organizing without organizations.* New York, NY: Penguin.

Siedel, J. V. (1998). *Qualitative data analysis. The ethnograph v5.0: A users' guide, Appendix E.* Colorado Springs, CO: Qualis.

Sinha, I. (1999). *The cyber gypsies: Love, life, and travels on the electronic frontier.* London, UK: Scribner.

Smith, A. (2013). *Smartphone ownership 2013.* Pew internet and American life project. Retrieved from http://pewinternet.org/Reports/2013/Smartphone-Ownership-2013.aspx

Smith, K. K., & Berg, D. N. (1988). *Paradoxes of group life.* San Francisco, CA: Jossey-Bass.

Stone, L. (2009, August 24). *The impacts of smartphones in society*. [Web log post]. Retrieved from www.lindastone.net

Swanson, R. A., & Holton, E. F. (2005). *Research in organizations: Foundations and methods of inquiry*. San Francisco, CA: Berrett-Koehler.

Tarafdar, M., Tu, Q., Ragu-Nathan, B. S., & Ragu-Nathan, T. S. (2007). The impact of technostress on role stress and productivity. *Journal of Management Information Systems*, *24*(1), 301–328. doi:10.2753/ MIS0742-1222240109

Taylor, S. J., & Bogdan, R. (1998). *Introduction to qualitative research methods: A guide and resource* (3rd ed.). New York, NY: John Wiley.

Trochim, W. M. K. (2006). Qualitative validity. *Social Research Methods*. Retrieved from http://www. socialresearchmethods.net/kb/qualval.htm

Turkle, S. (2011). *Alone together: Why we expect more from technology and less from each other*. New York, NY: Basic.

van Maanen, M. (1990). *Researching lived experience: Human science for an action sensitive pedagogy*. London, Ontario, Canada: The University of Western Ontario.

Vernon, M. (1998, June 4). Directors buckle under work pressures. *Computer Weekly*, p. 30.

Virilio, P. (1998). *The virilio reader*. Malden, MA: Blackwell.

Waite, A. (2010, June 6). *Re: InfoSec triads: Security / functionality / ease of use*. [Web log post]. Retrieved from: http://.infosanity.co.uk/2010/06/12/infosec-triads-securityfunctionalityease-of-use/

Wang, K., Shu, Q., & Tu, Q. (2008). Technostress under different organizational environments: An empirical investigation. *Computers in Human Behavior*, *24*(2), 3002–3013. doi:10.1016/j.chb.2008.05.007

Weber, L. (2013, April 24). Job hunt moves to mobile devices, *Wall Street Journal*, p. B8.

Weil, M. M., & Rosen, L. D. (1997). *Technostress: Coping with technology @WORK @HOME @PLAY*. New York, NY: John Wiley.

Westervelt, R. (2013, December 18). Mobile devices will pose the biggest risk in 2014, survey says. *Computing Resource Network*. Retrieved from http://www.crn.com/news/security/240164859/mobile-devices-will-pose-the-biggest-risk-in-2014-survey-says.htm

Wise, J. M. (1997). *Exploring technology and social space*. Thousand Oaks, CA: Sage.

Wolfe, T. (2000). *Hooking up*. New York, NY: McMillan.

Worthman, J. (2013, April 11). How to lighten the crush of e-mail. *New York Times*, p. B11.

Yarow, J. (2013, March 27). How people use facebook on smartphones. *Business Insider*. Retrieved from www.businessinsider.com/chart-of-the-day-facebook-usage-on-smartphones-2013-3

Yarow, J. (2014, April 3). We are spending a lot more time online thanks to smartphones and tablets. *Business Insider*. Retrieved from http://www.businessinsider.com/were-spending-a-lot-more-time-online-thanks-to-smartphones-and-tablets-2014-4?nr_email_referer=1&utm_source=Triggermail&utm_medium=email&utm_term=Tech%20Chart%20Of%20The%20Day&utm_campaign=SAI_COTD_040314

Young, P. (1998, September). Under fire. *CIO Magazine*, 15-20.

Yun, H., Kettinger, W., & Lee, C. (2012). A new open door: The smartphone's impact on work-to-life conflict, stress, and resistance. *International Journal of Electronic Commerce*, *16*(4), 121–151. doi:10.2753/JEC1086-4415160405

Chapter 6
Turning Weakness into Strength:
How to Learn From an IT Security Incident

Randy L. Burkhead
Capella University, USA

ABSTRACT

In today's culture organizations have come to expect that information security incidents and breaches are no longer a matter of if but when. This shifting paradigm has brought increased attention, not to the defenses in place to prevent an incident but, to how companies manage the aftermath. Using a phenomenological model, organizations can reconstruct events focused on the human aspects of security with forensic technology providing supporting information. This can be achieved by conducting an after action review for incidents using a phenomenological model. Through this approach the researcher can discover the common incident management cycle attributes and how these attributes have been applied in the organization. An interview guide and six steps are presented to accomplish this type of review. By understanding what happened, how it happened, and why it happened during incident response, organizations can turn their moment of weakness into a pillar of strength.

INTRODUCTION

A 21st Century individual must confront a new aspect of modern life – that information security incidents will happen and it could be anyone's fault. Anyone could be the person who loses a thumb drive, gives away someone's username and password, or anybody's identity might be the one someone steals. What happens when this happens? How can organizations respond to these various events? The research conducted in "A Phenomenological Study of Information Security Incidents Experienced by Information Security Professionals Providing Corporate Information Security Incident Management" (Burkhead, 2014) details how private companies located in the Pacific North West of the United States respond to these issues from a human perspective. Participants discussed experiences that ranged from working with small business clients to global firms dealing with threats large enough to take down the Internet around the world.

DOI: 10.4018/978-1-5225-0522-8.ch006

This chapter is designed to provide the reader with two essentials lessons to be learned. The first lesson is to inform the reader about this modern threat that can affect anyone around the world and how it is possible to assess and analyze a crisis situation in order to learn, mature, and grow over time. The second lesson is providing a moldable framework for conducting phenomenological research in various fields. Phenomenology models are designed to describe rather than explain experiences (Creswell, 2012). The focus of phenomenology is on the lived experiences of participants. The experiences, when analyzed, form a structure that reflects the essences of the phenomenon experienced. The media has remarked that security incidents are no longer a matter of if but a matter of when. This change makes what comes after an incident just as important, if not more so, than the protections placed around data to keep it safe.

The first part of this chapter is designed to provide the reader with some background information on the subject of information security incident management. Several terms are provided so that readers without an IT security background may have a better understanding of information security incidents. Once all readers have a common understanding of the terms used in this subject area, the results of some previous research using a phenomenological model are presented to provide the reader with a framework for the processes, procedures, and lessons learned in incident response. This common understanding of terms and pervious research is important in order to understand the processes and procedures involved in conducting reviews of information security incidents.

The second part of this chapter is designed to provide the reader with an explanation for conducting similar research. Prior to conducting a study it is important to establish the scope of the project. Once the scope has been established there are six steps to conducting an after action review using a phenomenological approach. Step one is to leave personal baggage at the door as it is important not to form biased opinions. Step two is to collect the data through interviews and technical analysis. Step three is to breakdown the data into its simplest components. Step four is to reconstruct the data in order to understand the themes that span all sources. Step five is to identify the essences of the reconstructed data in order to provide a strong basis for the final step. Step six is to recognize the conclusions and build recommendations. The end result of this assessment processes will allow organizations and individuals to learn from information security incidents.

PREVIOUS RESEARCH

There is a lot of existing research on the topic of cyber security ranging from war applications to criminal activities. There are published standards for IT security including industry regulations like the Payment Card Industry Data Security Standard (PCI-DSS), government sponsored standards like United States National Institute for Standards and Technology (NIST) special publication 800-53, laws and regulations such as the Health Information Privacy and Accountability Act (HIPAA), and international cyber security standards such as International Standard Organization (ISO) 2700 and Information Technology Infrastructure Library (ITIL). Each of these standards has processes and procedures for incident response; but they each have only limited instructions for how to build an incident response program. There is very little research into the phenomenon of IT security incidents and incident management in the field.

Despite being a problem that has existed for well over three decades most research has been focused on the attack methods, actors, and vectors rather than the actions, decisions, processes, and procedures used during information security incident management. A phenomenological model is uniquely suited for research designed to address this gap. In "A Phenomenological Study of Information Security Incidents Experienced by Information Security Professionals Providing Corporate Information Security Incident Management" the researcher built a model for assessing information security incidents in a phenomenological style (Burkhead, 2014). Ten themes were identified after analyzing the experiences of these incident responders. These ten themes address the flow of incident response activities and major decision making points, the importance of the attacker, the influence of third parties on incident response, and the importance of sharing information.

There are several common components to information security incident management. In previous research on information security incident management some form of diagnosis, containment, and recovery actions must occur in order to detect, stop the spread of an incident, and return systems to a secure state (Chu, Deng, & Chao, 2011; Lanter, 2011; Tammineedi, 2010). However, these parts of incident response and the steps used to address attacks are not represented as a holistic information security incident management process in previous literature. The purpose of previous research has primarily been focused on narrow aspects of incident response or on the prevention of incidents. This gap presents an incomplete picture of this sensitive and important information security process.

The gap can be addressed by conducting a phenomenological study on the lived experiences of responders during information security incidents. Burkhead's research sheds new light on information security incidents. Theme 1 specifically addresses the scope. The scope of an information security incident, based on the results of Burkhead's research (2014), can be defined using specific language including compromise, breach, attack, and attacker in the definition of an information security incident. Information security incidents are referenced in terms of technology, processes, and people according to various participants in the study. Establishing the scope provides a framework to discuss information security incidents.

Theme 2 specifically addresses the flow of incident response procedures in private organizations. Each incident starts with detection and progresses through an escalation procedure which start with an initial investigation designed to establish the scope and key critical elements (Burkhead, 2014). The key elements of information security incidents are the size, type, and probability of a data breach as well as the intention of the attacker as either malicious or benign. Once these elements are identified a decision is made regarding the next steps which are often different depending on the size and type of the incident. The flow of incident response is similar across descriptions of many information security incidents.

Theme 3 addresses the major decision points in incident response. This first decision point takes place after an initial investigation and is focused entirely on the scope of the situation in order to determine if the event is really an information security incident while the second major decision point involves the closure of a major incident (Burkhead, 2014). A formal decision is generally reached at the end of the secondary investigation. The technical context of this decision is based on the residual risk and impact of the incident. Themes 1, 2, and 3 each address how incidents are detected and managed in the field (Burkhead, 2014). These three themes together create a balanced and a holistic picture of how incidents are scoped and managed and how decisions are made during crisis situations.

There is a lack of empirical evidence in previous research demonstrating a holistic response process for incidents. While standards do exist for conducting incident response, such as standards contained in the NIST and ITIL frameworks, many organizations have not disclosed, and are reluctant to reveille, various parts of the incident response process to researchers to empirically evaluate (Ahmad, Hadgkiss, & Ruighaver, 2012; Werlinger et al., 2010). Organizations have not revealed parts of the incident response process to researchers for multiple reasons including the sensitive nature of these incidents, the potential negative customer impactions of public notification, and because due to the variances in organizational implementation of standards organizations many not collect or be required to report such incidents.

Theme 4 is about the analysis of how information about the attacker is addressed and managed in the field. The results of Burkhead's (2014) study indicate the importance of establishing who, what, and why to the incident response process. Direct questions about who an attacker was in any particular incident were generally answered by stating that the information was irrelevant to the response. Incident response will generally proceed according to the pattern established in the first three themes regardless of the source. However, in each description of a specific event, even accidental events, elements of the attacker and his or her identity are present. Despite being thought of as irrelevant to the investigation, identifying certain elements of the attacker is an innate and often unconscious process performed by the incident responders. Classifying the purpose of an attack in terms of criminal, espionage, or other overt effects of an information security incident helps responders when considering appropriate actions to remediate incidents. The purpose of the attack is a critical piece of information addressed before the first decision-making point in the incident response process and helps to establish the scope of the incident. Classifying the intention of an attacker focused only on if the attack was malicious or accidental. This is also a critical piece of information addressed by the first decision-making point in the incident response process and helps to establish the scope of the incident. Ultimately only the purpose and intention of an attacker are the two important elements to investigations since the identity of the attacker is often considered irrelevant.

Themes 6 and 7 each address recommendations based on the lived experiences of the participants in regards to improvements to incident response. These two themes together provide a direction for improvement in information security incident response operations based on past experiences (Burkhead, 2014). Theme 6 addresses the human element, which will always be a part of incident response. Humans are generally believed to be the weakest link in the security chain. The results of Burkhead's study of these lived experiences indicate a simple solution: Train people on incident response. Events are reported by users, management, and general IT staff internal to the organization and the initial incident response can be compromised if any of these people make poor decisions. Theme 7 addresses another component that is often missing from incident response based on the lived experiences of the participants in Burkhead's study. Her results indicate the importance of having a plan for information security incident management. Some of the participants had experiences that spanned the creation and maturation of an information security incident response program. These participants experiences demonstrated the benefits of a formal program with trained responders through decreased response times, better management decisions, and decreased losses as these programs became more mature. These two themes address the lessons learned based on the lived experiences of Burkhead's participants and how these lessoned influence current incident response practices.

Theme 10 addresses the perceived importance of offensive security. In theme 10 the importance of attack frameworks was addressed based on the lived experiences of information security professionals (Burkhead, 2014). The results of this analysis show that knowledge of attack frameworks is important for an information security professional such as knowledge about how to penetrate a system as an attacker. Knowledge about attack frameworks is of value to incident management. Knowing about the potential external threats via the Internet or internal threats inside an organization and how each type of attacker may try to attack a system gives a security professional additional knowledge with which to enact strong controls to prevent those known threat vectors and to set up alerts to detect and contain a threat quickly during an incident.

Additional layers of complexity mar the issue of incident response, particularly the global nature of the Internet. When an attacker can be anywhere in the world what hope do local authorities, bound by jurisdiction restraints, have to provide people with justice? Worse than that, what hope do citizens have against police, military, or state sponsored actors that cause incidents? As one participant in Burkhead's (2014) study asked, "How can you report an attack to your attacker?" (p. 122). Themes 5, 8, and 9 of her study each address how third-party organizations influence incident response for better or worse. These three themes together address a complex relationship between internal and external private organization politics.

Theme 5 addresses the relationship between private organizations and third-party organizations specifically law enforcement, military, and government agencies. The results of Burkhead's (2014) study indicate a negative impact on incident response in private organizations when these agencies become involved. Organization management often fears law enforcement due to the disruptions caused by investigations and the costs of criminal trails. Incident responders may fear law enforcement disrupting operations. Compounding this fear of law enforcement is a fear that the United States government may be one of the worst violators of information security. This indicates a very negative relationship between law enforcement, military, and government agencies with private organizations.

Theme 8 addresses the relationship between private organizations and general third-party organizations such as forensic organizations. The results of this theme, based on the experiences of Burkhead's (2014) participants, indicated a positive and almost necessary relationship for incident response. Third parties provided value to organizations during incident response by providing critical skills and, when necessary, they act as impartial expert witnesses. Theme 9 addresses the common theme of information sharing among the lived experiences of Burkhead's (2014) participants. Information sharing is extremely important to incident response in various ways including improving the change of detecting an incident based on information about recent attacks, trends, malicious sources, and common motivations experienced by others. However, discussing incidents is generally not authorized or encouraged in organizations due to fears of negative impacts to security, consumer confidence, and regulatory issues. These three themes together indicate a positive relationship and impact with third-party organizations that are not government, military, or law enforcement agencies.

In today's culture it has come to be expected that information security incidents and breaches are no longer a matter of if but when. This shifting paradigm has brought increased attention, not to the defenses in place to prevent an incident, but how companies manage the aftermath. Using a phenomenological model, organizations can reconstruct events focused on the human aspects of security with forensic technology providing supporting information. By understanding what happened, how it happened, and why it happened during incident response organizations can turn their moment of weakness into a pillar of strength.

Define the Research

Information security incidents are likely to develop as a result of targeted actions against sensitive resources. Symantec estimated that over $110 billion a year is lost to malicious cyber actions (Filshtinskiy, 2013). This number is only expected to grow. In addition to these types of monetary losses, there is an increasing culture of fear that military applications of technology could have a profound impact on modern life in the event of a military conflict (Butts, Rice, & Shenoi, 2012). As technology continues to grow and become integrated into modern life the threat from information security incidents becomes increasingly dire. Organizations can benefit from a better understanding of the experience of identifying and responding to these information security incidents as a means for supporting future professionals.

In the previous section several themes were identified in previous research. These themes provide the groundwork for future research in information security incident response. However, it is the way that the research was conducted that is unique. There are other standards such as the Verizon and Symantec incident data collection tools but these are focused on empirical data and thus provide only broad results such as 14% of attacks were for insiders (Verizon, 2013). The use of a phenomenological model shifts the focus away from statistical analysis of hard categories to qualitative inquiry. This unique process allows researchers to assess new areas.

The model designed by Burkhead for her study is of particular interested in the context of this chapter. The model she built is based on six steps (Burkhead, 2014). This has proven to be an effective way to do an after action review of an incident from a human perspective using a repeatable process. The methodological approach used by Burkhead in her study was structured around principles from multiple phenomenological sources that were used to create a unique creative phenomenological method. Phenomenology has many different forms and methods and phenomenologists have many outlooks on experience and how experience can be captured and analyzed (Van Manen, 2014). Each of the various phenomenology models addresses unique aspects of the overall method of phenomenological research. Each researcher ultimately uses different combinations and variations on the same central themes of phenomenology.

Prior to starting an investigation into information security incidents it is important to identify and understand the purpose of such a study. There are various different reasons for conducting a phenomenological study on information security incidents. The purpose of conducting a phenomenological study on incident response may be to answer a research question or it may be to discover the processes and procedures used in a specific organization and how they can be improved. Identifying these factors helps to keep the researcher on track throughout the study. The purpose of the study helps to inform the researcher on which questions should be emphasized during data collection and when drawing conclusions the purpose will provide context for the themes discovered during analysis. Identifying this critical element early is important to keeping this type of qualitative inquiry focused and on track.

The purpose of the study should be specific enough to provide the researcher with focus but broad enough to allow for some deviation in order to explore new possibilities during the course of the study. For example in the study conducted by Burkhead (2014) she had to redefine a research question based on participant feedback, "Based on the responses of the participants, which did indicate a common theme in regards to attack frameworks, this question should be addressed (rephrased) as: How does knowledge of attack frameworks influence decision making during information security incidents?" (p. 132). In her study the responses by participants went down an unexpected path that provided a new research question to answer within the scope of the project. This new research question provided value on the topic of information security incident management. Therefore, it is important to provide structure without eliminating the possibility of new directions.

STEP ONE: EPOCH

One of the most important elements of a phenomenological model is the epoche. This is the first step in the model presented in this chapter. The epoche, as described by Van Manen (2014) and Giorgi (2009), is a critical process used to bracket the researcher's experiences in a way that maintains the objectivity of the research process and results. As a researcher evaluating the lived experiences of others it is important that the researcher's experiences do not cloud her judgment. This identification phase provides the researcher with an opportunity to clearly identify her own experiences and views in order to set them aside during future analysis. Qualitative research is more subjective than quantitative research and the epoche process helps to identify potential bias so that the researcher is aware of their pre-existing opinions and experiences in order to put them aside when considering the experiences of others. This is a hard process to follow and requires the researcher to be self-aware.

One of the best manuals for reaching this type of awareness was written by the CIA in 1999. Heuer (1999) wrote about the importance of understanding one's own worldviews when considering alternative viewpoints, cultures, and experiences. In order to demonstrate this concept look closely at figure 1:

Based on the viewer's perception they would see either an old woman or a young lady in the picture. This type of image is a perceptual illusion because there are two images in the picture. The first impression represents the concept of bias. Now look at the picture again and try to see the other picture. Here is a hint, the young lady's chocker is the old woman's mouth and the old woman's nose is the young lady's chin. The second picture represents the viewpoints and experiences of others. Many people struggle to see past the first image just as many researchers struggle with bias. When the viewer can see past the first image to the second and back this represents being able to see things from both sides.

Prior to doing any of the other steps in this process it is important to conduct the epoche. The epoche is different for each researcher as everyone's experiences. The conclusions that they draw from those

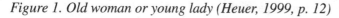

Figure 1. Old woman or young lady (Heuer, 1999, p. 12)

experiences are also different. In the context of learning about information security incidents it is important to list out ones experience with information security incidents. This should not just be a resume listing of jobs and experiences but a reflection on how those experiences impact ones current viewpoints.

For example the following is a summary of the author's epoche. The author is herself an information security professional in the American Northeast with over eight years of experience in information security. The author has a PhD degree in IT with a specialty in information assurance and security as well as the Certified Information Systems Security Professional (CISSP) and Certified Ethical Hacker (CeH) certifications. The author has also worked for the military as a Soldier and contractor, for other government agencies as a contractor, and for private organizations as a consultant over the past several years. The author has an extensive background in information security incident management including time spent as an incident manager for the military, along with researching incidents for her study, and responding to incidents as a contractor for private organizations. Given this background, the author has extensive knowledge and expertise on information security and the unique challenges of information security incident management.

In the author's experiences there are several common elements. In each information security incident detection was never accomplished with technical tools. Information security incidents were reported by users or administrators witnessing anomalous activities. In general, organizations have not developed the resources to respond to any information security incidents beyond returning systems to service. The only exception to this was the military which had the authority, responsibility, and resources to respond to attackers rather than just the information security incident. Even in these instances forensic investigations were rarely performed for the collection of criminal evidence. Due to the limited resources and immature processes and procedures at most organizations, with the exception of the military, there were no lessons learned from information security incidents. Since the vast majority of information security incidents never result in major breaches of protected data they are not reviewed. Based on the author's experience information security incidents from internal threat actors are more common than successful information security attacks from external threat sources. However, organizations spend more time and resources preventing external threats than internal threats. Information security incident response in private organizations is minimal and generally no prosecution occurs. Private organizations are not aggressive about information security incident response. These essences represent the author's unique experiences.

In this example the author's experiences in information security incident management can have an influence on her analysis. Documenting these issues allows her to set them aside and then to review them throughout the analysis process to ensure that they do not influence the analysis of participant experiences. This prepared the author to approach the collected participant experiences with a fresh outlook and an open mind when conducting these studies in the past. The focus of this type of study is, and should remain, on the participants. This process prepares a researcher to start gathering data from participants.

STEP TWO: DATA COLLECTION

The second step is the data collection process. The data collection process is primarily interview based. Technology may be limited in a given incident response situation. Logs may not be enabled or retained by systems and applications to demonstrate events recorded by technology. Logs may even be deleted as part of covering the attacker's tracks during an incident. Intrusion detection or prevention systems, anti-malware solutions, or other security systems may either not be in place or compromised as part of the incident. Thus technology is not always the best indicator of events. However, a person can also lie or forget certain events by the time the interview is conducted. Yet with multiple people involved in the process, and the iterative analysis of their experiences when broken down and reconstructed into a whole, the data collected through interviews provides a more reliable narrative.

The primary data collection instrument used by Burkhead in her study was a set of interview questions designed for her research. Interviewing as an instrument of data collection is appropriate for a phenomenology study (Creswell, 2012). The interview questions used by Burkhead were semi-structured and open ended in order to facilitate free exploration of the participant's experiences on the target issue. The questions she used were designed to elicit information, experiences, and opinions. The semi-structured nature of this framework allows the researcher to explore additional areas as necessary in each interview.

Creating or borrowing a set of standard questions including questions for demographics, qualifications, experiences, and expectations provides consistent structure to all the interviews. The framework established by Burkhead (2014) for these interview questions was approved by field testing with industry experts prior to being used in her research. The standard set of questions was field tested prior to data collection by a panel of industry experts. Each of the field-test participants had various qualifications and experiences related to information security. The experts all agreed that the questions were appropriate for the study. The results from Burkhead's research study were discussed earlier in this chapter.

Through the use of interviews the researcher can explore the individual experiences of each participant in relation to the scope of the project. Using established questions helps researchers to remain focused and not to influence the direction of the interviews with personal bias (Giorgi, 2009). However, it does not constrain the researcher from asking important questions that come up during discussions. The author has used Burkhead's interview guide multiple times since the original research was published in response to incidents and as a tool to build incident response programs based on the lessons learned from previous experiences. Burkhead's interview guide is a proven tool for reviewing incidents. The data from those reviews can be used for various purposes to improve an organization.

Interview guides can contain a variety of questions. The interview questions in Burkhead interview guide consist of several sections including questions related to the participant's icebreakers, information security incident experiences, and information security incident observations (Burkhead, 2014). The icebreaker questions are designed to explore general experiences in IT security and management and to place the participant at ease. These questions establish the pace of each interview. Once each individual had answered these general questions specific information security incidents were explored. Each information security incident related by the participant was explored with an emphasis on the participant's own experiences. After discussing the lived experiences of the participant during information security incidents, questions in the observations section are designed to give the participant an opportunity to discuss what they have learned from their own experiences.

The first set of questions is the icebreaker questions. These questions help the researcher, the one asking the questions, to understand the position, qualifications, and general processes related to each participant. These questions include,

Question 1: How many years of experience do you have responding to information security incidents?

Question 2: Let's continue, how do you define an information security incident? There are many different definitions but what is yours?

Question 3: In your response you mention specifically {repeat key elements}. Are these the key elements of your definition of an information security incident?

Question 4: What is your role during an information security incident?

Question 5: In general what is your procedure for identifying and addressing a potential information security incident?

Question 6: In general what is the balance between human and automated reporting?

Question 7: What are some things you do to prepare for incident response?

Question 8: How often do you need to respond to a potential information security incident? (Burkhead, 2014)

The first question establishes the participant's qualifications in regards to information security incidents. Those with more years of experience are likely to have multiple events to discuss. Those with little to no experience in this area, other than with the incident being reviewed, may have trouble with technical explanations.

Question 2 and 3 establish common ground. Each participant is asked to establish what they consider to be an information security incident. It would be difficult to proceed if the researcher and participant each had different definitions for the subject of the investigation. Questions 4 is designed to ensure the researcher understands the participant's position and daily duties. These may or may not be related to information security incident management. Question 5 and 6 are about how incidents are identified and classified. This helps the researcher to know which elements to focus on when asking questions in relation to pre-incident actions. The final two questions in this section, question 7 and 8, are designed to establish the maturity of the incident response program and abilities of the organization. Programs with prepared responses that are practiced regularly have established process and procedures that help the organization when responding to incidents. Organizations that have not established these elements are not likely to have certain processes and procedures such as a process for the classification of a potential information security incident or procedures for gathering and documenting the lessoned learned.

The second set of questions is designed to review a specific information security incident. These questions should all be answered from the perspective of each participant. The researcher should keep the interview focused on what the participant directly did or witnessed rather than on what the royal "we" was doing during each incident. While some exposition is necessary to understand what is happening around each participant during the incident, responses should be focused on their own lived experiences. These questions include,

Question 1: Think of a specific incident to discuss, what was the situation around that incident?

Question 2: What year did this incident take place?

Question 3: What role did you take during the incident and when were you notified?

Question 4: What steps did you use to detect and identify this potential incident?

Question 5: What was the time-lapse between the time the hack started and when it was detected?

Question 6: What steps did you take to classify this as an information security event?

Question 7: What was your decision making process in regards to the initial response steps for reviewing this incident?

Question 8: At that point what was the rest of the incident response?

Question 9: Did you discover any additional vulnerabilities when responding to this issue?

Question 10: At any time did you work with law enforcement or third party organizations?

Question 11: How important were elements of who the attacker was, their purpose, intent, tactics, and motivation to this investigation?

Question 12: At what point during the incident was the issue remediated?

Question 13: What if any compliance standards did you discover to be violated during this incident?

Question 14: At what point was the incident declared closed?

Question 15: What was the time-lapse between the start and close of this event?

Question 16: Did you conduct any additional investigations or follow-up following its closure?

Question 17: Were there any process improvements in incident response from this incident?

Question 18: Are there any additional incidents that you would like to discuss today that relate some of your unique experiences? (Burkhead, 2014)

Questions 1, 2, and 3 are designed to elicit responses about the situations around the incident and the context of the participant's lived experiences. These set the stage for the other 16 questions and their relevance. If the participant has no knowledge of the management aspects of the incident then those questions may not be able to be answered from her experiences. If the participant is not involved with the technical aspects of the incident she may not be able to answer those questions from her experiences.

Questions 4 through 7 are designed so that the researcher and participant can discuss elements of the incident detection and classification phase of incident response management. Every story has a beginning and these questions give the interview participant a place to start explaining their story. These questions cover the initial discovery or notification of the potential incident as well as the first responses. These questions do not just ask about what happened but what factors influenced certain elements. The next several questions build on these responses.

Questions 8 through 12 are designed to allow the participant to relate their experiences during the response phase of the incident management cycle. There are many different things that might happen during an incident response. These questions address the common elements such as searching for information about the attacker, involving law enforcement, notifications, and remediation steps. Questions 13 through 15 are designed to elicit responses about the end of the incident. The end of the incident is a semi-formal decision to close the activities related to the incident response. Some incidents have long-standing legal battles and other cleanup events that continue after the incidents have been remediated. Remediated in the context of this study means, that the issue, such as a breach, has been technically fixed, such as closing a port through a firewall rule change. The end of an incident might be months or even more than a year after the issues were technically remediated.

Finally, questions 16 through 17 get participants discussing what happened after the incident was closed. Just as each story has a beginning, these questions allow the participant to discuss the end of the incident response cycle. The true end of the incident response cycle includes the lessoned learned and improvements that were implemented as a result of the incident. Question 18 is used when there are more incidents to discuss. If the answer to this question starts another description of an event than the researcher would simply continue the interview with question 1 of this section. This process continues until there are no more unique incidents to discuss.

The last section of the structured interview guide is about how the participant has learned from their own experiences. These questions address program improvements and other support elements that the participant thinks are of value based on their experiences. These questions include,

Question 1: How strictly are process and procedures followed during an incident and how much freedom do you have to deviate when responding to incidents?

Question 2: Are there any processes or procedure improvements that you would recommend in regards to incident response?

Question 3: What types of support or training do you wish you had when responding to information security incidents?

Question 4: How useful has penetration testing knowledge, how to attack a machine, been in trying to respond to incidents?

Question 5: Do you feel that prior knowledge of threat and attack patterns is important to incident response?

Question 6: What, if any, aspects of the attacker are important to security incident response?

Question 7: If you worked with law enforcement in relation to information security incidents was this helpful and productive?

Question 8: Do you feel assistance from third party organizations is helpful in incident response?

Question 9: Do you feel that information sharing has been helpful?

Question 10: At this time I do not have any more questions do you have any additional thoughts?
(Burkhead, 2014)

Questions 1 through 3 allow the participant to openly remark on various improvements that they would recommend based on their experiences. These are broad and open-ended to allow the participant to expand on any given point related to incident response. However, questions 4 through 9 provide the participant the chance to address common incident response elements and how they might be specifically improved in the future. The final question, question 10, provides the participant with a final chance to remark on any element of the interview process.

One important skill to master in support of this type of data collection is active listening. Active listening is the art of listening and then interacting with the speaker to reconfirm understanding (Hoppe, 2011). For example, in the icebreaker questions, question 3, the researcher asks the interviewer to repeat the key components of the participant's definition of an information security incident. This type of active listening encourages clarity, understanding, and provides the participant an opportunity to clarify any confusion. Repeating key elements is a positive way to let each participant know that the researcher is paying attention to what they have to say and discussing these key elements may spark some additional conversations.

In order to facilitate these interviews it is recommended that each interview be recorded using voice recording software and encrypted for future transcription. As a backup a second hand-held recording device should also be used in the event of a failure in the primary recorder. Using a recording device frees the researcher to pay more attention to what is being said during the interviews; however, notes can still be taken during the interview process. Following the conclusion of each interview the researcher, if time and resources allow, should transcribe the recording with the researcher's notes into a single document. Once the transcription process is completed the document can be reviewed by the participant to ensure the accuracy of the information. This way each final document can be validated by each participant to ensure the accuracy of the transcript before analysis.

These narratives are the cornerstone of the phenomenological method. It is important to capture all of the data to make meaningful conclusions. However, there is a point known as data saturation. Data saturation is the point where new data is simply duplicating existing data without providing any new meaning (Walker, 2012). It may not be productive to interview every person involved in an information security incident if multiple people on the team performed the same actions leading to the same experiences. It may not be productive to continue to interview additional participants once similar experiences are frequently discussed during interviews. It is up the researcher to determine this point and when it is appropriate to move on to the next phase.

STEP THREE: PHENOMENOLOGICAL REDUCTION BREAKDOWN

Once data has been collected the next step is to breakdown each interview into its individual underlying themes. This is the first part of the phenomenological reduction. The phenomenological reduction is a two-part process of deconstruction and reconstruction that is used in order to identify meaningful units and themes (Van Manen, 2014). The reduction and breakdown of unique responses into coded themes allows for the reconstruction of the data during further analysis. Analysis of the data starts by deconstructing the data and identifying discrete units of meaning related to the phenomenon being studied. Each individual participant's experiences are deconstructed and coded. These coded responses allow the researcher to easily compare and note the similarities and differences in each participant's experiences.

Some data elements are facts stated as part of the interview process such as the type of incident and the people involved. Table 1-1 displays a mock breakdown of individual incidents discussed during data collection. In this example identifiers are listed for various types of information security incidents. The deconstruction happens when the researcher breaks down the narrative into the unique identifiers discussed by each participant. If participant 001 discussed a lost device that was lost by an internal employee on a business trip these elements can be pulled from the narrative and documented. Simple

Table 1. Phenomenological breakdown example

Identifier	P001 I1	P001 I2	P002 I1	P002 I2	P002 I3	P003 I1	P003 I2
Physical security	X			X			
Lost / stolen devices	X			X			X
Law suit			X				
Electronic		X	X		X	X	
Information security		X			X	X	X
Privacy				X			
Was the incident internal or external to the host organization?	Int	Ext	Int	Ext	Ext	Ext	Int
Breach method: Default username and password or simple vulnerability					X	X	
Breach method: phishing		X					
Breach method: Technical hacking or vulnerability exploit			X			X	
Breach method: Malware			X		X		X
Breach method: Lost or stolen device	X			X			X
Breach method: No encryption				X			
Breach method: Accidental disclosure / privacy			X				
Breach method: Not investigated							
Year incident occurred	2009	2010	2014	2013	2012	2012	2010

elements can be quickly and easily identified and documented based on the transcripts of the interviews. The columns contain marks to document the incidents reported. After reviewing all of the transcripts and documenting these facts patterns will start to emerge.

However, not all of the identifiers referenced in interviews are easily observed. Transforming a narrative into common elements is more subjective than documenting the fact that an incident took place in 2009. For example a transcript might read something like:

We started out by trying to determine how big the incident was and what systems were affected. John was trying to determine the volume of traffic but I was capturing packets and analyzing them to see what was going on with this traffic. I also pulled the logs from the boundary device to see the early signs of the incident. Everyone was down because of this huge volume of packets chocking the network. It was hard to coordinate anything because our primary communications systems, email and Lync, were not functioning. The help desk was swamped. We conducted a few scans on the border device and eventually we determined that we were being targeted for denial of service. Before we did anything else we tried to contact law enforcement but the local FBI office said they did not respond to these types of attacks. Thankfully I had some experience with this type of attack and suggested to the CIO that we contact our ISP and black hole the target IP.

This example is a short explanation of only a part of one incident but has many potential identifiers. Participants do not always speak plainly during interviews. When recalling an event a participant might jump around to different times during the incident, forget various elements, or embellish the story for personal reasons. This can make it hard to identify the common elements and break down the narratives.

Breaking down narratives and identifying each mechanism is subjective. Participants may use different words when discussing each information security incident to relate similar actions or the same meaning as another participant. It is up to the researcher to interpret these differences when categorizing common elements and terms. Table 1-2 shows a second example based on information security incident data. This example includes a breakdown of the initial responses conducted in each incident. The narrative above is documented in the column P001 I1. The primary focus of the example incident was on determining the size and impact of the incident rather than on the attacker or on containment. The actions discussed included reviewing logs, conducting scans, and notifying the Chief Information Officer (CIO), law enforcement, and third party partners.

When breaking down multiple lengthily interviews this process becomes harder. If another participant said that they contacted the president of the company because they do not have a CIO does this represent a significant difference? In many instances the answer might be no since they both represent notifying chief level representatives of major disruptions. Perhaps, another participant said that they conducted some captures of the problem to try and see how big it was rather than another that said they conducted captured focused on separating infected systems from the rest of the network. This would represent a significant difference in the primary focus of the initial response to the incident. The researcher has to balance between using the spoken words of each participant and their underlying meaning.

The researcher also has to balance emerging patterns during data collection and the breakdown of the data. In this phase of the phenomenology reduction the focus is on breaking down individual responses but the researcher may be tempted to start making conclusions based on emerging patterns. The researcher must remain aware of both their own experiences documented in the epoche and the purpose of this breakdown so that they can remain focused on the individual experiences. When subjectively

Table 2. Phenomenological Breakdown Example 2

Initial Response	P001 I1	P001 I2	P002 I1	P002 I2	P002 I3	P003 I1	P003 I2
Primacy focus: Resuming operations		X					
Primary focus: Establish scope, size, and impact	X			X	X		X
Primary focus: The attacker						X	
Primary focus: containment			X				
Interviews				X	X		
Review logs	X		X	X	X	X	
Conduct scans	X			X	X		
Notification: Law enforcement	X	X		X			
Notification: CIO	X					X	
Notification: Third party partners	X						X
Notification: Lawyers					X	X	

classifying and marking each identifier it is possible to force dissimilar responses together for the sake of easy comparisons or unintentional bias. These are important considerations to remember when data sets start to grow larger.

STEP FOUR: PHENOMENOLOGICAL REDUCTION RECONSTRUCTION

After breaking down the narratives these data elements are then reconsidered. The breakdown phase is focused on the individual whereas the reconstruction phase focuses on all of the experiences discussed during data collection. Reconstruction is the process of examining each individual experience in relation to the whole (Van Manen, 2014). A holistic review means that all of the data elements are compared with, and put into context against, all of the experiences recorded. This shift in perspective builds upon the breakdown performed in the first step of the phenomenological reduction. Common elements are noted and highlighted in each individual experience in the breakdown and then analyzed in relation to all the experiences during the reconstruction in order to identify themes. The researcher can then synthesize the identifiers together in order to reveal a structure that clarifies the phenomenon. This two-step phenomenological reduction promotes a deeper understanding of the experiences of each individual as well as the experiences of all participants.

The breakdown, as followed in the provided examples, ends with a chart detailing the identifiers related by each participant for each individual incident. When considering each element as part of a whole it may be necessary to review outliers and consolidate identifiers. Once these links have been forged, the researcher, following a suggestion from Van Manen (2014), returns to the raw data to look for variations. For instance, one of the categories listed in the example is lost and stolen devices. These two categories are very similar in that they both result in a missing device which may be an information security incident depending on the definitions used by participants. Since they each have the same result these two categories can be combined to make one category without changing the nature of the results.

The recombination of data into similar identifiers is subjective. As always it is important to remain aware of bias to prevent the researcher from improperly modifying datasets in order to fit potential conclusions.

A good rule to follow when considering consolidating identifiers is to consider if removing outliers or combining categories will change the nature of the information. If the answer is yes then it is probably not appropriate to consolidate or remove data from the findings. However, if changing the data does not modify the meaning of the finding or serves to clarify results than it may be an appropriate change to make to the data. For example, data may be collected by ten different participants that each experienced the same incident. However, one of the ten says the incident happened three days prior to the other nine participants. When reviewing this fact in relation to the others it may be appropriate to use the time related by the other nine participants. Yet if that one participant was involved three days prior to everyone else it might have been for good reason rather than a flaw in their memories. These types of decisions need to be made by the researcher when considering all of the data together.

One simple way to reconstruct the data is to total the number of times identifiers were referenced during participant interviews. Table 2-1 shows identifiers, totals, and averages from Burkhead's research study (2014). The totals are simply the total number of times the identifier was referenced and the average is the percentage of times the identifier was referenced in relation to all incidents reported during interviews. While constructing these totals and averages in relation to all incidents patterns may become visible. These patterns will be considered in the next step in order to determine the essences of the phenomenon.

However, some data may not be so easy to consolidate. As previously mentioned there may instances of major discrepancies between accounts of the same incident in relation to the timeline. While recording the type of incident is straightforward, recounting other aspects may be more difficult and abstract. For example the year an incident took place is not something that can be averaged between all incidents. However, the year an incident took place can be averaged between the types of incidents to determine the number of incidents in a year or the number of incident types in a year. It is up to each research to look into the data and see the obvious as well as the abstract relationships that tie each individual component together in relation to the whole in order to complete the phenomenological breakdown.

STEP FIVE: THE SEARCH FOR ESSENCES

What does all this information actually mean? The penultimate step of this research process is termed the search for essences. The search for essences is designed to synthesize meaningful units and themes gathered during the phenomenological reduction and then them into understanding that is unaffected by the researcher's perspectives (Giorgi, 2009). The synthesis of data may lead to various essences such as the average number of information security incidents per year or the most common procedures followed when identifying a potential information security incident. It is in this manner the supporting reconstructed data is linked to essences. These newly discovered essences identify the common themes and actions taken by IT security professionals in information security incidents. These various iterative reviews of the data, the breakdown, reconstruction, and developing essences, lead the researcher to logical conclusions based on the real-world data.

The search for essences starts upon the conclusion of the phenomenology reduction step. The researcher, once the data has been deconstructed and reconstructed, will map the themes in ways that lead to the greatest synthesis of the information provided from the interviews. In many cases this may be a straightforward process of reviewing the totals and averages in order to determine the most common approach and then use that information to make purposeful statements that define elements of the phenomenon. These relationships between themes and elements lead to the discovery of the essences related to the phenomenon.

The identifiers that are documented throughout the phenomenological breakdown are not the essences. Table 3-1 shows the identifiers for data related to after an incident is closed. This raw data still needs further analysis. In the context of this example these results would indicate that after an investigation is closed most organization do not conduct any follow up activities; but, those that do follow-up activities they include updating or create incident response procedures. Other data may indicate that few of the participants had formal plans and procedures prior to a major information security incident. Together these elements create an essence which indicates the importance of having a plan based on the lived experiences of the participants. Identifying these themes allows the researcher to address the topic of the investigation.

There may be any number of essences discovered during this phase. In the research conducted by Burkhead (2014) she documented 10 themes that each addressed elements of information security incidents and their management. These themes are independent of each other and alone do not indicate much about information security incidents. They are simply statements based on the lived experiences of the participants. In the next phase these statements are given meaning and context by relating them back to the purpose of the study.

Table 3. Phenomenological Breakdown Example

Identifier	Total	Average
Physical security	2	4.255319
Lost / stolen devices	5	10.6383
Law suit	5	10.6383
Electronic	47	100
Information security	44	93.61702
Privacy	9	19.14894
Was the incident internal or external to the host organization?	36 (Int)	76.59574
Breach method: Default username and password or simple vulnerability	6	12.76596
Breach method: phishing	6	12.76596
Breach method: Technical hacking or vulnerability exploit	16	34.04255
Breach method: Malware	16	34.04255
Breach method: Lost or stolen device	5	10.6383
Breach method: No encryption	4	8.510638
Breach method: Accidental disclosure / privacy	5	10.6383
Breach method: Not investigated	3	6.382979

Table 4. After Closure

After Closure	Total	Average
No additional investigation	26	55.31915
Discovered additional compromises	8	17.02128
Updated or created procedures	20	42.55319
Updated procedures: Trained help desk	6	12.76596
Updated technical controls	18	38.29787

STEP SIX: CONCLUSIONS

The final step in this phenomenology process is to draw the conclusions. Themes on their own make nice fact statements but provide very little in the way of answering any questions about the phenomenon. The purpose and the research question or questions should have been established at the start of the process. Now that the data has been individually reviewed and broken down, reconstructed in relation to the whole, and themes have been determined it is possible to finally match the themes against the stated purpose and any questions for the study. These answers are the conclusions.

The purpose of conducting these interviews is to accomplish some personal, research, or organizational goal. For example, one of the research questions proposed by Burkhead was, "What are the lived experiences of information security professionals in private organizations responding to information security incidents?" (2014, p. 8). This research question was answered by combining theme 1, which identified the processes used to identify the scope of incidents, theme 2, which was the flow of an incident response, and theme 3, which was the decision points reached in each incident, together to describe the common actions taken during an information security incident. The end result was a narrative description of how a typical information security incident is handled. This addressed the purpose of her study.

The results of a study can be used to fill gaps in organizational programs. Through identifying the essence of incident response, processes and procedures can be created to document and train staff on the appropriate responses. One of the conclusions reached by Burkhead (2014) stated that having a plan and training the plan was important to incident response. Through identifying the essence of incident response experiences, various lessoned learned can be applied to programs to make them better. The results can even be matched against other organizations to match up similarities and differences between programs and experiences. If this entire process is conducted multiple times results can be compared to previous years. There are many different gaps that this type of study can fill.

This chapter has been about learning how to conduct a phenomenological investigation within the context of IT security incident management. While conducting similar inquiries for organizations the purpose may be to create policy or procedures regarding incident response. That purpose becomes the research question being studied. The themes that are identified are given context by relating them to how the organization processes information security incidents. Through this analysis it is possible to gain the insight required to create or update policies and procedures on this subject. Thus by conducting this type of study a time of weakness can be made into a pillar of strength just as swords are tempered in fire.

CONCLUSION

In conclusion information security incidents will happen in modern society. In the first part of this chapter common terms and previous research on information security incidents was presented. Previous research has demonstrated this concept in action in relation to information security incidents. In the second part of this chapter the reader was provided with a framework for conducting similar research on information security incidents. There are six steps to transforming these moments of weakness into strength. By defining the purpose and questions for the research the project is given a scope. In step one the researcher identifies and puts aside personal thoughts and beliefs in order to focus on the pending collection and analysis. In step two the data is collected using the semi-structured interview guide provided. Then in steps three and four the data is broken down and reconstructed to complete the phenomenological reduction. This leads to essences and those essences are used to address the scope of the project with meaningful conclusions.

While this chapter has been framed within the context of learning how to conduct a phenomenological study into information security incidents, these same skills are transferable to any area of lived experiences. The lived experiences of people vary greatly and touch on all subjects. The true value of demonstrating how to review information security incidents is in learning the framework and phenomenological processes. Opportunities exist to use this same framework, with a different interview guide, to research anything from the experience of combat and military service to the experience of leadership in technology companies. It has been said that life is the best teacher and with these tools it is easy to learn not only from ones personal life experiences but the lives and experiences of everyone.

REFERENCES

Ahmad, A., Hadgkiss, J., & Ruighaver, A. (2012). Incident response teams—Challenges in supporting the organizational security function. *Computers & Security*, *31*(5), 643–652. doi:10.1016/j.cose.2012.04.001

Ayyagari, R. (2012). An exploratory analysis of data breaches from 2005-2011: Trends and insights. *Journal of Information Privacy & Security*, *8*(2), 33–56. doi:10.1080/15536548.2012.10845654

Bowles, M. (2012). The business of hacking and birth of an industry. *Bell Labs Technical Journal*, *17*(3), 5–16. doi:10.1002/bltj.21555

Brenner, S. W. (2004). U.S. cyber-crime law: Defining offenses. *Information Systems Frontiers*, *6*(2), 115–132. doi:10.1023/B:ISFI.0000025780.94350.79

Burkhead, R. L. (2014). *A phenomenological study of information security incidents experienced by information security professionals providing corporate information security incident management* (Doctoral dissertation). Retrieved from ProQuest Dissertations and Theses database. (UMI No. 3682325)

Butts, J., Rice, M., & Shenoi, S. (2012). An adversarial model for expressing attacks on control protocols. *Journal of Defense Modeling and Simulation: Applications, Methodology. Technology (Elmsford, N.Y.)*, *9*(3), 243–255.

Chan, A. K., Hyung, W. P., & Hoon, D. L. (2013). A study on the live forensic techniques for anomaly detection in user terminals. *International Journal of Security & its Applications, 7*(1), 181-188.

Chu, H., Deng, D., & Chao, H. (2011). An ontology-driven model for digital forensics investigations of computer incidents under the ubiquitous computing environments. *Wireless Personal Communications*, *56*(1), 5–19. doi:10.1007/s11277-009-9886-x

Creswell, J. W. (2012). *Qualitative inquiry and research design: Choosing among five approaches*. Los Angeles, CA: SAGE.

Drtil, J. (2013). Impact of information security incidents: Theory and reality. *Journal of Systems Integration*, *4*(1), 44–52.

Fenz, S., Ekelhart, A., & Neubauer, T. (2011). Information security risk management: In which security solutions is it worth investing? *Communications of the AIS*, *28*, 329–356.

Filshtinskiy, S. (2013). Cyber-crime, cyberweapons, cyber-wars: Is there too much of it in the air? *Communications of the ACM*, *56*(6), 28–30. doi:10.1145/2461256.2461266

Geers, K. (2010). Live fire exercise: Preparing for cyber war. *Journal of Homeland Security and Emergency Management*, *7*(1), 1–16. doi:10.2202/1547-7355.1780

Giorgi, A. P. (2009). *The descriptive phenomenological method in psychology: A modified Husserlian approach*. Pittsburgh, PA: Duquesne University Press.

Halfond, W. J., Choudhary, S., & Orso, A. (2011). Improving penetration testing through static and dynamic analysis. *Software Testing: Verification & Reliability*, *21*(3), 195–214.

Heuer, R. J. Jr. (1999). *Psychology of intelligence analysis*. Langley Falls, VA: Central Intelligence Agency.

Hoppe, M. (2011). *Active listening*. Hoboken, NJ: Pfeiffer.

Hua, J., & Bapna, S. (2013). Who can we trust? The economic impact of insider threats. *Journal of Global Information Technology Management*, *16*(4), 47–67. doi:10.1080/1097198X.2013.10845648

Kadlec, C., & Shropshire, J. (2010). Best practices in IT disaster recovery planning among US banks. *Journal of Internet Banking & Commerce*, *15*(1), 1–11.

Lanter, A. (2011). Are you ready? Getting back to business after a disaster. *Information Management Journal*, *45*(6), 4.

Pieters, W. (2011). The (social) construction of information security. *The Information Society*, *27*(5), 326–335. doi:10.1080/01972243.2011.607038

Rajakumar, M., & Shanthi, V. (2014). Security breach in trading system countermeasure using IPTraceback. *American Journal of Applied Sciences*, *11*(3), 492–498. doi:10.3844/ajassp.2014.492.498

Schuesster, J. H. (2013). Contemporary threats and countermeasures. *Journal of Information Privacy & Security*, *9*(2), 3–20. doi:10.1080/15536548.2013.10845676

Tammineedi, L. (2010). Business continuity management: A standards-based approach. *Information Security Journal: A Global Perspective, 1,* 36-49.

Thomas, M., & Dhillon, G. (2012). Interpreting deep structures of information systems security. *The Computer Journal*, *55*(10), 1148–1156. doi:10.1093/comjnl/bxr118

Tohidi, H. (2011). The role of risk management in IT systems of organizations. *Procedia Computer Science, 3*, 881–887. doi:10.1016/j.procs.2010.12.144

Van Manen, M. (2014). *Phenomenology of practice*. Walnut Creek, CA: Left Coast Press.

Verizon. (2013). *2013 data breach investigations report*. Basking Ridge, NJ: Author.

Vorobiev, A., & Bekmamedova, N. (2010). An ontology-driven approach applied to information security. *Journal of Research & Practice in Information Technology, 42*(1), 61–76.

Vuorinen, J., & Tetri, P. (2012). The order machine: The ontology of information security. *Journal of the Association for Information Systems, 13*(9), 695–713.

Walker, J. L. (2012). The use of saturation in qualitative research. *Canadian Journal of Cardiovascular Nursing, 22*(2), 37–41. PMID:22803288

Werlinger, R., Muldner, K., Hawkey, K., & Beznosov, K. (2010). Preparation, detection, and analysis: The diagnostic work of IT security incident response. *Information Management & Computer Security, 18*(1), 26–42. doi:10.1108/09685221011035241

KEY TERMS AND DEFINITIONS

Asset: There are many different targets that attackers may select during an information security incident. An asset can be a technology system or application, digital information, or the people associated with these elements (Pieters, 2011; Vuorinen & Tetri, 2012). All of these assets can be targeted and should be protected from attack.

Cyber Crime: Cyber crime is one potential classification of an information security incident. An information security incident is termed cyber crime when it is a combination of illegal actions such as those defined in Section 18 of the United States Code, part 1030, but the effects are less than the threshold of cyber war (Brenner, 2004). This definition encompasses a wide range of potential information security incidents.

Defensive Information Security: Defending information covers a wide area of preventive and reactive tasks that contribute to the security of information and systems. Defensive information security consists of the preventive management of risk as well as the reactive management of information security incidents (Fenz, Ekelhart, & Neubauer, 2011; Kadlec & Shropshire, 2010; Rajakumar & Shanthi, 2014; Schuesster, 2013; Tohidi, 2011; Werlinger et al., 2010). These defensive processes and procedures each cover a wide variety of tasks directly related to the security of information and systems.

Information Security: The field of information security contains many important elements that influence information security incident management. Information security is the identification of technology assets and targets, the processes of defending or attacking those technology assets and targets, and the social constructs influencing attackers and defenders (Pieters, 2011; Thomas & Dhillon, 2012; Vorobiev & Bekmamedova, 2010; Vuorinen & Tetri, 2012). These elements inform all aspects of information security as a common ontological framework.

Information Security Incident: Information security incidents come in many forms. An incident, an event that adversely affects technology systems or services, must relate to the elements of information security, including the identification of assets, processes for attack and defense, and human attackers and defenders, in order to be considered an information security incident (Ayyagari, 2012; Burkhead, 2014; Drtil, 2013). Incidents that meet these criteria can be termed information security incidents.

Information Security Incident Management: The management of information security incidents is the primary phenomenon under investigation. Information security incident management is identifying technology, processes, and people responsible for attacks and infiltrations against assets to violate the confidentiality, integrity, or availability of the asset and using that information to diagnose, contain, and recover from incidents (Burkhead, 2014; Kadlec & Shropshire, 2010; Rajakumar & Shanthi, 2014; Werlinger et al., 2010). The management of these incidents occurs at the intersection of offensive and defensive information security concepts.

Offensive Information Security: Offensive information security is just as broad as defensive information security. Offensive information security is the identification of targets, the processes of attacking those targets, and the social constructs influencing attackers (Bowles, 2012; Chan, Hyung, & Hoon, 2013; Geers, 2010). These elements are not well established but have an impact on information security incident management.

Perception: Perception and identification are important concepts in the decision-making process for information security incident management. Heuer (1999) described a process of intelligence analysis in which the analyst, through self-awareness, removes his or her worldviews and biases from the assessment of situations. The perception and identification of information security incidents leads to subsequent actions. The perception and identification of events is a central concept of this the phenomenological framework.

Phenomenology: Phenomenology is the qualitative research method presented in this chapter. Phenomenology is a research process that is focused on the unique lived experiences of participants using creative methods and processes to collect and analyze data (Van Manen, 2014; Gigori, 2009). Phenomenology in relation to the work presented in this chapter is a multipart process that starts with an epoche in order to identify and be aware of bias and includes the phenomenological reduction in which data is broken down and then reconstructed in order to answer the scope of the project with the discovered conclusions.

Risk Management: Risk management covers the implementation of information security in practice. Risk management is how information security is performed in modern organizations through the analysis and evaluation of vulnerabilities against threats to determine risk and the mitigation of that risk based on organizational priorities (Fenz et al., 2011; Schuesster, 2013; Tohidi, 2011). This is primarily a preventive framework designed to prevent information security incidents from occurring in secure networks.

Source and Intent: Identifying the source and intent of an information security incident may provide valuable information for the management of the information security incident. The source and intent of an information security incident is any combination of internal or external actors with purposeful or accidental intentions be they malicious or benign (Halfond, Choudhary, & Orso, 2011; Hua & Bapna, 2013). These two factors impact incident response in unique ways as each potential attacker and intention changes the course of investigations.

Section 2
Education

Chapter 7
Critical Thinking and Digital Technologies:
An Outcome Evaluation

Şahin Gökçearslan
Gazi University, Turkey

Ebru Solmaz
Gazi University, Turkey

Burcu Karabulut Coşkun
Gazi University, Turkey

ABSTRACT

The aim of this study is to identify the new trends on technology use in developing critical thinking skills. By this purpose, the researches published between 2008-2014 in Science Direct database were examined by using content analysis. Also study was completed in three main parts. The first part consists of the conceptual framework about, technology use in education, critical thinking, the effect of technology on critical thinking and new technologies used to develop critical thinking skills. In the second part the content analysis method was used to examine the researches published in Science Direct database. In the final part, the conclusion and recommendations were given about the research and future studies.

INTRODUCTION[1]

Today, critical thinking has an important place in the educational process. Analysis, self-regulation, making comments, identifying assumptions, giving explanations, and using evaluation are the main constituents of critical thinking. In the 21st century, technology has assumed a significant role in the critical thinking skills of students and teachers. A sharp increase has been observed in the use of IT, which enhances critical thinking and changes how it is used. Within the curriculum, critical thinking has been stated to include several sub-skills such as finding cause-and-effect relationships, getting similari-

DOI: 10.4018/978-1-5225-0522-8.ch007

ties and differences in details by using various criteria, assessing the acceptability and validity of the information provided, analyzing, evaluating, interpreting and making inference (MEB, 2005).

Technology changes how we think, gather and produce information. In particular, the Internet changes our life and ways of thinking. In a comparable study on the basic understanding of materials given to a class with and without Internet access, students were given access to the Internet within the class and encouraged to use the same in their studies to understand the material better compared to the students without Internet access. However, this research also shows that students who accessed the Internet during classes failed to process what the lecturer said. Test scores on the lecture showed that students without internet access performed better than students with internet access (Wolpert, 2009). The inclusion of real-time media like TVs and video games thus reduces the time that is allocated for critical thinking and contemplation (Wolpert, 2009). Yet sites such as Nings, wikis, blogs and discussion boards facilitate thinking and help students' present new ideas and contribute to discussions during the learning process (Thompson & Crompton, 2010).

As described by Glaser (1942, p.6) and by Fisher (2001), critical thinking is generally seen as the need to be able to recognize problems, to find workable means for solving those problems, to gather and marshal pertinent information, to recognize unstated assumptions and values, to comprehend and use language with accuracy, clarity, and discrimination, to interpret data, to appraise evidence and evaluate arguments, to recognize the existence (or non-existence) of logical relationships between propositions, to draw accurate conclusions and generalizations, to test these conclusions and the generalizations at which one arrives, to reconstruct one's patterns of beliefs on the basis of wider experience, and to render accurate judgments about specific things and qualities in everyday life.

In this study, following a presentation of a general framework for and about the use of technology in education, some aspects of critical thinking and its relationship to technology are addressed. Online discussion, web 2.0 tools, virtual learning environments, social networks, simulations, robotics and digital stories which provide an opportunity for learning, and most of which can be defined as new technologies, are explained. Moreover, a sub-framework including an assessment about the place of these technologies in critical thinking is presented. The main objective of this study is to assess the content, methodology and general outlook of studies into the relationship between critical thinking and technology that were published within a frequently used database between 2008 and 2014.

BACKGROUND

Technology Use in Education

The word 'technology' is a combination of the Ancient Greek words, "tekhne", meaning ability, and "logos", meaning science (Murphie & Potts, 2003). In defining technology, various opinions have been advanced. The current meanings of technology emerged in the modern age and started to be used in the second half of the 19th century. Kline (1985) defines technology as a term representing objects, actions, processes, methods and systems while the International Technology Education Association (ITEA) (2007) defines it as changing, renovating and transforming the natural environment to meet perceived human needs and requests. Demirel (2003) defines technology as using definite information in compliance with specific purposes. In general, technology is defined as a discipline formed with a combination of various items for a specific purpose in a particular pattern and functioning as a bridge between science and application thereof (Kosar, Yuksel, Ozkilic, Avci, Alyaz & Cigdem, 2003). There is no doubt that the community is the primary location influenced directly by technology. Individuals have started to take advantage of technological opportunities to create solutions suitable for their own needs (Reigeluth, 1991). In parallel to these improvements, education is required for individuals to benefit from the opportunities this environment gives and to gain the necessary information and skills (Alkan, 1997). In other words, the desire of individuals to learn about technology also causes the need for "teaching" to meet this changing situation.

Today, rapid developments in science and technology affect education as well as socio-economic structures. D'Ignazio (1993) likens technological developments in education to building electronic highways, and states that all aspects of society are now driven through these developing highways. From this perspective, technological developments have been the most important element for economic and social developments in knowledge-based society (Usun, 2003). The society that arises has been given various names based on the process of production and distribution of information. Some of these are "information society", "knowledge-based society", "informatics society" and "network society" (Castells, 2011). In knowledge-based societies, institutions go through a rapid transformation process in parallel to technological changes; the expectations placed on an educational institution also vary according to the changing needs (Çelik, 2000). In modern communities, there is a need for individuals who have lifelong learning skills, continuously refresh their knowledge, adapt themselves to change, and who can successfully manage and produce information. What is expected from educational institutions with the responsibility to educate qualified individuals is to produce individuals who are equipped with knowledge and abilities, use technology and have learned about the learning process itself (Akkoyunlu & Kurbanoğlu, 2003).

According to studies of students' motivation, it has also been found that the appropriate use of technology in education significantly increases students' academic achievements as well as their self-confidence, motivation and attendance in class (Balanskat, Blamire & Kefala, 2006; Uluyol, 2011). In schools where technology is used actively, it has been determined that students' motivation and academic achievements increase, the rate of truancy is reduced, and their attitudes towards learning become more positive because the course contents are enriched (Donmuş & Gürol, 2014). In another example, the use of technological tools during courses enabled students to participate more actively in classes (Sakız, Özden, Aksu & Şimşek, 2015). In another study, it has been revealed that the efficient use of technology in educational environments improves students' study skills, ability to implement what is learned to real-life situations, organizational skills, interest in the class and academic achievement, and enables them to gain critical thinking and problem-solving skills (Kırıkkaya, Bozkurt & İşeri, 2013).

According to the studies on general knowledge, skills and employment, the use of technology in education positively affects students' professional life after education (Cradler, McNabb, Freeman, & Burchett, 2002; Bimrose et al., 2014). The positive role of technology in women's employment has been specifically discussed (Webster, 2014). It is stated that in the end of the process of education, students attain higher individual achievements in their academic and professional lives due to qualified education served by technology. In addition they gain the ability that is appropriate for collaborative working principle (Cradler, McNabb, Freeman & Burchett, 2002; OECD, 2005). The contribution of technology during education in training the individuals to become part of a qualified labor force within society is enormous. Gaining the knowledge and ability to use technical tools (office programs, computer-aided drawing programs, Internet tools, website development programs, social network applications, etc.) provides individuals with an important advantage for their employment.

Given these findings, it is impossible not to use technology in education. It is clear that technology that facilitates daily life is essential for individuals. Technologies already used in many fields are frequently preferred due to their convenience for students, teachers and other factors in the learning environment (Baş, 2010; Watson & Tinsley, 2013). Furthermore, there are many studies about promoting the development of 21st century skills using technological tools. Today, the idea of '21st century learning' calls to mind specific skills such as problem-solving, critical thinking, and cooperation. The use of technological tools makes easier to learn these 21st century skills in the learning process. The following section explains what is meant by one of these skills, 'critical thinking', in a detailed way and discusses the relationship between learning and using this ability and technology.

CRITICAL THINKING

The word 'criticism' is used to indicate a judgment, discrimination and an assessment of general meaning. In other words, it can be described as evaluating a topic or commenting on a subject. There are many definitions for critical thinking. However, it is generally defined as the ability to comment on/about and evaluate things (Edward & Paul, 2014).

Critical thinking is a way of thinking in which a person combines, analyzes and evaluates information (Johnson, 2000). Insufficiency of merely formal education to attain increasingly enhancing fund of knowledge has arisen in individuals the necessity of attaining information on their own coping with problems on their own. The need for the ability to think critically to meet these latter demands has provoked a greater discussion of the concept. Critical thinking is composed of various elements and rules and is required to develop new ideas or different perspectives. When we analyze these features, Glaser (1985) suggests that critical thinking consists of three factors:

1. To tackle problems in a foresighted and thinking based way
2. To have information about methods of reasoning and to be able to query by reasoning
3. To have the ability to apply these methods in their daily life.

According to Demirel (1999), there are 5 rules of critical thinking:

1. Consistency: Contradictions in thoughts should be eliminated in the process of thinking critically.
2. Combination: Someone thinking critically should examine all dimensions of thinking and make connections between them.
3. Applicability: The person should combine his/her thoughts with what he/she has learned and practice it on a model.
4. Sufficiency: Someone thinking critically should base his/her understanding of experiences and their effects on realistic foundations.
5. Communication: Someone thinking critically should communicate his/her thoughts clearly and efficiently.

In the global world of the 21st century, life skills like critical thinking, creative thinking, innovation, problem solving, cooperation, communication, co-decision making, knowledge sharing, urgency, information and communication technology literacy, productivity and adaptation, which are the necessities of today, take the place of previously expected knowledge and abilities (Nagel, 2014).

That is why, in a world subject global events and in which ever more widely disseminated technological developments exist, defining education only as a process of providing desired behaviors will be wrong. In this view, it is important to assess educational activities as a process of implementing many models, which is far from rote learning, coercive or pacifying factors, and which is developed by individuals fully using their own potentials (Yang & Wu, 2012). This process should deal with teaching students how to think, not what to think. At this point, the focus of the educational process should be the development of critical thinking with the support of today's technology.

CRITICAL THINKING AND TECHNOLOGY

Individuals of the 21st century, which has sometimes been called the Informatics Age, have undergone an extensive transformation in their learning styles and social relationships. Achievement in social life is now seen as consisting of far more than rote learning. Instead, it involves cooperation and sharing, using knowledge in solving complex problems, adapting easily to new conditions, creating solutions, and benefiting from developing technology in creating solutions and knowledge. That is why the knowledge, abilities and skills previously expected from individuals have changed. Critical thinking, creative thinking, innovation, problem solving, cooperation, communication, co-decision making, and creating knowledge, which are the necessities of the 21st century, have taken their place (PPRC, 2011).

Critical thinking is considered a tool to allow individuals to be responsible for learning, thinking, and other parts of their lives and to be fulfilled in those (Paul & Elder, 2002). This skill is also one of the most important factors in the process of practicing necessary skills for this century such as acquiring and using advanced technology, using technology according to needs, being creative, analyzing, managing, storing and transferring information (PPRC, 2011; Thomson, 2001).

In a report about education in the NETS-S (National Educational Technology Standards for Students) preschool – the K12 (primary and secondary education) period, published by ISTE (International Society for. Technology in Education) in 2009, it was determined that students need to be able to use appropriate educational technologies for obtaining, evaluating knowledge; for developing new products; for making conscious decisions; for supporting their individual learning and for helping others to learn (ISTE, 2009). According to various studies about technology's effect on the ability to think critically: Students doing research on the Internet increase their self-confidence in communication and develop their critical thinking abilities (Arat, 2011). The most important reason for the web-based environments' contribution to the students' motivation is that today students are more familiar with computer culture (Owston, 1997). Therefore, this wide information network enables students to use critical thinking skills such as analysis, synthesis and evaluation (Uluyol, 2011).

It has been shown, as an example of the application of the internet, that when the teacher combines the use of web folio and traditional note-making, web folios enable students to gain critical thinking skills and provide them with a safe, permanent and an easily accessible tool as well as a physical environment (Aktay, 2011). In another example, it was found that computer programming training provided to seventh grade students positively affected their critical thinking skills. Furthermore, it has been stated that there is no gender difference in the critical thinking skills of students taking computer programming training (Coşar, 2013).

According to these studies, it has been concluded that developing technologies can support critical thinking skills by supporting individual learning activities, providing the opportunity for cooperative study, increasing motivation, enabling students to share and research easily, and by being not affected by physical working conditions. Some of the current technologies which are said to affect critical thinking skills are examined thoroughly below.

NEW TECHNOLOGIES USED IN EDUCATION FOR DEVELOPING CRITICAL THINKING

The following describes the new technologies which differentiate current forms of interaction and communication in learning environments from traditional class environments. The potential effect of these technologies on critical thinking is also evaluated.

ONLINE DISCUSSION

Discussion forums, one of the most popular technologies used in online education, are cooperative learning environments where people share their ideas with each other or with other groups (MacKnight, 2000). This technology was first used by academics to promote discussion and cooperation when the Internet was first developed. These tools, that enable learners to discuss issues in an open environment, provide an opportunity for online learning communities and learners to interact with other learners or teachers any time academically and socially (Corrich, Kinshuk & Hunt, 2004). In other words, these environments focus on students' understanding and how to interact with other people or ideas meaningfully (MacKnight, 2000). Moreover, conversations and discussions can be stored as the forum is web-based (Cheong & Cheung, 2008), and can be accessed by users everywhere and at any time.

Online discussions thus continue to support the learning environment both immediately and over an extended period of time. As a result of more people being online at the same time, synchronous discussion forums are spreading more and more, as mobile devices increasingly dominate our lives. Both synchronous and asynchronous discussions have different educational potentials, and they are very useful for students and teachers. Bach, Haynes and Smith (2006) state that online discussion relieves reluctant, shy and quiet students in oral class discussions. However, Cheong and Cheung (2008) indicate that these environments can decrease the shyness that students have with regard to face-to-face discussions as they are web-based, and that they also provide students more time to think and express themselves more clearly before answering. Markel (2001) suggests that courses with online discussions maximize learning and develop students' involvement. According to MacKnight (2000), this technology provides an opportunity to closely monitor student's learning and critical thinking skills through cooperation, reflection, discussion, peer tutoring, and it increases participation and cooperation in the learning process.

Bender (2012), supporting MacKnight's opinions (2001), states that online discussions provide open and broad opportunities for students to participate and cooperate actively. These environments create a cooperative learning environment by giving students the opportunity to communicate with other students and enable student-student interaction, which is an important part of online education (Hoffman, 2010). Gokhale (1995) states that the active exchange of ideas between small groups promotes critical thinking in cooperative learning. That is why online discussions can be used effectively to teach critical thinking and can provide a high level of understanding (Cheong & Cheung, 2008). MacKnight (2000) asserts that critical thinking is available in many online discussion groups, providing the opportunity for students to practice and participate. Furthermore, McLoughlin and Mynard (2009) argue that online discussion forums have the potential to support high level thinking processes. Environments in which elements such as the subject, relevant examples, and guidance are arranged carefully can give opportunities to the students to develop high-level thinking. In these studies, high level thinking and critical thinking are seen as synonymous. In conclusion, it can be clearly seen that online discussion forums promote critical thinking because they provide opportunities for active participation, cooperation and interaction.

WEB 2.0 TOOLS

From the invention of Internet to the late 90s, web applications consisted of static HTML codes, providing only information, and in which users were passive. Users obtained information from websites developed by others and technical skills (HTML codes) were required to create a website. When these applications, generally called Web 1.0, which were the first generation of the concept of the 'www' (world wide web) did not meet user needs, dynamic web applications, where users create and share content and engage in content-person interaction were developed in the 2000s.

These applications, generally called Web 2.0 tools, and comprising technologies such as the blog, wiki, podcast and social networks, provide more interactive and cooperative environments. McLoughlin and Lee (2007) define Web 2.0 as a communicative form of 'www', which underlines the sharing of ideas and information, participation and connectivity. While Web 1.0 enables the user to find and read information, Web 2.0 focuses on the development of material, online cooperation and knowledge sharing on the web, and this can be done without a high level know-how (Solomon & Schrum, 2011; Crane, 2012; Marcovitz, 2012). In the light of this information, it could be suggested that Web 2.0 reduces cost, provides flexibility and easy and fast access to information, and enables easy use without know-how, and saves time (Grosseck, 2009).

Web 2.0 tools provide interesting teaching and learning opportunities in terms of education. Educators can use these technologies to enhance and support teaching. The use of Web 2.0 technologies provides opportunities for information sharing and cooperation for learners and their learning activity (Ajjan & Hartshorne, 2008). Web 2.0 tools create an environment for educators to post their articles, videos, podcasts, wikis and presentations without any knowledge of programming skills. From these tools, educators can obtain new ideas by communicating with other educators. Students also can create online content, cooperate with other students around the world and display their studies to the whole world in these environments. Web 2.0 tools provide real learning experience for students and support the elements of communication, cooperation, critical thinking, creativity and the production of content required for 21st century learning (Crane, 2012). Students can learn how to acquire cooperation, communication and creativity skills with these tools, while they still usually need to focus on traditional skills in schools (Solomon & Schrum, 2011). For example, creating a personal blog, posting articles, preparing videos and sharing them through social media, asking questions related to the topic of their interest to experts in these topics while using these environments can help learners to develop their skills. The information received by students who use Web 2.0 technologies increases necessary communication and information literacy skills (Crane, 2012). Furthermore, Maloney (2007) states that Web 2.0 applications help course planners to focus on learners' needs. Anyone can create, combine, organize and share content using

Web 2.0 technologies to meet their own or others' needs (McLoughlin & Lee, 2007). Web 2.0 tools are easy to use, address a large audience and facilitate cooperation. By using these tools, learner-focused applications and learner-centered teaching activity to promote a constructivist approach can also be designed (Marcovitz, 2012).

A review of the literature shows that there are various studies discussing both Web 2.0 technologies and critical thinking (Mendenhall & Johnson, 2010). Among these technologies, blogs are said to provide the opportunity for commenting on and recognizing different opinions (Ocak, Gökçearslan, & Solmaz, 2014); wikis help project-based learning, group study, brainstorming, group portfolio presentation (Cole, 2009; Gokcearslan & Ozcan, 2011; Yukawa, 2006); podcasts increase student participation (Armstrong, Tucker & Massad, 2009). All these technologies are thus said to provide a serious potential for critical thinking. This potential can be actualized by using the Web 2.0's features of combination, communication and interaction of videos, images, audios and other media it allows, if the teaching process is designed and planned accordingly.

VIRTUAL LEARNING ENVIRONMENTS

Virtual learning environments are a Web 2.0 technology which can be evaluated as a new way of learning and teaching (Solomon & Schrum, 2011). Meadows (2008) defined virtual environments as online interactive systems where many people, sometimes millions of them, join to develop an interactive narrative. A virtual environment provides a series of experiences in a technological environment giving a user a strong feeling of being in the environment (Warburton, 2009). These environments are seen as richer, more creative and more impressive than other tools used during learning process, even other Web 2.0 tools by people (Solomon & Schrum, 2011).

The most well-known and popular virtual learning environment is Second Life (Warburton, 2009; Solomon & Schrum, 2011). Second Life is an Internet-based three-dimensional world created by users, and is used for various purposes involving social interaction. A person can join this environment by creating an avatar or a character. In this virtual world, the users can do many things they do in real life such as meeting people, joining groups, socializing, taking college education, buying consumer products, vehicles or houses. Some activities have to be paid for, but joining is free.

In terms of education, it is seen that virtual learning environments are used for different purposes. These environments that are easy for both learners and educators to explore, and can be used for the online distribution of course materials (O'Leary & Ramsden, 2002; Resta & Laferrière, 2007). Virtual learning environments can facilitate the access to learning materials and resources for students in or outside the campus, and provide flexible support for freelance educators (anytime and anywhere) to communicate with students and support them. Teachers can also benefit from these environments for their professional development and for communicating, cooperating and sharing information with colleagues and experts (Solomon & Schrum, 2011).

Virtual learning environments are thus of interest to the educational sector (Warburton, 2009) and contain the potential for new ways of learning and teaching, such as active and independent learning consisting of online communication, online evaluation and cooperative learning (O'Leary & Ramsden, 2002). These environments provide groups and people with opportunities for creativity, cooperation and communication. Solomon and Schrum (2011) state that multi-user virtual learning environments are designed for students in order to promote learning and creative thinking. Virtual environments can be used to support online cooperation (Resta & Laferrière, 2007) and enable students and educators to develop multiple relations with each other (Piccoli, Ahmad & Ives, 2001). These environments help students build creative lives in which they can interact with other people and explore the world (Solomon & Schrum, 2011). A high level of student control dominates in such environments; they support the connection with, and interaction of, the participants during the learning process, and provide an opportunity to restructure the learning experience in a way that cannot be practiced through computer-aided education alone (Piccoli, Ahmad & Ives, 2001).

SOCIAL NETWORKS

Thanks to the existence of online communication and communities, it is possible to connect electronically with people to share interests, problems and opinions rather than having the necessity of being in the same place geographically to communicate (Solomon & Schrum, 2011). Social networks have radically changed ways of connecting, interacting and sharing information (Towner & Munoz, 2011). Social networks, one of the Web 2.0 tools, can be defined as websites which gather people together with purposes such as having a conversation, sharing ideas, activities and interests, and making new friends (Crane, 2012). These environments enable users to build connections through friend lists and links, build direct connections with other users or join online groups (Green & Hannon, 2007).

Social networks have been a part of the education process because they address many people and have millions of users. Social networks can focus on supporting the mutual relationships between students, and students and teachers, can be used for learning, professional development and content sharing (Blankenship, 2011; Crane, 2012). Educators benefit from these environments to share relevant topics, problems and ideas with their colleagues. Teachers can also use them for sharing information with families and students, sharing files and for other class activities such as course videos, notes, and podcasts. Students can ask questions and explain their problems related to their courses (Solomon & Schrum, 2011).

In the literature, there is only a limited number of studies examining the effect of social media on critical thinking. According to the study by Saadé, Morin & Thomas (2012), online learning environments promote critical thinking, and in these environments critical thinking results from mutual interaction between the elements of content, interactivity and design (pedagogy and system) (Saadé, Morin & Thomas, 2012). Social networks can also be used as online learning environments, thereby offering the opportunity for critical thinking. According to another researcher, the key to using social media is the ability to evaluate the reliability of the information source without considering the real content (Pattison, 2012). Although it is important to practice this activity in traditional environments using traditional learning materials such as books, it is absolutely essential in social media environments. This is because information in social media environments does not go through the same process of validity-checking that official printed documents usually do. The skill of evaluating reliability/validity obviously requires critical thinking (Pattison, 2012).

SIMULATIONS

Simulations are one of the popular current learning methods using technology. They are software programs that transpose real life situations onto a virtual platform. A simulation is a presentation of real life events and actions in a simulated world (Laudrillard, 2013). Such platforms are used to allow learners, before they perform any specific skill in real life, to observe and experience factual events and situations.

Hence, simulations provide for the observation, testing and performance of situations, events and facts which are expensive, unsafe, time-consuming and not possible – or very rarely possible – to observe or perform in real life in a safe and an inexpensive way, and in a short span of time. For instance, experiencing the kind of systems failures and issues that may occur while aviating a real flight is unsafe; it is also impossible, in reality, to experience all the potential problems that may occur on a plane. In the field of genetics, it can also take time to observe effects and results in the real world. However, with a simulation, it is possible to immediately observe the results of an experiment that takes months in reality. Similarly, in medical science in general, it is not possible for prospective doctors encounter every disease or disorder during their actual training. With the simulations used during training, medical students can encounter many more patients and gain experience about various diseases including rare diseases. In simulations, a user encounters, within a specific scenario, similar situations to those that occur in real life. He/she analyzes them and then makes decisions. The platform changes according to users' decisions and there arise new situations that require new decisions to be made (Lockard & Abrams, 2003). The key to an effective simulation includes feeling that one is participating in real life activities and a high level of personal interaction (Lamb & Johnson, 2006).

Edwards (2012) indicates that simulations are effective tools to support teaching and learning. These platforms are one of the most flexible tools and can be used at all stages of training. They can be used to present a new topic during training, reinforce or revise topics being taught, and to evaluate students' performance. Simulations are platforms that can easily be adapted to different teaching approaches. These platforms can be designed in accordance with cognitive and constructivist approaches. Moreover, it is possible to design simulations that focus on behavioral objectives, problem solving, direct teaching, exploratory and experimental learning or individualized, cooperative and competitive learning. It is also possible to design platforms which include all these dimensions (Alessi & Trollip, 2001). In addition, simulations can also be used in teaching problem solving skills and role-playing (Barron & Orwig, 1997).

Given these properties of simulations, they are more interesting and motivating than many other technologies. A form of education or training which allows for students' active participation, rather than one in which the student is a passive observer, increases motivation. For instance, using a simulation of a plane is more interesting than a text-based course, which only teaches the theoretical aspect of how to fly. Simulations do not only attract attention, they also increase the transmission of information. For instance, while it is easier for a prospective teacher to apply what they have learned from simulations to reality, it will be harder for them to apply what they have learned solely from books (Alessi & Trollip, 2001).

Another contribution that simulations make is to concretize abstract concepts and make them visible, thus ensuring better reasoning and helping learners understand the topic at hand. Moreover, simulations allow learners to understand difficult concepts through experimentation. Variation of variables allows for the observation of the dynamic interactions between the components of a system (Wiske, Franz & Breit, 2010. Simulations also facilitate the development of creativity (Edwards, 2012). Moreover, as these platforms simulate real life activities, they are closer to the basic process of learning by doing and living (Alessi & Trollip, 2001). When the use of simulations in education is analyzed according to its significance critical thinking, it can be observed that these platforms are often currently used for teaching critical thinking in the field of health.

Research has recently been conducted in nursing education (Sullivan-Mann, Perron & Fellner, 2009; Cags, 2010; Fero, O'Donnell, Zullo, Dabbs, Kitutu, Samosky & Hoffman, 2010) on the effect of simulations on critical thinking. These studies have produced findings, which indicate that simulations develop critical thinking. It is obvious that a learner will deploy skills related to critical thinking, such as interpreting, judging, distinguishing, evaluating and making decisions to perform certain behaviors, in this context. These skills are needed in practical fields such as nursing education, medicine, teaching and law. Cady, Shea and Grenier (2011) thus indicate that in a virtual platform, cognitive presence encourages deep critical thinking processes.

ROBOTICS

Robots perform many functions such as, for example, searching the depths of oceans or seas and doing basic housework. Moreover, robot toys play with humans and follow their orders. Given their capacity for interaction, many children, as well as adults, are impressed with robots. Some consider robotic technology humorous.. This has brought an increase in the sales of robot toys and in robot production (Johnson, 2003; Ceceri, 2012). The science of designing, constructing, controlling and managing robots is called robotics (Ceceri, 2012). In the early 2000s, there has been an increasing interest in robotics and this technology has become more popular (Johnson, 2003). Given its popularity, robotics can also be considered a cost-effective (Alimisis & Kynigos, 2009) platform for learning

Educational robotics involves constructing small-scale robots, and programming and managing them with the help of computer programs, which should be written by the learners themselves (Denis & Hubert, 2001). Robotics is considered a developing field with a great potential in the teaching of technology, engineering and science at all levels from elementary school to graduate study (Mataric, 2004; Barker & Ansorge, 2007). Cheap robotics platforms are developing and being marketed; these can be accessed and used by anyone, without any knowledge in the fields of electrical, mechanical and computer engineering. This technology is used at the university level in various engineering courses, such as design courses in industrial engineering, microprocessor courses in electrical engineering, mechanical engineering dynamics and control courses, basic programming and artificial intelligence courses in computer science. Moreover, cheap robotic platforms are now being used in elementary, middle and high schools for teaching concepts related to the fields of computing, mechanics and electrical engineering and designing, and introducing technology to the students (Yu & Weinberg, 2003).

The reasons for using robots for educational purposes at all education levels are primarily that they attract students' attention and learners thus find them interesting and exciting. Robotics projects provide the opportunity to directly interact with technology, to design technology using the concepts appropriate for this science and apply them practically. This teaching and learning approach creates an active environment in which students can explore a certain design field, make hypotheses about how things work and produce experiments to justify newly-learned information and assumptions (Yu & Weinberg, 2003). Hence, this is considered an effective way to provide and promote education in many fields and motivate learners (children or adults) at every stage of the teaching and learning process (Johnson, 2003). Moreover, carrying out experiments with robots helps educators to effectively teach mathematical and scientific principles (Barker & Ansorge, 2007). Hence, students can easily learn abstract concepts and increase their levels of understanding (Nourbakhsh et al., 2005).

Constructing a robot requires students to integrate the systems of control, electronics and mechanics into a device which functions. In other words, constructing a robot and programming requires both the hardware and software skills that will ensure that these devices work (Beer, Chiel & Drushel, 1999).

Moreover, given that robotics focus on creating something new, learners are made to work together with their peers, teachers and experts to access the knowledge they need. Robotics thus provides a structure suitable for cooperative learning, project-based learning and team work (Denis & Huber, 2001). In this regard, robotics can improve the social skills of children and the process of constructing robots helps children develop skills of team work, problem solving, critical thinking and creative thinking (Johnson, 2003; Verner & Ahlgren, 2004; Goh & Aris, 2007). It also encourages them to use their powers of imagination and be innovative in design (Johnson, 2003). In addition, Ricca, Lulis and Bade (2006) indicate that platforms which include robotics can be appropriate for helping young students to develop critical thinking skills. This is because designing, constructing and programming robots require skills such as establishing relationships, and analyzing and interpreting data, which are the components of critical thinking. Beer, Chiel and Drushel (1999), whose study supports this view, also emphasize another dimension: Previous learning approaches used an environment in which students were passive listeners. Yet today, with the effect of constructivism, learning and teaching approaches have changed, and platforms which allow students' active participation help them learn by doing and thus to develop skills related to 21st century life. One of these platforms is robotics. Learning with robots is, accordingly, a tool which can aid the development of critical thinking as well as other skills.

DIGITAL STORIES

Storytelling, a natural component of culture and society, is an ancient art. Stories are an aspect of language use and are transmitted from human to human, society to society, and culture to culture using the tools available in a given period. Stories which were inscribed, painted or drawn on walls and then on stones in ancient times were ultimately written down and then printed on paper. Today, technological devices are increasingly used as a tool of transmission (Frazel, 2010). In other words, technology changes both the lives of people, and the nature of storytelling (Rossiter & Gartier, 2010). Digital storytelling can be defined as an art of storytelling, which uses multimedia components such as text, picture, digital graphic, voices and video (Robin, 2006). A digital story is a form of short story, which is displayed on television or computer screen as a short film (Davis, 2004).

Digital stories thus combine different media to contribute to the art of storytelling. In other words, digital storytelling is more than preparing simply a slide show (Drein, Kerper & Landis, 2011). In fact, creating a digital story requires a wide range of skills. The topic of story needs to be researched and developed as the story is created. A scenario and plot has to be written, and a file video, made up of a number of different media, has to be constructed and organized using a video organizing program and then transformed to an appropriate presentational format (Ohler, 2006).

Bringing together storytelling and technology has also attracted the interest of educators. The digital storytelling process allows students to be active participants in a society with an already intense media exposure rather than passive consumers (Ohler, 2006). Learners already use technologies needed for creating digital stories in their daily life. The active process of storytelling ensures that trainers and educators can meet the needs of different student groups, that learners are interested in and motivated by the issues presented, and that they thus develop their desire for learning (Frazel, 2010). Digital stories allow students to speak in their own language – that is, to express what they understand about topics in ways familiar to them (Ohler, 2013). This is because student's research, design, organize and present the story themselves. Accordingly, the media production process helps students develop the skills of critical thinking, problem solving, decision making, communication and cooperation, imagination, creativity, searching, planning and writing (Ohler, 2006; Frazel, 2010; Yang & Wu, 2012). Creating stories, presenting them, and sharing them with their peers also increases students' self-respect (Frazel, 2010) and self-confidence. Moreover, as creating a digital story requires the use of digital cameras and multimedia organizing programs, it provides great potential for innovative teaching and learning (Yang & Wu, 2012). The tools for creating and presenting multimedia such as PowerPoint, Movie Maker, iMovie, Illustrator promote cooperation, project management and learning by producing (Sadik, 2008). Moreover, digital stories are applicable to students at every level, and their content is applicable to every curriculum (Frazel, 2010).

With regard to critical thinking, multimedia presentations in digital storytelling allow learners to be engaged with many skills which require critical thinking (Jonassen, Myers & McKillop, 1996). Skills related to critical thinking include preparing a project's schedule, identifying any problems and organizing how to research and resolve them, data collection, data analysis, deciding how to present the data in order to capture people's attention, and evaluating the product and process. While creating their digital stories, students will research the topic of story, collect data, gather evidence to support the topic while developing an understanding of how others have handled similar problems, and be able to represent these problems in the characters of story. They will use hypermedia and multimedia components in these activities, and create a finished product from these (Yang & Wu, 2012). Jonassen, Myers & McKillop (1996) indicate that instead of using hypermedia and multimedia as data sources, producing hypermedia or databases will be more helpful for learners, and that researching, organizing and producing such databases will contribute notably to learner's critical thinking. Moreover, researchers suggest that storytellers should use the skills of interpreting, making conclusions (Sims, 2004) and decision-making (Maier & Fisher, 2006) to create a story and gain the audience's interest while telling a story. To conclude, digital storytelling can directly contribute to the development of critical thinking.

METHOD

To date, there have been several studies on critical thinking from various parts of the world. The present study intends to analyze these studies based on variable frequency, study group, data collection tools, research methods and distribution of studies among countries. The present study aims to assess the results of the publications included in the Science Direct database (a full-text scientific database including nearly 2500 journals about Physical Sciences and Engineering, Life Sciences, Health Sciences, Social Sciences and Humanities) under the keyword 'Critical thinking and technology' and published from 2008-2014. 2015 publications are not included. In applying it to the studies discussed, the present study will give an idea of the current studies and the deficiencies they have, and will serve as a guide for additional research. Future learning paradigms depend on technology. The present study aims to capture the importance of technology in teaching critical thinking.

The content analysis method has been used in this research in order to examine studies that include the keywords 'critical thinking and technology' in their abstracts, titles or keywords and that were published in the database of Science Direct. When the word 'technology' was searched for in the keyword sections alone, only some of the relevant articles could be found. Therefore, technology-related keywords such as 'online', 'web', 'media', 'distance education', 'e-learning', and 'social network' were also added as

Table 1. Distribution of the Publications by Year

Year	Publications
2008	1
2009	4
2010	5
2011	3
2012	13
2013	6
2014	10
Total	42

keywords. 42 relevant studies were found to be published in this database. The results of the study will be a guide to researchers for the importance of the technology on critical thinking.

Table 1 provides statistical data on the distribution of the studies according to the publishing year.

According to the Table 1, it is seen that yearly-published journal number has not shown any regular increase or decrease, however, the number of articles including said key words has increased in 2012 and 2014.

In line with the stated aim, the present study has been guided by the following research questions.

1. Which technologies were used in such studies and how frequently were they used?
2. Which variables were used in these studies and how frequently were they used?
3. Which scientific research methods were used in the studies?
4. Which data collection tools were used in the studies?
5. In which countries were the studies carried out?
6. What was the education level of participants in the studies?
7. Which type of publications were used in the studies?

RESULTS

In this section, 42 articles were examined in line with key words and the obtained results were explained in order of research questions.

The first question of the research is *"Which technologies were used in such studies and how frequently were they used?"*. Table 2 shows the technologies being used in the studies.

After the examination of the technologies being used in the studies related to critical thinking, online discussion (synchronous, asynchronous) environments were found to be the most frequently used technology (n=15, 29.4%). Online discussion environments were followed by web-based learning environments and LMS Tools (n=11, 21.6%) and Web 2.0 tools (n=9, 17.6%).

The second question of the research is *"Which variables were used in these studies and how frequently were they used?"*. Table 3 gives information related to the variables selected, their numbers and percentages.

Table 2. Technologies that were used

Technologies being used	N	%
Online discussions (synchronous, asynchronous)	15	29.4
Web-based learning environments and LMS tools	11	21.6
Web 2.0 tools (blog, wiki, social annotation, social networks)	9	17.6
Computer games	4	7.8
Simulations (web-based)	2	3.9
SMS, MMS, Messenger, Skype	2	3.9
Robotics	2	3.9
Videos	2	3.9
Virtual learning environments	1	2.0
Digital stories	1	2.0
Vtutor	1	2.0
Comics	1	2.0
Total	51	100

Table 3. Variables selected

Variables selected	N	%
Achievement, performance	6	12.8
Online learning environments	4	8.5
Teaching methods	4	8.5
Tools (robotic, simulation etc.)	4	8.5
Web 2.0 technologies	3	6.4
Skills (computer, problem solving etc.)	3	6.4
Learning type (mobile, blended, face-to-face)	3	6.4
Motivation	3	6.4
Satisfaction	2	4.3
Metacognition	2	4.3
Other	13	27.7
Total	**47**	**100**

An examination of the variables being used in the studies related to critical thinking shows that no specific variable was used predominantly. Among the variables, 'achievement and performance' (n=6, 12.8%) were found to be the most frequently used variables. 'Achievement and performance' were followed by online learning environments, teaching methods and tools (n=4, 8.5%).

The third question of the research is *"Which scientific research methods were used in the studies?"*. Table 4 shows the methods being used in the studies. These methods are quantitative, qualitative and mixed type. The numbers and percentages of these methods are also provided in the table.

Table 4. Methods that were used

Method	N	%
Quantitative	19	56.3
Qualitative	16	31.2
Mixed Type	7	12.5
Total	42	100

The quantitative method (n=19, 56.3%) was found to be the most frequently used method as a result of an examination of the methods used in the studies on critical thinking. This could be associated with the idea that experimental design is an appropriate way of examining the effects of technologies on critical thinking. The quantitative method was followed by qualitative method (n=16, 31.2%).

The forth question of the research is "*Which data collection tools were used in the studies?*". Data collection tools used for the studies are given in Table 5.

Qualitative data collection tools (n=18, 56.3%) were found to be the most frequently used tools. These were followed by the California Critical thinking test (n=6, 18.8%).

The fifth question of the research is "*In which countries were the studies carried out?*". Table 6 shows the countries where studies were carried out, and how the studies are distributed by country.

Table 5. Data collection tools

Tools	N	%
Qualitative data collection	18	56.3
California Critical Thinking Skills Test	6	18.8
Cornell Critical Thinking Test (Level Z), Watson-Glaser Critical Thinking appraisal scale	2	6.3
Other scales	6	18.8
Total	32	100

Table 6. Countries

Countries	N
USA	9
Malaysia	5
Turkey	5
Taiwan	4
Thailand	4
Canada	2
Australia	2
UK	2
Other	9
Total	42

According to Table 6, the highest number of studies was carried out in the USA (n=9). This was followed by Malaysia and Turkey (n=5), Taiwan and Thailand (n=4).

The sixth question of the research is *"What was the education level of participants in the studies?"*. Table 7 gives information about the education levels of students in the studies.

It was discovered that the majority of the subjects in the studies related to critical thinking were at the level of undergraduate students (n=29, 69%). According to Table 7, studies including other participants is less than the studies including undergraduate participants, so the studies including other participants can be focused in the future research.

The seventh question of the research is *"Which type of publications were used in the studies?"*. In Table 8, the distribution according to publication format is given.

The studies were found to have a balanced distribution in terms of articles (n=22, 52.4%) and procedia (n=20, 47.6%).

FUTURE RESEARCH DIRECTIONS

Considering the results of the current research, some advices are presented for future studies and researchers in this section. According to results, in the studies related to critical thinking and new technologies, online discussions, web-based learning environments and LMS tools, Web 2.0 tools are the most used technologies. So it can be suggested to researchers that the other technologies such as robotics, digital stories and virtual learning environments should be used in future studies. Besides online learning environments, new technologies, teaching methods and tools are the other most commonly used variables in the studies examined. It would be useful to promote the less frequently used variables in future studies.

Considering the methods used in the studies, it can be said that both qualitative and quantitative method should be used more in future studies. Also the studies are mainly focused on undergraduate level. In future research an increase in studies on this topic relating to lower age groups would be useful. Taking

Table 7. Participants

Participants	N	%
Undergraduate	29	69.0
Graduate	4	9.5
K12	3	7.1
Other	6	14.3
Total	42	100

Table 8. Publication Type

Publications	N	%
Article	22	52.4
Procedia	20	47.6
Total	42	100

into consideration the number of articles and procedias about critical thinking and new technologies, an increase in the number and proportion of both articles and procedias will be useful in the future.

CONCLUSION

When we face a problem, we often reflect on the issue and look for solutions. A student who handles a calculus problem, a computer programmer who designs a program, and an architect who designs a tower or plans a city, are initially uncertain of what to do and gain 'knowledge by thinking' (Halpern, 2014). People have faced many problems since the beginning of human history. Their degree of difficulty may either increase or decrease. It is obvious that in ancient times people had to think and act to solve problems in their fundamental struggle to survive. The need for education as a way of learning how to solve problems has always existed since ancient times and continues to do so now. Since the basic needs related to physiology and security according to Maslow's need hierarchy have mostly been satisfied, the requirements of education has changed. Yet until recently, only the most privileged people were educated. Today, in contrast, education is generally seen as a universal right. When historical developments in education field are examined, it is seen that education is also directly affected by technological developments as well as a variety of fields. Beginning of 21st century is a period of great educational changes. The question 'What happened at the beginning of this century to change the kinds and forms of education that were demanded or thought to be needed within advanced technological societies?' is highly challenging.

Libraries that have traditionally been one of the most important tools used for access to knowledge, have a five thousand year history. Clay tablets are the first written records, and their production was highly difficult as they are reproduced by hand (Toplu, 2010). Today, with electronic printing, the production, processing and spreading of knowledge has been highly accelerated. The so-called information society can be viewed as a result of certain stages of the development of civilization. In the 21st century, learners generally experience an early exposure to technology. They encounter information and technology at every stage of their lives. Those students who have been called 'digital natives' are considered to be individuals who access and analyze knowledge through information and communication technologies, realize their critical thinking interactively and cooperatively and perform multiple tasks actively (Prensky, 2001). To that end, the contemporary classroom environment is now designed to satisfy the needs of new learners (Prensky, 2005). The opportunities brought by internet for classrooms in the new century have provided various learning possibilities. In particular, Web 2.0 technologies have increased the capacity for interaction and mobile technologies have eliminated limitations of space (Trevor & Kevin, 2014).

It can be asserted that in many contemporary societies life has become relatively easier while questions about how best to live life have increased. When facing a problem, we now have the opportunity to access more knowledge and information about people from the ancient times, or indeed from any time and any place we wish. People have to develop some skills and use these skills to reach true information within this great information sources, to use technologies effectively and communicate with known or unknown people be means of new technologies. One of these skills called as 21st century skills is critical thinking. In contemporary society, people have developed their critical thinking through technologies and have more opportunity to think. The relationship of technology with critical thinking comprises the main focus of this study and this study evaluates them within the scope of critical thinking. This study evaluates research studies published within the specified database from 2008-2014.

It was observed that various technologies were used in the studies related to critical thinking. It was found that the most frequently used tools were online discussion environments, web-based learning environments, Web 2.0 tools and computer games. Online and co-education are common forms of learning with which we encounter recently. Now, with the new technologies, the limits of classrooms are exceeding the World limits. In online discussion platforms, people have the opportunity to share more ideas. The Web 2.0 tools and the use of social networks, which provide freedom of speech, are becoming widespread all over the world. From now on, it is inevitable that learning platforms will be affected. There are new tools for classroom atmosphere to realize constructivist learning. In particular, Web 2.0 tools, that do not require too much technical knowledge while being used, lead learners and teachers to these platforms. Even though they were rarely used, technologies related to simulation, robot and cyber learning environments were also among the technologies being used. The rare use of such technologies may have resulted from the fact that they have been only recently getting widespread. Considering the results of the current research, it can be said that critical thinking is commonly used in online learning environments. This situation can be alleged to be resulting from the fact that online learning environments provide opportunities and tools that may contribute to critical thinking.

The variables being used in the studies were found to be diverse. According to the results of the study, initial ranking of student success and performance among variables encountered in the study shows that critical thinking variable is mostly handled with these variables. Online learning environments, new technologies, teaching methods and tools are the other most commonly used variables in said studies.

While qualitative methods were found to be used slightly more frequently in studies related to critical thinking, quantitative methods were used with a nearly equal frequency. Producing more studies with mixed methods would be useful. As for the measurement tools being used, qualitative measurement tools were found to be more frequently used while the most frequently used quantitative tool was California Critical Thinking Skills test. The dominant use of both quantitative methods and qualitative measurement tools can be seen as a conflict. However, qualitative tools in the mixed type were also included in this number. Furthermore, this situation could be the result of using multiple qualitative measurement tools together.

While the USA ranked first by number among the countries where the studies were carried out, it was followed by Malaysia and Turkey respectively. There were also studies from many different countries. The majority of the participants were university students. Undergraduate level education can be too late for the acquisition of basic critical thinking, one of the human skills most required in the 21st century. This could be associated with the fact that this is the easiest group of people to access for research purposes. Therefore, an increase in studies on this topic relating to lower age groups would be useful. A balanced distribution was observed in the number of articles and procedia related to critical thinking.

REFERENCES

Ajjan, H., & Hartshorne, R. (2008). Investigating faculty decisions to adopt web 2.0 technologies: Theory and empirical tests. *The Internet and Higher Education*, *11*(2), 71–80.

Akkoyunlu, B., & Kurbanoğlu, S. (2003). Öğretmen adaylarının bilgi okuryazarlığı ve bilgisayar öz-yeterlilik algıları üzerine bir çalışma. *Hacettepe Üniversitesi Eğitim Fakültesi Dergisi*, *24*, 1–10.

Aktay, S. (2011). *İlköğretimde web tabanlı portfolyo (webfolyo) uygulaması.* (Unpublished doctoral dissertation). Anadolu University, Eskişehir, Turkey.

Alessi, S. M., & Trollip, S. R. (2001). *Multimedia for learning. Methods and development* (3rd ed.). Boston, MA: Allyn and Bacon.

Alimisis, D., & Kynigos, C. (2009). Constructionism and robotics in education. *Teacher Education on Robotic-Enhanced Constructivist Pedagogical Methods,* 11-26.

Alkan, C. (1997). *Eğitim teknolojisinin ikibinli yıllarda yapılandırılması.* Ankara: Anı Yayıncılık.

Arat, T. (2011). *İletişim teknolojilerinin yükseköğrenim kurumlarında öğretim amaçlı kullanımı: selçuk üniversitesi örneği.* (Unpublished doctoral dissertation). Selçuk University, Konya.

Armstrong, G., Tucker, J., & Massad, V. (2009). Interviewing the experts: Student produced podcast. *Journal of Information Technology Education: Innovations in Practice, 8*(1), 79–90.

Bach, S., Haynes, P., & Smith, J. L. (2006). *Online learning and teaching in higher education.* UK: McGraw-Hill Education.

Balanskat, A., Blamire, R., & Kefala, S. (2006). *The ICT impact report.* European Schoolnet.

Barker, B. S., & Ansorge, J. (2007). Robotics as means to increase achievement scores in an informal learning environment. *Journal of Research on Technology in Education, 39*(3), 229–243.

Barron, A. E., & Orwig, G. W. (1997). *New technologies for education: A beginner's guide.* USA: Libraries Unlimited.

Baş, G. (2010). Effects of brain-based learning on students' achievement levels and attitudes towards English lesson. *Elementary Education Online, 9*(2), 488–507.

Beer, R. D., Chiel, H. J., & Drushel, R. F. (1999). Using autonomous robotics to teach science and engineering. *Communications of the ACM, 42*(6), 85–92.

Bender, T. (2012). *Discussion-based online teaching to enhance student learning: Theory, practice, and assessment* (2nd ed.). Virginia: Stylus.

Bimrose, J., Brown, A., Holocher-Ertl, T., Kieslinger, B., Kunzmann, C., Prilla, M., & Wolf, C. et al. (2014). The role of facilitation in technology-enhanced learning for public employment services. *International Journal of Advanced Corporate Learning, 7*(3), 56–63.

Blankenship, M. (2011). How social media can and should impact higher education. *Education Digest, 76*(7), 39–42.

Cady, D., Olson, M., Shea, P., & Grenier, J. M. (2011). Part ii a pratical model and assignments for using virtual worlds in higher education. In R. Hinrichs & C. Wankel (Eds.), Cutting-edge Technologies in Higher Education: Transforming Virtual World Learning. Emerald Group Publishing.

Cags, M. (2010). New graduate nurses' perceptions of the effects of clinical simulation on their critical thinking, learning, and confidence. *Journal of Continuing Education in Nursing, 41*(11), 506–516. PMID:20672760

Castells, M. (2011). *The rise of the network society: The information age: Economy, society, and culture* (Vol. 1). Sussex, UK: Blackwell.

Ceceri, K. (2012). *Build it yourself robotics: Discover the science and technology of the future with 25 projects. White River Junction.* Ann Arbor, MI: Nomad.

Çelik, V. (2000). Eğitimsel liderlik (2nd ed.). Ankara, TR: Pegem A Yayıncılık.

Cheong, C. M., & Cheung, W. S. (2008). Online discussion and critical thinking skills: A case study in a Singapore secondary school. *Australasian Journal of Educational Technology*, 24(5), 556–573.

Cole, M. (2009). Using wiki technology to support student engagement: Lessons from the trenches. *Computers & Education*, 52(1), 141–146.

Coşar, M. (2013). *Problem temelli öğrenme ortamında bilgisayar programlama çalışmalarının akademik başarı, eleştirel düşünme eğilimi ve bilgisayara yönelik tutuma etkileri.* (Unpublished doctoral dissertation). Gazi University, Ankara, TR.

Cradler, J., McNabb, M., Freeman, M., & Burchett, R. (2002). How Does Technology Influence Student Learning? *Learning and Leading with Technology*, 29(8), 46–56.

Crane, B. E. (2012). *Using web 2.0 and social networking tools in the K-12 classroom.* American Library Association.

D'Ignazio, F. (1993). Electronic Highways and Classrooms of the Future. In T. Cannings & L. Finkle (Eds.), *The Technology Age Classroom. Wilsonville.* Franklin: Beedle.

Davis, A. (2004). Co-authoring identity: Digital storytelling in an urban middle school. *Technology, Humanities, Education, &. Narrative*, 1(1), 1.

Demirel, Ö. (1999). Öğretme sanatı. Ankara, TR: Pegem Yayınları.

Demirel, Ö. (2003). Eğitim terimleri sözlüğü (2. bs.). Ankara, TR: Pegem A Yayıncılık.

Denis, B., & Hubert, S. (2001). Collaborative learning in an educational robotics environment. *Computers in Human Behavior*, 17(5), 465–480.

Donmuş, A. G. V., & Gürol, M. (2014). The Effect of Educational Computer Games on Student Motivation in Learning English/İngilizce Öğrenmede Eğitsel Bilgisayar Oyunu Kullanmanın Motivasyona Etkisi. *International Journal of Educational Research*, 5(4), 1–16.

Edward, Z., & Paul, C. A. (2014). Critical thinking and computing project in computer studies postgraduate methods course: Technology perspective. *Education Research International*, 3(1), 88–102.

Edwards, A. (2012). *New technology and education: Contemporary issues in educational studies.* NY: Continuum International.

Fero, L. J., O'Donnell, J. M., Zullo, T. G., Dabbs, A. D., Kitutu, J., Samosky, J. T., & Hoffman, L. A. (2010). Critical thinking skills in nursing students: Comparison of simulation-based performance with metrics. *Journal of Advanced Nursing*, 66(10), 2182–2193. PMID:20636471

Fisher, A. (2001). *Critical thinking: An introduction.* London, UK: Cambridge University Press.

Frazel, M. (2010). *Digital storytelling guide for educators. Moorabbin.* International Society for Technology in Education.

Glaser, E. (1942). An experiment in the development of critical thinking. *Teachers College Record, 43*(5), 409–410.

Glaser, E. M. (1985). Critical thinking: Educating for responsible citizenship in a democracy. In *National Forum. Phi Kappa Phi Journal, 65*(1), 24–27.

Goh, H., & Aris, B. (2007). Using robotics in education: Lessons learned and learning experiences. *Smart Teaching & Learning: Re-engineering ID, Utilization and Innovation of Technology, 2.*

Gokcearslan, S., & Ozcan, S. (2011). Place of wikis in learning and teaching process. *Procedia: Social and Behavioral Sciences, 28,* 481–485.

Gokhale, A. A. (1995). Collaborative learning enhances critical thinking. *Journal of Technology Education, 7*(1). Retrieved from http://scholar.lib.vt.edu/ejournals/JTE/v7n1/gokhale.jte-v7n1.html?ref=Sawos.Org

Green, H., & Hannon, C. (2007). *Their space–education for a digital generation.* London, UK: Demos.

Grosseck, G. (2009). To use or not to use web 2.0 in higher education? *Procedia: Social and Behavioral Sciences, 1*(1), 478–482.

Halpern, D. F. (2014). *Critical thinking across the curriculum: A brief edition of thought & knowledge.* New York, NY: Routledge.

Hoffman, S. J. (2010). *Teaching the humanities online: A practical guide to the virtual classroom.* New York, NY: Routledge.

Johnson, J. (2003). Children, robotics, and education. *Artificial Life and Robotics, 7*(1-2), 16–21.

Jonassen, D. H., Myers, J. M., & McKillop, A. M. (1996). From constructivism to constructionism: Learning with hypermedia/multimedia rather than from it. In B. G. Wilson (Ed.), *Constructivist learning environments: Case studies in instructional design* (pp. 93–106). Educational Technology.

Kırıkkaya, E. B., Bozkurt, E., & İşeri, Ş. (2013). Fen ve teknoloji derslerinde gazetelerin kullanılması. *Ondokuz Mayıs Üniversitesi Eğitim Fakültesi Dergisi, 32*(2), 223–247.

Kline, S. J. (1985). What is technology? *Bulletin of Science, Technology & Society, 1,* 215–218. doi:10.1177/027046768500500301

Lamb, A. C., & Johnson, B. (2006). *Building treehouses for learning: Technology in today's classroom.* Recording for the Blind & Dyslexic.

Lockard, J., & Abrams, P. (2003). Computer assisted instruction fundamentals. In Computers for twenty-first century educators (6th ed.). Allyn and Bacon, Pearson Education.

MacKnight, C. B. (2000). Teaching critical thinking through online discussions. *EDUCAUSE Quarterly, 23*(4), 38–41.

Maier, R. B., & Fisher, M. (2006). Strategies for digital storytelling via tabletop video: Building decision making skills in middle school students in marginalized communities. *Journal of Educational Technology Systems, 35*(2), 175–192.

Maloney, E. (2007). What Web 2.0 can teach us about learning? *The Chronicle of Higher Education, 53*(18), B26.

Marcovitz, D. (2012). *Digital connections in the classroom.* Washington, DC: International Society for Technology in Education.

Markel, S. L. (2001). Technology and education online discussion forums: It's in the response. *Online Journal of Distance Learning Administration, 4*(2).

Mataric, M. J. (2004, March). *Robotics education for all ages.* Paper presented at AAAI Spring Symposium on Accessible, Hands-on AI and Robotics Education, San Jose, CA.

McLoughlin, C., & Lee, M. J. (2007, December). Social software and participatory learning: Pedagogical choices with technology affordances in the Web 2.0 era. In Proceedings of Ascilite Singapore 2007 ICT: Providing choices for learners and learning (pp. 664-675). Singapore.

McLoughlin, D., & Mynard, J. (2009). An analysis of higher order thinking in online discussions. *Innovations in Education and Teaching International, 46*(2), 147–160.

Meadows, M. S. (2008). *I, avatar: The culture and consequences of having a second life.* Berkeley, CA: New Riders.

MEB. (2005). *İlköğretim matematik dersi (6, 7, 8. Sınıflar) öğretim programı.* Ankara: Devlet Kitapları Müdürlüğü.

Mendenhall, A., & Johnson, T. E. (2010). Fostering the development of critical thinking skills, and reading comprehension of undergraduates using a Web 2.0 tool coupled with a learning system. *Interactive Learning Environments, 18*(3), 263–276.

Murphie, A., & Potts, J. (2003). *Culture and technology.* Basingstoke, UK: Palgrave Macmillan.

Nagel, P. (2014). Critical thinking and technology. *Social Studies and the Young Learner, 26*(4), 1–4.

Nourbakhsh, I. R., Crowley, K., Bhave, A., Hamner, E., Hsiu, T., Perez-Bergquist, A., & Wilkinson, K. et al. (2005). The robotic autonomy mobile robotics course: Robot design, curriculum design and educational assessment. *Autonomous Robots, 18*(1), 103–127.

O'Leary, R., & Ramsden, A. (2002). Virtual learning environments. Learning and Teaching. *Support Network Generic Centre/ALT Guides, LTSN.* Retrieved July 12, 2005, from ftp://www.bioscience.heacademy.ac.uk/Resources/gc/elearn2.pdf

Ocak, M. A., Gökçearslan, Ş., & Solmaz, E. (2014). Investigating Turkish pre-service teachers' perceptions of blogs: Implications for the FATIH project. *Contemporary Educational Technology, 5*(1), 22–38.

OECD. (2005). *Are students ready for a technology-rich world? What PISA studies tell us.* OECD.

Ohler, J. (2006). The world of digital storytelling. *Educational Leadership, 63*(4), 44–47.

Ohler, J. B. (2013). *Digital storytelling in the classroom: New media pathways to literacy, learning, and creativity.* Corwin.

Owston, R. D. (1997). The world wide web: A technology to enhance teaching and learning. *Educational Researcher, 26*(2), 27–33.

Pacific Policy Research Center (PPRC). (2010). *21st century skills for students and teachers.* Honolulu, HI: Kamehameha Schools, Research & Evaluation Division.

Pattison, D. (2012). Participating in the online social culture. *Knowledge Quest, 41*(1), 70–72.

Paul, R. W., & Elder, L. B. (2002). *Critical thinking: tools for taking charge of your professional and personal Life.* Upper Saddle River, NJ: Financial Times/Prentice Hall.

Piccoli, G., Ahmad, R., & Ives, B. (2001). Web-based virtual learning environments: A research framework and a preliminary assessment of effectiveness in basic IT skills training. *Management Information Systems Quarterly*, 401–426.

Prensky, M. (2001). Digital natives, digital immigrants part 2. Do they really think differently? *On the Horizon, 9*(6), 1–6.

Prensky, M. (2005). *Shaping tech for the classroom: 21st-century schools need 21st-century technology.* Edutopia.

Reigeluth, C. (1991). Principles of educational systems design. *International Journal of Education and Research, 19*(2), 117–131.

Ricca, B., Lulis, E., & Bade, D. (2006). Lego mindstorms and the growth of critical thinking. In *Proceedings of Intelligent Tutoring Systems Workshop on Teaching With Robots, Agents, and NLP.*

Robin, B. (2006, March). The educational uses of digital storytelling. In *Society for Information Technology & Teacher Education International Conference* (Vol. 2006, No. 1, pp. 709-716).

Rossiter, M., & Garcia, P. A. (2010). Digital storytelling: A new player on the narrative field. *New Directions for Adult and Continuing Education, 126*, 37–48.

Saadé, R. G., Morin, D., & Thomas, J. D. (2012). Critical thinking in E-learning environments. *Computers in Human Behavior, 28*(5), 1608–1617.

Sadik, A. (2008). Digital storytelling: A meaningful technology-integrated approach for engaged student learning. *Educational Technology Research and Development, 56*(4), 487–506.

Sakız, G., Özden, B., Aksu, D., & Şimşek, Ö. (2015). Fen ve Teknoloji Dersinde Akıllı Tahta Kullanımının Öğrenci Başarısına ve Dersin İşlenişine Yönelik Tutuma Etkisi. *Atatürk Üniversitesi Sosyal Bilimler Enstitüsü Dergisi, 18*(3), 257–274.

Sims, D. (2004). Management learning as a critical process: The practice of storying. In P. Jeffcutt (Ed.), *The foundations of management knowledge* (pp. 152–166). London, UK: Routledge.

Solomon, G., & Schrum, L. (2011). *Web 2.0 how-to for educators.* Washington, DC: International Society for Technology in Education.

Sullivan-Mann, J., Perron, C. A., & Fellner, A. N. (2009). The effects of simulation on nursing students' critical thinking scores: A quantitative study. *Newborn and Infant Nursing Reviews; NAINR, 9*(2), 111–116.

Thompson, A., & Crompton, H. (2010). Point/Counterpoint is technology killing critical thinking? *Learning and Leading with Technology, 38*(1), 6.

Toplu, M. (2010). Kil tabletlerden elektronik yayıncılığa kütüphanecilik felsefesinin gelişimi ve dönüşümü. *Türk Kütüphaneciliği, 24*(4), 644–684.

Towner, T. L., & Munoz, C. L. (2011). Facebook and education: a classroom collection? In C. Wankel (Ed.), *Educating Educators with Social Media, Cutting-edge Technologies in Higher Education* (pp. 33–57). Emerald Group Publishing.

Trevor, M., & Kevin, B. (2014). Access denied? Twenty-firstcentury technology in schools. *Technology, Pedagogy and Education, 23*(4), 423–437. doi:10.1080/1475939X.2013.864697

Uluyol, Ç. (2011). *Web destekli örnek olay yönteminde çoklu bakış açısı ve yüz yüze etkileşimin öğrencilerin eleştirel düşünme becerilerine etkisi.* (Unpublished doctoral dissertation). Gazi University, Ankara, Turkey.

Warburton, S. (2009). Second life in higher education: Assessing the potential for and the barriers to deploying virtual worlds in learning and teaching. *British Journal of Educational Technology, 40*(3), 414–426.

Watson, D., & Tinsley, D. (Eds.). (2013). *Integrating information technology into education.* London, UK: Springer.

Webster, J. (2014). *Shaping women's work: Gender, employment and information technology.* New York, NY: Routledge.

Wiske, M. S., Franz, K. R., & Breit, L. (2010). *Teaching for understanding with technology.* San Francisco, CA: John Wiley & Sons.

Wolpert, S. (2009). *Is technology producing a decline in critical thinking and analysis?* UCLA Newsroom.

Yang, Y. T. C., & Wu, W. C. I. (2012). Digital storytelling for enhancing student academic achievement, critical thinking, and learning motivation: A year-long experimental study. *Computers & Education, 59*(2), 339–352.

Yu, X., & Weinberg, J., B. (2003, October). Robotics in education: New platforms and environments. *IEEE Robotics & Automation Magazine.*

Yukawa, J. (2006). Co-reflection in online learning: Collaborative critical thinking as narrative. *International Journal of Computer-Supported Collaborative Learning, 1*(2), 203–228.

ADDITIONAL READING

Berry, D. M. (2011). The computational turn: Thinking about the digital humanities. *Culture Machine, 12*, 1–22.

Cottrell, S. (2011). *Critical thinking skills: Developing effective analysis and argument.* Palgrave Macmillan.

Hew, K. F., & Brush, T. (2007). Integrating technology into K-12 teaching and learning: Current knowledge gaps and recommendations for future research. *Educational Technology Research and Development*, *55*(3), 223–252.

Higgins, S. (2014). Critical thinking for 21st-century education: A cyber-tooth curriculum? *Prospects*, *44*(4), 559–574.

Laurillard, D. (2013). *Rethinking University teaching: A conversational framework for the effective use of learning technologies.* Routledge.

Malita, L., & Martin, C. (2010). Digital storytelling as web passport to success in the 21st century. *Procedia: Social and Behavioral Sciences*, *2*(2), 3060–3064.

Tadros, M. (2011). Part II. A social media approach to higher education. In C. Wankel (Ed.), *Educating educators with social media, cutting-edge technologies in higher education* (pp. 83–105). UK: Emerald Group Publishing.

KEY TERMS AND DEFINITIONS

Critical Thinking: It is one of 21st century skills which is a way of thinking including combining, analyzing, commenting and evaluating information.

Digital Stories: These are stories which are told by using multimedia such as text, picture, digital graphic, voices and video.

Digital Technologies: These tools are technologies relating to computers or the "Computer Age".

Online Discussion: It is defined as comparing views or gathering for a specific purpose in an online environment.

Robotics: It is a science related to designing, conducting, programming, operating and applying robots.

Simulation: This technology is a digital platform allowing users to experience situations, which are expensive, insecure, requiring a lot of time and not possible – or very rarely possible – to observe or perform in real life in a secure and an cheap way, in a virtual world.

Social Network: Social network is one of Web 2.0 tools which is a website where people meet to have a talk, share interests, ideas and activities.

Technology: It is a concept including tools that are used to find, create, learn, analyze, and present information.

Virtual Learning Environment: It is a Web 2.0 technology that presents interactive virtual world to users and provides opportunity to experience in a narrative.

Web 2.0: This is second generation web including more interactive and cooperative environments such as blogs, wiki, social networks and podcast.

ENDNOTE

[1]   Part of this study was presented by first author at the ATEE Spring Conference (2014), 'Innovation and Challenges in Education', Vilnius, Lithuania. The study has not been previously published.

Chapter 8

Academic Mobility Programs as Part of Individual and Professional Development in a Globalized World:
Uncovering Cultural Dimensions

Irina Khoutyz
Kuban State University, Russia

ABSTRACT

The purpose of this research is to establish a connection between the effects of globalization on contemporary societies and the increase in individualist attributes in former collectivist societies. To achieve it, the chapter presents the study of the experiences of Russian students participating in academic mobility programs. A two-step survey conducted among the Russian university students reveals, by means of cultural dimension analysis, individualist attributes in their academic behavior while studying overseas and at a home university. The interest towards academic mobility programs expressed by the students of various years of study, their desire for independence and self-development as well as an enjoyable process of acquiring a diploma are examples of individualist attributes. The conclusion is made that individuals trying to find their place in a globalized world acquire more individualist attributes in their behavior and world perception.

INTRODUCTION: GLOBALIZATION AND PROFESSIONAL MOBILITY

The purpose of this research was to establish a connection between the effects of globalization (academic mobility programs in this case) on contemporary societies and the increase in individualist attributes in former collectivist societies. This purpose was achieved by studying the experiences of several Russian students participating in academic mobility programs and uncovering cultural dimensions in their perceptions of an academic environment (see, for instance, Hofstede & Hofstede, 2005). The analysis

DOI: 10.4018/978-1-5225-0522-8.ch008

of individualist attributes in Russian students' academic behavior in an overseas academic institution and in a home university shows interconnection between modern students' desire for independence and self-development and their interest in academic mobility programs.

The goal of this research is accomplished through a case study based on the experiences of Russian students who took part in an academic mobility program established between Kuban State University (Krasnodar, Russia) and Katholieke Universiteit Leuven (Belgium). The research led to the conclusion that, on the one hand, despite unification processes and some changes in the national character, numerous practices within societies continue to maintain their local flavor: although an attempt has been made to make the process of education similar all over the world to enhance international cooperation, notions of what constitutes the process of learning and how it can be organized still differ. Yet, on the other hand, the students' (those who participated in academic mobility programs as well as those who never opted for them) expectations from academic processes illustrate the increased number of individualist attributes in their decisions and choices.

Whereas *globalization* may be described in so many words, one expression that captures the essence of such a phenomenon as globalization is *connectivity*. Prior to increases in the transnational transfer of knowledge, human and financial capital, technology, culture, and so on, entire nations were isolated. As Tomlinson (1999) observed, globalization connected otherwise remote, isolated, and inaccessible communities and entire nations. Twenty-first century technology has enabled intercultural-international communication and increased mobility and connectivity to "the centre of our lives" (p. 42).

A 21st-century individual enjoys the "right to unlimited travel and cultural consumption" (Urry, 1995, p. 200), although it is important to note that such rights do not globally extend to all communities or societies, given the prohibitive costs associated with the use of such technologies. Nonetheless, the fact that some societies have yet to partake in such a right of unlimited mobility, due to the associated costs of the enabling technologies, the most appropriate term would be *privilege* rather than *right*, as characterized by Tomlinson (1999).

Globalization, through media and increased cultural contact, makes nations more open to each other. The availability of numeral sources of information makes connectivity and travel easy for individuals in the current globalized world. Pretravel arrangements are easily made by accessing numerous Internet resources that provide information about travel destinations. Apart from Internet websites, other sources of information include, TV programs, printed media—newspapers, magazines, flyers, and the like. These sources of information make connectivity easy for the 21st-century individual.

Globalization has, in no uncertain terms, assured continuous prosperity even for rich and powerful countries. Industrialized economies are not absolved from economic instabilities that characterize capitalism. In a *Newsweek* magazine article, Sharkov (2015) elucidated such impermanence as applied to job losses and economic stress and strains in Germany, Spain, France, Italy, and the United Kingdom partially induced by the trade sanctions imposed on Russia by Western governments using the political conflict in Ukraine as justification. Once again, it testifies to the interconnectedness of the modern world.

Mobility has always been a sign of progress and literacy. Isolation and immobility are characteristics of social life before the modern era, typical of, for instance, small rural communities (Tomlinson, 1999). However, even in faraway times, there existed a small, but more mobile literate elite. Beginning in the ninth century, a semblance of prosperity became manifest as a product of mobility. Long-distance trading facilitated the establishment of cultural and economic links between the Christian and Muslim worlds. Citing Morris, Tomlinson (1999) explained the economic prosperity enjoyed by such mercantile cities as Venice, Genoa, or Constantinople resulting from trade that was accelerated by connectivity.

Increased international and intercultural connectivity (travel), which is one of the many benefits of globalization, enhances individual "awareness of the wider world as significant for us in our locality, the sense of connection with other cultures and even, perhaps, an increasing openness to cultural difference" (Tomlinson, 1999, p. 200). In the era of globalization, mobility is not limited to traveling, it also entails openness to intercultural experiences and, more importantly, to the feeling or perception of interconnection. Depending on the particular country in terms of, economic or technological prosperity, globalization is clearly experienced by some individuals who stay home and venture overseas less, if at all, for either business or pleasure.

Economic and technological disparity among nations is the antithesis of compatibility, a reality that exposes some of the defects of globalization. The dawning of the 21st century has shown a tendency to accentuate such inequalities, as poorer nations seem cut out or remain disconnected from the benefits of globalization and the Information Age that are bestowed upon richer nations. Whereas individuals in developed countries are able to experience the semblance of other cultures and even engage in intercultural communications by means of the Internet, those in poorer countries are left behind.

Professional mobility and interconnection with international colleagues constitute an essential part of living in the so-called *global village*. Partaking in any kind of mobility is an integral element of a global experience. Professional mobility in Europe is, for instance, supported by the Professional Qualifications Directive adopted by the EP Internal Market and Consumer Protection Committee. The directive unifies professional qualifications for 800 professions and provides people with a European professional card (European People's Party, 2013).

The purpose of this directive is to promote a more secured professional mobility in Europe making it easier for doctors, pharmacists, architects, and other professionals to move to and practice in another European Union country. One way of expediting expatriate relocation is the eradication of the bureaucratic bottlenecks that are associated with the process (European People's Party, 2013). According to an European Union Plenary Session press release, the European Union will establish "an alert system, to make it harder for those barred from a profession at home to do likewise" (European Parliament, 2013, para. 1).

As an inducement for potential employees, information about opportunities for the mobility of specialists can be found on the websites of some companies. *Professional mobility* is described by the Peugeot automobile manufacturer group as one of their main job management incentives of the company, as "a key lever to career development and as a means for employees to improve and enhance capabilities" (PSA Peugeot Citroën, n.d., para. 1). As indicated on their website, professional mobility allows Peugeot to support its four key ambitions: "(a) taking the lead on services and products; (b) becoming a global group; (c) becoming a standard setter on operational efficiency, and (d) focusing on social responsible development" (PSA Peugeot Citroën, n.d., para. 3).

These professional ambitions, which are supposed to be achieved by means of professional mobility, clearly describe the essence of the mobility phenomenon. Corporations that operate in various sectors and industries—for instance, education (see, for instance, information on the Education Charter Initiative enhancing stronger ties between academicians, professors, and educators worldwide) (Education Charter International, n.d.), IT, architecture, and so on—strive to enhance professional mobility via unified certification as well as the introduction of directives (decisions) aimed at removing bureaucratic obstacles that might appear on the specialists' way.

Professional mobility occurs globally. It is not specific to the European Union, which is often described as a single market. For instance, in order for the Australian Public Service to function efficiently, both the government and the Australian community see the professional mobility program as a way of strengthening its workforce and, according to its website, is an important part of the employees' professional development, of the organization's talent management strategy, as well as "a cost effective means of diversifying and enhancing an employee's knowledge, experience, and skills through immersion and learning" (Australian Public Service Commission, 2015, para. 7).

One of the prerequisites for professional mobility is the knowledge of English. This is why many European universities offer bachelor and master degree programs in English. According to the Institute of International Educations, the number of courses taught in English at master degree level more than quadrupled in the last 10 years in Europe. Such programs, commonly known as Study Abroad, are taught in Denmark, Finland, Belgium, France, Spain, Germany, and elsewhere (Study abroad: Where to study in Europe . . . in English, n.d.).

Professional mobility seems to be an inseparable part of globalization, which, according to Steger's (as cited in Fairclough, 2006) viewing of globalism, besides promoting the spread of democracy in the world, "benefits everyone" (p. 40). What is often forgotten, however, when speaking about professional mobility, is that despite a certain degree of unification and increased knowledge about other cultures, national professional environments continue to preserve their unique nature. The latter is often intensified by globalization itself: to withstand its darker side leading to cultural duplication, such as the same fast food chains, soap operas and sitcoms, and pop stars all over the world (Cronin, 2003), nations strive to preserve their unique features, thus creating duality, reflected in symbiosis of local and global aspects (Khoutyz, 2013a). Managing to balance one's cultural identity with a new cultural context requires people to have patience, tolerance and, as a result, self-growth achieved by means of raising cultural awareness and improved knowledge of a foreign language (usually English). Therefore, as modern cultures are becoming more interconnected, a certain degree of unification is unavoidable. As far as education is concerned, the Bologna Process is an example of how educational systems in different countries can be unified in order to promote knowledge exchange among students and academics.

BACKGROUND: STUDIES ON ACADEMIC MOBILITY

As academic mobility has become a part of successful degree acquirement and sometimes a requirement for completing a major (when mastering in foreign languages, for instance), researchers from different types of universities study how to make the process of academic exchange more efficient.

Most of the research devoted to the issues of academic mobility views the latter as a prerequisite for having competitive educational programs and graduates who are capable of succeeding in the globalized world. Often the authors of the research on academic mobility discuss the levels of internationalization of education in their countries and propose ways of improving the situation.

For instance, researchers from Mexico Codina, Nicolás, López, and Hernán (2013) described *academic mobility* as part of the overall internationalization of higher education together with student exchange, distance education programs, joint projects and seminars, international research agreements, and international journals. Although, according to Codina et al., academic mobility has a long history, in the age of globalization, it has evolved into a way of preparing successful professionals. The benefits of participating in academic mobility programs, among the obvious ones such as increased language proficiency and cultural awareness, include an ability to apply skillfully new information technologies, generating internationally competitive ideas and knowledge, up-to-date attitudes to teamwork, negotiation, increased professional adaptability, and an important ability to "think globally, act locally; ability to negotiate, establish partnerships, share and exploit knowledge" (Codina et al., 2013, p. 57).

Codina et al. (2013) expressed concern that Latin America is lagging behind Europe and Asia in the number of academic mobility programs and connect the low level of the overall internationalization of higher education in Latin America with the low level of investment in research and development. The authors conclude that for Latin America, obviously, as well as for other countries that want to create educational programs meeting the requirements of the globalized world, a competitive strategy of internationalization of education is necessary. This will allow us to establish new ways of teaching and producing knowledge in society.

Asanova and Ryssaldy (2013) researched the benefits of academic mobility programs based on the experiences of the students studying at Kazakh Ablai khan University of International Relations and World Languages in Kazakhstan. The students who participated in the research (55 all together) helped to identify numerous pros and, what is not usual, cons of academic mobility programs. Among the benefits of academic mobility programs, the researchers pointed out their positive influence on improving program participants' interpersonal, work-related and language skills, and increasing their self-esteem and self-assessment. These skills, as Asanova and Ryssaldy pointed out, will help future graduates to become active citizens and introduce progressive ideas into various areas of life in society. A similar idea is expressed by the Russian scholar Sergeev (2015), who stressed the importance of academic mobility programs for developing soft skills that can make university graduates more competitive in the job market; a study-abroad experience enhances communication skills (both in one's native and a foreign, usually English, language) and makes individuals more creative, open-minded, and welcoming of change.

Among the disadvantages of taking part in academic mobility programs, Asanova and Ryssaldy (2013) listed a culture shock and communication difficulties. However, not returning to a home country may be considered as the main disadvantage as the knowledge and experience acquired as a result of studying abroad are not brought back home. Asanova and Ryssaldy concluded that academic mobility programs have a great practical value for their participants and their societies and should be further developed and improved.

Bazhenova (2013), from Kazakh National University in Kazakhstan, came up with an idea to analyze the term *academic mobility* and determine its sometimes-ambiguous meaning: the term still can be interpreted differently depending on a university and geographic area. Having studied the meaning of the term in various discourses (the Bologna Declaration, the Great Charter of Universities, *United Nations Education, Scientific, and Cultural Organization Study Abroad Guide*, etc.), the author concluded, "It is worth noting that in addition to the act of moving from country to country, the academic mobility also requires a multifaceted process of personal development, self-realization and acquisition of professional and key competencies" (p. 484). The author stressed the need of Kazakhstan students to acquire access to European universities and, as a result, enhance the quality of higher education in Kazakhstan.

As having academic mobility programs is one of the signs of an effective educational process in Russia, universities present detailed information about available programs on their websites. The topic of academic mobility is actively discussed by Russian scholars. They agree that academic mobility programs are an instrument of integration into the international educational environment that is essential for improving the quality of education (Sergeev, 2015; Volodina, 2014) and raising the professional level of future graduates (Volodina, 2014); academic mobility might also increase international competitiveness of Russian universities (Kharitonova, 2012). Volodina (2014) attempted to classify the types of academic mobility programs that currently are available for Russian students and professors—for instance, short-term and long-term, individual and group, international and local, and so on.

The problems that programs of academic mobility are encountering in Russia include insufficient financial resources that can be provided to those participating in these programs and a lack of uniform procedures ensuring efficient academic exchange. It is also pointed out that Russian students participation in academic mobility programs can be complicated due to the incompatibility of their curricula with the curricula in similar academic programs abroad, as well as the differences in methods of teaching and knowledge assessment, integrating research into the study process, unpredictability of whether the transcripts from an international university will be accepted at the home university and, most importantly, the inability to communicate (and study) in a foreign language (Kharitonova, 2012). All in all, there is a great variety of research conducted by Russian scholars and devoted to academic mobility – starting with general analysis and classifications of the forms of available programs and ending with discussion of specific programs, for instance, in Spain (offered for postgraduate students of social sciences; Valeeva & Babukh, 2013).

Obviously, the issue of how to adapt to a new academic environment is an important one when speaking about academic mobility. Indeed, previous research has suggested that the adjustment of international students differs according to the country of origin and country of study (Mustaffa & Ilias, 2013, pp. 279-280). Academics from the Northern University of Malaysia analyzed cross-cultural variables that affect foreign students' adjustment in a new academic setting. For instance, these are such variables as the amount of contact with host nationals, length of residence, finance and accommodation. Using their own university as an example, Mustaffa and Ilias (2013) examined "the relationship between academic style, sociocultural factors, personal emotion, environment and intercultural communication apprehension with cross-cultural adjustment among foreign students" (p. 280). They concluded that language proficiency and previous travel experience play a key role in students' success during an academic mobility program.

The analysis of the research on academic mobility shows that special attention should be paid on how to make the integration of students and professors into a new educational setting more efficient. It has been mentioned that the interpretation of roles of those involved in the academic process can differ (Epstein & Kheimets, 2000). This certainly can cause difficulties for those trying to integrate into a new academic environment. Epstein and Kheimets (2000), for instance, discovered that in Israel, Russian immigrant students expect their teachers to be well prepared for the class, which is different from Israeli students' expectations:

The immigrant students' expectations that their teacher be competent in the instrumental aspect of his/her role (namely instruction and classroom control) are distinctly higher than those of their nonimmigrant peers. The veteran Israeli students, on the other hand, have somewhat higher expectations in the interpersonal domains of the teacher's role. (p. 194)

Hui and Triandis (1986) discovered that depending on cultural background researchers can differ in their attitudes to work and colleagues. They used the dimension of individualism and collectivism as a measuring tool for describing researchers' professional qualities. They claimed that researchers from collectivist societies tend to share more actively their resources with their colleagues, more willingly adopt other opinions, worry about self-presentation and loss of face, and so on. The researchers from individualist societies demonstrated, according to Hui and Triandis, a strong focus on individual goals (rather than common goals) and a sense of independence.

Different attitudes toward work and colleagues can certainly cause difficulties when adjusting to a new academic environment. These attitudes are molded by a specific social context that affects how people living in this society interpret the role of knowledge and education in their lives. In cultures that demonstrate more individualistic qualities, education is often understood as a way of becoming self-sufficient and independent. In individualist societies, education prepares an individual "for a place in a society of other individuals. This means learning to cope with new, unknown, unforeseen situations" (Hofstede & Hofstede, 2005, p. 98). The diploma in the individualist society testifies to a person's economic worth, "his or her self-respect: it provides a sense of achievement" (Hofstede & Hofstede, 2005, p. 99). For collectivists, education provides skills necessary to be accepted as a group member. "This leads to a premium on the products of tradition" (Hofstede & Hofstede, 2005, p. 98). A diploma means a great honor to its holder and the holder's family (in-group):

The social acceptance that comes with the diploma is more important than the individual self-respect that comes with mastering a subject, so that in collectivist societies the temptation is stronger to obtain diplomas in some irregular way, such as on the black market. (Hofstede & Hofstede, 2005, p. 99)

Obviously, the study of academic mobility programs and their implications on an individual and society should not be limited to the description of their advantages in the globalized era. In order to be successful, academic mobility programs have to provide their participants with a hospitable environment. For this purpose, more research should be devoted to cross-cultural differences and their manifestation in academic settings. This was one of the objectives of this research: to identify the possible differences (and difficulties) that students can experience while studying in an overseas university by means of the cultural dimensions analysis. The ultimate goal of this research was the development of a short training course to prepare students for differences they might encounter when studying abroad.

CONNECTING CULTURAL DIMENSIONS WITH ACADEMIC MOBILITY

In 1980, the Dutch social psychologist and former IBM employee Geert Hofstedein, in his book *Culture's Consequences*, published his research devoted to five dimensions that can be used to describe cultures to better understand and forecast behavior both of cross-cultural groups and organizations. These cultural dimensions are power distance (small and large), individualism/collectivism, uncertainty avoidance (high and low), masculinity/femininity, and orientation (long- and short-term). While working at IBM, he collected from its over 70 national subsidiaries around the world the largest cross-cultural database that he used later in his research.

The dimensions that are relevant for this research are collectivism/individualism as well as power distance and uncertainty avoidance.

The power distance index shows how society deals with inequalities. In the business environment of cultures with a small power distance index, inequalities are not expected as there is a preference for consultation and subordinates can more easily approach their bosses. In societies with a large power distance, "the emotional distance between subordinates and their bosses is large: subordinates are unlikely to approach and contradict their boss directly" (Hofstede & Hofstede, 2005, p. 46). The power distance factor affects the nature of the relationship between the students and their professors. In Asian cultures, a professor is viewed with reverence, which in an overseas environment, especially a U.S. one, can create a "deference barrier" (Cain, 2012, p. 185) and impede successful interaction. A professor in a high power distance culture cannot admit that they must look something up or check something. Adler (2007) described an Iranian student's experiences in the United States:

The first time . . . my [American] professor told me, "I don't know the answer, I will have to look it up," I was shocked. I asked myself, "Why is he teaching me?" In my country a professor would give the wrong answer rather than admit ignorance. (p. 70)

Specific features, such as the country's geographic position, population size, and national wealth can affect the power distance dimension in any sphere of people's life.

The uncertainty avoidance dimension shows how cultures tolerate ambiguity and unpredictable situations. The feelings that nations have about new unknown situations are related to their cultural heritage. Uncertainty avoidance demonstrates "the extent to which the members of a culture feel threatened by ambiguous or unknown situations" (Hofstede & Hofstede, 2005, p. 167). Wars, poverty, and social disturbances play a role in increasing the uncertainty avoidance dimension.

The dimension classifying cultures as collectivist and individualist focuses on the nature of the relationship between the individual and the group. When the interest of the group prevails over the interest of the individual, that society can be described as collectivist. *Collectivism* is described as "a social pattern consisting of closely linked individuals who see themselves as parts of one or more collectives . . . are primarily motivated by the norms of . . . and duties imposed by those collectives" (Triandis, 1995, p. 2). When speaking about individualism, one thinks about "a social pattern that consists of loosely linked individuals who view themselves as independent of collectives; are primarily motivated by their own preferences, needs, rights and the contacts they have established with ours" (Triandis, 1995, p. 2). The focus on the relationship between the individual and the group can be observed in all spheres of life, even in a classroom:

It often happens that teachers from a more individualist culture move to a more collectivist environment. A typical complaint from such teachers is that students do not speak up, not even when the teacher puts a question to the class. (Hofstede & Hofstede, 2005, p. 96)

Peetz (2010) observed that

Collectivist attitudes promote cooperation with other members of a group (or society). Individualistic attitudes, by contrast, are based on predominantly individual rather than predominantly group reference points and encourage self-referential rather than collective behaviour. At the individualist extreme all decisions are egocentric with no reference to any persons other than the selfish individual. (p. 385)

The previously mentioned cultural dimensions have been applied by scholars in various fields and in various kinds of research. For instance, André Laurent (1983), in his paper "The Cultural Diversity of Western Conceptions of Management," analyzed the perception of the role of a manager in various cultures relying mostly on a power distance dimension and claimed that "managers translate into behavior some of their basic, implicit beliefs about effective action in organization" (p. 75). Laurent composed a questionnaire consisting of 56 statements about the management process and administered it to 60 managers. Well aware of his colleague Geert Hofstede's work, he decided to compare the results between French and non-French managers.

As a result, Laurent (1983) came to a hypothesis about the connection between the national origin of European managers and their views of what proper management should be. Viewing organizations as authority systems, he discovered that "organizations are seen significantly more frequently as authority systems by French management (65% . . .) than by American managers (30% . . .)" (p. 83):

French, Italian, and Belgian managers report a more personal concept of authority that regulates relationships among individuals in organizations. American, Swiss, and German managers seem to report a more rational and instrumental view of authority that regulates interaction among tasks or functions. (p. 83)

Thus, organizations are "symbolic systems of social representation" (Laurent, 1983, p. 87-88).

Having studied national and cross national data on trends in dimensions of collectivism over periods of up to 2 decades, Peetz (2010), an Australian scholar who tried to answer the question whether individualistic attitudes are killing collectivism, noted that dimensions of collectivism/individualism are stimulated by the state's laws (or, better to say, by the whole legislative system); the behaviors of corporations and employers; and the condition of the labor market. Moreover, individualism is actively glamorized by advertisers and marketers. Peetz referred to the research stating that individualism is currently enhanced by inequality created by welfare state institutions such as education. As a result, "individuals are embedded in market relations, increasingly making their own choices (experiencing 'individuation'), fashioning their own identities, and are isolated, autonomous and egocentric" (p. 384).

However, proving that individualist attitudes are displacing collectivist attitudes and values is not so simple. Peetz (2010), for instance, brought the results of the World Values Survey that was conducted in the time period of over 2 decades. Participants of this survey were asked just two questions that showed whether they valued more their personal freedom (individualist attitude) or social equality (collectivist attitude). Americans scored the highest in individualist attitude as they consider freedom very important. However, what is essential in this survey is that it shows a change of people's attitudes over the time period: as time goes, support for personal freedom increased in seven countries, but, at the same time, nine countries increased support for social equality. Thus, the results of this survey cannot be used to prove that the spread of individualist values is killing collectivism.

What can be used to prove this hypothesis is the nature of the relationship between individuals and businesses, or, according to Peetz (2010), overall "individualization in the employment relationship," (p. 394) by which he meant the following:

The diminution or removal of collective mechanisms for determining the employment contract—that is, of collective bargaining, union representation and labour laws that provide collective protections for workers, so that wages and conditions are individually "negotiated" or, more commonly, unilaterally determined by management. (p. 394)

New work technology and an increasing role of work in the life of an individual increase one's dependence on the employer, thus making the current workforce find its own ways for professional (and financial) survival. This, as a result, together with structural changes in labor markets decreased the role of trade unions to organize collective action and defend the interests of workers (Peetz, 2010). Hence, the question that needs further elaboration is how the unions can place the interests of their members at the center of their activity, how to respond to their needs. Interestingly, a similar question is often posed currently by educators from the societies typically considered as collectivist (Russia, for instance), where it is strongly felt that old methods of class organization, knowledge assessment, and so on are not working anymore.

Hui, Yee, and Eastman (1995), in their study of 14 different countries aimed at establishing the relationship between collectivism/individualism and job satisfaction, observed that collectivists put more emphasis on social relationships at work rather than personal gains. As a result, the authors concluded that collectivism leads to greater job satisfaction. This stems from collectivists' striving to preserve interpersonal harmony, to establish and strengthen amicable relations among colleagues. The differences between collectivism and individualism, according to this research, can be observed even at the individual level in feelings and beliefs, intentions, and "behaviour related to solidarity and concern for others" (Hui et al., 1995, p. 277).

Since the 1950s, extensive research of collectivism/individualism has been conducted proving that this dimension is a valid measuring tool to understand cultural behavior. Contemporary research in this area has established a connection between the collectivism/individualism pattern and business behavior (Smith et al., 2011), occupational plans and work values (Hartung, Fouad, Leong, & Hardin, 2010), reward allocation (Fischer & Smith, 2003), implications for investment (Power, Schoenherr, & Samson, 2010), and education (Realo & Allik, 1999). Basabe and Ros (2005) established a connection between individualism and low population density, urbanization, migration, and a shift from extended to nuclear family structures. The authors concluded that as society becomes more affluent, people's need for independence, privacy, and individual choices increases. This idea—that societies are changing by demonstrating more individualist attributes—is frequently featured in the latest research.

Further to increased wealth and stability, members of societies undoubtedly crave more independent and interesting lifestyles. Moreover, individualism often seems to be more appealing as its attributes are aimed at providing more comfort. Air Mauritius (2014) advertises luxurious resorts in Mauritius and one of the reasons why people should travel there and stay at one of these hotels is

It's no longer enough for hotels to simply rest on the laurels of their five-star rating—they must recognise that more and more visitors value stylish individualism and independent thinking, and find ways to set themselves apart from the crowd.

At the best hotels and resorts in Mauritius, this is being achieved through a relentless focus on the personalisation of guest experiences, recognising that travellers are keen to try new things, and embracing unconventionality in all its forms. (para. 2, 3)

The positive connotation of such words and expressions as *stylish individualism, independent thinking, apart from the crowd*, and *personalization* illustrates that wealth is associated with individualism, which is becoming more and more widespread and is something that might be aspiring to individuals as well as to whole cultures. According to Richard Koch (2010), author of *The Star Principle: How It Can Make You Rich* and a highly successful entrepreneur and investor, individualism, indeed, has been stimulated by the overall growth of wealth all over the world (Koch, 2013).

At the same time, the adjective *cookie-cutter* has acquired, according to Reid (2014), a negative meaning as more and more people crave personalized services and goods. Individualism is stimulated by modern businesses which, apart from mass-produced products and services, provide modern consumers with a unique one-of-a-kind product or service. In all areas of activity (music, publishing, personal life), people are craving independence—"out of necessity or through evolution. Whatever independence means, for a nation, a person, an artist, it's becoming more and more important. We want community, certainly, but we also seek autonomy, on many levels" (Drew, 2014, para. 11). The advantages of individualism include a perceived right of personal freedom, feeling in control of one's destiny. More importantly, individualism provides people with numerous choices of personal development by offering unique educational experiences, bolstered by a modern person's desire for self-realization and, as a result, motivation for lifelong improvement (Reid, 2014). As Koch (2013) noted, "individualism has been an enormous success in encouraging ordinary people to realize their potential and their inner depths. . . . We develop ourselves for a higher cause, because that is the route to happiness and meaning" (para. 11, 16).

Based on Schwartz's (1992) extensive study of cultural values in which he identified those serving the interests of an individual, Konsky, Eguchi, Blue, and Kapoor (2002) further explored these values in individualist and collectivist cultures. Konsky et al. identified self-direction, stimulation, hedonism, and achievement as typical values of individualist societies (the study was based on U.S., Indian, and Japanese societies). Another piece of research in collectivism/individualism devoted to the study of values and lifestyles by means of U.S. and Taiwanese consumers' behavior, revealed that consumers of individualist societies (such as the United States) "were more brand-savvy, innovative, satisfied with their lives, financially satisfied and optimistic" (Tao, n.d., p. 411).

As can be seen from all these studies, collectivism/individualism is the dimension often used to identify, systematize and explain cultures' behavior in various aspects of people's life. As Tao (n.d.) noted, "this dimension has been identified as one of the major aspects of culture (e.g., Hofstede, 1980) and is perhaps one of the most significant ways in which societies differ" (p. 413). Such attributes as self-fulfillment, achievement, hedonism, and wanting everything to be personalized and tailored to one's specific needs and desires are usually associated with individualism.

Researchers from different cultural and professional backgrounds have shown an increasing interest in the study of the collectivism/individualism attributes, thus proving that a connection between the collectivism/individualism dimension and the academic environment can be further explored. In particular, the phenomenon of academic mobility, which has became a part of successful academic programs and/or education of a future graduate, deserves further attention. Several cultural studies have found that professional mobility increases individualistic attributes in modern societies along with the desire for self-improvement and self-fulfillment (Hofstede & McCrae, 2004; Triandis, 1995). Academic mobility programs are aimed at a future graduate's self-improvement and acquiring new experiences at the same time enjoying oneself and preparing for future professional (hopefully, successful) life. Therefore, they can be perceived as an impetus of attributes of individualism even in those societies which were considered to be collectivist (Russia, in this case).

This work attempted to study the experiences of students enrolled in academic mobility programs and to describe the distribution of collectivism/individualism attributes in their academic behavior. For this purpose, 10 students from the Department of Romance–Germanic Philology (Theoretical and Applied Linguistics Division), who took part in academic mobility programs for at least one semester, were surveyed. Before leaving their home institution, these students had demonstrated a good command of the English language and had theoretical knowledge of possible intercultural differences and communication skills necessary to overcome communication barriers.

It is important to stress that they all had a similar level of language proficiency and had successfully passed a required language test to participate in the program. Therefore, they did not feel overwhelmed by language difficulties or unexpected intercultural discoveries, which play an important role in adapting to a new academic environment (Mustaffa & Ilias, 2013, p. 292). These students were academically successful and enjoyed their intercultural experience although, at the same time, they also recorded differences between the Russian and the overseas academic environment. For the purpose of this research, these students were provided with essay questions about their experience abroad.

The similarities observed in the students' responses were highlighted and further analyzed from an intercultural perspective. Five main associative fields were identified in their answers, such as independence, freedom, choices, relationship with professors and exams. Their essays showed that these students enjoyed their independence and freedom to make their own choices while studying abroad. The fact that they decided to enroll in an academic mobility program demonstrates their desire for self-improvement and interest in traveling. These facts correlate with attributes of individualism and the lower index of uncertainty avoidance.

To test the results obtained from their questionnaires, a second survey was conducted with other students from the Department of Romance–Germanic Philology (years 2–5). They had to complete a multiple-choice questionnaire where the answer choices reflected collectivism/individualism patterns of behavior (these were borrowed from the previous research mentioned earlier in this section). The purpose of this second survey was to see whether the students, when answering the questions, demonstrated similar cultural dimensions to the students in Group 1. The analysis relied on the cultural dimensions, described by Hofstede and Hofstede (2005), and research on attributes of individualist and collectivist societies (such as Gudykunst et al., 1996; Schwartz, 1992; Triandis, 1995). At this stage of the analysis, 56 students were involved: 2nd-year students (34 people), 3rd-year students (10 people), and 4th- and 5th-year students (final year; 12 people). The students answered eight multiple-choice questions reflecting collectivism/individualism patterns of behavior in academic contexts.

The results proved the hypothesis that globalization increases the number of individualistic attributes in societies. The interconnection of cultures and the Bologna Process made it possible for Russian students to participate more actively in academic mobility programs, thus showing their desire for self-development and independence as well as demonstrating a lower uncertainty avoidance index in their behavior.

CASE STUDY: STUDENTS' EXPERIENCES IN ACADEMIC MOBILITY PROGRAMS

Previous research on collectivism/individualism usually identifies Russia as a collectivist society with high power distance and a high uncertainty avoidance index (see, for instance, Elenkov, 1998). Triandis (1995), in his book *Individualism and Collectivism*, described Russia in the following way:

In Russia it is assumed that the whole country is responsible for child rearing. If the parent is not doing an adequate job, an older person is responsible for upholding community standards. "Putting one's nose in another person's business" is perfectly natural and expected. (p. 3)

Hofstede and Hofstede, in their 2005 book, noted that Russia usually scores high on collectivism and it is "more collectivist than Western countries" (p. 103) with large power distance. More recently, in 2011, a group of academics, Tu, Lin, and Chang, conducted a cross-cultural comparison based on the collectivism/individualism dimension among Brazil, Russia, India, and China that included employees from public companies. Russia was again described as a collectivist society very similar to Brazil (Tu et al., 2011, p. 179).

However, globalization has brought about changes in Russian society that had already been transformed after the Perestroika. These changes also affected the academic environment. In 2003, Russia joined the Bologna Process and embarked on a very controversial road of reforms within its educational system. The main reason for this decision, according to the Russian government, was the necessity to promote academic mobility for both students and professors and create educational standards similar to those in Western countries.

In 2012, the Russian government attempted to reevaluate the readiness of Russian universities to compete successfully in the international arena (a so-called *effectiveness* factor). The introduction of successful academic mobility programs was one of the important factors (along with incoming students' test scores, employability of graduates and incomes from scientific projects) to evaluate the effectiveness of Russian universities. The Russian government implied that academic mobility programs were the result of a good educational and scientific environment able to attract overseas students and specialists and, at the same time, allow Russian students to integrate successfully in an international environment, thus bringing back home new experience and professional knowledge (Khoutyz, 2013b).

Since 2003, the number of academic exchange programs has peaked and become a matter of pride for Russian universities. Globalization provided Russian university students and professors with more academic mobility opportunities. Russian universities proudly present the information about the increased international contacts on their websites. For instance, Kuban State University (n.d.)—one of the largest universities in the South of Russia—pointed out in its English-language website that the university is establishing international links in its main sphere, education. There are more than 350 foreign students from all over the world presently studying at Kuban State University. Academic mobility programs do not include only students but also teaching and administrative staff members. Kuban State University cooperates with 55 foreign educational and scientific centers, and 13 partnership agreements were signed in 2014. According to Kuban State University (n.d.), in 2014, about 400 foreign students from 55 countries were studying at Kuban State University. Thanks to partnership agreements and contracts with 16 universities from Belgium, South Korea, Portugal, France, Germany, China, Sweden, Great Britain, the Netherlands, Austria, and the United States, 45 Kuban State University students were allowed to study abroad. Russian students are given an opportunity to acquire a double degree by simultaneously studying at Kuban State University and its partner universities, Berlin University of Applied Sciences and Czech University of Life Sciences. Supposedly, this offer is very lucrative for future Russian graduates. It is obvious that Kuban State University, just like other Russian universities, takes pride in its academic mobility programs, which are greatly advertised on its website.

Traveling abroad has certainly become more widespread and appealing to Russians in general and Russian students in particular. One hundred percent of the surveyed students (studying at the theoretical and applied linguistics division of Kuban State University) showed a great interest in enrolling in an academic mobility program (28 students participated in the survey from 1–4 years of studying) (Khoutyz, 2013b). The most popular reasons to study abroad were found to be to improve the knowledge of a foreign language (78%) followed by the desire to see a new country and find new friends (75%) and further personal development (68%). Thirty-nine percent of students considered this experience as an important aspect of their future career. Their answers demonstrated a great interest in other cultures and desire to combine the process of studying (personal development) with personal enjoyment and new life experiences. These choices reflect the presence of individualistic attributes in a modern student's character stimulated by such values as self-direction, achievement, and hedonism (values identified by Schwartz, 1992).

This is not surprising at all as the analysis of students' experience in Study Abroad programs showed an increased number of individualistic attributes in students' characters and in their perception of an academic environment. As was mentioned previously, the distribution of individualistic attributes has been revealed by means of a two-step survey.

Survey Step 1

The students who participated in the first part of the survey had to answer essay questions describing their experiences in a Study Abroad program. The focus was on the answers about what the students mostly liked and disliked in an overseas academic environment. All the students noted that most of all they liked the fact that they were treated as independent adults who could make their own decisions. The whole academic process was carefully organized to take student's interests into consideration: they could choose the classes they would take during the semester; nobody was supervising their progress; they felt responsible only to themselves. Following are excerpts from their answers in this respect as translated by the author; the age of the students reflects their age at the time of their participation in the academic mobility program.

Alexey, 20 Years

The student is regarded as an independent person who can choose their own program and classes. Students organize their time the way they like and create their own timetable. For instance, if I choose to study linguistics, besides the required courses, I can take the courses which I am interested in—for instance, management. Attendance is not a key factor in student performance assessment.

Ella, 20 Years

I liked best the opportunity to choose courses out of a great variety of classes at the beginning of the semester. I especially liked the fact that I had 2 weeks to make sure I made the right choice. I could attend any classes to make sure that the course would be useful (or interesting) for me.

Polina, 20 Years

I liked the fact that more attention is paid to the exam and knowledge per se rather than student attendance. The academic process is aimed at critical thinking: What is important is not how well a student learned the information but how well a student can use this information to test what they already know, analyze a point of view, and support or criticize it.

Anastasia, 18 Years

Students have a chance to choose their optional (secondary) courses. This allows students to create their own schedule. The university website lists all the available courses, their timetable, and all the professors who teach them. Students have their profiles on the university website. These profiles are created immediately after a student enters the university: They receive a student ID, which gives them access to all libraries and university sports centers in the city. Nobody makes you attend physical education classes; a student chooses which sports groups to attend.

In general, students answered that they liked almost everything in their Study Abroad experience. They underlined the importance of choice and independence as well as the opportunity of using rather than learning information. However, Polina (who liked the fact that the attendance did not matter as much as at her home university) wrote that she did not like the professors' complete lack of supervision of their students' progress; exam questions, which could have helped students focus on the most important aspects of the class, were not given in advance (Russian students are used to getting these questions at the beginning of a course). Anastasia wrote that the great focus on students' independent work with just a few "real" in-person classes made it harder for her to succeed:

I would like to mention a difference between Russian and, in my case, Belgian students. This is just my opinion. It seemed to me that Belgian students were more mature and better organized. They are expected to do most of the work independently: There is just one class per week.

Anastasia thought that this approach was because students are actually different: "For Russian students, a professor has to spoon-feed them the material and then make sure that they swallow it."

Among other things they did not like, the students mentioned the absence of so-called *advance exams* (Russian students get them in advance provided that they attend all the classes and demonstrate a good working knowledge during the semester), a difficult grading system, and too much focus on independent work with only 2 academic hours per class each week. Interestingly, in some cases, students contradict themselves: Polina liked the freedom she experienced in a Belgian university yet she found it to be a disadvantage that professors in no way supervised the progress of their students and did not liberate "hardworking students" from a final exam.

Students' answers reveal an association between the advantages of the mobility programs with their independence and freedom to make their own choices. The disadvantages included lack of supervision, absence of emotional involvement in their progress, and a strong emphasis on independent, out-of-class work.

Survey Step 2

In order to determine whether all Russian students demonstrate individualistic attributes (or only those who participated in academic mobility programs), a second party of the survey was conducted.

At this stage of the analysis, 56 students had to answer eight multiple-choice questions reflecting collectivism/individualism patterns of behavior within an academic environment (the nature of the survey is similar to the one conducted by the World Values Survey mentioned previously). The questionnaire was designed so as to take patterns of collectivism/individualism behavior described in previous research into consideration (see Basabe & Ros, 2005; Hofstede & Hofstede, 2005; Schwartz, 1992; Triandis, 1995): Self-development, financial stability, and independence are features of individualistic behavior whereas receiving respect in society or pleasing a family are patterns of collectivistic behavior. For instance, in Question 4, students were asked which pattern of relationship with their professors they considered to be appropriate: (a) The role of the professor is to clearly and interestingly inform on the subject, it is a formal, distant relationship; or (b) The role of the professor is to support and encourage students, help them with choices, and let them know when and how they need to improve their results. Obviously, the first option is consistent with individualist behavior whereas the second option is more typical of collectivist behavior. Other questions in the survey were aimed at assessing why students were studying at university, how they made the decision about where and what to study, which type of classes they enjoyed (lectures or seminars), what aspects of student activities are essential for grading, and so forth.

Results showed that all of the students demonstrated mostly features of individualistic behavior. For instance, the goal of their university study was self-development and self-realization: 73.5% for 2nd-year students and 67% for 4th- and 5th-year students. The majority of the 3rd-year students chose two individualistic patterns of behavior: They study for self-development (40%) and future financial stability (40%). Very few students chose patterns of collectivist behavior, such as respect in society and looking for new connections and possibly a future spouse. Preference was also shown for individualistic patterns of behavior on points of the questionnaire asking students about the type of classes they enjoy the most, which activities should matter the most when grading students, and the most important personal qualities which they wished to develop while studying at the university. Yet, students preferred their professors to act as collectivists towards them; they expected to be provided with all kinds of support and guidance.

The second phase of the survey explains the observations made by the Russian students enrolled in Study Abroad programs who responded in Phase 1 of the survey. They enjoyed their independence, freedom, and choices provided at the university, yet they were disappointed by how distant professors seemed and how much they had to do on their own without their professors' help. The results show that there are mostly individualist attributes in modern students' behavior, yet in their relationship with their professors, they continue to be collectivist. For instance, Russian students often congratulate their professors on their birthdays and on the students' graduation day; they give them gifts and flowers. Students will ask professors for life advice and sometimes even invite them to their weddings (as in Greek culture, according to Triandis, 1995).

FUTURE RESEARCH DIRECTIONS

Academic mobility programs are becoming a prerequisite for the survival of modern universities. Successful academic mobility programs attract new students and experienced academics. The programs also allow educational institutions to sustain competition and contribute to the international academic community. Processes relating to academic mobility are reinforced by opportunities for professional mobility. This kind of situation offers interesting perspectives for further research. For instance, research can bridge the gap between the needs of students, academics, as well as other professionals, and adequate intercultural awareness training programs. This can be achieved by identifying and explaining differences in cultural dimensions in several sociocultural contexts as well as showing how they are reflected in the attitude of individuals. The results of the survey presented and analyzed in this chapter also testify to the growing need to restructure the educational process in Russian universities by entrusting students with more personal choices and changing the methods of knowledge assessment. Thus, more research should be invested in developing new educational methods that meet the needs of a modern student.

CONCLUSION

Globalization brings about the interconnection of modern societies, which is reflected in intercultural awareness, coupled with an improvement in communicative competence in the lingua franca of the 21st century—the English language. As a result, new professional opportunities appear; professional mobility being an example. Professional mobility allows specialists to share their knowledge and compete at an international level. In academic environments, professional mobility is replaced by academic mobility programs. The programs are promoted by the Bologna Process.

Globalization and new professional opportunities leading to life-long self-improvement and the education process initiate changes in modern societies. In particular, as it has been illustrated in this chapter, collectivist societies begin to demonstrate more individualist attributes.

These attributes, such as desire for independence, self-perfection and self-development, present new choices, the acquisition of education for success, professional well-being, along with the opportunity to have interesting and enjoyable academic experiences were expressed by Russian students from both groups—those opting for academic mobility programs and those who have not experienced studying abroad (although they all find this experience very desirable). The results of the survey conducted among the students studying at the Department of Romance–Germanic Philology (Kuban State University) show that contemporary Russian students exhibit numerous patterns of individualist behavior. They independently choose the place and subject of their study; the purpose of their education is self-realization and self-improvement and financial stability; while at university, they try to study hard to get a good job in the future; they enjoy class participation and are fond of voicing their opinions; and they think that class participation should be the most important aspect in grading their work.

Furthermore, Russian university students are interested in communicative competence and how to be able to find a common language in any situation. Finally, this study found that students, in Russia, strive to achieve successful planning skills to be used outside the academic environment in order to maximize their time-management skills in all aspects of their daily lives. The only collectivist pattern in their thinking was found in their expectations about their professors' behaviour. This means that, in the opinion of students, professors should always be personally involved not only in teaching but also in the learning process. Students also expect teachers to be helpful and supportive in order to carefully guide them through all the stages of knowledge acquisition (Khoutyz, 2013b).

Modern Russian society, typically classified as collectivist, has undergone deep changes since the Perestroika years. Thanks to a stable political situation and increased international opportunities. Present-day Russia has undoubtedly become more prosperous. As a result, the Russian people, at least the younger generation, who partake in those opportunities generated by globalization, acquire more individualist attributes. It is reasonable to assume that all these changes decrease the index of uncertainty avoidance (reflected, for instance, in increased travel and professional mobility) and the index of power distance (less formal communication in certain professional environments expressed, for instance, by the use of the first name only).

REFERENCES

Adler, N. J. (2007). *International dimensions of organizational behavior*. Mason, OH: Thomson.

Air. (2014). *Travel trends 2014: Stylish individualism*. Retrieved from http://blog. airmauritius.com/travel-trends-2014-stylish-individualism/

Asanova, G., & Ryssaldy, K. (2013). Academic mobility as the source of scientific-educational cooperation. *CBU International Conference Proceedings, 3*, 174–181. doi:10.12955/cbup.v1.675

Australian Public Service Commission. (2015). *Employee mobility: Principles for advancing professional development*. Retrieved from http://www.apsc.gov.au/working-in-the-aps/applying-for-jobs/employee-mobility-principles-for-advancing-professional-development

Basabe, N., & Ros, M. (2005). Cultural dimensions and social behavior correlates: Individualism-collectivism and power distance. *Revue Internationale de Psychologie Sociale. PressesUniversitaires de Grenoble, 18*(1), 189–225.

Bazhenova, E. D. (2013). Content analysis of the category "Academic Mobility of Students.". *Middle-East Journal of Scientific Research, 13*(4), 483–488. doi:10.5829/idosi.mejsr.2013.13.4.2914

Cain, S. (2012). *Quiet: The power of introverts in a world that can't stop talking*. New York, NY: Broadway Books.

Codina, B., Nicolás, J., López, L., & Hernán, R. (2013). The importance of student mobility, academic exchange and internationalization of higher education for college students in a globalized world: The Mexican and Latin American case. *International Journal of Good Conscience, 8*(2), 48–63. Retrieved from http://www.spentamexico.org/v8-n2/A3.8%282%2948-63.pdf

Cronin, M. (2003). *Translation and globalization*. London: Routledge.

Drew, M. (2014, September 17). Intimations of independence. *Huffington Post*. Retrieved from http://www.huffingtonpost.com/michael-drew/intimations-of-independen_b_5829236. html

Education Charter International. (n.d.). *Global initiative*. Retrieved from http://cclpworldwide.com/eci/view-content/14/Global-Initiative.html

Elenkov, D. S. (1998). Can American management concepts work in? A cross-cultural comparative study. *Management Review, 40*(4), 133–156. doi:10.2307/ 41165968

Epstein, A., & Kheimets, N. (2000). Cultural clash and educational diversity: Immigrant teachers' efforts to rescue the education of immigrant children in Israel. *International Studies in Sociology of Education, 10*(2), 191–210. doi:10.1080/09620210000200055

European Parliament. (2013, September 10). *MEPs pave the way for greater professional mobility in the EU* [Press release]. Retrieved from http://www.europarl.europa.eu/news/ en/news-room/content/20131008IPR21711/html/MEPs-pave-the-way-for-greater-professional-mobility-in-the-EU

European People's Party. (2013, January 23). *Yes to professional mobility in Europe!* [Press release]. Retrieved http://www.eppgroup.eu/press-release/Yes-to-professional-mobility-in-Europe!

Fairclough, N. (2006). *Language and globalization*. London: Routledge.

Fischer, R., & Smith, P. B. (2003). Reward allocation and culture: A meta-analysis. *Journal of Cross-Cultural Psychology, 34*(3), 251–268. doi:10.1177/0022022103034003001

Gudykunst, W. B., Matsumoto, W., Nishida, T., Kim, K., Heyman, S., & Ting-Toomey, S. (1996). The influence of cultural individualism-collectivism, self-construals, and individual values on communication styles across cultures. *Human Communication Research, 22*(4), 510–543. doi:10.1111/j.1468-2958.1996.tb00377.x

Hartung, P. J., Fouad, N. A., Leong, F. T. L., & Hardin, E. E. (2010). Individualism-collectivism: Links to occupational plans and work values. *Journal of Career Assessment, 18*(1), 34–45. doi:10.1177/1069072709340526

Hofstede, G. (1980). *Culture's consequences: international differences in work-related values*. Thousand Oaks, CA: Sage.

Hofstede, G., & Hofstede, G. J. (2005). *Cultures and organization: Software of the mind*. McGraw-Hill.

Hofstede, G., & McCrae, R. (2004). Personality and culture revisited: Linking traits and dimensions of culture. *Cross-Cultural Research Journal, 38*(1), 52–88. doi:10.1177/1069397103259443

Hui, H. C., & Triandis, H. C. (1986). Individualism-collectivism: A study of cross-cultural researchers. *Journal of Cross-Cultural Psychology, 17*(2), 225–248. doi:10.1177/0022002186017002006

Hui, H. C., Yee, C., & Eastman, K. L. (1995). The relationship between individualism-collectivism and job satisfaction. *Applied Psychology, 44*(3), 276–282. doi:10.1111/j.1464-0597.1995.tb01080.x

International Cooperation. (n.d.). Retrieved from http://www.kubsu.ru/ en/node/1989

Kharitonova, O. V. (2012). Akademicheskaya mobil'nost v prostranstve visshego obrazovanija. [Academic mobility in high education]. *Chelovek i obrazovanie, 2*, 41–44. Retrieved from http://cyberleninka.ru/article/n/akademicheskaya-mobilnost-v-prostranstve-vysshego-obrazovaniya

Khoutyz, I. (2013a). Globalisation and English as a lingua franca: Does the future promise culturally homogenous or inimitable societies? In R. Fisher, L. Howard, K. Monteith, & D. Riha (Eds.), *Interculturalism, meaning and identity* (pp. 3–13). Oxford, UK: Inter-Disciplinary Press.

Khoutyz, I. (2013b). Multicultural perspectives in academic communication: Academic mobility and teaching practices. In *Proceedings of the 6th International Conference of Education, Research and Innovation* (pp. 6150–6169). Seville, Spain: International Academy of Technology, Education and Development.

Koch, R. (2010). *The star principle: How it can make you rich*. London: Piatkus.

Koch, R. (2013, October 7). Is individualism good or bad? *Huffington Post*. Retrieved from http://www.huffingtonpost.com/richard-koch/is-individualism-good-or-_b_4056305.html

Konsky, C., Eguchi, M., Blue, J., & Kapoor, S. (2002). Individualist-collectivist values: American, Indian and Japanese cross-cultural study. *Intercultural Communication Studies, 9*(1), 69–83. Retrieved from http://web.uri.edu/iaics/files/07-Catherine-Konsky-Mariko-Eguchi-Janet-Blue-Suraj-Kapoor.pdf

Laurent, A. (1983). The cultural diversity of Western conceptions of management. *International Studies of Management & Organization, 13*(1/2), 75–96. doi:10.1080/00208825.1983.11656359

Morris, R. (1988). Northern Europe invades the Mediterranean, 900–1200. In G. Holmes (Ed.), The Oxford history of medieval Europe (pp. 165–221). Oxford, UK: Oxford University Press.

Mustaffa, C., & Ilias, M. (2013). Relationship between students' adjustment factors and cross-cultural adjustment: A survey at the Northern University of Malaysia. *Intercultural Communication Studies, 22*(1), 279–300. Retrieved from http://web.uri.edu/iaics/files/19Che-Su-Mustaffa-Munirah-Ilias.pdf

Peetz, D. (2010). Are individualistic attitudes killing collectivism? *Transfer: European Review of Labour and Research, 16*(3), 383–398. doi:10.1177/1024258910373869

Peugeot Citroën, P. S. A. (n.d.). *Professional mobility: A chance to grow within the group.* Retrieved from http://www.psa-peugeot-citroen.com/en/inside-our-industrial-environment/a-socially-responsible-business/professional-mobility-chance-grow-within-group-article

Power, D., Schoenherr, T., & Samson, D. (2010). The cultural characteristic of individualism/collectivism: A comparative study of implications for investment in operations between emerging Asian and industrialized Western countries. *Journal of Operations Management, 28*(3), 206–222. doi:10.1016/j.jom.2009.11.002

Realo, A., & Allik, J. (1999). A cross-cultural study of collectivism: A comparison of American, Estonian, and Russian students. *The Journal of Social Psychology, 139*(2), 133–142. doi:10.1080/00224549909598367

Reid, B. (2014, October 3). Individualized just-in-time products and services should be a leadership priority. *Huffington Post.* Retrieved from http://www.huffingtonpost.com/

Schwartz, S. (1992). Universals in the content and structure of values: Theoretical advances and empirical advances in 20 countries. In J. M. Olson & M. P. Zanna (Eds.), *Advances in experimental psychology* (Vol. 25, pp. 1–65). Cambridge, MA: Academic Press. doi:10.1016/S0065-2601(08)60281-6

Sergeev, S. O. (2015). Akademicheskaya mobil'nost' kak instrument mjagkoi sili nauki. [Academic mobility as an instrument of power of soft science]. *Gumanitarnie, sotsial'no-ekonomicheskie i obshchestvennie nauki, 6*(1), 198–201.

Sharkov, D. (2015, June 19). Russian sanctions to 'cost Europe €100bn'. *Newsweek.* Retrieved from http://europe.newsweek.com/russian-sanctions-could-cost-europe-100-billion-328999

Smith, P. B., Torres, C. V., Hecke, J., Chua, C. H., Chudzikova, A., Degirmencioglu, S., & Yanchuk, V. (2011). Individualism-collectivism and business context as predictors of behaviors in cross-national work settings: Incidence and outcomes. *International Journal of Intercultural Relations, 35*(4), 440–451. doi:10.1016/j.ijintrel.2011.02.001

Steger, M. (2005). *Globalism: Market ideology meets terrorism.* Lanham, MD: Rowman & Littlefield.

Study abroad: Where to study in Europe . . . in English. (n.d.). *The Telegraph.* Retrieved from http://www.telegraph.co.uk/education/universityeducation/9447458/Study-abroad-Where-to-study-in-Europe...-in-English.html

Tao, S.-P. (n.d.). *Values and lifestyles of individualists and collectivists: A cross-culture study on Taiwanese and US consumers*. Retrieved from http://www.mnd.gov.tw/upload/16--%E9%99%B6%E8%81%96%E5%B1%8F.pdf

Tomlinson, J. (1999). *Globalization and culture*. University of Chicago Press.

Triandis, H. C. (1995). *Individualism and collectivism*. Oxford, UK: Westview Press.

Tu, Y., Lin, S., & Chang, Y. (2011). A cross-cultural comparison by individualism/collectivism among Brazil, Russia, India and China. *International Business Research, 4*(2), 175–182. doi:10.5539/ibr.v4n2p175

Urry, J. (1995). *Consuming places*. London: Routledge.

Valeeva, E. R., & Babukh, V. A. (2013). Izuchenie problem sotsial'noi politiki Ispanii i Rossii v protsesse prepodavanija pravovikh distsiplin studentam magistraturi v ramkakh programmi dvoinih diplomov. [The study of the social policy problems in Spain and in Russia when teaching law courses to post graduate students acquiring a double degree]. *Vestnik Kazanskogo tekhnologicheskogo universiteta, 1*, 302–306. Retrieved from http://cyberleninka.ru/article/n/izuchenie-problem-sotsialnoy-politiki-ispanii-i-rossii-v-protsesse-prepodavaniya-pravovyh-distsiplin-studentam-magistratury-v-ramkah

Volodina, E. D. (2014). Sistematizatsija form mezhdunarodnoi academicheskoy mobil'nosti studentov. [Classifying forms of academic mobility programs for students]. *Vestnik Chelyabinskogo gosudarstvennogo pedagogicheskogo universiteta, 2*, 93–102. Retrieved from http://cyberleninka.ru/article/n/sistematizatsiya-form-mezhdunarodnoy-akademicheskoy-mobilnosti-studentov

ADDITIONAL READING

Blumenthal, P. (Ed.). (1996). *Academic mobility in a changing world: Regional and global trends*. Bristol, England: Jessica Kingsley.

Braman, O. R. (1998). *The cultural dimension of individualism and collectivism as a factor of adult self-learning readiness*. Unpublished doctoral dissertation, The University of Southern Mississippi, Hattiesburg.

Byram, M., & Devin, F. (Eds.). (2008). *Students, staff and academic mobility in higher education*. Newcastle upon Tyne, England: Cambridge Scholars.

Devin, F. (Ed.). (2011). *Analyzing the consequences of academic mobility and migration*. Newcastle upon Tyne, England: Cambridge Scholars.

Fahey, J., & Kenway, J. (2010). International academic mobility: Problematic and possible paradigms. *Discourse (Abingdon), 31*(5), 563–575. doi:10.1080/01596306.2010.516937

Hoffman, D. (2009). Changing academic mobility patterns and international migration: What will academic mobility mean in the 21st century? *Journal of Studies in International Education, 13*(3), 347–364. doi:10.1177/1028315308321374

Holden, N. (2001). Knowledge management: Raising the spectre of the cross-cultural dimension. *Knowledge and Process Management*, 8(3), 155–163. doi:10.1002/kpm.117

Isernhagen, J. C., & Bulkin, N. (2011). The impact of mobility on student performance and teacher practice. *The Journal of At-Risk Issues*, 16(1), 17–24. Retrieved from http://files.eric.ed.gov/fulltext/EJ942895.pdf

Jöns, H. (2011). Transnational academic mobility and gender. *Globalisation, Societies and Education*, 9(2), 183–209. doi:10.1080/14767724.2011.577199

Kim, T. (2009). Transnational academic mobility, internationalization and interculturality in higher education. *Intercultural Education*, 20(5), 395–405. doi:10.1080/14675980903371241

Kim, T. (2010). Transnational academic mobility, knowledge, and identity capital. *Discourse: Studies in the Cultural Politics of Education*, 31(5), 577–591. doi:. 2010.51693910.1080/01596306

Musselin, C. (2004). Towards a European academic labour market? Some lessons drawn from empirical studies on academic mobility. *Higher Education*, 48(1), 55–78. doi:: high.0000033770.24848.4110.1023/b

Tower, R. K., Kelly, C., & Richards, A. (1997). Individualism, collectivism and reward allocation: A cross-cultural study in Russia and Britain. *The British Journal of Social Psychology*, 36(3), 331–345. doi:10.1111/j.2044-8309.1997.tb01135.x

Ulrich, K. (1993). Flexibility and mobility of academic staff. *Higher Education Management*, 5(2), 141–150. ERIC: EJ469003.

KEY TERMS AND DEFINITIONS

Academic Environment: A context interconnecting various agents and processes in academia.

Associative Field: Notions and concepts united by some general idea.

Attributes: Qualities—for instance, indirectness—typical of certain cultures.

Bologna Process: A European reform in education aimed at establishing similar educational processes to promote international cooperation and academic exchange.

Cultural Dimensions: Measurement instruments used for uncovering cultural differences.

Cultural Values: Norms and ways of behavior conditioning attitudes and reactions to events and various phenomena in a context of a culture.

Patterns of Behavior: Recurrent ways of behavior.

Chapter 9
Early Identification of Transformation in the Proficiency Level of Critical Thinking:
In the Associate Degree Nursing Student

Velmarie King Swing
Southern Nazarene University, USA

ABSTRACT

Critical Thinking (CT) in the nurse graduate continues to be a topic of concern in the academic and acute care settings. Few studies focus on early evaluation of Critical Thinking Skills (CTS). The purpose of this chapter is to show how the non-experimental, explanatory, quantitative study, the Kaplan CTIT, was employed to determine if a transformation in the level of CTS occurs within the first semester of associate degree nursing students. Participants completed the pretest in the first three weeks of classes. Posttests were given after course finals. A significant transformation in the level of CT occurred. The estimated change in CT test scores was 2.04, with 95% confidence. Implications for early measurement of CTS in nursing programs reveals if teaching methodology is providing the necessary input for developing CTS or if evaluation and changes are needed.

INTRODUCTION

Incorporating and implementing critical thinking skills (CTS), regardless of individual ethnicity, cultural background or nursing position should be every entry level nursing student's goal in order to provide accurate and safe patient care (Romeo, 2010). Critical thinking (CT), allows an individual to face a challenge and systematically work out a solution for the best possible resolution (Paul & Elder, 2006). Learning CTS can be arduous. The task requires guidance, assessment, and evaluation of skills to ensure appropriate efficacy and outcomes. Continuous monitoring of CTS throughout the nursing program can

DOI: 10.4018/978-1-5225-0522-8.ch009

support and ensure the student becoming licensed upon successful completion of an approved nursing program (Romeo, 2010).

Achievement in the academic and patient care settings are diametrically affected by the lack of or inability of critical thinking (Oermann, Poole-Dawkins, Alvarez, Foster, & O'Sullivan, 2010). Consistent reporting of newly graduated nurses in the acute care setting stated a lack of adequate CTS (Oermann, et al., 2010; Romeo, 2010). While there is a superfluity of comparison between the beginning and end of nursing programs CTS competence, little research has addressed the thorough evaluation of CTS proficiency in the first semester of nursing school. Early identification of CTS proficiency or lack thereof should be addressed and student learning needs met to ensure the nursing graduate has the essential tools to function safely in the acute care setting. The topic of the study was early identification of transformation in CTS in the first semester of the associate degree nursing (ADN) student. The objectives of this chapter include illustration of: (1) proof that computerized pre and posttests are effective in measuring transformation levels of CT in the first semester ADN student; (2) identification of affecting attributes that influence CTS; and (3) evidence that early assessment of CT can enhance the promotion of CTS.

BACKGROUND

Paul and Elder (2012) discussed the history and the roots of critical thinking, which was traced back to Socrates. Socrates challenged others by asking inquisitive questions in the attempt to prove or disprove individual claims of knowledge. It is important for the nursing student to understand the need for critical thinking and to have continuous growth of critical thinking in order to become a safe, effective nurse (Romeo, 2010). The Oklahoma Board of Nursing (Oklahoma, 2011) requires nursing programs to provide lecture, labs, and clinical experiences that facilitate the growth of or enhancement of CTS for the enrolled nursing student. While nursing programs provide the experiences as dictated by the nursing board, few new graduates adequately think critically in the acute care setting, despite the students' successful completion of the program and National Council Licensure Examination (NCLEX) to achieve licensure (Oermann et al., 2010).

Ensuring adequate growth in CTS may also affect student ability to provide safe, effective patient care (Romeo, 2010). Insufficient CTS may cause the new graduate nurse to miss an assessment and the identification of signs and symptoms regarding disease processes, which can further a hospital stay or even result in death. Evaluating the students' ability to think critically while in the nursing program continues to be problematic (Deschênes, Charlin, Gagnon, & Goudreau, 2011). In a 2000 study, Diede, McNish, and Coose indicated that new graduates barely met competencies required for the job according to nursing directors surveyed. The new graduate nurse continues to fall short in CTS despite the available studies that address the importance of having the ability to think critically.

THEORETICAL FRAMEWORK

The theoretical framework utilized was the Roy Adaptation Model (RAM), which asserted that all aspects of life affect the learner (Roy, 2009). A change in the level of CTS would further the assertion of RAM that human systems are affected by the environment, which allows for adaptation that can affect decisions and reactions in future situations. Roy identified a system as a set of parts that rely on each other to function and experience feedback, control, outputs and inputs (2009). The culture of an individual can influence how the elements of the RAM become expressed (Roy, 2009). Culture can also guide all or part of the RAM to a lesser or greater extent and evolve over time, which can require continuous evaluation for needed changes in nursing assessments, and further research and education. The cultural assumption represents a simple system comprised of inputs, controls, outputs, and feedback. In the study, the adaptation stimuli were the nursing curriculum, clinical, and lab activities that assisted the nursing student in cultivating critical thinking skills. The feedback was the students' clinical skills, exam grades, and simulation exercises in the lab that can lead back to the stimuli, which evoked change (Roy, 2009). Additionally, Roy concluded that life experiences outside of the learning arena affected responses to stimuli. In the study, the adaption stimuli were the nursing curriculum, clinical, and lab activities that assisted the nursing student in improvement of CTS.

LITERATURE REVIEW

(Search engines utilized were ProQuest, EBSCO host, ERIC, CINAHL, Ovid, and the websites of NLN, STTI, and OBN.)

Critical thinking has been in nursing literature since the 1980's. The majority of literature continues to indicate the lack of a concrete definition for critical thinking and the concept of critical thinking. Newly graduated nurses from Associate Degree (ADN) and Baccalaureate (BSN) programs consistently lack adequate critical thinking skills (CTS) in the acute care setting (Oermann et al., 2010; Romeo, 2010). Providing early identification of CTS proficiency or the lack thereof can help guide the educator in meeting student learning needs. Critical thinking is a requirement of the National Council of State Boards of Nursing (NCSBN) and an element tested by the National Council Licensure Examination (Romeo, 2010). When an educator strives to meet the learning needs of a student and ensures the use of essential tools to enhance CTS are utilized, safe patient care can be positively affected (Hopkins, 2008).

Review of Research Regarding Growth in the Level of Critical Thinking

Several themes surfaced regarding critical thinking (CT) during the literature review. Eight specific themes developed which will be discussed at length in this section. The themes were identified as: concept and definition of critical thinking; affecting attributes; educational strategies to promote CTS; educator responsibility; environment of learning; measurement and evaluation of CTS; expected level of ADN critical thinking skills; and review of methodological issues.

Critical Thinking: Concept and Definition

A simple definition of *concept* is a general idea inferred or derived from specific occurrences or instances. Although each term can be defined, the nursing profession has yet to agree on a unified and clear definition and concept of critical thinking. Many have used or found critical literacy, critical thinking, reflective thinking, clinical judgment, and clinical reasoning to be used synonymously (Clarke, 2009; Dykstra, 2008; Jones, 2010; Turner, 2005). Most of the reviewed literature revealed many definitions for critical thinking. A theoretical definition has yet to be accepted and defined in the nursing profession (Romeo, 2010). Brunt (2005) stated that critical thinking (CT) was a process of being practical and considered

CT to be "the process of purposeful thinking and reflective reasoning where practitioners examine ideas, assumptions, principles, conclusions, beliefs, and actions in the context of nursing practice" (p. 61).

Scheffer and Rubenfeld (2000) conducted a Delphi study and came to a consensus on cluster labels for skills of CT in nursing and for habits of the mind in an attempt to define critical thinking. The Delphi study was conducted to define critical thinking, specifically from experts in nursing practice to come to an agreement about CT. An international panel of nurses completed five rounds of sequenced questions to arrive at a consensus definition. While the definition was formed, more than a decade has passed and there continues to be a quandary about CT and the lack of a unified definition among health care educators.

Some of the common attributes of CT definitions included cognitive skills, reasoning, knowledge, logic, and the means of processing information (Jones, 2010). Another intangible definition described by Jones was the ability to prove the existence of, operationalize, or measure CT value. Facione (2011) indicated that education affected thinking critically and that CT was more than memorization. Until a unified, adopted definition of critical thinking for nurses can be reached, the concept of critical thinking will continue to be equally elusive. Paul and Elder (2012) offered a beginning definition of critical thinking as the art of thinking that encompasses three entwined segments of analyzing, evaluating, and improving thinking. Effective and productive thinking are produced when critical and creative thinking processes are used in tandem (Chaffee, 2012). Chaffee defined critical and creative thinking as exploring and using the thinking process to clarify and develop personal understanding and ideas to make intelligent decisions that are distinctive, applicable, and meaningful.

The critical thinking concept lacks clarity of margins or values despite the maturation of a critical thinking definition (Turner, 2005). Clarke (2009) presented Jones's Framework of deconstruction, reconstruction and social action regarding critical literacy. In order to understand the meaning of a scenario, having a different vantage point can assist one in finding meaning when looking at the layers of a situation. Nursing educators are charged with identifying, implementing, and teaching critical thinking skills (CTS) to nursing students, yet how to identify the concept and definition of critical thinking is often elusive.

Several studies used an amalgamation of different published definitions to create yet another definition of critical thinking. Brunt (2005) indicated that each study should clearly identify the definition used due to the ambiguous definition of critical thinking. The fast pace and increase of complexity faced in today's work place, requires the ability to critically think (Dykstra, 2008). Facione (2011) indicated that the definition of critical thinking was more than a definition for rote memorization and that CT can become incredulous without being derisive. Further concern discussed the importance of CTS for the practicing nurse, however, with all the multiple descriptions, how to instruct and evaluate CTS continues to be difficult due to the lack of clarity (Turner, 2005). The definition of CT continues to be influx, partially due to educators going in various directions when teaching CTS (Riddell, 2007). Clarifying the definition and limiting surrogate terms may improve the process of teaching CTS (Turner, 2005).

Many studies identified a clear definition of critical thinking for the respective study; however, several studies failed to identify a clear, universal definition for critical thinking. This study used the CT definition presented in Scheffer and Rubenfeld (2000):

Critical thinking in nursing is an essential component of professional accountability and quality nursing care. Critical thinkers in nursing exhibit these habits of the mind: confidence, contextual perspective, creativity, flexibility, inquisitiveness, intellectual integrity, intuitions, open-mindedness, perseverance, and reflections. Critical thinkers in nursing practice the cognitive skills of analyzing, applying standards, discriminating, information seeking, logical reasoning, predicting, and transforming knowledge (p. 357).

A clear definition and concept of critical thinking is needed for accurate measurement of a student's ability for CT. Until the nursing profession can come to a unified definition and concept, teaching CTS will continue to be a challenge.

Affecting Attributes in Critical Thinking

The literature review regarding characteristics that affect the development of, evaluation, and measurement of CT was identified by researchers as attributing factors, which affect the students' ability for CT (Carrick, 2011; Dykstra, 2008; Hopkins, 2008; Killam, Luhanga, & Bakker, 2011; Rogers, 2009; Rugutt & Chemosit, 2009; West, Toplak, & Stanovich, 2008). The attributing factors are common, yet are often overlooked or left out of the measurement and evaluation process. Attributing factors included the attitude, motivation, accountability, and commitment of students and faculty. Additional attributing factors were confidence of skills or lack of confidence and anxiety, age, experience, ability to connect lecture to practice, well-being, student health and wellness, beliefs, ability to communicate, frequent evaluation and success of CTS, and environment of learning.

Attitude. The attitude of the educator and student can hinder or enhance the growth and maturation of CTS (Carrick, 2011). When the attitude of involved parties evades consideration, the educator may assume the student is at fault for lack of achievement. When reviewing the systems viewpoint, student achievement was connected to the educator teaching methodology and individual learning systems. In other words, the input and personal influences from both parties should be considered while avoiding assumptions. Waiting to sit for the NCLEX may lead to failure, which would postpone an individual from beginning work as a nurse and greatly affect CT in the new nurse.

How individual students process information affects reasoning. Student attitude affects CTS and assessments of in-training skills are more effective when frequently and consistently administered (Deschênes et al., 2011). Further implications for quality care were that individual actions, attitudes, and reflective processes associated with personal philosophy of care are affected by the nurse's' beliefs and values. Equally essential was the need for frequent assessment in clinical training as related to classroom lecture.

Unsafe clinical practice has been tied to poor knowledge, poor skills, and attitude (Luhanga, Yonge, & Myrick, 2008). The unsafe nursing student was characterized as lacking clinical practice competence, having poor psychomotor skills, inadequate motivation and/or interpersonal skills. Additional concerns were poor time and organizational skills, inability to follow instructions which resulted in mistakes, lack of or poor clinical skills and knowledge, and failure to provide or implement basic safe care such as aseptic procedure. The educator who is diligent in checking personal attitude and assessing the student attitude may have a better experience in teaching CTS efficiently.

Motivation. Rugutt and Chemosit (2009) asked if motivation and CTS were affected and if there was a connection of the relationship between students and faculty to student collaboration. Motivation and academic performance was expressively related. When the educator and student have an advantageous relationship, learning and CT are more likely to occur. Equally significant was the student-to-student interaction for enhanced motivation and CTS. The study found that CTS and motivation were bonded.

Accountability. Killam, Luhanga, and Bakker (2011) found that professional image had three categories; attitudes, inappropriate behavior, and lack of accountability. These characteristics halted the ability of the student to provide the patient with an environment of safety and caring, which often led to overlooking patient needs. Students with inappropriate attitudes displayed repetitive errors, anger, disrespect, overconfidence, low confidence, apathy, and defensiveness. Lack of CTS may keep the student from questioning personal practice choices and choosing improper treatment plans when caring for patients. Lack of accountability (Killam et al., 2011; Ranse & Grealish, 2007) for actions or lack of appropriate actions overall influenced the ability for CT in nursing students.

Commitment. Student commitment to learning affects the ability for CT (Hopkins, 2008). Commitment requires dedicated time for thinking through situations and scenarios, a crucial element in the clinical setting for safe patient care. Nonacademic and academic variables affect the success of the nursing student. The five variables identified in a 2008 study that affected the success of ADN students were the students' ability to reason, learning style, analytic ability, level of anxiety, and commitment to learning (2008).

Confidence. Confidence can be considered another component of CT. For example, Kaddoura (2010) reported that through lab simulation, students voiced improved skills and confidence in CT in the clinical setting. When a nursing student becomes confident in clinical skills, the ability to apply classroom lecture to the clinical experience increases CTS. Through simulation lab, which reviews activities completed with and without errors, the student can receive meaningful feedback and discussion. The ability to review errors and practice skills increase individual confidence. Educators can assist the self-doubting student in CT development by utilizing group projects, which allow students to question each other's assumptions, activities, and interpretations and help with progressiveness. Lack of confidence and practice expertise can decrease the ability to traverse through the increasing patient acuity workload (Duchscher, 2008).

The professional and personal journey allow for personal evolution of CTS through the identified stages of being, knowing, and doing (Duchscher, 2008). Low confidence in skills was correlated to making clinical errors (Killam et al., 2011). Additionally, lack of CT, insight, and knowledge of personal practice affected cognitive ability. The lack of accountability was associated to failure of reporting vital patient information, being dishonest, ignoring professional boundaries, taking risks, and participation in illegal activities. Thus, the lack of accountability was linked to displaying poor CTS and placing patients in an unsafe environment. When new graduate nursing students felt unprepared for practice, overwhelmed, and lacked self-confidence, turnover rate and burn out occurred (Oermann et al., 2010).

Connection of theory and practice. Connecting the theory to the clinical practice can take time for the first semester nursing student. When the theory and clinical event fail to connect, categorizing, prioritizing, and interpreting the meanings of patient situations become difficult (Jones, 2008). When surveyed, 80 percent of senior nursing students reported feeling disappointed, disillusioned, and frustrated with progression in his/her respective nursing program. Additionally, students lacked consistency with categorizing and ranking patient needs or were unable to translate or clarify meaning when given scenarios of patient information.

Anxiety. Anxiety can derail confidence and prevent the student from learning how to think critically (Hopkins, 2008). When anxiety is decreased, CT is more likely to occur, which can directly affect clinical skills and confidence. Mentors, educators, and preceptors have the power to positively influence nursing students, augment confidence, and decrease anxiety in the work place. When the nursing faculty address and assist the student in recognizing and eliminating anxiety, resulting confidence for the nursing student can be the rebar needed for a solid foundation in CTS.

Age and experience. Previous experience and student age can influence or affect critical thinking ability due to learned coping skills of past situations. Experiential education has two distinguishing features requiring the directly engaged learner to experience an occurrence related to the study reviewed and to reflect on that experience. The learner then draws valuable CTS from the analysis of information (Hedin, 2010). The reflection of life situations or experiences can hinder or enhance CTS. Additionally, individual concepts can be modified or added to, based on lived experience.

Life experiences can allow an increase in the foundation of responses, in future circumstances (West et al., 2008). Additionally, individual's opinions and beliefs regarding the results the subject of CT can be negatively influenced when evaluating CT. In order for critical thinking to occur, an individual should have a healthy ability to think rationally and reflect on the experience to determine the outcome and/or analyze if the goal was met.

Well-being. The ability to present independent reasoning separate from previous beliefs was considered an element of CT. Some educators indicated that student happiness affected the ability to think critically and carry CTS beyond nursing knowledge. Additionally, some students stated that thinking for themselves and being able to discuss ideas with instructors created happiness (Jenkins, 2011).

Student health and wellness. Personal well-being, especially adequate sleep and nutrition, can affect the ability for CT (Rogers, 2009). Sleep deprivation can hinder thinking clearly, thus encumber the process of thinking critically. Poor nutrition and dehydration also affect the thought process, reaction to a situation, and retention of information, which in turn can affect the ability to form and implement efficient CTS.

Communication. Communication continues to be vital in learning CTS, yet few have mastered the ability to communicate effectively. When valuable interaction with peers, faculty, educators, and patients occur, the clinical experience can be positively shaped (Killam et al., 2011). Deficient communication skills were correlated to unsafe clinical practice along with poor work ethic, lack of motivation to learn or work, and unprofessional behaviors (Luhanga et al., 2008). Addressing the lack of or poor communication skills can require extra time with the student. Confidence in communication and CTS are connected and considered life skills that faculty are charged with conveying to students. Safe and effective patient care outcomes are connected to effective communication, CT, and adequate nursing judgment. Critical thinking was listed as a developing tool that assists in well-constructed solutions needed in the fast paced and complex world (Dykstra, 2008; Jones, 2008). Written and oral communications are important when selecting new employees, which can affect the student's future career. Additionally, memorandum-writing assignments may improve critical thinking among students. Productive communication with others and being confident in performing skills were associated with the enhancement of CTS.

Educational Strategies to Promote CTS

A variety of teaching strategies are available to promote CT. Case studies, journaling experiences, care plans, concept mapping, lab simulation, problem-based learning, and clinical post conferences can aid the educator in promoting CTS (Beyer, 2011; Oja, 2011; Ruthman, Jackson, Cluskey, Flannigan, Folse, & Bunten, 2004; Welk, 2001). Many of these teaching strategies were described as methods utilized in active learning (Johnson, 2011). The method of active learning can assist the educator to utilize more than the routine lecture method, which can be more successful in the engagement of students, thus developing CTS. With the many strategies and recommended tools available to promote CTS, educators may continue to use outdated methods of teaching and are resistant to change (Johnson, 2011). Outdated teaching methodology and resisting change can stifle the ability to learn at a higher level (Shell, 2001). Conversely, when an educator embraces change in teaching strategies to meet the need of the learner, growth and maturation in CT can occur for students. Students have a variety of learning skills and styles, thus nursing educators need to use more than one teaching methodology (Yildirim & Özkahraman, 2011).

Simulation. Simulation lab has become an integral part of nursing programs. Created vignettes that were designed by faculty and involved student interactions within the simulation were considered a good predictor of clinical performance (Van Eerden, 2001). Additionally, student comments indicated that communication, CT, and assessment skills improved when participating in the vignettes. Kaddoura (2010) studied the perception of the new nursing graduate in relation to clinical simulation and the development of personal CTS and confidence. Student confidence, learning ability, communication, leadership, development of CTS, and stress management improved after incorporation of simulation and feedback from the faculty. Some students considered the simulation lab a safe environment, which increased ability to learn. Armed with the knowledge of simulation and the possible learning effects, simulations could standardize nursing training (Kaddoura, 2010). The practice of debriefing was utilized after simulation activities were completed in an effort to enhance student understanding of simulation activities. After the completion of assigned activities, an informal information session was conducted with the group to review the performance of team members (McHugh Schuster & Nykolyn, 2010). Debriefing can be time-consuming and require educator effort. After a simulation or clinical experience, the breakdown of a care plan or case study with the educator can assist the student in recalling actions taken and the significance of each step which can expand the CTS of the student.

Care plans and journaling. Care plans have been the standard for nursing students since the early 1980's (Welk, 2001). The act of writing down patient information can allow the student to contemplate the most appropriate care for the assigned patient. The educator can utilize the care plan for discussion with the student in an attempt to assess CTS. If weak areas or the lack of clarity exists within the care plan, educators can assist the student with the review of information and think critically about patient care outcomes. Care plans continue to evolve with the use of concept mapping and journaling.

Journaling has been shown to link knowledge and experiences by written expression (Ruthman et al., 2004). Journal logs were kept by nursing students, which allowed reflective time to discuss clinical activities and how the relationship to nursing practice was affected. While journaling was utilized to improve writing skills, faculty found grading the logs to be challenging. Journaling required the student to examine personal feelings and actions taken in a clinical setting, and faculty felt that journaling assisted the student to CT by connecting practice to theory (2004). When looking at the written care plan versus journaling, students indicated a preference to journaling because of the shorter time required for completion (Marchigiano, Eduljee, & Harvey, 2011). The emphasis on less time needed to journal came into focus when the percentage of working college students was discovered during the study. Students reported the journaling task assisted with making the connection between theory and clinical, thus promoting CT. In the care plan new knowledge became easier to retain when the educator and student talked through the plan (Welk, 2001). Care plans and journaling are ways to teach CTS. The nursing process can promote CT in decision-making situations.

Problem based learning. Problem Based Learning (PBL) is composed of a non-lecture format. PBL was described as an inquiry-based method of instruction that is student-centered and steers students to resolutions of real-world issues by working in groups (Oja, 2011). When utilizing PBL, the educator acts as a facilitator, presents real-world situations, which expand past learning, involve group discussion, and student-guided problem solving. Group discussion or group format can be helpful for the students discussing the events of clinical or understanding theory. The use of a group format by recruiting seasoned nurses to assist in discussions about specific decision making can aid nursing students by hearing different approaches to solving an issue. A systematic review of several articles addressing how PBL within the teaching methodology would affect the CTS of nursing students yielded information that PBL was delivered differently. Therefore, comparing the efficacy of PBL strategies proved difficult (Oja, 2011).

Case studies. Utilization of case studies as a means to enhance CTS by the educator in the classroom or clinical setting was considered a viable tool, yet few researchers used case studies as a part of teaching methodology to enhance CT (Beyer, 2011). A patient case study can provide a scenario with specific details of a disease process, signs and symptoms presented, medication information, and lab results; usually created by the educator. The patient case study can be presented in a group setting allowing students and faculty to discuss and probe possible issues and nursing care to provide the safest and most effective patient care. Beyer used a 'reverse-case study', which is a combination of a case study and researcher modified concept map. A specific problem arose when students failed to understand that there could be more than one correct answer and how to make the decision of needed steps in order to arrive at a solution. The students who participated in Beyer's study indicated that talking through patient focused case studies enhanced CT through the process and stated, "This exercise helped pull it all together—I felt like it made me think like a nurse" (p. 50). The reverse case study tool utilized provided information, which assisted students to understand the process, relate the information to the nursing practice, and envisage the plan of care.

Educator Responsibility

Facione (2011) has written about critical thinking for decades. How an individual learns the art of CT can be affected by many venues of life experiences and not rote memorization, thus, a plausible reason why the definition of CT is difficult to find. CTS improved when students learned to write out experiences. This action was greatly enhanced when English and nursing departments teamed up to teach writing skills (Ruthman et al., 2004). Learning encompasses the educator and the student. Additionally, personal life can interfere with the ability to learn, comprehend, and retain information. Assuming the student has failed to study or prepare can lead to a poor experience and impede learning (Carrick, 2011). Frequent assessment and consideration of the learning environment can have positive outcomes in CTS. When a student feels 'safe' and supported in the learning environment, confidence can improve (Jones, 2010). Marchigiano, Eduljee, and Harvey (2011) indicated that the service provider and the nurse educator should share responsibility in cultivating a positive atmosphere for effective CTS.

Several authors discussed a common concern: the educators' inability to teach CTS (Broadbear, 2003; Del Bueno, 2005; Shell, 2001). Romeo (2010) investigated the need for nurse educators to reconcile on a critical thinking application theory for curricula development framework. Educators need to evolve and provide more than traditional teaching methodology. Too often the focus in the classroom is related to high stakes standard testing, which fails to nurture CTS (Tsai, 2012). In order for CTS to blossom, both creative and critical thinking should be used in tandem. Enhanced student CTS occurs when educators talk through created simulations in faculty guided CT vignettes (Van Eerden, 2001). Identifying the educators' CT concepts, knowledge, and perception of how CTS can be presented was as varied as the definition of CT (Stedman & Adams, 2012). Different teaching methods can allow educators to get nursing concepts across to students.

Educators face the challenge of and may find that many students want to be entertained during class (Walsh & Seldomridge, 2006). Students may have the expectation of the faculty being the only participant in the preparation and planning of the topic(s) for presentation and lack the understanding of the need to prepare for class and experience engagement during class. The push to use technology in the classroom can cause the faculty to become the entertainment during class (Walsh & Seldomridge, 2006). Understanding how and when to use technology in the classroom can affect the effectiveness of the educator.

Environment of Learning

Learning requires an environment that will nurture growth in the nursing student. When a student fails to learn new concepts, there may be several causes. The educator should be compelled to assess and investigate why a student lacks the ability to learn or understand concepts presented. Providing a safe environment for learning can allow the student to learn from mistakes and retain new knowledge.

Classroom climate. Classroom nuances substantially affect student learning. Specific nuances include the comfort of the classroom specifically temperature, lighting, air quality, noise, comfort of desk and chairs, relationships with other students and educators, and color of the classroom (Özay, Kaya, & Sezek, 2004). Additionally, the educator should maintain control in the classroom and be successful in the prevention of bullying or taunting in order for the student to engage (Ogundokun, 2011). Creating and sustaining a positive academic environment was linked to increased knowledge. When the educator can generate and preserve the positive environment, the students' skill development, knowledge, and faculty support perceptions are all influenced (Sherrod, Houser, Odom-Bartel, Packa, Wright, Dunn, Tomlinson, 2012).

Course design. Course design (Schaber & Shanedling, 2012) and a safe learning environment affect CTS. Educators should challenge the student in CT and analysis of information. A cyclical online course was designed to increase CT in students, which required students to analyze course content. The study showed that students gained CTS after the completion of the online course, which utilized focus groups who shared specific traits of the course that helped develop CT. The traits of the online course were well-structured and paced learning, active engagement with the course material, progressive and sequenced assignments, and timely and clear feedback from the instructor (Schaber & Shanedling). When the course design has a combination of CT and creative thinking, CTS can flourish (Tsai, 2012).

Another style of course design, which provided an alternative to traditional or online classroom, was simulation lab activities. Simulation labs have been instrumental in helping the novice nursing student learn in a safe environment, where mistakes are used as learning or teaching opportunities (Kaddoura, 2010; Martin, 2002; Van Eerden, 2001). With the increase of clinical expertise through simulation, advanced decision making and CTS develop in the nursing student (Martin, 2002). Simulation can assist the inexperienced student to avoid inappropriate decisions in the safe environment of the lab with educators present. Simulations provide psychomotor and cognitive skills for just-in-time learning (Kaddoura, 2010). Real patient situations in simulation provide learned critical care knowledge, role-playing aids in learned clinical skills, the consideration of total patient care, and promotion of CT as the gap of theory to practice becomes bridged. Additionally, simulation feedback cultivates CTS and leadership skills, as well as, the development of communication skills through collaborative teamwork. The simulation should be well planned and have clarity in objectives (Van Eerden, 2001). An essential task for the student wasis to come prepared for the simulation in order to glean as much knowledge as possible from the experience.

Measurement and Evaluation of CTS

Critical thinking skills are an integral aspect of nursing, which has the foundation laid during nursing school. Teaching CTS is a requirement of the National Council of State Boards of Nursing for nursing programs (Romeo, 2010). Measurement and evaluation of CTS are coupled with teaching CTS, yet identifying adequate tools to complete the task of evaluation and measurement of CTS can be as elusive as finding a unified definition and concept of critical thinking. An emerging question from a 2000 study questioned the identification of an instrument that would effectively measure nursing CT (Scheffer & Rubenfeld, 2000). The lack of a uniform concept and definition of CT can make measuring and evaluating CTS difficult (Nair & Stamler, 2013). Additionally, studies have shown an inconsistency with familiar tools such as the California Critical Thinking Skills Test and the Watson-Glaser Critical Thinking Appraisal Tool. Evaluations of CTS were considered by educators to include the students' ability to think as evidenced by the quality of written examinations, by educator-student collaborations, and emotional maturity (Jenkins, 2011). The following section will address the various tools used or reviewed in studies for measurement and evaluation of CTS.

Romeo (2010) utilized the California Critical Thinking Skills Test and the Watson-Glaser Critical Thinking Appraisal Tool (WGCTA) to resolve CT framework for curricular development. Similarly, Walsh and Seldomridge (2006) used the California Critical Thinking Dispositions Inventory and the Watson-Glaser Critical Thinking Appraisal Tool to review past studies that asked if nursing education affected critical thinking. Study findings mentioned the need for educators to improve oral questioning and allow nursing students to face the consequences of actions while avoiding being over protective (2006). The WGCTA explored five separate items, which included education, inference, interpretation, deduction, and evaluation of an argument to measure CT (West et al., 2008).

The California Critical Thinking Skills Test (CCTST) was utilized to determine if CTS had improved. While some literature showed that the students who were taught by problem based learning (PBL) scored higher on the CCTST, evidence was lacking that connected PBL to higher CT scores (Oja, 2011). Another CT measuring tool was the Pesut and Herman's Outcome-Present State test (OPT) model created in 1998 (Bartlett, Bland, Rossen, Kautz, Benfield & Carnevale, 2008). The OPT model was used as a teaching tool in a 2009 study where case studies were developed to test the model (Bland, Rossen, Bartlett, Kautz, Carnevale, & Benfield, 2009). The findings identified that students were able to learn with proper or adequate training and support from faculty.

Other measuring tools to assess CTS are the S.O.A.P. better known as 'subjective', 'objective', 'assessment', and 'plan' (Welk, 2001); and the nursing process, which is a problem solving activity and a linear process known as 'APIE', which represents 'assess', 'planning', 'intervention, and 'evaluation' (Yildirim & Özkahraman, 2011). The process of breaking down information, getting through the layers of an issue and rebuilding the information while getting input from others provided a different vantage point and is considered a method to measure CTS (Clark & Whitney, 2009). Brunt (2005) found that teaching to develop CT came through prominence on inquiry, reasoning, and process, and educators should apply theories for adult learning concepts to enable meaningful learning to connect theory and practice. Learning shared between the novice and seasoned nurse can hone and enhance CTS for safer patient care. Finally, Brunt asked the question of why seasoned nurses fail to share insight with novice nurses and why there was a gap between the two. The generation gap was examined to determine if there was a lack of encouragement to reflect on the actions of the novice nurse (2005). Understanding how each generation viewed situations and learning opportunities can assist in communication, which can enhance patient care.

Evaluation is a necessary component of any program to ensure a working process. Any concept taught should have an evaluation in place for the determination of efficacy. The evaluation tool should address personal beliefs and opinions, which might affect or skew the results (West et al., 2008). Additionally, caution should be used with the assumption that CTS can be taught (Riddell, 2007). Measuring and evaluating CTS is vital to safe patient care. Frequent evaluations of students in the clinical setting help to identify weak students and allow the educator to provide different methods of teaching to affect the ability in CT (Brunt, 2005; Killam et al., 2011; Romeo, 2010; Turner, 2005). Evaluation can open venues to meet the learning needs of the student and should occur frequently throughout the nursing program. Personal life experience, attitude of both educator and student, and motivation affects one's ability for CT. These factors should be considered when teaching and evaluating levels of CTS.

Expected Level of ADN Critical Thinking Skills

A smaller yet crucial theme, which surfaced was the expected level of CTS for nursing students and newly graduated nurses. The baccalaureate nursing program provides leadership and management skills, whereas the associate nursing degree is more task oriented. The difference in these degree programs can affect the level of CTS (Diede, McNish, & Coose, 2000; Orsolini-Hain & Waters, 2009). Some studies included the consideration that established the premise that nurses viewed newly graduated nurses as having or lacking clinical competence (Diede et al., 2000; Marshburn, Englke, & Swanson, 2009; Orsolini-Hain & Waters, 2009). Moreover, employers, nurse educators, and new ADN and BSN graduate nurses have varied expectations of clinical skills. When new nurses have confidence in clinical skills, CTS have been shown to flourish. Another possible correlation was questioned regarding the relationship between CT and competencies and confidence in personal skills and CT (Marshburn et al., 2009).

When examining the entire perspective of CTS, educators may pause when considering how to teach, assess, evaluate, and improve CTS if there continues to be a deficit in the expected level of the nursing student or new nursing graduates. Martin (2002) found that CTS or decision-making abilities were similar between the associate and baccalaureate subjects. The accelerated nursing student graduate had similar clinical skills and knowledge yet brought maturity and experience, which assisted with individual transition to the new role of nursing (Oermann et al., 2010). Minimal studies are available that address the topic of CT expectations of the nursing student and warrant further investigation.

Review of Methodological Issues

The literature review yielded information that indicated research designs used for studies regarding CT varied. Several articles were an overview of different topics concerning CTS, which included the evaluation and measurement of CT, or how to teach CT to nursing students. The vast majority of the articles were qualitative design with variations, which included exploratory (Kaddoura, 2010; Ranse, 2007) and descriptive (Martin, 2002; Oja, 2011) studies. Other types of quantitative studies utilized were quasi-experimental and correlational (Jones, 2008; Marshburn et al., 2009; Oja, 2011). Studies enlisted the use of interviews, surveys, focus groups, and Delphi approach. Three of the articles provided a review and analysis of quantitative research findings that addressed measuring tools for CTS (Brunt, 2005; Killam et al., 2011; Romeo, 2010). Mixed method and cross sectionals using journals and surveys were represented within the literature review (Diede et al., 2000; Ruthman et al., 2004; Shell, 2001). The surprising part of analyzing the literature review was the few quantitative studies available regarding measuring CTS.

The study sought to answer if there was a significant difference between critical thinking scores obtained at the beginning of the semester and critical thinking scores obtained at the end of the semester for first semester associate degree nursing students. The ability for CT has a direct effect on safe patient care, thus early evaluation to determine if a student's CTS has changed is crucial (Hopkins, 2008). A quantitative, non-experimental, explanatory approach was used for the study. A quantitative research study utilizes statistical analyses to attain results for studies (Marczyk et al., 2005). Explanatory method was described as non-experimental in which the question of why the phenomenon operates or works and tests the phenomenon theory and assists in the validation of a theory (Belli, 2009). Additionally, the explanatory method was described as a means of clarifying relationships among phenomenon, which recognized why events occur and the possible reason for the occurrences (Lapan & Quartaroli, 2009; Norwood, 2010). When educators take into consideration personal experiences of the study (both past and present) and can relate said experiences to the level of CTS, teaching methodologies can be molded to meet the students' learning needs.

The instrument selected for the study was the Kaplan Critical Thinking Integrated Test (KCTIT). The KCTIT test identified any change in the level of critical thinking from the beginning to the end of the first semester in the ADN program. The rationale behind the selected tool was to measure the level of CTS at the beginning and end of the first semester nursing student. The critical thinking instrument utilized evaluation of the student's knowledge base at the beginning of the nursing program, as well as, how the student gained knowledge was utilized by the end of the semester. The KCTIT consisted of 85 questions, has been in use approximately six years, and is currently used at ADN, BSN, and diploma nursing programs nationwide. The exam is one-dimensional and analyzed routinely to ensure evidence-based validity and reliability (Kaplan, 2012). Test developers in conjunction with subject matter experts collaborated to ensure the validity of test. Students' test scores were assessed for predictive validity that was in relation to the success rate in nursing school.

Evidence-based reliability of the exam was controlled by using students enrolled in ADN, BSN, and diploma-nursing programs. Further, these nursing students were in research studies performed, which consisted of a collection of the data from the schools and students on the exam scores for norming, item analysis, etc. Programs were dispersed geographically across the U.S. Group sizes ranged from 250-800, and measures were taken to ensure that participants accurately represented the population of enrolled nursing students nationwide (Kaplan, 2012).

Synthesis of Research Findings

The literature review provided information, which revealed a consensus that the concept and definition of CT lack clarity. Teaching the concept, measuring, and evaluating CTS of the students are difficult for the educator to navigate without needed lucidity. The review of literature revealed educators lack the ability to teach CT (Del Bueno, 2005). Most researchers agreed that each research study should provide a clear definition of CT (Clarke & Whitney, 2009; Dykstra, 2008; Facione, 2011; Jones, 2010; Romeo, 2010; Scheffer & Rubenfeld, 2000; Turner, 2005). Even with a clear definition, few, if any of the studies had the same definition, had a small sample size, and had a non-diversified population, which prevented generalization on many occasions.

There are superfluities of qualitative research articles, whereas quantitative research articles are few. Interviews, surveys, focus groups, and review or analyses of quantitative research findings represented the majority of methodology used in the literature reviewed. The limitation of measuring tools for CTS is as inconsistent as the definition and concept. Without validity, the soundness of the utilized research method and reliability, which is a consistent measurement in a tool, measuring and evaluation of the desired topic can be difficult (Marczyk et al., 2005).

Affecting attributes can enhance or hinder growth and maturation of CTS (Hedin, 2010; Rogers, 2009). The expectations for CT can vary significantly between the ADN student, the educator, the faculty, and the employer (Diede et al., 2000; Marshburn et al., 2009). Equally essential to building CTS is the attitude, motivation, learning environment, and expected behavior of the educator and student. Life situations also affect both the educator and student. While addressing all aspects of what affects the student's ability for CT may be difficult, the educator should attend to the characteristics that would assist the student progression towards mature CTS.

The study used a pre and post CT test to identify the beginning level of CT in the new ADN student early in the program. This study could help struggling students, thereby meeting the needs of the student and increasing program progression. There is an apparent necessity to conduct more quantitative studies reviewing CTS. Clarification of the concept and definition of CT, as well as, how to measure the level of CT of students can be affected or enhanced through further research.

METHODOLOGY

The methodology used for the study was a quantitative, non-experimental, explanatory approach to investigate a change in CTS among first semester ADN nursing students. Few quantitative studies have addressed CTS.

DATA ANALYSIS AND RESULTS

Data was collected using a computerized 85 item KCTIT exam, which was employed to measure the pre and posttest scores of critical thinking skills (CTS) and to determine the transformation in the first semester ADN nursing student. The number assigned to each participant for confidentiality purposes identified the demographic characteristics collected. The characteristics collected allowed the researcher to determine any connections between score differences. Additionally, affecting variables were identified.

The planned analysis incorporated a dependent *t* test where the participants' beginning pretest score was compared to the posttest score. The paired *t* test controlled for subject variability. Additionally, independent *t tests* or Mann-Whitney U tests were used to assess associations between students' characteristics and transformation in critical thinking skills (Gall, Gall, & Borg, 2006).

The independent variables were defined as the demographic characteristics of age, gender, race/ethnicity, and other characteristics of English as a Second Language (ESL), second career, and first attempt in the first semester. The dependent variable was defined as the scores of the pre and posttests. The goal was to ascertain if a significant transformation in the level of critical thinking occurred in the first semester ADN nursing student. The study utilized the method of purposeful sampling.

TARGET POPULATION AND SAMPLE

The target population included associate degree-nursing (ADN) programs in a Midwestern area with similar curricula, accreditation, and semester versus quarters. Four ADN programs received invitations to participate in the study after Internal Review Board (IRB) approval was received from all entities, information sessions and examinations were scheduled. The non-random, purposeful, convenience sample of nursing students defined the sample selected. Only those who met the inclusion criteria and in the first semester ADN Program were invited to participate in the study. A viable sample of 74 participants was determined by a power analysis. The setting consisted of college classrooms for information sessions and computer labs for completion of the pre and post exam.

All first semester nursing students at four accredited ADN programs were invited to participate in the study. Due to poor participation, the study was offered twice, spring and fall semester of 2013. Information sessions reached 332 potential participants. Of the 332, 58 took the pretest, representing 17.46%. Out of the 58 initial participants, 43 completed both the pre and posttests and 42 met the inclusion criteria.

SUMMARY AND DISCUSSION OF THE RESULTS

The 85-question KCTIT was utilized for the pre and posttest. The research question was addressed by analyzing the results of the test. A statistically significant transformation (change) was found in scores for first semester associate degree nursing students, as measured through a pretest and a posttest at the beginning and at the end of the semester respectively. The sample represented four metropolitan associate nursing programs with similar curriculum and the majority of the sample were females and whites with a mean age of 31.9 years.

The Statistical Packages for the Social Sciences (SPSS) 21.0 version program was utilized to analyze the data from the pre and post exams in addition to the demographic variables of age, gender, race/ethnicity, ESL, and second career. The mean score for the critical thinking test was higher by 2 points at the end of the semester compared with the test at the beginning of the semester (mean difference = 2.04, 95% CI 0.15, 3.94, $p = .035$). None of the demographic variables or the students' characteristics listed above were associated with the change in scores.

The data supported generalization of the results in relation to the population of associate nursing students in a Midwestern metropolitan city with a 95% confidence interval. A significant transformation in the level of critical thinking from the beginning to the end of the first semester associate degree nursing student occurred. The estimated change in critical thinking test scores was 2.04, with 95% confidence. The confidence was the true difference in critical thinking scores for first semester associate degree nursing students. It was between 0.15 and 3.94, which indicated a statistically significant increase in critical thinking ability. An unexpected finding was that age and experience lacked connection to the significant change in the level of critical thinking. One possible explanation for the finding could be the mean age was 31.9 years. Hedin (2010) noted that reflection and life experiences affect learning.

IMPLICATION OF THE RESULTS FOR PRACTICE

The results of the study demonstrated an improvement in the level of critical thinking in the first semester associate degree nursing (ADN) student and were suggestive of adequate CTS training in the classroom, skills lab and clinical setting. Early evaluation of CTS throughout the nursing program can increase confidence and assist the nursing student to make better decisions in the clinical setting for safer patient care (Del Bueno, 2005; Duchscher, 2008; Jones, 2008; & Killam et al., 2011).

While the study demonstrated an increase in CTS during the first semester, the same increase may not be present in all programs. Educators are encouraged to measure CTS early in nursing programs for identification of students having difficulty in learning CTS that can allow the educator to review or revise teaching methodologies, curricula, or student learning needs. Improved CTS in the new graduate directly affects patient care (Del Bueno, 2005). Positive solutions for nursing students and better learning tools for educators can assist in the empowerment of educators to address critical areas of student weakness and learning needs.

Issues, Controversies, Problems

Clinical CTS are deficient in the new nursing graduate student (Oermann et al., 2010), yet few studies investigate the CTS growth within the first semester. Identifying the lack of growth in CTS at the end of the first semester could help determine holes in the curriculum, teaching methodologies, student learning styles or disabilities, thereby provide a potential means to enhance the learning process. Investigating the presence of the fundamental foundation of and a change in the level of CTS in the new nursing student upon entering and completing the first semester in the associate nursing program, could affect student success in the completion of the nursing program and the ability to provide safe, effective patient care (Romeo, 2010). Insufficient CTS may cause the new graduate nurse to miss an assessment and identification of signs and symptoms of disease processes, which can further a hospital stay or even lead to patient death. The problem addressed in the study was the lack of early evaluation of transformation in the level of CTS during the first semester of the associate degree nursing student.

LIMITATIONS AND ASSUMPTIONS

Limitations can affect generalizability, therefore accurate identification is imperative (Norwood, 2010). An essential component of any study is generalizability in order for the body of knowledge to expand. Generalization to all ADN students may not be applicable, due to low participation and minimal diversity for practice. An adequate sample size is required in order to demonstrate significant differences after comparisons (Burns & Grove, 2011). One limitation of this study was related to the sample size of 42 participants. Poor participation could possibly be connected to the lack of faculty/peer support and evidenced based practice buy-in. Faculty are required to fill many roles in the academic setting and a tight schedule could prevent faculty from devoting time and support needed in the assistance of a study.

A convenience sample was utilized for the study, which could have caused a bias of self-select or students who were more motivated to be a part of the study. Stress of a first semester nursing program can be overwhelming, which may increase the attrition rate. The many requirements of a nursing program at the end of the semester may cause some participants to fail in providing a good effort in taking the exam. Life situations and/or poor achievements during the semester may cause lack of confidence to take the post exam. The demographics of predominantly white and female may have influenced the study outcomes.

The selected methodology may have missed the elimination of potential covariance(s). Another limitation was the number of sites selected. Selecting only the metropolitan area programs provided a smaller number of potential participants. Finally, the low number of participants prevented the collection of substantial data for analysis.

FUTURE RESEARCH DIRECTIONS

The small number of participants for the study lacked the diversity originally anticipated. A future study with a larger sample size could help to determine if age and experience make a significant difference in the scores. A difference exists between academia and acute care expectations about where the new graduate should be when considering level of CTS (Marchigiano et al., 2011). An additional recommendation is to examine the effect of various learning strategies on the development of CTS among nursing students.

CONCLUSION

The study was conducted to identify if the associate degree nursing student had a significant change in the level of critical thinking from the beginning to the end of the first semester. A total of 42 nursing students participated in the study. The KCTIT was utilized for both the pre and posttest. The estimated change in critical thinking mean score was 2.04 (95% CI 0.15, 3.94). The study included a pre and post-test during the first semester and the analyzed data indicated a significant increase in the scores on the critical thinking exam. The independent variables of age ($p = .865$), gender ($p = .287$), race ($p = .678$), ESL ($p = .486$), and experience ($p = .545$) were not associated with the change in critical thinking scores.

Data analysis indicated a significant increase in critical thinking scores of a pre and posttest. The RAM served as the guiding framework for the study (Roy, 2009). The theoretic framework was confirmed and expanded in that stimuli from the classroom, skills lab, and clinical settings affected the participant response, which demonstrated a significant increase in the test scores.

The implication of results for practice illuminated adequate instruction in the first semester showing a significant increase in critical thinking, which did not align with many of the studies reviewed. The participants' commitment, attitude, and motivation in improving CTS supported several studies (Carrick, 2011; Deschênes et al., 2011; Hopkins, 2008; & Luhanga, Yonge, & Myrick, 2008). When the environment is conducive to learning, in the classroom, skills lab, or clinical setting, CTS can grow. The study demonstrated that the first semester nursing student improved individual levels of critical thinking. Implications for practice suggested that having a unified definition and concept of CT could assist the educator with teaching and evaluating the progression of CTS appropriately.

REFERENCES

Bartlett, R., Bland, A. R., Rossen, E., Kautz, D. D., Benfield, S., & Carnevale, T. (2008). Evaluation of the outcome-present state test model as a way to teach clinical reasoning. *The Journal of Nursing Education, 47*(8), 337–344. doi:10.3928/01484834-20080801-01 PMID:18751647

Belli, G. (2009). Nonexperimental quantitative research. In S. D. Lapan & M. T. Quartaroli (Eds.), *Research essentials: An introduction to designs and practices* (pp. 59–77). San Francisco, CA: John Wiley & Sons, Inc.

Beyer, D. A. (2011). Reverse case study: To think like a nurse. *The Journal of Nursing Education, 50*(1), 48–50. doi:10.3928/01484834-20101029-06 PMID:21053856

Bland, A. R., Rossen, E. K., Bartlett, R., Kautz, D. D., Carnevale, T., & Benfield, S. (2009). Implementation and testing of the OPT model as a teaching strategy in an undergraduate psychiatric nursing course. *Nursing Education Perspectives*, *30*(1), 14–21. doi:10.1016/j.apnu.2005.08.002 PMID:19331034

Broadbear, J. T. (2003). Essential elements of lessons designed to promote critical thinking.[JoSoTL]. *The Journal of Scholarship of Teaching and Learning*, *3*(3), 1–8.

Brunt, B. (2005). Critical thinking in nursing: An integrated review. *Journal of Continuing Education in Nursing*, *36*(2), 60–67. PMID:15835580

Burns, N., & Grove, S. K. (2011). *Understanding nursing research* (5th ed.). Maryland Heights, MO: Elsevier Saunders.

Carrick, J. (2011). Student achievement and NCLEX-RN success: Problems that persist. *Nursing Education Perspectives*, *32*(2), 78–83. doi:10.5480/1536-5026-32.2.78 PMID:21667787

Chaffee, J. (2012). *Thinking critically* (10th ed.). Boston, MA: Wadsworth CENGAGE Learning.

Clarke, L. W., & Whitney, E. (2009). Walking in their shoes: Using multiple-perspectives texts as a bridge to critical literacy. *The Reading Teacher*, *62*(6), 530–534. doi:10.1598/RT.62.6.7

Del Bueno, D. (2005). A crisis in critical thinking. *Nursing Education Perspectives*, *26*(3), 278–282. PMID:16295306

Deschênes, M., Charlin, B., Gagnon, R., & Goudreau, J. (2011). Use of a script concordance test to assess development of clinical reasoning in nursing students. *The Journal of Nursing Education*, *50*(7), 381–387. doi:10.3928/01484834-20110331-03 PMID:21449528

Diede, N., McNish, G., & Coose, C. (2000). Performance expectations of the associate degree nurse graduate within the first six months. *The Journal of Nursing Education*, *39*(7), 302–307. PMID:11052652

Duchscher, J. B. (2008). A process of becoming: The stages of new nursing graduate professions role transition. *Journal of Continuing Education in Nursing*, *39*(10), 441–450. doi:10.3928/00220124-20081001-03 PMID:18990890

Dykstra, D. (2008). Integrating critical thinking and memorandum writing into course curriculum using the internet as a research tool. *College Student Journal*, *42*(3), 920–929. doi:10.1007/s10551-010-0477-2

Facione, P. A. (2011). Critical thinking: What it is and why it counts. Millbrae, CA: The California Academic Press. Available at www.insightassessment.com/pdf_files/what&why2006.pdf

Gall, M. D., Gall, W. R., & Borg, J. P. (2006). *Educational research: An introduction* (8th ed.). White Plains, N.Y: Longman.

Hedin, N. (2010). Experiential learning: Theory and challenges. *Christian Education Journal*, *7*(1), 107–117.

Hopkins, T. (2008). Early identification of at-risk nursing students: A student support model. *The Journal of Nursing Education*, *47*(6), 254–259. doi:10.3928/01484834-20080601-05 PMID:18557312

Jenkins, S. D. (2011). Cross-cultural perspectives on critical thinking. *The Journal of Nursing Education, 50*(5), 268–274. doi:10.3928/01484834-20110228-02 PMID:21366168

Johnson, P. A. (2011). Actively pursuing knowledge in the college classroom. *Journal of College Teaching and Learning, 8*(6), 17–30. doi:10.19030/tlc.v8i6.4279

Jones, J. H. (2010). Developing critical thinking in the perioperative environment. *AORN Journal, 91*(2), 248–256. doi:10.1016/j.aorn.2009.09.025 PMID:20152198

Jones, M. (2008). Developing clinically savvy nursing students: An evaluation of problem-based learning in an associate degree program. *Nursing Education Perspectives, 29*(5), 278–283. PMID:18834057

Kaddoura, M. A. (2010). New graduate nurses' perceptions of the effects of clinical simulation on their critical thinking, learning, and confidence. *Journal of Continuing Education in Nursing, 41*(11), 506–516. doi:10.3928/00220124-20100701-02 PMID:20672760

Kaplan. (2012). *Kaplan nursing integrated testing program faculty manual.* New York: Kaplan Nursing.

Killam, L. A., Luhanga, F., & Bakker, D. (2011). Characteristics of unsafe undergraduate nursing students in clinical practice: An integrative literature review. *The Journal of Nursing Education, 50*(8), 437–446. doi:10.3928/01484834-20110517-05 PMID:21598859

Lapan, S. D., & Quartaroli, M. T. (Eds.). (2009). *Research essentials: An introduction to designs and practices.* San Francisco, CA: John Wiley & Sons, Inc.

Luhanga, F., Yonge, O., & Myrick, F. (2008). Hallmarks of unsafe practice: What preceptors know. *Journal for Nurses in Staff Development, 24*(6), 257–264. doi:10.1097/01.NND.0000342233.74753. ad PMID:19060655

Marchigiano, G., Eduljee, N., & Harvey, K. (2011). Developing critical thinking skills from clinical assignments: A pilot study on nursing students' self-reported perceptions. *Journal of Nursing Management, 19*(1), 143–152. doi:10.1111/j.1365-2834.2010.01191.x PMID:21223414

Marczyk, G., DeMatteo, D., & Festinger, D. (2005). *Essentials of research design and methodology.* Hoboken, NJ: John Wiley & Sons, Inc.

Marshburn, D. M., Engelke, M. K., & Swanson, M. S. (2009). Relationships of new nurses' perceptions and measured performance-based clinical competence. *Journal of Continuing Education in Nursing, 40*(9), 426–432. doi:10.3928/00220124-20090824-02 PMID:19754030

Martin, C. (2002). The theory of critical thinking of nursing. *Nursing Education Perspectives, 23*(5), 243–247. PMID:12483815

McHugh Schuster, P., & Nykolyn, L. (2010). *Communication for nurses: How to prevent harmful events and promote patient safety.* Philadelphia, PA: F. A. Davis Company.

Nair, G. G., & Stamler, L. L. (2013). A conceptual framework for developing a critical thinking self-assessment scale. *The Journal of Nursing Education, 52*(3), 131–138. doi:10.3928/01484834-20120215-01 PMID:23402245

Norwood, S. L. (2010). *Research essentials: Foundations for evidence-based practice.* Upper Saddle River, NJ: Pearson Education, Inc.

Oermann, M., Poole-Dawkins, K., Alvarez, M., Foster, B., & O'Sullivan, R. (2010). Managers' perspectives of new graduates of accelerated nursing programs: How do they compare with other graduates? *Journal of Continuing Education in Nursing, 41*(9), 394–400. doi:10.3928/00220124-20100601-01 PMID:20540465

Ogundokun, M. O. (2011). Learning style, school environment and test anxiety as correlates of learning outcomes among secondary school students. *Ife Psychologia, 19*(2), 321–336. doi:10.4314/ifep.v19i2.69555

Oja, K. (2011). Using problem-based learning in the clinical setting to improve nursing students' critical thinking: An evidence review. *The Journal of Nursing Education, 50*(3), 145–151. doi:10.3928/01484834-20101230-10 PMID:21210603

Oklahoma Board of Nursing. (2011). *Rules.* Retrieved from http://www.ok.gov/nursing/ed-schls2.pdf

Orsolini-Hain, L., & Waters, V. (2009). Education evolution: A historical perspective of associate degree nursing. *The Journal of Nursing Education, 48*(5), 266–271. doi:10.9999/0144834-20090416-05 PMID:19476031

Özay, E., Kaya, E., & Sezek, F. (2004). Application of a questionnaire to describe teacher communication behaviour and its association with students in science in Turkey. *Journal of Baltic Science Education, 3*(2), 15–21.

Paul, R., & Elder, L. (2006). *Critical thinking: Tools for taking charge of your learning and your life* (2nd ed.). Upper Saddle River, NJ: Pearson/Prentice Hall.

Paul, R., & Elder, L. (2012). *Critical thinking: Tools for taking charge of your learning and your life* (3rd ed.). Boston, MA: Pearson/Prentice Hall.

Ranse, K., & Grealish, L. (2007). Nursing students' perceptions of learning in the clinical setting of the dedicated education unit. *Journal of Advanced Nursing, 58*(2), 171–179. doi:10.1111/j.1365-2648.2007.04220.x PMID:17445020

Riddell, T. (2007). Critical assumptions: Thinking critically about critical thinking. *The Journal of Nursing Education, 46*(3), 121–126. PMID:17396551

Rogers, T. L. (2009). Prescription for success in an associate degree nursing program. *The Journal of Nursing Education, 49*(2), 96–100. doi:10.3928/01484834-20091022-03 PMID:19877570

Romeo, E. M. (2010). Quantitative research on critical thinking and predicting nursing students' NCLEX-RN performance. *The Journal of Nursing Education, 49*(7), 378–386. doi:10.3928/01484834-20100331-05 PMID:20411861

Roy, C. (2009). *Roy adaptation model* (3rd ed.). Upper Saddle River, NJ: Pearson.

Roy, C., & Andrews, H. (1999). *Roy adaptation model* (2nd ed.). Stamford, CT: Appleton & Lange.

Rugutt, J., & Chemosit, C. (2009). What motivates students to learn? Contribution of student-to-student relations, student-faculty interaction and critical thinking skills. *Educational Research Quarterly, 32*(3), 16–28.

Ruthman, J., Jackson, J., Cluskey, M., Flannigan, P., Folse, V. N., & Bunten, J. (2004). Using clinical journaling to capture critical thinking across the curriculum. *Nursing Education Perspectives, 25*(3), 120–123. PMID:15301459

Schaber, P., & Shanedling, J. (2012). Online course design for teaching critical thinking. *Journal of Allied Health, 41*(1), e9–e14. PMID:22544412

Scheffer, B. K., & Rubenfeld, M. G. (2000). A consensus statement on critical thinking in nursing. *The Journal of Nursing Education, 39*(8), 352–359. PMID:11103973

Shell, R. (2001). Perceived barriers to teaching for critical thinking by BSN nursing faculty. *Nursing and Health Care Perspectives, 22*(6), 286–291. PMID:16370252

Sherrod, R. A., Houser, R., Odom-Bartel, B., Packa, D., Wright, V., Dunn, L., & Tomlinson, S. et al. (2012). Creating a successful environment for preparing doctoral-level nurse educators. *The Journal of Nursing Education, 51*(9), 481–488. doi:10.3928/01484834-20120706-01 PMID:22766073

Stedman, N. L. P., & Adams, B. L. (2012). Identifying faculty's knowledge of critical thinking concepts and perceptions of critical thinking instruction in higher education1. *NACTA Journal, 56*(2), 9–14.

Tsai, K. C. (2012). Dance with critical thinking and creative thinking in the classroom. *Journal of Sociological Research, 3*(2), 312–324. doi:10.5296/jsr.v3i2.2323

Turner, P. (2005). Critical thinking in nursing education and practice as defined in the literature. *Nursing Education Perspectives, 26*(5), 272–277. PMID:16295305

Van Eerden, K. (2001). Using critical thinking vignettes to evaluate student learning. *Nursing and Health Care Perspectives, 22*(5), 231–234. PMID:15957399

Walsh, C. M., & Seldomridge, L. A. (2006). Critical thinking: Back to square two. *The Journal of Nursing Education, 45*(6), 212–219. PMID:16780009

Welk, D. E. (2001). Clinical strategies: Teaching students a pattern of reversals eases the care plan process. *Nurse Educator, 26*(1), 43–45. doi:10.1097/00006223-200101000-00017 PMID:16372456

West, R., Toplak, M., & Stanovich, K. (2008). Heuristics and biases as measures of critical thinking: Associations with cognitive ability and thinking dispositions. *Journal of Educational Psychology, 100*(4), 930–941. doi:10.1037/a0012842

Yildirim, B., & Özkahraman, S. (2011). Critical thinking in nursing process and education. *International Journal of Humanities and Social Science, 1*(13), 257–262.

ADDITIONAL READING

Crenshaw, P., Hale, E., & Harper, S. L. (2011). Producing intellectual labor in the classroom: The utilization of a critical thinking model to help students take command of their thinking. *Journal of College Teaching and Learning*, *8*(7), 13–26. doi:10.19030/tlc.v8i7.4848

Ejiwale, J. A. (2012). Facilitating teaching and learning across STEM fields. *Journal of STEM Education: Innovations and Research*, *13*(3), 87–94.

Georgiou, I. (2000). The ontological constitution of bounding-judging in the phenomenological epistemology of von Bertalanffy's general system theory. *Systemic Practice and Action Research*, *13*(3), 391–424. doi:10.1023/A:1009567111785

Jenkins, S. D. (2011). Cross-cultural perspectives on critical thinking. *The Journal of Nursing Education*, *50*(5), 268–274. doi:10.3928/01484834-20110228-02 PMID:21366168

Karabudak Pucer, P., Trobec, I., & Žvanut, B. (2014). An information communication technology based approach for the acquisition of critical thinking skills. *Nurse Education Today*, *34*(6), 964–970. doi:10.1016/j.nedt.2014.01.011 PMID:24581890

Tomey, A. M., & Alligood, M. R. (2006). *Nursing theorists and their work* (6th ed.). St. Louis: Mosby.

Toofany, S. (2008). Critical thinking among nurses. *Nursing Management*, *14*(9), 28–31. doi:10.7748/nm2008.02.14.9.28.c6344 PMID:18372840

Yildirim, B., Özkahraman, S., & Karabudak, S. (2011). The critical thinking teaching methods in nursing students. *International Journal of Business and Social Science*, *2*(24), 174–182.

KEY TERMS AND DEFINITIONS

Adaptation: Creating human and environmental integration by choice and conscious awareness by feeling and thinking people, as individuals or in groups.

Antecedents: Before the occurrence of a concept, situations, which must occur.

Attributes: Are a feature or good quality that something or someone has.

Critical Thinking Skills: Nursing requires the component of critical thinking, exhibiting mind habits and cognitive skills of analyzing. Some characteristics are creativity, flexibility, confidence, open-mindedness, reflections, transforming knowledge, information seeking, logical reasoning and analyzing.

Stimuli: When the environment and human system interact and provokes a response.

System: Interdependence of parts functioning required as a set of for some purpose.

Veritivity: Human existence affirmed by a commonness of human nature.

Chapter 10
The Need for Global Standards in Biomedical Ethics and the Qualitative Methodology

F. Sigmund Topor
Keio University, Japan

ABSTRACT

The unity of humanity has placed the role of culture in maintaining wellness and coping with illness under examination in biomedical research. The qualitative methodology, which is the method most widely used in healthcare research, been placed under the globalization microscope for its role in intercultural biomedical research. Neither does the etiology of diseases such as, for example, the common cold, the adenovirus and influenza respiratory viruses, among others, nor treatments of such ailments distinguish between the religious, geographic, and linguistic dissimilarities that violate the unity of humanity. The subjectivity that clods investigators of various cultural backgrounds and disciplinary stripes, deems it expedient that stakeholders be provided with the means to ontologically verify research findings. Researchers employing the qualitative methodology can mitigate subjectivity and enhance objectivity by being culturally cognizant. The unity of humanity is manifested in healthcare and transcends national borders, laws, ethics, and customs.

INTRODUCTION

Cross-cultural research employing qualitative methodology presents challenges that were not contemplated in a preglobalized world. This chapter discusses the need for a global standard in biomedical research given the global unity of the human condition. All human activities conditionally arise from ethical convictions that are nurtured and enshrined by their respective sociocultural institutions. As humans, researchers see the world through culturally conditioned perceptibility. Given differences exemplified by empirical vs. holistic epistemologies, the need to balance local or cultural research prescriptions against those of a global or universal regimen becomes ever-pressing. The use of technology such as robots also incorporates moral standards in healthcare.

DOI: 10.4018/978-1-5225-0522-8.ch010

The individualism of Western cultures counters collectivism in Eastern cultures of China, Japan, Korea, and other countries. Collectivist societies prefer group harmony to individual initiatives. Whereas egalitarianism is advocated and practiced in Western cultures (e.g., North America and Europe), hierarchy based on social class, age, gender, and other attributes may inform qualitative data in, for instance, Japan (Cockerham, Lueschen, Kunz, & Spaeth, 1986; Ishikawa & Yamazaki, 2005). In contrast to Japan's venerated social hierarchy and status quo, change is encouraged and sought in Western societies. Belonging to a group-oriented society, individuals in Japan typically adhere to customs, tradition, and the status quo unremittingly (Hofstede, Hofstede, & Minkov, 1997), as opposed to the dynamic individualism in Western societies. However, such differences need not prevail at the peril of the health and welfare of humanity. The background, pathophysiology, and epidemiology of diseases clearly indicate the similarities of humans everywhere (Centers for Disease Control and Prevention, 2007).

Neither does the etiology of diseases such as, for example, the common cold, the adenovirus, and influenza respiratory viruses (Couch, 2001; Heikkinen & Järvinen, 2003; Lee et al., 2007; Ljungman et al., 2001; Marcone et al., 2013; Wright et al., 2007; Yuen et al., 1998), nor treatment of such ailments distinguish between the geographic, licit, ethical, and linguistic dissimilarities that violate the human condition (Heron, 1996; Kleinman, 1988), herein referred to as the *unity of humanity*. One of the most troubling phenomena that tend to annul the unity of humanity pertains to epistemological differences that both inform and invalidate research methodologies adopted in Eastern and Western civilizations.

In high-context cultures such as Japan (Hofstede et al., 1997; Kim, Pan, & Park, 1998), informants are often needed for translation purposes. As the Japanese language is imbued with multiple layers of politeness and other distinctive differences based on age (Hinds, 1971, 1975; Topor, 2013), syntactic and lexical distinctions between male and female speech (Loveday, 1981; Miller, 1967; Neustupny, 1978), and social status (Hidaka, 2010; Hinds, 1971, 1975; Ide, 1982; Inoue, 2002; Loveday, 1981; Suzuki, 1976, 1978), interpretative precision often depends on the social hierarchical juxtaposition of the interpreter and the informant. An informant–interpreter mismatch can potentially distort the data obtained in such scenarios (Hirano, 1999).

Given the burgeoning array of multiculturalism engendered by globalization, the need for global research has never been greater. Globalization can be summed up in one word: transfer—(a) of labor or skills (Berman & Machin, 2000; Taplin, 1997), (b) of knowledge or information (Inkpen & Tsang, 2005; Rodrik, 1997), (c) of capital or wealth (Tobin, 2000), and (d) of technology or dexterity (Bresnahan & Trajtenberg, 1995; Selinger, 2009) across continents and national borders. All attributes associated with globalization have had socioeconomic implications for all nations, cultures, and individuals. Globalization has facilitated the dissolution of trade barriers that were erected by national laws to safeguard and protect local manufacturing, technology, labor, skills—all financial and human capital.

The transcultural transplantation of human capital, a natural consequence of globalization, continues to accompany all the transfers subsumed under the globalization marvel. Universities continue to lead such transfers (Bouchard & Lemmens, 2008). Harmonization requires agreeable operationalization of variables through clear identifications, definitions, measurements, and so on (Calder, Phillips, & Tybout, 1981; Kazdin, 1998). Global results from research that are beneficial to humanity are generalizable only when intentions and conclusions are obviously well defined and transcend the locality of the research. Consistent with the unity of humanity, local healthcare needs are no less different from global requirements, even as societies and philosophies differ—Confucianism and Cartesianism being examples of Eastern and Western notions of ethics.

Globalization has empowered multinational pharmaceutical corporations (Ferreira, 2002; Spilker, 1994; Woo, Wolfgang, & Batista, 2008) to conduct research in one country, manufacture products in another, and orchestrate the distribution of products in yet another. Legal and ethical challenges regarding the validity and cost of drugs (Bond, 1999; Stewart, 2006) continue to exist between nation-states and powerful neoliberal pharmaceutical corporations. Drug price fixing is discussed in Chen (2013) and Mendelsohn (1980). For the socioeconomic impact on and international power struggle regarding drugs and their prices between countries, see Bond (1999) and Giordano (2013).

Morality and the cognitive processes that accompany validity and reasoning have been shown to differ culturally (Davies, 2007; Ennis, 2005; Nisbett, Peng, Choi, & Norenzayan, 2001; Peng, Nisbett, & Wong, 1997) and linguistically (Hoijer, 1954; Kay & Kempton, 1984). The comingling of intercultural healthcare research and practice is more than likely to induce ethical hemorrhaging for healthcare practitioners and scholars alike.

BACKGROUND

The search for answers to questions regarding right and wrong, and distinctions between knowledge and belief, science and fiction, and religion and spirituality (Casarez & Engebretson, 2012)—all of which may impact the administration of healthcare services and research, has now come to the fore in light of globalization. The adoption of a lingua franca highlights the effect of globalization and the need to adopt a single epistemology that facilitates understanding for the benefit of humanity.

Cultural diversities threaten to challenge global medical research even as stabilizing means of transcultural and international communication are harmonized by a global lingua franca in the English language. Diversions of epistemologies belie global scientific and academic endeavors. This paper elucidates real problems and difficulties likely to be faced by scholars interested in conducting cross-cultural biomedical research.

Culture is defined as a system comprising beliefs, values, assumptions, and other attributes about life that guides behavior and is shared by a group of people (Inglehart & Baker, 2000; Kern, 2003; Kuntz, Kuntz, Elenkov, & Nabirukhina, 2013), albeit Bargiela-Chiappini and Nickerson (2003) were less rapt with such a definition. Cultural values are transmitted across generations with belief systems kept intact (Suen, 2002). Different views and interpretations of culture can potentially lead to misunderstanding (Ziegahn, 2001). Ziegahn (2001) identified three cultural attributes that influence adult communication in a cross-cultural setting: individualism, egalitarianism, and change.

Harmonization of products and processes has become increasingly crucial as national borders are digitally erased, healthcare services are globally integrated, and medical tourism (Connell, 2006; Horowitz, Rosensweig, & Jones, 2007) becomes a normal phenomenon. Sex change, abortion, and drug habilitation are among some of the reasons both patients and physicians engage in medical tourism (Horowitz et al., 2007). Local healthcare systems and personnel incur stress and strain when expatriates from advanced economies are admitted for treatment otherwise available in their home countries. Treatment of post-surgery complications is among the leading services requiring the expertise of local physicians (Birch, Caulfield, & Ramakrishnan, 2007; Melendez & Alizadeh, 2011). Medical tourism is another example of the globalization of healthcare and medicine for which a universal standard is needed.

Contentious issues such as the definition of *death*; the notion of informed consent; the use, reuse, and potential abuse of qualitative data by third-party investigators, and other divergent cultural attributes demand standardization to ensure equal treatment for all of humanity. Debates about these issues oftentimes underscore divergence in humanity's one converging world. Standards are nullified by epistemological and cultural individualisms (Edelman & Hombach, 2008; Kligfield et al., 2007; Parfitt et al., 1987; World Health Organization, 2005), as if the social harmony profoundly esteemed in Confucian civilizations need not apply globally. Nevertheless, such deviations are purely superficial given the veracity of the unity of humankind. Cultures are only peculiar to the extent that they remain unacquainted.

Humans' ability to rationalize unfamiliar concepts or things (e.g., flying white elephants, unicorns, deities) depends on their sensuous experience and capability of balancing the appropriateness of acceptance with rejection of such concepts (McGaughey, 2006, p. 730). Cultural epistemology affects a range of research issues including methodology and translation. Camfield and Ruta (2007) cited Herdman, Fox-Rushby, and Badia in affirming the "difficulty of ensuring that translated measures preserve conceptual, item, semantic, operational, measurement[,] and functional equivalence" (p. 1039). Less affluent countries in the developing world tend to experience traumatic effects from demands on scarce expertise and other resources (Chinai & Goswami, 2007).

Giordano (2013,) argued that biomedical research in the age of globalization entails the implementation of Kantian declaration to "treat living beings as ends unto themselves, and not merely as means" (p. 1). Ethical issues of global concern are the principles of beneficence, nonharm, and respect for the autonomy of research subjects as outlined in the Nuremberg Code (1949), Declaration of Helsinki (Saif, 2000; World Medical Association General Assembly, 2004), and the (National Commission for the Protection of Human Subjects of Biomedical and Behavioral Research, 1979). Cultural differences are among the causes that submit global research to, in Clark's (2012) terms, the "perils and pitfalls" (p. 28) that have befallen qualitative research methodology.

Qualitative Research Methodology

The methodology of choice for most nursing research is qualitative (Clark, 2012; Glaser & Strauss, 1967). According to Denzin and Lincoln (2005), qualitative methodology has been the choice in healthcare research since the 1970s. According to Mills, Bonner, and Francis (2006), Glaser and Strauss first employed grounded theory as a string of qualitative methodology in nursing research "as a general method of comparative analysis" (p. 1). Whether or not the practice of grounded theory remains practically intact has been the subject of great scholarly debate (Duchscher & Morgan, 2004; Heath & Cowley, 2004). The original goal of consistent comparative analysis of qualitative data was the derivation of a theory from qualitative data, an accomplishment that has not been achieved as deviations from the original intention ensue (Corbin as cited in Mills et al., 2006).

Ponterotto (2005) cited literature (Camic, Rhodes, & Yardley, 2003; Denzin & Lincoln, 2000b; McLeod, 2001; Morrow & Smith, 2000; Rennie, 2002) affirming that the qualitative approach is often "anchored in positivist and postpositivist research paradigms" (p. 126), thereby ensuring methodological diversification through triangulation (Guba & Lincoln, 1994; Jick, 1979; Malterud, 2001; Morrow, 2005). Examples of triangulation includes multiple comparisons of research groups to establish internal consistency and reliability (Glaser & Strauss, 2009; Yin, 2009). Studies that employ both qualitative and quantitative methodologies would typically involve triangulation to assess external validity, that is—the transferability and generalizability of a particular study to the larger population (Malterud, 2001; van Maanen, 1988).

No single methodology provides the keel for either holistic or empirical epistemology in biomedical research (Y. Chen & Chen, 2012; Hackett & Lindsay, 2008; Morse, Barrett, Mayan, Olson, & Spiers, 2008; Nelson, 2009, 2012; Slife & Gantt, 1999; Wulff, 1997). Qualitative research explores phenomena with a holistic epistemology by looking at multiple variables, including historical events that may have impacted contemporary outcome in a given case under consideration (Regan, 1989; Yin, 2003, 2009). Contextually meaningful interpretation and process-oriented cases typically require a qualitative approach (Pawson & Tilley, 1997).

Some authors have suggested that presentation, rather than methodology, ascribes a given research its quality (Koch & Harrington as cited in Rolfe, 2006; Sandelowski & Barroso, 2003). By adopting such a qualitative attitude, these authors stand to attribute a qualitative appraisal to a quantitative methodology and effectively nullify any objective accounts contained in the quantitative method. Short of triangulation, it seems problematic how such a view might be applicable to statistical inference with hypothesis testing involving a large-scale pattern of behavior (Creswell, 2012; McLafferty, Slate, & Onwuegbuzie, 2010). Triangulation seems necessary in situations in which a given disease may have few or no symptoms (Hsieh et al., 2014). Patients suffering from certain maladies are said to display no symptoms. Examples of asymptomatic bacteriuria include chronic pulmonary disease and dementia (Marschall et al., 2013).

One may advocate the reconceptualization of the research methodologies that are currently in place; however, such advocacy is not the same as a blanket declaration that "there is no qualitative paradigm at all" (Rolfe, 2006, p. 310). Denying the existence of any research methodology is tantamount to exposing a misconception of the meaning of *methodology*. *Methodology* refers to the epistemology underlying data collection (Creswell, 2012).

Contextual understanding involves knowledge and experience, both of which cannot be quantified. Qualitative methodology comes into play in such a situation (Ives & Draper, 2009; Ives & Dunn, 2010). Regan (1989) explained that historical generalizations are made by comparing "complex combinatorial explanations" (p. 13) that are difficult to prove quantitatively. Nonetheless, qualitative methodology is used in quantitative epistemology to generate hypotheses, develop and implement trials, and interpret results.

The dearth of acceptable criteria to evaluate qualitative research has long beleaguered researchers and stakeholders alike (Sandelowski & Barroso, 2002). Others have suggested that the ability to definitively establish reliability and validity, and the assessment of the credibility of researchers remains elusive for qualitative methodology (Devers, 1999; Emden & Sandelowski, 1998, 1999; Engel & Kuzel, 1992; Maxwell, 1992; Seale, 1999; Sparkes, 2001; Whittemore, Chase, & Mandle, 2001).

Leaving ethics aside, issues of appropriateness concerning qualitative methodology include sample selection, methods of data collection, and data analysis (Kuper, Lingard, & Levinson, 2008). Unlike quantitative methodology, the sample size in qualitative research is not predetermined (Kuper et al., 2008). Termination of interviews may occur when experienced and knowledgeable (Norman, 2002; Rashid, 2013) researchers are able to conclude that a given sample is saturated (Carlsen & Glenton, 2011).

A qualitative research methodology of global applicability cannot disregard the instrumental role of language and other cultural practices such as power–distance (Hofstede et al., 1997) in medical decisions involving such issues as euthanasia, justice, autonomy, and benevolence (Beauchamp & Childress, 2001). When linguistics considerations are included, data collection and analysis more often than not involve extra layers of complication due to cultural and linguistic differences in the pragmatics of research participants.

Challenges faced by nursing students in qualitative analysis (Li & Seale, 2007; Milne & Oberle, 2005) have led to a search for solutions. Poetry reading has been identified as a pedagogical tool in the appreciation of personal individualities and epistemological diversifications in qualitative analysis (Reece, 2000). According to Raingruber (2009), "by using poetry reading assignments, nurse educators can teach students the skills needed for interpretive analysis in a nonthreatening, engaging manner" (p. 1754). In globalized medicine, poetry can help medical professionals identify and relate to cultural hermeneutics (Reece, 2000).

Validity and Qualitative Methodology

Validity of the qualitative method is ascertained severally through (a) the interaction and iteration between informants and the researcher, (b) the link between designs and implementation (Morse, Barrett, Mayan, Olson, & Spiers, 2002), and (c) the ability to foreswear the influence of culture and religion, and the appropriation or misappropriation of terminology. Morse et al. (2002) argued against the use of parallel or duplicate terminology and that "terms reliability and validity remain pertinent in qualitative inquiry and should be maintained" (p. 8). Ceci, Peters, and Plokin (1985) claimed that "funding agencies frequently dictate the form of research that is eventually submitted for journal review" (p. 994). Given that such agencies are not restricted to any particular country, industry, or culture, it behooves researchers to ensure strict adherence to reliability and validity.

The end does not always justify the means. Morse et al. (2002) argued against the gratuitous reliance on "tangible outcomes of the research" (p. 8) and encouraged researchers to instead focus on the verifiability process and strategies employed in the research. In certain instances, the means is used as the standard for authentication.

Apart from knowledge, assessment of the investigator's qualification comes into focus as a given phenomenon is explored and explained in qualitative terms (Creswell, 2012; Johnson & Onwuegbuzie, 2004; McLafferty et al., 2010). Kuper et al. (2008) raised the issue of the appropriateness of selected samples in relation to a given research question—that is, "whom or what to include in the sample—whom to interview, whom to observe, what texts to analyze" (p. 687). Interviews of relatives about the conditions of a patient should be regarded with wariness when such interviews are devoid of the patient's direct input.

The Unity of Humanity

Human organ transplantation and blood transfusion constitute common medical solutions that are applicable to humans everywhere. These solutions epitomize the unity of humanity. Global disagreements regarding end-of-life treatment persist (Beširevi, 2010; Eriksen, 2001; Li, 2005).

Whereas all humans are variously defined by dissimilarities (e.g., race, nationalities, gender), the unity of humanity is exemplified by similarities of conditions such as birth/death (Charlesworth & Partridge, 1997; Weitz & Fraser, 2001), wellness/illness, good/bad, right/wrong, and the like. The impermanence of mortality (Brooks, Lithgow, & Johnson, 1994), a prime defining character of humans, transcends national borders, geographic localities, political institutions, and religious and/or spiritual orientations. Dissimilarities promulgated by such human attributes as religious beliefs, spirituality (Dickerson, 2011), and national laws, culture, customs, and traditions have led to different perceptions of right and wrong, thus resulting in diversities of explanations or interpretations of qualitative data.

According to René, Lucas, Henk, and Doeke (2007), patients are the same everywhere. They are all initially shocked when they learn about the diagnosis and prognosis of their ailments. Younger patients repeatedly show more resilience and resistance than older patients. All patients have relationships (e.g., family, friends, and others). The ability to return to work, school, or home from the hospital is among questions that concern all patients, regardless of nationality, race, religion, and other superficial differences. These issues often do not cease even as patients receive support from their social environments.

Healthcare personnel also show common human characteristics. Nurses everywhere distinguish between younger and older patients. They also have emotions, which often play a role in their response and treatment of patients (René et al., 2007). All healthcare professionals respond more emotionally to the death of younger patients than of older patients. Studies reveal that moral distress can lead to low morale among healthcare providers everywhere (Gaudine & Beaton, 2002; Gaudine & Thorne, 2000; Rodney & Starzomski, 1993). Low morale has been identified as one of the leading causes of employee turnover (Batt & Valcour, 2003; Hayes et al., 2006; Janssen, de Jonge, & Bakker, 1999; Larrabee et al., 2003).

Ethical Climate in Healthcare

Perceptions that influence actions, behavior, and services provided by individuals in organizations comprise ethical climate (Olson, 1998). Ethical sensitivity entails the perception, discernment, and provision of appropriate response to linguistic as well as paralinguistic cues of patients by attending physicians and/or caregivers (Donnelly, 2000; Kim, Park, You, Seo, & Han, 2005; Schluter, Winch, Holzhauser, & Henderson, 2008). According to Schluter et al. (2008), "one of the most important issues in moral decision making is an ethically sensitive environment" (p. 306).

Ethical issues of global proportions abound. Monetary remuneration to research participants respecting risk (Giordano, 2013) encompass moral, legal, and ethical issues in some jurisdictions. Other ethical matters involve the effect of culture and customs on information and the consent of research subjects (Calloway, 2009; Gostin, 1995; Leach et al., 1999), the effect of the religious beliefs and spirituality of researchers and/or healthcare practitioners (Curlin & Hall, 2005; Curlin, Lantos, Roach, Sellergren, & Chin, 2005; Curlin, Lawrence, Chin, & Lantos, 2007; Glass, Chen, Hwang, Ono, & Nahapetyan, 2010), and the application of technology in the treatment of patients (Enerstvedt, 1999; Esposito, 2001).

Epistemological Diversities

Renewed focus on qualitative epistemology is necessitated by its intrinsic designs, which are rooted in social constructivism (Ponterotto, 2005). This is exemplified by such activities as interviews, observations, phenomenology, and grounded theory and are no longer restricted to the localized perspectives of individual researchers. The global community would be better served by a research paradigm that ensures the incorporation of both "local factors with global perspectives" (Sanchez-Arias, Calmeyn, Driesen, & Pruis, 2013, p. 34) on the one hand along with global factors with local perspectives in biomedical or healthcare research on the other.

There are divergences in the epistemological approaches employed by different cultures. The two foremost important paradigms are Eastern and Western epistemologies (X. Chen, 2004; Riddell & Iwafuchi, 1998; Shweder & Bourne, 1982). Whereas the Eastern paradigm is oriented toward holistic epistemology (Dale, 2005; Dewey, 1929; Douglas & Moustakas, 1985), Western epistemology is portrayed in quantitative research methodology, often referred to as *scientific realism* or *positivism*. The philosophical postulation of scientific inquiry, which is adopted in the West, is the assumptions that nature can reveal itself to scientific inquiry by breaking down complex natural phenomena into smaller parts or variables (Creswell, 2009; Lodico, Spaulding, & Voegtle, 2010; Tashakkori & Teddlie, 2003).

Epistemology entails knowledge whereas ethics entails action or doing (McGaughey, 2006; Quine, 2013). Demeter (2012) contended that individual cognition is shaped by sociological factors of which the individual is not necessarily cognizant. For Demeter, "[t]he question pertaining to the sociological conditioning of perception became central in philosophy of science starting with Kuhn's work on the role the socialization of scientists plays in the formation of their perceptual sensibilities" (p. 2). Kant (as cited in McGaughey, 2006) argued that all knowledge is related to humans' intuition of the empirical world. In Kant's view, intuition and knowledge are complementary, not mutually exclusive, even as he believed that some things are unknowable. In his explication of Kant, McGaughey (2006) stated that "[a] ny understanding that we might have of the physical world is the consequence of our mental capacity to match sensations of the physical world (appearances) with their appropriate concepts (abstractions of the things themselves)" (p. 729).

Some cultures such as Iran and India are classified as past oriented and more tactile than others whereas the United States and Canada are said to be present and future oriented (LeBaron, 2003). For example, cross-gender touching is allowed among friends in North America while discouraging the same outside of a close friendly relationship. In Japan, women can be seen holding hands (LeBaron, 2003), which indicates a cross-gender touching practice, whereas men in Japan are hardly ever seen holding hands. *Power–distance* refers to the degree to which deference is given to those perceived to be in position of power, and the degree or extent to which the powerful tolerate the powerless (Hofstede & Hofstede, 2001).

Western ethics is based on reason in Kantian terms (Korsgaard, 2012). Behaviors of ethical consequences are condemned and condoned depending on how and/or where they arise. Timmermann (2006) stated that actions are damnable when they are internally induced—for example, actions based on emotions whereas actions arising from exterior stimuli in response to practical reasons are condoned. Western culture, influenced by Kantian autonomy, places the basic requirements for moral judgment on individual discretion while concomitantly adhering to universal moral standards (Timmermann, 2006). Universality denotes standards that apply to all people in all cases at all times.

Cultural divergence appears to have afflicted the principle of informed consent in Confucian cultures such as Japan. Long (1999) noted that the concept of informed consent is so alien to the Japanese medical ethics that a parallel term is wanting in the language. However, Long noted the translated katakana version of informed consent as *setsumei to doi* (explanation and agreement). Leflar (1996) described the Japanese medical system as one infected with paternalism. The ability to actualize the incision required to eradicate the ailing system of benevolent paternalism, while concurrently retaining its effect, remains an outstanding challenge.

Ensuring a responsive research methodology coupled with informed professional regimens in healthcare remains a challenge. Ethical sensitivity, which encompasses the moral code, laws, culture, and customs of a particular country, are adjuvant to the setting in which researchers and practicing healthcare professionals engage as they administer services to recipients (American Nurses Association, 2001; Fry & Johnstone, 2008). Thus, Japan has a code of ethics that is distinct from that of Korea (Kim et al., 2005), the United States (American Nurses Association, 2001), China (Pang et al., 2003), and elsewhere.

The Case of the Japanese Language

Japan is referenced as exemplifying the East–West epistemic dichotomy for a number of reasons, of which two suffice as follows. Apart from the Japanese language being the most distinct from the global lingua franca, English (S. X. Chen, Benet-Martínez, & Ng, 2014; Chiswick & Miller, 2005; Iwawaki,

Eysenck, & Eysenck, 1977; Yoshida & Smith, 2003), Japan is the only Group of Seven country in which qualitative methodology is informed by the Confucius-influenced epistemology, which as applied in almost all Eastern cultures (i.e., China, Korea, Taiwan, Singapore, and others). Another reason to focus on Japan is the fact that the most recent 2012 recipient of the Nobel Prize in Biomedical Research is from Japan (Ochi, 2013).

The Japanese language and Confucian-oriented cultural traits present epistemological challenges to researchers employing qualitative methodology in biomedical research. According to Chiswick and Miller (2005), Japanese is "the most distant" (p. 7) language from English. Communication across cultures requires each interlocutor to be aware of these important differences in order to avoid communication breakdown and the problems that typically attend. Cross-cultural communications can be improved when negotiators are informed about the attributes that contribute to cultural differences. These attributes include time and space orientation, power–distance, and risk avoidance (Hofstede et al., 1997; LeBaron, 2003). English speakers are perceived as more articulate than Japanese speakers, who typically speak with more sentience (Ishii, Thompson, & Klopf, 1990).

Japanese has lexical and syntactic distinctions between male and female speech. Very formal and elaborate speech is as much a marker as a portrayal of femininity in Japanese (Miller, 1967, pp. 289–296; Neustupny, 1978, p. 235). Distinctions between the Japanese and English language have attracted ample scholarly interests. For research on sociocultural differences, see Hinds (1983); Kondo (1990), Martin (1988), Miller (1967), Morita (2003), and Suzuki (1976, 1978). For research on gender differences, see Hirose (2000), Inoue (2002), Kondo (1990), Kuroda (1965, 1973), Martin (1988), Miller (1967, 1977), Shibatani (1990), Suzuki (1976, 1978), and Wetzel (1994). Hasegawa and Hirose (2005) discussed the Japanese language in relation to the self.

According to LeBaron (2003), power–distance relations include social status, gender, race, age, education, birth, personal achievements, and family background, among others. The Japanese society, for example, is said to observe a high power–distance and less equality among people, a practice that promotes harmony (De Mente, 1990, 2003; Kelley, 2008), whereas some cultures such as those in North America and Europe tolerate risk and uncertainty. Intercultural communication is further characterized by fate, face, and personal responsibilities that are based on individual initiative vs. acceptance of the way things are ordered in Confusions societies (Adair & Brett, 2005; Hawrysh & Zaichkowsky, 1990; LeBaron, 2003; Walker, 2004).

CONCLUSION

The Internet, which is a derivative of the Information Age, has promoted the use and reuse of secondary qualitative data from storage repositories such as iClouds (Heinemann, Kangasharju, Lyardet, & Mühlhäuser, 2003), the Economic & Social Research Council Timescapes Archive of qualitative data (Irwin, Bornat, & Winterton, 2012; Neale & Bishop, 2012), and the like. Both iClouds and Timescapes are Internet-related digital data storages. Whereas iClouds is used for all types of data, the Timescapes Archive is a specialist resource for qualitative longitudinal data designed to entice researchers to store their data for their own use and reuse. Drawing on Hofstede (1980), Koeszegi, Vetschera, and Kersten (2004) explained that "differences in cultural dimensions such as individualism, masculinity, uncertainty avoidance, or power–distance" (p. 20) may explain the adoption or use of technology by different cultures.

The unity of humanity is symptomized by the capacity to interculturally share components such as, for example, vital organs through transplantation; blood through transfusion (Ainley, 2011; Banks, 1995; Matesanz, 1998; Miranda & Matesanz, 1998); and other medical services. Debate still rages regarding the definition of *death* (Halevy & Brody, 1993; Truog & Robinson, 2003; Zeiler, 2009).

The individualism of Western cultures counters collectivism in Eastern cultures such as Japan, where group harmony is preferred over individual initiative. Unlike in Japan, qualities of egalitarianism are espoused and practiced in Western cultures. Social class, age, gender, and other attributes may inform qualitative data from the Japanese setting (Cockerham et al., 1986; Ishikawa & Yamazaki, 2005). Although a recent study indicates that Japanese are becoming less group-oriented (Tafarodi et al., 2012), individuals in Japan adhere to customs, tradition, and the status quo more assiduously given a group-oriented approach (Hofstede et al., 1997).

Healthcare professionals in China, Japan, and Taiwan are said to be conflicted by ethical gridlocks induced by Confucian ethics (Davis, 1983; Oberle & Hughes, 2001; Pang, 2003; Parker, 1990; Penticuff, 2000; Söderberg & Norberg, 1993; Wagner & Hendel, 2000). Problems present opportunities to seek creative solutions within the scope of both natural as well as manmade laws. According to Kant (as cited in McGaughey, 2006), all humans have the ability or capacity, through practical knowledge, to transform *what is* into *what should be*.

A global code of ethics in biomedical research is needed to prevent moral distress, the condition that arises due to the failure or inability of healthcare professionals to solve (Corley, Minick, Elswick, & Jacobs, 2005) or feel prevented from solving (Mitton, Peacock, Storch, Smith, & Cornelissen, 2010) complex ethical problems. The consequences of failure are grave. Examples include inadequate patient-to-staff ratios, misapprehension of cultural values, inordinate reliance on high technology characterized by the use of robots where humans are expected, and so on.

The issue of migration and cross-border labor transfer raises questions in the ethics sphere as local hospitals accommodate a growing number of multicultural patients and international medical personnel responding to international natural disasters such as tsunamis and earthquakes (Mimura, Yasuhara, Kawagoe, Yokoki, & Kazama, 2011; Nelson et al., 2008; Srinivas & Nakagawa, 2008; Telford, Cosgrave, & Houghton, 2006), nuclear accidents (Baverstock, & Williams, 2007; World Health Organization, 2005), and the like. As Clark (2012) stated, "even within nations, there is a growing diversity of populations, and health status disparities are increasingly found among members of nondominant cultural groups" (p. 28).

Eastern epistemology is influenced by Confucianism and Buddhism (Bond & Hofstede, 1989; Hofstede, 1991). Attempts are made by Western scholars to exclude religion or spirituality from research (Nelson, 2009; Nelson & Slife, 2012; Slife & Reber, 2012). Western striving for empiricism appears to parallel Eastern atheism. To promote objectivity and attenuate the likelihood of presupposed acceptance or bias, Western scholars are dissuaded from the influence of religion and/or spirituality (Nelson & Slife, 2012).

The sequela of globalization presents a host of issues in biomedical research involving qualitative methodology. Among them is the marketization of higher education (Jones, 1999); internationalization of research policy (Enders, 2004; Jones & Oleksiyenko, 2011; Marginson & Rhoades, 2002); and socioeconomic (Pratt & Loff, 2012; Sassen, 1994; Smeral, 1998), technological (Archibugi & Iammarino, 2002; Archibugi & Michie, 1995; Tanzi, 2000), political, and cultural ramifications (Held, McGrew, Goldblatt, & Perraton, 1999; Nicholson & Sahay, 2001).

FUTURE RESEARCH DIRECTIONS

Qualitative data sharing raises several ethical questions, the least of which include data abuse. There is no known remedial protocol to prevent data abuse (Beaton, Bombardier, Guillemin, & Ferraz, 2000; Bowden & Fox-Rushby, 2003; De Haes & Olschewski, 1998; Wagner et al., 1998). Yet, as Irwin (2013) noted, there are already calls for the sharing of primary qualitative data with other researchers for secondary analysis (Bishop, 2009; Neale & Bishop, 2012; Van Den Eynden et al., 2011). Various proposals and guidelines for the adaptation of qualitative data exist (Beaton et al., 2000; Guillemin, Bombardier, & Beaton, 1993). However, these do not cover the use of secondary qualitative data. Thus, the potential for data abuse remains a real prospect.

A collectivist orientation, which supposes that qualitative data are communal resources, espouses the sharing of such data (Fry et al., 2009). Fry et al. (2009) claimed that the benefits of data curation and sharing include the diminution of research duplication and the burden research poses on participants.

Medical and healthcare robots also represent the need for a global code of ethics, not only because robots employ ethical corollaries but also because linguistic emanations are discharged alongside, if not because of, their employment. Specific areas of future research include the use of robots in surgery (Gerhardus, 2002; Kim et al., 2002; Taylor & Stoianovici, 2003), reproductive medicine (Dharia & Falconw, 2005), and other medical procedures. Robots can perform multiple tasks such as monitoring, managing, preventing hazards for, and facilitating and enhancing the independence of the weak and the elderly. Robots have the ability to fetch and carry heavy or bulky objects (Pigini, Facal, Blasi, & Andrich, 2012); however, robots can neither entirely replace the human touch nor provide the social and psychological needs that are fulfilled by religion and spirituality (Daaleman & VandeCreek, 2000). Moreover, Pigini et al. (2012) highlighted the emotional rancor induced by remote-control operations conducted by family members in cases in which a patient is incapacitated and unable to carry out such functions.

REFERENCES

Adair, W. L., & Brett, J. M. (2005). The negotiation dance: Time, culture, and behavioral sequences in negotiation. *Organization Science*, *16*(1), 33–51.

Ainley, R. (2011). Organ transploitation: A model law approach to combat human trafficking and transplant tourism. *Oregon Review of International Law*, *13*, 427.

American Nurses Association. (2001). *Code of ethics for nurses with interpretive statements*. Silver Spring, MD: Nursesbooks.

Archibugi, D., & Iammarino, S. (2002). The globalization of technological innovation: Definition and evidence. *Review of International Political Economy*, *9*(1), 98–122.

Archibugi, D., & Michie, J. (1995). The globalisation of technology: A new taxonomy. *Cambridge Journal of Economics*, *19*(1), 121–140.

Banks, G. J. (1995). Legal and ethical safeguards: Protection of society's most vulnerable participants in a commercialized organ transplantation system. *American Journal of Law & Medicine*, *21*, 45. PMID:7573083

Bargiela-Chiappini, F., & Nickerson, C. (2003). Intercultural business communication: A rich field of studies. *Journal of Intercultural Studies (Melbourne, Vic.)*, *24*(1), 3–15.

Batt, R., & Valcour, P. M. (2003). Human resources practices as predictors of work-family outcomes and employee turnover. *Industrial Relations*, *42*(2), 189–220.

Baverstock, K., & Williams, D. (2007). The Chernobyl accident 20 years on: An assessment of the health consequences and the international response. *Ciencia & Saude Coletiva*, *12*(3), 689–698. PMID:17680126

Beaton, D. E., Bombardier, C., Guillemin, F., & Ferraz, M. B. (2000). Guidelines for the process of cross-cultural adaptation of self-report measures. *Spine*, *25*(24), 3186–3191. PMID:11124735

Beauchamp, T. L., & Childress, J. F. (2001). *Principles of Biomedical Ethics*. New York, NY: Oxford University Press.

Berman, E., & Machin, S. (2000). *Skill-biased technology transfer: Evidence of factor biased technological change in developing countries. Mimeograph*. Boston University.

Beširevi, V. (2010). End-of-life care in the 21st century: Advance directives in universal rights discourse. *Bioethics*, *24*(3), 105–112. PMID:20136818

Birch, J., Caulfield, R., & Ramakrishnan, V. (2007). The complications of 'cosmetic tourism:–An avoidable burden on the NHS. *Journal of Plastic, Reconstructive & Aesthetic Surgery; JPRAS*, *60*(9), 1075–1077. PMID:17482899

Bishop, L. (2009). Ethical sharing and reuse of qualitative data. *The Australian Journal of Social Issues*, *44*(3), 255–272.

Bond, M. H., & Hofstede, G. (1989). The cash value of Confucian values. *Human Systems Management*, *8*(3), 195–199.

Bond, P. (1999). Globalization, pharmaceutical pricing and South African health policy: Managing confrontation with U.S. firms and politicians. *International Journal of Health Services*, *29*(4), 765–792. PMID:10615573

Bouchard, R. A., & Lemmens, T. (2008). Privatizing biomedical research: A 'third way'. *Nature Biotechnology*, *26*(1), 31–36. PMID:18183013

Bowden, A., & Fox-Rushby, J. A. (2003). A systematic and critical review of the process of translation and adaptation of generic health-related quality of life measures in Africa, Asia, Eastern Europe, the Middle East, South America. *Social Science & Medicine*, *57*(7), 1289–1306. PMID:12899911

Bresnahan, T. F., & Trajtenberg, M. (1995). General purpose technologies 'Engines of growth'? *Journal of Econometrics*, *65*(1), 83–108.

Brooks, A., Lithgow, G. J., & Johnson, T. E. (1994). Mortality rates in a genetically heterogeneous population of Caenorhabditis elegans. *Science*, *263*, 668–671. PMID:8303273

Calder, B. J., Phillips, L. W., & Tybout, A. M. (1981). Designing research for application. *The Journal of Consumer Research*, 197–207.

Calloway, S. J. (2009). The effect of culture on beliefs related to autonomy and informed consent. *Journal of Cultural Diversity, 16*(2), 68–70.

Camfield, L., & Ruta, D. (2007). Translation is not enough: Using the global person generated index (GPGI) to assess individual quality of life in Bangladesh, Thailand, and Ethiopia. *Quality of Life Research: An International Journal of Quality of Life Aspects of Treatment, Care and Rehabilitation, 16*(6), 1039–1051. PMID:17487570

Camic, P. M., Rhodes, J. E., & Yardley, L. (Eds.). (2003). *Qualitative research in psychology: Expanding perspectives in methodology and design.* Washington, DC: American Psychological Association.

Carlsen, B., & Glenton, C. (2011). What about N? A methodological study of sample-size reporting in focus group studies. *BMC Medical Research Methodology, 11*(1), 26–35. PMID:21396104

Casarez, R. L. P., & Engebretson, J. (2012). Ethical issues of incorporating spiritual care into clinical practice. *Journal of Clinical Nursing, 21*(15/16), 2099–2107. PMID:22788552

Ceci, S. J., Peters, D., & Plotkin, J. (1985). Human subjects review, personal values, and the regulation of social science research. *The American Psychologist, 40*(9), 994.

Centers for Disease Control and Prevention (CDC). (2007). Acute respiratory disease associated with adenovirus serotype 14--four states, 2006-2007. (*MMWR.*). *Morbidity and Mortality Weekly Report, 56*(45), 1181. PMID:18004235

Charlesworth, B., & Partridge, L. (1997). Ageing: Leveling of the grim reaper. *Current Biology, 7*(7), R440–R442. PMID:9210361

Chen, M. (2013). Patents against people: How drug companies price patients out of survival. *Dissent, 60*(4), 71–77.

Chen, S. X., Benet-Martínez, V., & Ng, J. K. (2014). Does Language Affect Personality Perception? A Functional Approach to Testing the Whorfian Hypothesis. *Journal of Personality, 82*(2), 130–143. doi:10.1111/jopy.12040 PMID:23607801

Chen, X. (2004). Culture and understanding: The Cartesian suspicion, The Gadamerian response, and the Confucian outcome. *Journal of Chinese Philosophy, 31*(3), 389–403.

Chen, Y., & Chen, X. (2012). Methodological issues in psychology of religion research in the Chinese context. *Pastoral Psychology, 61*(5-6), 671–683.

Chinai, R., & Goswami, R. (2007). Medical visas mark growth of Indian medical tourism. *Bulletin of the World Health Organization, 85*(3), 164–165. PMID:17486202

Chiswick, B. R., & Miller, P. W. (2005). Linguistic distance: A quantitative measure of the distance between English and other languages. *Journal of Multilingual and Multicultural Development, 26*(1), 1–11.

Clark, M. (2012). Cross-cultural research: Challenge and competence. *International Journal of Nursing Practice,* 1828–1837. PMID:22776530

Clark, M. (2012). Cross-cultural research: Challenge and competence. *International Journal of Nursing Practice,* 1828–1837. PMID:22776530

Cockerham, W. C., Lueschen, G., Kunz, G., & Spaeth, J. L. (1986). Social stratification and self-management of health. *Journal of Health and Social Behavior, 27*, 1–14. PMID:3711631

Connell, J. (2006). Medical tourism: Sea, sun, sand and… surgery. *Tourism Management, 27*(6), 1093–1100.

Corbin, J. M. (1998). Alternative Interpretations Valid or not? *Theory & Psychology, 8*(1), 121–128.

Corley, M. C., Minick, P., Elswick, R. K., & Jacobs, M. (2005). Nurse moral distress and ethical work environment. *Nursing Ethics, 12*(4), 381–390. PMID:16045246

Couch, R. B. (2001). Rhinoviruses. In D. M. Knipe & P. M. Howley (Eds.), *Fields Virology* (4th ed.; pp. 777–797). Philadelphia, PA: Lippincott Williams and Wilkins.

Creswell, J. W. (2009). Editorial: Mapping the field of mixed methods research. *Journal of Mixed Methods Research, 3*(2), 95–108.

Creswell, J. W. (2012). *Research design: Qualitative, quantitative, and mixed methods approaches.* Thousand Oaks, CA: Sage.

Curlin, F. A., & Hall, D. E. (2005). Strangers or friends? A proposal for a new spirituality-in- medicine ethic. *Journal of General Internal Medicine, 20*, 370–374. PMID:15857497

Curlin, F. A., Lantos, J. D., Roach, C. J., Sellergren, S. A., & Chin, M. H. (2005). Religious characteristics of U.S. physicians: A national survey. *Journal of General Internal Medicine, 20*, 629–634. PMID:16050858

Curlin, F. A., Lawrence, R. E., Chin, M. H., & Lantos, J. D. (2007). Religion, conscience, and controversial clinical practices. *The New England Journal of Medicine, 356*(6), 593–600. PMID:17287479

Daaleman, T. P., & VandeCreek, L. (2000). Placing religion and spirituality in end-of-life care.[JAMA]. *Journal of the American Medical Association, 284*(19), 2514–2517. PMID:11074785

Dale, J. L. (2005). Reflective judgment: Seminarians' epistemology in a world of relativism. *Journal of Psychology and Theology, 33*(1), 56–64.

Davis, A. J., & Aroskar, M. A. (1983). *Ethical dilemmas and nursing practice* (2nd ed.). Norwalk, CT: Appleton-Century-Crofts.

De Haes, J. C. J. M., & Olschewski, M. (1998). Quality of life assessment in a cross-cultural context: Use of the Rotterdam Symptom Checklist in a multinational randomised trial comparing CMF and Zoladex (Goserlin) treatment in early breast cancer. *Annals of Oncology, 9*(7), 745–750. PMID:9739441

De Mente, B. L. (1990). Japan's secret weapon: The kata factor: The cultural programming that made the Japanese a superior people. Phoenix, AZ: Phoenix.

De Mente, B. L. (2003). *Kata: The key to understanding and dealing with the Japanese!* Boston, MA: Tuttle.

Demeter, T. (2012). Introduction. *Studies in East European Thought, 64*(1/2), 1–4. PMID:22213720

Denzin, N. K., & Lincoln, Y. S. (2000b). Introduction: The discipline and practice of qualitative research. In N. K. Denzin & Y. S. Lincoln (Eds.), *Handbook of Qualitative Research* (2nd ed.; pp. 1–28). Thousand Oaks, CA: Sage.

Denzin, N. K., & Lincoln, Y. S. (Eds.). (2005). *The Sage handbook of qualitative research* (3rd ed., pp. 1–32). Thousand Oaks, CA: Sage.

Devers, K. J. (1999). How will we know "good" qualitative research when we see it? Beginning the dialogue in health services research. HSR. *Health Services Research, 34*(5 Pt. 2), 1153–1188. PMID:10591278

Dewey, J. (1929). *The quest for certainty: A study of the relation of knowledge and action.* New York, NY: Minton.

Dharia, S. P., & Falcone, T. (2005). Robotics in reproductive medicine. *Fertility and Sterility, 84*(1), 1–11. PMID:16009146

Dickerson, M. (2011). *The mind and the machine: What it means to be human and why it matters.* Grand Rapids, MI: Brazos.

Donnelly, P. L. (2000). Ethics and cross-cultural nursing. *Journal of Transcultural Nursing, 11*(2), 119–126. PMID:11982044

Douglas, B. G., & Moustakas, C. (1985). Heuristic inquiry: The internal search to know. *Journal of Humanistic Psychology, 25,* 39–55.

Duchscher, J. E. B., & Morgan, D. (2004). Grounded theory: Reflections on the emergence vs. forcing debate. *Journal of Advanced Nursing, 48*(6), 605–612. PMID:15548251

Edelman, R., & Hombach, J. (2008). "Guidelines for the clinical evaluation of dengue vaccines in endemic areas": Summary of a World Health Organization technical consultation. *Vaccine, 26*(33), 4113–4119. PMID:18597906

Emden, C., & Sandelowski, M. (1998). The good, the bad, and the relative, part 1: Conceptions of goodness in qualitative research. *International Journal of Nursing Practice, 4*(4), 206–212. PMID:10095513

Emden, C., & Sandelowski, M. (1999). The good, the bad, and the relative, part 2: Goodness and the criterion problem in qualitative research. *International Journal of Nursing Practice, 5*(1), 2–7. PMID:10455610

Enders, J. (2004). Higher education, internationalisation, and the nation-state: Recent developments and challenges to governance theory. *Higher Education, 47*(3), 361–382.

Enerstvedt, R. T. (1999). New medical technology: To what does it lead? *American Annals of the Deaf, 144,* 242–249. PMID:10423891

Engel, J. D., & Kuzel, A. J. (1992). On the idea of what constitutes good qualitative inquiry. *Qualitative Health Research, 2*(4), 504–510.

Ennis, M. (2005). Now I know in part: Holistic and analytic reasoning and their contribution to fuller knowing in theological education. *Evangelical Review Of Theology, 29*(3), 251–269.

Eriksen, T. H. (2001). Between universalism and relativism: A critique of the UNESCO concepts of culture. In J. Cowan, M. Dembour, & R. Wilson (Eds.), *Culture and Rights: Anthropological Perspectives* (pp. 127–148). Cambridge, UK: Cambridge University Press.

Esposito, N. (2001). From meaning to meaning: The influence of translation techniques on non- English focus group research. *Qualitative Health Research, 11*(4), 568–579. PMID:11521612

Ferreira, L. (2002). Access to affordable HIV/AIDS drugs: The human rights obligations of multinational pharmaceutical corporations. *Fordham Law Review, 71*, 1133. PMID:12523370

Fry, J., Lockyer, S., Oppenheim, C., Houghton, J., & Rasmussen, B. (2009). *Identifying benefits arising the curation from and open sharing of research data produced by UK higher education and research institutes.* Retrieved from JISC Repository: http://repository.jisc.ac.uk/279/2/JISC_data_sharing_final-report.pdf

Fry, S. T., & Johnstone, M. J. (2008). *Ethics in nursing practice: A guide to ethical decision making.* Oxford, UK: Blackwe.

Gaudine, A. P., & Beaton, M. R. (2002). Employed to go against one's values: nurse managers' accounts of ethical conflict with their organizations. *The Canadian Journal of Nursing Research= Revue Canadienne de Recherche en Sciences Infirmieres, 34*(2), 17-34.

Gaudine, A. P., & Thorne, L. (2000). Ethical conflict in professionals: Nurses' accounts of ethical conflict with organizations. *Research in Ethical Issues in Organizations, 2*, 41–58.

Gerhardus, D. (2002). Robot-assisted surgery: The future is here. *Journal of healthcare management/ American College of Healthcare Executives, 48*(4), 242-251.

Giordano, J. (2013). Ethical considerations in the globalization of medicine - An interview with James Giordano. *BMC Medicine, 11*(1), 1–5. PMID:23496884

Glaser, B. G., & Strauss, A. (1967). *The discovery of grounded theory: Strategies for qualitative research.* Chicago, IL: Aldine.

Glaser, B. G., & Strauss, A. L. (2009). *The discovery of grounded theory: Strategies for qualitative research.* Piscataway, NJ: Transaction.

Glass, A. P., Chen, L., Hwang, E., Ono, Y., & Nahapetyan, L. (2010). A cross-cultural comparison of hospice development in Japan, South Korea, and Taiwan. *Journal of Cross-Cultural Gerontology, 25*(1), 1–19. PMID:20054707

Gostin, L. (1995). Informed consent, cultural sensitivity, and respect for persons. *Journal of the American Medical Association, 27a*, 844–845. PMID:7650810

Guba, E. G., & Lincoln, Y. S. (1994). Competing paradigms in qualitative research. Handbook of Qualitative Research, 2, 163-194.

Guillemin, F., Bombardier, C., & Beaton, D. (1993). Cross-cultural adaptation of health-related quality of life measures: Literature review and proposed guidelines. *Journal of Clinical Epidemiology, 46*(12), 1417–1432. PMID:8263569

Hackett, C., & Lindsay, D. M. (2008). Measuring evangelicalism: Consequences of different operationalization strategies. *Journal for the Scientific Study of Religion, 47*(3), 499–514.

Halevy, A., & Brody, B. (1993). Brain death: Reconciling definitions, criteria, and tests. *Annals of Internal Medicine, 119*(6), 519–525. PMID:8357120

Hasegawa, Y., & Hirose, Y. (2005). What the Japanese language tells us about the alleged Japanese relational self. *Australian Journal of Linguistics, 25*(2), 219–251.

Hawrysh, B. M., & Zaichkowsky, J. L. (1990). Cultural approaches to negotiations: Understanding the Japanese. *International Marketing Review, 7*(2).

Hayes, L. J., O'Brien-Pallas, L., Duffield, C., Shamian, J., Buchan, J., Hughes, F., & Stone, P. W. et al. (2006). Nurse turnover: A literature review. *International Journal of Nursing Studies, 43*(2), 237–263. PMID:15878771

Heath, H., & Cowley, S. (2004). Developing a grounded theory approach: A comparison of Glaser and Strauss. *International Journal of Nursing Studies, 41*, 141–150. PMID:14725778

Heikkinen, T., & Järvinen, A. (2003). The common cold. *Lancet, 361*(9351), 51–59. PMID:12517470

Heinemann, A., Kangasharju, J., Lyardet, F., & Mühlhäuser, M. (2003). iclouds–peer-to-peer information sharing in mobile environments. In Euro-Par 2003 Parallel Processing (pp. 1038-1045). Springer.

Held, D., McGrew, A. G., Goldblatt, D., & Perraton, J. (1999). *Global trasformations: politics, economics and culture*. Stanford, CA: Stanford University Press.

Herdman, M., Fox-Rushby, J., & Badia, X. (1998). A model of equivalence in the cultural adaptation of HRQL instruments: The universalist approach. *Quality of Life Research: An International Journal of Quality of Life Aspects of Treatment, Care and Rehabilitation, 7*, 323–355. PMID:9610216

Heron, J. (1996). *Co-operative inquiry: Research into the human condition*. London, UK: Sage.

Hidaka, T. (2010). How Japanese language has been used and transformed-focused on social-cultural context and the use in communication. *Integrative Psychological & Behavioral Science, 44*(2), 156–161. PMID:20401549

Hinds, J. (1971). Personal pronouns in Japanese. *Glossa, 5*(2), 146–155.

Hinds, J. (1975). Third person pronouns in Japanese. *Language in Japanese Society*, 129-157.

Hinds, J. (1983). Contrastive rhetoric: Japanese and English. *Text-Interdisciplinary Journal for the Study of Discourse, 3*(2), 183–196.

Hirano, C. (1999). Eight ways to say you: The challenges of translation. *Horn Book Magazine, 75*(1), 34–41.

Hirose, Y. (2000). Public and private self as two aspects of the speaker: A contrastive study of Japanese and English. *Journal of Pragmatics, 32*, 1623–1656.

Hofstede, G. (1980). Culture's consequences, international differences in work-related values (Vol. 5). London, UK: SAGE.

Hofstede, G. (1991). *Cultures and organizations: Software of the mind*. London, UK: McGraw-Hill.

Hofstede, G., Hofstede, G. J., & Minkov, M. (1997). *Cultures and organizations*. New York, NY: McGraw-Hill.

Hofstede, G. H., & Hofstede, G. (2001). Culture's consequences: Comparing values, behaviors, institutions and organizations across nations. *Sage (Atlanta, Ga.)*.

Hoijer, H. (1954). The Sapir-Whorf Hypothesis. *Language in Culture*, 92-105.

Horowitz, M. D., Rosensweig, J. A., & Jones, C. A. (2007). Medical tourism: Globalization of the healthcare marketplace. *Medscape General Medicine*, *9*(4), 33. PMID:18311383

Hsieh, Y. H., Tsai, C. A., Lin, C. Y., Chen, J. H., King, C. C., Chao, D. Y., & Cheng, K. F. (2014). Asymptomatic ratio for seasonal H1N1 influenza infection among schoolchildren in Taiwan. *BMC Infectious Diseases*, *14*(1), 80. PMID:24520993

Ide, S. (1982). Japanese sociolinguistics politeness and women's language. *Lingua*, *57*(2), 357–385.

Inglehart, R., & Baker, W. E. (2000). Modernization, cultural change, and the persistence of traditional values. *American Sociological Review*, 19–51.

Inkpen, A. C., & Tsang, E. W. (2005). Social capital, networks, and knowledge transfer. *Academy of Management Review*, *30*(1), 146–165.

Inoue, M. (2002). Gender, language, and modernity: Toward an effective history of Japanese women's language. *American Ethnologist*, *29*(2), 392–422.

Irwin, S. (2013). Qualitative secondary data analysis: Ethics, epistemology and context. *Progress in Development Studies*, *13*(4), 295–306.

Irwin, S., Bornat, J., & Winterton, M. (2012). Timescapes secondary analysis: Comparison, context and working across data sets. *Qualitative Research*, *12*(1), 66–80.

Ishii, S., Thompson, C. A., & Klopf, D. W. (1990). A Comparison of the assertiveness: Responsiveness construct between Japanese and Americans. *Otsuma Review*, *23*, 63–71.

Ishikawa, H., & Yamazaki, Y. (2005). How applicable are western models of patient-physician relationship in Asia? Changing patient-physician relationship in contemporary Japan. *International Journal of Japanese Sociology*, *14*(1), 84–93.

Ives, J., & Draper, H. (2009). Appropriate methodologies for empirical bioethics: It's all relative. *Bioethics*, *23*(4), 249–258. PMID:19338525

Ives, J., & Dunn, M. (2010). Who's arguing? A call for reflexivity in bioethics. *Bioethics*, *24*(5), 256–265. PMID:20500762

Iwawaki, S., Eysenck, S. B. G., & Eysenck, H. J. (1977). Differences in personality between Japanese and English. *The Journal of Social Psychology*, *102*(1), 27–33. PMID:881807

Janssen, P. P. M., de Jonge, J., & Bakker, A. B. (1999). Specific determinants of intrinsic work motivation, burnout and turnover intentions: A study among nurses. *Journal of Advanced Nursing*, *29*(6), 1360–1369. PMID:10354230

Jick, T. D. (1979). Mixing qualitative and quantitative methods: Triangulation in action. *Administrative Science Quarterly*, 602–611.

Johnson, R. B., & Onwuegbuzie, A. J. (2004). Mixed methods research: A research paradigm whose time has come. *Educational Researcher, 33*(7), 14–26.

Jones, G. A., & Oleksiyenko, A. (2011). The internationalization of Canadian university research: A global higher education matrix analysis of multi-level governance. *Higher Education, 61*(1), 41–57.

Jones, M. (1999). Structuration theory. In W. Currie & R. Galliers (Eds.), *Rethinking management information systems* (pp. 103–135). New York, NY: Oxford University Press.

Kant, I. (1878). *Prolegomena zu einer jeden Künftigen Metaphysik: die als Wissenschaft wird auftreten konnen.* Verlag von Leopold Voss.

Kant, I. [1783] (1998). Prolegomena zu einer jeden konftigen Metaphysik, die als Wissenschaft wird auftreten konnen, Vol. III of Immanuel Kant: Werke. In S. Bonden (Ed.), Wilhelm Weischedel (pp. 109–264). Darmstadt: Wissenschaftliche Buchgesellschaft.

Kay, P., & Kempton, W. (1984). What is the sapir-whorf hypothesis? *American Anthropologist, 86*(1), 65–79.

Kazdin, A. E. (1998). *Research design in clinical psychology* (3rd ed.). Boston, MA: Allyn & Bacon.

Kelley, J. E. (2008). Harmony, empathy, loyalty, and patience in Japanese children's literature. *Social Studies, 99*(2), 61–70.

Kern, S. (2003). *The culture of time and space, 1880-1918: with a new preface.* Cambridge, MA: Harvard University Press.

Kim, D., Pan, Y., & Park, H. S. (1998). High-versus low-context culture: A comparison of Chinese, Korean, and American cultures. *Psychology and Marketing, 15*(6), 507–521.

Kim, V. B., Chapman Iii, W. H., Albrecht, R. J., Bailey, B. M., Young, J. A., Nifong, L. W., & Chitwood Jr, W. R. (2002). Early experience with telemanipulative robot-assisted laparoscopic cholecystectomy using da Vinci. *Surgical Laparoscopy, Endoscopy & Percutaneous Techniques, 12*(1), 33–40. PMID:12008760

Kim, Y. S., Park, J. W., You, M. A., Seo, Y. S., & Han, S. S. (2005). Sensitivity to ethical issues confronted by Korean hospital staff nurses. *Nursing Ethics, 12*(6), 595–605. PMID:16312088

Kleinman, A. (1988). *The illness narratives: Suffering, healing, and the human condition.* New York, NY: Basic books.

Kligfield, P., Gettes, L. S., Bailey, J. J., Childers, R., Deal, B. J., Hancock, E. W., & Wagner, G. S. et al. (2007). Recommendations for the Standardization and Interpretation of the Electrocardiogram Part I: The Electrocardiogram and Its Technology A Scientific Statement From the American Heart Association Electrocardiography and Arrhythmias Committee, Council on Clinical Cardiology; the American College of Cardiology Foundation; and the Heart Rhythm Society Endorsed by the International Society for Computerized Electrocardiology. *Journal of the American College of Cardiology, 49*(10), 1109–1127. PMID:17349896

Koch, T., & Harrington, A. (1998). Reconceptualizing rigour: The case for reflexivity. *Journal of Advanced Nursing*, *28*(4), 882–890. PMID:9829678

Koeszegi, S., Vetschera, R., & Kersten, G. (2004). National cultural differences in the use and perception of internet-based NSS: Does high or low context matter? *International Negotiation*, *9*(1), 79–109.

Kondo, D. K. (1990). *Crafting selves: Power, gender, and discourses of identity in a Japanese workplace.* Chicago, IL: University of Chicago Press.

Korsgaard, C. M. (2012). The right to lie: Kant on dealing with evil. *Philosophy & Public Affairs*, *15*(4), 325–349.

Kuntz, J. R. C., Kuntz, J. R., Elenkov, D., & Nabirukhina, A. (2013). Characterizing ethical cases: A cross-cultural investigation of individual differences, organisational climate, and leadership on ethical decision-making. *Journal of Business Ethics*, *113*(2), 317–331.

Kuper, A., Lingard, L., & Levinson, W. (2008). Critically appraising qualitative research. *British Medical Journal*, *337*(7671), 687–689. PMID:18687726

Kuroda, S. Y. (1965). Causative forms in Japanese. *Foundations of Language*, *1*(1), 30–50.

Kuroda, S. Y. (1973). Where epistemology, style, and grammar meet. In S. R. Anderson & P. Kipirsky (Eds.), *A Festschrift for Morris Halle* (pp. 337–391). New York, NY: Holt Rinehart and Willson.

Larrabee, J. H., Janney, M. A., Ostrow, C. L., Withrow, M. L., Hobbs, G. R. Jr, & Burant, C. (2003). Predicting registered nurse job satisfaction and intent to leave. *The Journal of Nursing Administration*, *33*(5), 271–283. PMID:12792282

Leach, A., Hilton, S., Greenwood, B. M., Manneh, E., Dibba, B., Wilkins, A., & Mulholland, E. K. (1999). An evaluation of the informed consent procedure used during a trial of a haemophilis influenzae Type B conjugate vaccine undertaken in the Gambia, West Africa. *Social Science & Medicine*, *48*(2), 139–148. PMID:10048773

LeBaron, M. (2003). *Bridging cultural conflicts: A new approach for a changing world.* San Francisco, CA: Jossey-Bass.

Lee, W. M., Kiesner, C., Pappas, T., Lee, I., Grindle, K., Jartti, T., & Gern, J. E. et al. (2007). A diverse group of previously unrecognized human rhinoviruses are common causes of respiratory illnesses in infants. *PLoS ONE*, *2*(10), e966. PMID:17912345

Leflar, R. B. (1996). Informed consent and patients' rights in Japan. *Houston Law Review/University of Houston*, *33*(1), 1-112.

Li, S., & Seale, O. (2007). Learning to do qualitative data analysis: An observational study of doctoral work. *Qualitative Health Research*, *17*(10), 1442–1452. PMID:18000083

Li, X. (2005). *Ethics, human rights, and culture: Beyond relativism and universalism.* New York, NY: Palgrave.

Ljungman, P., Ward, K. N., Crooks, B. N. A., Parker, A., Martino, R., Shaw, P. J., & Cordonnier, C. et al. (2001). VIRAL INFECTIONS-Respiratory virus infections after stem cell transplantation: A prospective study from the Infectious Diseases Working Party of the European Group for Blood and Marrow. *Bone Marrow Transplantation*, *28*(5), 479–484. PMID:11593321

Lodico, M. G., Spaulding, D. T., & Voegtle, K. H. (2010). *Methods in educational research: From theory to practice* (Vol. 28). San Francisco, CA: Wiley.

Long, S. O. (1999). Family surrogacy and cancer disclosure- Physician-family negotiation of an ethical dilemma in Japan. *Journal of Palliative Care*, *15*(3), 31–42. PMID:10540796

Loveday, L. (1981). Pitch, politeness and sexual role: An exploratory investigation into the pitch correlates of English and Japanese politeness formulae. *Language and Speech*, *24*(1), 71–89.

Malterud, K. (2001). Qualitative research: Standards, challenges, and guidelines. *Lancet*, *358*(9280), 483–488. PMID:11513933

Marcone, D. N., Ellis, A., Videla, C., Ekstrom, J., Ricarte, C., Carballal, G., & Echavarría, M. et al. (2013). Viral etiology of acute respiratory infections in hospitalized and outpatient children in Buenos Aires, Argentina. *The Pediatric Infectious Disease Journal*, *32*(3), e105–e110. PMID:23190781

Marginson, S., & Rhoades, G. (2002). Beyond national states, markets, and systems of higher education: A glonacal agency heuristic. *Higher Education*, *43*(3), 281–309.

Marschall, J., Piccirillo, M. L., Foxman, B., Lixin, Z., Warren, D. K., & Henderson, J. P. (2013). Patient characteristics but not virulence factors discriminate between asymptomatic and symptomatic E. coli bacteriuria in the hospital. *BMC Infectious Diseases*, *13*(1), 1–7. PMID:23663267

Martin, S. E. (1988). *A reference grammar of Japanese*. Rutland, VT: Tuttle.

Matesanz, R. (1998). Cadaveric organ donation: Comparison of legislation in various countries of Europe. *Nephrology, Dialysis, Transplantation*, *13*(7), 1632–1635. PMID:9681702

Maxwell, J. A. (1992). Understanding and validity in qualitative research. *Harvard Educational Review*, *62*(3), 279–301.

McGaughey, D. R. (2006). Kant on religion and science: Independence or integration? Zygon. *Journal Of Religion & Science*, *41*(3), 727–746.

McLafferty, C. L. Jr, Slate, J. R., & Onwuegbuzie, A. J. (2010). Transcending the quantitative-qualitative divide with mixed methods research: A multidimensional framework for understanding congruence and completeness in the study of values. *Counseling and Values*, *55*(1), 46–62.

McLeod, J. (2001). *Qualitative research in counseling and psychotherapy*. London, UK: Sage.

Melendez, M. M., & Alizadeh, K. (2011). Complications from international surgery tourism. *Aesthetic Surgery Journal*, *31*(6), 694–697. PMID:21813883

Mendelsohn, R. S. (1980). *Confessions of a medical heretic*. IN, Lebanon: Warner.

Miller, R. A. (1967). *The Japanese language*. Chicago, IL: University of Chicago Press.

Mills, J., Bonner, A., & Francis, K. (2008). The development of constructivist grounded theory. *International Journal of Qualitative Methods*, *5*(1), 25–35.

Milne, J., & Oberle, K. (2005). Enhancing rigor in qualitative description. *Journal of Wound, Ostomy, and Continence Nursing*, *32*(6), 413–420. PMID:16301909

Mimura, N., Yasuhara, K., Kawagoe, S., Yokoki, H., & Kazama, S. (2011). Damage from the Great East Japan Earthquake and Tsunami-a quick report. *Mitigation and Adaptation Strategies for Global Change*, *16*(7), 803–818.

Miranda, B., & Matesanz, R. (1998). International issues in transplantation: Setting the scene and flagging the most urgent and controversial issues. *Annals of the New York Academy of Sciences*, *862*(1), 129–143. PMID:9928215

Mitton, C., Peacock, S., Storch, J., Smith, N., & Cornelissen, E. (2010). Moral distress among healthcare managers: Conditions, consequences and potential responses. *Health Policy (Amsterdam)*, *6*(2), 99. PMID:22043226

Morita, E. (2003). Children's use of address and reference terms: Language socialization in a Japanese-English bilingual environment. *Multilingua*, *22*(4), 367–396.

Morrow, S. L. (2005). Quality and trustworthiness in qualitative research in counseling psychology. *Journal of Counseling Psychology*, *52*(2), 250.

Morrow, S. L., & Smith, M. L. (2000). Qualitative research for counseling psychology. In S. D. Brown & R. W. Lent (Eds.), *Handbook of Counseling Psychology* (3rd ed.; pp. 199–230). New York, NY: Wiley.

Morse, J. M., Barrett, M., Mayan, M., Olson, K., & Spiers, J. (2002). Verification strategies for establishing reliability and validity in qualitative research. *International Journal of Qualitative Methods, 1*(2), Article 2. Retrieved July 4 2002 from http://www.ualberta.ca/~ijqm/

Morse, J. M., Barrett, M., Mayan, M., Olson, K., & Spiers, J. (2008). Verification Strategies for Establishing Reliability and Validity in Qualitative Research. *International Journal of Qualitative Methods*, *1*(2), 13–22.

National Commission for the Protection of Human Subjects of Biomedical and Behavioral Research. (1979). *The Belmont report: Ethical principles and guidelines for the protection of human subjects of research*. Retrieved from http://www.hhs.gov/ohrp/humansubjects/guidance/belmont.html

Neale, B., & Bishop, L. (2012). The timescapes archive: A stakeholder approach to archiving qualitative longitudinal data. *Qualitative Research*, *12*(1), 53–65.

Nelson, A. R., Sawai, Y., Jennings, A. E., Bradley, L. A., Gerson, L., Sherrod, B. L., & Horton, B. P. et al. (2008). Great-earthquake paleogeodesy and tsunamis of the past 2000 years at Alsea Bay, central Oregon coast, USA. *Quaternary Science Reviews*, *27*(7), 747–768.

Nelson, J. M. (2009). Psychology, religion, and spirituality. New York, NY: Springer.

Nelson, J. M. (2012). A history of psychology of religion in the West: Implications for theory and method. *Pastoral Psychology*, *61*(5-6), 685–710.

Nelson, J. M., & Slife, B. D. (2012). Theoretical and epistemological foundations. In L. J. Miller (Ed.), *The Oxford handbook of psychology and spirituality* (pp. 21–35). Oxford, UK: Oxford University Press.

Neustupny, J. V. (1978). *Post-structural approaches to language: Language theory in a Japanese context.* Tokyo, Japan: University of Tokyo Press.

Nicholson, B., & Sahay, S. (2001). Some political and cultural issues in the globalisation of software development: Case experience from Britain and India. *Information and Organization*, *11*(1), 25–43.

Nisbett, R. E., Peng, K., Choi, I., & Norenzayan, A. (2001). Culture and systems of thought: Holistic versus analytic cognition. *Psychological Review*, *108*(2), 291–310. PMID:11381831

Norman, D. A. (2002). *The design of everyday things*. New York, NY: Basic.

Nuremberg Code. (1949). *The Nuremberg Code. Trials of war criminals before the Nuremberg military tribunals under control council law*. Washington, DC: U.S. Government Printing Office. Retrieved from: http://ora.georgetown.edu/irb/BioMedManual/AppendixIV.pdf

Oberle, K., & Hughes, D. (2001). Doctors' and nurses' perceptions of ethical problems in end-of-life decisions. *Journal of Advanced Nursing*, *33*(6), 707–715. PMID:11298208

Ochi, M. (2013). Shinya Yamanaka's 2012 Nobel Prize and the radical change in orthopedic strategy thanks to his discovery of iPS cells. *Acta Orthopaedica*, *84*(1), 1–3. PMID:23343378

Olson, L. L. (1998). Hospital nurses' perceptions of the ethical climate of their work setting. *Journal of Nursing Scholarship*, *30*(4), 345–349. PMID:9866295

Pang, M. C. S. (2003). *Nursing ethics in modern China: Conflicting values and competing role requirements*. Amsterdam, NL: Rodopi.

Pang, S. M., Sawada, A., Konishi, E., Olsen, D. P., Yu, P. L. H., Chan, M., & Mayumi, N. (2003). A comparative study of Chinese, American and Japanese nurses' perceptions of ethical role responsibilities. *Nursing Ethics*, *10*(3), 295–311. PMID:12762463

Parfitt, A. M., Drezner, M. K., Glorieux, F. H., Kanis, J. A., Malluche, H., Meunier, P. J., & Recker, R. R. et al. (1987). Bone histomorphometry: standardization of nomenclature, symbols, and units: report of the ASBMR Histomorphometry Nomenclature Committee. *Journal of Bone and Mineral Research*, *2*(6), 595–610. PMID:3455637

Parker, R. S. (1990). Nurses' stories: The search for a relational ethic of care. *ANS. Advances in Nursing Science*, *13*(1), 31–40. PMID:2122799

Pawson, R., & Tilley, N. (1997). *Realistic evaluation*. Thousand Oaks, CA: Sage.

Peng, K., Nisbett, R. E., & Wong, N. Y. C. (1997). Validity problems comparing values across cultures and possible solutions. *Psychological Methods*, *2*, 329–344.

Penticuff, J. H., & Walden, M. (2000). Influence of practice environment and nurse characteristics on perinatal nurses' responses to ethical dilemmas. *Nursing Research*, *49*(2), 64–72. PMID:10768582

Pigini, L., Facal, D., Blasi, L., & Andrich, R. (2012). Service robots in elderly care at home: Users' needs and perceptions as a basis for concept development. *Technology and Disability*, *24*(4), 303–311.

Ponterotto, J. G. (2005). Qualitative research in counseling psychology- A primer on research paradigms and philosophy of science. *Journal of Counseling Psychology*, *52*(2), 126.

Pratt, B., & Loff, B. (2012). Health research systems: Promoting health equity or economic competitiveness? *Bulletin of the World Health Organization*, *90*(1), 55–62. PMID:22271965

Quine, W. V. O. (2013). *Word and Object*. Cambridge, MA: MIT Press.

Raingruber, B. (2009). Assigning poetry reading as a way of introducing students to qualitative data analysis. *Journal of Advanced Nursing*, *65*(8), 1753–1761. PMID:19493139

Rashid, M. (2013). The question of knowledge in evidence-based design for healthcare facilities: Limitations and suggestions. *Health Environments Research & Design Journal*, *6*(4), 101–126. PMID:24089184

Reece, R. L. (2000, March-April). Preserving the soul of medicine and physicians: A talk with David Whyte. *Physician Executive*, *26*(2), 14–19. PMID:10847937

Regan, D. (1989). *Human brain electrophysiology: evoked potentials and evoked magnetic fields in science and medicine*. New York, NY: Elsevier.

René, V. L., Lucas, J., Henk, J., & Doeke, P. (2007). Aspects of spirituality concerning illness. *Scandinavian Journal of Caring Sciences*, *21*(4), 482–489. PMID:18036011

Rennie, D. L. (Ed.). (2002). Qualitative research: History, theory and practice[Special issue]. *Canadian Psychology*, *43*(3).

Riddell, R., & Iwafuchi, M. (1998). Problems arising from Eastern and Western classification systems for gastrointestinal dysplasia and carcinoma: Are they resolvable? *Histopathology*, *33*(3), 197–202. PMID:9777384

Rodney, P., & Starzomski, R. (1993). Constraints on the moral agency of nurses. *The Canadian Nurse*, *89*(9), 23–26. PMID:8221594

Rodrik, D. (1997). Has globalization gone too far? *California Management Review*, *39*(3), 29–53.

Rolfe, G. (2006). Validity, trustworthiness and rigor: Quality and the idea of qualitative research. *Journal of Advanced Nursing*, *53*(3), 304–310. PMID:16441535

Saif, M. (2000). World medical association declaration of Helsinki: Ethical principles for medical research involving human subjects. *The Journal of the American Medical Association, 284*, 3043-3045.

Sanchez-Arias, F., Calmeyn, H., Driesen, G., & Pruis, E. (2013, February 8). Human capital realities pose challenges across the globe. *Association for talent Development*. Retrieved from: https://www.td.org/Publications/Magazines/TD/TD-Archive/2013/02/Human-Capital-Realities-Pose-Challenges-Across-the-Globe

Sandelowski, M., & Barroso, J. (2002). Finding the findings in qualitative studies. *Journal of Nursing Scholarship*, *34*(3), 213–219. PMID:12237982

Sandelowski, M., & Barroso, J. (2003). Classifying the findings in qualitative studies. *Qualitative Health Research*, *13*(7), 905–923. PMID:14502957

Sassen, S. (1994). *Cities in a world economy* (Vol. 3). Thousand Oaks, CA: Pine Forge.

Schluter, J., Winch, S., Holzhauser, K., & Henderson, A. (2008). Nurses' moral sensitivity and hospital ethical climate: A literature review. *Nursing Ethics*, *15*(3), 304–321. PMID:18388166

Seale, C. (1999). *The quality of qualitative research*. London, UK: Sage.

Selinger, E. (2009). Technology transfer and globalization. In D. M. Kaplan (Ed.), Readings in the Philosophy of Technology, (pp. 321-344). Lanham, MD: Rowman & Littlefield.

Shibatani, M. (1990). *The languages of Japan*. Cambridge, UK: Cambridge University Press.

Shweder, R. A., & Bourne, E. J. (1982). Does the concept of the person vary cross-culturally? In A. J. Marsela & G. White (Eds.), *Cultural concepts of mental health and therapy* (pp. 97–137). Springer.

Slife, B. D., & Gantt, E. E. (1999). Methodological pluralism: A framework for psychotherapy research. *Journal of Clinical Psychology*, *55*(12), 1453–1465. PMID:10855480

Slife, B. D., & Reber, J. S. (2012). Conceptualizing religious practices in psychological research: Problems and prospects. *Pastoral Psychology*, *61*(5-6), 735–746.

Smeral, E. (1998). The impact of globalization on small and medium enterprises: New challenges for tourism policies in European countries. *Tourism Management*, *19*(4), 371–380.

Soderberg, A., & Norberg, A. (1993). Intensive care: Situations of ethical difficulty. *Journal of Advanced Nursing*, *18*(12), 2008–2014. PMID:8132934

Sparkes, A. C. (2001). Myth 94: Qualitative health researchers will agree about validity. *Qualitative Health Research*, *11*, 538–552. PMID:11521610

Spilker, B. (1993). *Multinational Pharmaceutical Companies: principles and practices*. Lippincott Williams & Wilkins.

Spilker, B. (1994). Multinational pharmaceutical companies: Principles and practices. Raven.

Srinivas, H., & Nakagawa, Y. (2008). Environmental implications for disaster preparedness: Lessons learnt from the Indian Ocean Tsunami. *Journal of Environmental Management*, *89*(1), 4–13. PMID:17904271

Stewart, K. A. (2006). Can a human rights framework improve biomedical and social scientific HIV/AIDS research for African women? *Human Rights Review (Piscataway, N.J.)*, *7*(2), 130–136.

Suen, A. (2002). *The Peace Corps*. New York, NY: Rosen.

Suzuki, T. (1976). Language and behavior in Japan: The conceptualization of personal relations. *Japan Quarterly (Asahi Shinbunsha)*, *23*(3), 255–266.

Suzuki, T. (1978). *Japanese and the Japanese: Words in culture*. Tokyo, Japan: Kodansha.

Tafarodi, R., Nishikawa, Y., Bonn, G., Morio, H., Fukuzawa, A., & Lee, J. (2012). Wishing for Change in Japan and Canada. *Journal of Happiness Studies*, *13*(6), 969–983.

Tanzi, M. V. (2000). Globalization and the future of social protection (No. 0-12). International Monetary Fund.

Taplin, I. M. (1997). Struggling to compete: Post-war changes in the U.S. clothing Industry. *Textile History*, *28*(1), 90–104.

Tashakkori, A., & Teddlie, C. (Eds.). (2003). *Handbook of mixed methods in social & behavioral research*. Thousand Oaks, CA: Sage.

Taylor, R. H., & Stoianovici, D. (2003). Medical robotics in computer-integrated surgery. *Robotics and Automation. IEEE Transactions on*, *19*(5), 765–781.

Telford, J., Cosgrave, J., & Houghton, R. (2006). *Joint evaluation of the international response to the Indian Ocean tsunami*. London, UK: Tsunami Evaluation Coalition.

Timmermann, A. (2006). Forecast combinations. In G. Elliot, C.W.J. Granger, & A. Timmermann (Eds.), *Handbook of Economic Forecasting* (Vol. 1, pp. 135-196). Retrieved from: http://management.ucsd.edu/faculty/directory/timmermann/pub/docs/forecast-combinations.pdf

Tobin, J. (2000). Financial globalization. *World Development*, *28*(6), 1101–1104.

Topor, F. S. (2013). *The predictive validity of a sentence repetition test for Japanese learners of English* (Doctoral dissertation). Capella University.

Truog, R. D., & Robinson, W. M. (2003). Role of brain death and the dead-donor rule in the ethics of organ transplantation. *Critical Care Medicine*, *31*(9), 2391–2396. PMID:14501972

Van Den Eynden, V., Corti, L., Woollard, M., Bishop, L., & Horton, L. (2011). *Managing and sharing data. Best practice for researchers*. University of Essex. Retrieved from: http://www. dataarchive. ac.uk/media/2894/managingsharing. pdf.

van Maanen, J. (1988). *Tales of the field*. Chicago, IL: University of Chicago Press.

Wagner, A. K., Gandek, B., Aaronson, N. K., Acquadro, C., Alonso, J., Apolone, G., & Ware, J. E. Jr et al.. (1998). Cross-cultural comparisons of the content of SF-36 translations across 10 countries: Results from the IQOLA project. *Journal of Clinical Epidemiology*, *51*(11), 925–932. PMID:9817109

Wagner, N., & Hendel, T. (2000). Ethics in pediatric nursing: An international perspective. *Journal of Pediatric Nursing*, *15*(1), 54–59. PMID:10714039

Walker, P. O. (2004). Decolonizing Conflict Resolution: Addressing the Ontological Violence of Westernization. *American Indian Quarterly*, *28*(3/4), 527–549.

Weitz, J. S., & Fraser, H. B. (2001). Explaining mortality rate plateaus. *Proceedings of the National Academy of Sciences of the United States of America*, *98*(26), 15383–15386. PMID:11752476

Wetzel, P. J. (1994). A movable self: the linguistic indexing of *uchi* and *soto*. Situated Meaning: Inside and Outside. In J. Bachnik & C. J. Quinn (Eds.), *Japanese Self, Society, and Language* (pp. 78–87). Princeton, NJ: Princeton University Press.

Whittemore, R., Chase, S. K., & Mandle, C. L. (2001). Validity in qualitative research. *Qualitative Health Research, 11*, 522–537. PMID:11521609

Woo, J., Wolfgang, S., & Batista, H. (2008). The effect of globalization of drug manufacturing, production, and sourcing and challenges for American drug safety. *Clinical Pharmacology and Therapeutics, 83*(3), 494–497. PMID:18253142

World Health Organization. (2005). *WHO guidelines on nonclinical evaluation of vaccines. In WHO Expert Committee on Biological Standardization. Fifty-fourth report* (Vol. 927). Geneva: World Health Organization.

World Health Organization. (2005). *Chernobyl: The true scale of the accident; 20 years later a UN report provides definitive answers and ways to repair lives*. Available at: http://www.who. int/mediacentre/news/releases/2005/pr38/en/index. html

World Medical Association General Assembly. (2004). World Medical Association Declaration of Helsinki: Ethical principles for medical research involving human subjects. *International Journal of Bioethics, 15*(1), 124. PMID:15835069

Wright, P. F., Deatly, A. M., Karron, R. A., Belshe, R. B., Shi, J. R., Gruber, W. C., & Randolph, V. B. et al. (2007). Comparison of results of detection of rhinovirus by PCR and viral culture in human nasal wash specimens from subjects with and without clinical symptoms of respiratory illness. *Journal of Clinical Microbiology, 45*(7), 2126–2129. PMID:17475758

Wulff, D. M. (1997). *Psychology of religion: Classic and contemporary*. New York, NY: Wiley.

Yin, R. K. (2003). *Case study research: Design and methods* (3rd ed.). Thousand Oaks, CA: Sage.

Yin, R. K. (2009). Case study research: Design and methods (Vol. 5). Thousand Oaks, CA: Sage.

Yoshida, H., & Smith, L. B. (2003). Shifting ontological boundaries: How Japanese-and English-speaking children generalize names for animals and artifacts. *Developmental Science, 6*(1), 1–17.

Yuen, K. Y., Chan, P. K. S., Peiris, M., Tsang, D. N. C., Que, T. L., & Shortridge, K. F. et al. H5N1 Study Group. (1998). Clinical features and rapid viral diagnosis of human disease associated with avian influenza A H5N1 virus. *Lancet, 351*(9101), 467–471. PMID:9482437

Zeiler, K. (2009). Deadly pluralism? Why death-concept, death-definition, death-criterion and death-test pluralism should be allowed, even though it creates some problems. *Bioethics, 23*(8), 450–459. PMID:18554277

Ziegahn, L. (2001). Talk about culture online: The potential for transformation. *Distance Education, 22*(1), 144–150.

ADDITIONAL READING

Andorno, R. (2002). Biomedicine and international human rights law: In search of a global consensus. *Bulletin of the World Health Organization, 80*(12), 959–963. PMID:12571724

Andorno, R. (2009). Human dignity and human rights as a common ground for a global bioethics. *The Journal of Medicine and Philosophy, 34*(3), 223–240. PMID:19386998

Düwell, M. (2012). *Bioethics: methods, theories, domains*. New York, NY: Routledge.

Engelhardt, H. T. (2011). Confronting moral pluralism in posttraditional Western societies: Bioethics critically reassessed. *The Journal of Medicine and Philosophy*. PMID:21724971

Hanssen, I. (2004). An intercultural nursing perspective on autonomy. *Nursing Ethics, 11*(1), 28–41. PMID:14763648

Macklin, R. (1999). *Against relativism: cultural diversity and the search for ethical universals in medicine*. New York, NY: Oxford University Press.

Nie, J. B. (2013). *Medical ethics in China: A transcultural interpretation*. New York, NY: Routledge.

KEY TERMS AND DEFINITIONS

Appropriation: Taking and converting something from another person for one's own use without the permission of the owner.

Collectivism: Entails duties rather than right. Individuals selflessly identify themselves in terms of others; group decision affect individuals.

Egalitarianism: Espouses the equality of all people and deserve equal rights and opportunities.

Empirical Epistemology: The acquisition or assessment of knowledge base on practical or observable first-hand experience rather than theoretical explanation.

Individualism: Entails rights rather than duties accrued to individual; it ascribes the right to make decisions pertaining to oneself; personal freedom of choice, wellbeing and independent thinking.

Instrumental Role: Agent or function that contributes to the achievement of objective.

Medical Tourism: Foreign travels meanly for medical or cosmetic surgery.

Perceptual Sensibility: The capacity to conceive and interpret phenomena through cognition.

Transcultural Transplantation: Transfer of organs from one person (donor) to another person (receiver) across cultures.

Chapter 11

Evaluating the "Flipped" Face to Face Classroom and the Online Classroom in Teacher Education

Lori Severino
Drexel University, USA

Mary Jean Tecce DeCarlo
Drexel University, USA

ABSTRACT

This chapter will discuss a study that set out to determine if knowledge of the structure of language and self-efficacy of pre-service and in-service teachers was impacted by whether the course was taken in a face to face or online format. Results of the study showed there was a statistically significant change in the Teacher Knowledge Assessment: Structure of Language (TKA: SL) for participants in the online courses, but not for students taking the course face to face. To determine whether or not self-efficacy increased, the Teacher Efficacy Scale: short form (TES) was used, The TES includes two subscales: teacher efficacy and personal efficacy. Results showed no statistical significance on the overall TES score between participants; however, on the personal efficacy score, there was a statistically significant change in pre and post test scores of participants who took the course face to face.

INTRODUCTION

Many people are turning to online degree programs to complete their coursework for teacher certification. Distance education has become an option for students that live far away from a university and for those who either do not have the time and or money to attend on campus. In the United States hybrid courses, flipped classrooms, and fully online classes are new options for those interested in becoming teachers. There has been concern over whether or not eLearning can provide the same opportunities and experiences necessary to develop successful teachers as face to face formats (Downing & Dyment, 2013; Fogle & Elliot, 2013). These online learning options raise several questions. Can pre-service teachers taking online courses gain the knowledge to become effective teachers in the classroom? Do university

DOI: 10.4018/978-1-5225-0522-8.ch011

students engaged in eLearning gain similar content knowledge to students in face to face courses? Do the on line students experience gains in self-efficacy? Are they provided with similar opportunities as their peers receiving instruction face to face? A set of university professors had these same questions and designed a study to investigate them. The study was completed at a university in the Northeast, United States. This School of Education has a well-regarded, online teacher education program as well as traditional face to face programs on campus. The professors wanted to explore the learning experiences, the knowledge gains and the feelings of self-efficacy between and among participants taking a course either in a "flipped" face to face class or an online class. This chapter will examine the similarities and differences in participant outcomes and experiences when a field-based, special education course geared toward struggling readers is offered online and also as a "flipped" face to face course on campus.

BACKGROUND

In the United States the majority of elementary and secondary teachers are trained through traditional four year undergraduate programs in colleges and universities (U.S. Department of Education Office of Postsecondary Education, 2013). Graduate degrees are also offered for those who wish to get an additional certification or deepen skills in a particular subject area. Degrees can be earned in early childhood education, elementary education, middle school education, secondary subject specific education, arts and physical education and special education. All of these programs include general academic coursework as well as classes in educational psychology, learning theory, teaching methods, and education law. Teacher education programs also provide pre-service educators with time in the field observing and working with students in elementary and secondary schools.

Successful program completers then apply for a teaching credential from a specific state. Each state has a Board or Department of Education, which requires educators to obtain a teaching license. All fifty states have standards for elementary and secondary classroom teachers, and 44 have specific teacher standards for all levels of special education (U.S. Department of Education Office of Postsecondary Education, 2013). Institutions of higher education submit plans of study to the state that demonstrate that the university coursework aligns with these standards.

Teacher education programs are now being influenced by the growth in eLearning. Some universities offer some or all of their courses online in synchronous or asynchronous formats. Even while attending on campus, students can choose to take some of their courses online. Flipped classrooms are also being incorporated into on campus programs. In a flipped classroom design, direct instruction moves from the group learning space to the individual learning space (What Is Flipped Learning, 2014). Content is delivered via online lectures and learning activities and face-to-face classroom time is devoted to applied learning such as problem sets, lab activities or field experiences. In this study, the "flipped" classroom involved field experiences and hands on learning in elementary or secondary schools.

Concerns have been raised about online learning and online teacher preparation specifically. Individual studies have found that online students can have lower graduation rates than on campus students (Grau-Valldosera & Minguillón, 2014; Jaggar & Hu, 2010). Fogle and Elliot (2013) found that school administrators who had not experienced online learning themselves were reluctant to hire teachers whose coursework was exclusively taken online. However larger meta-analyses have concluded that students from primary school through university can and do learn effectively in online formats (Means, Toyama, Murphy, Bakia, & Jones, 2009; The Future of State Universities, 2011).

The quality of teacher education programs in general has been challenged in recent years (Levine, 2006). Levine raised concerns about the balance of academic and clinical coursework in teacher education. Field experiences provide much of the clinical coursework. Levine (2006) stated, "Time in clinical settings is too short and involvement of university professors in the schools is insufficient (p.29)." Cochran-Smith and Zeichner (2015) argued that effective fieldwork requires "planned, guided, and sustained interactions with pupils (children and adolescents) within early field and student teaching settings (p. 317)."

Debates over teacher preparation align with specific fears about preparing teachers for reading instruction. There have been concerns not only about the lack of knowledge teachers have in teaching beginning readers (Josh et al., 2009), but also in the amount of practice the preservice teachers have in working with students to implement best practices while learning the theories that underpin effective reading instruction (Baumann, Ro, Duffy-Hester, Hoffman, 2000). Studies have shown that there is a positive relationship between quality teacher preparation programs and student outcomes (National Reading Panel, 2000). The practice in postsecondary institutions has been to provide the pedagogical instruction in one term and offer field experience at a different time. When teacher preparation programs include planned clinical field experiences it is better for student achievement (Darling-Hammond, 1997). It was the belief of the researchers in this study if participants could practice literacy instruction in a real-life situation while also learning best practices in teaching reading, they would grasp the knowledge concepts at a deeper level and would have more positive outlook on their own ability to teach reading, especially to struggling readers. The courses being examined in this study incorporated reading pedagogy instruction and applied fieldwork within the same course.

Issues in The Field

Both special education teachers and regular education teachers must be prepared to work with all levels of students. Teachers need to understand the reasons student struggle with reading in order to be able to provide the best instruction to meet students' needs. Of the students with diagnosed learning disabilities, most have issues with reading (Shaywitz & Shaywitz, 2004). "Prevalence estimates of reading problems in the population of those with learning disabilities range from 75% to 85% nationwide" (Moats, 1994, p. 82). Over the past 20 years, brain research has explored the difficulty students with learning disabilities have in reading. The research has shown that reading and spelling issues are due to issues in language processing (Shaywitz & Shaywitz, 2004; Moats, 1994). Since language processing is critically important in learning to read, this study set to explore the knowledge base of preservice and inservice teachers in relation to the structure of language. Teachers should be trained on what high quality reading instruction is and how to effectively deliver that instruction. However, studies have demonstrated that teachers, during their university coursework, are not learning the knowledge and skills necessary to effectively teach struggling readers (Moats, 1994). There has been controversy over the best way to teach reading, and related discussions about the best ways to prepare preservice teachers to be successful reading teachers (Chall, 1992; Stanovich & Stanovich, 1995). One side of the controversy called for a *whole language* approach which involved immersing children in print, while the other side called for a more *alphabetic principle* approach which involved direct teaching of letter sound relationships (Cunningham & O'Donnell, 2015). In 2000, the National Reading Panel Report concluded that research supported teaching reading required explicit instruction in phonemic awareness, systematic phonics instruction, methods to improve fluency, teaching vocabulary, and methods to improve comprehension. Moats (1994) states, the "degree of awareness of the phonological structure of words is the best predictor of a child's subsequent reading success" (p.84), therefore, it is of vital importance for teachers to acquire the knowledge necessary to understand and be able to teach the structure of the language. The National Research Council (NRC) (1998) report notes, teachers must be able to provide quality instruction in those five areas, but studies have shown that teachers are not always aware of ways to explicitly teach phonemic awareness and phonics (Moats, 1994; Fielding-Barnsley, 2010).

"To reach a satisfactory level of content knowledge and procedural expertise, teachers deserve intensive theoretical and practical training that needs to include demonstration and supervised practice" (Moats, 1994, p.86). This study sought to compare the difference in knowledge when participants had exposure to the same content, but one group had supervised practice and the other had practice, but no direct supervision by the university professor. To measure teacher knowledge of language participants were given the Teacher Knowledge Assessment: Structure of Language (TKA: SL) (Mather, Bos, & Babur, 2001) in the first week of the course and the last week of the course. This assessment would allow the professors to evaluate whether or not the content in the course and the experience in field placement had an impact on the knowledge of the structure of language for either/both the face to face and online participants.

Teachers' sense of efficacy is partly affected by the knowledge base of the teacher. "Without adequate training, teachers' sense of efficacy in their job is most certainly diminished" (Moats, 1994). Self-efficacy refers to the concept that "people's level of motivation, affective states, and actions are based more on what they believe than on what is objectively true" (Bandura, 1997, p. 2). Self-efficacy for teachers is defined by Guo (2012) as "teachers' judgment about whether or not they are capable of promoting students' learning (p.4)." In other words, teacher who feel they can make a difference through their instructional practices are more likely to actually impact student learning through their instructional practices. Teacher efficacy is believed, theoretically, to influence teachers' performance (e.g., instructional practices, motivating styles, pedagogical beliefs, effort), which in turn affects student outcomes such as motivation and achievement (Duffin, French & Patrick, 2012). The researchers chose to investigate this variable because self-efficacy has been shown to be a reliable predictor of teacher effectiveness in literacy instruction (Guo, Piasta, Justice, & Kaderavek, 2010; Justice, Mashburn, Hamre, & Pianta, 2008). The challenge for teacher educators is to find ways to engender this feeling of self-efficacy in their university students. Narkom and Black (2008) found that students who did fieldwork in literacy demonstrated strong feelings of self-efficacy with regards to teaching both proficient and struggling readers. Haverback and Parault (2008) completed a study demonstrating that preservice teachers had an increase in their feelings of self-efficacy when they tutored struggling readers during their field experiences.

For the study described in this chapter pre and posttests of both teacher knowledge of the structures of language and teacher self-efficacy were administered to university students in both the online and "flipped" face to face classes. In order to determine what knowledge the university students knew about the ways that the English language is encoded, the Teacher Knowledge Assessment of the Structure of Language (TKA:SL) (Mather, Bos, & Babur, 2001) was given in week one and week ten of the courses. The TKA: SL was adapted by Mather, Bos, & Babur (2001) from previous assessments of Lerner (1997), Moats (1994), and Rath (1994). All students were also asked to take a Teacher Efficacy Scale (Hoy & Woolfolk, 1993) survey in week two and week ten of the course.

METHODOLOGY

This study intended to answer the question of whether or not knowledge of the structure of language and/or self-efficacy improved for either/both flipped classroom and online participants over the course of the ten week term. The United States is moving in the direction of tying student achievement to teacher evaluation. Schools of Education need to be sure the teachers they are preparing are able to work with all types of learners and can impact student learning. Teacher knowledge and teacher efficacy can both have an effect on student achievement. Measuring these skills while participants are still under the direction of the university is critical. With the information obtained, professors can determine the gaps in knowledge and provide more direct instruction where necessary. Professors can also work with participants struggling with efficacy and provide more opportunities for them to feel more confident in the field. This study also wanted to identify if there were differences in knowledge and efficacy between participants taking the courses face to face and those taking the courses online. This information will be important to the course developers, but also to the field, as there has been controversy over whether or not students in online courses receive the same content and experiences.

Course Description

The courses involved in this study engaged participants in tutoring struggling readers. Participants were supported by classwork and instructor feedback on tutoring lesson plans. In this study, all university students, whether in the flipped course or online, had to tutor a struggling reader during the 10-week term. The undergraduate students tutor a minimum of 10 hours and the graduate students tutor a minimum of 15 hours. The difference in time is based on the number of courses the students take that include field experiences. In this study, the state Department of Education requires a different amount of field experience hours depending on undergraduate or graduate course. The undergraduates are required more hours total, but also have a much higher number of courses with field experiences and therefore, each course with field experience requires less hours than at the graduate level. The additional hours for the graduate level students may have an impact on both their self-efficacy and knowledge base since they are spending more hours in a one on one tutoring situation.

The courses discussed in this research study included two courses: one in instructing struggling readers from the ages of five to ten and a second course in teaching content area literacy to struggling readers ages 11 to 18. The courses have similar content, but focus on the age of the student in providing interventions to help the struggling reader. Both courses used eLearning applications to deliver content. The on campus courses were taught mostly in a local school near the university in which the face to face participants tutored struggling readers with the support of a university professor. The tutees were brought to a classroom to work with the university participants. The researchers deemed this a "flipped" classroom as participants did the coursework online and spent class time in the field and practicing skills. The online courses also had a field component; however, the participant tutored a student without the support of a faculty member or any other participant on site.

For the "flipped" face to face courses, all participants were assigned to the same school to work one on one with a student identified as having reading issues or at least two grade levels below his/her peers. The course content was delivered in the online environment and the field or practicum component was the actual instructional time with the professor; hence the "flipped" environment. In the field, participants would work one on one in tutoring a student in an area of concern: decoding, fluency or comprehension. The university professor was available during that time to observe, coach and provide immediate feedback.

The researchers embedded a pre/post knowledge assessment and a pre/post self-efficacy survey in both the "flipped" face to face courses and the online courses. The university was on the quarter system and classes were ten weeks with another week for final exams. Students were also required to do 10 hours (undergraduate level) or 15 hours (graduate level) of field experience with this course. The participants in the on-line course were sent to a school in their local area based on whether they were focusing on elementary or secondary. They worked with the school to set up a consistent time to work individually with a struggling reader. In both cases, the participants received the instruction for how to support struggling readers, how to assess a student, and how to provide appropriate interventions in an online format. The main difference between the courses was in how the field placement was implemented.

The research team sought to determine whether there was a difference in teacher knowledge or feelings of self-efficacy when a student took a flipped classroom course or a strictly online course. With so many universities adopting digital teaching strategies, it is important to understand if students are receiving similar instruction and support in these environments. The researchers focused on measures of teacher knowledge and teacher efficacy in order to explore the effectiveness of both methods of eLearning instruction. In the particular courses that were part of this study, the focus was to ensure that teachers gain the knowledge of the English language necessary to understand how that relates to teaching reading. Although the university course encompassed participants preparing to teach in all grade levels, the courses were specifically related to helping struggling readers. Even teachers at the secondary level may encounter adolescents that are still having difficulty with aspects of decoding. The researchers believed that all teachers need to be aware of the alphabetic code and to have awareness of how to help students who struggle with breaking or figuring out the code.

In the online courses, the participants participated in weekly lectures, multimedia experiences, discussion boards, and readings in an online environment. The same content was covered in the flipped classroom and online classroom. In the online courses, participants could ask for help through the discussion boards and receive feedback on lesson plans prior to teaching their lessons. Table 1 represents the models for the course.

Table 1. Model of courses

	Flipped Model	**Online Model**
Courses	EDEX 246 Elementary	EDEX 246 & EDEX 546 Elementary
	EDEX 266 Secondary	EDEX 566 Secondary
Content Delivery	Online and face to face	Online Only
Class Assignments	Online	Online
Field Hours Spent in Intervention	EDEX 246: 10	EDEX 246:10
	EDEX 266: 10	EDEX 546 & EDEX 566: 15
Supervisor Onsite for Interventions	Yes	No

Design

This study used a mixed-methods design. Quantitative analyses were performed using SPSS 23. Reliability analyses were performed first on both instruments to determine if the results would be reliable for these particular participants. Descriptive statistics and mean scores of all pre and post instruments were performed and analyzed. Then Paired Sample T tests were performed for each instrument to determine if there was a statistical difference in scores between participants in a face to face courses and participants in the online courses. Qualitative analyses included focus groups and interviews. All university students were invited to participate in the focus groups and interviews. Four students volunteered to participate in the face to face focus group and one student from the online course volunteered to be interviewed. Participants in all courses also completed a written field experience reflection. Reflections were randomly selected from all courses to add to the qualitative analysis. Four closed codes were created based upon the central research questions of the study:

- Student (struggling reader/writer) factors
- University student factors
- University student self-efficacy
- University student knowledge of language/literacy components.

After the interview transcripts and selected written field reflections were analyzed, a second set of codes was developed to expand on the initial set. The second set of codes was then applied to the original data set. These codes were:

- University student knowledge of literacy assessment and instructional strategies.
- Cooperating teacher factors.
- Course instructor factors.
- Filed placement setting factors.
- Coursework factors.

Instruments

In order to determine if there were changes in knowledge and efficacy, pre and posttests of both teacher knowledge and teacher self-efficacy were administered to university students in both the online and flipped classes. In order to assess the knowledge the university students knew about the structure of the English language, the Teacher Knowledge Assessment of the Structure of Language (TKA:SL) (Mather, Bos, & Babur, 2001) was given in week one and week ten of the courses. The entire assessment can be found in Appendix 1. In this assessment participants were asked for definitions of terms, to analyze speech sounds of words, to count the number of syllables in words, to analyze morphemic units and to identify concepts of language.

This study also used the Teacher Efficacy Scale: Short Form, developed by Woolfolk and Hoy (1993), to measure efficacy. This scale was chosen because it provides data on two subscales: teacher efficacy and personal efficacy. The subscale of teacher efficacy "appears to reflect a general belief about the power of teaching to reach difficult children and has more in common with teachers' conservative or liberal attitudes toward education" (Hoy & Woolfolk, 1990, p. 283). The second subscale "appears to be the more accurate indicator of the teachers' personal sense of efficacy" (Hoy & Woolfolk, 1993 p. 283). Examples of questions regarding teacher efficacy were: "A teacher is very limited in what he/she can achieve because a student's home environment is a large influence on his/her achievement," and "If parents would do more for their children, I could do more." Examples of questions regarding personal efficacy were: "When I really try, I can get through to most difficult students," and "If a student in my class becomes disruptive and noisy, I feel assured that I know some techniques to redirect him/her quickly." The entire scale can be found in Appendix 2. The responses to the statements were based on a Likert scale that ranged from one to six:

1. Strongly Agree
2. Moderately Agree
3. Agree slightly more than disagree
4. Disagree slightly more than agree
5. Moderately Disagree
6. Strongly Disagree

RESULTS

The participants in this study were seeking an undergraduate degree or a master's degree. The Teachers Knowledge Assessment of the Structure of Language (TKA: SL) was given to determine if there was a change in participants' knowledge of language from the beginning of the course to the end of the course. The researchers hypothesized that the participants' knowledge would increase over the course of the term due to the content provided in the course and the practice of the strategies in the field; however, the course covered more content than only the structure of language. In the elementary version of the course, three weeks of the ten weeks covered content on language structure specifically. In the course for secondary preparation, one week is specifically devoted to the structure of the language and other weeks included some information on the structure of language. It was presumed that the participants in the elementary preparation course would have a higher change in score than the participants in the secondary focused course due to the increase in content. Table 2 has a breakdown of the types of courses offered in this program. There appears to be more emphasis placed on elementary teachers understanding phonics and phonemic awareness in order to teach beginning readers the skills necessary to become skilled readers (National Reading Panel, 2000).

Table 2. Mean scores for pre and post TKA: SL for each course

Course	Pre TKA:SL	Post TKA:SL
Edex 246 face to face	13.1818	13.8000
Edex 246 online	13.1429	13.7143
Edex 546 online	13.2308	15.6552
Edex 266 face to face	13.2000	13.5556
Edex 566 online	12.3333	14.7692

TKA:SL

Reliability of the instrument was performed first. The original TKA: SL had an overall reliability using Cronbach's coefficient alpha of .83 in its initial field test (Mather, et al. 2001). In this study, the research team expected lower reliability in the pretest than the posttest. Students at the beginning of the term would not have the content knowledge necessary to answer the questions. Although the posttest score reliability was deemed more important, the analysis for reliability on the pretest was performed (.593 Cronbach's Alpha). Analysis of reliability for the posttest showed stronger reliability (.663 Cronbach's Alpha), but slightly below acceptable reliability of .70 (UCLA, 2015). The researchers deemed this an acceptable reliability analysis for the purposes of this study.

Table 2 shows the breakdown of mean pre and post TKA: SL scores for all of the courses in this study. The undergraduate courses were EDEX 246 (elementary) and EDEX 266 (secondary). The graduate level courses were EDEX 546 (elementary) and EDEX 566 (secondary). The mean scores for the pre TKA in all classes were similar ranging from 12.34 to 13.23. It did not appear to matter that some of the students were undergraduate and some of the students were graduate. It is not surprising that the lowest mean score on the pretest was from students in the graduate course that were teaching at the secondary level. The TKA: SL focuses on skills and knowledge traditionally expected of elementary teachers. The secondary teachers are more focused on learning specific content for the area in which they teach: social studies, science, math and English. The greatest gains in TKA: SL scores were with the online courses. There was a statistically significant change from pre to post TKA: SL scores for the participants in the online courses (p = .000). A Paired Sample T test was performed and the results are displayed in Table 3. The mean score during the pretest was 12.86 and on the posttest was 15.14. This significant change in scores may be due to the fact that many of the university students in the online classes were classroom teachers and were able to practice the content material every day; whereas, the flipped classroom university students were only working with five to 18 year old students for 10 hours during the term. In an analysis of interview data from this group the only elements of the TKS: SL that were specifically identified were *blending* and *segmenting*. Katrina, a student in the flipped class, commented in a focus group interview at the completion of the course that she didn't feel she had a strong knowledge base about the structure of language, saying, "Some of the more content knowledge from the course, I feel like I don't have as strong of an understanding. I feel like I can support them (the students) with my experiences. It would also have been nice to have more of a course where I could kind of get that background knowledge."

In a paired samples analysis of pre and post TKA: SL of the face to face participants, there was no statistically significant difference in pre and posttest (p= .264). This group had a small sample size of only 13 and the majority of those students were preservice teachers who have yet to have teaching experiences in their own classrooms. This may have had an impact on the minimal change in mean scores

Table 3. Paired samples t test for pre and post TKA: SL for online students

	N	Mean	Sig. (2-tailed)
Pre/Post TKA:SL for online participants	49	-2.28571	.000

from pretest to posttest. However, the posttest scores of the online participants are still not in the range necessary to demonstrate expertise in knowledge of the structure of language. An average mean score of 15.66 for the highest gains is only 70% of the knowledge assessed.

There were a few questions on the TKA: SL in which both students in the flipped classroom and in the online classes struggled. Question 8: A voiced consonant digraph is in the word: a. think b: ship c: whip d: the e: photo, had a mean score of .27 for the flipped classes and .24 for the online classes. To answer this question correctly, the examinee would need to understand the difference between voiced and unvoiced, what a consonant is, and what a digraph is. Consonants and digraphs are discussed in class; however, whether or not the consonant is voiced or unvoiced is not part of the instruction. This is certainly a term that can easily be added to the coursework. Question 11 also had a low correct response among both groups: How many speech sounds are in the word box? This is a tricky question to answer. Most people would respond that there are three speech sounds in box; however, the /x/ has two speech sounds- /k/ and /s/. This information will be used to update the courses with more direct instruction in the vocabulary necessary to improve knowledge in order to increase scores in future courses.

TES: Short Form Factor Analysis and Reliability

The researchers used Woolfolk and Hoy's (1993) Teacher Efficacy Scale (TES) Short Form which has two sets of variables: one set to focus on teacher efficacy and one set to focus on personal efficacy. The entire survey can be found in Appendix 2. In order to verify that our study found the same set of factors, a factor analysis was completed on the TES both for the pretest given to students in week two of the term and the posttest given in week ten of the term. In addition to identifying the latent variables, the researchers wanted to identify if any items were performing better or worse than others, which can be done through factor analysis. The recommended number of participants for an adequate factor analysis is a ratio of five to ten per item in the sample (Tinsley & Tinsley, 1987). In the factor analysis of the pre-TES, the N =68 is an appropriate size for a ten item scale. It should be noted that there was not a large sample size for this study and the results may not be generalizable. The initial factor analysis using Varimax rotation method yielded three factors with questions one, two, four, five and ten aligning with teaching efficacy. Questions six, seven, eight, and nine aligned with personal efficacy. Question three, "When I really try, I can get through to most difficult students" fell into a third factor. The scree plot from the factor analysis revealed that the questions really fell into two main factors and so another analysis was completed declaring only two factors (teaching and personal efficacy); the data revealed that the factor analysis matched the Woolfolk and Hoy (1993) factors. Question three now aligned with personal efficacy. The results of the factor analysis with the two determined factors can be seen in Table 4. In this second iteration of the factor analysis, the first factor (teacher efficacy) accounted for 31.146 percent of the variance and the second factor (personal efficacy) accounted for 28.041 percent of the variance.

The same analyses were performed with the post TES survey given in week ten of the term. The scree plot of this analysis showed there were three factors that played an important determination in the ten questions. During the first iteration of factor analysis using Varimax, questions one, two, four, five and ten represented factor one (teacher efficacy). Questions six, seven and eight represented the second factor (personal efficacy). This time, two questions were more closely related to a third factor: question three, which was the same question as in the pre TES and also question nine, "If I really try hard, I can get through to even the most difficult or unmotivated students". Question nine asked the same question as question three, but added "unmotivated students" with "most difficult" students. Both questions re-

Table 4. Results of factor analysis of the TES pre survey with two determined factors

	Teacher Efficacy	Personal Efficacy
Pre TES Question 1	**.666**	.020
Pre TES Question 2	**.632**	-.131
Pre TES Question 3	-.311	**.377**
Pre TES Question 4	**.882**	.102
Pre TES Question 5	**.918**	.090
Pre TES Question 6	.059	**.784**
Pre TES Question 7	.036	**.829**
Pre TES Question 8	.035	**.834**
Pre TES Question 9	-.126	**.778**
Pre TES Question 10	**.718**	-.147

lated to "I" statements in the beginning part of the questions and the researchers considered that a third factor may be involved in the post TES survey with this particular group of undergraduate and graduate students. The data that includes the third factor, can be found in Table 5. To be consistent with the pre TES analyses, a second analysis specifically using two determined factors was performed. The results of that analysis can be found in Table 6. Questions one, two, four, five and ten contributed to the teacher efficacy factor while questions three, six, seven, eight and nine contributed to the personal efficacy factor. This is consistent with the work done previously on the TES short form (Woolfolk and Hoy, 1993).

Table 5. Results of factor analysis of the TES post survey with three factors

	Teacher Eff	Personal Eff	Factor 3
Post TES Question 1	**.780**	.112	-.057
Post TES Question 2	**.542**	.030	-.045
Post TES Question 3	-.086	-.091	**.903**
Post TES Question 4	**.854**	-.209	-.200
Post TES Question 5	**.858**	-.212	-.161
Post TES Question 6	-.244	**.671**	-.084
Post TES Question 7	.182	**.771**	.051
Post TES Question 8	-.236	**.735**	.373
Post TES Question 9	-.244	.378	**.740**
Post TES Question 10	**.856**	-.239	-.104

Table 6. Results of factor analysis of TES post survey with two determined factors

	Teacher Efficacy	Personal Efficacy
Post TES Question 1	**.789**	.031
Post TES Question 2	**.543**	-.022
Post TES Question 3	-.186	**.379**
Post TES Question 4	**.841**	-.321
Post TES Question 5	**.840**	-.304
Post TES Question 6	-.157	**.549**
Post TES Question 7	.261	**.683**
Post TES Question 8	-.189	**.833**
Post TES Question 9	-.274	**.709**
Post TES Question 10	**.630**	-.298

Although reliability of the TES had been shown in other studies, it was necessary to ensure that there was consistency in the reliability in using the same survey with this group as well. Reliability of using this survey with this particular group of students was conducted using Chronbach's Alpha for each of the subscales (teacher efficacy and personal efficacy) to see if the questions for each of the subscales is consistent. In a previous study by Hoy and Woolfolk (1990), the alpha coefficients of reliability for teacher efficacy was 0.72 and for personal efficacy 0.84. The Cronbach's Alpha scores can be found in Table 7. A Cronbach's Alpha of .70 is considered to be consistent and reliable in most cases. The teacher efficacy subscale for both the pre and post TES are considered to be consistent and reliable with .828 and .857 respectively. Although the pre personal efficacy subscale was considered consistent and reliable (.774), the posttest of the personal efficacy subscale (.654) did not meet the required score for reliability. This may be explained by the information retrieved from the factor analysis. In the factor analysis for the posttest of personal efficacy, there were two questions that could have been connected to a third factor and this may have affected the reliability. To be consistent between the pre and posttest, the researchers accepted the reliability of the post test for personal efficacy as acceptable for this particular study.

TES: Short Form (Teacher Efficacy)

After the reliability was evaluated, an analysis of pre and post mean scores on the two subscales was performed to determine if there was a difference in mean scores between the students in the flipped classes and the on-line classes. Data analysis of the mean scores of the pre survey and post survey for the *teacher* efficacy subscale for students in flipped instruction and online instruction revealed there was no

Table 7. Reliability for teacher and personal efficacy subscales pre and post TES

Cronbach's Alpha	Teacher Efficacy Pre	Teacher Efficacy Post	Personal Efficacy Pre	Personal Efficacy Post
	.828	.857	.774	.654

statistically significant difference in the participants. Participants in the flipped instruction began with a mean of 4.0667 on the pre survey and a 4.3077 on the post survey of *teacher* efficacy. Participants in online instruction began with a mean teacher efficacy of 4.4080 and ended with 4.4107. There was a larger increase in the mean for students in the flipped classes than for the online classes; and the end of the term survey scores, both groups had similar scores with no statistical significance between the two. See Table 8 for the results of the teacher efficacy mean and results of the ANOVA. While the flipped participants did see more of an increase in their teacher efficacy, it was not statistically significant. A Paired Samples T test was run to determine if there was a statistically significant change in the flipped class student scores on the *teacher* efficacy subscale. There was no statistically significant change (p=.441). The undergraduate students may have had the increase in teacher efficacy due to exposure to working with a student and practicing the skills needed to improve under the supervision of the university professor. The online university students did not experience much of a change in teacher efficacy. The lack of university supervision may have contributed to this result. However, it is the intent of the courses to provide the knowledge that would then transfer into higher teacher efficacy. This did not happen with this particular group of participants.

TES: Short Form (Personal Efficacy)

The same analysis was used to determine if there was a difference in mean values of the *personal* efficacy subscale (questions three, six, seven, eight, and nine). The questions that relate to *personal* efficacy are worded so that a lower score (closer to one) translates to increased *personal* efficacy. The participants in flipped instruction had a pre mean score of 2.4526 and a post score of 1.9077. The participants in the online instruction had a pre mean score of 2.2680 and a post score of 2.1962. Similar to the *teacher* efficacy, results of the means of *personal* efficacy showed a larger increase in students in the flipped instruction; however, there was no statistically significant difference between the two groups on the post survey (p=.119). See Table 9 for results of the analysis of mean scores and ANOVA for the pre/post personal efficacy subscale. There were no statistically significant differences between the face to face participants and the online participants on either the pre or post *personal* efficacy. Both groups were similar at the beginning of the course in *personal* efficacy and at the end of the course. However, there is an increase in mean scores of the students face to face, which prompted further analysis.

Since there were data to support a larger increase in the pre and post personal efficacy scores, a Paired Samples T test was run to see if there was a statistically significant difference in pre and posttest scores

Table 8. Mean scores and ANOVA results for pre and post teacher efficacy scores

	Mean Pre Teacher Efficacy	Mean Post Teacher Efficacy	Significance
Face to Face	4.0667	4.3077	
Online	4.4080	4.4107	
Total	4.3176	4.3913	
ANOVA pre teaching efficacy between groups			.193
ANOVA post teaching efficacy between groups			.725

Table 9. Mean scores and ANOVA results for pre and post personal efficacy subscale

	Mean Pre Personal Efficacy	Mean Post Personal Efficacy	Significance
Face to Face	2.4526	1.9077	
Online	2.2680	2.1962	
Total	2.3188	2.1394	
ANOVA pre personal efficacy between groups			.395
ANOVA post personal efficacy between groups			.119

Table 10. Paired samples t test for pre and post personal efficacy scores for "flipped" participants

	N	Mean	Sig. (2-tailed)
Pre/Post Personal Efficacy	13	.92542	**.042**

of the flipped classroom participants. Thirteen students, a very small sample, showed a statistically significant difference from pre to post survey scores of *personal* efficacy (p = .042). Table 10 shows the results of the Paired T test of the pre and post *personal* efficacy for the flipped class participants.

There was a statistically significant difference in scores for the students in the face to face on the *personal* efficacy subscale. Participants in the flipped courses had a statistically significant change in their pre to post scores in *personal* efficacy. The change in participants in the online courses did not show such a change. This change for the flipped classroom participants may be contributed to having experience in working with a struggling reader while a university supervisor was present to assist and help them gain the knowledge and skills necessary to feel confident in affecting change.

This increase in feelings of personal efficacy were reflected in both interview data for students in the flipped courses and written reflections for online students. Athena, a student in a flipped class, shared, "...this was a successful field placement that I had. From that little bit of success, I now have the confidence and motivation to move forward." Katrina, a student who took the course as a flipped class was even stronger in her statement: "My experience with my student was really rewarding. He couldn't read much when we first started. Then, by the end he was reading these mini books that I made for him. He was really excited about it. I've done it with one student. I feel confident that I'll be able to do it with others." Online university student, Maria, talked about how the course helped her to see how she can better meet the needs of her students, stating "I also learned as a general education teacher, who to adapt, modify, and incorporate accommodations for [in order to] best ensure their success in my classroom."

Summary of Results

There was a statistically significant change from pretest to posttest in the TKA: SL for participants taking the course online. It is a positive step that these participants had an increase in scores, but there is still more work to be done. It is surprising and enlightening that the flipped classroom participants did not have much of an increase in overall mean scores from pre TKA: SL to post TKA: SL. The posttest scores for all participants reflect similar data found in previous studies which indicate teachers do not have the knowledge base necessary to effectively help struggling readers (Moats, 1994). Even with the increase in scores, the online students were only achieving an average of 70% on the assessment. The data provides information that will help the course developers update the courses to provide more specific instruction in the structure of language.

Overall, there was no statistically significant change in efficacy scores for the TES: Short form; however, when looking at the subscales, teacher and personal efficacy, there was a statistically significant change from pre survey to post survey in the participants who took the "flipped" face to face course. This was reflected in the qualitative data from that group of university students as well. For example, at the completion of EDEX 246, Amanda wrote this summary of her field experience:

At first, I did not know what to expect from the 246 course. I did not have prior tutoring experience with children. I was apprehensive because I thought I would not be an effective teacher for Jim. During the initial tests, his results were low for the passage reading, as well as, the Dolch Pre-Primer Sight Words. In the beginning of the quarter, Jim knew 15 out of 40 Pre-Primer words. However, I learned he did not have a problem with acquiring the sounds of letters because he scored over 80% reading nonsense words. His challenges included developing reading accuracy and fluency. Throughout the term, I created lesson plans, in order, to increase these skills. At the conclusion of the quarter, Jim reached the long term goal of being able to read all 40 Pre-Primer Sight Words. He is now ready to learn the Dolch Primer Sight Words. My intervention proved successful, but I wish I had the opportunity to continue to work with Jim.

She shares how she began the course with little confidence in her abilities and ended it with a desire to continue to work with her student and help him to continue to make progress.

These participants were supervised by the university professor while implementing reading instruction one on one with a student. The opportunity to receive immediate feedback from the professor while working with a student may have provided the support needed to increase personal efficacy. This is supported by additional information gathered in the face to face focus group. Katrina gave a specific example of how the university professor was able to provide support in a situation that helped her tutoring:

Then Professor walked around and took anecdotal notes, and then she would share them with us. She even offered feedback about things as we were doing it. I remember my student had trouble with the /p/ sound, and she showed him how to make the sound with his mouth. That was really helpful to get that immediate feedback.

SOLUTIONS AND RECOMMENDATIONS

The results of this study showed that for this particular group of undergraduate students and graduate students, online instruction is a place for participants to increase knowledge of the structure of language; however, more direct instruction in the vocabulary surrounding phonics and phonemic awareness is needed for even deeper understanding of the course content. The online course was effective in increasing the knowledge of the participants, but not to the degree expected to eventually effect student achievement of struggling readers. It is recommended the online courses be updated to include lecture, readings and weekly quizzes specifically targeting knowledge of the structure of the English language. Interactive games could also be incorporated into the weeks to review the information presented.

The results of this study also showed the personal efficacy of participants in the face to face courses improved significantly. This may have been due to the university supervisor being present during the field experience. If that is the case, it would be extremely difficult to replicate that type of experience for the online students. Online participants can be in any country or any state and there may only be one participant in that area. However, with the capability to incorporate synchronous sessions in the virtual environment, the university professor could be with the participant and tutee during a learning session. This virtual observation could be considered for the online courses to provide immediate feedback to the participant. In addition, participants could be required to submit video of the one on one sessions with the tutee. This would also provide the opportunity for participants to receive feedback and encouragement on their ability to provide needed instruction in literacy. Feedback is important for participants to hear while they are still engaged in the topic and when they can do something or change something after the feedback (Brookhart, 2008). University students in the flipped class appreciated feedback from their professor even if it occurred after their tutoring session. Carol described meeting after class with her professor, saying,

You could go up and say, "This is what we did today. I have a question about this. I didn't quite understand what to do." Or, "What should I do next with my student because this wasn't working." She was really helpful, and always open to answer questions.

Adding synchronous tutoring sessions or recorded tutoring sessions could create a similar level of feedback regarding the field experience for the online participant as already provided to the "flipped" face to face student.

FUTURE RESEARCH DIRECTIONS

Access to effective eLearning technologies will continue to be a key to the education and empowerment of information-oriented 21st century individuals. Globalization now requires that institutions of higher learning embrace multiple pathways to knowledge that will support the needs of these individuals. As digital learning environments, such as online courses and flipped classes, continue to open doors for learners across contexts, it will be critically important that researchers carefully explore the effectiveness of these environments.

The data in this study find that there is little significant difference between students who learn online exclusively and those who learn in a flipped class where direct instruction is delivered online and face to face time with the university professor is used to support the application of the new content in the field. This chapter shows that content can be effectively delivered to teacher education students using eLearning strategies such as slides with recorded lectures, carefully selected training videos, and online discussions and shared lesson plans. This chapter also demonstrates that both online coursework and flipped classes can be used to help preservice and inservice teachers preparing to teach struggling readers. The data from this small study suggests that courses that pair online direct instruction with coordinated fieldwork can increase the feelings of self-efficacy. The differences in learning between the university students in these two kinds of learning environments revealed that each format has its strengths.

Further research about the strengths in each of these digital learning environments is necessary. The online students in this study experienced greater growth in content knowledge than those students taking the course as a flipped class. Prior research has shown an advantage in online learning (Means, Toyama, Murphy, Bakia, & Jones, 2009) and replication of the study would be needed to know if the findings in this study align with that trend. The students in the flipped class experienced greater gains in their feelings of personal efficacy when it came to teaching struggling readers. This finding is supported by experts in the field who have been calling for teacher educators to increase the effectiveness of the fieldwork by creating more meaningful and supported experiences that align with content instruction (Cochran-Smith and Zeichner, 2005; Levine, 2006). Would flipped classes in other areas of teacher education such as mathematics instruction or classroom management also see higher personal efficacy outcomes for preservice educators?

Another direction for future research would be to investigate these same digital learning environments and eLearning strategies with university students in other fields of study. In the United States students can major in the humanities, the sciences and the professions. Teaching is considered a profession. Would other professional majors such as medicine and law find similar results? How do students in the humanities or the sciences perform in online courses and flipped classes?

Technology and education will remain closely intertwined as globalization opens the doors to skills and information in places and in formats that were not possible before the advent of eLearning. Scholars need to carefully document and investigate the ways that learning takes place in digital spaces and the outcomes for students who learn in those spaces. Best practices can then be identified and shared leading to successful individuals who can innovate, collaborate, and lead in the 21st century.

CONCLUSION

This study of a literacy course in a school of education in the Northeast, United States, demonstrates the need for more specific instruction for teachers responsible for teaching all students to read. The surprising result of the data collected in this specific study was that participants in the online courses had statistically significant increases in their scores on the TKA: SL, a test of knowledge about language and literacy, from pretest to posttest. Online courses have been scrutinized for not offering the same type of instruction as face to face courses. In this study, online participants appeared to learn more knowledge about the language structure than their on campus counterparts. There may be multiple explanations for this occurrence. Perhaps the online participants studied all of the material available in the course; whereas the face to face students relied more heavily on the instruction in the presentation and did not spend the allotted time also accessing the related websites associated with each week's content. Another explanation could be the increased time the online participants spent tutoring a struggling reader as compared to the time the face to face students spend tutoring a struggling reader. The post test scores of both cohorts of participants was not to the expected level of the researchers. In order for teachers to be able to help a student who is having difficulty learning to read, the teacher needs to understand the structure of language and how to translate that knowledge into effective instruction.

Teacher self-efficacy is an important aspect in becoming an effective teacher. In this study, participants did have slight increases in *teacher* efficacy; however, the increase was not statistically significant. It was expected that participants in the face to face courses would experience an increase in teacher efficacy due to the fact that these participants had an expert in the field available to provide feedback. Though there was no statistical significance in the *teacher* efficacy subscale score of the TES, there was a statistical significance in the pre to posttest scores of the *personal* efficacy subscale of the TES for the "flipped" face to face students. During this course, the participants are able to work with a student and apply new knowledge and skills in order to teach the student the necessary reading skills. This appeared to have a positive effect on the students in the flipped classroom learning environment. It is not surprising that the participants in the online courses did not have the same results as the face to face participants on the TES as they were tutoring on their own and in many instances had to wait a week for feedback on a lesson.

Although this was a small study in one school of education and the results may not be generalizable, it does provide a starting point for future research. As online learning becomes accessible around the globe, more research in the ways that teacher education programs can best train preservice and inservice teachers in digital spaces to become highly effective teachers of literacy will be needed.

REFERENCES

Bandura, A. (1997). *Self-efficacy: The exercise of control.* New York: Freeman.

Baumann, J. F., Ro, J. M., Duffy-Hester, A. M., & Hoffman, J. M. (2000). Then and now: Perspectives on the status of elementary reading instruction by prominent reading educators. *Reading Research and Instruction, 39*(3), 236–264. doi:10.1080/19388070009558324

Brookhart, S. M. (2008). *How to Give Effective Feedback to your Students.* ASCD.

Chall, J. S. (1992). The new reading debates: Evidence from science, art, and ideology. *Teachers College Record, 94,* 315–328.

Cunningham, A. E., & O'Donnell, C. R. (2015). Teachers' knowledge about beginning reading development and instruction. In A. Pollatsek & R. Treiman (Eds.), *The Oxford Handbook of Reading* (pp. 447–462). Oxford: Oxford University Press.

Darling-Hammond, L. (1997). *Doing what matters most: Investing in teacher quality.* Kutztown, PA: National Commission on Teaching and America's Future.

Downing, J. J., & Dyment, J. E. (2013). Teacher Educators' Readiness, Preparation, and Perceptions of Preparing Preservice Teachers in a Fully Online Environment: An Exploratory Study. *Teacher Educator, 48*(2), 96–109. doi:10.1080/08878730.2012.760023

Duffin, L., French, B., & Patrick, H. (2012). The teachers' sense of efficacy scale: Confirming the factor structure with beginning pre-service teachers. *Teaching and Teacher Education, 28*(6), 827–834. doi:10.1016/j.tate.2012.03.004

Fielding-Barnsley, R. (2010). Australian pre-service teachers' knowledge of phonemic awareness and phonics in the process of learning to read. *Australian Journal of Learning Disabilities, 15*(1), 99–110.

Fogle, C. D., & Elliott, D. (2013). The Market Value of Online Degrees as a Credible Credential. *Global Education Journal, 2013*(3), 67-95.

Grau-Valldosera, J., & Minguillón, J. (2014). Rethinking dropout in online higher education: The case of the Universitat Oberta de Catalunya. *The International Review of Research in Open and Distributed Learning, 15*(1).

Guo, Y., Piasta, S. B., Justice, L. M., & Kaderavek, J. N. (2010). Relations among preschool teachers' self-efficacy, classroom quality and children's language and literacy gains. *Teaching and Teacher Education, 26*(4), 1094–1103. doi:10.1016/j.tate.2009.11.005

Guo, Y., Connor, C. M., Yang, Y., Roehrig, A. D., & Morrison, F. J. (2012). The effects of teacher qualification, teacher self-efficacy, and classroom practices on fifth graders' literacy outcomes. *The Elementary School Journal, 113*(1), 3–24. doi:10.1086/665816

Haverback, H. R., & Parault, S. J. (2008). Pre-service reading teacher efficacy and tutoring: A review. *Educational Psychology Review, 20*(3), 237–255. doi:10.1007/s10648-008-9077-4

Hoy, W. K., & Woolfolk, A. E. (1990). Socialization of student teachers. *American Educational Research Journal, 27*(2), 279–300. doi:10.3102/00028312027002279

Hoy, W. K., & Woolfolk, A. E. (1993). Teachers' sense of efficacy and the organizational health of schools. *The Elementary School Journal, 93*(4), 356–372. doi:10.1086/461729

Jaggars, S. S., & Xu, D. (2010). Online learning in the Virginia community college system (CCRC Working Paper). New York, NY: Columbia University, Teachers College, Community College Research Center. Retrieved from http://ccrc.tc.columbia.edu/publications/online-learning-virginia.html

Joshi, R. M., Binks, E., Hougen, M., Dahlgren, M. E., Ocker-Dean, E., & Smith, D. L. (2009). Why Elementary Teachers Might Be Inadequately Prepared to Teach Reading. *Journal of Learning Disabilities, 42*(5), 392–402. doi:10.1177/0022219409338736 PMID:19542350

Justice, L. M., Mashburn, A. J., Hamre, B. K., & Pianta, R. C. (2008). Quality of language literacy instruction in preschool classrooms serving at-risk pupils. *Early Childhood Research Quarterly, 23*(1), 51–68. doi:10.1016/j.ecresq.2007.09.004 PMID:22773887

Haverback, H., & Parault, S. (2008). Pre-Service Reading Teacher Efficacy and Tutoring: A Review. *Educational Psychology Review, 20*(3), 237–255. doi:10.1007/s10648-008-9077-4

Levine, A. (2006). Educating school teachers. Washington, DC: The Education Schools Project. Retrieved from http://www.edschools.org/pdf/Educating_Teachers_Report.pdf

Mather, N., Bos, C., & Babur, N. (2001). Perceptions and knowledge of preservice and inservice teachers about early literacy instruction. *Journal of Learning Disabilities, 34*(5), 472–482. doi:10.1177/002221940103400508 PMID:15503595

Means, B., Toyama, Y., Murphy, R., Bakia, M., & Jones, K. (2009). *Evaluation of evidence-based practices in online learning: A meta-analysis and review of online-learning studies.* Washington, DC: U.S. Department of Education.

Moats, L. (1994). The missing foundation in teacher education: Knowledge of the structure of spoken and written language. *Annals of Dyslexia, 44*, 81–102.

Narkon, D. E., & Black, R. S. (2008). Pre-Service teachers' confidence in teaching reading acquisition skills to struggling readers and readers in general. *Electronic Journal for Inclusive Education, 2*(3).

National Reading Panel. (2000). *Teaching children to read: An evidence-based assessment of the scientific research literature on reading and its implications for reading instruction (NIH Publication No. 00-4769).* Bethesda, MD: National Institute of Child Health & Human Development.

National Research Council (NRC). (1998). *Preventing reading difficulties in young children.* Washington, DC: National Academy Press.

Shaywitz, S., & Shaywitz, B. (2004). Reading disability and the brain. *Educational Leadership, 61*(6), 6–11.

Stanovich, K. E., & Stanovich, P. J. (1995). How research might inform the debate about early reading acquisition. *Journal of Research in Reading, 18*(2), 87–105. doi:10.1111/j.1467-9817.1995.tb00075.x

The Future of State Universities. (2011, September). *Research on the effectiveness of online learning: A compilation of research on online learning.* Paper presented at The Future of State Universities Conference, Dallas, TX. Retrieved from http://www.academicpartnerships.com/sites/default/files/Research%20 on%20the%20Effectiveness%20of%20Online%20Learning.pdf

Tinsley, H. E. A., & Tinsley, D. J. (1987). Uses of factor analysis in counseling psychology research. *Journal of Counseling Psychology, 34*(4), 414–424. doi:10.1037/0022-0167.34.4.414

What does Cronbach's alpha mean? (2015). UCLA: Statistical Consulting Group. Retrieved July 29, 2015, from http:// http://www.ats.ucla.edu/stat/spss/faq/alpha.html

What is flipped learning. (2014). Retrieved from http://www.flippedlearning.org/definition

KEY TERMS AND DEFINITIONS

Asynchronous: Online class time in which students watch weekly presentations and complete assignments at times that meet their schedule. Students are not necessarily online at the same time.

Face to Face Class: A class in which students meet with the professor in a brick and mortar classroom during scheduled class time.

Flipped Class: For the purpose of this study, a class in which the instruction is delivered online and the field work is face to face with the university professor.

Hybrid Class: A class in which students meet face to face on occasion and also take part of the course online.

In-Service Teacher: A person who has already obtained a teaching certificate and teaching in a classroom.

Online Class: For the purpose of this study, a college level class delivered completely online in an asynchronous manner.

Preservice Teacher: A person who is an undergraduate student and taking courses to become a certified teacher.

Self- Efficacy: The belief that the individual has the ability to influence a situation and bring about a desired result.

Struggling Reader: For the purposes of this study, a struggling reader was a student aged five to 18 who was not keeping up with peers in learning to read (elementary grades) or at least two age levels behind peers (secondary level).

Synchronous: Online class time in which all students attend the session at the same time.

ENDNOTE

[1]   All names of university students are pseudonyms.

APPENDIX 1

Teacher Knowledge Assessment: Structure of Language (TKA:SL)*

1. Which word contains a short vowel sound?
    a. treat   b. start c. slip   d. paw   e. father
2. A *phoneme* refers to:
    a. a single letter   b. a single speech sound   c. a single unit of meaning   d. grapheme
3. A pronounceable group of letters containing a vowel sound is a
    a. phoneme   b. grapheme   c. syllable morpheme
4. If *tife* were a word, the letter *i* would probably sound like the *i* in:
    a. if b. beautiful c. find   d. ceiling   e. sing
5. A combination of two or three consonants pronounced so that each letter keeps its own identity is called a
    a. silent consonant b. consonant digraph   c. diphthong   d. consonant blend
6. A schwa sound is found in the word
    a. cotton b. phoneme   c. stopping   d. preview e. grouping
7. A diphthong is found in the word
    a. coat   b. boy   c. battle   d. sing e. been
8. A voiced consonant digraph is in the word
    a. think   b. ship   c. whip   d. the   e. photo
9. Two combined letters that represent one single speech sound are
    a. schwa   b. consonant blend   c. phonetic   d. digraph   e. diphthong
10. How many speech sounds are in the word eight?
    a. two   b. three   c. four   d. five
11. How many speech sounds are in the word box?
    a. one   b. two   c. three   d. four
12. How many speech sounds are in the word grass?
    a. two   b. three.   c. four   d. five
13. Why may students confuse the sounds/b/ and /p/ or /f/ and /v/?
    a.   students are visually scanning the letters in a way that letters are misperceived.
    b.   the students can't remember the letter sounds so they are randomly guessing.
    c.   the speech sounds within each pair are produced in the same place and in the same way, but one is voiced and the other is not.
    d.   the speech sounds within each pair are both voiced and produced in the back of the mouth.
14. What type of task would this be? "I am going to say a word and then I want you to break the word apart. Tell me each of the sounds in the word *dog*."
    a. blending   b. rhyming   c. segmentation   d. manipulation
15. What type of task would this be? "I am going to say some sounds that will make one word when you put them together. What does /sh/ /oe/ say?
    a. blending   b. rhyming   c. segmentation   d. manipulation

16. Mark the statement that is false
    a. Phonological awareness is a precursor to phonics
    b. phonological awareness is an oral language activity
    c. Phonological awareness is a method of reading instruction that begins with individual letters and sounds
    d. Many children acquire phonological awareness from language activities and reading
17. A reading method that focuses on teaching the application of speech sound to letters is called
    a. phonics   b. phonemics   c. orthography   d. phonetics   e. either (a) or (d)
18. What is the rule for using *ck* in spelling?
    a. when the vowel sound is a diphthong
    b. when the vowel sound is short
    c. when the vowel sound is long
    d. any of the above
19. Count the number of syllables for the word unbelievable
    a. 4   b. 5   c. 6   d. 7
20. Count the number of syllables in the word pies
    a. 1   b. 2   c. 3   d. 4

* In Mather, N., Bos, C., & Babur, N. (2001). Perceptions and knowledge of preservice and inservice teachers about early literacy instruction. *Journal of Learning Disabilities*, 34(5), 472-482.

APPENDIX 2

Teacher Efficacy Scale (Short Form)*

A number of statements about organizations, people, and teaching are presented in Table 11. The purpose is to gather information regarding the actual attitudes of educators concerning these statements. There are no correct or incorrect answers. We are interested only in your frank opinions. Your responses will remain confidential.

INSTRUCTIONS: Please indicate your personal opinion about each statement by circling the appropriate response at the right of each statement.

KEY: 1=Strongly Agree 2=Moderately Agree 3=Agree slightly more than disagree 4=Disagree slightly more than agree 5=Moderately Disagree 6=Strongly Disagree

Table 11. Teacher Efficacy Scale (Short Form)*

1.	The amount a student can learn is primarily related to family background.	1	2	3	4	5	6
2.	If students aren't disciplined at home, they aren't likely to accept any discipline.	1	2	3	4	5	6
3.	When I really try, I can get through to most difficult students.	1	2	3	4	5	6
4.	A teacher is very limited in what he/she can achieve because a student's home environment is a large influence on his/her achievement.	1	2	3	4	5	6
5.	If parents would do more for their children, I could do more.	1	2	3	4	5	6
6.	If a student did not remember information I gave in a previous lesson, I would know how to increase his/her retention in the next lesson.	1	2	3	4	5	6
7.	If a student in my class becomes disruptive and noisy, I feel assured that I know some techniques to redirect him/her quickly.	1	2	3	4	5	6
8.	If one of my students couldn't do a class assignment, I would be able to accurately assess whether the assignment was at the correct level of difficulty.	1	2	3	4	5	6
9.	If I really try hard, I can get through to even the most difficult or unmotivated students.	1	2	3	4	5	6
10.	When it comes right down to it, a teacher really can't do much because most of a student's motivation and performance depends on his or her home environment.	1	2	3	4	5	6

*In Hoy, W.K. & Woolfolk, A.E. (1993). Teachers' sense of efficacy and the organizational health of schools. *The Elementary School Journal 93*, 356-372.

Section 3
Individualism

Chapter 12
Special Education Leadership and the Implementation of Response to Intervention

Derek Cooley
Godwin Heights Public Schools, USA

Elizabeth Whitten
Western Michigan University, USA

ABSTRACT

Special education administrators provide leadership to guide the identification of learners with exceptionalities and ensure that staff working with special education students delivers instructional best practice. In order to execute these responsibilities, special education administrators must be effective leaders who collaborate with a variety of stakeholder including. Contrary to their general education counterparts, special education administrators must possess a specific body of procedural knowledge to identify low-performing groups of students. These procedures are often referred to Response to Intervention (RTI) or Multi-Tier Systems of Support (MTSS). Under IDEA (2004), students with and without disabilities can benefit from the same system of interventions and supports. This intersection has necessitated coordination of RTI models by both general and special education administrators. Special education and general education leaders will be challenged to blend models of leadership to address the high-stakes environment in our K-12 schools.

INTRODUCTION

Many decades ago, Berry (1941) stated that the differences in philosophy and administration between general and special education were only in that the emphasis was placed on students with disabilities. Today, there are more than 20,000 special education administrators practicing in the U.S. who continue to emphasize the importance of programs and services for students with disabilities. Although the difference some 70 years ago was merely between those students with and those student without disabilities,

DOI: 10.4018/978-1-5225-0522-8.ch012

special education administrators are now charged with providing equal educational opportunities for *all* students (Boscardin, 2007; Crockett, 2011; Crockett, Becker, & Quinn, 2009).

The practice of special education leadership is primarily responsible for the leadership and administration of programs and services for students with disabilities. Special education administrators provide leadership to guide the identification of learners with exceptionalities and ensure that staff working with special education students delivers instructional best practice. In order to execute these responsibilities, special education administrators must be effective problem-solvers who collaborate with a variety of stakeholders including parents, teachers, administrators, and the community.

Central to the practice of special education leadership is the "finely tuned recognition of and response to individual learning needs" (Crockett, 2011, p. 351). Effective special education administrators juxtapose the needs of all students with the needs of each individual learner. These administrators must navigate policy, ensure the delivery of instructional best practice, and understand the context in which they administer programs and services. Special education administrators ensure that students with disabilities benefit from educational programs in both the general and special education settings. As a result, special education administrators are being held responsible for educational access and accountability not only for students with disabilities but also for students without disabilities.

Crockett (2011) states that although once driven primarily by district-wide compliance, the administration of special education is now focused on delivering effective and responsive instructional models at all district levels. Crockett (2011) continues that the practice of special education administration includes:

(a) setting expectations for recognizing the individual capabilities of students with disabilities, (b) developing personnel who work collaboratively and effectively in responding to students' unique educational needs and (c) making the organization of schools work more flexibly on their behalf. (p. 359)

Of these three tasks, the process of identifying students with disabilities and the provision of coordinating special and general education programs is likely to be the most difficult challenge for special education administrators in public schools today (Boscardin, 2007; Crockett, 2011; Crockett et al., 2009; McHatton, Gordon, Glenn, & Sue, 2012; Passman, 2008).

Contrary to their general education counterparts, special education administrators must possess a *specific* body of procedural knowledge to identify low-performing groups of students (Crockett et al., 2009; Passman, 2008). Much of this specific knowledge is needed to provide early intervention services for at-risk students and to develop procedures for identifying students who are at-risk of being identified with a disability (Werts, Lambert, & Carpenter, 2009). These procedures are often referred to as Response to Intervention (RTI) or Multi-tier Systems of Support (MTSS).

BACKGROUND

Response to Intervention is a multi-tiered model of instruction designed to foster academic achievement for *all* students. It is based upon the use of evidence-based interventions and research-based curriculum, which are intended to address unique learning needs. If implemented successfully, RTI can serve as a model to prevent severe academic problems and provide a means to identify students with disabilities (Whitten, Esteves, & Woodrow, 2009).

Response to Intervention is often organized into a three-tiered model. Tier I is high-quality instruction in which approximately 85% of all students participate. Tier I instruction is often referred to as the general education curriculum. Tier II includes supplemental instruction for small groups of students, representing approximately 10% of the student population. Tier III includes specially designed instruction and interventions for approximately 5% of the student population. If students fail to make progress in one tier, they move on to the next tier of more intensive interventions. If students fail to respond to instruction in all three tiers, a referral for special education can be made. As a result, RTI is both a diagnostic tool and instructional model in which the needs of struggling learners can be met.

Among all administrators in education, special education administrators have primarily taken the lead to make certain that RTI is successfully implemented in schools at both the building and district levels. Given that there is no "right way" to implement RTI (Esteves & Whitten, 2014), special education administrators are faced with the complexity of designing the procedures, policies, and protocols to effectively implement RTI (Werts et al., 2009)

RTI AND LEADERSHIP

A number of recent federal, state, and local policies have included programs for decreasing or eliminating the number of students who qualify for special education services. The No Child Left Behind Act (NCLB), which was passed in 2001, mandates that schools provide high-quality instruction using evidence-based practices for all students. The reauthorization of Individuals and Disabilities Education Act (IDEA) in 2004 allowed for the creation of Multi-tier Systems of Support (MTSS) to address the needs of struggling learners and to identify students with disabilities. Coupled together, these two laws have created systematic reforms by merging general and special education to meet the needs of both general and special education students in one unified system (Sansosti & Noltemeyer, 2008).

Given that special education administrators have historically been responsible for the provision of programs and services for students with disabilities, they are uniquely positioned to take responsibility for implementing RTI for groups of students who similarly lack adequate academic achievement. Students who are non-disabled and underachieving are also likely to benefit from the mandates of IDEA (2004), which calls for the use of research-based interventions delivered in an RTI model. Under IDEA (2004), students with and without disabilities can benefit from the same system of interventions and supports. This intersection has necessitated coordination of RTI models by both general and special education administrators. Boscardin, McCarthy, and Delgado (2009) state that "as inclusive practices and accountability continue to shape American education, special education and general education leaders will be challenged to join together in solving the problems of practice inherent in a diverse, complex, high-stakes environment" (p. 68).

Special education administrators must determine which factors for implementing RTI are most effective. Although there is an abundance of literature that defines RTI and how its practiced in schools, there is less research on how to successfully implement it (Harlacher & Siler, 2011; O'Connor & Freeman, 2012; Sansosti, Goss, & Noltemeyer, 2011; Sansosti & Noltemeyer, 2008; Werts et al., 2009). Thus, special education administrators are more likely to be challenged with determining the "how" of RTI as opposed to the "what." Special education administrators encounter a number of challenges related to the implementation of RTI that includes the fidelity in which research-based instruction and evidence-based intervention is delivered, effective professional development supporting RTI practices, staff collaboration and buy-in, and the availability of resources and/or materials.

The ability for special education administrators to effectively implement RTI is dependent upon the leadership skills they possess. Thus, special education administrators are further confronted with selecting administrative interventions that lead to the successful implementation of RTI. Such interventions for managing school reform often rely upon theoretical models for change (Sansosti & Noltemeyer, 2008).

One such model of change is Fullan's (2001) Framework for Leadership. Frequently cited in the educational reform literature, Fullan (2001) describes his work as a set of dimensions that can improve leadership in education. Within his framework, Fullan (2001) stresses that effective leaders must understand the process of change, rely on relationships with and among staff, collaborate with stakeholders to create and share knowledge, and depend on a sense of moral purpose. Although there are a number of theoretical models for educational reform, Fullan's (2001) model is well suited to support special education administrators in that it directly applies to the implementation of RTI (Datnow, 2006; Sansosti & Noltemeyer, 2008).

Special Education Leadership

The practice of special education administration has been described as the "intersection" of special education, general education, and educational leadership (Lashley & Boscardin, 2003). Collaborating with many school personnel to achieve the shared intentions and goals of schools, special education administrators work on behalf of students with disabilities to provide equal access and high quality programming to ensure sufficient outcomes (Crockett, Billingsley, & Boscardin, 2012).

The skills special education administrators must possess in order to be successful are complex and multi-faceted. Special education administrators must possess a specific body of procedural knowledge, an in-depth knowledge of learner characteristics, disability criteria, and accommodations, modifications, and intervention plans. Special education administrators must also have the skills to successfully facilitate the problem-solving process, including mediation and negotiation skills. Working with a variety of school staff, parents, and the community, special education administrators must possess dispositions including compassion, flexibility, sensitivity to differences, and an ability to build relationships with others (Passman, 2008).

In a review of special education administration literature, Crockett, Becker, and Quinn (2009) found that a significant body of the literature is primarily focused on leadership roles and responsibilities. They define these roles and responsibilities as the "dimensions of the work of special education administrators and the programmatic issues they address in their positions" (p. 58). Central to this theme is a focus on providing support for improving instruction for both general and special education students. In order to provide this support, special education administrators must promote a collaborative partnership with teachers and administrators within general education. Effective special education administrators recognize that such partnerships are critical in meeting the needs of all students through high quality programming and equal educational access (Lashley & Boscardin, 2003).

Similar to other educational administrators, the roles and responsibilities of special education administrators are changing. The onset of higher standards and increased accountability necessitates the need for special education administrators to provide reliable and valid assessment data for students with disabilities (Baaken et al., 2007; Lashley & Boscardin, 2003; Voltz & Collins, 2010). Broadening this responsibility to all students, "special education and general education leaders will be challenged to join together to solve the problems inherent in a diverse, complex, high-stakes education environment" (Lashley & Boscardin, 2003, p. 73).

Boscardin (2007) provides a framework for the practice of special education administration based upon the premise that evidence-based leadership practices are needed to improve educational opportunities for students with disabilities. Within this framework, special education administrators employ leadership approaches and responsive leadership interventions that mimic the concepts applied to RTI. These concepts include:

1. The concept of multiple stages of administrative interventions to improve teaching in ways that lead to improved student achievement.
2. The implementation of differentiated administrative approaches.
3. Leadership provided by staff other than designated personnel.
4. Varied duration, frequency, and time of administrative interventions.
5. Traditional and non-traditional administrative decisions.
6. Situational conditions for decisions.
7. Urgency for administrative decisions.
8. The use of standard protocols for determining the use of specific administrative approaches or interventions. (p. 191)

This framework is not based upon a set of prescriptive actions, per se, but a set of conceptual processes that are guided by progress monitoring and problem solving at the building and district level. Within Boscardin's framework for leadership, *student*-progress monitoring is replaced with *system*-progress monitoring by using leadership interventions to respond rapidly to system needs.

Standards for Preparation and Practice

Several studies highlight the importance of articulated standards for the practice and preparation of special education administrations. Although there are a number of standards for educational administration in general, the standards authored by the Council for Exceptional Children are most frequently cited among special education administration and leadership.

Boscardin, McCarthy, and Delgado (2009) used an integrative approach to engage special education administrators to validate major knowledge and skill statements in special education leadership. Triangulating data from a literature review, Q-sort analysis, and surveys, the authors were able to prioritize and rate domains that are associated with special education leadership. Their work resulted in the 2009 edition of the Council for Exceptional Children's (CEC) Advanced Knowledge and Skills for Administrators of Special Education (2009). The standards are:

1. Leadership and Policy
2. Program Development and Organization
3. Research and Inquiry
4. Evaluation
5. Professional Development and Ethical Practice
6. Collaboration

These standards are intended to guide universities in developing standards for preservice programs as well as professional development opportunities for practitioners in the field.

In a similar study, Wigle and Wilcox (2002) investigated the competencies of special education directors by developing a survey based upon an earlier set of CEC standards. The results of this survey suggest that special education directors perceived themselves as having high levels of competence in the following areas: program development, collaboration, communication and advocacy, technology, and behavior management. The CEC standards provide a strong foundation to guide preparation and practice within this field.

Based upon historical themes in special education such as free appropriate public education (FAPE) and least restrictive environment (LRE), Crockett (2002) developed a framework for special education leadership. Crockett's (2002) five core principles are intended to guide institutions of higher education in the development and preparation of special education administrators. The core principles are:

1. Ethical practice: Ensuring universal educational access and accountability.
2. Individual consideration: Addressing individuality and exceptionality in learning.
3. Equity under law: Providing an appropriate education through equitable public policies.
4. Effective programming: Providing individualized programming designed to enhance student performance.
5. Establishing productive partnerships. (p. 163)

In sum, the literature on special education administration is quite limited. It is primarily based upon explanations, observations, and experiences of both practitioners and researchers in the field. Further explained, "the special education administrative knowledge base is informed primarily by theoretical or interpretive professional commentary rather than by data-based research studies that could guide effective leadership practice" (Crockett et al., 2009, p. 65). Some recommend a stronger empirical foundation to support this body of literature.

Response to Intervention

Since the first passage of the Individuals with Disabilities Education Act (IDEA) more than 30 years ago, the number of students identified as having a Learning Disability (LD) has increased more than 200% (Bradley, Danielson, & Doolittle, 2005). This dramatic increase has caused concern for the method in which students are identified as having learning disabilities (D. Fuchs, Fuchs, & Compton, 2004; Kavale, Kauffman, Bachmeier, & LeFever, 2008).

Traditional methods for identifying students as having LD rely upon "wait-to-fail" models in which the discrepancy between academic achievement and intelligence determines eligibility (D. Fuchs et al., 2004; Kavale et al., 2008). This discrepancy model has been criticized for an over-reliance on a single testing point and a wide variability in LD assessment procedures (Fletcher, Denton, & Francis, 2005; Mellard, Deshler, & Barth, 2004).

Resulting from mandates passed in IDEA (2004), one of the most commonly used methods for identifying students with LD is Response to Intervention (RTI). As a tiered model, RTI is designed to move poorly performing students through a series of increasingly intensive academic interventions. If students fail to respond to all tiers of intervention, schools must consider a referral for eligibility for special education services (Hollenbeck, 2007).

Background

The process for identifying students with LD dates to the original passage of the Education for All Handicapped Children Act of 1975. This law was renewed in 1991 as the Individuals with Disabilities Education Act (IDEA). Under IDEA (1991), the process for identifying students with LD was largely unchanged. This process relied heavily upon the use of a discrepancy formula, which is calculated on the difference between a student's actual performance and expected academic achievement (Mellard et al., 2004). Before the reauthorization of IDEA in 2004, school districts were allowed to individually define the formulas they used within their districts. As a result, inconsistencies in formula definitions allowed for a variation in LD identification procedures and prevalence rates not only from state to state but from school district to school district (Kratochwill, Clements, & Kalymon, 2007). Because of these inconsistencies and lack of student progress, the reauthorization of IDEA in 2004 included major reform efforts that provided states and districts the option to replace the "wait-to-fail method" with a response to intervention model of support. Such models identify students who are not working at grade level, whereby the use of evidence-based instruction is immediately implemented (D. Fuchs, Fuchs, & Compton, 2012).

In 2002, the President's Commission on Excellence in Special Education concluded that the entitlement of special education services was based upon waiting for a student to experience academic failure. Subsequently, it was recommended that special education services should be provided only after a student had the opportunity to participate in instructional programs that were designed to prevent failure (Gresham, 2007). Along with the President's Commission, the National Summit on Learning Disabilities (2002) concluded that little evidence supported a continued reliance on the IQ-discrepancy model as a means for LD identification. Both groups determined that a preventative model such as RTI could provide an alternative for LD identification (Kavale et al., 2008). Based upon the recommendations from these national groups and others, congress included provisions for RTI as a method for the identification of students with LD in the reauthorization of IDEA (2004). Specifically, IDEA outlines that states, "may permit the use of a process based on the child's response to scientific, research-based intervention" (IDEA, § 300.307(a)(2)). These words gave way to the term "Response to Intervention".

Definitions and Components of RTI

The literature outlines a number of components that define RTI. Among these definitions, the most common component is the use of outcome data for decision-making regarding the effectiveness of an academic intervention (L. S. Fuchs & Vaughn, 2012; Gresham, 2007; Knotek, 2007; Kratochwill et al., 2007). Such decisions can be made about the academic achievement of individual students and groups of students within schools and districts. These decisions can also include eligibility determination of special education for students who fail to respond to interventions. The National Association of State Directors of Special Education (NASDSE) defines RTI as "the practice of (1) providing high-quality instruction/intervention matched to student needs and (2) using learning rate over time and level of performance to (3) make important education decisions" (Batsche et al., 2005, p. 5). Outlining similar components to the NASDSE definition, the Council for Exceptional Children (CEC; 2008) states that RTI shall include universal screening, high quality research based instruction, and progress monitoring. CEC organizes these core components within a tiered system of instructional delivery.

Using a practical application of RTI components, Fletcher and Vaughn (2009) recommend that school personnel implement universal screening and assessment of academic progress at regular intervals, progress monitoring using curriculum-based measurement and, the provision of increasingly intense interventions for students who do not respond to instruction. Those students who do not adequately respond to instruction may be referred for evaluations for special education, which most often includes eligibility determinations of LD.

A Multi-Tiered System

RTI is most frequently structured around a three-tier system of interventions. Tier I is the core academic curriculum. Effective for 80% to 85% of all students, these core instructional interventions are preventative and proactive. Tier II consists of targeted group interventions for approximately 10% to 15% of students who are at-risk for academic failure. Comprising the most intensive interventions, tier III is tailored for 5% to 10% of students on an individual basis or small group basis. Longer in duration than tier I and II, tier III interventions utilize assessment measures most frequently to monitor student achievement (Batsche et al., 2005; Whitten et al., 2009).

When using RTI as a framework to establish LD identification, poor instruction is ruled out and student failure is more likely to be attributed to the result of a disability. Inadequate growth "suggests that disability is responsible and that specialized instruction is necessary to boost academic achievement" (D. Fuchs et al., 2004, p. 217). Although originally intended as a framework for early reading intervention, RTI is widely used to ensure that high-quality instruction and interventions are matched to students needs (Mellard, Stern, & Woods, 2011).

RTI has been found to increase student achievement and decrease the number of students identified as having a disability (Burns, Appleton, & Stehouwer, 2005; Hughes & Dexter, 2011). In a review of 13 published field studies, Hughes and Dexter (2011) report that schools implementing RTI report academic improvement. In a separate review of 21 studies, Burns, Appleton, and Stehouwer (2005) conclude that within existing RTI models, less than 2% of the student population was identified as LD, whereas national LD prevalence rates are higher than 5%

Response to Intervention Models

RTI is often constructed into two different, yet related, models – the problem-solving model and the standard treatment protocol (D. Fuchs et al., 2004; Hollenbeck, 2007; Marston, 2005; Mellard et al., 2011). Implementing an RTI framework requires choosing one of these models or establishing a hybrid between the two. Problem-solving models are associated with a shared decision-making team that identifies a problem. These teams are responsible for choosing interventions to address the problem, evaluating the outcome of the intervention, and monitoring progress to ensure the effectiveness of the intervention that was chosen (Fletcher & Vaughn, 2009).

Problems are defined as the difference between the actual and desired level of academic performance (Gresham, 2007). As the difference between the actual and desired levels of performance gets larger, so does the problem.

The second type of model uses a standardized protocol to deliver instruction. Implemented with validated interventions, standard protocols are delivered in a fixed- duration trial (e.g. 10-15 weeks) to allow for more control. Typically scripted, these interventions guarantee the integrity of delivery (Gresham, 2007). The standard protocol "approaches feature the use of tightly structured teaching using commercially available instructional packages" (Kovaleski, 2007, p. 83) These protocols have a high probability of producing outcomes for larger numbers of students (Batsche et al., 2005).

Some consider the use of both models, combined into one hybrid approach, preferable to the exclusive use of one model. Batsche et al. (2005) state, "in considering problem-solving teams and standard protocol interventions, it appears that a merger of the two approaches at tier 2 is most desirable" (p. 24). Within a hybrid model, problem solving teams utilizing standard protocols can increase treatment fidelity with specific interventions (e.g. reading fluency) to counteract less precise methods such as brainstorming (Batsche et al., 2005).

Universal Screening and Progress Monitoring.

Fuchs and Vaughn (2012) state, "RTI's greatest accomplishment to date may be the dramatic increase in schools' routine reliance on screening to identify students at risk for reading and increasing math difficulties" (p. 196). As the principle means for identifying struggling students, screening consists of brief assessments targeted at skills, such as reading and math, that are predictive of future academic achievement (Jenkins, Hudson, & Johnson, 2007). Universal screening tools, typically conducted three times per year, are administered to all students and intend to provide information to staff that allows for efficiently identifying academic problems (Fletcher & Vaughn, 2009; Hughes & Dexter, 2011; Whitten et al., 2009).

After universal screening is completed and student are receiving tier I instruction, progress monitoring is needed to frequently assess student performance to gauge the effectiveness of the interventions (Hughes & Dexter, 2011; Whitten et al., 2009). Stecker, Fuchs, and Fuchs (2008) define progress monitoring as "a system of brief assessments that are given frequently, at least monthly, to determine whether students are progressing through the curriculum in desired fashion and are likely to meet long-term goals" (p. 11).

Currently, the recommended time period for progress monitoring is 8-10 weeks (McMaster & Wagner, 2007). One of the most well-known and widely used techniques for progress monitoring is curriculum-based measurement (CBM). Similar to techniques used for universal screening, CBM can determine whether a student is learning and it can determine at what rate the learning is occurring. CBM is highly standardized, requires a small amount of time to be administered, and can be repeated multiple times during a school year (McMaster & Wagner, 2007; Whitten et al., 2009).

Implementation of RTI

Since the reauthorization of IDEA in 2004, School districts across the country have begun to implement RTI. Castillo and Batsche (2012) report that "district implementation of the response to intervention (RTI) model has occurred at a surprising rate" (p. 14). Findings from a survey by Spectrum K12 Solutions (2011) show that RTI implementation continues to rise nationally with 94% of districts reporting some level of RTI implementation (up from 72% in 2009). Eighty-eight percent of districts use RTI to identify students for early intervention and 66% of districts use RTI to identify students for special education services.

The National Association of State Directors of Special Education (NASDSE) published one of the most widely cited models for district-wide implementation of RTI (Elliott & Morrison, 2008). Designed to provide concrete guidance to school districts, these "Blueprints" define three steps for implementing RTI. Districts engage in district level consensus and infrastructure building, followed by specific implementation, evaluation, and professional development plans.

Although a number of states have implemented RTI in various ways, despite recommmendations from national organziations, no single model has been widely accepted.

Professional Development

Professional development has been cited as the most frequent factor leading to the successful implementation of RTI. School personnel should have many opportunities to practice new skills with ongoing feedback (Harlacher & Siler, 2011). School personnel participating in district-level professional development should understand the relationship between RTI and achievement, empirically validated instructional practices, use of the problem solving model, and evaluation strategies for student performance difference, which include continuous progress monitoring methods (Batsche et al., 2005; Harlacher & Siler, 2011).

Special Education Leadership and RTI Implementation

Administrative support has been cited as one of the most critical components for the successful implementation of RTI (O'Connor & Freeman, 2012; Sansosti et al., 2011; Werts et al., 2009; Wiener & Soodak, 2008). Specifically, Sansosti, Goss, and Noltemeyer (2011) state that the "role of the special education director as a leader and change agent is critical to successful implementation of RTI" (p. 16). When implementing RTI, special education administrators must assign staff roles and responsibilities, develop and implement district policies, and carefully consider the use of time and resources when overseeing programs (O'Connor & Freeman, 2012; Werts et al., 2009).

Having influence on decisions that impact student learning, special education administrators play key roles in data-based decision making processes that impact RTI. Special education administrators must be knowledgeable about concepts, principles, and communicate a rationale for a school-wide process for making data-based decisions. Working at the district level, special education administrators must establish and maintain structures for sustaining data-based decision making processes that align with school improvement goals and objectives.

Special education administrators consider a number of factors when implementing RTI. Wiener and Soodak (2008) found that special education administrators attributed RTI success to "access to professional development, resources and materials for training and implementation, and guidelines for implementation" (p. 43). Further, special education administrators are generally optimistic about the results of RTI in terms of impact on instruction and collaboration. Viewing the primary benefit of RTI as the improvement of instruction, rather than decreasing the number of student classified as LD, special education administrators concede that additional benefits will be realized through ongoing implementation and change (Wiener & Soodak, 2008). Creating a shared knowledge and understanding of RTI, special education administrators must provide clear and specific support to staff during RTI implementation (O'Connor & Freeman, 2012).

Implementing Educational Change

Duke (2004) defines educational change as "any intentional change designed to improve teaching and learning" (p. 30). As an ambiguous term, change may refer to the process in which change is initiated or the change as an artifact itself. Thus, not only is the study of educational change concerned with the process of change, but also the product of change (Duke, 2004).

The volume of educational change research is immense. A recent search of the literature revealed an astounding 461,000 journal articles referring to the topic. In order to conceptualize, organize, and make meaning of this amount of information, a number of researchers associate change within a particular perspective, or schema. From these perspectives, models and/or frameworks for educational change are created. The terms educational reform, educational change, and school reform are used interchangeably.

House and McQuillan (2005) conceptualize the literature on school reform into three perspectives: technological, political, and cultural. Researchers who subscribe to the technological perspective of school reform focus on specific goals and tasks, efficiency, outcomes, and systemic rational processes. This perspective is based on how to complete a specific set of steps to efficiently complete a job. Emphasis is largely placed upon the economics of the market as a means to frame the need for change. The political perspective of education reform relies heavily on negotiation. Concepts such as power, authority, group conflict and compromise, and competing interests make up this perspective. Lastly, theorists who rely on a cultural perspective focus on a school system as a community. Concepts include shared meaning, values, and the importance of relationships. Each of these perspectives points to a different set of factors that are responsible for change. Schools do not operate within one of these perspectives exclusively. The interaction among all three perspectives explains the complexity in which change occurs in schools. These models are typically prescriptive, in which a set of specific steps or actions are followed in order to implement, manage, and lead change.

Ellsworth (2000) makes three assumptions about the nature of educational change. First, educational change can be understood and managed. When approached as such, it is often referred to as *planned* change. Second, educational change can be understood and managed when practitioners apply a set of tools from a number of different models of change. Such models can be referred to as a "toolbox" that allows leaders to effectively match certain tools with certain innovations of change. Lastly, effective and lasting change must address the concerns and priorities of multiple stakeholder groups. The success of an initiative is a direct result of the willingness of staff, parents, and the community to change themselves as individuals (Edgehouse et al., 2007).

Educational change models are used by leaders to gain a better understanding of the process of change. These models describe *why* change occurs, *how* change occurs, and *what* will occur as a result of the change (Duke, 2004; Edgehouse et al., 2007). Certain models concentrate on a specific part of the process of change such as problem solving, innovation, the change agent, or the intended users of change. Ellsworth (2000) presents an overview of each of the major models of educational change. Instead of defining each model by the steps or components within them, questions that each model is most likely to answer are presented:

- What attributes can I build into the innovation or its implementation strategy to facilitate its acceptance by the intended adopter? – Roger's (1995) Diffusion of Innovations
- What are the conditions that should exist or be created in the environment where the innovation is being introduced to facilitate its adoption? – Ely's (1990) Conditions of Change
- What are the implications of change for people or organizations promoting or opposing it at particular levels? – Fullan and Stiegelbauer's (1991) Meaning of Educational Change
- What are the essential stages of the facilitation process and what activities should the change agent be engaged during the each stage? - Havelock's (1995) Change Agent's Guide

- What stages will stakeholders go through during implementation and what will be the major concerns at each stage? – Hall, Hord, and Newlove's (1973) Concerns-Based Adoption Model
- What are the cultural, social, organizational, and psychological *barriers* to change that can promote resistance to the innovation and what can I do to lower these barriers and encourage adoption? – Zaltman and Duncan's (1997) Strategies for Planned Change
- What are the factors *outside* the immediate environment in which the innovation is being introduced that can affect its adoption? Reigeluth and Garfinkle's (1994) Systemic Change in Education (p. 37)

Although each question is intended to guide a user to a specific model, many have suggested that school leaders draw on relevant components from all of the models to build one holistic strategy to approach change (Edgehouse et al., 2007; Ellsworth, 2000; Fullan, 2001). When special education administrators choose a selected model, for example, they must begin by determining which of the answers they are seeking. Each innovation or initiative comes with a different set of challenges, and as a result, may present with a new set of questions. Educational change cannot be achieved in a linear systematic process. Schools work on many different goals and initiatives at the same time, which require levels of concurrent management and coordination, which must all be integrated simultaneously (Hargreaves, 2005).

Even with an immense knowledge base for guidance in the field, efforts to lead change are often ineffective. Hargreaves (2005) mentions several factors that make leading change difficult. Some of these factors include:

- The reasons for the change is poorly conceptualized or not clearly demonstrated.
- The change is too broad and ambitious.
- The change is too fast or too slow for people to cope with.
- The change is poorly resourced.
- There is no long-term commitment to the change.
- Key staff are not committed to the change.
- Leaders are too controlling or ineffectual.
- The change is pursued in isolation and gets undermined by other unchanged structures (p. 2).

These factors highlight that educational change is not simply a technical process, nor is it based only upon an understanding of the culture and people of an organization. "People fear change not just because it presents them with something new, uncertain, or unclear – because it has no obvious or common meaning for them" (Hargreaves, 2005; p. 2). In sum, special education administrators must master the technical process of change, understand the culture in which they attempt to lead change, and ensure that stakeholders involved in change find meaning and purpose.

School Improvement and RTI

After the need for change has been identified and a design has been selected, the next phase involves developing an implementation plan. An implementation plan is a set of guidelines that ensures that the design itself is put into place. Such plans are often called school improvement plans or continuous school improvement. School improvement plans "are not the designs themselves, but the provisions for moving the designs from the drawing board to the school" (Duke, 2004, p. 123).

School improvement is based upon strategies that focus on curriculum and instruction, organization development, and the decentralization of decision making (Hopkins, 2005). Such efforts have led to a focus on the process of how to effect change, which is based upon school-selected priorities for improvement. This process often emphasizes the roles and perspectives of teachers and other stakeholders. School improvement also stresses the importance of a school culture, teacher collegiality, and staff relationships (Fink & Stoll, 2005). Such relationships are productive when the interactions between leaders and the people they work with produce desirable results for all stakeholders within a school (Cardno, 2012).

School improvement is an effective model when used to implement RTI because both processes focus on student outcomes. Further, both school improvement and RTI use planning and frequent review of system-level effectiveness to determine progress toward goals. Both models utilize system-wide decision making and progress monitoring to improve schools (Bernhardt & Hebert, 2011; O'Connor & Freeman, 2012).

Not only does school improvement focus on enhancing educational outcomes for students, it also strengthens the capacity for schools to understand and manage change (Bernhardt & Hebert, 2011). School improvement allows schools to take control of change. Thus, schools that use school improvement are "no longer the 'victims' of change, but can take more control of the process." (Hopkins, 2005, p. 3). Similarly, the implementation of RTI also allows for special education administrators to take control of change.

The literature often highlights that leading change is a complex and difficult task. Special education administrators must consider that change takes place in a world of chaos, and that the process of change is a complex chaotic process in and of itself. In addition to an understanding of the process of change, and the application of selected models that assist in leading it, special education administrators should consider societal change forces, the political factors that influence or mandate change, and the emotional aspects of teaching, learning and leading change (Hargreaves, 2005).

RTI and the Process of Change

Response to Intervention is often viewed as an educational reform initiative. Sansosti and Noltemeyer (2008) state that, "RTI cannot be characterized by one educational program or curriculum, but rather a transformation in the way that systems, schools, and professionals operate" (p. 56). Key to the success of reform initiatives such as RTI is a need for school leaders to understand the process of change and how to manage it. The literature fails to adequately identify factors that contribute to the successful implementation of RTI. As a result, it is important to review models and theories of educational change in order to improve future practice (Hargreaves, 2005; (Ellsworth, 2000; Sansosti & Noltemeyer, 2008).

Fullan's Model for Educational Change

Examining the process of change, Fullan (2001) provides a framework for leaders to define and implement change. Fullan suggests that "*leading* in a culture of change means *creating* a culture of change" (emphasis added, p. 44). Leaders who create a culture of change produce "the capacity to seek, critically assess, and selectively incorporate new ideas and practices" (Fullan, 2001, p. 44). Change is not addressed with step-by-step manuals or protocols. Rather, Fullan (2001) places emphasis on an understanding and an insight of change, rather than steps for taking action. His model, called A Framework for Leadership, is organized into five domains.

The first domain of Fullan's framework is *moral purpose*. Moral purpose is simply defined as the drive to make a difference in the lives of students. Leaders exhibiting moral purpose possess characteristics such as integrity, conviction, responsibility, moral excellence, and trust. Fullan states, "leaders in all organizations, whether they know it or not, contribute for better or for worse to moral purpose in their own organizations and in society as a whole" (p. 15). If leaders use moral purpose to lead change effectively, Fullan (2001) states they must:

(1) have an explicit 'making-a-difference' sense of purpose, (2) use strategies that mobilize many people to tackle tough problems, (3) be held accountable by measured and debatable indicators of success, and (4) be ultimately assessed by the extent to which it awakens people's intrinsic commitment, which is none other than the mobilizing of everyone's sense of moral purpose. (pg. 20)

Fullan's second domain of his framework for leadership is *understanding change*. Fullan summarizes the concept of understanding change into six parts:

1. The goal is not to innovate the most.
2. It is not enough to have the best ideas.
3. Appreciate the implementation dip.
4. Redefine resistance.
5. Reculturing is the name of the game.
6. Never a checklist, always complexity.

Leaders who implement initiatives do not always make progress. Without buy-in from staff, good ideas are nothing more than ideas. Effective leaders must not only possess good ideas, but be able to implement them as well. After implementing a new initiative, leaders find themselves and their staff lacking skills to sustain innovation because they don't have the new skills to accompany it. Fullan (2001) describes this as the implementation dip. Building in differences and offsetting equilibrium creates capacity for change. Leaders should foster organizations that have creativity to get through this implementation dip. As leaders understand the process of change, they realize that if everyone thinks exactly alike, no one will be able to make suggestions as how to move forward.

The third domain to Fullan's (2001) model is *relationships*. Fullan states that to implement change effectively, "it is actually the relationships that make the difference" (p. 51). Fullan (2001) articulates that although the development of people is important, it is not enough to successfully lead change. The creation of relationships is crucial, but only if the result is greater coherence among staff, programs, and schools. Relationships should lead to the creation of additional resources, which can be accessed by staff, parents, and the community. The role of leadership is to "cause" a greater capacity among the individuals in the organization. Professional relationships are bolstered with the use of professional development to improve teaching and learning. Fullan (2001) proposes professional development that focuses on system-wide change to improve instruction.

The fourth domain of Fullan's model is *knowledge creation and sharing*. The process of knowledge creation and sharing is built upon the development of relationships among staff. Ultimately, the purpose of relationships is to then create and share knowledge for the betterment of the organization. Fullan describes schools as being in the business of learning, yet he states that districts are inept at learning from one other. Using what Fullan calls intervisitation and peer advising, administrators and teachers can learn best practice from colleagues within their own schools and in neighboring schools.

Through inter-visitation, groups of teachers and administrators visit to observe instructional best practice in other schools. Districts participate in instructional consulting services in which both in-house consultants and out-of-house consultants work with staff to improve instruction. When staff shares information about best practices, they express a need for more knowledge, including the practical implications when implementing a new project or initiative. Administrators and teachers should also request time to reflect on newly implemented practices, policies, and protocols. During peer advising, administrators and teachers participate in a mentor-mentee program in which experienced administrators collaborate with new administrators.

The last domain of Fullan's framework for leadership is *coherence making*. Based upon the premise that complex systems such as schools are continually generating overload and fragmentation, the act of maintaining coherence is necessary to lead change. Fullan describes this coherence making by using the work Pascale, Millemann, and Gioja (2000, p. 6, emphasis in original):

1. *Equilibrium* is a precursor to *death*. When a living system is in a state of equilibrium, it is less responsive to changes occurring around it. This places it at maximum risk.
2. In the face of threat, or when galvanized by a compelling opportunity, living things move toward the *edge of chaos*. This condition evokes higher levels of mutation and experimentation, and fresh new solutions are more likely to be found.
3. When this excitation takes place, the components of living systems *self-organize* and new forms of *repertoires* emerge from the turmoil.
4. Living systems cannot be *directed* along a linear path. Unforeseen consequences are inevitable. The challenge is to *disturb* them in a manner that approximates the desired outcome.

In schools, "the main problem is not the absence of innovations but the presence of too many disconnected, episodic, piecemeal, superficially adorned projects (Fullan, 2001, p. 109). The result is that staff becomes frustrated, disenchanted, and complacent to change. Leaders must ensure organizational coherence to successfully implement new initiatives.

When applying each of Fullan's (2001) five domains to lead change, leaders should be patient and deliberate by absorbing challenges and redefining new patterns along the path of change. Learning in context, leaders are able to attain specific knowledge because the learning takes place with the group of an organization. Thus, commitment from staff cannot be activated from top-level leadership. Leadership at many levels within the organization is needed for sustainable success. Fullan (2001) concludes that "ultimately, leadership in a culture of change will be judged as effective or ineffective not by who you are as a leaders, but by *what leadership you produce in others*" (emphasis in original, p. 137).

SOLUTIONS AND RECOMMENDATIONS

In the non-stop pursuit to improve school systems and school personnel, understanding the process of change is important for special education administrators to successfully implement RTI. Fullan (2007) describes this structure as a hierarchy of successive levels. That is, students cannot be successful without successful teachers; teachers cannot be successful without successful leaders; and leaders must sustain the betterment of all stakeholders through sustaining meaningful educational change. When organizations change, leaders are required to link of all the parts of the system together (Fullan, 2006). Given the lack of research on what makes the implementation of RTI successful, theoretical models of change can serve to guide future educational practice. Specifically, Fullan's (2001) model for change has been pivotal in guiding practitioners and researchers through the process of educational change (Datnow, 2006; Sansosti & Noltemeyer, 2008; Stoll, 2006). Within the study of RTI, Sansosti and Noltemeyer (2008) purport that "Fullan's model appears to have direct applicability to the current practice of RTI" (p. 57).

FUTURE RESEARCH DIRECTIONS

A number of topics can be further explored using this chapter as a basis. Research including a large population could provide insight and comparisons among states and possibly larger geographic regions as well as a means to determine differences among subgroups of the sample population. Analysis could also include a review of policies and laws that are specific to each state within the region.

Understanding the perceptions of staff working under the authority of special education administrators during the implementation of RTI could be explored. Future research could address the interactions among special education administrators and their staff to determine the effectiveness of NASDE's steps to implement RTI in greater detail.

Furthermore, a study that includes an analysis of actual practices during implementation, qualitative methods such as direct observation, interviews, and focus groups could allow for a comparison between self-reported perceptions and actual practice in the field. These methods could also provide analysis to determine where challenges arise during each step of implementation.

CONCLUSION

This chapter provides information for special education administrators and others who are responsible for leading the implementation of RTI in schools and districts. Special education administrators will need a set of skills to successfully implement RTI, to understand the process of change, and to identify challenges during implementation. Special education administrators should have an in depth knowledge of the process of change, implement a strategic and prescriptive process for RTI based upon a systematic plan to address all district structures, and recognize the challenges that may impede the process along the way.

REFERENCES

Baaken, J. P., O'Brian, M. O., & Shelden, D. L. (2007). Changeing roles and responsibilities of special education administrators. *Advances in Special Education, 17*, 1–15. doi:10.1016/S0270-4013(06)17001-4

Batsche, G. M., Elliot, J., Graden, J. L., Grimes, J., Kovaleski, J. F., Prasse, D., & Tilly, W. D. (2005). *Response to intervention: Policy considerations and implementation*. Alexandria, VA: National Association of State Directors of Special Education.

Bergstrom, M. K. (2008). Professional development in response to intervention: Implementation of a model in a rural region. *Rural Special Education Quarterly, 27*(4), 27–36.

Berkeley, S., Bender, W. N., Peaster, L. G., & Saunders, L. (2009). Implementation of response to intervention. *Journal of Learning Disabilities, 42*(1), 85–95. doi:10.1177/0022219408326214 PMID:19103800

Bernhardt, V. L., & Hebert, C. L. (2011). *Response to intervention (RtI) and continuous school improvement (SCI) using data, vision, and leadership to design, implement, and evaluate a schoolwide prevention system.* Larchmont, NY: Eye on Education.

Berry, C. S. (1941). General problems of philosophy and administration in the education of exceptional children. *Review of Educational Research, 11*(3), 252–260.

Betts, F. (1992). How systems thinking applies to education. *Educational Leadership, 50*(3), 38–41.

Boscardin, M. L. (2007). What is special about special education administration? Considerations for school leadership. *Exceptionality, 15*(3), 189–200. doi:10.1080/09362830701503537

Boscardin, M. L., McCarthy, E., & Delgado, R. (2009). An integrated research-based approach to creating standards for special education leadership. *Journal of Special Education Leadership, 22*(2), 68–84.

Bradley, R., Danielson, L., & Doolittle, J. (2005). Response to intervention. *Journal of Learning Disabilities, 38*(6), 485–486. doi:10.1177/00222194050380060201 PMID:16392688

Burns, M. K., Appleton, J. J., & Stehouwer, J. D. (2005). Meta-analytic review of responsiveness-to-intervention research: Examining field-based and research-implemented models. *Journal of Psychoeducational Assessment, 23*(4), 381–394. doi:10.1177/073428290502300406

Cardno, C. (2012). *Managing effetive relationships in education.* London, GRB. Sage *(Atlanta, Ga.).*

Castillo, J. M., & Batsche, G. M. (2012). Scaling up response to intervention: The influence of policy and research and the role of program evaluation. *Communique, 40*, 14–16.

Creswell, J. W. (2007). *Qualitative inquiry and research design: Choosing among five approaches.* Thousand Oaks, CA: Sage.

Crockett, J. B. (2002). Special education's role in preparing responsive leaders for inclusive schools. *Remedial and Special Education, 23*(3), 157–168. doi:10.1177/07419325020230030401

Crockett, J. B. (2007). The changing landscape of special education administration. *Exceptionality, 15*(3), 139–142. doi:10.1080/09362830701503487

Crockett, J. B. (2011). Conceptual models for leading and administrating special education. In J. M. Kauffman & D. P. Hallahan (Eds.), *Handbook of special education.* New York, NY: Routledge.

Crockett, J. B., Becker, M. K., & Quinn, D. (2009). Reviewing the knowledge base of special education leadership and administration from 1970-2009. *Journal of Special Education Leadership, 22*(2), 55–67.

Crockett, J. B., Billingsley, B. S., & Boscardin, M. L. (Eds.). (2012). *Handbook of leadership and administration for special education.* New York, NY: Routledge.

Datnow, A. (2006). Comments on Michael Fullan's "The future of educational change: System thinkers in action". *Journal of Educational Change, 7*(3), 133–135. doi:10.1007/s10833-006-0005-4

Detgen, A., Yamashita, M., Davis, B., & Wraight, S. (2011). State policies and procedures on response to intervention in the Midwest Region. U.S. Department of Education, Institute of Education Sciences, National Center for Education Evaluation and Regional Assistance, Regional Education Laboratory Midwest.

Dillman, D. A., Smyth, J. D., & Christian, L. M. (2009). *Internet, mail, and mixed-mode surveys: The tailored design method* (3rd ed.). Hoboken, NJ: Wiley.

Duke, D. (2004). *The challenges of educational change*. Boston, MA: Pearson Education, Inc.

Edgehouse, M. A., Edwards, A., Gore, S., Harrison, S., & Zimmerman, J. (2007). Initiating and leading change: A consideration of four new models. *The Catalyst, 36*(2), 3–12.

Elliott, J., & Morrison, D. (2008). *Reponse to intervention blueprints: District level edition*. Alexandria, VA: National Association of State Directors of Special Education.

Ellsworth, J. B. (2000). *Surviving change: A survey of educational change models*. Syracuse, NY: ERIC Clearinghouse on Information and Technology.

Ervin, R. A., Schaughency, E., Goodman, S. D., McGlinchey, M. T., & Matthews, A. (2007). Moving from a model demonstration project to a statewide initiative in Michigan: Lessons learned from merging research-based agendas to address reading and behavior. In S. R. Jimerson, M. K. Burns, & A. M. VanDerHeyden (Eds.), *Handbook of response to intervention*. New York, NY: Springer. doi:10.1007/978-0-387-49053-3_27

Fanning, E. (2005). Formatting a paper-based survey questionnaire: Best practices. *Practical Assessment, Research & Evaluation, 10*(12).

Fink, D., & Stoll, L. (2005). Educational change: Easier said than done. In A. Hargreaves (Ed.), *Extending educational change* (pp. 17–41). New York, NY: Springer. doi:10.1007/1-4020-4453-4_2

Fletcher, J. M., Denton, C., & Francis, D. J. (2005). Validity of alternative approaches for the identification of learning disabilities: Operationalizing unexpected underachievement. *Journal of Learning Disabilities, 38*(6), 545–552. doi:10.1177/00222194050380061101 PMID:16392697

Fletcher, J. M., & Vaughn, S. (2009). Response to intervention: Preventing and remediating academic difficulties. *Child Development Perspectives, 3*(1), 30–37. doi:10.1111/j.1750-8606.2008.00072.x PMID:21765862

Fraenkel, J. R., & Wallen, N. E. (2006). *How to design and evaluate research in education* (6th ed.). New York, NY: McGraw-Hill.

Fuchs, D., & Fuchs, L. S. (2008). Implementing RTI: Response-to-intervention is an ambitious and complex process that requires administrators choose the right model. *District Administration, 44*, 73–76.

Fuchs, D., Fuchs, L. S., & Compton, D. L. (2004). Identifying reading disabilities by responsiveness-to-instruction: Specifying measures and criteria. *Learning Disability Quarterly, 27*(4), 216–227. doi:10.2307/1593674

Fuchs, D., Fuchs, L. S., & Compton, D. L. (2012). Smart RTI: A next-generation approach to multilevel prevention. *Exceptional Children, 78*(3), 263–279. doi:10.1177/001440291207800301 PMID:22736805

Fuchs, L. S., & Fuchs, D. (2007). A model for implementing responsiveness to intervention. *Teaching Exceptional Children, 39*(5), 14–20. doi:10.1177/004005990703900503

Fuchs, L. S., & Vaughn, S. (2012). Responsiveness-to-intervention: A decade later. *Journal of Learning Disabilities, 45*(3), 195–203. doi:10.1177/0022219412442150 PMID:22539056

Fullan, M. (2001). *Leading in a culture of change* (1st ed.). San Francisco, CA: Jossey-Bass.

Fullan, M. (2006). The future of educational change: System thinkers in action. *Journal of Educational Change, 7*(3), 113–122. doi:10.1007/s10833-006-9003-9

Gresham, F. M. (2007). Evolution of the response-to-intervention concept: Empirical foundations. In S. R. Jimerson, M. K. Burns, & A. M. VanDerHeyden (Eds.), *Handbook of response to intervention*. New York, NY: Springer. doi:10.1007/978-0-387-49053-3_2

Hackett, J. (2010). Developing state regulations to implement the response-to-intervention requirements of IDEA: The Illinois plan. *Perspectives on Language and Literacy, 36*(2), 36–39.

Hamel, G. (2000). *Leading the revolution*. Boston, MA: Harvard Business School Press.

Hargreaves, A. (2005). Pushing the boundaries of educational change. In A. Hargreaves (Ed.), *Extending educational change* (pp. 1–16). New York, NY: Springer. doi:10.1007/1-4020-4453-4_1

Harlacher, J. E., & Siler, C. E. (2011). Factors related to successful RTI implementation. *Communique, 39*, 20–22.

Hollenbeck, A. F. (2007). From IDEA to implementation: A discussion of foundational and future responsiveness-to-intervention research. *Learning Disabilities Research & Practice, 22*(2), 137–146. doi:10.1111/j.1540-5826.2007.00238.x

Hopkins, D. (2005). Tensions in and prospects for school improvement. In D. Hopkins (Ed.), *Practice and theory of school improvement* (pp. 1–21). New York, NY: Springer. doi:10.1007/1-4020-4452-6_1

House, E. R., & McQuillan, P. J. (2005). Three perspective on school reform. In A. Lieberman (Ed.), *The roots of educational change* (pp. 186–201). New York, NY: Springer. doi:10.1007/1-4020-4451-8_11

Hughes, C. A., & Dexter, D. D. (2011). Response to intervention: A research-based summary. *Theory into Practice, 50*(1), 4–11. doi:10.1080/00405841.2011.534909

Individuals With Disabilities Education Act, 20 U.S.C. § 1400 (2004).

Jenkins, J. R., Hudson, R. F., & Johnson, E. S. (2007). Screening for at-risk readers in a response to intervention framework. *School Psychology Review, 36*(4), 582–600.

Kavale, K. A., Kauffman, J. M., Bachmeier, R. J., & LeFever, G. B. (2008). Response-to-intervention: Seperating the rhetoric of self-congratulation from the reality of specific learning disability identification. *Learning Disability Quarterly*, *31*(3), 135–150.

Knotek, S. E. (2007). Consultation within response to intervention models. In S. R. Jimerson, M. K. Burns, & A. M. VanDerHeyden (Eds.), *Handbook of respoonse to intervention*. New York, NY: Springer. doi:10.1007/978-0-387-49053-3_4

Kotter, J. (1996). *Leading change*. Boston, MA: Harvard Business School Press.

Kovaleski, J. F. (2007). Potential pitfalls of response to intervention. In S. R. Jimerson, M. K. Burns, & A. M. VanDerHeyden (Eds.), *Handbook of response to intervention*. New York: Springer. doi:10.1007/978-0-387-49053-3_6

Kratochwill, T. R., Clements, M. A., & Kalymon, K. M. (2007). Response to intervention: Conceptual and methodological issues in implementation. In S. R. Jimerson, M. K. Burns, & A. M. VanDerHeyden (Eds.), *Handbook of response to intervention*. New York, NY: Springer. doi:10.1007/978-0-387-49053-3_3

Lashley, C., & Boscardin, M. L. (2003). Special education administration at a crossroads. *Journal of Special Education Leadership*, *16*(2), 63–75.

Marston, D. (2005). Tiers of intervention in responsiveness to intervention: Prevention outcomes and learning disabilities identification patterns. *Journal of Learning Disabilities*, *38*(6), 539–544. doi:10.1 177/00222194050380061001 PMID:16392696

McHatton, P.A., Gordon, K.D., & Glenn, T.L., & Sue. (2012). Troubling special education leadership: Finding purpose, potential, and possibility in challenging contexts. *Journal of Special Education Leadership*, *25*(1), 38–47.

McMaster, K. L., & Wagner, D. (2007). Monitoring response to general education instruction. In S. R. Jimerson, M. K. Burns, & A. M. VanDerHeyden (Eds.), *Handbook of response to intervention*. New York, NY: Springer. doi:10.1007/978-0-387-49053-3_16

Mellard, D. F., Deshler, D. D., & Barth, A. (2004). LD identification: It's not simply a matter of building a better mousetrap. *Learning Disability Quarterly*, *27*(4), 229–242. doi:10.2307/1593675

Mellard, D. F., Stern, A., & Woods, K. (2011). RTI school-based practices and evidence-based models. *Focus on Exceptional Children*, *43*(6), 1–15.

O'Connor, E. P., & Freeman, E. W. (2012). District-level considerations in supporting and sustaining RtI implementation. *Psychology in the Schools*, *49*(3), 297–310. doi:10.1002/pits.21598

Passman, B. (2008). Case in point: Knowledge, skills, and dispositions. *Journal of Special Education Leadership*, *21*(1), 46–47.

Pazey, B. L., & Yates, J. R. (2012). Conceptual and historical foundations of special education administration. In J. B. Crockett, B. S. Billingsley, & M. L. Boscardin (Eds.), *Handbook of leadership and administration of special education* (pp. 17–36). New York, NY: Routledge.

Sansosti, F. J., Goss, S., & Noltemeyer, A. (2011). Perspectives of special education directors on response to intervention in secondary schools. *Contemporary School Psychology*, 9-20.

Sansosti, F. J., & Noltemeyer, A. (2008). Viewing response-to-intervention through an educational change paradigm: What can we learn? *California School Psychologist*, *13*(1), 55–66. doi:10.1007/BF03340942

Skyttner, L. (2005). *General systems theory: Problems, persepctives, and practice* (2nd ed.). Hackensack, NJ: World Scientific Publishing Co.

Stoll, L. (2006). The future of educational change: System thinkers in action: Response to Michael Fullan. *Journal of Educational Change*, *7*(3), 123–127. doi:10.1007/s10833-006-0004-5

Tilly, W. D. (2002). Best practices in school psychology as a problem as a problem-solving enterprise. In A. Thomas & J. Grimes (Eds.), *Best practices in school psychology* (Vol. 4, pp. 21–36). Bethesda, MD: National Association of School Psychologists.

Voltz, D. L., & Collins, L. (2010). Preparing special education administrators for inclusion in diverse, standards-based contexts: Beyond the council for exceptional children and the Interstate School Leaders Licensure Consortium. *Teacher Education and Special Education*, *33*(1), 70–82. doi:10.1177/0888406409356676

Werts, M. G., Lambert, M., & Carpenter, E. (2009). What special education directors say about RTI. *Learning Disability Quarterly*, *32*(4), 245–254. doi:10.2307/27740376

Whitten, E., Esteves, K. J., & Woodrow, A. (2009). *RTI success: Proven tools and strategies for schools and classrooms*. Minneapolis, MN: Free Spirit.

Wiener, R. M., & Soodak, L. C. (2008). Special education administrators' perspectives on response to intervention. *Journal of Special Education Leadership*, *21*(1), 39–45.

Wigle, S. E., & Wilcox, D. J. (2002). Special education directors and their competencies on CEC-identified skills. *Education*, *123*(2), 276–288.

Yell, M. L., & Walker, D. W. (2010). The legal basis of response to intervention: Analysis and implications. *Exceptionality*, *18*(3), 124–137. doi:10.1080/09362835.2010.491741

Zirkel, P. A., & Thomas, L. B. (2010). State laws and guidelines implementing RTI. *Teaching Exceptional Children*, *43*(1), 60–73. doi:10.1177/004005991004300107

KEY TERMS AND DEFINITIONS

Fullan's Framework for Leadership: This framework defines the process in which leaders can address change themes that will result in effective leadership (Fullan, 2001).

Implementation: "The process of achieving intended change" (Duke, 2004, p. 158).

Implementation of Response to Intervention: The process of putting systematic supports and structures, often organized into successive components or steps, into place to establish a comprehensive model of Response to Intervention. This primarily takes place at the school district level, but may also include a focus on individual school buildings (Elliott & Morrison, 2008; O'Connor & Freeman, 2012).

Individuals with Disabilities Education Act (IDEA) of 2004: Federal law that influences education regarding the determination of individuals with disabilities using response to intervention (Yell & Walker, 2010).

Response to Intervention: The practice of (1) providing high-quality instruction/intervention matched to student needs and (2) using learning rate over time and level of performance to (3) make important education decisions (Batsche et al., 2005).

Special Education: Instruction that is specifically designed, at no cost to parents, to address the unique needs of a child with a disability to ensure access to and progress toward the general education curriculum ("Individuals With Disabilities Education Act," 2004).

Special Education Administrator: A school administrator whose primary responsibility is leading, supervising, and managing the delivery of special education and related services (Crockett, 2007).

Student with a Disability: A child having mental retardation, a hearing impairment, a speech or language impairment, a visual impairment, an emotional disturbance, an orthopedic impairment, autism, a traumatic brain injury, an other health impairment, a specific learning disability, deaf- blindness, or multiple disabilities needing special education and related services ("Individuals With Disabilities Education Act," 2004).

Chapter 13

The Lived Experiences of Authentic Leaders:
A Phenomenological Study Exploring the Defining Experiences that Informed Their Development

Sandra J. Aguirre
George Washington University, USA

ABSTRACT

Globalization presents an array of challenges and opportunities for today's leaders. Recurring corporate and government malfeasance on a global scale as well as the morally complex environments of organizations are imposing more significant demands on organizational actors. Authentic leadership is an emerging leadership category that is gaining much interest due to the demand for more authentic leaders. Authentic leaders attain greater performance from their followers and this is considered a leadership multiplier that produces a virtuous cycle of performance and learning for leaders, followers, and organizations. This chapter discusses a completed study that addresses the following research question: How do experiences inform authentic leadership development across the 4 dimensions of the authentic leadership multidimensional construct of self-awareness, balanced processing, relational transparency, and internalized moral/ethical perspectives?

INTRODUCTION

The demand and expansion of global leadership is dramatically changing the leadership development roadmap. Our understanding of how leadership develops is being eclipsed by the rush to implement global leadership competencies to meet the demand of globalization. According to Hannah, Avolio, and Walumbwa (2011), the morally complex environments of organizations are imposing significant demands and challenges on organizational actors. Recurring corporate and government malfeasance on a global scale has resulted in a demand for more authentic leaders. Authentic leadership is an emerging

DOI: 10.4018/978-1-5225-0522-8.ch013

leadership category that is gaining much interest not only because of the demand for more authentic leaders but also given that authentic leaders attain greater performance from their followers. This latter point is considered a leadership multiplier that produces a virtuous cycle of performance and learning for leaders, followers, and organizations (Chan, Hannah, & Gardner, 2005).

Authentic leadership is also becoming part of a broader social change not only in the way leaders are thought about but also in what society is demanding in their leaders—leaders they can trust and who maintain an unshakeable ethical fabric when the going gets tough, leaders who are driven by the greater good and not just for their ego. *Outlook on the Global Agenda 2015*, published by the World Economic Forum (2014), reported that there is a lack of leadership across the globe along with a growing collective sense around the world that citizens have become fearful, distrustful, and impatient of leaders.

Authentic leadership will remain a growing field as society calls for ethical and inspirational leaders (Witt, 2011). The crisis in confidence in leaders continues to grow on a national and global scale. According to the National Leadership Index report (Rosenthal, 2012), Americans' confidence in their leaders was below average for the 5th year in a row. In 2014, the Global Leadership Index, published by the World Economic Forum, reported 42% of global respondents do not have confidence in leaders of international organizations to be independent and not influenced by some political, partisan or national interests. International organizations in North America have the least confidence in leaders whereas Latin America has the greatest confidence in leaders. Overall, Pakistan (3.57) and the United States (3.93) have the lowest Global Leadership Index respectively and Switzerland has the highest (5.21).

Leadership remains a skill sought by organizations to improve their bottom line (Boatman & Wellins, 2011; Northouse, 2010). Organizations with high-quality leaders out perform their competitors 13 times more in financial performance in which organizational leadership quality was rated as excellent (Boatman & Wellins, 2011). Boatman and Wellins's (2011) Development Dimensions International (DDI) leadership forecast report had an overarching theme indicating that it is time for a *leadership revolution* in this time when change is rapidly occurring. The economic crisis of 2008 catapulted the global economy into an economic crisis not seen since the great depression. The financial crisis caused businesses to go into damage-control mode, focusing on minimal strategies to keep their businesses viable, and budgets were cut across the board adversely affecting talent investment (Boatman & Wellins, 2011). From a commercial perspective, organizational survival in a globally competitive environment depends on organizations being "keenly aware of their leadership talent and how to best develop it across all levels" (Day, 2007, p. 13). From a military perspective, the focus is on "developing people and ideas, and building organizations" (O'Bryant, 2012, para. 5) to meet the new challenges that the military is faced with now and in the future.

The problems presented by the world of today are huge, complex, and not always predictable, and at times seem unimaginable. Globalization has led to drastic organizational changes that are occurring within a complex, uncertain and turbulent business environment (Akella, 2008, p. 219). Corporate scandals continue to occur that are having global impact. The U.S. housing market debacle crippled a global economy, today the global economy remains weak. The United States military is promoting the concept of ethical and adaptive leadership to improve global agility to operate in a complex and fiscally constrained environment. Arab Spring-type social revolutions continue to occur in which there is a demand to end oppressive leadership and seek a forward strategy of freedom eliminating authoritarian resilience. Political instability is on a global scale. Most recently, the 2015 Volkswagen emission scandal highlights unethical leadership behavior on a global scale. Volkswagen leaders knowingly put into place a well-thought-out scheme for their emissions systems to cheat emissions tests. The lack of trust in leadership is beginning to loom large, casting a negative shadow across the globe.

While the study of authentic leadership is inverting the ways in which leadership is viewed and studied, the globalized digital age is inverting the way leaders are developed and changing the environment in which they practice. The study of leadership has transitioned from understanding associated behaviors, styles, and garden-variety forms of leadership to obtaining a deeper understanding of the processes that develop good leaders. Extraordinary leaders may be the products of chance, opportunity, talent, or expertise but the development of authentic leaders also requires a view into their human history to broaden the understanding of authentic leadership. The global digital age is moving leadership development from a traditional classroom to a virtual classroom and leadership practitioners operate in an organizational environment that is global and digitally connected. No longer are face-to-face interactions the norm in organizations; interactions have moved to virtual spaces that are global and digitally connected. Whereas traditional adult learning and leadership studies focus on the reflection of experiences and paths that one travels, which shapes their identity and the leader they are today.

While the globalized digital age brings to light pedagogical implications for leadership development, there remains a nascent understanding on how leadership develops across many conventional theoretical concepts of leadership, such as authentic leadership and the psychology based topics of self and identity that are critical in understanding leadership development. The global and digital world will certainly impact and change the view and understanding of leadership; this emerging paradigm will make both the study and practice of leadership more complex.

The ongoing conversation about authentic leadership touches on the notion of experience, and how experience informs the development of leaders into authentic leaders; yet there are no studies that focus explicitly on the experiences of authentic leaders. This is remarkable given that the concept of authentic leadership has been theoretically explored for nearly 20 years. Additionally, expanding leadership experiences that occur in a global context utilizing a primarily digital platform remains nascent as well and begs the question if conventional conceptions of leadership are overly simplistic and ineffective (Jennings & Dooley 2007).

As a step toward bringing to light current leadership development research while keeping in mind the global and digital world that will influence leadership development, practice, and research, this chapter provides an overview of seminal works, contemporary theories and models, and emerging perspectives of authentic leadership in past and present organizations that emphasize physical social connectedness, rather than virtual social connectedness. As such, the goal of this chapter is to expose the reader to the various ways in which authentic leadership has been conceptualized over the last 10 years and to discuss possibilities for shaping its future conceptualizations and outlining a research agenda for leadership in the context of a globalized digital age.

BACKGROUND

The following is a review of the authentic leadership literature that identifies key areas for understanding leadership development to aid the reader in understanding the different aspects of authentic leadership development that will have implications for future leadership theory, practice, and research that focus on the globalization and the digital age of leadership.

Luthans and Avolio (2003) postulated that to advance their theoretical model of authentic leadership, a comprehensive proactive strategy needs to include building taxonomies of trigger events that would be expected to promote the development of positive leadership to fully understand the constructs and events that influence this development. Without this understanding, Luthans and Avolio noted, humans will remain subject to life as the best alternative to producing the next generation of authentic leaders. Authentic leaders' personal history must be explored to unearth the internal and external sources of turbulence that challenge leaders' abilities in their life. Luthans and Avolio stated that experiences foster growth and development as humans, and they also foster the development of authenticity from within.

May, Chan, Hodges, and Avolio (2003) emphasized how authentic leaders learn from past experiences to determine how they might best deal with moral dilemmas at work. It is through the capability and capacity to learn that authentic leaders develop. Avolio, Gardner, Walumbwa, Luthans, and May (2004) called for more research that examines the relationship between authentic leadership and experienced meaning at work. These experiences can serve as sources to help researchers understand how authentic leadership emerges (Luthans & Avolio, 2003).

Even though the concept of experiences is a defining factor regarding how authentic leadership emerges in leaders, which is an idea that is shared by many authors (both scholars and practitioners), it is necessary to bear in mind that the points discussed herein are theoretical in nature and are not based on empirical evidence. From an empirical perspective, it seems important to explore the lived experiences of authentic leaders to help provide empirical insight into the question of how experiences inform authentic leadership, which remains unexplored.

Given that authenticity is at the core of authentic leadership theory, many theoretical conceptions regarding authentic leadership detail how authenticity within authentic leaders is an emergent, long-term, and individual process. Kernis (2003) defined *authenticity* as "the unobstructed operation of one's true core self in one's daily enterprise" (p. 16). Avolio and Gardner (2005) proposed that authentic leaders develop as part of a dynamic lifespan process, whereby trigger events at various points in their life strata shape their development over time.

Based on these propositions, it would seem most useful to examine the experiences of authentic leaders to increase our scholarly knowledge of how experiences play a role in the transition from being a leader to an authentic leader. This empirical study increased our knowledge of authentic leaders by exploring their lived experiences, specifically with respect to the defining experiences/moments in their lives that informed their development.

Although a variety of definitions of *authentic leadership* have been advanced over the years, there is no single accepted definition of authentic leadership among leadership scholars (Gardner, Cogliser, Davis, & Dickens, 2011; Northouse, 2010). Instead, there remains multiple definitions, each written from various viewpoints and with a different emphasis (Gardner et al., 2011; Northouse, 2010). Additionally, formulations of authentic leadership have evolved from a practical approach, which evolved from real-life examples and the training and development literature, and the theoretical approach, which is based on findings from social science research (Northouse, 2010).

In an attempt to more fully explore authentic leadership, researchers set out to identify its parameters and more clearly conceptualize this concept; in fact, the efforts continue today (Northouse, 2010). Although important work has been accomplished regarding authentic leadership, such as theory building, propositions, and empirical studies, the construct of authentic leadership has yet to be fully rationalized (Pittinsky & Tyson, 2005) and explored from a holistic perspective. What is meant by authentic leadership is not clear and the conceptualization of its four dimensions is equally as ambiguous (Pittinsky &

Tyson, 2005). Therefore, there may be missing components in the overall construct of authentic leadership (Walumbwa, Avolio, Gardner, Wernsing, & Peterson, 2008). This may be due, in part, to the idea that authentic leadership is in its nascent form and it is still in what some might consider a theory-building phase. There is much to explore, understand, and reconcile in regards to authentic leadership. Additionally, we still do not know the specifics of how it develops, yet we do know that experiences plays a role (Avolio et al., 2004; Eigel & Kuhnert, 2005; Hannah, Lester, & Vogelgesang, 2005; Luthans & Avolio, 2003; May et al., 2003; Shamir & Eilam, 2005).

Gardner, Avolio, Luthans, May, and Walumbwa (2005) argued that an authentic leader must achieve individual authenticity first and foremost, yet studies of authentic leadership do not fully comprehend how individual authenticity is achieved, nor do they uncover leaders' authentic relations with their followers, which is a critical part of becoming an authentic leader. Luthans and Avolio (2003) approached authentic leadership as a process that results in an individual's greater self-awareness and self-regulated positive behaviors, ultimately fostering positive self-development. Avolio and Wernsing (2008) further stated that this level of self-awareness, at the core of authentic leadership, requires substantial time and effort that is invested over many years; this translates into self-discovery to distinguish between inner conscience and external programming. That authentic leaders can recognize and accept that people in a group are at different levels in developing their self-awareness and authenticity, and that these individuals may not be able to see paradoxical possibilities, is suggested by the stories of authentic leaders presented thus far.

Walumbwa et al. (2008) identified a number of components that constitute authentic leadership and subsequently developed and tested a theory-based measure to assess it. The Authentic Leadership Questionnaire is the only valid measure of the construct. There continues to be an interest in what constitutes authentic leadership and how it evolves within the applied, academic management, and leadership literature (Walumbwa et al., 2008). Similarly, leadership development programs are currently focusing on the authentic leader (Pittinsky & Tyson, 2005), yet, as these and other authors suggest, there is more to authentic leadership than being true to oneself. Understanding how leader authenticity develops and evolves over time remains elusive in the domains of theory, practice, and research.

Authentic leadership is one of the emerging pillars of interest in the field of leadership (Avolio, Walumbwa, & Weber, 2009; Gardner, Lowe, Moss, Mahoney, & Cogliser, 2010), and it appears to hold great promise for theory and practice. Consensus continues to exist across the authentic leadership literature whereby additional empirical research is needed to further understand this construct, and to identify what precedes and/or influences the development of authentic leaders. Empirically increasing our understanding of authentic leadership can aid in the development of strategies to select and develop these leaders (Gardner et al., 2011). In this vein, there remains an enduring question: "What actually develops genuinely good leaders?" (Gardner, Avolio, & Walumbwa, 2005, p. xxii).

Collectively, what forms the basis of authentic leadership are components that are evolutionary and developmental by nature: self-awareness, values, convictions, self-knowledge, balanced processing, relational transparency, authenticity, identity, resiliency, self-concept, spirituality, vicarious learning, meaning, self-efficacy, self-transcendent values, self-view, self-concept, self-confidence, self-authorship, emotional regulation, psychological-capital (hope, optimism, resilience), self-monitoring, and so on. Historically, these types of developmental components are used to answer the question of, Who am I? However, answering this question begins with understanding, what one knows, which is influenced by one's experiences and social interactions with the world, along with the development and processing of knowledge and ideas (Luthans, Luthans, & Luthans, 2004). Meindl (1990) asserted that leadership behavior may be acquired through social contagion processes whereby followers of a given leader spontaneously spread their leadership experiences. In all, these theoretical perspectives argue that one's immediate social context and experiences are likely to influence a leader's subjective norms and perceived behavioral control.

If an individuals' leadership style is grounded in their personal knowledge that was gained from their life-long experiences, then it becomes critical to hear those personal stories to understand what unique experiences and events informed their authentic leadership development. It is these inner qualities that develop over time as well as the processes that individuals go through on their journey to become an authentic leader that need to be uncovered.

Authentic leadership acknowledges a developmental perspective that exists on a continuum and is open to development (Avolio et al., 2004). Authentic leaders have a learning capacity that fosters their ability to see their role as including an ethical responsibility and moral perspective, as they have learned how to deal with moral dilemmas from past experiences (May et al., 2003). Morality is, in part, a function of one's memories as encoded and stored from one's moral experiences and reflections, in which leaders manifest their authentic moral self during leadership episodes (Hannah et al., 2005). Furthermore, adaptability allows a leader to develop morally and to execute moral control over the leadership influence process; this largely stems from the plasticity of schemas and scripts that evolve over time through defining developmental "trigger events" (Hannah et al., 2005, p. 45). Authentic leaders become authentic leaders through experiences, trigger events, and the plasticity of schemas and scripts that evolve over time (Hannah et al., 2005).

The epistemological perspective and learning theory orientation adopted in this study are from a constructivist perspective, in which the process by which one constructs meaning is taken from experience (Merriam, Cafarella, & Baumgartner, 2007). Within the adult learning paradigm, social constructivism argues that although the mind constructs reality in its relationship to the world, this process is significantly informed and influenced by social relationships (Gergen, 1999). Merriam et al. (2007) illustrated the many dimensions of experience that shape learning. For example, one can learn from a direct embodied experience that engages an individual mentally, physically, and emotionally in a single moment; from a simulated experience or a relived past experience; by making sense of experience through collaboration with others in a community; or through introspective experiences, such as during meditation or dreaming.

The constructivist approach to learning emphasizes reflection on one's experience (Fenwick, 2003; Merriam et al., 2007). According to Merriam et al. (2007, p. 160), people have concrete experiences; they reflect on these experiences and construct new knowledge as a result of these reflections. In this view, the focus in on the learner's ability to derive meaning from a given experience. The concept of experiences in these seminal discussions is in the physical social world rather than in a globalized digital world. Cross-disciplinary and integrative views of leadership in the global and digital realm are beginning to emerge, yet there are limited empirical studies using the constructivist approach in this new context. The organizational domain has become a global organization and the organizational business has changed from a historical capital blue-collar-type work environment to a white-collar knowledge worker environment that requires a different type of leadership. Additionally, today's leaders need to know how to tap into and make use of the resources that exist across a corporation in which there are no physical boundaries. The business acumen and level of knowledge routinely far exceed the knowledge of the leader. Understanding how leaders will construct knowledge in today's new complex paradigm is yet to be seen and understood. The next section discusses the evolution of thought and the major perspectives of authentic leadership, learning, and adult learning to provide a theoretical understanding for future research focused on leadership in the globalized digital age. Understanding these seminal concepts is critical for future leadership development because relational interaction is inherent to leadership development. Therefore, if relational interactions primarily occur in the digital world, scholars and practitioners will need to understand what will be the implication for leadership development.

Seminal constructivist development scholars such as John Dewey, George Herbert Mead, and Lev Vygotsky view learning through an experiential lens, in which experiential learning emphasizes situations, not subjects, and adult education takes place in the context of concrete situations. What matters in this perspective is that people learn; it is not about what they learn, as truth and knowledge are provisional. In this way, learning is a product of the relationship/transaction between the subject and the world.

Experiential learning resonates and aligns with authentic leadership theory, whereby both perspectives acknowledge the importance of reflection on experiences as a process for development, resulting in congruence between the epistemology, theoretical perspectives, and methodology used in this study (Crotty, 1998).

Authentic Leadership

Although a variety of definitions of *leader authenticity*, or *authentic leadership*, have been advanced over the years, this study concentrates on Walumbwa et al.'s (2008) multidimensional model and definition of *authentic leadership*. Authentic leadership is a pattern of leader behavior that draws upon and promotes both positive psychological capacities and a positive ethical climate to foster greater self-awareness, the balanced processing of information, relational transparency, and an internalized moral/ethical perspective on the part of leaders working with followers, facilitating positive self-development.

Learning

Peter Jarvis's concept of learning is a multidisciplinary phenomenon that focuses on the whole person and takes into account the existential nature of philosophy: "the process of transforming experience into knowledge and skills, that results in a changed person" (Jarvis as cited in Illeris, 2009, p. 11). Jarvis (2009) posited that learning is a lifelong journey and discussed how lifelong learning is an intrinsic part of living itself; it is the combination of processes throughout a lifetime whereby the whole person—body (genetic, physical, and biological) and mind (knowledge, skills, attitudes, values, emotions, beliefs, and senses)—experiences social situations, the perceived content of which is then transformed cognitively, emotively, or practically (or through any combination thereof). These experiences are then integrated into the individual's biography resulting in a continually changing (or more experienced) person. According to Jarvis, learning occurs through encounters with life and the world, in which human experiences initially have no meaning; humans are confronted with novel situations that occur between experience of a situation and biography, which provides the knowledge and skills that enable humans to act meaningfully. This is the beginning of the learning process, as one has to learn something new and one is forced to ask questions such as (a) What do I do now? (b) What does this mean? and so on.

Adult Learning

Malcolm Knowles, a central figure in U.S. adult education in the second half of the 20th century (Smith, 2002), believed that adult education was a central need for the survival of civilization, so that man did not become obsolete due the new kind of world that was beginning to evolve in the late 1960s. Knowles

(1968) used the term andragogy to distinguish between adult learning and pre-adult learning; he then focused on developing a distinctive conceptual basis for adult education and learning via this notion of andragogy (Smith, 2002).

Knowles strongly believed that the art and science of teaching children (pedagogy) were extremely different from the art and science of helping adults learn (andragogy). In the concept of andragogy, to be adult means to be self-directing—a child psychologically becomes an adult when his self-concept changes from one of dependency to one of autonomy (Knowles, 1968). At this point, according to Knowles (1968), adults develop a deep psychological need to be perceived by themselves and by others as self-directing, as humans tend to resent and resist being put into situations in which they feel that others are imposing their will on them. Knowles believed that this self-concept lies at the heart of the "new technology" (p. 351) of andragogy, with andragogy based upon the insight that the deepest need that an adult has is to be treated as an adult, as a self-directing person, and with respect. According to Knowles, a curious phenomenon occurs regarding how individuals feel about their experience; adults define themselves in terms of their experiences and an adult's ability to self-identity is derived from what they have done, which is in contrast to a child, whose self-identity is formed in terms of family, school, community, and so on. According to Knowles, if people are not paying attention to their experiences and they are not incorporating them in their educational plans, adults feel rejected and devalued as people because "my experience is me" (p. 352).

Identity

Lord and Hall (2005) posited that leadership identity is constructed in organizations when individuals claim and grant leader and follower identities in their social interactions. According to Lord and Hall, identity is a central focus because it (a) provides an important structure around which relevant knowledge can be organized, (b) is a source of motivational and directional forces that determine the extent to which leaders voluntarily put themselves in developmental situations, and (c) may provide access to personal material (i.e., stories, core values, etc.) that can be used to understand and motivate subordinates. Their model suggests that as leaders' progress from novice to expert, they become increasingly capable of flexibly drawing on internal resources such as identities, values, and mental representations of subordinates and situations.

UNDERSTANDING THE DEVELOPMENT OF AUTHENTIC LEADERS

Issues, Controversies, Problems

Although the understanding of authentic leadership has been emerging over the past 30 years, there remains a dearth of empirical research explaining the many dimensions of what constitutes authentic leadership, how authentic leadership emerges, and how authentic leaders are developed. This lack of knowledge inhibits the ability to develop authentic leaders not only in the physical world but also in the globalized digital world.

Furthermore, given the limitations of the various research designs used in the study of authentic leadership, Gardner et al. (2011) suggested that the supportive evidence generated to date must be considered tentative, and further research using more rigorous and diverse methods is needed to strengthen confidence in the nomological validity of authentic leadership.

The central foreshadowed problem around authentic leadership is the understanding of how authentic leadership develops within leaders. Avolio and Gardner (2005) stated that over 100 years of leadership theories have originated without focusing on the core processes that result in the development of leadership; consequently, this remains true for authentic leadership.

Although there have been many novel, intriguing, and promising propositions on how authentic leadership develops, many are in early states of theory development. As such, additional empirical studies are needed to develop a deeper understanding of what motivates the development of an authentic leader (Avolio & Gardner, 2005).

The purpose of this phenomenological study is to understand the development of authentic leaders. This study analyzes data at the individual level and focuses on how authentic leaders are developed by exploring the lived experience of authentic leaders, including what defining experiences and moments informed their development.

Authenticity and Leadership

The concepts of authenticity and leadership are fundamental to understanding authentic leadership. Linking the constructs of authenticity and leadership is relatively new and during the past 10 years, there has been an increase in the interest and advancement of authentic leadership as a concept; however, this idea remains at its initial theory-building phase due to the small number of empirical studies performed and the limited number of methods used to date. Although there are several touchstones and distinguishing elements of authentic leadership, authenticity remains at the core of authentic leadership and underlies what it means to be a good leader, regardless of leadership theory (Gardner et al., 2011; Roche, 2010).

Authenticity

Authenticity is rooted in ancient Greek lore and philosophy, and the modern concept of authenticity has evolved over the past 80 years (Erickson, 1995; Gardner et al., 2011). The essence of authenticity in relation to authentic leadership is simply leaders who are true to their own inner self regardless of the challenges and ethical demands placed upon them and who are ultimately authentic and genuine. The authenticity of a leader is predicated on the authenticity of the person, in which authenticity in a person is an emergent property (Chan et al., 2005). Kernis (2003) defined authenticity as the unobstructed operation of one's true core self in one's daily enterprise. Kernis (2003) identified four components of authenticity—(a) awareness, (b) unbiased processing, (c) authentic action, and (d) relational transparency, which have served as the theoretical underpinnings of the concept of authentic leadership as it is known today.

Leadership

Contemporary views of leadership describe leadership as a process. It is not a trait or characteristic that resides in the leader; rather, it is a transactional event that occurs between the leader and the followers (Northouse, 2010). Northouse (2010) described how process implies that leaders affect and are affected by their followers, emphasizing that leadership is not a linear one-way event but rather an interactive event.

Defining leadership as a process implies that it becomes available to everyone and it is not restricted to the formally designated leader in a group (Northouse, 2010). Although there are a wide variety of different theoretical approaches to explain the complexities of the leadership process, leadership continues to be a complex process that has multiple dimensions and has been conceptualized in a multitude of ways.

For the purpose of this study, Northouse's (2010) definition of leadership is used: leadership is a process whereby one person influences a group of individuals to achieve a common goal. The concept that leadership is a process has emerged over time. Prior to looking at leadership as a process, the five areas of leadership theory that have historically dominated the leadership literature have included trait and skill, behavior, situation, transformational and transactional, and visionary.

As vibrancy in the field of leadership continues, there remains a resurgence of interest around ethical, servant, spiritual, and authentic leadership, suggesting that the past 10 years have represented a fertile time for the development of new theories and perspectives on leadership (Gardner et al., 2010). The past decade has seen a dramatic increase in scholarly interest on the topic of authentic leadership, primarily due to deep-rooted concerns about the ethical conduct of today's leaders. In these challenging and turbulent times, there is a growing recognition among scholars (Luthans & Avolio, 2003) and practitioners (George, 2003) alike, in which a more authentic leadership development strategy becomes relevant and urgently needed for desirable outcomes for leaders, followers, and organizations.

Authentic Leadership

Before reviewing the broad theoretical landscape of authentic leadership, it is critical to begin with an understanding of this concept. Authentic leadership is about the authenticity of leaders and their leadership practices, and it represents one of the newest areas of leadership research (Northouse, 2010). Authentic leadership remains in the formative phase of development and current research must be considered as tentative because new research about the theory is being published (Gardner et al., 2011; Northouse, 2010). Researchers today continue to explore the concept of authentic leadership to identify its parameters and to more clearly conceptualize it (Northouse, 2010).

The disconcerting action taken by leaders worldwide as well as the complexity of issues facing leaders today have given rise to the notion that authentic leaders are needed (Avolio & Gardner, 2005; Branson, 2007; Gardner et al., 2010; Roche, 2010). Authentic leadership is represented as an antidote to a leadership crisis, and it is posited that authentic leaders will be able to address the complex and unpredictable leadership demands of the present day (Branson, 2007; Luthans & Avolio, 2003; Roche, 2010). Authentic leadership is also becoming part of a broader social change not only in the way leaders are thought about but also in terms of what Americans want in their leaders—leaders they can trust and who maintain an unshakeable ethical fabric when the going gets tough. Finally, Americans want leaders who are driven by the greater good and not by their ego alone. Never before has so much attention been paid to the study of leadership; at this time, the understanding of authentic leadership has slightly advanced.

Although authentic leadership has been recognized as a prominent leadership theory over the past 10 years (Gardner et al., 2010), a shortfall of empirical studies remains and inhibits our understanding of authentic leadership, authentic leaders, and how authentic leadership develops. In essence, theoretical understanding of authentic leadership is emerging and the literature discussed here is only the beginning of the truly evolutionary scientific process.

SOLUTIONS AND RECOMMENDATIONS

Based on the findings of the study, it appears that the process of becoming an authentic leader is one of human cognition (learning) and applying what individuals learn from their experiences. The literary offerings on the concept of authenticity continually refer back to ancient Greek philosophy as well as to popular evocations such as Know thyself, The unexamined life is not worth living, and most popularly, To thine own self be true. What is missing in these concepts of authenticity and what this study particularly uncovered is the depth of compassion and caring that authentic leaders have for the people they lead as well as their own strong emotional and psychological functioning to endure the many challenging and traumatic events they experienced as a leaders. Moreover, this study brings to light several key factors that aided the participants in their development of becoming an authentic leader; this will be discussed in more detail below as follows.

The Process of Becoming an Authentic Leader

The process of becoming an authentic leader is based on the process of human cognition (learning) and applying what an individual learns from experiences over time. The results suggest that those experiences inform each of the authentic leadership constructs over the lifetime of an authentic leader. Several phases of the participants' lived experiences during childhood, throughout young adulthood, and in their professional lives shape and inform the analysis and findings of this study. The significant experiences that participants faced during their childhood or adolescence were influential in (a) shaping their values, (b) changing their behaviors, and (c) influencing who they want to be as a person and as a leader. Career experiences over a participant's adult lifetime—particularly during new, challenging, dangerous, life-or-death, and heartfelt experiences—reveal critical moments that informed their authentic leadership development across one or all four constructs. Additionally, the participants expressed how experiences with a good or poor leader (in the eyes of the participant) during adulthood were extremely influential in shaping who they want to be and who they do not want to be as a leader. Many times, these career experiences occurred within a short time period, between 1 to 3 years. Additionally, none of these experiences occurred within a global or digital context; they were all face-to-face interactions between leaders and followers.

Thematic Study Results

The analysis of the data resulted in the identification of four themes that inform authentic leadership development. These themes are listed and described in detail below.

Theme 1

Experiences are the primary sources of learning that inform authentic leadership development. This research revealed an array of experiences from childhood to adulthood that informed the participants' authentic leadership development. These experiences included being a supervisor during potential life-and-death situations, such as being in a typhoon or war (e.g., Desert Storm); dealing with the multiple deaths of subordinates (e.g., accidental and suicide); moving to a culturally different neighborhood during childhood; attending a military academy, in which expectations and feedback are engrained in each individual; being responsible for a nuclear weapons arsenal that could blow up the world three times; walking down a Indian reservation road holding one's grandfather's hand while the grandfather is teaching a grandson a lifelong lesson; being raised in an American Indian tribal environment and living communally rather than individually; being lost in the desert and being responsible for troops in a location where one can potentially be captured by terrorists or die of dehydration; taking over a leadership position from a toxic leader; having one's grandfather teach a lesson in ethics and morality (e.g., stealing); growing up in an environment in which kids are doing bad things; or having a single experience with a good or poor leader.

List of Experiences that Impact Authentic Leadership Development

Participants noted the following experiences that had the greatest impact on their leadership development:

- Observing leaders
- Interacting with many different people in different career fields
- Being mentored by great leaders
- Working under positive leadership
- Working under negative leadership
- Negative mentoring – meaning there was no one mentoring them
- Being placed in a great role
- Continually increasing the number of subordinates that leaders were in charge of
- Having a role model to follow, learn from, and someone who would take them under their wing regarding all aspects of development (e.g. putting the participants in challenging positions or advocating for the participants to apply for a higher-level position)
- Working for leaders who recognized the value of their followers, and who would facilitate their skill development and identify the areas in which to apply their skills
- Social contexts, such as church, that helped to develop a sense of right and wrong
- Significant emotional events in the eyes of the participants that occurred at different points in their lives (e.g. when they were a child, a young adult, an adult)
- Being given advice at the right time when it was needed
- Receiving words of wisdom from different family members (e.g. mother, father, grandfather, grandmother, mother-in-law)
- Getting over a difficult moment (e.g. suicides, accidental deaths, unexpected deaths, dysfunctional family issues)
- Leading in an extreme chaotic environment (e.g. typhoon, war)

When reviewing the transcripts of this study, it was clear that becoming an authentic leader is a lifelong journey and a process that is dependent upon dyadic relationships between leaders and followers. Each participant developed their leadership skills and knowledge by interacting face-to-face with leaders and colleagues that allowed them to change their behaviors and shape their leadership styles based on those interactions. It will be interesting to see how the globalized digital age will impact an individual's ability to learn from their mistakes that occur in a virtual context and how or if changes in their behavior can be translated in the digital world.

Theme 2

Feedback is essential in authentic leadership development. This study brought to light the idea that feedback is a critical factor in the development of an authentic leader. All participants (12 out of 12) felt strongly that if one is interested in improving one's self as a leader, one needs to consider all feedback. Each of the participants provided detailed accounts about how they incorporated feedback into their daily practice as a leader over their leadership career and how they continue to do so today. The data suggest that all participants have an interest in continually developing themselves.

The concept of self-awareness is central to the discussion of authentic leadership (Gardner, Avolio, & Walumbwa, 2005; Kernis, 2003; Luthans & Avolio, 2003; Shamir & Eilam, 2005; Sparrowe, 2005) and when participants responded to interview questions that focused on the construct of self-awareness, feedback was the most common theme that every participant discussed as being a critical factor in their development. The participants coupled feedback with a deep introspective look at themselves on a fairly ongoing basis to check and see how they were doing in their role as a leader and to make adjustments in their behaviors along the way.

The research data show a clear association between the dyadic relationships of leaders and followers, and feedback. Specifically, the participants discussed how real and raw feedback from subordinates informed the development of the participants' self-awareness.

The data also revealed that the participants typically had one defining experience in which they became aware that their words and behaviors impacted others. Once the participants made this realization, they would work on changing their words and behaviors. This suggests that the participants learned new behaviors and integrated them into their knowledge schemas.

The defining experiences included such things as being placed in a great role with critical responsibility in which they did not have any previous experience. Stumbling as a leader in front of subordinates, taking action to remedy their errors, and learning through immersion on an unfamiliar topic served as examples of these experiences. The participants described how these incidents prompted unexpected feedback from subordinates or led to the realization that these leaders had to depend on others; these experiences had a profound awakening effect on the participants' self-awareness. Typically, these experiences occurred early on in their leadership careers, and once the participants became aware of the value and importance of feedback and of the need for reflection and to modify their behaviors, many began to actively seek feedback. There was a sense among all the participants that it is important to focus on weaknesses and strive to continually improve, and they depend on feedback to make those improvements.

Participants described the different types of face-to-face feedback that influenced and appeared to help them develop their sense of self-awareness and included immediate unsolicited feedback from subordinates, solicited feedback from trusted advisors, and formal feedback as part of an institutional system, such as the military. Feedback from a virtual or digital perspective was not discussed and is an area for future research.

Theme 3

Authentic leadership development requires reliance on interactions with and fostering potential in others. Authentic followership and its association with authentic leadership is a primary area of focus within the authentic leadership literature (Avolio et al., 2004; Cianci, Hannah, Roberts, & Tsakumis, 2014; Eagly, 2005; Hinojosa, McCauley, Randolph-Seng, & Gardner, 2014; Zhu, May, & Avolio, 2004).

A common thread noted across the entire dataset of this study is that each of the participants had significant experiences with their leaders and subordinates throughout their careers; these moments were instrumental in developing who they are as leaders today. Moreover, what is not discussed in the authentic leadership literature is that many of the participants described how their family members greatly influenced them when they talked about how they gained knowledge that was most instrumental in shaping their current leadership style; they also described the people and experiences in their early adult and professional lives that had the greatest impact on them during the development of their current approach to leadership. The reliance on interactions with others informed authentic leadership constructs of self-awareness, interpersonal relationships, balanced processing, and ethics/morals. This finding demonstrates how the constructs of authentic leadership are interrelated and how experiences can inform more than one construct at a time.

When analyzing the data, there appears to be a clear reliance on interactions with others when it comes to authentic leadership development. This finding strongly supports the interpersonal lens adopted by a number of scholars (Eagly, 2005; Gardner, Avolio, & Walumbwa, 2005; Ilies, Morgeson, & Nahrgang, 2005; Luthans & Avolio, 2003). According to the participants, such interactions with positive/active role models who served as teachers early in their careers (when they themselves were followers) enabled them to glean positive attributes and knowledge that informed their leadership development and, in some cases, impacted their professional acumen in a specific career field. The participants learned how to be a leader and they also further developed their particular business acumen by working side-by-side with positive leaders. The descriptions that participants provided of their role models and mentors commonly illustrated an individual who was vested in the participants' careers and skill development, offering guidance and critical feedback because they believed in the participants, taking them under their wing to help with their development. Based on how the participants described their experiences, and on how the participants viewed this type of leader–follower relationship, the participants were viewed as "protégés" and the leader was considered more of a teacher than a mentor because of his/her active role in the participants' development – i.e. actively teaching rather than engaging in more passive mentoring. The teacher–protégé relationship that was identified in this study is unique and not currently reflected in the authentic leadership literature. Participant 12, a 50-year-old female who now works for the U.S. government, started out by working in the commercial bank industry; she recalls her experience with her first boss straight out of college and how he hired and trained her. The experience she described was one of a teacher–protégé relationship, she recalls how her boss (the teacher) saw something in her (the protégé) and took an active interest in her development. This experience was priceless and critically informed her development into an authentic leader.

Theme 4

Authentic leadership development occurred when participants worked with a positive leader, serving as a role model who would foster their potential. Every participant described an experience that involved learning from an expert in the field or a person that was a mentor or role model who acted as a teacher to foster their development. According to the participants, such interactions with positive/active role models who served as teachers early in their careers enabled them to glean positive attributes and knowledge that informed their leadership development and, in some cases, impacted their professional acumen in a specific career field. The participants learned how to be a leader and they also developed their particular business discipline. The descriptions that participants provided of their role models and mentors commonly illustrated an individual who was vested in the participants' careers and skill development, offering guidance and critical feedback because they believed in the participants, taking them under their wing to help with their development. Based on how the participants described their experiences and how the participants viewed this type of leader–follower relationship, the participants were viewed as protégés and the leaders were considered more of a teacher than a mentor because of their active role in the participants' development - that is, actively teaching rather than engaging in more passive mentoring. Although this study did not reveal any type of virtual mentoring, as a new age of mentoring is likely to emerge, this is an area for future leadership development research. E-mentoring, a concept that uses virtual technology to foster developmental relationships, is beginning to emerge. Increasing scholarly knowledge in this new discipline will be critical to future leadership development programs.

Theme 5

Throughout the authentic leadership literature, there are many conceptions regarding the moral foundation and values of authentic leaders. What the data suggest is that the moral foundation and values that are inherent in authentic leaders are developed during the childhood/adolescent phase, which is consistent with concepts of authentic leadership in which moral standards are primarily developed via cultural and societal influences (Hannah et al., 2005). The data suggest that the development of a moral standard and values was triggered by a significant experience in the eyes of the participant. The collective values of the participants appear to have developed into more of a value system that guides their actions and decision making. This value system may align with what scholars refer to as a moral foundation that authentic leaders possess (Luthans & Avolio, 2003; May et al., 2003). It is unknown what differentiates between these two concepts; this is an area for further research.

The concept that values are consistent over time once they are developed is also in alignment with the arguments presented by Ryan and Deci (2003), whereby authenticity is achieved when individuals enact an internalized self-regulation process. In this way, authentic leaders' conduct is guided by internal values as opposed to external threats, inducements, social expectations, and rewards. Participants appear to be anchored in the values that they hold; these values were established at a young age and influenced primarily by an immediate family member, such as a father, grandfather, mother, or mother-in-law, or were rooted in a specific social context.

Whereas the top global leadership skills reported by the 2015 Global National Index include global perspective, collaboration, and communication, global leadership competency models must consider an ethical/moral perspective in order to increase leader confidence levels. Global leadership competency models can build upon exiting leadership competency models and focus on a global multicultural perspective. Inceoglu and Bartram (2012) noted that such a context adds to the heterogeneity and complexity that leaders experience but is not different in kind to the other aspects of complexity with which leaders have to cope (e.g., different markets, stakeholders, and different levels of the organization). Broadening leadership competencies for a global context can work by providing examples from leadership models that are apply successfully in practice today (Inceoglu & Bartram, 2012).

FUTURE RESEARCH DIRECTIONS

The purpose of this study was to increase our empirical knowledge of how authentic leadership develops in leaders by exploring their lifelong experiences. By further drawing upon contemporary leadership and adult learning theories, this study helped to understand which defining experiences and moments informed leaders' development in becoming authentic leaders. As a result of the findings of this study, it provides an empirical perspective to help shape future conceptualizations of leadership development through the lens of a globalized digital age.

This research increased scholarly knowledge on the topic of authentic leadership and brought to light findings to advance the topic's current discourse. From a practice perspective, the results of this study can inform leadership and followership development programs in the digital and non-digital world to incorporate the findings of feedback, retrospection, leader–follower relationships, the intertwining nature of the authentic leadership multidimensional construct, leader–follower protégé relationships, bottom-up learning through subordinates, developing emotional connections in the leader–follower relationship, leveraging high levels of emotional and psychological functioning, and viewing leadership development through an interpersonal and digital lens. Finally, due to the nascent nature of authentic leadership research these findings have implications for global leadership theory and practice.

As leadership theory, research, and practice adapt their efforts to address a globalized and digital future, there are several emerging areas for further research that can draw on the findings of this study.

1. **Study how will the global digital age impact the leadership dichotomies of: doing more with less, balancing local interests with global interests, and working among apposing cultural norms and values:** Global leadership competencies is an emerging field, particularly, assessing, developing and managing global leadership competencies. According to Wang, James, Denyer, and Bailey (2014), the truly transnational—or global—leader needs to take a global perspective and have a different set of competencies from peers who may work as an expat in a single country. The recommendation for research is to explore the difference between traditional and global leadership competencies.

2. **Study how digital technologies trigger a different type of relationship between leaders and followers:** Gardner et al. (2011) considered that further exploration of the affective processes underlying authentic leader–follower relationships are crucial for the advancement of the field. This study brought to light (a) an emotional connection that exists between the leader–follower dyadic that informed participants' perceptions of authentic leaders and (b) how authentic leadership requires reliance on interaction with others. Therefore, it becomes increasingly more important as leaders work in a globalized digital age to explore the dyadic relationship. A subsequent study would focus on understanding the reciprocal relationship that occurs in a leader–follower dyadic in a global and digital context.

3. **Study leader effectiveness with dispersed teams:** With globalization comes dispersed teams. Allen and Ofahengau Vakalahi (2013) noted that literature is sparse on workforce expansion in the form of dispersed teams and that dispersed teams have unique dynamics and require leaders with unique skills and characteristics. They further posited that the success of dispersed teams is dependent on its leadership. As globalization fragments teams, it is increasing important to understand what informs the effective functioning of dispersed teams from a leadership perspective.

4. **Study the emerging concept of e-mentoring:** The global digital age is changing the dynamics of many interconnected relationships, including mentoring. Understanding how nontraditional relational interactions lead to learning for individuals is important to understand. E-mentoring is an emerging concept with multiple conceptualizations. While little is known about its implementation and results, the possibilities for e-mentoring are as endless as the Internet (Bierema & Merriam, 2002). A study would focus on the effectiveness in developing individuals through a nontraditional methods, such as e-mentoring, as understand how digital mediated technologies inform or impede e-mentoring.

CONCLUSION

Authentic leadership is one of the emerging pillars of interest in the field of leadership today (Avolio et al., 2009; Gardner et al., 2010), and it appears to hold great promise for theory and practice. The results of this study demonstrated the importance of unique and situational experiences that were instrumental in developing participants' current leadership style and provide a basis for future leadership theory, research, and practice.

As the landscape of leadership practice and developments transitions in the global and digital age, the enduring question of how effective leaders are developed will remain. This study identified five key factors that can inform authentic leadership development. These findings do not suggest that these are the only factors that inform authentic leadership; however, they represent significant factors in its development. Moreover, this study provides reasonable assurance that these factors are critical in the development of authentic leadership because of the diverse age, gender, ethnicities, and career fields of the participants involved in this study. It should be noted that 7 out of the 12 participants had previous military experience, so future research should broaden the scope of participants.

The Five Key Factors in the Development of Authentic Leaders

1. **Authentic Experiences:** Every participant discussed how learning in the workplace through real situational social experiences was most influential in their development as a leader; being part of a group with shared interests to learn and develop new skills and learning from multiple unique situations were also factors that fostered their development.
2. **Feedback:** Every participant mentioned that feedback was a critical factor in their development. A key factor is receiving candid feedback directly from subordinates. Moreover, feedback resulted in immediate reflection as well as changes in leadership behavior and practice. Feedback, reflection, and action on the feedback are lifelong activities for the participants. The participants were not afraid to implement change in their words, actions, or behaviors. All participants were oriented toward learning and self-improvement, and continually and actively sought out feedback to encourage learning and self-improvement.
3. **Reliance on Interactions with Others:** Every participant discussed an experience that involved learning from what Lev Vygotsky refers to as a more knowledgeable other. This included having a positive/negative role model and interacting with different leaders and subordinates that informed who they wanted to be and where they needed to improve.

4. **Fostering Potential:** Every participant described experiences with a good leader who saw their potential and fostered that potential. By working side by side with good leaders, participants were able to glean positive attributes that informed their development as leaders and, in turn, they carried on the tradition of fostering other people's potential.

5. **Value System:** Every participant discussed a value system that served as a guidepost throughout their careers. Participants appear to be anchored in the values that they already hold; these values were established at a young age and were influenced primarily by an immediate family member, such as a father, grandfather, mother, or mother-in-law, or they were established within a social context. The participants' values have evolved into a value system that serves as a guidepost throughout their life and career, by which they make decisions and interact with people, and that they use while presenting themselves.

This qualitative phenomenological research study adds to the body of literature on authentic leadership in the context of how experiences inform this construct. Throughout the authentic leadership literature, there are many propositions regarding how experiences inform the development of leaders into authentic leaders. This study brought to light the significance of lifelong experiences and how these experiences foster the development of authentic leadership over one's lifetime. Moreover, although leadership is inherently dependent upon the dyadic leader–follower relationship, this study revealed the interactive and delicate nature of this relationship through the following: (a) how experiences with positive and negative leadership can influence a follower's future leadership style and (b) how followers can influence a leader's future leadership style. This study demonstrated how authentic leaders take an active role in learning from their experiences. Each positive and negative experience matters to authentic leaders and they are willing to dissect and analyze each experience so that they can learn and pass along those lessons to the next generation of leaders. The uniqueness of experience is that it only takes one good or bad experience to impact a person in a positive or negative way. Therefore, it is important that leaders are aware that just one word or action can make either a positive or negative impact on their followers. This will be a critical understanding for leader effectiveness in the global digital age, in which words and actions can be virtual or occur in different social contexts.

REFERENCES

Akella, D. (2008). Discipline and negotiation: Power in learning organizations. *Global Business Review in Social Work, 9*(2), 219–241. doi:10.1177/097215090800900204

Allen, S. A., & Ofahengaue Vakalahi, H. F. (2013). My team members are everywhere! A critical analysis of the emerging literature on dispersed teams. *Administration in Social Work, 37*(5), 486–493. doi:10.1080/03643107.2013.828002

Avolio, B. J., & Gardner, W. L. (2005, June). Authentic leadership development: Getting to the root of positive forms of leadership. *The Leadership Quarterly, 16*(3), 315–338. doi:10.1016/j.leaqua.2005.03.001

Avolio, B. J., Gardner, W. L., Walumbwa, F. O., Luthans, F., & May, D. R. (2004, December). Unlocking the mask: A look at the process by which authentic leaders impact follower attitudes and behaviors. *The Leadership Quarterly, 15*(6), 801–823. doi:.2004.09.00310.1016/j.leaqua

Avolio, B. J., Walumbwa, F. O., & Weber, T. J. (2009). Leadership: Current theories, research, and future directions. *Annual Review of Psychology, 60*(1), 421–449. doi:10.1146/annurev.psych.60.110707.163621 PMID:18651820

Avolio, B. J., & Wernsing, T. S. (2008). Practicing authentic leadership. In S. J. Lopez (Ed.), *Positive psychology: Exploring the best in people, Volume 4: Pursuing human flourishing* (pp. 147–166). Retrieved from http://www.academia.edu/2319524/Practicing_authentic_leadership

Bierema, L. L., & Merriam, S. G. (2002). E-mentoring: Using computer-mediated communication to enhance the mentoring process. *Innovative Higher Education, 26*(3), 211–227. doi:10.1023/A:1017921023103

Boatman, J., & Wellins, R. S. (2011). *Time for a leadership revolution: Global leadership forecast 2011.* Retrieved from http://www.ddiworld.com/ddi/media/trend-research/ globalleadershipforecast2011_globalreport_ddi.pdf

Branson, C. (2007). Effects of structured self-reflection and on the development of authentic leadership practices among Queensland primary school participants. *Educational Management Administration & Leadership, 35*(2), 225–246. doi:10.1177/1741143207075390

Chan, A., Hannah, S. T., & Gardner, W. L. (2005). Veritable authentic leadership: Emergence, functioning, and impacts. In W. J. Gardner, B. J. Avolio, & F. O. Walumbwa (Eds.), *Authentic leadership theory and practice: Origins, effects and development* (pp. 3–41). Bingley, UK: Emerald Group.

Cianci, A. M., Hannah, S. T., Roberts, R. P., & Tsakumis, G. T. (2014). The effects of authentic leadership on followers' ethical decision-making in the face of temptation: An experimental study. *The Leadership Quarterly, 25*(3), 581–594.

Crotty, M. (1998). *The foundations of social research: Meaning and perspective in the research process.* Thousand Oaks, CA: Sage.

Day, D. V. (2007). *Developing leadership talent.* Retrieved from http://www.shrm.org/about/foundation/ research/documents/developing%20lead%20talent-%20final.pdf

Eagly, A. (2005, June). Achieving relational authenticity in leadership: Does gender matter? *The Leadership Quarterly, 16*(2), 459–474. doi:10.1016/j.leaqua.2005.03.007

Eigel, K. M., & Kuhnert, K. W. (2005). Authentic development: Leadership development level and executive effectiveness. In W. J. Gardner, B. J. Avolio, & F. O. Walumbwa (Eds.), *Authentic leadership theory and practice: Origins, effects and development* (pp. 357–385). Bingley, UK: Emerald Group.

Erickson, R. J. (1995). The importance of authenticity for self and society. *Symbolic Interaction, 18*(2), 121–144. doi:10.1525/si.1995.18.2.121

Fenwick, T. J. (2003). *Learning through experience: Troubling orthodoxies and intersecting questions.* Malabar, FL: Krieger.

Gardner, W. L., Avolio, B. J., Luthans, F., May, D. R., & Walumbwa, F. (2005, June). "Can you see the real me?" A self-based model of authentic leader and follower development. *The Leadership Quarterly, 16*(3), 343–372. doi:10.1016/j.leaqua.2005.03.003

Gardner, W. L., Avolio, B. J., & Walumbwa, F. O. (2005). Authentic leadership development: Emergent themes and future directions. In W. J. Gardner, B. J. Avolio, & F. O. Walumbwa (Eds.), *Authentic leadership theory and practice: Origins, effects and development* (pp. 387–406). Bingley, UK: Emerald Group.

Gardner, W. L., Cogliser, C. C., Davis, K. M., & Dickens, M. P. (2011, December). Authentic leadership: A review of the literature and research agenda. *The Leadership Quarterly, 22*(6), 1120–1145. doi:10.1016/j.leaqua.2011.09.007

Gardner, W. L., Lowe, K. B., Moss, T. W., Mahoney, K. T., & Cogliser, C. C. (2010, December). Scholarly leadership of the study of leadership: A review of the last decade, 2000-2009. *The Leadership Quarterly, 21*(6), 922–958. doi:10.1016/j.leaqua.2010.10.003

George, W. (2003). *Authentic leadership: Rediscovering the secrets to creating lasting value.* San Francisco, CA: Jossey-Bass.

Gergen, K. J. (2009). *An invitation to social construction* (2nd ed.). San Francisco, CA: Sage.

Hannah, S. T., Avolio, B. J., & Walumbwa, F. O. (2011, October). Relationships between authentic leadership, moral courage, and ethical and pro-social behaviors. *Business Ethics Quarterly, 21*(4), 555–578. doi:10.5840/beq201121436

Hannah, S. T., Lester, P. B., & Vogelgesang, G. R. (2005). Moral leadership: Explicating the moral component of authentic leadership. In W. J. Gardner, B. J. Avolio, & F. O. Walumbwa (Eds.), *Authentic leadership theory and practice: Origins, effects and development* (pp. 43–81). Bingley, UK: Emerald Group.

Hinojosa, A. S., McCauley, K. D., Randolph-Seng, B., & Gardner, W. L. (2014, June). Leader and follower attachment styles: Implications for authentic leader–follower relationships. *The Leadership Quarterly, 25*(3), 595–610. doi:10.1016/j.leaqua.2013.12.002

Ilies, R., Morgeson, F. P., & Nahrgang, J. D. (2005, June). Authentic leadership and eudaemonic well-being: Understanding leader–follower outcomes. *The Leadership Quarterly, 16*(3), 373–394. doi:10.1016/j.leaqua.2005.03.002

Illeris, K. (Ed.). (2009). *Contemporary theories of learning.* London: Routledge.

Inceoglu, I., & Bartram, D. (2012). Global leadership: The myth of multicultural competency. *Industrial and Organizational Psychology, 5*(2), 216–218. doi:.2012.01432.x10.1111/j.1754-9434

Jarvis, P. (2009). Lifelong learning: A social ambiguity. In P. Jarvis (Ed.), *The Routledge international handbook of lifelong learning* (pp. 9–18). New York, NY: Routledge.

Jennings, P. L., & Dooley, K. J. (2007). An emerging complexity paradigm in leadership research. In J. K. Hazy, J. A. Goldstein, & B. B. Lichtenstein (Eds.), *Complex systems leadership theory: New perspectives from complexity science on social and organizational effectiveness* (pp. 17–61). Mansfield, MA: ISCE.

Kernis, M. H. (2003). Toward a conceptualization of optimal self-esteem. *Psychological Inquiry, 14*(2), 1–26. doi:10.1207/S15327965PLI1401_01

Knowles, M. S. (1968). Andragogy, not pedagogy. *Adult Leadership, 16*(10), 350–352.

Lord, R. G., & Hall, R. J. (2005, August). Identity, deep structure and the development of leadership skill. *The Leadership Quarterly, 16*(4), 591–615. doi:.06.00310.1016/j.leaqua.2005

Luthans, F., & Avolio, B. J. (2003). Authentic leadership development. In K. S. Cameron, J. E. Dutton, & R. E. Quinn (Eds.), *Positive organizational scholarship: Foundations of a new discipline* (pp. 241–258). San Francisco, CA: Berrett-Koehler.

Luthans, F., Luthans, K. W., & Luthans, B. C. (2004). Positive psychological capital: Beyond human and social capital. *Business Horizons, 47*(1), 45–50. doi:.11.00710.1016/j.bushor.2003

May, D., Chan, A., Hodges, T. D., & Avolio, B. J. (2003). Developing the moral component of authentic leadership. *Organizational Dynamics, 21*(3), 247–260. doi:(03)00032-910.1016/s0090-2616

Meindl, J. R. (1990). On leadership: An alternative to the conventional wisdom. In B. M. Staw & L. L. Cummings (Eds.), *Research in organizational behavior* (Vol. 12, pp. 159–203). Greenwich, CT: JAI.

Merriam, S. B., Cafarella, R. S., & Baumgartner, L. M. (2007). *Learning in adulthood: A comprehensive guide*. San Francisco, CA: Jossey-Bass.

Northouse, P. G. (2010). *Leadership: Theory and practice*. Thousand Oaks, CA: Sage.

O'Bryant, A. (2012). *Cone discusses how TRADOC is shaping army of the future*. Retrieved from http://www.army.mil/article/74403

Pittinsky, T., & Tyson, C. J. (2005). Leader authenticity markers: Findings from a study of perceptions of African American political leaders. In W. L. Gardner, B. J. Avolio, & F. O. Walumbwa (Eds.), *Authentic leadership theory and practice: Origins, effects and development* (pp. 253–280). Bingley, UK: Emerald Group.

Roche, M. (2010). Learning authentic leadership in New Zealand: A learner-centered methodology and evaluation. *American Journal of Business Education, 3*(3), 7–79. Retrieved from http://www.cluteinstitute.com/ojs/index.php/AJBE/article/view/401/390

Rosenthal, S. A. (2012). *National Leadership Index 2012: A national study of confidence in leadership*. Cambridge, MA: Harvard University, Harvard Kennedy School, Center for Public Leadership.

Ryan, R. M., & Deci, E. L. (2002). On assimilating identities to the self: A self-determination theory perspective on internalization and integrity within cultures. In M. R. Leary & J. P. Tangney (Eds.), *Handbook of self and identity* (pp. 255–273). New York, NY: The Guilford Press.

Shamir, B., & Eilam, G. (2005, June). "What's your story?" A life-stories approach to authentic leadership development. *The Leadership Quarterly, 16*(3), 395–417. doi:. leaqua.2005.03.00510.1016/j

Smith, J. K. (2002). Malcolm Knowles, informal adult education, self-direction and andragogy. In *The encyclopedia of informal education*. Retrieved from http://www.infed.org/ thinkers/et-knowl.htm

Sparrowe, R. T. (2005, June). Authentic leadership and the narrative self. *The Leadership Quarterly, 16*(3), 419–439. doi:10.1016/j.leaqua.2005.03.004

Walumbwa, F. O., Avolio, B. J., Gardner, W. L., Wernsing, T. S., & Peterson, S. J. (2008). Authentic leadership: Development and validation of a theory-based measure. *Journal of Management, 34*(1), 89–126. doi:10.1177/0149206307308913

Wang, L., James, K. T., Denyer, D., & Bailey, C. (2014). Western views and Chinese whispers: Rethinking global leadership competency in multi-national corporations. *Leadership, 10*(4), 471–495. doi:10.1177/1742715013510340

Witt, E. (2011). *Authentic leadership in the college setting* [Review of the book *Authentic leadership theory and practice: Origins, effects, and development*, by W. L. Gardner, B. J. Avolio, & F. O. Walumbwa]. Retrieved from https://nclp.umd.edu/resources/bookreviews/bookreview-authentic_leadership-witt-2011.pdf

World Economic Forum. (2014). *Global agenda councils: Outlook on the global agenda 2015*. Retrieved from http://reports.weforum.org/outlook-global-agenda-2015/wp-content/ blogs.dir/59/mp/files/pages/files/outlook-2015-a4-downloadable.pdf

Zhu, W., May, D. R., & Avolio, B. J. (2004). The impact of ethical leadership behavior on employee outcomes: The roles of psychological empowerment and authenticity. *Journal of Leadership & Organizational Studies, 11*(1), 16–26. doi:10.1177/107179190401100104

ADDITIONAL READING

Begley, P. T. (2001). In pursuit of authentic school leadership practices. *International Journal of Leadership in Education, 4*(4), 353–365. doi:10.1080/13603120110078043

Clayton, H. (2012). The changing leadership landscape. *Strategic HR Review, 11*(2), 78–83. doi:10.1108/14754391211202134

Derue, S. D., & Ashford, S. J. (2010). Who will lead and who will follow? A social process of leadership identity construction in organizations. *Academy of Management Review, 35*(4), 627–647. doi:10.5465/AMR.2010.53503267

Hoy, W., & Henderson, J. (1983). Principal authenticity, school climate, and pupil-control orientation. *Alberta Journal of Educational Research, 29*(2), 123–130. Retrieved from ERIC database. (EJ28575)

Ryan, R. M., & Deci, E. L. (2003). On assimilating identities to the self: A self-determination theory perspective on internalization and integrity within cultures. In M. R. Leary & J. P. Tangney (Eds.), *Handbook of self and identity* (pp. 253–272). New York, NY: The Guilford Press.

Yammarino, F. J., Dionne, S. D., Schriesheim, C. A., & Dansereau, F. (2008, December). Authentic leadership and positive organizational behavior: A meso, multi-level perspective. *The Leadership Quarterly, 19*(6), 693–707. doi:. 00410.1016/j.leaqua.2008.09

KEY TERMS AND DEFINITIONS

Adult Learning: The art and science of helping adults learn through self-directed methods.

Authentic Experience: An experience that is emergent, unscripted, and unique, and when reflected upon serves as a learning tool for adults.

Authentic Leadership: An emerging and popular leadership style that is based on the premise that a leader has an authentic core that guides their actions, behaviors, and decisions.

Authentic Leadership Development: An adult learning perspective whereby authentic leadership, as a leadership style, can be developed over time primarily through experiences.

Authenticity: The belief that one's inner thoughts, beliefs, and feelings align with outer presentation and behaviors and guides an individual's daily action.

E-Mentoring: Mentoring using a computer-mediated relationship between a more skilled individual who is the mentor, and a lesser skilled individual who is the protégé.

Feedback: The process of one person reacting to another person's behavior, performance, or actions and verbalizing the reaction.

Globalization: The concept of businesses, technologies, and resources being spread across the world.

Informal Learning: An adult learning concept, which recognizes that learning can occur through everyday experiences.

Value System: A collection of personal and social values that exists in an individual's mind that guides their daily action.

Chapter 14
Investigating the Adult Learners' Experience when Solving Mathematical Word Problems

Ellen Brook
Cuyahoga Community College, USA

ABSTRACT

The purpose of the study was to describe the experiences adult learners have while solving mathematical word problems. The focus of the study was on how these adult students used prior mathematical knowledge and how their past experiences with mathematics influenced their solving of mathematics word problems. The study found that the attitudes, feelings and beliefs that adult students in the study hold toward mathematics and problem solving are an integral part of their mathematics learning experience. This study also reports on the particular pattern observed within the participants' attitude toward mathematics education during their schooling years beginning from elementary school till college. The adult students participated in the study lacked the necessary knowledge of such concepts as motion and concentration. Finally, the study found that even after learning the topic during the college class, the participants had difficulties with applying algebraic approaches to word problem solving.

Because learning transforms who we are and what we can do, it is an experience of identity. It is not just an accumulation of skills and information, but a process of becoming. (Wenger, 2004, p. 215)

The single most important reason to teach mathematics is that it is an ideal discipline for training students how to think. (Schoenfeld, 1982, p. 32)

DOI: 10.4018/978-1-5225-0522-8.ch014

INTRODUCTION

Difficulties Experienced by Adults Learning Mathematics

I would like to begin with providing some information on the studies in adult mathematics education. These studies found that the numeracy proficiency of 58.6% of U.S. adults was below level 3, the minimum level needed for managing today's working and living requirements (Statistic Canada and OECD, 2005). Furthermore, the quantitative literacy skills of 55% of U.S. adults are at a Basic or Below Basic level (NCES, 2006). The economic impact of having low numeracy skills has been reported by the Adult Literacy and Lifeskills Survey (ALL). U. S. adults performing at numeracy levels 1 and 2 (the lowest of five levels) are about three times more likely to receive social assistance payments from the state than those who score in levels 3, 4, or 5 (Statistics Canada and OECD, 2005). The Adult Literacy and Lifeskills Survey (OECD, 2005), examined adults numeracy skills in the context of daily life and work across seven countries, including the United State, and showed that those with low numeracy skill levels are more likely to be unemployed for six months longer that those at higher levels and three times more likely to receive social assistance payments. In 2009, passing rates on the GED mathematics exam were the lowest among the five academic subjects tests (American Council on Education, 2010).

Additionally, about 60 percent of community college students in the United States are referred to take developmental courses since these students are deemed insufficiently prepared to start college-level work (Attewell, Lavin, Domina, & Levey, 2006; Bailey, Jeong, & Cho, 2010). Mathematics classes in particular are a common roadblock for a large proportion of the community college student population (Achieving the Dream, 2006c). Approximately two of three community college students referred to a remedial mathematics sequence do not complete it (Bailey et al., 2010). According to a U.S. Department of Education study (Adelman, 2004), the three courses with the highest rates of failure and withdrawal in postsecondary education are developmental mathematics courses. About 50% of the thousands of individuals interviewed for the National Adult Literacy Survey, including numerous persons holding high school and college credentials, have major difficulties with quantitative literacy (Nesbit, 1996). This data reveals that the adult numeracy issue in the United States is severe, and its negative effects fall far beyond the classroom.

BACKGROUND

The Importance and Necessity of Teaching Mathematics to Adult Learners

I began working with adults in mathematics education a decade ago. During this time, as a teacher, I experienced both success and failure. My aspiration to help my adult students gain knowledge in mathematics and apply it in their lives influenced my decision to research adult mathematics education.

John Dewey began writing about the concept of adult education in 1916 (FitzSimons, 2001). Since that time, the quickly changing aspects of modern society, the more public existence led by individuals, and the increasing educational demands of employers have elevated the topic's significance. Educationally, adult learning is seen as a foundation of personal development and growth, a way of enhancing an individual's life. Economically, adult education is the way to become commercially competitive and to provide sufficiently for one's life style. Politically, lifelong learning can be seen as a carrier for social strength and integrity.

My personal and professional beliefs and inspirations resonate with the 1996 UNESCO Report *Learning: The Treasure Within* in which the following observation was made: "Education is at the heart of both personal and community development; its mission is to enable each of us, without exceptions, to develop all our talents to the full and to realize our creative potentials, including responsibility for our own lives and achievement of our personal aims" (FitzSimons, 2001, p.1).

It is imperative that mathematics education should be part of adult education since there is hardly a single human being around the world who is not using quantitative reasoning in everyday life (Gal, 2000; Ginsburg, Manly, & Schmitt, 2006). Thus, the importance of research in adult math education is growing constantly. Johansen (2002) presented the following grounds for teaching mathematics to adults: (a) to assure the demands of the modern information society, (b) to satisfy the demands of the labor market, (c) to provide individuals with the skills needed to lead an adequate social and private life. All the reasons stated above are clearly connected to the main motive for providing an education to any individual – to contribute to the development of the human society. The United States National Literacy Act of 1991 stated that literacy is an "individual ability to read, write, and speak, and to compute and solve problems at levels of proficiency necessary to function on the job and in society, to achieve one's goals, and develop one's knowledge and potential" (Gal, 2000, p. 9).

It is also vital to understand that many adult learners report negative attitudes about learning mathematics that affect their mathematics education (Gal, 2000; Tobias, 1993; Evans, 2000; DeBellis & Goldin, 2006). Those perceptions are generally attributed to the negative prior experiences they have had in a mathematics classroom (Tobias, 1993). As I have seen during my years of teaching adults, such attitudes and beliefs commonly obstruct the development of new math-related skills and severely affect test performance. The negative attitudes also impact the metacognitive habits. Consequently, one of the goals of adult mathematics education is to overcome our students' math anxiety, unproductive beliefs about the relevance of mathematics to real-life, and negative self-perceptions.

Mathematical Problem Solving

The NCTM *Standards* (1989, 2000) and the reform movement that followed emphasized that the view of "mathematics as problem solving" should be a key process standard in mathematics education. A number of years ago, a taskforce of the Adult Numeracy Practitioners Network (ANN) in the United States presented a framework describing numeracy skills needed to "equip learners for the future" (Curry, 1996). Building on the NCTM *Standards,* this project indentified seven themes that should serve as fundamentals or standards for adult numeracy (the term used for adult mathematics education) as well as a consequential need for adults to become confident in their knowledge. One of them is Problem Solving. This idea has also been expressed by the American Mathematical Association of two-Year Colleges (AMATYC), whose *Crossroads in Mathematics: Standards for Introductory College Mathematics before Calculus* (1995) named Problem Solving as the first standard for intellectual development. Nevertheless, according to Lester (1994):

It is safe to say that since the publication of the Agenda (An Agenda for Action, NCTM, 1980), problem solving has been the most written about, but possibly the least understood, topic in the mathematics curriculum in the United States (p.661).

Word Problem Solving

Within the general topic of problem solving much recent attention has been paid to the ubiquitous tradition of word problems. A word problem in mathematics teaching refers to an authentic or possible situation in an everyday context (Wyndhamn & Saljo, 1997). In spite of this long tradition in educational practice, the international research in the field of school mathematics filled with evidence that word problems do not fulfill these functions well. By the end of elementary school, many students do not see the applicability of their formal mathematical knowledge to real-world situations (Nesher, 1980); they do not have adequate use of heuristic and metacognitive strategies (De Corte, 1992; Greer, 1993); lastly they seem to dislike mathematics in general and word problems in particular (McLeod, 1992). The National Council of Teachers of Mathematics in their three standard documents (NCTM 1980, 1989, 2000), deemphasize traditional "word problems" where formulas and tables provide formulaic solutions. Instead they recommend a well-developed "operational sense" for deciding which procedures should be applied for practical problem solving.

Purpose of the Research

The purpose of the study was to understand and describe the experiences adult learners have while solving mathematical word problems in order to better understand the diverse beliefs and cognitive meanings of algebraic thinking of adult learners when attempting to solve word problems in order to provide teachers with new approaches to teach algebra in general and solving mathematical word problems in particular.

Research Questions

1. What attitudes and beliefs do adult students hold regarding mathematics education in general and word problem solving in particular?
2. What mathematical content knowledge do adult learners access when solving word problems?
3. What strategies do adult learners use to solve word problems?

LITERATURE REVIEW

In developing this chapter, information was sought from authors with background in mathematics education, adult education, problem solving, and word problems.

Adult Mathematics Education

Due to the progress of modern society, more and more attention is focused on adult mathematics education (Ginsburg, Manly, & Schmitt, 2006). At the same time, overwhelming public opinion of the discipline labels it as exclusive, abstract, inhuman and cold (Cockcroft, 1982). Very often it is viewed as importance- and culture-free. In addition, the subject is perceived as difficult and having significance relevant only to itself.

The method of instruction in the field of adult mathematics education focuses on technique, thus being deficient in connectedness or historicity (Tobias, 1990). Adult math education that is based on rote-learning and drill and practice is unrelated to real world application and to the learners' experience (Nesbit, 1995). In addition, there is a breach between the application-based, problem-solving approach required on the job and the traditional basic set of skills in educational curriculum (Buckingham, 1997; FitzSimons, 1998; Strasser, 1998).

As regards socio-psychological issues, there are a number of studies (Swindell, 1995; Kasworm, 1990; Gal, 2000) reporting on indirect deficiency of adult learners such as negative prior educational experiences, lack of motivation, and study skills. Kasworm (1990) also reported that chronological age of a learner is not the crucial variable. He stated that rather life experience, previous education, socio-cultural context, and attitude are more important. Considering affective domain to be one of the most important variables in the learning process, it is vital to see that at the same time surveys of attitude and beliefs of adult students showed that it may not be possible for many people to ever learn mathematics easily and effectively, or to find it interesting (Davis, 1996; Taylor, 1995; Agar & Knopfmacher, 1995). In addition, Wedege (2003) reported the apparent contradiction demonstrated by adults having difficulties with mathematics in formal educational settings, but who perform competently in everyday quantitative situations.

Teaching Mathematics to Adult Learners

To discuss teaching mathematics to adults, I want to recall that according to Knowles (1990), the term andragogy, which was coined in Europe in 1833, is understood as the "art and science of helping adults learn" (p. 54). Knowles argued that there is a distinction between pedagogy and andragogy. The first one is the theory of teaching children or youth, in which the teachers traditionally would assume full responsibility for making decisions about the learning process. His model of andragogy may include some conjectures from pedagogy, but not vice versa. Knowles (1990) recommended that teachers of adults become aware of their students' backgrounds, readiness to learn, previous experiences, self-concept, and motivation. Barnes (1994) suggested considering students' goals, values, and beliefs about the nature and purpose of mathematics. Ginsburg and Gal (1997) argued for the importance of developing students' reasoning skills, built on their extensive informal knowledge of mathematics and suggested authentic real-life problems to solve.

Baker (2001) presented two main theories of pedagogy being used in the field of adult mathematics education. The first is the traditional model. This model originated with the work of John B. Watson and of Ivan Pavlov. Behaviorists defined learning as an acquisition of a new behavior. According to this theory, knowledge exists outside of individuals and can be conveyed from an instructor to a student. In spite of the fact that this model has been in practice for decades, many math educators recognized the flaws in the Behaviorist movement. Behaviorists degraded such attributes of a human mind as uniqueness, perception, and construction. The traditional approach still widely used by educators and publishers, works for only an insignificant portion of the population who easily learn by "abstraction and symbolic manipulation" (Baker, 2001, p. 394). According to Gordon (1993), the traditional lecture approach and assessment practices prevented non-traditional students from learning efficiently. So, the second model, constructivism, came to light.

Constructivism is a philosophy of learning founded on the premise that human beings construct their own understanding by reflecting on their experience (Baker, 2001; Goldin, 1990, 2004; Lerman, 1989). Constructivism can be traced to the eighteenth century and the work of the philosopher Giambattista

Vico, who maintained that humans could understand only what they have themselves constructed. A great many philosophers and educationalists have worked with these ideas, but the first major contemporaries to develop a clear scheme of what constructivism involves were Jean Piaget, Lev Vygotsky, and John Dewey. Under Constructivism educators teach their students to analyze, understand, and predict information. Within the paradigm, the accent is on the learner rather than the teacher. In 1989, The National Council of Teachers of Mathematics (NCTM) took steps towards reform, releasing the new standards in mathematics education for K-12. Such reform was extended in 1995 to adult learners with the publication of *Crossroads in Mathematics: Standards for Introductory Mathematics before Calculus*. This work is based on the modern constructivist theory.

Study of Affect

When we approach the problem of the interrelation between thought and language and other aspects of the mind, the first question that arises is that of intellect and affect. Their separation as subjects of study is a major weakness of traditional psychology. (Vygotsky, 1962, p.10)

Affect includes different feelings (conscious as well as unconscious) during mathematical problem solving. McLeod (1992) presented three types of affect: beliefs, attitudes, and emotions. The major finding of the research was that the individual emotional state can enhance cognition (for example, through mathematical curiosity) or impede it (for example, through math anxiety).

In regard to beliefs and dispositions, Schoenfeld (1992) presented the following list of common beliefs that have strong (often negative) influences on mathematical thinking:

- Math problems have one and only one right answer.
- There is only one correct way to solve any mathematics problem –usually the rule the teacher has most recently demonstrated to the class.
- Ordinary students cannot expect to understand mathematics; they expect simply to memorize it and apply what they have learned mechanically without understanding.
- Math is a solitary activity, done by individuals in isolation.
- Students who have understood the mathematics they have studied will be able to solve any assigned problem in three minutes or less.
- The mathematics learned in school has little or nothing to do with the real world.
- Formal proof is irrelevant to the processes of discovery or invention.

Schoenfeld (1992) also argued that the students' beliefs about formal mathematics and their sense of the discipline are based in large measure on their experiences in the classroom. Those beliefs shape students' behavior in very powerful ways that have extraordinary consequences.

In relation to affective issues of adult students, Gal (2000) and McLeod (1992) argued that how well a numeracy situation is managed depends not only on the knowledge of mathematical rules and operations and linguistic skills, but also on the students' beliefs, attitudes, metacognitive habits and skills, self-concept, and feelings about the situation. According to Evans (2000), affect in general, and mathematical anxiety in particular, were considered as relatively established characteristics of an adult learner which have an ongoing effect on mathematical thinking, performance, and participation in mathematics courses. He argued that there is a positive correlation between affect and cognitive outcomes across all students.

Mathematical Problem Solving

Research in mathematics education is relatively young with the earliest work being conducted in the mid-1930s (Lesh & Zawojewski, 2006). Furthermore, the work directed at mathematical problem solving (word problems in particular) began in 1960s. Even considering not such a long period of time, the field of problem solving went through some considerable changes. Polya's ideas, presenting a whole problem solving strategy a while ago, now became only a part of a much bigger picture. The change in the field in mathematics education as well the change in the perception of problem solving goes parallels the changes in people's lives in modern society. According to the National Research Council (1999, cited in Lesh & Zawojewski, 2006),

Changing technologies will continue to alter skills and eliminate jobs at a rapid rate. Although skill requirements for some jobs may be reused, the net effects of changing technologies are more likely to raise skill requirements and change them in ways that give greater emphasis to cognitive, communications and interactive. (p.780)

There is a necessity for people to adapt and create mathematics for use in everyday environment. Consequently, there is a new perspective on problem solving that emerges. There is also evidence growing on de-emphasizing "transfer" of learning but moving instead toward dynamically interrelated and complex intellectual, emotional, and social processes of acquiring quantitative understanding and developing mathematical problem solving skills. Part of it is instinctive thinking skills available to all normal adults. There is no movement of intellectual resources. It is the individual learner that moves from one intellectual level to another. The environment within which the problem-solving abilities grow is always socially interactive and emotionally charged.

There is also the difference between the mathematics of school and of the workplace that is critical to a new perspective to problem solving (MSEB, 1998; Oakes, Rud, & Gainsburg, 2003; Magajna & Monaghan, 2003, cited in Lesh and Zawojewski). This difference is leading to mathematics modeling consistently emerging as one of the most important types of activities.

Research on Word Problem Solving

There are two major types of research on word problems. The first one focuses on individual cognition and competences for decoding textual information into symbols and obtaining correct answers. The second one focuses on the connection of word problem-solving and real-life quantitative situations.

From the cognitive perspective, mathematical word problem-solving processes begin with reading of the problem's text (Nathan et al., 1992). The next step is forming an object-based or mental model based on prior knowledge and continuing processing of the text elements. Those models may involve real or pictorial external representations that facilitate the development of mental images or internal representations of problem elements and their relationships. Thus, an active model is constructed through active transformation of the text base, activation of problem-type schemas, and integration of the problem elements within those schemas. Success or failure depends largely on the coherence of the mental representation formed (Pape, 2004; Kintsch & Greeno, 1985; Nathan et al., 1992) and the ability to control and change the problem-solving process (Schoenfeld, 1992). In addition, when solving word problems, people are required to move between diverse linguistic and symbolic codes (Wyndhamn & Saljo, 1997).

The research shows that students experience difficulties with aligning the semantics and syntactic of everyday language with the structure of formal mathematical reasoning (Wyndhamn & Saljo, 1997).

There are several factors (variables) in constituting difficulties students encounter with algebraic and arithmetic word problems and consequently impacting students' performance. One of them is the classification of word problems or the type of problem situation (De Corte & Verschaffel, 1988; Greeno & Heller, 1983; Greer, 1993; Nesher, 1982; Riley & Fuson, 1992; Vergnaud, 1982; Dewolf, Van Dooren, & Verschaffel, 2011; Verschaffel, 2012). The other factors are the exact phrasing of the problem, the particular numbers used, and the age and instructional background of the students. According to De Corte, Verschaffel, and De Win (1985), linguistic knowledge of a student is one of the variables of the word problem-solving outcome. They stated that rewording a problem so that the described relation is made more explicit makes the construction of an appropriate problem representation easier. Cummins (1991), Okamoto (1996), and Pape (2004) stated that students' failure to solve certain types of word problems is related to students' difficulties in comprehending the abstract language of mathematics. Moyer, Sowder, Threadgill and Moyer (1984) reported that readers of high ability in grades 3 through 7, as measured by a reading test, are more successful when solving word problems than low-ability readers. Ballew and Cunningham (1982) did a study that involved sixth graders solving word problems. The profile of each student consisted of the following four scores: computation score, problem interpretation score, reading-problem interpretation, and reading problem-solving score. Ballew and Cunningham (1982) stated that since all four components are vital for successful word problem solving, the lack of at least one leads to a failure. In the study only 19 of the 217 students had all four scores thus having solved the problems correctly.

When studying junior high school students solving algebraic word problems, Koedinger and Nathan (2004) observed that using multiple representations such as tables, graphs, and equations increases the possibility of obtaining the right answer. While doing similar research, Kieran (2007) added that generating an equation to represent the relationships is the area of difficulty for algebra students across the ages. Middle and high school students' preference for arithmetic reasoning and their difficulties with equations while solving algebraic word problems were reported by Bednarz and Janvier (1996), Cortes (1998), and Swafford and Langrall (2000).

Stacey and MacGregor (2000) propose that a major reason for difficulty is not misunderstanding the logic of solving a problem by algebra, but the deflection from the algebraic path grounded in arithmetic problem solving methods. Students in their study (aged 13-16) comprehended the problems but most did not formulate equations. Instead they tried to use a sequence of calculations to obtain the answer. The same has been reported by Herskovics and Linchevski (1994). Stacey and MacGregor (2000) also reported on difficulties students have with understanding the concept of 'an equation" as an equivalent relationship, not just a formula or a procedure (p.151). There is a students' belief that problems are solved by direct calculation instead of applying analytic methods. This impulse prevents students from looking for, selecting, and naming the appropriate unknown (s) and, consequently, in formulating an equation. Algebraic thinking does not develop spontaneously and students are unlikely to switch from an arithmetic approach unless they are specifically taught (Stacey & MacGregor, 2000; Verschaffel, 2012). Johanning (2004) when reporting on students' informal strategies while solving word problems observed systematic guess and check along with unwinding (working backwards).

There is evidence that adult students experience difficulties solving word problems as well (Ginsburg, et al., 2006). Working with science-oriented college students, Clement (1982) reported that a large proportion of the students were unable to solve a very simple kind of algebra word problem. While 99% of a group of freshmen engineering students solved the linear equation $5x = 50$ and $6/4=30/x$ correctly, only 27% of them did ratio/proportion word problem. Data obtained from the group testing indicated that a significant number of college students produce reversal errors in formulating algebraic equations of this kind. The sources for those errors are syntactic, that is, word order matching and semantic that is a static symbolization process. Those results lead to a concern about the extent to which students understand how equations are used to symbolize meanings.

In addition, Lee (1996) argued that the children's and adults' word problems solving techniques are not identical. When looking at the behavior of adults as well as high school students during word problem solving, she concluded that for both groups observed, using the algebraic language was extremely difficult. The qualitative responses of the adult students and those of the high school students were almost identical as well. Nevertheless, it was the interview behavior of the adult students that revealed some differences with their high school counterparts. During the interview, adults showed less concern about putting some algebra down on their papers and did not go off on meaningless algebraic manipulations to the same extent as high school students. Adults demonstrated a similar, if not greater, inability to use algebra and to do generalization. None were able to let X be any number while attempting to solve word problems and were troubled by word associations or misunderstandings.

Word Problems Solving and Informal Real Life Mathematics

According to Lave (1988), Saxe (1991), and Schliemann and Acioly (1989), there is evidence that individuals perform at lower levels of their ability when solving formal mathematical word problems rather than solving quantitative problems presented by real life situations. In a study by Verschaffel, De Corte, and Lazure (1994) seventy five 11to 12-year-old students were collectively given a word problem test involving multiplication and division problems in an ordinary mathematics classroom context. Besides standard problems in which the relationship between the situation and the corresponding mathematical operation is simple and straightforward, the test contained parallel versions of these problems in which the mathematical modeling assumptions are problematic. For this latter type of problem, only a small minority of the students was successful. Similar results for 13 to14-year-old students have been reported by Greer (1993). These findings convincingly demonstrated that considerable experience with traditional school mathematics word problems develops in students a strong inclination to exclude real world knowledge and reasonable contemplation from their solution process. The instructional implication of this finding is that "the impoverished diet of standard word problems currently offered in mathematics classrooms, should be replaced -- or at the least supplemented -- by a wide variety of problems that draw students' attention to realistic modeling, so that they do not implicitly learn that if there are two numbers in the problem, the answer will be found by adding, subtracting, multiplying or dividing these two numbers" (Greer, 1993, p. 292). Greer (1997) and Verschaffel (2012) also commented on a very widespread tendency of children to answer school mathematics word problems with evident disrespect for the reality of the situations described by the text of these problems. Analysis of this behavior strongly suggests that the reason for it is not a cognitive deficit of the children, but rather in the culture of the classroom where word problems are presented in stereotyped fashion, with an assumption that the application of one or more of the basic arithmetical or algebraic operations to the numbers given is appropriate.

METHODOLOGY AND FINDINGS OF THE STUDY

Qualitative Research and Multiple Case Studies as the Chosen Paradigm

Qualitative research focuses on processes, meanings, and the socially constituted nature of individual reality, and provides insights into the phenomena being studied that cannot be revealed by other types of inquiry. It is primarily concerned with human understanding, interpretation, intersubjectivity, and lived truth. Its aim is to record phenomena in terms of participant understanding (Teppo, 1998).

Case study is "an empirical inquiry that investigates a contemporary phenomenon within its real-life context, especially when the boundaries between phenomenon and context are not clearly evident (Yin, 1995). Merriam (2009) defined it in terms of the *end product*: "A qualitative case study is an intensive, holistic description and analysis of a single instance, phenomenon, or social unit". Qualitative case studies are *particularistic, descriptive,* and *heuristic*. This study is *particularistic* since it focuses on a particular phenomenon—adult students solving mathematical word problems. This study is *descriptive* since the end product is a "thick" description of the phenomenon under study. The description presents documentation of the events, artifacts, and quotes. This study is *heuristic* due to the fact that it concludes with my understanding of the phenomenon under study. Since the study offers a cross-case analysis suggesting generalizations about adult students and the process they use to solve word problems from the individual case studies, it results in a multiple case study format.

The research sample consisted of students taking a Beginning Algebra class at a Midwestern community college. The sample was *purposeful* as well as *convenient*.

Beginning Algebra was chosen for the study as the course where the topic of solving word problems is being taught.

Table 1. Participants in the Study

Name in the Study	Race, Gender	Age	Previous Degree	Prior Math Classes
Liz	BF	42	High School Diploma	Algebra and Geometry
Mina	WF	30	Licensure in the Massage Therapy	Algebra
John	BM	42	GED	Business Math
Ron	BM	46	High School Diploma	Business Math
Jana	BF	38	Associate Degree in Fashion Merchandizing	Algebra
Ken	WM	50	High School Diploma	Algebra
Rocky	BF	19	High School Diploma	Algebra, Geometry
Raul	BM	29	High School Diploma	Algebra, Geometry
Kate	BF	50	BA Psychology	Calculus (unfinished)
Martin	WM	26	High School Diploma	Algebra, Geometry
Tom	WM	31	High School Diploma	Algebra
Lora	BF	19	High School Diploma	Algebra, Geometry
Nell	WF	30	LNP	Business Math
Sarah	WF	19	High School Diploma	Algebra, Geometry
Tammy	BF	29	Associate in Culinary Art	Algebra and Geometry
Sal	WM	46	High School Diploma	Algebra

Data Collection

- In-depth, semi structured task-based (also called clinical) oral interviews about and during participants' problem solving activities. These interviews were video/audio tape recorded and then transcribed.
- Participant observation; that is, observing the participants in an actual problem-solving situation.
- A documentary study in which the writings, diagrams, graphs, etc. of the participants were reviewed to derive "meanings" from them. Examination of the artifacts was used in conjunction with the interviews and observations.

Word Problems Offered to the Participants during the Interviews

The two word problems were offered during the first interview (before the section on problem solving was taught) were:

Motion Problem I: *Two planes leave the same airport at the same time, flying in opposite directions. The rate of the faster plane is 300 miles per hour. The rate of the slower plane is 200 miles per hour. After how many hours will the planes be 1000 miles apart?*

and

Mixture Problem I: *How many ounces of a 50% alcohol solution must be mixed with 80 ounces of a 20% alcohol solution to make a 40% alcohol solution?*

The two word problems were offered during the second interview (after the section on problem solving was taught) were:

Motion Problem II: *How many ounces of a 15% alcohol solution must be mixed with 4 ounces of a 20% alcohol solution to make 17% alcohol solution?*

and

Mixture Problem II: *Two cities are 315 miles apart. A car leaves one of the cities traveling toward the second city at 50 miles per hour. At the same time, a bus leaves the second city bound for the first city at 55 miles per hour. How long will it take to for them to meet?*

Findings of the Study in Regard of the Attitudes and Beliefs of Adult Students toward Mathematics Education

- The attitudes, feelings and beliefs that the participants in the study hold toward mathematics and problem solving are an integral part of their mathematics learning experience.
- This relationship is rather dynamic, since there is a pattern in adult students' attitudes toward mathematics education that involves their experiences in adolescence and how those experiences transcend into their secondary education. Contentment and feelings of confidence while in an

elementary school arithmetic environment were replaced by discontent and lack of success in a secondary school algebraic environment. This feeling was ultimately replaced by determination in the college algebraic environment. This newfound commitment to academic success is often based on the students' need to improve their economic situation and the realization that the mathematics courses are the hoops they must jump through to obtain the degree and/or the life style they are striving for.

Data Supporting the Finding

When asked about their Elementary School/Arithmetic experience, the students replied:

Liz: *I remember my fourth grade; I was pretty good at math.*
Mina: *I was OK in class.*
John: *In elementary school I was pretty average in math.*
Jana: *When I was young, I liked math at that point of my life. Going to school and math was fine.*

When asked about their Middle/High School/Algebra, they commented:

Liz: *Math became more consuming. It was like I don't need this math. Friends meeting were more important.*
Mina: *It was negative experience...judgmental teacher's attitude... difficulty with algebraic concepts.*
Jana: *I started to dislike math. I didn't like school at all. I didn't see why I need it [mathematics] if we have calculators.*
Ken: *At that point I thought I was going to become a minister, so, why do I need it [algebra] in the field I am going to?*

The students' comments regarding the present time/Community College were:

Jan: *... I got embarrassed when was unable to help my niece with math homework... I feel excited and proud when I understand the material.*
Nell: *Having a goal is the reason I am succeeding in my math class.*

Findings of the Study in Regard to Adult Students' Attitudes toward Solving Word Problems

The participants expressed having difficulties with algebraic concepts in general and word problems in particular. Some students' comments were:

Mina: *It [solving word problems] was always difficult for me.*
Rocky: *Word problems are difficult...it requires a lot of concentration.*
Raul: *It [word problems] is sometimes difficult to understand.*
Martin: *It is easier with numbers. In my head a letter cannot be a number.*

Findings of the study in regard to the Content Knowledge Adult Learners Access Solving Word Problems

The majority of the participants in the study were not ready to tackle the traditional word problems offered in beginning algebra courses. The lack of cognitive resources (such as the deficiency of knowledge of basic science including the formula $D = RT$ and the concept of concentrations) and control strategies (such as metacognition) prevented further success for the participants. In addition, the majority of the participants displayed no transfer of learning between the classroom and everyday activities.

Some students' comments supporting this notion were:

Mina identified the formula D=RT as "distance, rate, and time."

John and Ron stated the formula, but failed to apply it correctly.

Jana said "I am sure there is a connection [between time, rate and the distance], but I don't know what the formula would be. It is probably distance times time equals speed."

Mina, Liz, Ron, Tammy, and John failed to see the problem as simultaneous motion of two vehicles and, consequently, attempted to calculate the time needed for each vehicle to cover the distance given. When asked to solve a concrete problem about the 50% alcohol solution, half of the participants were able to state that 50% means half, but were not able to define the ingredients of such a solution. When the entire participant group was asked to calculate the total amount and to approximate the possible concentration of the mixture of two given solutions, the students properly calculated the total amount as the sum of the original amounts, but only two participants approximated the resultant concentration as the average of the given ones. The rest of the group added the percentages as well and didn't express any concern about the consequential percentage being above 100%. When asked to approximate the concentration of the mixture of 50% and 70% solutions, Mina said, "I would say it would be between 20% and 30%". Ron identified percent as "[It is] a portion of, very small portion, point one zero, point zero one, one of a tenth." Tom identified "twenty percent alcohol solution" as "it is eighty and twenty, eighty is alcohol." Lora identified "50% alcohol solution" as "the whole bottle of alcohol solution, so it is 50% of that. I equated 50 with half, so it will be another 50 that we are not using."

This research project is unique because the participants showed weakness in solving word problems in the specific conceptual areas – motion and concentration. The concepts of motion and concentration are authentic to real life. The participants do drive and they do work with mixtures such as cooking and shopping in their everyday life.

Findings of the Study regarding the Evolution of the Answer

Most of the participants failed to obtain a reasonable answer when solving the word problems during the first interview. In addition, the participants who were able to solve the given problems by an equation during the second interview were not able to explain their method of solving the problem or why they chose the method.

During the first interview, Mina, John, Tina, and Tammy failed to use the formula D=RT and were not able to solve the problem. Liz, Rocky, Tom, Sarah, and Ron presented the formula but failed to apply it correctly, thus producing no correct answer either. Ken, Sal, and Jana presented the arithmetic value of the answer correctly, but were not able to explain logically how they derived it. Raul, Martin, John, Liz, and Lora failed to model the problem as the simultaneous motion of two moving objects, consequently obtaining an incorrect answer.

During the second interview half of the students solved the motion problem and obtained the correct answer. When students who solved the problem algebraically were asked to explain their equations, they cited the procedure instead of the meaning. The comments were:

Kate: *Because it is the equation. I don't really know. I just got it from class.*
Lora: *We were definitely told in class to put 55 times x.*
Mina: *I remember the formula shown in class.*

The exclusive findings of the study pointed out that the adult students, similar to the widespread tendency of children, also answer school mathematics word problems irrespective of the reality of the situations described by the text of these problems. In addition, they derive the answer by following a procedure rather than truly understanding a problem.

Findings of the Study Regarding the Approaches for Solving Word Problems and the Reasoning and Thinking when Solving Word Problems

- The data collected revealed that prior to any formal instruction in dealing with solving these types of problems, students used informal/arithmetic strategies in solving the problems.
- After formal instructions, some but not all students attempted to use the algebraic methods/solving by equation they were taught in class. The rest of the students still attempted to solve the problems arithmetically.
- The participants who attempted to employ the representations used letter-symbolic representations, such as variables and equations, over graphical, such as pictures and graphs.
- The students who used letter-symbolic representations and graphical ones failed to make a connection between the representations.
- As the data revealed, there was no evidence that the participants were able to analyze the situation given, construct a mental model, and set up and solve an equation. If, at times, the proper equation was set up, it was not interpreted properly afterwards. In summary, the participants of the study were not successful in their mathematical modeling.

When solving motion problem I, Mina, John, Liz, and Ron attempted to solve the problem arithmetically but failed to do it correctly as they presented the problem as an independent motion of two vehicles. Mina stated that, "To get the time, I guess I am trying to get it separate for each plane. I guess I took the rate of the first plane that is 300 miles per hour and I added the distance which is 1000 miles and I get 1300." In addition, neither participant used graphical representations such as diagrams, pictures, and/or graphs. Rocky was the only participant who set up the correct equation for the problem, but she failed to solve it correctly. She explained her approach as "We add two rates together and divide it by distance."

Raul stated that, "What I ended up finding out was that I needed to take 300 times two to check my answer, which gave me 600, so that gave me 400. Then 200 times two going that way is 400, and 600 plus 400 would be 1000, and it would take four hours for them to get there." Tom's explanation was, "I know it is ten hours. The way I did it is the rate of one plane is 300 miles per hour, the rate of another plane is 200 miles per hour, and the difference is 100. The question is how many hours it would take to get 1000 miles. So, I divided 1000 miles by 100 and got ten."

When solving mixture problem I, most of the participants didn't offer any logical approach. No graphical or algebraic representations were used. Ron stated: "They are diluted. Ok, if this one is 50%, so it must be mixed with 80 ounces to get twenty percent. No, to get 40% you need to dilute it, to break it down. With this one, I have no idea how to work this one."

Martin presented the problem it as the ratio of a percent of the agent to the percent of the solvent.

Sarah was the only participant who set up an equation when attempting to solve the first mixture problem. She properly represented the variable x as the amount of the 50% solution but failed to represent the amount of alcohol in the mixture as the product of its concentration and the amount. In addition, the majority of the participants had difficulties identifying and properly using such terms as *alcohol, alcohol solution, amount, ounces, solution, mixture, and concentration.*

When solving motion problem II, the participants presented the graphical representations--pictures-- only when I asked them to do so. The pictures were quite descriptive, presenting two cars moving, but didn't offer any connections between the distance and the rates.

John attempted to use a chart shown in class but then admitted that he didn't really know how to use it properly. He tried to use a ratio similarly to the first interview, stating that it might be needed since the problems solved by ratio are in the same section of the textbook. Jana and Sal solved the motion problem arithmetically similar to the first interview. Kate, Sarah, Lora, Rocky, and Martin solved the problem algebraically and were able to obtain the correct answer; nevertheless, they were not able to explain the reasoning beyond the fact that it was taught in class.

When solving mixture problem II, Mina, Ken, Kate, Nell, Sarah, Martin, and Rocky obtained the answers algebraically by equation. At the same time, when asked to explain the meanings of the products involved and the equation set, they restated the procedure (multiplication) without presenting the meaning of the products and added that it is based on the formula given in class. John, Jana, and Ron admitted that the wording of the problem was not clear. John attempted to solve the problem using ratios and a proportion.

The uniqueness of the study is in inimitably revealing that not only young students but adult students as well neither have had strong external representations constructed previously, such as knowledge of the concept of motion and /or concentration, nor had strong internal ones, such as an ability to draw on the intuitive ideas to help solve word problems. The participating adult students had trouble visualizing the stories, converting them into pictures, translating between the text and algebraic symbols and creating quantitative representations such as equations and charts. In addition, the participating adult students experienced difficulties with aligning the semantics and syntactic of ordinary language with the structure of formal mathematical reasoning. The findings of my study also revealed that if at times the participants were able to set and solve a correct equation, they were not able to explain either the concept of motion of two vehicles or the mixture concept logically, thus revealing that the crucial junctions in the development of algebraic thinking where a transition from one level to another takes place are missing.

Implications for Affective Domain

The uniqueness of this study is in revealing the pattern of adult students' affective domain within quite an extended period of time. Consequently, the implication of the study's findings is to help adult learners with understanding the pattern and with supporting the present determination to succeed in this often difficult but crucial endeavor.

Implications for Instruction

- In order to minimize the obvious discontent with personal experience of adult students, teaching algebra in general and teaching word problems solving in particular should strive to combine the formal approaches with informal/intuitive personal experience.

- The traditional teaching of standard word problems currently offered in mathematics classroom, should be replaced--or at the least supplemented--by a wide variety of problems that draw students' attention to realistic modeling. Students then would not implicitly learn to follow the directions given in class without actual comprehension. When modeling, using real or pseudo-real situations (such as visual objects, physical models, motion sensors and/or technology) would stimulate algebraic thinking.

- In order to achieve the necessary level of readiness of the learners, the algebraic approach to solving word problems should follow the teaching/learning of the scientific concepts the word problems are based upon (such as the attributes of motion and the formula that connects them and the concepts of concentration and percent).

- There is a need to improve the metacognition skills by teaching the learners how to analyze the problems and their components, establish inter-relations between the given and the unknown, estimate and analyze the validity of the answers obtained, and analyze similarities and differences between situations. When solving word problems, students should be required to check the answers obtained using common sense and the number line.

- The collaborative learning is advisable so the students would be put in a situation that requires asking/answering questions related to the problem.

- The participants of the study failed to use multi-representations; consequently, when teaching solving word problems, using a combination of representations such as tables, graphs, and equations, would increase the chances of success.

FUTURE RESEARCH DIRECTIONS

- In-depth studying of the informal ways adult students solve algebraic word problems would enhance the effort of math educators to help students make progress toward making sense of motion, mixture, and other related word problems.

- More research is needed in the area of adult students using single and multi-representations including binary quantitative representations such as charts, pictures, and graphs.

- Collaborative word problem solving for future research.

- Adult students' reading comprehension of mathematical texts/symbols/data.

- The long term impact of a graphing technology and function-based algebra on problem-solving abilities of the adult learners.

- A large scale quantitative research.

CONCLUSION

In the 21st century, an increasing number of adults will begin or continue their education. In addition, as society becomes increasingly dependent on technology, continuing mathematics education will be a necessity in every country (Bishop, 2000). Additionally, factors of researching adult mathematics education make it more difficult to research than school mathematics education. In the latter, the learning situation has been thoroughly explored by the literature, the goals are usually made explicit, it takes place at a specified location, the materials are publicly available, and the assessment results are readily accessible. In adult mathematics education, the situation is more complex (Bishop, 2000; Gal, 2000). Thus this is an important area to research, and this study aims to cover some of the open ground in the field. In addition, if solving mathematical word problems by children has been at the focus of research for a number of years, solving word problems by adults is yet to be thoroughly considered. By examining case studies of how adult students solve word problems, a more in-depth understanding can be obtained about mathematics adults need to know in the contexts of enrolling in postsecondary education, strategies for teaching adults the mathematics they need within these contexts, and the proper training necessary for adult education mathematics instructors.

REFERENCES

Achieving the Dream. (2006c, November/December). Developmental math students and college-level coursework. *Data Notes, 1*(8).

Adelman, C. (2004). *Principal indicators of student academic histories in postsecondary education, 1972-2000*. Washington, DC: U.S. Department of Education, Institute of Education Sciences.

Alter, P. (2012). Helping students with emotional and behavioral disorders solve mathematical word problems. *Preventing School Failure, 56*(1), 55–64. doi:10.1080/1045988X.2011.565283

American Council on Education. (2010). *2009 GED testing program statistical report*. Washington, DC: Author. Retrieved from http:www.acenet.edu/Content/NavigationMenu/ged/pubs/2009ASR.pdf

Asiala, M., Brown, A., DeVries, D. J., Dubinsky, E., Mathews, D., & Thomas, K. (2004). *A Framework for Research and Curriculum Development in Undergraduate Mathematics Education*.

Attewell, P., Lavin, D., Domina, T., & Levey, T. (2006). New evidence on college remediation. *The Journal of Higher Education, 77*(5), 886–924. doi:10.1353/jhe.2006.0037

Bailey, T., Jeong, D. W., & Cho, S. (2010). Referral, enrollment, and completion in developmental education sequences in community colleges. *Economics of Education Review, 29*(2), 255–270. doi:10.1016/j.econedurev.2009.09.002

Balacheff, N. (2001). Symbolic arithmetic vs. algebra: The core of a didactical dilemma. Postscript. In R. Sutherland, T. Rojano, A. Bell, & R. C. Lins (Eds.), *Perspectives on school algebra* (p. 249). Dordrecht, the Netherlands: Kluwer.

Ballew, H., & Cunningham, J. W. (1982). Diagnosing strengths and weaknesses of sixth-grade students in solving word problems. *Journal for Research in Mathematics Education, 13*(3), 202. doi:10.2307/748556

Buckingham, E. A. (1997). *Specific and generic numeracy of the workplace: How is numeracy learnt and used by workers in production industries, and what learning/working environments promote this?* Burswood, Vic.: Centre for Studies in Mathematics, Science, and Environmental Education, Deacon University.

Cockcroft, W. H. (1982). *Mathematics counts: Report of the committee of inquiry into the teaching of mathematics in school.* London: Her Majesty Stationery Office.

Cohen, D. (Ed.). (1995). *Crossroads in mathematics: Standards for introductory college mathematics before calculus.* American Mathematical Association of Two-Year Colleges.

Colleran, N., O'Donoghue, J., & Murphy, E. (2000). An educational program for enhancing adults' quantitative problem solving and decision making. In *Adults and Lifelong Education in Mathematics.* ALM.

Colleran, N., O'Donoghue, J., & Murphy, E. (2002). Adult problem solving and commonsense. Policies and practices for adults learning mathematics: Opportunities & risks. In *Proceedings of the 9ᵀʰ International Conference on Adult Learning Mathematics.* ALM.

Creswell, J. W. (2007). *Qualitative inquiry & research design.* Newbury Park, CA: Sage Publications.

Curry, D., Schmitt, M. J., & Waldon, S. (1996). *A Framework for Adult Numeracy Standards: The Mathematical Skills and Abilities Adults Need to be Equipped for the Future. ANN Standards.* Boston, MA: World Education.

De Corte, E., Verschaffel, L., & Depaepe, F. (2008). Unraveling the relationship between students' mathematics-related beliefs and the classroom culture. *European Psychologist, 13*(1), 24–36. doi:10.1027/1016-9040.13.1.24

DeBellis, V. A., & Goldin, G. (2006). Affect and meta-affect in mathematical problem solving: A representational perspective. *Educational Studies in Mathematics, 63*(2), 131–147. doi:10.1007/s10649-006-9026-4

Department of Education. National Center for Education Statistics. (2003). *National assessment of adult literacy.* Retrieved from http://nces.ed.gov/naal/glossary.asp

Dewolf, T., Van Dooren, W., & Verschaffel, L. (2011). Upper elementary school children's understanding and solution of a quantitative problem inside and outside the mathematics class. *Learning and Instruction, 21*(6), 770–780. doi:10.1016/j.learninstruc.2011.05.003

English, L. D., & Watters, J. (2005). Mathematical modeling in the early school years. *Mathematics Education Research Journal, 16*(3), 59. doi:10.1007/BF03217401

Evans, J. (2000a). *Adult mathematical thinking & emotions.* Routledgefalmer, London, UK: Evans, J. (2000b). Adult mathematics and everyday life. In D. Coben et al. (Eds.), *Perspective on adults learning mathematics. Research and practice* (p. 290). London: Kluwer.

FitzSimons, G., & Godden, G. L. (2000). Review on research on adult learning mathematics. In D. Coben et al. (Eds.), *Perspectives on adults learning mathematics* (p. 13). The Netherlands: Kluwer.

Gal, I. (2000a). Statistical literacy. In D. Coben et al. (Eds.), *Perspective on adults learning mathematics. Research and practice* (p. 135). London: Kluwer.

Gal, I. (2000b). The numeracy challenge. In I. Gal (Ed.), *Adult numeracy development* (p. 9). Hampton Press.

Ginsburg, L., Manly, M., & Schmitt, M. J. (2006). *The components of numeracy. NCSALL occasional paper. Harvard Graduate School of Education*. Cambridge, MA: National Center for the Study of Adults Learning and Literacy.

Goldin, G. A. (2008). Perspectives on representation in mathematical learning and problem solving. In L. D. English (Ed.), *Handbook of International Research in Mathematics Education*. New York, London: Rutledge.

Greer, B. (1993). The modeling perspective on world problems. *The Journal of Mathematical Behavior, 12*(3), 239. Retrieved from http://www.sciencedirect.com/science/journal/07323123

Greer, B. (1997). Modeling reality in mathematics classrooms: The case of word problems. *Learning and Instruction, 7*(4), 293–307. doi:10.1016/S0959-4752(97)00006-6

Johanning, D. I. (2004). Supporting the development of algebraic thinking in middle school: A closer look at students' informal strategies. *The Journal of Mathematical Behavior, 23*(4), 371–388. doi:10.1016/j.jmathb.2004.09.001

Kasworm, C. E. (1990). Adult undergraduates in higher education: A review of past research perspectives. *Review of Educational Research, 60*(3), 345–372. doi:10.3102/00346543060003345

Kieran, C. (2007). Learning and teaching of algebra at the middle school through college level: Building meaning for symbols and their manipulation. In F. K. Lester (Ed.), *Second handbook of research on mathematics teaching and learning* (p. 707).

Knowles, M. S. (1990). *The adult learner: A neglected species* (4th ed.). Houston, TX: Gulf Publishing Company.

Koedinger, K. R., & Nathan, M. J. (2004). The real story behind story problems: Effects of representations on quantitative reasoning. *Journal of the Learning Sciences, 13*(2), 129. doi:10.1207/s15327809jls1302_1

Koedinger, K. R., & Nathan, M. J. (2004). The real story behind story problems: Effects of representations on quantitative reasoning. *Journal of the Learning Sciences, 13*(2), 129–164. doi:10.1207/s15327809jls1302_1

Lesh, R. A., & Zawojewski, J. (2007). Problem solving and modeling. In F. K. Lester (Ed.), *Second handbook of research on mathematics teaching and learning*. NCTM.

Lester, F. K. (1994). Musing about mathematical problem solving research: 1970-1994. *Journal for Research in Mathematics Education, 25*(6), 660. doi:10.2307/749578

McLeod, D. B. (1992). Research on affect in mathematics education: A reconceptualization. In D. A. Grouws (Ed.), *Handbook of research on mathematics teaching and learning* (p. 575). New York: Macmillan.

Merriam, S. B. (2009). *Qualitative research and case study applications in education*. Jossey-Bass.

Mevarech, Z. R., & Fridkin, S. (2006). The effects of IMPROV on mathematical knowledge, mathematical reasoning, and meta-cognition. *Metacognition and Learning*, *1*(1), 85–97. doi:10.1007/s11409-006-6584-x

National Council of Teachers of Mathematics (NCTM). (2000). *Principles and standards for school mathematics*. Reston, VA: Author.

National Council of Teachers of Mathematics (NCTM). (2010). *Common core state standards*. Reston, VA: Author.

National Mathematics Advisory Panel (NMAP). (2008). *Foundations for success: The final report of the national Mathematics Advisory Panel*. Washington, DC: U.S. Department of Education.

National Center for Education Statistics. (2003). *Remedial education at degree-granting postsecondary institutions in fall 2000* (NCÉS 2004-010). Retrieved from U.S. Department of Education website: http://nces.ed.gov/pubsearch/pubsinfo.asp?pubid=2004010

Nesbit, T. (1995). *Teaching mathematics to adults*. Paper presented at the annual meeting of the American educational research association, San Francisco, CA.

Okamoto, Y. (1996). Modeling children's understanding of quantitative relations in texts: A developmental perspective. *Cognition and Instruction*, *14*(4), 409–440. doi:10.1207/s1532690xci1404_1

Palm, T. (2008). Impact of authenticity on sense making in word problems solving. *Educational Studies in Mathematics*, *67*(1), 37–58. doi:10.1007/s10649-007-9083-3

Pantziara, M., Gagatsis, A., & Elia, I. (2009). Using diagrams as tools for the solution of non- routine mathematical problems. *Educational Studies in Mathematics*, *72*(1), 39–60. doi:10.1007/s10649-009-9181-5

Pape, S. J. (2004). Middle school children's problem-solving behavior; a cognitive analysis from a reading comprehension perspective. *Journal for Research in Mathematics Education*, *35*(3), 187. doi:10.2307/30034912

Polya, G. (1957). *How to solve it*. Princeton, NJ: Princeton University Press.

Pressley, M., Burkell, J., & Schneider, B. (1995). Mathematical problem solving. In M. Pressley & V. Woloshyn (Eds.), *Cognitive strategy instruction* (p. 185). Brookline Books.

Schoenfeld, A. H. (1985). *Mathematical problem solving*. Orlando, FL: Academic Press.

Schoenfeld, A. H. (1987). A brief and biased history of problem solving. In F. R. Curcio (Ed.), *Teaching and learning: A problem-solving focus* (p. 27). Reston, VA: National Council of Teachers of Mathematics.

Schoenfeld, A. H. (1992). Learning to think mathematically: Problem solving, metacognition, and sense making in mathematics. In D. A. Grouws (Ed.), *Handbook of research on mathematics teaching and learning* (p. 334). New York: Macmillan.

Sfard, A. (2013). Almost 20 years after: Developments in research on language and mathematics. Review of J. N. Moschkovich (Ed.) (2010) Language and mathematics education: Multiple perspectives and directions for research. Educational Studies in Mathematics, 82(2). doi:10.1007/s10649-012-9446-2

Siegler, R. S. (1989). Hazards of mental chronometry: An example from children's subtraction. *Journal of Educational Psychology, 81*(4), 497–506. doi:10.1037/0022-0663.81.4.497

Stacey, K., & MacGregor, M. (2000). Learning the algebraic methods of solving problems. *The Journal of Mathematical Behavior, 18*(2), 149–167. doi:10.1016/S0732-3123(99)00026-7

Swafford, J. O., & Langrall, C. W. (2000). Grade 6th students' preinstructional use of equations to describe and represent problem situations. *Journal for Research in Mathematics Education, 31*(1), 89. doi:10.2307/749821

Teppo, A. R. (1998). *Diverse ways of knowing*. Philadelphia, PA: NCTM.

Tobias, S. (1990). *They are not dumb, they are different: Stalking the second tier*. Tucson, AZ: Research Corporation.

Verschaffel, L., & De Corte, E. (1997). Word problems: A vehicle for promoting authentic mathematical understanding and problem solving in the primary school? In T. Nunes & P. Bryant (Eds.), *Learning and teaching mathematics: An international perspective*. Psychology Press.

Verschaffel, L., De Corte, E., & Lasure, S. (1994). Realistic considerations in mathematical modeling of school arithmetic word problems. *Learning and Instruction, 4*(4), 273–294. doi:10.1016/0959-4752(94)90002-7

Verschaffel, L., Greer, B., & De Corte, E. (2000). *Making sense of word problems*. Lisse, The Netherlands: Swets & Zeitlinger.

Vygotsky, L. S. (1978). *Mind and society: The development of higher mental processes*. Cambridge, MA: Harvard University Press.

Wyndhamn, J., & Saljo, R. (1997). Word problems and mathematical reasoning - a study of children's mastery of reference and meaning in textual realities. *Learning and Instruction, 7*(4), 361–382. doi:10.1016/S0959-4752(97)00009-1

Yerushalmy, M. (2000). Problem solving strategies and mathematical resources: A longitudinal view on problem solving in function-based approach to algebra. *Educational Studies in Mathematics, 43*(2), 125–147. doi:10.1023/A:1017566031373

Yin, R. K. (2003). *Case study research: Design and methods*. Thousand Oaks, CA: Sage Publications.

KEY TERMS AND DEFINITIONS

A Coherent External Representation: Means a drawing, an equation, or a graph (Goldin, 1998).

A Complete and Coherent Verbal Reason: Means one based on a described pattern (Goldin, 1998).

Adult Learner: The definition revolves around the learner, not the level of mathematics being studied. Knowles (1990) argued that there four definitions of the term adult: biological, legal, social, and psychological. The last occurs at a point where self-direction comes into function and is the most central from the point of learning. In this study, adults are individuals of 18 years or older and continue their education intentionally. For some of them, it is a continuation of their school experience; for others there may be a break of a few years or more since their last formal mathematics course.

Affect: Is a combination of three dimensions: beliefs, attitudes, and emotions (Evans, 2000).

Internal Cognitive Representations: Include five kinds of mutually interacting systems which are (Goldin, 1987): (a) a verbal/syntactic system (use of language), (b) imagistic systems (visual/spatial, auditory, kinesthetic encoding), (c) formal notational systems (use of mathematical notation), (d) planning, monitoring, and executive control (use of heuristic strategies), and (e) affective representation (changing moods and emotions during problem, solving).

Mathematical Problems: Can be defined in many different ways. In the study, mathematical problems will consist of problems in which the individual would analyze the situation (s), draw diagrams, pose questions, search for patterns and solutions, use reasoning, and illustrate and interpret results.

Mathematics: Is a living subject which seeks to understand patterns that permeate both the world around us and the mind within us. Now much more than arithmetic and geometry, mathematics today is a diverse discipline that deals with data, measurements and observations from science; with inference, deduction and proof; and with mathematical models of natural phenomena, of human behavior, and of social systems. Although the language of mathematics is based on rules that must be learned, it is important for motivation that students move beyond rules to be able to express things in the language of mathematics (National Research Council, 1989; NCTM Standards, 1989).

Mathematics Education: In the study is a field defined by a multiplicity of practices including: (1) The teaching and learning of mathematics at all levels in school and college (2) Out of school learning of mathematics (3) The design, writing and construction of texts and learning material (4) Research in mathematics education (Coben, D., O'Donoghue, J., & FitzSimons, G. E., 2000).

Numeracy: Describes an accumulation of skills, knowledge, beliefs, dispositions, communication resources, and problem-solving skills that individuals need in order to separately engage and effectively manage numeracy situations that involve numbers, quantitative or quantifiable information, and visual or textual information, that are based on mathematical ideas or have embedded mathematical elements (Gal, 2000).

Problem Solving: In the study is defined as "…finding a way where no way is known off-hand, to find a way out of a difficulty, to find a way around an obstacle, to attain a desired end, that is not immediately attainable, by appropriate means" (Polya, 1980, p. 1). Problem solving is a process through which individuals utilize the knowledge they have gained previously and applied it to a new unique situation or condition.

Symbolic Language: Includes words, symbols, and notations used (Goldin, 1987).

Word Problems (or Story Problems): Is the traditional format of application problems intended to develop in students the skills of knowing when and how to apply their mathematics effectively in diverse problem situations encountered in everyday life. Word problems are also defined as verbal descriptions of problem situations wherein one or more questions are raised, the answer to which can be obtained by the application of mathematical operations to numerical data available in the problem statement (Verschaffel, Greer, & De Corte, 2000).

Section 4
Globalization

Chapter 15
Cultural Hemorrhage of Religion and Spirituality on Healthcare and Wellness

F. Sigmund Topor
Keio University, Japan

ABSTRACT

As life approaches expectancy and senescence actualizes, the regenerative capacity of the vital organs and their functionality is reduced. Such a reality gives rise the need to identify with a better purpose in life. Religion and spirituality assume a central role in the wellness and healthcare in such circumstances. Although societies and civilizations differ in their religious and spiritual orientations, all peoples everywhere ascribe to some God or gods. The globalization of religion was initiated sometime between the late Bronze Age and late classical antiquity. The pivotal point was characterized by a conversion from polytheism, or primary religions as practiced by the Ancient Egyptians; Phoenicians; Babylonians; Greek; and Romans on the one hand, to monotheism—secondary religions characterized by the worship of one supreme God. Religion and spirituality has now become the one and remaining source of solace for the terminally ill.

As life approaches expectancy and senescence actualizes, religion and spirituality assume a central role in the wellness and health care regimen of those who grow old. With reduced regenerative capacity of the vital organs, along with the diminishing function and appreciation of the senses (i.e., sight, taste, touch, and the like), reliance on medication gives way to increased spirituality and religiosity (Bauer & Barron, 1995; Dunn & Horgas, 2000; Touhy, 2001) as a means of accepting the inevitability of mortality. This trend takes on a global proportion as practiced in all countries and cultures. For example, demographic changes in Japan ensure an imminently overriding need for holistic services for the burgeoning elderly population that is becoming the majority of the population (Bloom, Canning, & Sevilla, 2003; Chen et al., 2013; Ogawa & Retherford, 1993).

The conversion from ancient polytheism to modern monotheism can be characterized as ignorance supplanted by knowledge. This is precisely what happened in Ancient Egypt with the transformation

DOI: 10.4018/978-1-5225-0522-8.ch015

from falsehood, which was characterized by localized, cultic, and narrowly focused worship of multitudinous totemic gods, to the dawning of monotheism, which was characterized by the emancipation of the Hebrew people as they were imbued with knowledge or truth. The change amounted to a revolution of biblical importance involving the codification and decodification of sacred texts—literacy. As a result, secondary religions, such as Buddhism, Christianity, Islam, and Hinduism (Bülow et al., 2008; W. H. Clark, 1958; Evans, 2006; Jonsen, 2006; Parrinder, 1999), are supported by sacred texts.

The globalization of religion was initiated sometime between the late Bronze Age and late classical antiquity (Masojć & Bech, 2011; Nigosian, 2010). The pivotal point was characterized by a conversion from polytheism, or primary religions as practiced by the Ancient Egyptians, Phoenicians, Babylonians; Greek, and Romans on the one hand, to monotheism—secondary religions characterized by the worship of one supreme God. Polytheistic cultures practice a cultlike religion, which posits the existence of a separate god, if totemistically, for almost every conceivable object, event, or phenomenon—for example, a separate god of fire, water, wind, earth, sorrow, and more. Monotheism, conversely, without denying the existence of other gods, acknowledges that all other gods exist in thrall to one omnipresent, omnipotent, and omniscient God.

In the globalized world of converging economies, technologies, and other human services, diverging views of health and wellness have added to notions of religion and spirituality in rendering intercultural–international research a global challenge. Apart from globalization, European and American societies that exhibit multicultural, multiethnic, and multiracial characteristics have foregrounded health care services. Globalization highlights the function of culture in the maintenance of wellness and the management of illness under the microscope.

Religion and spirituality, and their influence or dearth of influence on wellness have received a great deal of scholarly interest (George, Ellison, & Larson, 2002; P. C. Hill & Pargament, 2008; J. Jung, 2012; Koenig, McCullough, & Larson, 2001; D. B. Larson, Swyers, & McCullough, 1998; Plante & Sherman, 2001; Powell, Shahabi, & Thoresen, 2003; Seeman, Dubin, & Seeman, 2003; Seybold & Hill, 2001; Thoresen, 1999; Thoresen, Harris, & Oman, 2001). Extensive literature on religious fundamentalism is provided in Aten, Mangis, and Campbell (2010); Blogowska and Saroglou (2011); Bradley (2009); and E. D. Hill, Cohen, Terrell, and Nagoshi (2010). For religion and sexual prejudice, see Herek (2009), Rowatt et al. (2006), and Tsang and Rowatt (2007).

Attempts are made by Western researchers to exclude any semblance of religion or spirituality from research (J. M. Nelson, 2009; J. M. Nelson & Slife, 2012; Slife & Reber, 2012). The Western strive for empiricism seems to parallel Eastern-oriented atheism. To promote objectivity and attenuate the likelihood of presupposed acceptance or bias, Western researchers are dissuaded against the influence of religion and/or spirituality (J. M. Nelson & Slife, 2012).

Distinctive interpretations of illness and wellness among countries depict confusion. Such confusion arises from the cornucopia of cases, instances, or types of illness. Stress and other psychological maladies are examples of instances of unwellness emerging from sociocultural contexts (Donelson, 1999; Prior & Bond, 2008; Salsman, Brown, Brechting, & Carlson, 2005). Classification of such health conditions varies among countries or cultures. Suicide, for example, is morally wrong in Western societies; however, Confucian societies that practice Buddhism deem the practice acceptable (Coward & Ratanakul, 1999).

Duriez (2004a) alleged that religiosity in nowise ensures eleemosynary deeds. Wars have been fought, won, and lost on religious footing (Batson, 1983; Benedict, 1975; Ring, 2000; Seul, 1999). Universal attributes such as rigidity, insensitivity, insincerity, mercilessness, meanness, and heartlessness cannot be remedied through religiousness. Attention is drawn to the effect of religious motivations as catalyst for wars and atrocities committed against people of different religious or spiritual convictions. For example, in reference to Russian imperial history, Hellie (2005) claimed that "the subservience of organized religion to the state was enhanced after 1480 by the willingness of the state to put to death any clergyman who dared express an independent mind" (p. 89).

BACKGROUND

The term *religion*, as defined in *Merriam-Webster's Dictionary*, connotes an institutionalized canonical orthodoxy. Religion is broadly and universally used by social institutions such as the Church (Fouka, Plakas, Taket, Boudioni, & Dandoulakis, 2012) for a variety of purposes. For example, religion facilitates ritualistic ceremonies to cope with death (Mantala-Bozos, 2003; J. M. Nelson, 2009; Sor-hoon, 2011; Zinnbauer, Pargament, & Scott, 1999), the establishment of rules for the preservation of authority (Watts, 2005) over congregants, and a physical place of worship. This is different from spirituality, which denotes the personal individualistic approach to religion. *Spirituality* is defined variously depending on the culture. Religion and spirituality have threatened the positivist methodology and created a chasm between qualitative and quantitative methodologies in research (P. C. Hill & Pargament, 2008). Kant (1785/1949, 1797/1964, 1793/2004) believed that science and religion are not mutually exclusive but rather complementary. Religion is not separate from science. Barbour (1997) cited McGaughey in his claim that Kant justified the role of religion and faith based on limitations to what humans can know through science. (See also Dickerson [2011]).

There is ample medical research connecting spirituality and health or wellness (Koenig et al., 2001); however, more research is needed in nursing (Narayanasamy, 2001). It is important to distinguish between spirituality and religion (van Leeuwen, Tiesinga, Jochemasen, & Post, 2007) as the two are different (Narayanasamy, 2001; Taylor, 2003). Van Leeuwen et al. (2007) argued that the spiritual aspect of patients is foregrounded as they contemplate their conditions and relationships when faced with the prospect of death or permanent psychical deformity.

Such increased emphasis on holiness and spiritual revival has progressively become a major ingredient in health care. Contempt for prayers is rapidly becoming a thing of the past, as modern medical practices fail to address the spiritual and religious needs of the sick (Meraviglia, 2004, 2006; Walton, 1999; Walton & Sullivan, 2004). Studies show a holistic evolution in healthcare, with more people finding solace in prayers even as they endure remediation with modern medical technology. A 2002 survey of 31,044 U.S. adults age 18 years and over found that 62% used some form of complementary and alternative medicine therapy including prayers for health reasons (Barnes, Powell-Griner, McFann, & Nahin, 2002).

A survey conducted by Curlin, Sellergren, Lantos, and Chin (2007) found majority of Christians identify spirituality and religion as contributing factors to wellness. Sixty-nine percent, 58%, and 68% of physicians from Protestant, Catholic, and other religious groups respectively professed their belief in spirituality. The number of Jewish physicians with similar views was 20%. Whereas largely limited to the Christian faith—Roman Catholics, Anglicans, Orthodox, and the like, scholars in the United States, Europe, and elsewhere have described the influence of religion and spirituality as a mechanism of coping with illness and maintaining good health (Curlin et al., 2006; Curlin et al., 2007; Post, Puchalski, & Larson, 2000; Sloan, Bagiella, & Powell, 1999; Sloan et al., 2000). S. S. Larson and Larson (1992) argued that going to church promotes good health. Prayer and Prozac will be the medicine of the future

(Sides, 1997) as faith promotes healing (Yankelovich Partners, 1996). Physicians are as affected by religion and spirituality as their patients.

Christological exclusivity recorded in John 14:6 in the Cambridge edition of the 21st century King James version of the Christian Bible reads, "Jesus saith unto him, I am the way, the truth, and the life: no man cometh unto the Father, but by me." For more readings on the Christian doctrine, see Bonhoeffer (1959), Gibran (1997), and Hatfield (2004). Nevertheless, Largen (2006) assured the rest of humanity that Christological salvation is in nowise exclusive to Christians "but rather extends to the redemption of the whole human person, and even the whole physical universe" (p. 271). Curlin, Lantos, Roach, Sellergren, and Chin (2005) stated that the religious characteristics are dissimilar to the public at large. With respect to practicing physicians in the United States, Curlin et al. found the following:

Fifty-five percent of physicians say their religious beliefs influence their practice of medicine. Compared with the general population, physicians are more likely to be affiliated with religions that are under-represented in the United States, less likely to say they try to carry their religious beliefs over into all other dealings in life (58% vs. 73%), twice as likely to consider themselves spiritual but not religious (20% vs. 9%), and twice as likely to cope with major problems in life without relying on God (61% vs. 29%). (p. 629)

SINFUL PUNISHMENT

A punishment ought to be sinful if it causes pain and suffering, regardless of the transgressor and/or transgressee—the subject of transgression. Illness and disease are regarded as punishment for sin against God. The primeval sex of Adam and Eve constituted the first and original sin (Clifton, 1990; Delumeau & O'Connell, 2000). In the real world encompassing the totality of all religious faiths, punishment should be sinful if it is disproportionately applied. In the 13th century, emphasis on punishment (Johnson, 2005), as displayed by the story of Adam's expulsion from the Garden of Eden, was extolled (Kelly, 2000). A moral taxonomy emerged for the restoration of salvation by which those who believe in Jesus, as Christ, would be saved from incessant suffering (Carson, 1992; Couenhoven, 2010). What might be considered violence and aggression in layman terms is not necessarily so considered in the religious and spiritual realm.

Fretheim (2000) suggested that natural disasters such as earthquakes, floods, volcanic eruptions, plagues, and other conditions affecting human deformities are examples of violence visited upon humans by God. Buddhists and Christians hold that such aggressions are God's way of punishing humans for evil or sin (Fretheim, 2000; Thang Moe, 2015). The global nature of religion and spirituality, together with advances in medical science and technology, is referenced by Bishop Gianfranco Girotti (as cited in D. R. Nelson, 2009) as follows: "While sin used to concern mostly the individual, today it has mainly a social resonance, due to the phenomenon of globalization" (p. 1).

Sachs (1993) observed that God's love and mercy might be tarnished by the persistent insistence on divine justice, which may be actualized by hell. On account of the prospect of stern and sturdy condemnation by the magisterium, Sachs argued that refusal of most Roman Catholic theologians to embrace "a doctrine of universal salvation outright" (p. 617) necessitates counteractive measures against such "pessimistic and threatening exaggerations" (p. 617).

The doctrine of apocatastasis, which is commonly attributed to a Christian scholar and theologian (Chadwick, 1966), upholds that the entire creation, including sinners, the damned, and the devil, will eventually be restored to a condition of eternal happiness and salvation. This was an important theme in early Christian eschatology. Hate (Baird & Rosenbaum, 1999) and fear (Neuberg, Kenrick, & Schaller, 2011) are human emotions that inspire action.

It seems apparent that humans are more sensitive or affected by fear than by love. For example, the Christian doctrine of eternal punishment, which posits that individual sinners may face eternal damnation (Davies, 1971; Sachs, 1991) instead of salvation (Daley, 1991; Oestigaard, 2009), has had more impact on individual behavior than the doctrine of deliverance from harm or suffering either during earthly existence or eternally after death.

Whereas religion is confined to the realm of social institutions, spirituality transcends them; it pertains, more out of this world, to the supernatural. As Boyer (2008) stated, "Unlike other social animals, humans are very good at establishing and maintaining relations with agents beyond their physical presence; social hierarchies and coalitions, for instance, include temporarily absent members" (p. 1038). Authoritative clarity regarding the effect of the interplay between religiosity and human emotions (i.e., empathy) is wanting. All humans desire and appreciate kindness, relationships, and the attainment of happiness, love, and affection. It must henceforth be understood that human nature is not confined to positive or constructive wanders—deeds or strays.

Unfamiliarity propagates uncertainty. Uncertainties about a patient's condition add to treatment disparities by physicians, not discounting disparities in knowledge, experience, and technologies. Smedley, Stith, and Nelson (2009) stated that a physician must rely on cognitive heuristics—a patient's prior conditions including socioeconomic status, race, and gender. The physician's medical decision regarding the patient is then influenced by inferences about the patient's *prior* (history of activities) and the information from clinical encounter. When a physician's inferences are incongruent with reality, Smedley et al. explained, "treatment decisions and the patients' needs are potentially less well matched" (p .9). Inequalities between the familiar and the unfamiliar occur thus.

At times, disease may induce unequal treatment for different people, granted that the defining conditions propelling a global push towards religiosity and/or spirituality do not necessarily respond to medical or surgical treatment (Ejaz, Schur, & Noelker, 1997). Examples of such conditions include socioeconomic policies, education, employment, lifestyle, and others (Ejaz et al., 1997; Ferreira, Matsudo, Ribeiro, & Ramos, 2010; Masel, Raji, & Peek, 2010). The Organisation for Economic Co-operation and Development (2013) attributed health cost differentials among member countries to demographic structure, disease pattern, institutional arrangements, and clinical guidelines for treatment. Japan provides an example of conditions under which unequal treatments are administered in health care.

HOLISTIC DEMANDS ON MEDICAL PRACTITIONERS

All of humanity is epitomized by the increasing holistic demands that are placing more requirements on nursing practitioners to deliver religious and spiritual therapy to patients (Bauer & Barron, 1995; Grant, 2004; King & Bushwick, 1994) across cultures and geopolitical boundaries. Many authors have begun to demand medical personnel to do some soul searching, a feat that requires self-reflection about their own religiosity and/or spiritual orientation (Cavendish, Konecny, Luise, & Lanza, 2004; Nagai-Jacobson & Burkhardt, 1989; Treolar, 2000).

THE HUMAN CONDITION

The human condition of unwellness from illness is typified by morbidity. Religion and/or spirituality have proven to be a source of solace in dealing with human weaknesses and idiocies. The anguish of illness has no limit for all of humanity. Whereas language serves as a standard of demarcation, mortality is a unifying phenomenon for all humans. It transcends culture, customs, language, food, and all that tend to differentiate peoples. The dread of mortality is endogenous to morbidity, which is typically experienced when an individual's life or health is threatened with illness.

Consequential vulnerability and disempowerment from protracted pain and discomfort underlie the human condition (Kleinman, 1988) that transcends culture, customs, and language. To ascribe meaning to their life, patients generally seek religious or spiritual remediation when it is determined that physicians cannot palliate their condition and euthanasia is not in consideration. The soteriological teleology of the world's religions (Christians, Buddhists, Hindus, Muslims, and Jews) is apparent in their doctrinal pedagogies. This is more so for terminally ill patients who consider the afterlife as a true prospect. Religion and spirituality are thus considered the only hope for an afterlife salvation and to achieve *nirvana,* the transcendent state of attainment when one is released from the cycle of birth, death, and rebirth. Other eschatological goals of the Buddhist faith include the alleviation of ignorance and liberation of the sick from pain and suffering (Bayly, 2004; Kleinman, 1988; Perry, 1963).

Attributes such as hopelessness, helplessness, fear, and so on are common to all humans, and they represent human emotions that have never been controlled by any civilization or cultural institutions. Such conditions expose the immortality of humans, of which many have sought solace and protection from other sources (Batson, 1983; Dunbar, 2009; Johnson & Bering, 2006). All individuals need to attain and retain health and peace of mind, and to protect against conditions that are often attributed to a supernatural power (Atran & Henrich, 2010; Boyer, 1994, 2008; Gervais, Willard, Norenzayan, & Henrich, 2011). Membership to specific social institutions such as the church or religious organizations serves the need for protection against perceived supernatural forces.

SOCIETAL DIFFERENCES

Being cultural-specific, spirituality and religiosity are emphasized in dissimilar terms across cultures (Lewer & Van den Berg, 2007; Malota, 2012; B. G. Smith, 2012) including national laws, moral codes, and customs. Duriez (2004b) concluded that the manner in which religious content is processed impacts the behavior of followers (see also Batson and Gray [1981], Darley and Batson [1973], Donahue [1981], Francis and Pearson [1987], Greenwald, [1975], and Watson, Hood, Morris, and Hall [1984]). In this vein, it is fitting to conclude that the liturgy or the teleological process, which is the means to the end, is more effectual than the end, (i.e., salvation). All of the world's religions seek the same end—salvation (Moses, 2007). Eastern philosophy, the like of which is practiced in Japan (i.e., Buddhism), is more spiritual than ecclesial, which is a Western philosophical tenet.

Neither Eastern nor Western paradigms of moral rectitude are free of inconsistencies or *disunderstandings.* Although all Christians share a common believe in "Jesus Christ as their personal savior" (Aoanan, 2014; J. E. Clark, 2010; Qin, 2015; C. Smith & Emerson, 1998; Trelstad, 2014; Warner, 1979), both doctrinal and liturgical disagreements have resulted in multitudes of sects or denominations. According to Delkeskamp-Hayes (2009), "Roman Catholic, Reformed Protestant, Evangelical, and Orthodox are divided because of their greater or smaller distance from the Tradition of the Apostolic Church" (pp. 1-2). And, although their moral code is based on Christian values (Delkeskamp-Hayes, 2009), disagreements persist as to such social issues as capital punishment, birth control, sexuality, and the like (Hackett & Lindsay, 2008).

Eastern morality also encompasses multifaceted canons such as Confucianism, Shintoism, Taoism, and Buddhism, all of which are not necessarily in concordance (Fang & Faure, 2011; Hsiao, Jen, & Lee, 1990). Western religion, which is mostly Christian, frowns upon suicide (Dervic et al., 2004; Wright, 2010) and considers individuals with suicidal tendencies to be mentally ill. Dervic et al. (2004) claimed that religion helps to decrease the rate of suicide in religious countries. Nevertheless, the veracity of such claim lies in the distinction between religion and spirituality. If, for instance, the level of spirituality as observed by the Japanese could be translated in religious terms, the high rate of suicide in Japan (Picone, 2012; Pinguet, 1993; Takahashi, 2001; Ueno, 2005) would defy the claim that religion helps to reduces suicide rates.

For Hindus, salvation is a collective phenomenon applicable to all of humankind. Salvation is attained by achieving *moksha*—a transcendental state reached by being released from *samsara,* the cycle of birth, death, and rebirth. According to W. C. Smith (1993), following the day of judgment, believers of the Islamic faith escape punishment and receive salvation, although the soteriological criteria differ widely for Sunni and Twelver Shi'ite Muslims (Madelung, 1985; Madelung & Schmidtke, 2013; Mohamed, 2015; Morewedge, 1979; Sprochi, 2010).

Hindus and Jews are the most educated religious groups in the Untied States, with more than 1 in 10 immigrants affiliating with a non-Christian faith (e.g., Islam or Hinduism). The Pew Research Center (2011) stated that 77% and 59% of Hindus and Jews respectively are college graduates, compared with 27% of all U.S. adults. Christians include Catholics, Protestants, Episcopalians, Evangelicals, Mainlines, Historical Blacks, Orthodox Christians, Mormons, Jehovah's Witnesses, and Seventh-Day Adventists, among others. Non-Christians include Buddhists, Hindus, Jews, and Muslims.

Coward and Ratanakul (1999) expressed the belief that all living organisms, humans as well as animals, go through a round of birth and death in a phenomenon referred to as *samsara.* However, a Buddhist belief is that humans are the only sentient beings with the power to commit suicide, or "to terminate this endless cycle by obtaining release—*nibbana*" (p. 126).

The literature on religiosity and altruism specifies a universal human predisposition to employ empathetic emotions in reacting to others in sympathy, compassion, sadness, warmth, and so on (Batson, 1983; Hoffman, 1975, 1977, 1981; Krebs, 1975). Whoqol (2006) cited research affirming the universal pacifying function of religion, which includes the management of human desire (Atkinson & Bourrat, 2011; Atran & Henrich, 2010; Monsma, 2007; Snarey, 1996)—that is, to attain and retain good health, and protect one's future livelihood. These are among the basic needs of all individuals globally. Cultural epistemologies differentiate humanity through socialization.

For Buddhists, ignorance and desire tend to thwart emancipation from an individual's earthly burden (Mason, 2002). Believers advocate wisdom and *chi* (knowledge), whereas Christianity espouses love. Buddhist children indulge in large-group activities to avoid personal individuality. In post–World War II Japan, the abolition of state Shinto and the rise of religious freedom led to the parturition of the so-called *Rush Hour of the Gods*—some 2,000 new sects and cults (McFarland, 1967). Reader (2012) confirmed organized religion has "petered out" (p. 7) in Japan. Buddhists regard humans as having six senses, "the sixth being the subjective experience of the mind" (Coward & Ratanakul, 1999, p. 126). Sentience is simply awareness prior to the arising of *skandhas*—the five transitory personal elements of body, perception, conception, volition, and consciousness whose temporary concatenation forms the individual self.

JAPAN AS DISTINCT FROM THE UNITED STATES

Japan's extensive childhood education system, with the goal of installing *toku* (virtue), ensures at least 2 years of a licensed *youchien* (preschool) or *hoikuen* (child care center; Boocock, 1989) for preschoolers. Japanese preschoolers have had an opulent tapestry of Shinto and Buddhism enshrined in their curriculum for over a century (Wollons, 1993). Japanese Buddhism and Shinto teach followers to be virtuous, *itawari no kokoro*—kind and accommodating to all living things, including animals and plant life as well as humans (Holloway, 1999). Thus, preschool children didactically nurture the plants in their classrooms. Japanese Buddhism explicitly advocates a sense of duty and responsibility coupled with wisdom and esthetic refinement in order to lessen human suffering (Mason, 2002; Takakusu, 2002). The Japanese people may be keen on the telos of eschaton as exemplified by the presence of temples and shrines. However, given that most Japanese individuals profess to be nonreligious (Ama, 2005; Tanaka, 2010), Japan's multitudinous temples and shrines may point to the phenomenon described by Davie's (1990) book entitled *Believing Without Belonging*.

Many U.S. adults had a religious upbringing. However, the Pew Research Center (2011) reported that 18% of U.S. adults confess to have no religion albeit being raised in a religion in childhood and 9% adopted a religion, having been raised with no religious affiliation. Christianity has been losing the most adherents through switching, with Catholics being the largest religious group losing. The religion gaining the most adherents is the evangelical Protestant tradition.

About 95% of Americans have affirmed their belief in God. According to Miller and Thoresen (2003), the number of Americans professing their belief in God has never dropped below 90% in the last fifty years. Gallup and Lindsay (1999) also found that 9 out of 10 people stated that they pray to God daily and 40% attended church regularly. Gallup (1985, 1995) reported the centrality of faith in the daily lives of Americans; more than two thirds (69%) stated that they were members in a church or synagogue.

Uniqueness is an important attribute amid heterogeneous cultures, languages, and other human characteristics. Unless one is prepared to remain insular in a heretofore unitary insular system, the price of uniqueness can be enormous. The end of the 20th century and the beginning of the 21st have engendered a new reality in globalization, which, like monotheism, impels everyone to recognize the unity of humanity in such areas as wellness, illness, communication, and education, among others. Being in harmony with the world entails synchronicity (Cambray, 2009; C. G. Jung & Main, 1997; Stein & Jung, 1985), which connotes that nothing stays the same and everything must change (Blow, 2011; Kirk, 1951).

GLOBAL COPING MECHANISMS OF UNWELLNESS

Religion and spirituality are psychological measures (Lin & Bauer-Wu, 2003) that aid the remedial and recovery process and impart hope (Clayton et al., 2008; Duggleby, Holtslander, Steeves, Duggleby-Wenzel, & Cunningham 2010; Kylmä, Duggleby, Cooper, & Molander, 2009) to the sick. Religion and spirituality also improve the prospects of wellness and recovery in patients. Clayton et al. (2008) claimed that hope and its psychological effects not only transcend the domain of patients but also the psychological effects of religion and spirituality extend to medical professionals.

Spiritual care is typically desired in health care in the absence of beneficence, which, according to Polzer Casarez and Engebreston (2012), amounts to omission when holistic care is denied. For terminally ill patients, spiritual care can possibly fill a gap that is created with the absence of holistic care. To preserve wellness and promote longevity, Eastern civilizations including China and Japan have for centuries used physical activities and holistic healthcare principles to prevent certain environmental or lifestyle ailments (Congress & Lyons, 1992; Peng & Nisbett, 1999). Twenty-first-century environmental diseases include anxiety (Endler & Kocoviski, 2001; Kantor et al., 2001), lung cancer, and malignant mesothelioma caused by asbestos (Nicholson, Perkel, & Selikoff, 1982). Westerners are rapidly becoming holistically oriented. Western adoption of Eastern health practices such as careful attention to diet and other activities including meditation, breathing exercise, therapeutic massages, acupuncture, shiatsu, naturopathy, and so on (Barnes et al., 2002; J. M. Smith, Sullivan, & Baxter, 2011) affirms human nature as the same regardless of nationality, race, or creed.

HEALTH-PROMOTING EXTRASPIRITED ACTIVITIES

Prayers alone are not enough for a healthy life. A study by Lee, Rexrode, Cook, Manson, and Buring (2001) found health benefits attainable from light-to-moderate activities for women. The researchers found that overweight women with a high risk of coronary heart disease and women who smoked and had high levels of cholesterol benefited from at least 1 hour of walking per week. As if the adage avowing gain from pain would work as a maxim for long and healthy life, a recent study conducted by Albert et al. (1995, p. 585) found that higher levels of household daily chores involving strenuous activity and pulmonary peak expiratory flow were associated with smaller declines in cognitive performance (t value $= 2.5, p < .05$). For parallel conclusions (i.e., active older adults maintain better cognitive functions from physical exercise), see Dustman et al. (1990); Rogers, Myer, and Mortel (1990); and Seeman, Rodin, and Albert (1993). Other studies have taken a race and gender (*raciogender*) distinction in the illness–wellness discourse. According to the World Health Organization (2009), physical inactivity is among eight factors causing death, including use/abuse of alcohol and use of tobacco.

SOCIOLOGICAL IMPACT ON SPIRITUALITY

Physiological illness or psychological unwellness may be held to be tied to the wrath of God—as avowed by Christians, Jews, Muslims, Hindus, and other religions—for humans' improper deeds. Indeed, prior to Western-oriented empiricism, all unknown phenomena were attributed to a god. Prayers and supplications were undertaken to please the gods and restore and/or maintain good health (ap Siôn & Nash, 2013; Bounds, 2004). Research shows that diminished emphasis on theory or high academic achievement coupled with enhanced socialization (e.g., work habits, cleanliness, and other preventive practices) wont the Japanese people to wellness and longevity (Ishikawa, Nishiuchi, Hayashi, & Viswanath, 2012). Thus, it is empirically vetted that wellness is enhanced by fitness and fitness enhances wellness.

Although considered one of the most important modifiable risk factors for noncommunicable diseases (e.g., diabetes and others), physical inactivity was reported by the World Health Organization (2010) as the fourth-leading mortality factor globally (see also Dumith, Hallal, Reis, & Kohl, 2011; Kohl et al., 2012). Light-intensity exercise has been cited to improve wellness for the elderly (Fransson, Alfredsson, Ulf, Knutsson, & Westerholm, 2003) by improving muscle strength, reducing the number of falls (Nowalk, Prendergast, Bayles, D'Amico, & Colvin, 2001), and improving cognitive functions (Ejaz et al., 1997).

On a microlevel or household level, the ramification of wellness can be a function of the family (Bertelli, Bianco, Rossi, Scuticchio, & Brown, 2011; Wrzus, Wagner, & Neyer, 2012), taking into account financial resources, social status, education, and other factors. On a macrolevel, the state of a country's economic, political, and social policies is consequential in the well-being of individuals. The Japanese healthcare system routinely maximizes medical costs to patients through extended hospitalization (Ogawa & Retherford, 1997). Japanese patients stay the longest in hospital of all Organization for Economic Co-operation and Development member countries.

The extent to which a family line extends also plays a role in wellness, especially when there is disparity in the longevity among family members. The status of the childless elderly is less certain than those with children and grandchildren. Some cultures continue to observe the extended family model whereas others such as Japan have done away with it (Raikhola & Kuroki, 2009).

Although the spread of the intensity of religiousness in the United States seems on the wan, religious tolerance is on the rise notwithstanding. There is also growth in diverse religious neighborhoods, accompanied by a decline in religious homogeneity in the family (Putnam, Campbell, & Garrett, 2012). Religious scholars have found interdenominational marital increases, yet the children of such marriages tend to either express or show indifference to the religions of their parents. According to the Pew Research Center (2015a), 28% of adults switched from their parents' or childhood religion to one of their own choosing. This liminal phenomenon can best be understood in terms of the preference for spirituality, which is devoid of the institutional particularities that are characteristics of religion (Marler & Hadaway, 2002). It is apparent, therefore, that 21st-century Millennials are less interested in the liturgical and doctrinal modalities associated with salvation. Children of interdenominational wedded parents tend to express or show indifference to either parent's religions. It remains to be seen if such religious antipathy extends to health and wellness for Millennials.

Banchoff (2007) found 74% of Americans believe that other major world religions, including Hinduism, Buddhism, and Islam, contain some truth about God. According to the Pew Research Center (2015b), government restrictions on religion, which includes bans on certain faiths, increased in 39% of countries between 2012 and 2013. With China and India included in these countries, the Pew Research Center concluded that 5.5 billion, or 77%, of the world's population suffered from religious ban or restrictions by their governments in 2013.

FUTURE RESEARCH DIRECTION

Future research will have to determine the role of culture and effect of religiosity and spirituality in both wellness and ailments. What is already known is that life expectancy is highest in societies that emphasize holistic approach to wellness, which is probably akin to spirituality rather than the remediation regime championed in Western societies.

Wellness and *old age* will have to be distinctively defined in a universal sense. The current approach to wellness is overwhelmingly tilted toward remediation, which is antithetical to the World Health Organization's (1948) definition of *wellness*. The Eastern emphasis of illness prevention (Witmer &

Sweeney, 1992) will have to be incorporated in wellness as more centenarians inherit the earth in the 21st century, and happiness, lifestyle, and the wherewithal of individuals are considered elements of wellness. For over half a century, the World Health Organization's definition of *wellness* has expanded wellness beyond the mere absence of disease, aches, pains, or ailments to include individual lifestyle, physical and mental well-being, as well as socialization.

CONCLUSION

The soteriological teleology of the world's religions (Christians, Buddhists, Hindus, Muslims, and Jews) is apparent in their doctrinal pedagogies. This is more so for terminally ill patients who look to religion and spirituality as their only hope of afterlife salvation and to achieve *nirvana,* the transcendent state of attainment when one is released from the cycle of birth, death, and rebirth.

Culture can be both personal and social. This is more evident in health care, whereby an individual may have a priori determination of pain or illness whilst simultaneously connecting with the collective attribution of illness or wellness based on the shared values of culture. Wellness has to be the fulcrum of reality, which is characterized by the a priori discomfort of pain or unwellness, and the a posteriori reality characterized by the professional application of medication or therapy deemed acceptable by social orthodoxy. As Coward and Ratanakul (1999) stated, "Biomedicine is believed to be neutral, scientific, and an objective description of reality uninfluenced by social processes" (p. 71).

REFERENCES

Albert, M. S., Jones, K., Savage, C. R., Berkman, L., Seeman, T., Blazer, D., & Rowe, J. W. (1995). Predictors of cognitive change in older persons: MacArthur Studies of Successful Aging. *Psychology and Aging, 10*(4), 578–589. doi:10.1037/0882-7974.10.4.578 PMID:8749585

Ama, T. (2005). *Why are the Japanese non-religious? Japanese spirituality: Being non-religious in a religious culture.* Lanham, MD: University of Maryland.

Aoanan, M. L. (2014). Christ and the Filipino cultures: The changing faces of Christ in the Philippines. *Asia Journal of Theology, 28*(2), 283–299.

ap Siôn, T., & Nash, P. (2013). Coping through prayer: An empirical study in implicit religion concerning prayers for children in hospital. *Mental Health, Religion & Culture, 16*(9), 936–952. doi:10.1080/13674676.2012.756186

Aten, J. D., Mangis, M. W., & Campbell, C. (2010). Psychotherapy with rural religious fundamentalist clients. *Journal of Clinical Psychology, 66*(5), 513–523. doi:.2067710.1002/jclp

Atkinson, Q. D., & Bourrat, P. (2011). Beliefs about God, the afterlife and morality support the role of supernatural policing in human cooperation. *Evolution and Human Behavior, 32*(1), 41–49. doi:10.1016/j.evolhumbehav.2010.07.008

Atran, S., & Henrich, J. (2010). The evolution of religion: How cognitive by-products, adaptive learning heuristics, ritual displays, and group competition generate deep commitments to prosocial religion. *Biological Theory, 5*(1), 18–30. doi:10.1162/BIOT_a_00018

Baird, R. M., & Rosenbaum, S. E. (Eds.). (1999). *Hatred, bigotry, and prejudice: Definitions, causes, and solutions*. Amherst, NY: Prometheus.

Banchoff, T. (2007). *Democracy and the new religious pluralism*. Oxford, UK: Oxford University Press. doi:10.1093/acprof:oso/9780195307221.001.0001

Barbour, I. G. (1997). *Religion and science: Historical and contemporary issues*. San Francisco, CA: Harper.

Barnes, P. M., Powell-Griner, E., McFann, K., & Nahin, R. (2002). Complementary and alternative medicine use among adults: United States, 2002. *Seminars in Integrative Medicine, 2*(2), 54–71. doi:10.1016/j.sigm.2004.07.003

Batson, C. D. (1983). Sociobiology and the role of religion in promoting prosocial behavior: An alternative view. *Journal of Personality and Social Psychology, 45*(6), 1380–1385. doi:10.1037/0022-3514.45.6.1380

Batson, C. D., & Gray, R. A. (1981). Religious orientation and helping behavior: Responding to own or to the victim's needs? *Journal of Personality and Social Psychology, 40*(3), 511–520. doi:10.1037/0022-3514.40.3.511

Bauer, T., & Barron, C. R. (1995). Nursing interventions for spiritual care preferences of the community-based elderly. *Journal of Holistic Nursing, 13*(3), 268–279. doi:10.1177/089801019501300308 PMID:7650353

Bayly, C. A. (2004). *The birth of the modern world, 1780–1914: Global connections and comparisons*. Oxford, UK: Blackwell.

Benedict, P. (1975). Catholics and Huguenots in sixteenth-century Rouen: The demographic effects of the religious wars. *French Historical Studies, 9*(2), 209–234. doi:10.2307/286126

Bertelli, M., Bianco, A., Rossi, M., Scuticchio, D., & Brown, I. (2011). Relationship between individual quality of life and family quality of life for people with intellectual disability living in Italy. *Journal of Intellectual Disability Research, 55*(12), 1136–1150. doi:10.1111/j.1365-2788.2011.01464.x PMID:21883597

Blogowska, J., & Saroglou, V. (2011). Religious fundamentalism and limited prosociality as a function of the target. *Journal for the Scientific Study of Religion, 50*(1), 44–60. doi:10.1111/j.1468-5906.2010.01551.x

Bloom, D., Canning, D., & Sevilla, J. (2003). *The demographic dividend: A new perspective on the economic consequences of population change*. Santa Monica, CA: RAND.

Blow, F. (2011). "Everything flows and nothing stays": How students make sense of the historical concepts of change, continuity and development. *Teaching History, 145*, 47–55. Retrieved from ERIC database. (EJ960982)

Bonhoeffer, D. (1959). *The cost of discipleship*. Available from http://www.amazon.com/The-Cost-Discipleship-Dietrich-Bonhoeffer/dp/0684815001

Boocock, S. S. (1989). Controlled diversity: An overview of the Japanese preschool system. *Journal of Japanese Studies*, *15*(1), 41–65. doi:10.2307/132407

Bounds, E. M. (2004). *The complete works of E. M. Bounds on prayer: Experience the wonders of God through prayer*. Grand Rapids, MI: Baker.

Boyer, P. (1994). *The naturalness of religious ideas: A cognitive theory of religion*. Berkeley: University of California Press.

Boyer, P. (2008). Being human: Religion: Bound to believe? *Nature*, *455*(7216), 1038–1039. doi:10.1038/4551038a PMID:18948934

Bradley, C. (2009). The interconnection between religious fundamentalism, spirituality, and the four dimensions of empathy. *Review of Religious Research*, *51*(2), 201–219. Retrieved from http://www.jstor.org/stable/20697334?seq=1#fndtn-page_scan_tab_contents

Bülow, H. H., Sprung, C. L., Reinhart, K., Prayag, S., Du, B., Armaganidis, A., & Levy, M. M. et al. (2008). The world's major religions' points of view on end-of-life decisions in the intensive care unit. *Intensive Care Medicine*, *34*(3), 423–430. doi:10.1007/s00134-007-0973-8 PMID:18157484

Cambray, J. (2009). *Synchronicity: Nature and psyche in an interconnected universe*. College Station: Texas A&M University Press.

Carson, D. A. (1992). Reflections on Christian assurance. *Westminster Theological Journal*, *54*(1), 1–29. Retrieved from http://s3.amazonaws.com/tgc-documents/carson/1992_reflections_on_christian_assurance.pdf

Cavendish, R., Konecny, L., Luise, B. K., & Lanza, M. (2004). Nurses enhance performance through prayer. *Holistic Nursing Practice*, *18*(1), 26–31. doi:10.1097/00004650-200401000-00005 PMID:14765689

Chadwick, H. (1966). *Early Christian thought and the classical tradition: Studies in Justin, Clement, and Origen*. New York, NY: Oxford University Press.

Chen, W., Fukutomi, E., Wada, T., Ishimoto, Y., Kimura, Y., Kasahara, Y., & Matsubayashi, K. et al. (2013). Comprehensive geriatric functional analysis of elderly populations in four categories of the long-term care insurance system in a rural, depopulated and aging town in Japan. *Geriatrics & Gerontology International*, *13*(1), 63–69. doi:10.1111/j.1447-0594.2012.00859.x PMID:22672651

Clark, J. E. (2010). Reconceiving the doctrine of Jesus as savior in terms of the African understanding of an ancestor: A model for the Black Church. *Black Theology: An International Journal*, *8*(2), 140–159. doi:10.1558/blth.v8i2.140

Clark, W. H. (1958). The psychology of religion. *Pastoral Psychology*, *9*(4), 49–55. doi:10.1007/BF01741070

Clayton, J. M., Hancock, K., Parker, S., Butow, P. N., Walder, S., Carrick, S., & Olver, I. N. et al. (2008). Sustaining hope when communicating with terminally ill patients and their families: A systematic review. *Psycho-Oncology*, *17*(7), 641–659. doi:10.1002/pon.1288 PMID:18022831

Clifton, J. (1999). Gender and shame in Masaccio's expulsion from the Garden of Eden. *Art History*, *22*(5), 637–655. doi:10.1111/1467-8365.00180

Congress, E. P., & Lyons, B. P. (1992). Cultural differences in health beliefs: Implications for social work practice in health care settings. *Social Work in Health Care*, *17*(3), 81–96. doi:10.1300/J010v17n03_06 PMID:1465717

Couenhoven, J. (2010). Forgiveness and restoration: A theological exploration. *The Journal of Religion*, *90*(2), 148–170. doi:10.1086/649846

Coward, H. G., & Ratanakul, P. (1999). *A cross-cultural dialogue on health care ethics*. Waterloo, CA: Wilfrid Laurier University Press.

Curlin, F. A., Chin, M. H., Sellergren, S. A., Roach, C. J., & Lantos, J. D. (2006). The association of physicians' religious characteristics with their attitudes and self-reported behaviors regarding religion and spirituality in the clinical encounter. *Medical Care*, *44*(5), 446–453. doi:10.1097/01.mlr.0000207434.12450. ef PMID:16641663

Curlin, F. A., Lantos, J. D., Roach, C. J., Sellergren, S. A., & Chin, M. H. (2005). Religious characteristics of U.S. physicians: A national survey. *Journal of General Internal Medicine*, *20*(7), 629–634. doi:10.1111/j.1525-1497.2005.0119.x PMID:16050858

Curlin, F. A., Sellergren, S. A., Lantos, J. D., & Chin, M. H. (2007). Physicians' observations and interpretations of the influence of religion and spirituality on health. *Archives of Internal Medicine*, *167*(7), 649–654. doi:10.1001/archinte.167.7.649 PMID:17420422

Daley, B. (1991). *The hope of the early Church: A handbook of patristic eschatology*. New York, NY: Cambridge University Press.

Darley, J., & Batson, C. D. (1973). "From Jerusalem to Jericho": A study of situational and dispositional variables in helping behavior. *Journal of Personality and Social Psychology*, *27*(1), 100–108. doi:10.1037/h0034449

Davie, G. (1990). Believing without belonging: Is this the future of religion in Britain? *Social Compass*, *37*(4), 455–469. doi:10.1177/003776890037004004

Davies, P. C. (1971). The debate on eternal punishment in late seventeenth-and eighteenth-century English literature. *Eighteenth-Century Studies*, *4*(3), 257–276. doi:10.2307/2737732

Delkeskamp-Hayes, C. (2009). Diakonia, the state, and ecumenical collaboration: Theological pitfalls. *Christian Bioethics*, *15*(2), 173–198. doi:10.1093/cb/cbp013

Delumeau, J., & O'Connell, M. (2000). *History of paradise: The Garden of Eden in myth and tradition*. Chicago: University of Illinois Press.

Dervic, K., Oquendo, M. A., Grunebaum, M. F., Ellis, S., Burke, A. K., & Mann, J. J. (2004). Religious affiliation and suicide attempt. *The American Journal of Psychiatry*, *161*(12), 2303–2308. doi:10.1176/appi.ajp.161.12.2303 PMID:15569904

Dickerson, M. (2011). *The mind and the machine: What it means to be human and why it matters.* Grand Rapids, MI: Brazos.

Donahue, M. J. (1981). Intrinsic and extrinsic religiousness: Review and meta-analysis. *Journal of Personality and Social Psychology, 48*(2), 400–419. doi:10.1037/0022-3514.48.2.400

Donelson, E. (1999). Psychology of religion and adolescents in the United States: Past to present. *Journal of Adolescence, 22*(2), 187–204. doi:10.1006/jado.1999.0212 PMID:10089119

Duggleby, W., Holtslander, L., Steeves, M., Duggleby-Wenzel, S., & Cunningham, S. (2010). Discursive meaning of hope for older persons with advanced cancer and their caregivers. *Canadian Journal on Aging, 29*(3), 361–367. doi:10.1017/S0714980810000322 PMID:20731889

Dumith, S. C., Hallal, P. C., Reis, R. S., & Kohl, H. W. III. (2011). Worldwide prevalence of physical inactivity and its association with Human Development Index in 76 countries. *Preventive Medicine, 53*(1/2), 24–28. doi:10.1016/j.ypmed.2011.02.017 PMID:21371494

Dunbar, R. I. M. (2009). Mind the bonding gap: Constraints on the evolution of hominin societies. In S. Shennan (Ed.), *Pattern and process in cultural evolution* (pp. 223–234). Berkeley, CA: University of California Press.

Dunn, K. S., & Horgas, A. L. (2000). The prevalence of prayer as a spiritual self-care modality in elders. *Journal of Holistic Nursing, 18*(4), 337–351. doi:10.1177/089801010001800405 PMID:11847791

Duriez, B. (2004a). Are religious people nicer people? Taking a closer look at the religion–empathy relationship. *Mental Health, Religion & Culture, 7*(3), 249–254. doi:10.1080/13674670310001606450

Duriez, B. (2004b). Research: A research note on the relation between religiosity and racism: The importance of the way in which religious contents are being processed. *The International Journal for the Psychology of Religion, 14*(3), 177–191. doi:10.1207/s15327582ijpr1403_3

Dustman, R. E., Emmerson, R. Y., Ruhling, R. O., Shearer, D. E., Steinhaus, L. A., Johnson, S., . . . Shigeoka, J. W. (1990). Age and fitness effects on EEG, ERPs, visual sensitivity, and cognition. *Neurobiology of Aging, 11*(3), 193–200. doi: 90545-b10.1016/0197-4580(90)

Ejaz, F. K., Schur, D., & Noelker, L. S. (1997). The effect of activity involvement and social relationships on boredom among nursing home residents. *Activities, Adaptation and Aging, 21*(4), 53–66. doi:10.1300/J016v21n04_07

Endler, N. S., & Kocoviski, N. L. (2001). State and trait anxiety revisited. *Journal of Anxiety Disorders, 15*(3), 231–245. doi:10.1016/S0887-6185(01)00060-3 PMID:11442141

Evans, J. H. (2006). Who legitimately speaks for religion in public bioethics? In D. E. Guinn (Ed.), *Handbook of bioethics and religion* (pp. 61–80). Oxford, UK: Oxford University Press. doi:10.1093/0195178734.003.0004

Fang, T., & Faure, G. O. (2011). Chinese communication characteristics: A Yin Yang perspective. *International Journal of Intercultural Relations, 35*(3), 320–333. doi:10.1016/j.ijintrel.2010.06.005

Ferreira, M. T., Matsudo, S. M., Ribeiro, M. A., & Ramos, L. R. (2010). Health-related factors correlate with behavior trends in physical activity level in old age: Longitudinal results from a population in São Paulo, Brazil. *BMC Public Health*, *10*(1), 690–699. doi:10.1186/1471-2458-10-690 PMID:21067591

Fouka, G., Plakas, S., Taket, A., Boudioni, M., & Dandoulakis, M. (2012). Health-related religious rituals of the Greek Orthodox Church: Their uptake and meanings. *Journal of Nursing Management*, *20*(8), 1058–1068. doi:10.1111/jonm.12024 PMID:23151108

Francis, L. J., & Pearson, P. R. (1987). Empathic development during adolescence: Religiosity, the missing link? *Personality and Individual Differences*, *8*(1), 145–148. doi:10.1016/0191-8869(87)90024-9

Fransson, E. I., Alfredsson, L. S., Ulf, H., Knutsson, A., & Westerholm, P. J. (2003). Leisure time, occupational and household physical activity, and risk factors for cardiovascular disease in working men and women: The WOLF study. *Scandinavian Journal of Public Health*, *31*(5), 324–333. doi:10.1080/14034940210165055 PMID:14555368

Fretheim, T. E. (2000). Divine judgment and the warming of the world: An Old Testament perspective. *Word & World*, (Suppl. 4), 21–32. Available from https://wordandworld.luthersem.edu/supplement_4.aspx

Gallup, G. (1985). Religion in America. *The Annals of the American Academy of Political and Social Science*, *480*(1), 167–174. doi:10.1177/0002716285480001014

Gallup, G. Jr. (1995). Have attitudes toward homosexuals been shaped by natural selection? *Ethology and Sociobiology*, *16*(1), 53–70. doi:10.1016/0162-3095(94)00028-6

Gallup, G., & Lindsay, D. M. (1999). *Surveying the religious landscape: Trends in U.S. beliefs*. Harrisburg, PA: Morehouse.

George, L. K., Ellison, C. G., & Larson, D. B. (2002). Exploring the relationships between religious involvement and health. *Psychological Inquiry*, *13*(3), 190–200. doi:10.1207/S15327965PLI1303_04

Gervais, W. M., Willard, A. K., Norenzayan, A., & Henrich, J. (2011). The cultural transmission of faith: Why innate intuitions are necessary, but insufficient, to explain religious belief. *Religion*, *41*(3), 389–410. doi:10.1080/0048721X.2011.604510

Gibran, K. (1997). *The prophet*. Hertfordshire, UK: Wordsworth.

Grant, D. (2004). Spiritual interventions: How, when, and why nurses use them. *Holistic Nursing Practice*, *18*(1), 36–41. doi:10.1097/00004650-200401000-00007 PMID:14765691

Greenwald, A. G. (1975). Does the Good Samaritan parable increase helping? A comment on Darley and Batson's no-effect conclusion. *Journal of Personality and Social Psychology*, *32*(4), 578–583. doi:10.1037/0022-3514.32.4.578

Hackett, C., & Lindsay, D. M. (2008). Measuring evangelicalism: Consequences of different operationalization strategies. *Journal for the Scientific Study of Religion*, *47*(3), 499–514. doi:10.1111/j.1468-5906.2008.00423.x

Hatfield, R. (2004). What can I do when . . . I doubt there is a heaven and hell? In *Fourteenth Annual Truth in Love lectureship* (pp. 113–122). Retrieved from http://citeseerx.ist.psu. edu/viewdoc/downloa d?doi=10.1.1.465.9606&rep=rep1&type=pdf#page=111

Hellie, R. (2005). The structure of Russian imperial history. *History and Theory*, *44*(4), 88–112. doi:10.1111/j.1468-2303.2005.00344.x

Herek, G. M. (2009). Sexual stigma and sexual prejudice in the United States: A conceptual framework. In D. A. Hope (Ed.), *Contemporary perspectives on lesbian, gay and bisexual identities: The 54th Nebraska Symposium on Motivation* (pp. 65–111). New York, NY: Springer. doi:10.1007/978-0-387-09556-1_4

Hill, E. D., Cohen, A. B., Terrell, H. K., & Nagoshi, C. T. (2010). The role of social cognition in the religious fundamentalism-prejudice relationship. *Journal for the Scientific Study of Religion*, *49*(4), 724–739. doi:10.1111/j.1468-5906.2010.01542.x

Hill, P. C., & Pargament, K. I. (2008). Advances in the conceptualization and measurement of religion and spirituality: Implications for physical and mental health research. Psychology of Religion and Spirituality, S(1), 3–17. doi:10.1037/1941-1022.s.1.3

Hoffman, M. L. (1975). Developmental synthesis of affect and cognition and its implications for altruistic motivation. *Developmental Psychology*, *11*(5), 607–622. doi:10.1037/0012-1649.11.5.607

Hoffman, M. L. (1977). Empathy, its development and prosocial implications. In C. B. Keasey (Ed.), *Nebraska Symposium on Motivation* (Vol. 25, pp. 169–217). Lincoln: University of Nebraska Press.

Hoffman, M. L. (1981). Is altruism part of human nature?. *Journal of Personality and Social Psychology*, *40*(1), 121–137. doi:10.1037/0022-3514.40.1.121

Holloway, S. D. (1999). The role of religious beliefs in early childhood education: Christian and Buddhist preschools in Japan. *Early Childhood Research & Practice, 1*(2), 2–19. Retrieved from http://ecrp. uiuc.edu/v1n2/holloway.html

Hsiao, F. S. T., Jen, F. C., & Lee, C. F. (1990). Impacts of culture and communist Orthodoxy on Chinese management. In J. Child & M. Lockett (Eds.), Advances in Chinese industrial studies (Vol. 1, pp. 301–314). [Retrieved fromhttps://www.ideals.illinois.edu/bitstream/handle/2142/28848/impactsofculture1447hsia.pdf?sequence=1

Ishikawa, Y., Nishiuchi, H., Hayashi, H., & Viswanath, K. (2012). Socioeconomic status and health communication inequalities in Japan: A nationwide cross-sectional survey. *PLoS ONE, 7*(7), 1–9. doi:10.1371/journal.pone.0040664 PMID:22808229

Johnson, D. D. (2005). God's punishment and public goods. *Human Nature (Hawthorne, N.Y.)*, *16*(4), 410–446. doi:10.1007/s12110-005-1017-0 PMID:26189839

Johnson, D. D., & Bering, J. M. (2006). Hand of God, mind of man: Punishment and cognition in the evolution of cooperation. *Evolutionary Psychology*, *4*(1), 219–233. http://www.qub.ie/schools/InstituteofCognitionCulture/FileUploadPage/Filetoupload,90239,en.pdf doi:10.1177/147470490600400119

Jonsen, A. R. (2006). A history of religion and bioethics. In D. E. Guinn (Ed.), *Handbook of bioethics and religion* (pp. 23–36). Oxford, UK: Oxford University Press. doi:10.1093/0195178734.003.0002

Jung, C. G., & Main, R. (1997). *Jung on synchronicity and the paranormal.* London: Routledge.

Jung, J. (2012). Islamophobia? Religion, contact with Muslims, and the respect for Islam. *Review of Religious Research, 54*(1), 113–126. doi:10.1007/s13644-011-0033-2

Kant, I. (1949). *Fundamental principles of the metaphysic of morals* (T. K. Abbott, Trans.). (Original work published 1785). Retrieved from http://philosophy.eserver.org/kant/ metaphys-of-morals.txt

Kant, I. (1964). *The metaphysical principles of virtue: Part II of The Metaphysics of Morals* (J. Ellington, Trans.). New York, NY: The Library of Liberal Arts. (Original work published 1797)

Kant, I. (2004). *Religion within the boundaries of mere reason* (A. Wood & G. Di Viovanni, Trans.). Cambridge, UK: Cambridge University Press. (Original work published 1793)

Kantor, L., Endler, N. S., Heslegrave, R. J., & Kocovski, N. L. (2001). Validating self-report measures of state and trait anxiety against a physiological measure. *Current Psychology (New Brunswick, N.J.), 20*(3), 207–215. doi:10.1007/s12144-001-1007-2

Kelly, J. N. D. (2000). *Early Christian doctrines.* London: Continuum.

King, D. E., & Bushwick, B. (1994). Beliefs and attitudes of hospital inpatients about faith healing and prayer. *Journal of Family Practice, 39*(4), 349–352. Retrieved from EBSCOhost database. (Accession No. 24534177)

Kirk, G. S. (1951). Natural change in Heraclitus. *Mind, 55*(27), 35–42. doi:.3510.1093/mind/lx.237

Kleinman, A. (1988). *The illness narratives: Suffering, healing, and the human condition.* New York, NY: Basic.

Koenig, H. G., McCullough, M. E., & Larson, D. B. (2001). *Handbook of religion and health.* New York, NY: Oxford University Press. doi:10.1093/acprof:oso/9780195118667.001.0001

Kohl, H. W. III, Craig, C. L., Lambert, E. V., Inoue, S., Alkandari, J. R., Leetongin, G., & Kahlmeier, S. (2012). The pandemic of physical inactivity: Global action for public health. *Lancet, 380*(9838), 294–305. doi:10.1016/S0140-6736(12)60898-8 PMID:22818941

Krebs, D. L. (1975). Empathy and altruism. *Journal of Personality and Social Psychology, 32*(6), 1134–1146. doi:10.1037/0022-3514.32.6.1134 PMID:1214217

Kylmä, J., Duggleby, W., Cooper, D., & Molander, G. (2009). Hope in palliative care: An integrative review. *Palliative & Supportive Care, 7*(3), 365–377. doi:10.1017/S1478951509990307 PMID:19788779

Largen, K. J. (2006). Liberation, salvation, enlightenment: An exercise in comparative soteriology. *Dialog, 45*(3), 263–274. doi:10.1111/j.1540-6385.2006.00276.x

Larson, D. B., Swyers, J. P., & McCullough, M. E. (1998). *Scientific research on spirituality and health: A report based on the Scientific Progress in Spirituality Conferences.* Bethesda, MD: National Institute for Healthcare Research.

Larson, S. S., & Larson, D. B. (1992). Clinical religious research: How to enhance risk of disease: Don't go to church. *Christian Medical Dental Society Journal, 23*(3), 14–19. PMID:1298519

Lee, I. M., Rexrode, K. M., Cook, N. R., Manson, J. E., & Buring, J. E. (2001). Physical activity and coronary heart disease in women: Is "No pain, no gain" passé? *Journal of the American Medical Association*, *285*(11), 1447–1454. doi:10.1001/jama.285.11.1447 PMID:11255420

Lewer, J. J., & Van den Berg, H. (2007). Religion and international trade: Does the sharing of a religious culture facilitate the formation of trade networks? *American Journal of Economics and Sociology*, *66*(4), 765–794. doi:10.1111/j.1536-7150.2007.00539.x

Lin, H. R., & Bauer-Wu, S. M. (2003). Psycho-spiritual well-being in patients with advanced cancer: An integrative review of the literature. *Journal of Advanced Nursing*, *44*(1), 69–80. doi:10.1046/j.1365-2648.2003.02768.x PMID:12956671

Madelung, W. (1985). *Religious schools and sects in medieval Islam* (Vol. 213). Surrey, UK: Ashgate.

Madelung, W., & Schmidtke, S. (2013). *Studies in medieval Muslim thought and history*. Surrey, UK: Ashgate.

Malota, E. (2012). Global cultures? Consequences of globalization on cultural differences, a commentary approach. *International Journal of Business Insights & Transformation*, *5*(3), 94–100.

Mantala-Bozos, I. K. (2003). The role of religion and culture on bereavement: The example of the Orthodox Christian tradition. *Journal of Critical Psychology, Counselling and Psychotherapy, 3*(2), 96–110. Retrieved from https://www.hospicevolunteerassociation. org/HVANewsletter/Vol2No1_2003Mar03_The%20RoleOfReligion&CultureOnBereavement.pdf

Marler, P. L., & Hadaway, C. K. (2002). "Being religious" or "being spiritual" in America: A zero-sum proposition? *Journal for the Scientific Study of Religion*, *41*(2), 289–300. doi:10.1111/1468-5906.00117

Masel, M. C., Raji, M., & Peek, M. (2010). Education and physical activity mediate the relationship between ethnicity and cognitive function in late middle-aged adults. *Ethnicity & Health*, *15*(3), 283–302. doi:10.1080/13557851003681273 PMID:20401816

Masojć, M., & Bech, J. (2011). Introduction. *Acta Archaeologica, 82*(1), 203-204. doi:.1600-0390.2011.00460.x10.1111/j

Mason, J. W. T. (2002). *The meaning of Shinto*. Victoria, CA: Trafford.

McFarland, H. N. (1967). *The rush hour of the gods: A study of new religious movements in Japan* (Vol. 171). New York, NY: Macmillan.

Meraviglia, M. G. (2004). The effects of spirituality on well-being of people with lung cancer. *Oncology Nursing Forum*, *31*(1), 89–94. doi:10.1188/04.ONF.89-94 PMID:14722592

Meraviglia, M. G. (2006). Effects of spirituality in breast cancer survivors. *Oncology Nursing Forum*, *33*(1), E1–E7. doi:10.1188/06.ONF.E1-E7 PMID:16470229

Miller, W. R., & Thoresen, C. E. (2003). Spirituality, religion, and health: An emerging research field. *The American Psychologist*, *58*(1), 24–35. doi:10.1037/0003-066X.58.1.24 PMID:12674816

Mohamed, M. A. (2015). Classifying Muslims. *Cross Currents*, *65*(3), 334–345. doi:10.1111/cros.12143

Monsma, S. V. (2007). Religion and philanthropic giving and volunteering: Building blocks for civic responsibility. *Interdisciplinary Journal of Research on Religion, 3*, Art. 1. Available from http://www.religjournal.com/articles/article_view.php?id=19

Morewedge, P. (1979). *Islamic philosophical theology*. Albany, NY: State University of New York Press.

Moses, J. (2007). *Oneness: Great principles shared by all religions*. New York, NY: Random House.

Nagai-Jacobson, M. G., & Burkhardt, M. A. (1989). Spirituality: Cornerstone of holistic nursing practice. *Holistic Nursing Practice, 3*(3), 18–26. doi:10.1097/00004650-198905000-00006 PMID:2768352

Narayanasamy, A. (2001). *Spiritual care: A practical guide for nurses and health care practitioners*. Dunfermline, UK: Quay.

Nelson, D. R. (2009). *What's wrong with sin: Sin in individual and social perspective from Schleiermacher to theologies of liberation*. New York, NY: T & T Clark.

Nelson, J. M. (2009). Psychology, religion, and spirituality. New York, NY: Springer.

Nelson, J. M., & Slife, B. D. (2012). Theoretical and epistemological foundations. In L. J. Miller (Ed.), *The Oxford handbook of psychology and spirituality* (pp. 21–35). Oxford, UK: Oxford University Press.

Neuberg, S. L., Kenrick, D. T., & Schaller, M. (2011). Human threat management systems: Self-protection and disease avoidance. *Neuroscience and Biobehavioral Reviews, 35*(4), 1042–1051. doi:10.1016/j.neubiorev.2010.08.011 PMID:20833199

Nicholson, W. J., Perkel, G., & Selikoff, I. J. (1982). Occupational exposure to asbestos: Population at risk and projected mortality—1980–2030. *American Journal of Industrial Medicine, 3*(3), 259–311. doi:10.1002/ajim.4700030305 PMID:7171087

Nigosian, S. A. (2000). *World religions: A historical approach* (3rd ed.). New York, NY: Bedford/St. Martin's.

Nigosian, S. A. (2010). Religion through the ages. *Theological Review, 31*(2), 179–202. Retrieved from EBSCOhost database. (Accession No. 59664996) rfroebsco

Nowalk, M. P., Prendergast, J. M., Bayles, C. M., D'Amico, F. J., & Colvin, G. C. (2001). A randomized trial of exercise programs among older individuals living in two long-term care facilities: The FallsFREE program. *Journal of the American Geriatrics Society, 49*(7), 859–865. doi:10.1046/j.1532-5415.2001.49174.x PMID:11527475

Oestigaard, T. (2009). The materiality of hell: The Christian hell in a world religion context. *Material Religion, 5*(3), 312–331. doi:10.2752/175183409X12550007729941

Ogawa, N., & Retherford, R. D. (1993). Care of the elderly in Japan: Changing norms and expectations. *Journal of Marriage and the Family, 55*(3), 585–597. doi:10.2307/353340

Ogawa, N., & Retherford, R. D. (1997). Shifting costs of caring for the elderly back to families in Japan: Will it work? *Population and Development Review, 23*(1), 59–94. doi:10.2307/2137461

Organisation for Economic Co-operation and Development. (2013). *Health at a glance 2013: OECD indicators.* doi:10.1787/health_glance-2013-en

Parrinder, E. G. (1999). *World religions: From ancient history to the present.* New York, NY: Barnes & Noble.

Peng, K., & Nisbett, R. E. (1999). Culture, dialectics, and reasoning about contradiction. *The American Psychologist, 54*(9), 741–754. doi:10.1037/0003-066X.54.9.741

Perry, E. (1963). Interfaith encounter. *Journal of the American Academy of Religion, 31*(2), 160–162. doi:10.1093/jaarel/XXXI.2.160

Pew Research Center. (2011). *Table: Christian population as percentages of total population by country.* Retrieved from http://www.pewforum.org/2011/12/19/table-christian-population-as-percentages-of-total-population-by-country/

Pew Research Center. (2015a). *Latest trends in religious restrictions and hostilities.* Retrieved from http://www.pewforum.org/2015/02/26/religious-hostilities/

Pew Research Center. (2015b). *U.S. public becoming less religious.* Retrieved from http://www.pewforum.org/2015/11/03/u-s-public-becoming-less-religious/

Picone, M. (2012). Suicide and the afterlife: Popular religion and the standardisation of 'culture' in Japan. *Culture, Medicine and Psychiatry, 36*(2), 391–408. doi:10.1007/s11013-012-9261-3 PMID:22549663

Pinguet, M. (1993). *Voluntary death in Japan.* Cambridge, UK: Polity.

Plante, T. G., & Sherman, A. C. (Eds.). (2001). *Faith and health: Psychological perspectives.* New York, NY: Guilford.

Polzer Casarez, R. L., & Engebretson, J. C. (2012). Ethical issues of incorporating spiritual care into clinical practice. *Journal of Clinical Nursing, 21*(15/16), 2099–2107. doi:.1365-2702.2012.04168.x10.1111/j

Post, S. G., Puchalski, C. M., & Larson, D. B. (2000). Physicians and patient spirituality: Professional boundaries, competency, and ethics. *Annals of Internal Medicine, 132*(7), 578–583. doi:10.7326/0003-4819-132-7-200004040-00010 PMID:10744595

Powell, L. H., Shahabi, L., & Thoresen, C. E. (2003). Religion and spirituality: Linkages to physical health. *The American Psychologist, 58*(1), 36–52. doi:10.1037/0003-066X.58.1.36 PMID:12674817

Prior, K. N., & Bond, M. J. (2008). The measurement of abnormal illness behavior: Toward a new research agenda for the Illness Behavior Questionnaire. *Journal of Psychosomatic Research, 64*(3), 245–253. doi:10.1016/j.jpsychores.2007.10.013 PMID:18291238

Putnam, R. D., Campbell, D. E., & Garrett, S. R. (2012). *American grace: How religion divides and unites us.* New York, NY: Simon & Schuster.

Qin, D. (2015). The starting point of Christology: From below or from above? Part I. *Asian Journal of Pentecostal Studies, 18*(1), 21–37.

Raikhola, P. S., & Kuroki, Y. (2009). Aging and elderly care practice in Japan: Main issues, policy and program perspective; What lessons can be learned from Japanese experiences? *Dhaulagiri Journal of Sociology & Anthropology, 3*, 41–82. doi:10.3126/dsaj.v3i0.2781

Reader, I. (2012). Secularisation, R.I.P.? Nonsense! The 'rush hour away from the gods' and the decline of religion in contemporary Japan. *Journal of Religion in Japan, 1*(1), 7–36. doi:10.1163/221183412X628370

Ring, K. (2000). Religious wars in the NDE movement: Some personal reflections on Michael Sabom's *Light & Death. Journal of Near-Death Studies, 18*(4), 215–244. doi::102291670788710.1023/A

Rogers, R. L., Meyer, J. S., & Mortel, K. F. (1990). After reaching retirement age physical activity sustains cerebral perfusion and cognition. *Journal of the American Geriatrics Society, 38*(2), 123–128. doi:10.1111/j.1532-5415.1990.tb03472.x PMID:2299115

Rowatt, W. C., Tsang, J., Kelly, J., LaMartina, B., McCullers, M., & McKinley, A. (2006). Associations between religious personality dimensions and implicit homosexual prejudice. *Journal for the Scientific Study of Religion, 45*(3), 397–406. doi:.1468-5906.2006.00314.x10.1111/j

Sachs, J. R. (1991). Current eschatology: Universal salvation and the problem of hell. *Theological Studies, 52*(2), 227–254. doi:10.1177/004056399105200203

Sachs, J. R. (1993). Apocatastasis in patristic theology. *Theological Studies, 54*(4), 617–640. doi:10.1177/004056399305400402

Salsman, J. M., Brown, T. L., Brechting, E. H., & Carlson, C. R. (2005). The link between religion and spirituality and psychological adjustment: The mediating role of optimism and social support. *Personality and Social Psychology Bulletin, 31*(4), 522–535. doi:10.1177/0146167204271563 PMID:15743986

Seeman, T. E., Dubin, L. F., & Seeman, M. (2003). Religiosity/spirituality and health: A critical review of the evidence for biological pathways. *The American Psychologist, 58*(1), 53–63. doi:10.1037/0003-066X.58.1.53 PMID:12674818

Seeman, T. E., Rodin, J., & Albert, M. (1993). Self-efficacy and cognitive performance in high-functioning older individuals: MacArthur Studies of Successful Aging. *Journal of Aging and Health, 5*(4), 455–474. doi:10.1177/089826439300500403

Seul, J. R. (1999). 'Ours is the way of God': Religion, identity, and intergroup conflict. *Journal of Peace Research, 36*(5), 553–569. doi:10.1177/0022343399036005004

Seybold, K. S., & Hill, P. C. (2001). The role of religion and spirituality in mental and physical health. *Current Directions in Psychological Science, 10*(1), 21–24. doi:10.1111/1467-8721.00106

Sides, H. (1997). The calibration of belief. *New York Times Magazine, 7*, 16–21.

Slife, B. D., & Reber, J. S. (2012). Conceptualizing religious practices in psychological research: Problems and prospects. *Pastoral Psychology, 61*(5/6), 735–746. doi:10.1007/s11089-011-0397-9

Sloan, R. P., Bagiella, E., & Powell, T. (1999). Religion, spirituality, and medicine. *Lancet, 353*(9153), 664–667. doi:10.1016/S0140-6736(98)07376-0 PMID:10030348

Sloan, R. P., Bagiella, E., VandeCreek, L., Hover, M., Casalone, C., Jinpu Hirsch, T., & Poulos, P. et al. (2000). Should physicians prescribe religious activities? *The New England Journal of Medicine, 342*(25), 1913–1916. doi:10.1056/NEJM200006223422513 PMID:10861331

Smedley, B. D., Stith, A. Y., & Nelson, A. R. (Eds.). (2009). *Unequal treatment: Confronting racial and ethnic disparities in healthcare.* Washington, DC: National Academies.

Smith, B. G. (2012). The tangled web of Buddhism: An Internet analysis of religious doctrinal differences. *Contemporary Buddhism, 13*(2), 301–319. doi:. 71971110.1080/14639947.2012

Smith, C., & Emerson, M. (1998). *American evangelicalism: Embattled and thriving.* IL: University of Chicago Press.

Smith, J. M., Sullivan, S. J., & Baxter, G. D. (2011). Complementary and alternative medicine: Contemporary trends and issues. *The Physical Therapy Review, 16*(2), 91–95. doi:10.1179/1743288X1 1Y.0000000013

Smith, W. C. (1993). *What is scripture? A comparative approach.* Minneapolis, MN: Fortress.

Snarey, J. (1996). The natural environment's impact upon religious ethics: A cross-cultural study. *Journal for the Scientific Study of Religion, 35*(2), 85–96. doi:10.2307/1387077

Sor-hoon, T. (2011). The *Dao* of politics: *Li* (rituals/rites) and laws as pragmatic tools of government. *Philosophy East & West, 61*(3), 468–491. doi:10.1353/pew.2011.0043

Sprochi, A. K. (2010). Review of the book *Islam in the world today: A handbook of politics, religion, culture, and society,* by W. Ende & U. Steinbach, Eds. *Library Journal, 135*(12), 110–111.

Stein, M., & Jung, C. G. (1985). *Jung's treatment of Christianity: The psychotherapy of a religious tradition.* Asheville, NC: Chiron.

Takahashi, Y. (2001). *Jisatsu no sain wo yomitoru* [Reading a signal of suicide]. Tokyo, Japan: Kodansha.

Takakusu, J. (2002). *The essentials of Buddhist philosophy.* Honolulu, HI: Motilal Banarsidass.

Tanaka, K. (2010). Limitations for measuring religion in a different cultural context: The case of Japan. *The Social Science Journal, 47*(4), 845–852. doi:10.1016/j.soscij.2010.07.010 PMID:21113429

Taylor, E. J. (2003). Spiritual needs of patients with cancer and family caregivers. *Cancer Nursing, 26*(4), 260–266. doi:10.1097/00002820-200308000-00002 PMID:12886116

Thang Moe, D. (2015). Sin and evil in Christian and Buddhist perspectives: A quest for theodicy. *Asia Journal of Theology, 29*(1), 22–46.

Thoresen, C. E. (1999). Spirituality and health: Is there a relationship? *Journal of Health Psychology, 4*(3), 291–300. doi:10.1177/135910539900400314 PMID:22021598

Thoresen, C. E., Harris, A. H., & Oman, D. (2001). Spirituality, religion, and health: Evidence, issues, and concerns. In T. G. Plante & A. C. Sherman (Eds.), *Faith and health: Psychological perspectives* (pp. 15–52). New York, NY: Guilford.

Touhy, T. A. (2001). Nurturing hope and spirituality in the nursing home. *Holistic Nursing Practice, 15*(4), 45–56. doi:10.1097/00004650-200107000-00008 PMID:12120495

Trelstad, M. (2014). The many meanings of the only Christ. *Dialog: A Journal of Theology, 53*(3), 179–184. doi:10.1111/dial.12114

Treolar, L. L. (2000). Spiritual beliefs, response to disability, and the Church—Part 2. *Journal of Religion Disability & Health, 4*(1), 5–31. doi:10.1300/J095v04n01_02

Tsang, J. A., & Rowatt, W. C. (2007). The relationship between religious orientation, right-wing authoritarianism, and implicit sexual prejudice. *The International Journal for the Psychology of Religion, 17*(2), 99–120. doi:10.1080/10508610701244122

Ueno, K. (2005). Suicide as Japan's major export: A Note on Japanese suicide culture. *Revista Espaço Acadêmico, 44*. Retrieved from http://www.espacoacademico.com.br/044/ 44eueno_ing.htm

van Leeuwen, R., Tiesinga, L. J., Jochemasen, H., & Post, D. (2007). Aspects of spirituality concerning illness. *Scandinavian Journal of Caring Sciences, 21*(4), 482–489. doi:10.1111/j.1471-6712.2007.00502.x PMID:18036011

Walton, J. (1999). Spirituality of patients recovering from an acute myocardial infarction: A grounded theory study. *Journal of Holistic Nursing, 17*(1), 34–53. doi:10.1177/089801019901700104 PMID:10373841

Walton, J., & Sullivan, N. (2004). Men of prayer: Spirituality of men with prostate cancer a grounded theory study. *Journal of Holistic Nursing, 22*(2), 133–151. doi:10.1177/0898010104264778 PMID:15154989

Warner, R. S. (1979). Theoretical barriers to the understanding of evangelical Christianity. *Sociology of Religion, 40*(1), 1–9. doi:10.2307/3710492

Watson, P. J., Hood, R. W. Jr, Morris, R. J., & Hall, J. R. (1984). Empathy, religious orientation, and social desirability. *The Journal of Psychology, 117*(2), 211–216. doi:10.1080/00223980.1984.9923679

Watts, J. W. (2005). Ritual legitimacy and scriptural authority. *Journal of Biblical Literature, 124*(3), 401–417. doi:10.2307/30041032

Whoqol, G. (2006). A cross-cultural study of spirituality, religion, and personal beliefs as components of quality of life. *Social Science & Medicine, 62*(6), 1486–1497. doi:10.1016/j.socscimed.2005.08.001 PMID:16168541

Witmer, J. M., & Sweeney, T. J. (1992). A holistic model for wellness and prevention over the life span. *Journal of Counseling and Development, 71*(2), 140–148. doi:10.1002/j.1556-6676.1992.tb02189.x

Wollons, R. (1993, Spring). The Black Forest in a bamboo garden: Missionary kindergartens in Japan, 1868–1912. *History of Education Quarterly, 33*(1), 1–35. doi:10.2307/368518

World Health Organization. (1948). *Preamble to the Constitution of the World Health Organization as adopted by the International Health Conference, New York, 19–22 June, 1946.* Geneva, Switzerland: Author. Retrieved from http://www.ncbi.nlm.nih.gov/pmc/ articles/PMC2567708/

World Health Organization. (2009). *Interventions on diet and physical activity: What works: Summary report.* Retrieved from http://www.who.int/dietphysicalactivity/summary-report-09.pdf

World Health Organization. (2010). *World health statistics 2010*. Retrieved from http://www.who.int/gho/publications/world_health_statistics/EN_WHS10_Full.pdf

Wright, K. (2010). Employing spirituality and faith as a protective factor against suicide. *Mental Health Nursing, 30*(6), 14–15.

Wrzus, C., Wagner, J., & Neyer, F. J. (2012). The interdependence of horizontal family relationships and friendships relates to higher well-being. *Personal Relationships, 19*(3), 465–482. doi:10.1111/j.1475-6811.2011.01373.x

Yankelovich Partners. (1996). *Family Physician Survey*. Radnor, PA: John Templeton.

Zinnbauer, B. J., Pargament, K. I., Cole, B., Rye, M. S., Butter, E. M., Belavich, T. G., & Kadar, J. L. et al. (1997). Religion and spirituality: Unfuzzying the fuzzy. *Journal for the Scientific Study of Religion, 36*(4), 549–564. doi:10.2307/1387689

Zinnbauer, B. J., Pargament, K. I., & Scott, A. B. (1999). The emerging meanings of religiousness and spirituality: Problems and prospects. *Journal of Personality, 67*(6), 889–919. doi:10.1111/1467-6494.00077

ADDITIONAL READING

Al-Bar, M. A., & Chamsi-Pasha, H. (2015). *Contemporary bioethics: Islamic perspective*. New York, NY: Springer. doi:10.1007/978-3-319-18428-9

Anderson, G. (1989). Celibacy or consummation in the garden? Reflections on early Jewish and Christian interpretations of the Garden of Eden. *The Harvard Theological Review, 82*(2), 121–148. doi:10.1017/S0017816000016084

Chan, C. L. W. (2001). *An Eastern body-mind-spirit approach: A training manual with one-second techniques*. China: University of Hong Kong.

Chan, C. L. W., Ng, S. M., Ho, R. T., & Chow, A. Y. (2006). East meets West: Applying Eastern spirituality in clinical practice. *Journal of Clinical Nursing, 15*(7), 822–832. doi:10.1111/j.1365-2702.2006.01649.x PMID:16879375

Dyson, J., Cobb, M., & Forman, D. (1997). The meaning of spirituality: A literature review. *Journal of Advanced Nursing, 26*(6), 1183–1188. doi:10.1111/j.1365-2648.1997.tb00811.x PMID:9429969

Grasmick, H. G., Davenport, E., Chamlin, M. B., & Bursik, R. J. (1992). Protestant fundamentalism and the retributive doctrine of punishment. *Criminology, 30*(1), 21–46. doi:10.1111/j.1745-9125.1992.tb01092.x

Lucchetti, G., Lucchetti, A., & Puchalski, C. (2012). Spirituality in medical education: Global reality? *Journal of Religion and Health, 51*(1), 3–19. doi:10.1007/s10943-011-9557-6 PMID:22130583

McSherry, W. (2000). *Making sense of spirituality in nursing practice: An interactive approach*. London, England: Jessica Kingsley.

Narayanasamy, A. (1995). Spiritual care of chronically ill patients. *Journal of Clinical Nursing, 4*(6), 397–398. doi:10.1111/j.1365-2702.1995.tb00042.x PMID:8535582

Russell, B. (1957). *Why I am not a Christian and other essays on religion and related subjects.* Retrieved from https://books.google.com/

Sherman, A. C. (Ed.). (2001). *Faith and health: Psychological perspectives.* New York, NY: Guilford.

Unnever, J. D., & Cullen, F. T. (2006). Christian fundamentalism and support for capital punishment. *Journal of Research in Crime and Delinquency, 43*(2), 169–197. doi:10.1177/0022427805280067

KEY TERMS AND DEFINITIONS

Disunderstanding: Refusal to concede an idea. Unwillingness to acknowledge or attempt to understand a given concept, principle, act, or activity for fear that such understanding or acknowledgement is antithetical to one's own principles.

Eleemosynary: Relating to charity.

Empiricism: Information or knowledge that is based on hands-on or practical experience.

Eschatology: The field of theology that is concerned with death, judgment, salvation, and the final destiny of humans.

Nirvana: The final goal of Buddhists, which is a state of perfection and enlightenment in Buddhism in which an individual is free from wants or desire.

Orthodox: Traditional, conventional, or mainstream.

Samsara: A Hindu and Buddhist conception dealing with a cycle of birth, death, and rebirth that is characterized by the imperfection of individuals in the material world.

Sin: An offense in the Christian faith by which individuals are required to repent or be condemned by God and be punished and/or deprived of salvation.

Chapter 16
Employee Wellness Programs:
An International Examination

Jennifer Bandy
Independent Researcher, USA

ABSTRACT

The chapter purpose is to examine Employee Wellness Programs (EWP) internationally. The review of previous literature and discovery of outcomes and recommendations for future research are explored. Additionally, developing culturally competent international EWPs and training the development team are presented. The importance of intercultural communication, interpersonal and intrapersonal competence, and indigenous and cross-cultural psychology applications offer the foundation for the development of effective EWPs internationally. Issues, controversies, and problems, along with solutions and recommendations for the development of culturally competent EWPs are reviewed.

INTRODUCTION

Globalization has been defined in many ways and evokes diverse responses across cultures. Stevens and Gielen (2007) asserted globalization is not a new phenomenon, rather it has been around for thousands of years and can be described in two ways: unilateral and enlightened globalization. Unilateral globalization refers to the belief in superiority of its own culture, values, and ideals and the imposition of a single standard on all cultures.

However, enlightened globalization is based on understanding, dialogue, respect, and integrating knowledge to foster cultural development. This involves the recognition that each culture has a different set of values, beliefs, and resources and integrates information to transform the world. Fox et al. (2009) posited critical writers describe globalization as a form of continuing colonialism or imperialism, calling it 're-colonization' or neo'colonialism', due to the pattern of present-day global relationships follows that of the former European colonial empires.

Technology has aided in connecting individuals around the globe but internet technology is largely a privilege experienced by the affluent (Klopf & McCroskey, 2007). However, globalization, when con-

DOI: 10.4018/978-1-5225-0522-8.ch016

sidering general psychology, is considered an example of unilateral globalization that has been imposed in various parts of the world (Stevens & Gielen, 2007). There is a need for psychologists to move toward indigenous perspectives in order to prevent such criticism.

Indigenous psychologists are more focused on understanding each culture from its own frame of reference, including its own ecological, historical, philosophical, and religious or spiritual context (Stevens & Gielen, 2007). Further, Indigenous psychologists argue that general psychology ignores the wealth of both academic and cultural traditions of non-Western countries that may have enriched and advanced the field. Going beyond general psychology, scholars move past intra-individual processes and systematically analyze phenomena that are influenced by context, relationship, society, and culture. Gerstein et al. (2009) asserts indigenous psychology is based on knowledge which emerges from the target culture rather than either directly or indirectly from another location. There is an underlying premise which suggests psychological principles cannot be assumed to be universally similar. Typically, this knowledge stems from scholars located in the specific culture, has meaning within the specific culture, and is for the individuals within that culture.

Stevens and Gielen (2007) posit indigenous psychology advocates examining knowledge, skills, and beliefs individuals have about themselves and how they function in their cultural context. This is not restricted to the study of indigenous individuals or even the use of a particular method, rather indigenous psychology is in fact necessary for all cultural, indigenous, and ethnic groups, including economically developed countries. Moreover, some scholars argue that theories and strategies used in the United States are in fact indigenous to the U.S. cultures (Gerstein et al., 2009).

Multinational organizations employing international employee wellness programs (EWPs), however, may employ indigenous or cross-cultural perspectives. Multinational EWPs can be effective when a cross-cultural approach is engaged in the development and maintenance of the programs. Cross-cultural psychology encourages studying similarities and differences in individual psychological functioning in various cultural and ethnic groups and investigating variations in human behavior influenced by cultural context with data typically collected across many cultures (Vaughn 2010; Gerstein et al. 2009). In other words, the diversity of human behavior is explored and individual behavior is connected with the cultural environment in which it occurs, with a focus of the impact of culture on behavior.

What this means for international EWPs is that members of the EWP development team need to be mindful of the cultural context in which they are employing programs. Furthermore, there needs to be a great appreciation for the diversity which exists across locations and a desire to understand the distinct perspectives of wellness of the indigenous populations. Approaching EWP development with the idea that what works in one location, may not work in another location, and understanding, from the employee's perspective, what wellness involves in their culture is key.

The mission of this chapter is to explore how EWPs are defined, employed, and consider the individual within their cultural context. The concerns include the temptation of multinationals to export EWPs employed in Western settings without the consideration of the needs of indigenous employees across cultures and how these needs and wellness perspectives often vary widely. Approaches for employing EWPs internationally are provided. The international examination of employee wellness programs (EWPs) is limited in research and there is a need for the expansion of knowledge of sociocultural variances across and between nations, an important consideration for EWP research.

BACKGROUND

Chronic illnesses account for the majority of healthcare costs in developed markets and emerging markets (World Economic Forum, 2010). Illness impacts productivity in the workplace through absenteeism and presenteeism. Globally, chronic disease is estimated at U.S. $2 trillion in lost productivity each year. Organizations addressing wellness by targeting major risk factors, modifiable employee behaviors contributing to chronic disease, can save an average of U.S. $700 per employee per year in healthcare costs and productivity improvements. European organizations may save € 400 per employee, as a result of different healthcare and compensation patterns. However, in Asia, average potential savings are lower but the impact of a wellness program on company performance can be strong because in many parts of the world, companies do not benefit directly from savings in healthcare (because of out-of-pocket or public funding) but the productivity gains are available to all organizations.

Wellness programs have been instituted by organizations in an effort to improve the health of employees, control healthcare, absence and absenteeism costs and to provide an additional benefit to employees (Bly, Jones, & Richardson, 1986). Since the 1970s, employee wellness programs (EWPs) in the United States have been influenced in part by the occupational safety and health movement as well as worksite health promotion (Reardon, 1998). Many employers have progressed past safety measures and began to discover avenues for implementing a culture of health in the workplace in order to improve employee health, and reduce costs (Harlin, 2013).

Important to the implementation of an EWP is the portfolio of interventions that will have the greatest impact on a specific population (World Economic Forum, 2010). Specifically, the impact of an EWP and the variety of interventions that will make the biggest difference on productivity and costs will vary according to the profile of a workforce. This varies internationally across diverse workforces. Hofstede (1980) published *Culture's Consequences* in 1980 and a second edition in 2001. Both works examined the cultural dimensions of work values and have increased the interest in researching the impact of culture on organizational performance (Singh & Mohanty, 2011).

Many psychologists refer to Hofstede's work related to individualism/collectivism and more recently to masculinity/femininity (Hofstede, 2001). Much of the research conducted by Hofstede was conducted at the ecological level (country) level of analysis; however scholars have adapted his cultural value dimensions for work at the country, organization and individual levels of analysis (Kirkman, Lowe, & Gibson, 2006). Hansen and Brooks (1994) stated, "We must find new ways to understand and help organizations become functional and productive in the increasingly unpredictable and ambiguous circumstances of cross-cultural and cross-national enterprises" (p. 55).

Consequently, EWP positive outcomes are crucial for improvement, development and the implementation of EWP programs internationally. Berry, Mirabito, and Baun (2010) posited that managers have a responsibility to invest resources wisely and measure wellness program outcomes helps to connect investments in a program with short-and long-term results. Sophisticated companies set metrics-related goals and examine trends closely. Likewise, how differing and various cultural attributes are managed and leveraged across constituent groups within the organization has an impact on how well organizations are run and ultimately on the organization's success (Lundby & Jolton, 2010). Understanding cultural complexities is critical to business success. What works in the United States may not also work in other countries, for example.

Employee wellness programs are important interventions which protect and promote employee health (Michaels & Greene, 2013). Organizational development theories are central for the implementation of effective programs. Organizational development emphasizes planned organizational change, ideally with research and action linked (Austin & Bartunek, 2003). Specifically, organizational development is a "process of promoting positive, humanistically oriented, large system change" (Church, Waclawski, & Seigel, 1999, p.49). Lepak and Snell's (2002) commitment bundle theory places a premium on building human capital from within (e.g., promotion from within, extensive and continuous training and long-term employment incentives), enhancing workforce flexibility (e.g., job rotation and cross-training), promoting learning (e.g., developmental feedback), and empowering employees. This is one of four bundles presented by Lepak and Snell (2002), who advance a content-based approach to learning, training and development effectiveness. The four bundles include commitment, productivity, compliance, and collaboration.

This theory articulates a compilation style approach toward human resource management (HRM) systems. Further, the theory supports the empowerment of employees, promotion of learning and training and commitment of employees; all of which are vital components of EWPs. EWPs represent one approach to commitment and productivity, two of the bundles of the content-based approach to learning, training and development.

Implementing EWPs internationally, in various settings, requires consideration for effectiveness of the program as it relates to the culture of the employees. The need to understand EWP outcomes internationally is important for the successful deployment of effective programs that support organizational development as well as individual employee wellbeing, as implied by Hansen and Brooks (1994). For example, a study by the World Economic Forum (2010) found that for all companies, in all regions, regardless of employee age bracket, addressing physical activity and poor standard-of-care compliance ranked among the top three interventions for successful implementation of comprehensive EWPs. For companies in the European Union and Asia, a smoking-cessation initiative was among the top five interventions for reducing healthcare costs. In the United States, stress management was among the most cost-effective interventions.

MAIN FOCUS OF THE CHAPTER

International EWP Literature

EWPs have been adopted by organizations over the past 25 years in an attempt to develop high functioning employees (Parks & Steelman, 2008). Programs may occur within the organization or at external locations and offer various approaches to wellness. Some EWPs focus on physical health, such as gym membership incentives or healthy eating educational seminars. Lundby and Jolton (2010) posited organizational change is the sum of individuals' behavioral change. Consequently, EWPs are a central component for organizational change and development. EWP interventions may include preventative screening, immunizations, health risk appraisals, lifestyle classes, behavioral coaching or brief interventions, health education, and physical fitness. EWPs are particularly important for international organizations because of the added stress of conducting business across and between nations.

Organizational development encompasses many approaches to the development of employees. However, using data to inform organizational effectiveness and decision-making processes is vital (Waclawski &

Church, 2002). Because the world consists of individuals who think, feel and act differently, understanding the cultural differences in outcomes is important (Hofstede, Hofstede, & Minkov, 2010).

With globalization expanding and competition increasing, organizations have recognized that the knowledge, skills and abilities of their employees represent a major source of competitive advantage (Sheehan, 2012). One approach to developing employees is through EWPs, also termed worksite wellness programs (Michaels & Greene, 2013). Berry, Mirabito, and Baun (2010) defined EWPs as:

An organized, employer-sponsored program that is designed to support employees (and sometimes their families) as they adopt and sustain behaviors that reduce health risks, improve quality of life, enhance personal effectiveness and benefit the organization's bottom line. (p. 4)

EWPs have developed over the past 30 years. The goal of organizations adopting EWPs is to develop high functioning employees (Parks & Steelman, 2008), protect and promote employee health (Michaels & Greene, 2013), and provide preventative and rehabilitative interventions to address problems among workers (health; behavioral, mental, physical, workplace; stress, coworkers, manager and personal; social, family, financial, legal, gambling).

How an organization defines what exactly a high-functioning employee is, varies. However, much of the EWP research indicates participants improve their overall health and thus lower illness-related absenteeism rates and employers who provide EWPs are often viewed as having more concern for their employees and therefore have enhanced employee attitudes toward the organization (Parks & Steelman, 2008). Perceived Organizational Support (POS) may be one theoretical explanation for the impact of EWPs as POS influences various aspects of organizational treatment including rewards, benefits and in turn has been shown to impact job satisfaction (Rhoades & Eisenberger, 2002).

Additional goals of EWPs include reducing health care costs. For example, in 2003, Americans spent roughly $1.7 trillion on health care and employers paid one third of this expense (Finch, 2005). However, in 2012, the US spent an average of $8,915 per person on health care, rising to a total of $2.8 trillion (Wilson, 2014). Finch (2005) asserted comprehensive health promotion and disease prevention programs benefit employees and the organization in the short and long-term due to increased health, productivity and reduced medical costs. Within the European Union, 350 million work days are lost because of stress-related ill health, resulting in an overall cost of at least €20 billion each year and in the United States, businesses lose $300 billion annually as a result of lowered productivity, days absent and health-care costs due to stress (Limm et al., 2010).

Typically, organizations present employees with either a fitness wellness program, an educational wellness program, or a comprehensive wellness program including both (Parks & Steelman, 2008). However, not all employers provide wellness programs. Recent government incentives provided by federal health care legislation for U.S. companies offering wellness programs include tax incentives and grants (Berry, Mirabito, & Baun, 2010). The Workplace Wellness Alliance, in collaboration with FTI Consulting and the World Economic Forum offered a study examining workplace wellness programs and outcomes globally (World Economic Forum, 2013). The study included data collected across 40 countries in Europe, 31 in Asia, three across Oceania, 23 in Africa, ten in South America and twenty-one countries in North and Central America, all across a global coalition of over 150 organizations offering employee wellness programs.

The Workplace Wellness Alliance study results included recommendations for future EWPs globally, including three key characteristics of effective EWPs: the program needs to be based on robust analytics, guided by strategic vision and deep corporate engagement, and comprise a portfolio of activities focusing on individuals and their environment, at the workplace and elsewhere (World Economic Forum, 2013). Further, an online tool was developed to assist organizations. The Wellness App simulates the interplay among risk factors, chronic illness and specific interventions, including their implications for healthcare costs and potential productivity savings. Therefore, organizations that are sophisticated in their approach to EWPs, targeting risk factors accurately, engaging key decision makers and learning from experiences are seeing a rise in productivity and fall in per capita healthcare costs. The key is tracking strategic metrics for application in business and strategic decisions.

In the past 10 years, articles related to EWPs range from estimating the hard return (profits) for programs, the specific financial outcomes of investments, (Berry et al., 2010) to how to increase the adoption of workplace health promotion (Michaels & Greene, 2013), a meta-analysis of EWPs (Parks & Steelman, 2008), several evaluations of EWPs within the United States (Anshel, Brinthaupt, & Kang, 2010; Ballard, 2012; Berry, Mirabito, & Baun, 2010; Bright et al., 2012; Curd, Winter, & Connell, 2007; Drolet & Rodgers, 2010; Farrell & Geist-Martin, 2005; Finch, 2005; Gershon, 2013; Johnson, Lai, Rice, Rose, & Webber, 2010; Joslin, Lowe, & Peterson, 2006; Kocakülah, Cherry, & Morris, 2013; Middlestadt, Sheats, Geshnizjani, Sullivan, & Arvin, 2011; Ozminkowski et al., 2002; Person, Colby, Bulova, & Eubanks, 2010; Neville, Merrill, & Kumpfer, 2011; Srivastava, 2012; Perez, Phillips, Cornell, Mays, & Adams, 2009) and outside of the United States or international investigations (Blake, Zhou, & Batt, 2013; Kolbe, Tirozzi, Marx, Bobbitt-Cooke, Riedel, Jones, Schmoyer, 2005, & Bandy, 2015).

Research Outside of the US

EWP research outside of the United States includes a study conducted by Blake, Zhou, and Batt (2013); a longitudinal study assessing organizational commitment among EWP participants employed by National Health Service (NHS) in England. In this study, the authors examined the outcomes of an ecological workplace wellness intervention, which found improvements in health behaviors, reductions in sickness absence and improvements in job satisfaction and organizational commitment following five years of the workplace wellness intervention. The intervention included health campaigns, provision of facilities and health-promotion activities to encourage healthy lifestyle choices and sustained behavior change.

The results of the Blake, Zhou, and Batt (2013) study at a five-year follow-up, indicated appreciably more respondents actively traveled by walking or cycling both to work and for non-work trips and were more active while at work. Further, considerably more respondents met current recommendations for physical activity at five years than at baseline. Consequently, the results also showed lower sickness absence, greater job satisfaction and greater organizational commitment. However, the study only evaluated participants from England.

An article offering an international perspective on how to build or improve school employee health programs by school districts provides actions guiding readers seeking information to develop school health programs (Kolbe et al., 2005). The meta-analysis presented several international resources for readers to obtain more information regarding school health programs internationally. These included the worldwide education workers website, international school health programs websites, national school health program websites (United States) and U.S. worksite health promotion websites. Further, the authors suggested that in order to improve the quality of academic achievement of our students, we must improve the quality of life, health and productivity of school employees.

The Economical Insurance Group (TEIG) is a Canadian organization, which provided the case study sample for another study of EWPs. Hubbard and Singh (2009) stated that the wellness component included biometric clinics, wellness assessments and a new personal wellness account through the flexible benefit plan. The organization's program review detailed the evolution of the benefits offering to include greater choice, flexibility and control to better support the organizational and human resource strategy and to better meet the needs of its diverse workforce.

The Hubbard and Singh (2009) case study explored suggestions for the further development of their EWP, which included: alignment with and links to the overall HR strategy and the organizational strategy, values, mission and culture. Additionally, the study suggested the following for EWPs contemplating changing their fixed benefit plans: ensure alignment, understand that change is inevitable, conduct systematic diagnostic surveys on employee attitudes and desires, use technology wherever possible, understand the trade-offs, communication is vital and give the program time.

The World Economic Forum, an NGO based in Geneva, Switzerland, is an independent international organization committed to improving the state of the world by engaging leaders in partnerships to shape global, regional and industry agendas (World Economic Forum, 2010). The organization produced a report on EWPs internationally and presented results achieved by various organizations and multinationals. For example, Hindustan Unilever, Unilever's Indian subsidiary, launched a vitality initiative in 2006 focusing on biometric grading (body mass index [BMI], blood pressure, cholesterol levels, and sugar fasting). Over 14,000 employees participated and half of the more at-risk employees have been moved out of the danger zone and survey results reveal a boost in morale among participants.

US University Student Research

Additional studies focused on U.S. participants, including studies of university students in various regions and types of schools. Vanderbilt Medical School (VMS) developed a wellness program to promote student health and wellbeing through coordination of many new and existing resources among the three core components of the EWP: faculty, curriculum, and students (Drolet & Rodgers, 2010). The first published model of a comprehensive medical student wellness initiative suggests nearly every student has participated in at least two components of the VMS wellness program. Additionally, student response has been highly satisfactory, evidenced through positive feedback measured by participation and obtained through data collected as part of routine program evaluations.

The holistic wellness program's infrastructure included initiatives, activities, and resources, which were categorized into five comprehensive aspects of life: physical, psychological (emotional and spiritual), intellectual, social (interpersonal), and environmental. The wellness initiatives were programs such as the following: a mental health forum, yoga, Thai-Chi classes, health fairs, wellness curriculum, retreats, mentoring, lock-ins, student-student orientations, writing workshops, student assistance program, individual faculty advising, class Olympics, student wellness committee, faculty-student orientation, the College Cup, and the Commodore Challenge.

The program data was collected as part of routine program evaluations and illustrated systemic organizational development. For example, the wellness program consisted of collaboration with the Advisory College Program, the Student Wellness Committee, and the Vanderbilt Medical Student LIVE, thereby systemically approaching the design and implementation of the program. The mainstream business thinking model of learning organizations presented by Senge (1990), suggested learning organizations are organizations continually expanding their capacity to create their future and for which adaptive learning must be joined by generative learning, learning that enhances our capacity to create. This theory is particularly relevant to the scope of wellness programs instituted by the Vanderbilt University School of Medicine.

An additional university EWP study focused on physical fitness and mental wellbeing among employees of a university in the southeastern United States (Anshel, Brinthaupt, & Kang, 2010). The Disconnected Values Model (DVM) provided the framework for this research, with the goal to detect the inconsistencies between negative habits and values. The conclusions from the research were that when there was a disconnect among negative habits and values, it is considered problematic; an individual is prompted to change health behaviors. Participants included 164 full-time employees who participated in fitness coaching and a ninety-minute orientation based on the DVM over a ten-week program. Separate Multivariate Mixed Model (MMM) analyses with repeated measures on the time factor were performed in order to examine the effect of the intervention on fitness and mental well-being. Results, supporting both hypotheses, revealed that both pre- and post-intervention statistical comparisons indicated that all physical fitness measures were considerably improved, including reduced body fat and noteworthy improvements in cardiovascular and all strength measures.

Another U.S. university study was conducted to determine employee attitudes and barriers toward participation in a multidisciplinary work-site based health and wellness clinic (Bright et al., 2012). The survey was developed to determine patient preferences for specified pharmacist services as well as nutritional counseling options and exercise programs. The needs assessment survey consisted of 21 questions and was distributed electronically to all university employees, 880 total with a response rate of 34.7%, 303 participants. The survey questions consisted of the following topics: fitness initiatives, wellness seminars, nutrition, pharmacy initiatives, and general demographic questions. Survey methods were used to assess 303 respondents and the 34.7% response rate revealed 67.3% of participants indicated a desire to meet with a pharmacist to obtain medication information.

Additional findings included 43.2% of survey respondents reporting that they would be interested in meeting with a pharmacist for nutrition information and 89.8% of respondents indicating a desire to participate in exercise programming options on campus (Bright et al., 2012). Lastly, barriers to program participation included work schedule, lack of motivation, too busy at work, and a lack of ability to leave work to participate in the health and wellness clinic.

Additional US Research

Johnson & Johnson is the world's largest and most diverse medical devices and diagnostics company (Johnson & Johnson, 2015). The well-known organization revealed the long-term impact of their health and wellness program on health care utilization and expenditures in a study conducted by Ozminkowski et al. in 2002. Employees were evaluated for up to five years prior to program implementation and four years following program implementation. The medical care utilization and expenditures focus of the study concentrated on changing individual behavior and psychological risk factors instead of just focusing on symptom treatment. Further, emphasis was placed on awareness among employees through health education, prevention activities, self-responsibility, and self-care.

The EWP, termed health and wellness program, focused on providing appropriate intervention services before, during and after major health-related events (e.g., illness, accidents or injuries) occur. The pre-, at-event and post-event management techniques varied and included assessments, screening programs, emergency care, medical case management, and functional assessments to monitor progress. The analysis of health care utilization and expenditure analyses sought to determine whether the Johnson & Johnson EWP influenced various health care utilization measures such as emergency department visits and inpatient hospital days. The study sample ranged from 8, 927 participants 5 years before study implementation and 11,584 participants four years after study implementation. Results indicated a large reduction, approximately $224.66 per employee per year, in medical care expenditures over the four-year program period. These benefits were the result of reduced inpatient use, fewer mental health visits, and fewer outpatient visits compared to baseline.

An additional U.S. study investigated job satisfaction and absenteeism after participation in an EWP (Parks & Steelman, 2008). The researchers searched for published and unpublished studies that evaluated organizational wellness programs. Inclusion criteria for the studies reviewed included: conducted from 1980-2005, compared participation versus nonparticipation in an organizational wellness program, outcome variables examined absenteeism and/or job satisfaction, and the study reported empirical data. Consequently, seventeen studies met inclusion criteria; 15 published and two dissertations, yielding 7,705 participants with absenteeism data and 2,480 participants with job satisfaction data. The meta-analysis revealed that participation in an EWP was associated with decreased absenteeism and increased job satisfaction. No moderating effects were found although the type of EWP (fitness only or comprehensive) and the methodological rigor of the primary studies were examined as moderators.

Berry, Mirabito, and Baun (2010) presented an examination of existing research and a study of 10 organizations, across a variety of industries, whose wellness programs have systematically achieved measureable results. The methodology included group and individual interviews with over 300 participants, including CEOs and CFOs. The study investigated what works, what doesn't, and what overall impact the program had on the organization.

The findings resulted in the identification of six pillars of a successful, strategically integrated wellness program, regardless of an organization's size. The pillars are as follows: multilevel leadership, alignment, scope, relevance and quality, accessibility, partnerships, and communications.

Lastly, Bandy (2015) examined international employee wellness program (EWP) outcomes and specifically investigated stress, organizational commitment, and nationality. It was hypothesized that stress would decrease, organizational commitment would increase, and nationality would affect employee wellness program participation outcomes. A sample of individuals who have and who have not participated in an EWP ($N = 456$) was obtained from 27 countries. Results showed that there was not a meaningful difference between those who participated in an EWP and those who did not for perceived stress and organizational commitment.

However, there were noteworthy differences in levels of perceived stress and organizational commitment between participants whose nationality was outside of the United States and participants within the United States (Bandy, 2015). For participants whose self-reported nationality and passport nationality was outside of the United States, higher perceived stress was associated with lower organizational commitment. The scholar recommended that future studies include a more specific definition of EWPs in order to explore certain types of EWP programs.

Developing Culturally Competent EWPs

Understanding how an individual's political, spiritual, and legislative systems impact their behavior is vital to gain insight into how to best develop effective EWPs. Further, understanding how families function, the economic situation of the individuals, what the various ways of knowing and being involve, and other vital characteristics are necessary to gain awareness in order to effectively assist in EWP development and implementation.

These discussions support an indigenous and cultural psychology approach by understanding the population in historical and sociocultural contexts using concepts meaningful to their culture as well as discovering psychology which is local, constructed for the population, by scholars from the culture (Gerstein et al., 2009). Cultural psychology involves understanding individuals within their cultural context by employing concepts that are meaningful within a specific culture. The EWP development team may engage in conversations with indigenous wellness scholars and health practitioners in order to better understand wellness definitions, applications, and practice. This is an example of a bottom-up intervention strategy (Wessells & Dawes, 2007).

Prior to engaging in such conversations, however, organizations themselves need tremendous education and knowledge acquisition, not only about the cultures in which they deploy operations, but also about themselves. Cultural psychology approaches emphasize the context and culture that is inside the individual while cross-cultural psychology emphasizes content and culture outside of the person (Vaughn, 2010). Prior to obtaining interpersonal competence, thereby understanding the self and others and embodying the ability to relate with others who have different experiences, intrapersonal competence must be sought.

Training the EWP Development Team

The EWP development team members, therefore, will need to gain knowledge of the self, self awareness, and the ability to engage in reflection, or intrapersonal competence (Vaughn, 2010). Vital to gaining intrapersonal competence are specific personality characteristics. Therefore, even prior to the EWP development team assembly, members will need to be screened to manifest the following qualities: cultural empathy, action orientation, adventurousness/curiosity, flexibility, and extraversion.

Additional desired intrapersonal competence areas include: open-mindedness, emotional stability, emotional regulation, openness, and critical thinking. These individual qualities will assist each EWP development team member to contribute in a meaningful and effective manner both with other members and with fellow employees across diverse communities.

Important to the exploration of intrapersonal and interpersonal competence is embodying intercultural communication skills. Intercultural communication is not a new concept. Since the beginning of human history, there have been diverse groups in various parts of the world who have connected, interacted, and engaged in intercultural communication. Klopf and McCroskey (2007) assert intercultural communication or intercultural communication competence involves the knowledge, motivation, and skills to interact effectively and appropriately with members of different cultures. It is important to consider the key terms introduced in this definition.

Knowledge is considered to be the awareness or understanding of the necessary information and actions that are required to be interculturally competent (Klopf & McCroskey, 2007). This often entails an understanding of social norms or communication strategies, information about the culture of the individual(s), and basic rules, etiquette/netiquette involved in the social exchange. For example, an EWP development team member needs to learn many of the common wellness behaviors within a specific culture, how are they employed and discussed, and who may be involved.

Additionally, motivation encompasses drives, wants, needs, and desires of the individuals in communication. When considering motivation, thoughts of why another individual is communicating, what do they possibly want, are there underlying issues involved, or perhaps even prejudices subjugating the interaction. EWP development team members need an understanding of motivational communication factors across various cultures in order to effectively communicate with various populations and gather vital knowledge regarding a population's EWP perspective.

Skills involve the speaking behaviors that may be employed by the individuals communicating (Klopf & McCroskey, 2007). These behaviors may be socially appropriate or inappropriate and are often driven by the goals of the individual. Recognizing the speaker's goals when interacting across cultural groups contributes to the development of effective EWPs internationally. For example, when gathering information from participants about types of programming, etc., it is important to engage in active listening and to recognize what participant goals are. Is the individual attempting to change or re-direct program offerings? Is the individual hoping to acquire a new direction for the EWP to better match their cultural characteristics?

Interactions are noted to be particular circumstances in which the communicators are equally directing and coordinating their verbal and nonverbal behaviors to accomplish mutual goals. What is being said by a development team member and by the participant/employee in order to accomplish goals?

Effective refers to an individual's ability to identify the goals of speaking and the resources necessary to reach those goals (Klopf & McCroskey, 2007). This may involve the ability of the speaker to accurately predict responses of others involved in the interaction as well as finding solutions for successful communication. Lastly, appropriate refers to the word choice and mannerisms which are deemed socially acceptable in the cultures of the communicators. For example, when an EWP development team is gathering data across cultures in order to employ culturally sensitive EWPs, the team members need an understanding of what effective and appropriate communication strategies are within the particular culture.

Becoming a successful intercultural communicator involves a desire to learn about the cultural group memberships of the other individual(s) engaged in an interaction. Unfortunately, this is all too oftentimes overlooked and individuals will assume they know the intended meanings of ideas or thoughts without asking questions. The key for the EWP development team is inquiry and clarification when developing and maintaining EWPs internationally. When clarification is sought through inquisition, not only can clarity be obtained, but cultural awareness and sensitivity are brought to the forefront. Cultural competence and tolerance can then evolve, as well as a deeper, more meaningful interaction.

A key factor in achieving effective intercultural communication is perception. Perception is defined as the process by which "people select, organize, and interpret sensory stimulation into a meaningful and coherent picture of the world" (Klopf & McCroskey, 2007, p.74). Each individual perceives, even the exact experience, differently. Consequently, the meaning we afford experiences is quite unique and individual. Some factors which may influence our perceptions include, but are not limited to: psychological and physiological conditions, disconfirmed expectations, inaccurate attributions, and perhaps most importantly, our cultural memberships.

Cultural memberships contribute to our perceptions because cultural groups allow for diverse environments across individuals. These environments, and the norms of the cultural group, teach the members how to perceive various experiences (Klopf & McCroskey, 2007) . Communication across cultures is invariably rooted in diverse perceptions and clarification, or asking questions, aids in effective intercultural communication. EWP development team members need to be mindful of the effect of perceptions on communication and commit to ask questions for clarification.

Some of the inhibitors of effective intercultural communication previously mentioned include factors influencing perceptions. Disconfirmed expectations, or expectations which are not met in the way they may be expected, include concerns and anticipations that something may occur in a specific manner (Klopf & McCroskey, 2007). These expectations are largely based on previous experiences and involve the desire to know what will happen or what to expect. If outcomes have been personally experienced previously, or even by someone known to an individual, then anticipation that something will happen in this way again can interfere with reaching effective intercultural communication.

Often, these communication complications occur when individuals make assumptions, and then, for whatever reason, the expected outcome is not obtained. In other words, experiences are disconfirmed when the outcome does not coincide with anticipations. An EWP example of disconfirmed expectations might include participants expecting the same problems with programming as before, even though there may be a new, more culturally sensitive and aware team in place and then participants experience positive program changes which are more culturally appropriate.

Additionally, attribution often interferes in intercultural communication. Attribution entails making sense out of an individual's behavior (Klopf & McCroskey, 2007). Attributions involve assigning causes to an individual's behavior and are more accurate when effective intercultural communication transpires. In other words, when we are more culturally competent, our attributions may be more accurate. An EWP team member who is not culturally competent may think that low participation rates in an alcohol substance abuse program is due to disinterest whereas the reality is that the specific culture does not consider the consumption of alcohol problematic. The consumption amount of alcohol and what is considered a cultural norm varies internationally.

Understanding intercultural communication also encompasses an awareness of both verbal and nonverbal communications. Nonverbal communications are nonlinguistic ways of transmitting messages, are culturally acquired, and an essential component of social interaction (Klopf & McCroskey, 2007). Silence is also an important consideration for communications, a vital component within nonverbal communication. Culturally competent EWP development team members recognize the importance of understanding the meaning of silence when used in various contexts and cultures.

Pancultural, or the idea that nonverbal communication behaviors carry the same meanings across cultures, is yet another concept which is vital for the effective intercultural communicator. In other words, nonverbal communication does not carry the same meaning across cultures. EWP program team members engaging with program participants and evaluating programs internationally need to be mindful of the use of silence and other nonverbal behaviors.

While intrapersonal and interpersonal competence and intercultural communication skills are vital for the EWP development team, cultural competence is also imperative for each member of the group. Vaughn (2010) posits cultural competence is the ability to apply personal cultural knowledge to others' cultures. In other words, the EWP development team members need to be mindful of their actions prior to and after intercultural interactions. The EWP development team, therefore, is encouraged to debrief daily while training and in the specific location in order to reflect upon their actions and develop insightful ways to adjust behavior as necessary. Daily debriefing can become very important (Watters, 2010) for the group members to share in the processing of the thoughts and feelings which will invariably arise.

Taking the thought of cultural competence further, the EWP development team engages in the procurement of training in order for the team to sufficiently gain cultural competence about the diverse cultures in which they operate. The collaborative approach to cultural competence involves a training seminar in which the EWP team learns the ResCUE Model (Vaughn, 2010). The model consists of learning how to respectfully interact and negotiate with others. The Res = Respect, C = Communicate, U = Understand and E = Engage. The model encourages the respect for the individual, communicating with them about their needs and expectations, understanding where they are coming from in terms of their concerns and how that is grounded in the individual's cultural values. Lastly, this model extends the training in intercultural communication.

Next, personality approaches encourage developing characteristics which may need development. This portion of the seminar will include group work and role playing where the team members will be encouraged to reflect upon potential concerns or areas which they think need development. These activities also support interpersonal competence and prepare the members to communicate in a culturally sensitive and accepting manner.

An additional way for the development team members to more deeply prepare for their experiences with diverse cultural groups includes learning and considering Kleinman's medical anthropology questions (Vaughn, 2010; Lonner & Ibrahim, 2008) and existential questions (Comas-Diaz, 2012). Psychotherapists working with spiritually-oriented clients sometimes incorporate existential questions such as: Do you have a purpose in life? When do you feel most alive? Who are you in relation to your ancestors? This holistic approach to international work honors the collectivistic perspective and asserts that the only way to understand a system is to understand that entire system; the whole cannot be understood by examining the parts in isolation from the entire system (Strauch, 2003). Consequently, it is important to train the EWP development team to view the culture of the individual, thereby not embodying an us vs. them framework.

The main portion of the seminar will include historical, political, language, spiritual, family systems, marriage practices, economics, and birth and death rituals within the proposed cultural context. This knowledge will be vital to the EWP development team success as the understanding of as many cultural characteristics as possible will further support using cultural psychology and indigenous psychology approaches for the development of effective and meaningful EWP programs across diverse cultures.

As part of the EWP training curriculum, the team members are assigned homework to read EWP papers written by indigenous scholars. Gerstein et al. (2009) asserted that U.S. psychology literature is read by individuals around the world but that U.S. psychology and counseling professions rarely read publications in other languages. The EWP development team will support the translation of the materials prior to distributing the materials. This supports integration, not isolation of knowledge, as professionals who only read English journals are in fact isolated.

Vaughn (2010) asserted individuals and communities themselves are the experts about their cultural situations and that partnerships should be co-created toward interventions that meet the needs of the people involved. What is learned by the EWP development team members from the indigenous employees can be used to begin the process of developing a program which will be supportive at various levels in the community, and based on the needs as described by the indigenous population.

Knowledge of local idioms will likely result from conversations with the population once the EWP development team arrives at a particular location. Local idioms and how the individuals express their thoughts and feelings about wellness are vital for the team to understand. For example, the EWP development team cannot be effective if they do not understand the ways wellness is understood, experienced, and expressed in a distinct context. The team needs to view this effort as data gathering, a part of the bottom-up approach (Wessells and Dawes, 2007). The previously mentioned engagements with indigenous wellness scholars and health practitioners exemplifies a bottom-up approach.

For the EWP development team to approach a global EWP deployment, without considering the harm, on both individual and systemic levels, for each cultural group, would merely be an exercise in colonization. This exportation of Western ideologies and ideas of what an effective and meaningful EWP looks like and does not, contributes to globalization.

The EWP development team needs to prepare to engage in meaningful conversation and be prepared to receive any possible outcome. Western thoughts and ideas about EWPs cannot simply be exported because just as psychology is not universal, neither is the concept of the wellness. The meaning, function, and process of wellness is culturally rooted and defined. The EWP development team will serve the organization's operations across diverse cultures best by approaching the wellness topic from the population's perspective. Most importantly, the engagement in learning and serving the population as fellow humans, not as Westerners who "know better" will produce the most fruitful outcome for both parties.

Issues, Controversies, Problems

Intercultural communication presents issues for EWP development. Program administrators need an understanding of intercultural communication, how to effectively communicate across cultures, and how to best approach communication to encourage culturally competent EWP program design and deployment.

Further, organizational challenges, such as budget restrictions, may restrict the potential of developing culturally competent EWPs. However, sometimes there is simply not an interest or desire to engage in cultural competency and developing wellness programs which are meaningful to diverse workgroups.

SOLUTIONS AND RECOMMENDATIONS

When presented with intercultural communication issues, there are several paths to achieving effective intercultural communication. Perhaps most important to resolving issues related to intercultural communication is for individuals to release a dogmatic, or "instructor" position and placing an emphasis on the valuable position of lifelong learning. Additionally, listening is a primary consideration and involves being courteous to the speaker. Additionally, listening further involves active empathic and supportive behaviors (Klopf & McCroskey, 2007).

These behaviors encourage the speaker and provide optimal opportunity for comprehension. Avoiding defensive behaviors assists in developing intercultural communication and involves open, trusting, and supportive dialogue. Keeping the relationship at the center, as well as a mindful awareness for the communication can assist in eliminating defensive behaviors.

Additional solutions for intercultural communication issues encompass an openness to new and diverse experiences, by both parties. One way to achieve this involves avoiding evaluative talk. Evaluative talk involves judging the listener and descriptive talk offers a more collaborative approach. Descriptive talk is noted in the presentations of feelings, events, perceptions, or processes which do not imply that the listener alter behavior, perceptions, or attitudes (Klopf & McCroskey, 2007). Misunderstandings, criticism, insults, and offending others can be avoided when a problem-solving approach is offered, which includes descriptive talk.

Another type of communication which may help solve issues related to intercultural communication is problem-oriented talk. This type of communication encourages collaboration by defining a mutual problem and seeking a solution (Klopf & McCroskey, 2007). Attempting to control or change the listener is avoided, thereby decreasing resistance. The focus of problem-oriented talk is the relationship, not the stance of each individual on an issue. By focusing on the relationship, individuals are encouraged to create harmony and mutually beneficial exchanges. Oftentimes, this is noted when communicators convey feelings, focusing on individual perception rather than debating thoughts or ideas.

The issue of concerns with intercultural communication can further be reduced by the individuals generating an open mind combined with tolerance and acceptance. This often involves moving away from rigid thoughts and ways of knowing and considering the reality that there are many differences among human beings. Equality in speaking also assists in combating issues related to intercultural communication. When a speaker engages in equality in speaking, the speaker implies that the listener, regardless of their differences in education, experience, ability, power, etc., is similar (Klopf & McCroskey, 2007). Creating this sort of equal, or level ground, assists in diminishes the focus on the differences between the individuals and places the attention on generating mutual respect and trust.

Evaluating what is said and empathy offer solutions for intercultural communication problems as well. Oftentimes, listeners evaluate what is heard and then, if what is heard is determined to be unacceptable, the message is rejected (Klopf & McCroskey, 2007). However, in order to achieve affective intercultural communication, listeners are encouraged to first understand what is being said, then evaluate what is heard. This often involves separating thoughts from feelings, maintaining an objective attitude, clarify what has been said by asking questions, and separate fact from fiction.

Lastly, empathic listening skills are vital to combating intercultural communication issues. Empathic listening involves listening to the meanings rather than the words (Klopf & McCroskey, 2007). This can be seen when a listener uses paraphrasing, reflects feelings, reflects meaning, and summarizes what the speaker has said.

FUTURE RESEARCH DIRECTIONS

Additional recommendations, pertaining to future research, include the suggestion by Bandy (2015) to include a specific definition of EWPs in order to investigate certain types of EWP programs. Therefore, if the scope of the research is narrowed to EWP type, results may be narrowed and findings may be more concise. Further, the word choice of the assessment and participant interpretation of words and language across cultures are important considerations for future research. Longitudinal methodology may assist in capturing variances over time and better assist scholars to obtain progressive data.

Bandy (2015) also recommends a focus of a specific EWP program across cultures. Given a particular organization and even a certain segment of an EWP to investigate, scholars may be more likely to collect more specific program data. Additionally, the researcher also recommends considering assessment in multiple languages to obtain data from non-English speaking participants. Lastly, future research may also benefit from assessing participant history of mental illness, absenteeism, and job attitudes.

Lastly, using key metrics to analyze the EWP development team's cultural competence is imperative. When cultural competence training occurs, pre and post training assessment can provide valuable data to assist the entire EWP department. Future training, hiring, development, and more may be informed when metrics are employed.

CONCLUSION

EWPs employed internationally may be a mere extension of colonization if multinational organizations do not engage in indigenous or cross-cultural psychology practices. Learning what wellness looks like for each indigenous population is vital for effective EWPs internationally. The desire, openness, and tolerance of diversity among and across EWP development team members is paramount to the success of EWPs. The movement toward cultural competence by multinationals may provide the first steps in achieving truly meaningful EWPs for all benefitting parties.

REFERENCES

Anshel, M. H., Brinthaupt, T. M., & Kang, M. (2010). The disconnected values model improves mental well-being and fitness in an employee wellness program. *Behavioral Medicine (Washington, D.C.)*, *36*(4), 113–122. doi:10.1080/08964289.2010.489080 PMID:21186434

Austin, J. R., & Bartunek, J. M. (2002). Theories and practices of organizational development. In W. C. Parks, D. R. Ilgen, R. J. Klimoski, & I. B. Weiner (Eds.), Handbook of Psychology: Vol. 12. *Industrial and Organizational Psychology* (pp. 309–332). Hoboken, NJ: John Wiley & Sons, Inc.

Ballard, D. A. (2012). *Factors influencing acceptance of a worksite wellness program in a major urban healthcare system: A cross-sectional analysis.* (Unpublished master's thesis). University of Kentucky, Lexington, KY.

Bandy, J. (2015). *International evaluation of employee wellness program outcomes* (Doctoral dissertation). Available from ProQuest Dissertations and Theses database. (No. 10931)

Berry, L. L., Mirabito, A. M., & Baun, W. B. (2010, December). What's the hard return on employee wellness programs? *Harvard Business Review*. Retrieved from http://hbr.org/2010/12/whats-the-hard-return-on-employee-wellness-programs/ar/6

Blake, H., Zhou, D., & Batt, M. E. (2013). Five-year workplace wellness intervention in the NHS. *Perspectives in Public Health*, *133*(5), 262–271. doi:10.1177/1757913913489611 PMID:23771680

Bly, J. L., Jones, R. C., & Richardson, J. E. (1986). Impact of worksite health promotion on health care costs and utilization: Evaluation of Johnson & Johnson's live for life program. *Journal of the American Medical Association*, *23*(23), 3235–3240. doi:10.1001/jama.1986.03380230059026 PMID:3783867

Bright, D. R., Terrell, S. L., Rush, M. J., Kroustos, K. R., Stockert, A. L., Swanson, S. C., & DiPietro, N. A. (2012). Employee attitudes toward participation in a work-site based health and wellness clinic. *Journal of Pharmacy Practice*, *25*(5), 530–536. doi:10.1177/0897190012442719 PMID:22572221

Centers for Disease Control and Prevention. (n.d.). *Behavioral risk factor surveillance system*. Retrieved from http://www.cdc.gov/brfss/

Church, A. H., Waclawski, J., & Siegel, W. (1999). Will the real O.D. practitioner please stand up? A call for change in the field. *Organization Development Journal*, *17*(2), 49–59.

Comas-Diaz, L. (2012). Humanism and multiculturalism: An evolutionary alliance. *Psychotherapy (Chicago, Ill.)*, *49*(4), 437–441. doi:10.1037/a0027126 PMID:23205825

Curd, P. R., Winter, S. J., & Connell, A. (2007). Participative Planning to enhance inmate wellness: Preliminary report of a correctional wellness program. *Journal of Correctional Health Care*, *13*(4), 296–308. doi:10.1177/1078345807306754

Drolet, B. C., & Rodgers, S. (2010, January). A comprehensive medical student wellness program: Design and implementation at Vanderbilt School of Medicine. *Academic Medicine*, *85*(1), 103–110. doi:10.1097/ACM.0b013e3181c46963 PMID:20042835

Farrell, A., & Geist-Martin, P. (2005). Communicating social health: Perceptions of wellness at work. *Management Communication Quarterly*, *18*(4), 543–592. doi:10.1177/0893318904273691

Finch, R. (2005). Preventive services: Improving the bottom line for employers and employees. *Compensation and Benefits Review*, *37*(2), 18–22. doi:10.1177/0886368704274407

Fox, D., Prilleltensky, I., & Austin, S. (Eds.). (2009). *Critical Psychology: An introduction* (2nd ed.). London: SAGE Publications Ltd.

Gershon, J. C. (2014). Healing the healer: One step at a time. *Journal of Holistic Nursing*, *32*(1), 6–13. doi:10.1177/0898010113495976 PMID:24476909

Gerstein, L. H., Heppner, P. P., Aegisdottir, S., Seung-Ming, A., Leung, S.-M. A., & Norsworthy, K. L. (2009). Cross-cultural counseling. In L. H. Gerstein, P. P. Heppner, S. Aegisdottir, S-M. A., Leung, & K. L. Norsworthy (Eds.), International Handbook of Cross-Cultural Counseling: Cultural Assumptions and Practices Worldwide (pp. 3-32). Academic Press.

Hansen, C. D., & Brooks, A. K. (1994). A review of cross-cultural research on human resource development. *Human Resource Development Quarterly*, *5*(1), 55–74. doi:10.1002/hrdq.3920050107

Harlin, Z. (2013). *Employer perspectives of employee wellness programs* (Master's thesis). Available from ProQuest Dissertations and Theses database. (UMI No. 1547540).

Hofstede, G. (2001). Culture's recent consequences: Using dimension scores in theory and research. *International Journal of Cross Cultural Management*, *1*(1), 11–30. doi:10.1177/147059580111002

Hofstede, G., Hofstede, G. J., & Minkov, M. (2010). *Cultures and organizations: Software of the mind, intercultural cooperation and its importance for survival* (3rd ed.). New York, NY: McGraw Hill.

Hubbard, J., & Singh, P. (2009). The evolution of employee benefits at the Economical Insurance Group. *Compensation and Benefits Review*, *41*(6), 27–35. doi:10.1177/0886368709346683

Johnson, C. C., Lai, Y. L., Rice, J., Rose, D., & Webber, L. S. (2010). Action live: Using process evaluation to describe implementation of a worksite wellness program. *Journal of Occupational and Environmental Medicine*, *52*(1Supplement), S14–S21. doi:10.1097/JOM.0b013e3181c81ade PMID:20061882

Johnson & Johnson. (2015). *Our company*. Retrieved from http://www.jnj.com/about-jnj

Joslin, B., Lowe, J. B., & Peterson, N. A. (2006). Employee characteristics and participation in a worksite wellness programme. *Health Education Journal*, *65*(4), 308–319. doi:10.1177/0017896906069367

Kirkman, B. L., Lowe, K. B., & Gibson, C. (2006). A quarter century of Culture's Consequences: A review of the empirical research incorporating Hofstede's cultural value framework. *Journal of International Business Studies, 36*(3), 285–320. doi:10.1057/palgrave.jibs.8400202

Klopf, D., & McCroskey, J. C. (2007). *Intercultural communication encounters.* Boston, MA: Pearson Education, Inc.

Kocakülâh, M. C., Cherry, A., & Morris, J. T. (2013). Investing in company wellness programs: Does it make financial sense? *Journal of Health Management, 15*(3), 463–470. doi:10.1177/0972063413492041

Kolbe, L. J., Tirozzi, E. M., Bobbitt-Cooke, M. B., Riedel, S., Jones, J., & Schmoyer, M. (2005). Health programmes for school employees: Improving quality of life, health and productivity. *Promotion & Education, 12*(3-4), 157–161. doi:10.1177/10253823050120030115 PMID:16739507

Lepak, D. P., & Snell, S. A. (2002). Examining the human resource architecture: The relationships among human capital, employment, and human resource configurations. *Journal of Management, 28*(4), 517–543. doi:10.1177/014920630202800403

Limm, H., Angerer, P., Heinmueller, M., Marten-Mittag, B., Nater, U. M., & Guendel, H. (2010). Self-perceived stress reactivity is an indicator of psychosocial impairment at the workplace. *BMC Public Health, 10*(252), 1–10. doi:10.1186/1471-2458-10-252 PMID:20470413

Lonner, W. J., & Ibrahim, F. A. (2008). Appraisal and Assessment in cross cultural counseling. In P. B. Pedersen, J. G. Draguns, W. J. Lonner, & J. E. Trimble (Eds.), *Counseling across cultures* (pp. 37–55). doi:10.4135/9781483329314.n3

Lundby, K., & Jolton, J. (2010). *Going global: Practical applications and recommendations for HR and OD professional in the global workplace.* San Francisco, CA: Jossey-Bass, A Wiley Imprint.

Michaels, C. N., & Greene, A. M. (2013). Worksite wellness: Increasing adoption of workplace health promotion programs. *Health Promotion Practice, 14*(4), 473–479. doi:10.1177/1524839913480800 PMID:23545334

Middlestadt, S. E., Sheats, J. L., Geshnizjani, A., Sullivan, M. R., & Arvin, C. S. (2011). Factors associated with participation in work-site wellness programs: Implications for increasing willingness among rural service employees. *Health Education & Behavior, 38*(5), 502–509. doi:10.1177/1090198110384469 PMID:21482700

Neville, B. H., Merrill, R. M., & Kumpfer, K. L. (2011). Longitudinal outcomes of a comprehensive, incentivized worksite wellness program. *Evaluation & the Health Professions, 34*(1), 103–123. doi:10.1177/0163278710379222 PMID:20696740

Ozminkowski, R. J., Ling, D., Goetzel, R. Z., Bruno, J. A., Rutter, K. R., Isaac, F., & Wang, S. (2002, January). Long-term impact of Johnson & Johnson's health & wellness program on health care utilization and expenditures. *Journal of Occupational and Environmental Medicine, 44*(1), 21–29. doi:10.1097/00043764-200201000-00005 PMID:11802462

Parks, K. M., & Steelman, L. A. (2008). Organizational wellness programs: A meta-analysis. *Journal of Occupational Health Psychology, 13*(1), 58–68. doi:10.1037/1076-8998.13.1.58 PMID:18211169

Perez, A. P., Phillips, M. M., Cornell, C. E., Mays, G., & Adams, B. (2009, October). Promoting dietary change among state health employees in Arkansas through a worksite wellness program: The healthy employee lifestyle program (HELP). *Preventing Chronic Disease, Public Health Research, Practice and Policy, 6*(4). http://www.cdc.gov/pcd/issues/2009/oct/08_0136.htm

Person, A. L., Colby, S. E., Bulova, J. A., & Eubanks, J. W. (2010). Barriers to participation in a worksite wellness program. *Nutrition Research and Practice, 4*(2), 149–154. doi:10.4162/nrp.2010.4.2.149 PMID:20461204

Prochaska, J., & DiClemente, C. (1983). Stages and processes of self-change in smoking: Toward an integrative model of change. *Journal of Consulting and Clinical Psychology, 5*(3), 390–395. doi:10.1037/0022-006X.51.3.390 PMID:6863699

Quick, J. C., Macik-Frey, M., & Cooper, C. L. (2007). Guest Editor's Introduction: Managerial dimensions of organizational health: The healthy leader at work. *Journal of Management Studies, 44*(2), 189–205. doi:10.1111/j.1467-6486.2007.00684.x

Reardon, J. (1998). The history and impact of worksite wellness. *Nursing Economics, 16*(3), 117–121. PMID:9748973

Rhoades, L., & Eisenberger, R. (2002). Perceived organizational support: A review of the literature. *The Journal of Applied Psychology, 87*(4), 698–714. doi:10.1037/0021-9010.87.4.698 PMID:12184574

Senge, P. (1990). *The fifth discipline: The art and practice of the learning organization*. New York: Doubleday.

Sheehan, M. (2012). Investing in management development in turbulent times and perceived organisational performance: A study of UK MNCs and their subsidiaries. *International Journal of Human Resource Management, 23*(12), 2491–2513. doi:10.1080/09585192.2012.668400

Singh, R. N., & Mohanty, R. P. (2011). Participation satisfaction and organizational commitment: Moderating role of employee's cultural values. *Human Resource Development International, 14*(5), 583–603. doi:10.1080/13678868.2011.621286

Srivastava, P. (2012). Getting engaged: Giving employees a nudge toward better health. *Compensation and Benefits Review, 44*(2), 105–109. doi:10.1177/0886368712450982

Stevens, M. J., & Gielen, U. P. (2015). *Toward a global psychology: Theory, research, intervention, and pedagogy*. Mahwah, NJ: Lawrence Erlbaum Associates, Inc.

Strauch, I. (2003). Examining the nature of holism within lifestyle. *Journal of Individual Psychology, 59*(4), 452–460.

The Aster Awards. (2014, May 6). *About the Aster Awards*. Retrieved from http://www.asterawards.com/about-the-aster-awards/

Vaughn, L. (2010). *Psychology and culture: Thinking, feeling, and behaving in a global context*. East Sussex, UK: Psychology Press.

Waclawski, J., & Church, A. H. (Eds.). (2002). *Organizational development: A data-driven approach to organizational change (A professional practice series, a publication of the Society for Industrial and Organizational Psychology)*. San Francisco, CA: Jossey-Bass, A Wiley Company.

Ware, J. E. (2004). SF-36 Health survey update. In M. E. Maruish (Ed.), *The use of psychological testing for treatment planning and outcomes assessment* (3rd ed.). Lawrence Erlbaum Associates.

Watters, E. (2010). *Crazy like us: The globalization of the American psyche*. New York, NY: Free Press.

Wessells, G., & Dawes, A. (2007). Macro-level interventions: Psychology, social policy, and societal influence processes. In *Toward a global psychology: Theory, research, intervention, and pedagogy* (pp. 1–45). Lawrence Erlbaum Associates.

Wilson, K. B. (2014, July). Heath care costs 101: Slow growth persists. *California Health Care Costs*. Retrieved from http://www.chcf.org/publications/2014/07/health-care-costs-101

World Economic Forum. (2010). *The new discipline of workforce wellness: Enhancing corporate performance by tackling chronic disease* (2010 Report). Retrieved from the World Economic Forum website: http://www3.weforum.org/docs/WEF_HE_TacklingChronicDisease_Report_2010.pdf

KEY TERMS AND DEFINITIONS

Cross-Cultural Psychology: Encourages studying similarities and differences in individual psychological functioning in various cultural and ethnic groups and investigating variations in human behavior influenced by cultural context with data typically collected across many cultures; the diversity of human behavior is explored and individual behavior is connected with the cultural environment in which it occurs, with a focus of the impact of culture on behavior.

Employee Wellness Programs (EWPs): An organized employer-sponsored program that is designed to support employees (and sometimes their families) as they adopt and sustain behaviors that reduce health risks, improve quality of life, enhance personal effectiveness and benefit the organization's bottom line.

Enlightened Globalization: Is based on understanding, dialogue, respect, and integrating knowledge to foster cultural development. This involves the recognition that each culture has a different set of values, beliefs, and resources and integrates information to transform the world.

Globalization: A form of continuing colonialism or imperialism, 're-colonization' or neo'colonialism', due to the pattern of present-day global relationships follows that of the former European colonial empires.

Indigenous Psychology: Understanding each culture from its own frame of reference, including its own ecological, historical, philosophical, and religious or spiritual context; based on knowledge which emerges from the target culture rather than either directly or indirectly from another location; an underlying premise which suggests psychological principles cannot be assumed to be universally similar- this knowledge stems from scholars located in the specific culture, has meaning within the specific culture, and is for the individuals within that culture; advocates examining knowledge, skills, and beliefs individuals have about themselves and how they function in their cultural context, which is not restricted to the study of indigenous individuals or even the use of a particular method, rather indigenous psychology is in fact necessary for all cultural, indigenous, and ethnic groups, including economically developed countries; some scholars argue that theories and strategies used in the United States are in fact indigenous to the U.S. cultures.

Intercultural Communication Competence: The effective and appropriate reciprocal action with members of different cultures involving knowledge, motivation, and skills.

Unilateral Globalization: Unilateral globalization refers to the belief in superiority of its own culture, values, and ideals and the imposition of a single standard on all cultures.

Chapter 17
Health, Digitalization, and Individual Empowerment

Alena Lagumdzija
Karolinska University Hospital, Sweden

Velmarie King Swing
Southern Nazarene University, USA

ABSTRACT

Internet, eHealth and digitalization have opened information access for patients and medical health users. Digitalization provides an opportunity for telemedicine, storage of Electronic Patient Records (EPRs) and net communication for both medical staff and patients with access. Digitalization and technical improvement have increased the usage of Internet based technologies and telephones for positive health coaching and digital-learning applications for all medical users, school staff, and students. The effect of Information Technology on healthcare and medical services can be described as revolutionary. Increasingly, the utilization of digital equipment and medical technology are employed in patients' homes.

INTRODUCTION

The term 'information society', which encapsulates globalization and Information Technology (IT) phenomena, is often used to describe a society in which data production and consumption becomes increasingly vital in society functions. Many individuals are connected to different networks of one form or another in an information society. Such networks include cable and satellite television, telephone, computer-to-computer, person to computer communications and online information services (Webster, 2014). There are many benefits of IT in healthcare including the utilization of computer software application programs to enhance safety, efficiency, and real-time decision support to medical and healthcare practitioners (Blumenthal & Tavenner, 2010). IT presents solutions to current complex healthcare challenges. Progress from IT comes with higher medical expenses (Callahan, 2008; Deloitte Centre for health solutions, 2015; Wang et al., 2003). Also, long-term care of individuals and the cost of hospitalization are increasing significantly in different countries for different reasons (Callahan, 2008).

DOI: 10.4018/978-1-5225-0522-8.ch017

Several complementary investments are required for the integration of successful techniques in organizational, business, and educational developments. In other words, Information Technology does not simply mean the implementation of new technology. The need to adapt and integrate existing systems with care work operations and processes is essential. Equally essential is the education of clinical personnel, nurses, and physicians. Finally, an integrative approach to the resolution of legal issues and responsibilities associated with home and ambulatory care is essential.

The first objective of the chapter, from a Swedish perspective, is to explore the above issues and highlight the importance and difficulties involved in using information technology in globalized healthcare and medical services. These measures are concerns of politicians, policy-makers, healthcare authorities, schools, and private participants. The second objective is to explore how the information society has dealt with the challenge of integrating IT in healthcare in response to citizens' expectations and requirements.

Cost of Healthcare

Rapid development in medical science can offer new medical solutions, however, with potential high costs. Future development and improvement of medical techniques should relieve the currently overloaded primary healthcare system. Ethical concerns include justification of cost constrained solutions to the increasing complexity of individuals' health requirements. Technical progress is more than a prerequisite for the integration of information technology in healthcare and medicine.

Many countries are facing an aging population, which requires increased budgetary allocations for the elderly segment of the population due to disproportionate healthcare costs. For example, Sweden and Japan are countries known for low mortality. According to the World Health organization (WHO, 2014), Life expectancy for women in Japan is 87, the longest in the world. This is followed by Spain, Switzerland and Singapore. Men in Japan have a life expectancy of 80 years. life expectancy in Sweden it is 81.1 years (OECD, 2013). However, individuals with increased longevity can experience poor health from diseases such as dementia, mental health disorders, cancer, diabetes or other ailments. Possible chronic diseases or mental health illnesses may require multiple points of care by primary and specialist health care providers. Increased life expectancy drives the need for treatment capabilities in terms of long-term treatments and planning across complex care provider chains (Gröne, & Garcia-Barbero, 2001; Kodner, & Spreeuwenberg, 2002; Mur-Veeman, Raak van, & Paulus, 2008). Chronic diseases can require more than one point of care. The multiple care points can cause potential risks of errors that can cause additional health complications.

Information Technology

Documentation and regulatory compliance activities detract from actual face-to-face meeting between patient and medical staff. In the past years, technology push has been increasing. The term 'technology push' refers to new technology research and development that drives the production and sales of new products onto the market without market research or proper consideration of whether or not such products satisfy individual needs (Martin, 1994). Examples of technology push in medical care include wearable technologies such as bio-sensing wearables, digital hearing aids, blood pressure monitors and so on. Technology-Enabled Care (TEC), and collecting telemedicine, telecare, digital and mobile health are also examples of eHealth. Cultural and regulatory barriers to the adoption of TEC in different countries, the record keeping, digitalization, physician consultation problems as well as the national care agreements and guarantors are hot topics in the globalized world (Deloitte Centre for health solutions, 2015).

The effect of Information Technology on healthcare and medical services can be described as revolutionary. Increasingly, the utilization of digital equipment and medical technology are employed in patients' homes. The home environment would relieve nursing care, reduce transportation costs and the eventual medical intervention can occur at an earlier stage of the disease process. A study by Lindberg, Nilsson, Zotterman, Söderberg, and Skär, (2013) found that patients who utilized telecare at home preferred a combination of telecare and traditional healthcare delivery. Moreover, healthcare professionals could use Information and Communication Technology (ICT) applications in homecare as a tool to support people living with chronic illnesses (Lindberg et al. 2013). This brings up questions on how individuals can take advantage of technologies to improve their life and how digitalization of healthcare can help individuals become healthier?

The first indication of improvements is in the use of technology such as synchronized IT systems and centralized patients´ medical records to make the medical and healthcare system more efficient. Centralized medical records are necessary because many countries in the world, European and Japan are facing challenges of an aging society. A report by the Organization for Economic Cooperation and Development (OECD) showed that in 2011 the average life expectancy exceeded 80 years across OECD countries. Individual Swiss, Japanese, and Italians are expected to live longest among OECD countries (OECD, 2013).

Advancements in technology have caused greater availability of data for medical professionals and made data driven analysis possible for a variety of clinical methods. Data can be collected, processed into information, and accessed across the healthcare provider chain to effectively advance a patient´s status and treatment. However, digitalization of medical records has been developed using a top-down approach that affects the push of technology solutions in the medical industry.

A second response has been to engage people and help them take active and preventive care of their own health and to deal with current medical problems (OECD, 2013). With increased general welfare and rapid technology development, the Internet is currently considered as a basic standard service in everyday life. To facilitate communication between patients and clinicians, many health care providers have developed digital guides for those who need orientation in how to manage personal medical problem. The digital guides also connect patients with similar medical problems to collaborate in collecting relevant information. Swedish residents, for example, can study digitally available information about the medical treatment and results obtained by health providers in different areas (Sveriges Riksdag, 2012).

When prepared patients succeed in establishing a good dialog with the medical staff, increased understanding of the diagnosis can further motivated the patients to participate in the recommended treatment. As understanding of individual diagnosis increases, patients will more likely seek second and third opinions about treatment options. A third response is to develop technical and institutional solutions. Given the fact that many countries have aging societies, improved knowledge of IT and healthcare providers is essential in the development of technical and institutional solutions that connect providers and patients.

When considering the use of distance medical services, the legality of who is responsible should problems arise, need to be addressed. Additionally, retention of experienced personnel with technology and service provider activities may assist in the cost effectiveness of resolving issues.

In 2012 there were over 40,000 medical and health related apps, available for smartphones (Pelletier, 2012). This provides the opportunity for learning, but is also very important that everyone can share benefits regardless of the age and status. However, validation of information may become difficult and contextualizing within a particular situation. Enhanced individualized learning opportunities and searching in the 'overflow of information' is essential in discovering how to utilize available options and effectively evaluate information.

An example is the use of digital systems by a specialist while leading a surgery team at a distance. Teleconsultations are now widespread in almost all developed and developing countries (Jennett, et al., 2004) and empowers patients and facilitates disease management by allowing physicians and patients to confer on specific plans of care, specifically in cases where a control of a given disease, such as diabetes, depends on patients' self-care endeavour. Telemedicine technology is also useful in the identification of disaster victims and the administration of triage, which is typically the first step in pre-hospital medical treatment and transportation of casualties. As underdeveloped countries catch up with the digital requirements, i.e., the Internet and the World Wide Web, teleconsultations are certain to spread to such countries.

Individual Empowerment

As one of the world's most computer mature nations, Sweden is far ahead in terms of technology for the creation and implementation of e-courses at universities, secondary schools and companies. The Swedish schools are increasing applications of ICT as teaching tools needed to achieve their aims. The program, ICT for Everyone, which is a Digital Agenda for Sweden, proposed that Swedish school-children and teachers should have access to modern learning tools that are required for contemporary education and that every student, on completing primary and lower secondary school, should be able to use modern technology as a tool for knowledge-seeking, communication, creation and learning (Swedish Ministry of Enterprise, Energy and Communications [SMEEC], 2011). To apply knowledge, teachers need to be competent in usage of digital equipment and have a clear vision of how and why digital tools are used. Every individual learns in a different way. By using digital programs, teachers can customize pedagogical methods at different levels of school education and give students the tools, knowledge and digital skills required to understand the Internet and the digital environment (MEEC, 2011).

Moreover, present generations are accustomed to searching for new information and communicating with each other through computers, mobiles and digital games. Essary (2011) reported that 75% of millennials are connected to the Internet through Facebook. However, despite e-learning advantages, personal student-teacher contact can be lacking the relationships one develops with classmates in a classroom and school in the online setting. University students create social networks that are both personality stimulating and a place to make friends for life. It can also be difficult to replace the daily discussions with classmates, teachers or friends at campus.

The rapid IT and ICT progress that have so far been achieved could make traditional universities leery of e-learning. Sweden and other developed countries are facing revolutionary changes in high education. Although a large majority has not succumbed to it, many US universities currently provide courses online. Allen and Seaman (2013) have reported that by the fall of 2002, 1.6 million higher education students were taking courses online. Allen and Seaman also reported that 62.4% of higher education institutions began offering complete online programs in 2012 compared to 34.5% who did in 2002.

Unlike the United States, Japan, UK, Ireland, Australia (OECD, 2012), Swedes view higher education as a non-commercial product. Education in Sweden is a public practice with 40% of the population of 8.3 million enrolled (Boucher, 2014). For example, there are over a million 7-17 year-olds in compulsory basic education (*Grundskola*), 16-19 year-olds enrolled in integrated upper secondary school

(*Gymnasieskola*), and 270,000 adults taking school level courses administered by local governments (Swedish National Agency for Education, 2016). If the Swedish students in the future choose MOOC trainings it is likely that it will negatively affect the municipalities with higher education institutions. However, the use of online courses could have greater implications for developing countries when the cost of technology is calculated.

Distance learning and e-learning became popular concepts in the discussions on IT and educational issues. This concept in Sweden has been replaced by 'flexible learning'. A common international term, 'blended education' is a combination of e-learning and traditional learning, which address the different forms of teaching and learning. Perhaps the IT-health sector could learn from the education system so that the 'e-Health' is regarded as an integrated part of 'health' and not something outside or alternative to 'health'

Globalization

Globalization has allowed the transfer of patients, capital, knowledge, technology, and other services across borders. In recent years globalization has increased rapidly. Globalization has provided the ability for establishing stronger relationships between developed and developing nations. However, globalization can have positive and negative outcomes. A positive affect is increased accessibility to medical services, which promises to be one of the defining attributes of the 21st century. Apart from ethical considerations, the transmigration of medical personnel, from advanced economies to impoverished countries, is one of the benefits accruing to individuals the world over. Advancements in science have contributed to preventive healthcare by reducing the prospect of an individual acquiring severe and life-threatening illnesses. It is important to note that global communication technologies facilitate increases in scientific communications, information, knowledge sharing and the development of new techniques, methods, medicines, and vaccines. Tracking and monitoring outbreaks of particular diseases has been enhanced by IT.

Migration of highly trained medical specialists from thinly populated countries, e.g., Island (Solberg, et al., 2013) to other countries and cultures in reaction to economic conditions is one of the disadvantages of globalization. Another example of the disadvantages of globalization is the growing migration, tourism, and increased spread of infectious diseases such as, for instance, SARS and EBOLA, that can potentially exert a negative influence on both poor and rich countries (Pang & Guindon, 2004). Globalization can lead to increased exchange and influence of different cultures, customs, attitudes and philosophies of life. Regarding migration, a previous study explored the effects of poor working conditions and a desire for greater access to enhanced equipment and technology in medical care can be important (Astor, et al., 2005).

While longevity can reflect good health, ageing societies such as Japan, Germany, and Sweden are experiencing falling fertility rates, declining workforce, and increasing medical costs (Harper, 2013). Sweden's ageing society has increasing needs and associated costs for the medical services and emergency transportation (The Swedish Association of Local Authorities and Regions, 2014). For example, in 2014, the Swedish elderly care and nursing costs were approximately 25% of total costs (The Swedish Association of Local Authorities and Regions, 2014). In addition, most hospitals are overburdened and there is shortage of doctors, particularly in rural areas and in home care for elderly. However, elderly individuals prefer, as much as possible, to receive medical services at home (Burholt, & Naylor, 2005; Linhart, 2010; Dale, et al., 2008). In Sweden, the demographic aspect of an increasing aging population is only a partial portion of the burden on society. Providing an increased quality of life is becoming a higher priority.

While health-related quality of life in Sweden varies according to socio-economic status (Burström, Johannesson, & Diderichsen, 2001), elderly Swedes who manage to increased activity participation across domains perceived a beneficial effect in quality of life (Silverstein, & Parker, 2002). Active participation that contributes to productive personal growth includes culture-entertainment, outdoor physical activities, recreation, friendship, and so on.

Timely access to primary care depends on affordability and availability of medical care. Accordingly, since 2000, the number of doctors has grown in most OECD countries including Sweden with twice as many specialists as generalists (OECD, 2013). Inadequate numbers of primary healthcare physicians in comparison to secondary healthcare sectors is raising concerns regarding access to primary care (OECD, 2013). In addition, The Health Affairs research on access to primary care in seven different countries (Canada, Germany, Netherlands, New Zealand, Australia, U.K. and U.S.) indicated wide country differences.

The debate about the positive or negative consequences of globalization is an on-going one. Living in a globalized world with increased domestic and international movement of people can cause working people to immigrate to bigger towns causing acute manpower shortage in rural districts. In Sweden as an example, the population grew by more than one million in 2014 (Swedish Institute, 2013-2015). In a multicultural country, an influx of people with diverse language capabilities can cause challenges to communication as well as altered expectations in health service and other socio-economics sectors.

Providing quality care to culturally and linguistically diverse patients is often difficult. Barriers such as health illiteracy, culture, and language affect health outcomes. Such barriers result in poor understanding of medical diagnosis, recommendations for medication, treatment, and follow-up (Carrasquillo, Orav, Brennan, & Burstin, 1999; Crane, 1997; Sarver & Baker, 2000; Shapiro & Saltzer, 1981). According to Singelton and Krause (2009), understanding a patient´s level of health literacy requires an assessment of the patient`s linguistic skills and cultural norms. The challenges related to the integrative process into health literacy strategies are important for daily patient care.

To overcome the linguistic and cultural barriers, it becomes necessary to provide professional language services, which in many cases is not cheap. However, eHealth allows the mitigation of medical personnel shortages through the implementation of existing technologies such as videoconferencing, call centers and the Internet. Aadvance medical technology requires higher skills and complementary education that are becoming more essential in international competitiveness. However, finding ways to overcome linguistic, cultural or other social barriers may lead to enhanced care and more satisfied patients and medical providers (Singelton & Krause, 2009). Addressing any barriers is a global challenge. More research is needed to understand how cultural and linguistic concerns can guide quality improvement in healthcare.

Cross-Country Comparisons: Access to Primary Care

In Germany, Netherlands, and Australia, physicians offer early morning office hours and some hours beyond the typical workday. In Canada, New Zealand, U.K. and U.S, fewer than half of physicians offer early morning, evening, or weekend office hours and one-third or more reported no office hours during these times (Schoen, et al., 2006). Unlike the above-mentioned countries, there are very few physicians who offer either early morning, evening or weekend office hours in Sweden. Instead patients are required to contact nurses at on-call centers, or seek care at emergency wards. The lack of resources is a contributing factor to high workloads for physicians and long waiting time for patients.

Additionally, lack of resources indicate increased direct patient contact of hospital emergency wards (Glenngård, Hjalte, Svensson, Anell, & Bankauskaite, 2005). While emergency physicians are trained care givers, care may fail to meet the needs of patients due to longer wait time to meet a specialist. The health condition of patients commuting between vacant wards may worsens (Andersson & Karlberg, 2000; Glenngård et al., 2005; Swedish National Board of Health and Welfare, ([SNBHW], 2003).

Swedish patients are required to pay user-fees to visit a general practitioner in a public health centre (Glenngård et al., 2005; Gosden, et al., 2001). The monetary contribution may have created incentives to use other healthcare personnel than primary healthcare physicians. Nonetheless, waiting time, rather than user fees, may have a strong impact on patients' behaviour. Consequently, recondite or ineffective primary care and interdisciplinary care may increase the risk of patients' health complications and hospitalization resulting in increased costs of medical care.

Furthermore, many healthcare organizations currently suffer from poor and inefficient communication within healthcare organizations or between healthcare organizations and patients. The lack of effective communication can cause delays, errors, and failures in the application of vital resources. In accordance with different studies, lack of communication might be one of the major risks that could lead to patients´ morbidity or mortality (Ammenwerth, et al., 2006; Bates, & Gawande, 2003; Coiera, 1996, 2000, 2004; Coiera, & Tombs, 1998; Donchin, et al., 1995; Stetson et al., 2002).

Patient Empowerment and Healthcare-Associated Infections (HAIs)

An international studies reported that Healthcare-Associated Infections (HAIs) affected approximately 1,7 million hospitalized patients and caused around 100,000 deaths in 2002 in the United States alone (Klevens, et al., 2007) and in Europe 3.2 million hospitalized patients per year causing 110,000 deaths per year (Suetens, Hopkins, Kolman, & Diaz-Högberg, 2013). Moreover, in majority of low or average income countries, HAIs affected 5-19% with the prevalence of over 10% of all hospitalized patients (World Health Organization [WHO], 2010). Many HAIs are preventable through evidence-based infection control interventions and engagement of patients in the management of their own conditions. Empowering patients through different information sources may raise care standards by increasing well-being, reducing HAIs or unnecessary examinations and improving outcomes.

eHealth and Free Mobility Within the European Union

In light of a shortage of qualified medical personnel in Sweden (Stroetmann, Jones, Dobrev, & Stroetmann, 2006), a reality that continues on an increase worldwide, e-service may assist in providing adequate care. Currently, many people are moving to different locations both domestically and globally. One example is the administration of telemedicine to patients in Sweden by physicians in Spain (Stroetmann, et al, 2006).

The mobility of medical professionals and patients is one of the central points of European eHealth action plan (Maier et al, 2011). eHealth is aimed at improving efficiency and quality of public medical services, conforming to health professionals´ needs and placing patients at the centre of the health system while increasing safety and reducing medical costs. To be able to follow up, usage of 'Big data' is essential for collecting and storing individual patient records for future care decision-making, analysis or action. 'Big data' can allow medical providers to combine public life sciences data and clinical trial data, therefore, refining diagnosis and treatment protocols in order to provide enhanced care.

Since the early 1990's, EU implemented a high-quality eHealth to facilitate obtaining healthcare in other European member states. The program's goal was to secure infrastructure and coordinate communication between cross-border regions, healthcare stakeholders, the system and the citizen (European Commission, 2007).

An example of implemented projects is the European Health Insurance Card (EHIC) introduced across the European Union in 2004. The EHIC allows EU citizens to access healthcare while traveling and instantaneously assured participating hospitals accept the insurance of travellers and guaranteed fast reimbursement via electronic transfer of administrative data (European Commission, 2007, 2015). Additionally, the European eHealth initiated a commitment by all EU member states to develop eHealth schemes providing a transparent view of the eHealth national landscapes. The vision of EU was that European eHealth space should be able to deliver high quality healthcare to all European citizens independent of the location when in need of acute or medical care (European Commission, 2007).

The implementation of eHealth across Europe has progressed and an example is the EU project known as epSOS (Smart Open Services for European Patients). The epSOS was a European large-scale project financed and guaranteed by the EU and the 23 Member States. The project's goal was to implement cross-border exchanges of electronic medical information and connect EU member countries by eHealth. The connection can improve patient care by using the electronic patient record system when citizens traveling abroad are in need of help (Linden, 2009). The epSOS program will allow health professionals to access patient records and eHealth information in doctors' original languages with an original copy.

Currently, epSOS consists of patient summary and ePrescriptions. The patient summary contains information from the patients' home countries, i.e., patient's name, gender, birth, a list of the current medication. Crucial clinical patient data – current medical issues, allergies, major surgical procedures are also included in the epSOS. For security and protocol purposes, a recording of the information about whom and when treatment occurred is generated and updated. The epSOS and ePrescriptions contain the current prescriptions in patients' home countries and are transmitted electronically to pharmacies in countries using the epSOS system.

Primary Care vs. National Systems Computing

Sweden has provided digitalization and boosted personal empowerment through the common use of computers in Swedish homes. The rapid progress of digitalization occurred in the middle of the 1990s across diverse sectors of the society, including the medical segment. In 2010 Internet access in Sweden was 88.3% of all households, compared with Japan's 78% household Internet access in the same period (OECD, 2015).

Scandinavian countries (Denmark, Sweden, and Norway) are among the most advanced in terms of operational telecommunication infrastructure, broadband connection and fully operational national Information and Communication Technology infrastructures for communications support in the health sector (European Commission, 2007). In primary healthcare, providers are required to deliver preventive and acute care, thus facing the challenge of integrating and managing an enormous amount of information.

For enhanced coordination of patient care, Swedish healthcare providers have utilized Electronic Health Records (EHR) for prescriptions since 1997. In 2012, the EHR was fully implemented in Swedish primary care, hospitals, and psychiatry. EHR contain information from all providers involved in patient´s care. EHR allows a patient´s health record to move to other health care providers, hospitals, nursing homes and even across national borders. EHR allows instant access to information about patients' medical history, and became a valuable tool in crisis, enabling providers to reduce time in making treatment decisions.

Three factors that have contributed to the accessibility of information for both patients and medical professionals are: the Internet, eHealth, and digitalization. Digitalization provides an opportunity for many things including telemedicine, storage, retrieval of electronic patient records (EPRs), and communication among medical staff and patients. Digitalization and technical improvement have increased the usage of Internet based technologies and telephones for positive health coaching and digital-learning applications for all medical users, school staff, and students.

Beside advancements in Information and Communication technology (ICT) infrastructure, Sweden is unique in terms of citizens´ registration by personal identity number, utilizing the Modulus-10-system that is considered a very secure system and organized identification of citizens with very low or no risk for mixing people up (Ludvigsson, Otterblad-Olausson, Pettersson, & Ekbom, 2009). However, there is no single centralized national database for patients' medical records to date. An interesting note about Sweden is the ability to have centralized ePrescriptions, however, it lacks the centralized national patient records. A council of 21 counties, 290 municipalities, private organizations, and the central government share the centralization of records. There are no hierarchical relationships. Each county, council, and municipality can have individual self-governing local authorities and budgets for medical services with responsibility for different activities. The exception is the Swedish island of Gotland, where the municipality has the responsibilities and tasks normally associated with a county council.

The fractured structure can make communication and decision-making difficult. Part of the reason is that the system was constructed by IT specialists in the medical sector, who designed and developed a top-down system with inadequate knowledge or experience in business operations. Very few have a complete command over both information technologies and the business operations. Consequently, multiple IT medical record systems in use are difficult to connect to one common system.

There are advantages with an organizational structure such as the Swedish system, however, reaching a national or European level of connecting systems may be difficult. Undoubtedly, Swedish citizens are open-minded, however cautious. The government is focused on efforts to deploy various departments and authorities that would provide and control the future security of personal information access and transfer. This added complex hierarchy of authority renders the decision-making and implementation process more complicated. Examples of the supervisory authorities within the health sector are the Swedish Government Agency Health and Social Care Inspectorate and the Swedish eHealth Agency. The newly created authorities are aiming to increase the development of the national eHealth infrastructure, e.g. individuals' access to individual medical health records by personal health account and e-prescriptions.

Another authority that the Swedish government initiated was the National Patient Summary (*Nationell Patientöversikt, NPÖ*). The aim of NPÖ is to increase cooperation by making it possible for all health care providers, including private ones, to directly access a patient's medical records that are stored by other health care providers, provided all legal requirements are fulfilled (Jerlvall, & Pehrsson, 2012).

In contrast to Sweden, Norway and Denmark use national eHealth infrastructures that support electronic exchange of various healthcare related messaging and other services. Meanwhile, Finland's regional networks are allowing the exchange of various types of patient records (European Commission, 2007). However, there are many differences and common challenges between regions and countries in the delivery and founding of medical care (Hall & Walton, 2004; Haux, Ammenwerth, Herzog, & Knaup,

2002; Nytrø & Faxvaag, 2004). One example of a common challenge for both Sweden and Denmark is that hospitals are mainly public and are a part of the regional healthcare structure. Hospital departments and healthcare canters are responsible for individual facility budgetary control (Glenngård et al., 2005; Kjellberg et al., 2007). Facility budgets may create a limited initiative for increased activities in the healthcare centres or hospital departments.

The current payment system fails to reward cross-sectoral activities, which contributes to a lack of collaboration between hospital departments and healthcare centres (Glenngård et al., 2005; Vrangbaek & Christiansen, 2005). In turn, the lack of collaboration results in IT systems with different development levels and functional scopes.

Future points for consideration are the IT systems synchronizations and solutions. In order to respond effectively, the government has to find a balance between bottom-up and top-down dialog to identify common system requirements and goals. An essential aspect of the system development either in public, private, or medical sectors, is the application of preliminary solution plan known as 'Architectural principle' (Lindström, 2005). The architectural principle describes how to synchronize information content systems with each other. Systems that should communicate with other systems are also described, along with the person in charge of managing all systems. There is also the guidance required for specifications and evaluation of different alternatives that can affect decision making for IT product purchase and technique choices (Lindström, 2005).

Challenges of Digitalization

Addressing differences in healthcare between patients that have Internet access and those that lack connection is imperative to ensure that healthcare is provided for all. Sweden was identified as a world leader in the use of Information and Communication Technology (ICT), which contributed to the country's productivity growth. Since 2002, Sweden's 80 public hospitals, 800 primary care centres, 950 pharmacies and large number of private healthcare centres have been connected via *Sjunet*, a federated fibre-optical eHealth network (SMHSA, 2006; Stroetmann, Dobrev, Lilischkis, & Stroetmann, 2014). The Sjunet, which was developed as a regional project separated from the Internet, allows a secure exchange of confidential data, e.g., patient`s personal data, pictures and medical applications, images, e-prescription system and video conferencing. Additionally, Sjunet links regional administrations, pharmacies, health care, and county councils.

eHealth and the national social services efforts are focused on practical improvements in Swedish industries, healthcare, medical and social services. According to SMEEC (2011), the correct use of technology could allow physicians to receive all relevant information from the electronic patient medical record regarding severely ill patients that are admitted to the emergency or hospital wards.

On the other hand, beside positive Internet effects, privacy and identity security issues are some of problems that are often associated with being a member of a social network. There is also a new trend for bulling in schools or at working places thru mobile messages, social networking, or mails. Computers allow people to become victims of the so-called cyber-bullying (Hiduja, & Patchin, 2010). Internet access opens many ways for harassment and bullying that invade the lives of victims. Cyber-bullying can lead to more depression, discouragement, loneliness, and in the worst-case scenario, suicide (Hiduja, & Patchin, 2010).

Visiting social media Web sites are common activities of many technology savvy learners. However, dangers persist for those vulnerable children. Whereas many millennials are conversant with the Internet, some are exposed to cyber crimes, including bullying, extortion, and the like (Tokunaga, 2010). Children, 30 percent of whom use the Internet without parental supervision (ChildrenOnline, 2015), are exposed to the dangers of being dragged from home because they click with cyber tormenters. The number of children and teens that are exposed to crime on the Internet from home is rapidly growing. According to ChildrenOnline, one in every 25 teenagers has received online sexual solicitation and more than 70 percent between the ages of 12 and 17 have social media profile.

Cyber crime demands the attention of everyone, including patients, parents, school and medical administrators (Keith, & Martin, 2005). To prevent Internet harassment, it is crucial to teach users and creators of all ages early. Given that online education and telemedicine are here to stay as aspect of the 21st-Century culture, it is important to offer education that will help learners become aware of the pros and cons of online learning, including the ethics, safely, and legal issues at the early stages of schooling (*Digitaliseringskommissionen*, 2014).

The Wealth of Health (Medical Tourism)

The use of digital health across Europe has become increasingly globalized. Digital health has progressed from public discussions to applied eHealth and medical services. More patients, often from high-income EU countries, cross borders to developing countries in order to seek treatment and different types of medical services. The reasons are either shorter waiting time or lower cost of health service in developing countries. The trend has become known as medical tourism.

The definition of medical tourism takes into account the territorially bounded nature of health systems, where access to healthcare is often but not always limited to national boundaries (Carrera, & Bridges, 2006). Medical tourism constitutes an individual solution to what is traditionally considered a government concern in Sweden. Individuals, mostly from richer countries, basically try to solve their health problems by seeking cheaper and efficient treatment, mostly from relatively poorer countries in Asian and Latin America. In 2003, it is reported that nearly 350,000 patient travelled from developed countries as medical tourists to developing countries (Horowitz, Rosensweig, & Jones, 2007).

Notably, the health sector in Southeast Asia is expanding rapidly, attributable to rapid growth of the private sector and, medical tourism, which is emerging as a lucrative business opportunity (Pocock, & Phua, 2011). These countries combine high quality medical services and competitive pricing with tourist packages in capitalizing on the popularity of medical patients as tourist. Thailand, for example, has established cosmetic surgery and sex change operations, while Singapore is attracting patients at the high end of the market for advanced treatments such as cardiovascular and neurological surgeries and stem cell therapy (Pocock, & Phua, 2011; UNESCAP, 2007). In addition, Singapore, Malaysia and Thailand alone, had an estimated 2 million medical travellers visiting in 2006-2007 with earning of over US $ 3 billion in treatment costs (Pocock, & Phua, 2011). Many poor countries find it difficult to retain medical staff attracted by higher pay in rich countries.

Indeed, medical tourism can bring economic benefits to countries, including additional resources for investment in healthcare. However, unless properly managed and regulated on the policy side, the financial benefits of medical tourism for health systems may come at the expense of access and use of health services by local consumers. Pocock and Phua (2011) argued that governments and industry players would do well to remember that health is wealth for both foreign and local populations.

Generally speaking, the relationship among globalization, the medical sector, and education development is complex. Increased globalization makes it easier for medical workers to migrate to other countries (Mahroum, 2001). It can as well provide opportunities for high-income countries to increase economic investment and enhanced technology for developing countries. There is also potential to learn from countries that may be ahead in planning and development.

While it is important to observe recent improvements in telemedicine (Jennett, et al., 2004), especially in the treatment of prisoners, military personnel, and victims of natural disaster, at the same time it is necessary to be aware that more training is needed in order to extend the trend to more peoples of the world, including people in poorer countries. Although various studies suggest that telemedicine through teleconsultation is acceptable to a great number of patients, Perednia, and Allen (1995) found that further studies are needed to derive its precise health benefits.

Health, Linguistic and Cultural Divide

The progress in medical science and development of new therapies significantly reduced the need for hospital care. Nonetheless, it is predicted that there will not be enough resources for the healthcare sector due to rapid demographic changes (Anell, Glenngård, & Merkur, 2012). To accommodate the increased demand on healthcare, higher technical knowledge and further progress in development and usage of medical digital equipment are needed. For example, robots are being developed to assist family members or medical staff involved in homecare.

Patients do not always use the Emergency Department (ED) to conform to the original design and for the intended purpose. The ED is a specialized service equipped with specialized resources and personnel for the treatment of urgent and emergency life-threatening problems. However, research shows that Emergency Department personnel are routinely assigned to patients that do not meet the criteria of life-threatening emergency needs. According to Göransson, Ehrenberg, and Ehnfors (2005), 81% ED staff were assigned to patients who did not arrive at the hospital by ambulance.

Inequality happens to show a certain degree of pervasiveness in the Swedish health and medical system. While life expectancy for both men and women has improved, such improvement does not extend to people employed in menial jobs (Whitehead, Evandrou, Haglund, & Diderichsen, 1997). Apart from individual health conditions and wellbeing, attributes that determine the quality of a good health care system, from a European perspective, includes but not limited to, (a) the comfort of the physical environment, (b) availability of information, (c) adequate communication, (d), interpersonal relations between health care personnel–nurses, physicians, technicians, and the like (Johansson, Oleni, & Fridlund, 2002). If an individual were able to establish a dialogue with medical staff, she/he would be able to acquire a better understanding of his diagnosis, which in turn would help, to a large degree, his prognosis communication with a physician. It might help the patient become more motivated toward recommended treatment.

Individual empowerment is possible in health care due to the current Digital Age of the World Wide Web of Internet connections. The Internet allows the proliferation of apps that can collect and dispense medial information to promote and maintain healthy lifestyles as well as to treat various illnesses. Given the rampant nature of Internet provided information, it is important that patients are able to distinguish valuable and valueless information (Metzger, & Flanagin, 2013). As Cassel and Guest (2012) have suggested, the quantity of care and information is not necessarily equivalent to quality care and information. Nonetheless, well-informed patients should be capable of preventing or diagnosing disease by themselves.

Electronic health records enable the transfer and analysis of patient data among healthcare professionals. Despite the progress that have been made in Information and Communication Technology

(ICT), there is still planet of room for growth (Aarts, & Berg, 2006; Aarts, Doorewaard & Berg 2004; Littlejohns, Wyatt, & Garvican, 2003; Wears, & Berg 2005). In addition, ICT adoption by healthcare organizations is a slow process and Sweden is not the only country facing slow progression of ICT utilization. Professor emeritus K. Lundgren (2007) from Swedish Royal Institute of Technology claimed that approximately 70% of IT projects worldwide are unsuccessful. Electronic Health Record (EHR) systems are rarely successfully implemented in countries other than where they were developed (Kajbjer, Nordberg, & Klein, 2010).

What began as a series of pilot projects, computerized health support system has been available in Swedish hospitals as early as the mid-1960. The Karolinska Hospital in the Stockholm region gained notoriety due to the implementation of batch processing of medical records, limited in volume and scope nonetheless (Kajbjer et al, 2010). In the 1970s and early 1980s a system known as PAX was developed locally, in Gothenburg. A central mainframe computer with dumb terminals was developed to help manage patient invoicing and the allocation of hospital beds. Computerized in primary care medial records system was implemented in the mid-1980s. Among many commercialized computerized systems imported from Norway, Denmark, or Iceland in the 1990s, Journal III, Melior, and VAS were in use in Sweden. By 2009, approximately 85% of hospital wards were using Electronic Health Record (EHRs).

Kajbjer et al. (2010) explained that the popularity of these system is based on the fact that the clinical staff, nurses, and physicians were allowed to influence many of the details regarding how the system functions, although it took more than twenty years after the initial trials before EHR system was installed in the Swedish primary care. It is important that eHealth is based on a solid foundational structural where information processes are analyzed and management has established clear operational procedures. However, efforts to establish national information structures, standardizations, and the like, have either been delayed or failed to take hold. Many information systems have failed to communicate with each other because of technical, organizational, institutional, or frequent problems with security and reliability (Lundgren, 2007).

In many areas, including the home care environment, digitalization has neither contributed to improvements in working conditions, nor ensured better relationships with elderly patients. Digitalization in the home care environment has diminished individual autonomy and exerted increased external control over patients. In other words, rather than dialogues with the patient, digitalization has guaranteed bureaucratic demands. This is often the case in the medical sector. The organization is divided in autonomous island structures rather than a synchronized whole with clear goals and strategies.

The lack of dialog is partly one reason for many IT-projects to fail. According to previously published reports, large public sector IT-projects may experience failure because of inadequate dialog and knowledge transfer between management and IT-professionals, and because of unclear formulation of operational strategy development (Swedish National Audit Office, 2002). The famous American innovation researcher, von Hippel, stated that technical knowledge was more general, i.e., it was easier to communicate with a counterpart than it is for organizations to communicate its knowledge to suppliers (von Hippel, 1994, 1998). Knowledge of an organization´s goal, together with its customers, suppliers, as well as the knowledge and relationship among co-workers, are often based on specific company experience. For von Hippel (1994, 1998), the rational process is to make users solve problems and generate technical knowledge within an organization than to hire technicians from outside, who are not familiar with the organisation´s goal, to take that responsibility. von Hippel also pointed out that it would be more rational if more IT-technicians were hired by IT consuming organizations rather than within the

IT producing companies, wich could allow the development of competence of the IT users' information solutions (von Hippel, 1994, 1998).

eHealth can enhance individual wellbeing by making important information available to healthcare professionals, independent of their location. However, eHealth requires developmental demands, which include educating people and finding ways to reach those that are not so easy to reach. Because of the digital nature of data, which is transmitted over the Internet, monitoring patients involves issues relating to security and privacy (Atkinson & Gold, 2002). The balance between security and efficiency constitutes a challenging risk factor.

The current healthcare system in Sweden has long been known to suffer many problems (Hjern, Grindefjord, Sundberg, & Rosén, 2001; Wahlberg, Cedersund, & Wredling, 2003). There are problems of communication among government institutions, IT-professionals, patients and professional care providers. Effective and enduring solutions in healthcare are connected to leadership as an all-complex organization.

FUTURE RESEARCH DIRECTIONS

The role of patients in the healthcare sector is essential for a fully functional medical and healthcare system. Future challenges include a determination of the means by which citizens can effectively use Information Technology as a tool for managing their own health. Possible innovation processes in IT within the medical and healthcare sectors have been characterized by too much technology push and too little demand-pull. Clinical systems that have been developed in close cooperation with doctors and nurses have been more successful than systems developed with a top-down approach. Unfortunately, such systems are less prevalent.

It is important to be aware of the fact that the most essential user of any system is an individual. All future systems that do not include user input as part of the solution will likely fail. Hence, the success of any patient related healthcare system is probably measured in terms of the extent to which it facilitates the empowerment of patients. A necessary ingredient of a successful system is the development of the soft infrastructure, i.e., the structuring of information and tools that make it possible for people to understand and evaluate information and available services.

Early use of ICT and digital education can assist school students to increase knowledge transfer by using computers and technology. This could also promote students to increase self-discipline and select a preferred path towards learning. The best way of teaching ethics should be by combining knowledge and collaboration between schoolteachers and different area specialists such as medicine, computer scientists and engineers.

CONCLUSION

The lives of 21st Century individuals are expected to be vastly different from those of progenitors. It is in the 21st Century that life expectancy is expected to improve due to the development of newer effective drugs and the globalization of healthcare. The Information Age is also responsible for the digitization of healthcare documents to the advantage of patients, physicians, and researchers. The rapid development of technology needs to be matched with a rapid training and development of human resources that will be able to use the new technology in more areas that extend beyond medicine and healthcare.

Both developed and developing countries are faced with similar problems in terms of understanding the organization activities. Moreover, countries face problems with the establishment and implementation of Information Technology in healthcare. Organizational development and knowledge are strongly dependent on customer voices, which are the reference points in healthcare delivery. No consumer-oriented system can be constructed without such reference points. Sometimes decision-making is achieved more efficiently with top-down solutions and technology push. Other means of creating successful systems includes the ability to anticipate problems and to be ready to provide solutions as they develop. Solutions are more appropriate with input by consumers or end-users.

In order to successfully implement digitalization of the medical sector internationally both absorptive and sender capacities are needed. Evidently, building up and implementing new systems is a long-term project. For successful implementation of eHealth, governments should first consider and create new policies and strengthen laws for medical sector digitalization to better dialog on trade, education and health. An approach to match the patient with identifying data developed can assist in the follow up data in long-term, eHealth implementation to be institutionalised with clear contracts and trust in patients´ confidentiality.

REFERENCES

Aarts, J., & Berg, M. (2006). Same systems, different outcomes comparing the implementation of computerized physician order entry in two Dutch hospitals. *Methods of Information in Medicine*, *45*(1), 53–61. PMID:16482371

Aarts, J., Doorewaard, H., & Berg, M. (2004). Understanding implementation: The case of a computerized physician order entry system in a large Dutch university medical center. *Journal of the American Medical Informatics Association*, *11*(3), 207–216. doi:10.1197/jamia.M1372 PMID:14764612

Allen, I. E., & Seaman, J. (2013). Changing course: Ten years of tracking online education in the United States. Newburyport, MA: Sloan. Available from http://onlinelearningsurvey.com/reports/changing-course.pdf

Ammenwerth, E., Talmon, J., Ash, J. S., Bates, D. W., Beuscart-Zephir, M. C., Duhamel, A., & Geissbuhler, A. et al. (2006). Impact of CPOE on mortality rates-contradictory findings, important messages. *Methods of Information in Medicine*, *45*(6), 586–593. Available from http://www.lina-schwab.de/Publikationen/z42.pdf PMID:17149499

Andersson, G., & Karlberg, I. (2000). Integrated care for the elderly: The background and effects of the reform of Swedish care of the elderly. *International Journal of Integrated Care*, *1*(1), 1–10. Available from http://citeseerx.ist.psu.edu/viewdoc/download?doi=10.1.1.276.9726&rep=rep1&type=pdf PMID:16902694

Anell, A., Glenngård, A. H., & Merkur, S. (2012). Sweden: Health system review. Health systems in transition. *European Observatory on Health Systems and Policies, 14*(5), 1-159. Retrieved from http://www.euro.who.int/__data/assets/pdf_file/0008/164096/e96455.pdf

Astor, A., Akhtar, T., Matallana, M. A., Muthuswamy, V., Olowu, F. A., Tallo, V., & Lie, R. K. (2005). Physician migration: Views from professionals in Colombia, Nigeria, India, Pakistan and the Philippines. *Social Science & Medicine, 61*(12), 2492–2500. doi:10.1016/j.socscimed.2005.05.003 PMID:15953667

Atkinson, N. L., & Gold, R. S. (2002). The promise and challenge of eHealth interventions. *American Journal of Health Behavior, 26*(6), 494–503. doi:10.5993/AJHB.26.6.10 PMID:12437024

Bates, D. W., & Gawande, A. A. (2003). Improving safety with information technology. *The New England Journal of Medicine, 348*(25), 2526–2534. doi:10.1056/NEJMsa020847 PMID:12815139

Blumenthal, D., & Tavenner, M. (2010). The "meaningful use" regulation for electronic health records. *The New England Journal of Medicine, 363*(6), 501–504. doi:10.1056/NEJMp1006114 PMID:20647183

Boucher, L. (2014). *Tradition and change in Swedish education.* Oxford, UK: Elsevier.

Burholt, V., & Naylor, D. (2005). The relationship between rural community type and attachment to place for older people living in North Wales, UK. *European Journal of Ageing, 2*(2), 109–119. doi:10.1007/s10433-005-0028-3

Burström, K., Johannesson, M., & Diderichsen, F. (2001). Health-related quality of life by disease and socio-economic group in the general population in Sweden. *Health Policy (Amsterdam), 55*(1), 51–69. doi:10.1016/S0168-8510(00)00111-1 PMID:11137188

Callahan, D. (2008). *Health care costs and medical technology.* The Hastings Center. Available from http://healthcarecost-monitor.thehastingscenter.org/uploadedFiles/Publications/Briefing_Book/health%20care%20costs%20chapter.pdf

Carrasquillo, O., Orav, E. J., Brennan, T. A., & Burstin, H. R. (1999). Impact of language barriers on patient satisfaction in an emergency Department. *Journal of General Internal Medicine, 14*(2), 82–87. doi:10.1046/j.1525-1497.1999.00293.x PMID:10051778

Carrera, P. M., & Bridges, J. F. (2006). Health and medical tourism: What they mean and imply for health care systems. *Health and Ageing, 15.* Retrieved from https://www.genevaassociation.org/media/75240/ga2006-health15-carrerabridges.pdf

Cassel, C. K., & Guest, J. A. (2012). Choosing wisely: Helping physicians and patients make smart decisions about their care. *Journal of the American Medical Association, 307*(17), 1801–1802. doi:10.1001/jama.2012.476 PMID:22492759

ChildrenOnline. (2015). *Internet safety newsletter: Children online research 2007– 2008.* Retrieved from http://www.childrenonline.org

Coiera, E. (1996). Clinical communication: a new informatics paradigm. In Proceedings of the AMIA Annual Fall Symposium (pp. 17–21). American Medical Informatics Association. Available from http://www.ncbi.nlm.nih.gov/pmc/articles/PMC2233204/

Coiera, E. (2000). When conversation is better than computation. *Journal of the American Medical Informatics Association, 7*(3), 277–286. doi:10.1136/jamia.2000.0070277 PMID:10833164

Coiera, E. (2004). *Handbook of health information management: Integrating information and communication technology in health care work*. London, UK: Routledge.

Coiera, E., & Tombs, V. (1998). Communication behaviours in a hospital setting: An observational study. *British Medical Journal, 316*(7132), 673–676. doi:10.1136/bmj.316.7132.673 PMID:9522794

Crane, J. A. (1997). Patient comprehension of doctor-patient communication on discharge from the emergency department. *The Journal of Emergency Medicine, 15*(1), 1–7. doi:10.1016/S0736-4679(96)00261-2 PMID:9017479

Dale, B., Sævareid, H. I., Kirkevold, M., & Söderhamn, O. (2008). Formal and informal care in relation to activities of daily living and self-perceived health among older care-dependent individuals in Norway. *International Journal of Older People Nursing, 3*(3), 194–203. Doi: .10.1111/j.1748-3743.2008.00122.x

Deloitte Centre for health solutions. (2015). *Connected health. How digital technology is transforming health and social care*. London, UK: The creative studio at Deloitte. Retrieved from http://www2.deloitte.com/content/dam/Deloitte/uk/Documents/life-sciences-health-care/deloitte-uk-connected-health.pdf

Donchin, Y., Gopher, D., Olin, M., Badihi, Y., Biesky, M. R., Sprung, C. L., & Cotev, S. et al. (1995). A look into the nature and causes of human errors in the intensive care unit. *Critical Care Medicine, 23*(2), 294–300. doi:10.1097/00003246-199502000-00015 PMID:7867355

Essary, A. C. (2011). The impact of social media and technology on professionalism in medical education. *The Journal of Physician Assistant Education, 22*(4), 50–53. doi:10.1097/01367895-201122040-00009 PMID:22308935

European Commission. (2007). *eHealth ERA report. eHealth-priorities and strategies in European countries. Toward the establishment of a European eHealth research arena*. Retrieved from http://www.ehealth-era.org/documents/2007ehealth-era-countries.pdf

European-Commission. (2015). *European health insurance card*. Retrieved June 10, 2015 from http://ec.europa.eu/social/main.jsp?langId=en&catId=559&newsId=2281&furtherNews=yes

Glenngård, A. H., Hjalte, F., Svensson, M., Anell, A., & Bankauskaite, V. (2005). *Health systems in transition*. Retrieved from http://old.hpi.sk/cdata/Documents/HIT/Sweden_2005.pdf

Göransson, K. E., Ehrenberg, A., & Ehnfors, M. (2005). Triage in emergency departments: National survey. *Journal of Clinical Nursing, 14*(9), 1067–1074. doi:10.1111/j.1365-2702.2005.01191.x PMID:16164524

Gosden, T., Forland, F., Kristiansen, I. S., Sutton, M., Leese, B., Giuffrida, A., & Pedersen, L. et al. (2001). Impact of payment method on behaviour of primary care physicians: A systematic review. *Journal of Health Services Research & Policy, 6*(1), 44–55. doi:10.1258/1355819011927198 PMID:11219360

Gröne, O., & Garcia-Barbero, M. (2001). Integrated care: A position paper of the WHO European office for integrated health care services. *International Journal of Integrated Care, 1*(2), e21. doi:10.5334/ijic.28 PMID:16896400

Hall, A., & Walton, G. (2004). Information overload within the health care system: A literature review. *Health Information and Libraries Journal, 21*(2), 102–108. doi:10.1111/j.1471-1842.2004.00506.x PMID:15191601

Harper, S. (2013). *Ageing societies: Myths, challenges and opportunities*. New York, NY: Routledge.

Haux, R., Ammenwerth, E., Herzog, W., & Knaup, P. (2002). Health care in the information society. A prognosis for the year 2013. *International Journal of Medical Informatics, 66*(1-3), 3–21. doi:10.1016/S1386-5056(02)00030-8 PMID:12453552

Hiduja, S., & Patchin, J. W. (2010). Bullying, Cyberbullying, and Suicide. *Archives of Suicide Research, 14*(3), 206–221. doi:10.1080/13811118.2010.494133 PMID:20658375

Hjern, A., Grindefjord, M., Sundberg, H., & Rosén, M. (2001). Social inequality in oral health and use of dental care in Sweden. *Community Dentistry and Oral Epidemiology, 29*(3), 167–174. doi:10.1034/j.1600-0528.2001.290302.x PMID:11409675

Horowitz, M. D., Rosensweig, J. A., & Jones, C. A. (2007). Medical Tourism: Globalization of the healthcare marketplace. Medscape General Medicine. *The Medscape Journal of Medicine, 9*(4), 24–30. Available from http://www.ncbi.nlm.nih.gov/pmc/articles/PMC2234298/

Jennett, P. A., Scott, R. E., Affleck, H. L., Hailey, D., Ohinmaa, A., Anderson, C., & Lorenzetti, D. et al. (2004). Policy implications associated with the socioeconomic and health system impact of telehealth: A case study from Canada. *Telemedicine Journal and e-Health, 10*(1), 77–83. doi:10.1089/153056204773644616 PMID:15104919

Jerlvall, L., & Pehrsson, T. (2012). *eHealth in Swedish county councils*. Inventory comissioned by the SLIT group, CEHIS (swe: Center för eHälsa i Sverige/Eng: Center for eHealth in Sweden).

Johansson, P., Oleni, M., & Fridlund, B. (2002). Patient satisfaction with nursing care in the context of health care: A literature study. *Scandinavian Journal of Caring Sciences, 16*(4), 337–344. doi:10.1046/j.1471-6712.2002.00094.x PMID:12445102

Kajbjer, K., Nordberg, R., & Klein, G. O. (2010). Electronic health records in Sweden: from administrative management to clinical decision support. In History of Nordic Computing 3 (pp. 74–82). Springer Berlin Heidelberg. Available from http://dl.ifip.org/db/conf/hinc/hinc2010/KajbjerNK10.pdf

Keith, S., & Martin, M. E. (2005). Cyber-bullying: Creating a culture of respect in a cyber world. *Reclaiming Children and Youth, 13*(4), 224. Available from http://bienestaryproteccioninfantil.es/imagenes/tablaContenidos03SubSec/13_4_Keith_Martin.pdf

Kjellberg, J., Sørensen, J., Hansen, J., Andersen, S., Avnstrøm, L., & Borgstrøm, L. (2007). Almen praksis som koordinator—en international belysning. [General practice as coordinator—an international review]. *Copenhagen: Danish Institute for Health Services Research (DSI),* Report No. 02. [in Danish].

Klevens, R. M., Edwards, J. R., Richards, C. L., Horan, T. C. Jr, Gaynes, R. P., Pollock, D. A., & Cardo, D. M. (2007). Estimating health care-associated infections and deaths in US hospitals, 2002. *Public Health Reports, 122*(2), 160–166. PMID:17357358

Kodner, D. L., & Spreeuwenberg, C. (2002). Integrated care: Meaning, logic, applications, and implications–a discussion paper. *International Journal of Integrated Care, 2*(4), 1–6. doi:10.5334/ijic.67 PMID:16896389

Lindberg, B., Nilsson, C., Zotterman, D., Söderberg, S., & Skär, L. (2013). Using Information and Communication Technology in Home Care for Communication between Patients, Family Members, and Healthcare Professionals: A Systematic Review. *International Journal of Telemedicine and Applications*. doi: .10.1155/2013/461829

Linden, F. (2009). epSOS local data providers. *Acta Informatica Medica, 17*(3), 142. Retrieved from http://www.ejmanager.com/mnstemps/6/6-1299792486.pdf?t=1457826043

Lindström, Å. (2005). *On the Syntax, Semantics, and Pragmatics of Architectural Principles*. Working paper. Retrieved from http://www.ics.kth.se/Publikationer/Working%20Papers/EARP-WP-2005-03.pdf

Lindström, Å. (2006). *Using architectural principles to make the it-strategy come true* (Doctoral dissertation, KTH, Royal Institute of Technology Stockholm, Sweden). Retrieved from http://citeseerx.ist.psu.edu/viewdoc/download?doi=10.1.1.64.8686&rep=rep1&type=pdf

Linhart, M. (2010). *Independence in old age: Older German women living alone*. Saarbrücken: Lambert.

Littlejohns, P., Wyatt, J. C., & Garvican, L. (2003). Evaluating computerised health information systems: Hard lessons still to be learnt. *British Medical Journal, 326*(7394), 860–863. doi:10.1136/bmj.326.7394.860 PMID:12702622

Ludvigsson, J. F., Otterblad-Olausson, P., Pettersson, B. U., & Ekbom, A. (2009). The Swedish personal identity number: Possibilities and pitfalls in healthcare and medical research. *European Journal of Epidemiology, 24*(11), 659–667. doi:10.1007/s10654-009-9350-y PMID:19504049

Lundgren, K. (2007). *Draken i tiden: IT-nationen Sverige* [Dragon in time: IT-nation of Sweden]. Stockholm: Studieförbundet näringsliv och samhälle (SNS). [in Swedish]

Mahroum, S. (2001). Europe and the immigration of highly skilled labour. *International Migration (Geneva, Switzerland), 39*(1), 27–43. doi:10.1111/1468-2435.00170

Maier, C. B., Glinos, I. A., Wismar, M., Bremner, J., Dussault, G., & Figueras, J. (2011). Cross-country analysis of health professional mobility in Europe: the results. *Health professional mobility and health systems. Evidence from, 17*, 23-66. Available from http://apps.who.int/iris/bitstream/10665/170421/1/Health-Professional-Mobility-Health-Systems.pdf#page=36

Martin, M. J. C. (1994). Managing innovation and entrepreneurship in technology-based firms. New York: Wiley IEEE. Retrieved from https://books.google.se/books?id=fnE7R732COMC&printsec=frontcover&redir_esc=y#v=onepage&q&f=false

Metzger, M. J., & Flanagin, A. J. (2013). Credibility and trust of information in online environments: The use of cognitive heuristics. *Journal of Pragmatics, 59*, 210–220. doi:10.1016/j.pragma.2013.07.012

Mur-Veeman, I., van Raak, A., & Paulus, A. (2008). Comparing integrated care policy in Europe: Does policy matter? *Health Policy (Amsterdam), 85*(2), 172–183. doi:10.1016/j.healthpol.2007.07.008 PMID:17767975

Nytrø, Ø., & Faxvaag, A. (2004). *Healthcare informatics towards 2020. In Infosam 2020, Information Society of 2020* (pp. 127–133). Trondheim, Norway: NTNU.

OECD. (2012). *Education Indicators in focus*. Retrieved from http://www.oecd.org/education/skills-beyond-school/49729932.pdf

OECD. (2013). Health at a Glance 2013: OECD Indicators, OECD, Paris. OECD Publishing.

OECD (2015). *Internet access (indicator)*. doi: 10.1787/69c2b997-en

Pang, T., & Guindon, G. E. (2004). Globalization and risks for health. *EMBRO Rep, 5*(Supplement 1), S11–S16. doi:10.1038/sj.embor.7400226 PMID:15459728

Pelletier, S. G. (2012). *Explosive growth in health care apps raises oversight questions*. Association of American Medical Colleges. Retrieved from; https://www.aamc.org/newsroom/reporter/ october2012/308516/health-care-apps.html

Perednia, D. A., & Allen, A. (1995). Telemedicine technology and clinical applications. *Journal of the American Medical Association, 273*(6), 483–488. doi:10.1001/jama.1995.03520300057037 PMID:7837367

Pocock, N. S., & Phua, K. H. (2011). Medical tourism and policy implications for health systems: A conceptual framework from a comparative study of Thailand, Singapore and Malaysia. *Globalization and Health, 7*(12). doi:10.1186/1744-8603-7-12 PMID:21539751

Sarver, J., & Baker, D. W. (2000). Effect of language barriers on follow-up appointments after an emergency department visit. *Journal of General Internal Medicine, 15*(4), 256-264. Doi: .10.1111/j.1525-1497.2000.06469.x

Schoen, C., Osborn, R., Huynh, P. T., Doty, M., Peugh, J., & Zapert, K. (2006). On the front lines of care: Primary care doctors' office systems, experiences, and views in seven countries. *Health Affairs, 25*(6), w555–w571. doi:10.1377/hlthaff.25.w555 PMID:17102164

Shapiro, J., & Saltzer, E. (1981). Cross-cultural aspects of physician-patient communication patterns. *Urban Health, 10*, 10–15. Available from http://europepmc.org/abstract/med/10254342 PMID:10254342

Silverstein, M., & Parker, M. G. (2002). Leisure activities and quality of life among the oldest old in Sweden. *Research on Aging, 24*(5), 528–547. doi:10.1177/0164027502245003

Singleton, K., & Krause, E. (2009). Understanding cultural and linguistic barriers to health literacy. *OJIN: The Online Journal of Issues in Nursing, 14*(3). doi:10.3912/OJIN.Vol14No03Man04

SMEEC. (2011). *Swedish Ministry of Enterprise, Energy and Communications. ICT for everyone - A Digital Agenda for Sweden* (Reference No. N2011.19). Stockholm: Sweden. Åtta.45. Retrieved from http://www.government.se/reports/2011/12/ict-for-everyone---a-digital-agenda-for-sweden/

SNBHW. (2003). *Årsrapport NPS—En analys av barnmorskors, sjuksköterskors, läkares, tandhygienisters och tandläkares arbetsmarknad.* [Annual report NPS—an analysis of midwifes', nurses', doctors', dental hygienists' and dentists' labor market]. Stockholm, Sweden: Socialstyrelsen [Swedish National Board of Health and Welfare]]. Retrieved from http://www.socialstyrelsen.se

Solberg, I. B., Tómasson, K., Aasland, O., & Tyssen, R. (2013). The impact of economic factors on migration considerations among Icelandic specialist doctors: A cross-sectional study. *BMC Health Services Research, 13*(524), 7. PMID:24350577

Stetson, P. D., McKnight, L. K., Bakken, S., Curran, C., Kubose, T. T., & Cimino, J. J. (2002). Development of an ontology to model medical errors, information needs, and the clinical communication space. *Journal of the American Medical Informatics Association, 9*(Supplement 6), S86–S91. doi:10.1197/jamia.M1235

Stroetmann, K. A., Dobrev, A., Lilischkis, S., & Stroetmann, V. (2014). eHealth is worth it. *The economic benefits of implemented eHealth solutions at ten European sites. eHealth Impact.* Retrieved from http://www.ehealth-impact.org

Stroetmann, K. A., Jones, T., Dobrev, A., & Stroetmann, V. N. (2006). eHealth is Worth it. *The economic benefits of implemented eHealth solutions at ten European sites.* Available from http://www.ehealth-impact.org/download/documents/ehealthimpactsept2006.pdf

Suetens, C., Hopkins, S., Kolman, J., & Diaz Högberg, L. (2013). Point prevalence survey of healthcare associated infections and antimicrobial use in European acute care hospitals: 2011-2012. Stockholm, Sweden: European Centre for Disease Prevention and Control (ECDC). doi:10.2900/86011

Sveriges Riksdag. (2012). *Rapport från riksdagen 2011/12:RFR5. eHälsa-nytta och näring* [eHealth-advantage and industry]. Retrieved from https://www.riksdagen.se/sv/Dokument-Lagar/Utredningar/Rapporter-fran-riksdagen/eHalsa---nytta-och-naring_GZ0WRFR5/

Swedish Institute. (2013-2015). Retrieved from https://sweden.se/migration/#2013

Swedish Ministry of Health and Social Affairs. (2006). *National strategy for eHealth-Sweden.* Stockholm, Sweden: Socialdepartementet. Retrieved from http://sweden.gov.se/content/1/c6/06/43/24/f6405a1c.pdf

Swedish National Audit Office [Riksrevisionsverket]. (2002). *IT i verksamhetsutvecklingen-Bättre styrning av myndigheternas IT investeringar I IT-baserad verksamhetsutveckling.* Stockholm, Sweden: Riksrevisionens publikationsservice. Retrieved from http://www.riksrevisionen.se

Swedish National Agency for Education. (2016). Retrieved from http://www.skolverket.se/statistik-och-utvardering

The Swedish Association of Local Authorities and Regions. (2014). *Vägval för framtiden. Våra territoriella och kulturella gränser.* Retrieved from http://skl.se/download/18.547ffc53146c75fdec079e4b/1404478740292/skl-15-trender-vagval-for-framtiden-2025.pdf

Tokunaga, R. S. (2010). Following you home from school: A critical review and synthesis of research on cyberbullying victimization. *Computers in Human Behavior, 26*(3), 277–287. doi:10.1016/j.chb.2009.11.014

UNESCAP. (2007). *Medical travel in Asia and the Pacific: challenges and opportunities. Thailand.* Retrieved from http://www.unescap.org/ESID/hds/lastestadd/MedicalTourismReport09.pdf

von Hippel, E. (1994). Sticky information and the locus of problem solving: Implications for innovation. *Management Science, 40*(4), 429–439. doi:10.1287/mnsc.40.4.429

von Hippel, E. (1998). Economics of product development by users: The impact of "sticky" local information. *Management Science, 44*(5), 629–644. doi:10.1287/mnsc.44.5.629

Vrangbæk, K., & Christiansen, T. (2005). Health policy in Denmark: Leaving the decentralized welfare path? *Journal of Health Politics, Policy and Law, 30*(1-2), 29–52. doi:10.1215/03616878-30-1-2-29 PMID:15943386

Wahlberg, A. C., Cedersund, E., & Wredling, R. (2003). Telephone nurses' experience of problems with telephone advice in Sweden. *Journal of Clinical Nursing, 12*(1), 37–45. doi:10.1046/j.1365-2702.2003.00702.x PMID:12519248

Wang, S. J., Middleton, B., Prosser, L. A., Bardon, C. G., Spurr, C. D., Carchidi, P. J., & Bates, D. W. et al. (2003). A cost benefit analysis of electronic medical records in primary care. *The American Journal of Medicine, 114*(5), 397–403. doi:10.1016/S0002-9343(03)00057-3 PMID:12714130

Wears, R. L., & Berg, M. (2005). Computer technology and clinical work: Still waiting for Godot. *Journal of the American Medical Association, 293*(10), 1261–1263. doi:10.1001/jama.293.10.1261 PMID:15755949

Webster, F. (2014). *Theories of the Information Society*. New York: Routledge.

Whitehead, M., Evandrou, M., Haglund, B., & Diderichsen, F. (1997). As the health divide widens in Sweden and Britain, what's happening to access to care? *British Medical Journal, 315*(7114), 1006–1009. Retrieved from http://www.ncbi.nlm.nih.gov/pmc/articles/PMC2127673/pdf/9365303.pdf

WHO. (2014). *Large gains in life expectancy. World Health Statistics 2014*. Available from http://www.who.int/mediacentre/news/releases/2014/world-health-statistics-2014/en/

World Health Organization. (2010). *The burden of health care-associated infection worldwide: A summary*. Retrieved from http://www.who.int/gpsc/country_work/summary_20100430_en.pdf

ADDITIONAL READING

Anderson, C. L., & Agarwal, R. (2011). The digitization of healthcare: Boundary risks, emotion, and consumer willingness to disclose personal health information. *Information Systems Research, 22*(3), 469–490. doi:10.1287/isre.1100.0335

Angst, C. M., & Agarwal, R. (2009). Adoption of electronic health records in the presence of privacy concerns: The elaboration likelihood model and individual persuasion. *Management Information Systems Quarterly, 33*(2), 339–370. Available at http://www.jstor.org/stable/20650295

Baum, F. (2003). The new public health (No. Ed. 2). Oxford University Press.

Eysenbach, G. (2000). Consumer health informatics. *British Medical Journal, 320*(7251), 1713–1716. doi:10.1136/bmj.320.7251.1713 PMID:10864552

Tang, P. C., Ash, J. S., Bates, D. W., Overhage, J. M., & Sands, D. Z. (2006). Personal health records: Definitions, benefits, and strategies for overcoming barriers to adoption. *Journal of the American Medical Informatics Association*, *13*(2), 121–126. doi:10.1197/jamia.M2025 PMID:16357345

KEY TERMS AND DEFINITIONS

E-Health: The use of ICT (Information and Communications Technologies). It is used in support of health related fields.

EHIC: The European Health Insurance Card.

EHR: Electronic Health Records. A real-time longitudinal electronic record of patient's health information.

EPRs: Electronic patient records.

EpSOS: Smart Open Services for European Patients.

EU: European Union.

Globalization: the worldwide movement toward economic, financial, trade, and communications integration.

HAIs: Healthcare-associated infections.

ICT: Information and Communication Technology.

IT: Information Technology.

OECD: The Organization for Economic Co-operation and Development.

TEC: Technology-Enabled Care.

Chapter 18
Factors that Contribute to Continued Use of E–Training among Healthcare Professionals

Nilsa I. I. Elias
Capella University, USA

Terry W. Walker
Capella University, USA

ABSTRACT

The use of e-training in healthcare has experienced considerable growth. The results of this study provide insights regarding the importance of technology compatibility attributes to behavioral intentions to continue the use of e-training by healthcare professionals. A model based on the technology acceptance literature has been used. The model adds the construct of healthcare practice compatibility to the Technology Acceptance Model as a predictor of behavioral intention to continued use of e-training by healthcare professionals. Using Partial Least Squares Structural Equation Modeling (PLS-SEM), findings suggest that perceived practice compatibility, perceived workflow compatibility, and perceived task compatibility in e-training are essential to healthcare professionals' intent to continue use of e-training. The parsimonious model in this study is a more predictive model than the basic TAM model in explaining users' intentions to continue use of e-training.

INTRODUCTION

Though E-training has played a significant role in healthcare professionals' training and development, there is extensive evidence of numerous cases of underuse, resistance, workarounds, overrides, sabotage, and even abandonment of e-training (Bhattacherjee, 2001; Bhattachrjee & Hikmet, 2007; Holden & Karsh, 2010; Pai & Huang, 2011; Kamalzadeh Takhti, Abdul Rahman, & Abedini, 2013). Prior research studies have provided insight into participation in e-training; however, limited research exists on intention for continued use of e-training by healthcare professionals.

DOI: 10.4018/978-1-5225-0522-8.ch018

The ability to identify, predict, and manage employee acceptance and continued use of technology facilitates implementation efforts. The continued use of technology by users is essential to the success of healthcare IT (Schaper & Pervan, 2007a). Increased interest in the use of e-training by healthcare professionals has elevated the importance of theories that predict and explain e-training acceptance and use.

A fundamental approach to e-training in the workplace is practice compatibility: The concept that practice compatibility plays a significant role as a determinant of behavioral intention to continued use of e-training and that healthcare professionals need e-training technology that is perceived as being both useful and easy to use. Despite the large volume of research in technology acceptance and use, very little research has been conducted in the healthcare industry regarding factors specific to predicting and explaining healthcare professionals' continued use of e-training, which are thus not well understood. In this study, healthcare professionals in the U.S.A. were surveyed about their perceptions on the use of e-training for continuing education and professional development for the purpose of discerning how e-training technology might be revised to increase usage and user acceptance.

BACKGROUND

E-Training in Healthcare Organizations

The use of web-based tools, repositories, and environments have become popular delivery methods for workplace training (Arbaugh et al., 2009). In 2012, the Association for Talent Development reported that approximately 77% of American corporations were delivering training via technology, or e-training. E-training, which is anywhere, any-time instruction, delivered over the Internet or a corporate intranet to browser-equipped learners, provides a way to deliver specialized content, monitor employee participation, and assess performance and completion of courses required by an employer for the professional development of employees in an efficient and cost-effective manner.

Continued and mandatory training is a critical component for the development, maintenance, and improvement of healthcare practice and competence among healthcare professionals. E-training technology that fits within the general practice context defines roles and how healthcare practitioners understand their job functions, the clinical needs of patients, and standards for their professional activities (Cain & Haque, 2008; Chau & Hu, 2002; Tulu et al., 2006). In fact, research has demonstrated that e-training has a positive impact on healthcare delivery, reduces clinical errors, increases patient safety, and reduces expenses (Hung et al., 2009; Schaper & Pervan, 2007; Aggelidis & Chatzoglou, 2009).

Kim and Malhotra (2005) explained that the initial acceptance and adoption of an information system (IS) is an important indicator of system success; however, positive outcomes would be produced only if the technology is used. Research that investigates beyond the initial adoption or acceptance of technology has generally looked at IS continuance (Bhattacherjee, 2001; Bhattacherjee and Barfar, 2011). The goal of post-adoption research is to understand both "how" and "why" individuals use certain technologies to their fullest potential in the work place (Chin et al., 2008). The focus of IS continuance research—though grounded in the concepts and constructs of the Technology Acceptance Model (TAM) and the Unified Theory of Acceptance and Use of Technology (UTAUT)—has moved beyond the adoption stage of system use to look at the post-adoptive behaviors associated with information technology-enabled systems (Jasperson et al., 2005).

The attributes of healthcare users and technology differs from those in other business contexts (Davis, 1989). Thus, existing models developed to investigate technology acceptance and user behavior may not be valid in the healthcare environment. Studies of user's perceptions, intention to use, and system usage are essential to understanding the adoption and utilization of information technology.

Karahanna et al. (1999) explained that adoption and continued use of information technology have different behavioral attributes. Technology adoption is the initial usage (new behavior) of an IT innovation at the individual level, whereas technology usage is the subsequent continued usage after adoption at the individual level (Karahanna et al., 1999). Thus, the factors determining user acceptance of a new technology differ from those affecting users' attitudes toward continued usage of the technology. Consequently, distinguishing between initial and continuing usage of IT when studying factors that influence them is important.

Technology acceptance research involves understanding the factors that determine users' intentions to adopt a technology and their actual usage behaviors (Sun, Wang, Guo, & Peng, 2013). In particular, the technology acceptance model (Davis, 1989), a parsimonious theory of information technology adoption, has been successfully adopted to study technology usage in organizations (Holden & Karsh, 2010; Liao & Lu, 2008; Wu, Li, & Fu, 2011). This research study was based upon an adapted acceptance model that incorporated elements of both TAM and compatibility models to explain the continued use of e-training by healthcare professionals.

MAIN FOCUS OF THIS CHAPTER

Purpose of the Study

The purpose of the study was to test an adapted acceptance model that incorporates elements of TAM and compatibility models to explain the continued use of e-training by healthcare professionals. The research model employed the construct of Healthcare Practice Compatibility (HPC) based upon the Tulu et al. (2006) model of Workplace Practice Compatibility (WPC). HPC will be composed of the constructs of Healthcare Task Compatibility (TC), Healthcare Workflow Compatibility (WC) and Healthcare Professional Compatibility (PC). This study proposed to validate a causal model linking the constructs of HPC, Perceived Ease of Use (PEU), and Perceived Usefulness (PU). The model investigated the key assumption that healthcare professionals make choices about continued use of e-training long after the initial adoption decision was made.

Technology Acceptance Model

User behavior has long been a central and fundamental research topic in the IT field (Karahanna, Straub, & Chervany, 1999). IT researchers have used numerous perspectives to examine user acceptance and usage behavior of information technologies. The TAM was developed specifically for explaining the determinants of computer acceptance, as well as "explaining user behavior in many end-user information technologies and populations" (Davis et al., 1989, p. 985).

The TAM model is the most prevalent theory in the literature that has a strong record of predicting and explaining end-user reactions to information technology in organizations, including healthcare organizations (Moore & Benbasat, 1991). TAM researchers suggested that Behavioral Intention to Use (BIU) was the proximal precursor to information technology (IT) use. The TAM model proposed that BIU is thought to be influenced by users' attitudes toward IT and has two determinants: Perceived Usefulness (PU) and Perceived Ease of Use (PEU) (Bhattacherjee & Barfar, 2011; Davis, 1989).

TAM's key purpose was to provide a foundation and an explanation for the influence of external factors on internal beliefs and attitudes towards technology. TAM focuses Perceived Ease of Use and Perceived Usefulness as indicators of IT acceptance behaviors (Davis et al., 1989). According to TAM, a user will have a positive attitude if a system is perceived as easy to use and useful, thus creating a user's intention to use the system (Al-Gahtani, 2001; Chen, Park, & Putzer, 2010).

Perceived Usefulness (PU), the extent of belief that a technology will contribute to one's performance, and perceived ease of use (PEU), the belief that a technology will require low levels of effort, are hypothesized to have the strongest direct relationship to the goal of BIU. Research has demonstrated that the TAM constructs of perceived usefulness (PU) and perceived ease of use (PEU) are a subset of the Innovation Diffusion Theory (IDT) attributes of innovation (Lee, Hsieh, & Hsu, 2011).

IDT provided a set of innovation characteristics that appeared to affect an individuals' beliefs about adoption of a technology. They included relative advantage, compatibility, complexity, trialability, and result demonstrability. Rogers' Innovation Diffusion Theory (IDT) (Rogers, 2003) explored the relationship between work practices and information technology acceptance and use. Rogers (2003) explained that adoption and use of technology behavior is influenced by beliefs related to relative advantage, compatibility, complexity, trialability and observability.

Moore and Benbasat (1991) specifically examined the effect of usage on all innovation characteristics simultaneously and showed that compatibility, perceived usefulness, and ease of use were the most influential characteristics for continued use decisions. Moore and Benbasat (1991) refined the theoretical and operational definitions of IDT into a set of seven conceptually distinct constructs and investigated how users' perceptions influenced the adoption and use of an IT. In their study, only Perceived Usefulness (PU), Perceived Ease of Use (PEU), and compatibility were significantly related to continued use of technology (Moore & Benbasat, 1991).

Although research has demonstrated that TAM is useful in healthcare studies, these studies have not fully addressed the technological and behavioral aspects of continued use of technology. Research in social psychology has demonstrated that behavior is best predicted by an individual's attitude towards the behavior (such as using IT) rather than their behavior towards the objects involved in the behaviors (Mathieson, 1991). In particular, the Theory of Reasoned Action (TRA) suggested that the best predictor of continued use behavior is the intention to continue to use the IT (Karahanna et al., 1999).

The Technology Acceptance Model and Usage Behavior

During the last three decades, many researchers have adopted different theoretical approaches to explain, predict, and even increase user acceptance and use of information technology in the workplace. The intention-based theories of technology adoption (Technology Acceptance Model (TAM), Theory of Reasoned Action (TRA), Theory of Planned Behavior (TPB), and their extensions/modifications) have demonstrated that user adoption and continued use of information technologies are ultimately determined by individual beliefs and attitudes toward an IT system.

Technology acceptance studies have demonstrated that TAM is a good predictor of behavioral intent to accept and use technology in the healthcare sector, specifically among healthcare professionals (Bhattacherjee & Hikmet, 2007; Holden & Karsh, 2010; Schaper & Pervan, 2007). To better understand the emergence of TAM, a brief description of preceding theories TRA and TPB is required.

The Theory of Reasoned Action (TRA) is a well-established model that has been used to predict and explain human behavior in a variety of fields. Originating in the field of psychology, TRA assumed that an individual's actual behavior could be determined by studying prior intention together with personal beliefs about that behavior (Fishbein & Ajzen, 1975). According to TRA, the key predictor of a behavior is behavioral intention, and the intention is influenced by the attitude towards the behavior as well as subjective norms.

Subsequent social science research demonstrated that TRA was inadequate, especially when accounting for an individual's volitional control over the behavior (if the person can decide at will to perform or not perform the behavior). To balance these shortfalls, Ajzen (1991) added the construct of perceived behavioral control, thus resulting in a new theory known as the Theory of Planned Behavior (TPB). The TBP proposed that an individual's behavior is strongly influenced by "their confidence in their ability to perform that behavior or perceived behavioral control" (Ajzen, 1991, p. 181).

Accordingly, perceived behavioral control together with behavioral intention can be used to predict actual behavior. TPB may be used to explain behavior or technology adoption and usage by examining an individual's role and the organizational system involved in this process. Despite limitations, the Theory of Reasoned Action (TRA) demonstrated strong correlations between the model's variables that asked about trying to perform a given behavior and measures that dealt with actual performance of the behavior.

The Theory of Planned Behavior (TPB) is an extension of Theory of Reasoned Action (TRA) and proposed that behavioral beliefs have a favorable or unfavorable influence on the attitude towards a behavior (Ajzen, 1991). The TPB added the constructs of subjective norms and control beliefs as determinants of attitude and ultimately BIU. Research about attitude and IT have found that the predictive importance of attitude to BIU fluctuated, depending on conceptual, operational or contextual reasons.

At the conceptualization level, studies have shown that the roles of attitude towards IT did not have a direct effect on BIU (Zhang and Sun, 2009). At the operational level, the measures for attitude also varied. A review of the literature demonstrated that the operationalization and measurement of attitude is not consistent and subject to researcher determination. At the contextual level, attitude measurement is neither consistent of well defined (Zhang and Sun, 2009; Mathieson, 1991). Furthermore, there are no longitudinal studies about the effects of attitude on IT.

According to Karahanna et al. (1999), an individual's intention to continue to use technology is determined by personal interests or attitudes and social influences. Attitude towards continued use of technology is affected by the individual's beliefs that continued use of the IT will lead to certain consequences. Prior research studies have reported a persuasive and substantial causal linkage between behavioral intention and targeted behavior (Chau & Hu, 2001). As a result of this strong link, use of behavioral intention as a dependent variable to examine continued use of e-training is theoretically justifiable (Mathieson, 1991).

On the other hand, extant research in technology acceptance, particularly Rogers' Innovation Diffusion Theory (IDT), contends that a more comprehensive set of beliefs are predictors of both adoption and subsequent continued use of technology. Contrasting TAM with other findings in technology acceptance and use brought to light that compatibility is an important recurrent belief in IT acceptance studies, but is missing from TAM (e.g., Karahanna et al., 2006; Chau & Hu, 2002; Karahanna et al., 2006; Moore & Benbasat, 1991). Agarwal et al. (2006) explained that compatibility considers the degree of correspondence between a technology and several aspects of the user and the setting in which technology will be utilized.

One fundamental approach to e-training in the workplace is practice compatibility: The idea that practice compatibility plays a significant role as a determinant of behavioral intention to continued use of e-training and that healthcare professionals need e-training technology that is perceived as useful and easy to use. Specifically, the research study described in this chapter extended TAM to include three compatibility beliefs that were hypothesized to influence actual use behaviors, both directly and as mediated by usefulness and ease of use beliefs.

TAM Research

Developed by Davis (1989), the TAM is a comprehensive, stand-alone model that has been extensively studied in order to understand the behavioral intent to adopt and use a technology. TAM is an adaptation of TRA and TPB and is designed to model user acceptance of information technology. TAM focused on the technological aspects of IT with parsimony and high explanatory power (Wu, Li and Fu, 2011).

TAM combined the constructs PU and PEU, to predict the user's attitude toward the use of a technology (see Fig. 1 Basic TAM model). However, Davis (1989) did not take subjective norms into account in the prediction of actual behavior, as he believed that PU and PEU were sufficient to predict behavioral intention to use a system.

Empirical studies conducted to examine the explanatory power of TAM constructs have demonstrated relatively consistent results for the constructs that measure acceptance behaviors of IT end users (Venkatesh & Davis, 1996, 2000). Researchers agree that TAM provides a valid explanation of the determinants of technology acceptance which, in turn, enables explanations of user behavior for a wide scope of technologies and user populations. In order to address the rapid changes in IT, and to improve the understanding of predictors and the explanatory power of TAM, researchers have extended the model and incorporated new variables that identified factors with substantial influence (Marangunic & Granic, 2014).

The basic TAM model is composed of three main constructs: Perceived Ease of Use (PEU), Perceived Usefulness (PU) and Behavioral Intention to Use (BIU) (Davis, 1989). PEU and PU are the most dominant determinants for system use and PEU has a direct effect on PU (Davis et al., 1989). Venkatesh and Davis (2000) proposed an extended TAM where behavioral intent to use is jointly determined by PU and PEU.

Figure 1. Basic TAM Model

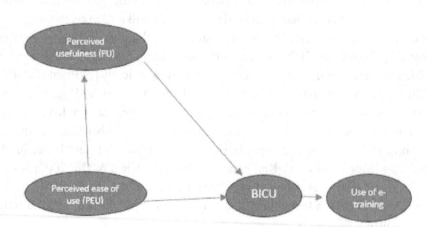

In this study, the TAM constructs of PU and PEU are hypothesized to have the strongest direct relationship with the endpoint of BIU of e-training. Additionally, the research model hypothesizes these relationships and that actual use of e-training technology is directly influenced by a person's behavioral intention to use. This means that healthcare professionals' perceptions of the degree to which e-training is easy to use influences both perception of usefulness and the professional's intention to use e-training.

In accordance with the reasoning of Yi, Jackson, Park, and Probst (2006) and Tulu et al. (2006), behavioral intent is selected as the dependent variable based on theoretical and practical grounds. For this study, Venkatech and Davis (1999) revised model (TAM without the attitude construct) was used. Also, included in the model are compatibility beliefs, which serve as antecedents of both PU and PEU on behavioral intention.

Compatibility and Innovation Diffusion Theory

Rogers' IDT proposed that "potential users make decisions to adopt or reject an innovation based on beliefs that they form about the innovation" (Agarwal & Prasad, 1997, p. 587). Accordingly, Rogers (2003) explained that "innovation" is equivalent to technology innovation, which in turn consists of computer hardware and software.

There are five attributes of an innovation that influence acceptance behavior: relative advantage, complexity, trialability, observability, and compatibility. Relative advantage is defined as the degree to which an innovation is considered an improvement or better than the idea or object replaced. Complexity is the perception that an innovation is understood and easy to use. Trialability is the degree to which an innovation can be tested prior to adoption. Observability is the degree of visibility of the innovation. Rogers (2003) proposed that these characteristics explain the decision-making process of adoption of an innovation technology.

Compatibility is defined as the degree to which an innovation is thought to be consistent with the users' existing values, prior experiences, and needs. Rogers (2003) was the first researcher to introduce and define the term compatibility in his Information Diffusion Theory (IDT). Compatibility, which is correlated with how a technology fit with prior experiences, was found to directly affect the constructs in the technology acceptance model.

Earlier studies indicated that compatibility had a strong direct impact in the variation in behavioral intention to adoption and use healthcare technology systems (Chau & HU, 2001). In research conducted by Agarwal and Prasad (1997), Chau and Hu (2002), Karahanna et al. (2006), compatibility was reported to significantly affect PU and behavioral intention. Chen, Guillenson, and Sherrell (2002) added the IDT construct of compatibility to TAM to evaluate and explain consumer's intention to adopt online e-commerce technology. They found that compatibility has a direct effect on PU and behavioral intention to use. These findings are consistent with other empirical evidence that the better e-training is matched with clinical and patient care working practices, the higher e-training continued use will be (Johnson & Turley, 2006).

Compatibility

Agarwal et al. (2006) suggested causal linkages between the TAM constructs of PU, PEU, and compatibility. However, the authors of this chapter asserted that limitations in prior research showed inadequate conceptualization and operationalization of compatibility, as well as the absence of theoretical linkages between the construct and other important technology acceptance beliefs. While compatibility studies defined the construct as multidimensional, they operationalized it as a unidimensional construct (i.e. Moore & Benbasat, 1991).

Agarwal et al. (2006) suggested a conceptual notion of compatibility as the perceived cognitive distance between an innovation and precursor methods for accomplishing tasks (p. 784). Accordingly, compatibility was hypothesized to evaluate the congruity between a new way of doing work facilitated by technology and the preceding methods, which are determined by an individual's cognitive processes which, in turn, have been influenced by the technology's predecessors, as well as by past experiences and beliefs (Agarwal & Prasad, 1997; Agarwal et al., 2006; Karahanna et al., 2006).

Karahanna et al. (2006) further segregated the operational concept of compatibility in three distinctive dimensions: compatibility with prior experience, compatibility with existing work practices, and compatibility with preferred work style. The authors hypothesized that the isolated dimensions of compatibility (p. 787) included: (1) compatibility with existing work practices, measuring the extent to which a technology "fits" with a user's current work process; (2) compatibility with preferred work style, capturing the possibility of the technology being consistent with a desired work style; (3) compatibility with prior experience, reflecting a fit between a technology and a variety of user's past encounters with technology; and (4) compatibility with values, epitomizing the match between the possibilities offered by the technology and the user's dominant value system.

The empirical results of the Karahanna et al. (2006) study supported the influential effect of compatibility beliefs in usefulness and ease of use. Most notably, the authors observed that compatibility with existing work practices, compatibility with preferred work style, and compatibility with prior experience, influenced usage behaviors directly, while compatibility with values was most influential in adoption behaviors. Fundamentally, this means that users are not only influenced by the precursor of the new technology but also by prior beliefs and task behaviors.

Chau and Hu (2001; 2002) conducted a conceptual replication of previous model comparison studies (e.g. Davis et al., 1989; Mathieson, 1991) to evaluate theoretical models of technology users in healthcare settings. Chau and Hu (2001) proposed a decomposed TPB model that incorporated the construct of compatibility, which was hypothesized as an antecedent of PU and PEU. Particularly, the authors focused on the concepts of job relevance and output quality to define compatibility as the degree to which the use of telemedicine technology was perceived by a physician to be consistent with his or her work practices (Chau & Hu, 2001, p. 704). The results implied that compatibility was a crucial antecedent of physicians' perceived technology usefulness and assumed an important role in their attitude towards using the technology.

Tulu et al. (2006) conducted a study to investigate physicians' intent for continued use of an online evaluation system. The authors used constructs from the Technology Acceptance Model and compatibility to explain the intent for continued use of a technology. Specifically, they used the concept of work-practice compatibility to understand continued use of technology within the healthcare and medical work system.

The proposed model included related factors known to contribute to physicians' adoption of information technologies, which included the TAM constructs of PU and PEU, and Behavioral Intent to Continue Use (BICU) (Tulu et al., 2006). Using the Chau and Hu (2001) construct of work practice compatibility as a theoretical foundation, Tulu et al. (2006) enhanced the model by including compatibility beliefs specific to medical work systems, including work-practice compatibility, medical-task compatibility, medical-work-flow compatibility, and medical-professional compatibility.

Moreover, Tulu et al.'s (2006) study highlighted the importance of the scope of professional activities, the healthcare professionals' perceptions of the appropriateness of an IT based technology for their professional role, and their influence on healthcare workflow. The authors concluded that a physician's intention to continue using a technology was a more accurate indicator of the potential success and effectiveness of an information technology system in the healthcare environment.

Compatibility as a multi-dimensional construct is thought to have significant effects on attitude towards technology, and research has demonstrated that attitudes of health care professionals can be a significant factor in the acceptance and efficiency of the use of IT in a medical practice (Agarwal & Karahanna, 1998; Karahanna et al., 1999). The Tulu et al. (2006) study was used to model this research, which aimed to investigate the construct of Behavioral Intent to Continue Use (BICU) of a technology in the medical informatics context and, more specifically, to investigate the construct of Healthcare Practice Compatibility (HPC).

Operationalizing Healthcare Practice Compatibility

For this research study, the TAM was enhanced by adding the construct of Healthcare Practice Compatibility (HPC), which is a composite of the constructs of Professional Compatibility (PC), Task Compatibility (TC), and Healthcare Workflow Compatibility (WC). Healthcare practice compatibility (HPC), was defined as the extent to which e-training technology fits with healthcare professionals' existing work processes, their professional medical role and was consistent with their desired work styles. In addition, this study proposed the concept of Healthcare Practice Compatibility as a multidimensional construct composed of three dimensions including healthcare workflow compatibility, healthcare task compatibility, and healthcare professional compatibility.

For this study, we defined Healthcare Workflow Compatibility (WC) as the healthcare professional's perception of the relationship of e-training technology, the flow of the healthcare systems and methods, and the healthcare team. Healthcare workflow compatibility is believed to have a positive influence in behavioral intention to continued use of e-training. We defined healthcare task compatibility (TC) as the healthcare professionals' perceptions that e-training technology fits with users' existing work processes, which in turn is related to the consistency of the technology with a desired work style. Healthcare Professional Compatibility (PC) was defined as the healthcare professionals' perceptions of the appropriateness of e-training for the professional healthcare practitioner role.

This study's intention was to further validate that compatibility is not an uncomplicated single measurable attribute. Tulu et al. (2006) theorized that behavioral intent for continued use of technology was the causal endpoint of the relationships between PU, PEU, and compatibility beliefs.

In this study, BICU of e-training was theorized to be influenced by the constructs of PU, PEU which in turn are mediated by Healthcare Practice Compatibility (see Fig. 3). Compatibility was added to the TAM model as a multidimensional construct and critical determinant of behavioral intent to continued use of e-training among healthcare professionals. Additionally, a set of causal linkage among the leading technology adoption and usage beliefs of perceived usefulness and perceived ease of use, and the three dimensions of Healthcare Practice Compatibility (TC, WC, and PC) were proposed for this research study.

The dimensions of work flow compatibility, task compatibility and professional compatibility were hypothesized to be direct determinants of healthcare practice compatibility. Healthcare practice compatibility in turn was hypothesized to have a positive influence in the behavioral intent to continued use of e-training among healthcare professionals. A major objective for this study was to find empirical support

Figure 2. Research Model

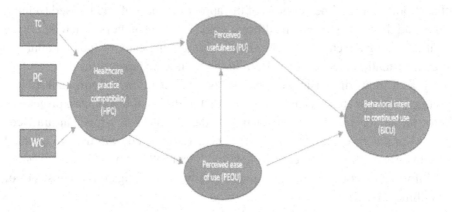

Figure 3. Extended TAM Model

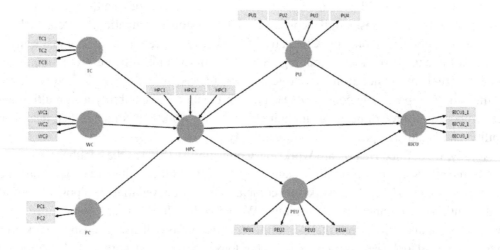

for the theorized consequents of behavioral intent to continued use of technology beliefs. Specifically, the compatibility dimensions were introduced as independent variables to measure healthcare practice compatibility as a key factor to predict continued use of e-training. The key research question to be answered by this study was: How well do healthcare practice compatibility factors (TC, PC, and WC) relate to BICU of e-training, as mediated by the variables of PU and PEU?

Methodology

This study used a confirmatory research approach and a quantitative research method involving a survey design and in accordance with the positivist philosophy. A quantitative survey design was used to collect data for the study. The survey instrument consisted of three validated constructs adapted from the studies of Chin et al. (2008) and Tulu et al. (2006). The dataset was analyzed using SmartPLS, a key multivariate analysis method for empirical research in international marketing and IT.

A single cross-sectional survey with questions from previously developed and validated surveys were collected using Survey Monkey Audience at a single point in time. In this research study, the research design incorporated the measurement and structural models for use of technology from the technology acceptance model developed by Davis (1989) and the medical technology continued use model developed by Tulu et al. (2006). The measurement items from both Davis (1989) and Tulu et al. (2006) consisted of five-point Likert-type scale items.

For this study, Partial Least Squares Structural Equation modeling analysis was used (PLS-SEM). PLS-SEM is a second generation statistical modeling methodology that takes a confirmatory approach (hypothesis testing) to the multivariate analysis of a structural theory. In this study, PLS-SEM was used to determine whether a hypothesized theoretical model for continued use of technology is consistent with the data collected to reflect the theory. For this study, we followed the PLS-SEM design proposed by Hair et al. (2014).

This PLS-SEM analysis involved a multi-stage process that included the specification of the inner and outer models, data collection and examination, the actual model estimation and the evaluation of results (Hair et al., 2014). For this study, the outer model (measurement model) specified the relationships among instrument items (exogenous latent variables) and their corresponding construct. The inner model specified the relationships between the constructs that were evaluated, HPC, PU, PEU and BICU (Figure 3).

The quality of the empirical data gathered during data collection was verified, including response rates and checks for nonresponse bias and common method bias. After verifying the quality of the data and applying reasonable actions to mitigate the effects of unmet assumptions, analysis of the models was performed. The first phase of analysis was designed to test the measurement model (outer model). This stage focused on discriminant validity and composite reliability of the instrument measures. The second phase evaluated the structural model (inner model) and calculated estimates in order to test the significance of the proposed hypotheses and the predictive power of the proposed research model.

The research model was comprised of structural models developed by Chau and Hu (2002) and Tulu et al. (2006). To answer the research questions, the model was tested using five first-order latent variable constructs, and two second-order latent variables: Behavioral Intent to Continue Use (BICU) of e-training and Healthcare Practice Compatibility (HPC). The second-order latent variable HPC consisted of three first-order latent variables: Healthcare Task Compatibility (TC), Healthcare Workflow Compatibility (WC), and Healthcare Professional Compatibility (PC). The other first-order latent variables were Perceived Usefulness (PU), and Perceived Ease of Use (PEU).

Research Question 1 with Hypotheses

Research Question 1 is: How well do healthcare practice compatibility factors (TC, PC, and WC) relate to Behavioral Intention to Continue Use (BICU) of e-training, as mediated by the variables of PU and PEU?

Hypotheses for Research Question 1 are:

H_0: There is not a statistically significant positive relationship between BICU of e-training and HPC, as mediated by PU, PEU.

H_A: There is a statistically significant positive relationship between BICU of e-training and HPC, as mediated by PU and PEU.

Research Question 2 with Hypotheses

What is the relationship between the independent variable healthcare practice compatibility (HPC) and the latent variables work task compatibility (TC), Healthcare Workflow Compatibility (WC), and professional compatibility (PC) of e-training?

The following hypotheses were tested:

H_0: There is not a statistically significant positive relationship between HPC and the latent variable TC of e-training.

H_A: There is a statistically significant positive relationship between HPC and the latent variable TC of e-training.

H_0: There is not a statistically significant positive relationship between HPC and WC of e-training.

H_A: There is a statistically significant positive relationship between HPC and WC of e-training.

H_0: There is not a statistically significant positive relationship between HPC and PC of e-training.

H_A: There is a statistically significant positive relationship between HPC and PC of e-training.

Population, Sampling Frame, and Sample Size

The population for this study was all clinical healthcare professionals practicing in the United States. The sampling frame consisted of clinical healthcare professionals practicing in the United States who were members of the Survey Monkey Audience panel. Survey Monkey sent email invitations to participate in this survey to a random sample of members of the sampling frame.

One hundred forty-two potential respondents opened the email invitation. Of the 142 who opened the survey, 104 participants indicated that they used e-training in their organizations. Of these initial 104 respondents, 22 (21.2%) chose not to complete the informed consent form, and 16 (15. 3%) submitted incomplete surveys that ended at various points in the question progression. Data from the 66 remaining

Figure 4. Research TAM Model with Hypothesized Relationships

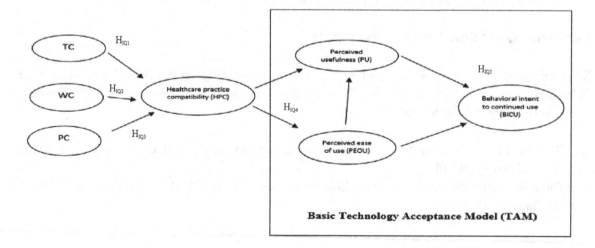

participants (63.5%) was analyzed for non-differentiation or straight-lining responses of the Likert-scale responses, which results in the elimination of three surveys. The final sample size of 63 resulted in a medium effect size of .35 ($p < .05$).

PLS ten times rule of thumb was used to meet PLS-SEM sample requirements (Barclay, Higgins & Thompson, 1995; as cited by Hair et al., 2014). The ten times rule indicates the sample size should be equal to the larger of (Hair et al., 2014, p. 20):

1.   Ten times the largest number of formative indicators used to measure a single construct or
2.   Ten times the largest number of structural paths directed at a particular construct in the structural model.

The proposed research model, the structural model had three exogenous constructs (PU, PEU, and HPC) to explain the single dependent construct BICU. The maximum number of arrows pointing at a particular latent variable was three. The rule of thumb for PLS-SEM indicates that for three indicators, a Power = .80, α = .05 and, a significance level of 5%, the sample size for this study should be 59 responses (calculations based on 3 indicators in the proposed model and using the ten times rule). The calculation of 59 responses represented a starting point for determining an appropriate sample size with an adequate level of accuracy and statistical power.

Power analysis was conducted using a subset of the research model using the impact of the three variables PU, PEU, and HPC on BICU. The power analysis results are reported in Table 1. Three power analyses were performed for a linear multiple regression with three predictors and one dependent variable, α = 0.05 (one tail), power = 0.80, and three different values for effect size (e.g., 0.02, 0.25, and 0.35). The a priori power analysis suggested sample sizes of 546, 48, and 36 for small, medium, and large effect size, respectively.

Instrumentation

The present research study extended the TAM model with the compatibility construct and the questions were taken directly from Tule et al. (2006) verbatim, except that the term "physician or medical professional," which was replaced by "healthcare professional." This research study was not a replica of Chau and Hu's (2001) or Tulu et al.'s (2006) studies. Chau and Hu's (2006) and Tulu et al.'s (2006) studies were one of the first to recognize the importance of the concept of compatibility when measuring TAM in the healthcare industry. These studies only researched the physician population and the compatibility construct was tested with that specific population. Conversely, this research study added the compat-

Table 1. Power Analysis Results

Approach	Power	A	Effect size	N
Linear multiple regression with three predictors	0.80	0.05	0.02	546
Linear multiple regression with three predictors	0.80	0.05	0.2	48
Linear multiple regression with three predictors	0.80	0.05	0.35	36

ibility construct as a mediator for PU and PEU and investigated the perceptions of the healthcare professional population. Thus, this study aimed to validate the same principles, in an attempt to generalize the applications of TAM and related behaviors, to the continued use of technology in a wider population.

Table 2 explains the latent variables, definitions, and survey items for the study. The level of measurement for each variable was ordinal. For Likert scale items, strongly disagree corresponded to value of 1, while strongly agree corresponded to 5. To maintain uniformity and facilitate statistical analysis, the labels for semantic differential scale were numbered in the same way as the Likert scales (i.e., *inefficient* corresponded to a value of 1, *efficient* corresponded to value of 5).

Data Analysis

The descriptive statistics focus on the study participant's gender and years of experience as healthcare professionals. Table 3 shows the frequency distribution of gender from survey responses; 74.2% were female and 25.8% were male participants.

Table 4 shows the frequency distribution of professional experience from the survey responses. Forty-one respondents, representing 62.1% of the participants, had more than 10 years of experience in healthcare.

The hypotheses were tested using PLS-SEM analysis. The software package SmartPLS v.3.1.5 (Ringle, Wende, & Becker, 2014) and SPSS version 21 were used for calculations. The data set was evaluated

Table 2. Operational Definitions and Values for Information Variables

Construct	Definition
BICU	Defined as a measure of the respondent's consisten, ongoing and routine e-training use behavior (Clay, Dennis, & Ko, 2005). For this research it was hypothesized that the construct of BICU would be predicted by the constructs of PU, PEU, and HPC.
PU	Definted as the degree to which a person believed that using a particular system would enhance his/her job performance (Davis, 1989).
PEU	The degree to which a person believed that using a particular system would be free of effort (Davis, 1989).
HPC	For this study, compatibility was defined as multidimensional construct that reflected the degree to which e-training was perceived as being consistent with healthcare professionals' existing work processes (Karahanna et al., 2006).
WC	Defined as the healthcare professional's perception of the relationship of e-training to the flow of the healthcare organization's work processes (Tulu et al., 2006).
TC	Defined as the healthcare professional's perceived compatability of e-training to specific user's medical tasks (Tulu et al., 2006).
PC	Defined as the healthcare professional's perceived appropriateness of e-training for the healthcare professional role (Tulu et al., 2006).

Table 3. Gender Distribution

Gender	Frequency	Valid Percent	Cumulative Percent
Female	49	74.2	74.2
Male	17	25.8	100.0
Total	66	100.0	100.0

Table 4. Experience Distribution

Experience	Frequency	Valid Percent	Cumulative Percent
< than 1 year	4	6.1	6.1
At least 1 year but less than 3 years	7	10.6	16.7
At least 3 but less than 5 years	4	6.1	22.8
At least 5 but less than 10 years	10	15.2	37.9
More than 10 years	41	62.1	100.0
Total	**66**	**100.0**	

for missing values, invalid observations, or outliers. Missing data for an observation that exceeded 15% was removed from the data set. When less than 5% of values per indicator were missing, mean value replacement was used. Otherwise, case-wise deletion was used. When outliers were identified, they were removed from the data.

Data was examined for skewness or kurtosis values greater than 1, which indicated non-normal data. This study followed Hair et al.'s (2014) recommendation to use bootstrapping in highly skewed data, which can cause issues in estimations of significance levels. After the data were prepared, the path model was created in the SmartPLS software and the PLS algorithm was run in order to obtain model estimation. The PLS-SEM algorithm estimated the standardized outer loading, outer weights, and structural model path coefficients.

Using SmartPLS version 3.1.5 (Ringle et al., 2014), the research model was specified and reflective and formative indicators were specified. According to Petter, Straub, and Rai (2007) when indicators are incorrectly specified, there is an increase in both Type I and Type II errors. The model depicted in Figure 5 expresses reflective indicators. In this model, HPC was a second-order reflective factor composed of the formative constructs task compatibility, workflow compatibility and, professional compatibility. BICU was a formative factor composed of the constructs of HPC, PU, and, PEU.

The structural model was assessed for collinearity of indicators using the criteria of indicator's tolerance levels lower than 0.20 (VIF above 5). If collinearity was determined based on tolerance or VIF levels, the constructs were eliminated or merged into a single index to treat these issues (Hair et al., 2014). Estimated path coefficients were evaluated for standardized values between -1 and +1. Path coefficients closer to +1 were considered to have strong positive relationships (and vice versa for negative values). Bootstrapping was used to assess the empirical t values for significance levels of 0.05 and 0.10. Hair et al. (2014) recommended 0.10 for exploratory research. Once the empirical *t values* were calculated, a one-tailed test was used to calculate p values to test the hypotheses. The confidence interval was also calculated.

To evaluate the predictive accuracy of the structural model, the standardized coefficient of determination, R^2 values, were assessed. The R^2 value ranges from 0 to 1, where higher levels indicated higher levels of predictive accuracy for the model. The adjusted R^2 value were used to avoid bias towards complex models by reducing the number of explaining constructs from the sample size to compensate for non-significant exogenous constructs (Hair et al., 2014).

The effect size, f^2, was calculated to evaluate whether an omitted construct had a substantive impact on the endogenous constructs of the model. Effect size values of 0.02, 0.15, and 0.35 respectively represent small, medium, and large effects (Hair et al., 2014). The predictive relevance, Q^2 values, were

Figure 5. Basic Model from Smart PLS

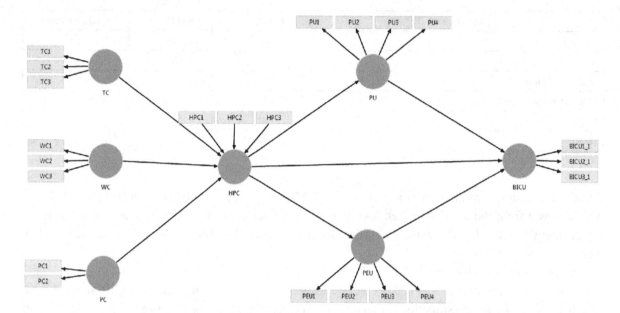

examined. Relative predictive relevance, q^2 values, for each endogenous construct were also calculated. Relative predictive relevance, q^2 values of 0.02, 0.15, and 0.35, respectively indicated that an exogenous construct had a small, medium, or large predictive relevance (Hair et al., 2014).

According to Hair et al. (2014), when examining reflective indicators in the measurement models, researchers should focus on establishing indicators reliability and validity. SmartPLS measurement of reliability of indicators included indicator loadings. Measures of internal consistency included Cronbach's alpha and composite reliability. Evidence of convergent validity was provided by average variance extracted measures (AVE). Discriminant validity was measured by examining the cross-loadings of the indicators.

The study followed the approach suggested by Hair, et al. (2014a) to assess collinearity of the constructs. This approach involved testing the multicollinearity among the indicators using regression. To detect multicollinearity, the collinearity statistic or variance inflation factor (VIF) for the inner and outer models was examined in SmartPLS.

According to Lowry and Gaskin (2014) a VIF value of 10 is acceptable, however, a VIF below 3.3 indicates sufficient construct validity for formative or reflective factors. Hair et al. (2014) suggested that tolerance levels below 0.20 (VIF above 5.00) in the predictor constructs were indicative of collinearity. All indicators in the inner and outer model exhibited VIF below 5.00, therefore confirming absence of collinearity. Table 5 shows the results Collinearity tests for inner and outer models in Smart PLS.

The estimation of the measurement model in SmartPLS provided three important results in the modeling window. These were (1) the outer weights or outer loadings for the measurement model (there are only outer loadings and no outer weights in this study's model as it only included formative measured constructs), (2) the path coefficients for the structural model relationships, and (3) the R^2 values for the latent endogenous variables HPC, PU, PEU, and BICU.

There were four basic evaluation types conducted to assess a reflective measurement model including indicator reliability, construct reliability, convergent validity, and discriminant validity (Chin (2010); Hair

Table 5. Results of Inner VIF Values

	BICU	HPC	PC	PEU	PU	TC	WC
BICU							
HPC	2.476			1	1.811		
PC		3.471					
PEU	1.822				1.811		
PU	1.79						
TC		4.332					
WC		2.591					

et al. (2014). Table 6 presents the measurement model results, including information about reliability, validity, correlations and factor loadings.

Loadings and cross-loadings are evidence of discriminant validity among indicators in the model. According to Hair et al. (2014), the outer loadings and cross-loadings should be higher than 0.708, and indicators with outer loading between 0.40 and 0.70 should be considered for removal only if the deletion leads to increased composite reliability. The AVE value above suggested threshold value (0.50).

The pattern of loadings and cross-loadings supported internal consistency and discriminant validity, with three exceptions: two work practice compatibility item (WC2), three work practice compatibility item (WC3), and two perceived ease of use (PEU2), with low loadings and crossloadings-0257, -0.640 and, 0.480 respectively. The deletion of the indicators WC2, WC3, and PEU2 led to an increase in composite reliability for the construct of HWC from 0.00 to 1.00, and an increase in AVE value above the suggested threshold value from 0.444 to 1.00. The indicator PEU2 was not deleted due to the lack of increase in composite reliability (from 0.877 to 0.922) and the lack of increase in AVE above the threshold of 0.50.

The path coefficients and the coefficients' significance were used for hypothesis testing. Hair et al. (2014) explained that hypothesis tests in SmartPLS involve the evaluation of t-values. All p significance levels (p < .01, p < .05 and p < .10) were addressed and the larger p value of less than .10 was appropriate for exploratory research. Table 8 presents a summary of the significance testing of the structural model path coefficients in SmartPLS.

Table 6. Overview of Model Measures of Reliability and Validity of the Indicators

	AVE	Composite Reliability	Cronbach's α
BICU	0.84	0.94	0.90
HPC	0.81	0.93	0.88
PC	0.73	0.87	0.64
PEU	0.65	0.88	0.82
PU	0.75	0.92	0.89
TC	0.80	0.92	0.87
WC	0.44	0.00	0.11

Table 7. Path Coefficients (Original Sample)

	BICU	**HPC**	**PC**	**PEU**	**PU**	**TC**	**WC**
BICU							
HPC	0.333			0.669	0.609		
PC		0.076					
PEU	0.291				0.078		
PU	0.254						
TC		0.346					
WC		0.501					

Table 8. Summary of Significant Testing Results of the Structural Model Path Coefficients

Path Description	**Path Coeffirient B**	***t* Values**	***p* Values**
HPC -> BICU	0.33***	2.49	0.01
HPC -> PEU	0.76***	8.67	0.00
HPC -> PU	0.61***	5.47	0.00
PC -> HPC	0.08 NS	0.86	0.19
PEU -> BICU	0.29**	2.73	0.00
PEU -> PU	0.08 NS	0.878	0.19
PU -> BICU	0.25**	2.12	0.02
TC -> HPC	0.35**	2.59	0.01
WC -> HPC	0.50**	4.49	0.00

Note: NS= not significant *p<.10, **p<.05, ***p<.01

The Structural Model Relationships

To assess the significance and relevance of the structural model relationships, the Hair et al. (2014) approach was followed. The sizes of the path coefficients (the relevance of the relationships) were obtained after running the PLS algorithm (Hair et al., 2014). The t values for the path coefficients (the significance of the relationships) were obtained after running the bootstrapping option in SmartPLS.

The relevance of significant relationships was explained as the relative importance of the exogenous driver constructs in predicting the dependent construct (Hair et al., 2014). The relevance of BICU (original sample) was evaluated by examining the path coefficients. Hair et al. (2014) explained that, as a rule, path coefficients with standardized values above 0.20 are usually significant, while those with values below 0.10 are usually not significant. Table 7 presents the path coefficients (original sample).

Based on their sizes, the results showed that HPC had the strongest effect on BICU (0.33), followed by PEU (0.29). PU (0.25) had the least effect on BICU. In the extended TAM model for this study, HPC was confirmed to have strong relationships with BICU (0.333), whereas PU and PEU had a moderate relationship to BICU (0.254 and 0.291, respectively). Additionally, the relative importance of the exogenous constructs predicting the dependent construct HPC showed that WC had the strongest effect on HPC (0.50), followed by TC (0.35). PC (0.08) had the least effect on HPC.

According to Hair et al. (2014), the significance testing is the process of testing whether a certain result has occurred by chance. Table 8 presents the path coefficients and their associated *t*-values. Critical *t*-values for significance levels ($\alpha = 0.05$) are $t > 1.96$ is significant for a two-tailed test, and $t > .98$ is significant for a one-tailed test (Hair et al., 2014). The results indicated that all paths were statistically significant using a one-tailed test except for PC-HPC and PEU-PU. However, seven of the nine structural paths were significant based on a two-tailed test.

The path coefficients and the coefficients significance were used for hypotheses testing. Hair et al. (2014) explained that hypothesis tests in SmartPLS involve the evaluation of t-values. All p significance levels ($p < .01$, $p < .05$ and $p < .10$) were addressed, as Hair et al. (2014) explained that the larger p value of less than .10 was appropriate for exploratory research. Table 8 presents a summary of the significance testing of the structural model path coefficients in SmartPLS.

The adjusted coefficient of determination R^2 was calculated using SmartPLS. This coefficient was the measure of the variance in the endogenous constructs that was explained by all the exogenous constructs with a path to the target construct. According to Hair et al. (2014), R^2 values of 0.75, 0.50, or 0.25 for the endogenous constructs can be described as respectively substantial, moderate, and weak. Additionally, R^2 values explain the model's ability to explain and predict the endogenous latent variables (dependent variables) and "can be used as the criterion to avoid bias towards complex models" (Hair et al., 2014, p. 176).

Table 9 presents the R^2 values for the exogenous constructs. The R^2 value of HPC is considered strong, whereas the R^2 values of BICU (0.573), PEU (0.448), and PU (0.441) are considered moderate. Based on the results, healthcare practice compatibility (HPC) exhibited strong predictive accuracy. PEU and PU exhibited moderate predictive accuracy.

SOLUTIONS AND RECOMMENDATIONS

This study demonstrated that HPC had a positive relationship with BICU ($\beta = 0.33$, $p = .01^- < \alpha = 0.05$). When considering the three variables contained in the HPC construct, the results demonstrated that TC had a positive relationship with HPC ($\beta = 0.35$, $p = .01^- < \alpha = 0.05$), WC had a positive relationship with HPC ($\beta = 0.50$, $p = .01^- < \alpha = 0.05$) and, PC did not have a positive relationship with HPC ($\beta = 0.08$, $p = .10 > \alpha = 0.05$). In addition, PU and PEU had positive relationships with HPC ($\beta = 0.67$, $p = .01^- < \alpha = 0.05$ and $\beta = 0.61$, $p = .01^- < \alpha = 0.05$, respectively).

Table 9. Results of R2 and Q2 Values

Endogenous Variables	R² Values	Q² Values
BICU	0.573	0.450
HPC	0.745	0.582
PC	0.000	
PEU	0.448	0.265
PU	0.441	0.306
TC	0.000	
WC	0.000	

These results supported the study's hypotheses and previous research results that behavioral intention is a reasonable predictor of behavior in contexts where users were already using the technology (Bhattacherjee & Barfar, 2011). Additionally, the research results supported the concept that behavioral intention is important in healthcare organizations because the expected benefits of technologies, such as e-training, could not be realized and their implementation could not be considered successful if usage is not sustained. Furthermore, this study's model introduced the construct of BICU of e-training and reinforced continued use as an important behavioral outcome influenced by compatibility and the context of healthcare task and work practices.

Based on these research findings, healthcare managers should increase their awareness of the benefits of (a) e-training that is compatible with users' work habits, (b) increased development in employees' skills, (c) improvement in patient care quality and outcomes and patient satisfaction, (d) decreased clinical errors, and (e) improved organizational performance and competitiveness. The increased use of e-training for healthcare professionals highlights the importance of understanding the determinants essential to e-training systems and their continued use. This study offered insight into whether organizational benefits could be achieved through the successful planning, design and implementation of e-training systems that consider users' perceptions and needs thus promoting continued use.

This study proposed a revised TAM that integrated healthcare practice compatibility, task compatibility, professional compatibility, and work compatibility with TAM to investigate what determined healthcare professionals' continued use of e-training. Findings from the study indicated that the extended TAM model was able to provide a reasonable assessment of healthcare professionals' behavioral intention to continue use of e-training. The study confirmed the validity of the TAM model in the context of predicting and explaining individual behaviors towards continued usage of e-training in the healthcare community. The overall predictive model explained 57.3% of the variance in BICU of e-training. Additionally, the predictive model explained 74.5% of the variance of the influence of healthcare practice compatibility in the BICU of e-training.

The results indicated that perceived usefulness, perceived ease of use, and healthcare practice compatibility were important determinants to users' behavioral intent. Among these, tests of the structural model indicated that healthcare practice compatibility had the strongest total effect on the intention to use, whereas perceived ease of use had a moderate total effect and perceived usefulness had a small total effect on behavioral intent. In addition, healthcare practice compatibility had a very strong total effect on both perceived ease of use and perceived usefulness.

The results showed that a healthcare professional's intention to continue to use e-training could be explained or predicted through perceived usefulness and perceived ease of use, and the professional perception of e-training usefulness was also influenced by the perception of e-training ease of use (Chau & Hu, 2001; Venkatesh & Davis, 2000). Consistent with prior studies (Chau & Hu, 2002; Horan et al., 2004), this study found that compatibility not only directly affected behavioral intent, perceived usefulness, and perceived ease of use, but also had the highest contribution (total effect) to a healthcare professional's intention to use e-training. These implied that work compatibility was the most significant antecedent of continued use of e-training and must be considered when promoting and implementing e-training technology.

Reuss, Menozzi, Buchi, Koller, and Krueger (2004) stated that although healthcare professionals would like to use technology for training, the acceptance and continued use of e-training were rather low because user demands were not necessarily analyzed carefully or considered. While e-training was more consistent with healthcare professionals' existing values, prior experiences, and practice needs, they would only feel more confident in using e-training if they did not have to exert a lot of effort to learn or become familiar with the system. Additionally, healthcare professionals would have a higher perception of e-training use benefits (Reuss et al., 2004). As a result, they would be more likely to use e-training on a continuing basis.

When developing useful and easy-to-use e-training systems, designers should also pay more attention to user requirements, conduct analysis to determine their expectations, and assess needs for e-training application content. The relevant materials and functions could then be incorporated into the systems. Only when participants had higher perceptions in compatibility with their previous or current practice processes would there be an increased possibility to achieve continued use of e-training.

The descriptive statistics from this research study indicated that 62% of respondents had 10 or more years of experience and 38% had less than 10 years of experience. The ratio of more than 10 years to less than 10 years of experience was 2 to 1. The role of professional experience in BICU of e-training was found to be significant. This suggested that managers needed to ensure e-training systems were compatible with clinical and patient care working practices to promote continued use of e-training by experienced employees. The descriptive statistics from this study indicated that 49% of respondents were female compared with 17% of male respondents. Previous research demonstrated that gender was not significant in explaining technology use attitude (Davis, 1989; Venkatesh & Davis, 2000; Ward et al., 2008). Therefore, this study did not focus on experience or gender.

Theoretical and Practical Implications

This research demonstrated that TAM predictors and healthcare compatibility played important roles in predicting and explaining individual behavior towards the continued use of e-training. Work practice compatibility was found to be the strongest predictor of healthcare compatibility. Previous research found that compatibility with an individual's work style and skills was strongly associated with satisfaction and continued use of a technology system (Tulu et al., 2006; Ward et al., 2008). Therefore, healthcare professionals were more likely to continue to use e-training that was compatible with their work styles and skills and that was aligned with an organization's work processes.

The significance of the effect workflow compatibility in healthcare practice compatibility and BICU of e-training was important from the perspective of a healthcare organization. This suggested that healthcare professionals are more likely to accept and continue using e-training that accommodates their workflows. Good workflow helps accomplish healthcare organizational goals in a timely manner and leads to the delivery of consistent, reliable, safe healthcare that was compliant with standards of practice (Cain & Haque, 2008). On the other hand, e-training that is not compatible with the user's workflow does not support the healthcare professional's goals and causes alternate workflows, which often has negative effects on patient outcomes and safety (Cain & Haque, 2008).

This study also confirmed that task compatibility had a significant effect on healthcare practice compatibility and behavioral intent to continued use of e-training, which was consistent with prior research. Goodhue and Thompson (1995) found that a technology system that fits work tasks was a strong predictor of work station continued use. This suggests that e-training that supports tasks results in continued usage and, in turn, has a positive impact on individual performance. Furthermore, the compatibility between e-training work tasks, the intention to continue use, and the clinical priorities of healthcare professionals are essential for the delivery of positive outcomes for patients. Conclusively, e-training which is perceived to be incompatible with the therapeutic relationship between healthcare professional and patient, or is incompatible with the goal of improved patient outcome, would eventually lead to rejection or underuse of e-training by healthcare professionals.

Further analysis of the structural model revealed several interesting findings. The significance and strength of the effects of professional compatibility on healthcare compatibility and BICU of e-training were very small. In contrast, another study found that compatibility between technology and professional practice compatibility was highly desirable (Tulu et al., 2006). Another study found that the technological requirements varied by healthcare professional groups (Ward et al., 2008).

Goodhue and Thompson (1995) also explained that the technological requirements for nurses and physicians were found to be different and these influenced healthcare professionals' attitudes toward acceptance and continued use of e-training technology. Goodhue and Thompson's (1995) study also found that the relationship between technology and users' professional role could lead to challenges to the healthcare professionals' role and traditional practice. Consequently, this study's results only confirmed that the constructs and relationships of the constructs of professional compatibility and BICU of e-training are complex and clearly require a sociotechnical approach to understand the views of those who work in healthcare.

At the heart of this study's extended TAM model was the assertion that perceived usefulness and perceived ease of use had a significant predictive effect on BICU of e-training. The confirmation of the effects of these constructs pointed to the general agreement that, at best, an e-training system with poor usability would result in increased user time and effort while, at worst, the e-training system would not be used at all.

The predictive capability of the research model was confirmed by the observed values above zero for the predictive relevance values obtained for the constructs of healthcare practice compatibility, perceived ease of use, perceived usefulness, and BICU of e-training. The results of this study confirmed the predictive capability of the research model to support findings in studies by Ward et al. (2008) and Tulu et al. (2006), who claimed that healthcare professionals' continued use of e-training was not the only factor of behavioral attitudes towards e-training based on the usefulness or ease-of-use of a system. Reasonably, this study concluded that continued use of e-training is based on complex social and technical factors that are challenged when e-training technology is integrated into the workplace.

FUTURE RESEARCH DIRECTIONS

Although this study provided important insights into the factors affecting the intention toward continued use of e-training, three main limitations were identified. First, the study was a cross-sectional, quantitative look at BICU of e-training that measured perceptions and intentions of individuals at a single point in time. The cross-sectional nature of the study provided a snapshot in time. Second, the study investigated BICU of e-training and did not investigate actual use of e-training. This limitation may raise issues as to the validity of the results regarding BICU of healthcare e-training. Third, the data for the study was self-reported. Ward et al. (2008) conducted a study that concluded that self-reported measures may be viewed as relative indicators of actual behaviors and intentions. Fourth, the study used a small sample size. Although the PLS-SEM algorithm used in the study can produce statistically significant results using small sample sizes, the sampling size may have limited the ability to make broader generalizations.

To help overcome these limitations, future longitudinal studies should be conducted that may add a new perspective to the results. Second, a qualitative study involving healthcare professionals' e-training use perceptions may help reflect local constituencies' understanding. Third, a larger sample size might be used to increase the precision of PLS-SEM estimations.

CONCLUSION

The results of this research indicated that three antecedents of TAM played a role in the continued use of e-training. The implications for e-training practitioners included: (a) the attitudes of healthcare professionals could be a significant factor in the efficient use of e-training, (b) e-training technology that failed to accommodate organizational workflow and users' work practices became a burden to the organization that led to rejection or underuse of e-training technology by healthcare professionals, (c) if the e-training system could not be used easily and efficiently, users became frustrated or lost interest in the training material, and (d) if users did not use e-training as intended, their organizations had suboptimal return on e-training investment.

The ability to identify, predict, and manage employee acceptance and continued use of e-training technology facilitates implementation efforts. In addition, the continued use of e-training technology by users is necessary for the ultimate success of healthcare IT (Schaper & Pervan, 2007a). Increasing interest in end-user reactions to e-training for healthcare professionals has elevated the importance of theories that predict and explain e-training acceptance and continued use. One fundamental approach to e-training in the workplace is practice compatibility: The results of this study indicated that practice compatibility played a significant role as a determinant of behavioral intention to continued use of e-training and that healthcare professionals need e-training technology that is perceived as useful and easy to use.

The benefits associated with continued use of e-training in a healthcare organization cannot be ignored. The effectiveness and efficiency of a healthcare organization is highly dependent on the competence of its healthcare professionals. When e-training is not accepted and used, a financial burden is placed on the organization and the quality of healthcare received suffers for patients who depends on health care professionals' knowledge and expertise. Burdens related to medical errors and low-quality medical care can be measured in economic terms, suboptimal outcomes, and even increased medical fatalities. Finally, with accelerated hospital competition and the growing popularity of e-training technology, understanding the determinants that encourage continued use of e-training could provide important insights for hospital administrators to develop opportunities and value for patients, increase the efficiency and effectiveness of healthcare personnel, and could increase hospital competitiveness.

REFERENCES

Agarwal, R., & Karahanna, E. (1998). On the multi-dimensional nature of compatibility beliefs in technology acceptance. In *Proceedings of the 19th Annual International Conference on Information Systems.* DIGIT. Retrieved from http://disc-nt.cba. uh.edu/chin/digit98/first.pdf

Agarwal, R., & Prasad, J. (1997). The role of innovation characteristics and perceived voluntariness in the acceptance of information technologies. *Decision Sciences, 28*(3), 557–582. doi:10.1111/j.1540-5915.1997.tb01322.x

Agarwal, V., Dasgupta, K., Karnik, N. M., Kumar, A., Kundu, A., Mittal, S., & Srivastava, B. (2005). A service creation environment based on end to end composition of web services. In *International Conference World Wide Web. WWW.*

Aggelidis, V. P., & Chatzoglou, P. D. (2009). Using a modified technology acceptance model in hospitals. *International Journal of Medical Informatics, 78*(2), 115–126. doi:10.1016/j.ijmedinf.2008.06.006 PMID:18675583

Ajzen, I. (1991). The theory of planned behavior. *Organizational Behavior and Human Decision Processes, 50*(2), 179–211. doi:10.1016/0749-5978(91)90020-T

Al-Gahtani, S. (2001). The applicability of TAM outside North America: An empirical test in the United Kingdom. *Information Resources Management Journal, 14*(3), 37-46. doi:10.418/irmj.20010700104

Arbaugh, J. B., Godfrey, M. R., Johnson, J., Pollack, B. I., Niendorf, B., & Wresch, W. (2009). Research in online and blended learning in the business disciplines: Key findings and possible future directions. *The Internet and Higher Education, 12*, 71-87. 10.1016/j.iheduc.2009.06.006

Association for Talent Development (ASTD-AST). (2013, October 30). *Workplace learning remains a key organizational investment Results from ASTD's 2013 of the Industry Report.* Retrieved from http://www.astd.org/Publications/Magazines/TD/TD-Archive/2013/11/Workplace-Learning-Remains-a-Key-Organizational-Investment

Bhattacherjee, A. (2001). Understanding Information Systems continuance: An expectation-confirmation model. *Management Information Systems Quarterly, 25*(3), 351–370. doi:10.2307/3250921

Bhattacherjee, A., & Barfar, A. (2011). Information Technology continuance research: Current state and future directions. *Asia Pacific Journal of Information Systems, 21*(2), 1–18.

Bhattacherjee, A., & Hikmet, N. (2007). Physicians' resistance toward healthcare information technology: a theoretical model and empirical test. *European Journal of Information Systems, 16*(6), 725-737. doi:.ejis.300071710.1057/palgrave

Cain, C., & Haque, S. (2008). Organizational workflow and its impact on work quality. In R. G. Hughes (Ed.), *Patient safety and quality: An evidence-based handbook for nurses* (pp. 217-244). Retrieved from Agency for Healthcare Research and Quality website: http://www.ncbi.nlm.nih.gov/books/NBK2638/pdf/ch31.pdf

Chau, P. K. & Hu, P. J-H (2002). Investigating healthcare professional's decision to accept telemedicine technology: an empirical test of competing theories. *Information & Management, 39*(4), 279-311. (01)00098-210.1016/S0378-7206

Chau, P. Y., & Hu, P. J.-H. (2001). Information technology acceptance by individual professionals: A model comparison approach. *Decision Sciences, 32*(4), 699–719. doi:10.1111/j.1540-5915.2001.tb00978.x

Chen, J., Park, Y., & Putzer, G. J. (2010). An examination of the components that increase acceptance of smartphones among healthcare professionals. *Electronic Journal of Health Informatics, 15*(2), 1-12. Retrieved from http://www.ejhi.net

Chen, L. D., Guillenson, M. L., & Sherrell, D. L. (2002). Enticing online consumers: An extended technology acceptance perspective. *Information and Management, 39*(8), 705-719. doi:(01)00127-610.1016/S0378-7206

Chin, W. W., Johnson, N., & Schwartz, A. (2008). A fast form approach to measuring technology acceptance and other constructs. *Management Information Systems Quarterly, 32*(4), 687–703. Retrieved from http://web.ffos.hr/oziz/tam/Chin_2008.pdf

Davis, F. D. (1989). Perceived usefulness, perceived ease of use, and user acceptance of Information Technology. *Management Information Systems Quarterly, 13*(3), 319–340. doi:10.2307/249008

Fishbein, M., & Ajzen, I. (1975). *Belief, attitude, intention and behavior: An introduction to theory and Research*. Reading, MA: Addison-Wesley.

Goodhue, D. L., & Thompson, R. L. (1995). Task-technology fit and individual performance. *Management Information Systems Quarterly, 19*(2), 213–236. doi:10.2307/249689

Hair, J. F., Sarstedt, M., Hopkins, L., & Kuppelweiser, V. G. (2014). Partial least squares structural equation modeling (PLS-SEM): An emerging tool in business research. *European Business Review, 26*(2), 106–121. doi:10.1108/EBR-10-2013-0128

Holden, R. J., & Karsh, B. T. (2010). The technology acceptance model: Its past and its future in healthcare. *Journal of Biomedical Informatics, 43*(1), 159–172. doi:10.1016/j.jbi.2009.07.002 PMID:19615467

Horan, T. A., Tulu, B., Hilton, B., & Burton, J. (2004). Use of online systems in clinical medical assessments: An analysis of physician acceptance of online disability evaluation systems. In *Proceedings of the 37th Annual Hawaii International Conference on System Sciences*. IEEE. doi:10.1109/HICSS.2004.1265364

Hung, S.-Y., Chen, C. C., & Lee, W.-J. (2009). Moving hospitals toward e-learning adoption: An empirical investigation. *Journal of Organizational Change Management, 22*(3), 239–256. doi:10.1108/09534810910951041

Jasperson, J. S., Carter, P. E., & Zmud, R. W. (2005). A comprehensive conceptualization of post-adoptive behaviors associated with technology enabled work systems. *Management Information Systems Quarterly, 29*(3), 525–557.

Kamalzadeh Takhti, H., Abdul Rahman, S. B., & Abedini, S. (2013). Factors determining nurses' hospital information systems. *International Journal of Management & Information Technology, 3*(3), 37–44. Retrieved from http://www.ijmit.com

Karahanna, E., Agarwal, R., & Angst, C. M. (2006). Reconceptualizing compatibility beliefs in technology acceptance research. *MIS Quarterly, 30*(4), 781-804. Retrieved from http://www.jstor.org/stable/25148754

Karahanna, E., Straub, D. W., & Chervany, N. L. (1999). Information technology adoption across time: A cross-sectional comparison of pre-adoption and post-adoption beliefs. *MIS Quarterly, 23*(2), 183-213. Retrieved from http://web.ffos.hr/oziz/tam/Karahanna_1999++++PRE-POST.pdf

Kim, S. S., & Malhotra, N. K. (2005). A Longitudinal Model of Continued IS Use: An Integrative View of Four Mechanisms Underlying Postadoption Phenomena. *Management Science, 51*(5), 741-755. doi:10.1287/mnsc.1040.326

Lee, Y. H., Hsieh, Y. C., & Hsu, C. N. (2011). Adding innovation diffusion theory to the technology acceptance model: Supporting employees' intentions to use e-learning systems. *Journal of Educational Technology & Society, 14*(4), 124–137. Retrieved from http://www.editlib.org/p/75487

Liao, H. L., & Lu, H. P. (2008). The role of the experience and innovation characteristics in adoption and continued use of e-learning websites. *Computers & Education, 51*(4), 1405–1416. doi:10.1016/j.compedu.2007.11.006

Marangunic, N., & Granic, A. (2014). Technology acceptance model: A literature review from 1986 to 2013. *International Journal of Universal Access in the Information Society,* 1-15. doi:10.1007/s10209-014-0348-1

Mathieson, K. (1991). Predicting user intentions: Comparing the technology acceptance model with the theory of planned behavior. *Information Systems Research, 2*(3), 173–191. doi:10.1287/isre.2.3.173

Moore, G. C., & Benbasat, I. (1991). Development of an instrument to measure perceptions of adopting an information technology innovation. *Information Systems Research, 2*(3), 192-222. Retrieved from 10.1287/isre.2.3.192

Mosby's. (n.d.). *Mosby's Medical Dictionary* (8th ed.). Elsevier.

Pai, F.-Y., & Huang, K.-I. (2011). Applying the technology acceptance model to the introduction of healthcare information systems. *Technological Forecasting and Social Change, 78*(4), 650–660. doi:10.1016/j.techfore.2010.11.007

Petter, S., Straub, D. W., & Rai, A. (2007). Specifying formative constructs in information systems research. *Management Information Systems Quarterly, 31*, 623–656.

Reuss, E., Menozzi, M., Buchi, M., Koller, J., & Krueger, H. (2004). Information access at the point of care: What can we learn for designing mobile CPR system? *International Journal of Medical Informatics, 73*(4), 363–369. doi:10.1016/j.ijmedinf.2004.02.003 PMID:15135755

Ringle, C. M., Sardest, M., & Straub, D. W. (2012). A critical look at the use of PLS-SEM in MIS Quarterly. *MIS Quarterly, 36*(1), iii-xiv. Retrieved from http://dl.acm.org/citation.cfm?id=2208956

Ringle, C. M., Wende, S., & Becker, J-M. (2014). *SmartPLS 3*. Retrieved from http://www.smartpls.com

Rogers, E. M. (2003). *Diffusion of innovations* (5th ed.). New York, NY: Free Press.

Schaper, L. K., & Pervan, G. P. (2007a). ICT and OT's: A model of information and communication technology acceptance and utilization by occupational therapists (Part 1). *International Journal of Medical Informatics, 76*(1), S212–S221. doi:10.1016/j.ijmedinf.2006.05.028 PMID:16828335

Sloman, M. (2002). *The e-learning revolution How technology is driving a new training paradigm*. New York, NY: AMACOM.

Sun, Y., Wang, N., Guo, X., & Peng, Z. (2013). Understanding the acceptance of mobile health services: A comparison and integration alternative models. *Journal of Electronic Commerce Research, 114*(2), 183–200. Retrieved from http://www.csulb.edu/journals/jecr/issues/20132/paper4.pdf

Tsai, A. (2012). An integrated e-learning solution for healthcare professionals. *Journal of Business Management, 6*(27), 8163–8177. doi:10.5897/AJBM11.2927

Tulu, B., Burkhard, R. J., & Horan, T. A. (2006). Continuing use of medical information systems by medical professionals: Empirical evaluation of a work system model. *Communications of the Association for Information Systems, 18*, 641–656. Retrieved from http://www.cgu.edu/pdffiles/KayCenter/journal_version_tulu_etal_cais2006@20@282@29.pdf

Venkatesh, V., & Davis, F. D. (1996). A model of antecedents of perceived ease of use: Development and test. *Decision Sciences, 27*(3), 451–481. doi:10.1111/j.1540-5915.1996.tb01822.x

Venkatesh, V., & Davis, F. D. (2000). A theoretical extension of the technology acceptance model: Four longitudinal field studies. *Management Science, 46*(2), 186–204. doi:10.1287/mnsc.46.2.186.11926

Ward, R., Stevens, C., Brentnall, P., & Briddon, J. (2008). The attitudes of healthcare staff to information technology: A comprehensive review of the research literature. *Health Information and Libraries Journal, 25*(2), 81–97. doi:10.1111/j.1471-1842.2008.00777.x PMID:18494643

Wu, I. L., Li, J. Y., & Fu, C. Y. (2011). The adoption of mobile healthcare by hospital's professionals: An integrative perspective. *Decision Support Systems, 51*(3), 587–596. doi:10.1016/j.dss.2011.03.003

Yi, M. Y., Jackson, J. D., Park, J. S., & Probst, J. C. (2006). Understanding information technology acceptance by individual professionals: Toward an integrative view. *Information & Management, 3*(3), 350–363. http://web.ffos.hr/oziz/tam/Yi_2006.pdf doi:10.1016/j.im.2005.08.006

Zhang, P., & Sung, H. (2009). The complexity of different types of attitudes in initial and continued use of ICT. *Journal of American Society for Information Science and Technology, 60*(10), 2048-2063. doi:10.1002/asi.21116

Section 5
Wellness and Healthcare

Chapter 19
Global Studies Impact:
A Case Study of the International School of the Americas

Donna Reed
Southwest Independent School District, USA

ABSTRACT

This qualitative case study describes global studies education and curriculum, global citizenship, and the impact of a global studies education and curriculum on students after graduation. What life choices might be influenced by what the students learned through global studies? Did they choose their university studies based on globalized thinking? These are difficult questions to answer, because there are so many variables in the life of an adolescent when making choices after high school graduation. This study discovers the impact of a global studies education with a global citizenship emphasis on graduates of a global studies high school through student voice and experience—backwards mapping.

Despite the existence of copious literature on global education since the mid-1800s, there remains a dearth of literature on assessment and the impact of a global education on students after graduation (Davies, 2006; Gaudelli, 2003; Mansilla & Gardner, 2007; Marshall, 2007; Wray-Lake, Flanagan, & Osgood, 2008). Will a globalized education produce people with a global worldview? Future adults need to know the world, not just from the myopic vision of the United States, but also from a panorama that encompasses outside views of the United States and how the interdependent world works (Boyer et al., 2007; Gibson et al., 2008; Sanchez, 2007; Tye, 2003).

If, as Davies (2006) wrote, the eventual aim of a global citizenship programme is a collection of "global citizens" who will challenge injustice and promote rights, how do we track these individuals and groups during and after their school life, and, conversely, how do we engage in "backwards mapping" to work out what caused people to act as global citizens, and what "percentage" was due to exposure to a global citizenship programme in a school? (p. 23)

This study begins a discussion of a global studies education and assessing the impact on graduates from a global studies high school in the United States by *backwards mapping,* as Davies suggested. There

DOI: 10.4018/978-1-5225-0522-8.ch019

is a need for global education (Gibson et al., 2008; Hanvey, 1976; Hayden et al., 2002; Jackson, 2004, 2008; Manzilla & Jackson, 2011; Roberts, 2007; Scott, 2005). It is important to consider the graduates and how they have benefitted from a global studies curriculum.

Talking to students can determine what is effective in education (Boyer et al., 2007). In this qualitative case study, global studies high school graduates confirmed the outcomes of educational researchers of global studies curriculum.

BACKGROUND

Giving our young people the tools to think globally in our local environment in order to compete in the global workforce within the world today is essential (Jackson, 2004, 2008; Roberts, 2007). This global workforce necessitates young adults work in diverse circumstances to solve problems and to create the future for themselves and their children, which, in turn, requires them to possess a global worldview (Davies, Evans & Reed, 2005; Jackson, 2008; Mansilla & Gardner, 2007). This encompasses "education for responsible participation in an interdependent global society" (Anderson & Anderson, 1979, p. 7). Future adults need to know the world, not just from the myopic vision of the United States, but also from a panorama that encompasses outside views of the United States and how the interdependent world works (Boyer et al., 2007; Gibson et al., 2008; Sanchez, 2007; Tye, 2003).

A global studies education concept has been written about since the Victorian era, when the first school of its kind opened in London in 1866 (Hayden et al., 2002). Although this school only lasted 16 years, the discussion of international education in its various forms and formats has continued. The next notable venture into international education came from Switzerland in 1924 with the International School of Geneva (Hayden et al., 2002). Global war and depression halted the "vision of international harmony by the creation of a new type of education" facilitating the idea of being "a citizen of the world at large," and the discussion waned until after the Second World War (Hayden et al., 2002, p. 30). After the Second World War, the "United States developed markedly more interest in the international community and in the 1950s encouraged international education for its school children" (Cook, 2008, p. 897). The words *international* and *global* were making their way into the national consciousness again. In the 1950s, other nations called for the United States to lead the world in ending hunger. In the 1960s, communication theorist Marshall McLuhan coined the phrase "global village" when speaking of electronic technology and how it had created a smaller world (McLuhan, 1964/1994, p. 5). And, in the 1970s, Robert Hanvey (1976) wrote his *An Attainable Global Perspective,* calling for young people to acquire a global perspective on education. As a result world history was added to most curriculums to bring about this "formation of a global perspective" (p. 1).

Life in the 21st century connects the world through instant media (Azmitia, Syed, & Radmacher, 2008; Boyer et al., 2007; Webber & Robertson, 2004). Global media causes a huge shift in the way young people see the world; it brings a global community into their home (Boyer et al., 2007). The United States education system lags behind this shift, which is triggering the impetus for education with a more global view (Scott, 2005).

The most recent impetus for international education emphasizing cultural differences has been the war on terror, beginning with the terrorist attacks against the United States on September 11, 2001. Those terrorist attacks motivated an increase in educational research in knowing more about the world outside the United States and the West (Cook, 2008). This time knowing the world outside the United States and the West, however, is not necessarily about global citizenship and understanding, but, maybe, about knowing one's enemy and trying to achieve economic superiority (Boyer et al., 2007; Cook, 2008; Frey & Whitehead, 2009).

THEORETICAL FRAMEWORK

Two theories comprised the framework of this study: (a) theory of adolescent development of identity, and (b) worldview theory.

Adolescent development of identity. Erik Erikson's theory of psychosocial development is key, especially Identity and Repudiation versus Identity Confusion (12– 18 years old) (Erikson, 1968). For Erikson, adolescents' main task is to create a self-identity. During that time of life, adolescents "try on" or testing and discard identities, thus repudiating what they were not (Erikson, 1968). Along with Erikson, Richard Lerner's contextualism, also includes adolescent environment into the equations of adolescent identity by "emphasizing the interaction that always occurs between adolescents and the environment in which they are growing" (as cited in Margolis, Dacey, & Kenny, 2007, p. 56).

The educational environment influences the testing and discarding of adolescent identity (Margolis et al., 2007). Erikson's theory, coupled with Lerner's contextualism, provided the framework for studying how adolescents secure their identity in the world (Cornbleth, 2003; Margolis et al., 2007). Adolescents' vision of who they are depends upon their context, and within that context, adolescents will repudiate various identities and select their own. Lerner's theory is especially important here, because of its consideration for developmental diversity, which highlights the idea of individual differences and focuses on "diversity that exists among ethnic groups" (Margolis et al., 2007, p. 59). It is important to include Lerner's theory, since the participants of this study were multicultural and classroom population demographics have grown in diversity to include multiple races and nationalities (Allison & Rehm, 2007; Cornbleth, 2003; Dalhouse & Dalhouse, 2006; Whitfield, Klug, & Whitney, 2007).

Cultural identity formation. Further, today cultural identity formation is important in adolescents' world (Jensen, 2003; Tatum, 1999). Exponential globalization, such as we have experienced in the twenty-first century, affects the way adolescents see themselves culturally (Azmitia et al., 2008). And "globalization ethos is in many ways Western and an American ethos, often emphasizes individual autonomy and secular values," which are not always the cultural values of our students (Jensen, 2003, p. 190). We have taught through one cultural lens, negating other cultures, even while students are exposed to other cultures on a daily basis. Jensen (2003) wrote that our cultural identity is passed on generationally, and we see the world through that cultural lens, which becomes our worldview. As adults, we are entrenched, but adolescence "may also be a time of life with a more pronounced openness to diverse cultural beliefs and behaviors" (Jensen, 2003, p. 191). With a global studies curriculum, students' self-image can be determined by the local culture and the global culture concurrently resulting in students seeing themselves as larger in the world (Phinney, 2008).

Worldview theory. Additionally, this research study is framed around the worldview theory of Aerts, Apostel, De Moor, Hellemans, Maex, Van Belle, and Van der Veken suggesting that a global worldview is necessary in today's world of globalization (Aerts et al., 2007; Boyer et al., 2007). These theorists contend a worldview is needed to exist in the world of globalization to "help us find our way and act coherently in this world" (Aerts et al., 2007, p. 7). It is most uncommon in our world today to interact only with persons of one culture, race, heritage, or nationality in our everyday life. "There is an unmistakable trend towards pluralisation of culture and individualization of human behavior" that affects adolescents (Aerts et al., 2007, p. 7).

Looking at adolescent development of identity theory, along with worldview theory, pointed to the necessity for adolescents to include a worldview in their identity. For the same reasons as Lerner cited of developmental diversity and the Aerts et al. idea that a worldview helped us find our way and act coherently, adolescents need a worldview. If we want to assess the idea of global education and global-mindedness, then we must talk with students about their worldview. Our students are our decision makers in the future and "will in fact determine society's future governance structurally and procedurally" (Boyer et al., 2007, p. 6). Listening to our young peoples' voice in education is essential to determine effective pedagogy (Boyer et al., 2007).

Young people are concerned about the world, in a large sense, as in war, destruction, the environment, violence, dehumanization, and inequality. This is of concern, since in this age of technology, adolescents are more isolated through technology. Many young people feel powerless to make a difference in their community, let alone the world (Hicks & Holden, 2007). There is a lack of "a shared vision…and broader sense of community" (Ziebertz & Kay, 2009). A broadening perspective and sense of community can be derived from a global studies education. A global studies curriculum works to bring students beyond stereotyping and guides them on ways to think about the world (Azmitia et al., 2008; Hicks & Holden, 2007; Phinney, 2008). Students need to see that what happens locally is a part of what happens globally (Ziebertz & Kay, 2009). What our youth need today is the knowledge to "address the fundamental issue of how we are to live" within cultures, but also a framework to see the world and their place in it (Eckersley, 2008, p. 18).

SETTING OF THE STUDY

The study focus was graduates from a public magnet high school located on a comprehensive inner-city high school campus, the International School of the Americas (ISA). Learning takes place through an internationally focused curriculum developed by faculty and has met the standards of the Texas Education Agency. The public high school is also a professional development school for a university located in the same metropolitan community. The mission statement is based on the Oxfam's *Education for Global Citizenship: A Guide for Schools* (Oxfam, 2006).

This public magnet campus housed approximately 460 high school students grade 9 through 12, with a faculty and staff of 35. Students were chosen by lottery after applying to attend their freshman year, creating an equal playing field for all students (Jackson, 2004). There is some natural attrition, especially between the 9th and 10th grades and the 10th and 11th grades, so the school does accept new students during those time frames to fill the vacancies. At the 11th and 12th grade, there are relatively few new students, since most families try to refrain from having their children change schools at the end of the secondary education experience in the United States. The school has been in existence since 1995, has won numerous state and national awards, and is a member of the International Studies School Network.

Demographically the student body included 4.33% Asian, 1.73% AfricanAmerican, 47.62% Hispanic, and 46.32% White, which is a reflection of the community in which the public school is located (Northeast Independent School District, 2013, para. 1). The magnet high school "is interdisciplinary with an emphasis placed upon a real world application of skills and content" (Northeast Independent School District, 2013, para. 1). All former ISA students in the study participated in academic travel, community service, a career exploration internship, and portfolio assessment.

Portfolio assessment took place at the end of each year for every grade, with the culminating portfolio at the end of the 12th grade. Each graduating senior demonstrated "knowledge, skills and values" as defined in the Graduate Profile (Appendix A), which included academic preparation, technological proficiency, problem solving proficiency, effective communication, personal wellness, collaboration and leadership, and global awareness. At the end of the senior year, all graduates presented a digital portfolio as a culmination of their education at the magnet school. Global education at this school is manifested through "critical thinking, participatory and holistic teaching and learning, values relating to human rights and social justice and issues relating to global interdependence" (Marshall, 2007, p. 358).

Each grade level was led by a team of teachers at ISA. All participants in the study shared the same teachers at the 9th and 10th grade level. That became increasingly difficult during the 11th and 12th grades, as student choice in curriculum became wider. At the 11th grade, students shared the same English teacher, American history teacher, and physics teacher. At the 12th grade level, students shared the same English teacher and social studies teacher. It was through these grade level teams that all school activities were directed, as well as the academic travel experiences. The team teachers met on a regular basis to discuss student improvement, discipline issues, and the planning of curriculum or grade level activities. From the inception of the school until 2009, the eight class academic school schedule was based on an A/B class schedule with four 90-minute classes each day, which allowed teacher team meetings every other day in addition to individual preparation periods. In 2009, with district public school budget cuts, the student academic schedule changed to a seven class day, which somewhat curtailed regular team meeting options.

There is an extensive Model United Nations (MUN) program in which all study participants were involved during their time at the school. Model United Nations is an academic simulation to educate students about the United Nations and its agendas, international relations, diplomacy, and current international events. Each year, this school organizes an extensive MUN conference that is attended by schools all over the United States, Canada, and Mexico. All 9th and 10th grade students and teachers are involved with this process, along with many of the 11th and 12th grade students.

This public school also maintains educational travel experiences at each grade level. These travel experiences involve key academic curriculum designed to enhance and is developed throughout the educational year through the travel event. Academic travel themes and locations included the following:

- **Ninth Grade:** Sustainable Development and Environment (Heifer International, Heifer Ranch, Perryville, Arkansas): Here students experienced a simulation of life in a developing country, involving lessons in economics, culture, poverty, foreign trade, and hardship conditions.
- **Tenth Grade:** Cultural Identities and Sense of Place (Mexico): That trip explored cultural identity by traveling to Zacatecas, Mexico. Zacatecas was founded by the same Catholic priests who eventually moved into the area where the ISA is now located. Studies included cultural development, architecture, and city development. However, since 2009, this academic travel experience has no longer been viable due to violence and unrest in Mexico. The academic travel experience was changed to New Mexico, with a focus on locations along the Camino Real. Students studied

how the resources of the Camino Real were used pre- and post-Spanish colonization and how that shaped the way people lived. (This is noted because some participants in this study may have experienced the Mexico trip or the New Mexico trip.)

- **Eleventh Grade:** Civil Rights and Justice (Birmingham/Montgomery, Alabama): This academic travel experience included travel to Alabama on buses to visit Birmingham, Montgomery, and Selma, key cities in the African American Civil Rights movement of the1950s and 1960s in the United States. Students studied social justice through history and current events.
- **Twelfth Grade:** Government and international affairs based on the United Nations Millennium Development Goals (2002 to present) (Washington, DC): Students were given more freedom and independence because of their age and traveled in small groups with adult chaperones during the 4- to 5-day trip. The students chose their small group based on the UN Millennium Development Goals topic and organized their itinerary to complete a project based on the selected topic

In addition to the grade level academic travel opportunities above, ISA maintains an active relationship with the Takayama Nishi High School in Takayama, Japan. This relationship includes a homestay exchange between Takayama Nishi High School students and ISA students. The exchange takes place on alternate years, with Japanese students and teachers traveling to ISA in San Antonio, and ISA students and teachers traveling to Takayama Nishi High School in Japan. Not all students participated in this travel opportunity.

This public magnet school provides four years of Spanish language studies, since Spanish is the majority language, other than English, in the area of the school. Because the magnet school is housed on a comprehensive high school campus, participants of the study had access to other international language studies, such as Chinese, Japanese, French, Latin, and German.

This global education school, which opened in 1996, was also chosen because of its track record. This public high school has won numerous state and national awards, including the Goldman Sachs Prize for Excellence in International Education. The school is partnered with international organizations and policy centers, reinforcing the mission and aims, such as the International Studies Schools Network (Jackson, 2004). The administration provides training and intense support to all staff with globalized curriculum. Torney-Purta (1986) suggested that "effective [global education] programs appear to be those which have been established for several years" (p. 23). With this in mind, this secondary school provided a reliable research base.

DATA COLLECTION AND PROCEDURE

Interviews. "Stories are a way of knowing" (Seidman, 2006, p. 7). The interviewing process is a way of letting people tell their stories, which, in turn, creates the meaning of what happened. We articulate our lives through language to solidify the meaning in an experience. So "interviewing is a basic mode of inquiry" (Seidman, 2006, p. 8). An interview process was used as the mode of inquiry, in addition to a demographic questionnaire which gave the participant the opportunity to put the topic into context, to add detail, and to reflect on the topic (Seidman, 2006). The questionnaire was followed by an in-depth interview of selected participants, based on the information obtained by the two open-ended questions included in the demographic questionnaire.

REPORT ON DEMOGRAPHIC INFORMATION OF ISA ALUMNI

Part I of the Questionnaire were questions dedicated to information about higher education attainment, study abroad, work abroad, and additional learned languages.

STUDY PARTICIPANTS

The following table reports the number of participants and the year they graduated from ISA.

Participant education attainment level. Out of 102 participants, 98 answered the question of education attainment level. ISA prides itself on the fact that all seniors have enrolled in a university or college upon graduation. According to the questionnaire findings, 47 of 98 ISA alumni completed a bachelor's degree, with 12 master's completions, and 2 PhD completions. Figure 2 provides the data. Since the closure of the study and questionnaire, three more participants have completed their bachelor's degree.

Study abroad and/or work abroad. Of 98 participants who answered this question, 18.4% had studied abroad in countries including United Kingdom, Belize, Italy, Republic of Macedonia, South Africa, Czech Republic, China, Chile, Mexico, Hungary, Australia, India, Germany, South Korea, Switzerland, and Spain. Five to six percent of the participants had lived and/or worked abroad in various countries, such as Republic of Macedonia, Germany, Cambodia, China, Malaysia, Mexico, Japan, Australia, Hungary, England, South Korea, Mexico, Singapore, United Kingdom, France, Kenya, Chile, the Netherlands, Austria, Belgium, Thailand, Bahrain, and United Arab Emirates.

Language learning. Language learning is also an important requirement at ISA, as students are required to take four years of language. Language learning also includes cultural knowledge and involves seeing through a global lens (Torney-Purta, 1986). This emphasis on international languages is impressed upon the ISA students with many choices, including Chinese, Japanese, German, Spanish, and French. The diverse student population also brings other languages to ISA. The participating alumni reported proficiency in the languages demonstrated in Figure 3, which also includes participants who are multi-lingual.

Figure 1. Participants by class year.

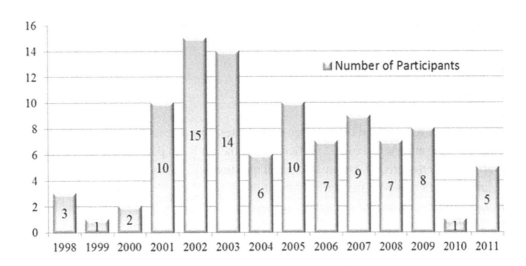

Figure 2. Participant education attainment level.

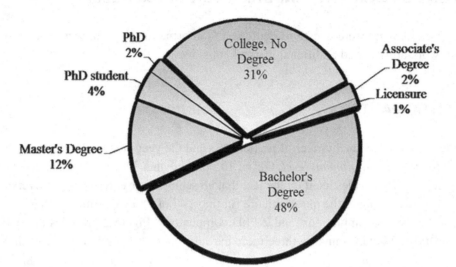

Figure 3. Second languages spoken by participants (89 respondents).

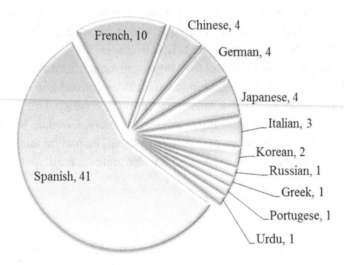

ANALYSIS AND FINDINGS OF TWO OPEN-ENDED QUESTIONS FROM ISA ALUMNI

Part II of the Questionnaire consisted of two open-ended questions pertaining to the global studies curriculum during their time at ISA. Out of 102 participants in the study, 84 participants answered Question One and 83 participants answered Question Two. Each question will be discussed individually at length, revealing the emergent themes with participant quotations.

Question one: describe a memorable event, classroom lesson, or experience you had while attending ISA that broadened your global awareness. The data analysis revealed three major themes of how global awareness was broadened. The three major themes included the Model United Nations experience, a classroom lesson, and an academic travel experience.

Model United Nations. Twenty-eight participants cited the Model United Nations (MUN) as a pivotal event that broadened their global awareness. ISA's extensive MUN program took place in the fall of each academic year. MUN was implemented during through the sophomore year, with junior and senior student staff organizing the event. Of the approximately 450 students at the high school, as many as 300 were involved in the event each year. Many of the former students cited MUN as the milestone that led to their understanding of how our complex world works politically and economically:

Model United Nations was a big part of my time at ISA...the event really helped me understand international politics on a much deeper level. (Participant 4)

Representing countries like China and Iran in MUN forced me to see the complexity of world affairs, and taught me to analyze situations holistically and to analyze bias. (Participant 6)

I loved learning about the ways in which other countries operate and make important decisions to better (or not) the people of their country and how that, in turn, effects their decisions to interact (or not) with other countries around the world. (Participant 27)

Students also keyed into the idea of a worldview that encompassed more than the United States. Those new worldviews also included how other countries or peoples view citizens of the United States. Students envisioned themselves through the eyes of others:

We were able to see things from a global perspective, rather than what we were used to seeing in our own "American tunnel vision." (Participant 8)

Model United Nations was, by far, the most memorable event for global awareness. We learned to know the views of the rest of the world on important issues. It was eye opening! (Participant 70)

I was able to see life beyond the [United States], and other peoples' struggles. (Participant 65)

ISA always challenged my worldview, and because of that, I always find ways to serve the local community, but also the global community. (Participant 47)

As a simulation, Model United Nations was most effective with former students consistently discussed how they were put into a situation of thinking outside the box. In the simulation, students must think and make decisions as someone from a country other than the United States concerning an issue of international importance. The recurring theme of "being in another's shoes" emerged as an important way of broadening global awareness:

Learning to put myself in other people's shoes to try and understand the cultural differences, as well as the things that make us all the similar. (Participant 69)

You had to pretend you were from the chosen country...It meant walking in their shoes. (Participant 32)

I was completely unfamiliar with global politics before this, and this gave me a pretty good overview of how countries interact with and affect one another. (Participant 48)

Academic travel. The evolution of the International School of the Americas included academic thematic travel experiences being introduced into each class level over time. The first trip to be incorporated into the curriculum was the sophomore trip to Zacatecas, Mexico, focusing on identity and culture, since Zacatecas, Mexico, and the home city of ISA, were settled by the same group of Catholic priests. The students studied the architecture and community development of Zacatecas and how that same community development translated to their hometown.

Going to Mexico in tenth grade...I loved seeing where the founders of _____ came from. It gave me a great understanding of the city I grew up in. (Participant 47)

The trip to Zacatecas is always the event I go back to that created a 'small world' mentality. It was hours away, but there were so many similarities to the city I grew up in. It changed the way I looked at the world. I look for similarities instead of differences. It caused me to look further into world events to understand why they happen. (Participant 58)

Many former ISA students had never traveled to Mexico or any other international country prior to that experience. Margolis, Dacey, and Kenny (2007) pointed out that developmental diversity, which explored ethnic diversity as well, was rich and beneficial. Since the majority of the multicultural students were hometown natives or had lived there most of their lives, study participants were able to examine a broader identity through the Mexico travel experience. Most of the participants agreed that the Zacatecas trip opened their eyes to cultural inequalities between Mexico and the United States, even though they are neighboring countries, and even the disparities that existed in the Mexican culture itself.

The sophomore class trip to Zacatecas, Mexico...We experienced strong culture shock and were able to see what it might be like living outside of the [United States]. (Participant 13)

The sophomore trip to Zacatecas, Mexico, really opened my eyes to how culture can be so different and vibrant...It made me realize what things are easily taken for granted in the United States that are hard to come by in Mexico. (Participant 19)

Our lessons on culture and our trip to Zacatecas really opened my eyes to the many different ways of life people live. (Participant 66)

The Zacatecas trip. It was a total immersion into a way of life that was unlike our own. (Participant 74)

During our trip to Zacatecas, I was made aware of an indigenous population that were greatly neglected. (Participant 37)

The freshman academic trip to Heifer International, where sustainable development and environment issues were studied in Arkansas, as well, had a great impact on the participants. Here students experienced a simulation of life in a developing country, involving lessons in economics, culture, poverty, foreign trade, and hardship conditions. Although the simulation lasted only 3 days, the experience placed students in that situation where they were in someone else's shoes.

I feel the trip to Heifer International was a major event that led to my learning of my global awareness. I was able to learn what other countries go through trying to get basic things they need to live. (Participant 41)

I felt as though the [Heifer] trip helped open our naïve minds to what the rest of the world was like. It was the perfect timing in our lives to be exposed to what other countries and cultures face, because we were at a stage in our life where we didn't necessarily have a set mindset of who we were; we were still able to be molded into a different, better person. (Participant 49)

In the junior year, some of the participants traveled to Alabama, studying the Civil Rights Movement in the United States as a gateway to learning about global civil disobedience. In the United States, many students believe that civil rights is something that happened in our country a long time ago, and they do not see it as a universal issue. This trip brought the issue of civil rights home and connected it to the world.

The Alabama trip my junior year! Even though it was a domestic trip, the notion of collective struggle is present all around the world, and always will be, whether it be on issues of class, gender, or race. (Participant 14)

It is evident the academic travel experiences created global awareness and a new way of thinking for the study participants.

Classroom experiences. Several participants recounted classroom lessons remembered long after graduation as broadening global awareness. As Gaudelli (2003) pointed out, critical thinking and participatory teaching methods were as important as globally minded teachers. Teachers at ISA seemed to create positive global studies lessons that created a situation where student perceptions were changed. Students were challenged on their ways of seeing the world, which led to a broader worldview.

In freshman world geography, we were told to peel an orange in one piece and then to flatten it as a map in 2D. This showed how distorted our perceptions of the world can be. (Participant 35)

Mr._____ gave a presentation using food as an eye opener to what other kids were eating around the world. In some cases, it was all those kids were eating all day. Sure, it was something I'd have known about before, but this moment really got the message across and had a lasting impact on me. (Participant 17)

Other important classroom lessons were simulations, including the Olympic Project,

Freshmen year, we all did a project called the Olympic Project, where we came up with a presentation promoting our assigned country to a panel of judges trying to convince them to hold the event in our country, (Participant 24) and the Global Environmental Project,

Global Environmental Project has always stuck with me. Having to take a position and present to our peers and teachers made students take it seriously. Since students were also talking about it with class-mates in and out of the classroom, GEP became more than a project, but something students actually became interested in. (Participant 29)

Those simulations required students to identify with a culture or country other than the United States and to represent that culture's or country's views in the classroom lesson. That kind of critical thinking and classroom curriculum appeared to play an essential part in promoting the global awareness of students.

Question two: what impact do you think your increased global awareness from your education at ISA has had on your life since graduation? The purpose of this question was to ascertain the impact of global studies on the participants' choices after high school. Previous researchers have written consistently that educators need to prepare our young people for globalization and dealing with the 21st century (Asia Society, 2007, Mansilla & Jackson, 2011; Roberts, 2007; Scott, 2005). I investigated the impact of global studies education on the adult life of the participants.

The data analysis revealed three central themes of how increased global awareness from attending ISA had impacted adult life and decisions after graduation. The four major themes included developing cultural understanding and tolerance, being better equipped for college and professional life, a desire to travel and/or study abroad, and igniting a desire to be politically active and aware locally and globally.

Cultural understanding and tolerance. A common thread throughout the data included cultural understanding and tolerance of others. It was Hanvey (1976) who said the "emergence of a global cognition" (p. 38) would create young people who made choices based on a broader worldview. Decisions and choices of participants were expressed by some in very personal terms. The participants understood how the world was connected and the effect it had had on their worldview.

Taught me to have a bigger worldview. We are all connected, and we need to help each other. (Participant 2)

I think ISA has made me a more tolerant and accepting person. Without having to look at the world critically and understand many social issues, I would be a lot more close minded. (Participant 10)

Having increased global awareness has made more me empathetic to other people that have different cultures and religions...I see the impact of lack of global awareness, not only in my students, but also with my coworkers, and it scares me that not everyone is as blessed as I was to learn at ISA. (Participant 15)

I am more thoughtful in my discussions and the way that I treat others around me...I feel I can still make objective observations about communities and societies. (Participant 28)

Not all issues are black and white. (Participant 30)

My increased global awareness informs the way I think, how I process information, and with what assumptions and biases. (Participant 35)

I tend to think in big picture terms now, so with this global awareness, I find myself consciously trying to figure out how my actions affect others around me, and how the actions of others affect me on both a global and local scale. (Participant 48)

Other participants expressed the ideas of tolerance and cultural understanding in a more general way, referring to societies as a whole.

I am more apt to embrace cultures for their uniqueness than judge them because they are not like me. (Participant 22)

I now not only respect the differences, but also appreciate the differences, and enjoy getting to know others from around the world. (Participant 25)

I'm more open to the idea that the way other people in the world live is valuable, and just because we're different does [not] mean we're better or worse than others. (Participant 31)

Cultural understanding and tolerance seemed to lead young people to create lives reflective of a broad worldview and way of thinking.

Better equipped for college and/or professional life. It seemed evident that ISA created an "education for responsible participation in an interdependent global society" (Anderson & Anderson, 1979, p. 3). Some participants of the study had entered the work world. The broad spectrums of careers represented by participants were police, military, international consulting, teaching, business, and research. Some alumni chose a career directly because of involvement at ISA, or noted that a globally-focused curriculum still assisted them in their work choices.

I majored in anthropology in college, with a specialization in medical and cultural anthropology. Understanding how different people from different cultures view issues of health and wellness affects me every day as I work with individuals with disabilities and their families...ISA helped me develop the early stages of my cultural understanding and emphasized the importance of broadening my understanding in this area. (Participant 1)

I learned that I am not just a citizen of the United States, but a citizen of the world...I learned how to respect and be friends with people from other cultures and nations through the many exchange students we had at ISA. I have taken these lessons with me through my college career, the Peace Corps, and my professional career. (Participant 71)

As a cop, I see people from all walks of life and have a better understanding of what makes them tick. (Participant 12)

My internship at the Esperanza Peace and Justice Center my senior year helped me see the beauty of community organizing and grassroots building. Since I graduated from ISA, I've been very involved in grassroots efforts around immigration issues in San Antonio, Boston, and when I studied abroad in Chile. (Participant 33)

It has made me a better leader in the sense that I am aware of current events, past world events, and can use this knowledge to better plan for my troops. (Participant 38)

As a current teacher, I try to incorporate global issues into my curriculum to enhance the learning experiences of my students, and I feel compelled to grant them the same ownership I had in my education. (Participant 63)

I am far more open and understanding of our customers' and suppliers' varying cultural backgrounds and needs. (Participant 64)

ISA set the stage for what has become a life as a global citizen...now I speak nearly 12 languages with very high levels of fluency. I have worked at the top consultancies and attended the world's finest universities, Harvard and Oxford, but nothing prepared me for the outside world like ISA...all of it was critical in making me the person I am today. (Participant 67)

Because I am more attuned to global and cultural differences, this has helped me in my career to think about how my research results may differ for different groups or countries of people. (Participant 74)

The influence of a global studies curriculum in high school seemed to impact the choices and decisions of the participants as professionals aware of how global and cultural issues fit into their career paths.

Desire to travel and/or study abroad. Some participants shared how they were inspired to study abroad after graduation from ISA, and while attending university or college. And others had traveled to work and sought an understanding of the cultural history of places.

I have no doubt that ISA played a large role in my massively global education and experiences...I have traveled to every continent (besides Antarctica) and continue to live, work, and study outside of the United States. Compared with many others I have met, I have to say that my education at ISA was unique in all the right ways. (Participant 39)

The global perspective of ISA has led me to discover a world of different cultures...[and] to pursue a study abroad program in Germany as well. (Participant 50)

I am known to be world traveler now...ISA prepared me for college and the world. (Participant 68)

It's made me see traveling to foreign countries in a different way. I've returned to Mexico several times, and always use that trip [Sophomore Zacatecas trip] as a benchmark. (Participant 71)

I studied abroad in China, an experience that changed my life. I am happy I went to ISA. (Participant 46)

A byproduct of a global studies curriculum appeared to be the aspiration to travel or study abroad.

Being politically active and/or aware locally and globally. Torney-Purta's (1989, 2001) research outcome suggested that reading international news in newspapers created globally aware students. Not many high school students read a newspaper today; however, the participants were exposed to current events and their impact on the world through classroom curriculum, internet research, Model United Nations, and academic travel. Some participants revealed how they continued to be very interested in what goes on politically in the world on a global basis.

I think I am more interested in the news of other countries. (Participant 3)

I feel more comfortable discussing current events in general. (Participant 6)

I'm more aware of what goes on in the world and I can't stop reading the news. (Participant 17)

As I learn about new events and try to form an opinion, I think beyond the context of the US and include the global community. (Participant 26)

I believe we have to be active participants in the global community, to know where [the United States] stand on current foreign policy, and understand our economic relationship with other countries. (Participant 33)

I believe I had become more politically aware, and also generally more interested in issues around the world. (Participant 45)

I certainly have a thirst to understand other cultures, political systems, and beliefs of people across the globe. (Participant 73)

ISA seemed to inspire students to be more connected globally and actively involved in the political world.

In-Depth Participant Interviews

Part III of the International School of the Americas Graduate Questionnaire asked participants if they would be willing to be interviewed for the study. As Marshall and Rossman (2006) said, the interview helped the researcher "delve into the complexities and process" of participants (pp. 98–103), and as Torney-Purta (1986) pointed out, it was the advantage of a qualitative model. Sixty-four participants out of 86 were willing to be interviewed. It was my goal to interview at least one representative from each graduate year from 2001 through 2011. Out of 27 alumni contacted for an interview, 12 responded. Each graduate year was represented, except 2010. The only 2010 alumni who participated in the study did not respond to the interview request.

Four major themes emerged from the in-depth interviews: Nonprofit Work and Volunteerism beyond ISA, Global Awareness and Life beyond ISA, Confidence and Critical Thinking, and Academic Curriculum and Academic Travel. In the following paragraphs, each theme is explored through participant response.

Nonprofit work and volunteerism beyond ISA. As Davies (2006) pointed out, one of the factors of global citizen education was "the experience of doing some form of community service," which is a path that ISA encourages (p. 17). ISA graduates are required to complete 120 hours of community service throughout their four years. For many study participants, volunteerism had continued into their lives after ISA. A number of students participating in the study related their experiences in the nonprofit sector of society. Some of the participants were strictly volunteers, working at a nonprofit during their college or university study, while others completed volunteer internships with a nonprofit organization.

So starting with my internship at ISA with the Esperanza Peace and Justice Center, I got introduced to immigrant rights, and then here in Boston, I found a group called the Student Immigrant Movement... then when I was a grad in Chile last year, I decided to intern with an organization called Collective Without Borders. (Participant 29)

[2-year] career in the Peace Corp...whenever I get the chance, I try to do grant writing for other non-profits. (Participant 18)

In college I worked for a bunch of nonprofits...I figure I have a lot of the artistic background, but I need the business savvy to be able to run a theatre or an arts nonprofit. (Participant 94)

Other participants who had volunteered while in high school and college went on to make nonprofit work a career.

Since I graduated from college, I've been working for a nonprofit... called the Presbyterian Border Ministry, and I'm their only [United States] employee. (Participant 97)

I literally got hired at the USO strictly because of all the event planning I have done, and then slowly but surely, I got a promotion, which launched me to the career I have today. So, I definitely owe that background I started at ISA...I work for another nonprofit. It's a partner with the USO, called the Comfort Crew for Military Kids. (Participant 35)

Community service seemed to have become an integral part of the participants' adult lives.

Global awareness and life beyond ISA. In the interviews, the meaning of global awareness emerged for several participants. The complex connection between global and local, as Ziebertz and Kay (2009) pointed out, had been revealed by attending ISA for participants. Phinney (2008) also contended that with a global studies education, students would see themselves as larger in the world. Questions about how global awareness affected their lives now as young adults rendered responses about how global issues and local issues were tied together.

It helped me to be aware of a world beyond _____. A world beyond _____, and it helped me to feel like I was a part of the rest of the world that was beyond my circle and to be interested in...what was going on and to understand that it affected my life as well. (Participant 97)

Kind of thinking about how poverty and the economy and all these issues would impact education and also literature. That is sort of one thing that I think started at ISA and grew over time, you know, about how things going on in the world sort of impact things on a smaller level. (Participant 77)

To be interested in what was going on and to understand that it affected my life as well. (Participant 97)

Some participants discussed how global concepts learned at ISA had led them in their current career.

ISA was really good about accepting people for who they were. I think dealing with people is one of the biggest jobs you need to have going into the real world. (Participant 49)

I'm working for an ethical company. I don't think I truly would understand that if I hadn't done that Model UN project. (Participant 46)

I was really interested in...being a global citizen...and then transitioned into wanting to do grant writing. (Participant 4)

I deal with confrontation all the time, and I guess global awareness is all about confrontation, because it's so many different ideals and life styles coming together. (Participant 75)

ISA really kind of brought me into a more real world practical kind of application for those things, so that kind of...I guess, that was when my interest in sociology really started, was of drawing me out of this abstract, and drawing me into a more concrete application. (Participant 77)

The idea of having a broader cultural view of the world and how it affected their lives emerged from others.

I started becoming more aware of the differences between us, and then I guess you could say, and...I think that it kind of helps me come to terms with my identity to who I am...it helps me appreciate other cultures a little bit more...I can take a look at the subtle differences and just appreciate the small things. (Participant 28)

I can see where not having attended a place like ISA and having a much more narrow view of culture and society...ISA sort of pads you to understand that it's going to be different wherever you go, and be ready for it, and be ready to accept it, because there's good that can come out of it. Don't freak out. (Participant 94)

You know, do we [United States] need to be in that country...do we need to really help shape it differently, or is it something what we are imposing on them? I think a lot of times I don't jump to the conclusion that whatever we are doing is the correct way of doing something. I think that was stemmed a lot from my time at ISA, just because it was so community based. (Participant 46)

It appeared that the ISA graduates had revealed their education was, as Becker (1979) wrote, "[an] education for responsible participation in an interdependent global society" (p. 40)

Confidence and critical thinking. Many participants spoke of the impact of curriculum and the teachers at ISA. Marshall (2007) declared that teaching critical thinking skills was important in a global studies curriculum. Along with critical thinking comes confidence in thinking resulting in the confidence as students to become involved in their own education. Many participants related how teachers encouraged independent and critical thinking.

I would say, yes, in the beginning, definitely, that I felt that I went into the [college or university] classes I had a confidence that other freshmen and sophomores, depending on the class...but because I have the experience at ISA, I feel like, yeah, I felt like I knew more. (Participant 97)

Confidence in my own opinion, because I feel like all of the classes that I had there [ISA] really encouraged me to think for myself. (Participant 77) I feel like my teachers, despite of the fact that I was a teenager, never told me or made me feel like something that I wanted to do wasn't possible. And like that sort of trust just inspired me to look at school differently. (Participant 4)

It was very fast paced...but it was fast paced with a purpose, which obviously you guys [teachers and staff] at ISA were always teaching us to do things with a purpose. (Participant 35)

I guess I didn't know how ISA had shaped me until I was halfway through college. You know, it's kind of hard to explain, but I remember my first English class in college, and we were discussing poetry, and this is, oh, this is just everyday life [for me], but the kids in the class were like...they didn't know how to talk about poetry. It's just like things like that, that you guys [ISA teachers] did for us that made us all better people. (Participant 35)

Well one thing for sure was confidence in my own opinion, because I feel like all of the classes that I had there [ISA] really encouraged me to think for myself. (Participant 77)

I entered an ISA classroom where the teacher became a facilitator. (Participant 55)

That confidence also led participants to have increased critical thinking skills beyond high school. Those critical thinking skills had served them well into adulthood.

Ah...you know, I'd say, yes, it probably opened me up to being a little more critical of everything. I think because I was exposed to so much [that] 'why' became a more common word in my grammar, I guess. You know, I started to question a lot of things of why is this, like, what causes that. (Participant 28)

Just being forced to be out of my comfort zone, arguing against my own ideas, and things like that. So those were a lot of specific examples, and so that just, I think, kind of snowballed and made me into a more critical thinker since ISA. (Participant 55)

I genuinely believe the only reason why I'm sitting here right now is because I went to ISA, and that whole mission as approaching education outside of the box sort of inspired me to be an archeologist. (Participant 4) I guess I can pinpoint a lot of my understanding on ethics, I guess I would say. The root from it, or I guess the seed that was planted, was at ISA, because I think, you know, a lot of times it was why, why do we do this, not is it right or is it wrong, but why. (Participant 46)

Academic curriculum and academic travel. Some participants discussed in detail about certain academic classroom or academic travel experiences and what lessons they took with them from ISA.

End of the semester with economics, and we were given some countries, and we were told, like, to help people. And that was it. It was help people use economics, and here's your country. We did a lot of research, and it was really cool to take that, take economics to such a higher degree, you know, and it literally felt like every meeting we had with the team...It felt like a business meeting. It just felt so real world. (Participant 49)

I think that was one thing that ISA really did was to help me draw all these connections to experiences that I had had in the past and make them bigger...ISA really kind of brought me into a more real world practical kind of application. (Participant 77)

And then, back in high school, that was like my thing,....I listened to certain bands...to see what they were talking about, and I think, you know,...that combined with ISA, you know, the mock election and...we looked at...immigration into the United States,...the depression...it just complimented that sense of urgency that I heard in my music, and it showed me, I guess, a few different ways that change can happen, beyond just, you know, writing a song about it...You know, we took a trip down to Mexico the sophomore year. That was my first real...the first time I was really faced with poverty. (Participant 28)

A commitment to introduce interdisciplinary projects, because we hadthat project that was both English and history final projects, and you had to analyze books from a historical perspective and talk about how history influenced them. I remember how to do that...And things like Ellis Island Immigration Simulation. (Participant 77)

I remember World Geography the freshman year with_____. And we peeled an orange and did that world map thing, the projection, and that just highlights for me the distortion that we face when we are trying to learn about the world and not just a map, but in any sort of situation, the distortion that happens when you are talking internationally, and you're trying to understand places far from you. (Participant 55)

But I really enjoyed the trip to Alabama. I think that was very significant for...like now that I reflect on it. Reflection! But, I really enjoyed that. It gave me a perspective for...civil rights and people, like, coming together for like a cause. (Participant 29)

I ended up doing classics, and I think a lot of it is because we had to read so much in ISA, and we had to read things that were challenging, like, or like, we had the option to read things that were challenging, like my senior year I read Ulysses and The Sound of the Fury. (Participant 4)

That [curriculum] innovation is what made a lot of us, me personally, interested in getting a PhD or really pursuing academics, not as a chore, not something you have to do, but something that I really love. (Participant 4)

I mean, you can go to a museum, you can go read about other cultures, but until you are actually doing what that culture does, I don't think you actually have an understanding, so that's what it [ISA curriculum] did for me. (Participant 75)

These participant quotations from the questionnaire and in-depth interviews represented the impact of a global studies curriculum following the ISA alumni into their adult lives. The participants' global studies had resulted in career choices, deeper critical thinking about the way the world works, the part they each played in this world, and how they had used their voices in adult life.

Discussion

In his *TED* talk, published on May 8, 2013, Geoffrey Canada, head of Harlem Children's Zone, asked, "Why is it that when we had rotary phones, when we were having folks being crippled by polio, that we were teaching the same way then that we're doing right now?" If we apply this same challenge to the idea of global studies education, which has been written about and tested since the Victorian Era, the question is the same: Why are educators still teaching the same conventional way? If past research has shown the importance of a global studies education, then why are we not practicing it more? What has been missing is definitive research providing an answer to the outcome of a global studies education. With this research, part of that gap has been filled.

This research case study provides an impact assessment of a global studies curriculum on graduates from the International School of the Americas, a public high school. Past educators and researchers have proposed the benefits of a global studies education as a broadening worldview, encouraging global citizenship in the world, and creating a way to meet the challenges of a global economy (Jackson, 2004, 2008; Roberts, 2007). Research depicting the influence of a global studies education on students, however, has been slow in coming. Davies (2006) called for a backwards mapping of students who had benefitted from a global studies secondary education to evaluate the impact through students (p. 23). Davies's challenge of backwards mapping inspired this research.

When asked what memorable event, classroom lesson, or experience while a student at ISA, the study participants, by and large, referred to Model United Nations as an experience that opened their minds globally, along with the academic travel. Model United Nations provided a goal that was "*authentic* in terms of the content area" (Gibson et al., p. 14). Academic travel experiences that placed students out of their comfort zone in another culture had the greatest impact. Classroom lessons were also cited as experiences that created global awareness, but several different lessons were cited by several participants. Lessons that involved students adopting a point of view foreign to their own, "a cultural contrast," and using that point of view in a given classroom task had the greatest impact (Gibson et al., p. 13).

I was able to gain a perspective and respect for other cultures and religions that I didn't have before. (Participant 5)

I learned to look at the history of the world in a more objective way, rather than through the lens of a "Westerner." (Participant 28)

Global awareness permeated the ISA experience in the classroom, during travel experiences, and at whole school events, producing "knowledge of globalization and the resulting issues and problems that affect everyone's lives" (Gibson et al., p. 15).

If I have learned anything from my time at ISA, it is that we need to be active participants in both local and global communities. (Participant 33)

Participants were emphatic as to the positive impact of their learning experience at the International School of the Americas.

Most participants felt they were more prepared for the college or university setting than their peers:

And so, for me, that was something that really helped me, and when I got to college I was a lot more willing to give my opinions in classrooms and argue over literature history and ask questions, and I don't think I would have been as willing to if ISA hadn't given me that big difference. So, and I've gotten more confident over the years. That really started at ISA. (Participant 77)

Global learning skills "require numerous critical thinking skills in order to generate possible solutions [and] make decisions" (Gibson et al., 2008, p. 17). Some participants said the importance of global studies curriculum had continued to make a difference in their professional lives.

Introduction to Heifer and other nonprofits likely led fairly directly to my current employment with Heifer International. (Participant 16)

I majored in international relations directly as a result of my attending ISA. (Participant 46)

This research seemed to confirm that "global learning provides opportunities that nurture a global consciousness and develop knowledge, skills, and attitudes necessary to be an effective world citizen" (Gibson et al., 2008, p. 18).

CONCLUSION

A summation of research regarding a global studies education and curriculum includes the following premises:

- A globalized curriculum uses globalization as the backdrop to lesson plans and learning objectives across the broad spectrum of the typical high school curriculum, including math, science, humanities, social studies, art, sports, and language arts.
- A global studies school is a school that espouses a globalized curriculum that encourages students to become global citizens, provides global problem solving skills, creates a global consciousness among young people, shapes ways of global conflict resolution for the future, and generates a global workforce.

These premises are evident in ISA and its graduates. ISA graduates consistently expressed increasing global awareness resulting from curriculum, academic travel, and school-wide events, such as Model United Nations. That global awareness resulted in life choices, including serving in the Peace Corps; careers including international travel; college or university choices, including majors with international components and study abroad experiences; careers involving international nonprofits and community service, along with volunteerism; a belief in citizenship locally and globally; and a desire to continue learning about the world economically and politically. These young people are prepared for a global workplace.

Aerts et al. (1994) indicated that young people need a worldview. The theory of Aerts et al., taken with Erikson's adolescent identity (12–18 years old) theory of donning and casting off identities, revealed the time to incorporate a global identity and a global worldview was during the years of secondary education.

Our trip to Mexico sophomore year was particularly memorable. It was my first major exposure to a completely foreign culture. Experiencing different ways commerce takes place, in contrast to what I was used to, was particularly interesting. It was also a great bonding experience with my friends at the time and put me in a position where I was compelled to interact with members of my class I never communicated with otherwise. So it also broadened my ability to socialize and relate to people outside my "clique," which was valuable at the age. (Participant 34)

Our trip to Heifer International [freshman year]…It was perfect timing in our lives to be exposed to what other countries and cultures face, because we were at a stage in our life where we didn't necessarily have a…mindset of who we were, were still able to be molded. (Participant 49)

The secondary educational years are key to the development of identity and worldview, as indicated by research and by the participants of this study. McCabe (1997) said, "We first have to identify where students are…and then create educational experiences that can move them forward towards an enhanced global perspective" (p. 45). ISA seems to be effective in creating educational experiences for students that foster a global perspective that becomes intrinsic in student lives who will live in a globally interdependent society.

Mansilla and Gardner suggested the efficient assessment of global education was to study "young individuals of demonstrated global consciousness," such as those working for international nongovernmental organizations (NGOs) (2007, Chapter 1, para. 51). Some ISA graduates work or have worked for international NGOs. While working with an international NGO is applauded, most American young people do not follow this path. An empirical study of young people who have worked internationally for an NGO seems rather narrow. Most American young people will live in the United States most of their lives. It would be more common for an American young person to work in a diverse population in the United States, rather than to work internationally. It is also possible for many American young people to never experience international travel in the course of their life. Many of the study participants have chosen to study and work in the United States. This does not mean they are immune to a global mindset:

I was actually explaining to somebody the other night something I learned in one of my classes at ISA… for somebody in my situation, you know, a white officer living on the outskirts of _____, it would be a culture shock, but I've been on the Civil Rights trip and thanks a lot. (Participant 75)

It is this global mindset that can create effectiveness in the workplace (McCabe, 1997). It is this global mindset than can shape global conflict resolution. It is this global mindset that can create solutions to global problems.

It must be acknowledged that it was impossible to conduct a large-scale study of global studies schools and graduates of such a school. As the studies of Gaudelli (2003) revealed, global studies programs were not always equal. To make this study feasible, it was necessary to conduct it as a case study. This study was unique to the case and cannot be construed as a performance indicator for all global studies schools. However, this research revealed a global studies school that is effective in its mission of creating young people with a global consciousness.

This study revealed the outcome of one public high school global studies program that can be implemented at the secondary education level. Since participants in the ISA questionnaire and in-depth interviews spanned a 12-year period of time, not all participants had the same educational experience at

ISA. Education is an organic experience; change is inevitable. There were staff and leadership changes, academic evolution refining the global studies component of the curriculum, integration of academic travel, and the school moved to a new location on the same campus in school year 2007–2008. Even with those changes over time, the participants consistently cited positive outcomes of a global studies program and its impact on life after high school. Several study participants found it hard to pinpoint one individual experience as the key to global awareness, but described their ISA experience as a *total immersion* of global awareness during their years at ISA:

It's hard to pinpoint one major experience…The goal of becoming globally aware was so entrenched in the overall goal of ISA, that it happened in almost every class and experience. (Participant 75)

Rather than one specific event, it was the summation of world events, culture, and experiences being incorporated into daily activities that stuck with me most. It was a constant point of discussion and awareness that shaped how I think about my community and my world. (Participant 1)

Those two participants encompassed the purpose of this global studies school in their description of what happened at ISA to broaden their global awareness. At The International School of the Americas, the global studies emphasis girds the entire educational process of the school.

REFERENCES

Aerts, D., Apostel, L., De Moor, B., Hellemans, S., Maex, E., Van Belle, H., & Van der Veken, J. (Eds.). (1994). Worldviews from fragmentation to integration. Brussels: VUB Press. Retrieved from http://pespmc1.vub.ac.be/clea/reports/worldviewsbook.html

Allison, B., & Rehm, B. L. (2007). Effective teaching strategies for middle school learners in multicultural, multilingual classrooms. *Middle School Journal*, *39*(2), 12–18. doi:10.1080/00940771.2007.11461619

Anderson, L., & Anderson, C. (1979). A visit to Middleston's world-centered schools: A scenario. In J. Becker (Ed.), *Schooling for a Global Age* (pp. 3–30). New York, NY: McGraw-Hill.

Asia Society. (2007). Learning in a global age: Knowledge and skills for a flat world. New York: Author.

Azmitia, M., Syed, M., & Radmacher, K. (2008). On the intersection of personal and social identities: Introduction and evidence from a longitudinal study of emerging adults. *New Directions for Child and Adolescent Development*, *120*(120), 1–6. doi:10.1002/cd.212 PMID:18521867

Becker, J. M. (Ed.). (1979). *Schooling for a global age*. New York, NY: McGraw-Hill.

Boyer, M. A., Brown, S. W., Butler, M. J., Niv-Solomon, A., Urlacher, B., Hudson, N., & Lima, C. O. et al. (2007). Experimenting with global governance: Understanding the potential for generational change. *Globalisation, Societies and Education*, *5*(2), 153–180. doi:10.1080/14767720701425727

Canada, G. (2013, May 8). Our failing schools: Enough is enough! *TED Talk*. Retrieved from http://www.youtube.com/watch?v=vY2l2xfDBcE

Cook, S. A. (2008). Give peace a chance: The diminution of peace in global education in the United States, United Kingdom and Canada. *Canadian Journal of Education, 31*(4), 889–914. Retrieved from http://files.eric.ed.gov/fulltext/EJ830504.pdf

Cornbleth, C. (2003). *Hearing America's youth: Social identities in uncertain times*. New York, NY: Peter Lang.

Creswell, J. W. (2005). *Educational research: Planning, conducting, and evaluating quantitative and qualitative research* (2nd ed.). Upper Saddle River, NJ: Pearson Merrill Prentice Hall.

Dalhouse, D. W., & Dalhouse, A. D. (2006). Investigating white preservice teachers' beliefs about teaching in culturally diverse classrooms. *Negro Educational Review, 57*, 69–84. Retrieved from http://www.oma.osu.edu/vice_provost/ner/index.html

Davies, I., Evans, M., & Reid, A. (2005). Globalising citizenship education? A critique of "global education" and "citizenship education". *British Journal of Educational Studies, 53*(1), 66–89. doi:10.1111/j.1467-8527.2005.00284.x

Davies, L. (2006). Global citizenship: Abstraction or framework for action? *Educational Review, 58*(1), 5–25. doi:10.1080/00131910500352523

Erikson, E. (1968). *Identity, Youth and Crisis*. New York, NY: W. W. Norton.

Frey, C. J., & Whitehead, D. M. (2009). International education policies and the boundaries of global citizenship in the US. *Journal of Curriculum Studies, 41*(2), 269–290. doi:10.1080/00220270802509730

Gaudelli, W. (2003). *World class: Teaching and learning in global times*. Retrieved from http://www.amazon.com/

Gibson, K. L., Rimmington, G. M., & Landwehr-Brown, M. (2008). Developing global awareness and responsible world citizenship with global learning. *Roeper Review, 30*(1), 11–23. doi:10.1080/02783190701836270

Hanvey, R. G. (1976). An attainable global perspective. *The American Forum for Global Education*. Retrieved from http://www.globaled.org

Hayden, M., Thompson, J., & Walker, G. (Eds.). (2002). *International education in practice: Dimensions for national and international schools*. Retrieved from http://www.Amazon.com

Jackson, A. (2004, November). Preparing urban youths to succeed in the interconnected world of the 21st century. *Phi Delta Kappan, 86*(3), 210–213. Retrieved from http://www.kappanmagazine.org/content/86/3/210

Jackson, A. (2008, May). High schools in the global age. *Educational Leadership, 65*(8), 58–62. Retrieved from http://www.ascd.org/publications/educationalleadership/may08/vol65/num08/High-Schools-in-the-Global-Age.aspx

Jensen, L. A. (2003). Coming of age in a multicultural world: Globalization and adolescent cultural identity formation. *Applied Developmental Science, 7*(3), 189–196. doi:10.1207/S1532480XADS0703_10

Mansilla, V. B., & Gardner, H. (2007). From teaching globalization to nurturing global consciousness. In M. M. Suarez-Orozco (Ed.), *Learning in the global era: International perspectives on globalization and education*. Berkeley: University of California Press. doi:10.1525/california/9780520254343.003.0002

Mansilla, V. B., & Jackson, A. (2011). *Educating for global competence: Preparing our youth to engage the world*. New York, NY: Asia Society.

Margolis, D., Dacey, J., & Kenny, M. (2007). *Adolescent development* (4th ed.). Mason, OH: Thomson.

Marshall, C., & Rossman, G. B. (2006). *Designing qualitative research* (4th ed.). Thousand Oaks, CA: Sage.

Marshall, H. (2007). Global education in perspective: Fostering global dimension in an English secondary school. *Cambridge Journal of Education*, *37*(3), 355–374. doi:10.1080/03057640701546672

McCabe, L. T. (1997). Global perspective development. *Education*, *118*(1), 41–46.

McLuhan, M. (1964). Understanding Media: The extensions of man. Cambridge, MA: MIT Press.

Merriam, S. B. (2001). *Qualitative research and case study applications in education: Revised and expanded from case study research in education*. San Francisco, CA: Jossey-Bass.

Oxfam. (2006). *Education for global citizenship: A guide for schools*. Retrieved July 30, 2011, from http://www.oxfam.org.uk/education/gc/files/education_for_global_citizenship_a_guide_for_schools.pdf

Phinney, J. S. (2008). Bridging identities and disciplines: Advances and challenges in understanding multiple identities. *New Directions for Child and Adolescent Development*, *2008*(120), 97–109. doi:10.1002/cd.218 PMID:18521863

Roberts, A. (2007, Winter). Global dimensions of schooling: Implications for internationalizing teacher education. *Teacher Education Quarterly*, 9–26. Retrieved from http://files.eric.ed.gov/fulltext/EJ795137.pdf

Sanchez, P. (2007). Urban immigrant students: How transnationalism shapes their world learning. *The Urban Review*, *39*(5), 489–517. doi:10.1007/s11256-007-0064-8

Schram, T. H. (2006). *Conceptualizing and proposing qualitative research* (2nd ed.). Upper Saddle River, NJ: Pearson.

Scott, R. A. (2005, Winter). Many calls, little action: Global illiteracy in the United States. *The Presidency*, 18–23. Retrieved from http://web.a.ebscohost.com.uiwtx.idm.oclc.org/ehost/pdfviewer/pdfviewer?vid=13&sid=0af845c8-1aaf-4546-a955-5d98456b18da%40sessionmgr4001&hid=4112

Seidman, I. (2006). *Interviewing as qualitative research: A guide for researchers in education and the social sciences* (3rd ed.). New York, NY: Teachers College Press.

Tatum, B. D. (1999). *"Why are all the black kids sitting together in the cafeteria?" and other conversations about race*. New York, NY: Basic Books.

Torney-Purta, J. (1986). *Predictors of global awareness and concern among secondary school students*. Columbus, OH: Citizen Development and Global Education Program.

Torney-Purta, J. (1989, March). *A research agenda for the study of global/international education in the United States.* Paper presented at the Annual Meeting of the American Educational Research Association, San Francisco, CA.

Torney-Purta, J. (2001). The global awareness survey: Implications for teacher education. *Theory into Practice, 21*(3), 200–205. doi:10.1080/00405848209543006

Tye, K. A. (2003, October). Global education as a worldwide movement. *Phi Delta Kappan, 85*(2), 165–168. doi:10.1177/003172170308500212

Webber, C. F., & Robertson, J. M. (2004). Internationalization and educators understanding of issues in educational leadership. *The Educational Forum, 68*(3), 264–275. doi:10.1080/00131720408984638

Whitfield, P., Klug, B. J., & Whitney, P. (2007). "Situative cognition" barrier to teaching across cultures. *Intercultural Education, 18*(3), 25. doi:10.1080/14675980701463604

Wray-Lake, L., Flanagan, C. A., & Osgood, D. W. (2008). Examining trends in adolescent environmental attitudes, beliefs, and behaviors across three decades. *Environment and Behavior, 42*(1), 61–85. doi:10.1177/0013916509335163 PMID:20046859

Ziebertz, H., & Kay, W. K. (2009). A key to the future: The attitudes and values of adolescent Europeans. *Globalisation, Societies and Education, 7*(2), 151–165. doi:10.1080/14767720902908000

Chapter 20
The Transformation of Russian Business Education and Its Outcomes:
How Russia Moved Away from Marxism toward a Market Economy through Revitalized Business Education

Elise Kiregian
TCI, USA

ABSTRACT

This chapter looks at the transformation of Post-Soviet Russian business education. The extraordinary metamorphosis shapes the new generation of Russians profoundly. Russians are now far more likely to speak English, to hold personal investment portfolios and to be able to work outside of Russia in global businesses. The old-fashioned idea of central control of every aspect of life is largely gone as are business courses extolling the virtues of Marxism. Research shows the wide acceptance of western business concepts such as strategic planning and case analysis and the rapid growth of the Master of Business Administration (MBA) degree. One unexpected outcome is the rise of Russian women to management positions in Russian corporations.

Since the fall of the Soviet Union more than 2 decades ago, massive change has enveloped Russia and the other Newly Independent States. The disappearance of the all-powerful central government armed with its trumpeted five-year plans left the new Russia without the financial resources and social control that held the nation together for decades. While most historians looked at the obvious upheavals—the shift of political power across the world, the plight of the ruble, the fate of Russian military power, and the push and pull of the free market system on the national economy, more subtle and far-reaching changes were underway. This chapter derives from a doctoral dissertation (Kiregian, 2015) that traced the transformation of Russian education and business. The results are astounding.

DOI: 10.4018/978-1-5225-0522-8.ch020

Two decades into the new Russia, its citizens are far more likely to speak English, work in a service-related job, hold personal investment portfolios, and be able to work outside of the homeland. These are massive changes compared to the years before the early 1990s. What brought about the transformation? The government played no direct role in the change as its power and its purse had shrunk. There were no political movements or public demonstrations moving the nation in this direction. That approach would only work if there had been a powerful government to listen to the demonstrations and take action.

As Russia moved into a market economy, old approaches to commerce and the attitudes toward work that developed through decades of Communist rule fell away. The cult of physical labor supported by the all-powerful central government offered little comfort in the emerging economy that challenged Russia's companies to produce attractive goods and services that outperformed international competition. The long-insulated Russian economy lost its protection. The rivals became all other countries in the market economy. As Russia's military might and its foreboding government dwindled, so did its xenophobic protection of domestic industry. Excellent insights are provided by Lucas (2008); Puffer, McCarthy, and Naumov (2000), and Aslund (1995). (See also "Putin Forges Higher Education Cooperation Deal With EU" [2005], Kuznetsov [2000], McCarthy and Puffer [1993], and Canel and Oldenziel [2000]).

For Western observers, educational reform meant that the old assumptions about a controlled economy had to give way before the fledgling Russian economy could stand on its own two feet. Russia's economic progress during these tumultuous years derives from adoption of Western business practices. This view is widely supported—for example, in Lane's (1997) review of "Russian Society in Transition" (p. 727). (See also Dash [1998], the United Nations Children's Fund International Child Development Centre [1999], and the United Nations Educational, Scientific and Cultural Organization Institute for Statistics [n.d.].) This book Studies . . . the shift from communist societies to capitalism and focuses on the political change from authoritarianism to democracy (in the sense of voting for competitive parties) and economic transformation from central planning to markets based on exchange and production for profit. (Lane, 1997, p. 727)

Note the strong link between democratic reform and economic transformation. This chapter does not advocate reform but reports what actually took place in Russia during the early post-Communist period (see R. Daniels, 2007).

Consider the social turmoil caused by these changes. Older Russians fretted about economic security. Younger Russians found few opportunities for government-supported labor, which had sustained earlier generations. On top of these developments, the poor performance of the Russian economy in the decade after the fall of Communism cut into the ready internal markets Russian companies enjoyed in the years of government control and protection of the status quo. People simply had less money to spend. Westerners saw reports of breadlines but did not feel the pain of ordinary Russians struggling to make do on small salaries (see Cherednichenko [2012], R. Daniels [2007], and Rutland [1998]).

Historians will see a curious parallel to the conditions of the early 20th century that led to the collapse of the government and the birth of Communist power. One difference stands out. The Russian Revolution brought about the replacement of the czar by a powerful Communist system. In the early 19902, there was no violent overthrow—simply a big fizzle. A power vacuum replaced the central government. This is the main reason that the momentous changes that took place were viewed so tentatively by historians, especially those outside Russia. The breadlines and the falling ruble were seen by Westerners as unfortunate and probably temporary events. Without a bloody revolution, the national condition lacked the drama of the Bolsheviks and full-blown civil war of an earlier era.

OTHER INVESTIGATIONS OF THESE TRENDS

Whereas this chapter highlights the changes in business education, many historians have commented on changes in the Russian economy and others have studied changes in the educational system. For example, Medvedev's (2000)*Post-Soviet Russia: A Journey Through the Yeltsin Era* traces the development of capitalism in Russia. Many scholarly works took a broad perspective on the state of the nation and its overall economy. These include Gaidar's (2003)*The Economics of Transition*, which looks at institutional reforms, monetary policy, and the transformation of the economy. Aslund, Guriev, and Kuchins's (2010)*Russia After the Global Economic Crisis* details economic challenges including corruption and the need for reform. Many other factors were looked at by historians and prove significant in seeing the transformation of business education. Scholars such as Clark (2003) in *Changing Attitudes Toward Economic Reform During the Yeltsin Era* looked at social transformation in Russia (also, see Dezhneva [as cited in Taylor, Mechitov, & Moshkovich, 1996], Kitaev [1994], and Mechitov and Peper [1998]). Changes in public opinion, support for economic reform, and the emerging middle class present critical factors underpinning the transformation of Russian business education. In addition, the development of capitalism provides significant insight into Russia's journey toward a market economy. A keen observer of statistics in Russia, Shcherbakova (2008), in her article, "The Trend of Education in Russia," catalogued facts about the educational level of Russians (p. 26ff). From a historical perspective, such studies demonstrate the large-scale advances in educational opportunities for all Russians prior to the period of study in this chapter. Similarly, the growing middle class and its desire for personal wealth prove significant. Zagrebina (2013), in her article, "Mechanisms of Upward Mobility as Perceived by Students in an Institution of Higher Learning," presented evidence about how Russian students see graduate education as a road to upward mobility, one of the driving forces behind educational change in post-Soviet Russia (Remington, 2010; Zagrebina, 2013).

The generations in Russia offer sharp differences in their attitudes about labor and the role of women (Bek, 2004; Brah, 1992; Chirikova, 1998). The evidence shows opportunities opening for women. In addition, adherence to the centrality of labor as an economic concept is falling away. Studies in this vein include Hahn and Logvinenko's (2008) "Generational Differences in Russian Attitudes Towards Democracy and the Economy." Combined with the statistical information available, such reviews provide an interesting panorama. Scholars (Adams, Middleton, & Ziderman, 1992) have catalogued the shift from vocational education toward market economy skills. These include Holmes, Read, and Voskresenskaya (1995) in *Russian Education: Tradition and Transition*, which looks at educational administration including curriculum, finances, and teacher preparation. (See also Dudgeon [1975], Grunberg [2011], and Johanson [1987].) During the late Communist period, engineering and vocational studies held the high ground. Western-style business education was viewed with disdain.

Criticism often proves a change catalyst. Among the most outspoken critics of Russian education is Gershunsky (1993) in *Russia in Darkness: On Education and the Future*. His open letter to Boris Yeltsin took issue with educational conditions including overcrowding and other issues that stifled learning. The decline of vocational education and the shrinking finances brought increased attention to the education of children.

Social forces also promote change. The expansion of economic self-interest has been well documented. For example, in *The Informal Post-Socialist Economy*, Morris and Polese (2013) told the stories of individuals across Eastern Europe who expressed their own ideas about labor and wealth. These secondary sources and others provide a valuable backdrop for the advance of business curriculum and for its increasing value as Russia's economy moves forward.

A BUSINESS CURRICULUM FOR RUSSIA

The development of business curriculum proves illuminating. The master of business administration (MBA), a clear Western import, has advanced in terms of enrollment and acceptance in the last 2 decades. As one might expect, the earlier MBA programs in Russia focused on areas of widespread interest: finance and marketing, for example. As more programs opened and as these programs matured, the content and areas of specialty began to link more closely to Russian business needs. For example, EDHEC, an international school offering an MBA in Russia, includes a trip to South Africa. Russia sees itself as a leader among the well-known BRICS, originally Brazil, Russia, India, and China. Now, the added *S* stands for *South Africa*. Russia and South Africa share a number of economic characteristics including their storehouses of natural resources and their challenges in distributing wealth to their populations. Russia and South Africa also share a concern for *sustainable development*. Generally associated with third-world or emerging economies, this term spans economic, social, infrastructure, and other aspects of societies trying to ensure that they will be able to provide the basics for current and future generations.

In July 2014, the BRICS launched a $100 billion development bank as a possible rival to the International Monetary Fund and World Bank. While economic progress in the BRICS has slowed in 2015, especially in Russia, they hold large populations and many natural resources. Russia is clearly vying for a leadership role in this loose grouping of nations.

Russia's designs on the BRICS arrangement may be viewed in political terms. However, all of these nations are joined by sobering economic issues. They need to provide for their citizens and compete effectively in the market economy (Hayoz, Jesień, & Koleva, 2011; Jha, 2002; Kortunov, 2009). Although members of the group may like the idea of controlled economies, the free market approach is clearly the favored alternative. The free market calls for business concepts that work in its environment. Historians are well aware that the days of the five-year plans are over. This staple of previous Russian governments has faded; Russian businesses seek more effective tools to map future success. The expansion of strategic planning is indeed significant as younger Russians develop the skills used by major Western corporations and governments. As expected, strategic planning has moved strongly into the MBA curricula in wide use across Russia (see Evenko [2003], J. Evans [2011], and L. Daniels [1988]).

Strategic planning takes into account the actions of one's competitors and evaluates various choices that will bring success in the market. Business students must be challenged to think through how companies will react to changes in the market. Western MBA programs have long used case writing as an important learning technique. Students are challenged to solve complex problems faced by actual companies. The Harvard Business School publishes a series of such cases and all business textbooks include some form of case studies. The EDHEC curriculum also refers to *action learning*. They offer students an opportunity to look closely at this list of leading companies: Amadeus, Microsoft, Philips, Ericsson, HP, IBM, Oracle, Nestlé, Danone, France Telecom, L'Oréal, EDF Energy, Thales, and Google. Several U.S. giants appear on the list as well as leading European companies, with a slight preference for global French-based corporations. A British, German, or Italian university might select a different list. For the purpose of this study, these companies confirm that Russian MBAs resemble what students are learning across the free world. Looking backward at Russian business education in previous decades, the case method is new.

THE MOSCOW INTERNATIONAL HIGHER BUSINESS SCHOOL

Master of Business Administration Program

Moscow International Higher Business School (MIRBIS), with headquarters in Moscow, Russia, also operates a master of business administration (MBA) program. As with EDHEC, they offer various business specialties. Their website shows that the banking and investment management MBA is new. Such an MBA specialty would be a Western staple, but this provides evidence that banking and investing are on the rise as needed business functions in Russia. It also shows that business students are asking for the skills that resonate in the new Russian economy. (See Bickerstaffe [2009], International University of Fundamental Studies [n.d.], and St. Petersburg University [n.d.].)

These examples confirm that the metamorphosis underway is transforming Russia in many spheres. The particular focus of this chapter is the massive changes in education—specifically business education—and their unexpected outcomes. As the old economic system fell away, new skills came into play. Russia's large corporations in which the government continues to play a significant role depend more fully on customers and governments outside the motherland. Russia's immense natural resources continue to attract customers across Europe. The pipeline stretching more than 2,500 miles supplying oil to Europe stands as a symbol of Russia's viability in the market economy.

The increasing focus on international business drew Russia into a business environment that placed new demands on the workforce. As is the case in the West, Russia's giant corporations that oversee huge supplies of oil and gas must negotiate, make deals, concede various demands, provide customer service, and agree to supply goods and services in a timely, competent and cost-effective manner. These rules determine success in the market economy. The Russian oil and gas giant Gazprom, for example, has adopted the management skills valued by ExxonMobil, Shell, and other giant international energy corporations. Although Russia holds massive natural resources, so do other parts of the world. These resources take on real value when they are mined, sold, delivered, and used effectively. The winners emerge from a competitive environment.

The long-term success of the sale of Russian energy has found Russia's energy giants opening more offices outside Russia and looking on the open market for candidates with skills in planning, accounting, and managing. These are the skills that younger Russians are developing in the newer curricula that have swept across Russia in the last 2 decades.

Historians are aware that Russia's economy has long operated on two tracks. One track rests on the immediate value of Russia's natural resources; oil and gas are the most visible. As is the case with the Organization of Petroleum Exporting Countries, Russia's natural resources can be sold to a ready market. Of course, oil must be refined, but the skills and equipment to refine fossil fuels are widely available. The other track in Russian commerce is its slate of domestically manufactured goods. Despite Russia's investment in technical education, it never put much effort or financial support into producing excellent consumer goods. Nor did it turn its technical skills to managing its agricultural productivity. The Leontief Paradox, named for the Russian Nobel laureate in economics, refers to the curious paradox of the United States importing technology, despite its place as the leading technology producer, and exporting agricultural products that appear to be low-technology. Russia was a huge importer of U.S. agricultural products. The reason for these imports was Russia's inability to produce and deliver food products. More specifically, it was often able to grow farm goods but had difficulty storing, processing, and delivering them. This demonstrates Russia's weakness in providing the level of expertise in manufacturing and management needed for a massive nation.

This two-pronged economy has opened the need for new business techniques on two fronts. Oil and gas require business skills for a market economy. Russia's long-protected manufacturing sector needs management and planning skills that will build quality and cost effectiveness.

ESTABLISHING EXCELLENCE IN THE AUTOMOBILE INDUSTRY

Post-Communist Russia was undergoing a sweeping series of changes affecting government, the economy, and education. Military might dominated Russia's governmental attention for decades. As impressive as its military was, the nation had little financial wherewithal to create and support organizations such as Procter & Gamble, General Electric, or General Motors. These U.S. consumer-oriented giants are masters of product excellence, innovation, and customer service. An excellent example of Russia's lag in consumer products is AvtoVAZ, the manufacturers of the Lada, an automobile prized inside Russia but unable to make its mark in the United States or Europe. The company is now partly owned by Renault, which bought 25% of the company in 2008 for $1 billion (Matlack, 2008). The small sum indicates that Lada is not a major force in its own sizeable home market, where approximately two and a half million cars were sold in 2014 (Matlack, 2008).

The rollout of new models, a dramatic event for such Western corporations as General Motors, Ford, and Volkswagen, has been held up by Renault in order to improve the quality of the vehicles. The slow transformation of Lada, engineered in part by its new European owner, reveals the need for managers who are able to focus on raising quality to compete in a market economy and for planners who will control the manufacturing cost and map the rollout date, number of vehicles available, and prices of new models.

NEW BUSINESS SKILLS NEEDED FOR A MARKET ECONOMY

This review of Russia's market economy prospects—strong natural resources and weak manufacturing—provides the backdrop for massive changes in business education. The need for new skills, new approaches to management, and a new sense of ensuring quality has proven a major barrier to progress since the fall of the Soviet Union. It would never suffice for Russian business to try to adopt manufacturing techniques provided directly by managers from other nations. For example, Russia's automobile manufacturing would not be able to hire managers from Japan to manage factories across Russia. Nor would it be sufficient to simply export oil and gas and import almost everything else. Thus, the need for effective business skills in the Russian workforce boiled up as a major concern during the tumultuous 1990s.

Educational reform can only take place where a strong base has been established. Historians have looked carefully at trends in Russian education going back for 2 centuries. Into the early 20th century, there simply was not much higher education available, especially for women. Just prior to the momentous 1990s, Russians had become accustomed to a range of educational opportunities. The post-Stalin period offered a virtual renaissance in higher education expansion. As valuable as this effort was, the content of higher education during these years focused on engineering and vocational skills. Engineering is critical to creating excellent products, but the Russian preference for military products diverted much talent away from the needs of a market economy. Vocational skills are also useful, but they work better where there is little or no competition as there is in a market economy. But a foundation of widely available higher education was in place.

NEW BUSINESS SKILLS EMERGE

All of these upheavals in the government and the economy opened the door for new ideas to take root. Partly through a search for effective business skills and partly by the collapse of Communist business ideology, Western business concepts began to take root inside the Russian academy. Beginning with a trickle, these new ideas soon became a powerful stream.

Russian business professors began to introduce newer, Western-based business concepts and teaching techniques. The early adoption of new techniques came about from a variety of academic events. Russian professors were exposed to Western ideas through scholarly interaction including visiting professors and international conferences, scientific research, the Internet, publications, and travel, all of which whetted the appetite of younger Russian professors for more contemporary concepts that were yielding results in successful corporations in the West. During the preceding decades, the flow of academic funding was more evenhanded in the United States than in Russia. Professors enjoyed more flexibility and more funding to pursue research interests. A sabbatical in Russia would offer a professor from a U.S. university a good deal of research and teaching material. And the sabbatical would bring about valuable interaction.

At the same time, younger Russians were exposed to an increasing flow of information about better living and greater freedom and wealth in the West. Attractive products and services appeared to be more accessible in the West. In addition, Russians of all ages saw the benefits of scientific and medical research and more effective production of agricultural products and manufactured goods. The fall of Russia's central government unleashed long-standing desires for better health care, higher quality manufactured products, international travel, personal wealth, better and more available food, and many other goods and services that were unavailable to the majority of Russians. (See Buckley [2006].)

The change inside Russian higher education might have come about through Russian colleges and faculties adopting attractive ideas from Western universities. In fact, the colleges and universities moved slowly. These long-standing institutions were rocked by the loss of central government funding, which led to the retirement of many professors who were tied closely to critique of the West, and by a general loss of faith in the Communist economic ideology. There were fewer exponents of Communist labor theory. (See F. Evans, Birch, and Nancy [1995].)

Imagine the shock and disappointment of seasoned professors inspired by the famous 1946 speech of Joseph Stalin in which he proclaimed the greatness of the Third Five-Year Plan. World War II was recently over; Russia was victorious. Stalin (1946) argued that "the Soviet social system has proved to be more capable of life and more stable than a non-Soviet social system, that the Soviet social system is a better form of organization of society than any non-Soviet social system" (p. 300). As the 1990s moved along, there were no new five-year plans, no planners, and no forceful advocates for the greatness of the last five-year plan. Russia had moved orthogonally from Stalin's words of 5 decades earlier.

Whereas an important subthesis in this chapter focuses on the shift in Russian higher education toward Western business principles, there was an effort to allow Soviet ideology to align more closely with the research needs of modern science. An interesting study in this area is Graham's (1972)*Science and Philosophy in the Soviet Union.* Graham's book reveals that through the 1960s—well before the period of focus in this study, the Soviets were concerned that scientific advancement not fall entirely under the sway of ideology. (See also Pokrosky [as cited in Taylor et al., 1996], Augustine [2007], and West and Frumina [2012].)

Mikhail Gorbachev played a role in these events as well, opening the door to a friendlier relationship with the West, which included more cooperation among educators. He made an effort to shift the Russian higher education establishment to provide more support for the emerging economy including a greater acceptance of innovation.

Attitudes about work were in motion. The generations in Russia offer sharp differences in their attitudes about labor and the role of women. Studies in this vein include Hahn and Logvinenko's (2008) "Generational Differences in Russian Attitudes Towards Democracy and the Economy" (pp. 1345–1360). Combined with the statistical information available, such reviews provide an interesting panorama. Several scholars have catalogued the shift from vocational education toward market economy skills. These include Holmes et al. (1995) in *Russian Education: Tradition and Transition*, which looks at educational administration including curriculum, finances, and teacher preparation. The mismatch did not go unobserved. Vucinich (1990) observed, "Step by step the Stalinist unity of science and ideology was dismantled" (p. 201). So, it is no surprise that the total collapse of the Soviet structure allowed educators to move in their own direction, a direction toward which they had been leaning for decades. This split was also known to the authorities and they took various actions to deal with the matter. The Russian government supported higher education, but they did not include modern business practices. The massive growth of engineers and other technicians demonstrates their commitment to building infrastructure and achieving other tangible outcomes. However, the period after the fall of the Soviet system damaged many of these efforts, which found institutions without financial support. As R. Daniels (2007) noted, "a wholesale approach was taken in developing higher education" (p. 343). Complained Afanasiev (1999), subsequently editor of *Pravda*, "Many universities that were hastily established for official reasons of prestige . . . have found themselves in a particularly difficult situation" (p. 294).

A powerful example of the proclivities of Soviet leaders is provided by L. Daniels (1988), who broke down data on the Twenty-Sixth Congress in 1981 and its 545 members, the last under Brezhnev. Of the members, 211 were (39%) from the full-time party apparatus, 179 (33%) were from the civil government (central and union republics), 40 (7%) from the military, six were from the police agencies, 21 were ambassadors (usually former party officials), 11 were trade union officials, 22 were cultural and scientific officials, four were heads of miscellaneous social organizations, and 51 (9%) were mass representatives (L. Daniels, 1988).

The breakdown makes clear that these officials were committed to the Soviet system and implies that they would be reluctant to support educational reform. No university officials were identified whereas the military and labor were well represented. Such were the priorities of the government. In R. Daniels's (2007) view, throughout the decade, the party leadership remained stable in outlook and in its general makeup—where they were from and what they represented. The 1986 congress was also voted in unanimously and offered a similar composition. It is certainly clear that education did not stand out in either group of selected leaders.

In addition to the bureaucratic outlook of these Soviet leaders, the battles between central control and the creative spirit that fits Western approaches to higher education were well known through several decades prior to the collapse of the Soviet system. Aleksandr Solzhenitsyn and others opposed to the Soviet system provided considerable evidence of the government's distaste for free expression. For the purpose of this study, it is clear that the central bureaucrats were in control until the 1990s and that new educational concepts or fields of study held little appeal to the hierarchy.

Slowly, younger professors armed with new ideas converged with younger Russian students who were willing to take on new skills that they sensed were working in Western business. These two forces—educators offering valuable ideas and students ready to pick up these skills—were already converging. The interaction among faculty and international colleagues and the expanded exposure to Western ideas prepared professors for a new direction.

Younger Russians were breaking out of the Communist skin. They also held high expectations of postsecondary education and a much stronger knowledge of English than their predecessors had. Spurred in part by the efforts of the U.S. Peace Corps, knowledge of English advanced rapidly among younger Russians through previous decades ("Will the Peace Corps Be Leaving Russia?" 2002). As the 1990s moved ahead, three major ingredients were reaching a boil in the Russian academic chowder: a pressing need for new skills in the market economy, widespread admiration for education, and increasing facility with the English language.

WESTERN CONCEPTS DRAW RUSSIANS IN

As Russia is drawn toward Western business practices and has embraced modern business thinking, led by its most successful industries and businesses holding sway on the world market, younger generations are clearly shifting from the views of their parents toward more Western attitudes about business. A number of studies have tracked basic attitudes of Russians about various aspects of life. Measuring a sense of the importance of personal well-being and education proves significant. Any discrepancies between generations or between men and women are also important for this chapter.

In the work done on the subject, one scholar reported that education represents an important factor affecting social well-being. According to 2008 data in a survey of young Russians reported by Shcherbakova (2008), 63.7% of respondents believed that a higher education is essential whereas 25.8% believed it is mostly essential. Only 5.1% said that a higher education is mostly or absolutely unnecessary. The difference is that the subject matter is shifting toward business skills.

A historian may look backward from today or look forward from the end of the Soviet period and find that Russians perceive higher education as very valuable. The major difference over these 2 decades can be found in the preferred courses of study and the heightened influence from Western sources. Kishkovsky (2000) pointed out that women reveal a greater preference for the trend:

The absolute importance of education is noted by the largest number of representatives of young people, which is entirely natural, by women more than by men, which is conditioned by the demand and competition in the labor market, and by those who are materially well-off. (p. 12)

YOUNGER RUSSIAN MEN AND WOMEN DIVERGE

This research verifies that Russians, specifically younger generations, believe in the importance of education. The research also shows a perceptible split between men and women. Why do young Russian men not share the same perceptions about higher education as women? Even following the end of the Soviet era, men are more likely to maintain a commitment to the older social structure, which glorified labor and the products of physical work. Surveys appear to confirm the idea that Russian men prefer to avoid uncertainty, adhering to older social norms at a time of significant change (Mikhailova, 2012).

Not surprisingly, this pattern of belief also holds in the Newly Independent States, which are also working through the post-Soviet period. In Bhat's (2011) article in the *Journal of Asian and African Studies*, the abstract states,

Women get less of the material resources, social status, power and opportunities for self-actualization than men do who share their social location—be it a location based on class, race, occupation, ethnicity, religion, education, nationality, or any intersection of these factors. (p. 12)

The study by Bhat (2011) looked at gender in the context of poverty reduction in Uzbekistan and takes a sociological approach. It opened a line of inquiry into cultural and institutional limitations that may put a ceiling on women's involvement in economic activity. So, the approach differs from the focus of this chapter. However, based on the information provided in this study, it does not appear that Russian women feel significant barriers to advancing through education. (See also Lapidus [1993], Ruane [1994], and Ashwin [2002].)

Curiously, as this study shows, even in this post-Soviet period, the change in attitudes between men and women in post-Soviet Russia relates less to women's liberation than to women taking new opportunities whereas men tending to refrain from embracing new ideas, preferring the comfort of the Communist ideology. Male uncertainty avoidance provides a possible explanation, but women seizing opportunity is shown by the evidence. This continued influence of Stalinist principles, specifically those expressed in *Economic Principles of Socialism in the U.S.S.R.*, Stalin's 1952 book in which he laid out the three preliminary conditions for the advent of the true Communist society, also accounts for some of the gender split. Stalin's third principle involved vocational education, which, in fact, related more to male aspirations.

In "The Cultural Preferences of Today's Russian College Students," Andreev (2011) pointed out a shift in the academic interests of young Russians. Science and mathematics are on the wane, another sign that the engineering and vocational emphasis is being replaced by other academic topics. (See also Mechitov and Schellenberger [1995] and Taylor et al. [1996].)

THE MASTER OF BUSINESS ADMINISTRATION TAKES HOLD

Many changes were underway in Russia's government, economy, and society. The Soviet Union placed a premium on scientific knowledge. The need for some degree of freedom for research runs counter to central control. A conflict is evident as the promise of the benefits of scientific research fit the Soviet plan. A critical development is Russia's shift toward Western teaching concepts. Among other writings, Tomusk's (2007)*Creating the European Area of Higher Education* provides insight into Russia's evolving educational relationship with Europe. A number of scholars inside Russia have studied trends and developments in this area. These include Smolentseva (2003) in "Challenges to the Russian Academic Profession." Articles such as F. Evans et al.'s (1995) "Business Education and Change in Russia and Eastern Europe" look at changes in the nature of business education. Research on these matters during the earlier period of study in this chapter (1993–2003) proves significant. All of these secondary works provide a framework of academic reform that was adapting to Western ideas.

The content and teaching methods of business education in Russia were also undergoing a significant transformation. Western academic degrees came into favor including the MBA degree. Rote learning gave way to problem solving, strategic planning, and critical thinking. Students began to tackle business cases by searching for the central problem and formulating a practical solution that would increase revenue and profit. Like their counterparts in the United States, Russian business students were grappling with the problems of maintaining the company's market capitalization, determining an effective price for a product, planning production levels, and defining measures of quality. More students were pursuing these studies using textbooks written in English. These business skills differ radically from the ideological studies that were common in previous generations.

The doctoral dissertation that fueled this chapter took a careful look at the curricula of MBA programs in Russia and compared them to programs in the United States, looking for changes in content and teaching methods. The similarities between U.S. and Russian approaches to learning are clear and growing. Russian and U.S. business students are trying to figure out a suitable business strategy for Google and are evaluating changes in stock prices on international exchanges. Graduates of these programs became more successful over time finding employment in Russia's burgeoning businesses, most of which maintained offices across Europe. This in turn attracted more applicants to study the new techniques.

These changes prove remarkable in a number of ways. First, they show the replacement of one ideology with newer ideas and a wide acceptance of the change. Of special interest to historians is the fact that these changes came about without a five-year plan and in the absence of the political or financial support of the government. In fact, these changes are so radical and so out of step with prevailing ideology, they prove more remarkable than Russia's military decline. Russian higher education was turned on its ear by the falloff of employment in Russian industry, which long thrived on engineering and vocational graduates.

Young Russians proved adept at grasping skills for jobs that would build their careers and personal wealth in the new market economy. Gazprom and other monoliths took on an aura of beauty never seen before. Those with Western-style business skills could find employment in large corporations with free-flowing products (gas and oil) across neighboring Europe.

A BUSINESS CURRICULUM FOR POST-SOVIET RUSSIA

It is interesting to ask which business specialties appealed most to Russian educators after the fall of the Soviet Union. For Russian collegians, management became the second most popular business major in the 1990s. It was offered only in a few universities before *perestroika*, but it rapidly earned almost the same popularity and scale it always held in U.S. colleges. Both existing state and new private schools opened many additional management departments and incorporated brand-new management courses into other business programs. The exceptional speed of the new programs' development, in addition to changes in the Russian economy's management styles, led Puffer (2003) to call it a management revolution in Russia.

The changeover found Russian business programs becoming less technical and more managerially oriented. Still requiring a solid mathematical and computer background, business schools have started to provide more courses on such previously Western topics as entrepreneurship, leadership, and organizational behavior, as well as requiring students to take more classes in liberal arts and foreign languages. Second, as Russian society becomes more dynamic and students more often have to combine their classes with their jobs, Russian schools strive to make their programs more flexible and consistent with one another.

So powerful is Western influence that observers note that only recently are textbooks in the Russian language being introduced. Since the 1990s, in many new academic areas such as management, finance, and marketing, Russian colleges have relied on Western textbooks, mostly written in English. Replacing them with Russian textbooks will help to combine theory with local business cases and make teaching more practically oriented. This will also make it easier for younger Russians to study management concepts.

This process of adapting is quite interesting and raises the question of which priorities emerged. In a paper, Czinkota (1997) noted what he called the "lack of relevance of the education offered" (p. 75) in Russia and identified the top four specific business concepts needed in order of importance: marketing; strategic planning, international business, and business law.

Czinkota (1997) also identified four business skills that relate more to the overall attitudes of students rather than the specific content of courses: problem solving, decision making, customer orientation, and team building and communication. The gap between U.S. business practices and the expectations of Russian students was considerable at the time. He pointed out that the expression *group discussion* struck students as something related to political indoctrination. Progress through the 1990s was remarkable.

This chapter reveals the foundational issues that had to be addressed as the business curriculum in Russia emerged. Students used to five-year plans and breadlines were not familiar with the idea of customer service or marketing (for example, Czinkota [1997]). This also offers powerful evidence of a virtual mimicking of U.S. courses and techniques.

Russia also boarded the European education reform bandwagon: "The Russian government has asked the European Union . . . for practical aid in advancing its participation in the Bologna process—the European educational harmonization project—which the country signed onto in 2003" (Pursiainen & Medvedev, 2005, p. 20). This European Union agreement focuses on higher education and builds on Russia's recent participation in the Tempus Programme. It was approved in Moscow by Vladimir Putin, European Commission President José Manuel Barroso and European Union Council of Ministers President Jean-Claude Juncker. So, Russia is shifting toward its neighbors in terms of educational content and technique. High quality knows no borders. (See Savickaya [2003], Alon & McIntyre [2005], Babenko [as cited in Taylor et al. [1996], Kerr [1996], "Putin Forges Higher Education Cooperation Deal With EU" [2005], and Dneprov [1998].)

WOMEN EMERGE AS CORPORATE LEADERS

One of the notable findings in this study is the advance of women during this tumultuous time. Education for women should also be seen in the context of its rather limited extent in earlier decades. More academic doors opened for women throughout the 20th century. Many historians have noted a significant expansion of higher education for women through the 1860s. These include the Lubjan Courses in 1869 and Bestuzhev Courses for Women in 1878. Bestuzhev proved quite significant because it survived many challenges and was integrated into the University of Petrograd in 1919. In their study of these events, Gouzevitch and Gouzevitch (2002) pointed out that at the turn of the 19th to the 20th century, business and industry were booming. This opened opportunities for women engineers. The St. Petersburg Polytechnic Institute for Women, founded in 1906, was the first higher technical school for women in any country. This parallels the evidence presented in this chapter that new business opportunities following the fall of the Soviet Union opened the door for Russian women to gain skill and move forward in new careers. However, relatively few Russian women were able to participate in these academic opportunities in the early 1900s (Gouzevitch & Gouzevitch, 2002). (See also Satina [1982] and Kligman [1996].)

The study identified an unexpected outcome of these transformations. Russian women embraced these new business concepts more readily than Russian men. As a result, Russian women are moving into the ranks of senior management in Russian-based corporations with extraordinary speed and agility. Consider a report by Grant Thornton (2015), which conducted a survey of 6,900 businesses in 26 countries regarding the employment of women in senior management and found that Russia ranked first with 89% of its businesses employing women in senior management. The Philippines ranked second with 85% and the United States third with 75%. Through this tumultuous period, Russian women moved from rare appearances in senior management to ranking first worldwide.

These accomplishments took place without the benefit of an organized movement. The weak central government also has not played a role in support of or in opposition to women attaining valuable business skills and advancing their careers. These findings, when shared by the author at international conferences, have been met with a combination of surprise and admiration. The default assumption about successful movements is the U.S. model, which begins with an organized movement for change. Next is to obtain the support of the government, which may pass laws to resolve grievances. Courts will interpret the law to extend new opportunities accordingly. But, Russian women have moved more aggressively into management positions and done so more quickly than women in other countries, and they have done so without government support and without the power of an organized movement.

From a historical perspective, Russia has undergone a rapid-fire industrial revolution. Aslund (1995) showed that in those years, Russia began to face the growing pains of modern industrialization. The United States and Western Europe had already undergone the transformation over many earlier decades. Russia was trying to accelerate its path and catch up to its rivals quickly. Much as China reels from the growth of its middle class and the attraction of manufacturing jobs that draw large numbers of people from the farms, Russia through the 1990s was struggling with issues of wealth, distribution of goods, currency valuation, and overall economic health.

Also of considerable historical interest is the peculiar difference between men and women. Whereas Russia offered considerable educational opportunities for women across many decades, one would reasonably expect men to latch onto the new business skills and move forward in their careers. It is the author's contention that the explanation for the male–female split is sociological. Russian men remain committed to the older Communist view that the value of labor is the most critical economic issue. Russian men have been instilled with the idea that physical labor is critical and that men are better equipped for workplace success than women are. Hence, they have proven reluctant to adopt new concepts and take advantage of new business opportunities. This hangover from the years of the five-year plans and the peculiar Russian approach to commerce has opened considerable opportunities for women. All of these factors explain why a total of 42% of senior management posts in Russia are held by women (Grant Thornton, 2015).

The findings in this chapter prove both unexpected and significant. The project started by looking for changes in business curriculum in Russian higher education. The massive changes affecting Russia called for new skills and business techniques. The expansion of English across Russia appeared to be a significant hurdle. By contrast, whereas Japan's economy recovered well from World War II after several decades of struggle, English fluency was not common. The relative ease with which English emerged as a Russian skill suggested that Russian business curriculum might adapt more readily to the market economy than one might have expected. Indeed, the research proved that the U.S.-style MBA degree moved expeditiously. The most unexpected discovery was the facility shown by Russian women in embracing new approaches to business. In turn, that discovery led the author to conduct further research, which showed that the rapid rise of Russian women in business came about in a manner not expected in the West: No women's movement, no sweeping court decisions, no conscious plans by companies to give women preference in hiring. And the Russian women's advance was greater than the advance of women in other countries.

It may be expected that in several years, Russian men will pick up the slack. The male reluctance to embrace newer business approaches represents a lingering social shadow of Communism. Conversely, the success of these women affirms the human spirit to adopt new ideas that carry significant benefits.

OLD WAYS PROVE A BARRIER TO WEALTH

Resistance to change can be seen in two ways. Resistance subsided because it took on the image of being a barrier to the new wealth offered by changing economic times. Curiously, resistance to democracy in Russia is standing up better than resistance to personal wealth. This means that events in Russia in the time period of this study offer interesting historical insights into how change actually occurs. Somewhat similar patterns took place in the former East Germany and are taking place through the Newly Independent States as well as China, which are improving their infrastructure and welcoming foreign investment. Personal wealth proves to be a motivator. Historians may expect similar patterns when the situations shift in Cuba and North Korea.

Russians are also *voting with their feet* by enrolling in academic programs that are personally interesting. With their newfound desire for wealth, they are inclined to enroll in programs that will yield a good paycheck. Whereas the advances made by women stand out, research indicates that the newer Western-influenced programs are perceived as more modern, diminishing the older Russian academy approach to business education. The article "Education as a Factor of Social Differentiation and Mobility" (2004) provided some interesting insight, noting that relatively few Russian students see the unified state examination as a positive force in modernizing education. This reveals a split in Russian higher education. The older system, which was closely tied to these exams, leaned toward the sciences and engineering, was male dominated, and did not charge tuition. The Western-style degrees lean toward business and the humanities, are more egalitarian, and some charge tuition. Naturally, the older generation resists. But younger Russians are latching on to the Western approach.

Even more expensive private education is booming in Russia. The post-Soviet era has seen the development of a parallel form of higher education that requires tuition, beginning in 1992, according to the article "Education as a Factor of Social Differentiation and Mobility" (2004). While the great state-funded, public Russian universities that concentrate on science and engineering remain, business programs are advancing rapidly. The growth of private colleges is also notable. This change contrasts sharply with the heavily state-run colleges and free education of the former era. The sheer number of institutions has risen dramatically as well. The 1990s witnessed a rapid and steady rise in the number of higher educational institutions as well as people enrolled in them. The total number of higher educational institutions stood at 514 in 1990, rising to 1,071 (including 662 state and municipal institutions, and 409 nonstate institutions) as of the end of 2004 (Shcherbakova, 2008). Note that these massive advances took place while the central government wobbled and the ruble flattened.

The evidence provided in this chapter demonstrates the importance of the events reported. From an educational perspective, revolution took hold of the techniques and content of Russian business education. The author contends that this alone carries massive significance. It is unlikely that these changes would have taken place had the other factors reviewed here not been at work. For example, the collapse of the central government and the decline of the ruble set Russians adrift from the economic system that had formed their outlook on life. Of great interest to historians is tracing how such cataclysms lead to change. The Russian proclivity for education and a growing desire for personal advancement and wealth—as a means of gaining many of the benefits held in the West—shaped educational and economic reform.

The absence of a well-funded and politically powerful central government means that these changes were not directed from above. For historians, this offers a view of how those who grew up in the Eastern side of Europe think and act when new freedom comes their way. This is further demonstrated by the rapid rise of Russian women in management. The new skills acquired through the renaissance of business skills and the clear demand for these skills confirms that the opportunities were real. Conversely, it is clear that Russian men adhere to the older system, which formed their outlooks, and which rested on the primacy of manual labor.

The value of human labor fared poorly in the waning years of the 20th century and opening decades of the 21st. The expansion of automation has reduced the number of laborers and the man-hours required for most manufacturing tasks. The shift of much manufacturing from the United States to China and other nations has been motivated by cost savings. The same man-hours can be completed outside the United States for a fraction of its domestic cost. This confirms what has been obvious for some time: that manual labor has become a readily available commodity. Thus, in future decades, the overhang of Marxist principles will continue to fade and the male–female split shown in this chapter will recede.

WOMEN EXCEL IN HIGHER EDUCATION

Whereas this chapter lays out various reasons, the advancement of women remains a remarkable occurrence. Russian women hold an edge over men in formal education: 24% of employed women have a higher education versus 19% of men, and 38% a secondary professional education versus 30% of men (Shcherbakova, 2008). One disturbing piece of evidence concerns younger Russian men. Whereas the general trend of education in Russia is upward and women are moving into a variety of positions that require these new skills, young Russian men are not progressing as well. The number of young Russians who have only a primary education rose 2.1 times between censuses in 1989 and 2002 (Shcherbakova, 2008). Some change is clearly evident in Russians between the ages of 25 and 29. In that cohort (as reflected in the 2002 census), 24.3% of women had achieved a higher education whereas men in the same group came in at 18.9% (Shcherbakova, 2008). Taken alone, this may not appear significant. But the sharper difference in the next younger cohort is indeed troubling. In fact, in the age ranges of 10 to 30, the number of male students in school has dropped below the levels for female students of the same age groups (Shcherbakova, 2008). Also, the evidence shows that young Russian male students are far more prone to drop out of school than they were previously (Shcherbakova, 2008). Whereas some commentators note that military service is a factor, it is hardly new to Russia, which has long had large numbers of young men in its military service. The problem is more severe among those in the ages of 15 to 19. Those who are age 20 and above are now the last group of Russians to reveal an upward trend in educational achievement (Shcherbakova, 2008). Others who looked at these trends include Bryans and Mavin (2003).

After they graduate, women make up 46.9% of the employed population in Russia (Paranyushkin, 2015). The greatest proportion of working women are in public health service (85%), education (81%), credit and finance (78%), and information and accounting services (75%; Paranyushkin, 2015). One area that still finds few women is politics. There have been only two female governors, and women make up a relatively small percentage of State Duma deputies. But note the dominance in business-related areas—accounting, credit, finance, and information. On the surface, these data reveal that women are advancing in the newer and more intellectually challenging professions. The statistics show that women are filling many positions in business that require the newer form of technical education. Women appear to have their feet planted firmly in the business arena of post-Communist Russia. These results also highlight the sharp contrast between the Women's Movement in the United States and the route traveled by Russian women since the early 1990s.

However, as pointed out by Hedlund (1999), who looked at Russia's transition to a market economy, its economic path is cluttered with intended systemic change that failed. This makes the post-Soviet experience even more painful because, as pointed out by Berglof, Kunov, Shvets, and Yudaeva (2003), Russia showed strong capability for applying economic analysis. It should have performed better than a number of its previous Socialist neighbors within and outside the former Soviet Union. This did not happen. Jha (2002) pointed out that "the market has to be created first and the state is the irreplaceable agent of its creation" (p. 5). The planning that followed the fall of the Soviet system appears to be no more successful than the five-year plans that preceded the fall.

The developments discussed in this chapter regard Russia and the former Soviet Union at a time of painful transition. It is clear that some expectations for the transition have not been achieved. Although Russia has moved forward into a new era, its economic and social challenges have not disappeared. The success of Russian women as demonstrated by the evidence provided here calls for insight and conclusions about the reasons for it.

REFERENCES

Adams, A., Middleton, J., & Ziderman, A. (1992). The World Bank's policy paper on vocational and technical education and training. *Prospects*, 22(2), 125–140. doi:10.1007/BF02195540

Afanasiev, V. (1999). *Scientific and technological revolution - Its impact on management and education*. Moscow, Russia: Progress.

Alon, I., & McIntyre, J. (Eds.). (2005). *Business education in emerging market economies: Perspectives and best practices*. Boston, MA: Kluwer Academic.

Andreev, L. (2011). The cultural preferences of today's Russian college students. *Russian Social Science Review*, *52*(4), 60–78. doi:10.2753/res1060-9393510905

Ashwin, S. (2002). The influence of the Soviet gender order on employment behavior in contemporary Russia. *Sociological Research*, *41*(1), 21–37. doi:10.2753/SOR1061-0154410121

Aslund, A. (1995). *How Russia became a market economy*. Washington, DC: Brookings Institution.

Aslund, A., Guriev, S., & Kuchins, A. (2010). *Russia after the global economic crisis*. Washington, DC: Peterson Institute for Internal Economics.

Augustine, D. (2007). *Red Prometheus: Engineering and dictatorship in East Germany, 1945–1990*. Cambridge, MA: The MIT Press.

Bek, A. (2004). *The life of a Russian woman doctor: A Siberian memoir, 1869–1954*. Bloomington: Indiana University Press.

Berglof, E., Kunov, A., Shvets, J., & Yudaeva, K. (2003). *The new political economy of Russia*. Cambridge, MA: The MIT Press.

Bhat, B. A. (2011). Gender earnings and poverty reduction: Post-Communist Uzbekistan. *Journal of Asian and African Studies*, *46*(6), 629–649. doi:10.1177/0021909611407584 PMID:22213880

Bickerstaffe, G. (2008). *Which MBA? 2009: Making the right choice of executive education*. Retrieved from http://graphics.eiu.com/whichmba/Which_MBA_20th_edition_2009.pdf

Brah, A. (1992). Questions of difference and international feminism. In J. Aaron & S. Walby (Eds.), *Out of the margins: Women's studies in the nineties* (pp. 111–134). London: Falmer Press.

Bryans, P., & Mavin, S. (2003). Women learning to become managers: Learning to fit in or to play a different game? *Management Learning*, *34*(1), 111–134. doi:10.1177/1350507603034001133

Buckley, N. (2006, October 30). Russia's middle class starts spending. *Financial Times*, p. 13.

Canel, A., & Oldenziel, R. (2000). *Crossing boundaries, building bridges*. Reading, UK: Harwood Academic.

Cherednichenko, G. A. (2012). The educational and professional trajectories of working young people. *Russian Education & Society*, *54*(11), 34–52. doi:10.2753/RES1060-9393541103

Chirikova, A. I. (1998). *A woman in charge of a firm*. Moscow, Russia: Institut Sotsiologii RAN.

Clark, T. (2003). *Changing attitudes toward economic reform during the Yeltsin Era*. Westport, CT: Praeger.

Czinkota, M. (1997). Russia's transition to a market economy. *Journal of International Marketing*, *5*(4), 73–93. Retrieved from EBSCOhost database. (Accession No. 6432650)

Daniels, L. (1988, May 2). Now Russia wants to learn the way U.S. managers do. *New York Times*. Retrieved from http://www.nytimes.com/1988/05/02/business/now-russia-wants-to-learn-the-way-us-managers-do.html

Daniels, R. (2007). *The rise and fall of Communism in Russia*. New Haven, CT: Yale University Press. doi:10.12987/yale/9780300106497.001.0001

Dash, P. L. (1998). Education in post-Soviet Russia: No more an obligation of the state. *Economic and Political Weekly*, *33*(21), 1232–1234. Available from https://www.econbiz. de/

Dneprov, E. D. (1998). *Contemporary school reform in Russia*. Moscow, Russia: Nauka.

Dudgeon, R. (1975). *Women and higher education in Russia, 1855–1905* (Doctoral dissertation). Available from ProQuest Dissertations and Theses database. (UMI No. 7526000)

Education as a factor of social differentiation and mobility (A roundtable). (2004). *Russian Education & Society, 46*(10), 7–30. doi:10.1080/10609393.2004.11056849

Evans, F., Birch, J., & Nancy, J. (1995). Business education and change in Russia and Eastern Europe. *Journal of Education for Business, 70*(3), 166–171. doi:. 1011774510.1080/08832323.1995

Evans, J. (2011, June 16). Why are they leaving? *Wall Street Journal*. Retrieved from http://www.wsj. com/articles/SB10001424052748704816604576333030245934982

Evenko, K. (2003, June 16). New MBA programs make first steps. *Independent Newspaper*, p. 7.

Gaidar, E. T. (2003). *The economics of transition*. Cambridge, MA: MIT Press.

Gershunsky, B. (1993). *Russia in darkness: On education and the future*. San Francisco, CA: Caddo Gap Press.

Gouzevitch, I., & Gouzevitch, D. (2000). Étudiants, savants et ingénieurs juifs originaires de l'Empire russe en France (1860–1940)[Students, scholars and Jewish engineers from the Russian Empire in France]. *Archives Juives*, *35*, 120–128. Retrieved from https://translate.google.com/translate?hl=en&sl=fr&u=https:// www.cairn.info/revue-archives-juives-2002-1-page-120.htm&prev=search

Graham, L. R. (1972). *Science and philosophy in the Soviet Union*. New York, NY: Knopf.

Grant Thornton. (2015). *Women in business: The path to leadership* [Press release]. Retrieved from http://news.grantthornton.com/press-release/us-businesses-show-little-progress-advancing-women-during-past-decade

Grunberg, L. (2011). *Access to gender-sensitive higher education in Eastern and Central Europe*. Bucharest, Romania: United Nations Educational, Scientific, and Cultural Organization.

Hahn, J. W., & Logvinenko, I. (2008). Generational differences in Russian attitudes towards democracy and the economy. *Europe-Asia Studies*, *60*(8), 1345–1369. doi:10.1080/09668130802292168

Hayoz, N., Jesień, L., & Koleva, D. (2011). *20 years after the collapse of Communism: Expectations, achievements and disillusions of 1989*. New York, NY: Peter Lang International Academic. doi:10.3726/978-3-0351-0273-4

Hedlund, S. (1999). *Russia's "market" economy. A bad case of predatory capitalism*. England: University College London Press.

Holmes, B., Read, G., & Voskresenskaya, N. (1995). *Russian education: Tradition and transition.* New York, NY: Routledge.

International University of Fundamental Studies. (n.d.). *Faculty of Economics & Management Master of Business Administration.* Retrieved from http://www.iufs.edu/MBA-Prog.htm

Jha, P. S. (2002). *The perilous road to the market: The political economy of reform in Russia, India and China.* London: Pluto Press.

Johanson, C. (1987). *Women's struggle for higher education in Russia, 1855–1900.* Kingston, Ontario, Canada: McGill-Queen's University Press.

Kerr, S. (1996, November). *The re-centering of Russian education.* Roundtable session at the American Association for the Advancement of Slavic Studies Annual Convention, Boston, MA.

Kiregian, E. (2015). *The transformation of Russian business education from 1993 to 2013* (Doctoral dissertation). Available from ProQuest Dissertations and Theses database. (UMI No. 3662550)

Kishkovsky, S. (2000). A bright future for Russian higher education. *Carnegie Reporter, 1*(1), 2–12. Retrieved from ERIC database. (EJ618192)

Kitaev, I. (1994). Russian education in transition: Transformation of labour market, attitudes of youth and changes in management of higher and lifelong education. *Oxford Review of Education, 20*(1), 111–130. doi:10.1080/0305498940200107

Kligman, G. (1996). Women and the negotiation of identity in post-Communist Eastern Europe. In V. Bonnell (Ed.), *Identities in transition: Eastern Europe and Russia after the collapse of Communism* (pp. 68–91). Oakland, CA: University of California Press.

Kortunov, A. (2009). Russian higher education social research. *Russia Today, 76*(1), 203–224. Retrieved from https://muse.jhu.edu/journals/social_research/v076/76.1.kortunov.pdf

Kuznetsov, A. (2000). Russia's "Market" Economy: A Bad Case of Predatory Capitalism[Book review]. *Europe-Asia Studies, 52*(2), 379–380.

Lane, D. (1997). Russian Society in Transition[Book review]. *Europe-Asia Studies, 49*(4), 727–728.

Lapidus, G. W. (1993). *Gender and restructuring: The impact of* perestroika *and its aftermath on Soviet women.* In V. M. Moghadam (Ed.), *Democratic reform and the position of women in transitional economies* (pp. 137–161). Oxford, UK: Clarendon Press.

Lucas, E. (2008). *The new Cold War.* Ann Arbor, MI: Palgrave Macmillan.

Matlack, C. (2008, February 29). Renault's Ghosn takes on a Russian relic. *Bloomberg Business.* Retrieved from http://www.bloomberg.com/bw/stories/2008-02-29/renaults-ghosn-takes-on-a-russian-relicbusinessweek-business-news-stock-market-and-financial-advice

McCarthy, D., Puffer, S., & Simmonds, P. J. (1993). Riding the Russian roller coaster: U.S. firms' recent experience and future plans in the former USSR. *California Management Review, 36*(1), 99–115. doi:10.2307/41165736

Mechitov, A., & Peper, M. J. (1998). Business education in free-market Russia: Opportunism or enlightened self-interest? *Convergence, 31*(4), 23–32.

Medvedev, R. (2000). *Post-Soviet Russia: A journey through the Yeltsin Era*. New York, NY: Columbia University Press.

Mikhailova, L. I. (2012). Russians' sense of social well-being and perception of the future. *Russian Social Science Review, 53*(1), 4–13. doi:10.1080/10611428.2012.11065461

Morris, J., & Polese, A. (2013). *The informal post-Socialist economy*. New York, NY: Routledge.

Paranyushkin, D. (2015). *Interesting facts about Russian women and women rights in Russia*. Retrieved from http://waytorussia.net/WhatIsRussia/Women/Facts.html

Puffer, S. M. (2003). *Russian management revolution: Preparing managers for a market economy*. Armonk, NY: M. E. Sharpe.

Puffer, S. M., McCarthy, D., & Naumov, A. (2000). *The Russian capitalist experiment: From state-owned organizations to entrepreneurships*. Northampton, MA: Edward Elgar.

Pursiainen, C., & Medvedev, S. A. (Eds.). (2005). *The Bologna Process and its implications for Russia: The European integration of higher education*. Retrieved from http://www.recep.ru/files/publ/bologna_en.pdf

Putin forges higher education cooperation deal with EU [Press release]. (2005). Retrieved from http://www.wes.org/ewenr/05july/russiacis.htm

Remington, T. (2010). *The Russian middle class as policy objective*. Retrieved from https://www.ucis.pitt.edu/nceeer/2010_825-06_Remington.pdf

Ruane, C. (1994). *Gender, class and the professionalization of Russian city teachers, 1860–1914*. University of Pittsburgh Press.

Rutland, P. (1998). *Annual Survey of Eastern Europe and the Former Soviet Union 1998*. New York, NY: EastWest Institute.

Satina, S. (1982). *Education of women in pre-revolutionary Russia*. Ann Arbor, MI: University of Michigan Press.

Savickaya, N. (2003, May 16). High-quality education is priceless. *Independent Newspaper*, p. 8.

Shcherbakova, E. M. (2008). The trend of education in Russia. *Russian Education & Society, 50*(4), 26–41. doi:10.2753/RES1060-9393500402

Smolentseva, A. (2003). Challenges to the Russian academic profession. *Higher Education, 45*(4), 391–424. doi:10.1023/A:1023954415569

St. Petersburg University. (2014). *Graduate School of Management*. Retrieved from http://gsom.spbu.ru/en/

Stalin, J. (1946, March1). New five-year plan for Russia. *Vital Speeches of the Day, 12*(10), 300–304.

Taylor, R., Mechitov, A., & Schellenberger, R. E. (1996). Transformation within the Russian academic community. *International Education,26*(1),29–39.

Tomusk, V. (Ed.). (2007). *Creating the European area of higher education*. Dordrecht, Netherlands: Springer. doi:10.1007/978-1-4020-4616-2

United Nations Children's Fund International Child Development Centre. (1999). *After the fall: The human impact of ten years of transition*. Retrieved from http://www.unicef-irc.org/ publications/pdf/ afterthefall.pdf

United Nations Educational, Scientific and Cultural Organization Institute for Statistics. (n.d.). *Russia Federation*. Retrieved from http://www.uis.unesco.org/DataCentre/Pages/country-profile. aspx?code=RUS&regioncode=40530

Vucinich, A. (1990). *Empire of knowledge: The Academy of Sciences of the USSR*. Oakland, CA: University of California Press.

West, R., & Frumina, E. (2012). European standards in Russian higher education and the role of English: A case study of the National University of Science and Technology, Moscow (MISiS). *European Journal of Education, 47*(1), 50–63. doi:.01507.x10.1111/j.1465-3435.2011

Will the Peace Corps be leaving Russia ? (2002, August 13). Retrieved from http://peacecorpsonline. org/messages/messages/2629/1008862.html

Zagrebina, A. V. (2013). Mechanisms of upward mobility as perceived by students in an institution of higher learning. *Russian Education & Society, 55*(66), 26–38. doi:10.2753/RES1060-9393550603

Chapter 21

Phraseology in English as an Academic Lingua Franca:
A Corpus-Based Study of Prepositional Verbs in Writing by Chinese, American, and British Students

Meilin Chen
City University of Hong Kong, China

ABSTRACT

Under the context of English as a Lingua Franca, this chapter explores the use of English prepositional verbs in writing by Chinese university students in comparison with that by their American and British counterparts. A written learner corpus compiled by the author and four native comparable corpora were used for both quantitative and qualitative analysis. The overall frequency of prepositional verbs in the five corpora shows that Chinese learners use fewer prepositional verbs in comparison with their American and British counterparts. Qualitative analysis, on the other hand, shows that Chinese learners are capable of producing an adequate number of prepositional verbs that stylistically appropriate. Moreover, differences are also found between the native novice writers in regard to both the frequency and the stylistic features of the prepositional verbs in the four native corpora. The results lead to critical discussion about the use of native corpora as the benchmark in learner corpus research.

INTRODUCTION: ENGLISH AS A LINGUA FRANCA

The worldwide spread of the English language dates back to the sixteenth century when it was used in the then colonies of the UK around the world. However, since the early 20th century, the phenomenon of English being the most commonly used language in international and intercultural communication has gradually been recognised by linguists as well as professionals in other domains. Such a phenomenon has generated a considerable debate since Kachru's (1985) tripartite classification of English as a world language, i.e. the inner, the otter and the expanding circles. The inner circle is made up of countries in

DOI: 10.4018/978-1-5225-0522-8.ch021

which English is used as native or the dominant language (e.g. the United Kingdom, Australia). The outter circle includes countries such as India and Malaysia where English serves as a lingua franca between ethnic and language groups, while the expanding circle encompasses countries such as China, Russia and Japan where English has no special administrative status. The second and third tiers in Kachru's (ibid) three-circle model, i.e. the outter and the expanding circles, led to a dramatic increase in investigations into localised varieties of English, which are often referred to as World Englishes.

However, due to the rapid development of globalisation in the past three decades, Kachru's model no longer seems to well represent the current use of English in the world. Kachru's model was pioneering, as it was one of the first attempts to recognise and legitimise the existence of English varieties in countries that belong to the outter and the expanding circles. Nevertheless, the differentiation of English varieties in the inner circle (e.g. British English, American English) as 'norm providers' from those in the outter and the expanding circles might suggest the linguistic privilege of the inner circle varieties and underrepresent the international status of varieties of English in the outter and the expanding circles.

Studies have shown that, as the population of users of English in the outer and the expanding circles is much bigger than that in the inner circle, around 80 per cent of communications in which English is used as a second or foreign language (ESL/EFL) do not involve any native speakers of English (Beneke, 1991; Gnutzmann, 2000). As Graddol (1997, p. 10) observes, native speakers of English "may feel the language 'belongs' to them, but it will be those who speak English as a second or foreign language who will determine its world future". Other World Englishes researchers (e.g. Chen & Hu, 2006; Hu, 2006) also start questioning the global dominance of the inner circle English varieties claiming that varieties of English in the outter and the expanding circles should be treated equally as their inner circle counterparts.

The debate about the global dominance of inner circle English has lad to an alternative, i.e. English as a Lingua Franca[1] (e.g., Gnutzmann, 2000; Jenkins, 1996, 1998; Knapp, 2002; Seidlhofer, 2001), which is used to replace the concepts of inner or outer circle English. Different from Kachru's model, which emphasises the geographical representation of English use in the world (focusing more on the nation, not the speakers), English as a Lingua Franca (ELF) focuses on the contexts of communication in which English serves as the common language among interlocutors who do not share the same first language (L1). Native speakers of English in these contexts therefore no longer set the linguistic agenda. Instead, speakers of all L1 backgrounds will need to make adjustments in order to achieve success in communication.

The notion of English as a Lingua Franca has also influenced learner corpus research. While the traditional practice of learner corpus research often involves a native English corpus serving as the benchmark against which the learner corpus is evaluated, in the past few years researchers began to question the use of native reference corpora (e.g. Chen, 2013b). Due to the growing internationalisation of educational institutes around the world, learners of English at the tertiary level in particular have been undergoing the transition from solely being English learners to being both learners and (future) users of English. If these learners will mostly communicate in English with people whose L1 is not English either, what is the point of benchmarking their English proficiency against native 'standards'? Should non-native features found in learner English always be taken as deficiency, or they could be considered as potential features of ELF?

Under the context of ELF, the present study aims to explore the use of multi-word verbs in writing by Chinese university students in comparison with that by their American and British counterparts. The rational for focusing on written data is that, although research into ELF is a relatively recent activity, it has witnessed considerable progress in studies of ELF in spoken communication (e.g. Baumgarten

& House, 2010; Björkman, 2011; Deterding & Kirkpatrick, 2006; House, 2002, 2013; Jenkins, 2000, 2002; Knapp, 2011; Osimk, 2009; Rajadurai, 2007). The increase of spoken ELF corpora is a further manifestation of such progress, for instance, the Vienna-Oxford International Corpus of English (VOICE, 2013) built by the research team led by Professor Seidlhofer, the Asian Corpus of English (Kirkpatrick, 2010) and The Corpus of English as a Lingua Franca in Academic Settings (ELFA, 2008). However, as Jenkins, Cogo and Dewey (2011) point out in their review of developments in ELF research, other areas, particularly relating to written communication and testing, have so far not been researched sufficiently. This study aims to narrow the gap in research into written ELF communication. The following section gives the rational for focusing on multi-word verbs in this study.

PHRASEOLOGY IN ENGLISH AS A LINGUA FRANCA

The essential role of phraseological units or multi-word expressions in successful language production has long been recognised in the field of applied linguistics based on both psycholinguistic (Conklin & Schmitt, 2008; Jiang & Nekrasova, 2007; Schmitt, Grandage, & Adolphs, 2004; Wray & Perkins, 2000) and corpus-based evidence (Biber & Barbiri, 2007; Biber, Conrad & Cortes, 2003, 2004; Biber, Johansson, Leech, Conrad, & Finegan, 1999; Sinclair, 1991, 1996, 2004).

In learner corpus research, a variety of multi-word expressions have been investigated using learner corpora. Studies have shown that multi-word expressions are notoriously difficult for English users of different L1 backgrounds (Chen & Baker, 2010; De Cock, Granger, Leech, & McEnery, 1998; De Cock, 2004; Granger, 1998; Li & Schmitt, 2009; Lorenz, 1998; Nesselhauf, 2004; Paquot & Granger, 2012). First, ESL/EFL learners generally use fewer phraseological units than native speakers of English (Granger, 1998; De Cock et al., 1998; De Cock, 2004; Wei, 2004). Second, learners tend to over-rely on certain structures and hence produce a smaller variety of phraseological units than native speakers (Granger, 1998; De Cock et al., 1998; Milton & Freeman, 1996; Li, 2004). Third, a complex picture of the impact of L1 on ESL/EFL learners' mastery of English phraseological units emerges (for French-speaking learners: see Granger, 1998; De Cock, 2003; Paquot, 2008; for German L1 learners: see Lorenz, 1998, 1999; Waibel, 2007; for Cantonese L1 learners: see Fan, 2009; and for Mandarin L1 learners: see Zhao, 2005).

Among the many different types of multi-word expressions, multi-word verbs have been a popular topic due to their high frequency in English and the semantic and syntactic complexities. Multi-word verbs are complex verbs that consist of two or more lexical items (a verb followed continuously or discontinuously by another or other lexical items) and yet function to some extent like "a single verb lexically or syntactically" (Quirk, Greenbaum, Leech, & Svartvik, 1985, p. 1150). They can be further divided into such sub-categories (Quirk et al., 1985) as phrasal verbs (a verb followed by an adverbial particle, *look up, turn out*), prepositional verbs (a verb followed by a preposition, *deal with, see through*), phrasal-prepositional verbs (a verb followed by an adverb and a preposition, *catch up with, look up to*), and verb-adjective combinations (a verb followed by an adjective, *put...straight, lay low*). They are very frequent in both spoken and written registers. In their investigation of a sub-type of multi-word verbs based on the 100-million-word British National Corpus (BNC), i.e. phrasal verbs, Gardner and Davies (2007, p. 347) found that multi-word verbs occur approximately "every 192 words, that is, almost two multi-word verbs per page of written text on average". Mastery of a large repertoire of multi-word verbs, together with other types of phraseological units, by native English speakers is considered an important difference between them and learners of English (Coxhead, 2008; Ellis, 2008; Wray, 2002).

Yet, multi-word verbs are difficult for non-native users of English because they are semantically non-compositional, very often polysemous, and syntactically more flexible than other types of phraseological units (e.g. variation of particle positions and pronoun or noun insertions are allowed in phrasal verbs). Among the sub-categories of multi-word verbs mentioned above, phrasal verbs have drawn considerable attention. Previous empirical studies have repeatedly found that non-native English users tend to avoid using phrasal verbs when there is a single-verb counterpart available (Dagut & Laufer, 1985; Hulstijn & Marchena, 1989; Laufer & Eliasson, 1993; Liao & Fukuya, 2004; Siyanova & Schmitt, 2007). Learner corpus studies, on the other hand, reveal a mixed picture of phrasal-verb use by ESL/ EFL learners, with learners of certain L1s using phrasal verbs as frequently as their native counterparts while others using them far less frequently than native writers (Chen, 2013a, 2013b; Gilquin, 2011; Waibel, 2007). Longitudinal research on EFL learners' acquisition of phrasal verbs does not reveal a promising linear progression (Chen, 2013a). The importance of phrasal verbs in second language acquisition (SLA) is also reflected in the lists of highly frequent phrasal verbs in British and American English generated by Gardner and Davies (2007) and Liu (2011) based on large corpora, i.e. the *British National Corpus* (BNC) and *Contemporary Corpus of American English* (COCA), which, according to them, can be useful for the teaching and learning of phrasal verbs.

Multi-Word Expressions Involving Prepositions in English as a Lingua Franca

While phrasal verbs have frequently been the focus of multi-word-verb research, another type of multi-word verbs, i.e. prepositional verbs, is investigated less frequently. I argue that prepositional verbs deserve more attention than they have received. There are two reasons for this. First, prepositional verbs are much more commonly used than phrasal verbs and other types of Multi-word verbs in English (Biber et al., 1999), especially in written English. On average, approximately every eighth word in an English text is a preposition (Mindt & Weber, 1989). Based on a 400-million-word corpus, Biber et al. (1999) compared the frequencies of different types of Multi-word verbs in both spoken and written English and found that, unlike phrasal verbs, which are highly frequent in spoken English, prepositional verbs are extremely common in academic written English. It is therefore crucial for learners of English to accumulate a large repertoire of prepositional verbs in order to write fluently in English.

Second, prepositional verbs or multi-word expressions involving prepositions are problematic for English learners of varying L1 backgrounds. They either underuse expressions involving prepositions or make more errors in writing than their native counterparts. Granger and her colleagues, among the first researchers to explore learner language using grammatical annotation, discovered the underuse of n-grams containing prepositions by English learners of different L1s (Aarts & Granger, 1998; Granger & Rayson, 1998). Aarts and Granger (1998) automatically retrieved grammatical sequences from part-of-speech-tagged (POS-tagged) learner corpora by Dutch, Finnish and French students and compared them with those in the *Louvain Corpus of Native English Essays* (LOCNESS) database. They found that, while only a minority of n-grams were similar in the native and non-native corpora, there were striking similarities between the three learner corpora. "Particularly noteworthy is the [learners'] consistent underuse of the four most common trigrams in NS writing, all of which contain prepositions (Aarts & Granger, 1998, p. 134)." Similar underuse was also found when Granger and Rayson (1998) compared English essays written by French learners with those by their native counterparts using lexical frequency software.

Such avoidance was also found in later studies with learners of other L1s. Tono (2002) examined the top trigrams in the sub-corpora of his *Japanese English as a Foreign Language Learner corpus* (JEFLL) with those in LOCNESS and found that of the nine trigrams present in LOCNESS but not in his learner data, seven contained prepositions. Japanese students, Tono concludes, also underuse multi-word expressions involving prepositions. This was further supported by empirical evidence. Kao (2001) tested Japanese students' knowledge of multi-word verbs by asking the students to judge the correctness of sentences in which the particle of the multi-word verb was missing. The students were also required to correct the sentence if they considered it wrong. The results show that the learners were not able to spot as many mistakes as the native English speakers did. When the students did notice the mistake, they tended to correct the mistake by using the preposition-stranded structure (e.g. "This is the house which John lived *in* for two years. Is this the house John lived *in* for two years?").

ESL/EFL learners' difficulties in learning prepositions are also reflected in their frequent mistakes with patterns that involve prepositions. For instance, during their exploration of the value of using error-tagged learner corpora in English learning and teaching, Cowan (2003) identified eight types of errors that are typical in Korean learners' English writing, three of which contain prepositions (i.e. prepositions following verbs, prepositions preceding noun phrases and prepositions which are not necessary with English verbs).

Moreover, investigations into factors that may influence the acquisition of prepositional patterns reveal a complex picture. Diez-Bedmar and Casas-Pedrosa (2011) carried out a longitudinal study on Spanish learners' acquisition of English prepositions and found that L1 transfer has a mixed impact on preposition acquisition. It shows positive influence where there is a one-to-one correspondence between English and Spanish but negative effects where a single preposition conveys a range of meanings in the other language. Groom (2009) investigated multi-word expressions in the *Uppsala Student English Corpus* (USE) by Swedish university students and found that learners' immersion in an English-speaking country seems not to be very helpful for the acquisition of multi-word expressions involving prepositions.

This study aims to explore prepositional verbs in a Chinese learner corpus in comparison with those in native English corpora by American and British university students respectively. While previous studies tend to focus on the group performance of different learners, this study takes the individual factor into consideration by examining the distribution of prepositional verbs across individual learners. The appropriateness of the learners' use of prepositional verbs was also investigated. As mentioned in the first section, native novice corpora in this study do not serve as a benchmark. Instead, the use of prepositional verbs by the three groups students are examined in order to reveal the phraseological profile of writing by novice writers of different L1s under the context of ELF. Therefore, the analysis of the results will focus more on differences rather than deficiencies.

THE STUDY

The Corpora

This study is based on a Chinese learner corpus compiled by the author and four native novice corpora obtained through different channels. The 188,628-word learner corpus consists of 780 argumentative essays written by 130 university students at a Chinese university. They were English language majors in their first three years of undergraduate studies when the data were collected. In the second semester of their second year, they all passed the Chinese national English proficiency exam for English majors: Test for English Majors-4 (TEM-4). This exam, which students are required to pass for the completion of their undergraduate studies, requires mastery of a 6,000-word vocabulary (which includes phraseological units such as idioms, multi-word expressions, etc.). A pass score from this exam is roughly equivalent to a 6.5 score for IELTS or 550 for paper-based TOEFL. The learners, therefore, could be considered upper intermediate EFL learners. The essays were written at the end of each semester (six time points over three years) under examination conditions with no access to writing aids such as reference tools.

The first two native corpora include argumentative essays written by American and British novice writers taken from: the LOCNESS corpus (Granger, Dagneaux, Meunier, & Paquot, 2009) and the *General Studies* corpus (Milton, 2001) respectively. The former consists of essays written by British and American university students on a variety of topics under different conditions (timed and mostly untimed). For this study, only essays by American students were included so that this corpus (LOCNESS-US hereafter) would represent argumentative writing by American students. The *General Studies* corpus (GS-UK hereafter) contains essays written by British secondary school leavers during the A-level examination. It represents argumentative writing by British students.

The second two native corpora consist of academic papers taken from the *Michigan Corpus of Upper-Level Student Papers* (MICUSP, 2009) and *British Academic Written English* (BAWE, Gardner & Nesi, 2012) respectively. While the reason for utilising the two native argumentative corpora is self-evident, the rationale for using the two academic corpora (MICUSP & BAWE) is the unexpected differences between American and British novice writing in the earlier stages of data analysis. This was discussed fully in Chen (2013b).

To make the four native novice corpora as comparable as possible to the Chinese learner corpus, many undesired texts were excluded from the four corpora, for instance, writing by science students or those at higher school levels (e.g. graduate students) and texts that do not belong to essay in terms of genre. Table 1 details the profiles of the five novice corpora.

Methodology

First, the five novice corpora were POS tagged by using the free online CLAWS 7 tagger provided by Lancaster University[2]. Next, all co-occurring lexical verbs and prepositions were extracted from the corpus using the *WordSmith Tools* 5.0 (Scott, 2008). However, the concordances automatically gener-

Table 1. Profiles of the five novice corpora used in the study

	CH	**LOCNESS-US**	**GS-UK**	**MICUSP**	**BAWE**
Tokens	188,628	227,972	398,279	88,217	211,929
L1	Chinese	AmE	BrE	AmE	BrE
Genre	argumentative essay	argumentative essay	argumentative essay	academic essay	academic essay
No. of topics	6	84	29	40	85
No. of essays	780	318	590	40	99

Note. CH = the Chinese learner corpus; AmE = American English; BrE = British English

ated by *WordSmith Tools* included not only prepositional verbs but also verb + prepositional phrase free combinations. For example, *look into* in "This accident should be *looked into*" is a prepositional verb meaning "to investigate", while *look* is used as a single-word verb followed by the prepositional phrase *into the cup* in "Jimmy *looked* **into the cup** and found nothing". The third step therefore involved a manual check in order to rule out verb + prepositional phrase free combinations.

After going through the aforementioned procedures, analyses were carried out to explore answers to the following questions:

1. Do Chinese students use fewer prepositional verbs like learners of other L1s did in previous studies when compared with their native counterparts?
2. Does the individual factor show any impact on the overall results of prepositional verbs in the learner and the native novice corpora? In other words, are the results affected by idiosyncratic use of prepositional verbs (e.g. extremely frequent or infrequent) by certain individuals?
3. Can Chinese students use prepositional verbs appropriately given that this type of multi-word verbs is more frequently used in the academic written register than other multi-word verbs?

The overall frequencies of prepositional verbs in the learner and the native novice corpora were calculated to explore answers to the first question. The significance of the differences between the corpora (if there were any) was then determined by using Chi-square tests. To further ensure the reliability of the differences observed between the corpora with respect to the overall results, an adjusted frequency test was carried out using Gries's (2008, 2009, 2012, p. 2) measure for dispersion: *DP* (for 'deviation of proportions'). The purpose of conducting this test was to decide whether the overall frequency of prepositional verbs in each corpus was affected by highly frequent use of this construction by certain individual writers and/or by text length. The distribution results thus provide answers to the second research question. As for the third question, the 30 most frequent prepositional verbs from the five novice corpora were searched in the four sub-corpora of COCA (Davis, 2008-) and the online version of the BNC (BNC, 2007) respectively. The four sub-corpora represent four different registers, i.e. news, fiction, spoken and academic. An adjusted frequency test was then carried out measuring the degree of dispersion (Gries, 2008, 2009, 2012, p. 2) to determine whether the prepositional verb is significantly more frequent in one register than in the others. By doing so, the stylistic profiles of the top 30 prepositional verbs in the learner and the native novice corpora were created. The following section presents findings from the analyses.

RESULTS AND DISCUSSION

Do Chinese Students Use Fewer Prepositional Verbs Than Their American and British Counterparts?

Analysis of the overall frequencies of prepositional verbs in the five novice corpora first reveals a difference between Chinese learners and their native counterparts regarding the first research question. As shown in Table 2, the frequency of prepositional verb tokens in the learner corpus is considerably lower than that in all the native novice corpora[3]. There are over 10,000 prepositional verbs per million words in the two academic novice corpora (MICUSP & BAWE) and more than 8,700 in the two native

Table 2. Frequencies of prepositional verbs in the learner and the native novice corpora

Corpus	Prepositional-Verb Types		Prepositional-Verb Tokens	
	Abs.	Rel.	Abs.	Rel.
CH	213	<u>1,129</u>	1,547	<u>8,201</u>
LOCNESS-US	304	2,101	1,439	9,944
GS-UK	432	1,085	3,499	8,785
MICUSP	231	2,619	913	10,349
BAWE	341	1,609	2,295	10,829

Note. Abs. = absolute frequency. Rel. = relative frequency. The relative frequency is acquired by normalising the absolute frequency to a one million token basis.

argumentative corpora (LOCNESS-US & GS-UK). However, only 8,201 prepositional verbs per million words were found in the learner corpus. Similarly, prepositional verb types in the learner corpus are also fewer than those in the native novice corpora, only slightly greater than in one native novice corpus (GS-UK). This indicates that, although the Chinese learners may know a variety of prepositional verbs, they do not use them as frequently as their native counterparts. The finding is in line with previous findings that ESL/EFL learners tend to use fewer multi-word expressions involving prepositions than their native counterparts (Aarts & Granger, 1998; Granger & Rayson, 1998; Tono, 2002).

Differences also emerge between native novice writers regarding prepositional verb use. First, greater prevalence of prepositional verbs in native academic writing (BAWE and MICUSP) compared to argumentative writing (GS-UK and LOCNESS-US) was found. This echoes Biber et al.'s (1999) finding that prepositional verbs are particularly frequent in the academic written register. Second, the American students tend to use a wider range of prepositional verbs than their British counterparts in both argumentative (LOCNESS-US vs. GS-UK; 2,101 vs. 1,085) and academic writing (MICUSP vs. BAWE; 2,619 vs. 1,609), while the British students use prepositional verbs much more frequently in academic writing (BAWE: 10,829 per million words) than in argumentative writing (GS-UK: 8,785 per million words). The American students also tend to use prepositional verbs more frequently in academic writing, but the difference is not so great (MICUSP vs. LOCNESS-US; 10,349 vs. 9,944). As for the Chinese EFL learners, since no academic writing by the learners was included in this study, it is not clear whether the Chinese learners would use more prepositional verbs in academic than in argumentative writing.

The American-British difference supports the Chen's (2013b) proposal that the English variety factor is as important as other factors in learner corpus studies. The discrepancy between the American and the British novice writing reveals that the traditional approach of involving a native corpus as the gatekeeper in learner corpus research might not be viable. Since differences do exist between the varieties of English in the inner circle, which native English variety should be selected as the benchmark in learner corpus research? The Chinese university students in this study are English language majors. The syllabus of their programme emphasises almost equal amount of input of both American and British English. For instance, they are required to take both British and American literature courses. American as well as British pronunciation is covered in the phonology course. Apart from local English teachers whose L1 is mostly mandarin, the students have the opportunity to communicate with international teachers from different countries. Most of these international teachers are from the inner circle countries such the United States, the UK, Australia and Canada. The students may also attend courses taught by teachers from the outter circle countries such as India or the expanding circle nations such as Germany. They are learners of English in the sense that they study English as a subject. In the meantime, they are ELF users who need to communicate with people of various L1 backgrounds and make use of different strategies to achieve success in communication. It may be too hasty to jump to the conclusion that the Chinese students are not competent in using prepositional verbs simply because of the difference observed between the learner corpus and native data.

Going back to the difference between the Chinese learner and their native counterparts regarding the number of prepositional verbs used in writing, it is worth noting that the frequency of prepositional verb tokens and types in the learner corpus is very close to that in GS-UK. The relative frequency of prepositional-verb types in the former is slightly higher than that in the latter. This shows that Chinese learners' mastery of prepositional verbs resembles that of British secondary school leavers most. The resemblance can be accounted for by several factors. The first factor is concerned with age and linguistic maturity level. Researchers such as Ringbom (1987) and Kaszubski (1998) have argued that it is more reasonable in interlanguage analysis to compare the learners of English with native speakers who are of the same age or slightly younger. The GS-UK corpus constitutes essays written by British secondary school leavers (aged 18) who are either of the same age or slightly younger than the Chinese EFL learners (aged 18-21). Essays in the remaining native novice corpora (LOCNESS-US, BAWE & MICUSP), nonetheless, were contributed by university students, many of whom were older than the Chinese EFL learners and had already received university education for from a few months up to two years.

The second is the condition of data collection. Only GS-UK and the learner corpus solely include essays written under examination conditions. The majority of the essays in the remaining native novice corpora, on the other hand, were written without time restriction and probably with the aid of secondary materials or reference tools. Such an impact of the condition of writing on the differences between learner and native English was also identified by Ädel (2008) regarding the use of metadiscourse. Taking this into consideration, although the difference between the Chinese learners and their native counterparts exists, their mastery of prepositional verbs is promising. They might perform better if they were given more time when writing essays.

Is the Overall Frequency Affected by Idiosyncratic use of Prepositional Verbs by Individual Writers?

To investigate the distribution of prepositional verbs across individual writers in the five novice corpora, the number of prepositional verbs used and the length of texts (tokens) written by each individual were calculated respectively. Gries's (2008, 2009, 2010) measure of dispersion, i.e. *DP* (deviation of proportions), was then used to determine whether the distribution is even in statistical terms. The rationale for choosing his method and the logic of this measure are explained as follows.

First, in his 2008 article, Gries gave a comprehensive review of different measures of dispersion to date and commented on the strengths and limits of different approaches. The *DP* approach proposed by him is a further development based on previous studies. Second, taking the findings of his review into consideration, Gries (2008) attempted to solve some of the problems that he enumerated in his article. Gries' *DP*, quoting his words, "does not rely on the unwarranted assumption of equally-sized corpus parts" and is "neither too nor too little sensitive" (2008, p. 415). Third, *DP* is conceptually a very simple measure. Following the detailed explanation of the steps, one could perform the calculation by simply using Microsoft Excel. And the interpretation of the result is fairly easy for anyone with a little knowledge of statistics.

The value of *DP*, which indicates the degree of dispersion, ranges from 0 to 1. Values near 0 indicate that the word or pattern in question is evenly distributed across the sub-sections of the corpora in proportion to the sizes of the sub-sections. In contrast, large values near 1 indicate that the word in question is not evenly distributed. Following Liu's (2011) categories, prepositional verbs with *DP* values below 0.25 are considered as evenly distributed across writers in this study. Prepositional verbs with values between 0.25 and 0.49 are not evenly distributed and those with values of 0.5 and above would be very unevenly distributed. The results of dispersion analysis are set out in Table 3.

The results show that prepositional verbs are evenly distributed across individuals in both the learner and the native novice corpora. As Table 3 shows, the values of distribution of prepositional verbs in all the five novice corpora are very close to zero (below 0.1). This indicates that the individual factor does not have much impact on the overall frequency of prepositional verbs in either the learner or the native novice writing. Even though a few students who contributed to the LOCNESS-US corpus did not use any prepositional verbs in their writing (see the fourth row of Table 3), these students only account for 1.8% of the whole group. The absence of prepositional verbs in their writing does not affect the overall distribution significantly. In a word, none of the novice corpora demonstrate any imbalanced distribution of prepositional verbs across individual writers.

The even distribution of prepositional verbs in the learner corpus displays a balanced picture of prepositional-verb-use across writers, which reflects consistent progress in phrasal verb acquisition. In other words, there are no students who "lagged behind" in the acquisition and production of prepositional verbs. The even distribution observed in the four native novice corpora shows that the overall frequencies from these corpora are reliable. They could serve as good reference corpora in this respect when one needs to compare learner writing with native data.

It is worth noting that, although individual idiosyncrasies were not found in this study, this points to the necessity of taking the individual factor into consideration in learner corpus research. In learner corpus studies, overall frequencies present a general picture of group performance. However, they may be raised to a false high level due to considerably frequent use of the item by a few individual learners. This may lead to a distorted image of the group performance and hence undermine the reliability of the results. The importance of exploring the distribution of the searched item across writers also applies to the native comparison corpus used in learner corpus studies, as the false high frequency of the search item in the native reference corpus caused by individual idiosyncrasies might enlarge the learner-native gap. This would not do ESL/EFL learners justice.

Table 3. Distribu tion of prepositional verbs in the five corpora

	CH	LOCNESS-US	GS-UK	MICUSP	BAWE
No. of writers	130	167	109	33	43
Length of essays (tokens)	133-333	212-2932	374-1068	647-6834	716-4005
No. of prepositional verbs per essay	0.5-4.67	0-36	2.33-11.5	6-49	9-60
DP value	0.053	0.032	0.054	0.112	0.098

Can Chinese Learners use Prepositional Verbs Appropriately?

To explore the appropriateness of prepositional verbs used in the learner and the native novice corpora, the 30 most frequent prepositional verbs were selected for analysis. The top 30 prepositional verbs were searched in the four sub-corpora (news, fiction, spoken and academic) of the online English general corpora, i.e. COCA and the BNC. The distribution of the prepositional verbs was then calculated by using the *DP* value of Gries (2008, 2009). Based on the frequency and distribution in both corpora, a stylistic label is given to the prepositional verb. Table 4 gives examples of the stylistic profile of a few prepositional verbs.

Associate with in Table 4 is labelled as an "academic" prepositional verb as it is not evenly distributed across the sub-corpora of both the BNC and COCA (DP code: 2) and appears much more frequently in the academic sub-corpus than in the other sub-corpora. *Begin with,* on the other hand, is considered evenly distributed across the four registers in both American and British English (*DP* code: 1). *Associate with* behaves differently in American and British varieties of English. It is evenly distributed across the four sub-corpora in the BNC but is more frequent in the spoken sub-corpus in COCA. Its stylistic feature is "different between varieties". Given that many grammatical items behave similarly in news and fiction registers (Biber et al., 1999), prepositional verbs that are considerably more frequent in either of these two registers are labelled as "Fiction/Spoken" in this study. *Know about* in Table 4 is an example. The stylistic profiles of the 30 most frequent prepositional verbs in the learner and the native novice corpora are summarised in Figure 1. Because no prepositional verbs from the five novice corpora were found to be very frequent in the news sub-corpus, the category of "News" prepositional verbs is missing in Figure 1.

The stylistic profiles presented in Figure 1 first show that most of the high-frequency prepositional verbs are more frequently used in the academic register than in the spoken or fiction registers. Given that prepositional verbs that are evenly distributed across the four registers are more or less stylistically neutral, hence, perfectly acceptable in the academic register, we could combine the two categories at the bottom (Academic and Evenly distributed). Prepositional verbs that belong to these two categories account for 66.67 to 87.51% of the top 30 prepositional verbs in the five novice corpora. Fiction/Spoken prepositional verbs, on the other hand, account for only 9.38 to 23.33%.

Table 4. E xamples of the stylistic profile of prepositional verbs

Prepositional Verb	Stylistic Feature	Corpus	Relative Frequencies in the Sub-Corpora				DP Code
			News	Fiction	Spoken	Academic	
associate with	Academic	BNC	19.89	8.65	17.29	208.78	2
		COCA	28.72	9.66	25.13	260.68	
agree with	Different between varieties	BNC	22.23	27.48	73.39	33.80	1
		COCA	25.38	15.51	117.50	26.13	2
begin with	Evenly distributed	BNC	15.57	15.52	14.60	37.65	1
		COCA	28.68	17.50	44.62	52.39	
know about	Fiction/Spoken	BNC	18.95	83.85	70.51	22.74	2
		COCA	30.48	78.14	91.36	28.83	

Note. DP code (1, 2, or 3) in the rightmost column indicates the distribution pattern of the verb across the four registers: 1 = fairly evenly distributed (*DP* value <0.25); 2 = not evenly distributed ($0.25 \leq DP$ value ≤ 0.49); 3 = very unevenly distributed (*DP* value ≥ 0.5).

Figure 1. Stylistic features of the high-frequency prepositional verbs in the learner and the native novice corpora

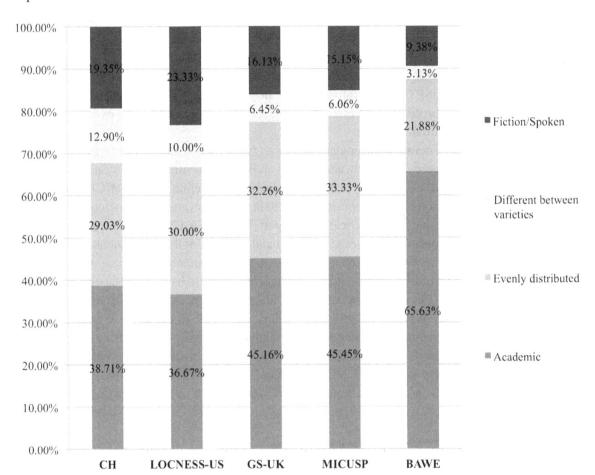

Such a concentration of academic items in the high frequency prepositional verbs in the five novice corpora parallels the findings from previous studies. Based on the 40-million-word *Longman Spoken and Written English Corpus* (LSWE) consisting of both American English and British English, Biber et al. (1999) generated a list of 75 highly frequent prepositional verbs in at least one of the four registers in LSWE, i.e. conversation, fiction, news and academic. In a later study, Liu (2011) created a list of multi-word constructions in academic written English by using the BNC and COCA, among which 37 are prepositional verbs. By putting the prepositional verbs from both studies together (29 prepositional verbs overlap), a list of 60 high-frequency prepositional verbs in the English language can be created. Out of the 60 prepositional verbs, 30 (50%) are more frequent in the academic register than in the other registers according to Biber et al. (1999) and Liu (2011). The consistent high-prevalence of prepositional verbs that are common in the academic register in both previous studies and this study points to the importance of knowing a sufficient number of prepositional verbs, especially those that are more frequently used in the academic register, in ESL/EFL learners' development of English writing if they wish to live up to the standard of professional academic writing.

Apart from the universally frequent use of academic prepositional verbs in the five novice corpora, differences between certain novice corpora were also found. The first difference is between native novice corpora of two genres: argumentative and academic. The proportion of academic prepositional verbs and those that are evenly distributed across registers in the British native academic corpus (BAWE: 87.51%) is much higher than that in the British native argumentative corpora (GS-UK: 77.42%). Following the same pattern, the percentage of academic and stylistically neutral (evenly distributed across registers) prepositional verbs in MICUSP (78.78%) is much higher than that in LOCNESS-US (66.67%). The difference between the native corpora of two genres shows the stylistic awareness, conscious or unconscious, of the two groups of native novice writers.

The second difference is between the novice corpora of two English varieties. As can be seen from Figure 1, there is a higher percentage of academic and stylistically neutral prepositional verbs in the British academic corpus (BAWE: 87.51%) than in the American academic corpus (MICUSP: 78.78%). In the same vein, the proportion of such prepositional verbs in the British argumentative corpus (GS-UK: 77.42%) is much greater than that in its American counterpart (LOCNESS-US: 66.67%). Such a difference echoes stylistic differences observed between American and British English in previous studies. Biber (1987, p. 99) also found in his corpus-based study that American written genres show more informal, colloquial and interactive features whereas British written genres "tend to have the surface characteristics of prescribed good writing". Phonetic, grammatical or syntactic differences were also found between the two varieties in other studies (e.g. Algeo, 1998, 2006; Johansson, 1979; Rohdenburg & Schlüter, 2009).

To better illustrate the difference, we can put the four native novice corpora on a scale of three points based on the use of academic and stylistically neutral prepositional verbs, with the British academic corpus (BAWE) on the top being most academic (87.51%) in style, GS-UK and MICUSP in the middle (around 78%) and the LOCNESS-US corpus at the bottom (66.67%) being most informal in style (see Figure 2).

Figure 2. The general stylistic feature of the top 30 prepositional verbs in the learner and native novice corpora

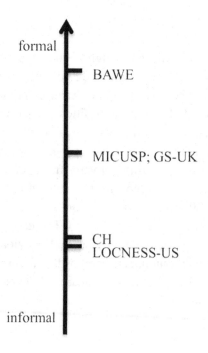

Judging by this scale, the learner corpus is slightly above the last-mentioned with 67.74% of the high-frequency prepositional verbs stylistically academic or neutral (see Figure 2). It seems that the Chinese learners have acquired a number of formal prepositional verbs. These stylistically academic or neutral prepositional verbs include: *attach to, base on, belong to, come from, come into, come to, contribute to, deal with, depend on, focus on, lead to, provide for, regard as, relate to* and *result in*. All of them have appeared in at least one of the four native novice corpora. On the other hand, if the Chinese students wish to reach a higher standard of native writing (e.g. BAWE), there is still room for improvement. For instance, the preposition *upon* is among the six most productive prepositions in all the native novice corpora but not in the learner corpus. It is especially productive in BAWE, the British academic corpus, appearing in prepositional verbs such as *act upon, build upon, decide upon, depend upon*, etc. However, *upon* is much less frequently used in the learner corpus. Its synonym, i.e. *on*, which is stylistically less formal, is more often used by the learners.

The fact that stylistic analysis yielded more striking differences between the native novice corpora than between the learner and the native novice corpora brings to light an important methodological issue in learner corpus studies, that is, the choice of native reference corpora in learner corpus studies may affect the results considerably.

However, one may not jump to the hasty conclusion that the Chinese learners in question seem to have mastered prepositional verbs just because they used slightly more stylistically academic or neutral prepositional verbs in argumentative writing than their American counterparts. First, the overall frequency of both prepositional verb tokens and types in both American novice corpora is considerably higher than that in the learner corpus. This indicates that American students do know more prepositional verbs than Chinese learners and they make more frequent use of such a type of verb in writing than the latter. Second, the proportion of stylistically academic or neutral prepositional verbs in the American academic corpus (MICUSP) is greater than that in the learner corpus. This shows that American students are capable of deploying such prepositional verbs to improve the formality of their writing. Third, as academic writing by the Chinese students is missing in this study, it is difficult to predict whether Chinese learners would use more prepositional verbs that are stylistically suitable for academic or formal writing.

CONCLUSION

This study investigated the use of prepositional verbs in writing by Chinese, American and British university students. The overall frequency of prepositional verbs in the five corpora shows that Chinese learners do use fewer prepositional verbs than their American and British counterparts. However, the numerical difference does not necessarily indicate that Chinese learners have failed to in English prepositional-verb acquisition. The difference can be caused by different factors such as age, linguistic maturity and educational background. It can also be affected by the input of English the learners receive in and out of the classroom. Moreover, the English variety factor plays an equally important role, as differences between native novice corpora have also been found. With regard to the frequency of prepositional verbs, Chinese learners' writing resembles argumentative writing by British secondary school leavers (GS-UK) most.

Differences also emerge between the American and British novice writing regarding prepositional-verb use. While more prepositional verbs were found in the American novice corpora than in the British novice corpora, more stylistically academic or neutral prepositional verbs were used in the latter than in the former. This points to an important methodological issue in learner corpus research, i.e. that the L1 variety factor should not be neglected in the selection of comparison corpora in learner corpus research. If a native corpus were used, it would better to use native data with texts from different L1 varieties separated, as utilising a native corpus with texts from different L1 varieties may lead to distorted results. This also indicates that it is important to ascertain different background information (e.g. learning experiences) of the learners, when one investigates or builds a learner corpus. Due to the rapid development of globalisation, learners of English nowadays are often at the same time users of English as a Lingua Franca. Evaluate their English performance with a randomly selected native corpus as the yardstick might not do the learners justice.

It is worth noting that emphasising the dual role of Chinese students in question being learners of English as well as users of ELF does not mean that native corpora should be completely excluded from learner corpus research. It, in fact, points to the importance of carefully selecting a native corpus if one is needed. Moreover, the dual role of the Chinese students also indicates that, if they wish to achieve higher proficiency level in English academic writing, they should have the freedom to choose the 'model' (native or nonnative) that they would like to follow. Under the context of English as a Lingua Franca, the success in communication might no longer be dependent on the nativeness of English, but more on the effective use of different strategies in order to overcome linguistic and pragmatic differences between different varieties of English and achieve mutual comprehension.

Another methodological issue was also raised based on the findings from this study. In not only learner corpus research but also any other corpus-based studies, one should take the individual factor into consideration when reporting the overall frequency of the searched items. While the overall figures can be quite useful for presenting a general picture, this picture might be distorted due to the idiosyncrasies of certain individual contributors to the corpus.

The findings are also of pedagogical value. The discrepancies observed between the inner circle English varieties suggest that the inner circle standard in English pedagogy may no longer be suitable for learners nowadays. Due to the accelerated pace of globalisation in the past few decades, these regionalised English varieties can no longer serve a leading role in communications in English internationally. English textbooks and reference tools should make changes accordingly to better suit the needs of English learners. The stylistic analysis of prepositional verbs indicates that the stylistic features are an indispensable part of multi-word-verb knowledge. This type of knowledge is usually missing in present reference tools. Learners should therefore be made aware of the importance of such knowledge in learning multi-word verbs.

REFERENCES

Aarts, J., & Granger, S. (1998). Tag sequences in learner corpora. In S. Granger (Ed.), *Learner English on computer* (pp. 132–141). London: Addison Wesley Longman.

Ädel, A. (2008). Metadiscourse across three Englishes: American, British, and advanced-learner English. In U. Connor, E. Nagelhout, & W. Rozycki (Eds.), *Contrastive rhetoric: Reaching to intercultural rhetoric* (pp. 45–62). London: Equinox. doi:10.1075/pbns.169.06ade

Algeo, J. (1988). British and American grammatical differences. *International Journal of Lexicography*, *1*(1), 1–31. doi:10.1093/ijl/1.1.1

Algeo, J. (2006). *British or American English? A handbook of word and grammar patterns*. Cambridge, UK: Cambridge University Press. doi:10.1017/CBO9780511607240

Baumgarten, N., & House, J. (2010). I think and I don't know in English as lingua franca and Beneke, J. (1991). Englisch als lingua franca oder als Medium interkultureller Kommunikation [English as lingua franca or as medium of intercultural communication]. In R. Grebing (Ed.), *Grenzenloses Sprachenlernen* (pp. 54–66). Berlin: Cornelsen.

Biber, D. (1987). A textual comparison between American and British writing. *American Speech*, *62*(2), 99–119. doi:10.2307/455273

Biber, D., & Barbieri, F. (2007). Lexical bundles in university spoken and written registers. *English for Specific Purposes*, *26*(3), 263–286. doi:10.1016/j.esp.2006.08.003

Biber, D., Conrad, S., & Cortes, V. (2003). Lexical bundles in speech and writing: an initial taxonomy. In A. Wilson, P. Rayson, & T. McEnery (Eds.), *Corpus linguistics by the Lune: A festschrift for Geoffrey Leech* (pp. 71–93). Frankfurt: Peter Lang.

Biber, D., Conrad, S., & Cortes, V. (2004). If you look at...: Lexical bundles in university teaching and textbooks. *Applied Linguistics*, *25*(3), 371–405. doi:10.1093/applin/25.3.371

Biber, D., Johansson, S., Leech, G., Conrad, S., & Finegan, E. (1999). *The Longman grammar of spoken and written English*. London: Longman.

Björkman, B. (2011). Pragmatic strategies in English as an academic lingua franca: Ways of achieving communicative effectiveness? *Journal of Pragmatics*, *43*(4), 950–964. doi:10.1016/j.pragma.2010.07.033

Chen, M. (2013a). Phrasal verbs in a longitudinal learner corpus: Quantitative findings. In S. Granger, G. Gilquin, & F. Meunier (Eds.), Twenty years of Learner Corpus Research: Looking back, moving ahead (pp. 89-101). Louvain-la-Neuve: Presses Universitaires de Louvain.

Chen, M. (2013b). Overuse or underuse: A corpus study of English phrasal verb use by Chinese, British and American university students. *International Journal of Corpus Linguistics*, *18*(3), 418–442. doi:10.1075/ijcl.18.3.07che

Chen, M., & Hu, X. (2006). Towards the acceptability of China English at home and abroad. *Changing English*, *13*(2), 231–240. doi:10.1080/13586840600833648

Chen, Y.-H., & Baker, P. (2010). Lexical Bundles in L1 and L2 Academic Writing. *Language Learning & Technology*, *14*(2), 30–49.

Conklin, K., & Schmitt, N. (2008). Formulaic sequences: Are they processed more quickly than non-formulaic language by native and nonnative speakers? *Applied Linguistics*, *29*(1), 72–89. doi:10.1093/applin/amm022

Cowan, R., Choi, H. E., & Kim, D. H. (2003). Four questions for error diagnosis and correction in CALL. *CALICO Journal*, *20*(3), 451–463.

Coxhead, A. (2008). Phraseology and English for academic purposes: Challenges and opportunities. In F. Meunier & G. Sylviane (Eds.), *Phraseology in Foreign Language Learning and Teaching* (pp. 149–161). Amsterdam: John Benjamins. doi:10.1075/z.138.12cox

Crystal, D. (1997). *English as a global language*. Cambridge, UK: Cambridge University Press.

Davies, M. (2008). *The Corpus of Contemporary American English: 450 million words, 1990-present.* Available at: http://corpus.byu.edu/coca/

De Cock, S. (2003). *Recurrent sequences of words in native speaker and advanced learner spoken and written English: A corpus-driven approach* (Doctoral dissertation). Louvain-la-Neuve: Université catholique de Louvain.

De Cock, S. (2004). Preferred sequences of words in NS and NNS speech. *Belgian Journal of English Language and Literatures (BELL). New Series, 2,* 225–246.

De Cock, S., Granger, S., Leech, G., & McEnery, T. (1998). An automated approach to the phrasicon of EFL learners. In S. Granger (Ed.), *Learner English on computer* (pp. 67–79). London: Longman.

Deterding, D., & Kirkpatrick, A. (2006). Intelligibility and an emerging ASEAN English lingua franca. *World Englishes, 25*(3), 391–410. doi:10.1111/j.1467-971X.2006.00478.x

Diez-Bedmar, M., & Casas-Pedrosa, A. (2011). The use of prepositions by Spanish learners of English at University level: A longitudinal analysis. In N. Kübler (Ed.), *Corpora, language, teaching, and resources: From theory to practice* (pp. 199–218). Bern: Peter Lang.

ELFA. (2008). *The Corpus of English as a Lingua Franca in Academic Settings.* Retrieved from http://www.helsinki.fi/elfa/elfacorpus

Ellis, N. C. (2008). Phraseology: The periphery and the heart of language. In F. Meunier & S. Grainger (Eds.), *Phraseology in language learning and teaching* (pp. 1–13). Amsterdam: John Benjamins. doi:10.1075/z.138.02ell

Fan, M. (2009). An Exploratory study of collocational use by ESL students: A task based approach. *System, 37*(1), 110–123. doi:10.1016/j.system.2008.06.004

Gardner, D., & Davies, M. (2007). Pointing out frequent phrasal verbs: A corpus-based analysis. *TESOL Quarterly, 41*(2), 339–360. doi:10.1002/j.1545-7249.2007.tb00062.x

Gilquin, G. (2011). *Corpus linguistics to bridge the gap between World Englishes and Learner Englishes.* Paper presented at the 12th International Symposium on Social Communication, Santiago, Cuba. Retrieved October 13, 2012, from http://hdl.handle.net/2078.1/112509

Gnutzmann, C. (1999). English as a global language: Perspectives for English language teaching and for teacher education in Germany. In C. Gnutzmann (Ed.), *Teaching and learning English as a global language: Native and non-native perspectives* (pp. 157–169). Tübingen: Stauffenburg.

Gnutzmann, C. (2000). Lingua franca. In M. Byram (Ed.), *The Routledge encyclopaedia of language teaching and learning* (pp. 356–359). London: Routledge.

Graddol, D. (1997). *The future of English?* London: British Council.

Granger, S. (1998). Prefabricated patterns in advanced EFL writing: Collocations and formulae. In A. Cowie (Ed.), *Phraseology: Theory, analysis, and applications* (pp. 145–160). Oxford, UK: Oxford University Press.

Granger, S., Dagneaux, E., Meunier, F., & Paquot, M. (Eds.). (2009). *The International Corpus of Learner English: Handbook and CD-ROM V2*. Louvain-la-Neuve: Presses Universitaires de Louvain.

Granger, S., & Rayson, P. (1998). Automatic profiling of learner texts. In S. Granger (Ed.), *Learner English on computer* (pp. 119–131). London: Addison Wesley Longman.

Gries, T. S. (2008). Dispersions and adjusted frequencies in corpora. *International Journal of Corpus Linguistics*, *13*(4), 403–437. doi:10.1075/ijcl.13.4.02gri

Gries, T. S. (2009). Dispersions and adjusted frequencies in corpora: further explorations. In T. S. Gries, S. Wulff, & M. Davies (Eds.), *corpus linguistic applications: Current studies, new directions* (pp. 197–212). Amsterdam: Rodopi.

Gries, T. S. (2012). Correction to 'Dispersions and adjusted frequencies in corpora'. *International Journal of Corpus Linguistics*, *171*, 147–149.

Groom, N. (2009). Effects of second language immersion on second language collocational development. In A. Barfield & II. Gyllstad (Eds.), *Researching collocations in another language: Multiple interpretations* (pp. 21–33). Basingstoke, UK: Palgrave Macmillan.

Hoffmann, S. (2005). *Grammaticalization and English complex prepositions: A corpus-based study*. London: Routledge.

House, J. (2002). Developing pragmatic competence in English as a Lingua Franca. In Knapp & Meierkord (Eds.), Lingua Franca communication (pp. 245–268). Frankfurt am Main: Peter Lang.

House, J. (2013). Developing pragmatic competence in English as a lingua franca: Using discourse markers to express (inter)subjectivity and connectivity. *Journal of Pragmatics*, *59*, 57–67. doi:10.1016/j.pragma.2013.03.001

Hu, X. (2004). Why China English should stand alongside British, American, and the other "World Englishes". *English Today*, *78*(20), 26–33.

Jenkins, J. (1996). Native speaker, non-native speaker and English as a Foreign Language: Time for a change. *IATEFL Newsletter*, *131*, 10–11.

Jenkins, J. (1998). Which pronunciation norms and models for English as an International Language? *ELT Journal*, *52*(2), 119–126. doi:10.1093/elt/52.2.119

Jenkins, J. (2000). *The phonology of English as an international language*. Oxford, UK: Oxford University Press.

Jenkins, J. (2002). A sociolinguistically based, empirically researched pronunciation syllabus for English as an International Language. *Applied Linguistics*, *23*(1), 83–103. doi:10.1093/applin/23.1.83

Jenkins, J., Cogo, A., & Dewey, M. (2011). Review of developments in research into English as a lingua franca. *Language Teaching*, *44*(3), 281–315. doi:10.1017/S0261444811000115

Jennifer, J. (2006). Current perspectives on teaching World Englishes and English as a lingua franca. *TESOL Quarterly, 40*(1), 157–181. doi:10.2307/40264515

Jiang, N., & Nekrasova, T. M. (2007). The processing of formulaic sequences by second language speakers. *Modern Language Journal, 91*(3), 433–445. doi:10.1111/j.1540-4781.2007.00589.x

Johansson, S. (1979). American and British English grammar: An elicitation experiment. *English Studies, 60*(2), 195–215. doi:10.1080/00138387908597961

Kachru, B. B. (1985). Standards, codification and sociolinguistic realism: the English language in the Outer Circle. In R. Quirk & H. G. Widdowson (Eds.), *English in the World: Teaching and learning the language and literatures* (pp. 11–30). Cambridge, UK: Cambridge University Press.

Kao, R. R. (2001). Where have the prepositions gone? A study of English prepositional verbs and input enhancement in instructed SLA. *IRAL, 39*(3), 195–215. doi:10.1515/iral.2001.002

Kaszubski, P. (1998) Learner corpora: the cross-roads of linguistic norm. Paper presented at the 1998 Teaching and language corpora conference, Oxford, UK.

Kirkpatrick, A. (2010). Researching English as a lingua franca in Asia: The Asian Corpus of English (ACE) project. *Asian Englishes, 31*(1), 4–18. doi:10.1080/13488678.2010.10801269

Knapp, A. (2011). Using English as a lingua franca for (mis-)managing conflict in an international university context: An example from a course in engineering. *Journal of Pragmatics, 43*(4), 978–990. doi:10.1016/j.pragma.2010.08.008

Knapp, K. (2002). The fading out of the non-native speaker. Native speaker dominance in lingua-franca situations. In K. Knapp & C. Meierkord (Eds.), *Lingua Franca communication* (pp. 217–244). Frankfurt: Peter Lang.

Li, J., & Schmitt, N. (2009). The acquisition of lexical phrases in academic writing: A longitudinal case study. *Journal of Second Language Writing, 18*(2), 85–102. doi:10.1016/j.jslw.2009.02.001

Li, X. H. (2004). Jiyuyuilaoku de effect dapeixingwei duibiyanjiu (A corpus-based study on the collocational behaviour of effect). *Foreign Language Education, 25*(6), 21–24.

Liu, D. (2011). The most-frequently used English phrasal verbs in American and British English: A multi-corpus examination. *TESOL Quarterly, 45*(4), 661–688. doi:10.5054/tq.2011.247707

Lorenz, G. (1998). Overstatement in advanced learners' writing: Stylistic aspects of adjective intensification. In S. Granger (Ed.), *Learner English on computer* (pp. 53–66). London: Addison Wesley Longman.

Lorenz, G. (1998). Overstatement in advanced learners' writing: Stylistic aspects of adjective intensification. In S. Granger (Ed.), *Learner English on Computer* (pp. 53–66).

Lorenz, G. (1999). *Adjective intensification: Learners versus native speakers. A corpus study of argumentative writing*. Amsterdam: Rodopi.

Lowenberg, P. H. (1993). Issues of validity in tests of English as a world language: Whose standards? *World Englishes, 12*(1), 95–106. doi:10.1111/j.1467-971X.1993.tb00011.x

Mair, C. (Ed.). (2003). *The politics of English as a world language: New horizons in postcolonial cultural studies*. Amsterdam: Rodopi.

McKay, S. (2002). *Teaching English as an international language: Rethinking goals and approaches*. Oxford, UK: Oxford University Press.

Michigan Corpus of Upper-level Student Papers. (2009). Ann Arbor, MI: The Regents of the University of Michigan. Available at: http://micusp.elicorpora.info/

Milton, J. (2001). *Research reports V2: Elements of a written interlanguage: A computational and corpus-based study of institutional influences on the acquisition of English by Hong Kong Chinese students*. Hong Kong: Hong Kong University of Science & Technology Press.

Milton, J., & Freeman, R. (1996). Lexical variation in the writing of Chinese learners of English. In C.E. Percy, C.F. Meyer, & I. Lancashire (Eds.), *Synchronic Corpus Linguistics: Papers from the sixteenth international conference on English language research on computerized corpora (ICAME 16)* (pp. 121-131). Amsterdam: Rodopi.

Mindt, D., & Weber, C. (1989). Prepositions in American and British English. *World Englishes, 8*(2), 229–238. doi:10.1111/j.1467-971X.1989.tb00658.x

Nesselhauf, N. (2003). The use of collocations by advanced learners of English and some implications for teaching. *Applied Linguistics, 24*(2), 223–242. doi:10.1093/applin/24.2.223

Osimk, R. (2009). Decoding sounds: An experimental approach to intelligibility in ELF. *Vienna English Working Papers, 18*, 64–89.

Paquot, M., & Granger, S. (2012). Formulaic language in learner corpora. *Annual Review of Applied Linguistics, 32*, 130–149. doi:10.1017/S0267190512000098

Prat Zagrebelsky, M. T. (2004). *Computer learner corpora. Theoretical issues and empirical case studies of Italian advanced EFL learners' interlanguage*. Alessandria: Edizioni dell'Orso.

Quirk, R., Greenbaum, S., Leech, G., & Svartvik, J. (1985). *A comprehensive grammar of the English language*. Harlow: Longman.

Rajadurai, J. (2007). Intelligibility studies: A consideration of empirical and ideological issues. *World Englishes, 26*(1), 87–98. doi:10.1111/j.1467-971X.2007.00490.x

Ringbom, H. (1998). Vocabulary frequencies in advanced learner English: A cross-linguistic approach. In S. Granger (Ed.), *Learner English on computer* (pp. 41–52). London, New York: Addison Wesley Longman.

Rohdenburg, G., & Schlüter, J. (2009). *One language, two grammars: differences between British and American English*. Cambridge, UK: Cambridge University Press. doi:10.1017/CBO9780511551970

Schmitt, N., Grandage, S., & Adolphs, S. (2004). Are corpus-derived recurrent clusters psycholinguistically valid? In N. Schmitt (Ed.), *Formulaic sequences* (pp. 127–152). Amsterdam: John Benjamins Publishing. doi:10.1075/lllt.9.08sch

Scott, M. (2008). *WordSmith Tools version 5*. Liverpool, UK: Lexical Analysis Software.

Seidlhofer, B. (2001). Closing a conceptual gap: The case for a description of English as a lingua franca. *International Journal of Applied Linguistics*, *11*(2), 133–158. doi:10.1111/1473-4192.00011

Simpson-Vlach, R., & Ellis, N. C. (2010). An Academic Formulas List: New methods in phraseology research. *Applied Linguistics*, *31*(4), 487–512. doi:10.1093/applin/amp058

Sinclair, J. (1991). *Corpus, concordance, collocation: Describing English language.* Oxford, UK: Oxford University Press.

Sinclair, J. (1996). The search for units of meaning. *TEXTUS*, *IX*, 75–106.

Sinclair, J. (2004). Meaning in the framework of corpus linguistics. *Lexicographica*, *20*, 20–32.

The British Academic Written English (BAWE) Corpus. (n.d.). Developed at the Universities of Warwick, Reading and Oxford Brookes under the directorship of Hilary Nesi, Sheena Gardner, Paul Thompson and Paul Wickens. Available at: http://www2.warwick.ac.uk/fac/soc/al/research/collect/bawe/

The British National Corpus, version 3 (BNC XML Edition). (2007). Distributed by Oxford University Computing Services on behalf of the BNC Consortium. Available at: http://www.natcorp.ox.ac.uk/

Tono, Y. (2002). *The role of learner corpora in SLA research and foreign language teaching: the multiple comparison approach.* (Unpublished doctoral dissertation). Lancaster University.

VOICE. (2013). *The Vienna-Oxford International Corpus of English* (version 2.0 online). Retrieved from http://voice.univie.ac.at

Waibel, B. (2007). *Phrasal verbs in learner English: A corpus-based study of German and Italian students.* (Unpublished PhD thesis). Albert-Ludwigs-Universität Freiburg.

Wei, N. X. (2004). Zhongguo xuexizhe yingyu kouyuyuliaoku chushi yanjiu[A preliminary study of the characteristics of Chinese learners' spoken English]. *Modern Foreign Languages*, *27*(2), 140–149.

Wray, A. (2002). *Formulaic sequences and the lexicon.* Cambridge, UK: Cambridge University Press. doi:10.1017/CBO9780511519772

Wray, A., & Perkins, M. (2000). The functions of formulaic language: An integrated model. *Language & Communication*, *20*(1), 1–28. doi:10.1016/S0271-5309(99)00015-4

Zhao, W. S. (2005). Cong dong/mingci dapei shiwu kan muyuqianyi dui eryuxide de yingxiang. [On the influence of L1 transfer on the verb-noun collocations in SLA] In H. Z. Yang, S. C. Gui, & D. F. Yang (Eds.), *Corpus-based analysis of Chinese learner English* (pp. 275–340). Shanghai: Shanghai Foreign Language Education Press.

ENDNOTES

[1] There are also other terms such as English as an International Language (EIL) (e.g., Jenkins, 2000; McKay, 2002), English as a Global Language (e.g., Crystal, 1997; Gnutzmann, 1999), English as

a World Language (e.g., Lowenberg, 1993; Mair, 2003). See Jenkins (2006) and Seidlhofer (2004) for detailed discussion about the nuances of the terminology.

[2]   The online free CLAWS POS tagger is available at http://ucrel.lancs.ac.uk/claws/.

[3]   The chi-square tests were performed based on absolute frequencies: CH vs. LOCNESS-US: $x^2 =$ 28.02, $p = .000$; CH vs. GS-UK: $x^2 = 5.12$, $p = .024$; CH vs. MICUSP: $x^2 = 31.49$, $p =.000$; CH vs. BAWE: $x^2 = 72.54$, $p =.000$.

Chapter 22

Tourism for Development in the Republic of Moldova:
Empowering Individuals and Extending the Reach of Globalization

Marc Pilkington
University of Burgundy, France

ABSTRACT

Can globalization be socially inclusive through new 2.0 digital initiatives? This is the thought-provoking question we ask in this article, with a special focus on the Republic of Moldova. Part 1 begins with a reflection on the intersection between globalization, development studies and the current Moldovan context. Part 2 is devoted to the promising field of emergent tourism, and more particularly, tourism 2.0, a blossoming concept that we try to uncover. Part 3 presents a concrete application with the example of Moldova Tours 2.0, a digital initiative in the field of tourism 2.0 in the Republic of Moldova. Various aspects of this project are highlighted and analyzed.

INTRODUCTION

The Republic of Moldova is a small (33,843 sq. km) relatively densely populated country with a rich History. She gained her independence, and became a sovereign country on 27 August 1991. Moldova is in South East Europe, sandwiched between Ukraine and Romania in the north of the Balkan Peninsula. The distance between the North and the South is 350 km, and between the West and the East, 150 km. The Republic of Moldova adopted her constitution in July 1994, and became a democratic republic (endorsing the separation of the legislative, executive and judicial powers), functioning under the Rule of Law. The legislative power is exercised by the Parliament, which is elected for four year-terms. There have been eight parliamentary elections since 1991. The latest parliamentary elections were held in Moldova on 30 November 2014. The elections were admittedly more a loss than a victory for the pro-European coalition, because center-right parties were obviously divided by sharp tensions. The pro-Russian So-

DOI: 10.4018/978-1-5225-0522-8.ch022

cialist Party, comprised of former communists, emerged as the winner of the 2014 elections. It was the strongest party in Parliament, with 20.51% of votes.

Yet, these facts are seldom known outside the small circles of specialists, journalists and commentators of this rather tormented region of the world. But what do people really know about the Republic of Moldova? Will they eventually book a flight to the capital Chisinau? Unfortunately, the Republic of Moldova does not quite enjoy a good reputation abroad: (oft-amplified) stories of poverty, trafficking of human organs, prostitution, and conflicts involving minorities abound.

As the BBC (2015, para12) states:

Moldova is one of the poorest countries in Europe, and has a large foreign debt and high unemployment. It is heavily dependent on Russia for energy supplies, and Russia has not hesitated to take advantage of this fact as a way of exerting economic pressure on Moldova.

In reality, Moldova presents a more appealing outlook and potential; small roads winding through the vineyards, sunflower fields and verdant pastures, bucolic and romantic waterfalls, beautiful monasteries carved into the limestone cliffs, not to forget the festive spirit that reigns in Chisinau, the capital. Part I will sketch out a synthesis between globalization trends and modern developments in the Republic of Moldova. Part II investigates the issue of tourism, and the underlying causes behind the disappointing figures in this small country. Part III puts forward a groundbreaking socially inclusive 2.0 digital initiative aimed at reconciling the dynamics of globalization with development trends in the Republic of Moldova.

THE REPUBLIC OF MOLDOVA AND GLOBALIZATION

Background

One Country at the Crossroads

Globalization is an umbrella term employed to describe a multi-factor causal process, which results in an increased level of interconnectedness between national economies, regional blocks, financial, capital, and information flows, and also people across the world. Globalization is a derivative of the terms "globe" and "global", which refer to an interconnected whole. It arguably originated with the industrial revolution in Great Britain in 1640, or with the French revolution in 1789. Other authors (O'Rourke & Williamson, 2002) date the phenomenon of globalization back to the nineteenth century. The common denominator of the often nebulous, definitions thereof, is a wide-ranging process of change that entails "social, cultural, economic, and political interdependencies and consequences" (Marsella, 2012, p. 456).

The Republic of Moldova signed an agreement of association with the European Union in Vilnius in 2014 (BBC, 2015). The EU being deeply involved in the globalization process, it is self-evident that the Republic of Moldova too is integral to globalization. The latter is not only circumscribed to the political and economic spheres, but also the cultural one. The results of the cultural integration of the Republic of Moldova into globalization may already be observed by the most vigilant observers. Thousands of Bessarabia's natives work abroad today. Some of them will eventually return, but others have decided to establish, to set new roots in their country of adoption. They do not leave Moldova alone, but often with their family, their traditions, and the cultural heritage they grew up with. They are the principal representatives of the Republic of Moldova abroad, which they incarnate in this complex globalization process.

Thanks to these emigrants, people from other nations are exposed to the culture of the Republic of Moldova, while Moldovans are also exposed to other cultures in a continuous process of cross-cultural interaction. What is taking place with this Moldovan cultural model being transposed to other people, traditions, models of existence and cultures? Is there any renunciation whatsoever to the essence of Moldovan culture? Moldova's very rich culture offers a wide range of activities to the interested visitor: literature, theater, music, plastic arts, architecture, radio and television broadcasting, library archives, design, book publishing, scientific research, cultural tourism... This diversity will be the coping stone of the novel thematic tours offered by our innovative 2.0 digital platform presented in section 3.

Globalization carries substantial changes in the international political sphere, thereby affecting all member countries of the international community, including, of course, the Republic of Moldova (Galben, 2011). On the one hand, world-systems analysis has shown that globalization goes hand in hand with the emergence of a world hegemonic power, the United States in the case at hand (Lechner, 2001), or more generally, a domination by Western advanced economies, thereby conferring a truly asymmetric nature to the globalization process. On the other hand, countries that appear to play a more passive role often point to cultural disruption, if not imperialism (Phillipson, 1992, 2000). All in all, globalization is never a zero-sum game. Corporate restructurings, mergers, bankruptcies, outsourcing, temporary employment are long-term societal trends affecting the lives of millions, thereby shaping anew the pattern of capital accumulation and technology transfers across the globe.

In spite of the unprecedented level of functional integration achieved by economic units that take part in the globalization process, the latter is characterized by a growing and multidimensional phenomenon of fragmentation. Interestingly enough, the different types of fragmentation "are not incompatible and indeed reinforce each other. They are specific: organizational fragmentation, geographical (by nation states) fragmentation; and fragmentation of the production process, which results in the international location of different components of manufacturing or services products in different countries" (Ietto-Gillies, 2005, p. 206). Moreover, another fundamental type of fragmentation is observed, that of the labor force itself through a "divide and rule strategy" (Cowling & Sugden, 1987), which can be seen as a mere by-product of the globalization process. Firms respond to attacks by rivals in the international arena by the search for cheaper labor and a divided labor force with a reduced bargaining power.

The 2007-2008 global turmoil sent shock waves throughout the world, thereby destabilizing the hard-fought configurations previously in place, and finally presiding over the emergence of a multipolar world, wherein the USA can no longer be seen as the single superpower in a globalized world. What we are witnessing, from a geopolitical standpoint, is an emerging plurality of centers of power. The recent creation of the New Development Bank in 2014 bears testimony to this shift towards a multipolar world, with the recognition of a rebalancing of power in favor of BRICS countries. The weight of this reconfiguration is particular acute in the Republic of Moldova where neighboring Russia exerts a pernicious influence on domestic economic affairs (BBC, 2015):

The fact that the Moldovan economy has traditionally been heavily dependent on the export of wine to Russia has also allowed Moscow to apply economic pressure by occasionally banning the import of Moldovan wine. In 2013-14, wine was among a broad range of Moldovan agricultural exports banned by Russia before and after the country's signing of an EU association agreement, along with Ukraine and Georgia.

What is so specific about the Republic of Moldova is the fact that globalization trends are superimposed on the unfinished agenda of modernization undergone by a country slowly moving in the direction of a functional democracy. At present, the Republic of Moldova needs its own geopolitical framework that would help her acquire more stability in our fast-changing world, having in mind long-term national interests of Moldovan society.

The Moldovan Economy

We present below a few select economic indicators for the Republic of Moldova, which are borrowed to the International Monetary Fund (2014) Country Report No 14/190.

Moldova's Development Strategy (Horizon 2025)

Devising a sound development strategy for the Republic of Moldova at the horizon 2025 is the safest way to overcome the global economic crisis that has plagued the world since 2007-2008, to stabilize the institutions, and ensure the modernization of the country. Since its independence in 1991, Moldova has undergone a wide-ranging transformation process. Yet, in spite of many important reforms in justice, education, and the economy that have helped achieve a more stable balance in key strategic areas, it remains unclear what exactly the nature of Moldova's development thread is. Delineating the development strategy of Moldova is made even more complex by the incomplete transition from the Soviet past toward a functional democracy with an efficient and sustainable model of economic growth and governance. The Republic of Moldova has suffered from the global crisis. In 2009, Moldova's economy experienced a massive recession (-6.5%), with a budget deficit amounting to 9% of GDP. The table below presents the evolution of nominal, real and per capita GDP between 2005 and 2009. After an impressive period of growth between 2005 and 2008, Moldova was hit violently by the global financial crisis.

Negative phenomena within the economic and political systems have been felt painfully in the most important areas of Moldovan life, thereby amplifying social issues, polarizing trends in society, and amplifying various expressions of alienation and intolerance in the social and political environment. It is increasingly clear that conventional (and often schematic) approaches to the Moldovan conundrum fail to provide the answer to the enduring question: where should we go from now? The political elite of the country, forming the state structures at all levels, tends to make electoral promises as part of ambitious development strategies, without being able to provide answers to the key questions for society, inter alia, how should the resources of the country be allocated, how can we attract foreign investment, and what should be the new priorities, in order to achieve a new qualitative level of development? Today, Moldovan society is characterized by a lack of consensus that further feeds internal and damaging contradictions, thereby hampering the potential of the country to set foot on the path toward development and prosperity.

The Bones of Contention that Characterize Moldova in 2015

The hybrid model of a democracy and a market economy, which has made the success of countless countries throughout the world, has proved largely ineffective in Moldova, due to limited knowledge of the modern world by the majority of the population, lack of sincerity at the upper echelons of power, faltering motivation to improve the lives of the Moldovans, irresponsibility on the part of politicians, who remain entangled in bureaucratic practices and finally corruption scandals (Pilkington, 2015).

Figure 1. Post-crisis economic performance in Moldova

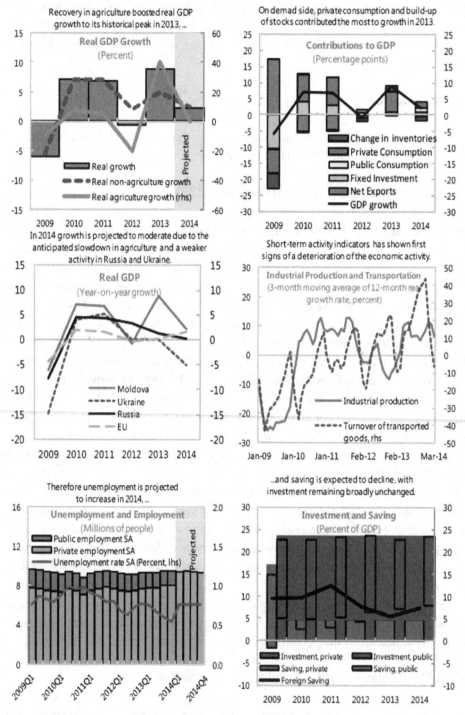

Sources: Moldovan authorities; National Bureau of Statistics of the Republic of Moldova; and IMF staff calculations.

Figure 2. Selected Economic Indicators for Moldova (2012 – 2019)

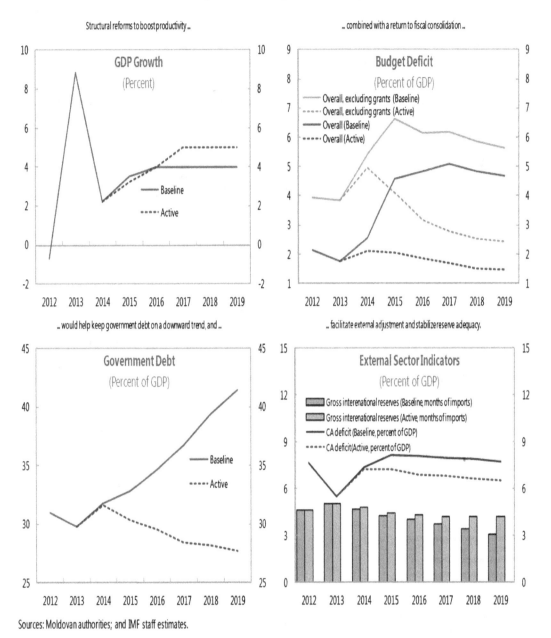

Sources: Moldovan authorities; and IMF staff estimates.

A contradiction persists between the oligarchic structure of the economy, and the need to develop a strong entrepreneurial base, without exacerbating the tensions between the dominant business and political groups. A pressure exists to develop broad international cooperation schemes. Yet the latter economic activities that would be supported should not be detrimental to the ecological configuration of the country, and should help maintain acceptable standards of food quality and health care for the citizens.

Moldova needs to consolidate the rule of Law, and move away from reform inertia, which has characterized the country for so long. It needs to put an end to the control of the judiciary power by politicians, thereby propelling judicial nihilism and corruption in Moldovan society.

Figure 3. Selected Economic Indicators for Moldova (2012-2019)

	2009	2010	2011	2012	2013	2014	2015	2016	2017	2018	2019
					Prel.			Projection			
I. Real sector indicators						(Percent change, unless otherwise indicated)					
Gross domestic product											
Real growth rate	-6.0	7.1	6.8	-0.7	8.9	2.2	3.5	4.0	4.0	4.0	4.0
Agricultural	-9.9	7.4	5.2	-20.1	40.6	0.0	4.0	4.0	4.0	4.0	4.0
Non-agricultural	-5.6	7.1	7.0	2.0	4.9	2.5	3.4	4.0	4.0	4.0	4.0
Demand	-15.1	9.2	8.3	0.4	6.2	2.1	2.4	2.6	3.2	3.2	3.3
Consumption	-6.9	7.3	7.5	0.9	5.2	2.8	3.0	2.8	3.1	3.2	3.2
Private	-8.0	9.6	9.4	1.0	6.5	1.9	1.9	2.6	2.9	3.1	3.1
Public	-2.0	-1.1	-0.7	0.6	-0.8	7.2	8.3	3.5	3.7	3.9	4.0
Gross capital formation	-30.9	17.2	13.0	1.8	3.3	3.8	2.2	1.5	4.0	2.7	3.4
Private	-32.1	18.5	11.3	-3.9	-3.7	0.5	1.0	3.5	4.0	4.0	4.0
Public	-26.4	12.4	19.3	21.6	22.4	11.0	4.5	-2.2	4.1	0.2	2.2
Nominal GDP (billions of Moldovan lei)	60.4	71.9	82.3	88.2	99.9	108.7	118.8	130.6	143.3	156.6	171.1
Nominal GDP (billions of U.S. dollars)	5.4	5.8	7.0	7.3	7.9	7.6	8.1	8.7	9.2	9.8	10.4
Consumer price index (average)	0.0	7.4	7.6	4.6	4.6	5.7	6.0	6.3	5.8	5.3	5.0
Consumer price index (end of period)	0.4	8.1	7.8	4.0	5.2	5.4	6.5	6.0	5.5	5.0	5.0
GDP deflator	2.2	11.1	7.3	7.9	4.0	6.5	5.6	5.7	5.5	5.1	5.0
Average monthly wage (Moldovan lei)	2,748	2,972	3,194	3,478	3,765	4,080	4,450	4,880	5,330	5,820	6,355
Average monthly wage (U.S. dollars)	247	240	272	287	299	286	304	325	344	364	387
Unemployment rate (annual average, percent)	6.4	7.4	6.7	5.6	5.1	6.0	5.8	5.6	5.5	5.5	5.5
Saving-investment balance						(Percent of GDP)					
Foreign saving	9.5	9.6	12.3	7.7	5.5	7.4	8.2	8.1	8.0	7.9	7.7
National saving	13.1	13.0	11.0	16.0	17.1	16.0	14.8	14.3	14.4	14.3	14.3
Private	14.8	10.4	8.1	11.7	11.7	10.6	11.5	11.7	12.1	11.9	11.9
Public	-1.7	2.6	2.9	4.3	5.3	5.4	3.3	2.6	2.4	2.3	2.4
Gross investment	22.6	22.6	23.3	23.6	22.6	23.3	23.0	22.4	22.4	22.2	22.0
Private	17.6	17.9	18.1	17.4	15.5	15.5	15.1	15.0	15.0	15.0	15.0
Public	5.0	4.8	5.2	6.3	7.1	7.9	7.9	7.4	7.4	7.2	7.1
II. Fiscal indicators (general government)											
Primary balance	-5.1	-1.8	-1.6	-1.4	-1.3	-1.9	-3.9	-4.0	-4.0	-3.7	-3.4
Overall balance	-6.3	-2.5	-2.4	-2.2	-1.8	-2.6	-4.6	-4.8	-5.1	-4.8	-4.7
Stock of public and publicly guaranteed debt	32.4	30.5	29.0	31.1	29.9	31.8	32.8	34.7	36.7	39.4	41.5
III. Financial indicators						(Percent change, unless otherwise indicated)					
Broad money (M3)	3.2	13.4	10.6	20.8	26.5	15.9	16.4	...	...	...	...
Velocity (GDP/end-period M3; ratio)	1.8	1.9	2.0	1.8	1.6	1.5	1.4	...	...	...	...
Reserve money	-10.1	15.9	18.4	22.9	31.9	13.4	14.0	...	...	...	...
Credit to the economy	-4.9	12.7	15.0	16.1	18.8	11.3	11.4	...	...	...	...
Credit to the economy, percent of GDP	39.5	37.4	37.6	40.7	42.7	43.7	44.6	...	...	...	...
IV. External sector indicators						(Millions of U.S. dollars, unless otherwise indicated)					
Current account balance	-516	-559	-863	-559	-438	-564	-662	-700	-737	-774	-806
Current account balance (percent of GDP)	-9.5	-9.6	-12.3	-7.7	-5.5	-7.4	-8.2	-8.1	-8.0	-7.9	-7.7
Remittances and compensation of employees (net)	1,124	1,273	1,549	1,745	1,913	1,864	1,839	1,892	1,950	2,010	2,073
Gross official reserves	1,480	1,718	1,965	2,515	2,820	2,751	2,621	2,599	2,551	2,511	2,409
Gross official reserves (months of imports)	3.9	3.4	3.9	4.7	5.0	4.7	4.3	4.0	3.7	3.4	3.1
Exchange rate (Moldovan lei per USD, period avge)	11.1	12.4	11.7	12.1	12.6	...	...	...	...	...	...
Exchange rate (Moldovan lei per USD, end of period)	12.3	12.2	11.7	12.1	13.1	...	...	...	...	...	...
Real effective exchrate (average, percent change)	5.4	-7.4	5.3	4.5	-3.4	-3.5	0.4	0.8	0.3	0.0	0.0
External debt (percent of GDP) 2/	80.2	82.0	77.6	82.5	83.6	90.0	87.8	86.2	84.9	84.2	82.3
Debt service (percent of exports of goods and services)	20.1	17.6	15.7	15.6	17.5	18.6	19.5	22.5	21.2	22.4	24.1

Sources: Moldovan authorities; and IMF staff estimates.
1/ Data exclude Transnistria.
2/ Includes private and public and publicly guaranteed debt.

At the time of writing, massive anti-government protests are taking place in Chisinau, structured around the Truth and Dignity platform (2015), led by notorious figures of civil society. Former Moldovan Prime Minister Vlad Filat was arrested on 15 October 2015 over allegations of corruption (Foy, 2015). Social peace and harmony is threatened by rising inequalities that are the widening gap between the rich minority and the poor majority of society of the country. Drawing on concepts of capability and justice (Sen,, 2010, 2012), the National Development Report (2014, p. 4) acknowledges that "recent economic

Table 1. Evolution of population income during 2005-2009

	2005	2006	2007	2008	2009
Nominal GDP per capita (MDL)	10488	12497	14955	17649	16260
Read GPD per capita (MDL, prices for year 2000)	6294	6613	6828	7379	6542
GDP per capita (USD)	832	952	1232	1699	1463

growth and social progress has disproportionately benefited the bigger cities, while people in rural areas continue to have fewer economic opportunities and only partial access services such as health, education, water and sanitation at best".

The apparent openness of society, and the pluralism of the Moldovan mass media in the developing civil society come in sharp contrast with opposing trends conducted through the same channels aiming at manipulation and concentration of power in the hands of a handful of public organizations and NGOs.

There is a growing tension between, on the one hand, the need to study the genuine History of Moldova, to develop a national identity, a true Moldovan patriotism with full respect for the interests of neighboring countries and, on the other hand, the absence of such a consciousness in the ranks of Moldovan citizens, on whom are imposed imaginary and manipulative versions as regards the origin and the History of the Moldovan people, whether consciously or unconsciously, often subordinated to intellectual elites and outside (foreign) influences.

Proposed Solutions for Moldova

The accumulation of contradictions leads to the continuous deformation of the socio-cultural context of the contemporary Moldovan society in its entirety, thereby turning it into a society with dual or even triple standards. This is why elements of the systemic crisis, the general crisis within which Moldova finds itself, requires a deep interpretative guidance, an analysis of reality from the same perspective as the problems and phenomena that society is currently faced with, inventing the modalities to solve the latter problems, and ensure a stable development of the country. The country's development strategy must ensure high quality, systemic and irreversible evolutions in key areas of social life supported by general democratic principles thanks to the real and enduring values of the Moldovan people, based on their tremendously rich culture and ancient history: "Moldova has a historic opportunity to modernize its economy and ensure inclusive sustainable development for all" (UNDP, Moldova National Development Report, 2014, p. 4).

Very modestly, we believe that our innovative project constitutes a step in the right direction on the path to the sustainable economic and human development.

TOURISM IN MOLDOVA: SOME ISSUES

Tourism and Poverty Alleviation: A Review of Literature

Although tourism in the Republic of Moldova is still embryonic, it could follow the example of other countries that have used tourism as a development engine with the implementation and monitoring of projects, which have contributed, at various degrees and levels, to the enhanced welfare of local populations.

The link between poverty alleviation and tourism was first acknowledged in 1999 during the seventh session of the UN Commission on Sustainable Development (CSD-7) which set the objective to "maximize the potential of tourism for eradicating poverty by developing appropriate strategies in cooperation with all major groups, and indigenous and local communities" (CSD7 1999, p. 39). Pro-poor tourism has been a flourishing research area ever since (Ashley, 2006; Ashley & Goodwin, 2007; Ashley & Haysom, 2008; Organisation Mondiale du Tourisme [OMT], 2002, 2005; Pro-Poor Tourism Partnership, 2004, 2005a, 2005b). SNV (i.e. Netherlands Development Organisation) is an international not-for-profit development organization that works on poverty alleviation schemes and sustainable development in twenty countries and five regions of the world. SNV has been very active in the tourism sector since 1994 (OMT & SNV, 2015, p. xv), in order to alleviate poverty through the increase in production, income and employment opportunities for underprivileged populations. Because the management of tourism destinations is paramount (OMT, 2007; Twining-Ward, 2007), SNV supervises field work and conducts ground-level studies to assess how financial flows that circulate in the tourism sector eventually reach the poor. Tourism projects in developing countries set the stage for innovative public-private partnerships (PPP).

In Western Ghana, SNV initiated in 2006 a tourism project (OMT & SNV, 2015, p.10) structured approximately twenty thermal stations, a NGO (Ghana Wildlife Society), a consulting company monitoring a poverty-alleviation scheme, the National Park of Ankasa, GTBank Ghana, and the Ministry of Finance and Economic Planning (MOFEP). The experiment successfully enabled the enhancement of tourism destinations on the West coast, thereby contributing to welfare, and reducing poverty levels.

Likewise, the Tourism Council of Bhutan in partnership with various actors of the private sector has been targeting specific actions aimed at the involvement of local communities, in order to derive economic benefits from tourism growth (ibid., p.18). Let us mention the creation of Nabji-Korphua (Dojri, 2007; Rinzi, Vermeulen & Glasbergen, 2007), a new marked trekking path that gave rise to the collection of data during its first year of existence. In spite of a very moderate number of visits (six groups accounting for 70 tourists in 2007), the initiative added US$4,000 to the income of the local communities, thus benefiting up to 72% of all households. Work includes drawing water, cooking, merchandising vegetables, and handicrafting (Rinzi, Vermeulen & Glasbergen, 2007)

In Albania, a country, which has, for a long time, shared with the Republic of Moldova the title of the poorest country in Europe, the role of tourism in promoting economing development has been analyzed by Bazini and Nedelea (2008, pp. 23-28).

A tourism project involves various communities in North Tanzania, who offer tourists to live in small villages, and share the genuine lifestyle of its inhabitants (Mitchell, Keane & Laidlaw, 2009; OMT & SNV, 2015). Accomodation and food catering services are offered, along with many types of excursions (by bicycle, boat, or on foot) in the forests near the waterfalls. Communities share cultural experiences, e.g., village tales, dances, handicrafts, and food, with the visitors (Mitchell, Keane, & Laidlaw, 2009). On-site training was provided by the project organizers. In Croatia, tourism is paramount in the rural development of the country, and its poverty reduction strategy (United Nations, 2008, p. 25):

Rural tourism plays an important role for the economic, social and cultural development of the rural areas. It is closely related to agricultural production, regional development, natural environment, and rural way of life showing traditional lifestyle, ambience, cultural and historical traditions.

A 2.0 Precedent: www.moldovenii.md

In our endeavor to understand the determinants and the potential of tourism in the Republic of Moldova, we draw on a benchmark in Moldovan cyberspace, a 2.0 role model so to speak, namely the breathtaking website www.moldovenii.md. It represents a platform that regroups the most significant news and information obtained from credible sources on History, culture, Diaspora and development programs of Moldova. A powerful search engine offers advanced access to a rich library that contains a wide variety of information that pertains to Moldovan music, films, literature, art, nature, architecture and so on. Independent of public authorities and political parties, www.moldovenii.md is a platform for discussions where opinion may be expressed, and where polls are available on topics of interest to Moldovans and foreigners. This makes www.moldovenii.md an innovative, collaborative, and interactive 2.0 platform promoting new projects, and empowering visitors of the website.

www.moldovenii.md (2015 para5) features a very interesting webpage on tourism:

Moldova is so small and diverse, so familiar and unfamiliar at the same time. There is no paradox, because even we, the majority of the Moldavian citizens, know too little about our country. Sometimes we think we know it well, but all of a sudden, one day, traveling outside Chisinau, Balti and Tiraspol somewhere into the country, on a picnic or to pay a visit, taking a tour or a hike with friends, having just moved from the central highway we start discovering those little wonders, which astonish us deeply.

Stakeholders in the Tourism Industry

For the UNWTO (2002), a local tourism destination is[a] physical space in which a visitor spends at least one overnight. It includes tourism products such as support services and attractions, and tourism resources within one day´s return travel time. It has physical and administrative boundaries defining its management, images and perceptions defining its market competitiveness. Local tourism destinations incorporate various stakeholders often including a host community, and can nest and network to form larger destinations.

The local tourism destination is (UNWTO, 2002)

- The fundamental unit, on which all the many complex dimensions of tourism are based,
- The focal point in the development and delivery of tourism products and implementation of tourism policy,
- The basic unit of analysis in tourism,
- Offers a broad range of products, experiences and services under the destination brand,
- Cluster: co-location of activities (products and services) that are linked horizontally, vertically or diagonally along the value chain and served by public and private sector,
- Physical, but also intangible (image, identity, personality).

Figure 4. Stakeholders in the tourism industry

Tourism in the Republic of Moldova

Now let us go into more detail, and assess the current situation of Moldova as regards its tourism industry, and its attractiveness potential. We reproduce below a brief outline of the country's administrative structure (PwC, 2014).

Moldova is currently divided into 37 first-tier units, including 32 districts (in Romanian - "raioane"), three municipalities (Chişinău, Bălţi, Bender), one autonomous territorial unit (Gagauzia) and one territorial unit (Transnistria). The capital and largest city is Chisinau. Moldova has 66 cities (towns), including the five with municipality status, and 917 communes. Some other 699 villages are too small to have separate administration, so are administratively part of either cities (40 of them) or communes (659). This makes for a total of 1,681 localities in Moldova (p.7).

Tourism Activities Offered by Tourism Agencies and Tour Operators of Moldova in 2014[1]

First and foremost, the Republic of Moldova has been a member of the World Tourism Organization (www2.unwto.org/), which is the United Nations agency responsible for the promotion of responsible, sustainable and universally accessible tourism. According to Moldova's national office of statistics, in 2014, tourism agencies and tour operators provided tourism services and excursions to 238100 tourists, a progression of +16.2% compared to 2013 (26% for domestic tourism i.e. Moldova for Moldovans, 14.7% for outward tourism and 9.2% for inward tourism). Let us note that inward tourism (attracting foreigners to Moldova) records the weakest increase in relative terms. Another way to look at the problem is to view potential inward tourism as being the highest, albeit still hampered by deficient infrastructures and a deficit in the perception of the country abroad.

Out of the 14,400 foreign tourists who visited the Republic of Moldova in 2014, and consumed the services of tourism agencies and tour operators, 58.2% traveled for leisure or recreational purposes, 34.5% for professional / business purposes, 3.9% to receive health care services. These tourists were respectively citizens of Romania (21,2%), Russian Federation (13,9%), Ukraine (10,7%), Germany

Figure 5. The administrative division of the Republic of Moldova

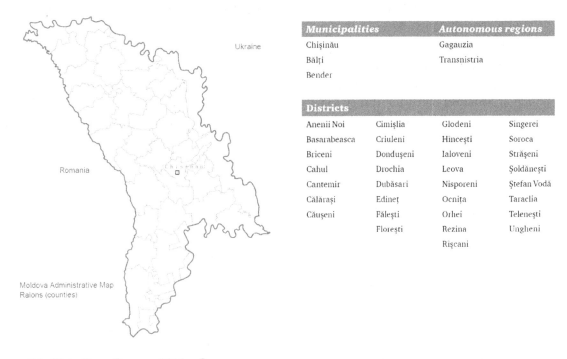

Municipalities		Autonomous regions
Chişinău		Gagauzia
Bălţi		Transnistria
Bender		

Districts			
Anenii Noi	Cimişlia	Glodeni	Sîngerei
Basarabeasca	Criuleni	Hinceşti	Soroca
Briceni	Donduşeni	Ialoveni	Străşeni
Cahul	Drochia	Leova	Şoldăneşti
Cantemir	Dubăsari	Nisporeni	Ştefan Vodă
Călăraşi	Edineţ	Ocniţa	Taraclia
Căuşeni	Făleşti	Orhei	Teleneşti
	Floreşti	Rezina	Ungheni
		Rişcani	

Moldova Administrative Map
Raions (counties)

Ukraine

Romania

Source: PriceWaterHouseCoopers, 2014, p.7

Table 2. The number of tourists and excursionists, participants in tourism services provided by tourism agencies and tour-operators, broken down by objective of the visit

	2014		% Variation (2013 = Basis 100)	
	Tourists and Excursionists	**Days of Tourism**	**Tourists and Excursionists**	**Days of Tourism**
TOTAL	238053	1631892	116,2	114,4
Inward tourism *(hosting foreign citizens in Moldova)* – total	14362	37050	109,2	88,3
Out of which whose objective was:				
Leisure, recreation	8355	14605	131,7	94,9
Professional / business	4952	13889	83,1	82,1
Health tourism	559	7586	93,8	93,7
Other objectives	496	970	199,2	62,5
Outward tourism *(trips of Moldovan citizens abroad)* - total	180646	1287340	114,7	117,0
Out of which whose objective was:				
Leisure, recreation	178260	1269617	115,5	118,1
Professional / business	1144	7412	79,9	114,9
Health tourism	1164	10042	77,3	61,0
Other objectives	78	269	25,3	9,8
Domestic tourism *(flows of Moldovan visitors in Moldova for tourism purposes)*	43045	307502	126,0	108,1

(4,9%), Turkey (4,8%), Italy (4,0%), USA (3,9%), Israel (3,7%), Poland (3,0%), United Kingdom Nord (2,9%), Bulgaria (2,7%), Belarus (2,5%), Netherlands (2,3%), Austria (1,9%), Sweden (1,7%), France (1,3%), Lithuania (1,2%).

Through tourism agencies and tour operators, 180,600 Moldovan tourists and excursionists went abroad in 2014 for tourism purposes, a 14.7% increase compared to 2013. An overwhelming majority of Moldovan citizens went abroad for leisure and recreational purposes (98.7%). Most citizens of the Republic of Moldova opted for Turkey (35.2% of the total went abroad), Bulgaria (33.4%), Romania (10.2%), Greece (8.5%), Egypt (2.1%), Ukraine and United Arab Emirates (both 1.6%), Spain (0.9%).

The number of tourists who took part in domestic tourism in 2014 amounted to 43,000, a 26% increase compared to 2013. Trips of Moldovan residents inside the country were organized by tourism agencies and tour operators of the municipality of Chisinau (49. 5%), the Centre (24.6%), and the South (21.0%).

Lonely Planet Depicting Moldova as Europe's Least-Visited Country in 2013

An online article by Leif Pettersen (2013) published by Lonely Planet depicts a bleak, albeit forward-looking, picture of the Moldovan tourism industry. Pettersen (2013) reminds us of the mere 9,000 international arrivals in the country in 2011. Instead of a defeatist attitude, Moldova is adopting a pro-active and forward-looking attitude towards tourism. In fact, the country was voted by Lonely Planet readers as the #2 off-the-beaten-path destination in the world (behind Bhutan) in the 2013 Traveler's Choice poll. Cooperative tourism sector is actively given support by USAID (www.usaid.gov) and CEED II (http://ceed.md/); Moldova's is telling the world how and why we must look at the other side of the coin of un/popularity. Numerous people have become jaded by the beaten path, and would certainly find the Republic of Moldova a land worth spending time in. Why not head toward a breathtaking cave monastery perched above a winding valley at Orheiul Vechi, taking a ride in a crowded minibus, and bounce down busted up roads squashed in the back row between villagers returning from a shopping afternoon in Chisinau?

Why not try a Soviet-loving, communist-era Moscow immersion in the breakaway republic of Transdniestra? This entails queuing up at a militarized border crossing, and sweating out tedious formalities, before entering a beautiful territory out of space and of time. Wine lovers will also get the chance to visit the wonder wine caves in Cricova (www.cricova.md), Purcari (www.purcari.md), Chateau Vartely (http://vartely.md), and Milestii Mici (www.milestii-mici.md) where rewarding tastings and tours can are already staged year-round. The 2012 legalization of small wine production was a milestone in Moldova. Prior to that, small producers were dependent on large, state-run producers, a legacy from the Soviet era, to bring their wine production to the market. Since then, the export wine market has experienced a second youth, as shown by the dynamism of Moldova's Wine Festival (www.facebook.com/moldovawineday), held during the first week of October, which is arguably the biggest event on the country's calendar. Close to the monastery at Orheiul Vechi, a sensorial agro-tourism experience can be found at Agro Pensiunea Butuceni (www.pensiuneabutuceni.md), a welcoming place that offers a variety of rooms, and can arrange meals, tours, cultural activities and performances. Interested observers will also be interested in the Consolidated Unit for Implementing and Monitoring the Wine Sector Monitoring Program, which offers an interesting Internet platform for all stakeholders in the wine industry (http://www.winemoldova.md/).

How about the capital Chisinau? First-time visitors are surprised by how green the city is, one of the leafiest capital cities in Europe. Chisinau's eating and drinking scene is an appealing place for gourmets. The nightlife too has a good reputation, not to forget the rich museums of the city.

Deficient Infrastructures, High Poverty Levels and Rising Geopolitical Tensions

In spite of the fast growth experienced by Moldova in the run-up to the global crisis, and the brevity of the recession that started in 2009, Moldova remains, as it is oft-quoted, a poor country (International Monetary Fund, 2014).

Despite a sharp decline in poverty in recent years, Moldova remains one of the poorest countries in Europe and structural reforms are needed to promote sustainable growth. Based on the Europe and Central Asia (ECA) regional poverty line of US$5/day (PPP), 55 percent of the population was poor in 2011. While this was significantly lower than 94 percent in 2002, Moldova's poverty rate is still more than double the ECA average of 25 percent (p.4).

Geopolitical tensions that originated with the Maidan revolution have triggered fears for Moldova. For the International Monetary Fund (2014, p.7), "the impact of recent regional geopolitical developments on the Moldovan economy will depend on whether the crisis spreads beyond Ukraine, trade tensions with Russia escalate, and trade routes and gas supply are disrupted". The International Monetary Fund believes that adverse consequences can be mitigated if external macroeconomic shocks are better absorbed, and if the Moldovan economy increases its levels of integration into global trade and energy markets over the medium term. The direct impact of the Ukrainian crisis on the Moldovan economy is likely to be fairly limited due to the modest trade and financial linkages between the two countries. Ukraine's share of Moldovan exports is about 6 percent, and remittances from Ukraine represent around 1 percent of GDP. Likewise, on the financial side, the direct impact would also be negligible due to the very limited cross-border financial relations.

Contrariwise, a further slowdown in the Russian economy, and/or an escalation of trade tensions with Russia, may prove harmful. Russia's share of Moldovan exports is roughly 26 percent, and remittances from Russia represent about 15 percent of Moldova's GDP (International Monetary Fund, 2014, p.7). Moreover, Russia is an important source of inward FDI to Moldova (about 10 percent of the total stock of FDI). A disruption of trade routes and gas supply would have harmful consequences on the Moldovan economy. The CIS's share in Moldovan exports is 40 percent, and most land routes to CIS countries pass through Ukraine. Similarly, Moldova is very reliant on Russian gas transported via pipelines in Ukraine (over 90 percent of total Moldovan gas consumption). Substituting gas imports from Russia will be problematic. Over the medium term, increased integration into global trade and energy markets would help reduce the impact of shocks in any single trading partner (International Monetary Fund, 2014, p.7). Furthermore, the Moldovan banking system is still heavily reliant on funding from Russian banks. A disruption of cross-bank funding between Russian and Moldovan banks could significantly destabilize the already fragile banking system of the country.

Furthermore, a major embarrassment has been caused for the ex-Soviet state on track for EU membership by a massive scandal that has severely destabilized the banking system (Pilkington, 2015). The Central Bank of Moldova shed light on the disappearance of a billion dollars (12.5% of the country's GDP) involving three banks (Banca de Economii, Banca Sociala and Unibank) that hold about a third of all bank assets of the country, including money for pension payments. The transactions allegedly happened just before the parliamentary elections in late November 2014.

Of course, these adverse socio-economic factors and geopolitical uncertainty do not create favorable conditions for the growth of tourism in the Republic of Moldova. Yet, as we will see, there might be a way out of this economic and geopolitical deadlock. Put differently, it might not be the end of History for tourism in Moldova.

A SOCIALLY INCLUSIVE 2.0 DIGITAL PLATFORM

Social Entrepreneurship and IT Skills in Moldova

The National Development Report (2014) states that,

Moldova needs a truly transformational change if it is to overcome these challenges. Such a change cannot be achieved by any one actor. However, the role of the private sector is essential in driving development; this report argues that the private sector's contribution to economic growth, technological change and general welfare has yet to be fully harnessed in Moldova (p.4).

As a matter of fact, the present era requires the enhancement of IT skills:

The implementation of new information technologies, which is a true revolution in the contemporary evolutionary process of science, and includes nano and biotechnologies, television laser, optical and quantum computers, depends heavily on the quality of resources and knowledge of contemporary specialists. In this regard, graduates in science of the Free International University of Moldova (ULIM) and the Technical University of Moldova, are highly appreciated not only in the United States and Canada, but are given to employment opportunities in universities, businesses and companies intercontinental and especially in scientific research centers (International Conference of Rectors, Shanghai, 2011).

The awareness of these societal needs coupled with the skills of these Moldovan graduates should ring a bell in favor of increased social entrepreneurship in the Republic of Moldova, by drawing upon innovative business techniques.

What Is Web 2.0 and Why Does It Matter for Tourism?

For many, the term web 2.0 was coined by O'Reilly on 30.9.2005 on his personal website. It amounted to a "business revolution in the computer industry caused by the move to the Internet as platform, and an attempt to understand the rules for success on that new platform". In fact, a year earlier, in 2004, the first web 2.0 conference was held October 5 - 7, 2004 at the Hotel Nikko in San Francisco[1]. The emergence of Web 2.0 is a revolution that has transformed the Internet landscape: "With more Internet users accessing broadband and surfing the web at higher speeds, social networking, user-generated content, social bookmarking, sharing of information, videos, images and opinions exponentially increased the amount of content on the Web" (Noti, 2013, p.116). The shift from Web 1.0 to Web 2.0 was essentially one from static to dynamic: "The beginning of the Web era, which than was mainly PC-based, enabled marketers to create static online brochures that later evolved into increasingly dynamic, multimedia resources" (Noti, 2013, p.115). This shift also impacted the business world for Internet technology has a direct impact on companies, customers, suppliers, distributors and potential entrants into an industry (Porter, 2001).

In the initial stages of mass Internet, in the late 1990s and early 2000s, until the advent of Web 2 .0, the online travel industry witnessed the development of new market dynamics and consumer behaviours (Werthner & Klein, 1999; Werthner & Ricci, 2004). Yet, the shift to web 2.0 was mirrored by a process of wide-ranging disintermediation in the tourism industry: "customers are able to purchase products/services or to make reservations in the tourism sector, directly online without having to deal with intermediary companies" (Noti, 2013, p.115). Tourists everywhere are looking for new experiences. They wish to retrieve on the Web all the relevant information about a particular destination (e.g. comments, videos, pictures, images, stories). Tourism 2.0 allows for the customization of tourism services by cherry-picking every detail, and comparing prices online. The Web 2.0 culture has paved the way for an interactive environment characterized by information sharing and feedback informational loops. Moreover, the implementation of Web 2.0 platforms and social media, have intensified social networking practices, giving the tourism experience an unprecedented interactive and collaborative nature.

Chief among our insights [at the first web 2.0 conference in 2004] was that "the network as platform" means far more than just offering old applications via the network ("software as a service"); it means building applications that literally get better the more people use them, harnessing network effects not only to acquire users, but also to learn from them and build on their contributions (O'Reilly, 2005).

Mobile Devices and Web 2.0

Another crucial evolution, which has accompanied the widespread use of Web 2.0, is the mass adoption of mobile devices encouraging tourism communication. Smartphones and tablets are easily portable and accessible devices that can be used by travellers whilst on holiday, in order to find and share information about tourist destinations.

The Transformative Power of Tourism 2.0

In tourism 1.0 (the current scenario), the user books on the Internet a range of services (hotel, travel agency, cultural site, museum…) that will form the thrust of the touristic experience. Yet, as Edu (2010) has argued:

The tourism model 1.0 guarantees neither access by SMEs nor equality of conditions to maintain the same level of competitiveness.

The tourism 1.0 model solves neither the problems of access to and transparency of information nor those of cooperation between businesses and destinations.

The tourism 1.0 model does not incorporate knowledge transfer as a factor determining the productivity of destinations and enterprises.

Figure 6. Number of mobile phone users worldwide (2012-2018) in Billions

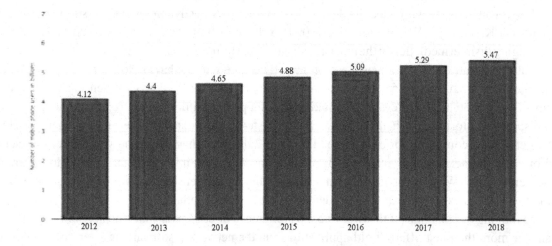

Based on the Te.S.C.He.T. (2003) project, tourism 2.0 is a new agent-based infrastructure enabling the handling and the organization of tourism-related information by the user, the creation of innovative services, and the dynamic, adaptive, intelligent, and autonomous composition of tourism services. The architecture of the tourism 2.0 solution allows for the integration of heterogeneous and distributed information sources as well as the interoperability among heterogeneous information systems. The guiding principle behind tourism 2.0 is to help the user access services and information over the Internet, through the use of smart mobile devices that evolve from being mere transmitter/receiver of information to full-fledged information-centric devices at the heart of a network containing active and pro-active elements.

Tourism 2.0 is the business revolution in the tourism and leisure industry caused by the move to the tourist ecosystem as platform, and an attempt to understand the rules for success on that new platform. Chief among those rules is this: build applications that harness network effects to get better the more people use them (Edu, 2010).

Tourism 2.0 or Tourism 3.0?

In the digital footprints of Web 2.0, Web 3.0 is the third stage of web development. Its comprehensive treatment is beyond the scope of the present chapter. Web 3.0 also called Semantic Web, allows the meaning of user-generated content to be recognized and understood by intelligent machines, thereby enabling computer to computer interaction (Mistilis & Bouhalis, 2012):

Web 3.0, frequently referred to as the Semantic Web, represents the evolution of Web 2.0 in key areas such as social networking and mobility, and introduces potentially revolutionary concepts including the use of intelligent agents, open data and semantic searches (HSMAI Foundation, 2015, p.6)

Figure 7. Tourism 1.0 vs. tourism 2.0

CURRENT SCENARIO (TOURISM 1.0)

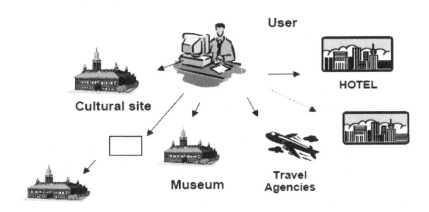

EXPECTED SCENARIO (TOURISM 2.0)

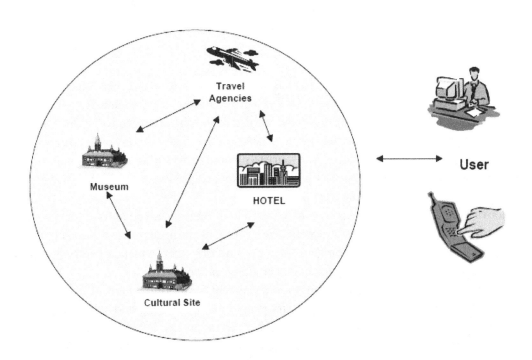

Source: Te.S.C.He.T. Technology System for Cultural Heritage in Tourism (2003)

517

Amongst the potentialities of tourism 3.0, we foresee two important trends:

- The use of blockchain technology (Pilkington, 2016) and crypto-currencies to pay for tourism services, as it is already the case for HolaCuba.de, a German vacation booking company, whose online customers can make payments for *casas particulares,* the Cuban versions of a "bed & breakfast," with Bitcoin[2].
- The use of connected object or the Internet of things, in order to enhance the collective intelligence enshrined in tourism services.

In the Internet of Things, smart objects are reading between the lines of our user data to deliver relevant information or experiences tailored to the time of day, the people we're with, the places we go and our current activities (pfsk labs, 2014).

For instance, by installing e-beacons sensors on Moldovan cultural sites, the interactive nature of visits is likely to be greatly improved. A precedent was successfully implemented in Belgium, a developed country.

To bring this contextual experience into the physical world, Prophets, a digital marketing and communication strategy firm, decided to create an *interactive experience* within the Rubens House in Antwerp, Belgium. By using iBeacon technology in key points around the museum, visitors are invited to use their tablets or phones to connect with artwork and exhibits in a whole new way. At first the Beacons serve as a guide through the different rooms, and then showcase relevant information as you approach a specific piece (pfsk labs, 2014).

Outline of the Project

These last decades, tourism expanded tremendously fast in comparison with other sectors of the economy, and it is developing countries that display the highest growth rates. Their revenue from international tourism has risen sixfold since 1990, while they only doubled in high-income countries (OMT & OND, 2015).

As shown on Figure 8, the Internet, whether accessed from a computer or a smartphone, was the predominant mode of decision-making for tourists planning to visit an emergent country in 2012. It will come as no surprise that the Internet will be a market penetration strategy of choice to successfully conquer the e-tourism market in the Republic of Moldova.

Moldova Tours 2.0 is a start-up company in the field of tourism aimed at foreigners with a thematic approach to its product-offer, to take into account the aspirations and needs of visitors travelling to Moldova.

Moldova Tours 2.0 is a start-up company of a new kind that offers a blend of entry points to discover beautiful Moldova so as to fill your personal aspirations and objectives.

The Republic Moldova is a young country in its current form, following notably the collapse of the Soviet Union and its independence in 1991. Its people are welcoming and often multilingual with a vibrant and dynamic culture, and a sense of openness to the world. It offers thematic tours on a wide range of levels to ensure that the visitors' experience will be an unforgettable one for themselves, their friends, their family and their colleagues. The country, bordered by Romania and Ukraine, was voted by readers of Lonely Planet in 2013 the number two off-the-beaten-path destination in the world. Following this assessment, only a customized formula can help visitors make the best of their visit. A platform will offer a fully secured transfer payment system in Dollars, Euros, Swiss francs, or even Bitcoin! Moldova Tours 2.0 plans to offer the following tours:

Figure 8. Main sources of decision-making to book a trip abroad

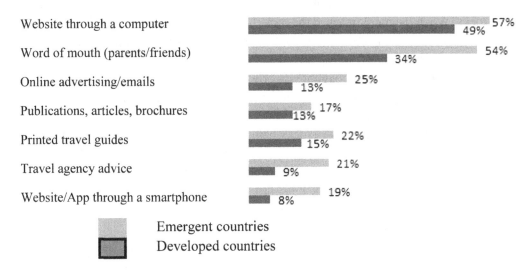

| | Emergent countries |
| | Developed countries |

<u>Source</u>:   PhoCusWright. Empowering Inspiration: The Future of Travel Search, février 2012

1.   The Monastery Tour
2.   The Wine Tour
3.   The History Tour (Art, History and Culture)
4.   The Outdoors Tour
5.   The Linguistic Tour (Romanian/Russian): stay in host families
6.   The Academic Tour
7.   The Social Business Tour
8.   The Corporate Tour (for potential investors)
9.   The Geopolitical Tour (guided tour to Transdniestria)
10. The Freedom Tour (entirely customized)

Highlights

The monastery tour is one of the highlights of the product offer. Notorious monasteries and churches in Moldova include the Capriana Monastery, the Hincu Monastery, the Rudi Monastery, the Saharna Monastery, the Tipova Monastery, the Curchi Monastery, the Frumoasa Monastery, the Cosauti Monastery, the Japca Monastery, and the Assumption of the Virgin Mary Church. They all represent the most valuable spiritual treasure of Moldova, symbols of the country's historical background. For first-time visitor, a tour with short trips to the Moldovan monasteries is offered.

The Capriana monastery is one of the oldest and most beautiful monuments in the Republic of Moldova. It is the cradle of the Moldovan literature, music and architecture. The Monastery is located in one of the most picturesque places of the Codry reserve, about 40 km from Chisinau. The Capriana Monastery dates back to the early 1420s. It was initially built of wood. It has been patronized by many rulers of Moldova, including Stefan cel Mare himself. The Holy Trinity Monastery of Saharna, situated about 110 km north of the capital Chisinau, is considered as one of Moldova's pilgrimage centres. One local legend says that once upon a time, a monk saw the shining figure of Maria on top of one of the highest rocks. When the monk reached the rock, he discovered the footsteps left by St. Maria.

The Frumoasa Monastery is a must-see in Moldova. *Frumoasa* in Romanian means beautiful. It was so named due to the beauty of the picturesque landscapes of the surrounding vineyards, orchards, and forests. Today, it is a convent, although it was originally founded as a monastery. The monastery founders first lived in earth-houses, and worked at the construction of the church, built of wood all day long. Today, a museum has opened in one of the restored buildings. Tipova Monastery is located about 100 km to the north from Chisinau city on a rocky bank of the Dniester River. It forms a marvellous complex of historical monuments and natural landscapes, an isle of preserved nature in Moldova. A small river flows into the Dniester River, and forms beautiful waterfalls of 10-16 meters height. There is a legend that the mythological poet Orpheus spent his last years in these rocks, and the remains of the poet rest in the niche of one of the cascades' gorge. The monastery complex is made of fifteen caves on dizzying height carved in a huge rock.

Let us finish with this small sample of Moldovan monasteries with Curchi Monastery founded in the times of Stefan Cel Mare. The monastery is made of three churches, one of them, the *Virgin's Assumption* Cathedral, is almost an exact replica of St. Andrew Cathedral in Kiev, built from the layouts of Bartolomeo Rastrelli. In all three churches, visitors enjoy extraordinary acoustics and beautiful ornaments.

The History Tour will take visitors through the rich cultural heritage of Moldova. Points of interest include the earliest visible remains of Geto-Dacian sites and Roman fortifications, the remains of medieval fortresses, archaeological complexes such as Orheiul Vechi, cave monasteries, nobles' mansions and peasant houses. Chisinau also features cultural heritage monuments that epitomize the domestic architecture from the 19th and 20th centuries.

The Republic of Moldova has eighty seven museums with rich collections of art. Many of them are of architectural significance. Notorious ones include Alexei Mateevici House & Museum, Alexandr Pushkin House & Museum, Constantin Stamati House & Museum, Igor Vieru House and Museum, Museum Complex Old Orhei, the National Museum of Ethnography and Natural History, the National Archaeology and History Museum of Moldova, the Museum of Popular Art, National Gagauz history and ethnographic museum Dumitru Cara-Ciobanu. The Republic of Moldova is a mosaic of nationalities and cultures with many traditions, languages, folklore, cooking, and so on. There are more than 880 folk music groups, reflecting the distinct traditions and ethnic origins. Moldova has made lots of progress in poverty alleviation over the last decade, and should be given credit for her accomplishments according to the International Monetary Fund and the World Bank. However, it is still the case that many people still live under the poverty threshold. Moldova Tours 2.0 wants to offer to its customers the possibility to make fully secured online donations to eminent grassroots-level NGOs through a payment platform.

Moldova Tours 2.0 offers a social business tour with visits guided by professionals in underprivileged areas. The visits have nothing to do with voyeurism or ill-spirited intentions. All the reverse, carry the hope that the social and development needs of Moldova will be better understood by foreigners. For instance, on the occasion of the International Roma Day, visitors will get the chance to meet the Roma community through concerts and special cultural events, which is an integral part of Moldovan society, and has long made important contributions to Moldova's history and culture.

The Wine tour runs through the vineyards, which are remarkable attractions of the Moldovan countryside. Throughout its history, Moldova has gained rich traditions of growing grapes, and wine production. There are now hundred and forty-two wineries, out of which twenty-three have experience and tourism capabilities to receive visitors. Visitors will experience and learn about the complex wine-making processes, including the bottling and sample the end-product. Moldovan wines enjoy an excellent international reputation for their quality. Moldova Tours 2.0 provides new opportunities to select itineraries: underground cellars and towns, wine storage facilities, wine processing factories, production processes of sparkling wine and so on. Along beautiful vineyards surrounding the Wine Road, visits to wineries such as Cricova Winery, Milestii Mici Winery, Purcari Winery, Cojusna Winery, are offered.

The Academic tour is a stunning innovation for customers. The founder of Moldova Tours 2.0, temporarily evolving away from academia, is connected to the local academic community. Academic visits and events in English are offered with, in mind, future collaborative initiatives

The Corporate tour is designed for potential investors. Knowing that the Moldovan workforce is young, skilled, dynamic, and multilingual, Moldova Tours 2.0 plans to offer investment services (on a consulting basis) for those willing to expand their activities in this promising country (PwC, 2014).

Due to its favorable geographical position, Moldova is an attractive location for international organizations and transnational corporations, and becoming increasingly important as a place to conduct business between western and eastern markets (p.9).

To the question 'why invest in Moldova?' answers include:

- Favorable geographical position at the crossroads of commercial routes
- Proximity to large world markets (European Union and Commonwealth of Independent States)
- Platform for manufacturing and exporting both to the CIS and to the EU
- Competitive general corporate income tax rate in the region – 12%
- Tax and customs framework similar to that of the EU
- Considerable network of operational Double Tax Treaties and Investment Protection Agreements
- Market access through three Free Trade Agreements including:
- WTO members (worldwide)
- Autonomous Trade Preferences (EU countries)
- Deep and Comprehensive Free Trade Area (DCFTA)
- CEFTA members (most Balkan countries)
- CIS members (with certain exceptions)
- Entrepreneurial activities under preferential terms and conditions developed in free economic zones
- Well-skilled multilingual workforce
- Relatively low employment costs
- Favorable visa regime
- Improved legal framework regulating entrepreneurial activity
- Starting a business – fast and easy to handle
- Investment opportunities through privatization of public property and public-private partnership (PwC, 2014, p.5)

The Corporate tour could become a flagship feature of the company in the future on the doorstep of future foreign direct investment projects.

In the short-run, the primary financial management objective (Brighham & Houston, 2015) of Moldova Tours 2.0 is to breakeven. However, as part of a renewed conception of the firm that espouses corporate social responsibility, Moldova Tours 2.0 is proud to set long-term aims to develop tourism in Moldova, and improve the global perception of the country abroad. Just like any business venture, Moldova Tours 2.0 must take cognizance of its environment, which features favourable characteristics, such as the pro-European policies adopted since 2009, likely to be reinforced by the Association of Agreement signed in Vilnius in 2014. It is true that tourism is embryonic in this post-soviet Republic and transition economy. Yet, increased attention is now placed on the Republic of Moldova by notorious tourist guides, such as Lonely Planet.

The economy in itself has great potential, as shown respectively by the 8.9% and 4.6% growth rates achieved in 2013 and 2014. Unfortunately, the Moldovan economy is projected to suffer a slight recession in 2015 as a consequence of the Ukrainian crisis, the Russian embargo bound to be detrimental to agriculture (BBC, 2015), and above all, following the gigantic banking scandal that has affected the country (Pilkington, 2015). Another encouraging sign is the improvement in the quality of the infrastructures, and the money recently invested by the European Investment Bank (2015). In spite of the Ukrainian crisis, there are valid reasons to be optimistic for this country. For instance, the quality of higher education is improving, which constitutes an increasing source of skilled workers in the form of dynamic, motivated and multilingual graduates. One must look at the drivers of growth for Moldova Tours 2.0, such as demographic changes, economic and legislative factors. Macro-benefits are uneasy to forecast, but one can envision the following socio-economic benefits in the medium term.

Poverty Alleviation

It is sometimes unclear whether tourism should somehow help the underprivileged fringe of society. More particularly, how should it benefit the poor, households who lack access to education and basic health care or people who suffer from disabilities or other health care problems? The latter are likely to be unable to participate directly in tourism activities. However, they might benefit from spill-over effects on other activities as well as from investment in social infrastructures promoted by tourism. Moreover, these weak segments of society should be protected from the adverse consequences of tourism. The UN has acknowledged the link between tourism and poverty alleviation in a context of sustainable development (CSD7, 1999). The following principles for pursuing poverty alleviation through tourism take into account previous, longstanding and relevant principles for 'pro-poor tourism' (Pro-Poor Tourism Partnership, 2005a).

1. All aspects and types of tourism should be concerned about poverty alleviation.
2. All governments should include poverty alleviation as a key aim of tourism development and consider tourism as a possible tool for reducing poverty.
3. The competitiveness and economic success of tourism businesses and destinations is critical to poverty alleviation.
4. All tourism businesses should be concerned about the impact of their activities on local communities and seek to benefit the poor through their actions.
5. Tourism destinations should be managed with poverty alleviation as a central aim that is built into strategies and action plans.
6. A sound understanding of how tourism functions in destinations is required, including how tourism income is distributed and who benefits from it.

7. Planning and development of tourism in destinations should involve a wide range of interests, including participation and representation from poor communities.
8. All potential impacts of tourism on the livelihood of communities should be considered, including current and future local and global impacts on natural and cultural resources.
9. Attention must be paid to the viability of all projects involving the poor, ensuring access to markets and maximising opportunities for beneficial links with local enterprises.
10. Impacts of tourism on poverty alleviation should be effectively monitored.

Tourism is endowed with characteristics that make it attractive to low-income countries and under-privileged communities. Tourism puts great emphasis on certain characteristics common to developing countries, such as warm weather, rich cultural heritage, beauty of landscapes and biodiversity. In this respect, let us note that *Orheiul Vechi Archaeological Landscape* meets all these conditions, and is currently part of the Tentative List, in order to qualify for inclusion in the World Heritage List by UNESCO[3]. Many of these advantages are often found in rural areas. This constitutes a competitive advantage for tourism, while a drawback for most other sectors. Tourism is accessible to the poor, as it is relatively labour intensive, and often composed of small and medium-sized enterprises, and micro-enterprises. Tourism activities lend themselves to women, young people, and underprivileged groups, such as ethnic minorities. The poor can find employment in the tourism sector, as the required skills need not be discouraging, and part-time work is often the norm. Tourism services are made of a wide array of activities and factors. Tourists spend their money on different types of goods and services, which benefit agriculture, craftsmanship, and transports. There will then be a multiplier effect, as economic agents benefiting from the consumption of tourists, make additional expenses in the rest of the economy.

Tourism bridges the gap between producers and consumers. The interaction between tourists and underprivileged communities gives rise to mutually advantageous exchanges between the two groups, such as enhanced awareness of social and environmental issues or benefits from improved social infrastructures. Social work can be consolidated by tourism enterprises, which are in a position to bridge the gap between an informal configuration wherein revenues barely cover the costs of a micro-enterprise, and a more formal and better-structured entity that attracts further investment potential.

The Enhanced Visibility of Moldova's Cultural Sites

The visibility of cultural sites could be improved, thanks to a fruitful collaboration with ICOM, the international organisation of museums and museum professionals. It is a NGO maintaining formal relations with UNESCO, committed to the conservation, continuation, and communication to society of the world's natural and cultural heritage, present and future, tangible and intangible. ICOM Moldova was registered in 2010. It is working on the national strategic plan, named Cultura-2020[4] aimed at the development of culture in Moldova. At the onset of the new millennium, ICOM Moldova has identified fifteen thousand monuments forming the historical and archaeological heritage of the country[5]. Museums funds count about 675 000 thousand exhibits preserved in six National museums, and one hundred local museums. ICOM Moldova aims to provide opportunities to museum professionals in Moldova to liaise with ICOM to keep up with the latest museological[6] trends in the world. ICOM Moldova is active in the area of development and improvement of museums, and their activity on par with world standards. ICOM Moldova plans to reach out, not only to all museum professionals, but also to the wider society. In this respect, Moldova Tours 2.0 could play a pivotal role at the interface between the stakeholders of the tourism ecosystem. ICOM Moldova also plans to cooperate with other institutions within the Eastern Partnership region and EU countries. The participation of ICOM Moldova in European financial assistance programs matters for the development of the cultural sector[7].

Potential for Social Inclusion of the Social Business Tour

This aspect involves active project management with eclectic actors in rural areas. Local residents must be taken into account as persons, but also community members, which might be defined from a geographic (towns, villages and the like), or socio-cultural (autochthon or ethnic groups, women, youngsters and so on) standpoint, or according to their areas of interest or activity. The social work conducted within local communities can be enriched by the development of representative organisations of the communities (OMT & OND, 2015, p.13). One can also promote socially inclusive businesses[8]. This term denotes those companies, which are sustainable, profitable, and act in favour of low-income communities. It pertains to tourism enterprises and associations, whenever they guide and assist the poor, by helping them gain access to specific markets (OMT & OND, 2015, p.48).

A Stepping Stone for FDI Initiatives in the Republic of Moldova

The corporate tour is designed with the help of a database of current and potential tourism sector investment opportunities in Moldova indicating their level of investment readiness. Up-to-date market intelligence and performance data sets will be provided, under the form of an annual tourism investment monitor highlighting trends within accommodation, transport and tourism-related services. Moldova Tours 2.0 will assemble an accessible PR and communications plan aimed at the international investment community. Moldova Tours 2.0 shall provide tourism sector specific facilitation services including introduction to local partners (B2B), and potential projects as well as tailored tourism research and market analysis. Moldova Tours 2.0 clients interested in the corporate tour might attend relevant tourism specific investment events and other investment conferences in key FDI source countries. They could express interest in hosting tourism investment opportunities conference/seminars as well as in potential source markets.

Academic Cross-Fertilization of Ideas

The academic tour should enable the cross-fertilization of ideas, and the development of new collaborative schemes between foreign academics, on the one hand, and Moldovan professors and higher education administrators on the other hand. Hopefully, this will contribute to the internationalization of the Moldovan higher education system (Pilkington, 2014), and eventually emphasize its newly established pro-European stance.

Geopolitical Awareness

Finally, a full geopolitical tour in Transdniestria will be proposed by Moldova Tours 2.0 in collaboration with official authorities. It is hoped that these off-the-beaten path tourism experiences will help raise awareness on issues that pertain to this autarchic and separatist region of Moldova at the interface between the West and the East.

FUTURE RESEARCH DIRECTIONS

The direct contributions of tourism consumption by foreign visitors in the Republic of Moldova could be apprehended through the use of Tourism Satellite Account (TSA), a standard statistical framework, and the main tool for the economic measurement of tourism (Frechtling, 2010, Dwyer et al., 2008; Cooper et al., 2008; United Nations, 2010).

One should also look at the policy strategies designed to modernize the education system, and enhance the skills and qualifications required by tourism growth in a globalized world: English proficiency, digital literacy, cross-cultural communication, and so on.

Another potential fruitful research direction could be to conduct qualitative field studies on the necessary compromises between the forces of globalization, and the growth of rural and sustainable tourism in the Republic of Moldova.

CONCLUSION

In this chapter, we have put into perspective the situation of the Republic of Moldova in the wider context of globalization. After briefly investigating the links between tourism and poverty alleviation, and precedents in other developing countries, we have outlined the idiosyncratic features and the transformative dimension of tourism 2.0.

Finally, we have unveiled an entrepreneurial project aimed at promoting tourism. Through the transformative power of tourism 2.0, Moldova Tours 2.0 marks a significant step towards enhanced human, economic and social development of the Republic of Moldova in a globalized world.

REFERENCES

Ashley, C. (2006). *How can governments boost the local economic impacts of tourism? Options and tools*. London: Overseas Development Institute.

Ashley, C., & Goodwin, H. (2007). *'Pro poor tourism': What's gone right and what's gone wrong?* London, UK: Overseas Development Institute.

Ashley, C., & Haysom, G. (2008). The development impacts of tourism supply chains: Increasing impact on poverty and decreasing our ignorance. In A. Spencely (Ed.), *Responsible tourism: Critical issues for conservation and development* (pp. 129–156). London, UK: Earthscan.

Bazini, E., & Nedelea, A. (2008). Impact of the tourism development on poverty reduction in Albania as a country in transition. *Revista de Turism*, *3*(5), 23–28.

BBC. (2015). Moldova country profile – Overview. *BBC News*. Retrieved from http://www.bbc.com/news/world-europe-17601580

Brigham, E. F., & Houston, J. (2015). *Fundamentals of Financial Management* (14th ed.). Boston, MA: Cengage Learning.

Commission on Sustainable Development 7. (1999). *Tourism and sustainable development*. Report of the Secretary-General (Document No. E/CN.17/1999/5). New York: United Nations. Retrieved from http://www.un.org/documents/ecosoc/docs/1999/e1999-29.htm

Cooper, C., Fletcher, J., Gilbert, D., & Wanhill, S. (2008). *Tourism: Principles and Practice* (4th ed.). Harlow: Pearson Education Limited.

Cowling, K., & Sugden, R. (1987). *Transitional Monopoly Capitalism*. New York, NY: Wheatsheaf.

Desvallées, A., & Mairesses, F. (Eds.). (2010). *Key concepts of museology*. Paris, FR: ICOM.

Dojri, P. (2007). *Nabji-Korphu Trek: The piloted community-based nature tourism in Bhutan*. Ministry of Tourism, Kingdom of Bhutan.

Dwyer, L., Forsyth, P., Spurr, R., & Van Ho, T. (2008). Tourism's economic contribution versus economic impact assessment: Differing roles for satellite accounts and economic modelling. In A. Woodside & D. Martin (Eds.), Tourism management (pp. 459–469). Wallingford, UK: CAB International.

Edu, W. (2010). *Tourism 2.0, definition and key concepts*. Video presentation. Retrieved from http://ofslides.com/eduwilliam-61600/presentation-64117

European Investment Bank. (2015). *Finance contracts signed - Republic of Moldova*. Retrieved from http://www.eib.org/projects/loans/regions/cei/md.htm?lang=en

Foy, H. (2015, October 15). Former Moldovan PM detained over alleged $1bn theft. *Financial Times*. Retrieved from http://www.ft.com/intl/cms/s/0/788aca7a-735d-11e5-a129-3fcc4f641d98.html#axzz3oqkRWshN

Frechtling, D. C. (2010). The Tourism Satellite Account: A Primer. *Annals of Tourism Research, 37*(1), 136–153. doi:10.1016/j.annals.2009.08.003

Galben, A. (2011). *Globalizarea învăţământului superior contemporan. Exemplul ULIM, Republica Moldova (Raport expus la Conferinţa Internaţională a Rectorilor de la Shanghai, 12 august 2011)*. Retrieved from http://agalben.ulim.md/wp-content/uploads/2013/12/Globalizarea-inv.-sup.-contemp.-final.pdf

Ietto-Gillies, G. (2012). *Transnational corporations and international production: concepts, theories and effects*. Cheltenham, UK: Edward Elgar.

International Monetary Fund. (2014). *IMF Country Report No 14/190*. IMF.

Lechner, F. (2001). Globalization Theories. World System's Theory. *The Globalization Website*. Retrieved from http://sociology.emory.edu/faculty/globalization/theories01.html

Marsella, A. (2012). Psychology and globalization: Understanding a complex relationship. *The Journal of Social Issues, 68*(3), 454–472. doi:10.1111/j.1540-4560.2012.01758.x

Michael, P. (2001). Strategy and the Internet. *Harvard Business Review, 79*(3), 62–78. PMID:11246925

Mitchell, J., Keane, J., & Laidlaw, J. (2009). *Making success work for the poor: Package tourism in Northern Tanzania*. London, UK: Overseas Development Institute.

Moldova Human Development Report. (2014). *Good Corporate Citizens: Public and Private Goals aligned for Human Development*. Chisinau: UNDP, Republic of Moldova. Retrieved from http://hdr. undp.org/sites/default/files/engleza_final.pdf

Moldovenii. (2011, November 1). *Tourism in Moldova*. Retrieved from http://www.moldovenii.md/en/ section/311

Morreale, V. (2003, February 10). *Te.S.C.He.T. (Technology System for Cultural Heritage in Tourism)*. FIPA Meeting, Palermo. Retrieved from http://docplayer.net/4172689-Te-s-c-he-t-technology-system-for-cultural-heritage-in-tourism-vito-morreale-engineering-ingegneria-informatica-s-p-a-fipa-meeting-palermo-10th.html

National Human Development Report. (2014) Good Corporate Citizens: Public and Private Goals Aligned for Human Development. Chisinau. http://hdr.undp.org/sites/ default/files/engleza_final.pdf. Accessed 21 July 2016

Noti, E. (2013). Web 2.0 and its influence in the tourism sector. *European Scientific Journal*, *9*(20), 115–123.

O'Reilly, R. (2005). *What is Web 2.0.? Design patterns and business models for the next generation of software*. Retrieved from www.oreillynet.com/ pub/a/oreilly/tim/news /2005/09/30/what-isweb-20.html

O'Rourke, K. H., & Williamson, J. G. (2002). When did globalisation begin? *European Review of Economic History*, *6*(1), 23–50. doi:10.1017/S1361491602000023

Organisation Mondiale du Tourisme. (2002). *Le Tourisme et la Réduction de la Pauvreté*. Madrid: OMT. Retrieved from http://www.gret.org/static/cdrom/bds/document_pdf/numero_6/Le%20tourisme%20et%20 la%20reduction%20de%20la%20pauvrete.pdf

Organisation Mondiale du Tourisme. (2005). *La Réduction de la Pauvreté par le Tourisme: un recueil de bonnes pratiques*. Madrid: OMT.

Organisation Mondiale du Tourisme and SNV (Netherlands Development Organisation). (2015). *Manuel sur le tourisme et la réduction de la pauvreté – Des mesures pratiques pour les destinations*. Madrid: OMT.

Organisation Mondiale du Tourisme (OMT). (2007). *Guide Pratique de Gestion des Destinations*. Madrid: OMT. Retrieved from http://pub.unwto.org/WebRoot/Store/Shops/Infoshop/4745/8BCE/AD9A/ ECA8/048B/C0A8/0164/0B7A/140529_guide_pratique_gestion_FR_excerpt.pdf

Pettersen, L. (2013, July 2). Moldova: embracing its status as Europe's least-visited country. *Lonely Planet*. Retrieved from http://www.lonelyplanet.com/moldova/travel-tips-and-articles/77774?lpaffil=lp-affiliates

Phillipson, R. (1992). *Linguistic imperialism*. Oxford, UK: Oxford University Press.

Phillipson, R. (Ed.). (2000). *Rights to language*. Mahwah, NJ: Lawrence Erlbaum.

Pilkington, M. (2007). The Concept of Social Marketing: From Local Development Initiatives to Global Integration-The Example of Health Care in Rural India. *International Review of Business Research Papers*, *3*(5), 328–346.

Pilkington, M. (2014). *Complementarities between the French and Moldovan higher education systems: Some implications for economic growth*. Retrieved from; doi:10.2139/ssrn.2529485

Pilkington, M. (2015). Where Did the Money Go? Endogenous Money Creation for International Fraudulent Purposes The Case of the 2015 Moldovan Banking Scandal. *International Journal of Pluralism and Economics Education*, 6(3), 251. doi:10.1504/IJPEE.2015.074355

Pilkington, M. 2016. Blockchain Technology: Principles and Applications, Handbook of Research on Digital Transformations'. edited by F. Xavier Olleros, and Majlinda Zhegu, Edward Elgar, Cheltenham, pp.225-253

PricewaterhouseCoopers. (2014). *Investing Guide Moldova 2014*. Retrieved from https://www.pwc.com/md/en/publications/assets/moldova-business-guide-2014.pdf

Pro-Poor Tourism Partnership. (2004). *Tourism in Poverty Reduction Strategy Papers (PRSPs). PPTP Sheet, No 9*. London: PPTP.

Pro-Poor Tourism Partnership. (2005a). *Annual Register 2005*. London: PPTP.

Pro-Poor Tourism Partnership. (2005b). *Key Principles and Strategies of Pro-Poor Tourism*. London: PPTP.

PSFK Labs. (2014, September 8). *Why 'Contexual' Is the New 'Search' Living Within the Internet of Things*. Retrieved from http://www.psfk.com/2014/09/contexual-new-search-living-within-internet-things.html

Rinzin, C., Vermeulen, W., & Glasbergen, P. (2007). Ecotourism as a Mechanism for Sustainable Development: The Case of Bhutan. *Environmental Sciences*, 4(2), 109–125. doi:10.1080/15693430701365420

Rosu, R. (2012). The impact of diaspora on political processess in republica Moldova. Administrarea Publica. *Revista motodico-stiintifica trimestriala*, 4(76), 103-111.

Sen, A. (2010). *The Idea of Justice*. London, UK: Penguin.

Sen, A. (2012). Development as capability expansion. In J. DeFilippis & S. Saegert, S. (Eds.), The community development reader. New York, NY: Routledge.

Stratan, A. (2010). Assessment of economic growth of the Republic of Moldova in the context of global economic crisis. *Journal for Economic Forecasting*, (5), 33-42.

Truth and Dignity Platform. (2015). Retrieved from http://moldovanpolitics.com/tag/truth-and-dignity-platform/

Twining-Ward, L. (2007). *A toolkit for monitoring and managing community-based tourism*. School of Travel Industry Management, University of Hawaii.

United Nations. (2008). *Rural Development, Croatia country report*. Retrieved from http://www.un.org/esa/agenda21/natlinfo/countr/croatia/ruralDevelopment.pdf

United Nations. (2010). *Tourism Satellite Account: Recommended methodological framework 2008.* Statistics Division, Statistical Office of the European Communities, Organisation for Economic Co-operation and Development & World Tourism Organization. Madrid: World Tourism Organization. Retrieved from http://unstats.un.org/unsd/publication/Seriesf/SeriesF_80rev1e.pdf

UNWTO Think Tank. (2002, April 2). *Destination Management - Conceptual Framework.* Retrieved from http://www.unwto.org/destination/conceptual/conceptual.php?lang=E

Vertovec, S. (2005). *The Political Importance of Diasporas.* Migration Policy Institute. Retrieved from www.migrationinformation.org/Feature/display.cfm?ID=313

Werthner, H., & Klein, S. (1999). *Information technology and tourism: a challenging ralationship.* New York, NY: Springer. doi:10.1007/978-3-7091-6363-4

Werthner, H., & Ricci, F. (2004). E-commerce and Tourism. *Communications of the ACM, 47*(12), 101–105. doi:10.1145/1035134.1035141

ADDITIONAL READING

Cárdenas-García, P.J., Sánchez-Rivero, M., & Pulido-Fernández, J. I. (2015). Does Tourism Growth Influence Economic Development? *Journal of Travel Research.* March, 54: 206-221. Published online before print December 18, 2013, doi: 10.1177/0047287513514297

Carter, M. (2015). The perfect place to escape other tourists: Moldova. *Financial Times.* May 22. http://www.ft.com/intl/cms/s/2/a1d3c85e-fd4d-11e4-9e96-00144feabdc0.html

Sava, L. (2012). La crise identitaire de la République de Moldavie dans le contexte de la globalisation. *Danubius,* Issue n°30/2012, pp. 397-411,

Silviana, S. C. (2015). Impact of European integration and globalization processes on tourism. PhD Thesis. World economy; International economic relations. Chişinău, Republica Moldova

Trofimov, A. (2015). Wine Tourism: An Opportunity to Increase International Awareness towards Moldova. Master in Tourism (thesis). Faculdade de letras. Universidade do Porto

Weiner, E. (2008). *The Geography of Bliss.* New York: Twelve, Hachette Book Group.

World Bank. (2013). *Moldova - Country partnership strategy for the period FY14-17.* Washington DC. World Bank. Retrieved from http://documents.worldbank.org/curated/en/2013/08/18114315/moldova-country-partnership-strategy-period-fy14-17

World Bank. (2015). *Briefing book from development partners of Moldova.* Washington, DC. World Bank Group. Retrieved from http://documents.worldbank.org/curated/en/2015/01/24203490/briefing-book-development-partners-moldova

KEY TERMS AND DEFINITIONS

Association Agreement: The Moldova–European Union Association Agreement is a treaty that establishes a political and economic association between the two parties. The association agreement commits Moldova to economic, judicial and financial reforms to converge its policies and legislation to those of the European Union. It was initialled on 29 November 2013 in Brussels. It was signed on 27 June 2014 in Vilnius, and has been provisionally applied since 1 September 2014.

Digital Platform: A digital platform refers to the software or hardware of a website allowing for the interaction of its users.

Economic Development: Economic development refers to the sustained, concerted actions of communities and policymakers that improve the standard of living and economic health of a given country. The overall concept of development is complex and multidimensional. It comprises social, economic, cultural, anthropological and technological aspects.

Empowerment: First introduced by Barbara Solomon in 1976 as a method of social work with oppressed Afro-American communities, empowerment refers to the ability to gain control over our lives either by ourselves or with the help of others.

Globalization: Globalization is a process of interaction and integration among the people, firms, and governments of different nations, a process driven by international trade and investment and aided by information technology. It has effects on the environment, on culture, on political systems, on economic development and prosperity, and on human well-being around the world.

Poverty Alleviation: Poverty alleviation is any process that reduces income fluctuation between poor and non-poor scenarios (Adongo and Deen-Swarray, 2006). This is different from poverty reduction, which aims to permanently move an individual or household from a poor to a non-poor scenario.

Social Inclusion: Social inclusion is the process of improving the terms for individuals and groups to take part in society by empowering poor and marginalized people to take advantage of global opportunities.

Tourism: 1. The practice of travelling for pleasure. 2. The business of providing tours and services for tourists.

Tourism 2.0: Tourism 2.0 is the business revolution in the tourism and leisure industry caused by the move to the tourist ecosystem as platform, and an attempt to understand the rules for success on that new platform. Chief among those rules is to build applications that harness network effects to get better the more people use them. (Edu, 2010).

Web 2.0: Web 2.0 is a business revolution in the computer industry caused by the move to the Internet as platform, and an attempt to understand the rules for success on that new platform (O'Reilly, 2005).

ENDNOTES

[1]   https://web.archive.org/web/20050312204307/http://www.web2con.com/web2con/
[2]   http://www.holacuba.de/reservation/payment-bitcoin.php
[3]   http://www.worldheritagesite.org/sites/t5937.html
[4]   http://lex.justice.md/index.php?action=view&view=doc&lang=1&id=352588

5   5698 monuments were included in the Register of Monuments of History and 7368 were included in the Register of Monuments of Archeology protected by the state.

6   http://icom.museum/fileadmin/user_upload/pdf/Key_Concepts_of_Museology/Museologie_Anglais_BD.pdf

7   http://network.icom.museum/icom-moldova/icom-moldova/who-we-are/L/10/

8   This resembles the concept of social marketing (Pilkington, 2007)

Compilation of References

Aerts, D., Apostel, L., De Moor, B., Hellemans, S., Maex, E., Van Belle, H., & Van der Veken, J. (Eds.). (1994). World-views from fragmentation to integration. Brussels: VUB Press. Retrieved from http://pespmc1.vub.ac.be/clea/reports/worldviewsbook.html

Aarts, J., & Berg, M. (2006). Same systems, different outcomes comparing the implementation of computerized physician order entry in two Dutch hospitals. *Methods of Information in Medicine*, *45*(1), 53–61. PMID:16482371

Aarts, J., Doorewaard, H., & Berg, M. (2004). Understanding implementation: The case of a computerized physician order entry system in a large Dutch university medical center. *Journal of the American Medical Informatics Association*, *11*(3), 207–216. doi:10.1197/jamia.M1372 PMID:14764612

Aarts, J., & Granger, S. (1998). Tag sequences in learner corpora. In S. Granger (Ed.), *Learner English on computer* (pp. 132–141). London: Addison Wesley Longman.

About, Saudi electronic university. (n.d.). Retrieved from https://www.seu.edu.sa/sites/en/AboutSEU/Pages/History-Timeline.aspx

Achieving the Dream. (2006c, November/December). Developmental math students and college-level coursework. *Data Notes*, *1*(8).

Ackerman, S. (2013, April). Army practices poor data hygiene on its new smartphones, tablets. *Wired*. Retrieved from www.wired.com/dangerroom/2013/04/army-data-hygiene

Ackoff, R. L. (1999). On learning and the systems that facilitate it. *Reflections: The SoL Journal*, *1*(1), 14–24. doi:10.1162/152417399570250

Adair, W. L., & Brett, J. M. (2005). The negotiation dance: Time, culture, and behavioral sequences in negotiation. *Organization Science*, *16*(1), 33–51.

Adams, A., Middleton, J., & Ziderman, A. (1992). The World Bank's policy paper on vocational and technical education and training. *Prospects*, *22*(2), 125–140. doi:10.1007/BF02195540

Adams, C. (2010). Cyberbullying: How to make it stop. *Instructor*, *120*(2), 44–49.

Addis, M., & Mahalik, J. (2003). Men, masculinity, and the contexts of help seeking. *The American Psychologist*, *58*(1), 5–14. doi:10.1037/0003-066X.58.1.5 PMID:12674814

Ädel, A. (2008). Metadiscourse across three Englishes: American, British, and advanced-learner English. In U. Connor, E. Nagelhout, & W. Rozycki (Eds.), *Contrastive rhetoric: Reaching to intercultural rhetoric* (pp. 45–62). London: Equinox. doi:10.1075/pbns.169.06ade

Adelman, C. (2004). *Principal indicators of student academic histories in postsecondary education, 1972-2000.* Washington, DC: U.S. Department of Education, Institute of Education Sciences.

Adler, N. J. (2007). *International dimensions of organizational behavior.* Mason, OH: Thomson.

Afanasiev, V. (1999). *Scientific and technological revolution - Its impact on management and education.* Moscow, Russia: Progress.

Agarwal, R., & Karahanna, E. (1998). On the multi-dimensional nature of compatibility beliefs in technology acceptance. In *Proceedings of the 19th Annual International Conference on Information Systems.* DIGIT. Retrieved from http://disc-nt.cba. uh.edu/chin/digit98/first.pdf

Agarwal, V., Dasgupta, K., Karnik, N. M., Kumar, A., Kundu, A., Mittal, S., & Srivastava, B. (2005). A service creation environment based on end to end composition of web services. In *International Conference World Wide Web. WWW.*

Agarwal, R., & Prasad, J. (1997). The role of innovation characteristics and perceived voluntariness in the acceptance of information technologies. *Decision Sciences, 28*(3), 557–582. doi:10.1111/j.1540-5915.1997.tb01322.x

Ageel, M. (2011). The ICT proficiencies of university teachers in Saudi Arabia: A case study to identify challenges and encouragements. *Hummingbird, University of Southampton's Doctoral Research Journal, 21*(8), 55–60.

Aggelidis, V. P., & Chatzoglou, P. D. (2009). Using a modified technology acceptance model in hospitals. *International Journal of Medical Informatics, 78*(2), 115–126. doi:10.1016/j.ijmedinf.2008.06.006 PMID:18675583

Ahmad, A., Hadgkiss, J., & Ruighaver, A. (2012). Incident response teams—Challenges in supporting the organizational security function. *Computers & Security, 31*(5), 643–652. doi:10.1016/j.cose.2012.04.001

Ainley, R. (2011). Organ transploitation: A model law approach to combat human trafficking and transplant tourism. *Oregon Review of International Law, 13,* 427.

Air. (2014). *Travel trends 2014: Stylish individualism.* Retrieved from http://blog. airmauritius.com/travel-trends-2014-stylish-individualism/

Ajjan, H., & Hartshorne, R. (2008). Investigating faculty decisions to adopt web 2.0 technologies: Theory and empirical tests. *The Internet and Higher Education, 11*(2), 71–80.

Ajjan, H., & Hartshorne, R. (2008). Investigating Faculty Decisions to Adopt Web 2.0 Technologies: Theory and Empirical Tests. *The Internet and Higher Education, 11*(2), 71–80. doi:10.1016/j.iheduc.2008.05.002

Ajzen, I. (1991). The theory of planned behavior. *Organizational Behavior and Human Decision Processes, 50*(2), 179–211. doi:10.1016/0749-5978(91)90020-T

Akbulut, Y., Sahin, T. L., & Eristi, B. (2010). Cyberbullying victimization among Turkish online social utility members. *Journal of Educational Technology & Society, 13,* 192–201.

Akella, D. (2008). Discipline and negotiation: Power in learning organizations. *Global Business Review in Social Work, 9*(2), 219–241. doi:10.1177/097215090800900204

Akkoyunlu, B., & Kurbanoğlu, S. (2003). Öğretmen adaylarının bilgi okuryazarlığı ve bilgisayar öz-yeterlilik algıları üzerine bir çalışma. *Hacettepe Üniversitesi Eğitim Fakültesi Dergisi, 24,* 1–10.

Aktay, S. (2011). *İlköğretimde web tabanlı portfolyo (webfolyo) uygulaması.* (Unpublished doctoral dissertation). Anadolu University, Eskişehir, Turkey.

Al Harbi, H. (2014). *Towards successful implementation of ICT in education.* Paper presented at the 2014 WEI International Academic Conference, Vienna, Austria. Retrieved from http://www.westeastinstitute.com/wp-content/uploads/2014/05/Hanaa-Eid-Al-harbi-Full-Paper.pdf

Al Mulhem, A. (2014). Common Barriers to E-learning Implementation in Saudi Higher Education Sector: A Review of Literature. In M. Searson & M. Ochoa (Eds.), *Proceedings of Society for Information Technology & Teacher Education International Conference 2014* (pp. 830-840). Chesapeake, VA: Association for the Advancement of Computing in Education (AACE).

Al Shaer, A. I. (2007). *Education for all programmes in the Kingdom of Saudi Arabia.* Paper commissioned for the EFA Global Monitoring Report 2008, Education for All by 2015: will we make it? Retrieved from http://unesdoc.unesco.org/images/0015/001554/155498e.pdf

Albert, M. S., Jones, K., Savage, C. R., Berkman, L., Seeman, T., Blazer, D., & Rowe, J. W. (1995). Predictors of cognitive change in older persons: MacArthur Studies of Successful Aging. *Psychology and Aging, 10*(4), 578–589. doi:10.1037/0882-7974.10.4.578 PMID:8749585

Albugami, S. & Ahmed, V. (2015). Success factors for ICT implementation in Saudi secondary schools: From the perspective of ICT directors, head teachers, teachers and students. *International Journal of Education and Development using Information and Communication Technology, 11*(1), 36-54.

Alebaikan, R., & Troudi, S. (2010). Blended learning in Saudi universities: Challenges and perspectives. *Research in Learning Technology, 18*(1), 49–59. doi:10.1080/09687761003657614

Alenzi, A. M. (2012). *Faculty members' perceptions of e-learning in the Kingdom of Saudi Arabia (KSA).* (Unpublished doctoral dissertation). Texas Tech University, Lubbock, TX.

Alessi, S. M., & Trollip, S. R. (2001). *Multimedia for learning. Methods and development* (3rd ed.). Boston, MA: Allyn and Bacon.

Al-Gahtani, S. (2001). The applicability of TAM outside North America: An empirical test in the United Kingdom. *Information Resources Management Journal, 14*(3), 37-46. doi:10.418/irmj.20010700104

Algeo, J. (1988). British and American grammatical differences. *International Journal of Lexicography, 1*(1), 1–31. doi:10.1093/ijl/1.1.1

Algeo, J. (2006). *British or American English? A handbook of word and grammar patterns.* Cambridge, UK: Cambridge University Press. doi:10.1017/CBO9780511607240

Alhareth, Y., McBride, N., Prior, M., Leigh, M., & Flick, C. (2013, July). *Saudi women and e-learning.* Paper presented at the third annual meeting of The Future of Education International Conference. Retrieved from http://conference.pixel-online.net/foe2013/common/download/Paper_pdf/142-ELE15-FP-Alhareth-FOE2013.pdf

Alimisis, D., & Kynigos, C. (2009). Constructionism and robotics in education. *Teacher Education on Robotic-Enhanced Constructivist Pedagogical Methods*, 11-26.

Aljabre, A. (2012). An exploration of distance learning in Saudi Arabian universities: Current practices and future possibilities. *International Journal of Business Human Technology, 2*(132), 132–137.

Al-Jarf, R. (2007). E-integration challenges for rectors and deans in higher education. *Computer and Advanced Technology in Education Conference Proceedings.* ACTA.

Al-Kahtani, N. K. M., Ryan, J. J. C. H., & Jefferson, T. I. (2006). How Saudi female faculty perceive internet technology usage and potential. *Information, Knowledge, Systems Management, 5*, 227–243.

Alkan, C. (1997). *Eğitim teknolojisinin ikibinli yıllarda yapılandırılması*. Ankara: Anı Yayıncılık.

Al-Khalifa, S. H. (2009, October). The state of distance education in Saudi Arabia. *eLearn Magazine*. Retrieved from http://elearnmag.acm.org/archive.cfm?aid=1642193

Allen, D. (2012, March 18), When technology overwhelms, get organized. *New York Times*, p. B4.

Allen, I. E., & Seaman, J. (2013). Changing course: Ten years of tracking online education in the United States. Newburyport, MA: Sloan. Available from http://onlinelearningsurvey.com/reports/changingcourse.pdf

Allen, E. I., & Seaman, J. (2015). *Grade level: Tracking online education in the United States, 2014*. Babson Park, MA: Babson Survey Research Group.

Allen, S. A., & Ofahengaue Vakalahi, H. F. (2013). My team members are everywhere! A critical analysis of the emerging literature on dispersed teams. *Administration in Social Work*, *37*(5), 486–493. doi:10.1080/03643107.2013.828002

Allison, B., & Rehm, B. L. (2007). Effective teaching strategies for middle school learners in multicultural, multilingual classrooms. *Middle School Journal*, *39*(2), 12–18. doi:10.1080/00940771.2007.11461619

Al-Maliki, S. (2013). Information and communication technology (ICT) investment in the kingdom of Saudi Arabia: Assessing strengths and weaknesses. *Journal of Knowledge Management*, *213*, 1–15.

Almalki, G., & Williams, N. (2012). A strategy to improve the usage of ICT in the kingdom of Saudi Arabia primary school. *International Journal of Advanced Computer Science & Application*, *3*(10), 42–49. doi:10.14569/IJACSA.2012.031007

Alon, I., & McIntyre, J. (Eds.). (2005). *Business education in emerging market economies: Perspectives and best practices*. Boston, MA: Kluwer Academic.

Al-Oteawi, S. (2002). *The perceptions of administrators and teachers in utilizing information technology in instruction, administrative work, technology planning and staff development in Saudi Arabia (Doctoral Dissertation)*. Ohio University.

Al-Shawi, A., & Al-Wabil, A. (2013). Internet usage by faculty in Saudi higher education. *International Journal of Computer Science Issue*, *10*(3), 81–87.

Altawil, A. N. (2012). The perceptions of Saudi students on using fully online courses at university level (Unpublished master's thesis). Chico, CA: California State University. Retrieved from http://www.academia.edu/8616172/The_perceptions_of_Saudi_students_on_using_fully_online_courses_at_university_level

Alter, P. (2012). Helping students with emotional and behavioral disorders solve mathematical word problems. *Preventing School Failure*, *56*(1), 55–64. doi:10.1080/1045988X.2011.565283

Alwani, A., & Soomro, S. (2010). Barriers to effective use of information technology in science education at Yanbu Kingdom of Saudi Arabia. In S. Soomro (Ed.), E-Learning Experiences and the Future. Rijeka, Croatia: InTech. doi:10.5772/8809

Al-Zaidiyeen, N. J., Mei, L. L., & Fook, F. S. (2010). Teachers' attitudes and levels of technology use in classrooms: The case of Jordan schools. *International Education Studies*, *3*(2), 211–218. doi:10.5539/ies.v3n2p211

Ama, T. (2005). *Why are the Japanese non-religious? Japanese spirituality: Being non-religious in a religious culture*. Lanham, MD: University of Maryland.

American Council on Education. (2010). *2009 GED testing program statistical report*. Washington, DC: Author. Retrieved from http:www.acenet.edu/Content/NavigationMenu/ged/pubs/2009ASR.pdf

American Educational Research Association, American Psychological Association, & National Council on Measurement in Education. (2014). *Standards for educational and psychological testing*. Washington, DC: Authors.

American Nurses Association. (2001). *Code of ethics for nurses with interpretive statements*. Silver Spring, MD: Nursesbooks.

Amicil, B. C., & Celentano, D. D. (1984). Human factors epidemiology: An integrated approach to the study of health issues in office work. In B. G. F. Cohen (Ed.), *Human aspects of office automation* (pp. 78–82). Amsterdam, The Netherlands: Elsevier.

Ammenwerth, E., Talmon, J., Ash, J. S., Bates, D. W., Beuscart-Zephir, M. C., Duhamel, A., & Geissbuhler, A. et al. (2006). Impact of CPOE on mortality rates-contradictory findings, important messages. *Methods of Information in Medicine*, *45*(6), 586–593. Available from http://www.lina-schwab.de/Publikationen/z42.pdf PMID:17149499

Anderson, S., & Rutherford, H. (2013, June). DoD's commercial mobile device implementation plan: Enabling the mobile workforce. *CHIPS*. Retrieved from http://www.privacy.navy.mil/CHIPS/ArticleDetails.aspx?id=4534

Anderson, L., & Anderson, C. (1979). A visit to Middleston's world-centered schools: A scenario. In J. Becker (Ed.), *Schooling for a Global Age* (pp. 3–30). New York, NY: McGraw-Hill.

Anderson, T. (2008). Toward a theory of online learning. In T. Anderson (Ed.), *The theory and practice of online learning* (pp. 45–74). Edmonton: AU Press.

Andersson, G., & Karlberg, I. (2000). Integrated care for the elderly: The background and effects of the reform of Swedish care of the elderly. *International Journal of Integrated Care*, *1*(1), 1–10. Available from http://citeseerx.ist.psu.edu/viewdoc/download?doi=10.1.1.276.9726&rep=rep1&type=pdf PMID:16902694

Andreev, L. (2011). The cultural preferences of today's Russian college students. *Russian Social Science Review*, *52*(4), 60–78. doi:10.2753/res1060-9393510905

Anell, A., Glenngård, A. H., & Merkur, S. (2012). Sweden: Health system review. Health systems in transition. *European Observatory on Health Systems and Policies*, *14*(5), 1-159. Retrieved from http://www.euro.who.int/__data/assets/pdf_file/0008/164096/e96455.pdf

Angelino, L. M., Williams, F. K., & Natvig, D. (2007). Strategies to engage online students and reduce attrition rates. *The Journal of Educators Online*, *4*(2). Retrieved from http://www.thejeo.com/Volume4Number2/Angelino%20Final.pdf

Ang, R. P., Kit-Aun, T., & Mansor, A. T. (2010). Normative beliefs about aggression as a mediator of narcissistic exploitativeness and cyberbullying. *Journal of Interpersonal Violence*, *26*(13), 2619–2634. doi:10.1177/0886260510388286 PMID:21156699

Anshel, M. H., Brinthaupt, T. M., & Kang, M. (2010). The disconnected values model improves mental well-being and fitness in an employee wellness program. *Behavioral Medicine (Washington, D.C.)*, *36*(4), 113–122. doi:10.1080/0896 4289.2010.489080 PMID:21186434

Aoanan, M. L. (2014). Christ and the Filipino cultures: The changing faces of Christ in the Philippines. *Asia Journal of Theology*, *28*(2), 283–299.

Aoyama, I., Barnard-Brak, L., & Talbert, T. L. (2011). Cyberbullying among high school students: Cluster analysis of sex and age differences and the level of parental monitoring. *International Journal of Cyber Behavior, Psychology and Learning*, *1*(1), 1–11. doi:10.4018/ijcbpl.2011010103

Aoyama, I., Utsumi, S., & Hasegawa, M. (2011). Cyberbullying in Japan: Cases, government reports, adolescent relational aggression and parental monitoring roles. In Q. Li, D. Cross, & P. K. Smith (Eds.), *Bullying in the global playground: Research from an international perspective*. Oxford, UK: Wiley-Blackwell.

ap Siôn, T., & Nash, P. (2013). Coping through prayer: An empirical study in implicit religion concerning prayers for children in hospital. *Mental Health, Religion & Culture, 16*(9), 936–952. doi:10.1080/13674676.2012.756186

Arat, T. (2011). *İletişim teknolojilerinin yükseköğrenim kurumlarında öğretim amaçlı kullanımı: selçuk üniversitesi örneği.* (Unpublished doctoral dissertation). Selçuk University, Konya.

Arbaugh, J. B., Godfrey, M. R., Johnson, J., Pollack, B. I., Niendorf, B., & Wresch, W. (2009). Research in online and blended learning in the business disciplines: Key findings and possible future directions. *The Internet and Higher Education, 12*, 71-87. 10.1016/j.iheduc.2009.06.006

Archibugi, D., & Iammarino, S. (2002). The globalization of technological innovation: Definition and evidence. *Review of International Political Economy, 9*(1), 98–122.

Archibugi, D., & Michie, J. (1995). The globalisation of technology: A new taxonomy. *Cambridge Journal of Economics, 19*(1), 121–140.

Aricak, T., Siyahhan, S., Uzunhasanoglu, A., Saribeyoglu, S., Ciplak, S., Yilmaz, N., & Memmedov, C. (2008). Cyberbullying among Turkish adolescents. *Cyberpsychology & Behavior, 11*(3), 253–261. doi:10.1089/cpb.2007.0016 PMID:18537493

Armstrong, G., Tucker, J., & Massad, V. (2009). Interviewing the experts: Student produced podcast. *Journal of Information Technology Education: Innovations in Practice, 8*(1), 79–90.

Arnold, M. (2003, October). On the phenomenology of technology: The "janus-faces" of mobile phones. *Information and Organization, 13*(4), 231–256. doi:10.1016/S1471-7727(03)00013-7

Arslan, S., Savaser, S., Hallett, V., & Balci, S. (2012). Cyberbullying among primary school students in Turkey: Self-reported prevalence and associations with home and school life. *Cyberpsychology, Behavior, and Social Networking, 15*(10), 527–533. doi:10.1089/cyber.2012.0207 PMID:23002988

Asanova, G., & Ryssaldy, K. (2013). Academic mobility as the source of scientific-educational cooperation. *CBU International Conference Proceedings, 3*, 174–181. doi:10.12955/cbup.v1.675

Ashley, C. (2006). *How can governments boost the local economic impacts of tourism? Options and tools.* London: Overseas Development Institute.

Ashley, C., & Goodwin, H. (2007). *'Pro poor tourism': What's gone right and what's gone wrong?* London, UK: Overseas Development Institute.

Ashley, C., & Haysom, G. (2008). The development impacts of tourism supply chains: Increasing impact on poverty and decreasing our ignorance. In A. Spencely (Ed.), *Responsible tourism: Critical issues for conservation and development* (pp. 129–156). London, UK: Earthscan.

Ashwin, S. (2002). The influence of the Soviet gender order on employment behavior in contemporary Russia. *Sociological Research, 41*(1), 21–37. doi:10.2753/SOR1061-0154410121

Asia Society. (2007). Learning in a global age: Knowledge and skills for a flat world. New York: Author.

Asiala, M., Brown, A., DeVries, D. J., Dubinsky, E., Mathews, D., & Thomas, K. (2004). *A Framework for Research and Curriculum Development in Undergraduate Mathematics Education.*

Aslund, A. (1995). *How Russia became a market economy.* Washington, DC: Brookings Institution.

Aslund, A., Guriev, S., & Kuchins, A. (2010). *Russia after the global economic crisis.* Washington, DC: Peterson Institute for Internal Economics.

Association for Talent Development (ASTD-AST). (2013, October 30). *Workplace learning remains a key organizational investment Results from ASTD's 2013 of the Industry Report*. Retrieved from http://www.astd.org/Publications/Magazines/TD/TD-Archive/2013/11/Workplace-Learning-Remains-a-Key-Organizational-Investment

Astor, A., Akhtar, T., Matallana, M. A., Muthuswamy, V., Olowu, F. A., Tallo, V., & Lie, R. K. (2005). Physician migration: Views from professionals in Colombia, Nigeria, India, Pakistan and the Philippines. *Social Science & Medicine*, *61*(12), 2492–2500. doi:10.1016/j.socscimed.2005.05.003 PMID:15953667

Aten, J. D., Mangis, M. W., & Campbell, C. (2010). Psychotherapy with rural religious fundamentalist clients. *Journal of Clinical Psychology*, *66*(5), 513–523. doi:.2067710.1002/jclp

Atkinson, N. L., & Gold, R. S. (2002). The promise and challenge of eHealth interventions. *American Journal of Health Behavior*, *26*(6), 494–503. doi:10.5993/AJHB.26.6.10 PMID:12437024

Atkinson, Q. D., & Bourrat, P. (2011). Beliefs about God, the afterlife and morality support the role of supernatural policing in human cooperation. *Evolution and Human Behavior*, *32*(1), 41–49. doi:10.1016/j.evolhumbehav.2010.07.008

ATLAS.ti. (2012). *Scientific software development corporation*. Retrieved from http://www.atlasti.com/index.html

Atran, S., & Henrich, J. (2010). The evolution of religion: How cognitive by-products, adaptive learning heuristics, ritual displays, and group competition generate deep commitments to prosocial religion. *Biological Theory*, *5*(1), 18–30. doi:10.1162/BIOT_a_00018

Attewell, P., Lavin, D., Domina, T., & Levey, T. (2006). New evidence on college remediation. *The Journal of Higher Education*, *77*(5), 886–924. doi:10.1353/jhe.2006.0037

Augustine, D. (2007). *Red Prometheus: Engineering and dictatorship in East Germany, 1945–1990*. Cambridge, MA: The MIT Press.

Austin, J. R., & Bartunek, J. M. (2002). Theories and practices of organizational development. In W. C. Parks, D. R. Ilgen, R. J. Klimoski, & I. B. Weiner (Eds.), Handbook of Psychology: Vol. 12. *Industrial and Organizational Psychology* (pp. 309–332). Hoboken, NJ: John Wiley & Sons, Inc.

Australian Public Service Commission. (2015). *Employee mobility: Principles for advancing professional development*. Retrieved from http://www.apsc.gov.au/working-in-the-aps/applying-for-jobs/employee-mobility-principles-for-advancing-professional-development

Avery, G. C., & Baker, E. (2002). Reframing he infomated household-workplace. *Information and Organization*, *12*(2), 109–134. doi:10.1016/S1471-7727(01)00013-6

Avolio, B. J., & Wernsing, T. S. (2008). Practicing authentic leadership. In S. J. Lopez (Ed.), *Positive psychology: Exploring the best in people, Volume 4: Pursuing human flourishing* (pp. 147–166). Retrieved from http://www.academia.edu/2319524/Practicing_authentic_leadership

Avolio, B. J., Gardner, W. L., Walumbwa, F. O., Luthans, F., & May, D. R. (2004, December). Unlocking the mask: A look at the process by which authentic leaders impact follower attitudes and behaviors. *The Leadership Quarterly*, *15*(6), 801–823. doi:.2004.09.00310.1016/j.leaqua

Avolio, B. J., & Gardner, W. L. (2005, June). Authentic leadership development: Getting to the root of positive forms of leadership. *The Leadership Quarterly*, *16*(3), 315–338. doi:10.1016/j.leaqua.2005.03.001

Avolio, B. J., Walumbwa, F. O., & Weber, T. J. (2009). Leadership: Current theories, research, and future directions. *Annual Review of Psychology*, *60*(1), 421–449. doi:10.1146/annurev.psych.60.110707.163621 PMID:18651820

Ayyagari, R. (2007). *What and why of technostress: Technology antecedents and implications.* (Unpublished doctoral dissertation). Clemson, SC: Clemson University.

Ayyagari, R. (2012). An exploratory analysis of data breaches from 2005-2011: Trends and insights. *Journal of Information Privacy & Security, 8*(2), 33–56. doi:10.1080/15536548.2012.10845654

Ayyagari, R., Grover, V., & Purvis, R. (2011). Technostress: Technological antecedents and implications. *Management Information Systems Quarterly, 35*(4), 831–858.

Azmitia, M., Syed, M., & Radmacher, K. (2008). On the intersection of personal and social identities: Introduction and evidence from a longitudinal study of emerging adults. *New Directions for Child and Adolescent Development, 120*(120), 1–6. doi:10.1002/cd.212 PMID:18521867

Baaken, J. P., O'Brian, M. O., & Shelden, D. L. (2007). Changeing roles and responsibilities of special education administrators. *Advances in Special Education, 17,* 1–15. doi:10.1016/S0270-4013(06)17001-4

Bach, S., Haynes, P., & Smith, J. L. (2006). *Online learning and teaching in higher education.* UK: McGraw-Hill Education.

Bailey, T., Jeong, D. W., & Cho, S. (2010). Referral, enrollment, and completion in developmental education sequences in community colleges. *Economics of Education Review, 29*(2), 255–270. doi:10.1016/j.econedurev.2009.09.002

Baird, R. M., & Rosenbaum, S. E. (Eds.). (1999). *Hatred, bigotry, and prejudice: Definitions, causes, and solutions.* Amherst, NY: Prometheus.

Balacheff, N. (2001). Symbolic arithmetic vs. algebra: The core of a didactical dilemma. Postscript. In R. Sutherland, T. Rojano, A. Bell, & R. C. Lins (Eds.), *Perspectives on school algebra* (p. 249). Dordrecht, the Netherlands: Kluwer.

Balanskat, A., Blamire, R., & Kefala, S. (2006). *The ICT impact report.* European Schoolnet.

Balch, T. (2013). *About MOOC completion rates: The importance of student investment* [Web log post]. Retrieved from http://augmentedtrader.wordpress.com/2013/01/06/about-mooc-completion-rates-the-importance-of-investment/

Ballard, D. A. (2012). *Factors influencing acceptance of a worksite wellness program in a major urban healthcare system: A cross-sectional analysis.* (Unpublished master's thesis). University of Kentucky, Lexington, KY.

Ballew, H., & Cunningham, J. W. (1982). Diagnosing strengths and weaknesses of sixth-grade students in solving word problems. *Journal for Research in Mathematics Education, 13*(3), 202. doi:10.2307/748556

Banchoff, T. (2007). *Democracy and the new religious pluralism.* Oxford, UK: Oxford University Press. doi:10.1093/acprof:oso/9780195307221.001.0001

Bandura, A. (1997). *Self-efficacy: The exercise of control.* New York: Freeman.

Bandy, J. (2015). *International evaluation of employee wellness program outcomes* (Doctoral dissertation). Available from ProQuest Dissertations and Theses database. (No. 10931)

Banks, G. J. (1995). Legal and ethical safeguards: Protection of society's most vulnerable participants in a commercialized organ transplantation system. *American Journal of Law & Medicine, 21,* 45. PMID:7573083

Banks-Wallace, J. (2000). Womanist ways of knowing: Theoretical considerations for research with African American women. *ANS. Advances in Nursing Science, 22*(3), 33–45. doi:10.1097/00012272-200003000-00004 PMID:10711803

Bannister, F., & Remenyi, D. (2009). Multitasking: The uncertain impact of technology on knowledge workers and managers. *The Electronic Journal Information Systems Evaluation, 12*(1), 1 – 12.

Barab, S., Goldstone, R., & Zulker, S. (2009). Transformational play as a curricular scaffold: Using videogames to support science education. *Journal of Educational Technology*, *18*(4), 305–320. doi:10.1007/s10956-009-9171-5

Barab, S., Gresalfi, M., & Ingram-Goble, A. (2010). Transformational play: Using games to position person, content, and context. *Educational Researcher*, *39*(7), 525–536. doi:10.3102/0013189X10386593

Barbour, I. G. (1997). *Religion and science: Historical and contemporary issues*. San Francisco, CA: Harper.

Bargiela-Chiappini, F., & Nickerson, C. (2003). Intercultural business communication: A rich field of studies. *Journal of Intercultural Studies (Melbourne, Vic.)*, *24*(1), 3–15.

Barker, B. S., & Ansorge, J. (2007). Robotics as means to increase achievement scores in an informal learning environment. *Journal of Research on Technology in Education*, *39*(3), 229–243.

Barlett, C. P., & Gentile, D. A. (2012). Long-term psychological predictors of cyber-bullying in late adolescence. *Psychology of Popular Media Culture*, *2*, 123–135. doi:10.1037/a0028113

Barlett, C. P., Gentile, D. A., Anderson, C. A., Suzuki, K., Sakamoto, A., Yamaoka, A., & Katsura, R. (2013). Cross-cultural differences in cyberbullying behavior: A short-term longitudinal study. *Journal of Cross-Cultural Psychology*, *45*(2), 300–313. doi:10.1177/0022022113504622

Barnes, P. M., Powell-Griner, E., McFann, K., & Nahin, R. (2002). Complementary and alternative medicine use among adults: United States, 2002. *Seminars in Integrative Medicine*, *2*(2), 54–71. doi:10.1016/j.sigm.2004.07.003

Barron, A. E., & Orwig, G. W. (1997). *New technologies for education: A beginner's guide*. USA: Libraries Unlimited.

Bartlett, R., Bland, A. R., Rossen, E., Kautz, D. D., Benfield, S., & Carnevale, T. (2008). Evaluation of the outcome-present state test model as a way to teach clinical reasoning. *The Journal of Nursing Education*, *47*(8), 337–344. doi:10.3928/01484834-20080801-01 PMID:18751647

Barzilai-Nahon, K., & Barzilai, G. (2005). Cultured technology: The Internet and religious fundamentalism. *The Information Society*, *21*(1), 25–40. doi:10.1080/01972240590895892

Basabe, N., & Ros, M. (2005). Cultural dimensions and social behavior correlates: Individualism-collectivism and power distance. *Revue Internationale de Psychologie Sociale. PressesUniversitaires de Grenoble*, *18*(1), 189–225.

Baş, G. (2010). Effects of brain-based learning on students' achievement levels and attitudes towards English lesson. *Elementary Education Online*, *9*(2), 488–507.

Bates, D. W., & Gawande, A. A. (2003). Improving safety with information technology. *The New England Journal of Medicine*, *348*(25), 2526–2534. doi:10.1056/NEJMsa020847 PMID:12815139

Batsche, G. M., Elliot, J., Graden, J. L., Grimes, J., Kovaleski, J. F., Prasse, D., & Tilly, W. D. (2005). *Response to intervention: Policy considerations and implementation*. Alexandria, VA: National Association of State Directors of Special Education.

Batson, C. D. (1983). Sociobiology and the role of religion in promoting prosocial behavior: An alternative view. *Journal of Personality and Social Psychology*, *45*(6), 1380–1385. doi:10.1037/0022-3514.45.6.1380

Batson, C. D., & Gray, R. A. (1981). Religious orientation and helping behavior: Responding to own or to the victim's needs? *Journal of Personality and Social Psychology*, *40*(3), 511–520. doi:10.1037/0022-3514.40.3.511

Batt, R., & Valcour, P. M. (2003). Human resources practices as predictors of work-family outcomes and employee turnover. *Industrial Relations*, *42*(2), 189–220.

Bauer, T., & Barron, C. R. (1995). Nursing interventions for spiritual care preferences of the community-based elderly. *Journal of Holistic Nursing*, *13*(3), 268–279. doi:10.1177/089801019501300308 PMID:7650353

Baumann, J. F., Ro, J. M., Duffy-Hester, A. M., & Hoffman, J. M. (2000). Then and now: Perspectives on the status of elementary reading instruction by prominent reading educators. *Reading Research and Instruction*, *39*(3), 236–264. doi:10.1080/19388070009558324

Bauman, S., Toomey, R. B., & Walker, J. L. (2013). Associations among bullying, cyberbullying, and suicide in high school students. *Journal of Adolescence*, *36*(2), 341–350. doi:10.1016/j.adolescence.2012.12.001 PMID:23332116

Baumgarten, N., & House, J. (2010). I think and I don't know in English as lingua franca and Beneke, J. (1991). Englisch als lingua franca oder als Medium interkultureller Kommunikation [English as lingua franca or as medium of intercultural communication]. In R. Grebing (Ed.), *Grenzenloses Sprachenlernen* (pp. 54–66). Berlin: Cornelsen.

Baverstock, K., & Williams, D. (2007). The Chernobyl accident 20 years on: An assessment of the health consequences and the international response. *Ciencia & Saude Coletiva*, *12*(3), 689–698. PMID:17680126

Bayar, Y., & Ucanok, Z. (2012). School social climate and generalized peer perception in traditional and cyberbullying status. *Educational Sciences: Theory and Practice*, *12*, 2352–2358.

Bayly, C. A. (2004). *The birth of the modern world, 1780–1914: Global connections and comparisons*. Oxford, UK: Blackwell.

Bazhenova, E. D. (2013). Content analysis of the category "Academic Mobility of Students.". *Middle-East Journal of Scientific Research*, *13*(4), 483–488. doi:10.5829/idosi.mejsr.2013.13.4.2914

Bazini, E., & Nedelea, A. (2008). Impact of the tourism development on poverty reduction in Albania as a country in transition. *Revista de Turism*, *3*(5), 23–28.

BBC. (2015). Moldova country profile – Overview. *BBC News*. Retrieved from http://www.bbc.com/news/world-europe-17601580

Beaton, D. E., Bombardier, C., Guillemin, F., & Ferraz, M. B. (2000). Guidelines for the process of cross-cultural adaptation of self-report measures. *Spine*, *25*(24), 3186–3191. PMID:11124735

Beauchamp, T. L., & Childress, J. F. (2001). *Principles of Biomedical Ethics*. New York, NY: Oxford University Press.

Becker, J. M. (Ed.). (1979). *Schooling for a global age*. New York, NY: McGraw-Hill.

Beckman, L., Hagquist, C., & Hellstrom, L. (2012). Does the association with psychosomatic health problems differ between cyberbullying and traditional bullying? *Emotional & Behavioural Difficulties*, *17*(3-4), 421–434. doi:10.1080/13632752.2012.704228

Beer, R. D., Chiel, H. J., & Drushel, R. F. (1999). Using autonomous robotics to teach science and engineering. *Communications of the ACM*, *42*(6), 85–92.

Bek, A. (2004). *The life of a Russian woman doctor: A Siberian memoir, 1869–1954*. Bloomington: Indiana University Press.

Belli, G. (2009). Nonexperimental quantitative research. In S. D. Lapan & M. T. Quartaroli (Eds.), *Research essentials: An introduction to designs and practices* (pp. 59–77). San Francisco, CA: John Wiley & Sons, Inc.

Bender, T. (2012). *Discussion-based online teaching to enhance student learning: Theory, practice, and assessment* (2nd ed.). Virginia: Stylus.

Benedict, P. (1975). Catholics and Huguenots in sixteenth-century Rouen: The demographic effects of the religious wars. *French Historical Studies, 9*(2), 209–234. doi:10.2307/286126

Benjamin, W. (2008). *The work of art in the age of mechanical reproduction and other essays on the media*. Cambridge, MA: Harvard UP.

Beran, T., & Li, Q. (2005). Cyber-harassment: A new method for an old behavior. *Journal of Educational Computing Research, 32*(3), 265–277. doi:10.2190/8YQM-B04H-PG4D-BLLH

Beran, T., & Li, Q. (2007). The relationship between cyberbullying and school bullying. *Journal of Student Wellbeing, 1*, 15–33.

Berglof, E., Kunov, A., Shvets, J., & Yudaeva, K. (2003). *The new political economy of Russia*. Cambridge, MA: The MIT Press.

Bergstrom, M. K. (2008). Professional development in response to intervention: Implementation of a model in a rural region. *Rural Special Education Quarterly, 27*(4), 27–36.

Berkeley, S., Bender, W. N., Peaster, L. G., & Saunders, L. (2009). Implementation of response to intervention. *Journal of Learning Disabilities, 42*(1), 85–95. doi:10.1177/0022219408326214 PMID:19103800

Berman, E., & Machin, S. (2000). *Skill-biased technology transfer: Evidence of factor biased technological change in developing countries. Mimeograph.* Boston University.

Bernhardt, V. L., & Hebert, C. L. (2011). *Response to intervention (RtI) and continuous school improvement (SCI) using data, vision, and leadership to design, implement, and evaluate a schoolwide prevention system.* Larchmont, NY: Eye on Education.

Berry, L. L., Mirabito, A. M., & Baun, W. B. (2010, December). What's the hard return on employee wellness programs? *Harvard Business Review*. Retrieved from http://hbr.org/2010/12/whats-the-hard-return-on-employee-wellness-programs/ar/6

Berry, C. S. (1941). General problems of philosophy and administration in the education of exceptional children. *Review of Educational Research, 11*(3), 252–260.

Bertelli, M., Bianco, A., Rossi, M., Scuticchio, D., & Brown, I. (2011). Relationship between individual quality of life and family quality of life for people with intellectual disability living in Italy. *Journal of Intellectual Disability Research, 55*(12), 1136–1150. doi:10.1111/j.1365-2788.2011.01464.x PMID:21883597

Beširevi, V. (2010). End-of-life care in the 21st century: Advance directives in universal rights discourse. *Bioethics, 24*(3), 105–112. PMID:20136818

Betts, F. (1992). How systems thinking applies to education. *Educational Leadership, 50*(3), 38–41.

Beyer, D. A. (2011). Reverse case study: To think like a nurse. *The Journal of Nursing Education, 50*(1), 48–50. doi:10.3928/01484834-20101029-06 PMID:21053856

Bhat, B. A. (2011). Gender earnings and poverty reduction: Post-Communist Uzbekistan. *Journal of Asian and African Studies, 46*(6), 629–649. doi:10.1177/0021909611407584 PMID:22213880

Bhattacherjee, A., & Hikmet, N. (2007). Physicians' resistance toward healthcare information technology: a theoretical model and empirical test. *European Journal of Information Systems, 16*(6), 725-737. doi:.ejis.300071710.1057/palgrave

Bhattacherjee, A. (2001). Understanding Information Systems continuance: An expectation-confirmation model. *Management Information Systems Quarterly, 25*(3), 351–370. doi:10.2307/3250921

Bhattacherjee, A., & Barfar, A. (2011). Information Technology continuance research: Current state and future directions. *Asia Pacific Journal of Information Systems*, *21*(2), 1–18.

Biber, D. (1987). A textual comparison between American and British writing. *American Speech*, *62*(2), 99–119. doi:10.2307/455273

Biber, D., & Barbieri, F. (2007). Lexical bundles in university spoken and written registers. *English for Specific Purposes*, *26*(3), 263–286. doi:10.1016/j.esp.2006.08.003

Biber, D., Conrad, S., & Cortes, V. (2003). Lexical bundles in speech and writing: an initial taxonomy. In A. Wilson, P. Rayson, & T. McEnery (Eds.), *Corpus linguistics by the Lune: A festschrift for Geoffrey Leech* (pp. 71–93). Frankfurt: Peter Lang.

Biber, D., Conrad, S., & Cortes, V. (2004). If you look at...: Lexical bundles in university teaching and textbooks. *Applied Linguistics*, *25*(3), 371–405. doi:10.1093/applin/25.3.371

Biber, D., Johansson, S., Leech, G., Conrad, S., & Finegan, E. (1999). *The Longman grammar of spoken and written English*. London: Longman.

Bichteler, J. (1987). Technostress in libraries: Causes, effects and solutions. *The Electronic Library*, *5*(5), 282–287. doi:10.1108/eb044766

Bickerstaffe, G. (2008). *Which MBA? 2009: Making the right choice of executive education*. Retrieved from http://graphics.eiu.com/whichmba/Which_MBA_20th_edition_2009.pdf

Bierema, L. L., & Merriam, S. G. (2002). E-mentoring: Using computer-mediated communication to enhance the mentoring process. *Innovative Higher Education*, *26*(3), 211–227. doi:10.1023/A:1017921023103

Bimrose, J., Brown, A., Holocher-Ertl, T., Kieslinger, B., Kunzmann, C., Prilla, M., & Wolf, C. et al. (2014). The role of facilitation in technology-enhanced learning for public employment services. *International Journal of Advanced Corporate Learning*, *7*(3), 56–63.

Bingimlas, K. A. (2010). *Evaluating the quality of science teachers' practices in ICT-supported learning and teaching environments in Saudi primary schools*. (Unpublished dissertation). RMIT University, Melbourne, Australia.

Birch, J., Caulfield, R., & Ramakrishnan, V. (2007). The complications of 'cosmetic tourism:–An avoidable burden on the NHS. *Journal of Plastic, Reconstructive & Aesthetic Surgery; JPRAS*, *60*(9), 1075–1077. PMID:17482899

Bishop, L. (2009). Ethical sharing and reuse of qualitative data. *The Australian Journal of Social Issues*, *44*(3), 255–272.

Björkman, B. (2011). Pragmatic strategies in English as an academic lingua franca: Ways of achieving communicative effectiveness? *Journal of Pragmatics*, *43*(4), 950–964. doi:10.1016/j.pragma.2010.07.033

Blake, H., Zhou, D., & Batt, M. E. (2013). Five-year workplace wellness intervention in the NHS. *Perspectives in Public Health*, *133*(5), 262–271. doi:10.1177/1757913913489611 PMID:23771680

Bland, A. R., Rossen, E. K., Bartlett, R., Kautz, D. D., Carnevale, T., & Benfield, S. (2009). Implementation and testing of the OPT model as a teaching strategy in an undergraduate psychiatric nursing course. *Nursing Education Perspectives*, *30*(1), 14–21. doi:10.1016/j.apnu.2005.08.002 PMID:19331034

Blankenship, M. (2011). How social media can and should impact higher education. *Education Digest*, *76*(7), 39–42.

Blazina, C., Settle, A., & Eddins, R. (2008). Gender role conflict and separation-individuation difficulties: Their impact on college men's loneliness. *Journal of Men's Studies*, *16*(1), 69–81. doi:10.3149/jms.1601.69

Blogowska, J., & Saroglou, V. (2011). Religious fundamentalism and limited prosociality as a function of the target. *Journal for the Scientific Study of Religion, 50*(1), 44–60. doi:10.1111/j.1468-5906.2010.01551.x

Bloom, D., Canning, D., & Sevilla, J. (2003). *The demographic dividend: A new perspective on the economic consequences of population change.* Santa Monica, CA: RAND.

Blow, F. (2011). "Everything flows and nothing stays": How students make sense of the historical concepts of change, continuity and development. *Teaching History, 145*, 47–55. Retrieved from ERIC database. (EJ960982)

Blumenthal, D., & Tavenner, M. (2010). The "meaningful use" regulation for electronic health records. *The New England Journal of Medicine, 363*(6), 501–504. doi:10.1056/NEJMp1006114 PMID:20647183

Bly, J. L., Jones, R. C., & Richardson, J. E. (1986). Impact of worksite health promotion on health care costs and utilization: Evaluation of Johnson & Johnson's live for life program. *Journal of the American Medical Association, 23*(23), 3235–3240. doi:10.1001/jama.1986.03380230059026 PMID:3783867

Boatman, J., & Wellins, R. S. (2011). *Time for a leadership revolution: Global leadership forecast 2011.* Retrieved from http://www.ddiworld.com/ddi/media/trend-research/ globalleadershipforecast2011_globalreport_ddi.pdf

Bonanno, R. A., & Hymel, S. (2013). Cyber bullying and internalizing difficulties: Above and beyond the impact of traditional forms of bullying. *Journal of Youth and Adolescence, 42*(5), 685–697. doi:10.1007/s10964-013-9937-1 PMID:23512485

Bond, M. H., & Hofstede, G. (1989). The cash value of Confucian values. *Human Systems Management, 8*(3), 195–199.

Bond, P. (1999). Globalization, pharmaceutical pricing and South African health policy: Managing confrontation with U.S. firms and politicians. *International Journal of Health Services, 29*(4), 765–792. PMID:10615573

Bonhoeffer, D. (1959). *The cost of discipleship.* Available from http://www.amazon.com/The-Cost-Discipleship-Dietrich-Bonhoeffer/dp/0684815001

Bonk, C. J., Lee, M. M., Sheu, F. R., & Kou, X. (2013). *Self-directed online learning: MOOCs, open education, and beyond.* Retrieved from http://www.courseshare.com/pdfs/Self-Directed_Lrng_MOOCs_Open_Ed_AECT_Bonk_et_al_Friday_paper_session.pdf

Bonk, C. J., & Kim, K. J. (2006). The future of online teaching and learning in higher education: The survey says…. *EDUCAUSE Quarterly, 4*, 22–30. Retrieved from http://www.educause.edu/ero/article/future-online-teaching-and-learning-higher-education-survey-says%E2%80%A6

Boocock, S. S. (1989). Controlled diversity: An overview of the Japanese preschool system. *Journal of Japanese Studies, 15*(1), 41–65. doi:10.2307/132407

Borg, J. (2010). Body language: 7 easy lessons to master the silent language. Upper Saddle River, NJ: FT.

Borgmann, A. (1987). *Technology and the character of contemporary life: A Philosophical inquiry.* Chicago, IL: University of Chicago Press.

Boscardin, M. L. (2007). What is special about special education administration? Considerations for school leadership. *Exceptionality, 15*(3), 189–200. doi:10.1080/09362830701503537

Boscardin, M. L., McCarthy, E., & Delgado, R. (2009). An integrated research-based approach to creating standards for special education leadership. *Journal of Special Education Leadership, 22*(2), 68–84.

Bouchard, R. A., & Lemmens, T. (2008). Privatizing biomedical research: A'third way'. *Nature Biotechnology, 26*(1), 31–36. PMID:18183013

Boucher, L. (2014). *Tradition and change in Swedish education*. Oxford, UK: Elsevier.

Boulton, M., Lloyd, J., Down, J., & Marx, H. (2012). Predicting undergraduates' self-reported engagement in traditional and cyberbullying from attitudes. *Cyberpsychology, Behavior, and Social Networking*, *15*(3), 141–147. doi:10.1089/cyber.2011.0369 PMID:22304402

Bounds, E. M. (2004). *The complete works of E. M. Bounds on prayer: Experience the wonders of God through prayer*. Grand Rapids, MI: Baker.

Bowden, A., & Fox-Rushby, J. A. (2003). A systematic and critical review of the process of translation and adaptation of generic health-related quality of life measures in Africa, Asia, Eastern Europe, the Middle East, South America. *Social Science & Medicine*, *57*(7), 1289–1306. PMID:12899911

Bowers, J. M. (1991). The janus face of design: Some critical questions for CSCW. In J. M. Bowers, & S. D. Benford (Eds.), Studies in computer supported cooperative work (pp. 333–350). Elsevier Science.

Bowles, M. (2012). The business of hacking and birth of an industry. *Bell Labs Technical Journal*, *17*(3), 5–16. doi:10.1002/bltj.21555

Bowman, R. J. (1997). High technology: Dream or nightmare? *Distribution*, *96*(13), 30–34.

Boyd, D. (2014, March). How to take an email sabbatical. *Fast Company*. Retrieved from http://www.fastcompany.com/3027058/work-smart/how-to-take-an-email-sabatical

Boyer, M. A., Brown, S. W., Butler, M. J., Niv-Solomon, A., Urlacher, B., Hudson, N., & Lima, C. O. et al. (2007). Experimenting with global governance: Understanding the potential for generational change. *Globalisation, Societies and Education*, *5*(2), 153–180. doi:10.1080/14767720701425727

Boyer, P. (1994). *The naturalness of religious ideas: A cognitive theory of religion*. Berkeley: University of California Press.

Boyer, P. (2008). Being human: Religion: Bound to believe? *Nature*, *455*(7216), 1038–1039. doi:10.1038/4551038a PMID:18948934

Bradford, C. (2010). Looking for my corpse: Video games and player positioning. *Australian Journal of Language and Literacy*, *33*(1), 54–64.

Bradley, C. (2009). The interconnection between religious fundamentalism, spirituality, and the four dimensions of empathy. *Review of Religious Research*, *51*(2), 201–219. Retrieved from http://www.jstor.org/stable/20697334?seq=1#fndtn-page_scan_tab_contents

Bradley, R., Danielson, L., & Doolittle, J. (2005). Response to intervention. *Journal of Learning Disabilities*, *38*(6), 485–486. doi:10.1177/00222194050380060201 PMID:16392688

Brah, A. (1992). Questions of difference and international feminism. In J. Aaron & S. Walby (Eds.), *Out of the margins: Women's studies in the nineties* (pp. 111–134). London: Falmer Press.

Branson, C. (2007). Effects of structured self-reflection and on the development of authentic leadership practices among Queensland primary school participants. *Educational Management Administration & Leadership*, *35*(2), 225–246. doi:10.1177/1741143207075390

Brenner, S. W. (2004). U.S. cyber-crime law: Defining offenses. *Information Systems Frontiers*, *6*(2), 115–132. doi:10.1023/B:ISFI.0000025780.94350.79

Bresnahan, T. F., & Trajtenberg, M. (1995). General purpose technologies 'Engines of growth'? *Journal of Econometrics*, *65*(1), 83–108.

Brewin, R. (2014, January). The army wants more smartphones on the battlefield. *Defense One*. Retrieved from http://www.defenseone.com/technology/2014/01/army-wants-more-smartphones-battlefield/77657/print/

Brigham, E. F., & Houston, J. (2015). *Fundamentals of Financial Management* (14th ed.). Boston, MA: Cengage Learning.

Brighi, A., Guarini, A., Melotti, G., Galli, S., & Genta, M. L. (2012). Predictors of victimisation across direct bullying, indirect bullying and cyberbullying. *Emotional & Behavioural Difficulties*, *17*(3-4), 375–388. doi:10.1080/13632752.2012.704684

Bright, D. R., Terrell, S. L., Rush, M. J., Kroustos, K. R., Stockert, A. L., Swanson, S. C., & DiPietro, N. A. (2012). Employee attitudes toward participation in a work-site based health and wellness clinic. *Journal of Pharmacy Practice*, *25*(5), 530–536. doi:10.1177/0897190012442719 PMID:22572221

Broadbear, J. T. (2003). Essential elements of lessons designed to promote critical thinking.[JoSoTL]. *The Journal of Scholarship of Teaching and Learning*, *3*(3), 1–8.

Brockett, R. G., & Donaghy, R. C. (2005, June). *Beyond the inquiring mind: Cyril Houle's contribution to self- directed learning*. Paper presented at the meeting of Proceedings of the 46th Annual Adult Education Research Conference, Athens, GA. Retrieved from http://www.sdlglobal.com/IJSDL/IJSDL9.2.pdf

Brod, C. (1984). *Technostress: The human cost of the computer revolution*. Reading, MA: Addison-Wesley.

Brookhart, S. M. (2008). *How to Give Effective Feedback to your Students*. ASCD.

Brooks, M. E. (2012, September). Death of secular saint Steve Jobs in a theologically devoid culture. *The Christian Post*. Retrieved from http://www.christianpost.com/news/death-of-secular-saint-steve-jobs-in-a-theologically-devoid-culture-59595/

Brooks, A., Lithgow, G. J., & Johnson, T. E. (1994). Mortality rates in a genetically heterogeneous population of Caenorhabditis elegans. *Science*, *263*, 668–671. PMID:8303273

Brown, S., & Macdonald, D. (2003). Masculinities in physical recreation: The (re)production of masculinist discourses in vocation education. *Sport Education and Society*, *13*(1), 19–37. doi:10.1080/13573320701780506

Brunt, B. (2005). Critical thinking in nursing: An integrated review. *Journal of Continuing Education in Nursing*, *36*(2), 60–67. PMID:15835580

Bryans, P., & Mavin, S. (2003). Women learning to become managers: Learning to fit in or to play a different game? *Management Learning*, *34*(1), 111–134. doi:10.1177/1350507603034001133

Buchanan, T., Sainter, P., & Saunders, G. (2013). Factors affecting faculty use of learning technologies: Implications for models of technology adoption. *Journal of Computing in Higher Education*, *25*(1), 1–11. doi:10.1007/s12528-013-9066-6

Buckingham, E. A. (1997). *Specific and generic numeracy of the workplace: How is numeracy learnt and used by workers in production industries, and what learning/working environments promote this?* Burswood, Vic.: Centre for Studies in Mathematics, Science, and Environmental Education, Deacon University.

Buckley, N. (2006, October 30). Russia's middle class starts spending. *Financial Times*, p. 13.

Bülow, H. H., Sprung, C. L., Reinhart, K., Prayag, S., Du, B., Armaganidis, A., & Levy, M. M. et al. (2008). The world's major religions' points of view on end-of-life decisions in the intensive care unit. *Intensive Care Medicine*, *34*(3), 423–430. doi:10.1007/s00134-007-0973-8 PMID:18157484

Burholt, V., & Naylor, D. (2005). The relationship between rural community type and attachment to place for older people living in North Wales, UK. *European Journal of Ageing*, *2*(2), 109–119. doi:10.1007/s10433-005-0028-3

Burkhart, G. E., & Older, S. (2003). *The information revolution in the Middle East and North Africa. National Defense Research Institute.* RAND.

Burkhead, R. L. (2014). *A phenomenological study of information security incidents experienced by information security professionals providing corporate information security incident management* (Doctoral dissertation). Retrieved from ProQuest Dissertations and Theses database. (UMI No. 3682325)

Burns, M. K., Appleton, J. J., & Stehouwer, J. D. (2005). Meta-analytic review of responsiveness-to- intervention research: Examining field-based and research-implemented models. *Journal of Psychoeducational Assessment, 23*(4), 381–394. doi:10.1177/073428290502300406

Burns, N., & Grove, S. K. (2011). *Understanding nursing research* (5th ed.). Maryland Heights, MO: Elsevier Saunders.

Burström, K., Johannesson, M., & Diderichsen, F. (2001). Health-related quality of life by disease and socio-economic group in the general population in Sweden. *Health Policy (Amsterdam), 55*(1), 51–69. doi:10.1016/S0168-8510(00)00111-1 PMID:11137188

Burton, K. A., Florell, D., & Wygant, D. B. (2013). The role of peer attachment and normative beliefs about aggression on traditional bullying and cyberbullying. *Psychology in the Schools, 50*(2), 103–114. doi:10.1002/pits.21663

Butts, J., Rice, M., & Shenoi, S. (2012). An adversarial model for expressing attacks on control protocols. *Journal of Defense Modeling and Simulation: Applications, Methodology. Technology (Elmsford, N.Y.), 9*(3), 243–255.

Cady, D., Olson, M., Shea, P., & Grenier, J. M. (2011). Part ii a pratical model and assignments for using virtual worlds in higher education. In R. Hinrichs & C. Wankel (Eds.), Cutting-edge Technologies in Higher Education: Transforming Virtual World Learning. Emerald Group Publishing.

Caelli, K., Ray, L., & Mill, J. (2003). Clear as mud: Toward greater clarity in generic qualitative research. *International Journal of Qualitative Methods, 2*(2). Article 1. Retrieved from http://www.ualberta.ca/~iiqm/backissues/pdf/caellietal.pdf

Cags, M. (2010). New graduate nurses' perceptions of the effects of clinical simulation on their critical thinking, learning, and confidence. *Journal of Continuing Education in Nursing, 41*(11), 506–516. PMID:20672760

Cain, C., & Haque, S. (2008). Organizational workflow and its impact on work quality. In R. G. Hughes (Ed.), *Patient safety and quality: An evidence-based handbook for nurses* (pp. 217-244). Retrieved from Agency for Healthcare Research and Quality website: http://www.ncbi.nlm.nih.gov/books/NBK2638/pdf/ch31.pdf

Cain, S. (2012). *Quiet: The power of introverts in a world that can't stop talking.* New York, NY: Broadway Books.

Calder, B. J., Phillips, L. W., & Tybout, A. M. (1981). Designing research for application. *The Journal of Consumer Research,* 197–207.

California Community Colleges Chancellor's Office, California Community Colleges Student Success Task Force. (2012). *Advancing Student Success in the California Community Colleges.* Retrieved from http://californiacommunitycolleges. cccco.edu/PolicyinAction/StudentSuccessTaskForce.aspx

Callahan, D. (2008). *Health care costs and medical technology.* The Hastings Center. Available from http://healthcarecost-monitor.thehastingscenter.org/uploadedFiles/Publications/Briefing_Book/health%20care%20costs%20chapter.pdf

Calloway, S. J. (2009). The effect of culture on beliefs related to autonomy and informed consent. *Journal of Cultural Diversity, 16*(2), 68–70.

Cambray, J. (2009). *Synchronicity: Nature and psyche in an interconnected universe.* College Station: Texas A&M University Press.

Camfield, L., & Ruta, D. (2007). Translation is not enough: Using the global person generated index (GPGI) to assess individual quality of life in Bangladesh, Thailand, and Ethiopia. *Quality of Life Research: An International Journal of Quality of Life Aspects of Treatment, Care and Rehabilitation, 16*(6), 1039–1051. PMID:17487570

Camic, P. M., Rhodes, J. E., & Yardley, L. (Eds.). (2003). *Qualitative research in psychology: Expanding perspectives in methodology and design*. Washington, DC: American Psychological Association.

Campbell, M., Spears, B., Slee, P. H., Butler, D., & Kift, S. (2012). Victims' perceptions of traditional and cyberbullying, and the psychosocial correlates of their victimisation. *Emotional & Behavioural Difficulties, 17*(3-4), 389–401. doi:10.1080/13632752.2012.704316

Canada, G. (2013, May 8). Our failing schools: Enough is enough! *TED Talk*. Retrieved from http://www.youtube.com/watch?v=vY2l2xfDBcE

Candy, P. (1991). *Self-direction for lifelong learning: A comprehensive guide to theory and practice*. San Francisco, CA: Jossey-Bass.

Canel, A., & Oldenziel, R. (2000). *Crossing boundaries, building bridges*. Reading, UK: Harwood Academic.

Cappadocia, M. C., Craig, W. M., & Pepler, D. (2013). Cyberbullying: Prevalence, stability and risk factors during adolescence. *Canadian Journal of School Psychology, 28*, 171–192.

Cardno, C. (2012). *Managing effetive relationships in education*. London, GRB. *Sage (Atlanta, Ga.)*.

Carey, R. J. (2014). *Response to TechAmerica CIO survey: IT in periods of rapid change*. Unpublished manuscript.

Carlsen, B., & Glenton, C. (2011). What about N? A methodological study of sample-size reporting in focus group studies. *BMC Medical Research Methodology, 11*(1), 26–35. PMID:21396104

Carrasquillo, O., Orav, E. J., Brennan, T. A., & Burstin, H. R. (1999). Impact of language barriers on patient satisfaction in an emergency Department. *Journal of General Internal Medicine, 14*(2), 82–87. doi:10.1046/j.1525-1497.1999.00293.x PMID:10051778

Carrera, P. M., & Bridges, J. F. (2006). Health and medical tourism: What they mean and imply for health care systems. *Health and Ageing, 15*. Retrieved from https://www.genevaassociation.org/media/75240/ga2006-health15-carrerabridges.pdf

Carrick, J. (2011). Student achievement and NCLEX-RN success: Problems that persist. *Nursing Education Perspectives, 32*(2), 78–83. doi:10.5480/1536-5026-32.2.78 PMID:21667787

Carr, N. (2010). *The shallows: What the internet is doing to our brains*. New York, NY: Norton.

Carr, S. (2000). As distance education comes of age, the challenge is keeping the students. *The Chronicle of Higher Education, 46*(23), A39–A41. Retrieved from http://chronicle.com/article/As-Distance-Education-Comes-of/14334

Carson, D. A. (1992). Reflections on Christian assurance. *Westminster Theological Journal, 54*(1), 1–29. Retrieved from http://s3.amazonaws.com/tgc-documents/carson/1992_ reflections_on_christian_assurance.pdf

Casarez, R. L. P., & Engebretson, J. (2012). Ethical issues of incorporating spiritual care into clinical practice. *Journal of Clinical Nursing, 21*(15/16), 2099–2107. PMID:22788552

Cassel, C. K., & Guest, J. A. (2012). Choosing wisely: Helping physicians and patients make smart decisions about their care. *Journal of the American Medical Association, 307*(17), 1801–1802. doi:10.1001/jama.2012.476 PMID:22492759

Cassidy, W., Brown, K., & Jackson, M. (2012a). "Making kind cool": Parents' suggestions for preventing cyber bullying and fostering cyber kindness. *Journal of Educational Computing Research*, *46*(4), 415–436. doi:10.2190/EC.46.4.f

Cassidy, W., Brown, K., & Jackson, M. (2012b). "Under the radar": Educators and cyberbullying in schools. *School Psychology International*, *33*(5), 520–532. doi:10.1177/0143034312445245

Castells, M. (2011). *The rise of the network society: The information age: Economy, society, and culture* (Vol. 1). Sussex, UK: Blackwell.

Castillo, J. M., & Batsche, G. M. (2012). Scaling up response to intervention: The influence of policy and research and the role of program evaluation. *Communique*, *40*, 14–16.

Cavendish, R., Konecny, L., Luise, B. K., & Lanza, M. (2004). Nurses enhance performance through prayer. *Holistic Nursing Practice*, *18*(1), 26–31. doi:10.1097/00004650-200401000-00005 PMID:14765689

Ceceri, K. (2012). *Build it yourself robotics: Discover the science and technology of the future with 25 projects. White River Junction*. Ann Arbor, MI: Nomad.

Ceci, S. J., Peters, D., & Plotkin, J. (1985). Human subjects review, personal values, and the regulation of social science research. *The American Psychologist*, *40*(9), 994.

Çelik, V. (2000). Eğitimsel liderlik (2nd ed.). Ankara, TR: Pegem A Yayıncılık.

Centers for Disease Control and Prevention (CDC). (2007). Acute respiratory disease associated with adenovirus serotype 14--four states, 2006-2007. (*MMWR.*). *Morbidity and Mortality Weekly Report*, *56*(45), 1181. PMID:18004235

Centers for Disease Control and Prevention. (n.d.). *Behavioral risk factor surveillance system*. Retrieved from http://www.cdc.gov/brfss/

Chadwick, H. (1966). *Early Christian thought and the classical tradition: Studies in Justin, Clement, and Origen*. New York, NY: Oxford University Press.

Chaffee, J. (2012). *Thinking critically* (10th ed.). Boston, MA: Wadsworth CENGAGE Learning.

Chall, J. S. (1992). The new reading debates: Evidence from science, art, and ideology. *Teachers College Record*, *94*, 315–328.

Chan, A. K., Hyung, W. P., & Hoon, D. L. (2013). A study on the live forensic techniques for anomaly detection in user terminals. *International Journal of Security & its Applications*, *7*(1), 181-188.

Chan, A., Hannah, S. T., & Gardner, W. L. (2005). Veritable authentic leadership: Emergence, functioning, and impacts. In W. J. Gardner, B. J. Avolio, & F. O. Walumbwa (Eds.), *Authentic leadership theory and practice: Origins, effects and development* (pp. 3–41). Bingley, UK: Emerald Group.

Chappuis, B., Gaffey, B., & Parvizi, P. (2011). Are your customers becoming digital junkies? *The McKinsey Quarterly*, (3): 20–23.

Charlesworth, B., & Partridge, L. (1997). Ageing: Leveling of the grim reaper. *Current Biology*, *7*(7), R440–R442. PMID:9210361

Chau, P. K. & Hu, P. J-H (2002). Investigating healthcare professional's decision to accept telemedicine technology: an empirical test of competing theories. *Information & Management, 39*(4), 279-311. (01)00098-210.1016/S0378-7206

Chau, P. Y., & Hu, P. J.-H. (2001). Information technology acceptance by individual professionals: A model comparison approach. *Decision Sciences*, *32*(4), 699–719. doi:10.1111/j.1540-5915.2001.tb00978.x

Chen, J., Park, Y., & Putzer, G. J. (2010). An examination of the components that increase acceptance of smartphones among healthcare professionals. *Electronic Journal of Health Informatics, 15*(2), 1-12. Retrieved from http://www.ejhi.net

Chen, M. (2013a). Phrasal verbs in a longitudinal learner corpus: Quantitative findings. In S. Granger, G. Gilquin, & F. Meunier (Eds.), Twenty years of Learner Corpus Research: Looking back, moving ahead (pp. 89-101). Louvain-la-Neuve: Presses Universitaires de Louvain.

Chen, M. (2013). Patents against people: How drug companies price patients out of survival. *Dissent, 60*(4), 71–77.

Chen, M. (2013b). Overuse or underuse: A corpus study of English phrasal verb use by Chinese, British and American university students. *International Journal of Corpus Linguistics, 18*(3), 418–442. doi:10.1075/ijcl.18.3.07che

Chen, M., & Hu, X. (2006). Towards the acceptability of China English at home and abroad. *Changing English, 13*(2), 231–240. doi:10.1080/13586840600833648

Chen, S. X., Benet-Martínez, V., & Ng, J. K. (2014). Does Language Affect Personality Perception? A Functional Approach to Testing the Whorfian Hypothesis. *Journal of Personality, 82*(2), 130–143. doi:10.1111/jopy.12040 PMID:23607801

Chen, W., Fukutomi, E., Wada, T., Ishimoto, Y., Kimura, Y., Kasahara, Y., & Matsubayashi, K. et al. (2013). Comprehensive geriatric functional analysis of elderly populations in four categories of the long-term care insurance system in a rural, depopulated and aging town in Japan. *Geriatrics & Gerontology International, 13*(1), 63–69. doi:10.1111/j.1447-0594.2012.00859.x PMID:22672651

Chen, X. (2004). Culture and understanding: The Cartesian suspicion, The Gadamerian response, and the Confucian outcome. *Journal of Chinese Philosophy, 31*(3), 389–403.

Chen, Y., & Chen, X. (2012). Methodological issues in psychology of religion research in the Chinese context. *Pastoral Psychology, 61*(5-6), 671–683.

Chen, Y.-H., & Baker, P. (2010). Lexical Bundles in L1 and L2 Academic Writing. *Language Learning & Technology, 14*(2), 30–49.

Cheong, C. M., & Cheung, W. S. (2008). Online discussion and critical thinking skills: A case study in a Singapore secondary school. *Australasian Journal of Educational Technology, 24*(5), 556–573.

Cherednichenko, G. A. (2012). The educational and professional trajectories of working young people. *Russian Education & Society, 54*(11), 34–52. doi:10.2753/RES1060-9393541103

ChildrenOnline. (2015). *Internet safety newsletter: Children online research 2007– 2008.* Retrieved from http://www.childrenonline.org

Chinai, R., & Goswami, R. (2007). Medical visas mark growth of Indian medical tourism. *Bulletin of the World Health Organization, 85*(3), 164–165. PMID:17486202

Chin, W. W., Johnson, N., & Schwartz, A. (2008). A fast form approach to measuring technology acceptance and other constructs. *Management Information Systems Quarterly, 32*(4), 687–703. Retrieved from http://web.ffos.hr/oziz/tam/Chin_2008.pdf

Chirikova, A. I. (1998). *A woman in charge of a firm.* Moscow, Russia: Institut Sotsiologii RAN.

Chisholm, J. F. (2006). Cyberspace violence against girls and adolescent females. *Annals of the New York Academy of Sciences, 1087*(1), 74–89. doi:10.1196/annals.1385.022 PMID:17189499

Chiswick, B. R., & Miller, P. W. (2005). Linguistic distance: A quantitative measure of the distance between English and other languages. *Journal of Multilingual and Multicultural Development, 26*(1), 1–11.

Christensen, C. M., & Overdorf, M. (2000, March-April). Meeting the challenge of disruptive change. *Harvard Business Review*, *2*(2), 88–101.

Chu, H., Deng, D., & Chao, H. (2011). An ontology-driven model for digital forensics investigations of computer incidents under the ubiquitous computing environments. *Wireless Personal Communications*, *56*(1), 5–19. doi:10.1007/s11277-009-9886-x

Church, A. H., Waclawski, J., & Siegel, W. (1999). Will the real O.D. practitioner please stand up? A call for change in the field. *Organization Development Journal*, *17*(2), 49–59.

Cianci, A. M., Hannah, S. T., Roberts, R. P., & Tsakumis, G. T. (2014). The effects of authentic leadership on followers' ethical decision-making in the face of temptation: An experimental study. *The Leadership Quarterly*, *25*(3), 581–594.

Clarke, L. W., & Whitney, E. (2009). Walking in their shoes: Using multiple-perspectives texts as a bridge to critical literacy. *The Reading Teacher*, *62*(6), 530–534. doi:10.1598/RT.62.6.7

Clark, J. E. (2010). Reconceiving the doctrine of Jesus as savior in terms of the African understanding of an ancestor: A model for the Black Church. *Black Theology: An International Journal*, *8*(2), 140–159. doi:10.1558/blth.v8i2.140

Clark, K., & Kalin, S. (1996). Technostressed out: How to cope in the digital age. *Library Journal*, *121*(13), 30–35.

Clark, M. (2012). Cross-cultural research: Challenge and competence. *International Journal of Nursing Practice*, 1828–1837. PMID:22776530

Clark, T. (2003). *Changing attitudes toward economic reform during the Yeltsin Era*. Westport, CT: Praeger.

Clark, W. H. (1958). The psychology of religion. *Pastoral Psychology*, *9*(4), 49–55. doi:10.1007/BF01741070

Clayton, J. M., Hancock, K., Parker, S., Butow, P. N., Walder, S., Carrick, S., & Olver, I. N. et al. (2008). Sustaining hope when communicating with terminally ill patients and their families: A systematic review. *Psycho-Oncology*, *17*(7), 641–659. doi:10.1002/pon.1288 PMID:18022831

Clifton, J. (1999). Gender and shame in Masaccio's expulsion from the Garden of Eden. *Art History*, *22*(5), 637–655. doi:10.1111/1467-8365.00180

Cobley, P. (2015). What the humanities are for: A semiotic perspective. *American Journal of Semiotics*, *30*(3/4), 205–228.

Cockcroft, W. H. (1982). *Mathematics counts: Report of the committee of inquiry into the teaching of mathematics in school*. London: Her Majesty Stationery Office.

Cockerham, W. C., Lueschen, G., Kunz, G., & Spaeth, J. L. (1986). Social stratification and self-management of health. *Journal of Health and Social Behavior*, *27*, 1–14. PMID:3711631

Codina, B., Nicolás, J., López, L., & Hernán, R. (2013). The importance of student mobility, academic exchange and internationalization of higher education for college students in a globalized world: The Mexican and Latin American case. *International Journal of Good Conscience*, *8*(2), 48–63. Retrieved from http://www.spentamexico.org/v8-n2/A3.8%282%2948-63.pdf

Cohen, A., & Brawer, F. (2008). *The American community college* (5th ed.). San Francisco, CA: Jossey Bass.

Cohen, D. (Ed.). (1995). *Crossroads in mathematics: Standards for introductory college mathematics before calculus*. American Mathematical Association of Two-Year Colleges.

Coiera, E. (1996). Clinical communication: a new informatics paradigm. In Proceedings of the AMIA Annual Fall Symposium (pp. 17–21). American Medical Informatics Association. Available from http://www.ncbi.nlm.nih.gov/pmc/articles/PMC2233204/

Coiera, E. (2000). When conversation is better than computation. *Journal of the American Medical Informatics Association, 7*(3), 277–286. doi:10.1136/jamia.2000.0070277 PMID:10833164

Coiera, E. (2004). *Handbook of health information management: Integrating information and communication technology in health care work*. London, UK: Routledge.

Coiera, E., & Tombs, V. (1998). Communication behaviours in a hospital setting: An observational study. *British Medical Journal, 316*(7132), 673–676. doi:10.1136/bmj.316.7132.673 PMID:9522794

Cole, M. (2009). Using wiki technology to support student engagement: Lessons from the trenches. *Computers & Education, 52*(1), 141–146.

Colleran, N., O'Donoghue, J., & Murphy, E. (2000). An educational program for enhancing adults' quantitative problem solving and decision making. In *Adults and Lifelong Education in Mathematics*. ALM.

Colleran, N., O'Donoghue, J., & Murphy, E. (2002). Adult problem solving and commonsense. Policies and practices for adults learning mathematics: Opportunities & risks. In *Proceedings of the 9Th International Conference on Adult Learning Mathematics*. ALM.

Columbus, L. (2013, September). IDC: 87% of connected devices sales by 2017 will be tablets and smartphones. *Forbes On-line Edition*. Retrieved from http://www.forbes.com/sites/louiscolumbus/2013/09/12/idc-87-of-connected-devices-by-2017-will-be-tablets-and-smartphones/

Comas-Diaz, L. (2012). Humanism and multiculturalism: An evolutionary alliance. *Psychotherapy (Chicago, Ill.), 49*(4), 437–441. doi:10.1037/a0027126 PMID:23205825

Commission on Sustainable Development 7. (1999). *Tourism and sustainable development*. Report of the Secretary-General (Document No. E/CN.17/1999/5). New York: United Nations. Retrieved from http://www.un.org/documents/ecosoc/docs/1999/e1999-29.htm

Congress, E. P., & Lyons, B. P. (1992). Cultural differences in health beliefs: Implications for social work practice in health care settings. *Social Work in Health Care, 17*(3), 81–96. doi:10.1300/J010v17n03_06 PMID:1465717

Conklin, K., & Schmitt, N. (2008). Formulaic sequences: Are they processed more quickly than nonformulaic language by native and nonnative speakers? *Applied Linguistics, 29*(1), 72–89. doi:10.1093/applin/amm022

Connell, J. (2006). Medical tourism: Sea, sun, sand and… surgery. *Tourism Management, 27*(6), 1093–1100.

Connell, R. W. (2005). *Masculinities* (2nd ed.). Berkeley, CA: UC Berkeley Press.

Cook, S. A. (2008). Give peace a chance: The diminution of peace in global education in the United States, United Kingdom and Canada. *Canadian Journal of Education, 31*(4), 889–914. Retrieved from http://files.eric.ed.gov/fulltext/EJ830504.pdf

Cooper, C. R., & Schindler, P. S. (2011). *Business research methods* (11th ed.). Boston, MA: McGraw-Hill.

Cooper, C., Fletcher, J., Gilbert, D., & Wanhill, S. (2008). *Tourism: Principles and Practice* (4th ed.). Harlow: Pearson Education Limited.

Cooper, S. (2002). *Technoculture and critical theory: In the service of the machine?* London, UK: Routledge. doi:10.4324/9780203167021

Corbin, J. M. (1998). Alternative Interpretations Valid or not? *Theory & Psychology*, *8*(1), 121–128.

Corcoran, L., Connolly, I., & O'Moore, M. (2012). Cyberbullying in Irish schools: An investigation of personality and self-concept. *The Irish Journal of Psychology*, *33*(4), 153–165. doi:10.1080/03033910.2012.677995

Corley, M. C., Minick, P., Elswick, R. K., & Jacobs, M. (2005). Nurse moral distress and ethical work environment. *Nursing Ethics*, *12*(4), 381–390. PMID:16045246

Cornbleth, C. (2003). *Hearing America's youth: Social identities in uncertain times*. New York, NY: Peter Lang.

Coşar, M. (2013). *Problem temelli öğrenme ortamında bilgisayar programlama çalışmalarının akademik başarı, eleştirel düşünme eğilimi ve bilgisayara yönelik tutuma etkileri*. (Unpublished doctoral dissertation). Gazi University, Ankara, TR.

Couch, R. B. (2001). Rhinoviruses. In D. M. Knipe & P. M. Howley (Eds.), *Fields Virology* (4th ed.; pp. 777–797). Philadelphia, PA: Lippincott Williams and Wilkins.

Couenhoven, J. (2010). Forgiveness and restoration: A theological exploration. *The Journal of Religion*, *90*(2), 148–170. doi:10.1086/649846

Cowan, R., Choi, H. E., & Kim, D. H. (2003). Four questions for error diagnosis and correction in CALL. *CALICO Journal*, *20*(3), 451–463.

Coward, H. G., & Ratanakul, P. (1999). *A cross-cultural dialogue on health care ethics*. Waterloo, CA: Wilfrid Laurier University Press.

Cowling, K., & Sugden, R. (1987). *Transitional Monopoly Capitalism*. New York, NY: Wheatsheaf.

Coxhead, A. (2008). Phraseology and English for academic purposes: Challenges and opportunities. In F. Meunier & G. Sylviane (Eds.), *Phraseology in Foreign Language Learning and Teaching* (pp. 149–161). Amsterdam: John Benjamins. doi:10.1075/z.138.12cox

Cradler, J., McNabb, M., Freeman, M., & Burchett, R. (2002). How Does Technology Influence Student Learning? *Learning and Leading with Technology*, *29*(8), 46–56.

Crane, B. E. (2012). *Using web 2.0 and social networking tools in the K-12 classroom*. American Library Association.

Crane, J. A. (1997). Patient comprehension of doctor-patient communication on discharge from the emergency department. *The Journal of Emergency Medicine*, *15*(1), 1–7. doi:10.1016/S0736-4679(96)00261-2 PMID:9017479

Creswell, J. W. (2003). *Research design: Qualitative, quantitative, and mixed-methods approaches* (2nd ed.). Thousand Oaks, CA: Sage.

Creswell, J. W. (2007). *Qualitative inquiry & research design*. Newbury Park, CA: Sage Publications.

Creswell, J. W. (2007). *Qualitative inquiry and research design: Choosing among five approaches*. Thousand Oaks, CA: Sage.

Creswell, J. W. (2008). *Educational research: Planning, conducting, and evaluating quantitative and qualitative research* (3rd ed.). Upper Saddle River, NJ: Pearson.

Creswell, J. W. (2009). Editorial: Mapping the field of mixed methods research. *Journal of Mixed Methods Research*, *3*(2), 95–108.

Creswell, J. W. (2009). *Research design: Qualitative, quantitative, and mixed methods approaches* (3rd ed.). Thousand Oaks, CA: Sage.

Crockett, J. B. (2002). Special education's role in preparing responsive leaders for inclusive schools. *Remedial and Special Education, 23*(3), 157–168. doi:10.1177/07419325020230030401

Crockett, J. B. (2007). The changing landscape of special education administration. *Exceptionality, 15*(3), 139–142. doi:10.1080/09362830701503487

Crockett, J. B. (2011). Conceptual models for leading and administrating special education. In J. M. Kauffman & D. P. Hallahan (Eds.), *Handbook of special education*. New York, NY: Routledge.

Crockett, J. B., Becker, M. K., & Quinn, D. (2009). Reviewing the knowledge base of special education leadership and administration from 1970-2009. *Journal of Special Education Leadership, 22*(2), 55–67.

Crockett, J. B., Billingsley, B. S., & Boscardin, M. L. (Eds.). (2012). *Handbook of leadership and administration for special education*. New York, NY: Routledge.

Cronin, M. (2003). *Translation and globalization*. London: Routledge.

Crotty, M. (1998). *The foundations of social research: Meaning and perspective in the research process*. Thousand Oaks, CA: Sage.

Crystal, D. (1997). *English as a global language*. Cambridge, UK: Cambridge University Press.

CTIA. (2014). *The wireless association: Policy and initiatives, accessibility and assistive technologies*. Retrieved from http://www.ctia.org/policy-initiatives/policy-topics/accessibility-and-assistive-technology

Cunningham, A. E., & O'Donnell, C. R. (2015). Teachers' knowledge about beginning reading development and instruction. In A. Pollatsek & R. Treiman (Eds.), *The Oxford Handbook of Reading* (pp. 447–462). Oxford: Oxford University Press.

Curd, P. R., Winter, S. J., & Connell, A. (2007). Participative Planning to enhance inmate wellness: Preliminary report of a correctional wellness program. *Journal of Correctional Health Care, 13*(4), 296–308. doi:10.1177/1078345807306754

Curlin, F. A., Chin, M. H., Sellergren, S. A., Roach, C. J., & Lantos, J. D. (2006). The association of physicians' religious characteristics with their attitudes and self-reported behaviors regarding religion and spirituality in the clinical encounter. *Medical Care, 44*(5), 446–453. doi:10.1097/01.mlr.0000207434.12450.ef PMID:16641663

Curlin, F. A., & Hall, D. E. (2005). Strangers or friends? A proposal for a new spirituality-in- medicine ethic. *Journal of General Internal Medicine, 20*, 370–374. PMID:15857497

Curlin, F. A., Lantos, J. D., Roach, C. J., Sellergren, S. A., & Chin, M. H. (2005). Religious characteristics of U.S. physicians: A national survey. *Journal of General Internal Medicine, 20*, 629–634. PMID:16050858

Curlin, F. A., Lawrence, R. E., Chin, M. H., & Lantos, J. D. (2007). Religion, conscience, and controversial clinical practices. *The New England Journal of Medicine, 356*(6), 593–600. PMID:17287479

Curlin, F. A., Sellergren, S. A., Lantos, J. D., & Chin, M. H. (2007). Physicians' observations and interpretations of the influence of religion and spirituality on health. *Archives of Internal Medicine, 167*(7), 649–654. doi:10.1001/archinte.167.7.649 PMID:17420422

Curry, D., Schmitt, M. J., & Waldon, S. (1996). *A Framework for Adult Numeracy Standards: The Mathematical Skills and Abilities Adults Need to be Equipped for the Future. ANN Standards*. Boston, MA: World Education.

Curseu, P. L., & Pluut, H. (2013). Student groups as learning entities: The effect of group diversity and teamwork quality on groups' cognitive complexity. *Studies in Higher Education, 38*(1), 87–103. doi:10.1080/03075079.2011.565122

Czinkota, M. (1997). Russia's transition to a market economy. *Journal of International Marketing, 5*(4), 73–93. Retrieved from EBSCOhost database. (Accession No. 6432650)

Daaleman, T. P., & VandeCreek, L. (2000). Placing religion and spirituality in end-of-life care.[JAMA]. *Journal of the American Medical Association, 284*(19), 2514–2517. PMID:11074785

Daher, T., & Lazarevic, B. (2014). Emerging instructional technologies: Exploring the extent of faculty use of web 2.0 tools at a midwestern community college. *TechTrends, 58*(6), 42–50. doi:10.1007/s11528-014-0802-1

Dale, B., Sævareid, H. I., Kirkevold, M., & Söderhamn, O. (2008). Formal and informal care in relation to activities of daily living and self-perceived health among older care-dependent individuals in Norway. *International Journal of Older People Nursing, 3*(3), 194–203. Doi: .10.1111/j.1748-3743.2008.00122.x

Dale, J. L. (2005). Reflective judgment: Seminarians' epistemology in a world of relativism. *Journal of Psychology and Theology, 33*(1), 56–64.

Daley, B. (1991). *The hope of the early Church: A handbook of patristic eschatology.* New York, NY: Cambridge University Press.

Dalhouse, D. W., & Dalhouse, A. D. (2006). Investigating white preservice teachers' beliefs about teaching in culturally diverse classrooms. *Negro Educational Review, 57*, 69–84. Retrieved from http://www.oma.osu.edu/vice_provost/ner/index.html

Daly, J. (2013, September 13). Mobility is about data, devices, and demand. *Fed Tech.* Retrieved from http://www.fedtechmagazine.com/article/2013/09/mobility-about-data-devices-and-demand

Daniels, L. (1988, May 2). Now Russia wants to learn the way U.S. managers do. *New York Times.* Retrieved from http://www.nytimes.com/1988/05/02/business/now-russia-wants-to-learn-the-way-us-managers-do.html

Daniels, R. (2007). *The rise and fall of Communism in Russia.* New Haven, CT: Yale University Press. doi:10.12987/yale/9780300106497.001.0001

Darley, J., & Batson, C. D. (1973). "From Jerusalem to Jericho": A study of situational and dispositional variables in helping behavior. *Journal of Personality and Social Psychology, 27*(1), 100–108. doi:10.1037/h0034449

Darling-Hammond, L. (1997). *Doing what matters most: Investing in teacher quality.* Kutztown, PA: National Commission on Teaching and America's Future.

Dash, P. L. (1998). Education in post-Soviet Russia: No more an obligation of the state. *Economic and Political Weekly, 33*(21), 1232–1234. Available from https://www.econbiz. de/

Datnow, A. (2006). Comments on Michael Fullan's "The future of educational change: System thinkers in action". *Journal of Educational Change, 7*(3), 133–135. doi:10.1007/s10833-006-0005-4

Davie, G. (1990). Believing without belonging: Is this the future of religion in Britain? *Social Compass, 37*(4), 455–469. doi:10.1177/003776890037004004

Davies, M. (2008). *The Corpus of Contemporary American English: 450 million words, 1990-present.* Available at: http://corpus.byu.edu/coca/

Davies, I., Evans, M., & Reid, A. (2005). Globalising citizenship education? A critique of "global education" and "citizenship education". *British Journal of Educational Studies, 53*(1), 66–89. doi:10.1111/j.1467-8527.2005.00284.x

Davies, L. (2006). Global citizenship: Abstraction or framework for action? *Educational Review, 58*(1), 5–25. doi:10.1080/00131910500352523

Davies, P. C. (1971). The debate on eternal punishment in late seventeenth-and eighteenth-century English literature. *Eighteenth-Century Studies, 4*(3), 257–276. doi:10.2307/2737732

Davis, A. (2004). Co-authoring identity: Digital storytelling in an urban middle school. *Technology, Humanities, Education, &. Narrative, 1*(1), 1.

Davis, A. J., & Aroskar, M. A. (1983). *Ethical dilemmas and nursing practice* (2nd ed.). Norwalk, CT: Appleton-Century-Crofts.

Davis, F. D. (1989). Perceived usefulness, perceived ease of use, and user acceptance of information technology. *Management Information Systems Quarterly, 13*(3), 319–340. doi:10.2307/249008

Davis, F. D. (1993). User acceptance of information technology: System characteristics, user perceptions and behavioral impacts. *International Journal of Man-Machine Studies, 38*(3), 475–487. doi:10.1006/imms.1993.1022

Davis, T. L. (2002). Voices of gender role conflict: The social construction of college men's identity. *Journal of College Student Development, 43*, 508–521.

Day, D. V. (2007). *Developing leadership talent.* Retrieved from http://www.shrm.org/about/foundation/research/documents/developing%20lead%20talent-%20final.pdf

De Cock, S. (2003). *Recurrent sequences of words in native speaker and advanced learner spoken and written English: A corpus-driven approach* (Doctoral dissertation). Louvain-la-Neuve: Université catholique de Louvain.

De Cock, S. (2004). Preferred sequences of words in NS and NNS speech. *Belgian Journal of English Language and Literatures (BELL). New Series, 2*, 225–246.

De Cock, S., Granger, S., Leech, G., & McEnery, T. (1998). An automated approach to the phrasicon of EFL learners. In S. Granger (Ed.), *Learner English on computer* (pp. 67–79). London: Longman.

De Corte, E., Verschaffel, L., & Depaepe, F. (2008). Unraveling the relationship between students' mathematics-related beliefs and the classroom culture. *European Psychologist, 13*(1), 24–36. doi:10.1027/1016-9040.13.1.24

De Haes, J. C. J. M., & Olschewski, M. (1998). Quality of life assessment in a cross-cultural context: Use of the Rotterdam Symptom Checklist in a multinational randomised trial comparing CMF and Zoladex (Goserlin) treatment in early breast cancer. *Annals of Oncology, 9*(7), 745–750. PMID:9739441

De Mente, B. L. (1990). Japan's secret weapon: The kata factor: The cultural programming that made the Japanese a superior people. Phoenix, AZ: Phoenix.

De Mente, B. L. (2003). *Kata: The key to understanding and dealing with the Japanese!* Boston, MA: Tuttle.

DeBellis, V. A., & Goldin, G. (2006). Affect and meta-affect in mathematical problem solving: A representational perspective. *Educational Studies in Mathematics, 63*(2), 131–147. doi:10.1007/s10649-006-9026-4

Defense Information Systems Agency. (2013). *Apple iOS 6 security technical implementation guide (STIG) Version 1.* Fort Meade, MD: Chief Information Assurance Executive.

Dehue, F., Bolman, C., & Vollink, T. (2008). Cyberbullying: Youngsters' experiences and parental perception. *CyberPscyhology & Behavior, 11*(2), 217–223. doi:10.1089/cpb.2007.0008 PMID:18422417

Dehue, F., Bolman, C., Vollink, T., & Pouwelse, M. (2012). Cyberbullying and traditional bullying in relation to adolescents' perceptions of parenting. *Journal of Cyber Therapy and Rehabilitation, 5*, 25–34.

Del Bueno, D. (2005). A crisis in critical thinking. *Nursing Education Perspectives, 26*(3), 278–282. PMID:16295306 deLara, E. W. (2012). Why adolescents don't disclose incidents of bullying and harassment. *Journal of School Violence*, *11*(4), 288–305. doi:10.1080/15388220.2012.705931

Delkeskamp-Hayes, C. (2009). Diakonia, the state, and ecumenical collaboration: Theological pitfalls. *Christian Bioethics*, *15*(2), 173–198. doi:10.1093/cb/cbp013

Deloitte Centre for health solutions. (2015). *Connected health. How digital technology is transforming health and social care*. London, UK: The creative studio at Deloitte. Retrieved from http://www2.deloitte.com/content/dam/Deloitte/uk/Documents/life-sciences-health-care/deloitte-uk-connected-health.pdf

Delumeau, J., & O'Connell, M. (2000). *History of paradise: The Garden of Eden in myth and tradition*. Chicago: University of Illinois Press.

Demeter, T. (2012). Introduction. *Studies in East European Thought*, *64*(1/2), 1–4. PMID:22213720

Demirel, Ö. (1999). Öğretme sanatı. Ankara, TR: Pegem Yayınları.

Demirel, Ö. (2003). Eğitim terimleri sözlüğü (2. bs.). Ankara, TR: Pegem A Yayıncılık.

Denis, B., & Hubert, S. (2001). Collaborative learning in an educational robotics environment. *Computers in Human Behavior*, *17*(5), 465–480.

Denzin, N. K., & Lincoln, Y. S. (1998). *Strategies of qualitative inquiry*. Thousand Oaks, CA: Sage.

Denzin, N. K., & Lincoln, Y. S. (2000b). Introduction: The discipline and practice of qualitative research. In N. K. Denzin & Y. S. Lincoln (Eds.), *Handbook of Qualitative Research* (2nd ed.; pp. 1–28). Thousand Oaks, CA: Sage.

Denzin, N. K., & Lincoln, Y. S. (Eds.). (2005). *The Sage handbook of qualitative research* (3rd ed., pp. 1–32). Thousand Oaks, CA: Sage.

Department of Defense. (2012a). *Managing for official use only information on commercial mobile devices*. Washington, DC: Office of the Chief Information Officer.

Department of Defense. (2012b). Capstone concept for joint operations: Joint force 2020. Washington, DC: Chairman of the Joint Chiefs of Staff.

Department of Defense. (2013). *Department of defense commercial mobile device implementation plan*. Washington, DC: Office of the Chief Information Officer.

Department of Education. National Center for Education Statistics. (2003). *National assessment of adult literacy*. Retrieved from http://nces.ed.gov/naal/glossary.asp

Department of the Army. (2013). *U.S Army guidance on the use of commercial mobile devices (CMD)*. Washington, DC: Office of the Secretary of the Army.

Department of the Army. (2014). *Army regulation 670-1 (Wear and appearance of Army uniforms and insignia)*. Washington, DC: Headquarters, Department of the Army.

Depraz, N., Varela, F., & Vermersch, P. (Eds.). (2003). *On becoming aware: Pragmatics of experiencing*. Philadelphia, PA: John Benjamins. doi:10.1075/aicr.43

Dervic, K., Oquendo, M. A., Grunebaum, M. F., Ellis, S., Burke, A. K., & Mann, J. J. (2004). Religious affiliation and suicide attempt. *The American Journal of Psychiatry*, *161*(12), 2303–2308. doi:10.1176/appi.ajp.161.12.2303 PMID:15569904

Deschênes, M., Charlin, B., Gagnon, R., & Goudreau, J. (2011). Use of a script concordance test to assess development of clinical reasoning in nursing students. *The Journal of Nursing Education*, *50*(7), 381–387. doi:10.3928/01484834-20110331-03 PMID:21449528

Desvallées, A., & Mairesses, F. (Eds.). (2010). *Key concepts of museology*. Paris, FR: ICOM.

Deterding, D., & Kirkpatrick, A. (2006). Intelligibility and an emerging ASEAN English lingua franca. *World Englishes*, *25*(3), 391–410. doi:10.1111/j.1467-971X.2006.00478.x

Detgen, A., Yamashita, M., Davis, B., & Wraight, S. (2011). State policies and procedures on response to intervention in the Midwest Region. U.S. Department of Education, Institute of Education Sciences, National Center for Education Evaluation and Regional Assistance, Regional Education Laboratory Midwest.

Devers, K. J. (1999). How will we know "good" qualitative research when we see it? Beginning the dialogue in health services research. HSR. *Health Services Research*, *34*(5 Pt. 2), 1153–1188. PMID:10591278

DeVillis, R. F. (2011). *Scale development: Theory and applications*. Thousand Oaks, CA: Sage.

Dewey, J. (1929). *The quest for certainty: A study of the relation of knowledge and action*. New York, NY: Minton.

Dewolf, T., Van Dooren, W., & Verschaffel, L. (2011). Upper elementary school children's understanding and solution of a quantitative problem inside and outside the mathematics class. *Learning and Instruction*, *21*(6), 770–780. doi:10.1016/j.learninstruc.2011.05.003

Dharia, S. P., & Falcone, T. (2005). Robotics in reproductive medicine. *Fertility and Sterility*, *84*(1), 1–11. PMID:16009146

Diamanduros, T., & Downs, E. (2011). Creating a safe school environment: How to prevent cyberbullying at your school. *Library Media Connection*, *30*(2), 36–38.

Dickerson, M. (2011), *The mind and the machine: What it means to be human and why it matters*. Grand Rapids, MI: Brazos.

Didden, R., Scholte, R. H. J., Korzilius, H., de Moor, J. M. H., Vermeulen, A., O'Reilly, M., & Lancioni, G. E. et al. (2009). Cyberbullying among students with intellectual and developmental disability in special education settings. *Developmental Neurorehabilitation*, *12*(3), 146–151. doi:10.1080/17518420902971356 PMID:19466622

Diede, N., McNish, G., & Coose, C. (2000). Performance expectations of the associate degree nurse graduate within the first six months. *The Journal of Nursing Education*, *39*(7), 302–307. PMID:11052652

Diez-Bedmar, M., & Casas-Pedrosa, A. (2011). The use of prepositions by Spanish learners of English at University level: A longitudinal analysis. In N. Kübler (Ed.), *Corpora, language, teaching, and resources: From theory to practice* (pp. 199–218). Bern: Peter Lang.

D'Ignazio, F. (1993). Electronic Highways and Classrooms of the Future. In T. Cannings & L. Finkle (Eds.), *The Technology Age Classroom. Wilsonville*. Franklin: Beedle.

Dillman, D. A., Smyth, J. D., & Christian, L. M. (2009). *Internet, mail, and mixed-mode surveys: The tailored design method* (3rd ed.). Hoboken, NJ: Wiley.

Dillon, A., & Gabbard, R. (1998). Hypermedia as an educational technology: A review of the quantitative research literature on learner comprehension, control, and style. *Review of Educational Research*, *68*(3), 322–349. doi:10.3102/00346543068003322

Dishion, T. J., & Tipsord, J. M. (2011). Peer contagion in child and adolescent social and emotional development. *Annual Review of Psychology*, *62*(1), 189–214. doi:10.1146/annurev.psych.093008.100412 PMID:19575606

Dneprov, E. D. (1998). *Contemporary school reform in Russia*. Moscow, Russia: Nauka.

Dojri, P. (2007). *Nabji-Korphu Trek: The piloted community-based nature tourism in Bhutan*. Ministry of Tourism, Kingdom of Bhutan.

Donahue, M. J. (1981). Intrinsic and extrinsic religiousness: Review and meta-analysis. *Journal of Personality and Social Psychology*, *48*(2), 400–419. doi:10.1037/0022-3514.48.2.400

Donchin, Y., Gopher, D., Olin, M., Badihi, Y., Biesky, M. R., Sprung, C. L., & Cotev, S. et al. (1995). A look into the nature and causes of human errors in the intensive care unit. *Critical Care Medicine*, *23*(2), 294–300. doi:10.1097/00003246-199502000-00015 PMID:7867355

Donelson, E. (1999). Psychology of religion and adolescents in the United States: Past to present. *Journal of Adolescence*, *22*(2), 187–204. doi:10.1006/jado.1999.0212 PMID:10089119

Donmuş, A. G. V., & Gürol, M. (2014). The Effect of Educational Computer Games on Student Motivation in Learning English/İngilizce Öğrenmede Eğitsel Bilgisayar Oyunu Kullanmanın Motivasyona Etkisi. *International Journal of Educational Research*, *5*(4), 1–16.

Donnelly, P. L. (2000). Ethics and cross-cultural nursing. *Journal of Transcultural Nursing*, *11*(2), 119–126. PMID:11982044

Douglas, B. G., & Moustakas, C. (1985). Heuristic inquiry: The internal search to know. *Journal of Humanistic Psychology*, *25*, 39–55.

Downing, J. J., & Dyment, J. E. (2013). Teacher Educators' Readiness, Preparation, and Perceptions of Preparing Preservice Teachers in a Fully Online Environment: An Exploratory Study. *Teacher Educator*, *48*(2), 96–109. doi:10.108 0/08878730.2012.760023

Drew, M. (2014, September 17). Intimations of independence. *Huffington Post*. Retrieved from http://www.huffingtonpost.com/michael-drew/intimations-of-independen_b_5829236. html

Drolet, B. C., & Rodgers, S. (2010, January). A comprehensive medical student wellness program: Design and implementation at Vanderbilt School of Medicine. *Academic Medicine*, *85*(1), 103–110. doi:10.1097/ACM.0b013e3181c46963 PMID:20042835

Drtil, J. (2013). Impact of information security incidents: Theory and reality. *Journal of Systems Integration*, *4*(1), 44–52.

Duchscher, J. B. (2008). A process of becoming: The stages of new nursing graduate professions role transition. *Journal of Continuing Education in Nursing*, *39*(10), 441–450. doi:10.3928/00220124-20081001-03 PMID:18990890

Duchscher, J. E. B., & Morgan, D. (2004). Grounded theory: Reflections on the emergence vs. forcing debate. *Journal of Advanced Nursing*, *48*(6), 605–612. PMID:15548251

Dudgeon, R. (1975). *Women and higher education in Russia, 1855–1905* (Doctoral dissertation). Available from ProQuest Dissertations and Theses database. (UMI No. 7526000)

Duffin, L., French, B., & Patrick, H. (2012). The teachers' sense of efficacy scale: Confirming the factor structure with beginning pre-service teachers. *Teaching and Teacher Education*, *28*(6), 827–834. doi:10.1016/j.tate.2012.03.004

Duggleby, W., Holtslander, L., Steeves, M., Duggleby-Wenzel, S., & Cunningham, S. (2010). Discursive meaning of hope for older persons with advanced cancer and their caregivers. *Canadian Journal on Aging*, *29*(3), 361–367. doi:10.1017/S0714980810000322 PMID:20731889

Duke, D. (2004). *The challenges of educational change*. Boston, MA: Pearson Education, Inc.

Dumith, S. C., Hallal, P. C., Reis, R. S., & Kohl, H. W. III. (2011). Worldwide prevalence of physical inactivity and its association with Human Development Index in 76 countries. *Preventive Medicine, 53*(1/2), 24–28. doi:10.1016/j.ypmed.2011.02.017 PMID:21371494

Dunbar, R. I. M. (2009). Mind the bonding gap: Constraints on the evolution of hominin societies. In S. Shennan (Ed.), *Pattern and process in cultural evolution* (pp. 223–234). Berkeley, CA: University of California Press.

Duncan, D. R. (2004). The impact of family relationships on school bullies and victims. In D. L. Espelage & S. M. Swearer (Eds.), *Bullying in American schools* (pp. 277–244). London: Lawrence Erlbaum Associates.

Dunn, K. S., & Horgas, A. L. (2000). The prevalence of prayer as a spiritual self-care modality in elders. *Journal of Holistic Nursing, 18*(4), 337–351. doi:10.1177/089801010001800405 PMID:11847791

Duriez, B. (2004a). Are religious people nicer people? Taking a closer look at the religion–empathy relationship. *Mental Health, Religion & Culture, 7*(3), 249–254. doi:10.1080/13674670310001606450

Duriez, B. (2004b). Research: A research note on the relation between religiosity and racism: The importance of the way in which religious contents are being processed. *The International Journal for the Psychology of Religion, 14*(3), 177–191. doi:10.1207/s15327582ijpr1403_3

Dustman, R. E., Emmerson, R. Y., Ruhling, R. O., Shearer, D. E., Steinhaus, L. A., Johnson, S., . . . Shigeoka, J. W. (1990). Age and fitness effects on EEG, ERPs, visual sensitivity, and cognition. *Neurobiology of Aging, 11*(3), 193–200. doi: 90545-b10.1016/0197-4580(90)

Dwyer, L., Forsyth, P., Spurr, R., & Van Ho, T. (2008). Tourism's economic contribution versus economic impact assessment: Differing roles for satellite accounts and economic modelling. In A. Woodside & D. Martin (Eds.), Tourism management (pp. 459–469). Wallingford, UK: CAB International.

Dykstra, D. (2008). Integrating critical thinking and memorandum writing into course curriculum using the internet as a research tool. *College Student Journal, 42*(3), 920–929. doi:10.1007/s10551-010-0477-2

Eagly, A. (2005, June). Achieving relational authenticity in leadership: Does gender matter? *The Leadership Quarterly, 16*(2), 459–474. doi:10.1016/j.leaqua.2005.03.007

Edelman, R., & Hombach, J. (2008). "Guidelines for the clinical evaluation of dengue vaccines in endemic areas": Summary of a World Health Organization technical consultation. *Vaccine, 26*(33), 4113–4119. PMID:18597906

Eden, S., Heiman, T., & Olenik-Shemesh, D. (2013). Teachers' perceptions, beliefs and concerns about cyberbullying. *British Journal of Educational Technology, 44*(6), 1036–1052. doi:10.1111/j.1467-8535.2012.01363.x

Edgehouse, M. A., Edwards, A., Gore, S., Harrison, S., & Zimmerman, J. (2007). Initiating and leading change: A consideration of four new models. *The Catalyst, 36*(2), 3–12.

Edu, W. (2010). *Tourism 2.0, definition and key concepts.* Video presentation. Retrieved from http://ofslides.com/edu-william-61600/presentation-64117

Education as a factor of social differentiation and mobility (A roundtable). (2004). *Russian Education & Society, 46*(10), 7–30. doi:10.1080/10609393.2004.11056849

Education Charter International. (n.d.). *Global initiative.* Retrieved from http://cclpworldwide.com/eci/view-content/14/Global-Initiative.html

Edwards, A. (2012). *New technology and education: Contemporary issues in educational studies.* NY: Continuum International.

Edwards, K., & Jones, S. (2009). "Putting my man face on": A grounded theory of college men's gender identity development. *Journal of College Student Development, 50*(2), 210–228. doi:10.1353/csd.0.0063

Edward, Z., & Paul, C. A. (2014). Critical thinking and computing project in computer studies postgraduate methods course: Technology perspective. *Education Research International, 3*(1), 88–102.

Ehrman, M. (1990). Psychological factors and distance education. *American Journal of Distance Education, 4*(1), 10–23. doi:10.1080/08923649009526688

Eigel, K. M., & Kuhnert, K. W. (2005). Authentic development: Leadership development level and executive effectiveness. In W. J. Gardner, B. J. Avolio, & F. O. Walumbwa (Eds.), *Authentic leadership theory and practice: Origins, effects and development* (pp. 357–385). Bingley, UK: Emerald Group.

Eisenberg, E., & Dowsett, T. (1990). Student dropout from a distance education project course: A new method analysis. *Distance Education, 11*(2), 231–253. http://files.eric.ed.gov/fulltext/EJ853871.pdf doi:10.1080/0158791900110205

Eisenhardt, K. M. (2000). Introduction to special topic forum: Paradox, spirals, ambivalence: The new language of change and pluralism. *Academy of Management Review, 25*(4), 703–705. doi:10.5465/AMR.2000.3707694

Ejaz, F. K., Schur, D., & Noelker, L. S. (1997). The effect of activity involvement and social relationships on boredom among nursing home residents. *Activities, Adaptation and Aging, 21*(4), 53–66. doi:10.1300/J016v21n04_07

Elenkov, D. S. (1998). Can American management concepts work in? A cross-cultural comparative study. *Management Review, 40*(4), 133–156. doi:10.2307/ 41165968

ELFA. (2008). *The Corpus of English as a Lingua Franca in Academic Settings*. Retrieved from http://www.helsinki.fi/elfa/elfacorpus

Elledge, L. C., Williford, A., Boulton, A. J., DePaolis, K. J., Little, T. D., & Salmivalli, C. (2013). Individual and contextual predictors of cyberbullying: The influence of children's provictim attitudes and teachers' ability to intervene. *Journal of Youth and Adolescence, 42*(5), 698–710. doi:10.1007/s10964-013-9920-x PMID:23371005

Elliot, J. (1998, June 2). Bill Gates calling or maybe not. *The Daily Telegraph*, p. 6.

Elliott, J., & Morrison, D. (2008). *Reponse to intervention blueprints: District level edition*. Alexandria, VA: National Association of State Directors of Special Education.

Ellis, N. C. (2008). Phraseology: The periphery and the heart of language. In F. Meunier & S. Grainger (Eds.), *Phraseology in language learning and teaching* (pp. 1–13). Amsterdam: John Benjamins. doi:10.1075/z.138.02ell

Ellsworth, J. B. (2000). *Surviving change: A survey of educational change models*. Syracuse, NY: ERIC Clearinghouse on Information and Technology.

Ellul, J. (1967). *The technological society* (J. Wilkinson, Trans.). New York, NY: Knopf/Vintage.

Emden, C., & Sandelowski, M. (1998). The good, the bad, and the relative, part 1: Conceptions of goodness in qualitative research. *International Journal of Nursing Practice, 4*(4), 206–212. PMID:10095513

Emden, C., & Sandelowski, M. (1999). The good, the bad, and the relative, part 2: Goodness and the criterion problem in qualitative research. *International Journal of Nursing Practice, 5*(1), 2–7. PMID:10455610

Enders, J. (2004). Higher education, internationalisation, and the nation-state: Recent developments and challenges to governance theory. *Higher Education, 47*(3), 361–382.

Endler, N. S., & Kocoviski, N. L. (2001). State and trait anxiety revisited. *Journal of Anxiety Disorders, 15*(3), 231–245. doi:10.1016/S0887-6185(01)00060-3 PMID:11442141

Enerstvedt, R. T. (1999). New medical technology: To what does it lead? *American Annals of the Deaf, 144*, 242–249. PMID:10423891

Engel, J. D., & Kuzel, A. J. (1992). On the idea of what constitutes good qualitative inquiry. *Qualitative Health Research, 2*(4), 504–510.

English, L. D., & Watters, J. (2005). Mathematical modeling in the early school years. *Mathematics Education Research Journal, 16*(3), 59. doi:10.1007/BF03217401

Ennis, M. (2005). Now I know in part: Holistic and analytic reasoning and their contribution to fuller knowing in theological education. *Evangelical Review Of Theology, 29*(3), 251–269.

Ephron, D. (2012, June 19). Upgrade hell. The *Wall Street Journal*, p. A13.

Epstein, A., & Kheimets, N. (2000). Cultural clash and educational diversity: Immigrant teachers' efforts to rescue the education of immigrant children in Israel. *International Studies in Sociology of Education, 10*(2), 191–210. doi:10.1080/09620210000200055

Erdur-Baker, O. (2010). Cyberbullying and its correlation to traditional bullying, gender and frequent and risky usage of internet-mediated communication tools. *New Media & Society, 12*(1), 109–125. doi:10.1177/1461444809341260

Erickson, R. J. (1995). The importance of authenticity for self and society. *Symbolic Interaction, 18*(2), 121–144. doi:10.1525/si.1995.18.2.121

Eriksen, T. H. (2001). Between universalism and relativism: A critique of the UNESCO concepts of culture. In J. Cowan, M. Dembour, & R. Wilson (Eds.), *Culture and Rights: Anthropological Perspectives* (pp. 127–148). Cambridge, UK: Cambridge University Press.

Erikson, E. (1968). *Identity, Youth and Crisis*. New York, NY: W. W. Norton.

Ervin, R. A., Schaughency, E., Goodman, S. D., McGlinchey, M. T., & Matthews, A. (2007). Moving from a model demonstration project to a statewide initiative in Michigan: Lessons learned from merging research-based agendas to address reading and behavior. In S. R. Jimerson, M. K. Burns, & A. M. VanDerHeyden (Eds.), *Handbook of response to intervention*. New York, NY: Springer. doi:10.1007/978-0-387-49053-3_27

Esposito, N. (2001). From meaning to meaning: The influence of translation techniques on non- English focus group research. *Qualitative Health Research, 11*(4), 568–579. PMID:11521612

Essary, A. C. (2011). The impact of social media and technology on professionalism in medical education. *The Journal of Physician Assistant Education, 22*(4), 50–53. doi:10.1097/01367895-201122040-00009 PMID:22308935

European Commission. (2007). *eHealth ERA report. eHealth-priorities and strategies in European countries. Toward the establishment of a European eHealth research arena*. Retrieved from http://www.ehealth-era.org/documents/2007ehealth-era-countries.pdf

European Investment Bank. (2015). *Finance contracts signed - Republic of Moldova*. Retrieved from http://www.eib.org/projects/loans/regions/cei/md.htm?lang=en

European Parliament. (2013, September 10). *MEPs pave the way for greater professional mobility in the EU* [Press release]. Retrieved from http://www.europarl.europa.eu/news/ en/news-room/content/20131008IPR21711/html/MEPs-pave-the-way-for-greater-professional-mobility-in-the-EU

European People's Party. (2013, January 23). *Yes to professional mobility in Europe!* [Press release]. Retrieved http://www.eppgroup.eu/press-release/Yes-to-professional-mobility-in-Europe!

European-Commission. (2015). *European health insurance card.* Retrieved June 10, 2015 from http://ec.europa.eu/social/main.jsp?langId=en&catId=559&newsId=2281&furtherNews=yes

Evans, B. (2013, December 13). *What does mobile scale mean?* [Web log comment]. Retrieved from http://ben-es.com/benedictevans/2013/12/18/what-does-mobile-scale-mean

Evans, F., Birch, J., & Nancy, J. (1995). Business education and change in Russia and Eastern Europe. *Journal of Education for Business, 70*(3), 166–171. doi:. 1011774510.1080/08832323.1995

Evans, J. (2011, June 16). Why are they leaving? *Wall Street Journal.* Retrieved from http://www.wsj.com/articles/SB1 0001424052748704816604576333030245934982

Evans, J. (2000a). *Adult mathematical thinking & emotions.* Routledgefalmer, London, UK: Evans, J. (2000b). Adult mathematics and everyday life. In D. Coben et al. (Eds.), *Perspective on adults learning mathematics. Research and practice* (p. 290). London: Kluwer.

Evans, J. H. (2006). Who legitimately speaks for religion in public bioethics? In D. E. Guinn (Ed.), *Handbook of bioethics and religion* (pp. 61–80). Oxford, UK: Oxford University Press. doi:10.1093/0195178734.003.0004

Evenko, K. (2003, June 16). New MBA programs make first steps. *Independent Newspaper,* p. 7.

Fabre, J., Jenkin, K., Thompson, C., & Senjen, R. (1999). *Trial of future wireless broadband services: Insights into customer behaviour* (Report 99–19). Retrieved from Telstra website: http://www.telstra.com.au/business-enterprise/

Facione, P. A. (2011). Critical thinking: What it is and why it counts. Millbrae, CA: The California Academic Press. Available at www.insightassessment.com/pdf_files/what&why2006.pdf

Fahrni, P., Rudolph, J., & De Schutter, A. (2004). Vendor-Assisted Evaluation of a Learning Management System. *International Review of Research in Open and Distance Learning, 5*(1), 1–4.

Fairclough, N. (2001). *Language and power* (2nd ed.). New York, NY: Longman Press.

Fairclough, N. (2006). *Language and globalization.* London: Routledge.

Fang, T., & Faure, G. O. (2011). Chinese communication characteristics: A Yin Yang perspective. *International Journal of Intercultural Relations, 35*(3), 320–333. doi:10.1016/j.ijintrel.2010.06.005

Fan, M. (2009). An Exploratory study of collocational use by ESL students: A task based approach. *System, 37*(1), 110–123. doi:10.1016/j.system.2008.06.004

Fanning, E. (2005). Formatting a paper-based survey questionnaire: Best practices. *Practical Assessment, Research & Evaluation, 10*(12).

Fanti, K. A., Demetriou, A. G., & Hawa, V. V. (2012). A longitudinal study of cyberbullying: Examining risk and protective factors. *European Journal of Developmental Psychology, 8*(2), 168–181. doi:10.1080/17405629.2011.643169

Farrell, A., & Geist-Martin, P. (2005). Communicating social health: Perceptions of wellness at work. *Management Communication Quarterly, 18*(4), 543–592. doi:10.1177/0893318904273691

Feenberg, A. (1999). *Questioning technology.* London, UK: Routledge.

Fenwick, T. J. (2003). *Learning through experience: Troubling orthodoxies and intersecting questions.* Malabar, FL: Krieger.

Fenz, S., Ekelhart, A., & Neubauer, T. (2011). Information security risk management: In which security solutions is it worth investing? *Communications of the AIS, 28*, 329–356.

Ferdon, C. D., & Hertz, M. F. (2007). Electronic media, violence, and adolescents. An emerging public health problem. *The Journal of Adolescent Health, 41*(6), 1–5. doi:10.1016/j.jadohealth.2007.08.020 PMID:17577527

Fero, L. J., O'Donnell, J. M., Zullo, T. G., Dabbs, A. D., Kitutu, J., Samosky, J. T., & Hoffman, L. A. (2010). Critical thinking skills in nursing students: Comparison of simulation-based performance with metrics. *Journal of Advanced Nursing, 66*(10), 2182–2193. PMID:20636471

Ferreira, L. (2002). Access to affordable HIV/AIDS drugs: The human rights obligations of multinational pharmaceutical corporations. *Fordham Law Review, 71*, 1133. PMID:12523370

Ferreira, M. T., Matsudo, S. M., Ribeiro, M. A., & Ramos, L. R. (2010). Health-related factors correlate with behavior trends in physical activity level in old age: Longitudinal results from a population in São Paulo, Brazil. *BMC Public Health, 10*(1), 690–699. doi:10.1186/1471-2458-10-690 PMID:21067591

Festl, R., Schwarkow, M., & Quandt, T. (2013). Peer influence, internet use and cyberbullying: A comparison of different context effects among German adolescents. *Journal of Children and Media, 7*(4), 446–462. doi:10.1080/17482798.2013.781514

Fielding-Barnsley, R. (2010). Australian pre-service teachers' knowledge of phonemic awareness and phonics in the process of learning to read. *Australian Journal of Learning Disabilities, 15*(1), 99–110.

Filshtinskiy, S. (2013). Cyber-crime, cyberweapons, cyber-wars: Is there too much of it in the air? *Communications of the ACM, 56*(6), 28–30. doi:10.1145/2461256.2461266

Finch, R. (2005). Preventive services: Improving the bottom line for employers and employees. *Compensation and Benefits Review, 37*(2), 18–22. doi:10.1177/0886368704274407

Fink, D., & Stoll, L. (2005). Educational change: Easier said than done. In A. Hargreaves (Ed.), *Extending educational change* (pp. 17–41). New York, NY: Springer. doi:10.1007/1-4020-4453-4_2

Fischer, R., & Smith, P. B. (2003). Reward allocation and culture: A meta-analysis. *Journal of Cross-Cultural Psychology, 34*(3), 251–268. doi:10.1177/0022022103034003001

Fishbein, M., & Ajzen, I. (1975). *Belief, attitude, intention and behavior: An introduction to theory and Research.* Reading, MA: Addison-Wesley.

Fisher, A. (2001). *Critical thinking: An introduction.* London, UK: Cambridge University Press.

Fisher, M., King, J., & Tague, G. (2001). Development of a self-directed learning readiness scale for nursing education. *Nurse Education Today, 21*(7), 516–525. doi:10.1054/nedt.2001.0589 PMID:11559005

FitzSimons, G., & Godden, G. L. (2000). Review on research on adult learning mathematics. In D. Coben et al. (Eds.), *Perspectives on adults learning mathematics* (p. 13). The Netherlands: Kluwer.

Fletcher, J. M., Denton, C., & Francis, D. J. (2005). Validity of alternative approaches for the identification of learning disabilities: Operationalizing unexpected underachievement. *Journal of Learning Disabilities, 38*(6), 545–552. doi:10.1177/00222194050380061101 PMID:16392697

Fletcher, J. M., & Vaughn, S. (2009). Response to intervention: Preventing and remediating academic difficulties. *Child Development Perspectives, 3*(1), 30–37. doi:10.1111/j.1750-8606.2008.00072.x PMID:21765862

Fogle, C. D., & Elliott, D. (2013). The Market Value of Online Degrees as a Credible Credential. *Global Education Journal, 2013*(3), 67-95.

Fouka, G., Plakas, S., Taket, A., Boudioni, M., & Dandoulakis, M. (2012). Health-related religious rituals of the Greek Orthodox Church: Their uptake and meanings. *Journal of Nursing Management, 20*(8), 1058–1068. doi:10.1111/jonm.12024 PMID:23151108

Fox, D., Prilleltensky, I., & Austin, S. (Eds.). (2009). *Critical Psychology: An introduction* (2nd ed.). London: SAGE Publications Ltd.

Foy, H. (2015, October 15). Former Moldovan PM detained over alleged $1bn theft. *Financial Times*. Retrieved from http://www.ft.com/intl/cms/s/0/788aca7a-735d-11e5-a129-3fcc4f641d98.html#axzz3oqkRWshN

Fraenkel, J. R., & Wallen, N. E. (2006). *How to design and evaluate research in education* (6th ed.). New York, NY: McGraw-Hill.

Francis, L. J., & Pearson, P. R. (1987). Empathic development during adolescence: Religiosity, the missing link? *Personality and Individual Differences, 8*(1), 145–148. doi:10.1016/0191-8869(87)90024-9

Fransson, E. I., Alfredsson, L. S., Ulf, H., Knutsson, A., & Westerholm, P. J. (2003). Leisure time, occupational and household physical activity, and risk factors for cardiovascular disease in working men and women: The WOLF study. *Scandinavian Journal of Public Health, 31*(5), 324–333. doi:10.1080/14034940210165055 PMID:14555368

Frazel, M. (2010). *Digital storytelling guide for educators. Moorabbin.* International Society for Technology in Education.

Frechtling, D. C. (2010). The Tourism Satellite Account: A Primer. *Annals of Tourism Research, 37*(1), 136–153. doi:10.1016/j.annals.2009.08.003

Fredrick, K. (2010). Mean girls (and boys): Cyberbullying and what can be done about it. *School Library Media Activities Monthly, 25*(8), 44–45.

Fretheim, T. E. (2000). Divine judgment and the warming of the world: An Old Testament perspective. *Word & World*, (Suppl. 4), 21–32. Available from https://wordandworld.luthersem.edu/supplement_4.aspx

Frey, C. J., & Whitehead, D. M. (2009). International education policies and the boundaries of global citizenship in the US. *Journal of Curriculum Studies, 41*(2), 269–290. doi:10.1080/00220270802509730

Friedman, T., & Mandelbaum, M. (2011). *That used to be us: How America fell behind the world it invented and how we can come back*. New York, NY: Farrar.

Friese, S. (2012). *Qualitative data analysis with ATLAS.ti*. Thousand Oaks, CA: SAGE.

Frissen, V. A. J. (2000). ICTs in the rush hour of life. *The Information Society, 16*(1), 65–75. doi:10.1080/019722400128338

Fry, J., Lockyer, S., Oppenheim, C., Houghton, J., & Rasmussen, B. (2009). *Identifying benefits arising the curation from and open sharing of research data produced by UK higher education and research institutes*. Retrieved from JISC Repository: http://repository.jisc.ac.uk/279/2/JISC_data_sharing_finalreport.pdf

Fry, S. T., & Johnstone, M. J. (2008). *Ethics in nursing practice: A guide to ethical decision making*. Oxford, UK: Blackwe.

Fuchs, D., & Fuchs, L. S. (2008). Implementing RTI: Response-to-intervention is an ambitious and complex process that requires administrators choose the right model. *District Administration, 44*, 73–76.

Fuchs, D., Fuchs, L. S., & Compton, D. L. (2004). Identifying reading disabilities by responsiveness-to-instruction: Specifying measures and criteria. *Learning Disability Quarterly, 27*(4), 216–227. doi:10.2307/1593674

Fuchs, D., Fuchs, L. S., & Compton, D. L. (2012). Smart RTI: A next-generation approach to multilevel prevention. *Exceptional Children*, *78*(3), 263–279. doi:10.1177/001440291207800301 PMID:22736805

Fuchs, L. S., & Fuchs, D. (2007). A model for implementing responsiveness to intervention. *Teaching Exceptional Children*, *39*(5), 14–20. doi:10.1177/004005990703900503

Fuchs, L. S., & Vaughn, S. (2012). Responsiveness-to-intervention: A decade later. *Journal of Learning Disabilities*, *45*(3), 195–203. doi:10.1177/0022219412442150 PMID:22539056

Fullan, M. (2001). *Leading in a culture of change* (1st ed.). San Francisco, CA: Jossey-Bass.

Fullan, M. (2006). The future of educational change: System thinkers in action. *Journal of Educational Change*, *7*(3), 113–122. doi:10.1007/s10833-006-9003-9

Gaidar, E. T. (2003). *The economics of transition*. Cambridge, MA: MIT Press.

Galben, A. (2011). *Globalizarea învățământului superior contemporan. Exemplul ULIM, Republica Moldova (Raport expus la Conferința Internațională a Rectorilor de la Shanghai, 12 august 2011)*. Retrieved from http://agalben.ulim.md/wp-content/uploads/2013/12/Globalizarea-inv.-sup.-contemp.-final.pdf

Gal, I. (2000a). Statistical literacy. In D. Coben et al. (Eds.), *Perspective on adults learning mathematics. Research and practice* (p. 135). London: Kluwer.

Gal, I. (2000b). The numeracy challenge. In I. Gal (Ed.), *Adult numeracy development* (p. 9). Hampton Press.

Gall, M. D., Gall, W. R., & Borg, J. P. (2006). *Educational research: An introduction* (8th ed.). White Plains, N.Y.: Longman.

Gallup, G. (1985). Religion in America. *The Annals of the American Academy of Political and Social Science*, *480*(1), 167–174. doi:10.1177/0002716285480001014

Gallup, G. Jr. (1995). Have attitudes toward homosexuals been shaped by natural selection? *Ethology and Sociobiology*, *16*(1), 53–70. doi:10.1016/0162-3095(94)00028-6

Gallup, G., & Lindsay, D. M. (1999). *Surveying the religious landscape: Trends in U.S. beliefs*. Harrisburg, PA: Morehouse.

Gamez-Guadix, M., Orue, I., Smith, P. K., & Calvete, E. (2013). Longitudinal and reciprocal relations of cyberbullying with depression, substance use, and problematic internet use among adolescents. *The Journal of Adolescent Health*, *53*(4), 446–452. doi:10.1016/j.jadohealth.2013.03.030 PMID:23721758

Ganzel, R. (1998). Feeling squeezed by technology? *Training (New York, N.Y.)*, *35*(4), 62–70.

Gardenshire-Crooks, A., Collado, H., Martin, K., & Castro, A. (2010). Terms of Engagement: Men of Color Discuss Their Experiences in Community College. *Achieving the Dream*, *I*, c.

Gardner, D., & Davies, M. (2007). Pointing out frequent phrasal verbs: A corpus-based analysis. *TESOL Quarterly*, *41*(2), 339–360. doi:10.1002/j.1545-7249.2007.tb00062.x

Gardner, W. L., Avolio, B. J., Luthans, F., May, D. R., & Walumbwa, F. (2005, June). "Can you see the real me?" A self-based model of authentic leader and follower development. *The Leadership Quarterly*, *16*(3), 343–372. doi:10.1016/j.leaqua.2005.03.003

Gardner, W. L., Avolio, B. J., & Walumbwa, F. O. (2005). Authentic leadership development: Emergent themes and future directions. In W. J. Gardner, B. J. Avolio, & F. O. Walumbwa (Eds.), *Authentic leadership theory and practice: Origins, effects and development* (pp. 387–406). Bingley, UK: Emerald Group.

Gardner, W. L., Cogliser, C. C., Davis, K. M., & Dickens, M. P. (2011, December). Authentic leadership: A review of the literature and research agenda. *The Leadership Quarterly, 22*(6), 1120–1145. doi:10.1016/j.leaqua.2011.09.007

Gardner, W. L., Lowe, K. B., Moss, T. W., Mahoney, K. T., & Cogliser, C. C. (2010, December). Scholarly leadership of the study of leadership: A review of the last decade, 2000-2009. *The Leadership Quarterly, 21*(6), 922–958. doi:10.1016/j.leaqua.2010.10.003

Garfinkel, S. (2005). *Design principles and patterns for computer systems that are simultaneously secure and usable.* (Doctoral Dissertation). Retrieved from http://hdl.handle.net/1721.1/33204

Garrison, D. R. (2003). Self-directed learning and distance education. In M. G. Moore & W. Anderson (Eds.), *Handbook of distance education* (pp. 161–168). Mahwah, NJ: Routledge.

Gatewood, B. (2012, November). The nuts and bolts of making BYOD work. *Information & Management, 46*(6), 26–30.

Gaudelli, W. (2003). *World class: Teaching and learning in global times.* Retrieved from http://www.amazon.com/

Gaudine, A. P., & Beaton, M. R. (2002). Employed to go against one's values: nurse managers' accounts of ethical conflict with their organizations. *The Canadian Journal of Nursing Research= Revue Canadienne de Recherche en Sciences Infirmieres, 34*(2), 17-34.

Gaudine, A. P., & Thorne, L. (2000). Ethical conflict in professionals: Nurses' accounts of ethical conflict with organizations. *Research in Ethical Issues in Organizations, 2,* 41–58.

Gay, L. R., Mills, G. E., & Airasian, P. (2012). *Educational research: Competencies for analysis and applications.* Boston, MA: Pearson.

Gayomali, C. (2014, April 10). The French move to protect workers from after-hours email. *Fast company.* Retrieved from http://www.fastcompany.com/3028945/work-smart/france-just-made-it-illegal-to-answer-work-emails-after-6pm

Gee, J. (2004). *What video games have to teach us about learning and literacy.* New York, NY: Palgrave Macmillan.

Gee, J. (2011). *Introduction to discourse analysis* (3rd ed.). New York, NY: Routledge.

Gee, J., & Hayes, E. (2010). *Women and gaming: The Sims and 21ˢᵗ century learning.* New York, NY: Palgrave Macmillan. doi:10.1057/9780230106734

Geers, K. (2010). Live fire exercise: Preparing for cyber war. *Journal of Homeland Security and Emergency Management, 7*(1), 1–16. doi:10.2202/1547-7355.1780

George, L. K., Ellison, C. G., & Larson, D. B. (2002). Exploring the relationships between religious involvement and health. *Psychological Inquiry, 13*(3), 190–200. doi:10.1207/S15327965PLI1303_04

George, W. (2003). *Authentic leadership: Rediscovering the secrets to creating lasting value.* San Francisco, CA: Jossey-Bass.

Gergen, K. J. (2009). *An invitation to social construction* (2nd ed.). San Francisco, CA: Sage.

Gerhardus, D. (2002). Robot-assisted surgery: The future is here. *Journal of healthcare management/American College of Healthcare Executives, 48*(4), 242-251.

Gershon, J. C. (2014). Healing the healer: One step at a time. *Journal of Holistic Nursing, 32*(1), 6–13. doi:10.1177/0898010113495976 PMID:24476909

Gershunsky, B. (1993). *Russia in darkness: On education and the future.* San Francisco, CA: Caddo Gap Press.

Gerstein, L. H., Heppner, P. P., Aegisdottir, S., Seung-Ming, A., Leung, S.-M. A., & Norsworthy, K. L. (2009). Cross-cultural counseling. In L. H. Gerstein, P. P. Heppner, S. Aegisdottir, S-M. A., Leung, & K. L. Norsworthy (Eds.), International Handbook of Cross-Cultural Counseling: Cultural Assumptions and Practices Worldwide (pp. 3-32). Academic Press.

Gervais, W. M., Willard, A. K., Norenzayan, A., & Henrich, J. (2011). The cultural transmission of faith: Why innate intuitions are necessary, but insufficient, to explain religious belief. *Religion, 41*(3), 389–410. doi:10.1080/004872 1X.2011.604510

Ghamraw, N. (2013). The relationship between the leadership styles of Lebanese public school principals and their attitudes toward ICT versus the level of ICT use by their teachers. *Open Journal of Leadership, 2*(1), 11–20. doi:10.4236/ojl.2013.21002

Ghannam, J. (2011). Social media in the Arab world: Leading up to the uprisings of 2011. Washington, DC: Center for International Media Assistance. Retrieved from http://www.databank.com.lb/docs/Social%20Media%20in%20the%20 Arab%20World%20Leading%20up%20to%20the%20Uprisings%20of%202011.pdf

Gharajedaghi, J. (2011). *Systems thinking, managing chaos and complexity: A platform for designing business architecture* (3rd ed.). Amsterdam: Elsevier.

Gibran, K. (1997). *The prophet*. Hertfordshire, UK: Wordsworth.

Gibson, K. L., Rimmington, G. M., & Landwehr-Brown, M. (2008). Developing global awareness and responsible world citizenship with global learning. *Roeper Review, 30*(1), 11–23. doi:10.1080/02783190701836270

Gillard, P., Wale, K., & Bow, A. (1997). Prediction of future demand from current telecommunications uses in the home. *Telecommunications Policy, 21*(4), 329–339. doi:10.1016/S0308-5961(97)00013-X

Gillespie, A. A. (2006). Cyber-bullying and harassment of teenagers: The legal response. *Journal of Social Welfare and Family Law, 28*(2), 123–136. doi:10.1080/09649060600973772

Gilquin, G. (2011). *Corpus linguistics to bridge the gap between World Englishes and Learner Englishes*. Paper presented at the 12th International Symposium on Social Communication, Santiago, Cuba. Retrieved October 13, 2012, from http://hdl.handle.net/2078.1/112509

Ginsburg, L., Manly, M., & Schmitt, M. J. (2006). *The components of numeracy. NCSALL occasional paper. Harvard Graduate School of Education*. Cambridge, MA: National Center for the Study of Adults Learning and Literacy.

Giordano, J. (2013). Ethical considerations in the globalization of medicine - An interview with James Giordano. *BMC Medicine, 11*(1), 1–5. PMID:23496884

Giorgi, A. (1997). The theory, practice and evaluation of phenomenological methods as a qualitative research procedure. *Journal of Phenomenological Psychology, 28*(2), 235–281. doi:10.1163/156916297X00103

Giorgi, A. P. (2009). *The descriptive phenomenological method in psychology: A modified Husserlian approach*. Pittsburgh, PA: Duquesne University Press.

Giorgi, A. P., & Giorgi, B. M. (2003). The descriptive phenomenological psychological method. In P. M. Camic, J. E. Rhodes, & L. Yardley (Eds.), *Qualitative research in psychology: Expanding perspectives in methodology and design* (pp. 243–273). Washington, DC: American Psychological Association. doi:10.1037/10595-013

Glaser, B. G., & Strauss, A. (1967). *The discovery of grounded theory: Strategies for qualitative research*. Chicago, IL: Aldine.

Glaser, E. (1942). An experiment in the development of critical thinking. *Teachers College Record, 43*(5), 409–410.

Glaser, E. M. (1985). Critical thinking: Educating for responsible citizenship in a democracy. In *National Forum. Phi Kappa Phi Journal, 65*(1), 24–27.

Glass, A. P., Chen, L., Hwang, E., Ono, Y., & Nahapetyan, L. (2010). A cross-cultural comparison of hospice development in Japan, South Korea, and Taiwan. *Journal of Cross-Cultural Gerontology, 25*(1), 1–19. PMID:20054707

Glenngård, A. H., Hjalte, F., Svensson, M., Anell, A., & Bankauskaite, V. (2005). *Health systems in transition.* Retrieved from http://old.hpi.sk/cdata/Documents/HIT/Sweden_2005.pdf

Gnutzmann, C. (1999). English as a global language: Perspectives for English language teaching and for teacher education in Germany. In C. Gnutzmann (Ed.), *Teaching and learning English as a global language: Native and non-native perspectives* (pp. 157–169). Tübingen: Stauffenburg.

Gnutzmann, C. (2000). Lingua franca. In M. Byram (Ed.), *The Routledge encyclopaedia of language teaching and learning* (pp. 356–359). London: Routledge.

Goebert, D., Else, I., Matsu, C., Chung-Do, J., & Chang, J. Y. (2011). The impact of cyberbullying on substance use and mental health in a multiethnic sample. *Maternal and Child Health Journal, 15*(8), 1282–1286. doi:10.1007/s10995-010-0672-x PMID:20824318

Goh, H., & Aris, B. (2007). Using robotics in education: Lessons learned and learning experiences. *Smart Teaching & Learning: Re-engineering ID, Utilization and Innovation of Technology, 2.*

Gokcearslan, S., & Ozcan, S. (2011). Place of wikis in learning and teaching process. *Procedia: Social and Behavioral Sciences, 28,* 481–485.

Gokhale, A. A. (1995). Collaborative learning enhances critical thinking. *Journal of Technology Education, 7*(1). Retrieved from http://scholar.lib.vt.edu/ejournals/JTE/v7n1/gokhale.jte-v7n1.html?ref=Sawos.Org

Goldin, G. A. (2008). Perspectives on representation in mathematical learning and problem solving. In L. D. English (Ed.), *Handbook of International Research in Mathematics Education.* New York, London: Rutledge.

Goodhue, D. L., & Thompson, R. L. (1995). Task-technology fit and individual performance. *Management Information Systems Quarterly, 19*(2), 213–236. doi:10.2307/249689

Göransson, K. E., Ehrenberg, A., & Ehnfors, M. (2005). Triage in emergency departments: National survey. *Journal of Clinical Nursing, 14*(9), 1067–1074. doi:10.1111/j.1365-2702.2005.01191.x PMID:16164524

Gosden, T., Forland, F., Kristiansen, I. S., Sutton, M., Leese, B., Giuffrida, A., & Pedersen, L. et al. (2001). Impact of payment method on behaviour of primary care physicians: A systematic review. *Journal of Health Services Research & Policy, 6*(1), 44–55. doi:10.1258/1355819011927198 PMID:11219360

Gostin, L. (1995). Informed consent, cultural sensitivity, and respect for persons. *Journal of the American Medical Association, 27a,* 844–845. PMID:7650810

Gouzevitch, I., & Gouzevitch, D. (2000). Étudiants, savants et ingénieurs juifs originaires de l'Empire russe en France (1860–1940)[Students, scholars and Jewish engineers from the Russian Empire in France]. *Archives Juives, 35,* 120–128. Retrieved from https://translate.google.com/translate?hl=en&sl=fr&u=https://www.cairn.info/revue-archives-juives-2002-1-page-120.htm&prev=search

Graddol, D. (1997). *The future of English?* London: British Council.

Gradinger, P., Strohmeier, D., & Spiel, C. (2009). Traditional bullying and cyberbullying. *The Journal of Psychology, 217,* 205–213.

Graham, L. R. (1972). *Science and philosophy in the Soviet Union*. New York, NY: Knopf.

Granger, S. (1998). Prefabricated patterns in advanced EFL writing: Collocations and formulae. In A. Cowie (Ed.), *Phraseology: Theory, analysis, and applications* (pp. 145–160). Oxford, UK: Oxford University Press.

Granger, S., Dagneaux, E., Meunier, F., & Paquot, M. (Eds.). (2009). *The International Corpus of Learner English: Handbook and CD-ROM V2*. Louvain-la-Neuve: Presses Universitaires de Louvain.

Granger, S., & Rayson, P. (1998). Automatic profiling of learner texts. In S. Granger (Ed.), *Learner English on computer* (pp. 119–131). London: Addison Wesley Longman.

Grant Thornton. (2015). *Women in business: The path to leadership* [Press release]. Retrieved from http://news.grant-thornton.com/press-release/us-businesses-show-little-progress-advancing-women-during-past-decade

Grant, D. (2004). Spiritual interventions: How, when, and why nurses use them. *Holistic Nursing Practice*, *18*(1), 36–41. doi:10.1097/00004650-200401000-00007 PMID:14765691

Grau-Valldosera, J., & Minguillón, J. (2014). Rethinking dropout in online higher education: The case of the Universitat Oberta de Catalunya. *The International Review of Research in Open and Distributed Learning*, *15*(1).

Green, H., & Hannon, C. (2007). *Their space–education for a digital generation*. London, UK: Demos.

Greenwald, A. G. (1975). Does the Good Samaritan parable increase helping? A comment on Darley and Batson's no-effect conclusion. *Journal of Personality and Social Psychology*, *32*(4), 578–583. doi:10.1037/0022-3514.32.4.578

Greer, B. (1993). The modeling perspective on world problems. *The Journal of Mathematical Behavior*, *12*(3), 239. Retrieved from http://www.sciencedirect.com/science/journal/07323123

Greer, B. (1997). Modeling reality in mathematics classrooms: The case of word problems. *Learning and Instruction*, *7*(4), 293–307. doi:10.1016/S0959-4752(97)00006-6

Gresham, F. M. (2007). Evolution of the response-to-intervention concept: Empirical foundations. In S. R. Jimerson, M. K. Burns, & A. M. VanDerHeyden (Eds.), *Handbook of response to intervention*. New York, NY: Springer. doi:10.1007/978-0-387-49053-3_2

Gries, T. S. (2008). Dispersions and adjusted frequencies in corpora. *International Journal of Corpus Linguistics*, *13*(4), 403–437. doi:10.1075/ijcl.13.4.02gri

Gries, T. S. (2009). Dispersions and adjusted frequencies in corpora: further explorations. In T. S. Gries, S. Wulff, & M. Davies (Eds.), *corpus linguistic applications: Current studies, new directions* (pp. 197–212). Amsterdam: Rodopi.

Gries, T. S. (2012). Correction to 'Dispersions and adjusted frequencies in corpora'. *International Journal of Corpus Linguistics*, *171*, 147–149.

Grigg, D. W. (2010). Cyber-aggression: Definition and concept of cyberbullying. *Australian Journal of Guidance & Counselling*, *20*(02), 143–156. doi:10.1375/ajgc.20.2.143

Grigg, D. W. (2012). Definitional constructs of cyberbullying and cyber aggression from a triagnulatory overview: A preliminary study into elements. *Journal of Aggression, Conflict and Peace Research*, *4*(4), 202–215. doi:10.1108/17596591211270699

Gröne, O., & Garcia-Barbero, M. (2001). Integrated care: A position paper of the WHO European office for integrated health care services. *International Journal of Integrated Care*, *1*(2), e21. doi:10.5334/ijic.28 PMID:16896400

Groom, N. (2009). Effects of second language immersion on second language collocational development. In A. Barfield & H. Gyllstad (Eds.), *Researching collocations in another language: Multiple interpretations* (pp. 21–33). Basingstoke, UK: Palgrave Macmillan.

Grosseck, G. (2009). To use or not to use web 2.0 in higher education? *Procedia: Social and Behavioral Sciences, 1*(1), 478–482.

Grow, G. (1991). Teaching learners to be self-directed: A stage approach. *Adult Education Quarterly, 41*(3), 125–149. doi:10.1177/0001848191041003001

Grunberg, L. (2011). *Access to gender-sensitive higher education in Eastern and Central Europe.* Bucharest, Romania: United Nations Educational, Scientific, and Cultural Organization.

Guba, E. G., & Lincoln, Y. S. (1994). Competing paradigms in qualitative research. Handbook of Qualitative Research, 2, 163-194.

Gudykunst, W. B., Matsumoto, W., Nishida, T., Kim, K., Heyman, S., & Ting-Toomey, S. (1996). The influence of cultural individualism-collectivism, self-construals, and individual values on communication styles across cultures. *Human Communication Research, 22*(4), 510–543. doi:10.1111/j.1468-2958.1996.tb00377.x

Guglielmino, L. M. (1977). *Development of the self-directed learning readiness scale* (Doctoral dissertation). Available from ProQuest Information & Learning. (No. 38)

Guillemin, F., Bombardier, C., & Beaton, D. (1993). Cross-cultural adaptation of health-related quality of life measures: Literature review and proposed guidelines. *Journal of Clinical Epidemiology, 46*(12), 1417–1432. PMID:8263569

Guo, Y., Connor, C. M., Yang, Y., Roehrig, A. D., & Morrison, F. J. (2012). The effects of teacher qualification, teacher self-efficacy, and classroom practices on fifth graders' literacy outcomes. *The Elementary School Journal, 113*(1), 3–24. doi:10.1086/665816

Guo, Y., Piasta, S. B., Justice, L. M., & Kaderavek, J. N. (2010). Relations among preschool teachers' self-efficacy, classroom quality and children's language and literacy gains. *Teaching and Teacher Education, 26*(4), 1094–1103. doi:10.1016/j.tate.2009.11.005

Habermas, J. (1984). The theory of communicative action: Vol. 1. *Reason and the rationalization of society.* Boston, MA: Beacon.

Habermas, J. (1985). The theory of communicative action: Vol. 2. *Lifeworld and system.* Beacon Press.

Hackett, C., & Lindsay, D. M. (2008). Measuring evangelicalism: Consequences of different operationalization strategies. *Journal for the Scientific Study of Religion, 47*(3), 499–514.

Hackett, J. (2010). Developing state regulations to implement the response-to-intervention requirements of IDEA: The Illinois plan. *Perspectives on Language and Literacy, 36*(2), 36–39.

Hahn, J. W., & Logvinenko, I. (2008). Generational differences in Russian attitudes towards democracy and the economy. *Europe-Asia Studies, 60*(8), 1345–1369. doi:10.1080/09668130802292168

Hair, J. F., Sarstedt, M., Hopkins, L., & Kuppelweiser, V. G. (2014). Partial least squares structural equation modeling (PLS-SEM): An emerging tool in business research. *European Business Review, 26*(2), 106–121. doi:10.1108/EBR-10-2013-0128

Halevy, A., & Brody, B. (1993). Brain death: Reconciling definitions, criteria, and tests. *Annals of Internal Medicine, 119*(6), 519–525. PMID:8357120

Halfond, W. J., Choudhary, S., & Orso, A. (2011). Improving penetration testing through static and dynamic analysis. *Software Testing: Verification & Reliability, 21*(3), 195–214.

Hall, A., & Walton, G. (2004). Information overload within the health care system: A literature review. *Health Information and Libraries Journal, 21*(2), 102–108. doi:10.1111/j.1471-1842.2004.00506.x PMID:15191601

Hallowell, E. (1999, January). The human moment at work. *Harvard Business Review, 77*(1), 58–152. PMID:10345392

Halpern, D. F. (2014). *Critical thinking across the curriculum: A brief edition of thought & knowledge.* New York, NY: Routledge.

Hamdan, A. (2014). The Reciprocal and correlative relationship between learning Culture and Online education: A case from Saudi Arabia. *The International Review of Research in Open and Distributed Learning, 15*(1). Retrieved from http://www.irrodl.org/index.php/irrodl/article/view/1408

Hamel, G. (2000). *Leading the revolution.* Boston, MA: Harvard Business School Press.

Hanley, M., & Boostrom, R. (2011). How the smartphone is changing college student mobile content usage and advertising acceptance: An IMC perspective. *International Journal of Integrated Marketing Communications*, 49-64.

Hannah, S. T., Avolio, B. J., & Walumbwa, F. O. (2011, October). Relationships between authentic leadership, moral courage, and ethical and pro-social behaviors. *Business Ethics Quarterly, 21*(4), 555–578. doi:10.5840/beq201121436

Hannah, S. T., Lester, P. B., & Vogelgesang, G. R. (2005). Moral leadership: Explicating the moral component of authentic leadership. In W. J. Gardner, B. J. Avolio, & F. O. Walumbwa (Eds.), *Authentic leadership theory and practice: Origins, effects and development* (pp. 43–81). Bingley, UK: Emerald Group.

Hannakaisa, L., Jose, M. P., & Mika, K. (2000). Collective stress and coping in the context of organizational culture. *European Journal of Work and Organizational Psychology, 9*(4), 527–559. doi:10.1080/13594320050203120

Hansen, C. D., & Brooks, A. K. (1994). A review of cross-cultural research on human resource development. *Human Resource Development Quarterly, 5*(1), 55–74. doi:10.1002/hrdq.3920050107

Hanvey, R. G. (1976). An attainable global perspective. *The American Forum for Global Education.* Retrieved from http://www.globaled.org

Haraway, D. (1985). A manifesto for cyborgs: Science, technology, and socialist feminism in the1980s. *Socialist Review, 80*, 65–107.

Haraway, D. (1991). *A cyborg manifesto in simians, cyborgs, and women: The reinvention of nature.* New York, NY: Rutledge.

Hargreaves, A. (2005). Pushing the boundaries of educational change. In A. Hargreaves (Ed.), *Extending educational change* (pp. 1–16). New York, NY: Springer. doi:10.1007/1-4020-4453-4_1

Harlacher, J. E., & Siler, C. E. (2011). Factors related to successful RTI implementation. *Communique, 39*, 20–22.

Harlin, Z. (2013). *Employer perspectives of employee wellness programs* (Master's thesis). Available from ProQuest Dissertations and Theses database. (UMI No. 1547540).

Harper, S. (2013). *Ageing societies: Myths, challenges and opportunities.* New York, NY: Routledge.

Harper, S., & Harris, F. (2010). *College men and masculinities: Theory, research, and implications for practice.* San Francisco, CA: Jossey-Bass.

Harris, F. (2008). Deconstructing masculinity: A qualitative study of college men's masculine conceptualizations and gender performance. *NASPA Journal*, *45*(4), 453–474.

Hartley, K., & Bendixen, L. D. (2001). Educational research in the Internet age: Examining the role of individual characteristics. *Educational Researcher*, *30*(9), 22–26. doi:10.3102/0013189X030009022

Hartung, P. J., Fouad, N. A., Leong, F. T. L., & Hardin, E. E. (2010). Individualism-collectivism: Links to occupational plans and work values. *Journal of Career Assessment*, *18*(1), 34–45. doi:10.1177/1069072709340526

Hasegawa, Y., & Hirose, Y. (2005). What the Japanese language tells us about the alleged Japanese relational self. *Australian Journal of Linguistics*, *25*(2), 219–251.

Hatch, J. A. (2002). *Doing qualitative research in educational settings*. Albany, NY: State University of New York Press.

Hatfield, R. (2004). What can I do when . . . I doubt there is a heaven and hell? In *Fourteenth Annual Truth in Love lectureship* (pp. 113–122). Retrieved from http://citeseerx.ist.psu. edu/viewdoc/download?doi=10.1.1.465.9606&rep= rep1&type=pdf#page=111

Haux, R., Ammenwerth, E., Herzog, W., & Knaup, P. (2002). Health care in the information society. A prognosis for the year 2013. *International Journal of Medical Informatics*, *66*(1-3), 3–21. doi:10.1016/S1386-5056(02)00030-8 PMID:12453552

Haverback, H. R., & Parault, S. J. (2008). Pre-service reading teacher efficacy and tutoring: A review. *Educational Psychology Review*, *20*(3), 237–255. doi:10.1007/s10648-008-9077-4

Hawrysh, B. M., & Zaichkowsky, J. L. (1990). Cultural approaches to negotiations: Understanding the Japanese. *International Marketing Review*, *7*(2).

Hayden, M., Thompson, J., & Walker, G. (Eds.). (2002). *International education in practice: Dimensions for national and international schools*. Retrieved from http://www.Amazon.com

Hayes, L. J., O'Brien-Pallas, L., Duffield, C., Shamian, J., Buchan, J., Hughes, F., & Stone, P. W. et al. (2006). Nurse turnover: A literature review. *International Journal of Nursing Studies*, *43*(2), 237–263. PMID:15878771

Hayoz, N., Jesień, L., & Koleva, D. (2011). *20 years after the collapse of Communism: Expectations, achievements and disillusions of 1989*. New York, NY: Peter Lang International Academic. doi:10.3726/978-3-0351-0273-4

Heath, H., & Cowley, S. (2004). Developing a grounded theory approach: A comparison of Glaser and Strauss. *International Journal of Nursing Studies*, *41*, 141–150. PMID:14725778

Hedin, N. (2010). Experiential learning: Theory and challenges. *Christian Education Journal*, *7*(1), 107–117.

Hedlund, S. (1999). *Russia's "market" economy. A bad case of predatory capitalism*. England: University College London Press.

Hehn, S. (2013, December 9). Teens dig digital privacy. *National Public Radio*. Retrieved from http://www.npr.org/blogs/alltechconsidered/2013/12/10/249731334/teens-dig-digital-privacy-if-snapchat-is-any-indication

Heidegger, M. (1950). *A question concerning technology*. New York, NY: Harper & Row.

Heidegger, M. (1969). *Discourse on thinking*. New York, NY: Harper & Row.

Heikkinen, T., & Järvinen, A. (2003). The common cold. *Lancet*, *361*(9351), 51–59. PMID:12517470

Heinemann, A., Kangasharju, J., Lyardet, F., & Mühlhäuser, M. (2003). iclouds–peer-to-peer information sharing in mobile environments. In Euro-Par 2003 Parallel Processing (pp. 1038-1045). Springer.

Heirdsfield, A., Walker, S., Tambyah, M., & Beutel, D. (2011). Blackboard as an Online Learning Environment: What Do Teacher Education Students and Staff Think? *Australian Journal Of Teacher Education*, *36*(7), 1–16. doi:10.14221/ajte.2011v36n7.4

Heirman, W., & Walrave, M. (2012). Predicting adolescent perpetration in cyberbullying: An application of the theory of planned behavior. *Psicothema*, *24*, 614–620. PMID:23079360

Held, D., McGrew, A. G., Goldblatt, D., & Perraton, J. (1999). *Global trasformations: politics, economics and culture.* Stanford, CA: Stanford University Press.

Heller, J. (2013, March). Call signs. *Hemispheres Magazine*, 15.

Hellie, R. (2005). The structure of Russian imperial history. *History and Theory*, *44*(4), 88–112. doi:10.1111/j.1468-2303.2005.00344.x

Herdman, M., Fox-Rushby, J., & Badia, X. (1998). A model of equivalence in the cultural adaptation of HRQL instruments: The universalist approach. *Quality of Life Research: An International Journal of Quality of Life Aspects of Treatment, Care and Rehabilitation*, *7*, 323–355. PMID:9610216

Herek, G. M. (2009). Sexual stigma and sexual prejudice in the United States: A conceptual framework. In D. A. Hope (Ed.), *Contemporary perspectives on lesbian, gay and bisexual identities: The 54th Nebraska Symposium on Motivation* (pp. 65–111). New York, NY: Springer. doi:10.1007/978-0-387-09556-1_4

Heron, J. (1996). *Co-operative inquiry: Research into the human condition.* London, UK: Sage.

Heron, J., & Reason, P. (1997). A participatory inquiry paradigm. *Qualitative Inquiry*, *3*(3), 274–279. doi:10.1177/107780049700300302

Herrmann, P. (1999). Electro-magnetic radiation. *International Well Being Magazine Annual*, *74*, 45–46.

Heuer, R. J. Jr. (1999). *Psychology of intelligence analysis.* Langley Falls, VA: Central Intelligence Agency.

Hew, K. F., & Brush, T. (2007). Integrating technology into k-12 teaching and learning: Current knowledge gaps and recommendations for future research. *Educational Technology Research and Development*, *55*(3), 223–252. doi:10.1007/s11423-006-9022-5

Hidaka, T. (2010). How Japanese language has been used and transformed-focused on social-cultural context and the use in communication. *Integrative Psychological & Behavioral Science*, *44*(2), 156–161. PMID:20401549

Hiemstra, R. (1994). Self-directed adult learning. In T. Husen & T. N. Postlethwaite (Eds.), *International encyclopedia of education* (2nd ed.; pp. 9–19). Oxford, UK: Pergamon Press.

High, P. (2013, October). Gartner: Top 10 strategic technology trends for 2014. *Forbes On-line*. Retrieved from http://www.forbes.com/sites/peterhigh/2013/10/14/gartner-top-10-strategic-technology-trends-for-2014/

Hill, P. C., & Pargament, K. I. (2008). Advances in the conceptualization and measurement of religion and spirituality: Implications for physical and mental health research. Psychology of Religion and Spirituality, S(1), 3–17. doi:10.1037/1941-1022.s.1.3

Hill, E. D., Cohen, A. B., Terrell, H. K., & Nagoshi, C. T. (2010). The role of social cognition in the religious fundamentalism-prejudice relationship. *Journal for the Scientific Study of Religion*, *49*(4), 724–739. doi:10.1111/j.1468-5906.2010.01542.x

Hillis, W. (2010, July 18). *Re: The knowledge web* [Web log comment]. Retrieved from http://edge.org/conversation/the-hillis-knowledge-web

Hilsop, G. W., & Ellis, H. C. J. (2004). A study of faculty effort in online teaching. *The Internet and Higher Education, 7*(1), 15–31. doi:10.1016/j.iheduc.2003.10.001

Hind, P. (1998, September). Captured by technology. *CIO Magazine*, 22-23.

Hinds, J. (1975). Third person pronouns in Japanese. *Language in Japanese Society*, 129-157.

Hinds, J. (1971). Personal pronouns in Japanese. *Glossa, 5*(2), 146–155.

Hinds, J. (1983). Contrastive rhetoric: Japanese and English. *Text-Interdisciplinary Journal for the Study of Discourse, 3*(2), 183–196.

Hinduja, S., & Patchin, J. W. (2007). Offline consequences of online victimization. *Journal of School Violence, 6*(3), 89–112. doi:10.1300/J202v06n03_06

Hinduja, S., & Patchin, J. W. (2008). Cyberbullying: An exploratory analysis of factors related to offending and victimization. *Deviant Behavior, 29*(2), 129–156. doi:10.1080/01639620701457816

Hinduja, S., & Patchin, J. W. (2010). Bullying, cyberbullying, and suicide. *Archives of Suicide Research, 14*(3), 206–221. doi:10.1080/13811118.2010.494133 PMID:20658375

Hinduja, S., & Patchin, J. W. (2012). Cyberbullying: Neither and epidemic nor a rarity. *European Journal of Developmental Psychology, 9*(5), 539–543. doi:10.1080/17405629.2012.706448

Hinduja, S., & Patchin, J. W. (2013). Social influences on cyberbullying behaviors among middle and high school students. *Journal of Youth and Adolescence, 42*(5), 711–722. doi:10.1007/s10964-012-9902-4 PMID:23296318

Hinojosa, A. S., McCauley, K. D., Randolph-Seng, B., & Gardner, W. L. (2014, June). Leader and follower attachment styles: Implications for authentic leader–follower relationships. *The Leadership Quarterly, 25*(3), 595–610. doi:10.1016/j.leaqua.2013.12.002

Hirano, C. (1999). Eight ways to say you: The challenges of translation. *Horn Book Magazine, 75*(1), 34–41.

Hirose, Y. (2000). Public and private self as two aspects of the speaker: A contrastive study of Japanese and English. *Journal of Pragmatics, 32*, 1623–1656.

Hjern, A., Grindefjord, M., Sundberg, H., & Rosén, M. (2001). Social inequality in oral health and use of dental care in Sweden. *Community Dentistry and Oral Epidemiology, 29*(3), 167–174. doi:10.1034/j.1600-0528.2001.290302.x PMID:11409675

Hoffman, M. L. (1975). Developmental synthesis of affect and cognition and its implications for altruistic motivation. *Developmental Psychology, 11*(5), 607–622. doi:10.1037/0012-1649.11.5.607

Hoffman, M. L. (1977). Empathy, its development and prosocial implications. In C. B. Keasey (Ed.), *Nebraska Symposium on Motivation* (Vol. 25, pp. 169–217). Lincoln: University of Nebraska Press.

Hoffman, M. L. (1981). Is altruism part of human nature?. *Journal of Personality and Social Psychology, 40*(1), 121–137. doi:10.1037/0022-3514.40.1.121

Hoffmann, S. (2005). *Grammaticalization and English complex prepositions: A corpus-based study*. London: Routledge.

Hoffman, S. J. (2010). *Teaching the humanities online: A practical guide to the virtual classroom*. New York, NY: Routledge.

Hofstede, G. (1980). *Culture's consequences, international differences in work-related values* (Vol. 5). London, UK: SAGE.

Hofstede, G. (1980). *Culture's consequences: international differences in work-related values.* Thousand Oaks, CA: Sage.

Hofstede, G. (1991). *Cultures and organizations: Software of the mind.* London, UK: McGraw-Hill.

Hofstede, G. (2001). Culture's recent consequences: Using dimension scores in theory and research. *International Journal of Cross Cultural Management, 1*(1), 11–30. doi:10.1177/147059580111002

Hofstede, G. H., & Hofstede, G. (2001). Culture's consequences: Comparing values, behaviors, institutions and organizations across nations. *Sage (Atlanta, Ga.).*

Hofstede, G., & Hofstede, G. J. (2005). *Cultures and organization: Software of the mind.* McGraw-Hill.

Hofstede, G., Hofstede, G. J., & Minkov, M. (1997). *Cultures and organizations.* New York, NY: McGraw-Hill.

Hofstede, G., Hofstede, G. J., & Minkov, M. (2010). *Cultures and organizations: Software of the mind, intercultural cooperation and its importance for survival* (3rd ed.). New York, NY: McGraw Hill.

Hofstede, G., & McCrae, R. (2004). Personality and culture revisited: Linking traits and dimensions of culture. *Cross-Cultural Research Journal, 38*(1), 52–88. doi:10.1177/1069397103259443

Hoijer, H. (1954). The Sapir-Whorf Hypothesis. *Language in Culture*, 92-105.

Holden, R. J., & Karsh, B. T. (2010). The technology acceptance model: Its past and its future in healthcare. *Journal of Biomedical Informatics, 43*(1), 159–172. doi:10.1016/j.jbi.2009.07.002 PMID:19615467

Hollenbeck, A. F. (2007). From IDEA to implementation: A discussion of foundational and future responsiveness-to-intervention research. *Learning Disabilities Research & Practice, 22*(2), 137–146. doi:10.1111/j.1540-5826.2007.00238.x

Holloway, S. D. (1999). The role of religious beliefs in early childhood education: Christian and Buddhist preschools in Japan. *Early Childhood Research & Practice, 1*(2), 2–19. Retrieved from http://ecrp.uiuc.edu/v1n2/holloway.html

Holmes, E. (2014, April 1). People for whom one cellphone isn't enough. *Wall Street Journal On-line.* Retrieved from http://online.wsj.com/news/article_email/SB10001424052702304432604579475303715000912-lMyQjAxMTA0M-DAwNzEwNDcyWj

Holmes, B., Read, G., & Voskresenskaya, N. (1995). *Russian education: Tradition and transition.* New York, NY: Routledge.

Hopkins, D. (2005). Tensions in and prospects for school improvement. In D. Hopkins (Ed.), *Practice and theory of school improvement* (pp. 1–21). New York, NY: Springer. doi:10.1007/1-4020-4452-6_1

Hopkins, T. (2008). Early identification of at-risk nursing students: A student support model. *The Journal of Nursing Education, 47*(6), 254–259. doi:10.3928/01484834-20080601-05 PMID:18557312

Hoppe, M. (2011). *Active listening.* Hoboken, NJ: Pfeiffer.

Horan, T. A., Tulu, B., Hilton, B., & Burton, J. (2004). Use of online systems in clinical medical assessments: An analysis of physician acceptance of online disability evaluation systems. In *Proceedings of the 37th Annual Hawaii International Conference on System Sciences.* IEEE. doi:10.1109/HICSS.2004.1265364

Horkheimer, T., & Adorno, M. (1999). *The dialectic of enlightenment.* New York, NY: Continuum.

Horn, R. E. (2001, May). *Knowledge mapping for complex social messes.* A presentation to the David and Lucile Packard Foundation, Stanford University, Palo Alto, CA.

Horowitz, M. D., Rosensweig, J. A., & Jones, C. A. (2007). Medical Tourism: Globalization of the healthcare marketplace. Medscape General Medicine. *The Medscape Journal of Medicine, 9*(4), 24–30. Available from http://www.ncbi.nlm.nih.gov/pmc/articles/PMC2234298/

Horowitz, M. D., Rosensweig, J. A., & Jones, C. A. (2007). Medical tourism: Globalization of the healthcare marketplace. *Medscape General Medicine, 9*(4), 33. PMID:18311383

House, J. (2002). Developing pragmatic competence in English as a Lingua Franca. In Knapp & Meierkord (Eds.), Lingua Franca communication (pp. 245–268). Frankfurt am Main: Peter Lang.

House, E. R., & McQuillan, P. J. (2005). Three perspective on school reform. In A. Lieberman (Ed.), *The roots of educational change* (pp. 186–201). New York, NY: Springer. doi:10.1007/1-4020-4451-8_11

House, J. (2013). Developing pragmatic competence in English as a lingua franca: Using discourse markers to express (inter)subjectivity and connectivity. *Journal of Pragmatics, 59*, 57–67. doi:10.1016/j.pragma.2013.03.001

Hoy, W. K., & Woolfolk, A. E. (1990). Socialization of student teachers. *American Educational Research Journal, 27*(2), 279–300. doi:10.3102/00028312027002279

Hoy, W. K., & Woolfolk, A. E. (1993). Teachers' sense of efficacy and the organizational health of schools. *The Elementary School Journal, 93*(4), 356–372. doi:10.1086/461729

Hsiao, F. S. T., Jen, F. C., & Lee, C. F. (1990). Impacts of culture and communist Orthodoxy on Chinese management. In J. Child & M. Lockett (Eds.), Advances in Chinese industrial studies (Vol. 1, pp. 301–314). [Retrieved fromhttps://www.ideals.illinois.edu/bitstream/handle/2142/28848/impactsofculture1447hsia.pdf?sequence=1

Hsieh, Y. H., Tsai, C. A., Lin, C. Y., Chen, J. H., King, C. C., Chao, D. Y., & Cheng, K. F. (2014). Asymptomatic ratio for seasonal H1N1 influenza infection among schoolchildren in Taiwan. *BMC Infectious Diseases, 14*(1), 80. PMID:24520993

Hu, E. (2013, September 5). Our cultural addiction to phones, in one disconcerting video. *National public radio*. Retrieved from http://www.npr.org/blogs/alltechconsidered/2013/09/05/219266779/our-cultural-addiction-to-phones-in-one-disconcerting-video

Hu, E. (2014, March 27). Pay attention: Your frustration over smartphone distraction. *National Public Radio*. Retrieved from http://www.npr.org/blogs/alltechconsidered/2014/03/27/294842209/pay-attention-your-frustration-over-smartphone-distraction

Hua, J., & Bapna, S. (2013). Who can we trust? The economic impact of insider threats. *Journal of Global Information Technology Management, 16*(4), 47–67. doi:10.1080/1097198X.2013.10845648

Huang, Y., & Chou, C. (2010). An analysis of multiple factors of cyberbullying among junior high school students in Taiwan. *Computers in Human Behavior, 26*(6), 1581–1590. doi:10.1016/j.chb.2010.06.005

Hubbard, J., & Singh, P. (2009). The evolution of employee benefits at the Economical Insurance Group. *Compensation and Benefits Review, 41*(6), 27–35. doi:10.1177/0886368709346683

Hughes, C. A., & Dexter, D. D. (2011). Response to intervention: A research-based summary. *Theory into Practice, 50*(1), 4–11. doi:10.1080/00405841.2011.534909

Hui, H. C., & Triandis, H. C. (1986). Individualism-collectivism: A study of cross-cultural researchers. *Journal of Cross-Cultural Psychology, 17*(2), 225–248. doi:10.1177/0022002186017002006

Hui, H. C., Yee, C., & Eastman, K. L. (1995). The relationship between individualism-collectivism and job satisfaction. *Applied Psychology, 44*(3), 276–282. doi:10.1111/j.1464-0597.1995.tb01080.x

Hung, A. C. Y. (2011). *The work of play: meaning-making in videogames.* New York, NY: Hill & Wang Press.

Hung, S.-Y., Chen, C. C., & Lee, W.-J. (2009). Moving hospitals toward e-learning adoption: An empirical investigation. *Journal of Organizational Change Management, 22*(3), 239–256. doi:10.1108/09534810910951041

Husserl, E. (1970). *Logical investigation.* New York, NY: Humanities.

Hu, X. (2004). Why China English should stand alongside British, American, and the other "World Englishes". *English Today, 78*(20), 26–33.

IDC Press Release. (2013, September 11). Tablet shipments forecast to top total PC shipments in the fourth quarter of 2013 and annually by 2015. *According to IDC.* Retrieved from http://www.idc.com/getdoc.jsp?containerId=prUS24314413

Ide, S. (1982). Japanese sociolinguistics politeness and women's language. *Lingua, 57*(2), 357–385.

Ietto-Gillies, G. (2012). *Transnational corporations and international production: concepts, theories and effects.* Cheltenham, UK: Edward Elgar.

Ihde, D. (1990). *Technology and the lifeworld: From garden to earth.* Bloomington, IN: Indiana University Press.

Iiyoshi, T., & Kumar, M. S. V. (2008). *Opening up education: The collective advancement of education through open technology, open content, and open knowledge.* MIT Press. Retrieved from https://mitpress.mit.edu/sites/default/files/titles/content/9780262515016_ Open_Access_Edition.pdf

Ilies, R., Morgeson, F. P., & Nahrgang, J. D. (2005, June). Authentic leadership and eudaemonic well-being: Understanding leader–follower outcomes. *The Leadership Quarterly, 16*(3), 373–394. doi:10.1016/j.leaqua.2005.03.002

Illeris, K. (Ed.). (2009). *Contemporary theories of learning.* London: Routledge.

Inceoglu, I., & Bartram, D. (2012). Global leadership: The myth of multicultural competency. *Industrial and Organizational Psychology, 5*(2), 216–218. doi:.2012.01432.x10.1111/j.1754-9434

Individuals With Disabilities Education Act, 20 U.S.C. § 1400 (2004).

Inglehart, R., & Baker, W. E. (2000). Modernization, cultural change, and the persistence of traditional values. *American Sociological Review,* 19–51.

Inkpen, A. C., & Tsang, E. W. (2005). Social capital, networks, and knowledge transfer. *Academy of Management Review, 30*(1), 146–165.

Inoue, M. (2002). Gender, language, and modernity: Toward an effective history of Japanese women's language. *American Ethnologist, 29*(2), 392–422.

International Cooperation. (n.d.). Retrieved from http://www.kubsu.ru/ en/node/1989

International Monetary Fund. (2014). *IMF Country Report No 14/190.* IMF.

International University of Fundamental Studies. (n.d.). *Faculty of Economics & Management Master of Business Administration.* Retrieved from http://www.iufs.edu/MBA-Prog.htm

Irwin, S. (2013). Qualitative secondary data analysis: Ethics, epistemology and context. *Progress in Development Studies, 13*(4), 295–306.

Irwin, S., Bornat, J., & Winterton, M. (2012). Timescapes secondary analysis: Comparison, context and working across data sets. *Qualitative Research, 12*(1), 66–80.

Ishii, S., Thompson, C. A., & Klopf, D. W. (1990). A Comparison of the assertiveness: Responsiveness construct between Japanese and Americans. *Otsuma Review, 23*, 63–71.

Ishikawa, H., & Yamazaki, Y. (2005). How applicable are western models of patient-physician relationship in Asia? Changing patient-physician relationship in contemporary Japan. *International Journal of Japanese Sociology, 14*(1), 84–93.

Ishikawa, Y., Nishiuchi, H., Hayashi, H., & Viswanath, K. (2012). Socioeconomic status and health communication inequalities in Japan: A nationwide cross-sectional survey. *PLoS ONE, 7*(7), 1–9. doi:10.1371/journal.pone.0040664 PMID:22808229

Ito, M. (2010). *Hanging out, messing around, and geeking out: Kids learning and living with new media.* Cambridge, MA: MIT Press.

Ives, J., & Draper, H. (2009). Appropriate methodologies for empirical bioethics: It's all relative. *Bioethics, 23*(4), 249–258. PMID:19338525

Ives, J., & Dunn, M. (2010). Who's arguing? A call for reflexivity in bioethics. *Bioethics, 24*(5), 256–265. PMID:20500762

Iwawaki, S., Eysenck, S. B. G., & Eysenck, H. J. (1977). Differences in personality between Japanese and English. *The Journal of Social Psychology, 102*(1), 27–33. PMID:881807

Jackson, A. (2004, November). Preparing urban youths to succeed in the interconnected world of the 21st century. *Phi Delta Kappan, 86*(3), 210–213. Retrieved from http://www.kappanmagazine.org/content/86/3/210

Jackson, A. (2008, May). High schools in the global age. *Educational Leadership, 65*(8), 58–62. Retrieved from http://www.ascd.org/publications/educationalleadership/may08/vol65/num08/High-Schools-in-the-Global-Age.aspx

Jackson, M. (2008). *Distracted: The erosion of attention and the coming dark age.* New York, NY: Prometheus.

Jaggars, S. S., & Xu, D. (2010). Online learning in the Virginia community college system (CCRC Working Paper). New York, NY: Columbia University, Teachers College, Community College Research Center. Retrieved from http://ccrc.tc.columbia.edu/publications/online-learning-virginia.html

Janssen, P. P. M., de Jonge, J., & Bakker, A. B. (1999). Specific determinants of intrinsic work motivation, burnout and turnover intentions: A study among nurses. *Journal of Advanced Nursing, 29*(6), 1360–1369. PMID:10354230

Jarvis, P. (2009). Lifelong learning: A social ambiguity. In P. Jarvis (Ed.), *The Routledge international handbook of lifelong learning* (pp. 9–18). New York, NY: Routledge.

Jasperson, J. S., Carter, P. E., & Zmud, R. W. (2005). A comprehensive conceptualization of post-adoptive behaviors associated with technology enabled work systems. *Management Information Systems Quarterly, 29*(3), 525–557.

Jendricke, U., & Markotten, D. (2005). *Usability meets security: The identity-manager as your personal security manager for the internet.* Unpublished paper, Albert-Ludwigs University of Freiberg, Germany.

Jenkins, H. (2009, November 16). The Skill of the future: In a word 'multitasking'. *Public Broadcasting Service.* Retrieved from www.pbs.org/wgbh/pages/frontline/digitalnation/living-faster/split-focus/the-skill-of-the-future.html

Jenkins, H. (2008). *Convergence culture.* New York, NY: New York University Press.

Jenkins, J. (1996). Native speaker, non-native speaker and English as a Foreign Language: Time for a change. *IATEFL Newsletter, 131*, 10–11.

Jenkins, J. (1998). Which pronunciation norms and models for English as an International Language? *ELT Journal, 52*(2), 119–126. doi:10.1093/elt/52.2.119

Jenkins, J. (2000). *The phonology of English as an international language*. Oxford, UK: Oxford University Press.

Jenkins, J. (2002). A sociolinguistically based, empirically researched pronunciation syllabus for English as an International Language. *Applied Linguistics*, *23*(1), 83–103. doi:10.1093/applin/23.1.83

Jenkins, J. R., Hudson, R. F., & Johnson, E. S. (2007). Screening for at-risk readers in a response to intervention framework. *School Psychology Review*, *36*(4), 582–600.

Jenkins, J., Cogo, A., & Dewey, M. (2011). Review of developments in research into English as a lingua franca. *Language Teaching*, *44*(3), 281–315. doi:10.1017/S0261444811000115

Jenkins, S. D. (2011). Cross-cultural perspectives on critical thinking. *The Journal of Nursing Education*, *50*(5), 268–274. doi:10.3928/01484834-20110228-02 PMID:21366168

Jenner, D., Reynolds, V., & Harrison, G. (1980). Catechlomine excretion rates and occupation. *Ergonomics*, *23*(2), 237–246. doi:10.1080/00140138008924737 PMID:7428768

Jennett, P. A., Scott, R. E., Affleck, H. L., Hailey, D., Ohinmaa, A., Anderson, C., & Lorenzetti, D. et al. (2004). Policy implications associated with the socioeconomic and health system impact of telehealth: A case study from Canada. *Telemedicine Journal and e-Health*, *10*(1), 77–83. doi:10.1089/153056204773644616 PMID:15104919

Jennifer, J. (2006). Current perspectives on teaching World Englishes and English as a lingua franca. *TESOL Quarterly*, *40*(1), 157–181. doi:10.2307/40264515

Jennings, P. L., & Dooley, K. J. (2007). An emerging complexity paradigm in leadership research. In J. K. Hazy, J. A. Goldstein, & B. B. Lichtenstein (Eds.), *Complex systems leadership theory: New perspectives from complexity science on social and organizational effectiveness* (pp. 17–61). Mansfield, MA: ISCE.

Jensen, L. A. (2003). Coming of age in a multicultural world: Globalization and adolescent cultural identity formation. *Applied Developmental Science*, *7*(3), 189–196. doi:10.1207/S1532480XADS0703_10

Jerlvall, L., & Pehrsson, T. (2012). *eHealth in Swedish county councils*. Inventory comissioned by the SLIT group, CEHIS (swe: Center för eHälsa i Sverige/Eng: Center for eHealth in Sweden).

Jha, P. S. (2002). *The perilous road to the market: The political economy of reform in Russia, India and China*. London: Pluto Press.

Jiang, N., & Nekrasova, T. M. (2007). The processing of formulaic sequences by second language speakers. *Modern Language Journal*, *91*(3), 433–445. doi:10.1111/j.1540-4781.2007.00589.x

Jick, T. D. (1979). Mixing qualitative and quantitative methods: Triangulation in action. *Administrative Science Quarterly*, 602–611.

Johanning, D. I. (2004). Supporting the development of algebraic thinking in middle school: A closer look at students' informal strategies. *The Journal of Mathematical Behavior*, *23*(4), 371–388. doi:10.1016/j.jmathb.2004.09.001

Johanson, C. (1987). *Women's struggle for higher education in Russia, 1855–1900*. Kingston, Ontario, Canada: McGill-Queen's University Press.

Johansson, P., Oleni, M., & Fridlund, B. (2002). Patient satisfaction with nursing care in the context of health care: A literature study. *Scandinavian Journal of Caring Sciences*, *16*(4), 337–344. doi:10.1046/j.1471-6712.2002.00094.x PMID:12445102

Johansson, S. (1979). American and British English grammar: An elicitation experiment. *English Studies*, *60*(2), 195–215. doi:10.1080/00138387908597961

Johnson & Johnson. (2015). *Our company*. Retrieved from http://www.jnj.com/about-jnj

Johnson, D. (2012, June 29). Making calls has become fifth most frequent use for smartphone for newly-networked generation of users. *The Blue*. Retrieved from http://news.o2.co.uk/?press-release=making-calls-has-become-fifth-most-frequent-use-for-a-smartphone-for-newly-networked-generation-of-users

Johnson, S. D., & Aragon, S. R. (2003). An instructional strategy framework for online learning environments. *Facilitating learning in online environments*, (pp. 31-43). San Francisco: Jossey-Bass. Retrieved from http://www.editlib.org/noaccess/15267

Johnson, C. C., Lai, Y. L., Rice, J., Rose, D., & Webber, L. S. (2010). Action live: Using process evaluation to describe implementation of a worksite wellness program. *Journal of Occupational and Environmental Medicine, 52*(1Supplement), S14–S21. doi:10.1097/JOM.0b013e3181c81ade PMID:20061882

Johnson, D. D. (2005). God's punishment and public goods. *Human Nature (Hawthorne, N.Y.), 16*(4), 410–446. doi:10.1007/s12110-005-1017-0 PMID:26189839

Johnson, D. D., & Bering, J. M. (2006). Hand of God, mind of man: Punishment and cognition in the evolution of cooperation. *Evolutionary Psychology, 4*(1), 219–233. http://www.qub.ie/schools/InstituteofCognitionCulture/FileUploadPage/Filetoupload,90239,en.pdf doi:10.1177/147470490600400119

Johnson, J. (2003). Children, robotics, and education. *Artificial Life and Robotics, 7*(1-2), 16–21.

Johnson, P. A. (2011). Actively pursuing knowledge in the college classroom. *Journal of College Teaching and Learning, 8*(6), 17–30. doi:10.19030/tlc.v8i6.4279

Johnson, R. B., & Onwuegbuzie, A. J. (2004). Mixed methods research: A research paradigm whose time has come. *Educational Researcher, 33*(7), 14–26.

Johnson, T., Wisniewski, M. A., Kuhlemeyer, G., Isaacs, G., & Kryzkowski, J. (2008). Technology adoption in higher education: Overcoming anxiety through faculty bootcamp. *Journal of Asynchronous Learning Networks, 16*(2), 63–72.

Joiner, R., Iacovides, J., Owen, M., Gavin, C., Clibbery, S., Darling, J., & Drew, B. (2011). Digital games, gender and learning in engineering: Do females benefit as much as males? *Journal of Science Education and Technology, 20*(2), 178–185. doi:10.1007/s10956-010-9244-5

Joinson, A. (1998). Causes and implications of behavior on the Internet. In J. Gackenbach (Ed.), *Psychology and the Internet: Intrapersonal, interpersonal, and transpersonal implications* (pp. 43–60). San Diego, CA: Academic Press.

Jonassen, D. H., Myers, J. M., & McKillop, A. M. (1996). From constructivism to constructionism: Learning with hypermedia/multimedia rather than from it. In B. G. Wilson (Ed.), *Constructivist learning environments: Case studies in instructional design* (pp. 93–106). Educational Technology.

Jones, G. A., & Oleksiyenko, A. (2011). The internationalization of Canadian university research: A global higher education matrix analysis of multi-level governance. *Higher Education, 61*(1), 41–57.

Jones, J. H. (2010). Developing critical thinking in the perioperative environment. *AORN Journal, 91*(2), 248–256. doi:10.1016/j.aorn.2009.09.025 PMID:20152198

Jones, M. (1999). Structuration theory. In W. Currie & R. Galliers (Eds.), *Rethinking management information systems* (pp. 103–135). New York, NY: Oxford University Press.

Jones, M. (2008). Developing clinically savvy nursing students: An evaluation of problem-based learning in an associate degree program. *Nursing Education Perspectives, 29*(5), 278–283. PMID:18834057

Jonsen, A. R. (2006). A history of religion and bioethics. In D. E. Guinn (Ed.), *Handbook of bioethics and religion* (pp. 23–36). Oxford, UK: Oxford University Press. doi:10.1093/0195178734.003.0002

Jordan, K. (2013). *MOOC completion rates: The data* [Web log post]. Retrieved from http://www.katyjordan.com/MOOCproject.html

Joshi, R. M., Binks, E., Hougen, M., Dahlgren, M. E., Ocker-Dean, E., & Smith, D. L. (2009). Why Elementary Teachers Might Be Inadequately Prepared to Teach Reading. *Journal of Learning Disabilities*, *42*(5), 392–402. doi:10.1177/0022219409338736 PMID:19542350

Joslin, B., Lowe, J. B., & Peterson, N. A. (2006). Employee characteristics and participation in a worksite wellness programme. *Health Education Journal*, *65*(4), 308–319. doi:10.1177/0017896906069367

Jung, C. G., & Main, R. (1997). *Jung on synchronicity and the paranormal*. London: Routledge.

Jung, J. (2012). Islamophobia? Religion, contact with Muslims, and the respect for Islam. *Review of Religious Research*, *54*(1), 113–126. doi:10.1007/s13644-011-0033-2

Justice, L. M., Mashburn, A. J., Hamre, B. K., & Pianta, R. C. (2008). Quality of language literacy instruction in preschool classrooms serving at-risk pupils. *Early Childhood Research Quarterly*, *23*(1), 51–68. doi:10.1016/j.ecresq.2007.09.004 PMID:22773887

Kachru, B. B. (1985). Standards, codification and sociolinguistic realism: the English language in the Outer Circle. In R. Quirk & H. G. Widdowson (Eds.), *English in the World: Teaching and learning the language and literatures* (pp. 11–30). Cambridge, UK: Cambridge University Press.

Kaddoura, M. A. (2010). New graduate nurses' perceptions of the effects of clinical simulation on their critical thinking, learning, and confidence. *Journal of Continuing Education in Nursing*, *41*(11), 506–516. doi:10.3928/00220124-20100701-02 PMID:20672760

Kadlec, C., & Shropshire, J. (2010). Best practices in IT disaster recovery planning among US banks. *Journal of Internet Banking & Commerce*, *15*(1), 1–11.

Kajbjer, K., Nordberg, R., & Klein, G. O. (2010). Electronic health records in Sweden: from administrative management to clinical decision support. In History of Nordic Computing 3 (pp. 74–82). Springer Berlin Heidelberg. Available from http://dl.ifip.org/db/conf/hinc/hinc2010/KajbjerNK10.pdf

Kakabadse, N. K., Kouzmin, A., & Kakabadse, A. K. (2000). Technostress: Over-Identification with information technology and its impact on employees and managerial effectiveness. In N. K. Kakabadse & A. K. Kakabadse (Eds.), *Creating futures: Leading change through information systems* (pp. 259–296). Hampshire, UK: Ashgate.

Kamalzadeh Takhti, H., Abdul Rahman, S. B., & Abedini, S. (2013). Factors determining nurses' hospital information systems. *International Journal of Management & Information Technology*, *3*(3), 37–44. Retrieved from http://www.ijmit.com

Kant, I. (1949). *Fundamental principles of the metaphysic of morals* (T. K. Abbott, Trans.). (Original work published 1785). Retrieved from http://philosophy.eserver.org/kant/ metaphys-of-morals.txt

Kant, I. [1783] (1998). Prolegomena zu einer jeden konftigen Metaphysik, die als Wissenschaft wird auftreten konnen, Vol. III of Immanuel Kant: Werke. In S. Bonden (Ed.), Wilhelm Weischedel (pp. 109–264). Darmstadt: Wissenschaftliche Buchgesellschaft.

Kant, I. (1878). *Prolegomena zu einer jeden Künftigen Metaphysik: die als Wissenschaft wird auftreten konnen*. Verlag von Leopold Voss.

Kant, I. (1964). *The metaphysical principles of virtue: Part II of The Metaphysics of Morals* (J. Ellington, Trans.). New York, NY: The Library of Liberal Arts. (Original work published 1797)

Kant, I. (2004). *Religion within the boundaries of mere reason* (A. Wood & G. Di Viovanni, Trans.). Cambridge, UK: Cambridge University Press. (Original work published 1793)

Kantor, L., Endler, N. S., Heslegrave, R. J., & Kocovski, N. L. (2001). Validating self-report measures of state and trait anxiety against a physiological measure. *Current Psychology (New Brunswick, N.J.), 20*(3), 207–215. doi:10.1007/s12144-001-1007-2

Kao, R. R. (2001). Where have the prepositions gone? A study of English prepositional verbs and input enhancement in instructed SLA. *IRAL, 39*(3), 195–215. doi:10.1515/iral.2001.002

Kaplan. (2012). *Kaplan nursing integrated testing program faculty manual*. New York: Kaplan Nursing.

Karahanna, E., Agarwal, R., & Angst, C. M. (2006). Reconceptualizing compatibility beliefs in technology acceptance research. *MIS Quarterly, 30*(4), 781-804. Retrieved from http://www.jstor.org/stable/25148754

Karahanna, E., Straub, D. W., & Chervany, N. L. (1999). Information technology adoption across time: A cross-sectional comparison of pre-adoption and post-adoption beliefs. *MIS Quarterly, 23*(2), 183-213. Retrieved from http://web.ffos.hr/oziz/tam/Karahanna_1999++++PRE-POST.pdf

Kasworm, C. E. (1990). Adult undergraduates in higher education: A review of past research perspectives. *Review of Educational Research, 60*(3), 345–372. doi:10.3102/00346543060003345

Kaszubski, P. (1998) Learner corpora: the cross-roads of linguistic norm. Paper presented at the 1998 Teaching and language corpora conference, Oxford, UK.

Kavale, K. A., Kauffman, J. M., Bachmeier, R. J., & LeFever, G. B. (2008). Response-to-intervention: Seperating the rhetoric of self-congratulation from the reality of specific learning disability identification. *Learning Disability Quarterly, 31*(3), 135–150.

Kay, P., & Kempton, W. (1984). What is the sapir-whorf hypothesis? *American Anthropologist, 86*(1), 65–79.

Kazdin, A. E. (1998). *Research design in clinical psychology* (3rd ed.). Boston, MA: Allyn & Bacon.

Keengwe, J. (2007). Faculty integration of technology into instruction and students' perceptions of computer technology to improve student learning. *Journal of Information Technology, 6*, 169–17.

Keengwe, J., Kidd, T., & Kyei-Blankson, L. (2009). Faculty and technology: Implications for faculty training and technology leadership. *Journal of Science Education and Technology, 18*(1), 23–28. doi:10.1007/s10956-008-9126-2

Keith, S., & Martin, M. E. (2005). Cyber-bullying: Creating a culture of respect in a cyber world. *Reclaiming Children and Youth, 13*(4), 224. Available from http://bienestaryproteccioninfantil.es/imagenes/tablaContenidos03SubSec/13_4_Keith_Martin.pdf

Kelley, J. E. (2008). Harmony, empathy, loyalty, and patience in Japanese children's literature. *Social Studies, 99*(2), 61–70.

Kelly, J. N. D. (2000). *Early Christian doctrines*. London: Continuum.

Kelly, T., & Erickson, C. (2007). An examination of gender role identity, sexual self-esteem, sexual coercion, and sexual victimization in a university sample. *Journal of Sexual Aggression, 13*(3), 235–245. doi:10.1080/13552600701794366

Kemmis, S., & Wilkinson, M. (1998). Participatory action research and the study of practice. In B. Atweh, S. Kemmis, & P. Weeks (Eds.), *Action research in practice: Partnerships for social justice in education* (pp. 21–36). New York, NY: Routledge.

Kernis, M. H. (2003). Toward a conceptualization of optimal self-esteem. *Psychological Inquiry, 14*(2), 1–26. doi:10.1207/S15327965PLI1401_01

Kern, S. (2003). *The culture of time and space, 1880-1918: with a new preface.* Cambridge, MA: Harvard University Press.

Kerr, S. (1996, November). *The re-centering of Russian education.* Roundtable session at the American Association for the Advancement of Slavic Studies Annual Convention, Boston, MA.

Khalaf, S. (2014, April 22). The Rise of the mobile addict. *Flurry Research.* Retrieved from http://www.flurry.com/bid/110166/the-rise-of-the-mobile-addict#.U2adya1dXMg

Kharitonova, O. V. (2012). Akademicheskaya mobil'nost v prostranstve visshego obrazovanija. [Academic mobility in high education]. *Chelovek i obrazovanie, 2*, 41–44. Retrieved from http://cyberleninka.ru/article/n/akademicheskaya-mobilnost-v-prostranstve-vysshego-obrazovaniya

Khoutyz, I. (2013a). Globalisation and English as a lingua franca: Does the future promise culturally homogenous or inimitable societies? In R. Fisher, L. Howard, K. Monteith, & D. Riha (Eds.), *Interculturalism, meaning and identity* (pp. 3–13). Oxford, UK: Inter-Disciplinary Press.

Khoutyz, I. (2013b). Multicultural perspectives in academic communication: Academic mobility and teaching practices. In *Proceedings of the 6th International Conference of Education, Research and Innovation* (pp. 6150–6169). Seville, Spain: International Academy of Technology, Education and Development.

Kieran, C. (2007). Learning and teaching of algebra at the middle school through college level: Building meaning for symbols and their manipulation. In F. K. Lester (Ed.), *Second handbook of research on mathematics teaching and learning* (p. 707).

Killam, L. A., Luhanga, F., & Bakker, D. (2011). Characteristics of unsafe undergraduate nursing students in clinical practice: An integrative literature review. *The Journal of Nursing Education, 50*(8), 437–446. doi:10.3928/01484834-20110517-05 PMID:21598859

Kim, S. S., & Malhotra, N. K. (2005). A Longitudinal Model of Continued IS Use: An Integrative View of Four Mechanisms Underlying Postadoption Phenomena. *Management Science, 51*(5), 741-755. doi:10.1287/mnsc.1040.326

Kim, D., Pan, Y., & Park, H. S. (1998). High-versus low-context culture: A comparison of Chinese, Korean, and American cultures. *Psychology and Marketing, 15*(6), 507–521.

Kimmel, M. (2008). *Guyland: The perilous place where boys become men.* New York, NY: Harper Collins.

Kimmel, M. (2011). *Manhood in America* (3rd ed.). Cambridge, UK: Oxford University Press.

Kim, V. B., Chapman Iii, W. H., Albrecht, R. J., Bailey, B. M., Young, J. A., Nifong, L. W., & Chitwood Jr, W. R. (2002). Early experience with telemanipulative robot-assisted laparoscopic cholecystectomy using da Vinci. *Surgical Laparoscopy, Endoscopy & Percutaneous Techniques, 12*(1), 33–40. PMID:12008760

Kim, Y. S., Park, J. W., You, M. A., Seo, Y. S., & Han, S. S. (2005). Sensitivity to ethical issues confronted by Korean hospital staff nurses. *Nursing Ethics, 12*(6), 595–605. PMID:16312088

King, D. E., & Bushwick, B. (1994). Beliefs and attitudes of hospital inpatients about faith healing and prayer. *Journal of Family Practice, 39*(4), 349–352. Retrieved from EBSCOhost database. (Accession No. 24534177)

Kiregian, E. (2015). *The transformation of Russian business education from 1993 to 2013* (Doctoral dissertation). Available from ProQuest Dissertations and Theses database. (UMI No. 3662550)

Kırıkkaya, E. B., Bozkurt, E., & İşeri, Ş. (2013). Fen ve teknoloji derslerinde gazetelerin kullanılması. *Ondokuz Mayıs Üniversitesi Eğitim Fakültesi Dergisi, 32*(2), 223–247.

Kirk, G. S. (1951). Natural change in Heraclitus. *Mind, 55*(27), 35–42. doi:.3510.1093/mind/lx.237

Kirkman, B. L., Lowe, K. B., & Gibson, C. (2006). A quarter century of Culture's Consequences: A review of the empirical research incorporating Hofstede's cultural value framework. *Journal of International Business Studies, 36*(3), 285–320. doi:10.1057/palgrave.jibs.8400202

Kirkpatrick, A. (2010). Researching English as a lingua franca in Asia: The Asian Corpus of English (ACE) project. *Asian Englishes, 31*(1), 4–18. doi:10.1080/13488678.2010.10801269

Kishkovsky, S. (2000). A bright future for Russian higher education. *Carnegie Reporter, 1*(1), 2–12. Retrieved from ERIC database. (EJ618192)

Kitaev, I. (1994). Russian education in transition: Transformation of labour market, attitudes of youth and changes in management of higher and lifelong education. *Oxford Review of Education, 20*(1), 111–130. doi:10.1080/0305498940200107

Kjellberg, J., Sørensen, J., Hansen, J., Andersen, S., Avnstrøm, L., & Borgstrøm, L. (2007). Almen praksis som koordinator—en international belysning. [General practice as coordinator—an international review]. *Copenhagen: Danish Institute for Health Services Research (DSI),* Report No. 02. [in Danish].

Klein, G. (2008). Naturalistic decision making. *Human Factors, 50*(3), 456–460. doi:10.1518/001872008X288385 PMID:18689053

Kleinman, A. (1988). *The illness narratives: Suffering, healing, and the human condition.* New York, NY: Basic books.

Klevens, R. M., Edwards, J. R., Richards, C. L., Horan, T. C. Jr, Gaynes, R. P., Pollock, D. A., & Cardo, D. M. (2007). Estimating health care-associated infections and deaths in US hospitals, 2002. *Public Health Reports, 122*(2), 160–166. PMID:17357358

Kligfield, P., Gettes, L. S., Bailey, J. J., Childers, R., Deal, B. J., Hancock, E. W., & Wagner, G. S. et al. (2007). Recommendations for the Standardization and Interpretation of the Electrocardiogram Part I: The Electrocardiogram and Its Technology A Scientific Statement From the American Heart Association Electrocardiography and Arrhythmias Committee, Council on Clinical Cardiology; the American College of Cardiology Foundation; and the Heart Rhythm Society Endorsed by the International Society for Computerized Electrocardiology. *Journal of the American College of Cardiology, 49*(10), 1109–1127. PMID:17349896

Kligman, G. (1996). Women and the negotiation of identity in post-Communist Eastern Europe. In V. Bonnell (Ed.), *Identities in transition: Eastern Europe and Russia after the collapse of Communism* (pp. 68–91). Oakland, CA: University of California Press.

Kline, S. J. (1985). What is technology? *Bulletin of Science, Technology & Society, 1,* 215–218. doi:10.1177/027046768500500301

Klopf, D., & McCroskey, J. C. (2007). *Intercultural communication encounters.* Boston, MA: Pearson Education, Inc.

Knapp, A. (2011). Using English as a lingua franca for (mis-)managing conflict in an international university context: An example from a course in engineering. *Journal of Pragmatics, 43*(4), 978–990. doi:10.1016/j.pragma.2010.08.008

Knapp, K. (2002). The fading out of the non-native speaker. Native speaker dominance in lingua-franca situations. In K. Knapp & C. Meierkord (Eds.), *Lingua Franca communication* (pp. 217–244). Frankfurt: Peter Lang.

Knotek, S. E. (2007). Consultation within response to intervention models. In S. R. Jimerson, M. K. Burns, & A. M. Van-DerHeyden (Eds.), *Handbook of respoonse to intervention*. New York, NY: Springer. doi:10.1007/978-0-387-49053-3_4

Knowles, M. S. (1968). Andragogy, not pedagogy. *Adult Leadership*, *16*(10), 350–352.

Knowles, M. S. (1975). *Self-directed learning*. New York, NY: Association Press.

Knowles, M. S. (1980). *The modern practice of adult education: From pedagogy to andragogy revised and updated*. New York, NY: The Adult Education Company.

Knowles, M. S. (1990).*The adult learner: A neglected species* (4th ed.). Houston, TX: Gulf Publishing Company.

Knowles, M. S., Holton, E. F., & Swanson, R. A. (2011). *The adult learner* (7th ed.). Oxford, UK: Elsevier.

Kocakülâh, M. C., Cherry, A., & Morris, J. T. (2013). Investing in company wellness programs: Does it make financial sense? *Journal of Health Management*, *15*(3), 463–470. doi:10.1177/0972063413492041

Koch, R. (2013, October 7). Is individualism good or bad? *Huffington Post*. Retrieved from http://www.huffingtonpost.com/richard-koch/is-individualism-good-or-_b_4056305.html

Kochenderfer-Ladd, B., & Pelletier, M. (2008). Teachers' views and beliefs about bullying: Influences on classroom management strategies and students' coping with peer victimization. *Journal of School Psychology*, *46*(4), 431–453. doi:10.1016/j.jsp.2007.07.005 PMID:19083367

Koch, R. (2010). *The star principle: How it can make you rich*. London: Piatkus.

Koch, T., & Harrington, A. (1998). Reconceptualizing rigour: The case for reflexivity. *Journal of Advanced Nursing*, *28*(4), 882–890. PMID:9829678

Kodner, D. L., & Spreeuwenberg, C. (2002). Integrated care: Meaning, logic, applications, and implications–a discussion paper. *International Journal of Integrated Care*, *2*(4), 1–6. doi:10.5334/ijic.67 PMID:16896389

Koedinger, K. R., & Nathan, M. J. (2004). The real story behind story problems: Effects of representations on quantitative reasoning. *Journal of the Learning Sciences*, *13*(2), 129. doi:10.1207/s15327809jls1302_1

Koenig, H. G., McCullough, M. E., & Larson, D. B. (2001). *Handbook of religion and health*. New York, NY: Oxford University Press. doi:10.1093/acprof:oso/9780195118667.001.0001

Koeszegi, S., Vetschera, R., & Kersten, G. (2004). National cultural differences in the use and perception of internet-based NSS: Does high or low context matter? *International Negotiation*, *9*(1), 79–109.

Kohl, H. W. III, Craig, C. L., Lambert, E. V., Inoue, S., Alkandari, J. R., Leetongin, G., & Kahlmeier, S. (2012). The pandemic of physical inactivity: Global action for public health. *Lancet*, *380*(9838), 294–305. doi:10.1016/S0140-6736(12)60898-8 PMID:22818941

Kolbe, L. J., Tirozzi, E. M., Bobbitt-Cooke, M. B., Riedel, S., Jones, J., & Schmoyer, M. (2005). Health programmes for school employees: Improving quality of life, health and productivity. *Promotion & Education*, *12*(3-4), 157–161. doi:10.1177/10253823050120030115 PMID:16739507

Kolowich, S. (2012, September). The MOOC survivors: edX explores demographics of most persistent MOOC students. *Inside Higher Education*. Retrieved from http://www.insidehighered.com/news/2012/09/12/edx-explores-demographics-most-persistent-mooc-students

Kolowich, S. (2014, January 22). *Completion rates aren't the best way to judge MOOCs, researchers say* [Web log post]. Retrieved from http://chronicle.com/blogs/wiredcampus/completion-rates-arent-the-best-way-to-judge-moocs-researchers-say/49721

Kondo, D. K. (1990). *Crafting selves: Power, gender, and discourses of identity in a Japanese workplace*. Chicago, IL: University of Chicago Press.

Konsky, C., Eguchi, M., Blue, J., & Kapoor, S. (2002). Individualist-collectivist values: American, Indian and Japanese cross-cultural study. *Intercultural Communication Studies, 9*(1), 69–83. Retrieved from http://web.uri.edu/iaics/files/07-Catherine-Konsky-Mariko-Eguchi-Janet-Blue-Suraj-Kapoor.pdf

Kop, R. (2011). The challenges to connectivist learning on open online networks: Learning experiences during a massive open online course. *International Review of Research in Open and Distance Learning, 12*(3), 19–38. Retrieved from http://www.irrodl.org/index.php/irrodl/article/view/882

Kop, R., & Fournier, H. (2010). New dimensions to self-directed learning in an open networked learning environment. *International Journal of Self-Directed Learning, 7*(2), 1–13. Retrieved from http://selfdirectedlearning.com/documents/Kop&Fournier2010.pdf

Korn, M. (2014, February 6). Smartphones make you tired and unproductive, study says. *Wall Street Journal Online*. Retrieved from http://blogs.wsj.com/atwork/2014/02/06/smartphones-make-you-tired-and-unproductive-study-says/?mod=e2fb

Korsgaard, C. M. (2012). The right to lie: Kant on dealing with evil. *Philosophy & Public Affairs, 15*(4), 325–349.

Kortunov, A. (2009). Russian higher education social research. *Russia Today, 76*(1), 203–224. Retrieved from https://muse.jhu.edu/journals/social_research/v076/76.1.kortunov.pdf

Kostere, K., & Percy, W. H. (2008). *Qualitative research approaches*. Unpublished manuscript, Capella University, Minneapolis, MN.

Kotter, J. (1996). *Leading change*. Boston, MA: Harvard Business School Press.

Koutropoulos, A., & Hogue, R. (2012). How to succeed in a MOOC: Massive online open course. *Learning Solutions Magazine*. Retrieved from http://www.learningsolutionsmag.com/articles/1023/how-to-succeed-in-a-massive-online-open-course-mooc

Kovaleski, J. F. (2007). Potential pitfalls of response to intervention. In S. R. Jimerson, M. K. Burns, & A. M. VanDerHeyden (Eds.), *Handbook of response to intervention*. New York: Springer. doi:10.1007/978-0-387-49053-3_6

Kowalski, R. M., & Limber, S. P. (2007). Electronic bullying among middle school students. *The Journal of Adolescent Health, 41*(6), 22–30. doi:10.1016/j.jadohealth.2007.08.017 PMID:18047942

Kratochwill, T. R., Clements, M. A., & Kalymon, K. M. (2007). Response to intervention: Conceptual and methodological issues in implementation. In S. R. Jimerson, M. K. Burns, & A. M. VanDerHeyden (Eds.), *Handbook of response to intervention*. New York, NY: Springer. doi:10.1007/978-0-387-49053-3_3

Krebs, D. L. (1975). Empathy and altruism. *Journal of Personality and Social Psychology, 32*(6), 1134–1146. doi:10.1037/0022-3514.32.6.1134 PMID:1214217

Kudya, S., & Diwan, R. (2002). The Impact of information technology on U.S. industry. *Japan and the World Economy, 14*(3), 321–333. doi:10.1016/S0922-1425(01)00074-3

Kuntz, J. R. C., Kuntz, J. R., Elenkov, D., & Nabirukhina, A. (2013). Characterizing ethical cases: A cross-cultural investigation of individual differences, organisational climate, and leadership on ethical decision-making. *Journal of Business Ethics, 113*(2), 317–331.

Kuper, A., Lingard, L., & Levinson, W. (2008). Critically appraising qualitative research. *British Medical Journal, 337*(7671), 687–689. PMID:18687726

Kuroda, S. Y. (1965). Causative forms in Japanese. *Foundations of Language, 1*(1), 30–50.

Kuroda, S. Y. (1973). Where epistemology, style, and grammar meet. In S. R. Anderson & P. Kipirsky (Eds.), *A Festschrift for Morris Halle* (pp. 337–391). New York, NY: Holt Rinehart and Willson.

Kuznetsov, A. (2000). Russia's "Market" Economy: A Bad Case of Predatory Capitalism[Book review]. *Europe-Asia Studies, 52*(2), 379–380.

Kvale, S. (1996). *InterViews: An introduction to qualitative research interviewing.* Thousand Oaks, CA: Sage.

Kylmä, J., Duggleby, W., Cooper, D., & Molander, G. (2009). Hope in palliative care: An integrative review. *Palliative & Supportive Care, 7*(3), 365–377. doi:10.1017/S1478951509990307 PMID:19788779

Lacroix, A. (1984). Occupational exposure to high demand / local control work and coronary heart disease incidence at the Framingham cohort. *Dissertation Abstracts International, 45*(2521B), 575–579.

Laftman, S. B., Modin, B., & Ostberg, V. (2013). Cyberbullying and subjective health: A large-scale study of students in Stockholm, Sweden. *Children and Youth Services Review, 35*(1), 112–119. doi:10.1016/j.childyouth.2012.10.020

Lamb, A. C., & Johnson, B. (2006). *Building treehouses for learning: Technology in today's classroom.* Recording for the Blind & Dyslexic.

Lane, D. (1997). Russian Society in Transition[Book review]. *Europe-Asia Studies, 49*(4), 727–728.

Lane, J. M. (2012). Developing the vision: Preparing teachers to deliver a digital world-class education system. *Australian Journal of Teacher Education, 37*(4), 59–74. doi:10.14221/ajte.2012v37n4.7

Lane, W., & Manner, C. (2011). The impact of personality traits on smartphone ownership and use. *International Journal of Business and Social Science, 2*(17), 22–28.

Lanter, A. (2011). Are you ready? Getting back to business after a disaster. *Information Management Journal, 45*(6), 4.

Lapan, S. D., & Quartaroli, M. T. (Eds.). (2009). *Research essentials: An introduction to designs and practices.* San Francisco, CA: John Wiley & Sons, Inc.

Lapidus, G. W. (1993). *Gender and restructuring: The impact of* perestroika *and its aftermath on Soviet women.* In V. M. Moghadam (Ed.), *Democratic reform and the position of women in transitional economies* (pp. 137–161). Oxford, UK: Clarendon Press.

Largen, K. J. (2006). Liberation, salvation, enlightenment: An exercise in comparative soteriology. *Dialog, 45*(3), 263–274. doi:10.1111/j.1540-6385.2006.00276.x

Larrabee, J. H., Janney, M. A., Ostrow, C. L., Withrow, M. L., Hobbs, G. R. Jr, & Burant, C. (2003). Predicting registered nurse job satisfaction and intent to leave. *The Journal of Nursing Administration, 33*(5), 271–283. PMID:12792282

Larson, D. B., Swyers, J. P., & McCullough, M. E. (1998). *Scientific research on spirituality and health: A report based on the Scientific Progress in Spirituality Conferences.* Bethesda, MD: National Institute for Healthcare Research.

Larson, S. S., & Larson, D. B. (1992). Clinical religious research: How to enhance risk of disease: Don't go to church. *Christian Medical Dental Society Journal, 23*(3), 14–19. PMID:1298519

Lashley, C., & Boscardin, M. L. (2003). Special education administration at a crossroads. *Journal of Special Education Leadership, 16*(2), 63–75.

Latour, B. (1987). *Science in action.* Milton Keynes, UK: Open University Press.

Laurent, A. (1983). The cultural diversity of Western conceptions of management. *International Studies of Management & Organization, 13*(1/2), 75–96. doi:10.1080/00208825.1983.11656359

Lazuras, L., Barkoukis, V., Ourda, D., & Tsorbatzoudis, H. (2013). A process model of cyberbullying in adolescence. *Computers in Human Behavior, 29*(3), 881–887. doi:10.1016/j.chb.2012.12.015

Leach, A., Hilton, S., Greenwood, B. M., Manneh, E., Dibba, B., Wilkins, A., & Mulholland, E. K. (1999). An evaluation of the informed consent procedure used during a trial of a haemophilis influenzae Type B conjugate vaccine undertaken in the Gambia, West Africa. *Social Science & Medicine, 48*(2), 139–148. PMID:10048773

LeBaron, M. (2003). *Bridging cultural conflicts: A new approach for a changing world.* San Francisco, CA: Jossey-Bass.

Lechner, F. (2001). Globalization Theories. World System's Theory. *The Globalization Website.* Retrieved from http://sociology.emory.edu/faculty/globalization/theories01.html

Lee, I. M., Rexrode, K. M., Cook, N. R., Manson, J. E., & Buring, J. E. (2001). Physical activity and coronary heart disease in women: Is "No pain, no gain" passé? *Journal of the American Medical Association, 285*(11), 1447–1454. doi:10.1001/jama.285.11.1447 PMID:11255420

Lee, W. M., Kiesner, C., Pappas, T., Lee, I., Grindle, K., Jartti, T., & Gern, J. E. et al. (2007). A diverse group of previously unrecognized human rhinoviruses are common causes of respiratory illnesses in infants. *PLoS ONE, 2*(10), e966. PMID:17912345

Lee, Y. H., Hsieh, Y. C., & Hsu, C. N. (2011). Adding innovation diffusion theory to the technology acceptance model: Supporting employees' intentions to use e-learning systems. *Journal of Educational Technology & Society, 14*(4), 124–137. Retrieved from http://www.editlib.org/p/75487

Leflar, R. B. (1996). Informed consent and patients' rights in Japan. *Houston Law Review/University of Houston, 33*(1), 1-112.

Lepak, D. P., & Snell, S. A. (2002). Examining the human resource architecture: The relationships among human capital, employment, and human resource configurations. *Journal of Management, 28*(4), 517–543. doi:10.1177/014920630202800403

Lesh, R. A., & Zawojewski, J. (2007). Problem solving and modeling. In F. K. Lester (Ed.), *Second handbook of research on mathematics teaching and learning.* NCTM.

Lester, F. K. (1994). Musing about mathematical problem solving research: 1970-1994. *Journal for Research in Mathematics Education, 25*(6), 660. doi:10.2307/749578

Levine, A. (2006). Educating school teachers. Washington, DC: The Education Schools Project. Retrieved from http://www.edschools.org/pdf/Educating_Teachers_Report.pdf

Levin, T., & Wadmany, R. (2005). Changes in educational beliefs and classroom practices of teachers and students in rich technology-based classrooms. *Technology, Pedagogy and Education, 14*(3), 281–307. doi:10.1080/14759390500200208

Lewer, J. J., & Van den Berg, H. (2007). Religion and international trade: Does the sharing of a religious culture facilitate the formation of trade networks? *American Journal of Economics and Sociology, 66*(4), 765–794. doi:10.1111/j.1536-7150.2007.00539.x

Lewis, M. W. (2000). Exploring paradox: Towards a more comprehensive guide. *Academy of Management Review, 25*(4), 760–766.

Liao, H. L., & Lu, H. P. (2008). The role of the experience and innovation characteristics in adoption and continued use of e-learning websites. *Computers & Education, 51*(4), 1405–1416. doi:10.1016/j.compedu.2007.11.006

Li, J., & Schmitt, N. (2009). The acquisition of lexical phrases in academic writing: A longitudinal case study. *Journal of Second Language Writing, 18*(2), 85–102. doi:10.1016/j.jslw.2009.02.001

Limm, H., Angerer, P., Heinmueller, M., Marten-Mittag, B., Nater, U. M., & Guendel, H. (2010). Self-perceived stress reactivity is an indicator of psychosocial impairment at the workplace. *BMC Public Health, 10*(252), 1–10. doi:10.1186/1471-2458-10-252 PMID:20470413

Lincoln, Y. S., & Guba, E. G. (1985). *Naturalistic Inquiry*. Beverly Hills, CA: Sage.

Lindberg, B., Nilsson, C., Zotterman, D., Söderberg, S., & Skär, L. (2013). Using Information and Communication Technology in Home Care for Communication between Patients, Family Members, and Healthcare Professionals: A Systematic Review. *International Journal of Telemedicine and Applications*. doi: .10.1155/2013/461829

Linden, F. (2009). epSOS local data providers. *Acta Informatica Medica, 17*(3), 142. Retrieved from http://www.ejmanager.com/mnstemps/6/6-1299792486.pdf?t=1457826043

Lindström, Å. (2005). *On the Syntax, Semantics, and Pragmatics of Architectural Principles*. Working paper. Retrieved from http://www.ics.kth.se/Publikationer/Working%20Papers/EARP-WP-2005-03.pdf

Lindström, Å. (2006). *Using architectural principles to make the it-strategy come true* (Doctoral dissertation, KTH, Royal Institute of Technology Stockholm, Sweden). Retrieved from http://citeseerx.ist.psu.edu/viewdoc/download?doi =10.1.1.64.8686&rep=rep1&type=pdf

Lin, H. R., & Bauer-Wu, S. M. (2003). Psycho-spiritual well-being in patients with advanced cancer: An integrative review of the literature. *Journal of Advanced Nursing, 44*(1), 69–80. doi:10.1046/j.1365-2648.2003.02768.x PMID:12956671

Linhart, M. (2010). *Independence in old age: Older German women living alone*. Saarbrücken: Lambert.

Li, Q. (2007). Bullying in the new playground: Research into cyberbullying and cybervictimization. *Australasian Journal of Educational Technology, 23*(4), 435–454. doi:10.14742/ajet.1245

Li, Q. (2008). A cross-cultural comparison of adolescents' experience related to cyberbullying. *Educational Research, 50*(3), 223–234. doi:10.1080/00131880802309333

Li, S., & Seale, O. (2007). Learning to do qualitative data analysis: An observational study of doctoral work. *Qualitative Health Research, 17*(10), 1442–1452. PMID:18000083

Littlejohns, P., Wyatt, J. C., & Garvican, L. (2003). Evaluating computerised health information systems: Hard lessons still to be learnt. *British Medical Journal, 326*(7394), 860–863. doi:10.1136/bmj.326.7394.860 PMID:12702622

Liu, D. (2011). The most-frequently used English phrasal verbs in American and British English: A multi-corpus examination. *TESOL Quarterly, 45*(4), 661–688. doi:10.5054/tq.2011.247707

Li, X. (2005). *Ethics, human rights, and culture: Beyond relativism and universalism*. New York, NY: Palgrave.

Li, X. H. (2004). Jiyuyuilaoku de effect dapeixingwei duibiyanjiu (A corpus-based study on the collocational behaviour of effect). *Foreign Language Education, 25*(6), 21–24.

Ljungman, P., Ward, K. N., Crooks, B. N. A., Parker, A., Martino, R., Shaw, P. J., & Cordonnier, C. et al. (2001). VI-RAL INFECTIONS-Respiratory virus infections after stem cell transplantation: A prospective study from the Infectious Diseases Working Party of the European Group for Blood and Marrow. *Bone Marrow Transplantation, 28*(5), 479–484. PMID:11593321

Lockard, J., & Abrams, P. (2003). Computer assisted instruction fundamentals. In Computers for twenty-first century educators (6th ed.). Allyn and Bacon, Pearson Education.

Lodico, M. G., Spaulding, D. T., & Voegtle, K. H. (2010). *Methods in educational research: From theory to practice* (Vol. 28). San Francisco, CA: Wiley.

Long, S. O. (1999). Family surrogacy and cancer disclosure- Physician-family negotiation of an ethical dilemma in Japan. *Journal of Palliative Care, 15*(3), 31–42. PMID:10540796

Lonner, W. J., & Ibrahim, F. A. (2008). Appraisal and Assessment in cross cultural counseling. In P. B. Pedersen, J. G. Draguns, W. J. Lonner, & J. E. Trimble (Eds.), *Counseling across cultures* (pp. 37–55). doi:10.4135/9781483329314.n3

Lord, R. G., & Hall, R. J. (2005, August). Identity, deep structure and the development of leadership skill. *The Leadership Quarterly, 16*(4), 591–615. doi:.06.00310.1016/j.leaqua.2005

Lorenz, G. (1998). Overstatement in advanced learners' writing: Stylistic aspects of adjective intensification. In S. Granger (Ed.), *Learner English on Computer* (pp. 53–66).

Lorenz, G. (1998). Overstatement in advanced learners' writing: Stylistic aspects of adjective intensification. In S. Granger (Ed.), *Learner English on computer* (pp. 53–66). London: Addison Wesley Longman.

Lorenz, G. (1999). *Adjective intensification: Learners versus native speakers. A corpus study of argumentative writing.* Amsterdam: Rodopi.

Loveday, L. (1981). Pitch, politeness and sexual role: An exploratory investigation into the pitch correlates of English and Japanese politeness formulae. *Language and Speech, 24*(1), 71–89.

Lowenberg, P. H. (1993). Issues of validity in tests of English as a world language: Whose standards? *World Englishes, 12*(1), 95–106. doi:10.1111/j.1467-971X.1993.tb00011.x

Lucas, E. (2008). *The new Cold War.* Ann Arbor, MI: Palgrave Macmillan.

Ludvigsson, J. F., Otterblad-Olausson, P., Pettersson, B. U., & Ekbom, A. (2009). The Swedish personal identity number: Possibilities and pitfalls in healthcare and medical research. *European Journal of Epidemiology, 24*(11), 659–667. doi:10.1007/s10654-009-9350-y PMID:19504049

Lue, R. (2013, December 16). *Massive Open Online Courses, MOOC's: The Future of Education?* [Audio podcast]. Retrieved from http://www.kcrw.com/news/programs/tp/tp131216massive_open_online_

Luhanga, F., Yonge, O., & Myrick, F. (2008). Hallmarks of unsafe practice: What preceptors know. *Journal for Nurses in Staff Development, 24*(6), 257–264. doi:10.1097/01.NND.0000342233.74753.ad PMID:19060655

Lundby, K., & Jolton, J. (2010). *Going global: Practical applications and recommendations for HR and OD professional in the global workplace.* San Francisco, CA: Jossey-Bass, A Wiley Imprint.

Lundgren, K. (2007). *Draken i tiden: IT-nationen Sverige* [Dragon in time: IT-nation of Sweden]. Stockholm: Studieförbundet näringsliv och samhälle (SNS). [in Swedish]

Luthans, F., Luthans, K. W., & Luthans, B. C. (2004). Positive psychological capital: Beyond human and social capital. *Business Horizons, 47*(1), 45–50. doi:.11.00710.1016/j.bushor.2003

Luthans, F., & Avolio, B. J. (2003). Authentic leadership development. In K. S. Cameron, J. E. Dutton, & R. E. Quinn (Eds.), *Positive organizational scholarship: Foundations of a new discipline* (pp. 241–258). San Francisco, CA: Berrett-Koehler.

Maani, K. E., & Cavana, R. Y. (2000). *Systems thinking and modeling: Understanding change and complexity*. Auckland, New Zealand: Pearson.

MacKenzie, D., & Wajcman, J. (1999). *The social shaping of technology* (2nd ed.). Buckingham, UK: Open University Press.

Mackness, J., Mak, S. F. J., & Williams, R. (2010). The ideals and reality of participating in a MOOC. Proceedings of the Seventh International Conference on Networked Learning. Lancaster, MI: University of Lancaster. Retrieved from http://www.lancs.ac.uk/fss/organisations/netlc/past/nlc2010/abstracts/Mackness.html

MacKnight, C. B. (2000). Teaching critical thinking through online discussions. *EDUCAUSE Quarterly, 23*(4), 38–41.

Macmillan, D. (2014, January 3). Andreessen: Bubble believers 'don't know what they're talking about'. *Wall Street Journal On-line.* Retrieved from http://online.wsj.com/news/articles/SB10001424052702303640604579298330921690014

Madden, M., Lenhart, A., Duggan, M., Cortesi, S., & Gasser, U. (2013). *Teens and technology 2013.* Retrieved from: http://www.pewinternet.org/2013/03/13/teens-and-technology-2013/

Madelung, W. (1985). *Religious schools and sects in medieval Islam* (Vol. 213). Surrey, UK: Ashgate.

Madelung, W., & Schmidtke, S. (2013). *Studies in medieval Muslim thought and history*. Surrey, UK: Ashgate.

Mahalik, J. R., Good, G. E., & Englar-Carlson, M. (2003). Masculinity scripts, presenting concerns, and help seeking: Implications for practice and training. *Professional Psychology, Research and Practice, 34*(2), 123–132. doi:10.1037/0735-7028.34.2.123

Mahroum, S. (2001). Europe and the immigration of highly skilled labour. *International Migration (Geneva, Switzerland), 39*(1), 27–43. doi:10.1111/1468-2435.00170

Maier, C. B., Glinos, I. A., Wismar, M., Bremner, J., Dussault, G., & Figueras, J. (2011). Cross-country analysis of health professional mobility in Europe: the results. *Health professional mobility and health systems. Evidence from, 17*, 23-66. Available from http://apps.who.int/iris/bitstream/10665/170421/1/Health-Professional-Mobility-Health-Systems.pdf#page=36

Maier, R. B., & Fisher, M. (2006). Strategies for digital storytelling via tabletop video: Building decision making skills in middle school students in marginalized communities. *Journal of Educational Technology Systems, 35*(2), 175–192.

Mair, C. (Ed.). (2003). *The politics of English as a world language: New horizons in postcolonial cultural studies.* Amsterdam: Rodopi.

Maloney, E. (2007). What Web 2.0 can teach us about learning? *The Chronicle of Higher Education, 53*(18), B26.

Malota, E. (2012). Global cultures? Consequences of globalization on cultural differences, a commentary approach. *International Journal of Business Insights & Transformation, 5*(3), 94–100.

Malterud, K. (2001). Qualitative research: Standards, challenges, and guidelines. *Lancet, 358*(9280), 483–488. PMID:11513933

Manjoo, F. (2013, December 31). Stop pouting about tech's next big thing, it's here, *Wall Street Journal On-line*. Retrieved from http://online.wsj.com/news/articles/SB10001424052702303640604579298330921690014

Mankin, D., Bikson, T., & Gutek, B. (1982). The office of the future: Prison or paradise? *The Futurist, 16*(3), 333–337.

Mansilla, V. B., & Gardner, H. (2007). From teaching globalization to nurturing global consciousness. In M. M. Suarez-Orozco (Ed.), *Learning in the global era: International perspectives on globalization and education*. Berkeley: University of California Press. doi:10.1525/california/9780520254343.003.0002

Mansilla, V. B., & Jackson, A. (2011). *Educating for global competence: Preparing our youth to engage the world*. New York, NY: Asia Society.

Mantala-Bozos, I. K. (2003). The role of religion and culture on bereavement: The example of the Orthodox Christian tradition. *Journal of Critical Psychology, Counselling and Psychotherapy, 3*(2), 96–110. Retrieved from https://www.hospicevolunteerassociation. org/HVANewsletter/Vol2No1_2003Mar03_The%20RoleOfReligion&CultureOnBereavement.pdf

Marangunic, N., & Granic, A. (2014). Technology acceptance model: A literature review from 1986 to 2013. *International Journal of Universal Access in the Information Society,* 1-15. doi:10.1007/s10209-014-0348-1

Marchigiano, G., Eduljee, N., & Harvey, K. (2011). Developing critical thinking skills from clinical assignments: A pilot study on nursing students' self-reported perceptions. *Journal of Nursing Management, 19*(1), 143–152. doi:10.1111/j.1365-2834.2010.01191.x PMID:21223414

Marcone, D. N., Ellis, A., Videla, C., Ekstrom, J., Ricarte, C., Carballal, G., & Echavarría, M. et al. (2013). Viral etiology of acute respiratory infections in hospitalized and outpatient children in Buenos Aires, Argentina. *The Pediatric Infectious Disease Journal, 32*(3), e105–e110. PMID:23190781

Marcovitz, D. (2012). *Digital connections in the classroom*. Washington, DC: International Society for Technology in Education.

Marcum, C. D., Higgins, G. E., Freiburger, T. L., & Ricketts, M. L. (2012). Battle of the sexes: An examination of male and female cyber bullying. *International Journal of Cyber Criminology, 6*(1), 904–911.

Marczyk, G., DeMatteo, D., & Festinger, D. (2005). *Essentials of research design and methodology*. Hoboken, NJ: John Wiley & Sons, Inc.

Marginson, S., & Rhoades, G. (2002). Beyond national states, markets, and systems of higher education: A glonacal agency heuristic. *Higher Education, 43*(3), 281–309.

Margolis, D., Dacey, J., & Kenny, M. (2007). *Adolescent development* (4th ed.). Mason, OH: Thomson.

Marini, Z., Dane, A., Bosacki, S., & Ylc-Cura, Y. (2006). Direct and indirect bully-victims: Differential psychosocial risk factors associated with adolescents involved in bullying and victimization. *Aggressive Behavior, 32*(6), 551–569. doi:10.1002/ab.20155

Markel, S. L. (2001). Technology and education online discussion forums: It's in the response. *Online Journal of Distance Learning Administration, 4*(2).

Marler, P. L., & Hadaway, C. K. (2002). "Being religious" or "being spiritual" in America: A zero-sum proposition? *Journal for the Scientific Study of Religion, 41*(2), 289–300. doi:10.1111/1468-5906.00117

Marschall, J., Piccirillo, M. L., Foxman, B., Lixin, Z., Warren, D. K., & Henderson, J. P. (2013). Patient characteristics but not virulence factors discriminate between asymptomatic and symptomatic E. coli bacteriuria in the hospital. *BMC Infectious Diseases*, *13*(1), 1–7. PMID:23663267

Marsella, A. (2012). Psychology and globalization: Understanding a complex relationship. *The Journal of Social Issues*, *68*(3), 454–472. doi:10.1111/j.1540-4560.2012.01758.x

Marshall, C., & Rossman, G. B. (2006). *Designing qualitative research* (4th ed.). Thousand Oaks, CA: Sage.

Marshall, E. (1995). *Transforming the way we work: The power of the collaborative workplace*. New York, NY: Amacom.

Marshall, H. (2007). Global education in perspective: Fostering global dimension in an English secondary school. *Cambridge Journal of Education*, *37*(3), 355–374. doi:10.1080/03057640701546672

Marshburn, D. M., Engelke, M. K., & Swanson, M. S. (2009). Relationships of new nurses' perceptions and measured performance-based clinical competence. *Journal of Continuing Education in Nursing*, *40*(9), 426–432. doi:10.3928/00220124-20090824-02 PMID:19754030

Marston, D. (2005). Tiers of intervention in responsiveness to intervention: Prevention outcomes and learning disabilities identification patterns. *Journal of Learning Disabilities*, *38*(6), 539–544. doi:10.1177/00222194050380061001 PMID:16392696

Martin, M. J. C. (1994). Managing innovation and entrepreneurship in technology-based firms. New York: Wiley IEEE. Retrieved from https://books.google.se/books?id=fnE7R732COMC&printsec=frontcover&redir_esc=y#v=onepage&q&f=false

Martin, C. (2002). The theory of critical thinking of nursing. *Nursing Education Perspectives*, *23*(5), 243–247. PMID:12483815

Martin, S. E. (1988). *A reference grammar of Japanese*. Rutland, VT: Tuttle.

Masel, M. C., Raji, M., & Peek, M. (2010). Education and physical activity mediate the relationship between ethnicity and cognitive function in late middle-aged adults. *Ethnicity & Health*, *15*(3), 283–302. doi:10.1080/13557851003681273 PMID:20401816

Masojć, M., & Bech, J. (2011). Introduction. *Acta Archaeologica*, *82*(1), 203-204. doi:.1600-0390.2011.00460.x10.1111/j

Mason, J. W. T. (2002). *The meaning of Shinto*. Victoria, CA: Trafford.

Mason, K. (2008). Cyberbullying: A preliminary assessment for school personnel. *Psychology in the Schools*, *45*(4), 323–348. doi:10.1002/pits.20301

Mataric, M. J. (2004, March). *Robotics education for all ages*. Paper presented at AAAI Spring Symposium on Accessible, Hands-on AI and Robotics Education, San Jose, CA.

Matesanz, R. (1998). Cadaveric organ donation: Comparison of legislation in various countries of Europe. *Nephrology, Dialysis, Transplantation*, *13*(7), 1632–1635. PMID:9681702

Mather, N., Bos, C., & Babur, N. (2001). Perceptions and knowledge of preservice and inservice teachers about early literacy instruction. *Journal of Learning Disabilities*, *34*(5), 472–482. doi:10.1177/002221940103400508 PMID:15503595

Mathieson, K. (1991). Predicting user intentions: Comparing the technology acceptance model with the theory of planned behavior. *Information Systems Research*, *2*(3), 173–191. doi:10.1287/isre.2.3.173

Matlack, C. (2008, February 29). Renault's Ghosn takes on a Russian relic. *Bloomberg Business*. Retrieved from http://www.bloomberg.com/bw/stories/2008-02-29/renaults-ghosn-takes-on-a-russian-relicbusinessweek-business-news-stock-market-and-financial-advice

Maxwell, J. A. (1992). Understanding and validity in qualitative research. *Harvard Educational Review, 62*(3), 279–301.

May, D., Chan, A., Hodges, T. D., & Avolio, B. J. (2003). Developing the moral component of authentic leadership. *Organizational Dynamics, 21*(3), 247–260. doi:(03)00032-910.1016/s0090-2616

McAuley, A., Stewart, B., Siemens, G., & Cormier, D. (2010). *The MOOC model for digital practice*. Unpublished manuscript, University of Prince Edward Island. Retrieved from http://www.elearnspace.org/Articles/MOOC_Final.pdf

McCabe, L. T. (1997). Global perspective development. *Education, 118*(1), 41–46.

McCarthy, D., Puffer, S., & Simmonds, P. J. (1993). Riding the Russian roller coaster: U.S. firms' recent experience and future plans in the former USSR. *California Management Review, 36*(1), 99–115. doi:10.2307/41165736

McCormick, P., & Elliston, F. (Eds.). (1981). *Husserl: Shorter works*. South Bend, IN: University of Notre Dame Press.

McFarland, H. N. (1967). *The rush hour of the gods: A study of new religious movements in Japan* (Vol. 171). New York, NY: Macmillan.

McGarry, B. (2013, March 27). Army set to introduce smartphones into combat. *Military.com*. Retrieved from www.military.com/daily-news/2013/03/27/army-set-to-introduce-smartphones-into-combat.html

McGaughey, D. R. (2006). Kant on religion and science: Independence or integration? Zygon. *Journal Of Religion & Science, 41*(3), 727–746.

McGee, M. K. (1996, March4). Burnout. *Information Week, 56*(9), 34–40.

McHatton, P.A., Gordon, K.D., & Glenn, T.L., & Sue. (2012). Troubling special education leadership: Finding purpose, potential, and possibility in challenging contexts. *Journal of Special Education Leadership, 25*(1), 38–47.

McHugh Schuster, P., & Nykolyn, L. (2010). *Communication for nurses: How to prevent harmful events and promote patient safety*. Philadelphia, PA: F. A. Davis Company.

McKay, S. (2002). *Teaching English as an international language: Rethinking goals and approaches*. Oxford, UK: Oxford University Press.

McKee, R. (1997). *Story, substance, style, and the principles of screenwriting*. New York, NY: Regan.

McLafferty, C. L. Jr, Slate, J. R., & Onwuegbuzie, A. J. (2010). Transcending the quantitative-qualitative divide with mixed methods research: A multidimensional framework for understanding congruence and completeness in the study of values. *Counseling and Values, 55*(1), 46–62.

McLeod, D. B. (1992). Research on affect in mathematics education: A reconceptualization. In D. A. Grouws (Ed.), *Handbook of research on mathematics teaching and learning* (p. 575). New York: Macmillan.

McLeod, J. (2001). *Qualitative research in counseling and psychotherapy*. London, UK: Sage.

McLoughlin, C., & Lee, M. J. (2007, December). Social software and participatory learning: Pedagogical choices with technology affordances in the Web 2.0 era. In Proceedings of Ascilite Singapore 2007 ICT: Providing choices for learners and learning (pp. 664-675). Singapore.

McLoughlin, D., & Mynard, J. (2009). An analysis of higher order thinking in online discussions. *Innovations in Education and Teaching International, 46*(2), 147–160.

McLuhan, M. (1964). Understanding Media: The extensions of man. Cambridge, MA: MIT Press.

McLuhan, M. (1967). *Understanding media: The extension of man.* London, UK: Sphere.

McMaster, K. L., & Wagner, D. (2007). Monitoring response to general education instruction. In S. R. Jimerson, M. K. Burns, & A. M. VanDerHeyden (Eds.), *Handbook of response to intervention.* New York, NY: Springer. doi:10.1007/978-0-387-49053-3_16

McQuade, C. S., Colt, P. J., & Meyer, B. N. (2009). *Cyber bullying: Protecting kids and adults from online bullies.* Westport: Praeger.

Meadows, M. S. (2008). *I, avatar: The culture and consequences of having a second life.* Berkeley, CA: New Riders.

Means, B., Toyama, Y., Murphy, R., Bakia, M., & Jones, K. (2009). *Evaluation of evidence-based practices in online learning: A meta-analysis and review of online-learning studies.* Washington, DC: U.S. Department of Education.

MEB. (2005). *İlköğretim matematik dersi (6, 7, 8. Sınıflar) öğretim programı.* Ankara: Devlet Kitapları Müdürlüğü.

Mechitov, A., & Peper, M. J. (1998). Business education in free-market Russia: Opportunism or enlightened self-interest? *Convergence, 31*(4), 23–32.

Medvedev, R. (2000). *Post-Soviet Russia: A journey through the Yeltsin Era.* New York, NY: Columbia University Press.

Meeker, M., & Wu, L. (2013, May 29). *Internet trends.* Presentation to the D11 conference. Abstract retrieved from http://www.kpcb.com/insights/2013-internet-trends

Meindl, J. R. (1990). On leadership: An alternative to the conventional wisdom. In B. M. Staw & L. L. Cummings (Eds.), *Research in organizational behavior* (Vol. 12, pp. 159–203). Greenwich, CT: JAI.

Mejiuni, O., & Obilade, O. (2006). The dialectics of poverty, educational opportunities, and ICTs. In A. Oduaran & H. S. Bhola (Eds.), *Widening Access to Education As Social Justice* (pp. 139–148). The Netherlands: Springer. doi:10.1007/1-4020-4324-4_9

Melendez, M. M., & Alizadeh, K. (2011). Complications from international surgery tourism. *Aesthetic Surgery Journal, 31*(6), 694–697. PMID:21813883

Mellard, D. F., Deshler, D. D., & Barth, A. (2004). LD identification: It's not simply a matter of building a better mouse-trap. *Learning Disability Quarterly, 27*(4), 229–242. doi:10.2307/1593675

Mellard, D. F., Stern, A., & Woods, K. (2011). RTI school-based practices and evidence-based models. *Focus on Exceptional Children, 43*(6), 1–15.

Mendelsohn, R. S. (1980). *Confessions of a medical heretic.* IN, Lebanon: Warner.

Mendenhall, A., & Johnson, T. E. (2010). Fostering the development of critical thinking skills, and reading comprehension of undergraduates using a Web 2.0 tool coupled with a learning system. *Interactive Learning Environments, 18*(3), 263–276.

Meraviglia, M. G. (2004). The effects of spirituality on well-being of people with lung cancer. *Oncology Nursing Forum, 31*(1), 89–94. doi:10.1188/04.ONF.89-94 PMID:14722592

Meraviglia, M. G. (2006). Effects of spirituality in breast cancer survivors. *Oncology Nursing Forum, 33*(1), E1–E7. doi:10.1188/06.ONF.E1-E7 PMID:16470229

Merleau-Ponty, M. (1962). *Phenomenology of perception.* London, UK: Routledge.

Merriam, S. B. (1993). Taking Stock. *New Directions for Adult and Continuing Education, 1993*(57), 105–110. doi:10.1002/ace.36719935712

Merriam, S. B. (2001). Andragogy and self-directed learning: Pillars of adult learning theory. *New Directions for Adult and Continuing Education, 2001*(89), 3–14. doi:10.1002/ace.3

Merriam, S. B. (2001). *Qualitative research and case study applications in education: Revised and expanded from case study research in education.* San Francisco, CA: Jossey-Bass.

Merriam, S. B. (2009). *Qualitative research and case study applications in education.* Jossey-Bass.

Merriam, S. B., Cafarella, R. S., & Baumgartner, L. M. (2007). *Learning in adulthood: A comprehensive guide.* San Francisco, CA: Jossey-Bass.

Mesch, G. S. (2009). Parental mediation, online activities, and cyberbullying. *Cyberpsychology & Behavior, 12*(4), 387–393. doi:10.1089/cpb.2009.0068 PMID:19630583

Meservy, T. (2013, September 5). *Re: Lying in a text message? Response delay trips people up.* [Web log post]. Retrieved from http://www.science20.com/news_articles/lying_text_message_response_delay_trips_people-119823

Metzger, M. J., & Flanagin, A. J. (2013). Credibility and trust of information in online environments: The use of cognitive heuristics. *Journal of Pragmatics, 59,* 210–220. doi:10.1016/j.pragma.2013.07.012

Mevarech, Z. R., & Fridkin, S. (2006). The effects of IMPROV on mathematical knowledge, mathematical reasoning, and meta-cognition. *Metacognition and Learning, 1*(1), 85–97. doi:10.1007/s11409-006-6584-x

Michael, P. (2001). Strategy and the Internet. *Harvard Business Review, 79*(3), 62–78. PMID:11246925

Michaels, C. N., & Greene, A. M. (2013). Worksite wellness: Increasing adoption of workplace health promotion programs. *Health Promotion Practice, 14*(4), 473–479. doi:10.1177/1524839913480800 PMID:23545334

Michigan Corpus of Upper-level Student Papers . (2009). Ann Arbor, MI: The Regents of the University of Michigan. Available at: http://micusp.elicorpora.info/

Middlestadt, S. E., Sheats, J. L., Geshnizjani, A., Sullivan, M. R., & Arvin, C. S. (2011). Factors associated with participation in work-site wellness programs: Implications for increasing willingness among rural service employees. *Health Education & Behavior, 38*(5), 502–509. doi:10.1177/1090198110384469 PMID:21482700

Mikhailova, L. I. (2012). Russians' sense of social well-being and perception of the future. *Russian Social Science Review, 53*(1), 4–13. doi:10.1080/10611428.2012.11065461

Miles, M. B., & Huberman, A. M. (1994). *Qualitative data analysis* (2nd ed.). Thousand Oaks, CA: Sage.

Miller, R. A. (1967). *The Japanese language.* Chicago, IL: University of Chicago Press.

Miller, W. R., & Thoresen, C. E. (2003). Spirituality, religion, and health: An emerging research field. *The American Psychologist, 58*(1), 24–35. doi:10.1037/0003-066X.58.1.24 PMID:12674816

Mills, J., Bonner, A., & Francis, K. (2008). The development of constructivist grounded theory. *International Journal of Qualitative Methods, 5*(1), 25–35.

Milne, J., & Oberle, K. (2005). Enhancing rigor in qualitative description. *Journal of Wound, Ostomy, and Continence Nursing, 32*(6), 413–420. PMID:16301909

Milton, J., & Freeman, R. (1996). Lexical variation in the writing of Chinese learners of English. In C.E. Percy, C.F. Meyer, & I. Lancashire (Eds.), *Synchronic Corpus Linguistics:Papers from the sixteenth international conference on English language research on computerized corpora (ICAME 16)* (pp. 121-131). Amsterdam: Rodopi.

Milton, J. (2001). *Research reports V2: Elements of a written interlanguage: A computational and corpus-based study of institutional influences on the acquisition of English by Hong Kong Chinese students*. Hong Kong: Hong Kong University of Science & Technology Press.

Mimura, N., Yasuhara, K., Kawagoe, S., Yokoki, H., & Kazama, S. (2011). Damage from the Great East Japan Earthquake and Tsunami-a quick report. *Mitigation and Adaptation Strategies for Global Change, 16*(7), 803–818.

Mindt, D., & Weber, C. (1989). Prepositions in American and British English. *World Englishes, 8*(2), 229–238. doi:10.1111/j.1467-971X.1989.tb00658.x

Miranda, B., & Matesanz, R. (1998). International issues in transplantation: Setting the scene and flagging the most urgent and controversial issues. *Annals of the New York Academy of Sciences, 862*(1), 129–143. PMID:9928215

Mitchell, J., Keane, J., & Laidlaw, J. (2009). *Making success work for the poor: Package tourism in Northern Tanzania*. London, UK: Overseas Development Institute.

Mitchell, K. J., Ybarra, M., & Finkelhor, D. (2007). The relative importance of online victimization in understanding depression, delinquency, and substance use. *Child Maltreatment, 12*(4), 314–324. doi:10.1177/1077559507305996 PMID:17954938

Mitton, C., Peacock, S., Storch, J., Smith, N., & Cornelissen, E. (2010). Moral distress among healthcare managers: Conditions, consequences and potential responses. *Health Policy (Amsterdam), 6*(2), 99. PMID:22043226

Moats, L. (1994). The missing foundation in teacher education: Knowledge of the structure of spoken and written language. *Annals of Dyslexia, 44*, 81–102.

Mohamed, M. A. (2015). Classifying Muslims. *Cross Currents, 65*(3), 334–345. doi:10.1111/cros.12143

Moldova Human Development Report. (2014). *Good Corporate Citizens: Public and Private Goals aligned for Human Development*. Chisinau: UNDP, Republic of Moldova. Retrieved from http://hdr.undp.org/sites/default/files/engleza_final.pdf

Moldovenii. (2011, November 1). *Tourism in Moldova*. Retrieved from http://www.moldovenii.md/en/section/311

Monsma, S. V. (2007). Religion and philanthropic giving and volunteering: Building blocks for civic responsibility. *Interdisciplinary Journal of Research on Religion, 3*, Art. 1. Available from http://www.religjournal.com/articles/article_view.php?id=19

Moore, G. C., & Benbasat, I. (1991). Development of an instrument to measure perceptions of adopting an information technology innovation. *Information Systems Research, 2*(3), 192-222. Retrieved from 10.1287/isre.2.3.192

Moore, M. J., Nakano, T. N., Enomoto, A., & Suda, T. (2012). Anonymity and roles associated with aggressive posts in an online forum. *Computers in Human Behavior, 28*(3), 861–867. doi:10.1016/j.chb.2011.12.005

Moran, M., Seaman, J., & Tinti-Kane, H. (2011). Teaching, learning, and sharing: How today's higher education faculty use social media. *The Educational Resources Information Center*. Retrieved from http://eric.ed.gov/?id=ED535130

Morewedge, P. (1979). *Islamic philosophical theology*. Albany, NY: State University of New York Press.

Morita, E. (2003). Children's use of address and reference terms: Language socialization in a Japanese-English bilingual environment. *Multilingua, 22*(4), 367–396.

Morreale, V. (2003, February 10). *Te.S.C.He.T. (Technology System for Cultural Heritage in Tourism).* FIPA Meeting, Palermo. Retrieved from http://docplayer.net/4172689-Te-s-c-he-t-technology-system-for-cultural-heritage-in-tourism-vito-morreale-engineering-ingegneria-informatica-s-p-a-fipa-meeting-palermo-10th.html

Morris, R. (1988). Northern Europe invades the Mediterranean, 900–1200. In G. Holmes (Ed.), The Oxford history of medieval Europe (pp. 165–221). Oxford, UK: Oxford University Press.

Morris, J., & Polese, A. (2013). *The informal post-Socialist economy.* New York, NY: Routledge.

Morrison, J. (2013, January 2). *MOOCs: Daphne Koller of Coursera shares insights* [Web log post]. Retrieved from http://digitalpresent.myblog.arts.ac.uk/2013/02/01/moocs-daphne-koller-of-coursera-shares-insights/

Morrow, S. L. (2005). Quality and trustworthiness in qualitative research in counseling psychology. *Journal of Counseling Psychology, 52*(2), 250.

Morrow, S. L., & Smith, M. L. (2000). Qualitative research for counseling psychology. In S. D. Brown & R. W. Lent (Eds.), *Handbook of Counseling Psychology* (3rd ed.; pp. 199–230). New York, NY: Wiley.

Morse, J. M., Barrett, M., Mayan, M., Olson, K., & Spiers, J. (2002). Verification strategies for establishing reliability and validity in qualitative research. *International Journal of Qualitative Methods, 1*(2), Article 2. Retrieved July 4 2002 from http://www.ualberta.ca/~ijqm/

Morse, J. M., Barrett, M., Mayan, M., Olson, K., & Spiers, J. (2008). Verification Strategies for Establishing Reliability and Validity in Qualitative Research. *International Journal of Qualitative Methods, 1*(2), 13–22.

Morse, J. M., & Richards, L. (2002). *Readme first for a users guide to qualitative methods.* Thousand Oaks, CA: Sage.

Mosby's. (n.d.). *Mosby's Medical Dictionary* (8th ed.). Elsevier.

Moses, J. (2007). *Oneness: Great principles shared by all religions.* New York, NY: Random House.

Mossberg, W. (2013, April 10). Facebook gets a hold on phones. *Wall Street Journal*, p. D1.

Moustakas, C. (1994). *Phenomenological research methods.* Thousand Oaks, CA: Sage.

Mouttapa, M., Valente, T., Gallagher, P., Rohrbach, L. A., & Unger, J. B. (2004). Social network predictor of bullying and victimization. *Adolescence, 39*, 315–335. PMID:15563041

Murphie, A., & Potts, J. (2003). *Culture and technology.* Basingstoke, UK: Palgrave Macmillan.

Murphy, L. R. (1987). A review of organizational stress management research: Methodological considerations. *Journal of Organizational Behavior Management, 8*(2), 215–227. doi:10.1300/J075v08n02_13

Mur-Veeman, I., van Raak, A., & Paulus, A. (2008). Comparing integrated care policy in Europe: Does policy matter? *Health Policy (Amsterdam), 85*(2), 172–183. doi:10.1016/j.healthpol.2007.07.008 PMID:17767975

Mustaffa, C., & Ilias, M. (2013). Relationship between students' adjustment factors and cross-cultural adjustment: A survey at the Northern University of Malaysia. *Intercultural Communication Studies, 22*(1), 279–300. Retrieved from http://web.uri.edu/iaics/files/19Che-Su-Mustaffa-Munirah-Ilias.pdf

Nagai-Jacobson, M. G., & Burkhardt, M. A. (1989). Spirituality: Cornerstone of holistic nursing practice. *Holistic Nursing Practice, 3*(3), 18–26. doi:10.1097/00004650-198905000-00006 PMID:2768352

Nagel, D. (2014, June). Spending on instructional tech to reach $19 billion within 5 years. *THE Journal.* Retrieved from https://thejournal.com/Articles/2014/06/11/Spending-on-Instructional-Tech-To-Reach-19-Billion-Within-5-Years.aspx?p=1

Nagel, P. (2014). Critical thinking and technology. *Social Studies and the Young Learner, 26*(4), 1–4.

Nair, G. G., & Stamler, L. L. (2013). A conceptual framework for developing a critical thinking self-assessment scale. *The Journal of Nursing Education, 52*(3), 131–138. doi:10.3928/01484834-20120215-01 PMID:23402245

Narayanasamy, A. (2001). *Spiritual care: A practical guide for nurses and health care practitioners.* Dunfermline, UK: Quay.

Narkon, D. E., & Black, R. S. (2008). Pre-Service teachers' confidence in teaching reading acquisition skills to struggling readers and readers in general. *Electronic Journal for Inclusive Education, 2*(3).

Natanson, M. (Ed.). (1973). *Phenomenology and the social sciences.* Evanston, IL: Northwestern University Press.

National Center for Education Statistics. (2003). *Remedial education at degree-granting postsecondary institutions in fall 2000* (NCÉS 2004-010). Retrieved from U.S. Department of Education website: http://nces.ed.gov/pubsearch/pubsinfo.asp?pubid=2004010

National Commission for the Protection of Human Subjects of Biomedical and Behavioral Research. (1979). *The Belmont report: Ethical principles and guidelines for the protection of human subjects of research.* Retrieved from http://www.hhs.gov/ohrp/humansubjects/guidance/belmont.html

National Council of Teachers of Mathematics (NCTM). (2000). *Principles and standards for school mathematics.* Reston, VA: Author.

National Council of Teachers of Mathematics (NCTM). (2010). *Common core state standards.* Reston, VA: Author.

National Human Development Report. (2014) Good Corporate Citizens: Public and Private Goals Aligned for Human Development. Chisinau. http://hdr.undp.org/sites/ default/files/engleza_final.pdf. Accessed 21 July 2016

National Mathematics Advisory Panel (NMAP). (2008). *Foundations for success: The final report of the national Mathematics Advisory Panel.* Washington, DC: U.S. Department of Education.

National Reading Panel. (2000). *Teaching children to read: An evidence-based assessment of the scientific research literature on reading and its implications for reading instruction (NIH Publication No. 00-4769).* Bethesda, MD: National Institute of Child Health & Human Development.

National Research Council (NRC). (1998). *Preventing reading difficulties in young children.* Washington, DC: National Academy Press.

Navarro, R., Serna, C., Martinez, V., & Ruiz-Oliva, R. (2013). The role of Internet use and parental mediation on cyberbullying victimization among Spanish children from rural public schools. *European Journal of Psychology of Education, 28*(3), 725–745. doi:10.1007/s10212-012-0137-2

Neale, B., & Bishop, L. (2012). The timescapes archive: A stakeholder approach to archiving qualitative longitudinal data. *Qualitative Research, 12*(1), 53–65.

Nelson, J. M. (2009). Psychology, religion, and spirituality. New York, NY: Springer.

Nelson, A. R., Sawai, Y., Jennings, A. E., Bradley, L. A., Gerson, L., Sherrod, B. L., & Horton, B. P. et al. (2008). Great-earthquake paleogeodesy and tsunamis of the past 2000 years at Alsea Bay, central Oregon coast, USA. *Quaternary Science Reviews, 27*(7), 747–768.

Nelson, D. R. (2009). *What's wrong with sin: Sin in individual and social perspective from Schleiermacher to theologies of liberation.* New York, NY: T & T Clark.

Nelson, J. M. (2012). A history of psychology of religion in the West: Implications for theory and method. *Pastoral Psychology, 61*(5-6), 685–710.

Nelson, J. M., & Slife, B. D. (2012). Theoretical and epistemological foundations. In L. J. Miller (Ed.), *The Oxford handbook of psychology and spirituality* (pp. 21–35). Oxford, UK: Oxford University Press.

Nesbit, T. (1995). *Teaching mathematics to adults.* Paper presented at the annual meeting of the American educational research association, San Francisco, CA.

Nesselhauf, N. (2003). The use of collocations by advanced learners of English and some implications for teaching. *Applied Linguistics, 24*(2), 223–242. doi:10.1093/applin/24.2.223

Neuberg, S. L., Kenrick, D. T., & Schaller, M. (2011). Human threat management systems: Self-protection and disease avoidance. *Neuroscience and Biobehavioral Reviews, 35*(4), 1042–1051. doi:10.1016/j.neubiorev.2010.08.011 PMID:20833199

Neustupny, J. V. (1978). *Post-structural approaches to language: Language theory in a Japanese context.* Tokyo, Japan: University of Tokyo Press.

Neville, B. H., Merrill, R. M., & Kumpfer, K. L. (2011). Longitudinal outcomes of a comprehensive, incentivized worksite wellness program. *Evaluation & the Health Professions, 34*(1), 103–123. doi:10.1177/0163278710379222 PMID:20696740

Nicholson, B., & Sahay, S. (2001). Some political and cultural issues in the globalisation of software development: Case experience from Britain and India. *Information and Organization, 11*(1), 25–43.

Nicholson, W. J., Perkel, G., & Selikoff, I. J. (1982). Occupational exposure to asbestos: Population at risk and projected mortality—1980–2030. *American Journal of Industrial Medicine, 3*(3), 259–311. doi:10.1002/ajim.4700030305 PMID:7171087

Nightengale, K. (2014, 14 February). *Re: The Army and IT.* [Online forum comment]. Retrieved from http://www.warlordloop.org/

Nigosian, S. A. (2010). Religion through the ages. *Theological Review, 31*(2), 179–202. Retrieved from EBSCOhost database. (Accession No. 59664996) rfroebsco

Nigosian, S. A. (2000). *World religions: A historical approach* (3rd ed.). New York, NY: Bedford/St. Martin's.

Nisbett, R. E., Peng, K., Choi, I., & Norenzayan, A. (2001). Culture and systems of thought: Holistic versus analytic cognition. *Psychological Review, 108*(2), 291–310. PMID:11381831

Nocentini, A., Calmaestra, J., Schultze-Krumbholz, A., Scheithauer, H., Ortega, R., & Menesini, E. (2010). Cyberbullying: Labels, behaviours and definition in three European countries. *Australian Journal of Guidance & Counselling, 20*(02), 129–142. doi:10.1375/ajgc.20.2.129

Noor-Ul-Amin, S. (2013). An effective use of ICT for education and learning by drawing on worldwide knowledge, research and experience: ICT as a change agent for education. *Scholarly Journal of Education, 2*(4), 38–54.

Norman, D. A. (2002). *The design of everyday things.* New York, NY: Basic.

Northouse, P. G. (2010). *Leadership: Theory and practice.* Thousand Oaks, CA: Sage.

Norwood, S. L. (2010). *Research essentials: Foundations for evidence-based practice.* Upper Saddle River, NJ: Pearson Education, Inc.

Noti, E. (2013). Web 2.0 and its influence in the tourism sector. *European Scientific Journal, 9*(20), 115–123.

Nourbakhsh, I. R., Crowley, K., Bhave, A., Hamner, E., Hsiu, T., Perez-Bergquist, A., & Wilkinson, K. et al. (2005). The robotic autonomy mobile robotics course: Robot design, curriculum design and educational assessment. *Autonomous Robots*, *18*(1), 103–127.

Nowalk, M. P., Prendergast, J. M., Bayles, C. M., D'Amico, F. J., & Colvin, G. C. (2001). A randomized trial of exercise programs among older individuals living in two long-term care facilities: The FallsFREE program. *Journal of the American Geriatrics Society*, *49*(7), 859–865. doi:10.1046/j.1532-5415.2001.49174.x PMID:11527475

Nuremberg Code. (1949). *The Nuremberg Code. Trials of war criminals before the Nuremberg military tribunals under control council law*. Washington, DC: U.S. Government Printing Office. Retrieved from: http://ora.georgetown.edu/irb/BioMedManual/AppendixIV.pdf

Nytrø, Ø., & Faxvaag, A. (2004). *Healthcare informatics towards 2020. In Infosam 2020, Information Society of 2020* (pp. 127–133). Trondheim, Norway: NTNU.

O'Bryant, A. (2012). *Cone discusses how TRADOC is shaping army of the future*. Retrieved from http://www.army.mil/article/74403

O'Kell, S. P. (1988). A study of the relationships between learning style, readiness for self-directed learning, and teaching preference of learner nurses in one health district. *Nurse Education Today*, *8*(4), 197–204. doi:10.1016/0260-6917(88)90149-9 PMID:3419409

O'Leary, R., & Ramsden, A. (2002). Virtual learning environments. Learning and Teaching. *Support Network Generic Centre/ALT Guides, LTSN*. Retrieved July 12, 2005, from ftp://www.bioscience.heacademy.ac.uk/Resources/gc/elearn2.pdf

O'Reilly, R. (2005). *What is Web 2.0.? Design patterns and business models for the next generation of software*. Retrieved from www.oreillynet.com/ pub/a/oreilly/tim/news /2005/09/30/what-isweb-20.html

Oberle, K., & Hughes, D. (2001). Doctors' and nurses' perceptions of ethical problems in end-of-life decisions. *Journal of Advanced Nursing*, *33*(6), 707–715. PMID:11298208

Ocak, M. A., Gökçearslan, Ş., & Solmaz, E. (2014). Investigating Turkish pre-service teachers' perceptions of blogs: Implications for the FATIH project. *Contemporary Educational Technology*, *5*(1), 22–38.

Ochi, M. (2013). Shinya Yamanaka's 2012 Nobel Prize and the radical change in orthopedic strategy thanks to his discovery of iPS cells. *Acta Orthopaedica*, *84*(1), 1–3. PMID:23343378

O'Connor, E. P., & Freeman, E. W. (2012). District-level considerations in supporting and sustaining RtI implementation. *Psychology in the Schools*, *49*(3), 297–310. doi:10.1002/pits.21598

OECD (2015). *Internet access (indicator)*. doi: 10.1787/69c2b997-en

OECD. (2005). *Are students ready for a technology-rich world? What PISA studies tell us*. OECD.

OECD. (2012). *Education Indicators in focus*. Retrieved from http://www.oecd.org/education/skills-beyond-school/49729932.pdf

OECD. (2013). Health at a Glance 2013: OECD Indicators, OECD, Paris. OECD Publishing.

Oermann, M., Poole-Dawkins, K., Alvarez, M., Foster, B., & O'Sullivan, R. (2010). Managers' perspectives of new graduates of accelerated nursing programs: How do they compare with other graduates? *Journal of Continuing Education in Nursing*, *41*(9), 394–400. doi:10.3928/00220124-20100601-01 PMID:20540465

Oestigaard, T. (2009). The materiality of hell: The Christian hell in a world religion context. *Material Religion*, *5*(3), 312–331. doi:10.2752/175183409X12550007729941

Ogawa, N., & Retherford, R. D. (1993). Care of the elderly in Japan: Changing norms and expectations. *Journal of Marriage and the Family*, *55*(3), 585–597. doi:10.2307/353340

Ogawa, N., & Retherford, R. D. (1997). Shifting costs of caring for the elderly back to families in Japan: Will it work? *Population and Development Review*, *23*(1), 59–94. doi:10.2307/2137461

Ogundokun, M. O. (2011). Learning style, school environment and test anxiety as correlates of learning outcomes among secondary school students. *Ife Psychologia*, *19*(2), 321–336. doi:10.4314/ifep.v19i2.69555

Ohler, J. (2006). The world of digital storytelling. *Educational Leadership*, *63*(4), 44–47.

Ohler, J. B. (2013). *Digital storytelling in the classroom: New media pathways to literacy, learning, and creativity*. Corwin.

Oja, K. (2011). Using problem-based learning in the clinical setting to improve nursing students' critical thinking: An evidence review. *The Journal of Nursing Education*, *50*(3), 145–151. doi:10.3928/01484834-20101230-10 PMID:21210603

Okamoto, Y. (1996). Modeling children's understanding of quantitative relations in texts: A developmental perspective. *Cognition and Instruction*, *14*(4), 409–440. doi:10.1207/s1532690xci1404_1

Oklahoma Board of Nursing. (2011). *Rules*. Retrieved from http://www.ok.gov/nursing/ed-schls2.pdf

Olenik-Shemesh, D., Heiman, T., & Eden, S. (2012). Cyberbullying victimisation in adolescence: Relationships with loneliness and depressive mood. *Emotional & Behavioural Difficulties*, *17*(3-4), 361–374. doi:10.1080/13632752.2012.704227

Olson, L. L. (1998). Hospital nurses' perceptions of the ethical climate of their work setting. *Journal of Nursing Scholarship*, *30*(4), 345–349. PMID:9866295

Olweus, D. (1999). Sweden. In K. Smith, Y. Morita, J. Junger-Tas, D. Olweus, R. Catalano, & P. Slee (Eds.), *The nature of school bullying: A cross-national perspective* (pp. 7–27). New York, NY: Routledge.

Organisation for Economic Co-operation and Development. (2013). *Health at a glance 2013: OECD indicators*. doi:10.1787/health_glance-2013-en

Organisation Mondiale du Tourisme (OMT). (2007). *Guide Pratique de Gestion des Destinations*. Madrid: OMT. Retrieved from http://pub.unwto.org/WebRoot/Store/Shops/Infoshop/4745/8BCE/AD9A/ECA8/048B/C0A8/0164/0B7A/140529_guide_pratique_gestion_FR_excerpt.pdf

Organisation Mondiale du Tourisme and SNV (Netherlands Development Organisation). (2015). *Manuel sur le tourisme et la réduction de la pauvreté – Des mesures pratiques pour les destinations*. Madrid: OMT.

Organisation Mondiale du Tourisme. (2002). *Le Tourisme et la Réduction de la Pauvreté*. Madrid: OMT. Retrieved from http://www.gret.org/static/cdrom/bds/document_pdf/numero_6/Le%20tourisme%20et%20la%20reduction%20de%20la%20pauvrete.pdf

Organisation Mondiale du Tourisme. (2005). *La Réduction de la Pauvreté par le Tourisme: un recueil de bonnes pratiques*. Madrid: OMT.

Orlikowski, W. J. (1991). Integrated information environment or matrix of control?: The contradictory implications of information technology. *Accounting, Management, and Information Technology*, *1*(1), 9–42. doi:10.1016/0959-8022(91)90011-3

O'Rourke, K. H., & Williamson, J. G. (2002). When did globalisation begin? *European Review of Economic History*, *6*(1), 23–50. doi:10.1017/S1361491602000023

Orsolini-Hain, L., & Waters, V. (2009). Education evolution: A historical perspective of associate degree nursing. *The Journal of Nursing Education, 48*(5), 266–271. doi:10.9999/0144834-20090416-05 PMID:19476031

Osimk, R. (2009). Decoding sounds: An experimental approach to intelligibility in ELF. *Vienna English Working Papers, 18*, 64–89.

Owston, R. D. (1997). The world wide web: A technology to enhance teaching and learning. *Educational Researcher, 26*(2), 27–33.

Oxfam. (2006). *Education for global citizenship: A guide for schools*. Retrieved July 30, 2011, from http://www.oxfam.org.uk/education/gc/files/ education_for_global_citizenship_a_guide_for_schools.pdf

Oyaid, A. (2009). *Education policy in Saudi Arabia and its relation to secondary school teachers' ICT use, perceptions, and views of the future of ICT in education*. (Unpublished dissertation). University of Exeter, Exeter, UK.

Özay, E., Kaya, E., & Sezek, F. (2004). Application of a questionnaire to describe teacher communication behaviour and its association with students in science in Turkey. *Journal of Baltic Science Education, 3*(2), 15–21.

Ozminkowski, R. J., Ling, D., Goetzel, R. Z., Bruno, J. A., Rutter, K. R., Isaac, F., & Wang, S. (2002, January). Long-term impact of Johnson & Johnson's health & wellness program on health care utilization and expenditures. *Journal of Occupational and Environmental Medicine, 44*(1), 21–29. doi:10.1097/00043764-200201000-00005 PMID:11802462

Pacific Policy Research Center (PPRC). (2010). *21st century skills for students and teachers*. Honolulu, HI: Kamehameha Schools, Research & Evaluation Division.

Pai, F.-Y., & Huang, K.-I. (2011). Applying the technology acceptance model to the introduction of healthcare information systems. *Technological Forecasting and Social Change, 78*(4), 650–660. doi:10.1016/j.techfore.2010.11.007

Palm, T. (2008). Impact of authenticity on sense making in word problems solving. *Educational Studies in Mathematics, 67*(1), 37–58. doi:10.1007/s10649-007-9083-3

Pang, M. C. S. (2003). *Nursing ethics in modern China: Conflicting values and competing role requirements*. Amsterdam, NL: Rodopi.

Pang, S. M., Sawada, A., Konishi, E., Olsen, D. P., Yu, P. L. H., Chan, M., & Mayumi, N. (2003). A comparative study of Chinese, American and Japanese nurses' perceptions of ethical role responsibilities. *Nursing Ethics, 10*(3), 295–311. PMID:12762463

Pang, T., & Guindon, G. E. (2004). Globalization and risks for health. *EMBRO Rep, 5*(Supplement 1), S11–S16. doi:10.1038/sj.embor.7400226 PMID:15459728

Pantziara, M., Gagatsis, A., & Elia, I. (2009). Using diagrams as tools for the solution of non- routine mathematical problems. *Educational Studies in Mathematics, 72*(1), 39–60. doi:10.1007/s10649-009-9181-5

Pape, S. J. (2004). Middle school children's problem-solving behavior; a cognitive analysis from a reading comprehension perspective. *Journal for Research in Mathematics Education, 35*(3), 187. doi:10.2307/30034912

Pappano, L. (2012, November 2). The year of the MOOC. *The New York Times*. Retrieved from http://www.nytimes.com/2012/11/04/education/edlife/massive-open-online-courses-are-multiplying-at-a-rapid-pace.html?pagewanted=all

Paquot, M., & Granger, S. (2012). Formulaic language in learner corpora. *Annual Review of Applied Linguistics, 32*, 130–149. doi:10.1017/S0267190512000098

Paranyushkin, D. (2015). *Interesting facts about Russian women and women rights in Russia*. Retrieved from http://waytorussia.net/WhatIsRussia/Women/Facts.html

Parfitt, A. M., Drezner, M. K., Glorieux, F. H., Kanis, J. A., Malluche, H., Meunier, P. J., & Recker, R. R. et al. (1987). Bone histomorphometry: standardization of nomenclature, symbols, and units: report of the ASBMR Histomorphometry Nomenclature Committee. *Journal of Bone and Mineral Research, 2*(6), 595–610. PMID:3455637

Parker, A. (1999). A Study of Variables that Predict Dropout from Distance Education. *International Journal of Educational Technology, 1*(2). Retrieved from http://www.ascilite.org.au/ajet/ijet/v1n2/parker/

Parker, R. S. (1990). Nurses' stories: The search for a relational ethic of care. *ANS. Advances in Nursing Science, 13*(1), 31–40. PMID:2122799

Park, N., & Lee, H. (2012). Social implications of smartphone use: Korean college students' smartphone use and psychological well-being. *Cyberpsychology, Behavior, and Social Networking, 15*(9), 491–497. doi:10.1089/cyber.2011.0580 PMID:22817650

Parks, K. M., & Steelman, L. A. (2008). Organizational wellness programs: A meta-analysis. *Journal of Occupational Health Psychology, 13*(1), 58–68. doi:10.1037/1076-8998.13.1.58 PMID:18211169

Parrinder, E. G. (1999). *World religions: From ancient history to the present.* New York, NY: Barnes & Noble.

Partington, A. (2010). Game literacy, gaming cultures, and media education. *English Teaching, 9*(1), 73–86.

Passman, B. (2008). Case in point: Knowledge, skills, and dispositions. *Journal of Special Education Leadership, 21*(1), 46–47.

Patchin, J. W., & Hinduja, S. (2006). Bullies move beyond the schoolyard: A preliminary look at cyberbullying. *Youth Violence and Juvenile Justice, 4*(2), 148–169. doi:10.1177/1541204006286288

Pattison, D. (2012). Participating in the online social culture. *Knowledge Quest, 41*(1), 70–72.

Patton, M. Q. (1987). *How to use qualitative methods in evaluation.* Thousand Oaks, CA: Sage.

Patton, M. Q. (1990). *Qualitative evaluation and research methods* (2nd ed.). Newbury Park, CA: Sage.

Paul, R. W., & Elder, L. B. (2002). *Critical thinking: tools for taking charge of your professional and personal Life.* Upper Saddle River, NJ: Financial Times/Prentice Hall.

Paul, R., & Elder, L. (2006). *Critical thinking: Tools for taking charge of your learning and your life* (2nd ed.). Upper Saddle River, NJ: Pearson/Prentice Hall.

Pawson, R., & Tilley, N. (1997). *Realistic evaluation.* Thousand Oaks, CA: Sage.

Payette, D. L., & Verreault, D. (2007). Teaching methods and technologies: Aggregated faculty analysis, conclusions and recommendations phase IV. *Journal of College Teaching and Learning, 4*(6), 43–60.

Pazey, B. L., & Yates, J. R. (2012). Conceptual and historical foundations of special education administration. In J. B. Crockett, B. S. Billingsley, & M. L. Boscardin (Eds.), *Handbook of leadership and administration of special education* (pp. 17–36). New York, NY: Routledge.

Pearson, E. J., & Koppi, T. (2002). Inclusion and online learning opportunities: Designing for a Accessibility. *ALT-J, 10*(2), 17–28. doi:10.1080/0968776020100203

Peetz, D. (2010). Are individualistic attitudes killing collectivism? *Transfer: European Review of Labour and Research, 16*(3), 383–398. doi:10.1177/1024258910373869

Pelletier, S. G. (2012). *Explosive growth in health care apps raises oversight questions.* Association of American Medical Colleges. Retrieved from; https://www.aamc.org/newsroom/reporter/ october2012/308516/health-care-apps.html

Peng, K., & Nisbett, R. E. (1999). Culture, dialectics, and reasoning about contradiction. *The American Psychologist*, *54*(9), 741–754. doi:10.1037/0003-066X.54.9.741

Peng, K., Nisbett, R. E., & Wong, N. Y. C. (1997). Validity problems comparing values across cultures and possible solutions. *Psychological Methods*, *2*, 329–344.

Penticuff, J. H., & Walden, M. (2000). Influence of practice environment and nurse characteristics on perinatal nurses' responses to ethical dilemmas. *Nursing Research*, *49*(2), 64–72. PMID:10768582

Perednia, D. A., & Allen, A. (1995). Telemedicine technology and clinical applications. *Journal of the American Medical Association*, *273*(6), 483–488. doi:10.1001/jama.1995.03520300057037 PMID:7837367

Perez, A. P., Phillips, M. M., Cornell, C. E., Mays, G., & Adams, B. (2009, October). Promoting dietary change among state health employees in Arkansas through a worksite wellness program: The healthy employee lifestyle program (HELP). *Preventing Chronic Disease, Public Health Research, Practice and Policy, 6*(4). http://www.cdc.gov/pcd/issues/2009/oct/08_0136.htm

Perren, S., Dooley, J., Shaw, T., & Cross, D. (2010). Bullying in school and cyberspace: Associations with depressive symptoms in Swiss and Australian adolescents. *Child and Adolescent Psychiatry and Mental Health*, *4*(1), 1–10. doi:10.1186/1753-2000-4-28 PMID:21092266

Perry, E. (1963). Interfaith encounter. *Journal of the American Academy of Religion*, *31*(2), 160–162. doi:10.1093/jaarel/XXXI.2.160

Person, A. L., Colby, S. E., Bulova, J. A., & Eubanks, J. W. (2010). Barriers to participation in a worksite wellness program. *Nutrition Research and Practice*, *4*(2), 149–154. doi:10.4162/nrp.2010.4.2.149 PMID:20461204

Petter, S., Straub, D. W., & Rai, A. (2007). Specifying formative constructs in information systems research. *Management Information Systems Quarterly*, *31*, 623–656.

Pettersen, L. (2013, July 2). Moldova: embracing its status as Europe's least-visited country. *Lonely Planet*. Retrieved from http://www.lonelyplanet.com/moldova/travel-tips-and-articles/77774?lpaffil=lp-affiliates

Peugeot Citroën, P. S. A. (n.d.). *Professional mobility: A chance to grow within the group*. Retrieved from http://www.psa-peugeot-citroen.com/en/inside-our-industrial-environment/a-socially-responsible-business/professional-mobility-chance-grow-within-group-article

Pew Research Center. (2011). *Table: Christian population as percentages of total population by country*. Retrieved from http://www.pewforum.org/2011/12/19/table-christian-population-as-percentages-of-total-population-by-country/

Pew Research Center. (2015a). *Latest trends in religious restrictions and hostilities*. Retrieved from http://www.pewforum.org/2015/02/26/religious-hostilities/

Pew Research Center. (2015b). *U.S. public becoming less religious*. Retrieved from http://www.pewforum.org/2015/11/03/u-s-public-becoming-less-religious/

Phillipson, R. (1992). *Linguistic imperialism*. Oxford, UK: Oxford University Press.

Phillipson, R. (Ed.). (2000). *Rights to language*. Mahwah, NJ: Lawrence Erlbaum.

Phinney, J. S. (2008). Bridging identities and disciplines: Advances and challenges in understanding multiple identities. *New Directions for Child and Adolescent Development*, *2008*(120), 97–109. doi:10.1002/cd.218 PMID:18521863

Piccoli, G., Ahmad, R., & Ives, B. (2001). Web-based virtual learning environments: A research framework and a preliminary assessment of effectiveness in basic IT skills training. *Management Information Systems Quarterly*, 401–426.

Picone, M. (2012). Suicide and the afterlife: Popular religion and the standardisation of 'culture' in Japan. *Culture, Medicine and Psychiatry*, *36*(2), 391–408. doi:10.1007/s11013-012-9261-3 PMID:22549663

Pieters, W. (2011). The (social) construction of information security. *The Information Society*, *27*(5), 326–335. doi:10.1080/01972243.2011.607038

Pigini, L., Facal, D., Blasi, L., & Andrich, R. (2012). Service robots in elderly care at home: Users' needs and perceptions as a basis for concept development. *Technology and Disability*, *24*(4), 303–311.

Pilkington, M. 2016. Blockchain Technology: Principles and Applications, Handbook of Research on Digital Transformations'. edited by F. Xavier Olleros, and Majlinda Zhegu, Edward Elgar, Cheltenham, pp.225-253

Pilkington, M. (2007). The Concept of Social Marketing: From Local Development Initiatives to Global Integration-The Example of Health Care in Rural India. *International Review of Business Research Papers*, *3*(5), 328–346.

Pilkington, M. (2014). *Complementarities between the French and Moldovan higher education systems: Some implications for economic growth.* Retrieved from; doi:10.2139/ssrn.2529485

Pilkington, M. (2015). Where Did the Money Go? Endogenous Money Creation for International Fraudulent Purposes The Case of the 2015 Moldovan Banking Scandal. *International Journal of Pluralism and Economics Education*, *6*(3), 251. doi:10.1504/IJPEE.2015.074355

Pinguet, M. (1993). *Voluntary death in Japan.* Cambridge, UK: Polity.

Pittinsky, T., & Tyson, C. J. (2005). Leader authenticity markers: Findings from a study of perceptions of African American political leaders. In W. L. Gardner, B. J. Avolio, & F. O. Walumbwa (Eds.), *Authentic leadership theory and practice: Origins, effects and development* (pp. 253–280). Bingley, UK: Emerald Group.

Plante, T. G., & Sherman, A. C. (Eds.). (2001). *Faith and health: Psychological perspectives.* New York, NY: Guilford.

Pocock, N. S., & Phua, K. H. (2011). Medical tourism and policy implications for health systems: A conceptual framework from a comparative study of Thailand, Singapore and Malaysia. *Globalization and Health*, *7*(12). doi:10.1186/1744-8603-7-12 PMID:21539751

Polya, G. (1957). *How to solve it.* Princeton, NJ: Princeton University Press.

Ponterotto, J. G. (2005). Qualitative research in counseling psychology- A primer on research paradigms and philosophy of science. *Journal of Counseling Psychology*, *52*(2), 126.

Poole, S. M., & Van De Ven, A. H. (1989). Using paradox to build management and organization theories. *Academy of Management Review*, *14*(4), 562–578.

Pornari, C. D., & Wood, J. (2010). Peer and cyber aggression in secondary school students: The role of moral disengagement, hostile attribution bias, and outcome expectancies. *Aggressive Behavior*, *36*(2), 81–94. doi:10.1002/ab.20336 PMID:20035548

Post, S. G., Puchalski, C. M., & Larson, D. B. (2000). Physicians and patient spirituality: Professional boundaries, competency, and ethics. *Annals of Internal Medicine*, *132*(7), 578–583. doi:10.7326/0003-4819-132-7-200004040-00010 PMID:10744595

Powell, L. H., Shahabi, L., & Thoresen, C. E. (2003). Religion and spirituality: Linkages to physical health. *The American Psychologist*, *58*(1), 36–52. doi:10.1037/0003-066X.58.1.36 PMID:12674817

Powell, T. C., & Dente-Micallef, A. (1997). Information technology as competitive advantage: The role of human, business, and technology resources. *Strategic Management Journal, 18*(5), 375–403. doi:10.1002/(SICI)1097-0266(199705)18:5<375::AID-SMJ876>3.0.CO;2-7

Power, D., Schoenherr, T., & Samson, D. (2010). The cultural characteristic of individualism/collectivism: A comparative study of implications for investment in operations between emerging Asian and industrialized Western countries. *Journal of Operations Management, 28*(3), 206–222. doi:10.1016/j.jom.2009.11.002

Powers, L., Alhussain, R., Averbeck, C., & Warner, A. (2012). Perspectives on distance education and social media. *Quarterly Review of Distance Education, 13*, 241–245.

Prahalad, C. K., & Krishnan, M. S. (2008). *The New Age of Innovation: Driving Co-Created Value Through Global Networks*. New York, NY: McGraw-Hill.

Prahalad, C. K., & Ramaswamy, V. (2004). Co-creating unique value with customers. *Strategy and Leadership, 32*(3), 4–9. doi:10.1108/10878570410699249

Prat Zagrebelsky, M. T. (2004). *Computer learner corpora. Theoretical issues and empirical case studies of Italian advanced EFL learners' interlanguage*. Alessandria: Edizioni dell'Orso.

Pratt, B., & Loff, B. (2012). Health research systems: Promoting health equity or economic competitiveness? *Bulletin of the World Health Organization, 90*(1), 55–62. PMID:22271965

Pratt, D. D. (1993). Andragogy after twenty-five years. In S. B. Merriam (Ed.), *An update on adult learning theory. New directions for adult and continuing education* (Vol. 57). San Francisco, CA: Jossey-Bass.

Prensky, M. (2001). Digital natives, digital immigrants part 2. Do they really think differently? *On the Horizon, 9*(6), 1–6.

Prensky, M. (2005). *Shaping tech for the classroom: 21st-century schools need 21st-century technology*. Edutopia.

Presencing Institute. (2010). *Theory u*. Retrieved from http://www.presencing.com/theoryu

Pressley, M., Burkell, J., & Schneider, B. (1995). Mathematical problem solving. In M. Pressley & V. Woloshyn (Eds.), *Cognitive strategy instruction* (p. 185). Brookline Books.

PricewaterhouseCoopers. (2014). *Investing Guide Moldova 2014*. Retrieved from https://www.pwc.com/md/en/publications/assets/moldova-business-guide-2014.pdf

Prior, K. N., & Bond, M. J. (2008). The measurement of abnormal illness behavior: Toward a new research agenda for the Illness Behavior Questionnaire. *Journal of Psychosomatic Research, 64*(3), 245–253. doi:10.1016/j.jpsychores.2007.10.013 PMID:18291238

Prochaska, J., & DiClemente, C. (1983). Stages and processes of self-change in smoking: Toward an integrative model of change. *Journal of Consulting and Clinical Psychology, 5*(3), 390–395. doi:10.1037/0022-006X.51.3.390 PMID:6863699

Pro-Poor Tourism Partnership. (2004). *Tourism in Poverty Reduction Strategy Papers (PRSPs). PPTP Sheet, No 9*. London: PPTP.

Pro-Poor Tourism Partnership. (2005a). *Annual Register 2005*. London: PPTP.

Pro-Poor Tourism Partnership. (2005b). *Key Principles and Strategies of Pro-Poor Tourism*. London: PPTP.

PSFK Labs. (2014, September 8). *Why 'Contexual' Is the New 'Search' Living Within the Internet of Things*. Retrieved from http://www.psfk.com/2014/09/contexual-new-search-living-within-internet-things.html

Puffer, S. M. (2003). *Russian management revolution: Preparing managers for a market economy*. Armonk, NY: M. E. Sharpe.

Puffer, S. M., McCarthy, D., & Naumov, A. (2000). *The Russian capitalist experiment: From state-owned organizations to entrepreneurships*. Northampton, MA: Edward Elgar.

Pursiainen, C., & Medvedev, S. A. (Eds.). (2005). *The Bologna Process and its implications for Russia: The European integration of higher education*. Retrieved from http://www.recep.ru/files/publ/bologna_en.pdf

Putin forges higher education cooperation deal with EU [Press release]. (2005). Retrieved from http://www.wes.org/ewenr/05july/russiacis.htm

Putnam, R. D., Campbell, D. E., & Garrett, S. R. (2012). *American grace: How religion divides and unites us*. New York, NY: Simon & Schuster.

Qin, D. (2015). The starting point of Christology: From below or from above? Part I. *Asian Journal of Pentecostal Studies*, *18*(1), 21–37.

Quick, J. C., Macik-Frey, M., & Cooper, C. L. (2007). Guest Editor's Introduction: Managerial dimensions of organizational health: The healthy leader at work. *Journal of Management Studies*, *44*(2), 189–205. doi:10.1111/j.1467-6486.2007.00684.x

Quine, W. V. O. (2013). *Word and Object*. Cambridge, MA: MIT Press.

Quirk, R., Greenbaum, S., Leech, G., & Svartvik, J. (1985). *A comprehensive grammar of the English language*. Harlow: Longman.

Ragu-Nathan, T. S., Tarafdar, M., Tu, Q., & Ragu-Nathan, B. S. (2008, December). The Consequences of technostress for end users in organizations: Conceptual development and empirical validation. *Information Systems Research*, *19*(4), 471–433. doi:10.1287/isre.1070.0165

Raikhola, P. S., & Kuroki, Y. (2009). Aging and elderly care practice in Japan: Main issues, policy and program perspective; What lessons can be learned from Japanese experiences? *Dhaulagiri Journal of Sociology & Anthropology*, *3*, 41–82. doi:10.3126/dsaj.v3i0.2781

Raingruber, B. (2009). Assigning poetry reading as a way of introducing students to qualitative data analysis. *Journal of Advanced Nursing*, *65*(8), 1753–1761. PMID:19493139

Rajadurai, J. (2007). Intelligibility studies: A consideration of empirical and ideological issues. *World Englishes*, *26*(1), 87–98. doi:10.1111/j.1467-971X.2007.00490.x

Rajakumar, M., & Shanthi, V. (2014). Security breach in trading system countermeasure using IPTraceback. *American Journal of Applied Sciences*, *11*(3), 492–498. doi:10.3844/ajassp.2014.492.498

Ranse, K., & Grealish, L. (2007). Nursing students' perceptions of learning in the clinical setting of the dedicated education unit. *Journal of Advanced Nursing*, *58*(2), 171–179. doi:10.1111/j.1365-2648.2007.04220.x PMID:17445020

Rashid, M. (2013). The question of knowledge in evidence-based design for healthcare facilities: Limitations and suggestions. *Health Environments Research & Design Journal*, *6*(4), 101–126. PMID:24089184

Reader, I. (2012). Secularisation, R.I.P.? Nonsense! The 'rush hour away from the gods' and the decline of religion in contemporary Japan. *Journal of Religion in Japan*, *1*(1), 7–36. doi:10.1163/221183412X628370

Realo, A., & Allik, J. (1999). A cross-cultural study of collectivism: A comparison of American, Estonian, and Russian students. *The Journal of Social Psychology*, *139*(2), 133–142. doi:10.1080/00224549909598367

Reardon, J. (1998). The history and impact of worksite wellness. *Nursing Economics*, *16*(3), 117–121. PMID:9748973

Reece, R. L. (2000, March-April). Preserving the soul of medicine and physicians: A talk with David Whyte. *Physician Executive*, *26*(2), 14–19. PMID:10847937

Regan, D. (1989). *Human brain electrophysiology: evoked potentials and evoked magnetic fields in science and medicine*. New York, NY: Elsevier.

Reid, B. (2014, October 3). Individualized just-in-time products and services should be a leadership priority. *Huffington Post*. Retrieved from http://www.huffingtonpost.com/

Reigeluth, C. (1991). Principles of educational systems design. *International Journal of Education and Research*, *19*(2), 117–131.

Remington, T. (2010). *The Russian middle class as policy objective*. Retrieved from https://www.ucis.pitt.edu/nceeer/2010_825-06_Remington.pdf

René, V. L., Lucas, J., Henk, J., & Doeke, P. (2007). Aspects of spirituality concerning illness. *Scandinavian Journal of Caring Sciences*, *21*(4), 482–489. PMID:18036011

Rennie, D. L. (Ed.). (2002). Qualitative research: History, theory and practice[Special issue]. *Canadian Psychology*, *43*(3).

Reuss, E., Menozzi, M., Buchi, M., Koller, J., & Krueger, H. (2004). Information access at the point of care: What can we learn for designing mobile CPR system? *International Journal of Medical Informatics*, *73*(4), 363–369. doi:10.1016/j.ijmedinf.2004.02.003 PMID:15135755

Rhoades, L., & Eisenberger, R. (2002). Perceived organizational support: A review of the literature. *The Journal of Applied Psychology*, *87*(4), 698–714. doi:10.1037/0021-9010.87.4.698 PMID:12184574

Ricca, B., Lulis, E., & Bade, D. (2006). Lego mindstorms and the growth of critical thinking. In *Proceedings of Intelligent Tutoring Systems Workshop on Teaching With Robots, Agents, and NLP*.

Richtel, M. (2010, July 7). Your brain on computers; Hooked on gadgets and paying a mental price. *New York Times*. Retrieved from http://community.nytimes.com/comments/www.nytimes.com/2010/06/07/technology/07brain.html

Riddell, R., & Iwafuchi, M. (1998). Problems arising from Eastern and Western classification systems for gastrointestinal dysplasia and carcinoma: Are they resolvable? *Histopathology*, *33*(3), 197–202. PMID:9777384

Riddell, T. (2007). Critical assumptions: Thinking critically about critical thinking. *The Journal of Nursing Education*, *46*(3), 121–126. PMID:17396551

Rideout, V. J., Roberts, D. F., & Foehr, U. G. (2005). *Generation M: Media in the lives of 8-18-year-olds: Executive summary*. Menlo Park, CA: Henry J. Kaiser Family Foundation.

Rifkin, J. (2011). *The third industrial revolution: How lateral power is transforming energy, the economy, and the world*. New York, NY: Palgrace Macmillan.

Ring, K. (2000). Religious wars in the NDE movement: Some personal reflections on Michael Sabom's *Light & Death*. *Journal of Near-Death Studies*, *18*(4), 215–244. doi::102291670788710.1023/A

Ringbom, H. (1998). Vocabulary frequencies in advanced learner English: A cross-linguistic approach. In S. Granger (Ed.), *Learner English on computer* (pp. 41–52). London, New York: Addison Wesley Longman.

Ringle, C. M., Sardest, M., & Straub, D. W. (2012). A critical look at the use of PLS-SEM in MIS Quarterly. *MIS Quarterly*, *36*(1), iii–xiv. Retrieved from http://dl.acm.org/citation.cfm?id=2208956

Ringle, C. M., Wende, S., & Becker, J-M. (2014). *SmartPLS 3*. Retrieved from http://www.smartpls.com

Rinzin, C., Vermeulen, W., & Glasbergen, P. (2007). Ecotourism as a Mechanism for Sustainable Development: The Case of Bhutan. *Environmental Sciences*, *4*(2), 109–125. doi:10.1080/15693430701365420

Rivard, R. (2013). The world is not flat. *Inside Higher Education*. Retrieved from http://www.insidehighered.com/news/2013/04/25/moocs-may-eye-world-market-does-world-want-them

Roberts, A. (2007, Winter). Global dimensions of schooling: Implications for internationalizing teacher education. *Teacher Education Quarterly*, 9–26. Retrieved from http://files.eric.ed.gov/fulltext/EJ795137.pdf

Robertson, M., & Al-Zahrani, A. (2012). Self-efficacy and ICT integration into initial teacher education in Saudi Arabia: Matching policy with practice. *Australasian Journal of Educational Technology*, *28*(7), 1136–1151. doi:10.14742/ajet.793

Robey, D., & Boudreau, M. C. (1999). Accounting for the contradictory organizational consequences of information technology: Theoretical directions and methodological implications. *Information Systems Research*, *10*(2), 167–185. doi:10.1287/isre.10.2.167

Robin, B. (2006, March). The educational uses of digital storytelling. In *Society for Information Technology & Teacher Education International Conference* (Vol. 2006, No. 1, pp. 709-716).

Roblyer, M. D., McDaniel, M., Webb, M., Herman, J., & Witty, J. V. (2010). Findings on Facebook in higher education: A comparison of college faculty and student uses and perceptions of social networking sites. *The Internet and Higher Education*, *13*(3), 134–140. doi:10.1016/j.iheduc.2010.03.002

Robson, C., & Witenberg, R. T. (2013). The influence of moral disengagement, morally based self-esteem, age, and gender on traditional bullying and cyberbullying. *Journal of School Violence*, *12*(2), 211–231. doi:10.1080/15388220.2012.762921

Roche, M. (2010). Learning authentic leadership in New Zealand: A learner-centered methodology and evaluation. *American Journal of Business Education*, *3*(3), 7–79. Retrieved from http://www.cluteinstitute.com/ojs/index.php/AJBE/article/view/401/390

Rodney, P., & Starzomski, R. (1993). Constraints on the moral agency of nurses. *The Canadian Nurse*, *89*(9), 23–26. PMID:8221594

Rodrik, D. (1997). Has globalization gone too far? *California Management Review*, *39*(3), 29–53.

Rogers, E. M. (1995). *Diffusion of innovations*. New York, NY: Free.

Rogers, R. L., Meyer, J. S., & Mortel, K. F. (1990). After reaching retirement age physical activity sustains cerebral perfusion and cognition. *Journal of the American Geriatrics Society*, *38*(2), 123–128. doi:10.1111/j.1532-5415.1990.tb03472.x PMID:2299115

Rogers, T. L. (2009). Prescription for success in an associate degree nursing program. *The Journal of Nursing Education*, *49*(2), 96–100. doi:10.3928/01484834-20091022-03 PMID:19877570

Rohdenburg, G., & Schlüter, J. (2009). *One language, two grammars: differences between British and American English*. Cambridge, UK: Cambridge University Press. doi:10.1017/CBO9780511551970

Rolfe, G. (2006). Validity, trustworthiness and rigor: Quality and the idea of qualitative research. *Journal of Advanced Nursing*, *53*(3), 304–310. PMID:16441535

Romeo, E. M. (2010). Quantitative research on critical thinking and predicting nursing students' NCLEX-RN performance. *The Journal of Nursing Education*, *49*(7), 378–386. doi:10.3928/01484834-20100331-05 PMID:20411861

Rosen, L. D. (2007). *Me, Myspace, and I: Parenting the Net Generation*. New York: Palgrave Macmillan.

Rosenthal, S. A. (2012). *National Leadership Index 2012: A national study of confidence in leadership*. Cambridge, MA: Harvard University, Harvard Kennedy School, Center for Public Leadership.

Rossiter, M., & Garcia, P. A. (2010). Digital storytelling: A new player on the narrative field. *New Directions for Adult and Continuing Education, 126*, 37–48.

Rosu, R. (2012). The impact of diaspora on political processess in republica Moldova. Administrarea Publica. *Revista motodico-stiintifica trimestriala, 4*(76), 103-111.

Rovai, A. (2002). Building sense of community at a distance. *International Review of Research in Open and Distance Learning, 4*(1), 1–9. Retrieved from http://www.irrodl.org/index.php/irrodl

Roy, C. (2009). *Roy adaptation model* (3rd ed.). Upper Saddle River, NJ: Pearson.

Ruane, C. (1994). *Gender, class and the professionalization of Russian city teachers, 1860–1914*. University of Pittsburgh Press.

Rugutt, J., & Chemosit, C. (2009). What motivates students to learn? Contribution of student-to-student relations, student-faculty interaction and critical thinking skills. *Educational Research Quarterly, 32*(3), 16–28.

Rushkoff, D. (2013). *Present shock: When everything happens now*. New York, NY: Penguin.

Ruthman, J., Jackson, J., Cluskey, M., Flannigan, P., Folse, V. N., & Bunten, J. (2004). Using clinical journaling to capture critical thinking across the curriculum. *Nursing Education Perspectives, 25*(3), 120–123. PMID:15301459

Rutland, P. (1998). *Annual Survey of Eastern Europe and the Former Soviet Union 1998*. New York, NY: EastWest Institute.

Ryan, R. M., & Deci, E. L. (2002). On assimilating identities to the self: A self-determination theory perspective on internalization and integrity within cultures. In M. R. Leary & J. P. Tangney (Eds.), *Handbook of self and identity* (pp. 255–273). New York, NY: The Guilford Press.

Saadé, R. G., Morin, D., & Thomas, J. D. (2012). Critical thinking in E-learning environments. *Computers in Human Behavior, 28*(5), 1608–1617.

Sachs, J. R. (1991). Current eschatology: Universal salvation and the problem of hell. *Theological Studies, 52*(2), 227–254. doi:10.1177/004056399105200203

Sachs, J. R. (1993). Apocatastasis in patristic theology. *Theological Studies, 54*(4), 617–640. doi:10.1177/004056399305400402

Sadik, A. (2008). Digital storytelling: A meaningful technology-integrated approach for engaged student learning. *Educational Technology Research and Development, 56*(4), 487–506.

Sahin, M. (2010). Teachers' perceptions of bullying in high schools: A Turkish study. *Social Behavior and Personality, 38*(1), 127–142. doi:10.2224/sbp.2010.38.1.127

Saif, M. (2000). World medical association declaration of Helsinki: Ethical principles for medical research involving human subjects. *The Journal of the American Medical Association, 284*, 3043-3045.

Sakız, G., Özden, B., Aksu, D., & Şimşek, Ö. (2015). Fen ve Teknoloji Dersinde Akıllı Tahta Kullanımının Öğrenci Başarısına ve Dersin İşlenişine Yönelik Tutuma Etkisi. *Atatürk Üniversitesi Sosyal Bilimler Enstitüsü Dergisi, 18*(3), 257–274.

Salsman, J. M., Brown, T. L., Brechting, E. H., & Carlson, C. R. (2005). The link between religion and spirituality and psychological adjustment: The mediating role of optimism and social support. *Personality and Social Psychology Bulletin*, *31*(4), 522–535. doi:10.1177/0146167204271563 PMID:15743986

Sami, L. K., & Pangannaiah, N. B. (2006). Technostress: A literature survey on the effect of information technology on library users. *Library Review*, *55*(7), 429–439. doi:10.1108/00242530610682146

Sanchez-Arias, F., Calmeyn, H., Driesen, G., & Pruis, E. (2013, February 8). Human capital realities pose challenges across the globe. *Association for talent Development*. Retrieved from: https://www.td.org/Publications/Magazines/TD/TD-Archive/2013/02/Human-Capital-Realities-Pose-Challenges-Across-the-Globe

Sanchez, P. (2007). Urban immigrant students: How transnationalism shapes their world learning. *The Urban Review*, *39*(5), 489–517. doi:10.1007/s11256-007-0064-8

Sanchez, S., Huerta, A., & Venesgas, K. (2012). Latino males and college preparation programs: Examples of increased access. *Metropolitan Universities*, *22*(3), 27–45.

Sandelowski, M., & Barroso, J. (2002). Finding the findings in qualitative studies. *Journal of Nursing Scholarship*, *34*(3), 213–219. PMID:12237982

Sandelowski, M., & Barroso, J. (2003). Classifying the findings in qualitative studies. *Qualitative Health Research*, *13*(7), 905–923. PMID:14502957

Sansosti, F. J., Goss, S., & Noltemeyer, A. (2011). Perspectives of special education directors on response to intervention in secondary schools. *Contemporary School Psychology*, 9-20.

Sansosti, F. J., & Noltemeyer, A. (2008). Viewing response-to-intervention through an educational change paradigm: What can we learn? *California School Psychologist*, *13*(1), 55–66. doi:10.1007/BF03340942

Sarver, J., & Baker, D. W. (2000). Effect of language barriers on follow-up appointments after an emergency department visit. *Journal of General Internal Medicine, 15*(4), 256-264. Doi: .10.1111/j.1525-1497.2000.06469.x

Sassen, S. (1994). *Cities in a world economy* (Vol. 3). Thousand Oaks, CA: Pine Forge.

Satina, S. (1982). *Education of women in pre-revolutionary Russia*. Ann Arbor, MI: University of Michigan Press.

Saudi Ministry of Higher Education. (n.d.). Retrieved from http://he.moe.gov.sa/en/default.aspx

Savickaya, N. (2003, May 16). High-quality education is priceless. *Independent Newspaper*, p. 8.

Sawyer, S., & Eschenfelder, K. R. (2002). Social informatics: Perspectives, examples, and trends. In B. Cronin (Ed.), Annual review of information science and technology. Medford, NJ: Information Today Inc./ASIST.

Sayman, D. (2007). The elimination of sexism and stereotyping in occupational education. *Journal of Men's Studies*, *15*(1), 19–30. doi:10.3149/jms.1501.19

Schaber, P., & Shanedling, J. (2012). Online course design for teaching critical thinking. *Journal of Allied Health*, *41*(1), e9–e14. PMID:22544412

Schaper, L. K., & Pervan, G. P. (2007a). ICT and OT's: A model of information and communication technology acceptance and utilization by occupational therapists (Part 1). *International Journal of Medical Informatics*, *76*(1), S212–S221. doi:10.1016/j.ijmedinf.2006.05.028 PMID:16828335

Scharmer, C. O. (2011). *The future of change management: 13 propositions draft 1.0*. Paper presented to the Zeitschrift fur Organisationsentwicklung, Berlin, Germany.

Scharmer, C. O. (2013, September 10). *Re: Implementation of theory u.* [Web log post]. Retrieved from http://www.blog.ottoscharmer.com/?p=557

Scharmer, C. O. (2009). *Theory u: Leading from the future as it emerges.* San Francisco, CA: Barrett-Koehler.

Scharmer, C. O., & Kaufer, K. (2013). *Leading from the emerging future: From ego-system to eco-system economies.* San Francisco, CA: Berrett-Koehler.

Scheffer, B. K., & Rubenfeld, M. G. (2000). A consensus statement on critical thinking in nursing. *The Journal of Nursing Education, 39*(8), 352–359. PMID:11103973

Schein, E. H. (2010). *Organizational culture and leadership.* San Francisco, CA: Jossey-Bass.

Schein, E. H. (2013). *Humble inquiry: The gentle art of asking instead of telling.* San Francisco, CA: Berrett-Kohler.

Schluter, J., Winch, S., Holzhauser, K., & Henderson, A. (2008). Nurses' moral sensitivity and hospital ethical climate: A literature review. *Nursing Ethics, 15*(3), 304–321. PMID:18388166

Schmitt, N., Grandage, S., & Adolphs, S. (2004). Are corpus-derived recurrent clusters psycholinguistically valid? In N. Schmitt (Ed.), *Formulaic sequences* (pp. 127–152). Amsterdam: John Benjamins Publishing. doi:10.1075/lllt.9.08sch

Schoen, C., Osborn, R., Huynh, P. T., Doty, M., Peugh, J., & Zapert, K. (2006). On the front lines of care: Primary care doctors' office systems, experiences, and views in seven countries. *Health Affairs, 25*(6), w555–w571. doi:10.1377/hlthaff.25.w555 PMID:17102164

Schoenfeld, A. H. (1985). *Mathematical problem solving.* Orlando, FL: Academic Press.

Schoenfeld, A. H. (1987). A brief and biased history of problem solving. In F. R. Curcio (Ed.), *Teaching and learning: A problem-solving focus* (p. 27). Reston, VA: National Council of Teachers of Mathematics.

Schoenfeld, A. H. (1992). Learning to think mathematically: Problem solving, metacognition, and sense making in mathematics. In D. A. Grouws (Ed.), *Handbook of research on mathematics teaching and learning* (p. 334). New York: Macmillan.

Schram, T. H. (2006). *Conceptualizing and proposing qualitative research* (2nd ed.). Upper Saddle River, NJ: Pearson.

Schuesster, J. H. (2013). Contemporary threats and countermeasures. *Journal of Information Privacy & Security, 9*(2), 3–20. doi:10.1080/15536548.2013.10845676

Schwartz, S. (1992). Universals in the content and structure of values: Theoretical advances and empirical advances in 20 countries. In J. M. Olson & M. P. Zanna (Eds.), *Advances in experimental psychology* (Vol. 25, pp. 1–65). Cambridge, MA: Academic Press. doi:10.1016/S0065-2601(08)60281-6

Scott, R. A. (2005, Winter). Many calls, little action: Global illiteracy in the United States. *The Presidency*, 18–23. Retrieved from http://web.a.ebscohost.com.uiwtx.idm.oclc.org/ehost/pdfviewer/pdfviewer?vid=13&sid=0af845c8-1aaf-4546-a955-5d98456b18da%40sessionmgr4001&hid=4112

Scott, M. (2008). *WordSmith Tools version 5.* Liverpool, UK: Lexical Analysis Software.

Seale, C. (1999). *The quality of qualitative research.* London, UK: Sage.

Seeman, T. E., Dubin, L. F., & Seeman, M. (2003). Religiosity/spirituality and health: A critical review of the evidence for biological pathways. *The American Psychologist, 58*(1), 53–63. doi:10.1037/0003-066X.58.1.53 PMID:12674818

Seeman, T. E., Rodin, J., & Albert, M. (1993). Self-efficacy and cognitive performance in high-functioning older individuals: MacArthur Studies of Successful Aging. *Journal of Aging and Health, 5*(4), 455–474. doi:10.1177/089826439300500403

Seidlhofer, B. (2001). Closing a conceptual gap: The case for a description of English as a lingua franca. *International Journal of Applied Linguistics*, *11*(2), 133–158. doi:10.1111/1473-4192.00011

Seidman, I. (2006). *Interviewing as qualitative research: A guide for researchers in education and the social sciences* (3rd ed.). New York, NY: Teachers College Press.

Selinger, E. (2009). Technology transfer and globalization. In D. M. Kaplan (Ed.), Readings in the Philosophy of Technology, (pp. 321-344). Lanham, MD: Rowman & Littlefield.

Sen, A. (2012). Development as capability expansion. In J. DeFilippis & S. Saegert, S. (Eds.), The community development reader. New York, NY: Routledge.

Sen, A. (2010). *The Idea of Justice*. London, UK: Penguin.

Senge, P. (1990). *The fifth discipline: The art and practice of the earning organization.* New York, NY: Random House.

Senge, P. (1990). *The fifth discipline: The art and practice of the learning organization.* New York: Doubleday.

Sergeev, S. O. (2015). Akademicheskaya mobil'nost' kak instrument mjagkoi sili nauki. [Academic mobility as an instrument of power of soft science]. *Gumanitarnie, sotsial'no-ekonomicheskie i obshchestvennie nauki, 6*(1), 198–201.

Seul, J. R. (1999). 'Ours is the way of God': Religion, identity, and intergroup conflict. *Journal of Peace Research, 36*(5), 553–569. doi:10.1177/0022343399036005004

Sevcikova, A., Machackova, H., Wright, M. F., Dedkova, L., & Cerna, A. (2015). Social support seeking in relation to parental attachment and peer relationships among victims of cyberbullying. *Australian Journal of Guidance & Counselling, 15*, 1–13. doi:10.1017/jgc.2015.1

Seybold, K. S., & Hill, P. C. (2001). The role of religion and spirituality in mental and physical health. *Current Directions in Psychological Science, 10*(1), 21–24. doi:10.1111/1467-8721.00106

Sfard, A. (2013). Almost 20 years after: Developments in research on language and mathematics. Review of J. N. Moschkovich (Ed.) (2010) Language and mathematics education: Multiple perspectives and directions for research. Educational Studies in Mathematics, 82(2). doi:10.1007/s10649-012-9446-2

Shamir, B., & Eilam, G. (2005, June). "What's your story?" A life-stories approach to authentic leadership development. *The Leadership Quarterly, 16*(3), 395–417. doi:. leaqua.2005.03.00510.1016/j

Shapiro, J., & Saltzer, E. (1981). Cross-cultural aspects of physician-patient communication patterns. *Urban Health, 10*, 10–15. Available from http://europepmc.org/abstract/med/10254342 PMID:10254342

Shapka, J. D., & Law, D. M. (2013). Does one size fit all? Ethnic differences in parenting behaviors and motivations for adolescent engagement in cyberbullying. *Journal of Youth and Adolescence, 42*(5), 723–738. doi:10.1007/s10964-013-9928-2 PMID:23479327

Shariff, S., & Hoff, D. L. (2007). Cyber bullying: Clarifying legal boundaries for school supervision in cyberspace. *International Journal of Cyber Criminology, 1*, 76–118.

Sharkov, D. (2015, June 19). Russian sanctions to 'cost Europe €100bn'. *Newsweek*. Retrieved from http://europe.newsweek.com/russian-sanctions-could-cost-europe-100-billion-328999

Shaywitz, S., & Shaywitz, B. (2004). Reading disability and the brain. *Educational Leadership, 61*(6), 6–11.

Shcherbakova, E. M. (2008). The trend of education in Russia. *Russian Education & Society, 50*(4), 26–41. doi:10.2753/RES1060-9393500402

Sheehan, M. (2012). Investing in management development in turbulent times and perceived organisational performance: A study of UK MNCs and their subsidiaries. *International Journal of Human Resource Management, 23*(12), 2491–2513. doi:10.1080/09585192.2012.668400

Shell, R. (2001). Perceived barriers to teaching for critical thinking by BSN nursing faculty. *Nursing and Health Care Perspectives, 22*(6), 286–291. PMID:16370252

Sherrod, R. A., Houser, R., Odom-Bartel, B., Packa, D., Wright, V., Dunn, L., & Tomlinson, S. et al. (2012). Creating a successful environment for preparing doctoral-level nurse educators. *The Journal of Nursing Education, 51*(9), 481–488. doi:10.3928/01484834-20120706-01 PMID:22766073

Shibatani, M. (1990). *The languages of Japan.* Cambridge, UK: Cambridge University Press.

Shih, P., Munoz, D., & Sanchez, F. (2006). The effect of previous experience with information and communication technologies on performance in a Web-based learning program. *Computers in Human Behavior, 22*(6), 962–970. doi:10.1016/j.chb.2004.03.016

Shirkey, C. (2008). *Here comes everybody: The power of organizing without organizations.* New York, NY: Penguin.

Shweder, R. A., & Bourne, E. J. (1982). Does the concept of the person vary cross-culturally? In A. J. Marsela & G. White (Eds.), *Cultural concepts of mental health and therapy* (pp. 97–137). Springer.

Sides, H. (1997). The calibration of belief. *New York Times Magazine, 7*, 16–21.

Siedel, J. V. (1998). *Qualitative data analysis. The ethnograph v5.0: A users' guide, Appendix E.* Colorado Springs, CO: Qualis.

Siegler, R. S. (1989). Hazards of mental chronometry: An example from children's subtraction. *Journal of Educational Psychology, 81*(4), 497–506. doi:10.1037/0022-0663.81.4.497

Sijtsema, J. J., Ashwin, R. J., Simona, C. S., & Gina, G. (2014). Friendship selection and influence in bullying and defending. *Effects of moral disengagement. Developmental Psychology, 50*(8), 2093–2104. doi:10.1037/a0037145 PMID:24911569

Silverstein, M., & Parker, M. G. (2002). Leisure activities and quality of life among the oldest old in Sweden. *Research on Aging, 24*(5), 528–547. doi:10.1177/0164027502245003

Simpson-Vlach, R., & Ellis, N. C. (2010). An Academic Formulas List: New methods in phraseology research. *Applied Linguistics, 31*(4), 487–512. doi:10.1093/applin/amp058

Sims, D. (2004). Management learning as a critical process: The practice of storying. In P. Jeffcutt (Ed.), *The foundations of management knowledge* (pp. 152–166). London, UK: Routledge.

Sinclair, J. (1991). *Corpus, concordance, collocation: Describing English language.* Oxford, UK: Oxford University Press.

Sinclair, J. (1996). The search for units of meaning. *TEXTUS, IX*, 75–106.

Sinclair, J. (2004). Meaning in the framework of corpus linguistics. *Lexicographica, 20*, 20–32.

Singh, R. N., & Mohanty, R. P. (2011). Participation satisfaction and organizational commitment: Moderating role of employee's cultural values. *Human Resource Development International, 14*(5), 583–603. doi:10.1080/13678868.2011.621286

Singleton, K., & Krause, E. (2009). Understanding cultural and linguistic barriers to health literacy. *OJIN: The Online Journal of Issues in Nursing, 14*(3). doi:10.3912/OJIN.Vol14No03Man04

Sinha, I. (1999). *The cyber gypsies: Love, life, and travels on the electronic frontier.* London, UK: Scribner.

Skyttner, L. (2005). *General systems theory: Problems, persepctives, and practice* (2nd ed.). Hackensack, NJ: World Scientific Publishing Co.

Slife, B. D., & Gantt, E. E. (1999). Methodological pluralism: A framework for psychotherapy research. *Journal of Clinical Psychology, 55*(12), 1453–1465. PMID:10855480

Slife, B. D., & Reber, J. S. (2012). Conceptualizing religious practices in psychological research: Problems and prospects. *Pastoral Psychology, 61*(5-6), 735–746.

Sloan, R. P., Bagiella, E., & Powell, T. (1999). Religion, spirituality, and medicine. *Lancet, 353*(9153), 664–667. doi:10.1016/S0140-6736(98)07376-0 PMID:10030348

Sloan, R. P., Bagiella, E., VandeCreek, L., Hover, M., Casalone, C., Jinpu Hirsch, T., & Poulos, P. et al. (2000). Should physicians prescribe religious activities? *The New England Journal of Medicine, 342*(25), 1913–1916. doi:10.1056/NEJM200006223422513 PMID:10861331

Sloman, M. (2002). *The e-learning revolution How technology is driving a new training paradigm.* New York, NY: AMACOM.

Slonje, R., & Smith, P. K. (2008). Cyberbullying another main type of bullying? *Scandinavian Journal of Psychology, 49*(2), 147–154. doi:10.1111/j.1467-9450.2007.00611.x PMID:18352984

Smedley, B. D., Stith, A. Y., & Nelson, A. R. (Eds.). (2009). *Unequal treatment: Confronting racial and ethnic disparities in healthcare.* Washington, DC: National Academies.

SMEEC. (2011). *Swedish Ministry of Enterprise, Energy and Communications. ICT for everyone - A Digital Agenda for Sweden* (Reference No. N2011.19). Stockholm: Sweden. Åtta.45. Retrieved from http://www.government.se/reports/2011/12/ict-for-everyone---a-digital-agenda-for-sweden/

Smeral, E. (1998). The impact of globalization on small and medium enterprises: New challenges for tourism policies in European countries. *Tourism Management, 19*(4), 371–380.

Smith, A. (2013). *Smartphone ownership 2013.* Pew internet and American life project. Retrieved from http://pewinternet.org/Reports/2013/Smartphone-Ownership-2013.aspx

Smith, B. G. (2012). The tangled web of Buddhism: An Internet analysis of religious doctrinal differences. *Contemporary Buddhism, 13*(2), 301–319. doi:. 71971110.1080/14639947.2012

Smith, J. K. (2002). Malcolm Knowles, informal adult education, self-direction and andragogy. In *The encyclopedia of informal education.* Retrieved from http://www.infed.org/ thinkers/et-knowl.htm

Smith, C., & Emerson, M. (1998). *American evangelicalism: Embattled and thriving.* IL: University of Chicago Press.

Smith, J. M., Sullivan, S. J., & Baxter, G. D. (2011). Complementary and alternative medicine: Contemporary trends and issues. *The Physical Therapy Review, 16*(2), 91–95. doi:10.1179/1743288X11Y.0000000013

Smith, K. K., & Berg, D. N. (1988). *Paradoxes of group life.* San Francisco, CA: Jossey-Bass.

Smith, P. B., Torres, C. V., Hecke, J., Chua, C. H., Chudzikova, A., Degirmencioglu, S., & Yanchuk, V. (2011). Individualism-collectivism and business context as predictors of behaviors in cross-national work settings: Incidence and outcomes. *International Journal of Intercultural Relations, 35*(4), 440–451. doi:10.1016/j.ijintrel.2011.02.001

Smith, P. K., Madsen, K. C., & Moody, J. C. (1999). What cause the age decline in reports of being bullied at school? Towards a developmental analysis of risks of being bullied. *Educational Research, 41*(3), 267–285. doi:10.1080/0013188990410303

Smith, P. K., Mahdavi, J., Carvalho, M., Fisher, S., Russell, S., & Tippett, N. (2008). Cyberbullying: Its nature and impact in secondary school pupils. *Journal of Child Psychology and Psychiatry, and Allied Disciplines, 49*(4), 376–385. doi:10.1111/j.1469-7610.2007.01846.x PMID:18363945

Smith, W. C. (1993). *What is scripture? A comparative approach.* Minneapolis, MN: Fortress.

Smolentseva, A. (2003). Challenges to the Russian academic profession. *Higher Education, 45*(4), 391–424. doi:10.1023/A:1023954415569

Snarey, J. (1996). The natural environment's impact upon religious ethics: A cross-cultural study. *Journal for the Scientific Study of Religion, 35*(2), 85–96. doi:10.2307/1387077

SNBHW. (2003). *Årsrapport NPS—En analys av barnmorskors, sjuksköterskors, läkares, tandhygienisters och tandläkares arbetsmarknad.* [Annual report NPS—an analysis of midwifes', nurses', doctors', dental hygienists' and dentists' labor market]. Stockholm, Sweden: Socialstyrelsen [Swedish National Board of Health and Welfare]]. Retrieved from http://www.socialstyrelsen.se

Soderberg, A., & Norberg, A. (1993). Intensive care: Situations of ethical difficulty. *Journal of Advanced Nursing, 18*(12), 2008–2014. PMID:8132934

Solberg, I. B., Tómasson, K., Aasland, O., & Tyssen, R. (2013). The impact of economic factors on migration considerations among Icelandic specialist doctors: A cross-sectional study. *BMC Health Services Research, 13*(524), 7. PMID:24350577

Solomon, G., & Schrum, L. (2011). *Web 2.0 how-to for educators.* Washington, DC: International Society for Technology in Education.

Sontam, V., & Gabiel, G. (2012). Student engagement at a large suburban community college: Gender and race differences. *Community College Journal of Research and Practice, 36*(10), 808–820. doi:10.1080/10668926.2010.491998

Sor-hoon, T. (2011). The *Dao* of politics: *Li* (rituals/rites) and laws as pragmatic tools of government. *Philosophy East & West, 61*(3), 468–491. doi:10.1353/pew.2011.0043

Sourander, A., Brunstein, A., Ikonen, M., Lindroos, J., Luntamo, T., Koskelainen, M., & Helenius, H. et al. (2010). Psychosocial risk factors associated with cyberbullying among adolescents: A population-based study. *Archives of General Psychiatry, 67*(7), 720–728. doi:10.1001/archgenpsychiatry.2010.79 PMID:20603453

Sparkes, A. C. (2001). Myth 94: Qualitative health researchers will agree about validity. *Qualitative Health Research, 11*, 538–552. PMID:11521610

Sparrowe, R. T. (2005, June). Authentic leadership and the narrative self. *The Leadership Quarterly, 16*(3), 419–439. doi:10.1016/j.leaqua.2005.03.004

Spilker, B. (1994). Multinational pharmaceutical companies: Principles and practices. Raven.

Spilker, B. (1993). *Multinational Pharmaceutical Companies: principles and practices.* Lippincott Williams & Wilkins.

Sprochi, A. K. (2010). Review of the book *Islam in the world today: A handbook of politics, religion, culture, and society,* by W. Ende & U. Steinbach, Eds. *Library Journal, 135*(12), 110–111.

Srinivas, H., & Nakagawa, Y. (2008). Environmental implications for disaster preparedness: Lessons learnt from the Indian Ocean Tsunami. *Journal of Environmental Management, 89*(1), 4–13. PMID:17904271

Srivastava, P. (2012). Getting engaged: Giving employees a nudge toward better health. *Compensation and Benefits Review, 44*(2), 105–109. doi:10.1177/0886368712450982

St. Petersburg University. (2014). *Graduate School of Management*. Retrieved from http://gsom.spbu.ru/en/

Stacey, K., & MacGregor, M. (2000). Learning the algebraic methods of solving problems. *The Journal of Mathematical Behavior, 18*(2), 149–167. doi:10.1016/S0732-3123(99)00026-7

Stalin, J. (1946, March1). New five-year plan for Russia. *Vital Speeches of the Day, 12*(10), 300–304.

Stanovich, K. E., & Stanovich, P. J. (1995). How research might inform the debate about early reading acquisition. *Journal of Research in Reading, 18*(2), 87–105. doi:10.1111/j.1467-9817.1995.tb00075.x

Stedman, N. L. P., & Adams, B. L. (2012). Identifying faculty's knowledge of critical thinking concepts and perceptions of critical thinking instruction in higher education1. *NACTA Journal, 56*(2), 9–14.

Steffgen, G., Konig, A., Pfetsch, J., & Melzer, A. (2011). Are cyberbullies less empathic? Adolescents' cyberbullying behavior and empathic responsiveness. *Cyberpsychology, Behavior, and Social Networking, 14*(11), 643–648. doi:10.1089/cyber.2010.0445 PMID:21554126

Steger, M. (2005). *Globalism: Market ideology meets terrorism*. Lanham, MD: Rowman & Littlefield.

Stein, M., & Jung, C. G. (1985). *Jung's treatment of Christianity: The psychotherapy of a religious tradition*. Asheville, NC: Chiron.

Stetson, P. D., McKnight, L. K., Bakken, S., Curran, C., Kubose, T. T., & Cimino, J. J. (2002). Development of an ontology to model medical errors, information needs, and the clinical communication space. *Journal of the American Medical Informatics Association, 9*(Supplement 6), S86–S91. doi:10.1197/jamia.M1235

Stevens, M. J., & Gielen, U. P. (2015). *Toward a global psychology: Theory, research, intervention, and pedagogy*. Mahwah, NJ: Lawrence Erlbaum Associates, Inc.

Stewart, K. A. (2006). Can a human rights framework improve biomedical and social scientific HIV/AIDS research for African women? *Human Rights Review (Piscataway, N.J.), 7*(2), 130–136.

Stoll, L. (2006). The future of educational change: System thinkers in action: Response to Michael Fullan. *Journal of Educational Change, 7*(3), 123–127. doi:10.1007/s10833-006-0004-5

Stone, L. (2009, August 24). *The impacts of smartphones in society*. [Web log post]. Retrieved from www.lindastone.net

Storey, J. (2009). *Cultural theory and popular culture: An introduction* (5th ed.). London, UK: Pearson.

Stratan, A. (2010). Assessment of economic growth of the Republic of Moldova in the context of global economic crisis. *Journal for Economic Forecasting*, (5), 33-42.

Strauch, I. (2003). Examining the nature of holism within lifestyle. *Journal of Individual Psychology, 59*(4), 452–460.

Strayhorn, T. (2013). Satisfaction and retention among African American Men at two-year community colleges. *Community College Journal of Research and Practice, 36*(5), 358–375. doi:10.1080/10668920902782508

Stroetmann, K. A., Dobrev, A., Lilischkis, S., & Stroetmann, V. (2014). eHealth is worth it. *The economic benefits of implemented eHealth solutions at ten European sites. eHealth Impact*. Retrieved from http://www.ehealth-impact.org

Stroetmann, K. A., Jones, T., Dobrev, A., & Stroetmann, V. N. (2006). eHealth is Worth it. *The economic benefits of implemented eHealth solutions at ten European sites*. Available from http://www.ehealth-impact.org/download/documents/ehealthimpactsept2006.pdf

Strohmeier, D., Aoyama, I., Gradinger, P., & Toda, Y. (2013). Cybervictimization and cyberaggression in Eastern and Western countries: Challenges of constructing a cross-cultural appropriate scale. In S. Bauman, D. Cross, & J. L. Walker (Eds.), *Principles of cyberbullying research: Definitions, measures, and methodology* (pp. 202–221). New York: Routledge.

Study abroad: Where to study in Europe . . . in English. (n.d.). *The Telegraph*. Retrieved from http://www.telegraph.co.uk/education/universityeducation/9447458/Study-abroad-Where-to-study-in-Europe...-in-English.html

Suen, A. (2002). *The Peace Corps*. New York, NY: Rosen.

Suetens, C., Hopkins, S., Kolman, J., & Diaz Högberg, L. (2013). Point prevalence survey of healthcare associated infections and antimicrobial use in European acute care hospitals: 2011-2012. Stockholm, Sweden: European Centre for Disease Prevention and Control (ECDC). doi:10.2900/86011

Suler, J. (2004). The online disinhibition effect. *Cyberpsychology & Behavior, 7*(3), 321–326. doi:10.1089/1094931041291295 PMID:15257832

Sullivan-Mann, J., Perron, C. A., & Fellner, A. N. (2009). The effects of simulation on nursing students' critical thinking scores: A quantitative study. *Newborn and Infant Nursing Reviews; NAINR, 9*(2), 111–116.

Sun, Y., Wang, N., Guo, X., & Peng, Z. (2013). Understanding the acceptance of mobile health services: A comparison and integration alternative models. *Journal of Electronic Commerce Research, 114*(2), 183–200. Retrieved from http://www.csulb.edu/journals/jecr/issues/20132/paper4.pdf

Suzuki, T. (1976). Language and behavior in Japan: The conceptualization of personal relations. *Japan Quarterly (Asahi Shinbunsha), 23*(3), 255–266.

Suzuki, T. (1978). *Japanese and the Japanese: Words in culture*. Tokyo, Japan: Kodansha.

Sveriges Riksdag. (2012). *Rapport från riksdagen 2011/12:RFR5. eHälsa-nytta och näring* [eHealth-advantage and industry]. Retrieved from https://www.riksdagen.se/sv/Dokument-Lagar/Utredningar/Rapporter-fran-riksdagen/eHalsa--nytta-och-naring_GZ0WRFR5/

Swafford, J. O., & Langrall, C. W. (2000). Grade 6th students' preinstructional use of equations to describe and represent problem situations. *Journal for Research in Mathematics Education, 31*(1), 89. doi:10.2307/749821

Swanson, R. A., & Holton, E. F. (2005). *Research in organizations: Foundations and methods of inquiry*. San Francisco, CA: Berrett-Koehler.

Swedish Institute. (2013-2015). Retrieved from https://sweden.se/migration/#2013

Swedish Ministry of Health and Social Affairs. (2006). *National strategy for eHealth-Sweden*. Stockholm, Sweden: Socialdepartementet. Retrieved from http://sweden.gov.se/content/1/c6/06/43/24/f6405a1c.pdf

Swedish National Agency for Education. (2016). Retrieved from http://www.skolverket.se/statistik-och-utvardering

Swedish National Audit Office [Riksrevisionsverket]. (2002). *IT i verksamhetsutvecklingen-Bättre styrning av myndigheternas IT investeringar I IT-baserad verksamhetsutveckling*. Stockholm, Sweden: Riksrevisionens publikationsservice. Retrieved from http://www.riksrevisionen.se

Tabata, L. N., & Johnsrud, L. K. (2008). The impact of faculty attitudes toward technology, distance education and innovation. *Research in Higher Education, 49*(7), 625–646. doi:10.1007/s11162-008-9094-7

Tafarodi, R., Nishikawa, Y., Bonn, G., Morio, H., Fukuzawa, A., & Lee, J. (2012). Wishing for Change in Japan and Canada. *Journal of Happiness Studies, 13*(6), 969–983.

Takahashi, Y. (2001). *Jisatsu no sain wo yomitoru* [Reading a signal of suicide]. Tokyo, Japan: Kodansha.

Takakusu, J. (2002). *The essentials of Buddhist philosophy*. Honolulu, HI: Motilal Banarsidass.

Tammineedi, L. (2010). Business continuity management: A standards-based approach. *Information Security Journal: A Global Perspective, 1,* 36-49.

Tanaka, K. (2010). Limitations for measuring religion in a different cultural context: The case of Japan. *The Social Science Journal, 47*(4), 845–852. doi:10.1016/j.soscij.2010.07.010 PMID:21113429

Tangen, D., & Campbell, M. (2010). Cyberbullying prevention: One primary school's approach. *Australian Journal of Guidance & Counselling, 20*(02), 225–234. doi:10.1375/ajgc.20.2.225

Tanner, J. R., Noser, T. C., & Totaro, M. W. (2009). Business faculty and undergraduate students' perceptions of online learning: A comparative study. *Journal of Information Systems, 20*(1), 29–40.

Tanzi, M. V. (2000). Globalization and the future of social protection (No. 0-12). International Monetary Fund.

Tao, S.-P. (n.d.). *Values and lifestyles of individualists and collectivists: A cross-culture study on Taiwanese and US consumers.* Retrieved from http://www.mnd.gov.tw/upload/16--%E9%99%B6%E8%81%96%E5%B1%8F.pdf

Taplin, I. M. (1997). Struggling to compete: Post-war changes in the U.S. clothing Industry. *Textile History, 28*(1), 90–104.

Tarafdar, M., Tu, Q., Ragu-Nathan, B. S., & Ragu-Nathan, T. S. (2007). The impact of technostress on role stress and productivity. *Journal of Management Information Systems, 24*(1), 301–328. doi:10.2753/MIS0742-1222240109

Tashakkori, A., & Teddlie, C. (Eds.). (2003). *Handbook of mixed methods in social & behavioral research.* Thousand Oaks, CA: Sage.

Tatum, B. D. (1999). *"Why are all the black kids sitting together in the cafeteria?" and other conversations about race.* New York, NY: Basic Books.

Taylor, E. J. (2003). Spiritual needs of patients with cancer and family caregivers. *Cancer Nursing, 26*(4), 260–266. doi:10.1097/00002820-200308000-00002 PMID:12886116

Taylor, R. H., & Stoianovici, D. (2003). Medical robotics in computer-integrated surgery. *Robotics and Automation. IEEE Transactions on, 19*(5), 765–781.

Taylor, R., Mechitov, A., & Schellenberger, R. E. (1996). Transformation within the Russian academic community. *International Education,26*(1),29–39.

Taylor, S. J., & Bogdan, R. (1998). *Introduction to qualitative research methods: A guide and resource* (3rd ed.). New York, NY: John Wiley.

Telford, J., Cosgrave, J., & Houghton, R. (2006). *Joint evaluation of the international response to the Indian Ocean tsunami.* London, UK: Tsunami Evaluation Coalition.

Teppo, A. R. (1998). *Diverse ways of knowing.* Philadelphia, PA: NCTM.

Thang Moe, D. (2015). Sin and evil in Christian and Buddhist perspectives: A quest for theodicy. *Asia Journal of Theology, 29*(1), 22–46.

The Aster Awards. (2014, May 6). *About the Aster Awards.* Retrieved from http://www.asterawards.com/about-the-aster-awards/

The big three, at a glance. (2012, November 2). *The New York Times*. Retrieved from http://www.nytimes.com/2012/11/04/education/edlife/the-big-three-mooc-providers.html

The British Academic Written English (BAWE) Corpus. (n.d.). Developed at the Universities of Warwick, Reading and Oxford Brookes under the directorship of Hilary Nesi, Sheena Gardner, Paul Thompson and Paul Wickens. Available at: http://www2.warwick.ac.uk/fac/soc/al/research/collect/bawe/

The British National Corpus, version 3 (BNC XML Edition) . (2007). Distributed by Oxford University Computing Services on behalf of the BNC Consortium. Available at: http://www.natcorp.ox.ac.uk/

The Future of State Universities. (2011, September). *Research on the effectiveness of online learning: A compilation of research on online learning*. Paper presented at The Future of State Universities Conference, Dallas, TX. Retrieved from http://www.academicpartnerships.com/sites/default/files/Research%20on%20the%20Effectiveness%20of%20Online%20Learning.pdf

The Swedish Association of Local Authorities and Regions. (2014). *Vägval för framtiden. Våra territoriella och kulturella gränser*. Retrieved from http://skl.se/download/18.547ffc53146c75fdec079e4b/1404478740292/skl-15-trender-vagval-for-framtiden-2025.pdf

Thomas, M., & Dhillon, G. (2012). Interpreting deep structures of information systems security. *The Computer Journal*, *55*(10), 1148–1156. doi:10.1093/comjnl/bxr118

Thompson, A., & Crompton, H. (2010). Point/Counterpoint is technology killing critical thinking? *Learning and Leading with Technology*, *38*(1), 6.

Thoresen, C. E. (1999). Spirituality and health: Is there a relationship? *Journal of Health Psychology*, *4*(3), 291–300. doi:10.1177/135910539900400314 PMID:22021598

Thoresen, C. E., Harris, A. H., & Oman, D. (2001). Spirituality, religion, and health: Evidence, issues, and concerns. In T. G. Plante & A. C. Sherman (Eds.), *Faith and health: Psychological perspectives* (pp. 15–52). New York, NY: Guilford.

Tilly, W. D. (2002). Best practices in school psychology as a problem as a problem-solving enterprise. In A. Thomas & J. Grimes (Eds.), *Best practices in school psychology* (Vol. 4, pp. 21–36). Bethesda, MD: National Association of School Psychologists.

Timmermann, A. (2006). Forecast combinations. In G. Elliot, C.W.J. Granger, & A. Timmermann (Eds.), *Handbook of Economic Forecasting* (Vol. 1, pp. 135-196). Retrieved from: http://management.ucsd.edu/faculty/directory/timmermann/pub/docs/forecast-combinations.pdf

Tinsley, H. E. A., & Tinsley, D. J. (1987). Uses of factor analysis in counseling psychology research. *Journal of Counseling Psychology*, *34*(4), 414–424. doi:10.1037/0022-0167.34.4.414

Tobias, S. (1990). *They are not dumb, they are different: Stalking the second tier*. Tucson, AZ: Research Corporation.

Tobin, J. (2000). Financial globalization. *World Development*, *28*(6), 1101–1104.

Tohidi, H. (2011). The role of risk management in IT systems of organizations. *Procedia Computer Science*, *3*, 881–887. doi:10.1016/j.procs.2010.12.144

Tokunaga, R. S. (2010). Following you home from school: A critical review and synthesis of research on cyberbullying victimization. *Computers in Human Behavior*, *26*(3), 277–287. doi:10.1016/j.chb.2009.11.014

Tomlinson, J. (1999). *Globalization and culture*. University of Chicago Press.

Tomusk, V. (Ed.). (2007). *Creating the European area of higher education*. Dordrecht, Netherlands: Springer. doi:10.1007/978-1-4020-4616-2

Tono, Y. (2002). *The role of learner corpora in SLA research and foreign language teaching: the multiple comparison approach*. (Unpublished doctoral dissertation). Lancaster University.

Topcu, C., Erdur-Baker, O., & Capa, A. Y. (2008). Examination of cyber-bullying experiences among Turkish students from different school types. *Cyberpsychology & Behavior*, *11*(6), 644–648. doi:10.1089/cpb.2007.0161 PMID:18783345

Toplu, M. (2010). Kil tabletlerden elektronik yayıncılığa kütüphanecilik felsefesinin gelişimi ve dönüşümü. *Türk Kütüphaneciliği*, *24*(4), 644–684.

Topor, F. S. (2013). *The predictive validity of a sentence repetition test for Japanese learners of English* (Doctoral dissertation). Capella University.

Torney-Purta, J. (1989, March). *A research agenda for the study of global/international education in the United States*. Paper presented at the Annual Meeting of the American Educational Research Association, San Francisco, CA.

Torney-Purta, J. (1986). *Predictors of global awareness and concern among secondary school students*. Columbus, OH: Citizen Development and Global Education Program.

Torney-Purta, J. (2001). The global awareness survey: Implications for teacher education. *Theory into Practice*, *21*(3), 200–205. doi:10.1080/00405848209543006

Totura, C. M. W., MacKinnon-Lewis, C., Gesten, E. L., Gadd, R., Divine, K. P., Dunham, S., & Kamboukos, D. (2009). Bullying and victimization among boys and girls in middle school: The influence of perceived family and school contexts. *The Journal of Early Adolescence*, *29*(4), 571–609. doi:10.1177/0272431608324190

Touhy, T. A. (2001). Nurturing hope and spirituality in the nursing home. *Holistic Nursing Practice*, *15*(4), 45–56. doi:10.1097/00004650-200107000-00008 PMID:12120495

Towner, T. L., & Munoz, C. L. (2011). Facebook and education: a classroom collection? In C. Wankel (Ed.), *Educating Educators with Social Media, Cutting-edge Technologies in Higher Education* (pp. 33–57). Emerald Group Publishing.

Trelstad, M. (2014). The many meanings of the only Christ. *Dialog: A Journal of Theology*, *53*(3), 179–184. doi:10.1111/dial.12114

Treolar, L. L. (2000). Spiritual beliefs, response to disability, and the Church—Part 2. *Journal of Religion Disability & Health*, *4*(1), 5–31. doi:10.1300/J095v04n01_02

Trevor, M., & Kevin, B. (2014). Access denied? Twenty-firstcentury technology in schools. *Technology, Pedagogy and Education*, *23*(4), 423–437. doi:10.1080/1475939X.2013.864697

Triandis, H. C. (1995). *Individualism and collectivism*. Oxford, UK: Westview Press.

Trochim, W. M. K. (2006). Qualitative validity. *Social Research Methods*. Retrieved from http://www.socialresearchmethods.net/kb/qualval.htm

Truog, R. D., & Robinson, W. M. (2003). Role of brain death and the dead-donor rule in the ethics of organ transplantation. *Critical Care Medicine*, *31*(9), 2391–2396. PMID:14501972

Truth and Dignity Platform. (2015). Retrieved from http://moldovanpolitics.com/tag/truth-and-dignity-platform/

Tsai, A. (2012). An integrated e-learning solution for healthcare professionals. *Journal of Business Management*, *6*(27), 8163–8177. doi:10.5897/AJBM11.2927

Tsai, K. C. (2012). Dance with critical thinking and creative thinking in the classroom. *Journal of Sociological Research, 3*(2), 312–324. doi:10.5296/jsr.v3i2.2323

Tsang, J. A., & Rowatt, W. C. (2007). The relationship between religious orientation, right-wing authoritarianism, and implicit sexual prejudice. *The International Journal for the Psychology of Religion, 17*(2), 99–120. doi:10.1080/10508610701244122

Tulu, B., Burkhard, R. J., & Horan, T. A. (2006). Continuing use of medical information systems by medical professionals: Empirical evaluation of a work system model. *Communications of the Association for Information Systems, 18,* 641–656. Retrieved from http://www.cgu.edu/pdffiles/KayCenter/journal_version_tulu_etal_cais2006@20@282@29.pdf

Tuman, M. C. (1988). Class, codes, and composition: Basil Bernstein and the critique of Pedagogy. *College Composition and Communication, 39*(1), 42. doi:10.2307/357815

Turkle, S. (2011). *Alone together: Why we expect more from technology and less from each other.* New York, NY: Basic.

Turner, P. (2005). Critical thinking in nursing education and practice as defined in the literature. *Nursing Education Perspectives, 26*(5), 272–277. PMID:16295305

Tu, Y., Lin, S., & Chang, Y. (2011). A cross-cultural comparison by individualism/collectivism among Brazil, Russia, India and China. *International Business Research, 4*(2), 175–182. doi:10.5539/ibr.v4n2p175

Twining-Ward, L. (2007). *A toolkit for monitoring and managing community-based tourism.* School of Travel Industry Management, University of Hawaii.

Tye, K. A. (2003, October). Global education as a worldwide movement. *Phi Delta Kappan, 85*(2), 165–168. doi:10.1177/003172170308500212

Ueno, K. (2005). Suicide as Japan's major export: A Note on Japanese suicide culture. *Revista Espaço Acadêmico, 44.* Retrieved from http://www.espacoacademico.com.br/044/ 44eueno_ing.htm

Uluyol, Ç. (2011). *Web destekli örnek olay yönteminde çoklu bakış açısı ve yüz yüze etkileşimin öğrencilerin eleştirel düşünme becerilerine etkisi.* (Unpublished doctoral dissertation). Gazi University, Ankara, Turkey.

UNESCAP. (2007). *Medical travel in Asia and the Pacific: challenges and opportunities. Thailand.* Retrieved from http://www.unescap.org/ESID/hds/lastestadd/MedicalTourismReport09.pdf

United Nations Children's Fund International Child Development Centre. (1999). *After the fall: The human impact of ten years of transition.* Retrieved from http://www.unicef-irc.org/ publications/pdf/afterthefall.pdf

United Nations Educational, Scientific and Cultural Organization Institute for Statistics. (n.d.). *Russia Federation.* Retrieved from http://www.uis.unesco.org/DataCentre/Pages/country-profile.aspx?code=RUS&regioncode=40530

United Nations. (2008). *Rural Development, Croatia country report.* Retrieved from http://www.un.org/esa/agenda21/natlinfo/countr/croatia/ruralDevelopment.pdf

United Nations. (2010). *Tourism Satellite Account: Recommended methodological framework 2008.* Statistics Division, Statistical Office of the European Communities, Organisation for Economic Co-operation and Development & World Tourism Organization. Madrid: World Tourism Organization. Retrieved from http://unstats.un.org/unsd/publication/Seriesf/SeriesF_80rev1e.pdf

UNWTO Think Tank. (2002, April 2). *Destination Management - Conceptual Framework.* Retrieved from http://www.unwto.org/destination/conceptual/conceptual.php?lang=E

Urry, J. (1995). *Consuming places.* London: Routledge.

Valeeva, E. R., & Babukh, V. A. (2013). Izuchenie problem sotsial'noi politiki Ispanii i Rossii v protsesse prepodavanija pravovikh distsiplin studentam magistraturi v ramkakh programmi dvoinih diplomov. [The study of the social policy problems in Spain and in Russia when teaching law courses to post graduate students acquiring a double degree]. *Vestnik Kazanskogo tekhnologicheskogo universiteta, 1,* 302–306. Retrieved from http://cyberleninka.ru/article/n/izuchenie-problem-sotsialnoy-politiki-ispanii-i-rossii-v-protsesse-prepodavaniya-pravovyh-distsiplin-studentam-magistratury-v-ramkah

Van Den Eynden, V., Corti, L., Woollard, M., Bishop, L., & Horton, L. (2011). *Managing and sharing data. Best practice for researchers.* University of Essex. Retrieved from: http://www. dataarchive. ac.uk/media/2894/managingsharing. pdf.

Van Eerden, K. (2001). Using critical thinking vignettes to evaluate student learning. *Nursing and Health Care Perspectives, 22*(5), 231–234. PMID:15957399

van Maanen, J. (1988). *Tales of the field.* Chicago, IL: University of Chicago Press.

van Maanen, M. (1990). *Researching lived experience: Human science for an action sensitive pedagogy.* London, Ontario, Canada: The University of Western Ontario.

Van Manen, M. (2014). *Phenomenology of practice.* Walnut Creek, CA: Left Coast Press.

Vandebosch, H., & van Cleemput, K. (2008). Defining cyberbullying: A qualitative research into the perceptions of youngsters. *Cyberpsychology & Behavior, 11*(4), 499–503. doi:10.1089/cpb.2007.0042 PMID:18721100

Vaughn, L. (2010). *Psychology and culture: Thinking, feeling, and behaving in a global context.* East Sussex, UK: Psychology Press.

Venkatesh, V., & Davis, F. D. (1996). A model of antecedents of perceived ease of use: Development and test. *Decision Sciences, 27*(3), 451–481. doi:10.1111/j.1540-5915.1996.tb01822.x

Venkatesh, V., & Davis, F. D. (2000). A theoretical extension of the technology acceptance model: Four longitudinal field studies. *Management Science, 46*(2), 186–204. doi:10.1287/mnsc.46.2.186.11926

Verizon. (2013). *2013 data breach investigations report.* Basking Ridge, NJ: Author.

Vernon, M. (1998, June 4). Directors buckle under work pressures. *Computer Weekly*, p. 30.

Verschaffel, L., & De Corte, E. (1997). Word problems: A vehicle for promoting authentic mathematical understanding and problem solving in the primary school? In T. Nunes & P. Bryant (Eds.), *Learning and teaching mathematics: An international perspective.* Psychology Press.

Verschaffel, L., De Corte, E., & Lasure, S. (1994). Realistic considerations in mathematical modeling of school arithmetic word problems. *Learning and Instruction, 4*(4), 273–294. doi:10.1016/0959-4752(94)90002-7

Verschaffel, L., Greer, B., & De Corte, E. (2000). *Making sense of word problems.* Lisse, The Netherlands: Swets & Zeitlinger.

Vertovec, S. (2005). *The Political Importance of Diasporas.* Migration Policy Institute. Retrieved from www.migrationinformation.org/Feature/display.cfm?ID=313

Virilio, P. (1998). *The virilio reader.* Malden, MA: Blackwell.

VOICE. (2013). *The Vienna-Oxford International Corpus of English* (version 2.0 online). Retrieved from http://voice.univie.ac.at

Volodina, E. D. (2014). Sistematizatsija form mezhdunarodnoi academicheskoy mobil'nosti studentov. [Classifying forms of academic mobility programs for students]. *Vestnik Chelyabinskogo gosudarstvennogo pedagogicheskogo universiteta, 2*, 93–102. Retrieved from http://cyberleninka.ru/article/n/sistematizatsiya-form-mezhdunarodnoy-akademicheskoy-mobilnosti-studentov

Voltz, D. L., & Collins, L. (2010). Preparing special education administrators for inclusion in diverse, standards-based contexts: Beyond the council for exceptional children and the Interstate School Leaders Licensure Consortium. *Teacher Education and Special Education, 33*(1), 70–82. doi:10.1177/0888406409356676

von Hippel, E. (1994). Sticky information and the locus of problem solving: Implications for innovation. *Management Science, 40*(4), 429–439. doi:10.1287/mnsc.40.4.429

von Hippel, E. (1998). Economics of product development by users: The impact of "sticky" local information. *Management Science, 44*(5), 629–644. doi:10.1287/mnsc.44.5.629

Vorobiev, A., & Bekmamedova, N. (2010). An ontology-driven approach applied to information security. *Journal of Research & Practice in Information Technology, 42*(1), 61–76.

Vrangbæk, K., & Christiansen, T. (2005). Health policy in Denmark: Leaving the decentralized welfare path? *Journal of Health Politics, Policy and Law, 30*(1-2), 29–52. doi:10.1215/03616878-30-1-2-29 PMID:15943386

Vucinich, A. (1990). *Empire of knowledge: The Academy of Sciences of the USSR*. Oakland, CA: University of California Press.

Vuorinen, J., & Tetri, P. (2012). The order machine: The ontology of information security. *Journal of the Association for Information Systems, 13*(9), 695–713.

Vygotsky, L. S. (1978). *Mind and society: The development of higher mental processes*. Cambridge, MA: Harvard University Press.

Waclawski, J., & Church, A. H. (Eds.). (2002). *Organizational development: A data-driven approach to organizational change (A professional practice series, a publication of the Society for Industrial and Organizational Psychology)*. San Francisco, CA: Jossey-Bass, A Wiley Company.

Wade, A., & Beran, T. (2011). Cyberbullying: The new era of bullying. *Canadian Journal of School Psychology, 26*(1), 44–61. doi:10.1177/0829573510396318

Wagner, A. K., Gandek, B., Aaronson, N. K., Acquadro, C., Alonso, J., Apolone, G., & Ware, J. E. Jr et al.. (1998). Cross-cultural comparisons of the content of SF-36 translations across 10 countries: Results from the IQOLA project. *Journal of Clinical Epidemiology, 51*(11), 925–932. PMID:9817109

Wagner, N., & Hendel, T. (2000). Ethics in pediatric nursing: An international perspective. *Journal of Pediatric Nursing, 15*(1), 54–59. PMID:10714039

Wahlberg, A. C., Cedersund, E., & Wredling, R. (2003). Telephone nurses' experience of problems with telephone advice in Sweden. *Journal of Clinical Nursing, 12*(1), 37–45. doi:10.1046/j.1365-2702.2003.00702.x PMID:12519248

Waibel, B. (2007). *Phrasal verbs in learner English: A corpus-based study of German and Italian students*. (Unpublished PhD thesis). Albert-Ludwigs-Universität Freiburg.

Waite, A. (2010, June 6). *Re: InfoSec triads: Security / functionality / ease of use*. [Web log post]. Retrieved from: http://.infosanity.co.uk/2010/06/12/infosec-triads-securityfunctionalityease-of-use/

Walker, J. L. (2012). The use of saturation in qualitative research. *Canadian Journal of Cardiovascular Nursing*, *22*(2), 37–41. PMID:22803288

Walker, P. O. (2004). Decolonizing Conflict Resolution: Addressing the Ontological Violence of Westernization. *American Indian Quarterly*, *28*(3/4), 527–549.

Walsh, C. M., & Seldomridge, L. A. (2006). Critical thinking: Back to square two. *The Journal of Nursing Education*, *45*(6), 212–219. PMID:16780009

Walton, J. (1999). Spirituality of patients recovering from an acute myocardial infarction: A grounded theory study. *Journal of Holistic Nursing*, *17*(1), 34–53. doi:10.1177/089801019901700104 PMID:10373841

Walton, J., & Sullivan, N. (2004). Men of prayer: Spirituality of men with prostate cancer a grounded theory study. *Journal of Holistic Nursing*, *22*(2), 133–151. doi:10.1177/0898010104264778 PMID:15154989

Walumbwa, F. O., Avolio, B. J., Gardner, W. L., Wernsing, T. S., & Peterson, S. J. (2008). Authentic leadership: Development and validation of a theory-based measure. *Journal of Management*, *34*(1), 89–126. doi:10.1177/0149206307308913

Wang, K., Shu, Q., & Tu, Q. (2008). Technostress under different organizational environments: An empirical investigation. *Computers in Human Behavior*, *24*(2), 3002–3013. doi:10.1016/j.chb.2008.05.007

Wang, L., James, K. T., Denyer, D., & Bailey, C. (2014). Western views and Chinese whispers: Re-thinking global leadership competency in multi-national corporations. *Leadership*, *10*(4), 471–495. doi:10.1177/1742715013510340

Wang, S. J., Middleton, B., Prosser, L. A., Bardon, C. G., Spurr, C. D., Carchidi, P. J., & Bates, D. W. et al. (2003). A cost benefit analysis of electronic medical records in primary care. *The American Journal of Medicine*, *114*(5), 397–403. doi:10.1016/S0002-9343(03)00057-3 PMID:12714130

Warburton, S. (2009). Second life in higher education: Assessing the potential for and the barriers to deploying virtual worlds in learning and teaching. *British Journal of Educational Technology*, *40*(3), 414–426.

Ward, M., Peters, G., & Shelley, K. (2010). Student and Faculty Perceptions of the Quality of Online Learning Experiences. *International Review of Research in Open and Distance Learning*, *11*(3), 57–77.

Ward, R., Stevens, C., Brentnall, P., & Briddon, J. (2008). The attitudes of healthcare staff to information technology: A comprehensive review of the research literature. *Health Information and Libraries Journal*, *25*(2), 81–97. doi:10.1111/j.1471-1842.2008.00777.x PMID:18494643

Ware, J. E. (2004). SF-36 Health survey update. In M. E. Maruish (Ed.), *The use of psychological testing for treatment planning and outcomes assessment* (3rd ed.). Lawrence Erlbaum Associates.

Wark, M. (2007). *Game Theory*. Cambridge, MA: Harvard University Press.

Warner, R. S. (1979). Theoretical barriers to the understanding of evangelical Christianity. *Sociology of Religion*, *40*(1), 1–9. doi:10.2307/3710492

Wasilik, O., & Bollinger, D. U. (2009). Faculty satisfaction in the online environment: An institutional study. *The Internet and Higher Education*, *12*(3-4), 173–178. doi:10.1016/j.iheduc.2009.05.001

Watson, D., & Tinsley, D. (Eds.). (2013). *Integrating information technology into education*. London, UK: Springer.

Watson, P. J., Hood, R. W. Jr, Morris, R. J., & Hall, J. R. (1984). Empathy, religious orientation, and social desirability. *The Journal of Psychology*, *117*(2), 211–216. doi:10.1080/00223980.1984.9923679

Watters, A. (2012a). *6.003z: A learner-created MOOC spins out of MITx* [Web log post]. Retrieved from http://www. hackeducation.com/2012/08/14/6.003z-learner-organized-mooc/

Watters, E. (2010). *Crazy like us: The globalization of the American psyche*. New York, NY: Free Press.

Watts, J. W. (2005). Ritual legitimacy and scriptural authority. *Journal of Biblical Literature, 124*(3), 401–417. doi:10.2307/30041032

Wears, R. L., & Berg, M. (2005). Computer technology and clinical work: Still waiting for Godot. *Journal of the American Medical Association, 293*(10), 1261–1263. doi:10.1001/jama.293.10.1261 PMID:15755949

Webber, C. F., & Robertson, J. M. (2004). Internationalization and educators understanding of issues in educational leadership. *The Educational Forum, 68*(3), 264–275. doi:10.1080/00131720408984638

Weber, L. (2013, April 24). Job hunt moves to mobile devices, *Wall Street Journal*, p. B8.

Webster, F. (2014). *Theories of the Information Society*. New York: Routledge.

Webster, J. (2014). *Shaping women's work: Gender, employment and information technology*. New York, NY: Routledge.

Weil, E. (2008). Teaching boys and girls separately. *New York Times*. Retrieved from http://nytimes. com/2008/03/02/magazine/02sex3-t. html

Weil, M. M., & Rosen, L. D. (1997). *Technostress: Coping with technology @WORK @HOME @PLAY*. New York, NY: John Wiley.

Wei, N. X. (2004). Zhongguo xuexizhe yingyu kouyuyuliaoku chushi yanjiu[A preliminary study of the characteristics of Chinese learners' spoken English]. *Modern Foreign Languages, 27*(2), 140–149.

Weitz, J. S., & Fraser, H. B. (2001). Explaining mortality rate plateaus. *Proceedings of the National Academy of Sciences of the United States of America, 98*(26), 15383–15386. PMID:11752476

Welk, D. E. (2001). Clinical strategies: Teaching students a pattern of reversals eases the care plan process. *Nurse Educator, 26*(1), 43–45. doi:10.1097/00006223-200101000-00017 PMID:16372456

Werlinger, R., Muldner, K., Hawkey, K., & Beznosov, K. (2010). Preparation, detection, and analysis: The diagnostic work of IT security incident response. *Information Management & Computer Security, 18*(1), 26–42. doi:10.1108/09685221011035241

Werthner, H., & Klein, S. (1999). *Information technology and tourism: a challenging ralationship*. New York, NY: Springer. doi:10.1007/978-3-7091-6363-4

Werthner, H., & Ricci, F. (2004). E-commerce and Tourism. *Communications of the ACM, 47*(12), 101–105. doi:10.1145/1035134.1035141

Werts, M. G., Lambert, M., & Carpenter, E. (2009). What special education directors say about RTI. *Learning Disability Quarterly, 32*(4), 245–254. doi:10.2307/27740376

Wessells, G., & Dawes, A. (2007). Macro-level interventions: Psychology, social policy, and societal influence processes. In *Toward a global psychology: Theory, research, intervention, and pedagogy* (pp. 1–45). Lawrence Erlbaum Associates.

West, R., & Frumina, E. (2012). European standards in Russian higher education and the role of English: A case study of the National University of Science and Technology, Moscow (MISiS). *European Journal of Education, 47*(1), 50–63. doi:.01507.x10.1111/j.1465-3435.2011

Westervelt, R. (2013, December 18). Mobile devices will pose the biggest risk in 2014, survey says. *Computing Resource Network.* Retrieved from http://www.crn.com/news/security/240164859/mobile-devices-will-pose-the-biggest-risk-in-2014-survey-says.htm

West, R., Toplak, M., & Stanovich, K. (2008). Heuristics and biases as measures of critical thinking: Associations with cognitive ability and thinking dispositions. *Journal of Educational Psychology, 100*(4), 930–941. doi:10.1037/a0012842

Wetzel, P. J. (1994). A movable self: the linguistic indexing of *uchi* and *soto.* Situated Meaning: Inside and Outside. In J. Bachnik & C. J. Quinn (Eds.), *Japanese Self, Society, and Language* (pp. 78–87). Princeton, NJ: Princeton University Press.

What does Cronbach's alpha mean? (2015). UCLA: Statistical Consulting Group. Retrieved July 29, 2015, from http://http://www.ats.ucla.edu/stat/spss/faq/alpha.html

What is flipped learning. (2014). Retrieved from http://www.flippedlearning.org/definition

Whitehead, M., Evandrou, M., Haglund, B., & Diderichsen, F. (1997). As the health divide widens in Sweden and Britain, what's happening to access to care? *British Medical Journal, 315*(7114), 1006–1009. Retrieved from http://www.ncbi.nlm.nih.gov/pmc/articles/PMC2127673/pdf/9365303.pdf

Whitfield, P., Klug, B. J., & Whitney, P. (2007). "Situative cognition" barrier to teaching across cultures. *Intercultural Education, 18*(3), 25. doi:10.1080/14675980701463604

Whittemore, R., Chase, S. K., & Mandle, C. L. (2001). Validity in qualitative research. *Qualitative Health Research, 11,* 522–537. PMID:11521609

Whitten, E., Esteves, K. J., & Woodrow, A. (2009). *RTI success: Proven tools and strategies for schools and classrooms.* Minneapolis, MN: Free Spirit.

WHO. (2014). *Large gains in life expectancy. World Health Statistics 2014.* Available from http://www.who.int/mediacentre/news/releases/2014/world-health-statistics-2014/en/

Whoqol, G. (2006). A cross-cultural study of spirituality, religion, and personal beliefs as components of quality of life. *Social Science & Medicine, 62*(6), 1486–1497. doi:10.1016/j.socscimed.2005.08.001 PMID:16168541

Wiener, R. M., & Soodak, L. C. (2008). Special education administrators' perspectives on response to intervention. *Journal of Special Education Leadership, 21*(1), 39–45.

Wigle, S. E., & Wilcox, D. J. (2002). Special education directors and their competencies on CEC-identified skills. *Education, 123*(2), 276–288.

Wiley, K. (1983). Effects of a self-directed learning project and preference for a structure on self-directed learning readiness. *Nursing Research, 32*(3), 181–185. doi:10.1097/00006199-198305000-00011 PMID:6551780

Will the Peace Corps be leaving Russia ? (2002, August 13). Retrieved from http://peacecorpsonline.org/messages/messages/2629/1008862.html

Wilson, K. B. (2014, July). Heath care costs 101: Slow growth persists. *California Health Care Costs.* Retrieved from http://www.chcf.org/publications/2014/07/health-care-costs-101

Winter, B. (2009). Gender related attitudes toward achievement in college. *Community College Enterprise, 15*(1), 83–91.

Wise, J. M. (1997). *Exploring technology and social space.* Thousand Oaks, CA: Sage.

Wiske, M. S., Franz, K. R., & Breit, L. (2010). *Teaching for understanding with technology.* San Francisco, CA: John Wiley & Sons.

Witmer, J. M., & Sweeney, T. J. (1992). A holistic model for wellness and prevention over the life span. *Journal of Counseling and Development, 71*(2), 140–148. doi:10.1002/j.1556-6676.1992.tb02189.x

Witt, E. (2011). *Authentic leadership in the college setting* [Review of the book *Authentic leadership theory and practice: Origins, effects, and development*, by W. L. Gardner, B. J. Avolio, & F. O. Walumbwa]. Retrieved from https://nclp.umd.edu/resources/ bookreviews/bookreview-authentic_leadership-witt-2011.pdf

Wolfe, T. (2000). *Hooking up*. New York, NY: McMillan.

Wollons, R. (1993, Spring). The Black Forest in a bamboo garden: Missionary kindergartens in Japan, 1868–1912. *History of Education Quarterly, 33*(1), 1–35. doi:10.2307/368518

Wolpert, S. (2009). *Is technology producing a decline in critical thinking and analysis?* UCLA Newsroom.

Woo, J., Wolfgang, S., & Batista, H. (2008). The effect of globalization of drug manufacturing, production, and sourcing and challenges for American drug safety. *Clinical Pharmacology and Therapeutics, 83*(3), 494–497. PMID:18253142

World Economic Forum. (2010). *The new discipline of workforce wellness: Enhancing corporate performance by tackling chronic disease* (2010 Report). Retrieved from the World Economic Forum website: http://www3.weforum.org/docs/WEF_HE_TacklingChronicDisease_Report_2010.pdf

World Economic Forum. (2014). *Global agenda councils: Outlook on the global agenda 2015*. Retrieved from http://reports.weforum.org/outlook-global-agenda-2015/wp-content/ blogs.dir/59/mp/files/pages/files/outlook-2015-a4-downloadable.pdf

World Health Organization. (1948). *Preamble to the Constitution of the World Health Organization as adopted by the International Health Conference, New York, 19–22 June, 1946*. Geneva, Switzerland: Author. Retrieved from http://www.ncbi.nlm.nih.gov/pmc/ articles/PMC2567708/

World Health Organization. (2005). *Chernobyl: The true scale of the accident; 20 years later a UN report provides definitive answers and ways to repair lives*. Available at: http://www.who. int/mediacentre/news/releases/2005/pr38/en/index. html

World Health Organization. (2005). *WHO guidelines on nonclinical evaluation of vaccines. In WHO Expert Committee on Biological Standardization. Fifty-fourth report* (Vol. 927). Geneva: World Health Organization.

World Health Organization. (2009). *Interventions on diet and physical activity: What works: Summary report*. Retrieved from http://www.who.int/dietphysicalactivity/summary-report-09.pdf

World Health Organization. (2010). *The burden of health care-associated infection worldwide: A summary*. Retrieved from http://www.who.int/gpsc/country_work/summary_20100430_en.pdf

World Health Organization. (2010). *World health statistics 2010*. Retrieved from http://www.who.int/gho/publications/world_health_statistics/EN_WHS10_Full.pdf

World Medical Association General Assembly. (2004). World Medical Association Declaration of Helsinki: Ethical principles for medical research involving human subjects. *International Journal of Bioethics, 15*(1), 124. PMID:15835069

Worthman, J. (2013, April 11). How to lighten the crush of e-mail. *New York Times*, p. B11.

Wray, A. (2002). *Formulaic sequences and the lexicon*. Cambridge, UK: Cambridge University Press. doi:10.1017/CBO9780511519772

Wray, A., & Perkins, M. (2000). The functions of formulaic language: An integrated model. *Language & Communication, 20*(1), 1–28. doi:10.1016/S0271-5309(99)00015-4

Wray-Lake, L., Flanagan, C. A., & Osgood, D. W. (2008). Examining trends in adolescent environmental attitudes, beliefs, and behaviors across three decades. *Environment and Behavior*, *42*(1), 61–85. doi:10.1177/0013916509335163 PMID:20046859

Wright, M. F. (2015b). Adolescents' cyber aggression perpetration and cyber victimization: The longitudinal associations with school functioning. Social Psychology of Education, 18(4), 653-666. doi: 10.1007/s11218-015-9318-6

Wright, M. F. (2015b). Cyber victimization and adjustment difficulties: The mediation of Chinese and American adolescents' digital technology usage. *CyberPsychology: Journal of Psychosocial Research in Cyberspace, 1*(1), article 1. Retrieved from: http://cyberpsychology.eu/view.php?cisloclanku=2015051102&article=1

Wright, K. (2010). Employing spirituality and faith as a protective factor against suicide. *Mental Health Nursing*, *30*(6), 14–15.

Wright, M. F. (2013). The relationship between young adults' beliefs about anonymity and subsequent cyber aggression. *Cyberpsychology, Behavior, and Social Networking*, *16*(12), 858–862. doi:10.1089/cyber.2013.0009 PMID:23849002

Wright, M. F. (2014a). Cyber victimization and perceived stress: Linkages to late adolescents' cyber aggression and psychological functioning. *Youth & Society*.

Wright, M. F. (2014b). Predictors of anonymous cyber aggression: The role of adolescents' beliefs about anonymity, aggression, and the permanency of digital content. *Cyberpsychology, Behavior, and Social Networking*, *17*(7), 431–438. doi:10.1089/cyber.2013.0457 PMID:24724731

Wright, M. F. (2014c). Longitudinal investigation of the associations between adolescents' popularity and cyber social behaviors. *Journal of School Violence*, *13*(3), 291–314. doi:10.1080/15388220.2013.849201

Wright, M. F., Kamble, S., Lei, K., Li, Z., Aoyama, I., & Shruti, S. (2015). Peer attachment and cyberbullying involvement among Chinese, Indian, and Japanese adolescents. *Societies*, *5*(2), 339–353. doi:10.3390/soc5020339

Wright, M. F., & Li, Y. (2012). Kicking the digital dog: A longitudinal investigation of young adults' victimization and cyber-displaced aggression. *Cyberpsychology, Behavior, and Social Networking*, *15*(9), 448–454. doi:10.1089/cyber.2012.0061 PMID:22974350

Wright, M. F., & Li, Y. (2013a). Normative beliefs about aggression and cyber aggression among young adults: A longitudinal investigation. *Aggressive Behavior*, *39*(3), 161–170. doi:10.1002/ab.21470 PMID:23440595

Wright, M. F., & Li, Y. (2013b). The association between cyber victimization and subsequent cyber aggression: The moderating effect of peer rejection. *Journal of Youth and Adolescence*, *42*(5), 662–674. doi:10.1007/s10964-012-9903-3 PMID:23299177

Wright, P. F., Deatly, A. M., Karron, R. A., Belshe, R. B., Shi, J. R., Gruber, W. C., & Randolph, V. B. et al. (2007). Comparison of results of detection of rhinovirus by PCR and viral culture in human nasal wash specimens from subjects with and without clinical symptoms of respiratory illness. *Journal of Clinical Microbiology*, *45*(7), 2126–2129. PMID:17475758

Wrzus, C., Wagner, J., & Neyer, F. J. (2012). The interdependence of horizontal family relationships and friendships relates to higher well-being. *Personal Relationships*, *19*(3), 465–482. doi:10.1111/j.1475-6811.2011.01373.x

Wu, I. L., Li, J. Y., & Fu, C. Y. (2011). The adoption of mobile healthcare by hospital's professionals: An integrative perspective. *Decision Support Systems*, *51*(3), 587–596. doi:10.1016/j.dss.2011.03.003

Wulff, D. M. (1997). *Psychology of religion: Classic and contemporary*. New York, NY: Wiley.

Wyndhamn, J., & Saljo, R. (1997). Word problems and mathematical reasoning - a study of children's mastery of reference and meaning in textual realities. *Learning and Instruction, 7*(4), 361–382. doi:10.1016/S0959-4752(97)00009-1

Yang, Y. T. C., & Wu, W. C. I. (2012). Digital storytelling for enhancing student academic achievement, critical thinking, and learning motivation: A year-long experimental study. *Computers & Education, 59*(2), 339–352.

Yankelovich Partners. (1996). *Family Physician Survey*. Radnor, PA: John Templeton.

Yarow, J. (2013, March 27). How people use facebook on smartphones. *Business Insider*. Retrieved from www.businessinsider.com/chart-of-the-day-facebook-usage-on-smartphones-2013-3

Yarow, J. (2014, April 3). We are spending a lot more time online thanks to smartphones and tablets. *Business Insider*. Retrieved from http://www.businessinsider.com/were-spending-a-lot-more-time-online-thanks-to-smartphones-and-tablets-2014-4?nr_email_referer=1&utm_source=Triggermail&utm_medium=email&utm_term=Tech%20Chart%20Of%20The%20Day&utm_campaign=SAI_COTD_040314

Yau, H. K., & Cheng, A. F. (2012). Gender difference of confidence in using technology for learning. *Journal Of Technology Studies, 38*(2), 74–79.

Ybarra, M. L., Diener-West, M., & Leaf, P. (2007). Examining the overlap in internet harassment and school bullying: Implications for school intervention. *The Journal of Adolescent Health, 1*(6), 42–50. doi:10.1016/j.jadohealth.2007.09.004 PMID:18047944

Ybarra, M. L., & Mitchell, K. J. (2004). Online aggressor/targets, aggressors, and targets: A comparison of associated youth characteristics. *Journal of Child Psychology and Psychiatry, and Allied Disciplines, 45*(7), 1308–1316. doi:10.1111/j.1469-7610.2004.00328.x PMID:15335350

Yell, M. L., & Walker, D. W. (2010). The legal basis of response to intervention: Analysis and implications. *Exceptionality, 18*(3), 124–137. doi:10.1080/09362835.2010.491741

Yerushalmy, M. (2000). Problem solving strategies and mathematical resources: A longitudinal view on problem solving in function-based approach to algebra. *Educational Studies in Mathematics, 43*(2), 125–147. doi:10.1023/A:1017566031373

Yildirim, B., & Özkahraman, S. (2011). Critical thinking in nursing process and education. *International Journal of Humanities and Social Science, 1*(13), 257–262.

Yi, M. Y., Jackson, J. D., Park, J. S., & Probst, J. C. (2006). Understanding information technology acceptance by individual professionals: Toward an integrative view. *Information & Management, 3*(3), 350–363. http://web.ffos.hr/oziz/tam/Yi_2006.pdf doi:10.1016/j.im.2005.08.006

Yin, R. K. (2009). Case study research: Design and methods (Vol. 5). Thousand Oaks, CA: Sage.

Yin, R. K. (2003). *Case study research: Design and methods* (3rd ed.). Thousand Oaks, CA: Sage.

Yoshida, H., & Smith, L. B. (2003). Shifting ontological boundaries: How Japanese-and English-speaking children generalize names for animals and artifacts. *Developmental Science, 6*(1), 1–17.

Young, J. R. (2013). *Coursera announces details for selling certificates and verifying identities*. [Web log post]. Retrieved from http://chronicle.com/blogs/wiredcampus/coursera-announces-details-for-selling-certificates-and-verifying-identities/41519

Young, P. (1998, September). Under fire. *CIO Magazine*, 15-20.

Yuan, L., & Powell, S. (2013). MOOCs and open education: Implications for higher education. *Center for Educational Technology & Interoperability Standards* [Whitepaper]. Retrieved from http://publications.cetis.ac.uk/wp-content/uploads/2013/03/MOOCs-and-Open-Education.pdf

Yuen, K. Y., Chan, P. K. S., Peiris, M., Tsang, D. N. C., Que, T. L., & Shortridge, K. F. et al. H5N1 Study Group. (1998). Clinical features and rapid viral diagnosis of human disease associated with avian influenza A H5N1 virus. *Lancet*, *351*(9101), 467–471. PMID:9482437

Yukawa, J. (2006). Co-reflection in online learning: Collaborative critical thinking as narrative. *International Journal of Computer-Supported Collaborative Learning*, *1*(2), 203–228.

Yun, H., Kettinger, W., & Lee, C. (2012). A new open door: The smartphone's impact on work-to-life conflict, stress, and resistance. *International Journal of Electronic Commerce*, *16*(4), 121–151. doi:10.2753/JEC1086-4415160405

Yu, X., & Weinberg, J., B. (2003, October). Robotics in education: New platforms and environments. *IEEE Robotics & Automation Magazine*.

Zagrebina, A. V. (2013). Mechanisms of upward mobility as perceived by students in an institution of higher learning. *Russian Education & Society*, *55*(66), 26–38. doi:10.2753/RES1060-9393550603

Zeiler, K. (2009). Deadly pluralism? Why death-concept, death-definition, death-criterion and death-test pluralism should be allowed, even though it creates some problems. *Bioethics*, *23*(8), 450–459. PMID:18554277

Zhang, P., & Sung, H. (2009). The complexity of different types of attitudes in initial and continued use of ICT. *Journal of American Society for Information Science and Technology*, *60*(10), 2048-2063. doi:10.1002/asi.21116

Zhao, W. S. (2005). Cong dong/mingci dapei shiwu kan muyuqianyi dui eryuxide de yingxiang. [On the influence of L1 transfer on the verb-noun collocations in SLA] In H. Z. Yang, S. C. Gui, & D. F. Yang (Eds.), *Corpus-based analysis of Chinese learner English* (pp. 275–340). Shanghai: Shanghai Foreign Language Education Press.

Zhu, W., May, D. R., & Avolio, B. J. (2004). The impact of ethical leadership behavior on employee outcomes: The roles of psychological empowerment and authenticity. *Journal of Leadership & Organizational Studies*, *11*(1), 16–26. doi:10.1177/107179190401100104

Ziebertz, H., & Kay, W. K. (2009). A key to the future: The attitudes and values of adolescent Europeans. *Globalisation, Societies and Education*, *7*(2), 151–165. doi:10.1080/14767720902908000

Ziegahn, L. (2001). Talk about culture online: The potential for transformation. *Distance Education*, *22*(1), 144–150.

Zinnbauer, B. J., Pargament, K. I., Cole, B., Rye, M. S., Butter, E. M., Belavich, T. G., & Kadar, J. L. et al. (1997). Religion and spirituality: Unfuzzying the fuzzy. *Journal for the Scientific Study of Religion*, *36*(4), 549–564. doi:10.2307/1387689

Zinnbauer, B. J., Pargament, K. I., & Scott, A. B. (1999). The emerging meanings of religiousness and spirituality: Problems and prospects. *Journal of Personality*, *67*(6), 889–919. doi:10.1111/1467-6494.00077

Zirkel, P. A., & Thomas, L. B. (2010). State laws and guidelines implementing RTI. *Teaching Exceptional Children*, *43*(1), 60–73. doi:10.1177/004005991004300107

About the Contributors

F. Sigmund Topor is a Scholar-Practitioner and President of International & Intercultural Communications, Francis Sigmund Topor conducts research and lecturers at a number of universities including Toyo and Keio, Universities in Tokyo, Japan. His expertise include Adult education, critical thinking, and Japanese Sociolinguistics and psycholinguistics. Dr. Topor also currently provides intercultural communicative competency to Japanese multinational corporations in Tokyo; haven provided educational services to the Tokyo Metropolitan Board of Education. He has an extensive portfolio of writings including A Sentence Repetition Placement Test For EFL/ESL Learners In Japan and the Empowerment of Japanese Women: What Will the Social Impact Be?

* * *

Sandra Aguirre has worked in the field of Leadership for over 20 years. She has worked in several technical and business leadership positions over her career and in 2015 completed her Doctor of Education from The George Washington University Executive Leadership Doctoral Program. Ms. Aguirre has a Bachelor of Science in Integrative Studies - Business Administration from George Mason University and a Master of Science in Systems Engineering from Johns Hopkins University.

Mabark Alshahri is an Associate professor at Imam Mohammed Ibn Saud Islamic University where he teaches courses in curriculum and instruction. His research interests include the use to technology for instruction in higher education contexts and curriculum design.

Jennifer Bandy holds a Doctor of Philosophy (Ph.D.) in International Psychology degree from The Chicago School of Professional Psychology. Her International Psychology degree program included two field experience requirements, in China and Japan. Dr. Bandy also holds a Master of Arts in Counseling degree and a Bachelor of Arts and Sciences in Psychology degree, both from Dallas Baptist University.

Arthur Bangert is an Associate Professor in the Department of Education at Montana State University where he teaches courses in Educational Research and Statistics. His research interests include online learning and student perceptions of their online learning experiences.

Ellen Brook was born and raised in the former Soviet Union and received her high school diploma as well as two graduate degrees in the former Soviet Union. Her family immigrated to the United States of America in 1990. Her teaching experience in this country consists of teaching high school mathematics for a few years and then teaching adults as a mathematics faculty of Cuyahoga Community College. Her responsibilities there include teaching mathematics courses ranging from developmental to calculus in a traditional classroom, non-traditional computerized environment, and online and developing new and improving established mathematics courses. In addition, she received the doctoral degree in Math education at Kent State University.

Randy L. Burkhead is a senior security engineer with JANUS Associates Inc. where she currently conducts penetration testing, audits, and other security tasks for clients. She has been working as a military, government, and civilian contractor in information security for 8 years. She has a PhD in Information Technology with a specialty in information security from Capella University. Her dissertation was a phenomenological study on information security incidents. In addition to her PhD she holds several industry certifications including the CISSP and CeH. Dr. Burkhead is also a prior service Army veteran. When she is not doing her research or at work she is often with her "dogter" running, hiking, or traveling. She also deeply enjoys movies, games, comics, novels, tabletop strategy games, RPGs, and the occasional TV show.

Meilin Chen is a Post-doctoral Research Fellow at City University of Hong Kong. Her research interests include learner corpus research, data-driven learning, corpus linguistics and English academic writing for ESL/EFL learners.

Derek Cooley has a Bachelor's Degree in special education from Central Michigan University, a Master's Degree in educational leadership from Grand Valley State University, and a Doctorate in special education from Western Michigan University. Before joining Godwin Heights Public Schools as Director of Special Education, Derek was the principal of a school for students with disabilities. Derek began his career as a special education teacher for students with emotional and behavioral disorders.

Mary Jean Tecce DeCarlo, EdD, is an Assistant Clinical Professor of Literacy Studies at Drexel University. Dr. DeCarlo designs and teaches courses in the Teacher Education Program and the Special Education program. She also serves as chair of School's Curriculum Committee. She earned her EdD in Reading, Writing and from the University of Pennsylvania. During her twenty years in education, Dr. DeCarlo has been a classroom teacher, a curriculum leader and a college professor in suburban and urban communities in the Philadelphia region. During her time at Drexel she has focused on issues and challenges regarding effective reading and writing instruction for delayed readers and writers and the development of information and digital literacy skills for children K-8. Dr. DeCarlo's work with delayed readers and writers includes work in the field in an urban elementary school. There she coaches in-service teachers and offers a special education literacy course for undergraduates. That class is offered as a "flipped classroom" model for training pre-service and in-service teachers in best practices for teaching struggling readers. Dr. DeCarlo, with her colleague Dr. Lori Severino, have an accepted book chapter on this topic in Handbook of Research on Individualism and Identity in the Globalized Digital Age, which will be published by IGI global. Dr. DeCarlo is also working with Dr. Severino to create ACE (Adolescent Comprehension Evaluation), a digital reading comprehension tool that will be used for progress monitoring reading comprehension growth for students in middle school. This work was begun with a seed grant from Drexel School of Education ($2000), which allowed Drs. DeCarlo and Severino, along with several undergraduate students, to begin creating ACE as an iPad app. The same research team, with Dr. DeCarlo as Co-PI, received a $100,000 award from the Drexel Venture Fund to complete the ACE sixth through eighth grade app and to build the app's teacher dashboard. Drexel University has applied for a provisional patent for the ACE. Dr. DeCarlo and Dr. Severino presented research on ACE at the Council for Educational Diagnostic Services Conference, a division of the Council for Exceptional Children, in October of 2014. She has partnered with the Philadelphia School District to pilot the ACE with sixth through eighth grade students during the 2015-16 school year in order to norm scores with the general population. Dr. DeCarlo also does research in the areas of information and digital literacy. She has created collaborative research projects with urban classroom teachers and a group of Drexel University researchers around the I-LEARN model created by Dr. Delia Neuman. A seed grant ($5,000) from the Drexel School of Education funded one of these projects. This work was presented at the European Conference on Information Literacy, Dubrovnik, Croatia in 2014, as well as the Hawaii International Conference on Education and American Education Research Association in 2015. Publications related to this work include Neuman, D., Grant, A., Lee, V., & Tecce DeCarlo, M.J. (2014). Information and digital literacy in a high-poverty urban school. School Libraries Worldwide. 21(1), 38-53. (peer reviewed) and DeCarlo, M.J., Grant, A., Lee, V., & Neuman, D. (2014). I-LEARN: Helping young children become information literate. Communications in Computer and Information Science (volume and pages 243-252). New York: Springer (peer reviewed).

Nilsa Elias graduated from Capella University with a PhD in Business Information Technology. She is the Chair of the Networking Technology Program at Virginia College in Macon, GA. Dr. Elias research interests include models of continued use of e-learning and e-training technology.

Greg Gardner, PhD, CISSP Chief Architect, Defense and Intelligence Solutions, NetApp And Senior Fellow, George Washington University's Center for Cyber/Homeland Security (CCHS) Greg leverages his decades of government service and IT experience to provide NetApp's U.S. Public Sector team with all aspects of defense and intelligence focused support. Greg came to NetApp from service as the Deputy Chief Information Officer (DCIO) for the Intelligence Community (IC). In that role, he assisted the IC CIO in developing the information management systems that enable our integrated, agile intelligence enterprise. Greg previously worked at Oracle Corporation where for five years he was Vice President of Homeland Security Solutions & Public Sector Strategy. He also served a career in the United States Army, retiring in 2004 as a Colonel with 30 years of commissioned service. During his final military assignment, Greg was responsible for Joint Command and Control in the Command, Control, Communications, and Computers Directorate of the Joint Staff. There he developed the prototype of the Joint Protected Enterprise Network (JPEN) that enables force protection information to be securely shared amongst Defense Department organizations. Greg's military assignments include leadership positions in infantry, airborne, and ranger units and command of the 1st Battalion, 504th Parachute Infantry Regiment, 82d Airborne Division, and the 3rd United States Infantry (The Old Guard). His military staff assignments include service as Operations Officer, 3rd Brigade Combat Team, 7th Infantry Division (Light) during Operation JUST CAUSE in Panama, G3, 25th Infantry Division (Light) in Hawaii, Executive Officer to the Commander in Chief, Pacific Command, and Chief of Staff, Ministry of National Security and Defense, Coalition Provisional Authority, Baghdad, Iraq. A 1974 graduate of the United States Military Academy with a Bachelor of Science degree in Electrical Engineering, Greg also holds Master's Degrees in Industrial Relations / Personnel Management from The Krannert School, Purdue University, Military Art and Science from the Army's School of Advanced Military Studies, and Strategy and Policy from the Naval War College. Greg earned a PhD in IT Management from Capella University and is an Adjunct Professor in the Volgenau School of Engineering at George Mason University. He is a Certified Information Systems Security Professional. Greg is a Senior Fellow of the George Washington University Center for Cyber and Homeland Security and a standing member of the Cybersecurity Task Force. He previously served as a consultant to the Defense Science Board. Recently, he was a Commissioner on the Commission on the Leadership Opportunity in U.S. Deployment of the Cloud (CLOUD2), the Big Data Commission, and the Federal Technology Convergence Commission.

Şahin Gökçearslan graduated from Hacettepe University, Computer Education and Instructional Technologies Department. After same department finished Master and PhD on Educational Technology. His Research interest is mainly about new web technologies, learning communities, computer programming, technology integration. Currently working on Gazi University Informatics and Distance Education R & D Center.

Irina Khoutyz is head of Theoretical and Applied Linguistics Division at the Department of Romance and Germanic Philology at Kuban State University. She is interested in intercultural communication, discourse analysis, social psychology and linguistics.

Elise Kiregian, J.D. St. Johns University, Queens, NY, M.A. Hunter College, NY, NY, B.A. Columbia University, has taught History and Humanities at TCI College in New York for over thirty years. She has also served as an adjunct Associate professor at LaGuardia Community College for eighteen years.

Alena Lagumdzija received PhD in Medical Cell Biology from the Karolinska Institutet (KI), (Sweden) in 2005, with research interest in effects of hormones and peptides on osteoblast-like cells. In 2005 she was recognized "Scientist of the month" from the Health Care Workers Union. Same year Dr Lagumdzija was hired by Unilabs where she worked at clinical laboratories. 2009 she joined, LifeGene, KI (the biggest National resource project for the future medical research studies) as Test leader/Project assistant. Year 2006 and between 2010 and 2014 Dr Lagumdzija did post-doc in Japan at RIKEN (studied: Bioactive small-molecule compounds effects on osteoblast-like cells); was visitor post-doc at School of Bionics, Tokyo University of Technology Research Centre of Advanced Bionics (studied: Coenzyme Q10 and antioxidants), and was consulting researcher for time limited project (studied: Development of a portable blood testing) at Nihon University School of Medicine. At present, she works at Karolinska University Laboratory, Sweden.

Doug Leigh, Ph.D., is a professor with Pepperdine University's Graduate School of Education. He earned his Ph.D. in instructional systems from Florida State University, where he served as a technical director for projects with various local, state, and federal agencies. His current research, publication, and lecture interests concern cause analysis, organizational trust, leadership visions, and dispute resolution. He is coeditor of The Handbook of Selecting and Implementing Performance Interventions (Wiley, 2010) and coauthor of The Assessment Book (HRD Press, 2008), Strategic Planning for Success (Jossey-Bass, 2003) and Useful Educational Results (Proactive Publishing, 2001). Leigh served on a two-year special assignment to the National Science Foundation, is two time chair of the American Evaluation Association's Needs Assessment Topic Interest Group, and past editor-in-chief the International Society for Performance Improvement's (ISPI) monthly professional journal, Performance Improvement. A lifetime member of ISPI, he is also a member of the editorial board for its peer-reviewed journal, Performance Improvement Quarterly.

Eric Niemi is a recent graduate of the Adult and Higher Education doctoral program at Northern Illinois University, and he currently teaches developmental writing and student success courses at Chippewa Valley Technical College.

Marc Pilkington is Associate Professor of Economics, at the University of Burgundy, France, and founder of Moldova Tours 2.0.

Donna Reed holds a PhD in International Education and Entrepreneurship from University of the Incarnate Word, San Antonio, Texas. She is currently an educator with Southwest Independent School District in San Antonio, Texas.

Amanda Sue Schulze is an innovative learning technology and education professional with over 15 years of experience. Her research interests include Massive Open Online Courses (MOOCs), instructional design, using technology to facilitate learning experiences, and informal learning through social media. She works with colleges and universities across the U.S. to design online education.

Lori Severino is an Assistant Clinical Professor at Drexel University. She is also the Program Director for Special Education in the School of Education. Her research interests include literacy, dyslexia, preservice teacher education, differentiated instruction, and professional learning communities. Prior to Drexel University, she worked in the public school system in the field of special education for 26 years.

Paul Sparks leads technology courses in the doctoral and master's programs at Pepperdine. Previously, he was director of training at Epoch Internet where he developed its curriculum. Dr. Sparks was also an educational technologist and information systems specialist for Rockwell International. He was previously a high school and adult education instructor in the Whittier Union High School District.

Elio Spinello is an adjunct professor in the Education Division at the Pepperdine University Graduate School of Education and Psychology, and he is also a partner in RPM Consulting, LLC, a consulting firm which provides research, training, and system development services to a variety of public and private organizations. He has published research examining the use of computer simulations in training health professionals, as well as examining the willingness and ability of K-12 teachers to perform CPR and emergency procedures in a classroom environment. In addition to teaching at Pepperdine, he also teaches at California State University Northridge College of Health and Human Development, and the University of Redlands Graduate School of Business. He has also been a consultant to the State of California Employment Development Department, assessing the outcomes of state-funded job training programs.

Velmarie K. Swing, PhD, RN, earned ADN at OSU-OKC in 1986, BS (Nursing) 1998, and MS (Nursing Education) 2008 from Southern Nazarene University, and PhD (Nursing Education) 2014 from Capella University. Entered into academia in 2003 and was Nursing Chair in 2011. Currently the program coordinator of three tracks for new RN graduates and adjunct in a graduate nursing program.

Elizabeth Whitten (Director) is a Professor in the Department of Special Education and Literacy Studies (SPLS) and teaches courses in teaming, curriculum and instruction, learning disabilities and leadership. Dr. Whitten has served as both a general and special education teacher, building principal, and director of special education. She has been a professor in higher education for the past 23 years and chaired the Department of Special Education at WMU for eight years. Dr. Whitten consults with numerous school districts, locally, nationally, and internationally providing PD in areas of collaboration and teaming, leadership, co-teaching, curriculum-based assessment and research-based instruction, and evidence-based strategies.

Michelle F. Wright is a postdoctoral research fellow at Masaryk University. Her research interests include the contextual factors, such as familial and cultural, which influence children's and adolescents' aggression and victimization as well as their pursuit, maintenance, and achievement of peer status. She also has an interest in peer rejection and unpopularity and how such statuses relate to insecurity with one's peer standing, aggression, and victimization.

Index

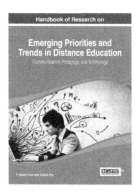
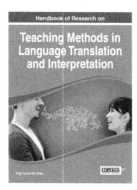
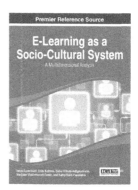

Printed in the United States
By Bookmasters